Chinese History

A Manual

Harvard-Yenching Institute Monograph Series, 46

CHINESE HISTORY

A MANUAL

Endymion Wilkinson

Published by the Harvard University Asia Center
and distributed by Harvard University Press
Cambridge (Massachusetts) and London
1998

Printed in the United States of America

The Harvard-Yenching Institute, founded in 1928 and headquartered at Harvard University, is a foundation dedicated to the advancement of higher education in the humanities and social sciences in East and Southeast Asia. The Institute supports advanced research at Harvard by faculty members of certain Asian universities and doctoral studies at Harvard and other universities by junior faculty at the same universities. It also supports East Asian studies at Harvard through contributions to the Harvard-Yenching Library and publication of the *Harvard Journal of Asiatic Studies* and books on premodern East Asian history and literature.

Library of Congress Cataloging-in-Publication Data

Wilkinson, Endymion Porter.

    Chinese history : a manual / Endymion Wilkinson.

       p.   cm. -- (Harvard-Yenching Institute monograph series ; 46)

    Includes bibliographical references and index.

    ISBN 0-674-12337-8 (alk. paper). -- ISBN 0-674-12378-6 (pbk. : alk. paper)

       1. China--History--Handbooks, manuals, etc.   I. Title.

II. Series.

DS735.W695   1998

951--dc21   98-14141

                                           CIP

Indexes by the author

Printed on acid-free paper

Last figure below indicates year of this printing

08 07 06 05 04 03 02 01 99

Printed from camera-ready copy supplied by the author

Acknowledgments

I am most grateful to Timothy Connor, who not only made many fruitful suggestions but also corrected an enormous number of mistaken characters and orthographic faults in a careful reading of the entire draft. Many others generously shared their learning, including William Jenner and Diana Lary, who commented on the entire first draft; Charles Aylmer, Beatrice S. Bartlett, Peter Bol, Hubert Durt, Roger Greatrex, Christian Lamouroux, John D. Langlois, D.C. Lau (Liu Dianjue 劉殿爵), James Z. Lee (Li Zhongqing 李中清), Liu Xueshun 劉學順, Michael Loewe, Alfreda Murck, Edwin Pulleyblank, Qi Wenxin 齊文心, Jessica Rawson, Shi Yanting 史延廷, Takashima Ken'ichi 高嶋謙一 and Yu Junfang 于君方, all of whom generously advised and corrected one or more chapters; An Zuozhang 安作璋, Chu Shibin 初世賓, Craig Clunas, Hu Pingsheng 胡平生, Roderick MacFarquar, Pavel Ostrov, Elisabeth Rochat de la Vallée, David Schaberg, Edward Shaughnessy, Frank Joseph Shulman, Song Zhenhao 宋鎮豪, Wang Lixing 王立興, Wang Weixin 王維新, Pierre-Etienne Will, Zhang Xiujun 張秀軍 and Zhao Keqin 趙克勤, who generously gave advice or sent materials.

John R. Ziemer not only edited the text, but showed me how to prepare the camera-copy pages ready for printing; Laura Carter patiently corrected my orthography. He Jin 何晋, Zhao Dongmei 趙冬梅 and Li Xinfeng 李新峰 proofread the final draft. Pornchai Mahaisavariya helped me compile the indexes.

At Cambridge (England) in the early 1960s I had the good fortune to sit at the feet of Chang Hsin-chang (Zhang Xinzhang 張新章), Cheng Te-k'un (Zheng Dekun 鄭德坤), Paul Kratochvil, Michael Loewe, Edwin G. Pulleyblank and Piet van der Loon. Later, as a Ph.D. student at Princeton, James T. C. Liu and Fritz Mote were my teachers. Yamane Yukio (山根幸夫) accepted me into his seminar on Ming law in Tokyo, despite my incompetence and the student struggles raging at that time (1968–9).

I should never have sustained a lasting interest in Chinese history without the inspiration of these exceptionally learned and generous teachers and I am therefore delighted to have this opportunity to express my thanks to them.

Contents

III. Historical Genres

IV. Literary and Other Primary Sources

V. Primary Sources by Period

Boxes

Tables

CONTENTS

Preface

The manual has four principal aims. The first two are straight-forward: to suggest solutions to basic problems encountered in doing research on traditional Chinese civilization and history; and to introduce the main primary sources and research tools for all periods from the Shang to the Qing.[1] Neither of these aims includes the desire to compile a bibliography of secondary scholarship.[2]

The third aim is to give readers some sense of the variety and of the changes that took place in Chinese history. Looking backwards from today it is easy to forget that the Chinese, their language and their culture were "ever in the process of becoming." The main reason that it is easy to overlook this is that the modern western image of China was not formed at different stages of the process but at the very end of the imperial era. Another reason is that Chinese culture itself stressed continuity, longevity and past precedent. Starting with the Tang, every dynasty paid immense care in writing the record of its predecessor. One of the duties of the official historians was to establish the legitimacy of the dynasty by showing that past precedent was respected. Because the literary style they used remained essentially unchanged, it is easy to gain the erroneous impression that Chinese civilization is not only ancient but also unchanging. It was an impression that influenced the first scholarly interpreters of China to the West, the Jesuits, who stressed literary and philosophical continuity. The view was re-

---

[1] A quarter of a century ago, I wrote *The History of Imperial China: A Research Guide*, HUP, 1973. It was intended for students of Chinese economic and social history. The present manual is a new and much larger work with different aims and coverage, and so it has a different title.

[2] Several bibliographies of secondary sources arranged by topic and by period are available. One of the best for Western scholarship is the chapter on China in the *American Historical Association Guide to Historical Literature*, Mary Beth Norton, ed., 2 vols., New York: OUP, 1995. It is periodically updated. See section 10.4.1.

inforced in the nineteenth century, because China, by comparison with the changes in the newly industrializing countries of the West, seemed like a country caught in an unchanging time warp. Seen from a distance the landscape appeared flat and, it was assumed, unchanging over time.

In the twentieth century, Chinese intellectuals and politicians were often impatient with their own past and completely rejected the old notion that it was a mirror for the present. Nevertheless, they continued to use it—selectively, anachronistically and teleologically—to legitimize the present. A practice that nationalism reinforces today (it is not unusual, for example, for contemporary historians to write about "national minorities" in the Shang dynasty even though neither China, let alone the concept of national minority, existed at that time).

For all these reasons it is easy to fall into ahistorical interpretations of Chinese history. So, my fourth and final aim in writing the manual is to suggest some of the ways to avoid this. For example, check the official written record with unofficial sources and newly discovered epigraphic evidence. Check written records of all kinds with the archaeological record. Above all, develop a sense of the changes in the Chinese language. The same words and terms meant different things in different hands and in different periods and places in China. This is not a plea for philology, but for historical imagination and accuracy. Finally, compare institutions and other phenomena in China with those found elsewhere in other civilizations.

In writing the book I had in mind to produce the sort of manual that I would have appreciated when I started Chinese studies in 1962. It is written, however, at a time of increasing specialization. This makes it difficult for students to have a good grasp of the primary sources and research tools for periods and fields outside of their own. I hope therefore that it may prove useful not only for beginners, but even for those more advanced.

The time span is from the late Shang to 1911, a period that represents just over 97 percent of China's recorded history. No attempt is made to deal in any detail with the new situation

brought about by the arrival of the foreign powers in the nineteenth century because that leads to different problems and to
different types of sources, already dealt with in several excellent
guides.[3]

It is possible to arrange a historical manual either by research problems, by the different types of primary sources, by
period or by subject—or by all four, which is the course followed here: research problems are dealt with mainly in Part I;
Parts III and IV are on genres and to a certain extent on subjects; Parts II and V are on periods, subdivided mainly by genres. Cross-referencing has been used throughout to avoid repetition.

Part I deals with basic knowledge. The historian of Chinese
civilization needs a good mastery of all forms of written Chinese, so the first chapter is on the language and the second is on
dictionaries. The rest of Part I covers people, places, time,
numbers and bibliography, including advice on how to master
the characters, how to convert dates, how to find places, how
to trace people and how to evaluate historical statistics. This is
followed by a discussion of where to find primary sources
(including rare, lost, recovered, forged and banned books),
what is in them and how to find the meanings of difficult titles.
The main index and concordance series are also introduced.
Part I concludes with chapters on the guides and bibliographies
for using and locating secondary sources in Chinese, Japanese
and Western languages and on the main libraries of Chinese
books in China, Japan, the United States, Europe and Russia.

Part II introduces the sources for the pre-Qin: archaeological, epigraphic and textual. There are also chapters on the early
script and its possible precursors.

---

[3] For example *Kindai Chûgoku kenkyû annai* 近代中國研究案内
(Guide to research on modern China), by Kojima Shinji 小島晋治 and
Namiki Yorihisa 並木賴壽, Iwanami, 1993, or the handy *Chûgoku sankô
tosho gaido Kingendaishi hen* 中國參考圖書ガイデ近現代史編, Ichiko
Kenji 市古健次, comp., Kyûko, 1997.

Part III describes the different branches of historical writing and compilation in imperial China (primary and secondary sources, annals, the Standard Histories, topically arranged histories, miscellaneous histories, official communications, government institutions, penal and administrative law, army administration and warfare).

Part IV deals with literary and other primary sources, including encyclopaedia of various kinds, literary anthologies and the collected works of individuals, women's studies, philosophy, myth and religion, popular literature, and particular subjects such as agriculture and the environment, technology and science, medicine, the fine arts, non-Han peoples (both inside and outside of the country), and foreign accounts of China.

Part V presents the main primary sources and research tools for each of seven historical periods from the Qin to the Qing.

The five parts of the manual are divided into fifty chapters. These are in turn subdivided into a total of two hundred sections and several dozen subsections.

Because some research problems addressed in Part I are already well-discussed in the literature (for example, biography and historical geography) these chapters are shorter than those on chronology and keeping the time, which are neglected subjects. Likewise, because some sources are important, others less so, and some are plentiful, while others are rare, the chapters in Parts II through V are sometimes long, sometimes short. For example, the chapter on the Standard Histories is much longer than the one dealing with topically-arranged histories and the chapter on the Qing is far longer than on any other period since there are more extant sources from the Qing than from all the rest of Chinese history put together. In other places more space has deliberately been given to newly discovered sources, such as documents on bamboo and wooden strips or from the archives, on the grounds that these are the sources with which students will be least familiar. Finally, in elaborating the thesis that China was ever in the process of becoming, I have deliberately gone into more detail in some chapters and sections, for example those on the diverse origins of the Chinese people and civilization (13.1); the expanding area brought under central control; changes in the language (chapter 1) and changes in the diet and cuisine (35.2).

I have brought together the scholarship of many generations of students of Chinese civilization. In doing so, my role has been "to compile and to transmit, not to innovate." I only hope that I have done so accurately and with due acknowledgment and that readers will send their comments and suggestions for improvement.

Endymion Wilkinson

Beijing

Conventions

Romanization

Today it is hard to imagine that not so long ago one of the main problems facing Western students of the Chinese language was the number of different systems of romanization that had to be mastered. British and American textbooks alone came in a bewildering variety of transcriptions of Chinese. Having mastered Wade-Giles, students had to learn the various modifications to it in Mathews' dictionary, in the *Postal Atlas of China* and in library catalogs.[4] Shortly thereafter they began to study spoken Chinese using the completely different American Army system as developed at Yale. Next, there were the Chinese systems to master, starting with *Gwoyeu Romatzyh* (*Guoyu luomazi* 國語羅馬字, National Romanization, 1928, 1986) and the *Zhuyin zimu* 注音字母 (Mandarin Phonetic Letters, 1918; name changed in 1930 to *Zhuyin fuhao* 注音符號, Mandarin Phonetic Symbols). When reading about China in the other European languages, they had to learn how to decode yet more systems of romanization.

To add insult to injury, there were always those scholars who invented personal modifications (and there are some still at it). Giles' own comment on the Wade-Giles system holds true today: "It is," he said, "anything but scientifically exact. In some respects it is cumbersome; in others it is inconsistent." The same could be said of *Hanyu pinyin* 漢語拼音 (Chinese Phonetic Alphabet, *pinyin* for short, 1958). But at least it is now the one system that is used by most scholars, both Chinese and foreign alike. Although sinological library collections in Europe and North America have still not completed the expensive process of converting to *pinyin*, they have begun.

So, *pinyin* is used throughout the manual. Not because it is linguistically superior to its numerous predecessors, but be-

---

[4] See Box 2, chap. 2; also 4.1, *Romanization of Chinese Place-Names*.

cause as the normative system, it has become the standard for the romanization of Chinese in English and for the other languages written in the roman alphabet.[5]

Characters

Characters are given in their complex form throughout.

Notes

Readers should not be surprised if the points made in the text are not necessarily the same as those made in the references cited in the footnotes.

Publishers

Publishers are indicated after every book title. In some cases, the name has been shortened (for example, by dropping the word *chubanshe* or *shuju*, so Hunan Renmin Chubanshe 湖南人民出版社 becomes Hunan renmin; Shangwu Yinshuguan 商務印書館 becomes Shangwu and Chengdu Chubanshe 成都出版社 appears as Chengdu.

Full names of all publishers, with principal place of business and Chinese or Japanese characters, where appropriate, are given in the Appendix. The only exceptions are a small number of Western publishers that if they are only referred to once are cited in full in the text. No attempt has been made to list pirated editions.

---

[5] There are a large number of concordances of the different ways of transliterating the sounds of Chinese into Western languages. The most comprehensive contains 50 different systems: Ireneus Laszlo Legeza, *Guide to Transliterated Chinese in the Modern Peking Dialect*, 2 vols., Brill, 1968-9. Vol. 1 shows equivalents in 21 current systems and vol. 2 lists equivalents in 29 defunct systems.

If you are uncertain of the orthography of *pinyin*, where, for example, to use spaces, hyphens or apostrophes (*zuqiu chang* or *zuqiuchang* 足球場? *Renyi daode* or *renyi-daode* 仁義道德? *Lao er wugong* or *lao' erwugong* 勞而無功?), look up the authoritative *Hanyu pinyin cihui* 漢語拼音詞匯, 1989; 2nd rev. ed., Yuwen, 1991; 2nd prnt., 1995. In the above three examples the second spelling is the recommended one.

Western university presses are abbreviated throughout as indicated in the following table:

ANU Press	Australian National University Press
CMC	Chinese Materials Center
Col. UP	Columbia University Press
Corn. UP	Cornell University Press
CUP	Cambridge University Press
HUP	Harvard University Press
IUP	Indiana University Press
HKCU Press	Hong Kong: Chinese University Press
HKU Press	Hong Kong University Press
OUP	Oxford University Press
PUF	Presses Universitaires de France
PUP	Princeton University Press
SUP	Stanford University Press
SUNY Press	State University of New York Press
UAP	University of Arizona Press
UBC Press	University of British Columbia Press
UChP	University of Chicago Press
UCP	University of California Press
UHP	University of Hawaii Press
UMP	University of Michigan Press
UWP	University of Washington Press
YUP	Yale University Press

Abbreviations of Institutions

Abbreviations of institutions in China and Japan are normally given in the manual according to the standard abbreviations used in Chinese and Japanese; not according to the many abbreviations for them sometimes found in Western languages.

Beitu 北圖	Beijing tushuguan 北京圖書館 (Peking Library)
CASS	See Shekeyuan 社科院
CCS	Center for Chinese Studies (various)
EFEO	Ecole française d'extrême orient, Paris
ICS	Institute of Chinese Studies, Chinese University of Hong Kong, Shatin
IEAS	Institute of East Asian Studies, University of California, Berkeley

Jimbun 人文	Kyôto daigaku, Jimbun kagaku kenkyûjo 京都大學人文科學研究所 (Institute for Humanistic Studies, Kyoto University)
Jinshisuo 近史所	Zhongyang yanjiuyuan Jindaishi yanjiusuo 中央研究院近代史研究所 (Institute of Modern History, Academia Sinica), Taibei
Kaogusuo 考古所	Zhongguo shehui kexueyuan, Kaogu yanjiusuo 中國社會科學院考古研究所 (Institute of Archaeology, Shekeyuan), Beijing
MFEA	Museum of Far Eastern Antiquities (Östasiatiska Samlingarna), Stockholm
Lishisuo 歷史所	Zhongguo shehui kexueyuan, Lishi yanjiusuo 中國社會科學院歷史研究所 (Institute of Historical Research, Shekeyuan), Beijing
Shekeyuan 社科院	Zhongguo shehui kexueyuan 中國社會科學院 (Chinese Academy of Social Sciences (CASS), Beijing
Shiyusuo 史語所	Zhongyang yanjiuyuan, Lishi yuyan yanjiusuo 中央研究院歷史語言研究所 (Institute of History and Philology, Academia Sinica), Taibei
SOAS	School of Oriental and African Studies, University of London
SSEC	Society for the Study of Early China, USA
Tôbunken 東文研	Tôkyo daigaku, Tôyô bunka kenkyûjo 東京大學東洋文化研究所 (The Institute of Oriental Studies, Tokyo University)
Wenkaosuo 文考所	Wenwu kaogu yanjiusuo 文物考古研究所 (Cultural Relics and Archaeology Institute)
Yishiguan 一史館	Zhongguo diyi lishi dang'an guan 中國第一歷史檔案館 (First Historical Archives, Beijing)

Book Titles

All Chinese book titles are given first in *pinyin* in *italics*, then in their original characters followed by an English translation in brackets. If the book has already been translated or has a widely used English title, it is usually put in italics. If not, not. For example, *Yijing* 易經 (*Book of Changes*), but *Wenshizhe gongju jianjie* 文史哲工具簡介 (Brief introduction to reference works for literature, history and philosophy). Often a work is identified by its title, for example, most of the Standard Histories, not by the author. For this reason, titles are frequently listed first, followed by the author.

Abbreviations of Book Titles

CHAC	*The Cambridge History of Ancient China*, Michael Loewe and Edward L. Shaughnessy, eds., New York: CUP, 1999
CHC	*The Cambridge History of China*, John K. Fairbank and Denis Twitchett, general editors, 15 vols., CUP, 1978– (chap. 43)
DMB	*Dictionary of Ming Biography 1368–1644*, Luther Carrington Goodrich and Chaoyang Fang, eds., 2 vols., Col. UP, 1976
DOTIC	Charles O. Hucker, *A Dictionary of Official Titles in Imperial China*, SUP, 1985; SMC rpnt., 1988
ECCP	*Eminent Chinese of the Ch'ing Period*, Arthur W. Hummel, ed., 2 vols., Washington, DC: Government Printing Office, 1943–44; SMC rpnt., 1991
ECTBG	*Early Chinese Texts: A Bibliographical Guide*, Michael Loewe, ed., *Early China* Special Monograph Series, SSEC and IEAS, 1993 (19.1)
H-Y Index	*Harvard-Yenching Institute Sinological Index Series* (9.10)
ICS Concordance	*Institute of Chinese Studies Ancient Chinese Texts Concordance Series* (9.10)
ISMH	*An Introduction to the Sources of Ming History*, Wolfgang Franke, ed., Kuala Lumpur and Singapore: University of Malaya Press, 1968
NSECH	*New Sources of Early Chinese History: An Introduction to the Reading of Inscriptions and Manuscripts*, Edward L. Shaughnessy, ed., SSEC and IEAS, 1997
SB	*A Sung Bibliography,* initiated by Etienne Balazs, Yves Hervouet, ed., HKCU Press, 1978
SCC	*Science and Civilisation in China*, Joseph Needham, ed., CUP, 1954–95; 1996– (chap. 38)

Conventions

Other Abbreviations

chap(s).	chapter(s)
comp(s).	compiler(s)
ed(s).	editor(s)
n.d.	no date (of publication)
prnt.	printing
rpnt.	reprint or reprinted
tr(s).	translator(s) or translated
vol(s).	volume(s) as in a modern book

CHINESE HISTORY

A MANUAL

Introduction

Recent Historiographical Trends

From 1949 to 1979, the writing of history in China became even more directly subordinate to politics than it had been in imperial China. However, the past was no longer regarded as a mirror for the present, but as the dark night at the end of which, following liberation in 1949, a new era had dawned. What happened during the course of the long night of Chinese "feudal" history (and even during the "pre-class" millennia before then) was analyzed in Marxist-Maoist terms. All other forms of historical studies were proscribed and the research agenda limited to five themes: peasant rebellions (because it was believed that peasant uprisings were the major driving force of the development of China's feudal society); the formation of the Han nation; the landholding systems of feudal China; capitalist sprouts in the Ming and Qing; periodization. Despite the fact that the research agenda had the backing of the state and was watched over by a handful of politically approved historians, not every question was resolved. For example, no final decision was reached on how to deal with Marx's slippery concept of the Asiatic mode of production. Nor is there to this day a consensus on periodization, a subject discussed below.

During the entire 1949–79 period Chinese historians were cut off from historical studies in the West. Foreign publications, if available at all, were severely restricted.

Much work of tremendous value was done, sometimes at the direct command of Mao Zedong, as when, for example, a group of leading historians were assigned to produce variorum punctuated editions of the *Zizhi tongjian* 資治通鑑 and of the Standard Histories.

Some of the varieties of historical writing that flourished during these years have since been labeled by Chinese historians as teleological history (*mudilun shixue* 目的論史學), according to which everything of value in the past was a preparation for the glorious present; weathervane history (*fengpai shixue* 風派史學), which was as influenced by present political fads as by historical evidence; hot-air history (*yilun shixue* 議論史學), another name for the previous genre; Aesopian history (*yingshe shixue* 影射史學), whose practitioners, following an old Chinese tradition, criticized the present indirectly by using historical precedents.

Many avoided controversy by engaging in compilation of excerpts on the approved themes or by writing pot-boiler history (*huiguorou shixue* 回鍋肉史學), rehashing other people's work (in the name of popularization, as acceptable an activity as independent research was suspicious). At times of heightened tension, such as during the Cultural Revolution, all forms of study and writing stopped.

The end of nation building in a Maoist framework in 1979 began to free Chinese historians from the necessity to work within such narrow margins. During the 1980s and early 1990s scholarship blossomed. New journals were founded. Manuscripts that had been unpublishable for decades saw the light of day. Pre-1949 works were for the first time given their due. The barriers that had previously divided historical studies abroad from those in China were removed. For the first time in a generation foreign journals and books started to become available. Travel abroad was allowed. Access for foreign scholars to colleagues in China opened up. Fruitful contacts multiplied. New interpretations began to emerge.

Regional and local history are now booming, as pride in local traditions is fortified and financed by economic growth and by the discovery of a huge variety of archaeological treasures, including whole settlements from villages to cities, attesting to distinct, and in many cases unsuspected, Neolithic and Bronze Age cultures.

Greater attention is being paid to the role of the non-Han peoples, both in the formation of Chinese civilization in its earliest stages and at later periods of Chinese history.

Gender studies are beginning to make their mark.

Previously Chinese history was either seen as part of world history in a Marxist-Leninist framework or as a statement of the unique genius of Chinese national identity. There are some signs that new cross-border and cross-cultural comparisons are now being made, even though many still have a predilection to regard history principally as a means to evoke national pride.

Historical archives have opened doors that until the 1980s were shut. Joint archaeological digs were allowed in the 1990s for the first time in forty years.

In these more open times, the volume and diversity of historical works, compilations and reprints of historical texts has increased enormously. Although there is more private wealth in society, there are ever diminishing public funds available to support scholarly research and publication. The use of the computer to edit, analyze, index and disseminate research results may mitigate such difficulties. For example, searching for bibliographic references has become much more efficient with the availability of online library catalogs, in some cases allowing access to major Chinese and Japanese collections all over the world. Hundreds of Chinese journals are distributed on CD-ROM, which allows checking current research trends much more rapidly and at less cost to the scholar or library than would have been thought possible only a few years ago.

Epigraphic sources, too, are becoming more accessible. Even if the originals may still be scattered in collections in many countries, transcriptions have been made and comprehensive editions published, and CD-ROM versions are becoming available. Ironically, greater ease of access comes just at the moment when the ability to handle Classical or Literary Chinese, not to speak of the difficult ancient scripts of the Shang and Zhou inscriptions, is declining.

Historians of imperial China (from Qin to Qing) in China itself, as well as in Japan and Korea, have usually concentrated on particular periods (such as the classical period or the more recent dynasties) and they continue to do so. Conversely they usually neglected periods of alien rule or division, except in special cases, for example the Manchu interest in the Jin dynasty because it was founded by their Jurchen (Nüzhen 女真) ancestors. Today, there are many more specialized fields and disciplines, covering not only the dynasties when China was strong, but also the periods of disunity.

That Chinese historical studies in the West should become more specialized is entirely fitting. In the study of European and American history it is considered normal for historians to concentrate on one period—the Tudors or the antebellum South, or even on a single event such as the French Revolution—and certainly to specialize in a discipline such as economic history or the history of science. The old idea that a historian of China should cover three or four thousand years of history in all its manifestations was an indication of the immaturity of the field, or simply a reliance on received interpretations.

One result of increased specialization is that works covering all of Chinese history are written by large teams. For example, more than two hundred historians contributed to the twenty-two volumes of *Zhongguo tongshi* 中國通史 (Shanghai renmin) covering Chinese history to the end of the Qing; seventy-five historians wrote the chapters in the four-volume *Chûgoku shigaku no kihon mondai* 中國史學の基本問題 (Kyûko) and more than one hundred scholars contributed to the most comprehensive and detailed account of Chinese history ever attempted in a Western language, the fifteen-volume *Cambridge History of China* (chap. 43).[1]

Today, although there is increased specialization, the periods covered are still vast. A historian who takes the Han as his special field is after all taking a period longer than that which separates the first Queen Elizabeth of England from the second, or the Pilgrim Fathers from the moon landing. No subsequent

---

[1] The collecting, writing and copying of large-scale reference books and compilations of all sorts by teams of scholars often working on behalf of, if not inspired by, prestigious editorial committees or powerful patrons, has been a feature of Chinese intellectual and official life since the Han dynasty, if not before.

dynasty lasted as long as the Han (although its predecessor, the Zhou, was twice as long), but the volume of extant primary sources grows larger as we approach the present, and even the Qing (the shortest of China's major dynasties) lasted for 267 years.

The blossoming of historical studies in the new, more open atmosphere of the 1980s and early 1990s in China was made possible by the contributions of scholars of an older generation many of whom for the first time in thirty years were left in peace to do their research. However, historical studies reached a watershed in the mid-1990s due to the near breakdown of the state-supported systems of academic and university scholarship and publication in a society where the pursuit of wealth made the slow acquisition of the skills to study ancient history seem beside the point.

Periodization

History since at least the Han dynasty has been broadly divided using the relative terms *gu* 古 and *jin* 近, ancient and modern, with the definitions changing as each new generation sees itself as modern and an ever larger stretch of the past as ancient. Currently in China political criteria are applied: ancient history (*gudaishi* 古代史) covers antiquity to the early nineteenth century; modern history (*jindaishi* 近代史) is from 1840 to 1919; and contemporary history (*dangdaishi* 當代史) is from 1919 to the present. As the "contemporary" inevitably fades into the "modern," and as the "modern" gradually becomes "ancient," these demarcation lines will no doubt shift again.[2]

Yuangu 遠古, remote antiquity, sometimes refers to the legendary time before the use of writing. Thereafter, within the vast time span of "ancient," divisions are usually made in one of three ways. By tradition, the *Sandai* 三代 (the three dynasties of Xia, Shang, and Zhou) are simply lumped together as *xian-*

---

[2] 1840 is the beginning of the Opium War; 1919 is the May Fourth Movement; 1949 is the founding of the People's Republic.

Qin 先秦 (pre-Qin, i.e., before the Qin unification) or *shanggu* 上古 (high antiquity; archaic China, ancient history), a period that covers in all about 1,900 years. Since the Han, this is usually divided into the Western and Eastern Zhou (following the forced removal of the dynasty from its principal to secondary capital, see the table of dynasties on pages 9–11). The Eastern Zhou is further subdivided into the Spring and Autumn and the Warring States periods. Thereafter, the following 2,200 years (often referred to as "imperial China") are divided into six or seven main dynastic periods, alternating between those that ruled over a united empire and those that existed in a period of weakness and disunity. The drawback of this convention is that it still leads to the uncritical acceptance of what might be called "the Zhou interpretation of history," whereby all of the Chinese past is seen as having originated from one (mythological) source leading inexorably to the Zhou and continuing thereafter in an unbroken succession of "legitimate" dynasties, each founded by an upright and capable ruler who gains the mandate of heaven as the result of the corruptness and disorder under the last ruler of the previous dynasty. This teleological approach to the past focused almost exclusively on court politics and the concerns of the imperial government ever conscious of the need to justify its actions in moral terms.[3]

The second way of dividing Chinese history is to use Freiderich Engels' stage theory (still applied in China) of primitive society (*yuanshi shehui* 原始社會),[4] slave society (*nuli shehui* 奴隸社會), feudal society (*fengjian* 封建社會),[5] semi-colonial, semi-feudal society (*banzhimindi, banfengjian shehui* 半殖民地

[3] See section 13.1 for the first challenges to the "Zhou interpretation of history."

[4] Primitive society is defined as pre-class society and sub-divided into pre-clan, matriarchal clan and patriarchal clan. What effect the application of these categories has had on Chinese archaeology is discussed in 13.3.

[5] Arif Dirlik, "Feudalism in 20th century Chinese Historiography," *China Report*, 33.1: 35–66 (1997); Cho-yun Hsu, "Early Chinese History: The State of the Field," *JAS* 38.3: 453–75 (1979).

半封建社會), and capitalist society (*ziben zhuyi shehui* 資本主義社會).[6] The timing of the transition to slave society varies according to the historian from different periods of the Longshan culture (third millennium BC), the Xia, or the Shang dynasties. The end of slave and the beginning of feudal society are variously placed in the Western Zhou, the Spring and Autumn, the Warring States, the Qin unification, the Later Han or the Wei-Jin periods. The beginnings of the end of the feudal are usually placed in the Ming and Qing with the appearance of capitalist sprouts (*ziben zhuyi mengya* 資本主義萌芽), nipped in the bud by the arrival of the imperialists.[7]

The third method of periodization (often used by Western and Japanese historians) is to apply the conventional categories of European history: ancient, medieval and modern.[8] The *Nan-Bei Chao* are usually taken to mark the transition to medieval, and the Song (or the Ming), the transition to modern.[9] The disadvantage is not so much that these categories cannot be made to fit the Chinese experience, but that their familiarity in the European context suggests false connotations.

A simplification found in many Western textbooks is to lump everything which happened before the Qin unification as the formative age, from the Qin to the Song as the early empire, and from the Song to the Qing as the later empire, thus

[6] Albert Feuerwerker, *History in Communist China*, MIT Press, 1968, covers the formative years up to 1959.

[7] Timothy Brook, "Capitalism, Modern History, and the Chinese Premodern," in *Culture and Economy: The Shaping of Capitalism in East Asia*, Timothy Brook and Hy V. Luong, eds., UCP, 1997.

[8] Joshua A. Vogel, *Naito Konan [1866–1934] and the Development of "Modernity" in China*, Sharpe, 1984; Tanigawa Michio, "Problems Concerning the Japanese Periodization of Chinese History," Joshua A. Fogel, tr., *Journal of Asian History* 21.2: 150–68 (1987). See also the same author's *Medieval Chinese Society and the Local Community*, Joshua A. Fogel, introduced and tr., UCP, 1985.

[9] In Japan, the Kyoto school regarded the Song as marking the transition to the modern; the Tokyo school identified the late Ming in this role. The Chinese orthodoxy chose the Ming.

creating three massive and rather indigestible slices of one thousand years each.

Controversies have raged as to which method to use and where the demarcation lines should be drawn, but periodization is not a science. Whichever method is chosen (and each has drawbacks and advantages), it should serve to clarify analysis, not to provide a straightjacket into which to fit the data.

The manual follows the first approach: the pre-Qin is taken as a whole, followed by seven main dynastic periods. The advantage is that most of the primary sources fit neatly into this scheme.

The Dynasties

Pre-Qin: The Three Dynasties (Sandai 三代)

	BC
Xia 夏[1]	ca. 21st–16th c.
Shang 商	ca. 1600–1045
Early Shang (Erligang 二里岡 period)	ca. 16th–14th c.
Yin Shang 殷商 (Anyang 安陽 period)	14th c.–1045
Zhou 周[2]	1045–256
Western Zhou 西周	1045–771
Eastern Zhou 東周	770–256
Spring and Autumn (*Chunqiu* 春秋)[3]	770–476
Warring States (*Zhanguo* 戰國)[4]	475–221
Six Kingdoms (*Liuguo* 六國)[5]	

[1] The historicity of the Xia is generally accepted in China although no contemporary written evidence has been found.

[2] 1045 is one of many estimates for the Zhou conquest of the Shang. In the year 256 Qin destroyed the Western Zhou whose last ruler was killed.

[3] The name *Chunqiu* 春秋 comes from the chronicle of that name (21.1) which covered the years 722–481 BC. By modern convention the *Chunqiu* period has been extended to cover the years 770–476, that is from the start of the Eastern Zhou (marked by the removal of the Zhou capital to Luoyi 雒邑, modern Luoyang) to the start of the Warring States period.

[4] The name *Zhanguo* 戰國 comes from the *Zhanguoce* 戰國策 (see Table 18, section 19.1). Its beginning was traditionally either put in 475 (*Shiji* 史記) or in 403 (*Zizhi tongjian* 資治通鑑; this latter date marks the formal recognition by the Zhou of the rulers of Han 韓, Zhao 趙 and Wei 魏, who had earlier dismembered Jin 晉). Modern convention normally uses 475.

[5] The Six Kingdoms at the end of the Warring States were Han 韓 (403–230), Zhao 趙 (403–222), Wei 魏 (403–225), Chu 楚 (?–223), Qi 齊

Footnote continued on next page

Dynasties of Imperial China

Qin 秦	221–206 BC
Han 漢	202 BC–AD 220
Former Han 前漢 (also called Western Han)	202 BC–AD 23
Xin 新 (Wang Mang 王莽 interregnum)	AD 9–23
Later Han 後漢 (also called Eastern Han)	25–220
Wei, Jin, *Nan-Bei Chao* 魏濬南北朝	220–589
Sanguo 三國 (Three Kingdoms)	220–280
Wei 魏 (commonly known as Cao Wei 曹魏)	220–265
Han 漢 (commonly known as Shu Han 蜀漢)	221–263
Wu 吳 (commonly known as Sun Wu 孫吳)	222–280
Jin 晉	265–420
Western Jin 西晉	265–316
Eastern Jin 東晉	317–420
Six Dynasties 六朝[6]	222–589
Sixteen Kingdoms 十六國[7]	304–439
Nan-Bei Chao 南北朝	420–589
Southern Dynasties 南朝	420–579
Liu Song 劉宋	420–479
Qi 齊	479–502
Liang 梁	502–557
Chen 陳	557–589

(11th c. BC–221) and Yan 燕 (11th c. BC–222). They were all conquered by Qin 秦.

[6] The Six Dynasties (*Liuchao* 六朝) of the years 222–589 were Wu 吳, Dong Jin 東晉 and the four Southern dynasties of Song 宋, Qi 齊, Liang 梁 and Chen 陳. They were grouped together because they had their capitals in the South at Jiankang 建康 (Nanjing). They are sometimes called the southern Six Dynasties to distinguish them from another definition of the term, the northern Six Dynasties (Wei 魏, Xi-Jin 西晉, Bei-Wei 北魏, Bei-Qi 北齊, Bei-Zhou 北周 and Sui 隋). Occasionally, too, the whole period of *Sanguo*, Jin, *Nan-Bei Chao* is called the Six Dynasties.

[7] Conventional term for the sixteen states established over most of North China and Sichuan between 304 and 439, of which five were Xianbei 鮮卑; three Han 漢; three Xiongnu 匈奴; two Di 氏 and one each Qiang 羌, Jie 羯 and Badi 巴氏. Collectively the non-Han peoples who ruled in the North at this time were known as the "five barbarians" (*wuhu* 五胡). They were not counted in the legitimate succession of dynasties (*zhengtong* 正統); on which see 20.4.

Northern Dynasties 北朝[8]	386–581
Northern Wei 北魏[9]	386–534
Eastern Wei 東魏	534–550
Western Wei 西魏	535–556
Northern Qi 北齊	550–577
Northern Zhou 北周	557–581
Sui 隋	581–618
Tang 唐	618–907
The Five Dynasties and Ten Kingdoms	
(*Wudai shiguo* 五代十國)	902–979
Five Dynasties 五代 (North China)[10]	907–960
Ten Kingdoms 十國 (South China)[11]	902–979
Song	960–1279
Northern Song 北宋 period	960–1127
Southern Song 南宋 period	1127–1279
Liao 遼 (*Qidan* 契丹, Khitan)	916–1125
Jin 金 (*Nüzhen* 女真, Jurchen)	1115–1234
Xia 夏 (*Dangxiang* 黨項, Tangut)[12]	1038–1227
Yuan 元 (*Menggu* 蒙古, Mongol)	1279–1368
Ming 明	1368–1644
Qing 清 (*Manzhou* 滿洲, Manchu)	1644–1911

[8] The founders and rulers of the Northern Dynasties were all Xianbei 鮮卑 (a non-Han people) with the exception of the Northern Qi whose ruling house was founded by a Han from Bohai 渤海. Another convention is to date the Northern dynasties to the years 439–581 (from the Wei unification of North China to the establishment of the Sui dynasty).

[9] Also called Tuoba Wei 拓拔魏.

[10] The Five Dynasties were Later Liang 後梁 (907–923); Later Tang 後唐 (*Shatuo* 沙陀, a Turkic people, 923–936); Later Jin 後晉 (*Shatuo* 沙陀, 936–946); Later Han 後漢 (*Shatuo* 沙陀, 947–950); and Later Zhou 後周 (951–960).

[11] The Ten Kingdoms were Wu 吳 (902–937); Nan Tang 南唐 (937–975); Wu-Yue 吳越 (907–978); Chu 楚 (907–951); Min 閩 (909–945); Nan Han 南漢 (917–971); Qian Shu 前蜀 (903–925); Hou Shu 後蜀 (933–965); Jingnan 荊南 (924–963); and Bei Han 北漢 (*Shatuo* 沙陀), 951–979. Most were conquered by the Song.

[12] Not counted in the legitimate succession.

Note on Cycles of Rule

The Chinese and steppe empires influenced each other in an interactive way. When there were strong dynasties in China, there were usually steppe empires to the North and Northwest:

Qin and Han: Xiongnu 匈奴 and Xianbei 鮮卑 empires;
Sui and Tang: Turkish and Uighur empires;
Ming and Qing: Oirats, Mongols and Zunghars.

When China was divided and weak, steppe peoples seized the opportunity and were often able to establish themselves in China:

Nan-Bei Chao: Tuoba Wei etc. in the North
Song: Jin and Xi-Xia in the North and Northwest; the Mongols in
the North
Yuan: Mongol rule
Qing: Manchu rule

At such times there was usually no strong steppe empire (the Mongols were the single exception).[13]

Note on Dynastic Names (Guohao 國號)

Nearly all the names of states and fiefs up to and including the Han were taken from place names. Between the fall of the Han and the establishment of the Jin in the twelfth century, the same names for dynasties were used over and over again. Most were taken from aristocratic titles, which in turn perpetuated the names and titles of Zhou dynasty states or fiefs (*guo* 國). There were also those states that claimed a restoration by using the dynastic title of an immediately previous dynasty (the Later Tang, 923–936, for example).

The Liao and the Jin followed the old traditions in that they took their *guohao* from place names, albeit not those of ancient

[13] See the Table in Thomas J. Barfield, *The Perilous Frontier: Nomadic Empires and China, 221 BC to AD 1757*, Blackwell, 1989; rpnt., 1996, 13; L. S. Yang (楊聯陞), "Toward a Study of Dynastic Configurations in Chinese History," in his *Studies in Chinese Institutional History*, HUP, 1963, 1–17.

states, but the names of rivers in the homelands of their dynastic founders. Thereafter, for reasons explained at the beginning of chap. 48, starting with the Yuan, an entirely new course was followed.

Khubilai Khan adopted the term "Fundamental force" (*Yuan* 元) for the name of his dynasty. It was taken not from history but from the beginning of the *Yijing* 易經 (*Book of Changes*).

The first emperor of the Ming 明 decided to perpetuate the title of the Red Turban leader Xiao Mingwang 小明王 (Young Prince of Radiance) whose mantle he inherited. The name had strong Messianic overtones (see chap. 49, note 1).

Huang Taiji 皇太極 (Abahai), the ruler of Da Jin 大金 (or Hou-Jin 後金) in 1636 changed his dynasty's name to Qing 清. The reasons why he did so are not known, but probably included *wuxing* 五行 beliefs (see Box 10, chap. 50).

To distinguish between dynasties with the same name later generations qualified them by time (Former and Later Han) or by place (often the relative situation of the capital, as Western and Eastern Han); or by the names of their ruling houses (Cao Wei 曹魏), which was in any event a common way to refer to dynasties as in Zhu Ming 朱明 or Man Qing 滿清.

Dynasties were often grouped together in sets that were revised as time went by. There were, for example, two different sets of Six Dynasties (Liuchao 六朝, see note 6), not to speak of four definitions of the Liudai 六代 (Six Dynasties), the fourth of which is the Liuchao.

Note on the Dates of Dynasties

The dynastic tables can be misleading because they suggest that each period followed the preceding one in an unbroken succession. In reality, this was not the case. New powers and contenders for power often overlapped with established rulers. It was only later that historians constructed a legitimate succession of dynasties, each neatly following its predecessor (20.4). This pattern was then projected into the pre-dynastic past. Thus according to convention, the Zhou succeeded the Shang, but modern historians suggest that the two powers probably coexisted for many centuries, each ruling over different parts of China. To take a later example, the Former Han is usually listed as beginning in 206 BC. That was the year in which the last Qin ruler died and Liu Bang, the founder of the Han, was marginalized with a provincial command. He did not become emperor until 202 BC. Yet many historical works list the Han dynasty as beginning in 206 BC. To take another example, the tables show the Song dynasty ending in 1279 and the Yuan beginning in the same year. But history was not nearly as simple or as swift as that. Starting in 1211, the Mongol conquest of China took over half a century. During that time they ruled for about 40 years over much of North China. The conquest of South China began in 1257. Khubilai Khan proclaimed in 1271 that the new dynasty of Da Yuan 大元 should begin the next year, but it was not until 1276 that the Southern Song capital at Hangzhou fell, and only three years later, in 1279, that the last Song emperor was drowned in the sea off an island near present-day Hong Kong. Historical convention has the Yuan dynasty starting that year.

Note that the date for the ending of a failed dynasty was often prolonged after it had ceased to rule over most of China. To avoid confusion when this happened the failed dynasty was sometimes given a new name (for example, the Southern Ming, Nan Ming 南明, 1644–1661).

I

Basics

1

Language

Language is one of the most sensitive barometers of change in society. It is also the basic tool for doing historical research. So, the manual begins with a brief overview of the history of the Chinese language (1.1). This is followed by an examination of two of the main problems in reading Chinese sources: the many meanings of a single word (1.2) and the large number of characters to be learned (1.3).

The discussion of the first problem covers multiple meanings (1.2.1); ways of creating new words (1.2.2); cognates (1.2.3); the shift from monosyllabic to polysyllabic words (1.2.4); compounds (1.2.5); affixes (1.2.6); loan words (1.2.7); and the relationship between words, syllables and characters (1.2.8).

The discussion of the second problem starts with the number of characters to be mastered (1.3.1) and then turns to how students learned them in old China (1.3.2); how to dissect the characters (1.3.3) and how to punctuate a text (1.3.4).

Dictionaries are the subject of chapter 2. The specialized subjects of the origins and changing structure of the characters are discussed in Part II (chaps. 14–17).

Note that all works to do with the study of language and the characters (*xiaoxue* 小學) were placed in the Classics branch of the traditional fourfold bibliographical classification (*Sibu* 四部, on which see 9.3).

1.1 Historical Changes

The official belief in an uninterrupted legitimate succession from ancient times to the dynasty of the day and the unbroken use of the same script for the literary language reinforced the impression of an unchanging China. It is a false impression. A good demonstration is the history of the changes that took place in the language itself.[1]

Over the course of the last three millennia, the pronunciation, for example, changed radically: initial consonantal clusters and consonantal finals virtually disappeared from the standard language; there was a general move toward homophony and tones were introduced. Monosyllabic words, usually with many meanings, account for about two thirds of the words in Classical Chinese texts. In Modern Chinese, both spoken and written, they have been largely replaced by polysyllabic words, usually having a clearly defined meaning. Old Chinese was an isolating language with fixed word order. Modern Chinese retains the same basic word order but has gained greater precision using many varieties of affixes.

There is no generally agreed way of describing the different stages of the Chinese language during its recorded history. A widely accepted convention is to divide its development before Modern Chinese (*Xiandai Hanyu* 現代漢語) into three stages. The terms are all modern:

> *Shanggu Hanyu* 上古漢語 (Old Chinese)
> *Zhonggu Hanyu* 中古漢語 (Middle Chinese)
> *Jindai Hanyu* 近代漢語 (Mandarin)

[1] For a comprehensive survey of the history of the Chinese language covering phonology, script, morphology, syntax, lexicon and the dialects, see Jerry Norman, *Chinese*, CUP, 1988; 5th prnt., 1997. Note Christoph Harbsmeier, *Language and Logic in Traditional China*, SCC Vol. VII, Part 1, CUP, 1998. The main trends of modern research on the Chinese language are introduced in *Ershi shiji de Zhongguo yuyanxue* 二十世紀的中國語言學 (The study of the Chinese language in the twentieth century), Liu Jian 劉堅, ed. in chief, Beijing daxue, 1998.

"Old," "Middle" and "Mandarin" refer to stages of spoken Chinese as reconstructed largely on the basis of extant written texts. The language of those that have survived from the period of Old Chinese—principally the Confucian Classics—is referred to as Classical Chinese.[2]

From the Han onward, Literary Chinese (*wenyanwen* 文言文) modeled on Classical Chinese developed. As time went by, like Latin in medieval Europe, it was left behind by developments in the standard vernacular and in the dialects. But it retained its importance because it was the standard written language of the educated elite and was used by the court and government for all official business. Its mastery was a matter of survival and advancement for every scholar and official in the empire. Almost without exception, the primary sources that the historian of imperial China will be handling are written in it. *Wenyanwen* was by no means immobile; indeed, it was reformed and refined in numerous literary movements. It was also influenced by developments in the spoken language and in the vernacular literature. Its styles differed. Private correspondence, for example, was less formal than an examination essay or a memorial addressed to the emperor. It remained in use well into the twentieth century.

Throughout the manual Classical Chinese is used to refer to the written language of the sixth to second century BC. Literary Chinese (*wenyanwen*) refers to the elite written language used from the Han to the mid-twentieth century. There is some risk of confusion because the modern Chinese expression *Gudai Hanyu* 古代漢語 in its broadest sense embraces all forms of Chinese before the twentieth century. Even in the narrow sense of the written language of the elite, it makes no distinction between Classical and Literary Chinese. Another possible source of confusion is that the term *guwen* is sometimes used as

---

[2] Chou Fa-kao (Zhou Fagao 周法高, 1915–94), "Stages in the Development of the Chinese Language," in *Papers in Chinese Linguistics and Epigraphy*, HKCUP, 1986, 1-3. Zhou uses the terms archaic, medieval and modern instead of Old, Middle and Mandarin.

a synonym for *Gudai Hanyu*, yet *guwen* has at least three other distinct meanings (see chapter 16, note 5).[3] The pre-modern written vernacular is called *baihua* 白話 or *baihuawen* 白話文 (like *wenyanwen* it is a twentieth-century term).

Modern Standard Chinese (*Xiandai Hanyu* 現代漢語) is the general term for the Chinese language of today and is commonly used to refer to both the spoken language and its written forms. It grew out of Mandarin (*guanhua* 官話) and has been extended to the whole country. It is often called *Beifang hua* 北方話. In the 1920s and 1930s, *Guoyu* 國語 (National-Language) referred to the standard form of Modern Chinese. The term is still used in Taiwan. In Singapore and elsewhere in Southeast Asia it is called *Huayu* 華語. The deliberately created *lingua franca* of the People's Republic, *Putonghua* 普通話 (common speech), was based on *Guoyu*. It is the current, standard spoken form of *Xiandai Hanyu*. In addition, Modern Chinese also includes the six major, mutually unintelligible, regional dialects. Because of the continuous history of the Chinese language and thanks to the late survival of *wenyanwen*, Modern Standard Chinese retains a far greater portion of its ancient roots than any other world language (most clearly seen in its written form, *shumianyu* 書面語).

[3] An enormous number of different and often overlapping terms have been used to describe and analyze the Chinese language. No less than 11,000 covering philology, phonology, graphology and grammar from ancient times to 1990 are briefly defined in *Hanyu zhishi cidian* 漢語知識辭典 (Dictionary of Chinese language knowledge), Dong Shaoke 董紹克 and Yan Junjie 閻俊杰, eds. in chief, Jingguan, 1996.

For definitions of the special terms relating to Classical Chinese, consult: *Gu Hanyu zhishi xiangjie cidian* 古漢語知識詳解辭典 (Dictionary of detailed definitions of Classical Chinese knowledge), Ma Wenxi 馬文熙 and Zhang Guibi 張歸壁, eds. in chief, Zhonghua, 1996. It contains 3,600 entries divided between philology (700); phonology (270); semantics (660); grammar (930); rhetorical and stylistic devices in literature (400); literary genres (168); and bibliography (484), as well as brief biographies of 298 linguists and philologists, both ancient and modern. The entries scrupulously quote the often contradictory theories and views of the leading authorities. There are four-corner and *pinyin* indexes.

1.1.1   Shanggu Hanyu 上古漢語 *(Old Chinese)*

Historical linguists have tried to identify the pre-Shang constituents of Old Chinese and its relationships with other languages and language groups. The evidence comes from a variety of scattered data derived from archaeology, genetics, comparative linguistics, inscriptions and early texts. Some have even hypothesized that an early form of Tibeto-Burman was the language of the Yangshao culture, at least in the middle and upper reaches of the Yellow river; the language of the Shang was descended from the Dongyi 東夷 peoples in Shandong and to the South, and early Miao-Yao was spoken in the middle Yangzi. Awaiting further research and more evidence, such hypotheses must remain tentative.[4] It is a controversial field with tantalizing pointers, for example, most of the languages of Central Asia right across to Japan have since they first appeared been subject-object-verb, agglutinating and polysyllabic. Chinese, on the other hand, along with most of the languages of the Sino-Tibetan family (but not Tibetan itself), has been predominantly a subject-verb-object, isolating, and in its earliest written, and possibly also in its earliest spoken forms, mainly monosyllabic, language.

The language of the Shang and early Western Zhou is recognizably Chinese, but incompletely known because it has been preserved only in the divinatory formulae carved on the Shang and early Zhou oracle bones (the longest no more than 200 characters), on the slightly longer inscriptions on bronze (the longest no more than 500 characters), and in the earliest parts of the *Shangshu* 尚書 (*Documents*) and of the *Shijing* 詩經 (*Odes*). These are the concise records of the shaman, the archivist or the minstrel, each representing quite different uses of the language. With the possible exception of the oracle bone inscriptions, they were far removed from the spoken languages of

---

[4] Wu Anqi 吳安其, "Han-Zangyu tongyuan wenti yanjiu 漢藏語同源問題研究" (A study of questions of genetic affinity in Sino-Tibetan languages), *Minzu yuwen* 2: 18–25 (1996). On the Yangshao and other Neolithic cultures, see section 13.1.

their day. Some scholars include these early traces of Chinese in the definition of Classical Chinese. Others prefer to classify them as *Yuangu* 遠古 or *Taigu* 太古 *Hanyu* 漢語 (Chinese of remote antiquity, pre-classical or archaic Chinese, ca. 1200–600 BC).

The *Shijing* and the main works of Classical Chinese circulated by word of mouth for years, if not for centuries, before being written down. Even after they were recorded, the practice of memorization and chanting of texts was the norm until the advent of printing in the Song. Classical Chinese is therefore probably a rather special form of the language whose short words and brief sentences were designed for easy memorization, a style closer to ritual poetry than prose. Indeed, many of the works of the pre-Qin thinkers are notable for their brevity and most are rhymed in whole or in part. The longest entry in the *Chunqiu* 春秋 (*Spring and Autumn Annals*) is only 47 characters; the entire *Lunyu* 論語 consists of short sections with a combined total of only 15,883 characters. The *Thirteen Classics* altogether only contain 589,283 characters (Table 19, section 19.2). New works written in the Han were beginning to become much longer, more like prose than poetry. The *Shiji* 史記, for example, is almost as long as the Classics and 33 times longer than the *Lunyu*. One reason that it is so much longer is that it is closer to the spoken language of the day. This resulted in more polysyllabic words than are found in the pre-Qin texts. The difference in styles can be seen clearly in Sima Qian's reworking of earlier texts such as the *Shangshu* in his "Benji 本紀" chapters and the *Zuozhuan* and *Guoyu* 國語 (Discourses of the states) in his "Shijia 世家" chapters.[5]

---

[5] Zhu Minche 祝敏徹, "Cong *Shiji Hanshu Lunheng* kan Hanyu duo-yinci de goucifa 從史記, 漢書, 論衡看漢語多音詞的構詞法," *Hanyuxue luncong*, 8, Shangwu, 1981, 142–56; *Liang Han Hanyu yanjiu* 兩漢漢語研究 (Research on the Chinese language during the Former and Later Han), Cheng Xiangqing 程湘清, ed. in chief, Shandong jiaoyu, 1992; rpnt., 1994, 262–364.

The idea that the need to memorize many of the early texts influenced their form is a hypothesis. It and other views as to the nature of the language of the pre-Qin texts needs to be further tested, a task made easier by the discovery of excavated works that pre-date, and in some cases differ from, the orthodox transmitted versions most of which were only written down and edited during the Han.[6]

Even if the pre-Qin texts may be far removed from the spoken language of their day, the rhymes they contain can be used as an indicator of the phonology of Old Chinese. Indeed, the method used by Qing philologists and modern historical linguists has been to reconstruct the pronunciation of Old Chinese by working back from the sounds of Middle Chinese (for which rhyme books are available).[7] The task is a controversial one because there are no rhyme books for Old Chinese, only the odes in the *Shijing*. These were written over a 500-year period in the dialects of the Central Yellow River states that were not necessarily the direct ancestors of the southern dialects of the Middle Chinese rhyme books. Indeed, in the present state of knowledge it is not possible to give a complete and reliable reconstruction of the sounds or other features of Old Chinese. All that can be said with any certainty is that it was different

---

[6] For an analysis of the role of reported dialog and speech in pre-Qin historical works, see David Schaberg, "Foundations of Chinese Historiography: Literary Representation in *Zuozhuan* and *Guoyu*," Ph.D., Harvard University, 1996.

[7] Bernhard Karlgren (Gao Benhan 高本漢, 1889–1978) summed up his reconstructions of the sounds of Old Chinese (which he and some others refer to as Archaic Chinese) in *Grammata Serica Recensa*, *BMFEA*, 29: 1–332 (1957). He did so by working backwards from his reconstruction of "Ancient Chinese" (based on the *Qieyun* 切韵, 600 AD). For an account of his work, see S. Robert Ramsey, *The Languages of China*, PUP, 1987; rpnt., with corrections, 1989, 136–48.

Jerry Norman and South Coblin argue that the rhyme tables cannot be used as the key to unlocking the stages in the history of Chinese phonology, as they were by the Qing phonologists and later by Karlgren and Pulleyblank and others. See Norman and Coblin, "A New Approach to Chinese Historical Linguistics," *JAOS* 115.4: 576–84 (1995).

from its written form, Classical Chinese. It was probably more prosaic and used more polysyllabic words.

The *yayan* 雅言 (cultivated speech or received pronunciation) of the Spring and Autumn period was based on *Zhongguo-yu* 中國語, the dialect of the Eastern Zhou royal domain whose center was Luoyi 雒邑 (modern Luoyang). As the prestige pronunciation of the day, it served as a standard for interstate diplomacy, as a means of communication across dialect boundaries and as the correct pronunciation for reciting the Classics (*Lun-yu* 論語, vii.18). The *yayan* in the sense of standard speech was contrasted with the regional languages, *fangyan* 方言 (conventionally regarded as "dialects"), found in other parts of China. In the sense of cultivated speech, *yayan* was contrasted with *suyan* 俗言 (everyday speech).

By the end of the Spring and Autumn period, the Austro-Asiatic Yi 夷 of Shandong and the Huai valley had mostly been sinicized, as had also the other early languages spoken along the Yangzi River, in Wu 吳 and Yue 越 and by the Man 蠻 of Chu 楚, a process accelerated by the forced migrations of northern speakers to the South and Southwest.[8]

By the Han, only a scattering of montagnards would have spoken in the old indigenous languages whether in the North or in the South. The exceptions were the peoples in the Southwest, many of whose languages belonged to the Tibeto-Burman branch of the Sino-Tibetan family. Their sinification was to come later. In the rest of the South, the six major regional dialects of today gradually began to take on their distinctive forms as the result of the language of the settlers from different parts of the North merging with the various sinicized and semi-sinicized languages of the places in which they settled. By the end of the Song the pattern of today's southern dialects had been established.

---

[8] Populations moved in and out and within the China area (and what are now its neighboring countries) for tens of thousands of years during prehistoric times. Forced migrations may have begun in the Shang and Zhou but the earliest records only date from the fourth century BC.

In the larger dialect areas, the main cities set the model or standard form of the dialect (as does, for example, Guangzhou for Cantonese). Each dialect also had (and still has) many sub-dialects and brogues (*tuhua* 土話, *difanghua* 地方話), which often coexist alongside non-Han tongues, such as the Zhuang-Tai dialects in Guangdong.[9]

In the North, Chinese was influenced by the Turkic and Altaic languages of the Xianbei 鮮卑, Khitan, Jurchen, Mongol and Manchu conquerors, all of whom made their languages the official language (*guoyu* 國語) while at the same time making lesser or greater efforts to master the language of their subjects.[10] In the South the dialects were less influenced by these northern conquerors and in some cases retain to this day traces

[9] The earliest dialect geography was written by Yang Xiong 揚雄 (53 BC–AD 18), *Fangyan* 方言. In it he listed words in use in various cities which differed from those in *tongyu* 通語 (the commonly used or standard language). Arrangement is by subject category. See Paul M. Serruys, *The Chinese Dialects of Han Times According to Fang Yan*, UCP, 1959, and Coblin in *ECTBG*, 94–99; not a few of the words included by Yang as dialects were probably from non-Han languages, see Li Jingzhong 李敬忠, "Fangyan zhong de shaoshu minzu yuci shixi 方言中的少數民族語詞試析" (Tentative analysis of national minority words in *Fangyan*), *Minzu yuwen* 3: 64–68 (1987).

Zhou Zhenhe 周振鶴 and You Rujie 游汝杰, *Fangyan yu Zhongguo wenhua* 方言與中國文化 (Dialects and Chinese Culture), Shanghai renmin, 1986; 3rd prnt., 1991. For a general introduction to the Chinese language with special emphasis on the non-Han languages and on dialects, see Ramsey (1989). For the modern distribution of the dialects, see *Language Atlas of China*, S. A. Wurm, B. K. Tsou and D. Bradley, eds., HK: Longmans, Parts 1 and 2, 1987 and 1991.

[10] Mantaro Hashimoto, "Language Diffusion on the Asian Continent—Problems of Typological Diversity in Sino-Tibetan," *Computer Analyses of Asian and African Languages* 3 (1976), 49–97, and the same author's "The Altaicization of Northern Chinese," in *Contributions to Sino-Tibetan Studies*, Brill, 1986, 76–97; Jerry Norman, "Four Notes on Chinese-Altaic Linguistic Contents," *Tsing Hua Journal of Chinese Studies* 14: 243–47 (1982); A. Rygaloff, "A Possible Argument for Altaicization of Chinese," *Proceedings of the International Conference on Chinese Border Area Studies*, Taibei, 1985.

of Old Chinese brought to the South by settlers in the previous millennium.[11]

As the power of the central state waxed and waned, the influence of the language of the capital (*jingyu* 京語) rose or fell. In the Han, apart from being called *tongyu* 通語, it was also known as *changyu* 常語 or *fanyu* 凡語 and remained centered on Luoyang, a direct descendant of the *yayan* of the Zhou. Again in the Tang, the Song, the Ming and the Qing, a common vernacular and literary standard grew up based on the dialect of the capital which eventually formed Modern Chinese.

1.1.2   Zhonggu Hanyu 中古漢語 *(Middle Chinese)*

Zhonggu Hanyu broadly refers to the Chinese as reconstructed using the *Qieyun* 切韻, a rhyming dictionary completed in AD 601.[12] It covers the mainstream cultivated spoken language from the end of the Han to the end of the Tang. It has been further divided by some scholars into Early Middle Chinese (the cultivated spoken language of the *Nan-Bei Chao* as represented in the *Qieyun*) and Late Middle Chinese (the standard spoken language of the Tang probably based on Chang'an as represented by the *Yunjing* 韻經 and other rhyme tables in the same tradition). During these centuries, many lexical items took on grammatical functions as new particles proliferated and noun classifiers were introduced.

---

[11] Cantonese and Southern Min (Fujian) are the dialects considered closest to Old Chinese because of the retention of the finals 'p', 't', 'k' and 'm' which had begun to disappear from Mandarin already in the Song. They also retain more tones and still use many Classical words and characters (see 1.2.7 for some examples).

[12] The *Qieyun* also systematized the *fanqie* 反切 method of indicating pronunciation by giving two characters, the first showing the *shengmu* 聲母 (initial), the second, the *yunmu* 韻母 (final). For example, *dan: de, an, qie* 旦: 得安切. Previously, homophones or near-homophones had been used. *Fanqie* remained the standard method until the twentieth century. For the phonology of Middle Chinese and Mandarin, see Edwin G. Pulleyblank, *Lexicon of Reconstructed Pronunciation in Early Middle Chinese, Late Middle Chinese and Early Mandarin*, UBC Press, 1991.

The translation of more than 55 million characters of Buddhist scriptures provided a powerful stimulus for linguistic innovation and change (1.2.7). The desire to propagate the faith to the general public (not just to the educated) led to the choice of the spoken language. A huge new lexicon was created (comparable in size to the 12,000 words having German etymologies in the English language). The new words were mainly polysyllabic reflecting both the Sanskrit from which they were translated and long-term trends in the Chinese language. Buddhist literature broke the monopoly of *wenyanwen* on written Chinese. This helped prepare the way for the growth of a vernacular literature in the Song (34.3). The desire to produce as many texts as possible to gain merit was also a major stimulus leading to the invention of printing (18.4).

Along with many other aspects of Chinese higher culture, the Chinese writing system was adopted by Korea, Japan and Vietnam during this period. Classical pronunciation of the characters in these languages therefore provides important clues as to the sounds of Middle Chinese.

1.1.3   Jindai Hanyu 近代漢語 *(Mandarin)*

Jindai Hanyu 近代漢語 covers the cultivated spoken language from the end of the Tang to the mid-Qing. Some scholars subdivide it into Early (Song to Yuan), Middle (Ming to Qing) and Late (nineteenth to twentieth century) Mandarin. Everyday speech was called *suyu* 俗語 or *liyu* 俚語.[13]

Guanhua 官話 (Mandarin) was the *luinga franca* of officials. It had begun to develop in the Liao, Jin and Yuan and was based on the spoken Chinese of north China, gradually shifting from the Central Plains to Nanjing in the Ming and to Beijing

---

[13] Jiang Jicheng 蔣冀騁 and Wu Fuxiang 吳福祥, *Jindai Hanyu gangyao* 近代漢語綱要 (Essentials of Modern Chinese), Hunan jiaoyu, 1997; Jiang Shaoyu 蔣紹愚, *Jindai Hanyu yanjiu gaikuang* 近代漢語研究概況 (Outline of research on Modern Chinese), Beijing daxue, 1996, summarizes the primary sources and research (1930s to 1990) under phonology, grammar and lexicon.

at the end of the Qing. This *jingyu* 京語 of the later empire formed the basis of Modern Standard Chinese. It was able to do so as the result of the North's having set the standard for so many centuries and also as the result of huge migrations to the South during the Qing.[14] Moreover, from the eighteenth century, examination candidates from Guangdong and Fujian were required to use *guanhua* and efforts were made to teach them.

Baihuawen 白話文 is the modern term for the written form of the post-Han spoken language of which first traces appear in the popular literature and vernacular stories of the Tang. It reached its most developed form in novels such as the *Honglou meng* 紅樓夢 (*Dream of the Red Chamber*). It was normally based on the relatively educated spoken language of north China (the *Hongloumeng* is the best available record of eighteenth-century Beijing dialect) although some *baihua* fiction uses the spoken tongues of the lower Yangzi.

1.2 Words

1.2.1   Multiple Meanings

One of the main difficulties in reading both Classical and Literary Chinese is that individual characters typically have many different meanings. They do so because there were always more words than characters, especially in early China, and the written language was not nearly as standardized as it later became, so a single character was pressed into use for many different words. This is most clearly seen in the oracle-bone script, which uses, to take but one example, the original form of the character *shi* 史 for the words whose basic meanings were later differentiated with *shi* 事 (carry out an official duty), *shi* 史 (record official acts), *li* 吏 (the person who does an official duty), and *shi* 使 (send somebody on an official errand).

[14] James Lee and R. Bin Wong, "Population Movements in Qing China and their Linguistic Legacy," in *Languages and Dialects of China*, William S. Y. Wang, ed., *Journal of Chinese Linguistics*, Monograph series 3: 52–77 (1991).

Another difficulty is that the same word was often used for different parts of speech, often with a different meaning. Sometimes the pronunciation or tone was changed or a new character was made to differentiate the meanings (1.2.2), but often only the context can help indicate which meaning is the correct one. For example, *lou* 漏 as a verb means to drip (*dilou* 滴漏); as a noun, it means clepsydra (*louhu* 漏壺).

A third difficulty, shared with all other languages, is that most Chinese words changed their meanings as time went by. But unlike other ancient languages, because words in Classical Chinese typically had many meanings and continued in use for such a long time, they accumulated an unusually large number of meanings. Many became more general, a few became more specialized; some lost their pejorative sense, some gained one, and some took on altogether new meanings. Some radically different, some only slightly so. Not infrequently a word in *wenyanwen* had a different nuance than the same word in *baihuawen*. Words and terms in *wenyanwen* not only changed their meanings as the centuries went by, but many were re-used to create the vocabulary of Modern Chinese (1.2.7). Many mistakes are made by assuming that the meaning of a word in Classical Chinese is the same as in Modern Chinese.[15]

A fourth difficulty is a graphic one: for the first thousand years of the script, there was no commonly accepted standard to ensure that a given character was written for a given word and individual characters had many variant forms (16.4).

Given the emphasis in Chinese culture on examinations based on memorization of past models of moral and literary excellence, it is hardly surprising that the literary language accumulated vast resources of set phrases (*chengyu* 成語) and quotations (*diangu* 典故), often drawn from the Confucian Classics. Some of these phrases entered the spoken language, often in abbreviated form (many four-character phrases were shortened

---

[15] For introductions to lexicology, see Zhao Keqin 趙克勤, *Gudai Hanyu cihuixue* 古代漢語詞匯學 (The lexicology of Classical Chinese), Shangwu, 1994.

to two characters, which in time became standard disyllabic
compounds. This was made easier by the fact that *chengyu* are
often composed of two balanced disyllabic compounds). For
the student of Literary Chinese who has already a good command of individual characters, the main problems of understanding arise from identifying and decoding such compounds
and phrases whose full meaning is derived from literary allusions. Large comprehensive dictionaries such as the *Hanyu da
cidian* 漢語大辭典 contain explanations of *diangu* and *chengyu*.
Specialized reference works are also available for their elucidation and to trace their origins (2.4, items 12–14 and 2.5).

The names of institutions and titles are also a trap for the
unwary because they often continued in use long after the reality which they had originally described had changed. *Baixing*
百姓, for example, in the earliest classical texts meant "the clan
leaders." It was then extended to mean the "the senior officials." During the Warring States, it took on the sense of "the
ordinary people," as in modern *laobaixing* 老百姓. In post-Han
texts it is also sometimes used to mean "many sons." The
changes in the meaning of *Zhongguo* 中國 or *Hanzi* 漢子 in
later Chinese history are other good examples (Box 3 and 42.1).

Another problem is to be able to decide when two characters are still two words or have become a compound. Take the
example of *baixing* 百姓. To translate it as "the hundred
names" is a mistake. Not only because *bai* 百 is used as a figurative number (7.1.2) meaning "many", but also because it had
early become a compound whose meaning had changed radically in the classical period and was more than the separate
meanings of its two constituent root morphemes. There are no
rules: the process leading from two separate words to one compound was not uniform (1.2.5).

The challenge for the student of Chinese history is to recognize the changed meanings of words and phrases in different
periods in different genres and in some cases, in different dialects, and having recognized them, to explain them. To repeat
the point: students should never assume that because a word,

character or compound is familiar from a modern context that its meaning in an earlier period was the same.

1.2.2 Ways of Creating New Words

The lexicon of the Shang already contains much of the core vocabulary of Chinese. Judging from the limited evidence available in oracle-bone script, it was mainly monosyllabic and words tended to have single meanings (16.3). As society became more complex, new words were needed. As literature became more sophisticated, greater precision was required. During the Zhou many new words were created, including for abstract concepts and for grammatical relations. The new words were formed on the basis of old ones. Typically, single words were extended to include related meanings (1.2.3). These new meanings were often indicated with different pronunciations, different tones and alterations to the original character and eventually, sometimes, with new characters. For example, the basic meaning of *hui* 會 is "to get together." When it was also extended to mean "to bring numbers together" the pronunciation changed to *kuai* 會.

Changes in sound signaling a change in meaning were sometimes indicated by slightly altering the character, for example, when *xiao* 小 [Old Chinese: *siô*, small] took on the meaning "few," the pronunciation shifted to *sjiô* and the new character *shao* 少 was created. When *lao* 老 [*lu*, old] took the meaning of father, the pronunciation changed to *ku* and the character was altered to *kao* 考 (later borrowed for *kao* (examine) as in *kao-zheng* 考證). In a similar way antonyms were also developed from each other, for example, water and fire; or ancient and modern (*shui* 水 [*siwei*] and *huo* 火 [*huai*]; *gu* 古 [*ka*] and *jin* 今 [*kiam*]). The next stage, starting in the early Zhou, was the addition of a signific to differentiate the characters for the extended or new meanings of monosyllabic words (16.2).

Another way of differentiating the meanings of a word was by changing the tone. For example, *hao* 好 as an adjective is read in its original (third) tone (*benyin* 本音), but as a verb, in the fourth tone; *dao* 道 in the fourth tone means "road;" it was extended to mean "to guide" (later this meaning was differentiated by creating the new character *dao* 導, now pronounced in the third tone). Linguists refer to this as *sisheng bieyi* 四聲別義 (derivation by tone change). Sometimes the change in meaning (and in part of speech) is indicated by changes in the sound, including changes in the tone: *chang* 長 in the second tone means "long" and *zhang* 長 in the third tone means "to grow." As more is discovered about the phonology of Old Chinese, it may be possible to discern the morphological rules governing such changes.[16] Different readings for different meanings of a character were often indicated by commentators, but most have been dropped in modern editions.

Bound compounds (formed according to rhyme) have been common in Chinese since the earliest Zhou texts (1.2.4). They predate compounds formed according to grammar. After the Han, new types of compounding became increasingly common—either by combining existing words to create new ones, (1.2.5) or by derivation (mainly by adding prefixes and suffixes to existing monosyllabic words, see 1.2.6). Loan words from non-Chinese languages were another source, but less important than the other methods until the late Qing (1.2.7). During these centuries new words continued to be created by extending and changing the meanings of old ones and by importing dialect words into the language of the capital.

1.2.3   Cognates

One result of creating new words in the Zhou and Han by extending the meanings of existing ones was the creation of cognates or word families (*tong yuanci* 同源詞, the characters for which are called *tong yuanzi* 同源字).[17] Cognates must have

---

[16] Norman (1988), 84–5; Luo Zhengjian 羅正堅, *Siyi yinshen daolun* 詞義引申導論 (Introduction to the extended meanings of words), Nanjing daxue, 1996.

[17] See Wang Li 王力 (1900–86), *Tongyuan zidian* 同源字典 (Dictionary of cognate words), Zhonghua, 1982; 4th prnt., 1997. Two interesting works have since extended the scope of Wang's dictionary by exam-

Footnote continued on next page

similar meanings and sounds, but need not have the same form. To reconstruct word families it is essential to go back to the Old Chinese pronunciation. In the six examples below, the cognates in each set were derived from the root words (placed at the beginning). In many cases, as the meanings of the root words were extended they had significs added to help differentiate the new meanings. Thus, the root came frequently to serve as the *shengfu* 聲府 (phonetic indicator, see 1.3.3), while continuing to carry the original meaning. In other cases completely different characters were used for the cognates (see the *rou* 柔 set):

Bing 并 (combine): 餅 *bing* (pancake; water and flour combined), *pian* 駢 (double-horses harnessed together), *pian* 胼 (callous, i.e., double skin on hands and feet), *pin* 姘 (man and woman living together out of wedlock).

Fen 分 (divide): *ban* 半 (half), *pian* 片 (one part; half), *pan* 泮 (half), *pan* 胖 (half a piece of meat), *pan* 判 (chop wood in half), *bie* 別 (separate; divide), *bian* 辨 (distinguish; separate), *bian* 辯 (distinguish).

Rou 柔 (soft): *ruo* 弱 (weak), *ruan* 軟 (soft), *rou* 揉 (knead; make malleable), *rou* 鞣 (tanning and dressing leather).

Xia 瑕 (red): *xia* 霞 (red sky at sunrise or sunset), *xia* 蝦 (shrimp; turns bright pink when cooked).

Zeng 曾 (add): *zeng* 增 (increase), *zeng* 甑 (double cooking vessel), *zeng* 罾 (extra high fishing net), *zeng* 贈 (contribute; add to someone's wealth), *ceng* 層 (second story of a building).

Zhang 長 (stretch): *Zhang* 張 (stretch a bow), *zhang* 帳 (canopy), *zhang* 漲 (increase of water), *zhang* 脹 (distended stomach).

---

ining the phonological basis and the structure of the characters respectively: Qi Chongtian 齊沖天, *Shengyun yuyuan zidian* 聲韵語源字典 (Dictionary of etymologies based on initials and rhymes), Qongqing, 1997; Wang Yunzhi 王蘊智, *Yin-Zhou guwen tongyuan fenhua xianxiang tansuo* 殷周古文同源分化現象探索 (Investigation of the phenomenon of the division of cognate characters in Yin-Zhou scripts), Jilin renmin, 1996. Liu Junjie 劉鈞杰, *Tongyuan zidian zaibu* 同源字典再補 (More additions to the *Tongyuan zidian*), Yuwen, 1998, adds 500 groups of cognates.

Not all characters sharing the same phonetic are *tong yuanzi*, nor are all synonyms necessarily derived from the same root. The various classifications of characters and their relationship with *tong yuanzi* are specialized subjects dealt with in Part II. Briefly, variant characters (*yitizi* 異體字, 16.4.1), correct and vulgar characters (*zhengsuzi* 正俗字, 16.4.3) and alternative characters (*tongjiazi* 通假字, 16.4.4), are not *tongyuanzi* because they are all different ways of writing the same character; *gujinzi* 古今字 (16.4.2), on the other hand, usually are *tongyuanzi*. Substituting one member of a word family for another happened more often than using alternative characters for which they are often mistaken.

1.2.4 Polysyllabic Words in Clasical Chinese

The use of polysyllabic words was quite advanced in Classical Chinese, up to 25–30 percent of whose lexicon is composed of them (most were disyllabic compounds; trisyllables are only occasionally found in nouns and adjectives, never in verbs). The earliest polysyllables were onomatopoeic reduplicates (e.g., *jiangjiang* 將將 for the sound of a carriage) or simple repetitions (*mama* 媽媽). Others include alliterative semi-reduplicates such as *pipa* 琵琶 (lute) or *linglong* 玲瓏 (nimble); rhyming ones, such as *paihuai* 徘佪 (waver), or those which are neither alliterative nor rhyming, such as *furong* 芙蓉 (cottonrose hibiscus). A number of this type of word are the names of plants, fruits, animals, birds, fish or insects and other things imported or absorbed into the areas where Old Chinese developed (including toponyms). They may be loans from the languages of non-Han tribes and peoples. With the exception of simple repetitions, all of the reduplicates and semi-reduplicates have one thing in common: their meaning cannot be deduced from the individual words. They are therefore termed bound compounds (*lianmianzi* 聯綿字; for a special dictionary, see 2.4). They were often written with various characters because these were used for their sounds, not their meanings. *Lianmian* (formed according to rhyme) preceded compounds (formed according to grammar). Another completely different category of disyllabic words was composed of proper names or official titles.

Disyllabic words occur much less frequently than monosyllabic words in Classical Chinese (which as a result score 80–90 percent in word frequency counts of early works such as the *Shijing* or the *Mengzi*).[18] In Middle Chinese, the number and frequency of disyllabic words increased greatly.

Some scholars argue that Old Chinese was close to the written language of the day, Classical Chinese, and therefore, like it, mainly monosyllabic. Further, the demand for new words in Old Chinese could only have been met with monosyllabic words if there had been a sufficiently large number of distinct syllables to cope with the problem of ambiguity caused by the new words having the same pronunciation as existing ones. In practice, according to this view, because the number of sounds was already declining in Old Chinese as the result of phonological attrition (*yuyin jianhua* 語音簡化), the only way to avoid ambiguity was to create polysyllabic words. Phonological attrition is a process found in all languages but which may have been accelerated in the case of Chinese because the standard language was spoken by more and more people as a second "dialect," all of whose distinctions they may not have found easy to master. Moreover, these speakers were soon to include northern conquerors for whom standard Chinese was a second language. Their own languages were polysyllabic. This too may have increased the weight of polysyllabic words in Chinese. The South also came under polysyllabic influence in these centuries through the creation of a huge new vocabulary of Buddhism.

[18] The *Mengzi* contains 713 polysyllabic compounds (of which 200 were proper names or titles) out of a total of 2,278 words, so 78 percent of its lexicon is monosyllabic. Many of the monosyllabic words occur more than 500 times while few of the disyllabic words occur more than 10 times. See "Xian-Qin shuangyinci yanjiu 先秦雙音詞研究" (Research on polysyllabic words in the Pre-Qin) in *Xian-Qin Hanyu yanjiu* 先秦漢語研究 (Research on the Chinese language in the Pre-Qin period), Cheng Xiangqing 程湘清, ed., Shandong jiaoyu, 1992; rpnt., 1994, 45–113.

Many disyllabic words also found their way into *wenyan-wen*. The lexicon of Modern Chinese is overwhelmingly disyllabic. Yet, as with nearly all other languages, including English and even German, most of the most frequently used words remain monosyllabic.[19]

1.2.5   Compounds

In the most common type of compound (which was already beginning to make an appearance in Classical Chinese), the two constituent words had equal weight and were usually synonyms or near synonyms, such as *daolu* 道路 (avenue + road = highway). Not infrequently, the two synonyms were also cognates (e.g., *rouruo* 柔弱 "weak" or *shaoxiao* 少小 "young"). Others were antonyms, e.g., *daxiao* 大小 (big + small = size); another common type was when the first word modified the second, as in *daji* 大計 (big + plan = strategy); *tiaozao* 跳蚤 (jump + flea = flea), or the second modified the first, as in *shuoming* 說明 (speak + clear = explain). Many of the compounds at first had more abstract meanings than their constituent parts (e.g., *pengyou* 朋友, *guojia* 國家). Synonym compounds, may have arisen as a means of avoiding ambiguity by identifying which word a speaker was referring to. For example, in order to avoid confusing *chu* 初 with another word having the same pronunciation, the speaker might have said (as did Xu Shen 許慎 in the *Shuowen jiezi* 說文解字), *chu shi ye* 初始也 (start is begin).[20] The two words gradually became linked to

---

[19] Of the 3,000 most commonly used words today, 1,337 are monosyllabic. Of the remaining 1,663 polysyllabic words, 724 contain characters from the monosyllabic list. The *Hanyu da cidian* 漢語大辭典 contains a total of 369,000 words from all periods of the language. Of these 94% are polysyllabic (and 80% of these are disyllabic). Only six percent are monosyllabic.

[20] The *Shuowen* was completed in AD 100 (2.2.1 and 16.2). Xu also defines many pairs of words in terms of each other: *sheng, yin ye* 聲,音也 and under the entry *yin* 音: *yin, sheng ye* 音, 聲也 probably indicating that whatever differences there may once have been between the two words they had been lost by his day. Other words defined by a synonym

Footnote continued on next page

form the compound *chushi* 初始. Likewise, a speaker would have avoided confusing *zao* 蚤 (flea) with other words having the same pronunciation (and for which 蚤 had been pressed into service to represent), by saying something along the lines of "*tiaozao zhi zao ye* 跳蚤之蚤也" (flea as in jumping flea). Eventually it was easier just to use the compound *tiaozao* for flea (this is sometimes called the clear identification of meaning theory of the origin of disyllabic words, *mingque biaoyi shuo* 明確表義説). Early dictionaries and glosses on the Classics in the Wei, Jin and *Nan-Bei Chao* used the same method. Since these works were intensively studied or even committed to memory by the wordsmiths (the literati), the definitions themselves may often have been the source of new disyllabic words or increased their currency.[21]

In Classical Chinese, disyllabic compounds usually had only one meaning and their constituent syllables were rather loosely connected, for example, *renmin* 人民 [A-B] could also be written *minren* 民人 [B-A] and both *ren* 人 and *min* 民 could represent independent words. In some cases, the reverse order of the syllables served to indicate different parts of speech, as in *yanyu* 言語 (speak, a verb) and *yuyan* 語言 (language, a noun). As time went by, the link between the words in a compound became stronger and their order irreversible. Today there are a still a number of A-B, B-A compounds. Usually the B-A alternative is less used (e.g., *zhishuang* 直爽 and *shuangzhi* 爽直, candid). Occasionally, a reverse order has been retained in a dialect, as in *huanxi* 歡喜 (to like) in the Wu dialect as opposed to the standard *xihuan* 喜歡.

---

or chain of near synonyms often emerge as compounds if they had not already done so.

[21] For example, *xing wei xingxiang* 形爲形象, gloss by Guo Pu 郭璞 (276–324) on *Erya*, II.1. Xu De'an 徐德庵 has a list of 839 examples of such disyllabic glosses by Guo on monosyllabic words in the *Erya* and in the *Fangyan* 方言 in his *Gudai Hanwen lunwenji* 古代漢文論文集, Ba-Shu, 1989, 225–74.

1.2.6   Affixes

Affixation became increasingly common from Middle Chinese onward. It was done by adding either prefixes (*a* 阿, *lao* 老) or suffixes (*tou* 頭, *zi* 子, *shi* 師, *jia* 家, *bian* 邊, *mian* 面) to a word. Many of these affixes were meaningless (e.g., *zi* 子 in *beizi* 杯子, *yizi* 椅子, *wenzi* 蚊子). They functioned to create a more balanced rhythm (and possibly to compensate for some lost feature such as a final). Being unstressed they enabled an alternation of stressed and unstressed syllables which are easier to speak than a string of stressed ones. They also functioned to differentiate the meanings of homonyms (for example, to distinguish *yi* 椅 from *yi* 衣 you said, *yizi* 椅子). There are many such affixes. The *Hanyu da cidian* lists 1,200 compounds ending in *zi* 子 (and *zi* is only the most common). Another large class of disyllabic words was formed using grammatical affixes, such as *liao* 了 (*laile* 來了), *li* 里 (*jiali* 家里) or *qu* 去 (*zouqu* 走去).

1.2.7   Loan Words

The third important source of new words were loans from other languages. The main types were *jieci* 借詞 (based on a transcription of the sound, *yinyi* 音譯, what could be termed "aliens"); *yici* 譯詞 (based on a translation of the meaning, *yiyi* 意譯); or hybrids, a mixture of both types (*banyin banyi* 半音半意). Over time, as an "alien" moved from the dialect of first transcription to general use, it often made the transition from the first to the second type (from "alien" to "denizen") and in doing so moved from the demotic to the literary language. The reason is that people found it easier to recognize and to pronounce a new word based on two familiar *wenyan* characters than a jumble of characters not necessarily even representing the foreign sounds because of dialect differences. Thus, for example, in the early twentieth century, *linggan* 靈感 (inspiration) quickly replaced its earlier transcription, *yanshipilichun* 烟士披里純 and *kexue* 科學 (science) prevailed over the earlier transcription *sai'ensi* 賽恩斯. In the course of time most loan words were gradually sinicized in this or in other ways. Today, given the prestige of Cantonese, the dialect word sometimes prevails over the translated term, e.g., *digxi* 的士 (taxi) over *chuzu qiche* 出租汽車, even though *digxi* in *putonghua* (*dishi* or *di* for short) gives no indication of the original sound. On Chinese loan words, see the refererences cited in section 2.6, item 5. Note that even with those words which remained transcriptions, some margin was possible in the choice of characters, allowing not only an approximation of the sound but also conveying a particular meaning. This can be seen in the flattering characters chosen for the transcriptions of the western powers in the nineteenth century (e.g., Meiguo 美國) as compared to the graphic pejoratives selected for aborigines and enemy peoples (40.2 and 41.2).

At the formative period of Chinese in prehistoric times, a huge amount of the vocabulary probably came from non-Huaxia tribes.[22] There are glimpses of foreign loans even in some of the basic vocabulary. The earliest forms of *jiang* 江 (river) and *hu* 虎 (tiger) are possibly derived from Austroasiatic; *he* 河 (river) from Altaic; and *xiang* 象 (elephant) from one of the early Southeast Asian languages. As pointed out in subsection 1.2.4, some of the early bound reduplicates may also have been loans. It is not easy to discern such pre-Qin loans because of the remoteness of the time and because they were assigned Chinese characters whose pronunciation has changed and whose phonetic origin has long since been forgotten.[23]

---

[22] Under the empire, most loan words were from non-Han languages spoken outside China; few were from the non-Han languages in the China area except proper names. For some examples of exceptions, see, D. Strecker and A. Haudricourt, "Hmong-Mien (Miao-Yao) Loans in Chinese," *TP* LXXVII 4-5: (1991); 4.1 on non-Han toponyms; 40.2 on the transcription of the ethnonyms of non-Han peoples in China into Chinese; and 36.2 for some examples of the dishes of non-Han peoples absorbed into the Han cuisine.

[23] Norman, 1988, 6–22; *The Ancestry of the Chinese Language*, William S. Y. Wang, ed., *Journal of Chinese Linguistics*, Monograph series 8 (1995), especially Edwin G. Pulleyblank, "The Historical and Prehistorical Relationships of Chinese," and the same author's "Zou and Lu and the Sinification of Shandong," in *Chinese, Language, Thought and Culture: Nivison*

Footnote continued on next page

The first easily identifiable wave of loan words date from
the Former Han dynasty, during which new goods and the new
words for them were imported from the Xiongnu and from
Western Asia. They are easily identifiable, not only because
many were listed, but also because they were formed in a similar way. Typically they were disyllabic transcriptions of the
sounds, e.g., *luotuo* 橐駝 (camel; standardized and hence sinicized in the Tang by writing it in the dictionaries with the appropriate signific (*ma* 馬) to form *luotuo* 駱駝); *musu* 目宿
(alfalfa; later standardized as *muxu* 苜蓿); *putao* 蒲陶 (grape;
later standardized as 葡萄). Another common way to make a
new word for a new product was to form a disyllabic compound consisting of the current word for barbarian (at this
time, *hu* 胡) tacked on to an existing Chinese word, e.g., *gua* 瓜
(generic for gourds), to form *hugua* 胡瓜 (cucumber). Centuries
later such compounds were often sinicized by replacing the *hu*
with a descriptive (the *hugua* 胡瓜 became a *huanggua* 黃瓜).

Sanskrit was the next major source of loans, not only for
things but also for ideas, mainly conveyed during the process of
translating the Buddhist scriptures between the Later Han and
the Tang.[24] They were in a rhythmic, polysyllabic form of Sanskrit intended for easy memorization. The translators emulated
the originals. Transcriptions circulated for centuries in a profu-
sion of phonetic approximations. *Futu* 浮屠 (the earliest Chi-

---

and his Critics, Philip J. Ivanhoe, ed., Open Court, 1996, 39–57; for the
possible connections of Chinese with Indo-European via the Tarim Basin, see 13.1, note 4.

[24] See Liang Xiaohong 梁曉虹, *Fojiao ciyu de gouzao yu Hanyu cihui
de fazhan* 佛教詞語的構造與漢語詞匯的發展 (The structure of Buddhist
words and the development of Chinese vocabulary), Beijing yuyan xueyuan, 1994; Zhu Qingzhi 朱慶之, *Fodian yu zhonggu Hanyu cihui yanjiu*
佛典與中古漢語詞匯研究 (Researches on the Buddhist Canon and the
vocabulary of Middle Chinese), Wenjin, 1992; rpnt., 1996; Victor H.
Mair, "Buddhism and the Rise of the Written Vernacular in East Asia:
the Making of National Languages," *JAS* 53.3; 707–51 (1994); *Xiyu fanyishi* 西域翻譯史 (History of translation in the Western Regions), Rez-
hake Maitiniyazi 熱扎克買提擬牙孜, ed. in chief, Xinjiang daxue, 1997.

nese loan for Buddha) was also written as *fotu* 佛圖, *futu* 浮圖 or *fotu* 佛屠. Eventually, *fotuo* 佛陀 emerged during the early Tang as the standard. Soon it was abbreviated as *fo* 佛 and then coupled with existing Chinese monosyllabic words to form dozens of new disyllabic compounds for Buddhist concepts such as *fofa* 佛法 (Buddha dharma), *fojiao* 佛教 (Buddhism), *fojing* 佛經 (sutra), *fosi* 佛寺 (Buddhist temple), and so forth; all of which are still in common use. Such words are readily identifiable as originally part-Sanskrit imports. Other Sanskrit loans were not transcribed, but translated using different combinations of sound and meaning as well as affixes, for example, *huashi* 畫師 (from *citara-kara*, painter). Many thousands of new words were created using existing Chinese words to invent new compounds, for example:

fangbian 方便 (*upâya* "skillful methods;" modern "convenient")
pingdeng 平等 (*upeksâ* "space and time have the same form;" modern "equal")
shiji 實際 (*koti*; *tathatâ* "the frontier of consciousness;" modern "real")
shijie 世界 (*loka-dhâtu* "time and space," replaces the old Chinese word *tianxia* 天下; modern "world")
zhongzi 種子 (*bîja* "the cause of things;" modern "seed")
guoqu 過去, *xianzai* 現在 and *weilai* 未來 ("past," "present" and "future")

Words like these have become so much part of the general language (often with extended meanings) that very few people have any idea of their non-Chinese origin.[25]

A thousand years went by before the next major wave of foreign loan words. It reached a high point at the end of the Qing and continues to this day. It started with the arrival of the Westerners in south China in the Ming. *Fan* 番 was often used

---

[25] Zhu Qingzhi (1996) lists 248 examples of Chinese words that began as loans from Sanskrit in the *Zhongbenqi jing* 中本起經 (Madhyametyukta-sutra, a life of Sakyamuni) of which only 128 are found in the *Hanyu da cidian* 漢語大詞典 and of these 128, 105 are from later, non-Buddhist sources. The translation of *Zhongbenqi jing* was made in AD 207. See Zhu (1996), 57–102.

to indicate foreign instead of *hu* 胡 (as in *fangua* 番瓜, pumpkin and *fanqie* 番茄, tomato). In the nineteenth century, the meaning of *xi* 西 was extended to mean "western" in general (previously it had meant "coming from the Western Regions," i.e., Central Asia). *Yang* 洋 served the same purpose. Both *yang* and *xi* 西 were typical of Shanghai coinages. As in previous periods, alien loan words became denizens, in this case by changing the prefixes for a descriptive with no sense of foreign. But the dialect into which they had been first introduced sometimes retained the original transcriptions (e.g., Cantonese *fanjian* 番梘 for soap instead of *feizao* 肥皂; see 35.2 for many more examples). There are even a few examples of reverse imports of words with *fan* into English: fangwei/fankwae (*fangui*) 蕃鬼 (foreigner) or fantan 蕃攤 (a card game).

The missionaries exerted a considerable influence in creating loan words. They would translate the text into spoken Chinese explaining it as they did so to a Chinese collaborator, who would then write down his understanding in *wenyanwen*. Some of the neologisms thus invented, even at the first arrival of the missionaries in the early seventeenth century, are still in use today—for example, the translations of geometrical terms such as "triangle" (*sanjiaoxing* 三角形) by Matteo Ricci (1552–1610) and Xu Guangqi 徐光啓 (1562–1633) in their Chinese version of Euclid's *Elements*. It was also Ricci and his Chinese collaborators who invented the translations for geographical terms such as Atlantic (Da Xiyang 大西洋), Mediterranean (Dizhonghai 地中海), North and South Pole 南北極, and equator (*chidao* 赤道). In the nineteenth century, the missionaries translated many more scientific and medical texts into Chinese using neologisms like *luosiding* 螺絲釘 (screw); *gongsi* 公司 (company) or calques such as *tielu* 鐵路 (railroad, from Fr. *chemin de fer*). Popular works by Chinese authors explaining one or other aspect of the West, such as the *Haiguo tuzhi* 海國圖志, were often based on these early translations thus giving them a wider circulation both in China and Japan (33.7.1 and 33.7.3).

Chinese scientific translators working alone or with the missionary educators or in the College of Interpreters, Tongwen guan 同文館, 1862–1902) or at the Jiangnan Arsenal (Jiangnan jiqi zhizao ju 江南機器制造局) also invented many words. Xu Shou 徐壽 (1818–84) was responsible, for example, for the characters for the chemical elements and Li Shanlan 李善蘭 (1810–82), coined hundreds of terms, including *daishuxue* 代數 學 (algebra) and *weifen* 微分 (differential). These were quickly adopted in Japan. Neologisms were also drawn from a number of early English-Chinese dictionaries, today completely forgotten, e.g., Wilhelm Lobschied, *Yinghua zidian* 英華字典, 1866– 69. Such works were used to compile English-Japanese dictionaries. These were then used as a source of neologisms for scientific and other new words in Japan.

Typically, in both China and in Japan, different versions of a loan word circulated for several decades before a winner emerged. In the case of the rival terms for mathematics (*suanxue* 算學 and *shuxue* 數學), the two were in use for a century before a national conference in China in 1938 decided by a narrow margin to settle for *shuxue*. *Kuangwu* 礦物 (minerals) was coined in 1853, but it only replaced *jinshi* 金石 (also used at this time for minerals) in 1902. These examples show that the establishment of a loan word was in two main stages: first, the coining or transcription of the new word; second, its gaining acceptance as the standard term for the new product or concept.

In many thousands of cases, those words that emerged as standard for new scientific, legal and other terms in Japan were then imported into China at the beginning of the twentieth century, where there too they became the standard replacing earlier translations or transcriptions. The reason that the Chinese readily accepted these loans was that they were "denizens" rather than "aliens." No doubt, too, the boom in China for things Japanese after the Japanese victory over Russia in 1905 and the resultant sense that Japan had successfully mastered western learning (*xixue* 西學) also played their part. Some of the loans were well established Japanese words, for example, *baai* 場合 (*changhe*) for occasion; or had just been created using old Chinese words such as *zu* 足 (foot) to form calques like *zu-qiu* 足球 (football); or were old phrases with a new meaning, for example *kagaku* 科學 (*kexue*) for science (original meaning in *wenyanwen*: "study for the official examinations") or *keizai* 經濟 (*jingji*) for economy (original meaning: "governing and assisting the people"). Many were taken from the Japanese versions of Chinese-English dictionaries, where they had first appeared in their modern sense, e.g., *guanxi* 關係 (relation, now used in the sense of "special connections"), *xingwei* 行爲 (action), *liyi* 利益 (profit), *lixi* 利息 (interest), *falü* 法律 (law). Hundreds of others were affix compounds, such as *yan* 炎 (*wei-yan* 胃炎, gastri̲t̲i̲s̲); *zhuyi* 主義 (*shehuizhuyi* 社會主義, social-i̲s̲m̲); *hua* 化 (*xiandaihua* 現代化, moderni̲z̲a̲t̲i̲o̲n̲). Only occasionally did Japanese supply aliens, such as the curious Chinese word *wasi* 瓦斯 for "gas" (from the Japanese pronunciation of *wa* as *ga*). European languages, chiefly English, on the other hand, provided large numbers of such loans.[26]

In a passage that captures the haphazard way in which new words were coined, the great educationist and popularizer of the West Fukuzawa Yukichi 福澤諭吉 (1835–1901), explains how he found the new word for steam: "Up to this time [ca. 1860], the English word 'steam' had been translated by *zhenqi* 蒸氣. But I thought, is it possible to shorten this to one character? So, I got out the *Kangxi zidian* and glanced over the characters with fire and water significs. There I came across the character *qi* 汽 with the annotation, 'the vapor of water.' I thought this was not bad, so, for the first time I used it [in *Seiyô jijô* 西洋事情, 1866]." Actually, *qiche* 汽車 had already appeared in China in 1855 and in Japan in 1864. But given the popularity of his works, Fukuzawa may have been right in claiming that he was the one who ensured that it became the standard in Japan (replacing the earlier loans, *kasha* 火車 and *karinsha* 火輪車).

---

[26] Masini (1993) and Liu (1995) have exellent appendixes with many examples of the different categories of missionary and Japanese loans. See also Gunn (1991). Full references to these works are given at 2.6, *Loan words*.

The picture is often more complicated than is sometimes presented in dictionaries and textbooks. Words flew backwards and forwards between China and Japan and the process by which, and at what time, one or other transcription or translation became the standard is often not clear. Not surprisingly, in many cases, the Chinese and Japanese eventually chose different neologisms, of which the words for train and automobile are but two of many examples (*huoche* 火車 and *qiche* 汽車, respectively in Chinese as opposed to *kisha* 汽車 and *jidôsha* 自動車 in Japanese).

Once a standard emerged, often assisted by national scientific associations, the variants gradually disappeared, although not infrequently in China some have been retained to this day in one or other of the southern dialects.

Throughout Chinese history large numbers of loan words fell out of use after the influence of the people who had introduced them declined. This was the fate of many Xiongnu, Xianbei, Khitan, Jurchen, Mongolian, Manchu and Russian loans. Finally, because translation of the meaning rather than transcription of the sound was the preferred form for loans, with the passage of time their foreign origin was often forgotten. One way of spotting a loan from earlier times (especially a proper name) is if it has an unusual pronunciation. For example, the kingdom of Kucha (618–732) is pronounced Qiuci 龜茲, not Guici. It is clearly a loan.

1.2.8 Words, Syllables and Characters

Languages were in use long before scripts were invented to record them. As with the other ancient writing systems, the Chinese script was used to record words or parts of words, not directly things or ideas: that is to say, even though many of the earliest characters were derived from symbols or drawings of things, they were neither pictographs nor ideographs, but logographs. This was pithily expressed in the late Warring States: "Writing cannot encompass all words, words cannot encompass all ideas" ("Shu bujin yan, yan bujin yi 書不盡言，言不盡意,"

Yijing 易經, i.12). Some of the definitions of the characters underlying these distinctions are given in Box 1.

Almost without exception classical philologists after the
Han called "words" characters (*zi* 字), a usage first recorded in
the *Shiji*. They did so because they were analyzing the literary
language in which most words were single morphemes represented by single characters (*ci* 詞, the modern word for "word"
was used for "grammatical particle", *xuci* 虛詞, empty word).
Characters are of course not the same as words. In a polysyllabic word they stand for syllables, not for the word; the same
character was not infrequently used for two quite different
words and likewise two or more characters were on different
occasions written for the same word.

Box 1: The Definition of Chinese Characters

There is no agreement on how to define Chinese characters. Some
stress their meaning, some their sound, some both. Some emphasize
the change from single-morpheme words in Classical Chinese to disyllabic words (*shuangyinci* 雙音詞) in Modern Chinese. All are
agreed that characters can be analyzed in terms of three essential
elements: form, meaning and sound. The main definitions follow:

Biaoyi wenzi 表義文字 (pictographic or ideographic writing).
Biaoyin wenzi 表音文字 (phonetic writing).
Yiyin biaoci he yinyi biaoci 意音表詞和音義表詞 (picto-phonetic
and phonetic-picto word writing).
Yanci wenzi 言詞文字 (logographic writing) in Classical Chinese.
Yusu wenzi 語素文字 (morphemic writing) in Modern Chinese.

The variety of the definitions is no doubt explained by the difficulty
of applying a single definition to a writing system which went
through major changes in its structure and in its relation with the
spoken language in the course of three millennia.

1.3   On Studying Chinese Characters

1.3.1   The Number of Characters

At first sight the most formidable hurdle in studying written Chinese, including Classical Chinese, is the large number of characters to be mastered. It has been on the rise since the second millennium BC. Fortunately, there were far fewer characters in general use at any one time than the figures in Table 1 suggest.

An unchanging core of no more than a few hundred basic characters have remained the most frequently used since the Shang dynasty to the present day. They account for up to 70 percent of all characters employed at any given time. Another 1,000 to 2,000 characters were in the frequently used category in any particular period, accounting for 30 percent and more of the total. Finally, a large number of characters only rarely make an appearance. They account for no more than five percent of all characters in use in a particular period. The remainder formed a growing pool of graphic variants (*yitizi* 異體字; 16.4.1) and dead characters (*sizi* 死字) long since discarded except in successive dictionaries or rhyme books, each of which not only added new characters but also cumulated the totals of its predecessors.

Table 1: The Number of Characters

1000 BC	4,500	*jiaguwen* 甲骨文 (15.3)
AD 100	9,353	*Shuowen* 說文 (2.2.1 and 16.2)
1066	31,319	*Leipian* 類篇[27]
1716	47,035	*Kangxi zidian* 康熙字典 (2.2.1)
1990	54,678	*Hanyu da zidian* 漢語大字典 (2.3)
1994	85,568	*Zhonghua zihai* 中華字海[28]

[27] The *Leipian* is a dictionary containing many characters newly coined in the Tang and Song. Final editing was done by Sima Guang 司馬光 (1019–86).

[28] *Zhonghua zihai*, Zhonghua, 1994. The large increase in characters in this dictionary is accounted for by the inclusion not only of all charac-

Footnote continued on next page

To get a sense of proportion, the *Lunyu* has only 1,382 different characters in a total of 15,883. Only about 10 percent of the different characters (not counting the 88 particles) appear more than 10 times, but they occur so frequently that they account for 70 percent of the total characters. Sixty-seven percent of the characters appear less than five times, but they account for only 10 percent of the total characters. Of the most common characters in the *Lunyu*, about 100 have remained among the most frequently used to this day, retaining the same forms and basic meanings (but not pronunciation). In addition, even some of the characters which appear infrequently in the *Lunyu* have in the meantime joined the core of most frequently used characters. There are 6,544 different characters in the *Thirteen Classics* (including 1,500 proper names).

A traditional scholar would have had an active knowledge (the ability to write) at least 6,000 or 7,000 characters.[29] His passive knowledge (the ability to read) on the other hand would have covered many more, because before the advent of Qing philology and modern scholarship, a considerable proportion of his reading ability depended on recognizing borrowed characters, graphic variants and changed meanings. The 6,000 or 7,000 characters could of course be arranged in different combinations to form tens of thousands of different words and phrases.[30]

---

ters listed in previous dictionaries, but also of variants found in Buddhist and Daoist texts and new epigraphic sources, such as vulgar and dialect characters as well as characters unique to Hong Kong, Taiwan, Singapore, Korea and Japan.

[29] In the Han dynasty, a knowledge of 9,000 characters was required as a condition to qualify as a scribe (*shi* 史).

[30] Since 1988, there has been an official listing of 3,500 frequently used characters of which primary school children have to learn 2,535 by the time they graduate at age 12 *sui*, the remaining 1,000 are acquired at junior high school along with a further 2,000 or so to bring the total to 5,000–6,000. Adult literacy is defined as having a knowledge of at least 3,000 characters (of which 45% are monosyllabic words and 44% are used in the most common 1,663 compounds).

Footnote continued on next page

1.3.2   Traditional Ways of Studying the Characters

Fu yu dushu bi xian shizi, yu shizi bi xian chaxing 夫欲讀書必先識字欲識字必先察形 (All those who wish to read books, must first be able to recognize characters; and to recognize characters, you must first scrutinize their forms), Gu Aiji 顧藹吉, in *Preface* to *Libian* 隸辨 (Analysis of chancery script), 1718.

Nowadays children in China begin to study the characters by learning to spell their sounds using an alphabetic writing system (*pinyin wenzi* 拼音文字). In the old days there was no such system, so they began by memorizing the characters for everyday words often using the equivalent of "flash cards" (individual characters on separate bits of paper or wood) with a homonym character, a picture or both on the back.[31] They usually began with pictographic characters such as those for sun and moon. They also used lists of characters in rhyming doggerel arranged by categories such as heaven and earth, trees and flowers, fruits and nuts, animals and birds, pots and pans, farm tools, place-names and official titles and much else besides. The first reference to such lists of miscellaneous characters (*zazi* 雜字) is in the Song. Normally they either circulated separately or were included in almanacs and encyclopaedia for everyday

---

A knowledge of 3,500 characters is enough to enable comprehension of 99 percent of everyday printed matter in modern China; knowledge of 3,800 would only enable comprehension to be increased to 99.9 percent, and of 5,200 to 99.99 percent, see the references cited in Qiu (1996), p. 39.

Character counts say nothing directly about the number of words (especially in modern Chinese) mastered by an individual since some frequently used characters (*xue* 學, for example) often reappear in different words, while others (*de* 的, for example) do not. Frequency counts have therefore to take into account not only how frequently a character is used, but also its "word formation capability." See "The Number of Chinese Characters," Yin (1994), chap. 2, 45–89.

[31] There is a good account in Evelyn Sakakida Rawski, "Elementary Education," and "Popular Education Materials," chaps. 2 and 6 of *Education and Popular Literacy in Ch'ing China*, UMP, 1979, 24–53; 125–54. Zhang Zhigong 張志公 contributed an important study on *Chuantong yuwen jiaoyu chutan* 傳統語文教育初談 (A Preliminary Study of Traditional Language Primers), rev. ed., Shanghai Jiaoyu, 1962; rpnt., 1979.

use (29.3). One of the first to survive dates from the fifteenth century. It is the earliest illustrated primer in the world.[32] Only one is known to have been written by a famous writer (Pu Songling 蒲松齡, 1640–1715, *Riyong suzi* 日用俗字).

Village children studied part-time in the winter slack season. No doubt they stopped their studies once they had learned enough basic characters for everyday use. But if they came from a wealthy or educated family, they continued fulltime at family or clan primary schools. Children began formal studies at the age of eight *sui* or even earlier. The first step was to memorize one of several of the famous character primers (*qimengshu* 啓蒙書), which not only listed characters but also contained a moral. Children chanted the primers aloud, either singly, in turn, or in unison. The primers (sometimes referred to as *cunshu* 村書, village school books) were used as copy-books for learning the characters. Dozens are extant. They are an important source for the history of education and the transmission of received ideas.[33] They were often written and rewritten by eminent scholars and statesmen or at least attributed to them. The chancellor of Qin, Li Si 李斯 (280–208 BC), was the author of *Cang Jie* 倉頡, the first primer of which fragments survive. More than a millennium later, Zhu Xi 朱熹 carried on the tra-

[32] Luther Carrington Goodrich introduces the *Xinbian duixiang siyan* 新編對象四言 (Newly compiled and illustrated four-word primer), 1436, in *15ᵗʰ Century Illustrated Chinese Primer*, HKU Press, 1967; rpnt., 1975. This contains 326 illustrations of 244 single-character words and 82 two-character compounds.

[33] *Zhongguo mengxue jicheng* 中國蒙學集成 (Anthology of Chinese elementary primers), Han Xiduo 韓錫鐸, ed., Liaoning jiaoyu, 1993. This massive tome contains the original texts of 74 primers with detailed notes on their content and language. The editor has also compiled a bibliography of the editions of all known extant primers, 2083–2098.

Zhongguo chuantong mengxue dadian 中國傳統蒙學大典 (Repository of traditional Chinese elementary primers), Mao Shuiqing 毛水清, Liang Yang 梁揚, eds. in chief, Guangxi renmin, 1993, prints 36 of the most famous primers of all types in the original and with *baihua* translations. There is also an appendix containing a bibliography of primers compiled by Zhang Zhigong 張志公.

dition with his *Tongmeng xuzhi* 童蒙須知 (What infants should know).[34] From the Han to the Six Dynasties, the most popular character primer was the *Jijiu pian* 急就篇 compiled by Shi You 史游 (fl. 43–33 BC). It introduced everyday characters for basic vocabulary arranged in groups.[35] By the Tang, this had been replaced by the *Qianziwen* 千字文 (Thousand character text). Another popular primer was the *Baijiaxing* 百家姓 (Myriad family names). It lists 438 of the most common surnames arranged in six-character rhyming couplets. Both the *Qianziwen* and the *Baijiaxing* were deliberately written so that almost no character they contain occurs more than once. They were memorized generation after generation for well over 1,000 years. Starting in the Song, the first eight characters of the *Qianziwen* were also used for archival classification (20.2).[36] From the Yuan to the Qing, the single most popular primer of all was the *Sanzijing* 三字經 (*Three Character Classic*).[37] In the later empire, these three primers—the *Sanzijing*, the *Baijiaxing*

[34] It was expanded under the title *Cang Jie pian* 倉頡篇. The fragments that survive were discovered in a tomb at Fuyang in Anhui; see 44.3.2.2; from Juyan, 44.3.2.3; and Dunhuang, 46.4), see Roger Greatrex, "An Early Western Han Synonymicon: the Fuyang Copy of the *Cang Jie Pian*," in *Outstretched Leaves on his Bamboo Staff: Essays in Honour of Göran Malmqvist on his 70th Birthday*, Joakim Enwall, ed., Stockholm: The Association of Oriental Studies, 1994, 97–113.

[35] *Jijiu pian* (Speed mastery of the characters), punctuated and collated edition, Zeng Zhongshan 曾仲珊, , Yuelu, 1989.

[36] The *Qianziwen* was written in the early sixth century. It consists of 250 four-character lines in which only one character appears more than once. See *Ch'ien tzu wen, The Thousand Character Classic, A Chinese Primer*, Francis W. Paar, ed., Frederick Ungar, 1963. This includes the original Chinese in several Chinese scripts plus English, French, German and Latin translations by various nineteenth-century hands.

[37] *San Tzu Ching*, Herbert A. Giles, tr. and annotated, 1900; 2nd ed., rev., Kelly and Walsh, 1910. The *Sanzijing* contains 356 alternating rhyming lines of three characters each. It has 514 separate characters. See James T. C. Liu, "The Classical Chinese Primer: Its Three-Character Style and Authorship ," *JAOS* 105.2: 191–96 (1985), who argues that the *Sanzijing* was probably not written by the Southern Song scholar Wang Yinglin 王應麟 to whom it is usually attributed.

and the *Qianziwen*—were known as the *San-Bai-Qian* 三百千. They were also known as the *San-Bai-Qian-Qian* 三百千千 (the *Sanbaiqian* plus the *Qianjiashi* 千家詩, the myriad poems). Some are still in use (albeit in rewritten versions).

Many other primers came into common use, sometimes on more specialized themes, such as history, poetry or uplifting stories. They are usually in rhyming, balanced phrases with very short lines to make them easy to memorize and to do away with the need for punctuation.[38] In the preface to his translation of the *Sanzijing*, the first professor of Chinese at Cambridge, Herbert Giles, stressed that "to foreigners who wish to study the book-language of China, and to be able to follow out Chinese trains of thought, [its importance] can hardly be over-estimated. Serious students would do well to imitate the schoolboy, and commit the whole to memory." The first professor of Chinese at Oxford, James Legge, used the *Sanzijing* to teach his beginning students who were required to memorize it. If this seems asking too much, then at least memorize the opening lines: 人之初性本善, 性相近習相遠, 苟不教性乃遷, 教之道貴以專 (At birth human nature is basically good; our natures are the same, but our behavior differs. If foolishly there is no teaching, nature will deteriorate. The right way of teaching is to pay attention to the details).[39]

The characters for numbers were memorized in the arithmatic lessons, which were an important part of the primary school curriculum.

Although girls did not attend government schools, they too used the same primers if they attended clan schools or were privately educated at home. In addition there were special

[38] *Meng Ch'iu: Famous Episodes from Chinese History and Legend*, Burton L. Watson, tr., Tuttle, 1979. The *Meng Qiu* 蒙求 is a primer in the form of a history story book. It was written by Li Han 李翰 (Tang).

[39] The first two lines were based on *Lunyu*, xvii. 2. It has been on the lips of every Chinese schoolchild ever since the Yuan dynasty. After 1949, a different message was taught: the class background of one's parents makes people different; the right way of teaching is to be expert (*zhuan* 專) and politically correct (*youhong youzhuan* 又紅又專).

primers with characters and sentiments considered appropriate for them (39.2).

As an integral part of learning to read the characters (*shizi* 識字), students also learned to write them (*xiezi* 寫字). They started, as they do today, with the strokes (*bihua* 筆畫) and the stroke order (*bishun* 筆順). They practiced them over and over again (*xizi* 習字); first by filling in ones written by the teacher, then by tracing from the primers, and finally by imitating rubbings of the calligraphy (*shufa* 書法) of accepted masters.

By the time they had memorized the primers (which between them contained from 400 to 1,500 different characters), students would have been seven or eight years old and ready to begin to read simple books. It was commonly held that a person's ability to memorize was at its strongest up to the age of 15 *sui*. So there was great pressure to pack in as much as possible by then. The technique used was constant repetition. First on the list was the *Xiaojing* 孝經 (Classic of filial piety) which was used as a character primer, soon followed by the *Sishu* 四書 (*Four Books*), specially selected for their brevity and correct Confucian thinking by Zhu Xi 朱熹 (see 19.2). Girls also had to memorize the *Xiaojing* as well as one or other of the ethical texts for women (39.2). Reading took several forms: explanations by the teacher (including the difficult characters, punctuation and key passages); reading aloud or silently by the students (*du* 讀 or *kan* 看), including punctuating the texts for themselves, and finally, and above all, memorization.. After the basic Classics and poetry came abbreviations of well-known works and famous texts from the Qin and the Han periods (*wen bi Qin Han* 文必秦漢). Students also memorized the classifiers (often also called radicals, 16.3). Composition of literary and moral essays and poetry was the final stage of study. Here the emphasis was on the imitation of the styles of the ancient masters with a premium on quotations from the Classics (*yongdian* 用典, *diangu* 典故).

A late Qing poet satirizes a village school:

一陣烏鴉噪晚風， 諸徒齊逞好喉嚨。
趙錢孫李周吳鄭， 天地元[玄]黃宇宙洪。

千字文完翻鑒略，百家姓畢理神音。
就中有個超群者，一日三行讀大中。

Like a flock of crows cawing in the evening breeze, the students
show the quality of their lungs: 'Zhao, Qian, Sun, Li, Zhou, Wu,
Zheng' [opening of the *Baijiaxing*], 'Heaven and earth, dark and yellow, the universe vast and great' [the beginning of the *Qianziwen*].
When the *Qianziwen* is finished, they go over the *Jianlüe* (*Abbreviated Mirror*), when the *Baijiaxing* is done, they do the *Shentong shi*
(Poems for infant prodigies). An outstanding student reads at high
speed the *Daxue* (*Great Learning*) and the *Zhongyong* (*Doctrine of the
Mean*)."[40]

From an early stage of learning the characters, Chinese students gained the habit of dissecting compound characters *hetizi*
合體字 into their component parts as a mnemonic, as a literary
device (*xizi* 析字), as an influential approach to etymology
(1.2.3) and as a popular form of fortune telling (*chaizi* 拆字, *cezi*
測字, *xiangzi* 相字).[41] These practices no doubt began when the
first *hetizi* were put together. The earliest references are in the
Zhou period. Several are recorded in the *Zuozhuan* 左傳, one
under the year 542 BC: *Yuwen min chong wei gu* 于文皿蟲爲蠱
("the character for 'ultra venomous insect' is made up of insects
[above the character for] bronze vessel"). Xu Shen in the *Postface* of the *Shuowen* deplores the faulty analyses of the component parts of characters, which were common in his day. He
cites several, for example, *ma tou ren wei chang* 馬頭人爲長

---

[40] *Cunxue shi* 村學詩 (Village school poem) from Guo Chenyao 郭
臣堯, *Pengfuji* 捧腹集 (Comic collection, early-nineteenth century) as
quoted by Liang Shaoren 梁紹壬 (1792–1837), *Liangban qiuyu an suibi* 兩
般秋雨庵隨筆 (Miscellaneous writings in autumn rain study), Shanghai
guji, 1982, p. 214; see Angela Leung, "Elementary Education in the Lower Yangtze Region in the Seventeenth and Eighteenth Centuries," in
Education and Social Change in Late Imperial China, Benjamin Elman and
Alexander Woodside, eds., UCP, 1994, p. 396.

[41] There is a thorough description of the different forms of *xizi* as a
literary device in Karl S. Y. Kao, "Rhetoric," in *The Indiana Companion
to Traditional Chinese Literature*, William H. Nienhauser Jr., ed., IUP,
1986, 134–5.

([The character for] "long" [is incorrectly] written with the [characters for the] top part of the horse and man), see 16.2. A modern example of a mnemonic is *Hong shi jiangbian niao* 鴻是江邊鳥 (The goose [character] is a bird beside the river) or, more succinctly, *jiangniao hong* 江鳥鴻. Character riddles (*zimi* 字謎) were also popular. You had to guess what character was being referred to. For example, *bange pengyou bu jianle* 半個朋友不見了 (answer: *yue* 月), or *dayu xia zai hengshan shang* 大雨下在橫山上 (answer: *xue* 雪).

It was not uncommon to refer to a particular character by its components, as in the expression so and so "*you qiubafeng* 有丘八風" (has the air of a grunt [*bing* 兵]). In a similar way, many proper names have long since had customary ways of using their components to distinguish them, e.g., *gongchang Zhang* 弓長張 or *muzi Li* 木子李. This is but one example of dissecting the characters into their constituent parts (of which there are many varieties as set out in Table 2).

Table 2: Component Parts of Characters
Example: zhang 蟑 as in zhanglang 蟑螂, *cockroach*

Bushou 部首 (classifiers or radicals)	虫
Pianpang 偏旁 (side components)[42]	虫 章
Xingfu 形符 (significs)[43]	虫
Shengfu 聲符 (phonetic indicators)[44]	章
Bujian 部件 (constituent parts)	虫 立 日 十
Zigen 字根 (roots)[45]	虫 立 日 十

[42] *Pianpang* (side components) is the collective way of referring to *xingfu* and *shengfu*. Although they can occur in any position in a character, they are referred to in this way because they occur on the left and right side of more than 60 percent of *xingsheng* compounds.

[43] Also called *xingpang* 形旁.

[44] Also called *shengpang* 聲旁.

[45] The *zigen* are used in computer coding. The concept is very similar to the *bujian*. There is no agreed count of the number of *zigen*. The Big-5 system uses 125.

1.3.3 Dissecting the Characters

Having learned the strokes and the stroke order, the next key to mastering Chinese characters is to learn how to dissect them. Although single-component characters (*dutizi* 獨體字) account for only three percent of all characters in use today, they are the oldest and they have been among the most frequently used at every stage of the language because they form the basic core of the vocabulary. Moreover, the most common ones feature as significs or phonetics in other characters. They are also used as classifiers in dictionaries so it makes good sense to begin by mastering them, starting with the classifiers (16.3).

All the classifiers in use today have customary descriptions. The easiest to remember are those classifiers which are also independent single-component characters. They are simply listed with an indication of their position in the character, e.g., *shanzitou* 山字頭 (as in *yan* 岩); *yanzipang* 言字旁 (as in *shuo* 説); *xinzidi* 心字底 (as in *ying* 應). Classifiers which cannot stand alone have their own nicknames, such as *liangdianshui* 兩點水 and *sandianshui* 三點水 (as in 冰 and 河). These ways of referring to classifiers are listed in the appendix of most good dictionaries. They are worth remembering because they are used in everyday life (to identify *ru* 汝 during a telephone call, you would say *sandianshui, yige nü zi* 三點水一個女字).

Having mastered the classifiers, the next step is to learn to recognize the *pianpang* 偏旁. The most common compound characters are the *xingshengzi* 形聲字 (see 16.1 on the structure of the characters). They are composed of a signific (*xingfu* 形符) and a phonetic indicator (*shengfu* 聲符). In *zhang* 蟑, the signific is *chong* 虫 and the phonetic indicator is *zhang* 章. Karlgren's *Grammata Serica Recensa* is a listing of *xingsheng* characters in Old Chinese by their phonetic indicators on the basis of their reconstructed sounds (2.5). Not infrequently, *xingsheng* series contain groups of cognate words (1.2.3) and their study is another way of learning the characters. *Lishi Zhongwen zidian* 李氏中文字典 is a dictionary of Modern Chinese words organized in the same way but using their modern pronunciations (2.7). Note that because the script by its nature was ill-suited to keep pace with changes in the spoken language, today the phonetic indicators of only about 18 percent of the charactersgive an exact indication of their pronunciation; 59 percent give a hint; and 23 percent give no indication at all. The scores would be slightly higher in Cantonese and much higher in Old Chinese.

Another method of dissecting characters into their component parts (used in computer coding) is to break them into smaller units than the *pianpang*. These are usually called *bujian* 部件 or sometimes *zigen* 字根.[46] They include graphemes (*zisu* 字素, *ziwei* 字位), defined as the smallest units in the script capable of causing a contrast in meaning. *Bujian* are sometimes single-component characters (*dutizi*) with which multiple-component characters (*hetizi*), were built. The most frequently used *bujian* are also classifiers. Most have been in use since the Shang.

In the case of *zhang* 嶂 in Table 2, the *bujian* are *chong* 虫, *li* 立, *ri* 日 and *shi* 十. The majority of characters consist of two *bujian* at each stage of assembly. For example, the first level of *zhang* brings together *ri* 日 and *shi* 十; next *li* 立 and *zao* 早 and finally *zhang* 章 and *chong* 虫.

There is no agreed number of *bujian*. It depends into how many graphic components the characters are split and for what period of the script the analysis is made. Throughout most of Chinese history there were something less than 400.[47]

There are, then, only limited numbers of component parts to be learned: the dozen or so basic strokes; the 214 classifiers;

---

[46] In one large sample of several million characters, the 10 most frequently used *bujian* were all classifiers, i.e., *kou* 口, *ren* 人, *tu* 土, *ri* 日, *huo* 火, *ren* 亻 (usually called *danliren* 單立人), *quan* 犬, *bai* 白, *gou* 勹 and *mu* 木. They accounted for 23 percent of the total sample.

[47] One scholar has counted 348 *bujian* in the oracle bones; modern characters are dissected into 623 *bujian* for electronic communications. See *Yitizi zidian* 體字異體字字典 (Dictionary of graphic variants), Li Pu 李圃, ed., Xuelin, 1995; rev., 1997, Introduction, 3) and *Hanzi xinxi zidian* 漢字信息字典 (A dictionary of Chinese character information), Kexue, 1988.

the 1,000 or so *pianpang* from which most compound characters are constructed and the 350 to 600 or so *bujian* into which all characters of whatever type can be dissected. Each method overlaps with the others, so the total number of component parts is much less than their sum.

Different memnomics have been used to help commit the characters and their component parts to memory. The student of Classical Chinese will want to avoid fanciful inventions such as *yao* 要: "what he <u>wants</u> is a Western (*xi* 西) girl (*nü* 女)," and instead learn the meanings of characters based wherever possible on their ancient forms.

1.3.4   Punctuating a Text

As with other ancient writing systems, Pre-Qin texts had no punctuation and most later ones had none either. It was left to each reader to mark pauses in a sentence (with a pause mark, *dou* 讀, inserted between characters), and the end of a sentence with a small circle " 。 " (*quan* 圈) or dot (*dian* 點) called *ju* 句 which was placed beside the last character. The process was called *judou* 句讀 from the Han onward (also *judou* 句度, *jujüe* 句絕, *juduan* 句斷). One of the hallmarks of a good scholar was how easily and accurately he could punctuate a text.

In everyday life, scribes or other writers did provide some punctuation, as can be seen even as early as the oracle bones, where sentences are sometimes divided by straight lines drawn under the last character. In imperial times, characters such as *ju* 句 or *dou* 逗 were occasionally used in place of the circles and dots. Sometimes only *quan* were used. Sometimes a blank space was left at the end of a sentence. Ticks were also used as a sort of paragraph indicator or sentence divider. Instead of repeating a phrase, or occasionally a character, an equals sign was used. Many other punctuation marks were inserted, as can be seen on excavated texts written on bamboo, wood and silk (see chap. 18). If the same character had several tones, this was often indicated by writing a little circle at the corners of the character: the level tone (*ping* 平) in the bottom left-hand corner; the rising tone (*shang* 上), top left; the departing tone (*qu* 去), top right; the entering tone (*ru* 入), bottom right.

Various clues can be used to help mark sentences and pauses. For example, introductory and final particles indicate the beginnings and endings of sentences and interlinear notes were always placed at the end of a sentence. Rhythm and parallelism are also important indicators.

There were, of course, no capital letters at the beginning of a sentence and proper nouns were not marked. A reader would emphasize a passage with a row of circles, one to the left of each character. Occasionally in the Song and more frequently in the Qing, editions were printed with punctuation already added.

The lack of punctuation is a real difficulty in reading an old text. Modified Western punctuation (*biaodian* 標點) was gradually introduced in the twentieth century. Fortunately, modern editions of old texts are usually punctuated. But there are many mistakes. They arise from failing to understand institutions, personal and place-names, book titles, grammar and special terms.

1.3.5   *Textbooks and Readers*

It is best to study Classical Chinese having mastered Modern Standard Chinese. A convenient way to start is to go through one of the many excellent annotated texts of the Classics which give the original text in complex characters, a translation into Modern Chinese and notes. Or use a good bilingual text of one of the Classics such as *Lunyu* 論語 or the *Mengzi* 孟子 (Table 18, chap, 19). While doing so be guided by a good grammar (such as Pulleyblank's *Outline of Classical Chinese Grammar*, UBC Press, 1995), and try one of the many beginner's dictionaries such as *Jianming gu Hanyu zidian* 簡明古漢語字典 or *Gu Hanyu changyongzi zidian* 古漢語常用字字典 (2.4). More structured approaches are available in the textbooks of Classical Chinese listed below.

Modern editions of Han and pre-Han works can help overcome many difficulties, such as indicating alternative characters

(16.4.4) or the special readings of a character in a particular context, and they invariably provide punctuation. But not all texts
which a historian will be reading will have modern editions or
translations.

To study different genres of Classical Chinese, start with a
textbook or reader. Each generation to visit China, from the
first missionaries through the consuls and customs inspectors
to modern scholars, has produced its own. Some are still worth
using; for example, there is much to interest the economic historian in a perusal of Friedrich Hirth (1845–1927), *Textbook*,
which includes 240 documents, including contracts with translation, notes and vocabularies.[48] There are plenty of more recent textbooks for non-Chinese students: for example, Harold
Shadick,[49] Raymond Dawson,[50] Donald Wagner[51] or Xu Zong-
cai 徐宗才.[52]

Note also the annotated readers with excerpts from historical texts of a particular dynasty or style, for example,

The History of the Han Dynasty: Selections with a Preface, Kan Lao, ed.
    (44.5.1).

A Handbook for T'ang History, Denis C. Twitchett and Howard L.
    Goodman, eds. (46.5.1).

Selected Readings in Yuan History, Lao Yanshan, ed. (48.1).

Ming History: An Introductory Guide to Research, Edward L. Farmer,
    Romeyn Taylor and Ann Waltner, eds. (49.6).

---

[48] *Textbook of Documentary Chinese*, 2 vols., Statistical Department of
the Inspectorate General of Customs, 1885; 2nd enlarged ed., 1909; rpnt.
in 1 vol., Ch'eng-wen, 1968.

[49] *First Course in Literary Chinese*, 3 vols., Corn. UP, 1968; 8th prnt.,
1992.

[50] *A New Introduction to Classical Chinese*, OUP, 1984; rpnt., 1986.

[51] *A Classical Chinese Reader: The Hanshu Biography of Huo Guang* [霍
光, d. 68 BC], Curzon, 1997.

[52] *Gudai Hanyu keben* 古代漢語課本 (Classical Chinese textbook), 3
vols., Beijing yuyan wenhua daxue, 1998. This contains carefully graded
excerpts ranging from the easy to the difficult, and from the short to the
long, with bilingual annotations in the first two volumes and Chinese
only in vol. 3.

Introduction to Ch'ing Documents, Philip Kuhn and John King Fairbank, eds. (50.8.2).

Note also the textbooks and readers compiled for Chinese students of Classical Chinese at all different levels and for different purposes. For example,

1. *Gaozhong guwen xuexi rumen* 高中古文學習入門 (Introduction to the study of Literary Chinese for senior high schools), Peng Geren, 彭格人, ed. in chief, Zhongguo renmin gongan daxue, 1997. Selected short readings with inter-textual "translations" into Modern Chinese and short notes on various aspects of basic knowledge about Classical Chinese.

2. *Gu Hanyu wenxian daodu* 古漢語文獻導讀 (Guide to reading Classical Chinese texts), Han Zhengrong 韓崢嶸, ed. in chief, Jilin daxue, 1994. The approach is to get back to the original texts and to encourage students to think for themselves, so excerpts for reading are given with their original commentaries and without punctuation. Replaces *Gudai Hanyu* 古代漢語 (Classical Chinese), Wang Li 王力, ed. in chief, 2 vols., Zhonghua, 1962–4; rev. ed., 4 vols., 1981; 26th printing, 1996; 2nd rev. ed., 1998. This textbook was for many years the standard for Chinese universities. Its threefold arrangement (selected readings, frequent words and general surveys of particular topics) is still the most widely used.

3. *Zhongguo lishi wenxuan* 中國歷史文選 (Selected readings in Chinese history), Zhang Yantian 張衍田, ed., Beijing daxue, 1996. This is the course book used for teaching Classical Chinese to students in the history department of Peking University. It contains brief introductions to primary sources arranged under archaeology and the four branches (*Sibu*). There are 80 excerpts. Part 6: *Gu Hanyu zici yufa zhishi* 古漢語字詞語法知識 (Vocabulary and grammar of ancient Chinese) is available as a separate volume within the History Department.

4. *Zhongguo jingji sixiangshi ziliao xuanji* 中國經濟思想史資料選輯 (Selected materials on the history of Chinese economic thought), Wu Baosan 巫寶三, ed. in chief, Shehui kexue, 1982–96: *Xian-Qin*, 2 vols., 1985; *Qin-Han*, 2 vols., 1982; *Sanguo, Liang-Jin, Nan-Bei Chao, Sui-Tang*, 2 vols., 1992; *Song, Jin, Yuan*, 2 vols., 1996; *Ming-Qing*, 2 vols., 1992. This series contains extracts from a wide variety of sources; each extract is followed by notes and a translation into Modern Chinese.

2

Dictionaries

There has been a great improvement in dictionaries of Classical Chinese thanks to the collaborative efforts of lexicographers and the use of computer databases (2.3 and 2.4). These modern efforts have been able to build on a tradition of dictionary making that goes back to the Han dynasty and beyond (2.1). There have also been many new dictionaries of particular types of Chinese, for example, the secret language of the trades or of the mantic arts. A selection is given in 2.6.

New insights on character formation and meanings have been gained from the study of epigraphic sources discovered in the twentieth century, but these have not yet been fully integrated with the pre-Qin textual sources, nor are they yet available on database (although the work is underway). Special dictionaries for oracle-bone inscriptions and other epigraphic sources are given in chaps. 15–17.

There has been no major dictionary of Classical or Literary Chinese into English or any other Western language (2.5) since those of the nineteenth century (some of which are still useful as repositories of late Qing Mandarin, but are outdated for other purposes, see Box 2 at the end of this chapter). Some excellent new Chinese-English dictionaries have been published and a major Chinese-French dictionary should be completed in the year 2001 (2.8).

Note that dictionaries, as with all works to do with the study of language and the characters (*xiaoxue* 小學), were placed in the Classics branch of the traditional fourfold bibliographical classification (*Sibu* 四部, on which see 9.3).

2.1 The Criteria for a Good Dictionary

The scope of the dictionary should be clearly indicated. For example, is it intended to be synchronic (that is to cover all genres of a particular period of the language); diachronic (all genres from the earliest times to the present); or restricted to a particular genre at or during a specific time? Whichever the case, the corpus of literature upon which it is based should be made clear.

Ideally, comprehensive diachronic dictionaries should be able to build on more specialized synchronic dictionaries. In China, this is not yet always the case, but publishers still produce diachronic dictionaries whose focus as a result is often fuzzy.

Having defined its scope and ambitions, a good dictionary will avoid putting definitions together in a single list, but will divide them into categories, starting with the root meaning or etymon (*benyi* 本義), then moving in a systematic and clearly indicated manner through the alternative (*tongjia* 通假), special (*tezhi* 特指), general (*fanzhi* 泛指), derived (*yinshenyi* 引申義) and metaphorical (*biyu* 比喻) meanings. It will also indicate variant, ancient and modern, and alternative characters (*yitizi* 異體字, *gujinzi* 古今字, *tongjiazi* 通假字) and different pronunciations. Parts of speech should be indicated, as also usage (for example, literary or spoken; Buddhist or Daoist). The definitions should be illustrated with citations (*yinzheng* 引證) whose sources should be clearly indicated. The date of first known appearance of a word or usage should be indicated.

One of the chief criteria for a good dictionary is not that it defines more characters and compounds than its predecessors.

Rather, it is how thoroughly, accurately and clearly the editors have been able to combine explanations of the forms, sounds and meanings (*jiexing* 解形, *zhuyin* 注音 and *shiyi* 釋義) of words (characters, compounds, phrases). Such explanations should include, but not be limited to, examples of usage.

If it is a comprehensive dictionary, it should give maximum help with compounds by providing examples of usage of a character whether it stands alone or at the head, middle or end of a compound or phrase.[1] It should also list homonyms and either quote or cross reference cognates.

A good dictionary will have several indexes (*pinyin*, classifiers and stroke count).

Last but not least, the dictionary should be available in both print form and on CD-ROM. The CD-ROM search engine should be powerful and flexible enough to allow searches not only on head-words, but also on etymologies and quotations. It should be possible to assemble cognates, synonyms and antonyms. If it is in print, the characters should be sufficiently large to ensure that those with many strokes are legible.

[1] The usual practice in Chinese dictionaries is to list multi-character compounds under their first character, e.g., *lishi* 歷史 appears under its head character *li*. In recent years, several *nixu* 逆序 or *daoxu* 倒序 (reverse-head character) dictionaries have been published listing compound words under their last character (2.4, 2.7 and 2.8). Thus *lishi* would be found under *shi* along with all the other compounds ending in *shi*. This has the advantage of showing the usage of characters in contexts which are not immediately apparent in normally arranged dictionaries. In traditional China, rhyming phrase books were also arranged in this manner. It is possible to list compounds under their head characters and to show in index when they appear at the end or middle of words and phrases (see for example, *Duo gongneng Hanyu da cidian suoyin* 多功能漢語大詞典索引, 2.3). Dictionaries on CD-ROM or other computer media open the possibility for the first time of instantaneously finding characters wherever they appear in words or phrases.

2.2 Ancient Dictionaries and Etymology

2.2.1 Ancient

Chinese dictionaries customarily concentrated on meanings, forms or phonology and were arranged by semantic category, by classifier or by rhyme.[2] The earliest lexicographical work, the *Erya* 爾雅 (Examples of refined usage), third century BC, contains brief definitions of some 4,300 words and phrases arranged by semantic category. It was made one of the Classics in the Tang in 837. This greatly enhanced the influence of the *Erya* on the interpretation of the Classics, and no doubt also on the development of the language itself since generations of scholars memorized it. Many supplements and corrections to the *Erya* were written,[3] but the thesaurus-like approach of the *Erya* was not developed. Later dictionaries were organized by rhyme or by classifier.

The earliest comprehensive dictionary of Chinese characters to have survived is the *Shuowen jiezi* 說文解字 by the Later Han scholar, Xu Shen 許慎.[4] Xu was the first to make system-

---

[2] The generic term for dictionary from the sixth to the eighteenth centuries was *zishu* 字書 (a term also applied to character primers). After the publication of the *Kangxi zidian* 康熙字典 (1716), the term *zidian* 字典 gradually replaced *zishu*. Both *cidian* 辭典 and *cidian* 詞典 are modern expressions for dictionary.

[3] *Erya jilin* 爾雅集林 (Collected glosses on the *Erya*), Zhu Zuyan 朱祖延, ed. in chief, 6 vols., Hubei jiaoyu, 1994– .

[4] *Shuowen jiezi* (Explanation of single component graphs and analyses of compound characters), completed in AD 100, but presented to the emperor only in 121. See Boltz in *ECTBG* (1993), 429–442. *Shuowen jiezi* 說文解字集注 (Collected commentaries on the *Shuowen jiezi*), Jiang Renjie 蔣人傑, comp., 3 vols., Shanghai guji, 1996, adds paleographic evidence and commentary since the last major edition, that of Ding Fubao 丁福保 (1874–1952): *Shuowen jiezi gulin* 說文解字詁林 (Collected commentaries on the *Shuowenjiezi*), Shangwu, 1930; 1932. For a convenient index by modern pronunciation to the *Shuowen* and the works of the four main Qing commentators (Duan Yucai 段玉裁, Gui Fu 桂馥, Zhu Junsheng 朱駿聲 and Wang Jun 王筠), see *Shuowen jindu ji wujia tongjian* 說文近讀暨五家通劍, Li Xingjie 李行杰, ed., Qi-Lu, 1997.

atic use of the significs as classifiers (*bushou* 部首).[5] This break-through was made possible by the predominant position by the Han of characters with both a signific (*xing* 形) and a phonetic indicator (*sheng* 聲), the *xingshengzi* 形聲字.[6] Had Xu had access to the earliest script forms such as the oracle bone and Zhou bronze inscriptions, and thus been better able to search out the basic significs, it is possible that he might have achieved more comprehensive and accurate results.[7] He might also have used a more simple classification scheme than that which he did (in principle he lists as separate classifiers the significs of all *xing-sheng* and *xingyi* characters, thus, for example, *zhui* 隹, *chou* 雔 and *za* 雥 he makes into three separate classifiers; moreover not all of his classifiers are significs).[8] Be that as it may, such was Xu Shen's influence that his system of 540 classifiers (under each of which words were grouped according to their meaning) was followed with minor modifications for the next 1,500 years up to the *Zihui* 字彙, a Ming dictionary completed in 1615 by Mei Yingzuo 梅膺祚 (fl. 1570–1615). Mei included 33,179 char-acters and turned the classifiers into an index tool by reducing their number to 214 and by listing characters under each classi-fier by the number of residual strokes, still today the most widely used system. In recent years, the simplification of the characters has enabled editors to further reduce the number of

[5] Earlier works had used the classifiers as a basis of organization; for example, the character primers, *Cang Jie* 倉頡 (third century BC or *Jijiu pian* 急就篇 (first century BC), see 1.3.2. Both were arranged by subject categories (*yilei fenbu* 義類分部), hence in practice by *xingpang* (classi-fiers).

[6] Xu's analysis of the structure of the characters and the development of their different types is traced in 16.2.

[7] A Qing scholar (Zhu Junsheng 朱駿聲) estimated that Xu had left out 1,844 characters from written texts available in his day. But Xu's aim was to analyze small seal characters, so he did not include many Han characters invented after small seal had fallen out of use.

[8] Paul L-M. Serruys, "On the System of the *Pu Shou* (部首) in the *Shuo-wen chieh-tzu* 説文解字," *SYSJK* 55: 651–754 (1984), translates Xu Shen's definitions of all 540 *bushou*.

classifiers (to 201, 200, 189 or even 180), but modern dictionaries of ancient scripts are still arranged by the *Shuowen* classifiers (chaps. 15–17).

After the *Shuowen* (containing 10,516 different characters, of which 1,163 are graphic variants), dozens of dictionaries were compiled over the following centuries, each drawing from its predecessors and also increasing the number of characters defined. The largest of all the character dictionaries, the *Kangxi zidian* 康熙字典 (1716), contains a total of 47,035 characters, out of which as many as 20,000 (40 percent) are graphic variants. There are also many dead characters or characters which were used rarely or only once. Leaving aside the graphic variants, the *Kangxi zidian* contains nearly three times as many characters as the *Shuowen*.

The most comprehensive premodern collection of phrases was compiled under imperial auspices and presented in 1711 (and with supplement, 1720): Zhang Yushu 張玉書 (1642–1711) et al., *Peiwen yunfu* 佩文韵府.[9] To this day no modern Chinese dictionary has included as many compounds. All 700,000 are arranged under the rhyme of their last character. Each compound is followed by quotations (with references) showing the different uses of the word or phrase, but no definitions as such are given. The *Peiwen yunfu* is an enlargement of Yuan and Ming dynasty predecessors and, like them, it was intended as an aid to literary composition. There are modern indexes available. Another (and complementary) eighteenth-century collection of literary phrases is the *Pianzi leibian* 駢字類編.[10]

---

[9] *Peiwen yunfu* (Yunfu additional repository of rhymes ["Yunfu," the storehouse of rhymes, was the name of the Kangxi emperor's library]), 1711 and (supplement) 1720; 7 vols., Wanyou wenku, 2nd series, 1937 (vol. 7 is an index); 4 vols., Shanghai guji, 1983 (vol. 4 is an index).

[10] *Pianzi leibian* (Compound phrases arranged by category), Zhang Tingyu 張廷玉 et al., 1726; 8 vols., Xuesheng, 1963. Zhuang Weisi 莊爲斯 (Wallace S. Johnson, Jr.), *Pianzi leibian yinde* 駢字類編引得 (Index to the *Pianzi leibian*), Taibei, 1966. There is also an index to rhyming groups: *Pianzi leibian yinxu suoyin* 駢字類編音序索引, Wuhan daxue, 1995, and to the Zhongguo shudian reprint (1988).

In the opinion of the *Siku* editors (9.5) there was no phrase or allusion which could not be found in either the *Peiwen yunfu* or in the *Pianzi leibian*. They were referring to *literary* phrases.

2.2.2   Etymology

Ever since the Han the meanings of words have been defined by analyzing the forms of the characters, reconstructing their sounds or tracing their usage in early texts (*xingxun* 形訓, *yinxun* 音訓, *yixun* 義訓). Scholars stressed now one, now the other method.

The analysis of single-component characters (whose origin was often pictographic) has customarily been based on the analysis of their graphic structure. The starting point has traditionally been the *Shuowen jiezi* 説文解字 with examples of usage drawn from the Classics (*xingxun* 形訓). The discovery of new epigraphic material (on the oracle bones and on bronze) has given a whole new life to the this approach. The same approach can be used for analyzing characters with significs, but it does not work for characters which were borrowed for their sounds and whose forms therefore usually bore no relation to their meaning (see 16.1 for the distinction between these different types of characters). Even when it was not good etymology, the breaking down of the characters into their component parts served as a way of committing them to memory (1.3.3).

The second method (*yinxun* 音訓) is based on the analysis of the sounds of a word and is summed up in the phrase *yinjin yitong* 音近義通 (if the sound is close, the meaning is the same). It was initiated by Liu Xi 劉熙, who compiled the first etymological dictionary, the *Shiming* 釋名, ca. 200.[11] The tracing of cognate words (*tong yuanci* 同源詞) that had the same or simi-

---

[11] *Shiming* (Explanation of words). Liu used rhyming puns and both the literary and spoken language of his day to trace the origins of 1,500 words under 27 subject categories. See *A Concordance to the Shiming and Jijiu pian* 釋名急救篇逐字索引, D.C. Lau and Chen Fongqing 陳方正, eds. HK: Shangwu, forthcoming.

lar sounds in Old Chinese and connected meanings derived from a common root is one of the best ways of finding the different shades of meanings of words. It also shows how characters were formed and reveals the connections between them (1.2.3).[12]

During the Qing, the great phonologist Duan Yucai 段玉裁 (1735–1815) recommended using both these approaches as well as tracing usage over time. Linguists today follow his advice, using both the pre-Qin *guwen* 古文 script forms of a character (Table 16, chap. 16), its reconstructed sounds in Old Chinese and examples of usage. The final step is to check that the meaning assigned to a character fits with other examples from similar contexts. The same approach is used for reading texts from later stages of the language, which often present their own particular difficulties (the more vernacular the style, the less fixed the characters). Linguists today have the advantage that a great deal more is now known about the ancient scripts. Comparative phonology has also contributed to improving the analysis of the sounds of Old Chinese.

The words whose meaning and usage have been most systematically studied are those traditionally classified as *xuzi* 虛字 (empty characters, that is to say particles for showing grammatical relationships).[13] All other words were classified as *shizi* 實字 (content words). Their changing meanings have been less intensively studied, although important dictionaries of Chinese along historical lines, notably the *Hanyu da cidian* 漢語大詞典, have been published (2.3 and 2.4). These are a great step

[12] Tsu-lin Mei, "Notes on the Morphology of Ideas in Ancient China," in *The Power of Culture: Studies in Chinese Cultural History*, Willard J. Peterson et al., eds., HKCU Press, 1994, 37–46, gives some fascinating examples of how essential this approach is to fully understanding the meanings of words in Classical Chinese.

[13] *Xuzi* were also called *ci* 詞. A comprehensive dictionary of Classical Chinese particles covering all styles of *wenyanwen* would contain about 800 of them; the core particles number between 150 to 200. They changed considerably over time. Pulleyblank examines 330 in his *Outline of Classical Chinese Grammar*, UBC Press, 1995.

forward because they illustrate with citations how words changed their meanings over time.

2.3   Modern Comprehensive Dictionaries

Modern Chinese dictionaries concentrate on characters, on compounds or on both. Some focus on the language of a specific work, style or period, for example, Classical Chinese in the strict sense, or are more general in scope trying to cover everything written between the *Shijing* 詩經 and the *Qingshi* 清史, or even more ambitiously, all varieties of written Chinese from the earliest times to the present day. Many publishers put out small, medium and large versions of a dictionary in order to cater for different segments of what is a lucrative market.

Table 3 gives a quantitative idea of the scope of many of the dictionaries discussed in the following sections.

The most comprehensive dictionary of Chinese available is the *Hanyu da cidian* 漢語大詞典.[14] It is a diachronic dictionary, that is to say, it defines not only the language of today, but also records usage at all periods and in all styles from the Zhou dynasty Confucian Classics to the speeches of Mao Zedong. It does so by means of definitions and quotations from a huge range of historical sources. In this sense it is comparable to the *Oxford English Dictionary on Historic Principles* and it was compiled in much the same way.[15]

---

[14] *Hanyu da cidian* (Great Chinese word dictionary), 13 vols., Hanyu da cidian, 1986–90; 1990–3; 5th prnt., 1995; 3-vol., small-print ed., 1997.

[15] Unlike the *OED*, the *Hanyu da cidian* had the support of the government and took 11, not 54, years to complete. The decision to compile it (as well as the *Hanyu da zidian* 漢語大字典, see 2.4) was taken at the highest levels in Beijing in 1975. Four hundred scholars worked on the former; three hundred on the latter. Real work was able to begin only in 1979.

Table 3: Definitions of Dao 道

Note: The reference in the left-hand column indicates in which section of this chapter the dictionary is discussed. The first figure after the title indicates the number of meanings each dictionary defines for *dao* 道. The second figure shows how many words it contains with *dao* as the head (or tail) character.

2.3	漢語大詞典	45	1,291	(345 head + 922 tail positions; 598 in disyllabic words and 324 in polysyllabic words and phrases. Available on CD-ROM)
	大漢和辭典	47	410	(+ 100 books, place-names etc.)
	中文大辭典	47	290	(+ 10 Western phrases)
2.4	漢語大字典	45	0	
	字通	7	204	(of which 62 have no citations)
	辭源	12	68	(of which 15 are book titles)
	使用古漢語大詞典	12	20	
	簡Â鞴藕河鎰值ä	28	0	
	古漢語常用字字典	9	2	
	逆序類聚古漢語辭典	6	86	
	連綿字典	0	15	
	古辭辨	4	0	(articles on the meanings of *dao*)
2.6	近代漢語辭典	7	21	
2.7	新華字典	11	0	
	現代漢語詞典	17	47	(192 if used with the next entry)
	倒序現代漢語詞典	17	145	
	李氏中文字典	8	9	
2.8	漢英詞典	13	46	
	漢英逆引詞典	7	134	
	Ricci (1976)	13	44	
	Le Grand Ricci	35	250	
Box 2	Morrison	0	11	
	Williams	0	33	(incl. 19 in which *dao* is a suffix; examples, but no citations)
	Couvreur	15	0	
	Giles	10	261	(no citations)
	Mathews	6	147	(+ 77 compounds in which *dao* is used as a suffix; no citations)

In one sense the editors of the *OED* had an easy task: they had only to cover the development of English over the relatively short time span of 850 years. The editors of the *Hanyu da cidian*, on the other hand had to record the changes in the Chinese language over nearly 3,000 years. Hundreds of scholars were assigned different words and given the task not only of defining them, but also of tracking their first and subsequent meanings and uses from ancient times to the present day. As a first step, words and examples of their usage were selected from over 10,000 works, both ancient and modern. These were then recorded on eight million filing cards from which a first selection of two million was made. Next, definitions and explanations were written for a total of some 370,000 words. These are arranged under 23,000 head characters whose definitions are no less copious than in the standard large-scale character dictionary, the *Hanyu da zidian* 漢語大字典 (2.4, item 1), but far fewer characters are included because obsolete ones have deliberately been excluded. Nor is any attempt made to trace the development of the forms of the characters using the ancient scripts (a feature of the *Hanyu da zidian*). Despite the fact that it weighs over 20 kilos and contains a total of 50 million characters spread over 20,000 large double-column pages, the *Hanyu da cidian* is an easy dictionary to use to the full because it is unusually well indexed and it is also available on CD-ROM.[16]

Overall arrangement is by 200 classifiers. Volume 13 contains convenient *pinyin* and stroke-count indexes. In addition, the full use of this important dictionary is greatly enhanced by the publication of a multi-purpose index in a separate volume, *Duo gongneng Hanyu da cidian suoyin* 多功能漢語大詞典索引. This lists the appearance of all characters whether they appear at the head, tail or middle positions of words or phrases. Alto-

---

[16] *Hanyu da cidian*, CD-ROM version, Hanyu da cidian and Hong Kong: Shangwu, 1998. This contains 29,920 different characters; 346,000 word entries and 23,250 *chengyu* and sayings, giving a total of 511,000 entries. There are many different search possibilities. Characters are given in both complex and simple forms.

gether the index contains 728,000 entries clearly arranged on 1,700 eight-column pages. There is a *pinyin* finding index.[17]

In the body of the dictionary head characters are given in *fanti* 繁體 (complex forms), although *jianti* 簡體 (simplified forms) are also indicated. Pronunciation of head characters is given in *fanqie* and in *pinyin*. Polysyllabic words are given in their complex forms and are arranged by order of the second character's stroke count and classifier. By far the quickest search method is to use the CD-ROM version. Otherwise, the separate multi-purpose index lists page references for every character and word. In the dictionary itself the number of strokes in the second character of a polysyllabic word is always given beside the first definition in the top left-hand column of each page and also beside the phrase when the number of strokes changes.

Definitions and explanations are in simplified characters. Fortunately, quotations from old Chinese works use the original complex characters (even if these are graphic variants) while modern works are quoted in simplified characters. Quotations are arranged chronologically. Sources are clearly indicated, although a full listing of authors and publications cited is only given in the CD-ROM version. Single- and multi-character words are included as well as phrases, idioms, *diangu* 典故 (classical allusions), proverbs, colloquial sayings, slang and important institutions from all periods. All genres of literature are included.

There are 2,503 illustrations of apparel, accouterments, and architectural detail. People and book titles, except for the most famous, are for the most part not included.[18] Modern specialist vocabulary is excluded unless it has become part of the general language.

---

[17] *Duo gongneng Hanyu da cidian suoyin* (General-purpose index to the *Hanyu da cidian*), Hanyu da cidian chubanshe and Zen bunka kenkyûjo, eds., Hanyu da cidian, 1997.

[18] To locate a book or check a title, see chap. 9.

Apart from the indexes to head characters, volume 13 contains detailed appendixes on the evolution of Chinese weights and measures using both archaeological and written evidence, as well as chronological tables giving era and reign-name years with their cyclical characters and Western year equivalents from 841 BC to 1909.

In a comprehensive dictionary which aims to cover all genres of Chinese from the Classics to the present there are bound to be some areas that are less well covered than others (one weakness noted in section 1.2.7 is the failure to incorporate thoroughly the language of Buddhism from the Han to the Tang, a time when its influence on the development of Chinese was particularly strong). Nor do the editors always give the first occurrence of words.[19] The quality of the volumes is not the same, reflecting the different standards of the volume editors. Nevertheless the *Hanyu da cidian* is the leading dictionary of the Chinese language. The fact that it is available on CD-ROM makes all its riches incomparably more accessible than any of its rivals. Students of Chinese history and civilization will no doubt wish to start their search for the changing meanings of words in this dictionary before proceeding to other more specialized ones.

The only other dictionary of Chinese on a similar scale (but different in scope), is Morohashi Tetsuji 諸橋轍次, *Dai Kan-Wa jiten* 大漢和辞典. This great work, usually referred to in Japan as *Dai Kan-Wa jiten*, and in the West simply as "Morohashi", includes 49,964 individual characters with many quotations, mainly from Classical Chinese, showing their usage. In addition there is a great deal of encyclopaedic information, especially on book titles, official titles and place-names, and

[19] For example, the *Hanyu da cidian*'s first citation of the phrase *Hanyu* 漢語 is from Yu Xin 庾信 (513–81), but this is at least 100 years after the first known occurrence of the term (in a story about the early fourth-century monk Srimitra (Gao Zuo 高座) of whom it was said that he did not speak in the language of the Han (*Hanyu* 漢語) in order to avoid being pestered by others (*Shishuo xinyu* 世説新語, see 45.2).

130,000 phrases mainly from Modern Chinese, including names of foreign people and places and Buddhist terms to give a grand total of 500,000 compounds (the original edition of 1955–60 contained 370,000 compounds). Despite these additions, Morohashi remains essentially a dictionary of Classical and Literary Chinese. Also, despite an attempt to add root meanings based on oracle-bone and bronze inscriptions, it remains weak in this area. Entries are arranged by classifiers and there are good indexes. Under each head character, compounds are arranged in the order of the Japanese pronunciation of the second character.[20]

In his autobiography, Morohashi explained his original motives in wanting to compile a Chinese-Japanese dictionary. As an overseas student in China in 1917–19, he had to spend between a third and a quarter of his study time trying to find the meanings of words and phrases. This tedium he felt could be avoided if there were a dictionary which provided both citations and definitions (the two largest Chinese dictionaries then available had their limitations: the *Kangxi zidian* gives definitions of characters but contains no phrases, while the *Peiwen yunfu* contains phrases but has no definitions). By the time he returned to Japan, he had filled 20 notebooks with vocabulary. It was in 1928 that he signed the contract to edit a Chinese-

---

[20] *Dai Kan-Wa jiten* (The great Chinese-Japanese dictionary), 13 vols., Taishûkan, 1955–60; rpnt., in smaller format and with revisions, 1966–88; rev. and enlarged ed., 1984–86; a 14th volume is a glossary indexing all words and phrases alphabetically according to Japanese syllabary, Taishûkan 1989; 5th prnt., 1997. A Chinese version of the first edition of Morohashi was produced in Taibei: *Zhongwen da cidian* 中文大辭典 (The encyclopaedic dictionary of the Chinese language), 38 vols., 2 vols. index, Zhongguo wenhua yanjiu suo, 1962–68; rev. ed., 10 vols., 1973.

The editing of Morohashi was completed in 1943, in which year the first volume was published to coincide with the editor's 60th birthday. Vol. 2 was in print and the remaining 11 vols. ready for print when along with all the fonts they were completely destroyed by firebombs in 1945. Morohashi had kept three sets of the proofs, so he and his fellow workers reedited these. They were soon ready, but it took the best part of 10 years to make another set of fonts and to print the dictionary.

Japanese dictionary. Within four years students under his direction had culled phrases from the main Han and pre-Han texts and filled 400,000 cards. It became clear to Morohashi and to his publisher (who fortunately by this time had become a personal friend) that this was going to be a very large dictionary. He spent the rest of his long life lecturing on Chinese literature, acting as curator of the Seikadô Library (11.3, item 6) and above all editing, reediting and revising his dictionary until his death in 1982 at the age of 99.

2.4 Dictionaries of Classical Chinese

There are a number of Chinese-Chinese or Chinese-Japanese dictionaries specializing in Classical and Literary Chinese. Each of the 14 introduced below is as different as the different varieties of the language it attempts to define. The first (*Hanyu da zidian* 漢語大字典) is the standard modern dictionary of characters; the second (*Jitsû* 字通), is a Japanese dictionary of Chinese characters and compounds. It innovates in a number of important ways, not least by incorporating insights gained from the analysis of the graphology and phonology of characters based on the corpus of newly discovered ancient inscriptions. Item 7 (*Gu Hanyu changyongzi ziyuan zidian* 古漢語常用字字源字典) is a similar effort but on a much smaller scale. Most of the remainder concentrate on the explanation of meanings. Number 3 (*Ciyuan* 辭源) was the first modern phrase dictionary but is now superseded. Number 4 (*Shiyong gu Hanyu da cidian* 實用古漢語大詞典) is a medium-large dictionary with definitions and citations both in Modern Chinese. Numbers 5 (*Jianming gu Hanyu zidian* 簡明古漢語字典) and 6 (*Gu Hanyu changyongzi zidian* 古漢語常用字字典) are among the best medium- and small-sized dictionaries of frequently used characters; number 8 (*Nixu leiju gu Hanyu cidian* 逆序類聚古漢語辭典) is a reverse-head character dictionary; number 9 (*Lianmian zidian* 聯綿字典) is the standard work on early bound compounds; and numbers 10 (*Gucibian* 古辭辨) and 11 (*Gu Hanyu tongshi yiming cidian* 古漢語同實異名辭典) are studies of near synonyms. There are also many other dictionaries of the classical language covering particular genres or periods. Many are listed in the relevant sections of the manual. Only two examples are included here (items 12–14 on four-character phrases and allusions). A sampling of special-purpose dictionaries for other branches of the language is given in section 2.6.[21]

1. The *Hanyu da zidian* 漢語大字典 is one of the largest *zidian* 字典 (character dictionaries) ever compiled; it contains explanations of the form, the sounds and the meanings of 54,678 characters.[22] Each head character is given in regular script, below which examples are drawn from oracle-bone, bronze, seal, jade, bamboo and chancery scripts. Pronunciation is given for Old Chinese (rhyme categories, *yun* 韵); Middle Chinese (*fanqie*); and Modern Chinese (*pinyin*). Characters were drawn from the main traditional *zidian* (although some modern characters, for example for the elements, are included). Definitions begin by citing the *Shuowen* and later classical dictionaries. Arrangement is by 200 classifiers. The index is by stroke count (vol. 1, 1–112).

2. *Jitsû* 字通 is a large, comprehensive dictionary that achieves a number of aims.[23] It defines the meanings of some 9,500 characters in depth by tracing the development of their forms, starting with oracle-bone and bronze scripts, as well as changes in their pronunciation. Next, compounds in which the character occurs in the head position are listed with brief definitions but no citations. This is followed by a simple listing of two-character compounds in which the character appears in the tail position (these compounds are

[21] For example, for dictionaries of ancient scripts, *guwenzi* 古文字, see chaps. 16 to 18.

[22] *Hanyu da zidian* (Dictionary of Chinese characters), 8 vols., Sichuan cishu and Hubei cishu, 1990; 3 vols., with corrections, 1995; reduced-size, one vol. rpnt., 1992; 3rd rpnt., 1996.

[23] *Jitsû* (Comprehensive character dictionary), Shirakawa Shizuka 白川靜, ed., Heibonsha, 1996.

mainly drawn from the *Peiwen yunfu*). Finally, the most important two-character compounds in which the character appears in the head position are defined. There are 223,000 such entries. Examples of usage are drawn from some 500 works from the Zhou Classics to the Qing (an appendix lists and describes each work and its author when known). The citations are given in Japanese translation, not in the original Chinese. Arrangement is by Japanese syllabary. There are indexes by classifier, stroke count and by the four-corner system. The innovations of this important dictionary include combining the best of the approaches normally found separately in character dictionaries and phrase dictionaries. In addition, the author has integrated much of the new work on Old Chinese based on the analysis of the expanding epigraphic record, to the interpretation of which he himself has made important contributions. This is a beautifully printed and presented work with over 2,000 pages each divided into four rows of text.

3. *Ciyuan* 辭源.[24] The editors of the 1979 edition of this, the first modern encyclopaedic phrase dictionary, deliberately cut out the technical and international words which had crept in during 60 years of revisions and updates (it was originally published as a classical phrase dictionary in 1915), so it now covers the Chinese language up to 1840. There are 12,980 head characters under which are defined 84,134

---

[24] *Ciyuan* (The roots of words), 4 vols., Shangwu, 1915; rev. ed., 4 vols., 1979–84; reduced-size, single vol. ed., 1988.

The *Cihai* 辭海 (Sea of words), 1936; 5th rpnt., 2 vols., 1994, began life as Zhonghua's answer to its rival, Shangwu's *Ciyuan*. Today, it serves a different purpose. The 2nd rev. ed. (1989), deliberately covers modern China and international matters as much as China's past. In other words, it has now become a general-purpose encyclopaedic dictionary of modern Chinese and as such is less useful than the *Ciyuan* for the purposes of historical research. It contains 13,587 head characters and 84,336 compounds. A CD-ROM version of a new revised edition of the *Cihai* is scheduled for publication in 1999.

compounds. Volume 4 has a *pinyin* index attached. The only reason for using this rather old-fashioned, classical dictionary rather than plunge straight into the riches of the *Hanyu da cidian*, *Jitsû* or Morohashi is that it is cheaper.

4. The *Shiyong gu Hanyu da cidian* 實用古漢語大詞典 was written for high-school teachers and their students with special attention to providing definitions of pre-Qin compounds and phrases in Modern Chinese.[25] *Pinyin* is used to indicate the pronunciation of the 11,000 head characters (shown in simplified and complex forms) and the 65,000 compounds defined. Usage of characters and words is shown by means of quotations, all of which, and this is the key distinctive feature, are translated into Modern Chinese. Despite this excellent feature, the dictionary risks falling into the category of "neither-nor:" a fraction the size of the *Hanyu da cidian*, it cannot begin to include the riches of that work, nor is it small enough to be as handy as the *Jianming gu Hanyu zidian*, let alone the *Gu Hanyu changyongzi zidian*. But if you want your citations translated into Modern Chinese, this is the work for you. In addition, it has large-size (B-5), triple-column, clearly printed pages and is arranged by *pinyin*.

5. The *Jianming gu Hanyu zidian* 簡明古漢語字典 contains 8,500 frequently used characters and also a small number of compounds. It uses examples not only from *wenyanwen*, but also from *baihua*. Pronunciation is given in *pinyin*. Accurate and handy. The complete text contains 1.7 million rather small characters.[26]

---

[25] *Shiyong gu Hanyu da cidian* (The large practical dictionary of Classical Chinese), Henan renmin, 1995.

[26] *Jianming gu Hanyu zidian* (Simplified dictionary of Classical Chinese), Zhang Yongyan 張永言 et al., eds., Sichuan daxue, 1986; 8th prnt., 1995.

6. *Gu Hanyu changyongzi zidian* 古漢語常用字字典 is a small
    dictionary of the most frequently used characters in Classi-
    cal Chinese which carries a surprising amount of informa-
    tion.[27] It almost succeeds in avoiding the weakness of most
    such dictionaries, namely, that they seem never to have the
    infrequently used character (it turns out) that you were
    looking up. Its success is based on a very long list of fre-
    quently used characters in Classical Chinese (a total of just
    over 4,100) and an appendix of an additional 2,500 "diffi-
    cult," less frequently used characters. It was written by lin-
    guists at Peking University working under Wang Li 王力 in
    the 1960s and 1970s and grew out of the list of 1,086 fre-
    quently used characters analyzed in a standard university
    textbook, *Gudai Hanyu* 古代漢語 (1.3.5). Modern pronun-
    ciations are indicated in *pinyin* and illustrative citations
    with references follow the definitions, as well as a limited
    number (2,500) of compounds. There is a 30-page appendix
    of tables of Chinese history. This is an excellent dictionary
    which contains an enormous amount of reliable informa-
    tion and manages to pack in 900,000 very small characters.
    Use with the next item.

7. The *Gu Hanyu changyongzi ziyuan zidian* 古漢語常用字字
    源字典[28] was compiled to complement *Gu Hanyu chang-
    yongzi zidian* (1979 edition) by giving the earliest forms of
    each character (oracle-bone, bronze, large seal, small seal);
    the basic meaning; the sound in Middle Chinese and Mod-
    ern Chinese; differentiated, vulgar, and alternative charac-
    ters. It does not quite meet its targets, but nevertheless it
    packs in an extraordinary amount of information (hand-
    written) in a tight space.

---

[27] *Gu Hanyu changyongzi zidian* (Dictionary of commonly used characters in Classical Chinese), Shangwu, 1979; rev. and enlarged ed., 1993;
30th prnt., 1997.
[28] *Gu Hanyu changyongzi ziyuan zidian*, Da Shiping 達世平 and Shen
Guanghai 沈光海, Shanghai shudian, 1989; 3rd prnt., 1997.

8. The *Nixu leiju gu Hanyu cidian* 逆序類聚古漢語辭典 is unique in being a reverse-head character dictionary of Classical Chinese.[29] It contains 2,500 head characters and 22,300 compounds, all of whose readings are given in *pinyin*. After a brief definition arranged by grammatical category, there are citations showing usage drawn from the main texts of the classical corpus. Arrangement is by classifiers. It carries more information than a conventional dictionary because in addition to the main 1,600-page text there is a 200-page index giving compounds by *pinyin* reading of head characters. This enables the reader to find, for example, 15 compounds in which *shi* 史 appears (in nine compounds as the second character under the main entry for *shi*, and in six compounds as the head character accessed through the index). This is a small-sized, fat work with a total of 1.9 million characters.

9. *Lianmian zidian* 聯綿字典.[30] The author, Fu Dingyi 符定一, spent 30 years compiling this unique dictionary. It contains about 15,000 bound disyllabic compounds from the Classics up to the Six Dynasties and about another 5,000 regular compounds. *Lianmianzi* (more correctly *lianmianci* 聯綿詞) are total or partial reduplicates and typically alliterative or rhyming. Pronunciations are given according to the *Shuowen* and rhyme books and variant characters listed (for example, eighty-three ways of writing *weiyi* 委蛇, meandering). One day when this rich data is put on computer it will be possible to arrange the entries by sound, which will be much more useful than the present arrangement by Kangxi classifiers. The strength of the dictionary lies in the amount of data gathered rather than in the explanations. Index: head characters by stroke count.

---

[29] *Nixu leiju gu Hanyu cidian*, An Deyi 安德義, ed. in chief, Hubei renmin, 1994.

[30] *Lianmian zidian* (Dictionary of reduplicate words), 11 *ce*, Beiping: Jinghua yinxuju, 1943; 2nd ed., 4 vols., Zhonghua, 1954; rpnt., 1983.

10. *Gucibian* 古辭辨 examines the sets of lexemes (usually characters) belonging to a particular area of meaning or semantic field.[31] This method is especially effective for Classical Chinese, in which characters were often used interchangeably so that the conventional approach of defining individual words in isolation is less helpful. The success of *Gucibian* also derives from its concentration on a specific lexicon (3,800 of the most frequently used characters based on the word counts in the concordances to 19 of the Han and pre-Qin texts). Near-synonyms are organized into 1,400 groups divided into 50 semantic fields such as movements of the hands (60 entries, each analyzing between two and six near-synonyms); of the eyes (12 entries); of the mouth (19); of the tongue (41); of the body (52); of the heart (46); and of time (21). One of the entries on time, to take an example, is a brief article of 1,500 characters analyzing the changing meanings and interrelations of *sui* 歲, *nian* 年, *si* 祀 and *zai* 載 (see 5.2, note 11 for a summary). The explanations are in clear Modern Chinese with plenty of examples of usage. Characters are in simplified form, but complex forms are given for the head characters. Finding your way around this excellent work is easy. In addition to a detailed table of contents, there are classifier and *pinyin* indexes. This is a large-size, clearly printed book containing a total of over 1.8 million characters.

11. *Gu Hanyu tongshi yiming cidian* 古漢語同實異名辭典[32] is useful both for historians and readers of Chinese literature. It is an attempt to put together in dictionary form a collec-

---

[31] *Gucibian* (An analysis of ancient near-synonyms), Wang Fengyang 王風陽, comp., Jilin wenshi, 1994.
[32] *Gu Hanyu tongshi yiming cidian* (Dictionary of alternative phrases for the same reality), Yang Shishou 楊士首 and Yang Beining 楊北寧, eds., Jilin jiaoyu, 1994; rpnt., 1995. Many such dictionaries were compiled in old China, see, for example, the Qing work, *Shiwu yiming lu* 事物異名錄 (Record of different words for events and things), Li Quan 厲荃, indexed ed., Shanxi guji, 1993.

tion of different phrases used to describe the same reality in Classical Chinese. There is a table of contents showing the 600 head phrases by *pinyin* and a stroke-count index of the 10,000 alternative phrases.

12. *Zhonghua chengyu cihai* 中華成語辭海 contains altogether 40,000 four-character or set phrases (*chengyu* 成語).[33] One of the largest of the many *chengyu* dictionaries.

13. *Hanyu chengyu kaoshi cidian* 漢語成語考釋詞典 (Dictionary of the origins of Chinese *chengyu*), Liu Jiexiu 劉潔修, comp., Shangwu, 1989; rpnt., 1996. Particularly careful examination of the origins and changing meanings of 7,600 *chengyu* and 10,000 of their variant forms. There is also an appendix of 5,000 special phrases of various types.

14. The *Zhonghua diangu quanshu* 中華典故全書 contains explanations and citations for 22,000 classical allusions (*diangu* 典故).[34]

2.5   Bilingual Dictionaries of Premodern Chinese

2.5.1   Classical and Wenyanwen Dictionaries

There has been no major new dictionary of Classical Chinese into English or other European languages since Séraphin Couvreur compiled his *Dictionnaire classique de la langue chinoise* at the end of the nineteenth century (see Box 2). The problem was less one of funding than of the very concept of trying to produce a comprehensive dictionary before detailed synchronic and genre dictionaries were available in China itself. There have, however, been important specialized works, for example:

A Dictionary of Early Zhou Chinese, Axel Schuessler, UHP, 1987. This is one of the very few attempts in the last hundred years to compile a

[33] *Zhonghua chengyu cihai* (Dictionary of Chinese four-character phrases), Jilin daxue, 1994; rpnt., 1995.

[34] *Zhonghua diangu quanshu* (Dictionary of Chinese classical allusions), Yu Changjiang 俞長江 et al., eds., Zhongguo guoji guangbo, 1994.

dictionary of Classical Chinese into a foreign language. It gives readings as reconstructed by Li Fanggui 李方桂 (1902–87), "Studies in Archaic Chinese Phonology," Gilbert L. Mattos, tr., of Li (1971), *University of Hawaii Working Papers in Linguistics* 6.1: 171–282 (1974).

Grammata Serica Recensa, Bernhard Karlgren, *BMFEA*, 29: 1–332 (1957); Elanders, 1964; rpnt., MFEA, 1974. Replaces the author's earlier *Grammata Serica*, *BMFEA*, 12 (1940). It contains his reconstruction of the pronunciation of Old Chinese (which he termed "Archaic Chinese"), and at the same time indicates the pronunciation of around AD 600 and Modern Chinese. Arrangement is by 1,260 phonetic indicators. There is a radical (i.e., classifier) index. There is a Chinese translation: *Han Wendian* 漢文典, Shanghai cishu, 1997. It has both a stroke count and a *pinyin* index. A pioneering monument in its day, *GSR* has been superseded by more recent works.

Dictionnaire Ricci des Caractères Singuliers, Ricci Institute, 1999. Defines 16,000 separate characters. One of the many excellent features of this unique work is that homophones are shown at the beginning of each section with their reference number, tone, classifier and frequency count and stroke count indicated. Simplified, alternative, vulgar and wrong forms are also given. Arrangement is by Wade transcription. The dictionary is fully indexed. It also traces in detail the semantic evolution of 2,000 of the characters from the late Shang to the Han. Changed meanings of these characters are defined, from the oracle-bone and bronze inscriptions and the main classical texts up to the *Shuowen* definition. Inscriptional forms of the characters are indicated with examples. The entire work was drawn from *Le Grand Dictionaire Ricci de la Langue Chinoise* (2.8).

Lexicon of Reconstructed Pronunciation in Early Middle Chinese, Late Middle Chinese and Early Mandarin, Edwin G. Pulleyblank, UBC Press, 1991.

Han-Ying duizhao chengyu cidian 漢英對照成語辭典 (Comparative dictionary of sayings in Chinese and English), Chen Yongzhen 陳永禎 and Chen Shanci 陳善慈, comps., HK: Shangwu, 1983 gives English equivalents of 4,000 *chengyu*. Synonyms and antonyms are also noted.

Chinese-English Dictionary of Chinese Historical Terminology, David Y. Hu (Hu Yingyuan 胡應元), 2 vols., Huaxiang yuan, 1992. The compiler translates and defines 11,811 historical terms, mainly famous sayings and allusions (*diangu* 典故), names, titles and institutions. Arrangement is by Wade-Giles with an index to terms used in the definitions.

Some of the difficulties of trying to produce a comprehensive dictionary of all styles of Classical and Literary Chinese are illustrated by the fate of a project initiated in 1936 at the Harvard-Yenching Institute to produce a Chinese-English dictionary covering all styles of Chinese. A trial fascicule was published in 1953, but the project was abandoned in 1955. Work on the H-Y dictionary project began by pasting together the contents of 16 dictionaries from the *Shuowen* to Karlgren (1940). The trial fascicule of the character *zi* 子 after defining 30 different meanings, gives 68 pages of compounds with *zi* as head character: *Chinese-English Dictionary, Preliminary Print*, Fascicle 39.0.1–3, H-Y Institute, 1953.

2.5.2 Bilingual Dictionaries of the Colloquial Language

Dictionary of Colloquial Terms and Expressions in Chinese Vernacular Fictions (*Zhongguo huaben xiaoshuo suyu cidian* 中國話本小説俗語辭典), Tian Zongyao 田宗堯, comp., Lianjing, 1983; rev. and enl., 1985. The first Chinese-English dictionary for old *baihua* ever published. It examines about 22,000 character combinations (the author claims 32,000) and gives an English translation, sometimes with a short explanation. Arrangement is by *pinyin*. There is a classifier index. References are noted to examples in *baihua* fiction, but there are no citations. This appears to be based on two earlier works by Lu Dan'an 陸澹安.[35]

For Chinese-Chinese dictionaries of vernacular Chinese, see 34.3, *Dictionaries*.

2.6 Special-Purpose Dictionaries

There are thousands of special purpose dictionaries, dictionary-like compilations and glossaries available. Their contents are

[35] *Xiaoshuo ciyu huishi* 小説詞語會釋 (Collected explanations of phrases found in Chinese novels), Zhonghua, 1964; HK: Zhonghua, 1973; Shanghai guji, 1981, and *Xiqu ciyu huishi* 戲曲詞語匯釋 (Collected explanations of phrases found in Chinese drama), Shanghai guji, 1981, but it does not entirely replace them, because Lu quotes examples of usage for all, or nearly all, the 8,000 entries. See 34.2 for other dictionaries of the colloquial language.

not necessarily included even in the largest of the comprehensive dictionaries. A dozen examples follow:

Dialects: *Hanyu fangyan da cidian* 漢語方言大辭典 (Dictionary of Chinese dialects), 5 vols., Zhonghua, 1998.

Economic terminology: *Zhongguo jingjishi cidian* 中國經濟史辭典 (Dictionary of Chinese economic history), Zhao Dexin 趙德馨, comp., Hubei cishu, 1990.

Economic and social history terminology (as found, for example, in the "Shihuozhi 食貨志," 22.3): *Chûgoku shakai keizaishi goi* 中國社會經濟史語彙 (Glossary of Chinese social and economic history), Hoshi Ayao 星斌夫, comp., Tôyô bunko, 1966; rev. ed., Kôbundô, 1976; continuation (*zokuhen* 曾編), Kôbundô, 1975; third collection (*sanhen* 三編), Kôbundô, 1988. The brief explanations are based on the major Japanese studies and translations of the *Shihuozhi* as well as on other important contributions of Japanese scholars to Chinese social and economic history.

Enigmatic folk similes (*Xiehouyu* 歇後語): John S. Rohsenow: *A Chinese-English Dictionary of Enigmatic Folk Similes (xiehouyu)*, UAP, 1991.

Euphemisms: *Hanyu weiwanyu cidian* 漢語委婉語辭典 (A dictionary of Chinese euphemisms), Zhang Gonggui 張拱貴, ed., Zhongguo wenhua yuyan daxue, 1996. This innovatory dictionary contains nearly 3,000 entries from classical and Modern Chinese arranged and indexed by category. For example, urine, excreta, toilets, menstruation, tears and sweat (117 entries). Examples of usage are given. There are stroke-count and *pinyin* indexes.

Loan words (*wailaici* 外來詞): see *Hanyu wailaici cidian* 漢語外來詞辭典 (Dictionary of loan words and hybrid words in Chinese), Gao Mingkai 高名凱 et al., eds., Shanghai cishu, 1984. This contains over 10,000 loan words ("aliens" and "hybrids", not "denizens," see 1.2.7 for a definition of these terms). Not always accurate. See also the following three studies:

Frederico Masini, *The Formation of Modern Chinese Lexicon and its Evolution Towards a National Language: The Period from 1840 to 1898*, Berkeley, 1993.

Edward Gunn, *Rewriting Chinese: Style and Innovation in Twentieth Century Chinese Prose*, SUP, 1991.

Lydia H. Liu, *Translingual Practice*, SUP, 1995, contains a good discussion of loan words in Chinese as well as appendixes showing neologisms derived from various sources, 265–378.

Mantic and medical arts (*fangshu* 方術): *Zhongguo fangshu da cidian* 中國 方術大辭典 (Dictionary of Chinese mantic arts), Chen Yongzheng 陳永正, ed. in chief, Zhongshan daxue, 1991. This contains 6,393 clear entries on the special phrases used in 25 mantic arts from *qixiang zhanbu* 氣象占卜 (aeromancy or divination by the weather) to *mengbu* 夢卜 (oneiromancy or divination by dreams); from *zhan-xingbu* 占星卜 (astrology) to *guxiangxue* 骨相學 (phrenology); from *bagua* 八卦 (Eight Trigrams) to *fengshui* 風水 (geomancy). Arrangement by topic. There is a thematic as well as a comprehensive index.

Myth and legend (*shenhua chuanshuo* 神話傳說): Yuan Ke 袁柯, *Zhongguo shenhua chuanshuo cidian* 中國神話傳說辭典 (A dictionary of Chinese myth and legend), Shanghai cishu, 1986. Contains 3,006 entries arranged by stroke count. There is a thematic index (men, things, heaven and earth, books, events, others). The 175 books listed (and briefly described) constitute the main primary sources for the study of Chinese myth and legend.

Numerical phrases; numerological correspondences (*shumuci* 數目詞): *Hanyu shumuci cidian* 漢語數目詞辭典 (A dictionary of Chinese numerical phrases), Yin Xiaolin 尹小林, comp., Zhonghua, 1993. From the Three Dynasties to the Four Modernizations; from the Five Drums to the *Five Classics*, from ancient times to the present day, the Chinese language is peppered with numerological correspondences and affinities at one end of the scale and numerical mnemonics intended for primary students at the other. The trouble is that there are so many, and not a few were used with different meanings in different periods. There is a rich tradition of dictionaries of numerical phrases written for children. The present dictionary goes a long way to sorting things out with its clear arrangement and definitions of 2,760 numerical phrases (including 700 different phrases beginning with "the three ...").[36]

Secret languages and tradesmen's jargon (*heihua* 黑話, *qiekou* 切口, *yinyu* 隱語, *hanghua* 行話): *Zhongguo yinyu hanghua da cidian* 中國隱語行話大辭典 (A comprehensive dictionary of China's enigmatic language and jargon), Qu Yanbin 曲嚴斌, ed., Liaoning jiaoyu, 1995; or the smaller *Yuhai: Mimi yu fence* 語海:秘密語分冊 (An encyclopaedia of

[36] One of the largest and most interesting was compiled by Wang Yinglin 王應麟, *Xiaoxue ganzhu* 小學紺珠 (Purple pearls for elementary studies), Zhonghua facs. ed., 1987. A 60-page table of contents has been added, showing each of the 2,257 entries divided by the author into 17 main subject categories.

Chinese folk language: volume 1, Chinese secret languages), Wenyi, 1994. Both have *pinyin* indexes.

Symbols (*xiangzheng* 象徵): Liu Xicheng 劉錫誠 and Wang Wenbao 王文寶, eds., *Zhongguo xiangzheng cidian* 中國象徵辭典 (Dictionary of Chinese symbols), Tianjin jiaoyu, 1991. The editors were able to call on more than 60 experts to help them define 2,900 symbols using not only book knowledge, but also recent archaeological findings and in some cases interviews. The results can be appreciated by comparing an entry (e.g., the three pages on "dragon") with the entries on dragon in two earlier dictionaries of Chinese symbols, Eberhard (1986) and Williams (1941).[37] There is no doubt that the interpretations in *Zhongguo xiangzheng cidian* are fuller and more rigorous. There are illustrations and a bibliography of works consulted. Arrangement is alphabetical by *pinyin* and the entries are also indexed by stroke count.

Vernacular literature: In addition to *A Dictionary of Colloquial Terms and Expressions in Chinese Vernacular Fictions* (item 5 of the previous section), note *Jindai Hanyu cidian* 近代漢語辭典, Xu Shaofeng 許少峰, Tuanjie, 1997. It covers the language of vernacular literature from the late Tang to the end of the Qing. All 25,000 entries include examples of usage with references cited. Arrangement is by *pinyin* with every phrase spelled out in full (chap. 34).

Many other special-purpose dictionaries, devoted to literary styles, to individual literary and historical works, to Buddhist and Daoist terminology or to specific periods are discussed in the appropriate sections. For biographical and geographical dictionaries, see chaps. 3 and 4 respectively.

---

[37] Wolfram Eberhard (1986) and Wolfram Eberhard, *A Dictionary of Chinese Symbols*, Routledge, 1988; 4th prnt., 1993; C. A. S. Williams, *Outlines of Chinese Symbolism and Art Motives*, 3rd rev. ed., Kelly and Walsh, 1941, rpnt., under the title *Chinese Symbolism and Art Motives*, Julian Press, 1960; Tuttle, 1974; Dover, 1976.

2.7 Dictionaries of Modern Standard Chinese

The standard medium-sized dictionary of *Putonghua* is the *Xiandai Hanyu cidian* 現代漢語詞典 (*XHC*, for short).[38] It is arranged by *pinyin* and gives authoritative pronunciations for all 61,000 entries (in *pinyin*). The definitions are noted for their accuracy. There is a "reverse-head character" version of the 2nd (1983) edition: *Daoxu XHC* 倒序現代漢語詞典. Arrangement is by rhymes (it is partly intended for those wishing to write poetry). There are also *pinyin* and classifier indexes.[39] The *Daoxu XHC* unlocks many of the riches of the original dictionary, for example, *XHC* only lists 47 words in which *dao* 道 features (as the head character). The *Daoxu XHC* lists an additional 145 words (in which *dao* is the end character). These words are in the *XHC*, but before the appearance of the *Daoxu XHC* there was no means of accessing them. The *Gudai Hanyu zidian* 古代漢語字典 published by Shangwu in 1998 is intended to be the classical companion to *Xiandai Hanyu cidian*.

The standard pocket dictionary of characters is the *Xinhua zidian* 新華字典.[40] Despite its small size, this dictionary has been immensely influential. Since the 1950s, more than 300 million copies have been printed. Two generations of Chinese primary and middle school students and their teachers have been brought up on it. *XHZD* is also useful to foreign students of

[38] *XHC* (Dictionary of modern Chinese), Shangwu, 1978; 2nd rev. ed., 1983; 3rd rev. ed., 1996; 186th prnt., 1996. The draft was completed in 1963. Between 1978 and 1995, 25 million copies were sold. The 1996 revision cut out 4,000 out-of-date phrases and added 9,000 new ones. As a sign of the times, the four-corner index was dropped. Arrangement is by 189 classifiers.

[39] *Daoxu XHC* (Reverse-order *XHC*), Shangwu, 1987; 5th prnt., 1997.

[40] *Xinhua zidian* (New Chinese character dictionary), Renmin jiaoyu, 1953; 6th rev. ed., Shangwu, 1998; 119th prnt. (in Beijing), 1998. The first edition was compiled in the early 1950s by veteran editors, some of whom had worked in the early part of the century on the *Zhonghua da zidian* 中華大字典, Zhonghua, 1915; 2 vols., 1995 (with over 48,000 separate characters, this was the first dictionary to contain more characters than the *Kangxi zidian*—and to correct 2,000 errors in it).

Chinese, and not only beginners. It contains authoritative pronunciations of its more than 10,000 head characters, and clear,
concise definitions of them (plus another 3,500 compounds and
phrases). Arrangement is by *pinyin*. Simple characters are used
throughout, but complex characters are also indicated (in
brackets after each head character), as well as alternative characters (16.4.1). *XHZD* has gone through six major revisions and
continuous minor ones. During the Cultural Revolution years,
as with all other standard dictionaries in China, it was heavily
influenced by changes in the political climate. The last major
revisions (1979, 1992 and 1998) have been more influenced by
the search for lexicographical perfection than politics.[41] The
1998 edition (the launch print run of which was 5 million copies) is printed on especially manufactured paper with a slightly
yellow hue to make it easier on the eyes.

    Lishi Zhongwen zidian 李氏中文字典[42] is an unusual dic-
tionary for a number of reasons: the 12,800 characters it defines
are organized under about 1,100 phonetic indicators (*shengfu* 聲
符) and 60 or so *xingfu* 形符. This is useful for seeing characters
which are pronunced in the same or a similar way. In addition
the Cantonese pronunciation is also given for every character
and compound. Definitions are short but include examples of
usage and common compounds. There are *pinyin*, Cantonese,

---

[41] The 1965 revised edition was ready and printed but not released. It
was only in 1970, on the direct orders of the prime minister, Zhou Enlai,
that a revised version was finally published, but only after Zhou had personally read over the draft and agreed on the inclusion of words related
to such conroversial matters as the *diwang-jiangxiang* 帝王將相 (emperors, kings, generals and prime ministers, i.e., the feudal rulers), e.g., *bixia*
陛下 (Your Majesty). After the fall of Lin Biao in 1971, all expressions
associated with him (e.g., *sige diyi* 四個第一; *wuhao zhanshi* 五好戰士;
xue Maozhu 學毛著) were weeded out (*wagai* 挖改), a process that continued between printings according to the changing political climate. In the
1979 revision most of the Cultural Revolution phrases were cut, a process completed in later revisions.

[42] Li Choh-ming (Li Zhuomin 李卓敏), *Lishi Zhongwen zidian* (Li's
Chinese dictionary), HKCU Press, 1980; Xuelin, 1980; 2nd ed., 1989.

stroke-count and *shengfu* indexes which obviate the necessity of mastering the author's unique "fan system" of arranging the phonetic indicators.

2.8   Bilingual Dictionaries of Modern Standard Chinese

General-purpose dictionaries of Modern Chinese into English and other languages have improved greatly in recent years:

Grand Dictionnaire Ricci de la Langue Chinoise (Chinese-French). This will be the main dictionary of Chinese into a foreign language (estimated publication, 2001). It is to be an encyclopaedic, diachronic dictionary containing 16,000 individual head characters and 300,000 compounds. It has been in the making on and off for 50 years.[43] The single characters and their definitions have been published as a separate dictionary (see 2.5). Some 200,000 of the words defined are from standard colloquial Chinese; the remainder range from ancient to modern Chinese culture. They cover many specialist vocabularies, from aviation to zoology; from Buddhism to television. There are a large number of appendixes with information on diverse subjects such as the 24 seasons of the year or the 64 hexagrams. One advantage of the *Grand Ricci* is that it will also be available on CD-ROM. Early on the editors decided to use Wade-Giles as the system of romanization, a decision that they have maintained.

Han-Ying da cidian 漢英大詞典 (Large Chinese-English dictionary), Wu Guanghua 吳光華, ed. in chief, 2 vols., Jiaotong daxue, 1993, translates no less than 220,000 Chinese words and characters, many of them modern scientific compounds. It is arranged alphabetically by *pinyin*. The *pinyin* readings for all compounds are given. In addition, it has the welcome luxury of three indexes: by *pinyin*, classifiers and stroke count.

ABC (Alphabetically Based Computerized) Chinese-English Dictionary, John DeFrancis, ed., UHP, 1996, is arranged by words in *pinyin* in strict alphabetic sequence. The advantage is that if you know the pronun-

---

[43] See the earlier *Dictionnaire français de la langue Chinoise*, Ricci Institute, ed., Paris: Institut Ricci - Kuangchi Press [Guangqi chubanshe 光啓出版社], 1976. This is a good medium-size Chinese-French dictionary. It contains 6,500 head characters under which are listed 50,000 polysyllabic words. Arrangement is by Wade (with *pinyin* and other transcriptions indicated).

ciation of the word you are looking for (but perhaps you cannot remember the characters), this is the fastest way to find it. On the
other hand, if you do not know the pronunciation of a word, you
are lost (there is no stroke-count or classifier index). If you only
know the first character of a two-character phrase, you are partially
lost. The *ABC* manages to pack its more than 71,300 entries into a
relatively small-sized book, partly by using exceptionally clear, small
typefaces, and partly by giving one-word, or very brief definitions
and almost no parts of speech or examples of usage. There are also 50
pages of appendixes containing orthography rules for *pinyin* etc. The
ABC is not up to the standard of the best Japanese bilingual dictionaries of Modern Chinese (see for example, the *Chû-Nichi jiten* below).

The *Han-Ying cidian* 漢英詞典 (Chinese-English dictionary), 1978; rev.
and enlarged ed., Waiyu jiaoxue yu yanjiu, 1995, is a good single-
volume dictionary of Modern Chinese which contains about 80,000
entries. Eight hundred new head characters and 18,000 phrases have
been added and much of the political jargon included previously has
been excised. Definitions are under head characters arranged by *pinyin*. Also includes *pinyin* readings for all compounds and examples of
usage. There is a classifier index.

The *Han-Ying niyin cidian* 漢英逆引詞典 (A Reverse Chinese-English
Dictionary), Shangwu, 1986; rpnt., 1993, is a reverse-head character
dictionary arranged by *pinyin* with *pinyin* readings for all 67,000 entries. It was based on the first (1978) edition of the *Xiandai Hanyu
cidian*.

Chû-Nichi jiten 中日辭典, Shogakukan and Shangwu, eds., 1992; 17th
prnt., 1998. This is probably the best available medium-sized bilingual dictionary of modern Chinese. It contains 80,000 entries and
over 60,000 examples of usage (giving both the Chinese original and a
Japanese translation). There are also many useful insets and line
drawings illustrating special vocabulary and various aspects of the
language, for example, the similarities and differences between words
used in Standard, Hong Kong and Taiwanese Chinese. There is a
CD-ROM version available. Shogakukan's *Chûnichi jiten* is more up-
to-date than Aichi University's *Chû-Nichi daijiten* 中日大辭典, 1968;
rev. and enl., 1994.

Box 2: Early Bilingual Dictionaries

The Classics contain references to interpreters facilitating the exchanges between northern tribes and the Hua-Xia in the Zhou period. There is no mention of any lists of equivalent words and none have survived. The earliest extant such reference works are the bilingual glossaries compiled to meet the needs of the alien dynasties in the North. They date from the twelfth century and are from Chinese to Tangut (40.2). More are extant from the Yuan, Ming and Qing. The Vietnamese, Koreans and Japanese compiled primers of Chinese and glossaries. Chinese scholars engaged in the detailed study of their own language including its lexicon, but they appear not to have been too interested in the languages of non-Han peoples.

The Jesuits were the first Westerners to compile bilingual dictionaries (from Chinese into Latin, Portuguese, Spanish, French and Manchu). They also made the first systematic attempts to devise systems of romanization and glossaries, such as Nicolas Trigault (1577–1628) and Wang Zheng 王徵, *Xiru ermuzi* 西儒耳目資 (Western literati materials for the eyes and ears), Hangzhou, 1626. Thereafter, sinologists gradually improved the quality of dictionaries of Chinese into Western languages.

The first Chinese-English, English-Chinese dictionary was compiled by the pioneer Protestant missionary to China, a young Englishman who started learning Chinese on arrival in Canton in 1807 aged 25: Robert Morrison, *Zhongguo yuwen zidian* 中國語文字典 (*A Dictionary of the Chinese Language in Three Parts*), 6 vols., Macao: East India Company Press, 1815–23. This contains more than 40,000 head characters and sold at the princely sum of 20 guineas. Arrangement was both by Kangxi classifiers (vols. 1–3) and by pronunciation (vols. 4–5). Aspirations were not shown.

Morrison was superseded by the work of a younger contemporary and one-time colleague, the American missionary and diplomat-scholar Samuel Wells Williams, whose *Syllabic Dictionary of the Chinese Language*, Kelly and Walsh, 1874, was less bulky (and cheaper). The organizing principle was to list characters under 858 phonetic indicators. Williams retired to become the first professor of Chinese at Yale, having earlier published an influential work, *The Middle Kingdom*, 1844, rev. ed., 2 vols., 1883.

A number of early English-Chinese dictionaries were translated into Japanese and played an important role as a source of neologisms for scientific and other words, see 1.2.7.

Box 2—Continued

Williams was overtaken by Herbert A. Giles, *Chinese-English Dictionary*, Kelly and Walsh, 1892; rev. and enl., 1912; rpnt., Ch'eng-wen, 1968. It is still interesting as a repository of late Qing documentary Chinese, although there is little or no indication of the citations (mainly from the *Kangxi zidian*). Giles was HBM Consul at Ningbo before becoming the second professor of Chinese at Cambridge in succession to Thomas Wade, the inventor of what became the Wade-Giles system of romanization (based on the Beijing pronunciation of Mandarin as recorded in the 1912 edition of his dictionary). Most libraries that still use Wade-Giles omit the diacriticals, breve and circumflex.

For French speakers there was Séraphin Couvreur SJ (1835–1919), *Dictionnaire classique de la langue chinoise*, 1890; 3rd rev., Ho Kien Fou: Imprimerie de la Mission Catholique, 1911. The author based his work on the Confucian Classics using works such as the *Peiwen yunfu*. Sources for the citations in the 21,400 entries are indicated. Arrangement is either alphabetic (3rd ed.) or by Kangxi classifier (2nd ed., 1904). The French romanization system reflects the Nanjing pronunciation of Mandarin as based on Joseph Prémare (1666–1736), *Notitia Linguae sinicae*, completed, 1730; published, Malacca, 1831.

Giles was replaced by Robert H. Mathews, *A Chinese-English Dictionary Compiled for the China Inland Mission*, Shanghai, 1931. Arrangement is by syllabic order of modified Wade-Giles under which 7,785 different characters and 104,000 character combinations are defined. Over 15,000 phrases were added for the revised US edition published under the title *Mathews' Chinese-English Dictionary*, HUP, 1943; 18th prnt., 1996; a *Revised English Index* was published as a separate volume by HUP in 1947. *Mathews'* continues in use, especially by students of *wenyanwen*. For other purposes it has been outdated by the many excellent dictionaries mentioned in 2.8.

3

People

The chapter begins by examining the ethnonyms (collective names) used by the Chinese people (Chinese names for China are summarized in Box 3, section 4.1; Chinese names for non-Han peoples and foreigners and foreign countries are dealt with in 40.2 and 41.2; foreign names for the Chinese and China are covered in 42.1).

Next come the personal and alternative names of men, women, and children from both the elite and the non-elite (3.2), as well as the names, forms of address, and titles of the ruler (3.3), and a selection of modern biographical dictionaries (3.4).

An enormous quantity of biographical writing is extant, especially from the last 500 years of imperial history. Published indexes alone refer to biographical materials on more than 250,000 people who lived from the Qin to the Qing (3.4). The greater part of these materials served a ritual or social function, to commemorate, praise, or commend deceased family members or personal friends. The main categories of biographical writing were genealogies, family instructions, and wills (3.5); diaries, autobiographies, and letters (3.6); commemorative writings (3.7); and various categories of biographical writing, including historical and other biographies; chronological biographies; biographies in local gazetteers and biographical collections (3.8). The chapter ends with a brief section on portraits (3.9).

Biographical works (*zhuanji* 傳記) were placed in the History branch of the traditional fourfold bibliographical classification (*Sibu* 四部, on which see 9.3).

3.1   The Chinese

The Xia 夏, Shang 商 and Zhou 周 dynasties (and later their peoples) were named after Xia, Shang and Zhou, the places which they counted as their homeland.[1] The Shang and the Zhou also referred to each other by these names. By the end of the Western Zhou, the practice had grown of calling the Shang dynasty and people, *Yin* 殷 (perhaps after the last Shang capital), or sometimes *Yi* 衣 (an alternative character for Yin) and their own people, Xia (after the first dynasty). The people of the Zhou fiefs were called collectively *Xia* 夏 or *Zhuxia* 諸夏 (also known as the *Hua* 華). Hua was probably originally the name of an earlier tribe, or possibly an alternative for Xia 夏, but was later glossed as meaning "cultivated" as in Huaxia 華夏."[2] *Hua* and *yi* 夷 were common adjectives in the Spring and Autumn period for Chinese and barbarian respectively. The words were linked from the early Tang in the phrase *Huayi* 華夷 (Chinese and barbarians). See 40.1 for some of the background to these and similar expressions.

During the Warring States, people referred to themselves by the name of their kingdom: *Songren* 宋人, *Weiren* 魏人 and so forth. After the Qin unification, for most of the rest of Chinese

---

[1] Kwang-chih Chang, "On the Meaning of *Shang* in the Shang Dynasty," *EC* 20: 69–77 (1995). Traditionally, the Xia were said to have come from Western Henan, and the Shang and Zhou from Shaanxi. Archaeological evidence is not conclusive but seems to point to either Western Henan or Southern Shanxi as being the original home of the Xia; the area encompassing the borders of Shanxi, Henan and Hebei, for the Shang, and the Western part of Shaanxi for the Zhou who in any event had prior to that been semi-nomads outside the China area. As yet there is no consensus whatsoever on these matters.

[2] Another similarly spurious gloss is on the character *Man* 蠻 (the southern tribes), said to be a cognate of *man* 慢 (slow, lazy).

history, the Chinese continued to refer to themselves collectively as the Xia (or Hua, Huaxia or Zhongxia 中夏). They also used the name of a dynasty to refer to the people of that dynasty. After the Tang, Han 漢 or *Hanren* 漢人 was used in this sense and also as an alternative for Huaxia (42.1).

People of the Ming and Qing sometimes referred to themselves as *Mingren* 明人 or *Qingren* 清人. *Qiren* 旗人 (bannermen) referred to members of the Manchu elite (although as the dynasty wore on, its meaning more readily included the Mongol and Han bannermen). The Manchu continued to call the Huaxia *Han'er* 漢兒 (see 42.1 on the changing nuances of this term). Zhongguoren 中國人 and Hanzu 漢族 are modern expressions.

3.2 Personal and Alternative Names

Over 8,000 surnames have been recorded in the course of Chinese history. This statistic, like that for the total number of Chinese characters, is true but misleading (on the total number of characters and of the much smaller number actually in use, see 1.3.1). At any given time, there were probably no more than a total of a couple of thousand surnames in use, even including the most obscure ones. And of these, the vast majority of the population used no more than a few hundred. This is a good example of a random drift trend by which many thousands of choices become narrowed down to a few, in this case, more and more people using fewer and fewer names. Today the total of Han surnames is about 3,000, of which the three most common (Li 李, Wang 王, and Zhang 張) account for something to the order of one quarter of the twenty most commonly used ones and hence 16 percent of the total. One reason for this is that for most of the twenty names, there is no other with an identical pronunciation. Conversely, the surnames that have many other names with an identical pronunciation are rarely used (e.g., *Ji* in the fourth tone: 計, 記, 季, 薊, 冀, 暨). Whatever the reasons, there are today, as there were in the past, an extraordinarily small number of names in use by a very large number of people. Some of the consequences of this imbalance are examined in the following pages.[3]

Most surnames were by origin the names of ancient states, topographical features, official titles or occupations. Given the large number of surnames that have accumulated over the centuries, it is not unusual to come across words once used as surnames, but now more familiar for their meaning, for example, Fu 父, Mu 母, Xiong 兄, and Di 弟. Such unexpected names are sometimes called *qixing* 奇姓 or *xixing* 希姓.[4] Fortunately modern punctuated texts of old Chinese books include conventions for indicating proper names.

Before the Qin unification, the possession of a clan name (*shi* 氏), a title (*jue* 爵), or a posthumous name (*shi* 謚), or even just a patronymic (family name, *xing* 姓), a cognomen (given name, *ming* 名), or a style (*zi* 字), was a mark of high status.[5] Ordinary people did not have names.[6] Thereafter, the use of surnames, at least for administrative records, seems to have quickly spread.

Since the Qin, the typical Chinese family name (*xing* 姓) has been a single character. Several thousand double-character *xing* are known to have existed, although they were not nearly as frequently used as single-character ones. Triple-character and

---

[3] The twenty most commonly used surnames in the 1990s were Li 李, Wang 王, Zhang 張, Liu 劉, Yang 楊, Chen 陳, Zhao 趙, Huang 黄, Zhou 周, Wu 吳, Xu 徐, Sun 孫, Hu 胡, Zhu 朱, Gao 高, Lin 林, He 何, Guo 郭, Ma 馬 and Luo 羅.

[4] Others include Dong* 東, Nan 南, Xi 西, Bei 北; Qian 前, Hou 後, Zuo* 左, You 右; Jin* 金, Mu* 木, Shui* 水, Huo 火, Tu 土 (those still in use as names are marked with an asterisk).

[5] Emblematic clan names typically found on the bronzes are conveniently listed in Gao Ming 高明, *Guwenzi leibian* 古文字類編 (Ancient Chinese characters arranged by type), Zhonghua, 1980, Tôhô, 1987; 5th prnt., 1990, 557–653.

[6] Li Xueqin 李學勤, "Xian-Qin renming de jige wenti 先秦人名的幾個問題" (Various questions concerning Pre-Qin personal names), in *Gu wenxian conglun* 古文獻叢論 (Collected essays on ancient documents), Shanghai yuandong, 1996, 128–36 (originally published in *Lishi yanjiu*, 1991.5).

above *xing* account for less than 1 percent and nearly always represent transcriptions of the names of non-Han peoples and foreign names. The long-term trend was for more and more people to have three character names (so people with a double-character *xing* tend to have a single-character given name (*ming* 名). The most common *xing* have often been those having a royal or imperial connection. Li 李, the most common of all, came to popularity during the early Tang, whose founding emperor was a Li (there are more than 100 million Li's in China today). In the Northern Song, Zhao 趙 became the most popular name for the same reason. Until modern times, it was comparatively easy to change one's surname, and so people reinforced the trend by choosing the most common ones.

The main given names which became the norm from the Han onward can be summarized in the following simple chart:

1. *Xiaoming* 小名 (for infants)
2. *Ming* 名 (for children)
3. *Zi* 字 (given on coming of age)
4. *Hao* 號 (nicknames for adults)
5. *Shihao* 謚號 (given after death)

In modern times, the *xiaoming* has been retained; the *ming* and the *zi* have been combined to form the *mingzi* 名字. The *hao* and *shihao* have fallen out of use.

Shortly after birth, children, from emperor to peasant without exception, were given a milk name (*ruming* 乳名, *xiaoming* 小名, or *xiaozi* 小字) by their parents or wet nurse. The *ruming* were the familiar terms for infants still used today such as Xiaobao 小寶 in Mandarin or Abao 阿寶 in Cantonese (little treasure); Xiaosanzi 小三子 or Asan 阿三 (little no. 3). A common type of *ruming* are those made up of a prefix such as *a* 阿 or *xiao* 小 plus the last character of the *ming*, as in A-lin 阿林 for Wang Hailin 王海林.

Three months after birth, it was the normal practice for the father to choose the given name (*ming*, sometimes called *xueming* 學名 or *daming* 大名 to distinguish it from the *xiaoming*). Within a family, the seniority among brothers or sisters was often indicated by using ranking characters in the *ming* or *zi* (a practice known as *paihang* 排行). For example, starting from the Zhou period, *bo* 伯 (*meng* 孟),[7] *zhong* 仲, *shu* 叔, and *ji* 季 were used for first, second, third and fourth. Thus Confucius's *zi*, Zhongni 仲尼, indicates that he was the second son. *Bo*, *zhong*, *shu* and *ji* were also used in the different terms for relatives, for example to distinguish between *bofu* 伯父 (elder brother of one's father) and *shufu* 叔父 (younger brother of one's father). Other series for ranking siblings are given under 7.1.1, *Ordinal Numbers*. In the Tang, numbers came into fashion among the literati who used them instead of given names in their poems to refer to junior friends of the same generation (who were therefore called *hangdi* 行第), a practice that had died out by the Southern Song.[8]

Numbers in earlier Chinese history were used by ordinary people in place of given names (a practice that declined as they began using *ming* and *zi* in the later empire). Numbers 1–10 were all used in the earlier centuries for surnames; Liu 六, Qi 七, Bai 百, Qian 千 and Wan 萬 were among the most common. They were also not infrequently used in given names by all types of people. The favorite was *jiu* 九, (nine). Parents often referred to their own children (as they still do) by order of birth, for example, *lao'er* 老二 or *laosan* 老三 (second or third born). The eldest is called *laoda* 老大.

A shared character in a two-character *ming* or *zi* was often used for all the brothers and fraternal cousins to indicate that they belonged to the same generation. If they had a single-character *ming*, then a character with the same classifier would often be used (as with the brothers Su Shi 蘇軾 and Su Zhe 蘇轍). In the Han it was a not uncommon practice to identify all males of the same generation with the same character in their *ming*. From the Tang, and increasingly from the Song, it became the common practice. After the Song, genealogies contained the rules (and the names) for use by later generations in a particular lineage.

---

[7] *Meng* was used for the eldest child of the secondary wife.
[8] See 46.5.2 for a special list identifying Tang *hangdi* 行第.

Throughout Chinese history not only the ranking, but also the choice of characters for given names was heavily influenced by *wuxing* 五行 (five elements) and *bagua* 八卦 (Eight Trigrams) beliefs and practices.[9]

The *ming* could be one character or two. Fashions changed. During the reign of Wang Mang (9 BC to AD 23) it was forbidden to use disyllabic given names. This prohibition lasted more or less until the third century. From then until the Ming both disyllabic and one-syllable given names were in use. In the Qing, disyllabic ones became more popular. Since the 1950s, one-syllable names have staged a come-back, especially since the 1970s.

Translating the meanings of given names (a common practice in Treaty-Port writing) almost invariably gives a false or cute impression. Do not translate them, although studio and other alternative names need explanations.

In addition to the *ming*, for people of social standing, at coming of age (15 *sui* for girls; 20 *sui* for boys) it was normal practice to receive a disyllabic courtesy name (*zi* 字). This was usually chosen to extend the meaning of the *ming* and was used outside the family.

The *ming* was used for referring to oneself when in the company of one's elders (to whom one showed normal politeness by invariably calling them by their *zi*). Superiors called their juniors by their *ming*. Those of equal status used each other's *zi* or *hao* (but never to refer to themselves). It was taboo to refer to a dead person by his name.

In addressing a contemporary or superior, it was normal practice to use the family name but always with a prefix or suffix similar to the modern "Lao Wang 老王!" or "Wang shifu 王師傅!" Juniors were often addressed with diminutive *xiao* 小

---

[9] On five-element theory, see Box 8, 20.4. On their influence on the choice of names, see Wolfgang Bauer (1930–97), *Der Chinesichen Personenname: Die Bildungsgesetze und hauptächlichsten Bedeutungsinhalte von Ming, Tzu und Hsiao-ming*, Harrassowitz, 1959.

as in "Xiao Wang 小王!" Among themselves, family members often used kinship terms rather than names.[10]

Given the minutely small stock of commonly used Chinese surnames and the habit of choosing again and again the same optimistic and fortunate given names, there are enormous numbers of people in Chinese history bearing the same names. Many lists of these were made over the ages. *Gujin tong xing-ming da cidian* 古今同姓名大辭典[11] contains 56,700 people with the same names from antiquity to 1936. Arrangement is by stroke count. Sources are given.

It may well have been that because so many people had the same name, people were eager to adopt additional alternative names. The literati gave themselves literary names (*hao* 號, *bie-hao* 別號), sometimes using several dozen in the course of a life. These could be a single character or more usually three or four. From the Tang, *shiming* 室名 (house names), or *zhaiming* 齋名 (studio names), became popular, and by the Qing studio names had overtaken *biehao*. The choice was personal and often whimsical. It had no special connection with a writer or pain-

[10] Han-yi Feng, *The Chinese Kinship System*, H-Y Institute Studies 22, 1948; rpnt., 1967. Han points out that the modern kinship terms took on their present form during the Tang after 1,000 years of constant transformation and confusion from the Qin to the Tang. He concludes his study with an invaluable "Historical Review of Terms," 64–125. See also the discussion of Chinese and English kinship terms in *Kinship Organization in Late Imperial China, 1000–1840*, Patricia B. Ebrey and James L. Watson eds., UCP, 1986, 4–10; Yuen Ren Chao (Zhao Yuanren 趙元仁, 1892–1982), "Chinese Terms of Address," *Language* 32: 217–41 (1956). For a dictionary of appellations, see Wu Hailin 吳海林, *Zhongguo gujin chengwei quanshu* 中國古今稱謂全書 (Dictionary of Chinese appellations, ancient and modern), Heilongjiang jiaoyu, 1991. This contains over 12,000 family, kin, professional, trade, and official appellations from the earliest times to the present day with citations and sources indicated. It is well indexed both by *pinyin* and by category.

[11] *Gujin tong xingming da cidian* (Large dictionary of ancient and modern same names), Peng Zuozhen 彭作楨, Beijing haowang shudian, 1936; rpnt., Shanghai shudian, 1983.

ter's *ming* or *zi*. *Shiming* or *zhaiming* were often used by a writer in the title of his collected works.

Nicknames or sobriquets (*chuohao* 綽號, *hunhao* 渾號, *hunming* 渾名, *waiming* 外名, or *waihao* 外號) were common. Unlike the *biehao*, they were not chosen by the individual, but given by others, and they were usually in direct, not refined, language. For example, the Han soldier Li Guang 李廣, famed for his rapid maneuvers, was given the nickname, the flying general (*fei jiangjun* 飛將軍); Zhuge Liang 諸葛亮, before his talents were given full rein, was known as the sleeping dragon (*wolong* 臥龍), and the Tang expert in the small seal script Li Yangbing 李陽冰 was known as the brush tiger (*bihu* 筆虎).

In addition, officials took official names (*guanming* 官名), Buddhist monks and nuns took religious names (*faming* 法名 or *fahao* 法號),[12] and kin groups frequently used ancestral hall names (*tangming* 堂名). Another important type of name was the posthumous name or title (*shi* 謚, *shihao* 謚號). For ranking officials this was bestowed by the court. For others by the family or clan. The practice may go back as far as the Shang.

3.2.1 Women's Names

It is a sign of the lower status of women that in general they had fewer names than men.[13] Within their own family, they were usually referred to by their *xiaoming* until they married. The Dunhuang manuscripts show that reduplicates such as Maomao 毛毛, Xinxin 心心, Dandan 丹丹, and so forth were popular for girls' *xiaoming*, as they have remained to this day.

---

[12] The surname of Buddhist monks was "*Shi* 釋" (derived from Shishi 釋氏, the abbreviated Chinese transcription of Sakyamuni 釋迦牟尼) plus a two-character personal name bestowed during ordination. Daoist masters and recluses sometimes took nicknames, *Daohao* 道號).

[13] For a discussion of women's given names, see Viviane Alleton, *Les Chinois et la passion des noms*, Aubier, 1993, 205-22. This fascinating study concentrates mainly on given names in Chinese society. See also Rubie S. Watson, "The Named and the Nameless: Gender and Person in Chinese Society," in *Gender in Cross Cultural Perspective*, Caroline B. Brettel and Carolyn F. Sargent, eds., Prentice Hall, 1993, 120-33.

Outsiders called them by their father's name, as in Zhang *nüzi* 張女子 (daughter of Zhang) or Zhang *ermei* 張二妹 (the second Zhang girl). Women high up in the social scale received a *ming* and a *zi*, but this was often not recorded for reasons explained in a much quoted passage from the *Yili*: "Women have no business outside the home, therefore their names are not known by outsiders." After marriage, they were ranked according to their husband's ranking among the brothers in his own family and called *dasao* 大嫂, *ersao* 二嫂, *sansao* 三嫂 ... and, when they became older, *daniang* 大娘, *erniang* 二娘, *sanniang* 三娘 ... Outside their household, they were referred to in formal documents by their original family name followed by a gender indicative, as in Zhang *nü* 張女, Zhang *mu* 張母, Zhang *qi* 張妻, or, most commonly, Zhang *shi* 張氏, or in everyday speech, Zhang *sao* 張嫂. To indicate seniority between women of the same generation, ranking characters were also sometimes used before the *xing*—for example, *shao* Zhang 少張 (Zhang Four) or afterward it, as in Zhang *sisao* 四嫂. Often the family name of the husband was also indicated (first), as in Liu Zhang *shi* 劉張氏, Miss Zhang, wife of Liu (or Mrs. Liu, née Zhang).

3.2.2 *Alternative Names*

Many of the biographical dictionaries contain lists of alternative names, but it usually saves time to turn directly to one of the comprehensive separate indexes of alternative names:

Gudai mingren zihao cidian 古代名人字號辭典 (Dictionary of alternative names of ancient personages), Zhongguo shudian, 1996. Over 40,000 alternative names are conveniently listed by *pinyin* and identified with their owners. There is also a *pinyin* index of regular names.

Gujin renwu bieming suoyin 古今人物別名索引 (An index to alternative names of personalities, ancient and modern), Chan Takwan (Chen Deyun 陳德蕓), comp., Lingnan, 1937; Xin wenfeng, 1965, 1978; Shanghai shudian, 1984; 1987. Lists 70,000 alternative names of some 40,000 people. Arrangement is by stroke count with index.

Shiming biehao suoyin (zengdingben) 室名別號索引 (增訂本), Chen Nai-qian 陳乃乾, Ding Ning 丁寧 et al., comps., Zhonghua, 1982 (this revised and enlarged a 1957 work that had combined two of the same author's previous books into one: *Shiming suoyin* 室名索引, 1933,

and *Bieming suoyin* 別名索引, 1936). Some 34,000 studio and alternative names are listed by stroke count, but only those containing three or more characters are included.

None of these works contains biographical information, and if you are looking up somebody reasonably famous, try *Lidai mingren shiming biehao cidian* 歷代名人室名別號辭典. It contains over 13,500 entries indexing alternative names as well as dates, domicile, and writings of about the same number of people from the Zhou to 1840.[14]

For the Qing, turn directly to *Qingren shiming biecheng zihao suoyin* 清人室名別稱字號索引.[15]

In the twentieth century, writers have used *biming* 筆名 (*nom de plume*) when in the past they would have used one or another type of *bieming*.

3.3 Emperors' Names

Leaving aside the mythical *Sanhuang* 三皇 (three sovereigns) and *Wudi* 五帝 (five emperors), from the Shang to the Qin, the normal title of the ruler was *wang* 王, originally, "big man," later "chief," and later still, "king".[16] They were referred to as Tianzi 天子 (son of heaven) although this expression is not found on the oracle bones, which suggests it may only have come into use from the Zhou. Rulers referred to themselves at least since the Shang as *yu yiren* 于[余]一人 or *yiren* 一人 (the one and only) and also used the self-deprecating terms *gu* 孤

[14] *Lidai mingren shiming biehao cidian* (Studio and alternative names of historical personages), Chi Xiuyun 池秀雲, ed., Shanxi guji, 1996; rev. ed., 1998.

[15] *Qingren shiming biecheng zihao suoyin* (Index to studio and alternative names of the Qing), Yang Tingfu 楊廷福 and Yang Tongfu 楊同甫, eds., 2 vols., Shanghai guji, 1988 (see chap. 50). See also *Zhongguo jin xiandai renwu minghao da cidian* 中國近現代人物名號大辭典, Chen Yutang 陳玉堂, ed., Zhejiang guji, 1993.

[16] Qi Wenxin, "An enquiry into the Original Meaning of the Chinese Character for King," *Chinese Studies in History* 25.2: 3–16 (1991).

(the solitary one), *gua* 寡 or *guaren* 寡人 (the impoverished one), or *bugu* 不穀 (the unfortunate one).

The First Emperor accepted the new title of *huangdi* 皇帝 (made by combining the titles of the *sanhuang* and the *wudi*). He also decided that he alone would refer to himself as *zhen* 朕 (previously this had been a common personal pronoun). Others had to call him *bixia* 陛下, and court historians in writing of his actions were to use the simple word *shang* 上. It is not recorded that he used a modest term to refer to himself. On the contrary, two years before his death in 210, he decided to call himself the *zhenren* 真人 (True Man) rather than *zhen* 朕. Apart from this change, the first emperor's innovations were to last until 1911, except during periods of disunion, when China broke up into kingdoms and local rulers went back to using the title of king. Later rulers continued to use the old expressions *gu*, *gua* and *bugu*, but *gua* fell out of use after the Han.

From the Shang dynasty to the Sui, rulers were normally referred to in later records by their posthumous name (*shihao* 謚號) and title, e.g., Zhou Liwang 周厲王 or Han Wudi 漢武帝. An index to these and to aristocratic titles is available.[17] Probably because the titles were getting too long, temple names (*miaohao* 廟號), which were inaugurated during the reign of Han Jingdi 漢景帝, were used from the Tang to the Ming, e.g., Tang Gaozu 唐高祖. From the beginning of the Ming it became customary to use one era name for the whole reign and thus to refer to emperors by their reign name (*nianhao* 年號); thus Zhu Yijun 朱翊鈞, the thirteenth emperor of the Ming, is today usually known as the Wanli emperor (Wanli *huangdi* 萬曆皇帝) rather than Ming Shenzong 明神宗 (temple name), or the emperor Xian 顯 (posthumous name). Occasionally, emperors

---

[17] *Lidai renwu shihao fengjue suoyin* 歷代人物謚號封爵索引 (An index of posthumous and conferred titles), Yang Zhenfang 楊震方 and Shui Laiyou 水賚佑, comps., Shanghai guji, 1996. See also Wang Shoukuan 汪受寬, *Shifa yanjiu* 謚法研究 (Research on the system of posthumous titles), Shanghai guji, 1996. The posthumous names of the Shang rulers were all taken from the *Tiangan* 天干 (5.2.2).

are mistakenly referred to in translation as if the reign name was their own name, for example, "the emperor Wanli" or "the emperor Qianlong." It is less misleading to put it the other way round: "the Wanli emperor" or "the Qianlong emperor."

The emperor had many other names and titles that he himself or his family and court used during the course of his lifetime. Use of the characters in the emperor's personal name became taboo upon his death (Qin-Han) and upon his accession thereafter.[18]

Chronological tables showing emperors' personal names, titles, and era names are given in 5.2.1. Dictionaries of official titles and posts are given in 22.3 and in each chapter of Part V.

3.4 Biographical Dictionaries

There are enormous amounts of biographical materials available. The various indexes to them include data on over 250,000 people who lived from the Qin to the Qing. Despite this wealth of detail, unmatched in any other historical tradition, there is as yet no satisfactory Chinese dictionary of national biography. The nearest is the *Ershiwushi renming da cidian* 二十

---

[18] There are several convenient listings: *Lidai bihuizi huidian* 歷代避諱字匯典 (Compendium of historical taboo characters), Wang Yankun 王彥坤, ed., Zhongzhou guji, 1997; Wang Jian 王建, *Shihui cidian* 史諱辭典 (Dictionary of historical taboo names), Aichi daigaku, 1997. The classic work is Chen Yuan 陳垣, *Shihui juli* 史諱舉例 (Examples of historical taboo names), Beijing, 1928; rev. ed., Kexue, 1958; rpnt., 1962; Shanghai shudian, 1998. B. J. Mansvelt Beck shows that the taboo took effect on an emperor's death in the Qin and Han: "The First Emperor's Taboo Character and the Reign of King Xiaowen," *TP* 73: 68–85 (1987). D.C. Lau shows the importance of taboo characters for dating Qin and Han texts: "Win hui chutan 秦諱初探" (Preliminary investigation of taboo characters in the Qin and Han), *The Journal of the Institute of Chinese Studies of the University of Hong Kong* 19: 217–289 (1988); Michel Soymié notes that the Dunhuang inscriptions show that writers of Buddhist works did not always respect the imperial taboos: "Observations sur les caractères interdits en Chine," *JA* 228 (3–4): 377–407 (1990).

五史人名大辭典.[19] But there are a number of works covering individual dynasties. If you know when the person you are looking for lived, these are the best starting place. Biographical dictionaries and indexes to biographical materials for specific periods are listed in Part V. Below are listed only the main English-language biographical references:

Qin, Former Han and Xin Dynasties Biographical Dictionary, Michael Loewe, forthcoming, Brill. To include some 5,000–6,000 entries.

Later Han Biographical Dictionary, Rafe de Crespigny, forthcoming, Brill. To include some 5,000–6,000 entries.

Sung Biographies, Herbert Franke, ed., 4 vols., Steiner, 1976. Includes 441 people.

In the Service of the Kahn: Eminent Personalities of the Early Mongol Yuan Period (1200–1300), Igor de Rachewiltz, Hok-lam Chan, Hsiao Ch'i-

[19] The *Ershiwushi renming da cidian* (Dictionary of personal names in the 25 Histories), Huang Huixian 黃惠賢, ed. in chief, 2 vols., Zhongzhou, 1997, summarizes and indexes all the nearly 30,000 biographies in the 25 Histories as well as biographical materials on the several thousand more people found in other sections of the Histories. It also includes dates of birth and death (see 22.2). This replaces earlier works such as the *Zhongguo renming da cidian* 中國人名大辭典 (Cyclopedia of Chinese biographical names), Zang Lihe 臧勵龢, ed. in chief, Shangwu, 1921, 1958; rpnt., Shanghai shudian, 1982; Zhongzhou guji, 1993. The editors managed to include brief biographical entries (mainly drawn from the biographies in the Standard Histories) for some 40,000 people. Neither exact dates nor sources are given, and it is none too reliable. The arrangement is by stroke count. There is a four-corner index and an appendix of alternative names of the personalities included in the body of the dictionary arranged by stroke number (*Yiming biao* 異名表, 1–34).

The *Zhonguo wenxuejia da cidian* 中國文學家大辭典 (Encyclopaedic dictionary of Chinese writers, Shangwu, 1934; HK, 1961; Taibei, 1962, gives more details than Zang (1921), including dates, but contains notices of only about 6,000 literati and is not too reliable.

A Chinese Biographical Dictionary, Herbert A. Giles, comp., Kelly and Walsh, 1898; Taibei rpnt., 1964, contains biographical sketches of about 2,500 people from the whole range of Chinese history, but it is full of inaccuracies, and the selection leaves much to be desired. To be avoided.

ch'in and Peter W. Grier, eds., Harrassowitz, 1993. Includes extensive biographies of 37 people.

Dictionary of Ming Biography 1368–1644, 2 vols., Luther Carrington
Goodrich and Chaoying Fang (Fang Zhaoying 房兆楹), eds., Col.
UP, 1976. The *DMB* contains some 659 biographies with biblio-
graphic notes. It has name, book title, and subject indexes.

Eminent Chinese of the Ch'ing Period, Arthur W. Hummel, ed., 2 vols.,
Washington: Government Printing Office, 1943–44; 1 volume, rpnt.,
SMC, 1991. The *ECCP* includes authoritative biographies (written by
50 scholars) of over 800 leading officials, writers, and personalities active during the Qing. There are detailed name, book title, and subject
indexes.

Biographical Dictionary of Republican China, Howard L. Boorman, ed.,
Richard C. Howard, associate ed., 5 vols., Col. UP, 1967–71. The 5th
vol. is a personal-name index compiled by Janet Krompart, Col. UP,
1979. Includes biographies of 600 leading personalities active in the
years 1911–49. There is some overlap with *ECCP* because almost all
the subjects of this dictionary were born at the end of the Qing and
some had already made their mark before the establishment of the
Republic. The editors have included cross-references to *ECCP*.

A quick way of finding someone's dates is to look in one of
the references giving the birth and death dates of famous people; the most comprehensive is the *Ershiwushi renming da cidian*.[20]

Note that there is no hard and fast rule as to where to classify people whose lives straddled two dynasties: *ECCP* includes
dozens who died before the Qing even started, but has no separate biographical notices for those dying after 1912. *DMB* does
not include figures with entries in *ECCP*. In old China people
were conventionally classified under the dynasty in which they
were born even if they lived many years into the succeeding

---

[20] See also the earlier *Lidai renwu nianli beizhuan zongbiao* 歷代人物
年里碑傳綜表 (A table of dates and places of birth, dates of death [with
epitaphs and biographical sketches referenced] of historical personalities),
Jiang Liangfu 姜亮夫, comp., Shangwu, 1937; rev. ed., Zhonghua, 1959;
HK, 1961; Taibei, 1963. This includes the dates of some 12,000 people
who lived between antiquity and 1919. The table is arranged chronologically, and there is also a surname index

one. For example, Yuan Haowen 元好問 (1190–1257) is normally referred to as a Jin poet although the last 23 years of his
life, during which he wrote much of his work, were spent in
the Yuan. This convention is however not always followed.
Wang Wei 王禕 (1323–74) spent 45 out of his 51 years under
the Yuan, but was classified as a Ming figure because of his
work for the founder of that dynasty. The conclusion is that in
searching for biographical details, as for other sources, cast the
net across the dynastic divides.

3.5   Genealogies, Family Instructions and Wills

3.5.1   Genealogies

Throughout Chinese history the genealogies (*pudie* 譜牒) or
descent lines (*xipu* 系譜, *shibiao* 世表) of royal houses were
kept. The earliest extant traces of genealogical records are those
of the Shang kings, which can be reconstructed from the oracle-
bone inscriptions and later written sources, notably the *Shiji*.
Sima Qian used pre-Qin *pudie* and the descent lines of Warring
States kingdoms (and aristocratic houses) for his own chapters
on *Benji* 本紀 (basic annals) and the genealogical lines of early
rulers (*Sandai shibiao* 三代世表; *Shi'er zhuhou nianbiao* 十二諸
侯年表) and *Shijia* 世家 (hereditary houses). Few of these early
sources were extant even in the Han. None survive today. One
source used by Sima Qian, the *Shiben* 世本, compiled by Liu
Xiang 劉向 (ca. 77–ca. 6 BC), is itself an archive of Warring
States descent lines. It was lost in the Song, but partially reconstructed by Qing scholars, eight of whose efforts have been republished: *Shiben bazhong* 世本八種, Shangwu, 1957.

There were many officially commissioned *pudie* in the
Tang. Only one survives today.[21]

---

[21] *Yuanhe xingzuan* 元和姓纂, Lin Bao 林寶, comp., 812; annotated
edition by Cen Zhongmian 岑仲勉, *Yuanhe xingzuan si jiaoji* 元和姓纂四
校記, *SYSJK* Special Issue 29, 1948; 1973. It was recovered by the *Siku*
editors from the *Yongle dadian* 永樂大典

After the Five Dynasties, the *pudie* ceased to have political significance, and many were lost. The Song court established a Yudiesuo 玉牒所 to compile the imperial genealogy (*Yudie* 玉牒). A draft of the years 1218 and 1219 survives in the collected works of the chief compiler, Liu Kezhuang 劉克莊 (1187–1269). The Qing Yudieguan 玉牒館 compiled *Zongshi yudie* 宗室玉牒 (Imperial clan genealogies) every 10 years starting from 1661. They are preserved in the Yishiguan 一史官 (50.1.1) and in the Shenyang Provincial Archives (50.1.4). They total 2,600 massive volumes (also available on microfilm, see 50.2.1).[22]

From the Han to the Tang the genealogical records (*pudie* 譜牒) of the powerful families (*shizu* 士族) became established as a recognized historical genre. After the revival of clan and family institutions in the Northern Song, the well-to-do began compiling clan (family) genealogies *zupu* 族譜 (*jiapu* 家譜). This trend was encouraged by the Qing court. *Zupu* have survived in considerable numbers, mainly dating from the Republic and late Qing and mainly from South China.[23] Many of the descent lines in the later genealogies are traced back to the Song. Apart from family and clan trees, they also include biographical details of all kinds, family covenants and family instructions, and details of commonly held property such as charitable estates. The *jiapu* are an essential source for family

[22] For a description of the Qing *Yudie*, see James Lee, Cameron Campbell, and Wang Feng, "The Last Emperors: An Introduction to the Demography of the Qing Imperial Lineage," in Roger Schofield and David Reher, eds., *Old and New Methods in Historical Demography*, OUP, 1993, 361–82

[23] Other terms included *zongpu* 宗譜 and *jiasheng* 家乘 (lit. "family history"). See the general introductions by Joanna M. Meskill, "The Chinese Genealogy as a Research Source," in *Family and Kinship in China*, Maurice Freeman, ed., SUP, 1970; and by Otto B. van der Sprenkel, "Genealogical Registers," *Essays on the Sources for Chinese History*, Donald Daniel Leslie et al., 1973 and 1975, 83–98. See also Ted A. Telford, "Survey of Social Demographic Data in Chinese Genealogies, *LIC* 7.2: 118–48 (1986), and by the same author, "Patching the Holes in Chinese Genealogies," *LIC* 11.2: 116–35 (1990). See also 7.2 for further references to micro-demographical studies based on *zupu*.

history, biography, local history, and micro-demography (7.2). Many were destroyed during the Cultural Revolution. A number of reprints and excerpts have been published. The Shanghai Library has a major collection and has established a special genealogical reading room. The main collections and catalogs are as follows:

Zhongguo jiapu zonghe mulu 中國家譜綜合目錄, Zhonghua, 1998. This is a union catalog of 14,761 genealogies compiled before 1949 held in 400 Chinese collections.

The largest collection by far in the United States (and in the world) is held on microfilm in the Genealogical Society of Utah (GSU) Family History Library. It contains more than 7,000 printed (woodblock or lead type) editions of genealogies and in addition 9,000 manuscript genealogies, mainly from private owners in Taiwan and Hong Kong. The holdings are described Melvin P. Telford, "Chinese Collection of the Genealogical Society of Utah," *LIC* June (1998). The printed genealogies contain more data of potential interest to the historian of late imperial China. The GSU also has nearly 5,000 local gazetteers on microfilm and various late Qing census and land taxation data from the Shenyang archives. GSU holdings may be viewed in any of its 2,000 libraries or reading rooms (family history centers) in more than 40 countries.[24]

Other collections outside China are in the Taiwan, the Tôyô bunko in Tokyo and the Chinese collections at the C. V. Starr East Asian Library at Columbia University in New York. For catalogs, see:

Fujian: Chen Zhiping 陳支平, *Fujian zupu* 福建族譜 (Fujian Genealogies), Fujian renmin, 1996. For an innovative selection, see *Min-Tai guanxi zupu ziliao xuanbian* 閩臺關係族譜資料選編 (Selected genealogical materials on Fujian-Taiwan relations), Zhuang Weiji 莊為璣 and Wang Lianmao 王連茂, comps., Fujian renmin, 1984.

[24] The earlier catalog of the GSU is now out of date but still useful for its annotations: *Chinese Genealogies at the Genealogical Society of Utah: An Annotated Bibliography*, Ted A. Telford et al., eds., Taibei, 1983; rprnt., Tôhô, 1988. It lists 3,105 genealogies then held on microfilm at the GSU. There are locality and name indexes.

Guangdong: the provincial library (Zhongshan library) has a catalog of its holdings of 390 Guangdong genealogies: *Guancang Guangdong zupu mulu* 館藏廣東族譜目錄), 1986.

Hong Kong: Luo Xianglin 羅香林, *Zhongguo zupu yanjiu* 中國族譜研究 (Studies on Chinese genealogies), HKCU Press, 1971, includes a list of holdings of the Chinese University of Hong Kong.

Huangshan: the municipal museum holds a rich collection of 170 genealogies of local Xin'an 新安 (modern Huangshan, Anhui) families, see Zhai Tunjian 翟屯建, "Huangshanshi bowuguan cang shanben jiapu shuyao" 黄山市博物館藏善本家譜述要 (Brief introduction to the rare genealogies held in the Huangshan municipal museum), *Wenxian* 文獻 3: 113–34 (1996).

Japan: Taga Akigorô 多賀秋五郎, *Sôfu no kenkyû: shiryôhen* 族譜の研究 史料編 (An analytical study of genealogical books: source materials), Tôyô bunko, 1960; and the same author's *Chûgoku sôfu no kenkyû* 中 國族譜の研究 (Research on Chinese genealogies), 2 vols., Tokyo, 1980–2. Vol. 2 contains detailed listings of (1) 1,276 genealogies in Japanese collections; (2) 1,247 genealogies held by Columbia, Harvard, Library of Congress, Berkeley, Stanford, and Chicago; (3) 873 genealogies held by six institutions in China, Hong Kong, and Taiwan. In each case call numbers are indicated. There are surname and title indexes, but no locality index, chronological index, or institution index (unlike the 1960 volume).

Taiwan: *Taiwanqu zupu mulu* 臺灣區族譜目錄 (Catalog of Chinese genealogies in Taiwan), Zhao Zhenji 趙振績 and Chen Meigui 陳美桂 eds., Taiwan sheng gexing lishi yuanyuan fazhan yanjiu xuehui 臺灣 省各姓歷史淵源發展研究學會, 1987. This is a union catalog of 10,613 genealogies (mainly Taiwanese) held in Taiwan.

A society for the study of genealogy was established in Taiyuan 太原 under the aegis of the Shanxi Shekeyuan 山西社科院 (Shanxi Academy of Social Sciences) in 1990. It puts out an annual journal: *Zhongguo pudie xue yanjiu* 中國譜牒學研究 (published by Shumu wenxian).

3.5.2   *Family Instructions*

Family instructions (*jiaxun* 家訓, *jiagui* 家規, *jiayue* 家約) are an important source for family and clan education and organization. They were either printed separately or also commonly in genealogies. The first such work extant is *Yanshi jiaxun* 顏

氏家訓| by Yan Zhitui 顏之推 (531–91).[25] There is a translation
into English.[26]

3.5.3   Wills

In Europe (and America) one of the main sources for biography and family history, not to speak of social and economic
history, are the last wills and testaments of individuals. They
have survived in huge quantities, dating back in some cases to
the twelfth and thirteenth centuries. Apart from the standard
homilies addressed to descendants, they deal with the division
of property. In China, property was also divided in wills
(*xianling quanshu* 先令券書, *fenjiadan* 分家單). The earliest to
survive dates from AD 5. It was excavated from a tomb in Jiangsu.[27] Wills were sometimes drawn up, but few have survived
(for some Anhui merchant wills, see 50.4.2). Most Chinese
wills do not deal with property, but are testaments in the sense
of final instructions (*yixun* 遺訓, *yiling* 遺令) or last words

---

[25] See Liu [Wang] Hui-chen, *The Traditional Chinese Clan Rules*, Col.
UP, 1959; also Liu, "An Analysis of Chinese Clan Rules: Confucian
Theories in Action," in Arthur F. Wright and David Nivison, eds., *Con-
fucianism in Action*, SUP, 1959, 63–96; also D. C. Twitchett, "Documents on the Clan Administration: 1. The Rules of Administration of
the Charitable Estate of the Fan Clan," *AM* 8: 1–35 (1960); Linda Walters,
"Charitable Estates as an Aspect of Statecraft in Southern Sung China,"
in *Ordering the World: Approaches to State and Society in Sung Dynasty
China*, UCP, 1993, 255–79. Patricia B. Ebrey, *Confucianism and Family
Rituals in Imperial China: A Social History of Writing about Rituals*, PUP,
1991; Patricia B. Ebrey, *Chu Hsi's Family Rituals*, PUP, 1991; Charlotte
Furth, "The Patriarch's Legacy: Household Instructions and the Transmission of Orthodox Values," in *Orthodoxy in Late Imperial China*, K. C.
Liu, ed., UCP, 1990, 125–46.
[26] Teng Ssu-yü, *Family Instructions for the Yen Clan*, Brill, 1968. Albert E. Dien, "Yen Chih-tui (531–591): A Buddho-Confucian," in *Confucian Personalities*, Arthur Wright and Denis Twitchett, eds., SUP, 1962,
43–64. For a Song example, see Patricia Buckley Ebrey, *Family and Property in Sung China: Yuan Ts'ai's Precepts for Social Life*, PUP, 1984.
[27] Bret Hinsch, "Women, Kinship, and Property as See in a Han Dynasty Will," *TP* 84 (1998), 1–3.

(*yiyan* 遺言) or self-composed epitaphs. For a collection of 289 last testaments from all periods of Chinese history, see Zhou Wu 周武, *Zhongguo yishu jingxuan* 中國遺書精選.[28]

3.6 *Diaries, Autobiographies and Letters*

Diaries, letters and autobiographies, not to speak of poems, postfaces and prefaces are all important biographical sources.

Diaries (Riji 日記)

If diaries were published separately they were usually classified under *Zibu* 子部 or *zajia* 雜家. Autobiographies may sometimes be found in a writer's collected works.[29] Note that many authors not infrequently talk about themselves or the reasons that they wrote what they did in postfaces or prefaces.[30]

---

[28] *Zhongguo yishu jingxuan* (A selection of Chinese last testaments), Huadong shifan daxue, 1994. The editor gathered these testamentary writings from all sorts of scattered biographical sources as well as collected works. He provides explanations and linguistic notes. See also Albert E. Dien, "Instructions for the Grave: The Case of Yan Zhitui," *Cahiers d'Extrême Orient*, 8: 41–58 (1995).

[29] For an example of an unusually frank autobiography, see Shen Fu, *Six Records of a Floating Life*, tr. with an introduction and notes by Leonard Pratt and Chiang Su-hui, Penguin, 1983. Arthur Waley translated excerpts from the diaries of Lin Zexu, which cover the years 1812 to 1845, in *The Opium War through Chinese Eyes*, Allen and Unwin, 1958. Zhang Dechang 張德昌, *Qingji yige jingguan de shenghuo* 清季一個京官的生活 (The life of a court official in the Qing Dynasty: A study of personal income and expenditure), HKCU Press, 1970, tabulates the personal expenditures of Li Ciming 李慈銘 over the years 1854–94. It is based on Li's diaries.

[30] Until the Song, authors placed their last words on completion of a work in a postface (*xu* 序) in the last bundle or scroll. With the advent of printing and the possibility for the first time of the whole work circulating in a single text or collection, authors began to put their last words at the beginning in a preface (for which the old word *xu* 序, or 敘, was now used), while *ba* 跋 was retained for colophon or postface. Both words had many synonyms: *tiji* 題記 or *qianyan* 前言 for *xu*; and *tiba* 題跋, *houxu* 后序, *bawei* 跋尾 or *houji* 后記 for *ba*.

For selections and references to several hundred notable diaries, see:

Mingren zizhuanwen chao 明人自傳文鈔 (Excerpts from the autobiographical works of Ming writers), Yiwen yinshuguan, 1977., Du Lianji 杜聯喆, ed., contains 180 autobiographical excerpts by Ming writers.

Qingdai riji huichao 清代日記匯抄 (Collection of excerpts from Qing diaries), Shanghai renmin, 1982.

Zhongguo jindaishi wenxian bibei shumu 中國近代史文獻必備書目 (Essential written sources for the history of modern China), Zhonghua, 1996, 291–301, lists over 200 Qing diaries written between 1840 and 1911.

Autobiographies (Zizhuan 自傳)

On autobiography as a genre, see:

Pei-yi Wu, *The Confucian's Progress: Autobiographical Writings in Traditional China*, PUP, 1990.

For a huge survey of all forms of autobiographical writings, see:

Wolfgang Bauer, *Das Antlitz chinas der autobiographische Selbstdarstellung in der chinesischen Literatur von ihren Anfänges bis Heute*, Hauser, 1990.

Letters (Shu 書)

Shu 書 was the most common word for letter for most of Chinese history. There were many others, of which *chidu* 尺牘 was the most common. The expression *shuxin* 書信 began to come into use in the *Nan-Bei Chao*, but only replaced *chidu* in the twentieth century. The earliest extant private letter so far discovered dates from the Qin (44.3.2.1, Shuihudi). Considerable numbers of private letters have been found in Han tombs, the best preserved is on silk. It was found near Dunhuang (44.3.2.3). The earliest extant manual of letter writing dates from the Western Jin; more than 100 such manuals were found among the Dunhuang manuscripts: Zhou Yiliang 周一良, *Tang*

Wudai shuyi yanjiu 唐五代書儀研究.[31] One of the Yuan popular encyclopaedic manuals of letter writing has been photographically reproduced: *Xinbian shiwen leiyao qizha qingqian* 新編事文類要啓扎青錢.[32]

It was forbidden to use official couriers to send private letters or other documents. For some interesting comments on how private letters circulated (in the Ming), see Timothy Brook, "The transmission of private documents," in his chapter entitled "Communications and Commerce," *CHC*, vol. 8, CUP, 1998, 639–41.

For a selection of 35 letters from all periods of Chinese history translated into English (with Chinese originals in annex), see *Renditions*, nos. 41 and 42, Spring and Autumn, 1994.

3.7 Commemorative Writings

The most important types of commemorative writings were those connected with the ancestral cult. These included epitaphs on tombstones (*mubei* 墓碑), which were carved on stelae and erected on the tomb (*mubiao* 墓表), or on the path or avenue leading to it (*shendaobei* 神道碑).[33] Starting from the end of the Later Han there were frequent regulations banning the use of *mubei*. Eventually they were reduced in size and buried in the grave and called *muzhi* 墓誌, *muzhiming* 墓誌銘 or *kuangming* 壙銘 (sometimes translated into English as "tomb epitaphs" to distinguish them from tombstones or "tomb tablets," the expression used in the manual). Similar inscriptions were also deposited in the ancestral temple (*miaozhi* 廟誌). About

[31] *Tang Wudai shuyi yanjiu* (Researches on letter-writing manuals of the Tang and Five Dynasties), Shehui kexue, 1996.

[32] *Xinbian shiwen leiyao qizha qingqian* (Newly edited forms of correspondence as good as ready cash arranged by categories), Koten kenkyûkai, 1963.

[33] Ann Paludan, *The Chinese Spirit Road: The Classical Tradition of Stone Statuary*, YUP, 1991. Construction works have turned up huge quantities of commemorative and other types of stelae, many of which have been transcribed and published (17.3).

7,000 *muzhi* have been indexed. In addition, there were funeral orations (*jiwen* 祭文, *diaowen* 吊文), eulogies to the dead (*lei* 誄), elegies (*aici* 哀詞), and funerary odes (*song* 頌 or *zansong* 贊 頌).

Tomb-Tablet Indexes

Collections by place: *Xin Zhongguo chutu muzhi* 新中國出土墓誌 (Tomb tablets excavated in New China) is a series containing inscriptions discovered since 1949, arranged by province, of which the first volume to appear was *Henan* 河南, vol. 1, parts 1 and 2, Wenwu, 1994. It includes illustrations of 461 tomb tablets from the fourth to twentieth centuries, with annotated transcriptions, many published for the first time. There is a chronological index.

Hedong chutu muzhi lu 河東出土墓誌錄 (Record of excavated tomb tablets from Shanxi), Chen Jiyu 陳繼瑜, Shanxi renmin, 1997.

Luoyang chutu lidai muzhi jisheng 洛陽出土歷代墓誌輯繩 (Collected historical tomb tablets from Luoyang), Shehui kexue, 1991. Includes 815 *muzhi*.

Luoyang xinhuo muzhi 洛陽新獲墓誌 (Newly discovered tomb tablets from Luoyang), Li Xianqi 李獻奇 and Guo Yinqiang 郭引強, eds., Wenwu, 1996.

Jiangxi chutu muzhi xuanbian 江西出土墓誌選編 (Selection of tomb tablets excavated in Jiangxi), Chen Baiquan 陳柏泉, ed., Jiangxi jiaoyu, 1991. The editor has added biographical notes on the individuals and appended 40 tomb contracts (for the afterlife). On this latter type of document, see Ina Asani, *Religiöse Landverträge aus der Song-Zeit*, Edition Forum, 1993; Valerie Hansen, "Why Bury Contracts in Tombs?" *Cahiers d'Extrême-Asie* 8: 59–66 (1995).

Collections by period: Part V of the manual contains references to published collections of tomb tablets dating from individual dynasties, for example transcriptions of well over 5,000 Sui, Tang, and Wudai funerary inscriptions held in collections all over China (46.5).

1949–1989 Sishi nian chutu muzhi mulu 四十年出土墓誌目錄 (Catalog of tomb tablets unearthed during the past 40 years), Rong Lihua 榮麗華, ed.; Wang Shimin 王世民, rev., Wenwu, 1993. This index lists 1,467 stelae and includes references to reports and an index of names appearing on the inscriptions.

Collections of individual libraries, most important, Beitu 北圖, which has published an index of its holdings of rubbings of 4,638 funerary inscriptions from the Former Han to 1949: *Beijing tushuguan cang muzhi tapian mulu* 北京圖書館藏墓誌拓片目錄, Xu Ziqiang 徐自強, Zhonghua, 1990. The *Qian-Tangzhi zhai* 千唐誌齋 in Xin'an county 新安縣 near Luoyang, is the only museum dedicated to ancient tombstones of which it has 1,413, the greater number (1,209) dating from the Tang (46.5).

> For two indexes edited by Mao Hanguang 毛漢光 of rubbings of stone inscriptions held at the Shiyusuo, see *Zhongyang yanjiu-yuan, Lishiyuyan yanjiusuo cang* 中央研究院歷史語言研究所藏, *Lidai muzhiming tapian mulu fu suoyin* 歷代墓誌銘拓片目錄附索引, Shiyusuo, 1985 (25,000 tomb tablets and inscriptions); *Zhongyang yanjiuyuan, Lishiyuyan yanjiusuo cang* 中央研究院歷史語言研究所藏, *Lidai beizhiming tazhiming zazhiming tapian mulu* 歷代碑誌銘塔誌銘雜誌銘拓片目錄 (stele, pagoda and miscellaneous epitaphs), Shiyusuo, 1987.

Biographies were not only prepared for tomb tablets, but also for family records or the family history (*jiazhuan* 家傳), or to substantiate claims for the subject's inclusion in officially compiled works, such as the local gazetteer, or, for senior officials, the Veritable Records of a reign, or even the Standard History of a dynasty, and also to make the case for the bestowal of posthumous titles and honors. Such claims or assessments were put in the standard form of accounts of conduct (*xingzhuang* 行狀, also called *zhuang* 狀, *xingshi* 行實, or *xingshu* 行述). It was upon these that the biographies in official historical works were usually based.

The classification and models for all these types of writing began to take shape during the Eastern Han, although their origins may be sought in the commemorative writings cast on bronze vessels in the Shang and Zhou. After the Han dynasty, ritual and social biographies are often found in the collected works (*wenji* 文集) of their authors or in the chronological biographies (*nianpu* 年譜) of their subjects. They were also included in literary anthologies. Special collections of commemorative writings have survived in great numbers from later periods.

Not surprisingly, the ritual and social biographies paint a somewhat stereotyped picture, since they were intended as a record of merit (*jigong* 記功) lauding the virtues and achievements of their subjects for the instruction of later generations. Despite this drawback, they provide a huge quantity of basic biographic material on many thousands of members of central and local elites in all periods of Chinese history from the Han down to the twentieth century.

There are some excellent introductory studies on the nature and methods of the different types of Chinese biographical writing, as well as some case studies that discuss the weaknesses of the sources.[34]

A major problem for the would-be biographer is that most of the biographical sources emphasize the moral, literary, scholarly, and official achievements of their subjects while drawing a veil of silence over their private lives, business interests, or financial dealings. In this sense they are not unlike the bland obituaries of civil servants and other public figures that used to appear in establishment newspapers in the West until quite recently.

The traditional biographical sources do not distort. They simply reflect the basic attitude that self-revelation, whether in action or in words, even in diaries, was not to be encouraged. Attainment lay in the fulfillment of one's familial and social roles. Not surprisingly, some of the best modern biographies

---

[34] Brian Moloughney discusses many of the earlier studies of Chinese biographical writing in "From Biographical History to Historical Biography: A Transformation in Chinese Historical Writing," *East Asian History* 4: 1–30 (1992). See also D. C. Twitchett, "Chinese Biographical Writing," in *Historians of China and Japan*, Beasley and Pulleyblank, eds., OUP, 1961, 95–114; and by the same author, "Problems of Chinese Biography," and Arthur F. Wright, "Values, Roles and Personalities," in *Confucian Personalities*, Wright and Twitchett, eds., SUP, 1962, 24–42; 3–23 respectively; David S. Nivison, "Traditional Chinese Biography," *JAS* 21: 451–63 (1962); Hans H. Frankel, "Objektivität und Parteilichkeit in der offiziellen chinesischen Geschichtsschreibung vom 3 bis 11 Jahrhundert," *Oriens Extremus* 5: 133–44 (1958). See also the studies cited in note 36.

have drawn on their subject's poetry or painting to try and get behind the social mask. See, for example, Frederick Mote, *Kao Ch'i*, Arthur Waley (1889–1968), *Yuan Mei*, Jonathan Spence, *K'ang-hsi*, or David S. Nivison, *Chang Hsüeh-ch'eng*.[35]

3.8 Biographies

3.8.1 Historical Biographies

Biographies included in official historical works were termed *shizhuan* 史傳. All other forms of biographical writing were lumped together in catalogs as *zazhuan* 雜傳. From the Song this began to be replaced with the term *zhuanji* 傳記. Biographies attached to genealogies were called *jiazhuan* 家傳. Apart from authorized biographies (the *shizhuan* and *jiazhuan*), less formal biographies were classified as *biezhuan* 別傳 and *waizhuan* 外傳, of which the latter, just like the *waishi* 外史, verged on fiction. The category *xiaozhuan* 小傳 (brief lives) was also fairly common. Most prestigious of all were the biographies included in the grouped biographies (*liezhuan* 列傳), which had been included in the Standard Histories ever since the *Shiji*. They were put in their final form by each new dynasty for its predecessor. It was also highly prestigious to have your obituary included in the Veritable Records.

For the most part, *liezhuan* were based on the various categories of commemorative and social writings introduced in 3.7. For senior officials they were based on the obituaries in the Veritable Records. Although official historians were expected to take a less eulogistic view of their subject, *liezhuan* were sometimes selected to form a group of exemplary lives of an age to illustrate some larger moral pattern or theme such as chastity of widows, filial conduct, or loyalty. Senior officials of a

---

[35] F. W. Mote, *The Poet Kao Ch'i, 1336–1374*, PUP, 1962; Arthur Waley, *Yuan Mei: Eighteenth Century Chinese Poet*, Macmillan, 1956; Jonathan D. Spence, *Emperor of China: Self-portrait of K'ang-hsi*, Knopf, 1974; David S. Nivison, *The Life and Thought of Chang Hsüeh-ch'eng (1738–1801)*, SUP, 1966.

dynasty or a particular reign were also put together (in chronological rather than moralistic groupings). The standards of historical criticism applied to the biographies were not the same as
those applied to other types of historical writing; thus again
and again the same clichés (often drawn from a famous literary
model) were used to round out the major stages of a subject's
life, which in the end appears two-dimensional, more ideal than
real. At times fiction took over altogether, as has been shown,
for example, not only in the earlier Histories, but also in the
later ones as well.[36]

Liezhuan account for over half the space in the Standard
Histories and contain individual biographies of nearly 30,000
people. In addition, the Histories contain biographical materials on several thousand more people found in other sections of
the Histories. Both the biographies and the biographical materials are summarized and indexed in *Ershiwushi renming da cidian* 二十五史人名大辭典. The dictionary also includes dates
of birth and death and identifies ancient place-names and it

---

[36] Twitchett (1992), 62–83; Herbert Franke, "Some Remarks on the
Interpretation of Chinese Dynastic Histories," *Oriens* 3: 113–22 (1950);
Ch'en Shih-hsiang, "An Innovation in Chinese Biographical Writing,"
FEQ 13: 49–62 (1953); James T. C. Liu, "Some Classifications of Bureau-
crats in Chinese Historiography," in *The Confucian Persuasion*, SUP, Ar-
thur F. Wright, ed., 1959, pp. 165–81; Liu Ts'un-yan, "Men of Letters in
the Light of Chinese Historiography," *BMFEA* 37: 137–65 (1965); Arthur
F. Wright, "Biography and Hagiography, Hui-chien's [Hui Jiao 慧皎,
497–544] *Lives of Eminent Monks* [*Gaoseng zhuan* 高僧傳]," in *Silver Jubilee Volume of the Zimbun-Kagaku-Kenkyusyo*, Kyoto, 1954, 383–432; Hans
H. Frankel, "T'ang Literati: A Composite Biography," in Wright and
Twitchett (1962), 65–83; Robert des Rotours, *Les inscriptions funeraires de
Ts'ouei Mien (673–739), de sa femme née Wang (685–734) et de Ts'ouei Yeou-
fou (721–780)*, Maisonneuve, 1975; Wang Gungwu, "The Rebel Reformer
and Modern Chinese Biography," in his *The Chineseness of China: Selected
Essays*, HKCU Press, 1991, 187–206; Kenneth DeWoskin, "Famous Chinese Childhoods," in *Chinese Views on Childhood*, Anne Behnke Kinney,
ed., HUP, 1995, 57–78; Anne Behnke Kinney, "The Theme of the Preco-
cious Child in Early Chinese Literature," *TP* 81.1–3: 1–24 (1995).

therefore replaces earlier indexes. The edition indexed is the Zhonghua punctuated edition.[37]

The biographies in the Ming Veritable Records have been excerpted in the series *Ming Shilu leizuan* 明實錄類纂 (49.1). An enormous number of official biographies survive in the Court Diaries (*qijuzhu* 起居注) and Veritable Records of each reign of the Qing (49.4.1 and 50.4.2). In addition, the biographical archives of the Qing Guoshi Guan 國史館 (National History Office) have survived. Their contents have been used (for example in the *Qingshi gao* 清史稿), but they have not yet been fully exploited.

3.8.2   *Lists of Degree Holders*

Examination lists of successful candidates for the *jinshi* 進士 degree were kept from 622 to the end of the Qing. These lists (*dengke lu* 登科錄) are useful for finding place of origin, paternal background, and approximate dates of individuals (and hence, for example, which local gazetteer to search for further details). Similar official registers (*timing lu* 題名錄) or Directories of Officials (*Jinshen quanshu* 縉紳全書) were also kept for other degrees (sometimes to be found in local gazetteers); and for candidates of the same year.

None of the Tang lists are extant, but an early nineteenth-century scholar, Xu Song 徐松, managed to piece together references to 3,326 successful candidates (including also those in the Five Dynasties).[38] There are also reconstructed lists of Hanlin members in the Tang. *Jinshi* lists for only three years of the Song and the Yuan have survived, namely those for 1148, 1256,

---

[37] *Ershiwushi renming da cidian* (Dictionary of personal names in the 25 Standard Histories), Huang Huixian 黃惠賢, ed. in chief, 2 vols., Zhongzhou, 1997.
[38] *Dengkeji kao* 登科記考, 1838; repr., 3 vols., Zhonghua, 1984. There is a short supplement with corrections and additions by Cen Zhongmian 岑仲勉. There is also a name index to this work as well as to the short supplement: *Tôkaki kô sakuin ichi, ni* 登科記考索引 一, 二, Jimbun, 1949.

and 1333.[39] From the Ming through the Qing complete lists have survived.[40] Most are available on microfilm either through the Family History Library of the Genealogical Society of Utah or directly from the Yishiguan in Beijing. See Table 22, chapter 22 for an outline of the examination system and its different degrees in the Qing dynasty.

3.8.3   Chronological Biography

From the Song onward, the application of annals style to biographical materials produced a more rigorous form of biographical writing than the ritual and social biographies and historical biographies discussed above. This new form was called *nianpu* 年譜 (chronological biography). These trace the subject's life, year by year, in great detail, particularly for personalities of the late Ming or Qing, for whose lives the source materials are more copious than for previous periods. An example is the recently compiled *nianpu* of the Ming loyalist, philosopher, writer, and painter Huang Daozhou 黄道周 (1585–1646).[41] The preliminaries include a study of the 32 alternative names used by Huang and an outline of his paternal and maternal ancestors (1–49). There follows a strictly chronological account of his activities in each year of his life (50–367). The

[39] See Edward A. Kracke, "Family vs. Merit in Chinese Civil Service Examinations under the Empire"*HJAS* 10: 103-23 (1947); reprinted in John L. Bishop, ed., *Studies of Governmental Institutions in Chinese History*, HUP, 1968, 171-94.

[40] *Ming-Qing jinshi timing beilu suoyin* 明清進士題名碑錄索引 (Index to Ming-Qing stele lists of *jinshi* degrees), Zhu Baojiong 朱保烱 and Xie Peilin 謝沛霖, eds., 3 vols., Shanghai guji, 1980; Taibei: Wenshizhe, 1982, gives the names of the 51,624 *jinshi* of the Ming and the Qing. Arranged by name. Gives native place, date of degree, and quality of degree (i.e., rank in that year's class). There is a *pinyin* index. Vol. 3 also lists those who passed by date, rank, and category and most usefully, also indicates where biographical sources on them may be found. On the examination system of the Qing, see Table 22, chap. 22.

[41] *Huang Daozhou jinian zhushu hua kao* 黄道周紀念著述畫考, Hou Zhenping 侯真平, ed., 2 vols., Xiamen daxue, 1996.

second volume contains an annotated bibliography of Huang's writings, inscriptions, paintings, and calligraphy (369–768).

Nianpu are available for over 4,000 outstanding historical figures.[42]

3.8.4   Biographies in Local Gazetteers

Local gazetteers contain considerable numbers of biographies usually grouped as in the Standard Histories. They also sometimes contain additional biographical materials such as epitaphs. In recent years more and more gazetteer indexes have been compiled, sometimes for biographies of people who lived in a particular period, increasingly for biographies of those from a particular region, province, or city. Biographies of people from a particular place are not necessarily published in a gazetteer (see below under Jiangsu for example):

Particular Periods

Song-Yuan fangzhi zhuanji suoyin 宋元方志傳記索引 (Index to the biographies in Song and Yuan local gazetteers), Zhu Shijia 朱士嘉, Shanghai guji, 1963; 1986.

Mingdai difangzhi zhuanji suoyin 明代地方誌傳記索引, 2 vols., Taibei, 1986, includes holdings of Taiwan and Japan and published material, thus expanding *Nihon genson* 日本現存 *Mindai chihôshi denki sakuin kô* 明代地方志傳記索引稿 (Draft index of people with biographies in Ming local gazetteers (extant in Japanese collections), Yamane Yukio 山根幸夫, ed., Tôyô bunko, Mindai kenkyû shitsu, 1964. Includes references to biographies of some 30,000 people in 299 Ming gazetteers.

---

[42] *Zhongguo lidai renwu nianpu kaolu* 中國歷代人物年譜考錄 (Catalog of chronological biographies of historical personalities), Xie Wei 謝巍, Zhonghua, 1992. Includes carefully arranged notes on 6,259 *nianpu* of 4,010 people. The author spent a lifetime collecting *nianpu* and has included the holdings of all major libraries in China and abroad. There are convenient indexes of personalities and authors arranged by *pinyin* and notes on editions and provenance of each *nianpu*. Replaces all previous *nianpu* catalogs.

Particular Places

Beijing: *Beijing Tianjin difangzhi renwu zhuanji suoyin* 北京天津地方志人物傳記索引, Gao Xiufang 高秀芳 et al., Beijing daxue, 1987. Indexes the biographies in 73 editions of local gazetteers of counties presently attached to Beijing and Tianjin. Each of the 14,608 entries gives name, alternative name(s), dynasty, native place, and biographical citations.

Guangdong: *Guangdong difangzhi zhuanji suoyin* 廣東地方志傳記索引, Pan Mingshen 潘銘燊, 2 vols., HKCU Press, 1989. Indexes the biographies of 10,222 persons in 11 Qing gazetteers.

Guangxi: *Guangxi difangzhi zhuanji renming suoyin* 廣西地方志傳記人名索引, Guangxi renmin, 1997.

Jiangsu: *Ming-Qing Jiangsu wenren nianbiao* 明清江蘇文人年表, Zhang Huijian 張慧劍, comp., Shanghai guji, 1986. Contains the names, dates, and works of 4,379 Ming and Qing (up to 1840) literati from Jiangsu arranged as a chronological table.

Shanxi: *Shanxi tongzhi renwu zhuan suoyin* 山西通志人物傳索引, Chi Xiuyun 池秀雲, Taiyuan, 1984. Indexes 15,808 people.

Northeast: *Dongbei fangzhi renwu zhuanji ziliao suoyin* 東北方志人物傳記資料索引 (Indexes to biographical materials in Northeastern gazetteers): (*Jilin juan* 吉林卷), Jilin sheng tushuguan 吉林省圖書館, eds., Jilin wenshi, 1989; (*Liaoning juan* 遼寧卷), Liaoning sheng tushuguan 遼寧省圖書館, eds., Liaoning renmin, 1991; (*Heilongjiang juan* 黑龍江卷), Heilongjiang sheng tushuguan 黑龍江省圖書館, eds., Heilongjiang renmin, 1989.

3.8.5   Biographical Collections

Far more extensive than the biographies in the Standard Histories and in the local gazetteers are the very large numbers of ritual, commemorative, and "unofficial biographies" (*biezhuan* 別傳), that is, those not included in an official historical work. They are usually contained in the collected works (*wenji* 文集) of their authors or in special biographical collections. The great bulk date from the last thousand years of Chinese history and are relatively well indexed (see appropriate sections of Part V for titles). Unfortunately the same is not true of the periods before the Song. For these earlier centuries the student should look first through the standard biographical indexes for each period, including indexes of stone inscriptions and tomb tablets (listed in Part V). Next, the collected works of individual authors as well as the great literary anthologies should be checked (many of these latter include commemorative biographical writings as a category).

Very large numbers of privately compiled collections of biographies of famous people are also extant. Frequently the organizing principle was the inclusion of all famous people living in a certain region or locality; other collections group the famous men of an age or of a certain type. For this last category a considerable number of modern biographical dictionaries have been compiled. If you know what the individual you are looking was or did, then it is usually quicker to check one of these special references, for example, for military men (chap. 28), doctors (chap. 36), non-Han peoples (40.2), women (chap. 39), artists, craftsmen, and musicians (38.3), writers and poets (chap. 30), philosophers (chap. 32) or Daoist and Buddhist monks and nuns (33.4 and 33.5).

To give an idea of the number of biographical collections available today: the section on biographies in the *Siku* (subbranch seven of the History branch) lists 460 collections while the much more comprehensive *Zhongguo congshu zonglu* 中國 叢書綜錄 contains references to over 2,000 biographical collections under 18 different categories. Fortunately the most important of these have been indexed in standard reference works such as the biographical indexes in the *H-Y Index Series* (which indexes a total of 199 biographical collections), but not always.[43]

---

[43] *H-Y Index* 34 (Song), 35 (Liao, Jin and Yuan), 24 (Ming), and 8 (Qing) index 47, 30, 89, and 33 of the most important biographical collections respectively. In several cases more comprehensive indexes to biographical collections are now available; see individual sections in Part V for references.

3.9 Portraits

The range of expression of prehistoric representations of the human face in China is astonishing. Two quite different types of features are shown on the prehistoric jades and again on the rare depictions of humans on bronzes. In one the eyes are slanted and often have stirated eyebrows. In the other, the eyes are depicted as deep round hollows. The former are found in the South and West, the latter at the Shang centers in Henan such as Anyang. Both types appear intended to strike fear and may have been used in battle or in sacrificial rituals.[44] The stylized painted faces of Peking opera come at the end of a long evolution of one branch of the history of masks, those used for dance.

From the fifth century BC to the later empire, it was a common practice to bury figurines (*yong* 俑) in tombs.[45] These have survived in large numbers and often have expressive, lifelike, non-stylized, albeit anonymous, features.

But these are exceptional. In many ways the aims of portrait painters and carvers of imperial China were not so different from the authors of biographies: their purpose was spiritual, bureaucratic, or social rather than individual. Good examples

[44] Jessica Rawson, "Some examples of Human or Human-like Faces on Shang and Western Zhou Bronzes," in *Proceedings of the International Conference on 'Chinese Archaeology Enters the Twenty-first Century'*, Kexue, 1998, 124–28; Li Jinshan 李錦山 and Li Guangyu 李光雨 also examine prehistoric contrasts, as well as others dating from the Shang, Zhou and Han in *Zhongguo gudai mianju yanjiu* 中國古代面具研究 (Research on ancient Chinese masks), Shandong daxue, 1994; see also the comic-book style faces on the prehistoric petroglyphs, closer to their contemporary cousins on the other continents than to their dynastic descendents. A good selection is in Song Yaoliang 宋耀良 *Zhongguo shiqian shenge renmian yanhua* 中國史前神格人面岩畫 (Mythical humans in China's prehistoric petroglyphs), HK: Sanlian, 1992. Xue Ruolin 薛若鄰 has edited a collection of ritual masks: *Zhongguo wunuo mianju yishu* 中國亞儺面具藝術 (The Art of Chinese Ritual Masks), 2 vols., SMC, 1996. The 2nd vol. contains a summary in English.

[45] Ann Paludan, *Chinese Tomb Figurines*, HK: OUP, 1994.

are the portrayal of children with their rosy cheeks, smiling faces, and fat little bodies or the ideal images of Confucius as an ancient sage embodying all those qualities society wished him to stand for but with no shred of evidence upon which to base a likeness. Therefore he is invariably shown as an immensely old sage, not unlike a Daoist hermit.[46]

On portrait painting in general, see Audrey Spiro, *Contemplating the Ancients: Aesthetic and Social Issues in Early Chinese Portraiture*, UCP, 1990. On portrait painting in the Ming, see "Man," in Craig Clunas, *Pictures and Visuality in Early Modern China*, Reaktion, 1997, 88-101. Many more portraits survive from the Qing; see Richard Vinograd, *Boundaries of the Self, Chinese Portraits, 1600-1900*, CUP, 1992. Check also exhibition catalogs.

Beitu 北圖 has published 10 volumes of rubbings of portraits in its collection of stone inscriptions.[47] For an index to 4,353 illustrations in a wide variety of historical sources in every conceivable medium, see *Zhongguo lishi renwu tuxiang suoyin* 中國歷史人物圖象索引.[48] Note that there are many portraits among the 7,000 illustrations contained in *Zhongguo gudaishi cankao tulu* 中國古代史參考圖錄 (8.2.1).

For missionary painters and embassy artists, see 42.3.1. Photographic portraits date from the 1850s (42.3.2).

[46] Michael Siggerstedt, "Forms of Fate: An Investigation of the Relationship Between Formal Portraiture, Especially Ancestor Portraits, and Physiognomy (*xiangshu*) in China," *International Colloquium on Chinese Art History, 1991: Proceedings, Painting and Calligraphy*, 2 vols., Taibei, 1992, 713-48.

[47] *Beijing tushuguan cang huaxiang taben huibian* 北京圖書館藏畫像拓本匯編, 10 vols., Shumu wenxian, 1993.

[48] *Zhongguo lishi renwu tuxiang suoyin* (Index to images of Chinese historical personages), Qu Guanqun 瞿冠群 et al., Jiangsu jiaoyu, 1994.

4

Geography

This chapter is concerned with domestic geography; Chinese geographical works on the rest of the world are dealt with in chapter 41.

Place-names carry a lot of history in them and are worth studying for that alone (4.1). They frequently changed, as did regional and local administrative units (4.2), and so it is essential to know how to trace the different names and boundaries of a place over time (4.3). There are place-name dictionaries (4.3.1) and historical maps (4.3.2) to help with these tasks.

The Chinese state and Chinese scholars produced all kinds of geographical works, for military and administrative purposes; for historical studies and for everyday life. These are examined in the rest of the chapter as follows: cartography (4.4); comprehensive geographical works (4.5), including early works (4.5.1), monographs in the Standard Histories (4.5.2), comprehensive gazetteers (4.5.3), geographical studies (4.5.4); local gazetteers and how to find them (4.6); descriptions of cities (4.7) and modern studies (4.7.1); merchant route books and manuals (4.7.2); diaries of travel inside China (4.8). The chapter concludes with bibliographies and textbooks of historical and economic geography (4.9).

Environmental history, including climate change, shifts in river courses, lakes and coasts, desertification and deforestation and their interaction with economic and social life are introduced in 35.4. Hydrographic works and water control are the subject of 35.3. Descriptions of border areas and the coasts are covered in 41.4.

Works on geography (*dili* 地理) were placed in the History branch of the traditional fourfold bibliographical classification (*Sibu* 四部, on which see 9.3).

4.1   Place-Names

Most Chinese place-names have two elements, the name itself and the geographic or administrative unit to which it belongs. This applies as well to the name of the country as to the smallest village. In Zhongguo 中國, Beijingshi 北京市 or Zhangjiabao 張家堡, *guo* 國, *shi* 市 and *bao* 堡 indicate the unit, just as *jiang* 江 and *shan* 山 in Changjiang 長江 and Lushan 廬山 indicate the geographic feature.

Amongst the oldest place-names are those for rivers, mountains and human settlements. Of these, the most numerous are the names of villages. Most of these were made up of a lineage or family name plus descriptor such as *cun* 村, *zhuang* 莊 (village), *li* 里 (village or lane), *zhen* 鎮 (market town), *ji* 集 (periodic market), *shi* 市 (market), *jie* 街 (street), *pu* 鋪 or *dian* 店 (shop), *fang* 坊 (quarter), *ping* 坪 (level ground), *wan* 灣 (bay), *qiao* 橋 (bridge), *kou* 口 or *zui* 嘴 (mouth of river), *gang* 港 (harbor), *du* 渡 (ford) and many others. Examples include names like Lijiacun 李家村 or Wangzhuang 王莊.

Given thousands of years of military settlements, village and other place-names often contain words for one kind or another of military encampment. These include *tun* 屯 (army settlement), *bao* 堡 (fort), *ying* 營 (encampment), *chang* 場 (field), *wei* 衛 (garrison), *guan* 關 (pass), *zhai* 寨 (camp; stockaded village) and many others. Typical examples would be Weihaiwei 威海衛, Sanlitun 三里屯 or Lijiaying 李家營.

Cities were not infrequently named after the era name in which they were founded (e.g., Shaoxing 紹興 in Zhejiang, after the Shaoxing era, 1131–1162).

Box 3: Zhongguo 中國

Under the Shang, the name for the royal cultic center, the earliest capital, was *Shang* 商, *Zhongshang* 中商, *Dayishang* 大邑商 or *Tianyishang* 天邑商. This was extended to mean the royal domain. The area indirectly ruled through royal relatives and senior officials was called *sifang* 四方 (the four quarters) or *situ* 四土. Beyond that lay the peoples outside Shang rule, the *duofang* 多方.

Under the Zhou, the phrase used for the royal domain was *Zhongguo* 中國 (*guo* 國 meaning a city and its surrounding area, traditionally translated as "state") as opposed to the area where the feudal lords had their lands, still called *sifang* (hence the expression *fangyan* 方言 "local speech," or today, "dialect"). After the Eastern Zhou was established at Luoyi 雒邑 (modern Luoyang) in 770, *Zhongguo* referred either to Luoyang or to the area around it, and thus came to refer to what is now known as the Central Plain (Zhongyuan 中原). *Zhongguoyu* 中國語 or *Zhong-Xiayu* 中夏語 was the dialect spoken in this area. Because of the weakness of the Zhou, *Zhongguo* was also used at this time to refer to the feudal states of the Zhongyuan. States such as Chu 楚 were not regarded as being one of the Zhongguo. Apart from Zhongguo, other expressions used during the Zhou were *Zhongtu* 中土, *Zhongzhou* 中州, *Qu-Xia* 區夏, *Zhong-Xia* 中夏, *Fang-Xia* 方夏, *You-Xia* 有夏 or *Tianxia* 天下. So, Zhongguo had different meanings for the first five centuries of its use under the Zhou.

In the Wei and Jin period, *Zhongguo* and *Hua-Xia* were abbreviated to form *Zhonghua* 中華, an expression which came into general use during the *Nan-Bei Chao*. It referred to either the area inhabited by the Zhonghua as opposed to the surrounding barbarian lands, or simply the Zhongyuan (Central Plain). There were at least a dozen other ways of referring to what we now call "China" (on the origins of this word, see 42.1). For example, *Jiuzhou* 九州 or *Shenzhou* 神州. It was only in the nineteenth century that Zhongguo 中國 emerged as the main name for the country (it appears in a formal document for the first time in the title of the chief Manchu negotiator at the Treaty of Nerchinsk, 1689).

It is sometimes implied that the Chinese were unique in regarding their country as central. Nothing could be further from the truth: the ancient Greeks, Romans, Indians, Japanese, Incas, Mayas and Aztecs all saw their countries as the center of the world—but only the Chinese used the concept for the name.

Names with characters symbolizing good fortune were very popular (Changchun 長春, Jinshan 金山, Longjing 龍井 and so on). Not surprisingly, the most common first characters in county names are for propitious qualities such as *xin* 新 (new, 39 counties); *nan* 南 (south, 38); *ping* 平, *an* 安 (peaceful, 31); (calm, 31); *yong* 永 (everlasting, 30); *jian* 堅 (firm, 30); *wu* 武 (valiant, 25); *dong* 東 (east, 25) and *ning* 寧 (peaceful, 25). Note that *yang* 陽 in place-names means south of the mountain (e.g., Guiyang 貴陽), but north of the river (e.g. Hanyang 漢陽) because these are the positions that catch the sun. Yin 陰 is used in the opposite sense (e.g., Huaiyin 淮陰, which is to the south of the river).

The names of the provinces are usually derived from topography (e.g., Henan); history (e.g., Sichuan); pre-existing non-Han names (e.g., Xizang); major cities (e.g., Jiangsu) or they are statements of imperial policy (e.g., Ningxia), see Table 4. Note that all of the provinces (and most cities, regions and counties) have simplified names, and sometimes several. These are usually a single character taken from the modern name or from the ancient kingdom in which the province is situated or from both. Thus Jing 京, Jin 津, Hu 滬 (or Shen 申) and Yu 渝 for Beijing, Tianjin, Shanghai and Chongqing. Single-character province and city names were not only used in literature, they are still used in everyday life today as a convenience, for example on automobile registration plates. They are also used in the spoken language, usually linked with another word to form a compound (it is normal, for example, to refer to northern Sichuan or to southern Fujian as Chuanbei 川北 and Minnan 閩南). In addition to their simplified names, many of the provinces, especially the older ones, have several alternative names, for example, Shanxi is known as San Jin 三晉; Sichuan, as Shu 蜀, or Ba-Shu 巴蜀. Some of common ones are shown in Table 4, which provides a brief summary of the origins of the province names (obviously the detailed historical changes in provincial place-names were a great deal more complex than can be shown in a table).

Table 4: The Origins of the Names of the Provinces

Province Name (Origin of Meaning); Simplified Name, also Alternative Name

Anhui 安徽 (Anqing 安慶 + Huizhou 徽州); Wan 皖

Fujian 福建 (Fuzhou 福州 + Jianning 建寧); Min 閩, also Ba Min 八閩

Gansu 甘肅 (Ganzhou 甘州 + Suzhou 肅州); Gan 甘, also Long 隴

Guangdong 廣東 (The enlarged territories to the [South] East); Yue 粵,
    also Nanhai 南海, Lingnan 嶺南 or Yuedong 越東

Guangxi 廣西 (The enlarged territories to the [South] West); Gui 桂

Guizhou 貴州 (named after the Tang prefecture Juzhou 矩州 (which then had
    the same pronunciation as Guizhou 貴州); the formal change from Ju to
    Gui was made in the Yuan; Qian 黔, also Gui 貴

Hainan 海南 (Hainan Isl., Hainan *dao* 海南島); Hai 海, also Zhuya 珠崖

Hebei 河北 (North of the Yellow River); Ji 冀, also Zhili 直隸

Heilongjiang 黑龍江 (named after the river Heilong); Hei 黑

Henan 河南 (S. of the Yellow River); Yu 豫, also Zhongzhou 中州

Hubei 湖北 (N. of the [Dongting] Lake 洞庭湖); E 鄂, also Jing 荊

Hunan 湖南 (S. of the [Dongting] Lake 洞庭湖); Xiang 湘

Jiangsu 江蘇 (Jiangning 江寧 + Suzhou 蘇州); Su 蘇

Jiangxi 江西 (from the Tang name Jiangnan xidao 江南西道, the Western cir-
    cuit south of the Yangzi); Gan 贛, also Yuzhang 豫章

Jilin 吉林 (Manchu *Jilin* [along] *wula* [the big river, i.e., the Songhua]); Ji 吉

Liaoning 遼寧 (Peaceful territories of the Liao River); Liao 遼

Nei Menggu 內蒙古 (Mongolian *Mongol*); Nei Menggu 內蒙古

Ningxia 寧夏 (Peaceful Xia [the ancient kingdom of Xi-Xia]); Ning 寧

Qinghai 青海 (tr. of Mongolian *Kokonor*, Blue Lake); Qing 青

Shaanxi 陝西 (W. of Shaanzhou 陝州); Shan 陝; also Qin 秦; Guanzhong 關中

Shandong 山東 (E. of the [Taihang 太行] Mts.); Lu 魯, also Qi-Lu 齊魯

Shanxi 山西 (W. of the [Taihang 太行] Mts.); Jin 晉, also San Jin 三晉

Sichuan 四川 (named after the four administrative regions of Tang Sichuan,
    by later convention sometimes associated with the rivers Changjiang 長江,
    Minjiang 岷江, Tuojiang 沱江, Jialingjiang 嘉陵江); Chuan 川; also Shu
    蜀 or Ba-Shu 巴蜀

Taiwan 臺灣 (known as Daoyi 島夷 in (Warring States); Yizhou 夷州 (in San-
    guo); Liuqiu 琉球 (Sui–Yuan); Taiwan (Ming–); possibly from S. Min pro-
    nunciation of Dayuan 大員 (the main city in Taiwan in the Ming); Tai 臺

Xinjiang 新疆 (The new frontier), 1884 (previously Xiyu 西域); Xin 新

Xizang 西藏 (from the administrative unit founded by the Yuan, dBus gTsang,
    itself based on the gTsang-bo River [see 41.2.2]); Zang 藏

Yunnan 雲南 (S. of the Yunling 雲嶺 Mts.); Dian 滇, also Yun 雲

Zhejiang 浙江 (Zhejiang was the old name for the Qiantang River 錢塘江);
    Zhe 浙, also Wu-Yue 吳越

Emperors started building their tombs shortly after acceeding to the throne. A common practice was to found a new county town at the tomb site and populate it with conscript laborers and craftsmen. Such "tomb counties" are identified with the character *ling* 陵 (Liu Bang is at Changlingxian 長陵縣; Han Wudi at Maolingxian 茂陵縣).

Non-Han languages were the source for many place-names. Usually the sounds were transcribed—for example:

Dunhuang 敦煌: (a transcription of Sogdian Draw"n).

Turpan: Tulufan 吐魯番 (a transcription of the Uighur name meaning "low-lying ground"), see 46.3, note 17.

Gobi: Gebi 戈壁 (a transcription of *gov*, the Mongolian for desert).

Hutong 胡同 (the name for the lanes in Beijing, Tianjin and the cities of the Northeast; from *khôtagh* (also transcribed as *gudum* or *hottôk*), the Mongolian for water well.

Zhan 站 (from Mongolian *jam*, post station. Found in many places named after Mongolian postal relay stations, for example, Huazhouzhan 華州站. Not infrequently such names were subsequently sinicized by using the older Chinese word for postal station (*yi* 驛) instead of the Mongolian loan-word *zhan* 站. *Zhan* itself survives in modern words such as *jiayouzhan* 加油站, gasoline station or *huochezhan* 火車站, railroad station).

Cities and temples changed their names frequently. One reason they did so is because when they were rebuilt after having been destroyed by fire or war a new name was considered a way of bringing better fortune. Another reason was political, as when 75 percent of the commandery, kingdom or county names were changed during the Wang Mang interregnum, or as when the character *an* 安 was removed from place-names after the rebellion of An Lushan 安祿山.

Often different words are used in place-names in different parts of the country. Traditionally, *jiang* 江 was the usual word for rivers in the South; *he* 河 in the North and *shui* 水 for those in between. The word for lane in the North is *hutong* 胡同; in the South, it is variations of *xiang* 巷, for example, *xiangdao* 巷道, *xiaoxiang* 小巷, or *xiangzi* 巷子. In Wu dialect it is *long* 弄 or *lilong* 里弄 (*longtang* 弄堂 in Shanghai).

Romanization of Chinese Place-Names

Western Europeans first came to China in modern times via the South and therefore they recorded many Chinese place-names (as well as personal and other names) according to Cantonese pronunciation: "Hong Kong" for Xianggang 香港; "Kiangnan" for Jiangnan 江南; and "Canton" for Guangdong 廣東 (presumably a transcription derived from the Cantonese pronunciation of the province of Guangdong 廣東, not from its capital of Guangzhou 廣州). These were the transcriptions incorporated into the late Qing *Postal Atlas of China*. In addition, this work also reflects the French system of romanization (based on the Nanjing pronunciation of Mandarin), for example, "Tsinan" for Jinan 濟南, and the British system (Wade-Giles), based on the Beijing pronunciation of Mandarin, for the names of smaller places. Other dialects also affected the romanizations used in the Post Office system, which continued to influence Chinese names in English (and many other languages, including for example, Japanese and Thai) until the 1970s. Thereafter the tendency has been to use *pinyin* based on Standard Modern Chinese pronunciation (e.g., Beijing 北京 instead of Post Office Cantonese, "Peking").

4.2 Administrative Units in Different Dynasties

One of the main problems for the central government throughout most of Chinese history was how to control threats to its authority at the regional level. Many dynasties were brought down by regional warlords, but bit by bit layers of centrally appointed supervision or centrally controlled regional government were installed. The result was that the center became ever stronger. New terms were constantly applied to what gradually evolved into the provincial governments. At the same time many of the older terms were pushed down the administrative hierarchy (*zhou* 州 for example began as the highest level regional unit in the Zhou 周 period and was even used in many synonyms for China (Box 3); from the Sui it was demoted to the second highest regional unit (prefecture); by the Qing it had become the second lowest level (department); today it is used only for self-governing administrative units in non-Han areas. Other terms, for example *xian* 縣, underwent a similar process of debasement covering ever smaller units as new organs of control were added above them.

At the top and in the center, the symbolic and sometimes effective head of the entire system, the emperor, resided in the palace (*da'nei* 大內, *jincheng* 禁城), the heart of the government structure in the capital (*jing* 京 or *du* 都 as in Beijing 北京 or Shangdu 上都). In many dynasties it was normal to have twin capitals. The lowest level to which the center appointed an official was the county (*xian* 縣, sometimes called district). They were governed by a magistrate (*xianling* 縣令 or *xianzhang* 縣長 in the Qin and Han; *xianling* to the Song and thereafter *zhixian* 知縣). Below the counties were various systems of locally regulated control and supervision down to the villages (*li* 里, *cun* 村) and urban wards (*fang* 坊).[1]

The Qin introduced regional government after it destroyed the last remaining independent, hereditary kingdoms and set up a total of 36 (later expanded to 48) commanderies (*jun* 郡) each responsible for between five to 20 counties (of which in all there were about 1,000).

The Han began by following the same system in about half the empire, but in the other half installed hereditary princedoms (*wangguo* 王國) at the commandery level and marquisates (*houguo* 侯國) the size of counties. Gradually these were brought under central control and by the end of the Later Han there were nearly 100 *jun*-level units (responsible for a total of 1,500 counties). To control the *jun*, 13 regional inspectorates (*zhou* 州) were established. Out of these eventually developed the provinces of the later empire.

---

[1] The clearest outline in English of the main administrative units at the center and in the provinces in each dynasty, as well as brief descriptions of military and personnel administration may be found in the Introduction to *DOTIC*, 3–96.

The *zhou-jun-xian* structure was retained by the smaller dynasties during the period of disunion. From the Tang, the term *jun* disappears and is replaced by *zhou* 州 (prefectures headed by prefects *cishi* 刺史). Above these, itinerant regional surveillance commissioners (*anchashi* 按察使) were appointed. Their unit of operation was the circuit (*dao* 道) of which there were 10 to 15. From 977, the *dao* were termed *lu* 路, and from the Yuan (by which time they were beginning to become more like a permanent provincial administration), they were called *xing zhongshu sheng* 行中書省 (branch secretariats), or *xingsheng* 行省 for short. As a consequence, the Song *lu* were downgraded to prefectural level. The *xingsheng* of the Yuan became the familiar provinces (*sheng* 省) of the Ming and Qing of which there were between 13 and 18 in China proper. The provincial yamen in the Ming supervised *fu* 府 (prefectures); under which in some cases came *zhou* 州 (subprefectures); and at the bottom some 1,500 *xian* 縣 (counties).

In the Qing, the provincial Governors-general or Viceroys were called *Zongdu* 總督 and the Governors, *Xunfu* 巡撫. The hierarchy below the province was *fu-ting-zhou-xian* 府廳州縣 (prefectures headed by prefects, *zhifu* 知府; subprefectures headed by subprefectural magistrates, *tongzhi* 同知; departments headed by department magistrates, *zhizhou* 知州; and counties headed by county magistrates, *zhixian* 知縣).

There were many other administrative units and direct and indirect links in every period. The metropolitan region surrounding the capital since the earliest historical records to the present day has always been directly administered by the central government. Special units were established to administer and control non-Han regions and to secure the frontiers (in the Qing, the subprefectures, *ting* 廳, were used for these functions). Starting in the Han, throughout the five centuries of the Xiongnu threat, the Western Regions (Xiyu 西域) were kept directly subordinate to the center (44.3.2.3).

The problem of changing territorial and administrative boundaries is a troublesome one; for example, statistics about a

circuit (provincial level unit) in the Tang dynasty are difficult
to compare with similar statistics for a region in the Han or a
province in the Ming since the boundaries may have changed.
One solution is to check that the same counties were included
but there is no guarantee that their borders were the same and
it is a laborious business because more often than not the
names changed. But it can be done. *Zhongguo lidai xingzheng
quhua* 中國歷代行政區劃 lists the names of all administrative
units including all counties in every period from 221 BC to the
end of 1991.[2] The many works tabling boundary changes in
specific periods are listed in the relevant sections of Part V.
Note that local gazetteers usually contain tables of administrative changes (*yan'ge biao* 沿革表) which show for example
when the area of a former locality (*xiang* 鄉) became upgraded
to a county (*xian* 縣) and was therefore no longer included in
the area of the county to which it had been attached previously.

4.3 How to Identify Historical Places

The first problem in identifying places referred to in historical
sources is that place-names changed over time. For example,
Beijing 北京 (the Northern Capital), was the name for nine
capital cities between the third and fifteenth centuries before it
was applied to the capital we now know by this name. Moreover, before that time, the city we know today as "Beijing" had
had at least seven different names in the course of its history.[3]

---

[2] *Zhongguo lidai xingzheng quhua* (Chinese historical administrative
units), Zhang Minggeng 張明庚 and Zhang Mingju 張明聚, eds. and
comps., Zhongguo Huaqiao, 1996.

[3] Ji 薊 (Shang), Yanguo ducheng 燕國都城 (*Chunqiu*), Yanjing 燕京
(Liao), Zhongdu 中都 (Jin), Dadu 大都 (Yuan), Jingshi 京師 or Beijing
北京 (1403–1927), Beiping 北平 (1927–1949), Beijing 北京 (1949–). For a
scholarly examination of the linguistic and historical origins of Beijing
street names, see Zhang Qingchang 張清常, *Beijing jiexiang mingcheng
shihua: shehui yuyanxue de zai tansuo* 北京街巷名稱史話: 社會語言學的
Footnote continued on next page

The second problem is to understand the many different terms used for administrative units at different times (4.2).

The third problem is that the administrative boundaries of places frequently shifted. These are conveniently traced in historical atlases and special tables (4.3.2).

Chinese scholars spent a great deal of time compiling reference tools in all branches of historical studies, not the least in historical geography. Modern place-name references and historical atlases are based on their labors.

4.3.1   Place-Name Dictionaries

Modern historical place-name dictionaries list the various names of a place and the periods in which these names were used as well as the modern equivalent. The most comprehensive of these works is *Zhongguo lishi diming da cidian* 中國歷史地名大辭典.[4] It contains 60,000 brief entries giving the original name and period of foundation and subsequent history of some 90,000 places (provinces, prefectures, cities, towns, rivers, and mountains) in use from earliest times up to 1949. The present location is given in terms of the provinces and administrative units as of the 1990s. Arrangement is by stroke count, but there

---

再探索 (Historical discussion of Beijing street names: a re-examination using socio-linguistics), Beijing yuyan wenhua daxue, 1997.

⁴ *Zhongguo lishi diming da cidian* (Dictionary of Chinese historical place-names), Wei Songshan 魏嵩山, ed. in chief, Guangdong jiaoyu, 1995. Before being superseded by Wei Songshan, the largest historical place-name dictionary was edited under the direction of the indefatigable Shangwu Press editor, Zang Lihe 臧勵龢, *Zhongguo gujin diming da cidian* 中國古今地名大辭典 (Dictionary of Chinese place-names, ancient and modern), Shangwu, 1931, rpnt., 1979, 1982). It contains 40,000 historical place-names, but it is none too accurate. There is another dictionary of historical place-names that has been reissued in an expanded edition in Japan: Liu Junren 劉鈞仁, *Chūgoku chimei dai jiten* or *Zhongguo diming da cidian* 中國地名大辭典, 6 vols., Tokyo, 1980. It contains about 34,000 names and has a *pinyin* index. It, too, has been superseded by Wei Songshan (1995).

is a handy *pinyin* index (as well as an appendix of chronological tables covering every year from 841 BC to 1949).

The volume on historical geography of the *Zhongguo lishi da cidian* 中國歷史大辭典 is broader in scope than a historical place-name dictionary, covering in 9,640 entries not only historical place-names (including some found on oracle-bone and bronze inscriptions), but also famous geographers from earliest times to 1911 and their works.[5]

Shangwu's *Zhonghua renmin gongheguo diming cidian* 中華人民共和國地名辭典 was not intended as a means of tracing historical place-names, but if all else fails, it is worth trying since it was based on detailed on-the-spot investigations as well as book research. It has over 180,000 place-names (including temples, bridges, roads, and other monuments and constructions) and a certain amount of historical information on them.[6]

There are a number of specialized historical place-name dictionaries, for example, for the Western Regions (Xiyu 西域, 41.3.1) or Southeast Asia (41.5.1). Reference to such works are given in the appropriate section of the manual.

For an annual handbook incorporating the latest administrative boundary changes, see *Zhonghua renmin gongheguo xingzheng quhua jiance* 中華人民共和國行政區劃簡冊, Ditu.

[5] *Lishi dili* 歷史地理, Tan Qixiang editorial chairman, Shanghai cishu, 1996. The work was compiled by historical geographers at Fudan and Hangzhou universities and the Academy of Social Sciences. One of the best volumes of the *Zhongguo lishi da cidian*, on which see 8.4.

[6] *Zhonghua renmin gonghe guo diming cidian* (The People's Republic of China place-name dictionary), Shangwu, one volume per province, 31 vols., 1984–99; also combined ed., 6 vols., 1998–2000. The United States Board on Geographic Names, *Mainland China*, 2 vols., Washington, DC: Government Printing Office, 1968, includes 108,000 names, including some village names, each identified by finding coordinates and regional code reference.

4.3.2   Historical Atlases

The most accurate maps of historical changes in China's external frontiers, internal administrative boundaries, and place-
names available is the *Zhongguo lishi dituji* 中國歷史地圖集.[7]
This eight-volume work covers from the earliest times to 1840
in 304 historical maps (plus a large number of inset maps).
Work on it began in 1954 and had proceeded far enough for an
restricted circulation edition to be put out in 1974. This was
then corrected and the new archaeological discoveries taken
into account before publication began in 1982. The *Lishi dituji*
is a summation of many centuries of detailed scholarship.[8] It
starts off where the previous largest map showing changing
boundaries and place-names, that of Yang Shoujing 楊守敬, left
off.[9] A total of 70,000 place-names are included. Each volume is
indexed. The relevant volume for each period is listed in Part
V. There is a one-volume, concise version with 33 maps: *Jianming Zhongguo lishi dituji* 簡明中國歷史地圖集.[10]

[7] *Zhongguo lishi dituji* (Collection of historical maps of China), Tan
Qixiang 譚其驤 (1911–91), ed. in chief, 8 vols., 2nd rev. ed., Zhonghua
ditu xueshe, 1974–76; rpnt., Ditu, 1985; HK: Sanlian, 1991–92.

[8] Six volumes of detailed additional materials that were too bulky to
be published in the *Zhongguo lishi dituji* are being separately published
under the title *Zhongguo lishi dituji shiwen huibian* 中國歷史地圖集釋文
匯編. To date, only vol. 5 on the Northeast, has appeared; Zhongyang
minzu xueyuan, 1988.

[9] *Lidai yudi yan'getu* 歷代輿地沿革圖 (Maps of changing places and
boundaries in different periods), 42 *ce* (Shanghai, 1878–1911; 10 vols.,
Lianjing, 1975; vol. 11, personal-name index, 1982). Tables of administrative boundary and place-name changes were compiled on an empire-wide
scale, especially in the Qing, culminating in the work of Yang. Part of
the information in this work is reproduced in map form, but not accurately, in Norton Ginsburg's *An Historical Atlas of China* (new ed.,
UChP, 1966). This does not include small places (county towns and below). It has a good index but there are no characters on the maps, only a
rather clumsy glossary of characters.

[10] *Jianming Zhongguo lishi dituji* (Concise atlas of Chinese history),
Gu Naifu 顧乃福, ed., Ditu, 1991.

For a historical atlas that shows military campaigns as well as administrative changes, see *Zhongguo gudai lishi dituji* 中國古代歷史地圖集 (Collection of historical maps of China), Liaoning jiaoyu, 1992.

Caroline Blunden and Mark Elvin, *Cultural Atlas of China*, Facts on File, 1983, is an attractive overview of Chinese history in map form.

Detailed maps of a province, prefecture, or county in a given period are available in most local gazetteers (4.6). In recent years historical atlases of individual provinces have begun to appear, for example *Guangdong lishi dituji* 廣東歷史地圖集.[11] City maps and plans are dealt with in 4.7.

4.4 Cartography

The best collection of ancient Chinese maps, including recent archaeological discoveries, is the three-volume *Zhongguo gudai dituji* 中國古代地圖集. Vol. 1 covers the Warring States to the Yuan dynasty; vol. 2, the Ming, and vol. 3, the Qing.[12] These large volumes contain over 650 reproductions both in color and in black and white. There are scholarly notes in both Chinese and English concerning each map as well as longer papers on various aspects of cartography in each period.[13]

---

[11] *Guangdong lishi dituji* (Collection of historical maps of Guangdong), Shenzhen: Guangdong sheng ditu, 1995.

[12] *Zhongguo gudai dituji* (A collection of ancient Chinese maps), vol. 1, *Zhanguo zhi Yuandai* 戰國至元代; vol. 2, *Mingdai* 明代; vol. 3, *Qingdai* 清代, Wenwu, 1990, 1995 and 1997. For a single volume collection, *Treasures of Map: A Collection of Maps in Ancient China*, Science Press, 1998.

[13] For a short introduction, see Richard J. Smith, *Chinese Maps: Images of All Under Heaven*, HK: OUP, 1996. The author discusses representations of barbarians in histories and encyclopaedias and discusses maps as marking the boundary between the self and the other.

See also Brian J. Harley and David Woodward, *The History of Cartography*, vol. 2, book 2, *Cartography in the Traditional East and Southeast Asian Societies*, UChP, 1994.

There are plenty of references to maps in pre-Qin works, but the earliest discovered so far date from the late Warring States. They have a good claim to be the most detailed, oldest maps in the world. Archaeologists have also discovered a handful of maps and plans drawn on wood or silk dating from the Qin and Han. We know from the early literature that they were used primarily for military, fiscal and administrative purposes, and secondarily for general information for settlement and travel. The modern phrase *bantu* 版圖 meaning domain or territory is derived from the pre-Qin practice of drawing maps on wooden tablets.

Qin: Tianshuishi Fangmatan 天水市放馬灘, Gansu: seven maps on four wooden tablets discovered in a late Qin tomb, 1986 (*Wenwu* 1989.2; 1989.12); fragment of one map on paper from a Former Han tomb, clearly illustrated with brief scholarly commentary in *Zhongguo gudai dituji*, vol. 1; Hsu Mei-ling, "The Qin Maps: A Clue to Later Chinese Cartographic Development," *Imago Mundi* 48: 90–100 (1993). These are the earliest Chinese maps discovered so far.

Warring States: Pingshan xian, Hebei 河北平山縣: Architectural blueprint (drawn to scale) of the mausoleum of the King of Zhongshan, 中山國兆域圖. Set in bronze and silver. Discovered in 1977; illustrated with transcriptions and scholarly commentary in *Zhongguo gudai dituji*, vol. 1. See also Song Zhongming 孫仲明, "Zhanguo Zhongshan wangmu 'Zhaoyu tu' de chubu tantao" 戰國中山王墓 '兆域圖' 的初步探討, *Dili yanjiu* 1982.1.

Han: Mawangdui, near Changsha 長沙馬王堆: three silk maps discovered in Mawangdui tomb No. 3 (168 BC). None of these maps bore names, but they are now referred to as (1) the *dixing tu* 地形圖 (Topographical map, 96 × 96 cm), which shows the southern part of the princedom of Changsha (covering northern Guangdong, northeastern Guangxi and southern Hunan) on a scale of 1:180,000; depicts with remarkable accuracy physical features such as mountains and rivers, towns, villages, and roads; (2) the *zhujun tu* 駐軍圖 (Garrison map, 98 × 78 cm), which is on a larger scale (1:80,000 to 1:100,000) and shows part of the area covered by the topographical map, with garrisons, strongholds, a castle, and lines of march; (3) the *chengyi tu* 城邑圖 (City map 52 × 52 cm), which is the oldest extant city map in the world. It may be of Linxiang 臨湘 (Changsha) and shows the city wall, streets, pavilions, and so forth. Each of the maps was based on surveying and uses standard symbols (e.g., a circle for villages and a square for towns). Illustrated with transcriptions, reconstruction of the place-names and symbols, and scholarly commentary in *Zhongguo gudai dituji*, vol. 1.

Few traces survive of the innovations in mapping made between the Han and the Song. The main ones are credited to Pei Xiu 裴秀 (AD 224–71) and to Jia Dan 賈耽 (729–805). Pei introduced the system of indicating distances using a grid, and he also made the first historical map showing changes in place-names and boundaries (*Jinshu* 晉書, *juan* 35, *Pei Xiu zhuan*). None of his maps survive, although the six principles he propounded are known. In the Tang, Jia is said to have used the grid system of Pei to draw a huge map entitled *Hainei Huayitu* 海内華夷圖 (Map of the Hua and barbarian territories between the seas). It was on the scale of one inch to one hundred *li* 里. Old place-names were shown in black; their current ones in red. This convention is still occasionally used (*Jiu Tangshu* 舊唐書, *juan* 138, *Jia Dan zhuan*).

Two maps carved on opposite sides of a stele in 1136 have survived (they may be seen in the *Beilin* 碑林 at Xi'an, see 17.3). The first is the *Huayitu* 華夷圖 (Map of the Hua and barbarian territories) which was based on and named after Jia's *Hainei Huayitu* 海内華夷圖. The other is a map of waterways, the *Yujitu* 禹迹圖 (Map of the tracks of Yu). It is the earliest extant map using a grid system. See the illustrations and commentary in *Zhongguo gudai dituji*, vol. 1. See also another three Song maps carved on stone held in the Suzhou Museum of Inscribed Stelae (17.3, *Collections of Stelae*).

After the mariner's compass came into use in the Song, navigational maps were drawn indicating compass courses. They were called *zhenlutu* 針路圖, *zhenjing* 針經 or *zhenshu* 針書 (needle guides). The earliest to survive shows the seventh voyage of Zheng He (1371–1434) to Ceylon (1430). It is partly reproduced in *Zhongguo gudai dituji*, 168–71.[14]

---

[14] The mariner's compass (*zhinanzhen* 指南針) was like the geomancer's *luopan* (37.3), indeed probably evolved from it, but retained

Footnote continued on next page

An important step was made in the thirteenth century by Zhu Siben 朱思本 (1273–1337).[15] He produced a new map of the empire (*Yuditu* 輿地圖) using the grid system and showing the Mongol conquests. Zhu's map has not survived, but a manuscript copy of it formed the basis for extant Ming maps.[16] The concept of measuring height based on the sea level was proposed by Guo Shoujing 郭守敬 (1231–1316).

A new stage in the development of Chinese mapping came in the eighteenth century when the Jesuits by imperial command conducted trigonometric surveys between 1708 and 1718 and drew a complete series of maps of China and its neighbors. These far surpass their earlier efforts of the seventeenth century and they remained the basis for all maps of China, both in China and abroad, down to the early twentieth century. The results were printed in various editions and with differing titles between 1717 and 1721.[17] The scale for the earlier editions was 1:1,400,000, but as the area covered grew larger, the scale was reduced to 1:2,000,000. These maps were printed in several publications in China, including in the imperially commis-

---

only the essential directional information on its dial (usually the 24 directions (*ershisi fang* 二十四方, *ershisi wei* 二十四位, *ershisi xiang* 二十四向). The 24 points were set at 15° intervals. They were indicated with the characters for the 12 earthly branches (*dizhi* 地支), eight of the heavenly stems (*tiangan* 天干) and four of the *bagua* 八卦 from the *Yijing* (the *siwei* 四維, four directions, namely *gen* 艮, *xun* 巽, *kun* 坤 and *qian* 乾 for the inter-cardinal points). Some compasses only showed the eight directions (the four cardinal and inter-cardinal points). At the end of the Qing, the Western 16-point compass card began to come into use.

[15] See Walter Fuchs, *The "Mongol Atlas" of China by Chu Ssu-pen and the Kuang yü t'u with 48 Facsimile Maps Dating from 1555*, *MS* Monograph 8, Catholic Univ., Beiping, 1946. Luo Hongxian 羅洪先 (1504–64), *Guang yutu* 廣輿圖 (Expanded edition of the *Yutu*), 1541, was one of the first works to be based on Zhu's "Mongol Atlas." It was printed in 1555.

[16] *Zhongguo gudai dituji*, vol. 2, contains an important, annotated collection of 248 Ming maps with excellent color reproductions and notes in Chinese and English on every map and research articles by the editors.

[17] *Huangyu quan lantu* 皇輿全[覽]圖 (Comprehensive atlas of the imperial territory of the Kangxi reign), 1718.

sioned encyclopaedia, the *Gujin tushu jicheng* (29.3). In Europe, the 1721 woodblock edition was revised and published by Jean-Baptiste du Halde to accompany his *Description géographique, historique, politique, et physique de l'Empire de la Chine*, Paris, 1735, and by his cartographer, J-B. D'Anville, as an atlas, *Nouvelle Atlas de la Chine*, The Hague, 1737.

By order of the Qianlong emperor a new survey was undertaken in 1756–59, and the original was revised to include his conquests, notably what was later to be called Xinjiang.[18] These maps were held in secret at the Neifu until used as the basis for printing the *Da Qing wannian yitong tianxia yutu* 大清萬年一統天下輿圖 during the Tongzhi reign.

Many maps of individual counties and provinces as well as plans of cities and towns are found in Ming-Qing gazetteers (4.7), while the comprehensive gazetteers of the empire from the Ming on also contain maps (4.5.3). The first extant frontier maps (after the stone-carved twelfth-century *Huayitu*), as well as route maps used by officials and merchants, also date from the Ming (50.4.3).[19]

The Yishiguan 一史官 has over 7,000 Qing maps, some of them over 400 square feet in area. Most use a grid system and were drawn to accompany specific reports of campaigns or border relations. Most are not available to the public (50.1.1.V). The *Zhongguo gudai dituji* (*Qingdai*), contains reproductions of 212 Qing maps, the largest published selection available.

For reproductions of 166 maps from the Warring States to the end of the Qing, see *Zhonghua gu ditu zhenpin xuanji* 中華古地圖集珍品選集 (A selection of original ancient Chinese maps), Harbin ditu, 1998.

[18] Walter Fuchs, *Der Jesuiten Atlas der Kanghsi Zeit, seine Entstehungsgeschichte nebst Namensindices für die Karten der Mandjurei, Mongolei, Ostturkestan und Tibet; mit Wiedergabe der Jesuiten-Karten in Original-grösse*, MS Monograph 4, 1943.

[19] See *SCC*, vol. III, *Mathematics and the Sciences of the Heavens and the Earth*, CUP, 1959, and also *Zhongguo cehuishi* 中國測繪史 (History of Chinese surveying and mapping), 2 vols., Cehui, 1995; Lu Liangzhi 盧良志, *Zhongguo dituxueshi* 中國地圖學史 (History of Chinese cartography), Cehui, 1984.

For a selection of 100 rare maps (mainly Qing) from the Dalian Library
(which was based on the South Manchuria Railway Co. Library), see
Liu Zhenwei 劉鎮偉, *Zhongguo gu dituji* 中國古地圖集 (A collection
of China's ancient maps), Zhongguo shijieyu, 1995.

Note the bilingual catalog of old Chinese maps in European collections:
Li Xiaocong 李孝聰, *A Descriptive Catalogue of Pre-1900 Chinese
Maps Seen in Europe*, Guoji wenhua, 1996.

A number of national sheet maps were made by the military authorities in the early Republic on the scale of 1:50,000
and 1:100,000, but the quality is uneven. The most accurate and
detailed maps of China in the first half of the twentieth century
were made by the survey department of the Japanese army:
Chûgoku hondo chizu 中國本土地圖.[20]

United States Army maps based on Landsat data are available on the scale of 1:200,000 with place-names in English and
Chinese. 1:100,000 also exists.

Soviet army maps based on original satellite surveys conducted in the 1980's to the scale of 1:25,000 are available.

4.5   Comprehensive Geographical Works

4.5.1   Early Works

The earliest extant work covering the whole of China, as it
then was, is the *Shanhaijing* 山海經 (Classic of mountains and
seas), a mythogeography, parts of which were written in the
Warring States period and part in the Han and Jin (33.1). The
Shangshu 尚書 (*Documents*) contains an early geographical

---

[20] *Chûgoku hondo chizu*, 1:25,000, 4 vols., Kagaku shoin, 1989–92;
separate index vol., 1993. 1:50,000, 5 vols., Kagaku shoin, 1994; separate
index vol., 1994. Manchuria, 2 vols., Kagaku shoin, 1985. These maps
have been reprinted from copies held in the American Geographical Society Collection at the Golda Meir Library, University of Wisconsin-
Milwaukee. There is also an index of the holdings of maps of China in
major collections in Japan: *Chûgoku hondo chizu mokuroku* 中國本土地
圖目錄, Nunome Chôfû 布目潮渢 and Matsuda Kôichi 松田孝一, eds.,
1967; rev. and enlarged ed., 1987.

work, the *Yugong* 禹貢 (The tribute of Yu), which describes the nine regions of China and their products.[21] The third important early geographic work, the *Shuijing*, is dealt with under water control (35.3.2).

4.5.2 Monographs on Geography in the Standard Histories

Most pre-Han geographical works as well as those from the Han to the Tang have been lost. Up to the Tang, therefore, the study of Chinese historical geography (including the study of place-names, changing boundaries, local products, and population) has to be based mainly on the early works (4.5.1), together with the summaries found in the *Dili zhi* 地理志 (also called *Junguo zhi* 郡國志, *Zhoujunzhi* 州郡志, or *Dixingzhi* 地形志 (monographs on administrative geography) in the Standard Histories of the Former Han, Later Han, Jin, Southern Qi, Wei, and Sui, the sections on foreign peoples (Table 27, chap. 41), and the monographs on rivers and canals in the *Shiji* and the *Hanshu* (35.3.2). These should also be supplemented with the monographs on financial administration (22.3).

The *Dilizhi* reflect much the same origins as were suggested for early Chinese maps; they contain information useful for tax gatherers (hearth and head counts; land under cultivation statistics) and administrators (names of administrative units, changes of place-names over time, distances between places, main topographical features).

The *Hanshu* 漢書 (Standard History of the Former Han) was the first to include a monograph on administrative geography (*juan* 28) and it is somewhat broader in scope than the monographs in the other Standard Histories. It includes historical introductions to the regions of China (quoting exten-

---

[21] *The Book of Documents*, Bernhard Karlgren, tr., *BMFEA* 22: 1–81 (1950), includes the Chinese text along with his annotated translation. The complete text with extensive commentary and explanations is included in Gu Jiegang 顧頡剛, *Zhongguo gudai dili mingzhu xuandu* 中國古代地理名著選讀 (Selected readings from famous ancient Chinese geographical works), vol. 1, Kexue, 1959.

sively form the *Yugong*); population figures (the census of AD 2) and the names and numbers of the counties in each province and fief; land under cultivation; and brief economic profiles of each region (following *Shiji, juan* 129).[22]

After the *Hanshu*, 18 of the Standard Histories included monographs on administrative geography. They follow much the same pattern as the monograph in the *Hanshu*, but are more narrowly focused on administrative matters. The Zhong-hua Shuju has published place-name indexes to each of the Standard Histories. These cover all place-names, including those in the monographs on administrative geography. In addition indexes are available to some of the monographs on geography (for titles for each period, see Part V). Failing these, the comprehensive indexes to the Standard Histories can be used (22.2). Even without an index it is not difficult to locate places in the monographs since their arrangement follows standard administrative hierarchies (4.2). In order to check changes in place-names (often recorded in the monographs) a modern place-name dictionary such as *Zhongguo lishi dili da cidian* (1995), that is based on the monographs, should be used (4.3.1).

After the Tang many more geographical works (including maps) are extant, and the monographs in the later Standard Histories become only one of many sources for Chinese historical geography. Later sources include the comprehensive gazetteers of the Empire, which contain similar information to the monographs (see below); the local gazetteers, which are filled with much greater detail (4.6); and the geographical chapters of the encyclopaedic histories of institutions (chap. 26), not to speak of the many private geographical works, travel books, and scholarly studies that have survived in great numbers.

[22] See Nancy Lee Swann, "An Analysis of Structure of the Treatise on Geography," *Food & Money in Ancient China*, PUP, 1950, 71–5.

4.5.3   Comprehensive Gazetteers

Very few geographic works from the Han to the Tang have survived.[23] The earliest extant geographical work covering the whole empire was compiled in the ninth century by Li Jifu 李吉甫 (758–814), *Yuanhe junxian tuzhi* 元和郡縣圖志.[24]

The next extant comprehensive geography was written by Yue Shi 樂史 to explain the geography of China and her neighbors newly unified under the emperor Taizong: *Taiping huanyu ji* [zhi] 太平寰宇記 [志] (Gazetteer of the world during the Taiping period, 976–83); late tenth century.[25] This was an influential work in that it set the trend toward the inclusion of biographies, literary works, etc. in geographical works, a trend that was taken up in the local gazetteers. It was highly praised by the *Siku* editors. Yue's gazetteer is largely based on Tang works, and it is therefore an important source for Tang geography. There is an index available.[26] Other important comprehensive Song geographical works are listed in 47.2.

Only fragments of the enormous *Da Yuan yitongzhi* 大元一統志 (Comprehensive gazetteer of the Yuan), rev. version, end of thirteenth century, are extant (35 or so *juan* out of 1,000). The title and arrangement of this work were followed, however, in the Ming and again in the Qing.

---

[23] *Han-Tang fangzhi jiyi* 漢唐方志輯佚 (Recovered fragments of Han and Tang gazetteers), Liu Weiyi 劉緯毅, comp., Beijing tushuguan, 1997. See also *Han-Tang dili shu chao* 漢唐地理書抄, Wang Mo 王謨 (*jinshi* 1778), Zhonghua, 1961, gathers together fragments of lost geographic works.

[24] *Yuanhe junxian tuzhi* (Maps and gazetteer of the provinces and counties in the Yuanhe period, 806–14), 2 vols., Zhonghua, 1983; rpnt., 1995. The maps in this work were lost in the Song, as were also *juan* 19, 20, 23–26, and parts of *juan* 5, 18, and 25, but the work is still an important supplement to the monographs on administrative geography in the Old and New Standard Histories of the Tang. It is indexed along with these works in Hiraoka (1956).

[25] *Taiping huanyu ji*, 3 vols., Wenhai, 1980.

[26] *Taiping huanyu ji suoyin* 太平寰宇記索引, Wang Hui 王恢 comp., Wenhai, 1975.

The comprehensive gazetteers of the empire are easy to use since they, like the monographs on administrative geography in the Standard Histories, are arranged according to well-established administrative hierarchies (4.2). Three were compiled during the Qing with the title provided by Kangxi, *Da Qing yitongzhi* 大清一統志. The third, the *Jiaqing chongxiu yitongzhi* 嘉慶重修一統志, was the largest and most accurate comprehensive gazetteer (see 50.6.1 for details).

4.5.4 Empire-wide Geographical Studies

The two outstanding Qing works on historical geography are:

Gu Yanwu 顧炎武 (1613–82) *Tianxia junguo libing shu* 天下郡國利病書 (The characteristics of each province in the empire).

Gu Zuyu 顧祖禹 (1631–92) *Dushi fangyu jiyao* 讀史方輿紀要 (Essentials of geography for reading history).[27]

Gu Yanwu was acknowledged as the founder of what was later termed the Hanxuepai 漢學派 (School of Han learning). Gu and like-minded scholars rejected the Song and Ming Neo-Confucian interpretation of the Classics to return to the Han texts and early commentators. The Hanxuepai used induction based on the careful accumulation of evidence. Typically, they applied evidential research (*kaozheng* 考證) to the study of history and textual criticism, phonetics, and etymology. Gu used it in all of his studies (as displayed, for example, in his notes, *Rizhilu* 日知錄, 50.6.7), including geography.[28] Emphasizing

---

[27] The *Tianxia junguo libing shu*, which included many maps, was written between 1639 and 1662 and printed for the first time in 1811; there are many modern editions and an old manuscript version was included in *Sibu congkan* 四部叢刊, 3rd series.

The *Dushi fangyu jiyao* was written between the 1630s and 1660s and first printed in 1811; many modern editions, including a punctuated six-volume ed., Zhonghua, 1955; rpnt. 1957, and an indexed edition in 12 vols., Shanghai guji, 1991.

[28] See Fang Chao-ying's masterly profile of Gu and the Hanxuepai in *ECCP* (421–426) or the biography by Willard J. Peterson, "The Life of Ku Yen-wu (1613–1682)," *HJAS* 28: 114–56 (1966); 29: 201–47 (1969); for

Footnote continued on next page

the effect of topography on political and economic developments, the *Tianxia junguo libing shu* is the most important
study of historical and natural geography and local conditions
throughout China to have been written up to that time. Gu
paid particular attention to strategic considerations (the title
literally means "the strategic advantages and disadvantages of
the topography of each province") and used not only books but
also the knowledge gained during his travels in China.

Like Gu Yanwu, Gu Zuyu (no relation) was influenced as a
young man by the collapse of the Ming and resentment at the
Manchu conquest. He concentrated all his life on historical
geography and is remembered for having identified the historical names of 30,000 places.[29] He also assisted in the
compilation of the *Da Qing yitongzhi*. Both Gu Yanwu and Gu
Zuyu stimulated the use of local gazetteers in historical and
geographical writing. The new interest soon gained imperial
sponsorship (more gazetteers were compiled in the Qing than
all previous periods put together).

4.6   Local Gazetteers

Local gazetteers (*difangzhi* 地方志 or *fangzhi* 方志 for short),
sometimes also called "local histories," are called "local" to differentiate them from the various kinds of comprehensive gazetteers (*zongzhi* 總志) discussed in 4.5.3. By the Qing (the period
in which most were compiled) local gazetteers contained materials arranged in all or some of the categories set out in Table 5.

---

the academic background to *kaozheng*, see Benjamin Elman, *From Philosophy to Philology: Intellectual Aspects of Change in Late Imperial China*,
Council on East Asian Studies, Harvard University, 1984, rpnt., 1990.

[29] For an index to the place-names identified by Gu Yanwu, see Aoyama Sadao 青山定雄, *Dokushi hôyo kiyô sakuin Shina rekidai chimei yôran* 讀史方輿紀要索引支那歷代地名要覽, Tôhô bunka gakuin, Tôkyô
kenkyûjo, 1933; rev. ed., 4th prnt., Shôshin, 1974.

Table 5: The Contents of Local Gazetteers

Preface and general rules (*fanli* 凡例) with compilers and editorial policy

Maps of the county, city plans, etc. (*yutu* 輿圖, *tukao* 圖考)

Changing borders, tables of changing administrative units included in the
   county, prefecture, etc. (*jiangyu* 疆域, *yan'ge* 沿革)

Main topographical features, rivers, mountains, etc. (*shanchuan* 山川)

Famous places, ruins, views (*mingsheng* 名勝, *guji* 古蹟)

Official buildings, city walls and moats, government offices (*gongshu* 公
   署, *chengchi* 城池, *jianzhi* 建置)

Passes, fords, and bridges (*guanjin qiaoliang* 關津橋梁)

Water conservancy, canals and rivers, hydraulics, irrigation works (*he-
   fang* 河防, *hequ* 河渠, *shuili* 水利)

Chronicle of natural and man-made disasters or omens: flood, drought,
   hail, snow, locusts; uprisings, soldiers, high prices, low prices, etc.
   (*zaiyi* 災異, *xiangyi* 祥異, *bing* 兵)

Academies (Shuyuan 書院)

Schools (*xuexiao* 學校)

Buddhist and Daoist temples (*siguan* 寺觀)

Office holders (*zhiguan* 職官)

Examinations and names of successful candidates (*xuanju* 選舉)

Fiscal information: household and head counts (*hukou* 戶口), land and
   other taxes (*fushui* 賦稅, *tianfu* 田賦)

Granary reserves (*cangzhu* 倉儲)

Markets, tolls, and barriers (*shizhen* 市鎮)

Products and crops (*wuchan* 物產)

Customs and festivals (*fengsu* 風俗)

Biographies of dignitaries, upright officials, chaste women, etc. (*renwu* 人
   物, *minghuan* 名宦, *lienü* 列女)

Military institutions and military men (*bingzhi* 兵制, *bingyi* 兵役, *junzhi*
   軍制); *bingshi* 兵事 (military events)

Biographies of technicians, including doctors; Buddhist and Daoist
   monks (*fangji* 方技, *shilao* 釋老)

Inscriptions and tombs (*jinshi* 金石, *lingmu* 陵墓)

Bibliographies and choice excerpts (*yiwen* 藝文)

Miscellaneous topics and records (*zalu* 雜錄)

The gazetteers were often compiled by members of the local
elite and were produced under the sponsorship of the local officials. Altogether about 8,000 local gazetteers are extant, in a
staggering total of 125,000 *juan*. They form one of the most
important sources for the study of Chinese history in the past

one thousand years, since they contain copious materials on local administration, local economies, local cultures, local officials, and local dignitaries, materials that often cannot be found elsewhere.

Gazetteers are usually subdivided into the gazetteers of provinces (*tongzhi* 通志), prefectures (*fuzhi* 府志), sub-prefectures (*zhouzhi* 州志), and counties (*xianzhi* 縣志). In addition, there are a number of gazetteers for market towns (*xiangzhenzhi* 鄉鎮志), garrisons (*weisuozhi* 衛所志 or *weizhi* 衛志), academies (*shuyuanzhi* 書院志), temples and shrines (*simiaozhi* 寺廟志), and famous mountains and rivers (*shanshuizhi* 山水志).

Usually the longest sections were the different categories of biographies, followed by various forms of fiscal information and tables of officeholders. Indexes to biographies in local gazetteers are listed in subsection 3.8.4.

In origin, local gazetteers derived from the practice of keeping basic information on local conditions, population, and revenue and submitting these together with maps and plans to the central government. At the same time they also derive from the practice, which became widespread in the third century AD, of collecting biographies of local worthies and their writings in order to celebrate local achievements. Many elements of the later gazetteers were in earlier periods copied and circulated as separate works (for example the records of local customs (*fengsu zhuan* 風俗傳) or the maps and records of rivers and mountains (*shanchuan tuji* 山川圖記). The local gazetteer as a work in its own right combining all these elements emerged in the Song (sometimes with the earlier name, *tujing* 圖經, the forerunner of the *zongzhi* 總志 first compiled in the Sui). On the earlier types of gazetteer (down to the Yuan), see Zhang Guogan 張國淦 (1876–1959), *Zhongguo gu fangzhi kao* 中國古方志考.[30] This is an annotated bibliography of well over 2,000 gazetteer-style works compiled to the end of the Yuan, about 99 percent of which are no longer extant. Titles are arranged by

---

[30] *Zhongguo gu fangzhi kao* (Critical notes on old Chinese gazetteers), Shanghai: Zhonghua, 1962. See also Aoyama (1963).

zongzhi 總志 and by *fangzhi* 方志, with the latter grouped by modern provinces. There is a stroke-count title index.

Nearly 200 local gazetteers are known to have been compiled in the Song (mainly in the Southern Song and therefore for localities in South China), of which only about 30 survive. Yuan scholars are known to have compiled 60, of which only 11 are extant. Thereafter, the number of available local gazetteers increases enormously; altogether 900 are extant mainly from the late Ming out of an unknown number compiled (49.8), while more than 5,600 Qing local gazetteers are extant. Approximately 650 were compiled during the Republican period, and many more are being compiled today (with the emphasis on the present conditions rather than on history).

The stimulus for gazetteer compilation in the Qing came in part from the practical school of geo-military and geo-historical Ming loyalists (the Zhexi group), whose influence was still felt long after the trend in scholarship had turned to critical philological studies (4.5.4). Official orders in 1672 and 1729 that every province compile a gazetteer also greatly stimulated local gazetteer production.

A great many Qing scholars, historians, and local officials took part in the compilation of local gazetteers, and there arose for the first time the phenomenon almost of the professional gazetteer-compiler. These trends were summed up by the historian Zhang Xuecheng 章學誠 (1738–1801), who was the first to discuss gazetteers as an important branch of historical writing on a par with the National Histories (*Guoshi* 國史).[31] He also suggested that local archives should be kept and that the editing and compilation of the gazetteers should be in the hands of specialists.

---

[31] On Zhang's writing on gazetteers and on the interesting gazetteers written by him, see David S. Nivison, *The Life and Thought of Chang Hsüeh-ch'eng (1738–1801)*, SUP, 1966, and in greater detail, Chu Shi-chia, "Chang Hsueh-ch'eng and His Contributions to Local Historiography," Ph.D., Columbia Univ., 1950.

The provincial gazetteers were compiled usually by summarizing the information in the prefectural gazetteers, which were in turn abridged from previous editions and from the individual county gazetteers. Not surprisingly, they vary greatly in quality.

As a general rule, richer areas could afford to pay better editors and produced a superior product to that published by poorer areas. So south China is better covered than the North. Gazetteers for the Northwest and the Northeast are particularly weak.

The author of a monumental study of rural China in the nineteenth century, Kung-chuan Hsiao (Xiao Gongquan 蕭公權), warns about the uneven quality of the gazetteers,

> The local gentry and in some instances the local officials who dictated the actual contents as well as the editorial policies of the works sponsored by them, were too often not above prejudice or selfishness. The fact that any single gazetteer was written by a number of persons whose scholarly qualifications were not uniformly high and who frequently executed their assignments with poor coordination and inadequate supervision, points to the possibility of unintentional errors and omissions, even where willful misrepresentation was not practiced. A well-known Chinese historian [Mao Qiling 毛奇齡, 1623–1716] went so far as to say that local gazetteers were among those categories of writings to which credence could not be lent. Most of the gazetteers contain sections dealing with geographical and related matters. Even there the data are too often inadequate and inaccurate. In many instances later editions of a gazetteer reproduced entries from editions compiled decades or centuries earlier without making necessary provisions to reflect whatever changes may have taken place during the interval and without warning the reader of the fact. Occasionally, in small or remote localities, a dearth of reliable information prevented even the most conscientious compilers from producing satisfactory records.[32]

For a good introduction to local gazetteers (with bibliography), see Pierre-Etienne Will "Chinese Local Gazetteers: An Historical and Practical Introduction," *Notes de Recherche du Centre*

---

[32] Kung-ch'üan Hsiao, *Rural Control in China in the Nineteenth Century*, UWP, 1960; rpnt., 1967, Preface, vii–viii.

Chine, No. 3, Paris: Centre de Recherches et de Documentation sur la Chine Contemporaine, 1992. See also Timothy Brook, *Geographical Sources of Ming Qing History*, Michigan Monographs in Chinese Studies No. 58, Ann Arbor, 1988.

Modern historians and scholars have combed the local gazetteers and collected excerpts on all kinds of topics, for example, on population,[33] on local customs,[34] on celestial phenomena,[35] or on coal mining.[36]

How to Find Local Gazetteers

The quickest way of finding out what gazetteers are extant for a particular county, prefecture, or province is to consult one of the two available union catalogs: *Zhongguo difangzhi lianhe mulu* 中國地方志聯合目錄[37] or *Zhongguo difangzhi zongmu tiyao*

---

[33] P. T. Ho, *Studies in the Population of China, 1368–1953*, HUP, 1958.

[34] *Zhongguo difangzhi minsu ziliao huibian* 中國地方志民俗資料匯編 (Collection of materials from Chinese gazetteers on popular customs), Ding Shiliang 丁世良 and Zhao Fang 趙放, eds., 11 vols., Shumu wenxian, 1989–95 (33.3).

[35] Zhuang Weifeng 莊威鳳 and Wang Lixing 王立興, eds., *Zhongguo gudai tianxiang jilu zongji* 中國古代天象記錄總集 (Comprehensive collection of records of celestial phenomena in ancient China), Jiangsu kexue jishu, 1988 (5.1.1).

[36] Qi Shouhua 祁守華, *Zhongguo difangzhi meitan shiliao xuanji* 中國地方志煤炭史料選輯 (Collected historical materials on coal from Chinese local gazetteers), Meitan gongye, 1990. Contains records from over 937 coal producing areas from various periods of Chinese history.

[37] *Zhongguo difangzhi lianhe mulu* (Union catalog of Chinese local gazetteers), edited at Zhongguo kexueyuan, Beijing tianwentai 中國科學院北京天文臺 (Chinese Academy of Sciences, Beijing Observatory), Zhuang Weifeng 莊威鳳, Zhu Shijia 朱士嘉, and Feng Baolin 馮寶琳, eds. in chief, Zhonghua, 1985. Based on Zhu Shijia (1962). This lists and gives brief bibliographic notes on 8,264 local gazetteers edited before 1949 held in 191 Chinese libraries and in Taiwan. There is a title index as well as an index of some 10,000 authors and compilers. Both indexes are arranged by stroke number. It was compiled as part of a huge project that listed celestial phenomena recorded in the Standard Histories, Veritable Records, and local gazetteers (5.1). The net was cast wide enough to in-

Footnote continued on next page

中國地方志總目提要, which is the larger of the two and contains more comprehensive notes on each of the 8,557 gazetteers it lists.[38] There are also more detailed studies of local gazetteers and "union catalogs" for individual provinces or regions.

Since gazetteers were usually compiled by committees of local officials and scholars, they are usually referred to by title (sometimes preceded by reign name to distinguish editions) except when the compiler was a well-known writer. The most convenient form of citation for gazetteers is title followed by date of compilation.

After finding the titles and compilers of gazetteers for a given locality or period, it is necessary to locate the libraries that hold them. The *Zhongguo difangzhi lianhe mulu* shows which of the major Chinese libraries holds each of the 8,264 gazetteers listed. But often you will be able to find the gazetteer you are looking for in one of the many multi-volume collections of facsimile reprints of local gazetteers. Indeed, the reprints of rare gazetteers (and their wide availability on microfilm), and the huge compilations of Ming and Qing gazetteers, have made the published catalogs of the holdings of original gazetteers by individual collections, both in China and elsewhere, somewhat out-of-date.[39]

---

clude all works functioning as gazetteers, so it includes, for example, geographical surveys and local investigation reports.

[38] *Zhongguo difangzhi zongmu tiyao* (Chinese local histories: a comprehensive annotated catalog), Jin Enhui 金恩輝 and Hu Shuzhao 胡述兆, eds., 3 vols., Sino-American publishers, 1996. It contains notes on 8,557 titles compiled up to 1949.

[39] *Zhongguo fangzhi congshu* 中國方志叢書, Chengwen, 1966–93; 1,370 titles. The Cambridge University Library Chinese collection online catalog contains detailed entries for each title in this series indicating, for example, the edition from which the reproduction was taken. *Zhongguo difangzhi jicheng*, 中國地方志集成, 160 sets, Jiangsu guji, 1993. Note also that reprints of historical materials on a particular province or region often contain many dozens of gazetteers, for example, the 203 volumes on Northwest China: *Zhongguo de xibei wenxian congshu* 中國的西北文獻叢書, Lanzhou, 1990, or the 1,110 vols. of Taiwan gazetteers: *Taiwan fangzhi* 臺灣方志, series A, 1–102 (440 vols.); series B, 103–345 (666

Footnote continued on next page

In 1982, a series of catalogs and studies of gazetteers for each province was begun under the general editorship of the Committee for Gazetteer Compilation of Jilin: *Zhongguo difangzhi xianglun congshu* 中國地方志詳論叢書. Some of these contain more information than can be found in the two union catalogs. Examples of titles published to date include:

Guangdong fangzhi yaolu 廣東方志要錄, Li Xian 李獻, ed., Guangdong sheng fangzhi bianzuan weiyuanhui bangongshi, 1988.

Liaoning difangzhi lunlüe, 遼寧地方志論略, 1982; rev. and enl., Chen Jia 陳加 et al., Liaoning tushuguan, 1986.

Shanghai fangzhi ziliao kaolu 上海方志資料考錄, Shanghai shifan daxue tushuguan, eds., Shanghai shudian, 1987. Detailed catalog of gazetteers on Shanghai compiled between the Song and 1984.

Shaoxing difang wenxian kaolu 紹興地方文獻考錄, Chen Qiaoyi 陳橋驛, ed., Zhejiang renmin, 1983.

Zhejiang fangzhi kaolu 浙江方志考錄, Hong Huanchun 洪煥椿 (1920–), ed., 1958; rev. and enl. under new title, *Zhejiang fangzhi kao* 浙江方志考, Zhejiang renmin, 1984, in which are listed about 1,800 gazetteers, including lost ones, for this province alone. There is a title index.

There are also comprehensive catalogs of gazetteers for most provinces and other administrative units, often compiled by the provincial or local library; for example:

Hebei sheng difangzhi zonglu, chugao 河北省地方志總錄初稿, 1982 (includes gazetteers of Beijing and Tianjin).

Dongbei difangzhi zonglu 東北地方志總錄, Guo Jun 郭君 and Sun Renkui 孫仁奎, eds., in *Zhongguo fangzhixue gailun* 中國方志學概論 (Survey of the study of Chinese local histories), Heilongjiang renmin, 1984.

Hu'nan sheng difangzhi zonghe mulu 湖南省地方志綜合目錄, 1987.

Shanghai difangzhi mulu 上海地方志目錄, 1979.

---

vols.), Chengwen. Series A covers from 1696 to 1893; series B, the Japanese occupation (1894–1942) or thirty-one rare gazetteers held in Japanese collections reprinted in *Riben cang Zhongguo hanjian difangzhi congkan* 日本藏中國罕見地方志叢刊, Shumu wenxian, 1990–92.

There are a number of published catalogs of holdings of local gazetteers in Europe and North America. These, too, have been outdated for the practical purpose of locating a gazetteer by the reprint collections.[40]

In recent years more and more indexes have been compiled for gazetteers, especially for the gazetteer biographies for a period or province (3.8.4). Some of the larger gazetteers should soon be available on computer disk.

In 1934 the Shangwu Press reprinted six late Qing provincial gazetteers with (four-corner) indexes attached:

Guangdong tongzhi 廣東通志, 1884
Hubei tongzhi 湖北通志, 1911
Hu'nan tongzhi 湖南通志, 1885
Jifu tongzhi 畿輔通志 (Metropolitan region), 1906
Shandong tongzhi 山東通志, 1911
Zhejiang tongzhi 浙江通志, 1736

Individuals and local institutions often compile collections of local data and historical materials or catalogs of these. These compilations are not necessarily intended for historians, and their value is often rather limited.

4.7 Cities

Many large-scale settlements (cities) from the Bronze Age to the earlier dynasties have now been excavated, and their plans pub-

---

[40] *Catalog des monographies locales chinoises dans les bibliothèques d'Europe*, Yves Hervouet, comp., Mouton et Cie, 1957. Lists 1,434 gazetteers in 17 European collections. *A Catalogue of Chinese Local Histories in the Library of Congress*, comp., Chu Shih Chia, Washington, DC: Government Printing Office, 1942, Xinwenfeng, 1985. *Nihon shûyô toshokan kenkyûjo shozô Chûgoku chihôshi sôgo mokuroku* 日本主要圖書館研究所所藏中國地方志綜合目錄 (Union catalog of Chinese local gazetteers in fourteen major libraries and research institutes in Japan), Tôyô bunko, 1969. *Zhonghua minguo Taiwan diqu gongcang fangzhi mulu* 中華民國臺灣地區公藏方志目錄 (Catalog of local gazetteers in the Republic of China [Taiwan District] public collections), Wang Deyi 王德毅, comp., Hanxue yanjiu ziliao ji fuwu zhongxin, 1985.

lished in the archaeological reports as well as in special studies. The influence of sun worship can be seen in the arrangement of most of these settlements with an inner area (symbolizing the sun) set within a larger square (symbolizing the earth), as, for example, at Sidun in Yuyao, Zhejiang. All later capitals followed this basic form with the palace eventually set in the central position (see section 39.2, *Architecture*).

The earliest city plan discovered so far is on silk and dates from the Former Han. It is probably of Changsha and was discovered in the Mawangdui tomb (4.4, item 3).

Local gazetteers are a major source for the history of cities and towns from the Song onward, including for schematic plans and maps. Ye Xiaojun 葉驍軍 in *Zhongguo ducheng lishi tulu* 中國都城歷史圖錄 has included many plans of capital cities as well as illustrations of artifacts in this four-volume collection.[41] There is a 90-page bibliography of books and articles on Chinese capitals at the end of vol. 4, as well as a table of all the dozens of capitals from the Xia dynasty to the present day, including even the capitals of minor kingdoms (for example that of Nan Zhao 南詔 and Dali 大理, which was Taihecheng 太和城, modern Dali 大理, Yunnan). Where possible the dates are given.

The largest, most detailed, and best-produced collection of modern historical maps of a Chinese city is *Xi'an lishi dituji* 西安歷史地圖集. The first of the 89 maps shows the Xi'an area at the time of Lantian Man 藍田人, and the last is of Xi'an in 1995. Pride of place is reserved for maps of Chang'an in the

---

[41] *Zhongguo ducheng lishi tulu* (An atlas of historical capitals of China), 4 vols., Lanzhou daxue, 1986–87. Vol. 1 covers from the Xia to the end of the Warring States; vol. 2, from Qin to the end of the Tang; vol. 3, from Song to the end of the Qing; vol. 4, the Republican period. The table of capitals has been corrected and enlarged in *Zhongguo lidai ducheng* 中國歷代都城 (Historical capitals of China), Li Jieping 李潔萍, Heilongjiang renmin, 1994, 407–18.

Zhou, Han, and Tang. There is extensive commentary and illustrations of artifacts found in the city in each period.[42]

The most detailed city plan known to have survived from the later empire is of Beijing in the mid-eighteenth century, *Qianlong jingcheng quantu* 乾隆京城全圖.[43] Illustrations of this and redrawings of many other historical maps of Beijing are reproduced in Hou Renzhi 候仁之, *Beijing lishi dituji* 北京歷史地圖集.[44] There are also collections of historical maps of many other cities, for example, *Wuhan lishi dituji* 武漢歷史地圖集, Zhongguo ditu, 1998. This contains more than 100 maps of the Wuhan cities from the Song to the People's Republic.

There are many fascinating, detailed, and more informal accounts of cities and city life (usually in the capitals) than can be found in the local gazetteers. They were classified either in the geography section of the History branch or among the miscellaneous notes (*biji* 筆記) in the Philosophers' or one of the other branches. Six of the better-known titles follow:

Luoyang qielan ji 洛陽伽藍記 (45.2)
Liang jing xinji 兩京新記 (46.2).
Dongjing menghua lu 東京夢華錄 (47.2, *Biji*).
Dijing jingwulue 帝京景物略 (49.2, *Local Gazetteers*).
Chunming mengyu lu 春明夢餘錄 (49.2, *Biji*)

---

[42]*Xi'an lishi dituji* (The historical atlas of Xi'an), Shi Nianhai 史念海 (1912–), ed. in chief, Xi'an ditu, 1996.

[43] Beijing Yanshan, 1994. The first study was put out by the Palace Museum: *Qianlongchao jingcheng quantu fangxiang gongdian kao* 乾隆朝京城全圖坊巷宮殿考 (A study of the Qianlong period map of the streets and wards of the capital), Gugong wenxianguan et al., Beida fashang xueyuan, 1936. The first modern print was under the title *Kenryô keisei zenzu fu kaisetsu sakuin* 乾隆京城全圖附解説索引 (Complete map of the capital in the Qianlong period with explanations and index), 1940, reprinted from a manuscript copy kept in the Imperial Household Archive with notes and an index by Imanishi Shunjû 今西春秋. Also reprinted by the Palace Museum under the title *Qing neiwufu cang jingcheng quantu* 清內務府藏京城全圖, Beijing, 1940.

[44] *Beijing lishi dituji* (Collection of historical maps of Beijing), Beijing, 1988; 2nd collection, 1997.

Rixia jiuwenkao 日下舊聞考 (50.6.1).

4.7.1 Modern Studies of Urban History

There are increasing numbers of histories written of individual cities, often of the capitals, for which there are more sources.[45] Not infrequently the primary sources for a given city are assembled.[46] Studies of the economic or demographic history of a

[45] See for example, Paul Wheatley, *The Pivot of the Four Quarters*, UChP, 1971; Hans Bielenstein, "Lo-yang in Later Han Times," *BMFEA* 48 (1976), 1–142; Ho Ping-ti, "Loyang, A.D. 495–534: A Study of the Physical and Socio-Economic Planning of a Metropolitan Area," *HJAS* 26: 52–101 (1966); William Jenner, *Memories of Loyang*, Oxford: Clarendon, 1981; *Tangdai Yangzhou shigao* 揚州史稿 (Draft history of Yangzhou in the Tang), Li Tingxian 李廷先, Jiangsu guji, 1992; *Songdai dongjing yanjiu* 宋代東京研究 (Researches on the eastern capital in the Song dynasty), Zhou Baozhu 周寶珠, ed., Henan daxue, 1992. A detailed study of many aspects of the history of the Northern Song capital of Kaifeng (from 960 to 1132); Jacques Gernet, *Daily Life in China on the Eve of the Mongol Invasion, 1250–1276*, Allen and Unwin, 1962; SUP, 1970; R. Stewart Johnston, "The Ancient City of Suzhou: Town Planning in the Song Dynasty," *Town Planning Review* 54.2: 194–222 (1983); Frederick W. Mote, "The Transformation of Nanking, 1350–1400," in G. William Skinner, ed., *The City in Late Imperial China*, SUP, 1977, 101–53; Han Dacheng 韓大成, *Mingdai chengshi yanjiu* 明代城市研究 (Researches on Ming dynasty towns), Renmin daxue, 1991; Frederick W. Mote, "A Millennium of Chinese Urban History: Form, Time and Space Concepts in Soochow," *Rice University Studies* 59.4: 35–65 (1973); "City Life," in Naquin and Rawski (1987), 55–64; Mark Elvin, "Market Towns and Waterways: the County of Shanghai from 1840 to 1910," in the author's *Another History: Essays on China from a European Perspective*, Wild Peony, 1996, 101–39 (originally appeared in 1977); *Shanghai: From Market Town to Treaty Port, 1074–1858*, Linda Cook Johnson, ed., SUP, 1995; William T. Rowe, *Hankow: Commerce and Society in a Chinese City, 1791–1889*, SUP, 1984; vol. 2, 1989; Victor F. S. Sit, *Beijing: The Nature and Planning of a Chinese Capital City*, Wiley, 1995. Contains chapters on the early history of Chinese cities and Beijing, 1–81.

[46] *Yandu guji kao* 燕都古籍考 (Examination of the ancient written sources on Beijing), Wang Canchi 王燦熾, Jinghua, 1995; rpnt., 1996, contains thorough notes and brief summaries of 151 primary sources on Beijing from the earliest times to 1912. Arrangement is by period.

particular town are beginning to appear.[47] Urban social life (apart from the life of the emperor and his court) is only just beginning to be studied in detail—see, for example, the studies of consumption patterns, leisurely tastes and pursuits of the urban literati in Ming and Qing China cited in subsection 50.4.3. A history of hoodlums and vagabonds can reveal one aspect of city life because they usually gathered in the cities.[48] The maintenance of security at night was a constant preoccupation of officials (6.4). Much detail can be gleaned from Ming-Qing vernacular fiction, for example, the action of *Jin Ping Mei* 金瓶梅 is set in a busy local town, Linqing 林清, on the Grand Canal in Shandong (34.3, item 2).

For an overview of recent secondary studies, see Frederick W. Mote, "Urban History in Late Imperial China," *Ming Studies* 34: 61–76 (1995).

A great deal of work has been done on marketing systems linking small economic towns and cities, much of it drawn from local gazetteers.[49]

Large cities today often publish encyclopaedias or dictionaries of the city which can sometimes contain an interesting selection of information not readily available elsewhere.

There is an association for the study of ancient Chinese cities, Zhongguo gudu xuehui 中國古都學會. Journal: *Zhongguo gudu yanjiu* 中國古都研究, 1985– , irregular.

---

[47] See for example, *Beijing gudai jingjishi* 北京古代經濟史 (Economic history of Beijing in ancient times), Sun Jian 孫健, Beijing Yanshan, 1996, or *Beijing lishi renkou dili* 北京歷史人口地理 (7.3).

[48] See Chen Baoliang 陳寶良, *Zhongguo liumangshi* 中國流氓史 (A history of vagabondism in China), Shehui kexue, 1993.

[49] G. William Skinner, ed., *The City in Late Imperial China*, SUP, 1977. On Skinner's application of central place theory to Chinese local and regional history, see the debate in *JAS* vols. 46 (1986) and 49 (1990). Linda Cook Johnson, ed., *Cities of Jiangnan in Late Imperial China*, SUNY Press, 1993.

4.7.2   Merchant Route Books and Manuals

Some twenty to thirty merchant manuals and route books are known to survive from the sixteenth to the late nineteenth century, no doubt reflecting the upsurge of trade at this time. These manuals form a unique source for trade routes, market location, business practices, and merchant ethics of the later empire. They usually contain information on trade routes including time taken between stopping points, location of tax barriers and markets, and so on, as well as general knowledge for merchants, including information on differences between regional weights and measures, notes on different goods, and ethical maxims. The sections of these works on routes were based on official administrative geographical works, and they are usually arranged according to the standard administrative hierarchy. Individual merchants using such works would, of course, have marked up their own copies with marginal notes. For Ming-Qing route books and studies of these sources, see 50.4.3.

Encyclopaedias for daily use of the late Ming and Qing (29.4) also not infrequently contain the same kind of materials as the merchant manuals.

4.8   Travel Inside China

Records of journeys and excursions (*youji* 遊記), often in chronological diary form with the personal observations of the writer, were established as a literary sub-genre in the Tang by Liu Zongyuan 柳宗元 (773–819) in his *Yongzhou baji* 永州八記, and by Li Ao 李翱 (772–841) in his *Lainan lu* 來南錄.[50] Frequently the travel was to take up a new bureaucratic post (or, as in the case of Liu, to go into exile), to return to the capital or to fulfill a foreign mission (for such embassy diaries, see

---

[50] Liu Zongyuan, *Yongzhou baji* (Eight records of Yongzhou, [southern Hunan]), and Li Ao, *Lainan lu*, which briefly records a journey from Luoyang to Guangdong in 819. On the *Yongzhou baji*, see William H. Nienhauser, Jr., *Liu Tsung-yuan*, Twayne, 1973, 66–79.

47.2). Several of the most famous Chinese travel diaries or records of excursions have been translated. Four are listed below.

There is a beautifully produced anthology in English of Chinese travel literature (*youji wenxue* 遊記文學) from ancient times to the present century by Richard E. Strassberg, *Inscribed Landscapes: Travel Writing from Imperial China*, UCP, 1994. There are introductions to the writer of each excerpt. There are many such anthologies in Chinese, sometimes arranged geographically by province, sometimes chronologically and sometimes containing poetry as well as prose.[51]

For studies of another more popular form of travel, the pilgrimage, see Susan Naquin and Chün-fang Yü eds., *Pilgrims and Sacred Sites in China*, UCP, 1992.

Song

On the Road in Twelfth-Century China: The Travel Diaries of Fan Chengda (1126–1193), James M. Hargett, tr., introduced and annotated, Steiner, 1989. In his *Canluan lu* 驂鸞錄 (Register of mounting a simurgh), Fan Chengda 範成大 recorded a four-month journey from his birthplace in Suzhou to take up a post in Guilin in 1171–72; the second Fan diary translated, the *Lanpeilu* 攬轡錄 (Register of grasping the carriage reigns), records the author's journey on an ambassadorial mission from the Southern Song capital of Lin'an (Hangzhou) to the Jin capital of Zhongdu (Beijing) in 1170–71.

South China in the Twelfth Century: A Translation of Lu Yu's Travel Diaries, July 3–December 6, 1170, Chang Chun-shu and Joan Smythe, tr., HKCU Press, 1981. A fully annotated translation of Lu You 陸游 (1125–1210), *Rushu ji* 入蜀記 (Record of entering Sichuan).

Yuan

Leaving for Mt. Hua: A Chinese Physician's Illustrated Travel Record and Painting Theory, Kathlyn Maureen Liscomb, tr., CUP, 1993. Translation of the travel journal of Wang Lü 王履 (d. early Ming).

---

[51] See *Zhongguo mingsheng shici da cidian* 中國名勝詩詞大辭典 (Dictionary of Chinese poems on scenic spots and historical sites), Yang Gang 楊鋼, comp., Wuhan daxue, 1992.

Ming

The Travel Diaries of Hsu Hsia-k'o, Li Chi, ed., HKCU Press, 1974. Xu
Hongzu 徐弘祖 (best known with his *hao* as Xu Xiake 徐霞客,
1587–1641) was China's most famous traveler inside the country. Between the years 1607 and 1640 he went on seventeen trips throughout China culminating in a four-year exploration of Guangxi, Guizhou and Yunnan. He left behind lengthy diaries of his travels
amounting to 404,000 characters of which the greater part is devoted
to his last great exploration in the Southwest.[52] Xu not only climbed
all the sacred mountains of China, but also explored the sources of
major rivers and made geographical and geological investigations despite the many hardships and mishaps along the way. Li Ji has translated and annotated those sections of the diaries covering the sacred
mountains and also supplied route maps for these journeys. There is
an appendix containing a short biography by Chun-shu Chang, 223–
31. The Ding Wenjiang edition (see footnote) contains a full chronological biography, 1–67. The clearest and most detailed maps of all
Xu's routes are in *Xu Xiake lüxing lucheng kaocha tuji* 徐霞客旅行路
程考察圖輯 (Atlas of Xu Xiake's travels), Zhu Shaotang 褚紹唐, ed.
in chief, Zhongguo ditu, 1991.

4.9 Bibliography

There is a convenient description of the main physical regions
of China in *SCC*, vol. I, *Introductory Orientations*, CUP, 1954,
55–72. The earlier work by Chi Ch'ao-ting (Ji Chaoding 冀朝
鼎), *Key Economic Areas in Chinese History as Revealed in Public
Works for Water Control*, Allen and Unwin, 1936; Paragon,
1963, is still worth reading. The Chinese version remains in
print. Frank Leeming, *The Changing Geography of China*, Blackwell, 1993; rpnt., 1995, is brief and covers the broad historical
changes; Zhou Shunwu's *China Provincial Geography*, FLP,
1992, is relatively up-to-date, as is Zhao Songqiao, *Geography of
China*, Wiley, 1994.

---

[52] The best edition is that of Ting Wen-chiang (Ding Wenjiang 丁文
江), *Xu Xiake [Xu Hongzu] youji* 徐霞客遊記 (The travel diaries of Xu
Xiake [Xu Hongzu]), 1928; rpnt., Shanghai guji, 1980; Zhonghua, 1988,
1996.

Zhongguo lishi dilixue lunzhu suoyin (1900–1980) 中國歷史地理學論著索引 (Index of articles and books on Chinese historical geography, 1900–80), Du Yu 杜瑜 and Zhu Lingling 朱玲玲, comps., Shumu wenxian, 1986, is a bibliography of secondary scholarship on Chinese historical geography, both Chinese and Japanese. In it are indexed 15,000 articles and 2,600 books. An appendix gives Japanese contributions (3,000 articles and 500 books).

Chûgoku shûrakushi no kenkyû [zôho] 中國聚落史の研究 [增補] (Research on Chinese settlements [rev. and enl.], Tôdaishi kenkyûkai 唐代史研究會, comp., Tôsui shobo, 1988; rev., 1990, is a bibliography of secondary works in Chinese and Japanese on the history of individual Chinese towns (in all periods, not just the Tang. The listing itself (Part 2) is culled from 20 previous bibliographies and studies. Arrangement is by city (or town) and period. Part 1 contains research articles on city and village settlements in various periods.

For modern studies of changing land-use patterns in Chinese history, see Kang Chao (Zhao Gang 趙岡), *Man and Land in Chinese History, An Economic Analysis*, SUP, 1986.

Zhongguo lishi dilixue 中國歷史地理學 (The study of Chinese historical geography), Li Enjun 李恩軍, Renmin jiaotong, 1995, is a textbook with succinct coverage of change over time and its effects on botanical regions; deserts and rivers, lakes and coasts; natural disasters of all kinds; border regions; historical economic geography, including changes in agricultural regions; military geography, including strategic regions; and military lines and historical routes.

5

Chronology

There are two main problems concerning dates in Chinese history:

1. The nature and verification of the Chinese lunar-solar calendars and dating systems in use in different periods. This is a complex subject (particularly for the pre-Qin period), which belongs to the history of Chinese calendrical sciences (5.1).

2. How to establish an absolute chronology for Chinese history before 841 BC.

The rest of the chapter focuses on the different methods of recording dates: years (5.2) and their division into seasons (seasons, festivals and holidays are also briefly introduced, 5.3); the *ganzhi* cycle (5.2.2); months and days (5.4), and the conversion of dates found in Chinese sources to the Western calendar (5.5). The Buddhist, Muslim, Tibetan, Dai and Yi calendars are presented plus special calendrical concordances for converting them to Chinese and Western dates (5.6). There are short sections on the Korean, Japanese and Vietnamese calendars and calendrical concordances (5.7), and tables of events (5.8).

Note that works on astronomy and mathematics (*tianwen, suanfa* 天文, 算法) were placed in the Philosophers' branch of the traditional fourfold bibliographical classification (*Sibu* 四部, see 9.3).

5.1 Calendars and Almanacs

A lunar-solar calendar (*yinyangli* 陰陽曆) has been used in China since at least the Shang dynasty. After this was abolished in 1911, it was referred to as the *jiuli* 舊曆 (the old calendar) or the moon calendar (*yinli* 陰曆). After 1949, it was also called the farmer's calendar (*nongli* 農曆). Nowadays all these terms are in use, as well as *Zhongli* 中曆 (Chinese calendar) or *Xiali* 夏曆 (the Xia calendar).

The annual task of establishing and promulgating the calendar (*zhili* 治曆, *shouli* 授曆) was the exclusive prerogative of the ruler. Each dynasty announced its own calendar, and some dynasties reformed the calendar several times. The work was done by the astronomical bureau, whose duties until the Han were conducted by the court historians (who also conducted divination). Right up to the end of the empire, the bureau also had the function of keeping the time.

The main purpose of premodern Chinese astronomy however, was not to set the calendar nor indeed to regulate the farming year, important though those these tasks were. The main purpose was to predict accurately and interpret heavenly signs, both periodic and nonperiodic, especially to predict eclipses and the movement of the planets for astrological divination. If this prerogative was carried out accurately, it demonstrated the emperor's right to rule.[1] The imperial monopoly on astronomy and the setting of the calendar was enforced by laws forbidding people to possess astronomical instruments, maps of the heavens or esoteric books; to study astronomy privately, or to publish calendars. Infringement was punished by two years of penal servitude.[2]

Already by the end of the Warring States, the calendar was remarkably accurate. It reached the basic form it was to retain

[1] Wolfram Eberhard, "The Political Function of Astronomy and Astronomers in Han China," in J. K. Fairbank, *Chinese Thought and Institutions*, UChP, 1957; rpnt., 1967.

[2] See, for example, Article 110 in *The T'ang Code: Vol. II, Specific Articles*, Wallace Johnson, tr., PUP, 1997, p. 78.

until modern times in 104 BC. Thereafter it was refined in over 100 reforms, the last of which was in 1742. All the Standard Histories contain treatises on astronomy (with the exception of the *Liaoshi*) and most also contain treatises on the calendar.[3]

Chinese traditional society was above all one in which the highest importance was attached to choosing the right time and the right place for activities both high and low, solemn and trivial. The selection was done using a myriad mantic arts. The first glimpse we have is in the oracle bones. Much later, despite the prohibitions, popular calendars and almanacs (*rishu* 日書, *lipu* 曆譜, *lishu* 曆書, *tongshu* 通書, and so forth) circulated in huge quantities. The earliest extant ones are the dozen or so that have been unearthed in the form of bamboo-strip manuscripts from Warring States, Qin, and Han tombs.[4] The phrase used at that time was *rishu* because their main purpose was for choosing an auspicious day for important activities. At first they were relatively simple. By the Song dynasty they had become increasingly elaborate with a wealth of information not only on lucky and unlucky days and hours but also on festivals, birthdays of legendary figures, and mantic lore of all kinds. The

[3] See Beijing Tianwentai (1975–76) and Chen Zunwei, vol. 3, 1984, pages 1336–1586. For a brief history, see Cui Zhenhua 崔振華, *Zhongguo gudai lifa yan'ge* 中國古代曆法沿革 (The evolution of the ancient Chinese calendar), Xinhua, 1992.

[4] Rao Zongyi 饒宗頤 and Zeng Xiantong 曾憲通, *Yunmeng Qinjian rishu yanjiu* 雲夢秦簡日書研究 (Researches on the Qin bamboo almanacs from Yunmeng), HKCU Press, 1982 (part 2 contains transcriptions); Michael Loewe, "The Almanacs (*jih-shu*) from Shui-hu-ti," *AM* 1.2: 1–28 (1988); Mu-chou Poo, "Popular Religion in Pre-Imperial China: Observations on the Almanacs of Shui-hu-ti," *TP* 79: 225–48 (1993); and Motô Kudô (工藤元男), "The Ch'in Bamboo Strip *Book of Divination (Jih-shu)* and Ch'in Legalism," *Acta Asiatica*, 58 (1990), 24–37. Liu Lexian 劉樂賢, *Shuihudi Qinjian rishu yanjiu* 睡虎地秦簡日書 研究 (Researches on the Qin bamboo almanacs at Shuihudi), Wenjin, 1994. The same author sums up research on this topic in "Shuihudi qinjian rishu yanjiu ershinian 睡虎地秦簡日書研究二十年" (Twenty years of research on the Qin bamboo almanacs at Shuihudi), *Zhongguoshi yanjiu dongtai*, 10: 2–10 (1996). The finds of Han bamboo almanacs are listed in 44.3.2.1.

first extant printed almanac dates from the Tang, the *Qianfu sinian lishu* 乾符四年曆書 (The almanac of 877).[5]

Sources for the History of Chinese Astronomy

Chinese records of eclipses, comets, and other celestial phenomena are more complete and continuous than those found in any other culture. There are many such records on the oracle bones. Modern astronomers have calculated the possible dates on which these observations could have been made, although there is no means as yet of situating them in an absolute chronology.[6] Later, for the Spring and Autumn period, it is possible to check the accuracy of the records: 33 out of the 37 solar eclipses recorded in the *Chunqiu Zuozhuan* have been verified.

A huge effort was made in the 1970s and 1980s by historians of science to collect all references to such phenomena from the Standard Histories, local gazetteers, and the Ming and Qing Veritable Records: *Zhongguo gudai tianxiang jilu zongji* 中國古代天象記錄總集.[7] More than 10,000 records of eclipses, sunspots, comets, meteors, etc., are excerpted. As part of the same scholarly effort, historians of astronomy at Peking Observatory compiled *Zhongguo tianwen shiliao huibian* 中國天文史料匯編. It was excerpted from the same sources and covered all

---

[5] See 18.3. On Qing almanacs, see Richard J. Smith, *Chinese Almanacs*, OUP, 1992, and for a translation of a modern Cantonese almanac, see Martin Palmer, *T'ung Shu: The Ancient Chinese Almanac*, Rider and Co., 1986. *Wannianshu* 萬年書 (multiannual almanac), *wannianli* 萬年曆 (perpetual calendar) or *rixianshu* 日憲書 (book of constant conformity with the heavens) were common terms for almanacs in the later empire.

[6] The main astronomical, calendrical, and meteorological records on the oracle bones are included in *Jiaguwen heji* 甲骨文合集 and indexed in *Jiaguwen tongjian* 甲骨文通檢, vol. 3 (16.4). Noel Barnard, "Astronomical Data from Ancient Chinese Records: The Requirements of Historical Research Methodology," *East Asian History* 6: 47–74 (1993).

[7] *Zhongguo gudai tianxiang jilu zongji* (Comprehensive collection of records of celestial phenomena in ancient China), Zhuang Weifeng 莊威鳳 and Wang Lixing 王立興, eds., Jiangsu kexue jishu, 1988.

those who wrote on astronomy.[8] There is a punctuated uniform edition of the monographs on astronomy and the calendar in the Standard Histories: *Lidai tianwen lüli deng zhi hui bian* 歷代天文律曆等志匯編.[9]

For a comprehensive reader on the early history and development of Chinese astronomy and the calendar, see Zheng Cisheng 鄭慧生, *Gudai tianwen lifa yanjiu* 古代天文曆法研究.[10] The sources excerpted cover a broad range, including the oracle bones and new epigraphic and archaeological materials and ancient texts down to the Han dynasty. Each is given in the original and translated into Modern Chinese. The book also contains a substantial introduction that concentrates on the background to the differences between the Xia, Shang, and Zhou calendars as well as 16 of the author's research articles on early Chinese astronomy and calendars.

On the history of Chinese astronomy, see

SCC, vol. III, *Mathematics and the Sciences of the Heavens and the Earth*, CUP, 1959. This is still the single best introduction in a Western language.

Christopher Cullen, *Astronomy and Mathematics in Ancient China: The Zhoubi suanjing* [周髀算經], CUP, 1996, 1–170.

Sun Xiaochun and Jacob Kristemaker, *The Chinese Sky During the Han: The Constellations Reconstructed and their Cultural Background Explored*, Brill, 1997.

Nathan Sivin, *Cosmos and Computation in Early Chinese Mathematical Astronomy*, in Sivin (1995), originally in *TP* 55: 1–73 (1969).

Chen Zunwei 陳遵媯, *Zhongguo tianwenxueshi* 中國天文學史 (A history of Chinese astronomy), 4 vols., Shanghai renmin, 1980–89; rpnt., Mingwen, 1984–89.

---

[8] *Zhongguo tianwen shiliao huibian* (Historical materials on Chinese astronomy), Kexue, 1989.

[9] *Lidai tianwen luli deng zhi huibian* (Collection of treatises on astronomy and the calendar from the Standard Histories), 10 vols., Zhonghua, 1975–76.

[10] *Gudai tianwen lifa yanjiu* (Research on ancient astronomy and the calendar), Henan daxue, 1995.

Jiang Xiaoyuan 江曉原, *Tianxue zhenyuan* 天學真原 (The real origins of the study of the heavens), Liaoning jiaoyu, 6th prnt., 1995. This a shorter and more skeptical introduction than Chen Zunwei.

For illustrations and articles on the history of astronomical instruments, including those newly excavated, see the following collections:

Zhongguo gudai tianwen wenwu tuji 中國古代天文文物圖集 (Collected illustrations of ancient astronomical artifacts), Kaogusuo, eds., Wenwu, 1980.

Zhongguo gudai tianwen wenwu tulu lunwenji 中國古代天文文物圖錄 論文集 (Collected articles and illustrations of ancient astronomical artifacts), Kaogusuo, eds., Wenwu, 1980.

Zhongguo gudai tianwen wenwu lunji 中國古代天文文物論集 (Collected articles on ancient astronomical artifacts), Wenwu, 1988.

Zhongguo tianwenxueshi wenji 中國天文學史文集 (Collected articles on the history of Chinese astronomy), 6 vols., Kexue, 1978–94. This series contains over 60 research articles, many on non-Han calendars used within China.

Kejishi wenji 科技史文集 (Papers on the history of science), vols. 1 (1978), 6 (1980), and 10 (1983) were special issues devoted to the history of astronomy.

Ziran kexueshi yanjiu 自然科學史研究 (see chap. 37) frequently carries articles on the history of astronomy.

5.2 Years

Four main words were used for year in early China. All had different origins, but came to be used interchangeably: *sui* 歲, *nian* 年, *zai* 載, and *si* 祀.[11]

---

[11] *Sui* 歲 originally meant Jupiter or a cycle of 12 years; in the Eastern Zhou, it was also used to mean a completed cycle of the four seasons, or full harvest, hence year; *nian* 年 originally meant *nian* 埝, a rich harvest or harvest year; *zai* 載 could mean to start and came to be used for the renewal of all things at springtime, hence year; *si* 祀 originally meant annual sacrifice, and in the Shang was also used to mean year. Already in the Warring States *nian* was normally used before numbers and referred

Footnote continued on next page

Absolute dating in Chinese history begins in 841 BC: *Xi-Zhou gonghe yuan nian* 西周共和元年 (the first year of the *gonghe* interregnum of Western Zhou). From then on Chinese chronology is on firm ground in an unbroken and confirmed record up to the present. Before 841 BC, many of the names and dates of rulers and particular events are known back to the Shang, but no absolute chronology has as yet been agreed upon.[12] The dating of an important event such as the Zhou defeat of the Shang has been since the Han dynasty and still is the subject of much controversy. Various hypotheses place the decisive battle at dates ranging from 1130 BC to 1018 BC with some 40 alternatives in between.[13]

5.2.1   Regnal Years, Era Names and Reign Names

The most common and the earliest method of recording years was by setting the year of accession of the ruler as year one (*ji-yuan* 紀元), the year after as year two, and so on successively. This system began in the late Shang and continued with certain

---

to the calendar year; *sui* was used after numbers to count an individual's age (years since year of birth).

[12] So important is the gap felt that a project was included in the ninth five-year plan (1996–2000) to establish an absolute chronology for Chinese history prior to 841 BC and to write annals-style histories of the Xia, Shang, and Zhou (*Xia-Shang-Zhou duandai gongcheng* 夏商周斷代工程). To get results, it will be necessary to improve archeometric techniques, including specially adapted radiocarbon dating for relatively late artifacts such as those of the Shang. For an outline of the project research tasks, see *Early China News*, vol. 9, 1996.

For the time being, the best introduction to the many problems of establishing an absolute chronology extending back from 841 BC to at least the fall of the Shang is Edward L. Shaughnessy, "Calendar and Chronology," *CHAC*, chap. 2.

[13] For a convenient collection of modern arguments supporting the different dates for the defeat of the Shang, see *Wu wang ke Shang zhi nian yanjiu* 武王克商之年研究 (Research on the year of King Wu's defeat of the Shang), Beijing shifan daxue, 1997. Ancient arguments are also summarized.

important modifications right up until 1911.[14] Before the mid-fourth century BC, the first year of the new reign begins in the same year as the previous ruler's death; after the mid-fourth century, it begins on the first day of the lunar New Year following the previous ruler's death, a practice that continued until the end of the Qing.[15]

The first modification to the reign period came during the Warring States when two rulers restarted the cycle from the first year (*yuannian* 元年) during the course of their reign, a practice referred to as *gengyuan* 更元 or *gaiyuan* 改元.[16] The next change was in the reign of Han Wendi 漢文帝, when the year was set to the beginning (*geng yuannian*) upon the adoption of a new calendar in 163 BC. His successor, Jingdi 景帝, after being on the throne six years, did the same in 149, and again after six years, in 143 BC. The next emperor, Han Wudi 漢武帝, followed suit, switching the year count back to the beginning every six years, six times in succession (the six-year gap between *gaiyuan* is a reflection of the Former Han belief that six was a particularly lucky number, a belief inherited from the Qin). Each new six-year period was simply numbered successively as *yuannian, eryuan* 二元, *sanyuan* 三元 and so on. By the time the system had reached *wuyuan sannian* 五元三年 (114

---

[14] In the Republic of China, years were counted successively from 1912. Thus 1935 was *Minguo 24 nian* 民國 24 年. After 1949, the People's Republic adopted the Western calendar, but in Taiwan years are still officially counted by the *Minguo* method. Japan alone retains the reign name count.

[15] For listings of *nianhao*, see A. C. Moule, *The Rulers of China, 221 BC–AD 1949*, Praeger, 1957. More thorough tables of China's rulers exist, for example, giving also families of empresses and names of offspring, see *Zhongguo diwang huanghou qinwang gongzhu shixilu* 中國帝王皇後親王公主世系錄 (Genealogical records of Chinese emperors and kings, empresses, princes and princesses), Bai Yang 柏楊, ed., 2 vols., Youyi, 1982.

[16] When Duke Hui of Wei (魏惠公) assumed the title of king and all the pretensions of that title in 334 BC, he started the year count from the beginning (*gaiyuan*), and 334 was termed *houyuan yuannian* (後元元年) likewise, when Duke Huiwen of Qin 秦惠文公 usurped the title of king in 324 BC, the year count was changed (to *gengyuan yuannian* 更元元年).

BC), it was found so inconvenient that an official proposed ret-rospectively renaming each "beginning" with single, mainly as-tronomical, characters (*jianyuan* 建元, *yuanguang* 元光, *yuan-shuo* 元朔). Han Wudi accepted this proposal only in 110 BC af-ter six years had gone by since the previous *gaiyuan*. Having just conducted the *feng* 封 rites at Taishan, he named the new era *yuanfeng* 元封. This is usually regarded as the first era name (*nianhao* 年號) in Chinese history.[17] Six years later in 104 BC, the Han inaugurated a new calendar (Taichu 太初) and the era name was changed mainly every four years (within reigns) up to the end of the Former Han.

Thereafter, no particular interval for *gaiyuan* was observed. Instead, new eras were frequently inaugurated to mark a new beginning for political reasons, often on the occasion of an aus-picious astronomical sign or splendid event such as a military victory, and always as an affirmation of the sovereignty of the ruler. Altogether more than 800 era names were used in Chi-nese history. Not only the emperors themselves but also lead-ers of non-Han and rebel governments adopted *nianhao*, as did the rulers of the kingdoms in Japan, Korea, and Vietnam. Cop-per coins, starting sporadically from the mid-fourth century, and systematically from the eighth century, bore the *nianhao* of the ruler in the standard four-character formulae of either *ni-anhao yuanbao* 年號元寶 (original treasure of such and such era) or *nianhao tongbao* 年號通寶 (circulating treasure of such and such era).[18]

With only a few exceptions, *nianhao* were composed of two characters, for example, the much-used *jianyuan* 建元 (estab-lishing the beginning) or *yong'an* 永安 (eternal peace). The most frequently used word was *tian* 天 (heaven). From the be-

---

[17] According to the *Shiji*, the first reign name was Yuanding 元鼎 (116–111 BC). However, *Yuanding* was also adopted retrospectively (in 113 BC), see *CHC*, vol. 1, 155–56.

[18] *Guqian xiao cidian* 古錢小辭典, Zhu Huo 朱活 comp., Zhonghua, 1995. In the Ming and Qing only the expression *tongbao* was used on coins since *yuanbao* had come to mean an ingot of shoe-shaped silver. See Lien-sheng Yang, *Money and Credit in China*, HUP, 1952, 24–25.

ginning of the Ming until the end of the Qing normally only one era name was used for the whole reign. As a result era names become synonymous with reign names. For most purposes era names and reign names need not be translated.[19]

5.2.2 *The* Ganzhi 干支 *Cycle*

The *ganzhi* 干支 cycle is one of the two basic counting systems in Chinese culture, the other being decimal.[20] The cycle was formed by combining two sets of counters, one denary (the *shigan* 十干, 10 stems) and the other duodenary (the *shi'erzhi* 十二支, 12 branches).[21]

Table 6: The Tiangan 天干 *and the* Dizhi 地支

	1	2	3	4	5	6	7	8	9	10	11	12
Gan 干	*jia*	*yi*	*bing*	*ding*	*wu*	*ji*	*geng*	*xin*	*ren*	*gui*		
	甲	乙	丙	丁	戊	己	庚	辛	壬	癸		
Zhi 支	*zi*	*chou*	*yin*	*mao*	*chen*	*si*	*wu*	*wei*	*shen*	*you*	*xu*	*hai*
	子	丑	寅	卯	辰	巳	午	未	申	酉	戌	亥

The 10 *gan* appear already on the oracle bones in the late Shang (1200–1045 BC) as a way of enumerating a 10-day "week" (*xun* 旬) and were then known as the 10 *ri* 日. They were usually

---

[19] For other points of view, see Edward H. Schafer, "Chinese Reign Names—Words or Non-sense Syllables," *Wennti Papers* 1: 33–40 (1954); Mary C. Wright, "What's in a Reign Name: The Use of History and Philology," *JAS* 18.1: 103–6 (1958); Also Schafer, "Reply to Readers' Comments," *Wennti Papers* 2: 75–77 (1954). See also A. F. Wright and E. Fagan, "Era Names and Zeitgeist," *Etudes asiatiques* 5: 113–21 (1951).

[20] Before the Han, the *ganzhi* were known as *richen* 日辰. During the Han they were also called *muzi* 母子. It was only after the Later Han that they became known by their present name *ganzhi* (the first reference is in *Baihu tong* 白虎通 (Comprehensive discussions in the White Tiger Hall), "Xingming pian 姓名篇" (Names chapter).

[21] The *shigan* came to be known as *tiangan* 天干 (heavenly stems) or *gan* for short, and the *shi'erzhi* as *dizhi* 地支 (earthly stems) or *zhi* for short.

used in combination with the 12 *zhi* (known as *chen* 辰) to count either three or six cycles of 10 days each. *Ganzhi* day dates are found on thousands of oracle-bone inscriptions. A number of complete tables of all 60 pairs of the cycle are also recorded. The best-preserved complete table dates from the last reigns of the Shang. It is reproduced as #37,986 in *Heji* 合集 (15.4), as well as in most of the readers of oracle-bone script.[22] During the millennium following the Shang, the sexagesimal cycle was gradually extended to count most of the other units of time including years, months, and hours. The cycle was not used for mathematical calculations.

Nobody knows the origin of the *richen* (*ganzhi*), but there have been many theories.[23] For example, it has been speculated

[22] E.g., Li Pu (1995), 54–63 (16.5). Table 10 of Keightley, *Sources* (1978) reproduces the table of 22 *ganzhi* characters as they were written in each of the five periods into which Dong Zuobin 董作賓 divided the evolution of the oracle bone script (15.1). For a concordance of all terms on the oracle bones relating to astronomy or the weather, see *Jiaguwen tongjian* 甲骨文通檢, vol. 3 (15.4).

[23] In Sumerian-Babylonian mathematics a decimal system was used for counting up to 60, thereafter the cycle began again. The influence of the Babylonian base-60 system is still felt today all over the world in the way we count units of time and measure angles. Until quite recently, the superficial similarity of the *ganzhi* cycle with the Babylonian system was taken as one of the "proofs" for the Western origin of early Chinese civilization. One of the earliest to do so was Terrein de Lacouperie (1845–94), who taught at University College, London, in the 1880s. His theories have long since been rejected, not least because the *ganzhi* are different from the Babylonian system both in concept and function. The *ganzhi* were derived by combining two separate cyclical systems, not from a base-60 numeral system (Chen Cheng-yih, *Early Chinese Work in Natural Science*, HKU Press, 1996, 187–90). Edwin Pulleyblank believes that the *ganzhi* represented the 22 consonants of the Chinese language at the time of the invention of the script: "The *Ganzhi* as Phonograms and Their Application to the Calendar," *EC* 16: 39–80 (1991), and "The *Ganzhi* as Phonograms," *Early China News* 8: 29–30 (1995). Gordon Whittaker summarizes some of the other speculations in his *Calendar and Script in Proto-historical China and Mesoamerica: A Comparative Study of Day Names and Their Signs*, Holos, 1990.

that in pre-Shang times, when every month may have been reckoned as having 30 days exactly, the 12 *zhi* may have originally been combined with the 10 *gan* in order to avoid the ambiguity of having three identical 10-day cycles within one month. By using a cycle of 60 days each with a unique date, the first repetition only came in the third month by which time seasonal change was sufficiently advanced to reduce the risk of confusion. Another speculation is that the decimal *gan* were used by one tribe and the duodecimal *zhi* by another. The two were combined when the tribes joined their forces. There is no evidence for these hypotheses. Given the importance of periodic sacrificial rituals at the Shang court and given the close connection between the origins of the characters and divination, a magico-religious origin would seem the most likely.[24]

In oracle-bone script, none of the 22 *ganzhi* share graphic elements with each other, which possibly suggests they were used as alteration-proof numbers, more secure than the common numerals, whose single straight lines (一, 二, 三) could easily be miswritten whether by accident or by design. They were changed only once in the course of 3,500 years: temporarily when the Taipings used three new *zhi* as part of their calendar reform.

The *ganzhi* have been among the most frequently used characters, not only because they were used for recording dates and counting the hours and times of the day, but also because they were borrowed as side elements in many other characters (six are used as classifiers and many more as phonetic indicators). They were also used as suffixes (e.g., *zi* 子) as well as in many common compounds (e.g., *zhongwu* 中午, midday).

---

[24] The 10 *ri* appear in the names attributed to the Xia rulers. They were used as the posthumous names of deceased Shang rulers (no doubt derived from the days on which sacrifices were performed in their honor).

5.2.3   A Cycle of Cathay

The *ganzhi* were used for counting a 60-year cycle (*liushi huajia* 六十花甲 or *liushi jiazi* 六十甲子) from at least the Former Han and during the reign of Wang Mang 王莽. In AD 85 government orders made their use official. Later they were extrapolated backwards to count years from the beginning of Chinese history. In Treaty Port English, the 60-year cycle was often called "a cycle of Cathay."

Between the Han and the Qing there are 25 cycles with the same *ganzhi*. Confusion is avoided because during the whole of imperial China, only one reign period lasted for more than 60 years (Kangxi). Moreover, the dynasty is either known from the context or is given, and era names are also usually written as part of a date. For example, *Yuan Zhongtong ernian xiyou* 元中統二年辛酉 refers to the *xiyou* year, the second year since the adoption of the era name Zhongtong by the Yuan emperor Shizu (Khubilai Khan), i.e., 1261.

Finding the equivalent year in the Western calendar is relatively easy. Most dictionaries and encyclopaedias such as the *Hanyu da cidian* or the *Cihai* contain tables of dynasties, names of emperors, accession dates, and era names and cyclical characters. In addition, dozens of chronological tables (*nianbiao* 年表) are available, for example, Fang Shiming 方詩銘, *Zhongguo lishi jinian biao* 中國歷史紀年表, which is short but accurate (it was originally published as the chronological appendix to the 1979 edition of the *Cihai*).[25] Chronological tables of the Warring States kingdoms and rebel dynasties are clearly indicated, as well as dates of accession and dates of adoption of *nianhao*. It covers 841 BC to AD 1911.

For chronological tables of non-Han regimes, see 5.6.

Zhongguo lishi niandai jianbiao 中國歷史年代簡表 is useful for looking up years and *nianhao* of all the main dynasties and convenient because of its small size, but it does not have clear

---

[25] *Zhongguo lishi jinian biao* (Tables of Chinese historical periods), Shanghai renmin, 1976, Shanghai cishu, 1980.

tables of complicated periods such as the Warring States and does not indicate the difference between accession and the adoption of the *nianhao*. It covers from 841 BC to AD 1911 and has an index of *nianhao*.[26]

There are also many chronological tables that show Chinese and Western equivalents for the era names of China's East Asian neighbors, most of which adopted their calendars from the Chinese.[27]

Apart from regnal years and *ganzhi*, the names of the 12 annual stations of Jupiter began to be used to count years in 365 BC. They were in turn replaced by the stations of Taisui 太歲 (the God of Time in later popular almanacs), an invisible counter-orbital correlate of Jupiter (*xingsui jinian* 星歲紀年). This method continued in use during the Warring States, the Qin, and the Former Han until replaced by the *ganzhi* in AD 54. It was occasionally used by literati in later periods.[28]

A popular way of counting years was by using the 12 Animals (*shengxiao* 生肖), each of which was associated with one of the 12 Taisui and one of the 12 earthly branches, *dizhi*. The practice was in common use by the Qin dynasty in the form in which it has continued to this day. The Chinese animal signs do not, however, correspond to the 12 signs of the Western zodiac.[29]

[26] *Zhongguo lishi niandai jianbiao* (Simplified tables of Chinese historical periods), Wenwu, 1973; 2nd ed., 5th prnt., 1994.

[27] *Zhongguo riben Chaoxian Yuenan siguo lishi niandai duizhaobiao* 中國日本朝鮮越南四國歷史年代對照表 (Comparative table of the historical periods of China, Japan, Korea and Vietnam), compiled and published by Shanxisheng tushuguan 山西省圖書館, 1979. Covers 660 BC to 1918 AD. Many Western libraries may still have older works such as Mathias Chang, *Synchronismes chinois: Chronologie complète et concordance avec l'ère chrétienne de toutes les dates concernant l'histoire de l'Extrême-Orient (Chine, Japon, Corée, Annam, Mongolie, etc.), (2375 av. J.C.–1904 apr. J.C.),* Variétés Sinologiques no. 24, Shanghai, 1905; Taipei rpnt., 1967.

[28] See Liu Tan 劉坦, *Zhongguo gudai zhi xingsui jinian* 中國古代之星歲紀年 (Ephemeris years in ancient China), Kexue, 1957.

[29] The classic study is Edouard Chavannes, "Le Cycle turc des douze animaux," *TP* 7: 51–122 (1906). One of the earliest pictures of mythical

Footnote continued on next page

Table 7: The Twelve Animal Signs

Zhi 支	Animal signs shengxiao 生肖	Zhi 支 (cont.'d)	Animal signs (cont.'d)
zi 子	shu 鼠 rat	wu 午	ma 馬 horse
chou 丑	niu 牛 ox	wei 未	yang 羊 sheep
yin 寅	hu 虎 tiger	shen 申	hou 猴 monkey
mao 卯	tu 兔 rabbit	you 酉	ji 鷄 cock
chen 辰	long 龍 dragon	xu 戌	quan 犬 dog
si 巳	she 蛇 snake	hai 亥	zhu 猪 pig

5.3   Seasons, Festivals and Vacations

5.3.1 Seasons

The year was divided according to the seasons (*shi* 時), which were accurately measured in ancient China. The oracle bones record spring and autumn (*chun* 春 and *qiu* 秋, also later used together as a compound meaning "time" and, later still, "year"). In the *Chunqiu* period, if not before, a more detailed system of four seasons (*sishi* 四時) developed based on the two solstices (*er zhi* 二至) and the two equinoxes (*erfen* 二分). The year itself was measured from winter solstice to winter solstice.

By the Former Han, each season was divided into six climatic periods (*qi* 氣) of fifteen days each (in Treaty Port English, "calendrical fortnights"). The 24 *qi* alternated between *zhongqi* 中氣 (the odd-numbered *qi* in Table 8, customarily translated as "medial *qi*") and *jieqi* 節氣 (the even-numbered joints, as of a bamboo, usually translated as "nodal *qi*"). The system as a whole was known as the 24 *jieqi* 節氣. The eight main climatic periods at the beginning and middle of each season were known as the *bajie* 八節 (marked in bold in Table 8).

---

creatures associated with the 12 months is on the Chu Silk Manuscript dating from the third century BC (18.2). See Liu Xinfang 劉信芳, "Zhongguo zuizao de wuhou liyue ming 中國最早的物候曆月明 (The

Footnote continued on next page

Table 8: The Jieqi 節氣 System

	Jieqi (the bajie are highlighted)	Translation	Western Calendar	Chinese Calendar
1	Dongzhi 冬至	Winter Solstice	22 or 23/Dec.	十一中
2	Xiaohan 小寒	Slight Cold	6 or 7/Jan.	十二節
3	Dahan 大寒	Great Cold	21 or 22/Jan.	十二中
4	Lichun 立春	Start of Spring	4 or 5/Feb.	正月節
5	Yushui 雨水	Rain Water	19 or 20/Feb.	正月中
6	Jingzhe 驚蟄	Waking of Insects	6 or 7/March	二月節
7	Chunfen 春分	Spring Equinox	21 or 22/March	二月中
8	Qingming 清明	Pure Brightness	5 or 6/Apr.	三 etc.
9	Guyu 穀雨	Grain Rain	20 or 21/Apr.	
10	Lixia 立夏	Start of Summer	6 or 7/May	四
11	Xiaoman 小滿	Forming of Grain	21 or 22/May	
12	Mangzhong 芒種	Grain in Ear	6 or 7/June	五
13	Xiazhi 夏至	Summer Solstice	22 or 23/June	
14	Xiaoshu 小暑	Slight Heat	7 or 8/July	六
15	Dashu 大暑	Great Heat	23 or 24/July	
16	Liqiu 立秋	Start of Autumn	8 or 9/Aug.	七
17	Chushu 處暑	Limit of Heat	23 or 24/Aug.	
18	Bailu 白露	White Dew	8 or 9/Sept.	八
19	Qiufen 秋分	Autumn Equinox	23 or 24/Sept.	
20	Hanlu 寒露	Cold Dew	9 or 10/Oct.	九
21	Shuangjiang 霜降	Frost's Descent	24 or 25/Oct.	
22	Lidong 立冬	Start of Winter	8 or 9/Nov.	十
23	Xiaoxue 小雪	Slight Snow	23 or 24/Nov.	
24	Daxue 大雪	Great Snow	7 or 8/Dec.	十一

From AD 520, a more refined system of dividing each *qi* into three periods of five days known as the 72 *hou* 候 was made part of the official calendar. On the phenological basis for the *jieqi* and the *hou*, and subsequent adjustments to them to take account of the shift of the center of farming to the different climatic conditions of southern China, see 35.1.1.

The *jieqi* system was adopted in Korea, Japan, and Vietnam along with the same terms for the four seasons and their subdivisions. In China, both *qihou* 氣候 and *shihou* 時候 were nor-

---

earliest names for Chinese signs for the months)," *Zhonghua wenshi luncong*, 53: 75–107 (1994).

mally used in the sense of "climate." *Shihou* was only used in the sense of "time" from about the Song.

5.3.2   *Festivals*

Festivals (*jieri* 節日) in China, as elsewhere, served to celebrate, commemorate, reenact, or preview great events whether agricultural, religious, social, or political. The timing of the earliest festivals was set by the seasons of the year and by the food production cycle of north China. There was thus a direct connection between the main *jieqi* 節氣 and the *jieri* 節日. The festivals were linked to the worship of the soil, of fertility, and of the ancestors. The ordering of the annual festivals which took place in the Han dynasty remained basically unaltered for the next 1,000 years.[30] The changes were in the form of additions and adaptations from Buddhism (and to a lesser extent, Daoism). Long after the Han, there were no fixed dates, only rough times according to season. Gradually the practice developed of holding the main festivals on odd days of odd-numbered months (these being considered male and lucky). The imperial government sought to truncate and adapt the festivals and also influenced them by fixing the civil calendar and announcing the dates of the main festival days. In addition to the better known festivals there were many others, both national and local, and a huge number of special days marking the birth of various gods.[31]

As the center of gravity of Chinese life shifted in the Song, many of the festivals were adapted once again, this time to the different customs and climate of the South. An obvious example is the association of Qu Yuan 屈原 and dragon-boat racing

[30] For the annual festivals observed in the Han, see Derke Bodde, *Festivals in Classical China: New Year and Other Annual Observations during the Han Dynasty, 206 BC–AD 220*, PUP, 1975.

[31] On the Hungry Ghosts Festival (7/15), see Stephen F. Teiser, *The Ghost Festival in Medieval China*, PUP, 1988; on a festival for warding off epidemics, see Paul R. Katz, *Demon Hordes and Burning Boats: the Cult of Marshall Wen in Late Imperial Chekiang*, SUNY, 1995.

with the Duanwu 端午 festival. The main festivals of today are the direct descendants of those of the Song. By the Ming and Qing, the three main festivals of the year were known as the *san dajie* 三大節 (marked with an asterisk in Box 4).

The literati not infrequently recorded their observations of annual festivals (*suishi* 歲時, *shiling* 時令) usually chronologically arranged for each of the 12 months of the year. They also recorded popular customs (*fengsu, fengtu ji* 風俗, 風土集). Such works were either printed separately for a locality or region or were included as a chapter or two of the local gazetteer or put in their *biji* (miscellaneous notes, see chap. 31).[32] The earliest extant example is the *Fengsu tongyi* 風俗通義 (*ICS Concordance* 43). An example from the Northern Song is found in the second part of Meng Yuanlao 孟元老 (fl. 1110–60), *Dongjing menghualu* 東京夢華錄, which is a *suishi ji* for the capital (see 47.2, under *Biji*). A late Qing example of the genre was translated by Derke Bodde, *Annual Customs and Festivals in Beijing as Recorded in the Yen-ching Suishi-chi* [燕京歲時記], Henri Vetch, 1936; repr., SMC, 1977; 1994.

Box 4: Seven Main Annual Festivals in Late Imperial China
1/1: *yuandan** 元旦 (Lunar New Year; *chunjie* 春節, Spring Festival)
1/15: *yuanxiao jie* 元宵節 (Lantern Festival)
3/early: *qingming jie* 清明 (grave sweeping)
5/5: *duanwu jie** 端午節 (Dragon Boat or Double Fifth Festival)
8/15: *zhongqiu jie** 中秋節 (Mid-autumn or Moon Festival)
12/23 (in the North); 12/24 (in the South): Zao Wangye 竈王爺
   (Kitchen God)
12/29 or 30: *chuxi* 除夕 (Lunar New Year's Eve)

---

[32] See for example Chao Weipang's translation of the description of the dragon-boat festival in Hunan by Yang Sichang 楊嗣昌 (1588–1641) "The Dragon Boat Race in Wuling, Hunan," *Folklore Studies* 2: 1–18 (1943). Also translated in Patricia Buckley Ebrey, *Chinese Civilization: A Sourcebook*, 1981; 2nd ed., rev. and expanded, Free Press, 1993, 208–10.

5.3.3   Vacations

The main festivals in traditional China extended over many days, sometimes for up to a month in winter (the slack farming season). Officially, the total varied from dynasty to dynasty and the practice in the countryside and in the administrative centers must also have been very different. In the Tang, the official total of festival days was 53 with a maximum of seven days off for any one festival. Periods of up to three years mourning were laid down at the death of a parent. Other periods of leave were granted for important family occasions such as the coming of age of a son. On official holidays and office hours as well as business and working hours, see Lien-sheng Yang, "Schedules of Work and Rest in Traditional China."[33] Yang shows that official days of rest were gradually reduced from one every five days in the Han to one in 10 in the Tang to the Yuan and none in the Ming and Qing.

5.4 Months and Days

The Chinese based their calendar, as did most other ancient civilizations, on observation of the rising and setting of the sun; the phases of the moon, and the movements of the stars, especially the pole star (hence day = *ri* 日; month = *yue* 月, and year = *sui* 歲).

Days had been named since the Shang using the *ganzhi* (cyclical characters), as explained in 5.2; months were named with the 12 *zhi* from the Spring and Autumn period. Both months and days were also increasingly referred to by number.[34] Thus the *Chunqiu* records a total solar eclipse on what is the earliest absolute day date in Chinese history: the beginning of the second month of the third year of the reign of Duke Yin [posthumous title] of Lu, i.e., February 22, 720 BC, in the West-

---

[33] *HJAS* 18: 301–25 (1955), rpnt. in his *Studies in Chinese Institutional History*, Harvard-Yenching, 1961, 3rd prnt., 1969; Hongqiao, 1975, 18–42.

[34] See also Marc Kalinowski, "The Use of the Twenty-eight 'Xiu' as a Day Count in Early China," *Chinese Science* 13: 55–81 (1997).

ern (Gregorian) calendar.[35] It is an absolute date because the eclipse has been corroborated by modern astronomical calculations (according to Zhang Peiyu, 1990, its magnitude was 0.50 and it could have been observed at Luoyang at 7.21 am). From this day onward all Chinese days can be precisely identified up to the present time.

During the pre-Qin period, various other naming systems were used for the months, including the 12 half-tones of the Chinese musical scale, 12 trees and flowers, and the 12 animal signs. Toward the end of the Warring States, the Five Elements were correlated with the months in an elaborate scheme.[36]

From the Later Han, however, in everyday life, it was numbers that were used for naming months and days of the month, although in official documents and records where accuracy was required, including horoscopes, the *ganzhi* tended to be used.

In addition, there were a large number of special terms for particular months and special days, many of which are still in use. For example:

Zhengyue 正月 (the first month of the year, which had at least 15 other names in the course of Chinese history); *layue* 臘月 (the last month of the year).

The four phases of the moon: *shuoyue* 朔月 (new moon), *shangxian* 上弦 (first quarter), *wangyue* 望月 (full moon), *xiaxian* 下弦 (last quarter).

Dayue 大月 (large month) is a lunar month of 30 days (or a solar month of 31 days); *xiaoyue* 小月 (small month) is a lunar month of 29 days (or a solar month of 30 days).

The month is divided into three 10-day periods, *sanxun* 三旬 (or *sanhuan* 三浣), referred to as *shangxun* 上旬, *zhongxun* 中旬, *xiaxun* 下旬.

---

[35] *Yingong sannian chun wang eryue jiyou ri you shi zhi* 隱公三年春王二月己巳日有食之 (*Chunqiu Gong yang zhuan* 春秋公羊傳).

[36] John B. Henderson, *The Development and Decline of Chinese Cosmology*, Col. UP, 1984, includes analysis of Chinese correlative thinking. See also A. C. Graham, "Yin-Yang and the Nature of Correlative Thinking," Institute of East Asian Philosophy, University of Singapore, Occasional Paper, 1986.

Chuxi 除夕 (New Year's Eve); *yuandan* 元旦 (New Year's Day); *yuanxiao* 元宵 is the night of the fifteenth of the first lunar month (i.e., the eve of the Lantern Festival); *nianye* 年夜 (evening of the last day of the year);

The first 10 days of each of the lunar months are known as *chuyi* 初一, *chu'er* 初二 … *chushi* 初十.

Shuo 朔 is the first day of the lunar month, *wang* 望 is the fifteenth day of "small" months and the sixteenth day of "large" months and *hui* 晦, the last day of both the large and small months.

During the Spring and Autumn and Warring States periods, three main calendars were in use at different times: the Xia, Yin (Shang), and Zhou calendars.[37] Each started the year in a different solar month: the Zhou calendar began in the first solar month (*ziyue* 子月, i.e., in the month containing the winter solstice). The Yin calendar began in the second solar month (*chouyue* 丑月) and the Xia began in the third solar month (*yinyue* 寅月). During the Warring States, each kingdom based its calendar with minor variations on one of the three calendars. In general, the states in the middle Yellow River used the Xia calendar, and the remainder used that of the Zhou. There were however important variations due mainly to different methods of reckoning intercalations.

At the Qin unification, the Yin calendar was adopted. This was continued by the Han until 104 BC, when the Xia calendar took its place. It remained the basis for all subsequent calendars until 1912 when the Gregorian calendar was promulgated. The Xia calendar is now called the *nongli* 農曆. Its New Year's Day has been renamed the Spring Festival.

Since 12 lunar months fall short of the solar year by about 11 days, extra months (*runyue* 閏月) were intercalated since at least the Shang dynasty to close the gap. By the seventh century BC, seven intercalations were made every 19 years.[38]

---

[37] On the different calendars used in pre-Qin times, see Zhang Peiyu's calendrical concordance cited in 12.2.

[38] A *zhang* 章 cycle in Chinese (called a Metonic cycle in English after the Greek astronomer Meton, who lived in the fifth century BC).

5.5 Date Conversion

Several calendrical concordances (*libiao* 曆表 or *liri duizhaobiao* 曆日對照表) are available. They give year, month, and days in cyclical characters and their equivalents in the Western calendar (using the modern Gregorian calendar even for pre-1582 dates). A good concordance will also indicate intercalations, *jieqi* (climatic periods, see Table 8), *nianhao* and Julian calendar days and much else besides.[39] Some concordances also record dates in the Buddhist, Muslim, Yi, Dai, and other calendars (5.6).

Before using any of the concordances, it is essential to read the compiler's introductory remarks to find out what conventions have been followed, for example, how to allow for the zero year between 1 BC and AD 1 in the Western calendar, which of the pre-Qin calendars have been used for calculating pre-Qin dates and where the intercalary months have been inserted. Three of the most comprehensive and accurate are:

1. *Xinbian Zhongguo sanqian nian liri jiansuobiao* 新編中國三千年曆日檢索表 (New search tables for 3,000 years of Chinese calendar days), Xu Xiqi 徐錫祺, ed., Renmin jiaoyu, 1992. This gives the cyclical characters for the year, *nianhao*, and first day of each month (Chinese calendar) from 1,500 to 2050 (between 1500 and 723 BC, the year is given starting with the month containing the winter solstice and ending with the thirteenth month). From 722 to AD 53, the *xingci* 星次 name is indicated and, from 402 BC, also the *sui* 歲 name. After AD 53, these were no longer used. Intercalary months are indicated throughout. There are additional columns for the rulers and reign names of Japan (660 BC–AD 1990), as well as for the different Korean (207–111 BC; 57 BC–AD 1910) and Vietnamese (208–109 BC; AD 544–1945) kingdoms. From 1500 BC to AD 616, each page has 12 years; from 616 to 2050, there are 10 years to a page (to fit in the Muslim calendar starting in 622). There are separate tables for the

[39] Julian day calendar dates are given throughout (the Julian day calendar system of astronomical dates counts day 1 as starting from noon of Jan. 1st, 4713 BC, a date which precedes all civil calendars. Conversion into Julian days enables comparison between different calendrical systems. Do not confuse Julian days *Rulüeri* 儒略日 with the Julian calendar, *Rulüeli* 儒略曆. Julian days were invented in 1582 when the Julian calendar was replaced with the Gregorian.

chronologies of the Spring and Autumn and Warring States duke-
doms and kingdoms, as well as for the later independent kingdoms in
China, including Rouran 柔然 (464–520), Gaochang 高昌 (Qoco,
531–640), Bohai 渤海 (698–925), Nanzhao 南詔 (748–975), Tubo
(Tibet, 815–?), Dali 大理 (986–1254), Northern Liao 北遼 (1122–23),
Western Liao 西遼 (1124–1211), and the Taiping 太平 (1851–68).
One of the appendixes gives the three different Yellow-Emperor dating systems used between 1903 and 1911. The archeoastronomer
Zhang Peiyu (the author of item 3 below) provides a table of calculated winter solstice dates between 1500 BC and AD 2050 (305–16).
The appendixes give detailed and useful supplementary information
often lacking from earlier calendrical concordances, e.g., tables of the
different names used for the months; festivals in the Buddhist, Daoist, Muslim, and Christian calendars; minor festivals in the Chinese
calendar; a table of different terms for dividing the day according to
14 different sources; a list of 94 calendars promulgated between the
third century BC and AD 1852 (including some which were not implemented); brief notes on 30 different era systems, including the
Christian, Muslim, Japanese, Korean, Buddhist, Burmese, Jewish,
Zoroastrian, Coptic, Egyptian, Babylonian, Olympian, Roman, Seleucid, Byzantine, Nepalese, and Saptashi; and a table of the dates of
adoption of the Gregorian calendar by 26 selected countries. There
are separate indexes (*pinyin*, stroke-count, and four-corner) of era
and reign names, both for China and for independent kingdoms and
neighboring states.

2. *Zhongguoshi liri he Zhong-Xi liri duizhao biao* 中國史曆日和中西曆
    日對照表 (Chinese historical calendar days and a calendrical concor-
    dance of Chinese and Western days), Fang Shiming 方詩銘 and Fang
    Xiaofen 方小芬 eds., Shanghai cishu, 1987. The compilers have made
    good use of earlier calendrical concordances, the mistakes in eight of
    which are noted at the date where they occur. They have also taken
    into account recent archaeological discoveries. Throughout all the
    tables, the format is the same: four years to the page with the first
    day of each of the three 10-day periods (*xun* 旬) of each lunar month
    shown (there is a table listing the 60 *ganzhi* on page 880 to assist find-
    ing the *ganzhi* for other days).[40] Part I covers the years 841 to 1 BC
    with the date (year, month, day) in the Chinese calendar and the *gan-*

---

[40] One of the earlier tables corrected by Fang and Fang is Dong Zuobin 董作賓, *Zhongguo nianli zongpu* 中國年曆總譜 (Chronological Tables of Chinese History), 2 vols., HKU Press, 1960. Vol. 1 contains tables
up to 1 BC and vol. 2 contains tables from AD 1 to 2000.

zhi equivalents. Appendixes contain a daily concordance for the Yin calendar covering 1384 to 1112 BC; for the Western Zhou calendar for the years 1111 to 842 and for the Former Han (Yin) calendar for the years 206–105 BC. Part II is arranged in the same way for the years AD 1 to 1949, but adds the Western calendar month and day equivalents. The dates of accession and adoption of *nianhao* are noted. The Taiping calendar is given. An appendix covers the years 1949 to 2,000 with the Western calendar as the base. There is an index of *nianhao* by stroke count.

3. *Sanqian wubai nian liri tianxiang* 三千五百年曆日天象 (3,500-year calendar of heavenly phenomena), Zhang Peiyu 張培瑜 comp., Henan jiaoyu, 1990; rpnt., Dajia, 1997. This enormous calendar cum astronomical table was compiled by a historian of Chinese astronomy. It is divided into two main parts. The first begins with a table of intercalary months for the Spring and Autumn period (AD 722–480, pp. 1–56). This is followed by a table of intercalary days for the years 221 BC to AD 2050. There are six years to a page showing the first day of every month and the dates of each of the eight nodal climatic periods (*bajie* 八節). From 104 BC, all 24 of the climatic periods are given (pp. 57–438). The second part (astronomical) has tables showing the date and time in hours and minutes of the new and full moons for every month from 1500 BC to AD 2000 (pp. 439–884); the date and time of the beginning of the eight nodal periods (pp. 885–958); the magnitude and different times at which the midpoint of solar eclipses could have been seen from 13 of the main cities of China from 1500 BC to AD 2500 (959–1052). Appendixes show the differences in intercalations used during the Three Kingdoms, the *Nan-Bei Chao*, and the Song, Liao, and Jin (pp. 1053–1083); lunar eclipses as they would have been seen from Anyang during the years 1500–1000 BC (pp. 1084–1184). There is an index of era and reign names.[41]

There are many calendrical concordances for particular periods that are usually more detailed than those covering the whole sweep of Chinese history (see under *Chronology* in sections 12.2; 44.5; 46.5; 49.5 and 50.6).

---

[41] For computer-generated maps of China for the extrapolated positions from which each solar eclipse could have been seen in China between 1,500 BC and AD 1900, see F. R. Stephenson and M. A. Houlden, *Atlas of Historical Eclipse Maps in East Asia*, CUP, 1986 and F. R. Stephenson, *Historical Eclipses and Earth's Rotation*, CUP, 1997.

5.6 Buddhist, Muslim, Dai, Yi, and Tibetan Calendars

The Buddhist era (*Buddhasakaraj*) begins in 543 BC (the year in which the Buddha attained Nirvana) and counts consecutively from then on: so the year 2,340 is 1796 (which following the Chinese Calendar began on the ninth of the second lunar month).

The Muslim calendar (Huili 回曆) is a lunar calendar. It begins with the day after the Flight (Hegira) of Mohammed to Medina, July 16, AD 622, and counts consecutively from then on. Because years in the Muslim character are shorter than in the Western or Chinese calendar, the year of Mohammed 1,211 (which began on the seventh of the seventh lunar month) is 1796.[42]

The Dai calendar (Daili 傣曆) starts on the first day of the seventh month (March 21) AD 638, and counts consecutively from then on, so the year 1,158 (which began on the sixth of the seventh Dai month, i.e., April 12) is 1796.

The Yi 彝 used two different calendars, one a 12-month lunar calendar, the other a 10-month solar calendar in both of which they counted years according to their own system. So 1796 is the Southwest Year (which began on the nineteenth [pig day] of the first Yi month).

Various calendars were used in Tibet based on Chinese and Indian models until the adoption in 1027 of a cycle of sixty based on the five elements (iron, wood, water, fire and earth) and the twelve animals. This dating system was extended backwards to the foundation of the first Tibetan kingdom in 627.

[42] The Muslim calendar is included in standard chronological concordances (see 5.8). There are also special concordances for converting Buddhist, Muslim, Tibetan, Dai, Yi, and other calendars. Two pioneering works often encountered in Western libraries are Dong Zuobin (1960) and *Zhong, Xi, Hui shi rili* 中西回史日曆 (A comparative daily calendar for Chinese, Western and Muslim history, AD 1 to 1940), Chen Yuan 陳垣, comp., Yanjing daxue, 1926; rev. ed., Zhonghua, 1962. Both have been superseded by the references at the end of this section.

The year 1796 is the fire dragon year (following the Chinese calendar it began on the ninth of the second lunar month).

Calendrical Concordances

Zhongguo minzushi renwu cidian 中國民族史人物辭典 contains a 150-page chronological concordance of non-Han dynasties and regimes that ruled in China, as well as their genealogical tables.[43]

Zhonghua tongshi da lidian 中華通史大曆典 (Calendrical compendium of Chinese history),Wang Kefu 王可夫 and Li Min 李民, eds., 3 vols., Sichuan minzu, 1996. This is the most detailed concordance for matching the main non-Han calendars with the Chinese and Western calendars. In the course of 4,600 pages and three large volumes it tabulates each day individually (from 1500 BC). There is a great deal of supplementary information, including notes on the major events each year for the years 717 BC to AD 1990. Intercalary months and Julian days are given throughout, as well as a finding code for the *ganzhi* characters for the first day of every month. In addition, the tables show for the legendary years 2674 to 1501 BC: *ganzhi*; traditional rulers; estimates from Dong Zuobin, Bamboo annals, and other sources (pp. 1–77); 1500 to 841 BC: traditional rulers; estimations of dates by various scholars; Zhou fiefs and their capitals; temple and posthumous names (pp. 78–643); 840 BC to AD 2000: rulers (including rulers of kingdoms and fiefs); capitals; temple and posthumous names; calculated days of the month and days of the week (pp. 644–4079). Muslim dates are added from 622 and Tibetan dates are added from 1027. There is table comparing dates in the Western, Taiping, Dai 傣, two Yi 彝 and Russian calendars for the years 1804–2000 (the Russian calendar is not shown from March, 1918 when the Western calendar was introduced in the newly established Soviet Republic). Appendixes contain very full tables of the rulers of each dynasty including those of lesser kingdoms and usurpers and leaders of armed uprisings. There are also annotated lists of tribes and non-Han peoples active in each dynasty with the names of all their rulers when known (pp. 4461–4591).

Gong, Nong, Hui, Dai, Yi, Zang, Fo he rulüeri duizhao biao 公農回傣彝藏佛和儒略日對照表 (A comparative calendar for Western, Chinese, Muslim, Hui, Dai, Yi, Tibetan, Buddhist calendars, and Julian day

---

[43] *Zhongguo minzushi renwu cidian* (Dictionary of personalities in ethnic minority history), Gao Wende 高文德, ed. in chief, Shehui kexue, 1990, 617–805.

numbers, AD 622 to 2050), Wang Huanchun 王煥春 et al., comps.,
Kexue, 1991. A convenient calendrical concordance especially for the
period 1840 to the present. The years 622 to 1839 are tabulated in the
seven different calendars of the title (taking the Western calendar as
the basis) plus the day on which New Years Day fell in the Chinese,
Muslim, Yi and Dai calendars (pp. 11–52). The main part shows day
equivalents (six months to a page) in the Western, Chinese, Muslim
and Dai calendars between 1840 and 2050 (pp. 53–475). In addition,
the Yi 10-month solar calendar New Year's Day Western calendar
equivalents are shown. Julian day calendar dates are given throughout. Given the clear layout, conversion from any one of the calendars to another is easily done for the modern period. *Ganzhi* characters, *jieqi* and days of the week are also shown. Appendix 1 gives
chronological tables of Chinese, Japanese, Korean and Vietnamese
reign names from 1516 to 1949 (478–91).

5.7   Japanese, Korean and Vietnamese Calendars

Japanese-style dating works in a similar manner to the Chinese
system. Lists of emperors' accession dates and era names (*nen-
gô*) can be found in most Japanese-English dictionaries and the
calendrical concordances introduced in 5.6. Japan switched
from its lunar-solar calendar to the Gregorian calendar on January 1, 1873.[44]

Korea adopted the Chinese calendar in the seventh century
and from the seventeenth to the nineteenth centuries used Chinese *nianhao* on official documents. From 1896 to 1900, Ko-

---

[44] The most popular pocket-sized Japanese chronological table giving
Chinese, Japanese and Korean equivalents to the Western calendar is the
long-lived *Tôhô nenpyô* 東方年表 (Chronological tables of Oriental history), comp., Fujishima Tatsurô 藤島達朗 and Nogami Shunjô 野上俊
静, Heirakuji, 1955; 3rpnt., 1996. A large-format edition was issued in
1996. This table covers dynasties which ruled in China, Korea and Japan
(including the kingdom of Bohai and Manchukuo), but not Warring
States kingdoms or rebel dynasties. It manages to indicate graphically
when there is a difference between the date of adoption of a *nianhao* and
the date of accession. Dates covered are 660 BC to AD 1995. There is an
index of rulers arranged chronologically as well as an index of *nianhao*
arranged by country.

rean *nyunho* were used. Thereafter, Japanese reign names and the Gregorian calendar were imposed until 1945, when the Gregorian calendar alone began to be used. The Korean calendar (*tanji* 檀紀, based on the accession of the mythical founder, King Tan, in 2333 BC), was also used until 1910 and again in 1945, and in South Korea after 1953 (to convert to Western years subtract 2,333 (e.g., 4332 is 1999).

Until 1306, the Vietnamese used the Chinese calendar and Chinese *nianhao*. After 1306, they used the Chinese calendar and their own *niên-hiêu*. From 1644 to 1812 they continued to use the Ming calendar. In 1812, they finally moved to the Qing calendar for lunar reckoning, having inaugurated the Western calendar for certain official purposes at the beginning of the Gia Long period in 1802.[45]

5.8 Events

One of the largest of the many chronological tables of important events listed year by year is *Zhongguo lishi dashi biannian* 中國歷史大事編年.[46]

Note that events in Chinese history are often referred to by their cyclical dates, e.g., the *Wuxu bianfa* 戊戌變法 (1898 reforms), the *Jiawu zhanzheng* 甲午戰爭 (Sino-Japanese war), or the *Xinhai geming* 辛亥革命 (the 1911 Revolution). In more recent times, dates are used, e.g., the *wusi yundong* 五四運動 (May Fourth Movement).

Even the best Western chronological tables of events tend to pay scant attention to China and the other countries of East Asia. So use a Chinese publication such as *Zhongwai lishi nianbiao, gongyuan qian 5000 nian–gongyuan 1918 nian* 中外歷史年表公元前 5000 年–公元 1918 年, which is one of the most

[45] Bui Quang Tung, "Tables synoptiques de chronologie vietnamienne," *BEFEO* 51: 1–78 (1963). See also the references given in note 27.

[46] *Zhongguo lishi dashi biannian* (Chronicle of main events in Chinese history), Zhang Xikong 張習孔 et al., eds., 5 vols., Beijing chubanshe, 1987; rpnt., 1988.

comprehensive chronological tables of important events in China and the rest of the world.[47]

Note that there are numerous chronological tables for special subjects whose range at the best is broader than any available work in a Western language. Take, for example, the *Shijie zhexueshi nianbiao* 世界哲學史年表, whose tables include not only all the main philosophers in the Western tradition, but also those in the Arabic, Chinese, Japanese, and Korean traditions. Apart from arranging year by year all world philosophers, including their works and their births and deaths, these tables add reference events under most years. The entries start with the birth of Thales in 624 BC and end in 1945. There is an index of names of non-Chinese philosophers with transcriptions into Chinese and another index by names in Chinese arranged by stroke count.[48]

Chronological tables of events for specific periods are listed in the appropriate section of Part V.

[47] *Zhongwai lishi nianbiao, gongyuan qian 5000 nian- gongyuan 1918 nian* (Chronological tables of Chinese and world history, 5000 BC to AD 1918), Qi Sihe 齊思和, Liu Qige 劉啓戈, Nie Chongqi 聶崇岐, and Jian Bozan 翦伯贊, comps., Zhonghua, 1958; 4th prnt., 1985.

[48] *Shijie zhexueshi nianbiao* (Chronological tables of the history of world philosophy), Ma Cai 馬采 and Chen Yun 陳雲 comps., Shehui kexue, 1992.

6

Telling the Time

Since how days were divided into smaller units of time during different periods of Chinese history attracted the attention of the leading Qing historians, it is strange that modern Chinese dictionaries and encyclopaedias, most of which contain chronological tables and appendixes on the weights and measures in use in each dynasty, pay little or no attention to the changing ways of counting the hours.

For these reasons the present chapter examines the matter in some detail. It is a task made possible by scholars who have not only collected and compared the references in historical and astronomical works with the new evidence unearthed by archaeology and exploration, but also reconstructed some of the main time keeping instruments, such as the various types of water clock.[1]

---

[1] On the pre-Qin period, see Song Zhenhao 宋鎮豪, "Xian-Qin shiqi shi ruhe jishi de? 先秦時期是如何記時的?" (How was time recorded in the pre-Qin period?), *Wenshi zhishi*, 6: 80–85 (1986). For imperial China from the Han to the Ming, see Wang Lixing 王立興, "Jishi zhidu kao 記時制度考" (An examination of the methods of recording the time), *Zhongguo tianwenxue wenji* 中國天文學文集 (Articles on Chinese astronomy), Kexue, vol. 4 (1988), 1–47. The author was joint editor in chief of the major collection of records of celestial phenomena in pre-modern China and bases his analysis on them (Zhuang Weifeng and Wang Lixing, 1988).

The chapter begins by examining the three main ways in which the passing hours were measured (6.1), then summarizes the way the day was divided in the Shang and Zhou (6.2), before turning in greater detail to the 100-unit system (6.3), which was used for the night watch (6.4) and the 12 "double-hour" system (6.5). There is also an explanation of the many ways of referring to the time during the empire (6.6) and a brief outline of the introduction of the Western hours-minutes-seconds system by the Qing (6.7).

6.1 Introduction

Three ways of dividing the day into smaller units were used in China before the introduction of the Western 24-hour system and mechanical clocks in the early seventeenth century:

1. Unequal divisions of the day (*shi* 時), mainly based on the position of the sun, but also set by daily routines such as mealtimes. The earliest evidence is on the Shang oracle bones. Time-telling would have been done by observing the position of the sun or of its shadow.

2. Ten watches; five during the daytime hours, five at night. The number of watches remained the same throughout the year; so they, too, were of unequal duration. The night watches were shorter, for example, in the summer than in the winter. The first evidence is from the Spring and Autumn period.

3. Twelve equal two-hour units based on the sun at noon. This was an absolute system, since the length of the hours was always the same. The hours were named after the 12 *chen* 辰 (mansions of the zodiac) and also after 12 of the ancient periods of the day (the *shi* of method 1). This system was in use by the end of the Warring States. It was officially promulgated during the Former Han, a time of improvements in

the instruments for measuring time and of major calendrical reform. The double "hours" were for many centuries called *chen* or *shi* and, from the Song, also *ke* 刻. Today the term is *shichen* 時辰.[2]

All three methods were in use together from at least the third century BC. After the Han, officials increasingly kept time by the *chen* during the day; officials as well as ordinary people in the towns and cities were kept aware of the time by the drum and gong beats of the watch patrols. But in the villages, as well as in the towns and cities, the position of the sun (or of its shadow) during the day and the stars and moon at night remained, as they had been at least since the Shang, the normal way of indicating the passage from one division of the day to the next.

The main instrument used for measuring time until the seventeenth century was the water clock (clepsydra), which counted 100 *ke* 刻 (eighths) every 24 hours (6.3). In addition, all sorts of other instruments were used for measuring the continuous passage of time (or for measuring lapsed time), such as incense sticks or coils, incense seals (*xiangyin* 香印), moondials (*yuegui* 月晷), sand clocks, and graduated candles (*kezhu* 刻烛). Sundials (*rigui* 日晷) were for the day. Typically, perpetual lamps (*changdeng* 長燈), lit with a wick floating in a sea of oil or butter, were used in temples and tombs.

---

[2] Joseph Needham, Wang Ling, and Derek Price, "Horary Systems," in *Heavenly Clockwork: The Great Astronomical Clocks of Medieval China–A Missing Link in Horological Research*, CUP, 1960; rev. ed., 1986, 199–205. The authors divide the Chinese horary systems into the double-hour system, the 100-unit system, and the five night watches. See also "Early East Asian Time Measurement"), chap. 1 of Silvio A. Bedini, *The Trail of Time: Time Measurement with Incense in East Asia*, CUP, 1994, 1–24. For the larger context, see David S. Landes, *Revolution in Time*, Belknap Press of HUP, 1985.

6.2 Divisions of the Day in the Shang and Zhou

日出而作日入而息 (When the sun comes out, work; when the sun goes down, rest), *Zhouli* 周禮

Box 5: Shang Time

1. *xi* 夕 (night)
2. *ming* 明 or *dan* 旦 (dawn)
3. *dacai* 大采 (great assembly) or *zhao* 朝 (early morning)
4. *dashi* 大食 (main meal)
5. *zhongri* 中日 or *rizhong* 日中 (midday)
6. *ze* 昃 [lit. the sun past the meridian] (early afternoon)
7. *xiaoshi* 小食 or *guoxi* 郭夕 (supper)
8. *hun* 昏 (dusk) or *xiaocai* 小采 (small assembly)
9. *mu* 暮 (night fall)

No doubt the earliest division of the day in China was into three unequal periods: morning, afternoon, and night, as measured by sunrise, noon, and sunset. By the late Shang, there is evidence on the oracle bones that the hours of light were divided into a number of unequal units (*shi* 時), but a trace of the basic threefold division remained, in that the night was still regarded as one unit (*xi* 夕). The daylight units were measured by the position of the sun and also based on the two mealtimes — *dashi* 大食 at about 0800–0900 and *xiaoshi* 小食 at about 1600–1700.

It was a seasonal system since the length of the time periods varied with the length of the day. Several of the periods seem to have fallen at the same or similar times to the daylight periods in common use in the Warring States and later fixed in the Former Han as beginning at 0700 and thereafter continuing at two-hour intervals until 1900 hours.[3]

---

[3] Historians dispute exactly how many time periods are shown on the oracle bones. The problem arises from the difficulty of distinguishing whether a time period is an established one in its own right or a variant

Footnote continued on next page

The Shang diviners based their calendar and divisions of the day on close observation of the sun and the moon and the stars. No Shang instrument for measuring time has as yet been deciphered on the oracle bones and none has ever been unearthed, so there is no means of knowing how accurately they fixed the beginning and ending of the daily divisions.

In the Zhou period, a similar way of dividing the day seems to have been used as in the late Shang except that the day began at midnight, not at dawn. This was continued into the Spring and Autumn and Warring States periods, whose texts contain many scattered references to the by then familiar divisions of the day. The first evidence for a standardized naming system dates from the end of the third century BC (6.5).

6.3 The 100-Unit System

The earliest mechanical method of measuring the passage of time was to divide the day and night into 100 equal units (*baike* 百刻). The instrument used was a simple water clock (clepsydra) consisting of a water jar with a small hole at the bottom. A measuring rod (*loujian* 漏箭) with a float at its base was slotted through the lid of the jar to indicate the time as it dropped with the water level. The first reference is in the *Zhouli*, which mentions (in the context of military logistics), a jar-filling official (*qiehu shi* 挈壺氏) charged with several functions, including

---

name for an existing one. The earlier oracle bones record fewer time periods than the later ones. This led Dong Zuobin 董作賓 to argue that there were two competing ways of dividing the day in the Shang; the earlier method used seven time periods; a later method used 15 (10 for the day and five for the night), the five for the night being an early form of the night watch; see Dong Zuobin, *Yin lipu* 殷曆譜 (Yin calendar tables), 2 vols., Nanqi, Sichuan: Shiyusuo, special publication, 1945; rpnt., 1992. Chen Mengjia 陳夢家 gives eight daylight periods in his *Yinxu buci zongshu* 殷墟卜辭綜述 (General explanation of the oracle script of the Wastes of Yin), Kexue, 1956, p. 235. Song Zhenhao (1986), p. 85, tabulates sixteen divisions of the day in the late Shang, a number he believes to have been the norm until the spread of twelve periods in the Warring States.

setting up a water clock to time maneuvers and short, fixed periods such as the length of the night watches or the wakes at funerals. The military orign of the instrument is also suggested by the use of the word for arrow for the measuring rod.[4]

The measure used for the 100-unit system was linear in origin. The Han clepsydras were about 23 centimeters in height, allowing the insertion of a float stick the same length as a standard Han foot rule, divided into 10 *cun* and subdivided into 100 *fen*. By the Han, one float stick was used for the daylight hours, another for nighttime. Altogether 100 units were carved (*ke* 刻) onto the two float sticks, hence the name *ke* 刻 (translated as "quarters" 2,000 years later when the Western hour with its four parts was introduced to China). From early days the practice developed of subdividing each *ke* at first into 100 *fen* 分 and later into 60 *fen*. Expressions like *cunyin* 寸陰 (an inch of shadow),[5] meaning a short period of time, were derived from the instrument used to set the clepsydras since at least the seventh century BC, the shadow gnomon whose rule was also measured in decimal units (*cun* 寸). The Han sundials (*rigui* 日晷) or gnomon chronometers (*ribiao* 日表) had 69 radial

[4] *Zhouli* 周禮, "Xiaguan sima 夏官司馬," 4. In the Qin and Han and in later dynasties, the official was called a *shuaigeng ling* [alt. *leigeng ling*] 率更令 (director of the watches). Outflow clepsydras were used in ancient Babylon and Egypt from the sixteenth century BC, and much later in Greece, and in Rome. The Greeks designed a clepsydra capable of running non-stop for 24 hours in the fourth century BC. Julius Caesar mentions his army's use of a clepsydra to measure the length of the British night (*De bello gallico*, v. 13).

[5] The expression first appears in the *Huainanzi*, "Nandaoxun" 南道訓: "The ancients did not value a foot of jade, but an inch of shadow, because time is difficult to get and easy to lose." The earliest known handheld device for measuring the length of the shadow of the sun (gnomon, *guibiao* 圭表) dates from the Later Han. It has a 15-inch measure divided into 150 subunits. See Che Yixiong 車一雄, Xu Zhentao 徐振韜, and You Zhenyao 尤振堯, "Yizheng Dong-Han mu chutu tong guibiao de chubu yanjiu" 儀征東漢墓出土銅圭表的初步研究 (Preliminary research on a bronze gnomon excavated from an Eastern Han tomb), in *Zhongguo gudai tianwen wenwu lunji* (1988), 156–61.

lines carved on two-thirds of their surface, making a total of 68 segments, each segment taking up one-hundredth of the dial. The 100 units measured by the clepsydra were identical to the time measured by one segment on the sundial, i.e., about 14.4 modern minutes.[6]

The first extant clepsydras are three from the Han dynasty that were recently unearthed (two more are known from illustrations).[7] The earliest of the three dates from some time before 113 BC. All except one are single-chamber, outflow clepsydra in which the float stick sank as the water dripped out. The exception is the "prime minister's office clepsydra," only illustrations of which have survived. It appears to have had two holes in the lid (one for water inflow and one for the float stick) and is therefore presumed to have been a two-chamber clepsydra capable of running continuously with constant refills to keep it going. At first it served as an inflow-type with the water dripping from a top chamber (which has not survived), then continued as an outflow-type after the spout was unblocked and the water was allowed to drip from it while the top chamber was filled again. In the Later Han and again in the Eastern Jin, more chambers were added to avoid the uneven water pressure of the old single- or double-chamber clepsydra and to enable the last chamber to serve as a more accurate inflow-type clepsydra (with the measuring rod rising as the water dripped in). The clepsydra was filled at dawn and at dusk. In winter, the water was heated in order to prevent it from freezing.

[6] See Yan Linshan 閻林山 and Quan Hejun 全和鈞, "Lun woguo de baike jishi zhi" 論我國的百刻計時制 (On China's 100-quarter system of keeping time), *Kejishi wenji* 6: 1–6 (1980). The earliest gnomon chronometers to have been unearthed are three dating from the Former Han, one of which is on display at the Historical Museum in Beijing, another at the Royal Ontario Museum, Toronto, Canada.

[7] Chen Meidong 陳美東, "Shilun Xi-Han louhu de ruogan wenti" 試論西漢漏壺的若干問題 (Preliminary discussion of the questions surrounding the Han clepsydras) in *Zhongguo gudai tianwen wenwu lunji* (1988), 137–44.

Officials at the Bureau of Astronomy in the capital from Han times to the early twentieth century were charged with the maintenance of the bureau's clepsydras, and the keeping and announcing of the hours (*shoushi* 授時, *baoshi* 報時). In most dynasties, after the sounding of the hour, its name was displayed on a tablet, either at the palace gates or at the drum tower or both.

Because there were always five watches during the night and five during the day, the length of the watch depended on the time of the year and on the place. Simple indicators were adopted as to the relative lengths of day and night according to the season.[8] In 130 BC, under Han Wudi, a more precise regulation was introduced, and the length of the float sticks had to be changed (*gaijian* 改箭) every 9 days (calculated on the basis that the length of the day varied by 20 *ke* over the 180 days between the winter and summer solstices). Then in AD 34, a second set of more precise rules were introduced requiring that a night float stick with an extra *ke* and a day stick with one less *ke* had to be used every 7.5 days. In 102, the 9-day rule was finally abolished, and a new regulation introduced to change the float sticks for every 2.4° declination of the sun. In 443, the regulation was made easier to apply by stipulating once again that the changes had to be made at each half-season (i.e., every 7.5 days), both for the day float stick and for the night one. The system therefore required 48 float sticks with different numbers of *ke* on each, but with the total on each night stick and its corresponding day stick always coming to 100. With minor modifications this method remained in use until the beginning of the Qing. One of the duties of the Bureau of Astronomy in drawing up the calendar was to calculate detailed tables of sunrise and sunset and the corresponding times of the night watches for each of the 24 climatic seasons (*jieqi* 節氣). These tables were published with the calendar.

---

[8] The pre-Qin formulation of summer (60:40), winter (40:60), spring and autumn (50:50) was gradually refined to eight adjustments (at the *ba-jie* nodal points).

In the history of Chinese time systems, just as in other spheres, it is worth asking the question to what extent were the regulations put into practice in different historical periods and in different places. During the Warring States, each kingdom no doubt kept its own time, just as it kept its own calendar. Strangely enough, time was one of the few measurements which the First Emperor of the Qin and his chancellor did not unify, but from the Han standardization onward, successive dynasties made every effort to apply the regulations and for three good reasons: astrological, security, and administrative. Accurate timekeeping was directly related to the precise recording and interpreting of celestial events. Second, the public announcement of the hours and an efficient watch system were basic to the security of the imperial palace and the area immediately surrounding it, as well as to the offices of the central administration, and of the capital itself. Dark, unlighted streets were considered so dangerous that throughout Chinese history, just as in medieval Europe, a night curfew was imposed (6.4). It was the same throughout the empire, where we know that in the provincial and county towns, efforts were made to keep the time and to enforce the curfew, as also by the army, whether on garrison duty at the border or on campaign. The third reason for accurate timekeeping was administrative: the wheels of the imperial bureaucracy required precise timing. How precise is revealed on the bamboo documents (*jiandu* 簡牘) discovered at the northwestern border and elsewhere.[9] These show that from the Han the exact time of the dispatch and arrival of documents even in remote outposts was meticulously recorded down to fractions of an hour (compare ancient Greece and Rome, where such accurate records were not kept except for astronomical observations). Office hours had also to be maintained. In some dynasties failure to arrive on time was punishable with a beating.

[9] Michael Loewe, *Records of Han Administration*, 2 vols., CUP, 1967, vol. 1 (44.5.2.2).

Nor was careful timekeeping limited to the civil and military administrations at the capital city and in the provincial and county towns. Simple clepsydras were used in the countryside: several poets wrote about the farm clepsydras (*tianlou* 田漏) in the eleventh century, including Wang Anshi, who also noted the use of drums and clepsydras in Sichuan to call villagers together and to set the rhythm for their collective work in the fields. Early in the fourteenth century, a county magistrate in north China compiled a farming manual that contains instructions on how to set up a field clepsydra "in order to time the work," i.e., to measure lapsed time, like an hourglass.[10]

But there were enormous practical difficulties. Even in the capital itself, as early as 762 the Tang official in charge of the security of the palace and the city memorialized that there was a gap of at least a *ke* between the announcement of the first night watch at the palace and the drum signaling its start in the suburbs.

Ever since the Warring States, the regulations stipulated different ways to adjust the watches to the different seasons. Given a recognized margin of error of at least 40 minutes in making these adjustments, given that local administrations, in many cases at different latitudes from the capital, had to set their own time; and given that the clepsydras, even after the Song improvements, cannot have been all that accurate, the empire must have been a huge patchwork quilt of local, idiorhythmic time zones even at the best of times.

Despite all the temporal and regional variations over 2,000 years, the general pattern for the announcement of time and the night watch patrols from the Han to the beginning of the Qing was maintained, in some cases right up to the 1930s.

[10] For Song and Yuan references to clepsydras, see *Dong-Lu Wangshi nongshu yizhu* 東魯王氏農書譯注 (Mr. Wang's of Eastern Lu [Wang Zhen 王禎] *Agricultural Treatise* translated [into modern Chinese] with notes), Miao Qiyu 繆啓愉, tr., Shanghai guji, 1994, *Nongqi tupu* 農器圖譜 14, 709–10.

During the day a drum was sounded five times: at dawn; at main mealtime (*xiagu* 下鼓, 13 *ke* after the lifting of the night curfew), at midday (*wugu* 午鼓 or *shigu* 市鼓), at the afternoon meal (*bugu* 晡鼓, 13 *ke* before the curfew drum), and at dusk. From at least the Tang, the official drum signaling the change of the hours was echoed in each ward or street corner. By the Song, the morning and afternoon meal drums had fallen into disuse except in the army. By the later empire, the 12-*chen* system had replaced the five day watches in most places, and only the dawn, noon, and dusk drums were sounded.

6.4 The Night Watch

Every dynasty enforced a strict curfew (*yan'geng* 嚴更, *yanye* 嚴夜, or *jinye* 禁夜), especially in the capital. The potential danger came not only from bandits, thieves, and other disturbers of law and order, but also from the constant risk of accidental fires. The curfew began at nightfall (about 45 minutes after the first night watch was sounded at dusk) and was announced by the dusk barriers drum (*muguan gu* 暮關鼓, *mugu* 暮鼓).[11] Thereafter, the city gates and the ward and street barriers were closed, and nobody was allowed to move about the town except the civil or military watch patrols. Exceptions were made in the summer months, when people were allowed to try and escape the heat indoors by sitting or sleeping outside, but only in their own street or ward. Exceptions for the pregnant or sick could be made throughout the year. There were strict prohibitions against climbing the city walls at night. During the curfew, no lighted fires were allowed (the night watch also performed the function of a fire patrol, part of its duties being to report those who kept a fire burning at night). Anyone found outside without an official lantern was challenged, "who goes there?" (*shei shei* 誰誰?). The curfew was lifted just before dawn

---

[11] In the Tang, 800 drumbeats were stipulated. In later dynasties, the number varied. By the Qing, showing the influence of Buddhism, it was 108.

by the sounding of the dawn barriers drum (*xiaoguan gu* 曉關鼓).[12]

The responsibility for the night watch patrols in the capital was in the hands of the official, usually military, in charge of security. In the county towns and villages it was the local magistrate. Implementation was carried out by the various local self-governing units set up in different periods. In certain dynasties, for example, in the Southern Song, much of the system appears to have broken down. But it was reinstated on the foundation of the Yuan, and it was implemented during the Ming and the Qing.

The night was divided into five watches (*wuye* 五夜, *wugeng* 五更, or *wugu* 五鼓). From the Han, each watch was subdivided into five smaller units called *dian* 點 (or *chou* 籌 or *chang* 唱).[13]

In the capital and larger cities, the watch was sounded at the drum or bell tower (*gulou* 鼓樓, *zhonglou* 鐘樓) and in the wards in smaller cities, outside the yamen, or at the post station, or watch tower (*genglou* 更樓); in even smaller places, simply by the night watchmen on their rounds.[14] The time of

---

[12] During the Tang, it was 3,000 drumbeats (to wake people up). The practice of blowing a trumpet or horn was also widespread. In the Southern Song capital at Hangzhou, it was the monks who woke people with clappers and announced the weather. From the Ming onward, a dawn cannon (*mingpao* 明炮) was fired at Nanjing, a practice that continued up to the 1930s.

[13] At first, the watches were counted using the *gan* characters (*jiaye* 甲夜, *yiye* 乙夜, *bingye* 丙夜 ...), but later numbers became more widespread (*chugeng* 初更, *ergeng* 二更, *sangeng* 三更 ...). For imaginative ways of keeping the watch operative in a county town and its surrounding villages in the 1670s, see Huang Liuhong 黃六鴻, *Fuhui quanshu* 福惠全書, Djang Chu (Zhang Chu 章楚), tr. and ed., *A Complete Book Concerning Happiness and Benevolence While in Office: A Manual for Local Magistrates in Seventeenth-Century China*, UAP, 1984, 486–94.

[14] Referred to in the *Zhouli* and in the earlier dynasties as *siwu shi* 司寤氏 and by the later empire more commonly as *gengfu* 更夫, *gengren* 更人, or *jiren* 鷄人. At the end of the eighteenth century, the draftsman attached to the Macartney embassy, William Alexander, sketched a watch-

Footnote continued on next page

the start of the first watch varied from about 1700 in winter to about 2000 (modern times) in the summer depending on the time of sunset.

The regulations laid down the number of drumbeats or bell tolls for each watch; local practice gave rise to different rhythms. By the end of the Qing, in Beijing, 108 drumbeats were sounded from the massive drum tower to the north of the palace at each of the five watches until the fifth watch (*wugeng* or *lianggeng* 亮更). The drumbeats were the signal for the 60-ton bell at the nearby bell tower to be tolled. This continued until 1924. Beijingers can still remember the characteristic pattern of "18 fast beats; 18 slow beats; 18 neither fast nor slow," which were repeated to make 108 beats in all. [15]

In large cities the clepsydra (*genglou* 更漏) was normally kept on the drum tower (*gulou* 鼓樓). In well-to-do private households as on the watch towers, the time was also measured with incense sticks (*gengxiang* 更香), one for each watch.

The watchmen sounded the changing of each watch (*gaigeng* 改更) with a drumbeat (*genggu* 更鼓) and the fifths of each watch with a clapper made of bamboo or wood (*tuo* 橐), or with a bell (*zhong* 鐘 or *zheng* 鉦), or gong (*luo* 鑼), or with a chanted phrase (*chang* 唱). Thereafter they remained in touch throughout the night by beating their bamboo clappers, striking their gongs, or calling out to one another.

---

man with his bamboo rattle, probably in Canton, and recorded that "the barricades at the end of each street are kept shut [at night]," *Views of 18th Century China*, Studio Editions, 1988, plate iv.

[15] The drum tower in Beijing still stands and is open to the public. It is a huge structure, 50 meters high. It was first built in 1272 and named the *qizheng lou* 齊整樓, "mustering for duty tower," because the morning drum was the signal for all government employees to assemble for the start of the workday. It housed 24 drums (2 meters high), one for each of the 24 seasons. Today only one remains, its skin slashed to shreds by the Allied forces at the time of the Boxers. The bronze clepsydra (dating from the Song), fell out of use early in the Qing when official time switched to the western twenty-four hour system.

When Du Fu 杜甫 (712–770) wrote the lines which every schoolchild has had to learn since then he was evoking ideal conditions, 好雨知時節, 當春乃發生; 隨風潛入夜, 潤物細無聲.[16] Neither the poet nor anybody else could have spent a quiet night in a Chinese city, in Chengdu in the eighth century (where these lines were written) or at any other time or place, either in town, on the outskirts or in the countryside. Quite apart from all the noises of a pre-industrial age, people were more likely to have been woken by the cacophony of drums, gongs, bells, trumpets, rattles, and the night watchmen's chant. These may have made Chinese cities and villages more secure, but this practice also made them very noisy places, a fact remarked upon by most visitors to China (from Ennin and Sulaiman in the ninth century to Marco Polo in the thirteenth, Magalhaes in the seventeenth, and Macartney in the eighteenth). The conventional image is of the poet lying awake in the depths of the night (*gengshen* 更深) as the moon slowly glides past his window. It is a lonely and silent scene, save for occasional evocative sounds such as the snatch of a song, the notes of a lute, the sighing of a cassia in the breeze, the whisper of the spring rain, or the distant tolling of the midnight bell. The poet's object in using these topoi was to trigger in his reader a refined and literary mood. It was not his intention to describe a particular, and therefore noisy, reality.

6.5 *The 12 Double-Hour System*

From the Warring States, if not before, the 12 *dizhi* were correlated not only with the 12 stations of Jupiter but also with the 12 directions. The positions of the sun were correlated with the cardinal points (*sifang* 四方), and so sunrise, noon, sunset, and midnight were associated with the *dizhi* characters for E, S, W,

---

[16] "A good rain knows its season, it brings things to life right in spring. It enters the night, unseen with the breeze; it moistens things gently and without sound," *An Anthology of Chinese Literature, Beginnings to 1911*, edited and tr. by Stephen Owen, Norton, 1996, p. 427.

and N, respectively, i.e., *mao* 卯, *wu* 午, *you* 酉 and *zi* 子 (Table 9). To this day the directions in Chinese follow the sun in this way (*dong* 東, *nan* 南, *xi* 西, *bei* 北). As a result, we refer, for example, to the *Nan-Bei Chao* 南北朝, not as we do in English to the "Northern and Southern Dynasties."

The first extant enumeration of the 12 periods of the day correlated with the 12 *chen* (named using the *dizhi*) is found in two popular almanacs dating from about 217 BC. Almanac 2 lists the *chen*, and almanac 1 has the first known list of the 12 animal signs linked to the 12 *chen* in almost the form still in use today. The almanacs were used for choosing lucky and avoiding unlucky days and hours. They were written on bamboo strips and discovered in 1975 at Yunmeng 雲夢 in the former kingdom of Chu in the central Yangzi region. Almanac 2 divides the day into 16, not 12, divisions. This may reflect a local Chu tradition or it may be further evidence that two systems of dividing the day coexisted from the Qin into the Han.[17] In any event, it is likely that for several centuries two or more variants of naming the periods of the day co-existed in different parts of China (just as different calendars were used in the different kingdoms of the Warring States). The various existing terms for the divisions of day and night were standardized in the *chen* system officially introduced as part of the Taichu 太初 calendar reform in 104 BC.

Alternative descriptive terms for the divisions of the day, many of them variants, had been widespread since the Shang, and many more developed over the centuries. A few are still in use today, although often with slightly different meanings, e.g.,

[17] Yu Haoliang 于豪亮, "Qinjian 'Rishu' jishi jiyue zhu wenti" 秦簡日書記時記月諸問題 (Questions relating to the recording of time and of months in the Qin almanacs on bamboo strips) in *Yunmeng Qin Hanjian yanjiu* 雲夢秦漢簡研究 (Researches on the Qin bamboo strips found at Yunmeng), Zhonghua, 1981, 351-57; Li Jiemin 李解民, "Qin-Han shiqi de yiri shiliu shi zhi 秦漢時期的一日十六時制" (The sixteen-hours per day system in the Qin and Han) in *Jianbo yanjiu* 簡帛研究, vol. 2, Falü, 1996, 80-88.

zaochen 早晨, zhongwu 中午, bangwan 傍晚. Many alternative terms, some of them ancient, have been retained in the dialects.

The day was reckoned from midnight (*yebanzi* 夜半子) to midnight, that is halfway through the first double-hour, which began at 2300.

On the whole, the Han reformed system seems to have become the normative system by the beginning of the first century AD among officials. By the Tang dynasty, the 16 *chen* had disappeared, and the 12 *chen* were being taught in rhyming couplets to far-off peoples at the edge of the empire, as evidenced by several of the popular songs found in the Dunhuang temple library.

Table 9: Chinese Hours in Imperial Times (12 chen 辰)

Chen 辰	Compass (solstices; months)	Descriptive terms	Animal signs for hours	Modern time
zi 子	NORTH (Winter solstice; 11th month)	*yeban* 夜半 (*wuye* 午夜 or (*yewu* 夜午) (*ziye* 子夜) (*yefen* 夜分) (*zhongye* 中夜 or (*yezhong* 夜中)	*shu* 鼠 rat	2300–0100
chou 丑	NNE	*jiming* 鷄鳴 (*huangji* 荒鷄)	*niu* 牛 ox	0100–0300
yin 寅	ENE	*pingdan* 平旦 (*pingming* 平明) (*danming* 旦明) (*liming* 黎明) (*zaodan* 早旦) (*ridan* 日旦) (*zaochen* 早晨) (*zaozhao* 早朝) (*meishuang* 昧爽)	*hu* 虎 tiger	0300–0500
mao 卯	EAST (Spring equinox; 2nd month)	*richu* 日出 (*dianmao* 點卯) (*rishang* 日上) (*risheng* 日生) (*rishi* 日始) (*rixi* 日唏) (*xuri* 旭日)	*tu* 兔 rabbit	0500–0700

Table Continues

Chen 辰	Compass (solstices; months)	Descriptive terms	Animal signs for hours	Modern time
chen 辰	ESE	*shishi* 食時 (*zaoshi* 早食) (*yanshi* 宴食)	*long* 龍 dragon	0700–0900
si 巳	SSE	*gezhong* 隔中 (*yuzhong* 禺中) (*riyu* 日禺) (*riyuzhong* 日禺中)	*she* 蛇 snake	0900–1100
wu 午	SOUTH (Summer solstice; 5th month)	*rizhong* 日中 (*rizheng* 日正) (*riwu* 日午) (*rigao* 日高) (*zhongwu* 中午) (*tingwu* 亭午) (*zhuowu* 卓午)	*ma* 馬 horse	1100–1300
wei 未	SSW	*ridie* 日昳 (*rice* 日側) (*rize* 日昃) (*rize* 日仄) (*ridie* 日昳)	*yang* 羊 sheep	1300–1500
shen 申	WSW	*bushi* 晡時 (*pushi* 鋪食) (*rixi* 日夕) (*xishi* 夕食)	*hou* 猴 monkey	1500–1700
you 酉	WEST (Autumn equinox; 8th month)	*riru* 日入 (*rimo* 日没) (*richen* 日沉) (*rixi* 日西) (*riluo* 日落) (*riwan* 日晚) (*bangwan* 傍晚)	*ji* 鷄 chicken	1700–1900
xu 戌	WNW	*huanghun* 黃昏 (*rimu* 日暮) (*rixun* 日曛) (*xunhuang* 曛黃)	*quan* 犬 dog	1900–2100
hai 亥	NNW	*rending* 人定 (*yinye* 夤夜)	*zhu* 猪 pig	2100–2300

From the Han, the division of the *chen* into two made a total of 24 small hours. The first was named *chu* 初; the second, *zheng* 正; and the end, *mo* 末. Thus *shenchu* 申出 (or *bushichu*

晡時初) meant 1500; *shenzheng* 申正 (or *bushizheng* 晡時正), 1600; and *shenmo* 申末 (or *bushimo* 晡時末), 1600–1700.

Another simplification was to use the 24 points of the compass to name each of the 24 hours (Table 10). This method was used for recording the times of celestial phenomena during the Wei, Jin, and *Nan-Bei Chao*. By the Tang it had been forgotten and was only used by geomancers for selecting the time and the place for burials. By the Ming, the system had come back into use for recording the time, but the 24-hour cycle usually began not at *zichu*, but at *zizheng* (2400). Thereafter it was a simple matter to adapt this system to the 24-hour Western clock.

Table 10: The Compass Names for the 24 Hours

renshi 壬時	2300	*bingshi* 丙時	1100
zishi 子時	2400	*wushi* 午時	1200
guishi 癸時	0100	*dingshi* 丁時	1300
choushi 丑時	0200	*weishi* 未時	1400
genshi 艮時	0300	*kunshi* 坤時	1500
yinshi 寅時	0400	*shenshi* 申時	1600
jiashi 甲時	0500	*gengshi* 庚時	1700
maoshi 卯時	0600	*youshi* 酉時	1800
yishi 乙時	0700	*xinshi* 辛時	1900
chenshi 辰時	0800	*xushi* 戌時	2000
xunshi 巽時	0900	*qianshi* 乾時	2100
sishi 巳時	1000	*haishi* 亥時	2200

From the third century, it became common to divide the *chen* into "quarters" by adding *shao* 少 [*xiao* 小], *ban* 半 and *tai* 太 [*da* 大] after the hour, e.g., *shenshichu ban* for 1630 and *shenshichu tai* for 1645.

One complication with the different systems of telling the time was that the 12 *chen* could not be divided into an equal number of *ke* (there being 100 *ke*, each *chen* lasted 9.3 *ke*). The *chen* themselves before the Tang were divided into 10 *fen* of 12 minutes each (one *ke* lasted 14.4 minutes). Clearly the 100-*ke* and the 12-*chen* were two systems of completely different origin. Not surprisingly, they coincided only four times in 24 hours (at midnight, 0600, midday and 1800). Efforts to resolve these problems by changing the number of *ke* to 120 (so every *chen* had exactly 10 *ke*), 96 (one *chen* equals eight *ke*) or 108 (one *chen* equals nine *ke*) failed on at least four separate occasions between 5 BC and AD 544. The grounds for refusal were not always the same, but the main argument was the conservative one: the 100-*ke* system had been used since time immemorial and therefore should not be tampered with. In the meantime, as in many other traditional societies, the different timekeeping systems ran in parallel and instead of reform, various compromises were found to make them work more easily together, each dynasty announcing a new system at the promulgation of its calendar.

From the Sui, it became common to place the odd one-third *ke* in every regular *chen* at the end of each *chen*. It was called a *xiaoke* 小刻. Another practice, again starting in the Sui, was to divide the *ke* into 60 *fen*, so that each *chen* had eight *ke* 20 *fen*. From the Han, and increasingly from the Tang, the *chen* were divided into two small hours (*xiaoshi* 小時), each of which had four regular *ke* of 14.4 minutes and 1 small *ke* of 2.4 minutes (popularly inserted at the beginning of the full hour, but officially placed at the end). In the Song, a clock was constructed that measured 96 intervals.[18] The practice also developed of showing both the 12 *chen* and the 100 *ke* on the clepsydra float stick. Thereafter the double-hour began to be called not only *shi*, but also *ke*. Eventually, 96 quarters (of 15 minutes each) replaced the 100 *ke* (of 14.4 minutes each) when the Western system was introduced by the Qing (6.5).

The history of time-keeping in China, as in other spheres, is a history of the official announcement and often official implementation of a new system while ordinary people continued to use previous ones to which they were accustomed. So in the Qing all official time records used the Western system but or-

[18] Needham, Wang, and Price (1986), 206–15, corrects accounts of Su Song's clock in *SCC*, vol. IV, Part 2, *Mechanical Engineering*, CUP, 1965, 461. For reasons unexplained, Needham is a proponent of the Babylonian origin of the 12 *shichen* system.

dinary people (and the writers of novels) continued to use the 100-*ke* and 12-*chen* as they had developed in the Ming.

The difference between the 100-*ke* and the 12-*chen* systems has led some scholars to suppose that the 100-*ke*, which was the older of the two, was indigenous, while the 12-*chen* were imported from Babylon. If this were indeed the case, it might help explain the refusal to adapt the Chinese system to the imported one. But there is no evidence one way or the other. Most cultures have used vestiges of several different counting systems as a matter of custom, and some continue to do so to this day, however inconvenient this may be.[19] A more likely explanation is that the 100-*ke* system was originally used for measuring the lapse of a fixed length of time, like the five watches of the day or night or a military patrol. It was not originally intended to measure continuous stretches of time since it was not until the Han that an instrument capable of doing so became available.

The main difficulty in understanding references to the time in Chinese sources is that there was no standard way of referring to it; dozens of terms were used, based on the three main systems of telling the time. Another difficulty is that it is not always clear whether the time phrase refers to a point in time or to a period of time. There were also special terms for special uses, such as recording the exact time of an eclipse or the hour of birth. Table 10 lists the names of the 24 hours, and section 6.6, different ways of referring to the time.

6.6 Telling the Time (Han to Qing)

There were no strict rules on how to tell the time, but to take the ninth double-hour, *shen* (15.00–17.00) as an example, it could be called:

[19] For example, in most parts of the world, units of time and angle measure inherited from a sexagesimal system coexist uneasily with a decimal system (and in America, they coexist with a third base unit system, the duodecimal, for linear measure). The French too, to take an-
Footnote continued on next page

bushishen 晡時中

shenshi 申時 (from the Ming, this could also mean 1600)

shenke 申刻 (the expression becomes common from the eleventh century when the clepsydra float stick also had *chen* carved on; from the Ming, this could also mean 1600)

shen paishi 申牌時 (1500–1700 hours; lit. the "shen [hour] as displayed on the hour tablets" [at the drum tower or on street corners]. This was a common way of referring to the hour in novels)

bushi 晡時

houshi 猴時 (the hour of the monkey)

and subdivided for greater accuracy, e.g.:

shenshichu 申時初 (*shenchu* 申初): 1500

shenshizheng 申時正 (*shenzheng* 申正): 1600

shenshimo 申時末 (*shenmo* 申末): 1600–1700

with further subdivisions up to the Tang, e.g.:

shen liuke 申六刻: 1626, approximately

shenshichu erke 申時初二刻: 1528 (and 48 seconds)

shenshichu liangge xiaofen 申時初兩個小分: 1520 (a *xiaofen* was 10 minutes)

and further subdivisions after the Tang, e.g.:

shenshichusanke 申時初三刻 (*shenchusanke* 申初三刻): 1543

shenshizhengsanke 申時正三刻 (*shenzhengsanke* 申正三刻): 1645

Gengdian 更點 (*Watch Hours*)

The night hours in the earlier dynasties up to the Tang were usually referred to by the watch (*wugeng*) count (as were daylight hours):

yelou shangshui shike 夜漏上水十刻: 2 hours 24.4 minutes after the filling of the night clepsydra (or *yelou shang shike* 夜漏上十刻); later could be simplified to *sangeng* 三更

yelou weijin sanke 夜漏未盡三刻: 45.2 minutes before the end of the nightwatch

Note the expressions *yeshaoban* 夜少半 (before midnight) and *yedaban* 夜大半 (after midnight).

---

other example, continue to use vestiges of a Celtic vegesimal system (87 is *quatre-vingt sept*, i.e., $4 \times 20 + 7$) alongside the decimal.

In order to convert nightwatch times to absolute times, you
need to know the season of the year and where the reading was
made. Instead of going through the monographs on the calendar in the Standard Histories (not all of which preserve full
nightwatch tables), a good shortcut is to use the charts for converting watch hours to absolute hours in Wang Lixing (1988).

After the Tang, it became common to refer to the night
hours using the *chen* system.

Other Ways of Measuring Time

At home or in the courtyard, no doubt the earliest method of
measuring the time in China was by observing the length and
direction of the shadow of the sun or the position of the sunbeams. There are references to the use in the Zhou of a stone
stele placed in front of a wall. The sun shone through a special
hole cut at the top of the stele marking the hours on the wall
behind. The Mongolians also used the sunbeams (see *Neighboring Countries* below, much as did the early American settlers
with their noon mark). Another practice was to look at the
eyes of a cat. According to a mid-nineteenth century writer on
cats quoting a Tang source, at dawn and dusk, a cat's pupils are
round like a mirror; at midmorning and midafternoon, they
are elliptical like the stone of a date, and at midnight and noon,
they are a slit.[20]

Outside the house, in the fields or on the road, as in other
peasant societies all over the world, to the question What time
is it? the answer would most likely have been "Look at the
sun." To the question How long does it take to the next village? the answer would have been, "The time it takes to eat a
bowl of rice (or [hot, cold] meal);" "The time taken to burn a
stick of incense;" "The time taken to smoke a pipe," or some

---

[20] I am grateful to Charles Aylmer for the reference to Huang Han
黄漢, *Maoyuan* 猫苑 (The garden of cats), 1853, *juan* 1: 8b. Han quotes
the ninth-century *Youyang zazu* 酉陽雜俎 (46.2) as saying that at dawn
and dusk a cat's eyes are round and at noon they are like a vertical line.
The Abbé Huc also recounts such a method of telling the time in his *The
Empire of China*, 303–304 (42.2, *Nineteenth Century*).

such phrase. At this level, China was until the twentieth century a task-discipline rather than a time-discipline society.

Horoscope Hours

Horoscopes required the *shengchen bazi* 生辰八字 (the Eight Characters), that is, the *ganzhi* for the year, month, day, and hour of birth, so a *gan* character was added to the *zhi* name of the hour according to the *ganzhi* for the day of birth (there were mnemonics to assist in this task). Population records sometimes give the hour of birth, in which case the *chen* hour was used.

Neighboring Countries

The Chinese systems of telling the time continue to leave their mark in East Asia, most of whose countries, including Korea, Japan, and Vietnam, adopted the 12 Chinese double-hours and still today use some of their names to describe different parts of the day and night.[21]

In Mongolia, the Chinese double-hours were introduced after the Yuan, although most Mongols continued to judge the time from the position of the sunbeams shining through the *toono* (the hole at the apex of the *ger* [*yurta*]). For example, at midday the sun shone on the uppermost part of the wall of the *ger* opposite the door (which was always aligned with the south). It was under this position that the head of the family sat, as he still sits today, at mealtimes and when receiving guests (the first reference to this practice is in the *Hanshu*). They also use observations of the behavior of the marmot as an indicator of the time.

[21] Bedini (1994), chap. 1, contains a good general account of the Chinese horary system and also of its later adaptation elsewhere in East Asia, mainly in Japan and Korea. For a book-length comparison of the variations on telling the time in Japan, China, and Korea, see Saitô Kuniji 齋藤國治, *Kodai no jikoku seidô* 古代の時刻制度, Yûzankaku, 1995.

In Thailand, the words for telling the time in use today reflect a system of Chinese origin, e.g., *thum* (drum sound) for the night hours and *mong* (gong sound) for the daylight hours.

6.7 Qing Reforms

It was Matteo Ricci [利瑪竇] (1552–1610), who introduced the first self-chiming clock (*ziming zhong* 自鳴鐘) to China in 1585. It was considered a great novelty. When he finally managed to reach Peking, in 1601, he presented two to the Wanli emperor.[22] On his death, Ricci became in some parts of China the tutelary deity of clocks and was known popularly as Limadou pusa 利瑪竇菩薩 (the Bodhisattva Ricci).

The government abandoned the 100-*ke* system and switched to Western 24-hour time in 1670. Thenceforward each hour officially had four quarters and 60 minutes (*fen* 分) and each minute, 60 seconds (*miao* 秒). But ordinary people continued to rely on the sun or to use the 100-*ke* system, and some Qing scholars continued to argue in favor of retaining the old system.[23]

The Kangxi emperor was an enthusiastic user of the new timepieces. He had a horological manufactory and repair works set up in the palace. It was closed down in 1796 by the Jiaqing emperor, who also banned the import of Western clocks and watches. By this time mechanical clocks (*chenzhong* 辰鐘) were being made in the main Chinese commercial centers. The old practice of naming 24 "small hours" (*xiaoshi* 小時) came into greater use (the word itself has been retained to this day for

[22] One of the criteria for selecting Jesuits for the Far Eastern mission was their horological skill. From the eighteenth century, European embassies took their cue from the Jesuits and brought clocks as presents for the emperors. The Palace Museum in Beijing has a collection of 1,000 magnificently elaborate timepieces presented to the court from the seventeenth century. Two hundred are on display.

[23] See Catherine Jami, "Western Devices for Measuring Time and Space," in *Time and Space in Chinese Culture*, Chun-chieh Huang and Erik Zürcher, eds., Brill, 1995, 169–200.

"hour"), but Western clocks remained a novelty for the rich, a gift or a toy rather than an essential instrument, because there was no felt need for the accurate measurement of time to the last minute or fraction of a minute at least in daily life.[24] It was not until cheap Western clocks and watches became available in the late nineteenth and early twentieth century that old habits began to change and the *chen* double-hours and the 100 *ke* were finally abandoned.

[24] "Why Are the Memorials Late?" Landes (1983), 37–52. The phrase is from the last line of a poem written by the Kangxi emperor in praise of Western clocks.

7

Statistics

No other country has such a wealth of extant historical statistics covering two millennia. Most important of all are the population statistics (7.2). Other statistical records were also gathered on a regular basis, for example, of astronomical phenomena (5.1.1), or from the Tang, rainfall and crop prices. Records of examination pass results were also kept and have been used for detailed studies of social mobility in the later empire.

Statistics of all sorts from the earliest periods mainly survive in summarized form in provincial or national totals. More detailed statistical records from lower levels of the reporting chain survive in much larger quantities from the later empire, especially from the Qing. Land and price statistics in contracts and other private records have survived in smaller numbers, also usually from the last centuries of the empire.

In interpreting Chinese historical statistics, the first essential is to understand what the numbers mean and do not mean in the sources (7.1). In order to appraise their reliability it is necessary to find out why they were reported. Population records are taken as an example (7.2). Temporal and regional variations in units and measures also have to be taken into account (7.3). Finally, sources on money and prices are introduced (7.4).

7.1   Numbers and Orders of Magnitude

Base 10 was the main way of counting in China. A sexagenary cycle was also used for recording dates and time (5.2.2). Both systems have existed since the first extant records (late Shang).

There were separate characters in the oracle-bone script for 13 numerals (1–10 and 100, 1,000 and 10,000). They are recognizably the same as those in use today. In addition, 21 oracle-bone compound characters (*hewen* 合文) have been deciphered for third power and above numerals. Only two of these have survived in Modern Chinese (MC), namely *nian* 廿 and *sa* 卅 (for 20 and 30; see section 14.1).[1]

The largest number in the oracle-bone script is 30,000 (*sanwan* 三萬). Very large numbers begin to appear in Zhou texts—*yi* 億, *zhao* 兆, *jing* 經 (京), for example, and many others for even larger ones—but there is some uncertainty as to what they mean, especially in Han and pre-Qin texts, since they could go up by tens, by 10,000s or by each unit multiplied by itself (Table 11). Sometimes this is indicated (as with *juwan* 巨萬 or *dawan* 大萬 meaning 10^8, as distinct from 10^4). Moreover, as with the mega numbers in Daoist and Buddhist scriptures, really big numbers are often not intended to be taken literally (7.1.2).

[1] For references on the history of Chinese mathematics, see 37.2. For an account of numbers in the Shang oracle bones, see Takashima Kenichi 高嶋謙一, "Noun plus Numeral plus Classifier or Measure-word," in Matsumaru Michio 松丸道雄 and Takashima Kenichi. *Studies in Early Chinese Civilization, Religion, Society, Language and Palaeography*, Hirakata, Osâka: Kansai Gaidai University, 2 vols., 1996, vol. 1, 204–22; Redouane Djamouri, "L'emploi des signes numériques dans les inscriptions Shang," *Sous les Nombres le Monde: Matériaux pour l'histoire culturelle du nombre en Chine ancienne, Extrême-Orient, Extrême-Occident* 16: 13–42 (1993); Zhao Cheng 趙誠, "Shuci he liangci 數詞和量詞" (Numbers and measure words) in *Jiaguwen jianming cidian–buci fenlei duben* 甲骨文簡明詞典–卜辭分類讀本 (Concise dictionary of oracle-bone characters with topically arranged readings), Zhonghua, 1988; 3rd prnt., 1996, 253–9.

Table 11: Big Numbers

Number	Pre-Qin	Post-Qin	Modern
100,000 (10^5) 十萬	*yi* 億		
1,000,000 (10^6) 百萬	*zhao* 兆	*baiwan* 百萬	*baiwan* 百萬
10,000,000 (10^7) 千萬	*jing* 經 (京)	*jing* 經 (京)	
100,000,000 (10^8) 萬萬	*yi* 億	*yi* 億	*yi* 億
1,000,000,000 (10^9) 十億	*zhao* 兆	*zhao* 兆	*zhao* 兆 (billion)

7.1.1   Numbers in Literary Chinese

Cardinal Numbers (jishuci 基數詞)

Numbers were used without counters in Literary Chinese. They can appear either before or after the noun: e.g., *Li you zui san* 李有罪三, which in MC would be *Li you santiao zuizhuang* 李有三條罪狀 (note that this could mean either that Li had three offenses or a few offenses, see below). If the number is linked to a verb, it often goes before the verb, whereas in MC it comes after. Number one is frequently left out: *lu shang you hu* 爐上有壺 (MC: *lu shang you yiba hu* 爐上有一把壺).

You 有 [or 又] is often used between digits, especially in pre-Qin texts, for example, *wushi you liu* 五十有六 is 56 and *bai you liu* 百有六 is 106. The zero (*ling* 零 or 0) was introduced to China in the Southern Song (the character *ling* had previously been used for the word meaning "a light fall of rain"). Sometimes characters with fewer strokes such as *dan* 單 or *ling* 另 were used in its place.

All the numbers have many derived meanings and connotations. *Yi* 一 (one), for example, can be used to mean the same as in *yiyang* 一樣, the whole as in *yi beizi* 一輩子, and independent as in *yiyi guxing* 一意孤行 (to insist on doing things one's own way); *shi* 十 can mean completely as in *shifen* 十分 (fully) or *shizu* 十足 (downright).

There were many alternative ways of writing numbers, perhaps the most important were the counting-rod numerals (one is one vertical rod; four is four rods, a method identical to the Babylonian, Egyptian and Roman counting systems). Counting-rod numbers are the only parts of the Chinese script

script written horizontally from left to right (see 18.1). Commercial numerals were similar to these and gradually evolved into the following set: 丨 丨丨 丨丨丨 Ⅹ 丩 丄 丄 亖 夂 十 . They are still in use today for keeping quick tallies.

The set of alteration-proof forms of 13 numbers (*changshu* 長數) for accounting or commercial transactions in use today date from the Tang (壹, 貳, 叄, 肆, 伍, 陸, 柒 [or 漆], 捌, 玖, 拾 [plus *bai* 佰, *qian* 仟, *qianbai* 仟佰 and *baiwan* 佰萬 for 100, 1,000, 100,000 and 1 million]). Half were borrowed for their sound (4, 6, 7, 8, 9, 10, 100), the remainder had been in use since the pre-Qin. There were commonly used in government documents.

Many trades used their own ways of writing alteration-proof numbers, for example, silversmiths counted from 1 to 10 using 錢, 衣, 寸, 許, 丁, 木, 才, 奇, 長, 田. The same trade in different provinces often used different characters corresponding to the local dialect.

The use of *yao* 幺 as an alternative for 1 in a series of numbers has been growing for many centuries but it only crept into the script (in telegraphic communications) at the end of the Qing. It is now normal in spoken Chinese.

Ordinal Numbers (xushuci 序數詞)

Cardinal numbers in Classical Chinese were also used as ordinal numbers. In Literary Chinese, words such as *di* 第 or *qi* 其 were placed before cardinal numbers to indicate the order of things in a series. The *ganzhi* 干支 were also used as well as many different series, for example, *bo* 伯, *zhong* 仲, *shu* 叔, and *ji* 季 for first, second, third, and fourth. From the Han, *zhang* 長, *yuan* 元, *ci* 次, *shao* 少, *you* 幼 and *zhi* 稚 indicated ranking from one to six and, along with many other sets, are still in use today.[2]

---

[2] For example, the five elements, the seasons or flowers and trees: wood, fire, earth, metal, water (*mu* 木, *huo* 火, *tu* 土, *jin* 金, *shui* 水); spring, summer, autumn, winter (*chun* 春, *xia* 夏, *qiu* 秋, *dong* 冬); plum, lotus, bamboo, chrysanthemum (*mei* 梅, *lan* 蘭, *zhu* 竹, *ju* 菊).

Fractions (fenshu 分數)

Ban 半, *daban* 大半 [*taiban* 太半], and *xiaoban* 小半 [*shaoban* 少半] (half, and more and less than half, respectively in MC) mean half, two-thirds and one-third in Literary Chinese. Sometimes *ban* was left out and *da* 大 [*tai* 太] and *xiao* 小 [*shao* 少] were used alone.

Percentages are expressed without indication following the numbers 10, 100, 1,000, or 10,000, e.g., *shi liu qi* 什 [十] 六七 means about 60 or 70 percent, not 16 or 17. Note that the earliest meaning of *wanyi* 萬一 was one ten-thousandth.

San fen er 三分二 in MC is *san fen zhi er* 三分之二 (two-thirds). A number before *fen* 分 indicates percentage; for example, *liufen* 六分 is 60 percent. The standard mathematical terms for subunits (i.e., *qiang* 强, *ruo* 弱, *ban* 半) are placed after the numeral, e.g., *wufen ruo* 五分弱 (less than 50 percent).

Yi 一 and *ban* 半 are often used together to indicate a few, or small amount, as in *yishi banke* 一時半刻 (a short time). Three and two are used in the same way, *sanyan liangyu* 三言兩語.

In multiplication, the smaller number usually comes first, as in *wu qi sanshiwu* 五七三十五 (5 × 7 = 35). Occasionally, numbers are referred to by their parts: *Zi jinnian er jiu* 子今年二九 means "the child is two 9s (i.e., 18 *sui*) this year," that is what we would call 16 or 17 years old (it does not mean 29 *sui*, which would be *zi jinnian ershi you jiu* 子今年二十有九).

7.1.2   Approximate, Figurative, and Auspicious Numbers

Approximate numbers (*yueshu* 約數) are expressed in various ways. *Wu liu ren* 五六人 means about five or six people. Sometimes the particles *ke* 可, *gai* 蓋, or the expression *wulü* 無慮 is used before the number or *xu* 許, *suo* 所, or *yu* 余 after it—for example, *wushi you liu xu* 五十有六許 (about 56); *shiren suo* 十人所 (*shiren zuoyou* 十人左右, about 10 people); or *wulü wushi* 無慮五十 (about 50).

The numbers 10, 100, 1,000, and 10,000 are frequently used as orders of magnitude, not numbers. In this usage they are called *xushu* 虛數 (figurative or pseudo numbers). Thus for example *baiyue* 百越 means "the Yue," not "the hundred Yue;" *baihuo* 百貨 means "general merchandise," not "100 goods;" the book title *Baijiaxing* 百家姓 is not the *Hundred Family Names* but the *Myriad Family Names* (it actually contains 438 names) and the Wanli changcheng 萬里長城 is not 10,000 *li*. Beware numbers such as 30, 300, or 3,000. They are often *xushu*.

The numbers 3, 9, and 12 are often used to mean several and many and a lot. So too is *ba* 八 (many) as in *babeizi* 八輩子 (many generations). Many other numbers were used as *xushu*, for example 18, 36, and 72.

At least from the Eastern Zhou, odd numbers were regarded as heavenly; even, as earthly. Later, the terms *yin* 陰 (even) and *yang* 陽 (odd) were used. The number 72 had a special meaning since it was the result of multiplying 8 and 9, the heaven and earth numbers immediately preceding 10. It also featured in everyday life in that the calendar itself was made up of 72 *hou* 候 (periods of five days, see 5.7). The belief in the power of mystical numbers was at its strongest in the pre-Qin and Han. Numbers appearing in works written during these centuries (e.g., the *Shiji*) should therefore be used with extreme caution.[3]

Numbers continued to permeate all areas of Chinese life up to the present, for example, for choosing lucky days and telling fortunes. Today, the belief in lucky and unlucky numbers is especially strong in south China: *si* 四 (four) is unlucky because of the similarity to *si* 死 (death), so the number 4,421 is particularly unfortunate (*sisi eryi* 死死而矣). Eight (*ba* 八) is fortunate because of its closeness to *fa* 發 (as in *facai* 發財, get rich). Such considerations weigh heavily in the choice of automobile regis-

---

[3] Yang Xizhang 楊希枚, "Zhongguo gudai de shenmi shuzi lungao 中國古代的神秘數字論稿" (Draft discussion of mystical numbers in ancient China), in his, *Xian-Qin wenhuashi lunji* 先秦文化史論集 (Collected essays on pre-Qin culture), Shehui kexue, 1995, 616–653. In the same collection, the author also discusses the mystical qualities of the number 72 (pp. 654–716 and 717–737).

tration plates; telephone numbers—and even the dates for important events, such as marriage or setting out on a long journey.

Numbers were often used for expressing numerological correspondences and affinities as well as for numerical mnemonics. There are an enormous number of these in Literary Chinese and an equally large number of different ones in the vernacular. The numbers one and three permeate the language more than any other (see the special dictionary of numerical phrases, 2.6, item 9).

Numbers are sometimes still used as a code based on their sounds as in *wu qi yi* 五七一 (*wu[zhuang] qiyi* 武裝起義, armed uprising).

7.1.3   *Wrong Numbers*

In every dynasty there were a range of punishments laid down in the codes for scribes who miscopied characters, especially numbers.[4] Nevertheless misprints and wrongly copied numbers are legion.

For an overview of the problems with Chinese historical statistics, see L. S. Yang (楊聯陞), "Numbers and Units in Chinese Economic History," in his *Studies in Chinese Institutional History*, HUP, 1963, 75–84. Yang warns against (1) copyists' errors, (2) figurative numbers, (3) under and over reporting depending on the matter reported on, and (4) regional variations in units. See also Peng Zeyi 彭澤益 (1916–94), "Quantification Problems in the Study of Chinese Economic History," *SSC* 7.3: 63–88 (1986). Derk Bodde has a brief discussion of some difficulties with the statistics in the *Shiji* in his chapter in the *CHC*, and Fang Chao-ying examines similar problems for the Qing in

---

[4] Hong Mai 洪邁 (1123–1202) tells the story of five Song woodblock-engravers who met an even worse fate: they were struck by lightning after changing the texts of prescriptions in a medical book they had been engraving, quoted in Susan Cherniack, "Book Culture and Textual Transmission in Sung China," *HJAS* 54.1 (1994), 5–6.

"A Technique for Estimating the Numerical Strength of the Early Manchu Military Forces."[5]

7.1.4 Misleading Statistics

Exaggerated and misleading statistics in modern statements about the Chinese past are another category against which the student should be on guard. They may not always be wrong, but they are misleading. Some common examples include:

The length of Chinese history (5,000 years is a common figure). A strange claim when the first written records date from 1200 BC and even if the historicity of the Xia is accepted, the length would only come to about 4,000 years (see Introduction, *The Dynasties*).

The total number of Chinese characters. Figures of 60,000 or even over 100,000 are given. On examination this turns out to include dead characters, graphic variants, Japanese characters, dialect characters and any number of other types of character long since forgotten (see 1.3.1).

The number of extant works written before modern publishing began in the 1890s is sometimes said to be between 70 and 100,000. The weakness of such statements is that "works" may cover anything from a slim volume of poems to a huge collection of thousands of memorials. Such statistics are therefore practically meaningless (see 9.1).

The size of library collections is usually given in volumes. It often turns out that Chinese *ce* are counted as one volume which gives the impression that the collection is far larger than it is. Another practice is to count each work in a collectanea separately. The number of works in the Buddhist Tripitaka, for example, is sometimes given as over 4,000 although the titles include anything from a brief recipe for toothache to a major life of Sakyamuni.

The number of Qing documents in particular archives is often given in precise figures when the definition of a "document" turns out to include everything from huge memorials to a fragment; from a single edict to a book summarizing at length a year of reports (see 50.1.2).

[5] "The State and Empire of Ch'in," *CHC*, vol. 1, CUP, 1986, rpnt., 1990, 98–102. The Fang article is in *HJAS* 13.1: 192–214 (1950).

7.2 Population

7.2.1 Registration and Policy

Throughout Chinese history, governments have attached enormous importance to registering the population. Taxes, tribute, and labor and military services were based on population counts. The registration of the population also served as the basis for social control and security. Families were grouped together and made responsible for registering their numbers and keeping a watch on each other and reporting any crimes. Travel was controlled. The earliest references to such a system go back to the Western Zhou. Traces of the system in action have been found on Qin documents (18.1.1 and 44.3.2), but the first actual registers to survive in manuscript form (on bamboo strips) date from the Han, as does the first extant census in the world, which was taken by Han officials in AD 2. Each register (made up of several bamboo strips) recorded one household, listing the head of the household (*huzhu* 戶主), his wife and adult children (*danan* 大男 and *danü* 大女), and the total number of dependents (mouths, *kou* 口). The registers often recorded much else, including health, domicile, occupation, and wealth.

Population figures (and indeed statistics of all sorts) were reported in summary form to the capital. In imperial times it was these summaries that were typically printed in historical works such as the Standard Histories (in the monographs on financial administration) and in government compendia. In the later empire they also survive in local gazetteers and in the Qing, sometimes in their original form (see the microfilm of crop price reports in 50.2.1).

Zhongguo lidai hukou, tiandi, tianfu tongji 中國歷代戶口田地田賦統計 compiled by Liang Fangzhong 梁方仲 (1908–70), is a large-scale handbook of Chinese historical statistics, containing 215 printed tables of China's population, acreage, and land-tax statistics from the Former Han to the end of the

Qing.[6] The data in the tables were drawn from nearly 300 traditional primary sources, including the Standard Histories, encyclopaedic works on government, and local gazetteers. The author was well aware of the pitfalls in traditional Chinese statistics and has added copious notes.[7] One problem is that there are few alternative figures with which to check the accuracy of the summary of the population counts in official works such as the Standard Histories or even the local gazetteers.[8]

Other sources for the study of historical demography include data culled from household registers and from Ming and Qing genealogies (3.5).[9] The most detailed records are those of the Qing imperial household.[10] For a study based on local banner household registers from Liaoning in the late Qing, see James Lee and Cameron Campbell, *Fate and Fortune in Rural China: Social Organization and Population Behavior in Liaoning, 1774–1883*, CUP, 1997. Appendix A sets out the sources and methods used in this important study.

For a history of traditional Chinese population policies, see Wang Yuesheng 王躍生, *Zhongguo renkou de shengshuai yu dui-*

[6] *Zhongguo lidai hukou, tiandi, tianfu tongji* (Chinese historical population, land, and land-tax statistics), Shangwu, 1980; 4th repr., 1993.

[7] On the problems of population statistics, see Chao Kang, *Man and Land in Chinese History: An Economic Analysis*, SUP, 1986.

[8] G. William Skinner, "Sichuan's Population in the 19th Century: Lessons for Disaggregated Data," *LIC* 8.1: 1–79 (1987), finds that the sum of the county figures are overestimates. Arthur P. Wolf and Chieh-shih Huang in *Marriage and Adoption in China, 1845–1945*, SUP, 1980, use Japanese imperial figures to check traditional Chinese head counts.

[9] On the genealogies, see Ted A. Telford, "Survey of Social Demographic Data in Chinese Genealogies," *LIC* 7.2: 118–48 (1986). And on new approaches using sources such as household registers, see the chapters in *Chinese Historical Micro-Demography*, Stevan Harrell, ed., UCP, 1995.

[10] *Qingdai huangzu renkou xingwei yu shehui huanjing* 清代皇族人口行為與社會環境 (The behavior and social background of the Qing royal clan), Li Zhongqing 李中清 and Guo Songyi 郭松義, Beijing daxue, 1994.

ce 中國人口的盛衰與對策 which also describes the systems used to register the population in different periods.[11]

For overall surveys of China's historical population trends, see Hans Bielenstein, "Chinese Historical Demography, AD 2–1982," *BMFEA* 59: 1–288 (1987). This updates an earlier survey by Michel Cartier and Pierre-Etienne Will.[12] See also Ge Jianxiong 葛劍雄, *Zhongguo renkou fazhanshi* 中國人口發展史, or Zhao Wenlin 趙文林 and Xie Shujin 謝書進, *Zhongguo renkoushi* 中國人口史.[13]

Archaeologists have recently made some interesting estimates of China's population and land use patterns at the dawn of history based on the analysis of burial sites.[14] Thereafter, there are a number of studies of the population of China in different historical periods:

Hans Bielenstein, "The Census of China During the Period 2–742 AD," *BMFEA* 19: 125–63 (1947).

Robert M. Hartwell (1932–96), "Demographic, Political and Social Transformations in China, 750–1550," *HJAS* 42.2: 365–442 (1982).

Ho Ping-ti (He Bingdi 何炳棣), "An Estimate of the Total Population in Sung-Chin China," in *Etudes Song in memoriam Etienne Balazs*, I (1970).

Ho Ping-ti, *Studies on the Population of China 1368–1953*, HUP, 1959. The classic study of population in late imperial China.

---

[11] *Zhongguo renkou de shengshuai yu duice* (The rise and fall of China's population and policy measures), Shehui kexue wenxian, 1995.

[12] "Demographie et institutions en Chine: Contribution à l'analyse des recensements de l'époque imperiale (2 ap. J.C.–1750)," *Annales de demographie historique* 1971: 161–245.

[13] *Zhongguo renkou fazhan shi* (A history of the development of China's population), Fujian renmin, 1991; *Zhongguo renkou shi* (China's population history), Beijing renmin, 1988. For further references, see William Lively, James Lee, and Wang Feng, "Chinese demography: The State of the Field," *JAS* 49.4: 807–34 (1990).

[14] See for example, Song Zhenhao 宋鎮豪, *Xia-Shang shehui shenghuo shi* 夏商社會生活史 (A history of social life in the Xia and Shang periods), Shehui kexue, 1994; rpnt., 1996.

Dwight H. Perkins, *Agricultural Development in China*, Aldine, 1969. An examination of population and land area estimates from an economist's point of view.

Liu Ts'ui-jung (Liu Cuirong 劉翠溶), "Agricultural Change and Population Growth: A Brief Survey on the Case of China in Historical Perspective," *Academia Economic Papers* 14.1: 29–68 (1986). Liu was the first to use genealogies to examine population trends at the micro-level (see next item).

Liu Ts'ui-jung, "The Demography of Two Chinese Clans in Hsiao-shen, Chekiang, 1650–1850," in Susan B. Hanley and Arthur P. Wolf, eds., *Family and Population in East Asian History*, SUP, 1985, 13–61.

Liu Cuirong 劉翠溶, *Ming-Qing shiqi jiazu renkou yu shehui jingji bianqian* 明清時期家族人口與社會經濟變遷 (Lineage population and socio-economic changes in the Ming and Qing periods), 2 vols., Nangang: Institute of Economics, Academia Sinica, 1992.

Studies of the historical demography of individual towns have begun to appear see, for example, Han Guanghui, 韓光輝 *Beijing lishi renkou dili* 北京歷史人口地理.[15]

7.2.2 Internal Migration

No doubt people were on the move in and throughout East Asia long before records become available. In China, one of the first recorded migrations was into Sichuan, when 50,000 Qin people were settled there following the conquest of the kingdom of Shu 蜀 in 316 BC. Shu loyalists fled south and eventually 60,000 of them settled in what is today the northern part of Vietnam. About 4,000 criminals from the North, along with their families were settled by Qin in Sichuan in 238.[16]

Even small numbers of migrants could have a big impact on the place they settled if they came with advanced techniques.

---

[15] *Beijing lishi renkou dili* (The historical geography of Beijing's population), Beijing daxue, 1996.

[16] Inward migration into Sichuan throughout Chinese history continued to influence the development of Sichuan dialect, see Cui Rongchang 崔榮昌, *Sichuan fangyan yu Ba-Shu wenhua* 四川方言與巴蜀文化 (The Sichuan dialect and Ba-Shu culture), Sichuan daxue, 1996.

The best detailed study of migration is by Ge Jianxiong 葛
劍雄, Cao Shuji 曹樹基 and Wu Songdi 吳松第, *Zhongguo yiminshi* 簡明中國移民史.[17]

For pioneering studies in English, see

James Lee, "Migration and Expansion in Chinese History," in *Human
Migration*, William McNeill and Ruth Adams, eds., IUP, 1977, 20–47.

Herold J. Wiens, *The Han Chinese Expansion in South China*.[18]

See also:

Edward H. Schafer, *The Vermilion Bird: T'ang Images of the South*, UCP,
1967; rpnt., 1985.

For the early colonization of Fujian, see

Hans Bielenstein, "The Chinese Colonization of Fukien until the End of
the T'ang," in *Studia Serica Berhard Karlgren dedicata*, Ejnar Munksgaard, 1959, 98–122.

Edward H. Schafer, *The Empire of Min*, Tuttle, for the H-Y Institute,
1954.

Hugh R. Clark, *Community, Trade and Networks: Southern Fujian Province from the 3rd to the 13th Centuries*, CUP, 1991.

For Fujian in the later empire, see *Development and Decline of Fukien
Province in the 17th and 18th Centuries*, E. B. Vermeer, ed., Brill, 1990.

For other regions, see, for example,

Zheng Xuemeng 鄭學檬, *Zhongguo gudai jingji zhongxin nanyi he Tang-
Song Jiangnan jingji yanjiu* 中國古代經濟重心南移和唐宋江南經濟
研究 (Research on the movement of ancient China's center of economic gravity and the economy of South China in the Tang-Song),
Yuelu, 1996.

Richard von Glahn, *The Country of Streams and Grottoes: Expansion, Settlement, and the Civilizing of the Sichuan Frontier in Song Times*,
Council on East Asia Studies, Harvard University, 1987.

---

[17] *Zhongguo yiminshi* (History of migrants in China), 6 vols., Fuzhou
renmin, 1997.

[18] Shoestring Press, 1954; Westview, 1967. Original title: *China's
March into the Tropics*, Washington, D.C.: United States Navy, Office of
Naval Research, 1952.

Li Bozhong 李伯重, *Tangdai Jiangnan nongye de fazhan* 唐代江南農業 的發展 (The development of agriculture in South China in the Tang), Nongye, 1990; and the same author's *Agricultural Development in Jiangnan, 1620–1850*, Macmillan, 1998. This is based on many of his more detailed studies.

Liu Cuirong 劉翠溶 "Ming-Qing renkou zhi zengzhi yu qianyi 明清人口 之增植與遷移" (The growth and migration of population during the Ming and Qing) in *Zhongguo shehui jingji shi yantao hui lunwenji* 中 國社會經濟史研討會論文集 (Papers for the seminar on Chinese social and economic history), Center for Chinese Cultural Studies, Taibei, 1983, 283–316.

For early Chinese expansion into the ancient kingdoms of Vietnam, see Jennifer Holmgren, *Chinese Colonization of Northern Vietnam: First to Sixth Centuries AD*, ANU, 1980, and the sources cited in Keith Weller Taylor, *The Birth of Vietnam*, UCP, 1983. For later Chinese migration to Southeast Asia, there are a number of special bibliographies available (41.5).

The effect of migration on the late formation of dialects is examined in James Lee and R. Bin Wong, "Population Movements in Qing China and Their Linguistic Legacy," in *Language and Dialects of China*, William S. Y. Wang, ed., *Journal of Chinese Linguistics* Monograph Series 3, Berkeley, 1991, 52–77.

7.3 Land Statistics, Weights and Measures

On traditional cultivated-land statistics, consult He Bingdi 何 炳棣, *Zhongguo lidai tudi shuzi kaoshi* 中國歷代土地數字考釋, in which he argues that the land acreage figures denominated in *mu* 畝 and the Ming and Qing *ding* 丁 figures are taxation units that underestimate the actual land and population.[19] Statistics of

---

[19] *Zhongguo lidai tudi shuzi kaoshi* (Research on Chinese historical land statistics), Lianjing chuban shiye gongsi, 1995. This is a revised version of the author's earlier work *Zhongguo gujin tudi shuzi de kaoshi he pingjia* 中國古今土地數字的考釋和評價 (Land statistics in ancient and modern China: Research, interpretation and evaluation), Shehui kexue, 1988.

military land were notoriously over-estimated. See also Liang Fangzhong (1980).

The standard comprehensive study of historical weights and measures is Qiu Guangming 丘光明, *Zhongguo lidai duliangheng kao* 中國歷代度量衡考.[20] This is a detailed, well-illustrated study based on both written and archaeological evidence. Note that the official measures increased over time thus the foot grew by 40 percent between the Qin and the Qing (from 23 to 32 cm). For routine conversions, the appendix on weights and measures in volume 13 of the *Hanyu da cidian* should be enough. The author, Wang Guanying 王冠英, was also able to make good use of recent archaeological discoveries.[21]

The above studies and summaries of changes in weights and measures cover the official records at a national level. They do not cover the variations between particular areas and commodities in different periods, which often differed from the national units. For example, see the land units used in the Huizhou rent contracts. In such cases there is no recourse but to work out the values on the basis of internal evidence.

Just as with numbers, there were alteration-proof characters for weights and measures (e.g., *sheng* 勝 for *sheng* 升).

Yan Zhongping 嚴中平 (1909–91), *Zhongguo jindai jingjishi tongji ziliao xuanji* 中國近代經濟史統計資料選輯, is mainly

---

[20] *Zhongguo lidai duliangheng kao* (Research on weights and measures through the ages in China), Kexue, 1992. See also Guo Zhengzhong 郭正忠, *Zhongguo quanheng duliang san zhi shisi shiji* 中國權衡度量三至十四世紀 *Zhongguo quanheng duliang san zhi shisi shiji* (Chinese weights and measures: fourth to 14th centuries), Shehui kexue, 1993.

[21] Studies of Chinese measures, especially the foot measure, have been made throughout Chinese history. Outstanding studies were made in the 1930s, mainly on the basis of literary evidence, by Wu Chengluo 吳承洛, *Zhongguo duliianghengshi* 中國度量衡史, (A history of Chinese weights and measures), 1937, 2nd ed., Shangwu, 1957, rpnt., 1993; Yang Kuan 楊寬, *Zhongguo lidai chidu kao* 中國歷代尺度考 (Historical study of the Chinese foot measure), 1938; rpnt., Shangwu, 1955, 1957. These studies have now been superseded by Qiu (1992) and Guo (1993).

on the late Qing and the Republic. A planned supplementary volume never appeared.[22]

7.4 Money and Prices

7.4.1 Money

The best introduction remains L. S. Yang (楊聯陞), *Money and Credit in China: A Short History*, HUP, 1952. In just over one hundred pages he covers from antiquity to the end of the Qing: coins, gold and silver, paper money, traditional credit institutions, old-style and modern banks, and loans and interest rates. Compare with Richard von Glahn, *Fountain of Fortune: Money and Monetary Policy in China, Tenth to Seventeenth Centuries*, UCP, 1996. Note also:

Peng Xinwei 彭信威 (1907–1965), *A Monetary History of China*, Edward H. Kaplan, tr., Western Washington Univ. Press, 1994. The original was *Zhongguo qianbishi* 中國錢幣史, 2 vols., 1965; 2nd ed., 1988, Shanghai renmin.

Zhongguo qianbi da cidian 中國錢幣大辭典 (Dictionary of Chinese coins), *Xian-Qin*, Zhonghua, 1995, is the most convenient recent work including archaeological discoveries since 1949. *Zhongguo guqian pu* 中國古錢譜 (Illustrated catalog of ancient Chinese coins), Wenwu, 1989; 4th reprint, 1995, is on a smaller scale.

Zhongguo lidai huobi daxi 中國歷代貨幣大繫 (Collection of Chinese historical currency), Wang Qingzheng 汪慶正, ed. in chief, 12 large folio vols., Shanghai renmin and Shanghai guji, 1988– . The first volume (1988) is on the pre-Qin.[23]

Zhongguo guchao tuji 中國古鈔圖輯 (Selected illustrations of Chinese paper money), *Nei-Menggu qianbi yanjiuhui* 內蒙古錢幣研究會 and *Zhongguo Qianbi* 中國錢幣, editorial dept., comps., Zhongguo jin-

---

[22] *Zhongguo jindai jingjishi tongji ziliao xuanji* (Selected statistical materials on modern Chinese economic history), 2 vols., Kexue, 1955. Covers the years 1796–1898.

[23] Both the *qianbi da cidian* and the *Lidai huobi daxi* replace the earlier Ding Fubao 丁福保, *Guqian da cidian* 古錢大辭典 (Encyclopaedia of ancient Chinese coins), Shanghai, 1937; latest rpnt., 2 vols., Zhonghua, 1989.

rong, 1992. This is a well-illustrated bilingual account of the history of paper money.

The Chinese Numismatic Society publishes the scholarly journal *Zhongguo qianbi* 中國錢幣 (China numismatics; 1983– , quarterly), which carries news of the discovery of ancient coins and articles on monetary history.

7.4.2   Prices

For a systematic survey of Chinese price history based on original sources see Tan Wenxi 譚文熙, *Zhongguo wujiashi* 中國物價史.[24] The author examines in each period of the empire the concept of price; changing prices as reflected in contemporary data, and government price policy. For the pre-Qin there is almost no price data, but many of the classical thinkers commented on prices and governments sought by various means to control the market. Prices of commodities in the early empire are occasionally recorded in traditional written sources, on stone inscriptions, or on newly discovered documents such as those on the bamboo strips.[25] Specialized works on mathematics also sometimes include problems based on real data and questions using prices.[26]

The most extensive price records relate to crops. Grain price reporting connected with the operation of the ever-normal granaries was in place at least from the Tang dynasty, although no records are extant. The Qing system was inherited

[24] *Zhongguo wujiashi* (A history of Chinese prices), Hubei renmin, 1994.

[25] Qin and Han commodity prices on the *hanjian* are excerpted in *Zhongguo gudai shehui jingjishi ziliao* 中國古代社會經濟史資料 (Materials on ancient Chinese socioeconomic history), Lishisuo, eds., 1st collection, Fujian renmin, 1985, 1–98.

[26] The Han work on mathematics, the *Jiuzhang suanshu* 九章算術 (Nine chapters on the mathematical arts), for example, records 68 prices for 27 different products. These have been studied and compared with other Han price data in Song Jie 宋傑, *Jiuzhang suanshu yu Handai shehui jingji* 九章算術與漢代社會經濟 (The *Jiuzhang suanshu* and the social economy of the Han), Shoudu shifan daxue, 1993.

from the Ming and installed during the reign of Kangxi. Reports were made every 10 days and summarized at provincial level for forwarding to the capital.[27] Tens of thousands of the reports have been preserved in the Qing archives and are available today on microfilm. They cover each of the 28 provinces from Kangxi to 1911. The reports were secretly held at the palace and used not only for the granary system, but as a sort of early warning of trouble. Occasional finds of them have been published, but this is the first time they have been made available in full.[28]

There are also fairly extensive price records for salt and other government monopolies, and for palace construction and maintenance, and court consumption.

[27] On the grain-price reporting system as it was practised in the Qing, see Wang Yejian 王業鍵, "Qingdai de liangjia chenbao zhidu 清代的糧價陳報制度," *Taibei gugong jikan* 13.1 (1978). The Qing grain-price reports were used by Han-sheng Chuan and Richard A. Kraus, *Mid-Ch'ing Rice Markets and Trade: An Essay in Price History*, East Asian Research Center, HUP, 1975; Robert B Marks, "Rice Prices, Food Supply, and Market Structure in Eighteenth-Century South China," *LIC* 12.2 (1991); Kishimoto Mio 岸本美緒, *Shindai Chûgoku buka to keizai henken* 清代中國物價經濟變遷, Kenbun, 1997.

[28] *Gongzhong liangjiadan* 宮中糧價單 (Grain-price reports in the palace archives), Yishiguan, comps., 328 reels, 1990. Other price materials from the Qing archives are listed in 50.4.1.

8

Guides and Encyclopaedias

This chapter introduces sinological and historical guides (8.1–2) and historical encyclopaedias (8.3) covering the whole of Chinese history. Chapters 43–50 cover guides and primary sources and to individual periods.

8.1 Sinological Guides

The best guide in English to reference works on all aspects of Chinese studies (sinology) covering most subjects and all periods from the first emperor to modern times is Harriet S. Zurndorfer *China Bibliography: A Research Guide to Reference Works about China Past and Present*, Brill, 1995. Zurndorfer supersedes previous general English-language guides to reference works.

Although not as up-to-date as Zurndorfer, Teng Ssu-yü (Deng Siyu 鄧嗣禹) and Knight Biggerstaff, *An Annotated Bibliography of Selected Chinese Reference Works*, 3rd rev. ed., H-Y Institute, 1971, contains fuller descriptions of earlier reference works.[1]

For an online Website bibliography, see *Classical Historiography for Chinese History*, Benjamin Elman, author, with the help of Ping-yu Chu, Xiaoping Cong, Miaw-fen Lu, Sam Gilbert and Adam Schorr, UCLA Social Science Computing Center, 1996. This is arranged as a series of bibliographic exercises

---

[1] Teng and Biggerstaff cover Chinese studies in general and arrange Chinese reference works of all periods up to about 1940 under the following categories: (1) bibliographies, (2) encyclopaedias, (3) dictionaries, (4) geographical works, (5) biographical works, (6) tables, (7) yearbooks, (8) sinological indexes.

intended to guide beginning students through the English language secondary literature on Chinese history and thought (unannotated). A number of Chinese primary sources and references are also listed, especially for the Ming and Qing and often with annotations. Wade-Giles romanization is used.[2]

There are large numbers of Chinese guides to modern reference works for students of Chinese literature and history. For example:

Zhongwen gongjushu jiaocheng 中文工具書教程 (A coursebook of Chinese reference books), Zhu Tianjun 朱天俊 and Li Guoxin 李國新, eds., Beijing daxue, 1991, contains the essentials and has reliable explanations.

Wenshizhe gongjushu jianjie 文史哲工具書簡介 (A brief introduction to reference works for literature, history, and philosophy), Chinese Dept. and History Depts., Nanjing University Library, eds., Tianjin jiaoyu, 1980. This is more bibliographic in approach. The compilers note different editions of primary sources from first appearance to the present day. There is a stroke-count index.

Zhongguo lishi gongjushu zhinan 中國歷史工具書指南 (A guide to reference books for Chinese history), Lin Tiesen 林鐵森, Beijing daxue, 1992, was written specifically for students of Chinese history; it also includes some Western and Japanese reference books and has a full *pinyin* index.

8.2 Historical Guides

8.2.1 Chinese

As China becomes more modern and as a result (at least in the early stages), more cut off from its history, Chinese students need guidebooks to help them in their studies, especially of ancient history. Since the 1980s, a large number have been published. The space allotted to primary sources, secondary scholarship and research problems differs in each. Some concentrate on a single period, others cover all of Chinese history. The following three cover the whole of Chinese history. Guides de-

[2] World Wide Web: < http://www.sscnet.ucla.edu/history/elman/ ClassBib/ > .

voted to individual periods are introduced in chapter 43 and the other chapters of Part V. Some good readers are mentioned in 1.3.5.

Zhongguoshi yanjiu zhinan 中國史研究指南 (Guide to research on Chinese history), Gao Mingshi 高明士, ed., 5 vols., Lianjing, 1990. One of the most comprehensive guides. It is a translation into Chinese of the leading Japanese guide to Chinese history (Yamane, 1983, see 8.2.2). The editor, Gao Mingshi, has added the contributions of Taiwan and Hong Kong scholars, and thus the guide covers secondary scholarship in all languages (as of the early 1980s) for every period of Chinese history as well as Chinese primary sources. About two-thirds of the guide goes to secondary scholarship and one third to primary sources and reference works. Secondary Western scholarship is only partially included. Just after this translation was published in 1990, Yamane and his team produced an update to their guide. There is a second Chinese translation of Yamane, this time of the updated version, Tian Renlong 田人隆, tr. *Zhongguoshi yanjiu rumen* 中國史研究入門, 2 vols., Shehuikexue wenxian, 1994.

Zhongguo gudaishi shiliaoxue 中國古代史史料學 (The study of the primary source materials for ancient Chinese history), Chen Gaohua 陳高華 and Chen Zhichao 陳智超 et al., Beijing, 1983; 6th prnt., 1991. This is a straightforward introduction to primary sources arranged by period from the late Shang to the mid-Qing. Each chapter was written by a specialist from the Lishisuo (not to be confused with the next item, which has an identical title but is arranged by genre, not by period). There is little attempt to include either reference books or secondary scholarship.

Zhongguo gudaishi shiliaoxue 中國古代史史料學 (The study of the primary source materials for ancient Chinese history), An Zuozhang 安作璋, ed., Fujian renmin, 1994. Complements the previous two items in that the arrangement is by type of primary source (as defined by a modern historian), not by period. There is no attempt to include either reference books or secondary scholarship.

Illustrations

A Journey into China's Antiquity, National Museum of Chinese History, eds., Morning Glory, 1997–8. This superb book of color photographs of the main exhibits of the Museum of Chinese History (after the reorganization which took place from 1988) includes newly excavated artifacts. There are excellent brief explanations. The four volumes in the series bring the story to the twentieth century:

Vol. 1: *Palaeolithic–Spring and Autumn Period*
Vol. 2: *Warring States–Northern and Southern Dynasties*
Vol. 3: *Sui-Tang–Song*
Vol. 4: *Yuan, Ming and Qing*

An earlier much longer Chinese version has many more illustrations but they are in rather poor black and white reproductions and are based on the museum's collections before the 1988 reorganization: *Zhongguo gudaishi cankao tulu* 中國古代史參考圖錄 (Reference illustrations for ancient Chinese history), Zhongguo lishi bowuguan 中國歷史博物館, eds., 9 vols., Shanghai jiaoyu, 1989–91. Altogether this series contains 7,000 annotated illustrations of objects of interest to a historian including people, tools, machinery, original editions of books and so forth.

8.2.2   *Japanese Historical Guides*

There are several Japanese guides to the study of Chinese history written for Japanese students. One of the more recent was edited by a team of Tokyo historians led by Yamane Yukio 山根幸夫, *Chûgokushi kenkyû nyûmon* 中國史研究入門.[3] The handbook is arranged by period. Vol. 1 covers from earliest times to the end of the Ming; vol. 2, the Qing up to the early 1990s. Each chapter is written by one or more specialists and includes lengthy discussions of the secondary scholarship on selected themes. The emphasis is on Japanese and Chinese scholarship, but English and other Western language work is included. There are also annotated bibliographies of selected primary sources. About two-thirds of the guide is devoted to secondary scholarship and one third to primary sources and reference works. The index includes titles of primary sources. The second edition includes a new essay at the end of each volume summarizing publications which appeared after the first edition, between 1982 and 1991 (vol. 1) and between 1982 and

---

[3] *Chûgokushi kenkyû nyûmon* (Handbook for research into Chinese history), 2 vols., Yamakawa, 1983; rev. and enl. ed., vol. 1, 1991; rpnt., 1996; vol. 2, rev. and enl., 1995.

1994 (vol. 2). The Yamane handbook is similar to the *Tôyô shiryô shûsei* 東洋史料集成, which it supersedes.[4]

It is interesting to compare the coverage in Yamane with another recent guide produced mainly by historians at Kyoto. Despite the interest of the topically arranged chapters in the Kyoto handbook, the Tokyo guide is more thorough and up-to-date:

Ajia rekishi kenkyû nyûmon アジア歴史研究入門 (Handbook for research into Asian history), Shimada Kenji 嶋田虔次, ed. in chief, 5 vols., Dôhôsha, 1983–4; vol. 6 (index), 1987. China is covered in vols. 1–3. Detailed bibliographical essays by specialists cover both primary and secondary sources (in all languages). Vol. 3 is topically arranged and covers catalogs, historical geography, archaeology, the history of thought, science and technology, customs, and women. A separate, sixth volume contains a comprehensive author-title index to the entire work.

8.3   Historical Encyclopaedias

8.3.1   English

China: A Cultural and Historical Dictionary, Michael Dillon, ed., Curzon, 1998, contains about 1,500 entries covering from earliest times to the present day.

8.3.2   Chinese

There are two main Chinese encyclopaedias of Chinese history:

Zhongguo da baike quanshu 中國大百科全書 (The great Chinese encyclopaedia), 74 vols., 1980–94; among which *Zhongguo lishi* 中國歷史 (Chinese history), 3 vols., Zhongguo da baike quanshu, 1992; 3rd prnt., 1995. The fairly long articles were written by China's leading historians. Arrangement is by *pinyin*. There is also a detailed *pinyin* index. Although there are only about 2,000 articles in the three history volumes, it is easier to separate the wheat from the chaff than in the 60,000 very short articles of the *Zhongguo lishi da cidian* (item 2, below). Well illustrated. There is an overall, alphabetically arranged

---

[4] *Tôyô shiryô shûsei* (Bibliography of primary and secondary sources for Oriental history), Heibonsha, 1956; 3rd prnt., 1992.

index in one volume to the entire encyclopaedia, which is useful if you are looking up, for example Chang'an, and want to find references, not only in the history volumes, but also in the separate volumes on archaeology, literature, and many others. The entire *Zhongguo da baike quanshu* is available on 24 CD-ROMs. There is also a CD-ROM version of the simplified version of the encyclopaedia (1994) which contains 8,000 entries and five million characters.

Zhongguo lishi da cidian 中國歷史大辭典 (The great encyclopaedia of Chinese history), 14 vols., Shanghai cishu, 1983– . The eight chronological volumes on the customary periods from pre-Qin through to Qing contain short factual entries of basic information on events, people, reign names, emperors, institutions, laws, regulations and book titles. Arrangement is by stroke count. The entire series contains over 12,000 double-column pages with a total of 60,000 entries. If the editors had added a little more detail and a *pinyin* index to each volume (as well as to the whole series) it would be both more useful and more convenient to use. The chronological vols. are as follows:

Pre-Qin (1996)   Song (1984)
Qin, Han (1990)   Liao, Xia Jin, Yuan (1986)
Wei, Jin, *Nan-Bei Chao* (1997)   Ming (1995)
Sui, Tang, Wudai (1995)   Qing vol. 1, 1644–1840; vol. 2, 1840–
                                  1912, (1992)

In addition, there are five separate volumes on:

1. Historiography (*Shixueshi* 史學史, 1983). Not a study of historiography but a somewhat skimpily annotated bibliography of traditional historical works arranged by book title (stroke-count index).

2. Historical geography (*Lishi dili* 歷史地理, 1996); over 9,000 entries. One of the best pocket-size introductions not only to historical place-names, but also to famous geographers from earliest times to 1911 and their works (4.5.3).

3. History of ethnic groups (*Minzu shi* 民族史, 1995).

4. History of thought (*Sixiang shi* 思想史, 1989).

5. History of science and technology (*Kejishi* 科技史, forthcoming).

Both the *Zhongguo da baike quanshu* (*Zhongguo lishi*) and the *Zhongguo lishi da cidian* are strong on historical personages, book titles, and other facts which would normally feature in an old-fashioned index of names, places, and titles, but not on generic terms or concepts. Thus, for example, if you want to look up a subject such as "price history," you will not find it. Even something as concrete as the "navy" merits not a single entry, but you will find references to individual admirals—if you know their names.

8.3.3 Japanese

There are a number of excellent historical encyclopaedias and historical dictionaries available that contain short articles on all aspects of Asian history, personalities, periods, places, institutions and events in a readily accessible form. The most recent is the single-volume *Tôyôshi jiten* 東洋史辞典.[5] Much larger but already 30 years old is *Ajia rekishi jiten* アジア歴史事典.[6] Its entries are comprehensive and easy to locate; arrangement is phonetically by Japanese syllabary. Vol. 10 contains tables and indexes, including a stroke-count index and a shorter Wade-Giles index.

[5] *Tôyôshi jiten* (Dictionary of Oriental history), rev. ed., Sôgensha, 1980.

[6] *Ajia rekishi jiten* (Encyclopaedia of Asian history), 10 vols., Heibonsha, 1959–62; rpnt., 1984. *Ajia rekishi jiten* replaced the same publisher's prewar historical enyclopaedia, *Tôyô rekishi daijiten* 東洋歴史大辞典 (Encyclopaedia of Oriental history), 9 vols., Heibonsha, 1937–39. This is now superseded, but the articles indicate the level reached by the textually-based studies of Chinese history in Japan before the war.

9

Locating Primary Sources

The chapter begins with a summary of the different ways of finding out what books were circulating in a given period (9.1). Chinese libraries have existed for at least 2,500 years (9.2). Various classification schemes were used. It was in the Han that the four main categories of Classics, History, Philosophy and Belles-lettres began to take shape (9.3). The largest collections were normally those of the emperor. Six of the imperial library catalogs are included in the Standard Histories (9.4). Book catalogs (*mulu* 目錄) were placed in the History branch of the traditional fourfold bibliographical classification (*Sibu* 四部, 9.3). The largest library of all was the especially commissioned collection of the Qianlong emperor, the *Siku quanshu* 四庫全書 (9.5). Works were often published in *congshu* 叢書 (series or collectanea, 9.6). One way of tracking down old books and finding what they contain is to use modern annotated bibliographies of primary sources (9.7). Throughout Chinese history there have been large numbers of rare, lost, recovered, forged, and banned books (9.8). This complicates the often tricky problem of alternative and difficult book titles (9.9). The index and the concordance were unknown in old China. Now many works, both the well-known and the obscure, have been indexed (9.10).

9.1   Overview: How to Locate a Work

Nobody knows exactly how many pre-twentieth-century Chinese works have survived. An estimate in the range of 40,000 to 50,000 is probably not too far wrong, but this includes such a wide range of different titles from the flimsiest collection of poetry to major philosophical works that it is a practically meaningless statistic. Most of the works which have survived date from the later empire, because before the widespread use of printing in the Song, books usually circulated only in a few manuscript copies and were therefore easily lost. There are a number of ways to find out what books were circulating in a given period (including the titles of those that have not survived). There are also shortcuts to finding out what the contents of a book are, and there are published catalogs to locate the whereabouts in modern libraries of those books that have survived. Many old Chinese books have been indexed, and there are an increasing number available on CD-ROM or computer disk which enables rapid subject searches. Note that books were very often dated at the end of the preface or in the colophon; sometimes, too, by the dedication or presentation to the emperor, and sometimes by the date of printing.

Dynastic bibliographies were included in many of the Standard Histories. They were normally based on the catalog of the imperial library of a given period. They were not annotated. Some have survived, and many have been reconstructed later. Both categories have been enlarged to include all books known to have circulated in a given period. Thus they include the titles of books written in a dynasty plus those that survived from previous dynasties. Altogether, the dynastic bibliographies contain the titles of at least 40,000 separate works (the majority of which have long since been lost). There is a combined index available in the *H-Y Index* 10 (9.4).

Annotated catalogs, usually of a particular library, are the quickest shortcut to the contents of a source without having to read through hundreds of pages of thousands of separate titles. The largest annotated catalog ever compiled in China before modern times was that for the Qianlong emperor's library, the *Siku quanshu zongmu tiyao* 四庫全書總目提要 (*Siku zongmu* 四庫總目 for short), 9.5. This catalog has now been superseded (unless you are specializing in Qing intellectual history) by a modern annotated catalog, the *Siku da cidian* 四庫大辭典 that was modeled after, and to a considerable extent based on, the *Siku zongmu*. Your starting point should be *Siku da cidian*, which contains abstracts of over 20,000 separate works and is by far the largest annotated catalog of traditional Chinese sources available (9.7).

It has been a common practice in China ever since the Song, to reprint separate books together in a *congshu* 叢書 (series, collectanea). A *congshu* can contain anything from a few dozen to a few thousand books. There is a union catalog available: *Zhongguo congshu zonglu* 中國叢書綜錄, which has a total of 70,000 entries listing in all 38,891 separate titles in 2,086 *congshu* (9.6).

Having found what you are looking for or stumbled across an unexpected title, you will want to check if a modern index is available, because old Chinese books were almost never indexed (9.10).

Major libraries are increasingly making their catalogs available on CD-ROM and also online for Internet searches (11.6). But very often older works are the last to be entered and few libraries have converted all their cards to one system of romanization hence printed library catalogs are still essential to locate books, especially old ones.

A few of the best collections have excellent published catalogs, notably those of Beitu 北圖 (Peking Library), Jimbun (the Research Institute for Humanistic Studies at Kyoto University), and Tôbunken (the Institute for Oriental Culture at Tokyo University), on whose collections, see 11.3.

An essential way of keeping up-to-date with reprints and new works is to skim through the catalogs of publishers and bookstores. There are not all that many specializing in Chinese history (see 11.6 for a brief introduction).

Despite the large numbers of different book titles in circulation and the large number of books that have survived, only a handful of references are essential:

1. To find a title in the dynastic bibliographies use the *Yiwenzhi ershi zhong zonghe yinde* 藝文志二十種綜合引得 (Combined indices to 20 dynastic bibliographies), *H-Y Index* 10 (9.4).

2. To check if there is an alternative title or if there is another book with the same title, use *Tongshu yiming tongjian* 同書異名通檢, which lists books with more than one title, or *Tongming yishu tongjian* 同名異書通檢, which lists books having the same title (9.9).

3. To help find the meaning of a difficult title: *Zhongguo gujin shuming shiyi cidian* 中國古今書名釋義辭典 (9.9).

4. To find the contents of a work: *Siku da cidian* 四庫大辭典 (9.7).

5. To find a title in a *congshu*, or author, or a *congshu*: *Zhongguo congshu zonglu* 中國叢書綜錄 (9.6).

6. Check the published catalogs of the Jimbun and Tôbunken, two of the world's leading collections of Chinese books (11.3).

7. Browse the bookstores specializing in old Chinese books and their reprints (11.6).

8. Browse the international databases of Chinese library collections (11.5).

9.2 Early Chinese Libraries

The earliest libraries in China for which there is any evidence date from the Spring and Autumn period. Not much is known about them except that they were official collections. They were called *cefu* 冊府, *cefu* 策府, or generically, *gufu* 故府. At the beginning of the Former Han a very famous central archive was established, the Shiquge 石渠閣 (20.2). Two others were also erected, the Tianluge 天祿閣 and Qilinge 麒麟閣. It was at the Shiquge that the *Five Classics* were edited. The first imperial library as such, the Mige 秘閣, was established in the palace for Han Wudi (140–88 BC), and it was for this collection that Liu Xiang 劉向 developed his influential library classification scheme, the *Qilüe* 七略 (9.3). He did the collating and editorial work in the Tianluge 天祿閣. There were other palace collections in the Han, most famously the Lantai 蘭臺 where the author of the Hanshu 漢書, Ban Gu (AD 32–92), worked (44.1). Later dynasties built up their own collections (and continued the tradition of calling the imperial library and archives the Mige, until the Northern Song, when it became known as the Mishu sheng 秘書省). An official was appointed as imperial librarian in AD 159 with the title Mishujian 秘書監. The imperial library catalogs of six dynasties were published in the Standard Histories of those dynasties (9.4).[1]

The first recorded book market was in Luoyang in the Former Han. In the Song, the book markets shifted to the woodblock centers. These were in Jianyang 建陽 (north Fujian), Hangzhou, and Sichuan. In the Ming and Qing, the book trade moved to Jiangsu and Zhejiang. The main markets were there as well in the capitals, Nanjing and Beijing.[2]

Academies in China were called Shuyuan 書院. The term dates from the Tang and referred at first to an official office for collecting and collating books. Later private Shuyuan were set up. Shuyuan book collections grew after printing became more common in the Song. By this time they had become schools, some of which were famous centers for the teaching of *Lixue* 理學 (neo-Confucianism). Their libraries held anything from 10,000 to 100,000 *juan*, which came from various sources including public and private donations. During the golden age of

---

[1] Jean-Pierre Drège, *Les Bibliothèques en Chine aux temps des manuscrits jusqu'au Xᵉ siècle*, EFEO and Maisonneuve, 1991; John Winkelman, "The imperial library in Southern Sung China, 1127–1279: A Study of the Organization and Operation of the Scholarly Agencies of the Central Government," *Transactions of the American Philosophical Society*, n.s. 64.8 (1974).

[2] Lai Xinxia 來新夏, *Zhongguo gudai tushu shiyeshi* 中國古代圖書事業史 (A history of the book trade in ancient China), Shanghai renmin, 1990; rpnt., 1991, is a good general introduction to the history of the Chinese book trade, which covers the collection, storage, editing, production and circulation of books in each period. For further references to the history of printing in China, see 18.4.

the Shuyuan in the Ming and the Qing, their collections grew, and catalogs of individual *shuyuan* libraries were published.[3] The Ming also saw the rise of prefectural and county school libraries.[4]

Private libraries had been in existence since at least the Han, if not before, but only the very rich could afford them because of the rarity and high price of books. There were 20 or 30 book collectors in the Tang, but private collections only became more common during the Song. The first extant private library catalog dates from ca. 1151.[5]

More than 500 private libraries flourished in the Qing, both of individual book collectors and academies.[6] Two Qing guides

[3] All extant catalogs of *shuyuan* and much other information will be found in *Zhongguo shuyuan cidian* 中國書院辭典 (A dictionary of academies in China), Ji Xiaofeng 季嘯鳳, ed. in chief, Zhejiang jiaoyu, 1996. Contains brief articles on over 1,500 Shuyuan by province; biographies of people connected with them; and primary and secondary sources. A listing in appendix contains the names of 7,300 known *shuyuan* and their founders. There is a *pinyin* index.

[4] Timothy Brook, "Edifying Knowledge: the Building of School Libraries in Ming China," *LIC* 17.1: 93–119 (1996)

[5] Chao Gongwu 晁公武 (ca. 1105–80), *Junzhai dushu zhi* 郡齋讀書志 (Record of reading books at the commandery study), *Sibu congkan*, 3rd series. Contains annotations on 1,468 books many of which were bought by the author when a magistrate at Rongzhou 榮州 in Sichuan (hence the title of the catalog). On the background to book collecting in the Song, see Cherniack (1994) and Thomas H. C. Lee, "Books and Bookworms in Song China: Book Collection and the Appreciation of Books, *JSY* 25: 193–218 (1995).

[6] Cheuk-woon Taam (Tan Zhuoyuan 譚卓垣), *The Development of Chinese Libraries under the Ch'ing Dynasty, 1644–1911*, Shanghai: Shangwu, 1935; rpnt., CMC, 1977; Nancy Lee Swann, "Seven Intimate Library Owners," *HJAS* 1: 363–90 (1936) discusses the private libraries of Hangzhou in the eighteenth century. Wu Han 吳晗, *Jiang-Zhe cangshujia shilüe* 江浙藏書家史略 (Brief history of the book collectors of Jiangsu and Zhejiang), Zhonghua, 1981, gives the biographies of 900 book collectors active from earliest times to 1911 in Jiangsu and Zhejiang; Wang Shaozeng 王紹曾, *Shandong cangshujia shilüe* 山東藏書家史略 (Brief history of the book collectors of Shandong), Shandong daxue, 1992, does the same for

Footnote continued on next page

for book collectors have been translated into English by Achilles Fang (1910–95).[7]

For excerpts from the prefaces, colophons, and postfaces of both public and private book catalogs from the Han to the Qing, as well as tables of contents and the comments of the *Siku zongmu* editors on each catalog, see *Zhongguo lidai tushu zhulu wenxuan* 中國歷代圖書著錄文選.[8]

The oldest extant private library building is the Tianyige 天一閣 at Ningbo (1532), which held one of the most famous Ming private collections.[9] The first modern public library (*tushuguan* 圖書館) was the Hunan gongli tushuguan 湖南公立圖書館 (1905).

Just as with archives, book collections, especially imperial libraries, led a precarious existence. In the 2,058 years between Xiang Yu's destruction of the Qin libraries (20.2) and the Taiping Rebellion, the imperial collections were deliberately and totally destroyed by fire on at least 14 occasions (an average of once every 150 years). Each time the buildings were rebuilt and

---

559 collectors from Shandong. *Lidai cangshujia cidian* 歷代藏書家辭典 (Dictionary of historical book collectors), Liang Zhan 梁戰 and Guo Qunyi 郭群一, eds., Shanxi renmin, 1991, contains brief biographies of book collectors, printers, copyists, collators, and woodblock-carvers from all over China. The series *Qingren shumu tiba congkan* 清人書目題跋叢刊 (Qing book catalog annotations), 10 vols., Zhonghua, 1990–93, reprints the most famous Qing book catalogs. *Zhongguo mulu xuejia cidian* 中國目錄學家辭典 (Dictionary of Chinese bibliographers), Shen Chang 申暢 et al., comps., Henan renmin, 1988, contains biographies and details of the contributions of 2,200 bibliographers up to 1949.

   [7] "Bookman's Decalogue (Ts'ang-shu shih-yüeh 藏書十約) Yeh Tê-hui 葉德輝 (1864–1927)," Achilles Fang, tr., HJAS 13: 132–73 (1950); also "Bookman's Manual," *HJAS* 14: 215–60 (1951), a translation of Sun Congtian 孫從添 (1702–22), *Cangshu jiyao*, Gudian wenxue, 1957.

   [8] *Zhongguo lidai tushu zhulu wenxuan* (Selection from historical records of Chinese book catalogs), Yuan Yongqiu 袁咏秋 and Zeng Jiguang 曾季光, comps., Beijing daxue, 1995. This contains the prefaces of the main public and private library catalogs from the Qin to the Qing, plus in many cases, their tables of contents.

   [9] *Tianyige shumu* 新編天一閣書目 (Newly edited *Tianyige* catalogs), Li Zhaoxiang 李肇翔, ed. in chief, Zhonghua, 1996.

the collections replenished, an interesting illustration of the fact that Chinese imperial institutions and culture did not simply continue, but had to be periodically reconstituted. Quite apart from deliberate acts of destruction, there were the deprivations brought about by insects, floods and accidental fires, and the losses due to neglect. For private collectors, there was the increasingly likelihood that their books would be destroyed for political reasons (9.8.4).

During the nineteenth century, the dispersal and destruction of Chinese printed books and manuscripts continued on a massive scale; the Taipings simply followed a well-established tradition, burning libraries, especially in Jiangsu and Zhejiang, where most of the main private collections were located. Foreign troops joined in the destruction and looting on several occasions (notably during the Anglo-French expedition in 1860 and the Boxer uprising in 1900). In the first half of the twentieth century, the destruction and dispersal continued. Thousands of the manuscripts, bamboo strips, and oracle bones newly discovered at Dunhuang, Anyang and elsewhere were sold for export. Famous collections were requisitioned or sold. Connoisseurs would buy books at Beijing's traditional book and antiques street, Liulichang 琉璃廠, not by the title, or even by the shelf, but by the wall to be dispatched directly to the shipping agent by trucks. Many Japanese and Western individuals and institutes built up their collections during these chaotic years. The last major movement of books took place in late 1948 and early 1949 when the Guomindang shipped to Taibei large numbers of rare books (plus about seven percent of the Qing central archives, 50.1.2).

9.3   Classification

Bibliography is the most important requirement for reading books. Only if bibliography is understood can you pursue your studies; if you don't understand it, you will not be able to find your way (目錄之學學中第一緊要事必從此問涂方能得其門而入), Wang Mingsheng 王鳴盛, *Shiqishi shangque* 十七史商榷 (A critical study of the *Seventeen Standard Histories*).

How knowledge was categorized is a good indicator of what was considered important and how Chinese priorities differed from our own. Also, to find sources produced or preserved in the old historical tradition it is, of course, necessary to know where a given type of source would be classified.

The Confucian *Six Classics* dealt with six broadly separate categories: philosophy (*Yi* 易, *Book of Changes*); government (*Shu* 書, *Documents*); literature (*Shi* 詩, *Odes*); society (*Li* 禮, *Rites*); history (*Chunqiu* 春秋, *Spring and Autumn Annals*); and the arts (*Yue* 樂, *Book of Music*).

The first bibliographic classification (known as the *Qilüe* 七略, Seven epitomes) was devised by Liu Xiang 劉向 (ca. 77–6 BC) as an annotated catalog for the imperial library at the end of the Former Han. It was modified by his son Liu Xin 劉歆 (d. AD 23). Apart from a general summary, they used six categories: Classics, philosophy, poetry, military writers, mathematics and sciences (including astronomy, the calendar and divination), and medicine (including the arts of the bedchamber). The *Qilüe* itself has not survived, but it was used as the basis of the "Yiwenzhi 藝文志" in the *Hanshu* (9.4).[10] A number of imperial librarians in the following centuries began to use a fourfold division, classifying all forms of literature into *sibu* 四部 (four branches), namely Classics (*jing* 經), History (*shi* 史), Philosophers (*zi* 子) and Belles-lettres (*ji* 集). This became the norm at the beginning of the Tang with the compilation of the dynastic catalog in the Standard History of the Sui.[11] During the Tang, the four branches were stored in four separate palace depositories (*siku* 四庫), so *siku* was used interchangeably with *sibu*. Color coding was used to distinguish the branches: yellow for Classics (the color symbolizing the center and the emperor); white for History; purple (*zi* 紫) for Philosophy; red for Belles-lettres. Tags were used for silk books and scrolls; later, colored

---

[10] In general, private libraries followed the same classification as that in the imperial catalogs. The different early bibliographic classifications are outlined in J.-P. Drège, *Les Bibliothèques en Chine* (1991).

[11] *Suishu jingjizhi* 隋書經籍志, 629–36, Shangwu, 1955–57.

covers or title slips were used for printed books. The phrase *siku quanshu* 四庫全書, or *siku* for short, was also used to mean "all books." In the Qing, it was taken as the title of the most famous of China's imperial library collections, the *Siku quanshu* (imperial library or complete library in four branches of literature, 9.5). In broad outline, these are the classifications still used in library catalogs of old Chinese books today. The first and fourth of the four branches of the *Siku quanshu* (Classics and Belles-lettres) present few difficulties as to their contents (chaps. 19 and 30). The subcategories in the history branch are shown in Table 12 (numbers in brackets after each entry in the lefthand column refer to chapter and section numbers in the manual).

Table 12: The History Branch in the Siku *Classification*

Standard Histories (chap. 22)	*zhengshi* 正史
Annals (21)	*biannian* 編年
Topically arranged histories (23)	*jishibenmo* 紀事本末
Unofficial histories (20.5)	*bieshi* 別史
Miscellaneous histories (24)	*zashi* 雜史
Edicts and memorials (25.1–2)	*zhaoling zouyi* 詔令奏議
Biographical works (3.7–8)	*zhuanji* 傳記
Historical excerpts (20.5)	*shichao* 史抄
Contemporary records (20.5)	*zaiji* 載記
Regulation of time (5, 6 and 35.1.1)	*shiling* 時令
Geography (4 and 41)	*dili* 地理
Government offices (22.3)	*zhiguan* 職官
Government Institutions (26)	*zhengshu* 政書
Bibliography; epigraphy (9 and 17)	*mulu* 目錄
Historiography (20.4)	*shiping* 史評

Within the History branch many different classification systems were used in different periods. In broad outline, however, most were similar to that employed by the *Siku* editors. The various changes in the subcategories are traced in *Zhongguo shibu mulu xue* 中國史部目錄學 (A study of the classifications of the History branch), Zheng Hesheng 鄭鶴聲, Shangwu, 1930; rev. ed., 1956.

The third branch of the *Siku*, Philosophers, also contains many works essential to the historian (Table 13; numbers in brackets after each entry in the lefthand column refer to chapter and section numbers in the manual).

Table 13: The Philosophers' Branch in the Siku *Classification*

Confucian writers (chaps. 19; 32)	*rujia* 儒家
Military experts (28)	*bingjia* 兵家
Legal writers (19, 27 and 32)	*fajia* 法家
Writers on agriculture (35)	*nongjia* 農家
Writers on medicine (36)	*yijia* 醫家
Astronomy and math (5, 37)	*tianwen suanfa* 天文算法
Mantic arts (36, 37)	*shushu* 術數
The fine arts (38)	*yishu* 藝術
Manuals, e.g., on cooking (35.2)	*pulu* 譜錄
Miscellaneous writers (32)	*zajia* 雜家
Encyclopaedias (29)	*leishu* 類書
Essays and misc. works (34.3)	*xiaoshuo* 小説
Buddhists (33.5)	*shijia* 釋家
Daoists (33.4)	*daojia* 道家

Note that it is unwise to assume that works will necessarily be where you would expect to find them. Take the example of agriculture. Many books classified under Agriculture (sub-branch four of Philosophy) cannot be considered agricultural works, while conversely a great many books connected with agriculture are found in other branches, as well as in other sub-branches of Philosophy (e.g., *pulu* 譜錄).

9.4 Dynastic Bibliographies

The simplest way to find what books were circulating in different periods is to check through one of the many library catalogs that have survived. Those of the imperial library were usually printed with, or as a supplement to, the Standard Histories as *yiwenzhi* 藝文志 or *jingjizhi* 經籍志 (dynastic bibliographies). Catalogs of private collections were also printed.

H-Y Index 10 is an index to the contents of seven dynastic bibliographies, eight supplements, four banned book lists, and one private library catalog shown in Table 14.[12]

Table 14: Dynastic Bibliographies

Title	Period Compiled	No. of titles
1. *Hanshu* 漢書 "Yiwenzhi 藝文志"	Han	596
2. *Hou Hanshu* 後漢書 "Yiwenzhi 藝文志"	Qing	
3. *Sanguo* 三國 "Yiwenzhi" 藝文志	Qing	
4. *Bu Jinshu* 補晉書 "Yiwenzhi 藝文志"	Qing	
5. *Suishu* 隋書 "Jingjizhi 經籍志"	Tang	6,520
6. *Jiu Tangshu* 舊唐書 "Jingjizhi 經籍志"	Later Jin	3,062
7. *Xin Tangshu* 新唐書 "Yiwenzhi 藝文志"	Song	3,277
8. *Bu Wudaishi* 補五代史 "Yiwenzhi 藝文志"	Qing	
9. *Songshi* 宋史 "Yiwenzhi 藝文志"	Yuan	9,819
10. *Songshi* 宋史 "Yiwenzhibu fubian 藝文志補附編"	Qing	
11. *Bu Liao Jin Yuan* 補遼金元 "Yiwenzhi 藝文志"	Qing	
12. *Bu sanshi* 補三史 "Yiwenzhi 藝文志"	Qing	
13. *Bu Yuanshi* 補元史 "Yiwenzhi 藝文志"	Qing	
14. *Mingshi* 明史 "Yiwenzhi 藝文志"	Qing	
15. *Jinshu zongmu* 禁書總目	Qing	
16. *Quanhui shumu* 全毀書目	Qing	
17. *Chouhui shumu* 抽毀書目	Qing	
18. *Wei'ai shumu* 違礙書目	Qing	
19. *Zhengfang Mingji yishumu* 徵訪明季遺書目	Rep.	
20. *Qingshigao* 清史稿 "Yiwenzhi 藝文志"	Rep.	54,880

Note: Items 15–18 are lists of forbidden books (see section 7.2.4). They were compiled during the Qing and reprinted in *Sibu congkan*, 1st series, vol. 42, Shangwu, 1937; rpnt., Zhonghua, 1985.

The count for item 20 is taken from *Qingshi gao yiwenzhi shiyi* 清史稿藝文志拾遺 (see below under *Recent Editions and Studies*).

---

[12] *Yiwenzhi ershi zhong zonghe yinde* 藝文志二十種綜合引得 (Combined indices to twenty dynastic bibliographies), *H-Y Index* 10, 4 vols., Beiping, 1933.

Items one and five of Table 14 give the nearest approximation to a complete summary of the books available at a particular time, i.e., the end of the Former Han and the beginning of the Tang. Item six is the first extant catalog to be arranged in strict four-branch categories. Since it was intended to show the splendor of the Kaiyuan period (713-741), no later works were included.

During the 1950s the Shangwu Press brought out a uniform edition of the *yiwenzhi* with Qing supplements printed with each one.[13] This edition has the added advantage of being indexed. The most complete collection of dynastic bibliographies and supplements can be found in the six volumes of corrections and additions to the monographs and tables in the Standard Histories published with the Kaiming shudian edition of the *Twenty-five Histories* (22.1), under the title *Ershiwushi bubian* 二十五史補編.[14]

Several of the *Shitong* 十通 (26.2) contain important bibliographies, for example "Yiwenlüe 藝文略" in Zheng Qiao 鄭樵, *Tongzhi* 通志, and the "Jingji kao 經籍考" in Ma Duanlin 馬端臨, *Wenxian tongkao* 文獻通考.[15]

Recent Editions and Studies

Hanshu yiwenzhi tongshi 漢書藝文志通釋 (Comprehensive studies of the *Hanshu* dynastic bibliography), Zhang Shunhui 張舜徽, Hubei jiaoyu, 1990.

Zuisho keisekishi shôkô 隋書經籍志詳考 (Detailed investigations of the *Suishu* dynastic bibliography), Kôzen Hiroshi 興膳宏 and Kawai Kôzô 川合康三, ed., Kyûko, 1995. Adds biographical notes on the authors and bibliographical comments to their works; also supplements the original by filling in contemporary works on Buddhism

---

[13] *Shishi yiwen jingjizhi* 十史藝文經籍志 (Dynastic bibliographies in 10 Standard Histories), Shangwu, 1955-9; rpnt., Shijie, 1963. Arrangement is by four-corner index. Each volume has an author/title index.
[14] *Ershiwushi bubian* (Supplements to the twenty-five histories), 6 vols., Shanghai, 1936–37; rpnt., 6 vols., Zhonghua, 1955; 1986.
[15] *Wenxian tongkao Jingji kao* 文獻通考經籍考 (The "Study of Bibliography" in *Wenxian tongkao*), 2 vols., Huadong shifan daxue, 1985.

and Daoism. Indexes of authors and titles. Based on the Zhonghua punctuated edition.

Qingshi gao yiwenzhi shiyi 清史稿藝文志拾遺 (Supplement to the dynastic bibliography of the *Qingshi gao*), Wang Shaozeng 王紹曾, vol. 1 (*shi* 史, *zi* 子), Zhonghua, 1997; vol. 2 (*jing* 經, *ji* 集); vol. 3 (index), forthcoming. The count is 20,071 titles in *Qingshi gao yiwenzhi ji bubian* 清史稿藝文志及補編 (The dynastic bibliography of the *Qingshi gao* with additions), Wu Zuocheng 武作成, 2 vols., Zhonghua, 1982. Vol. 2 is a four-corner index with a stroke-count finding index.

The *Siku jingji tiyao suoyin* 四庫經籍提要索引 Indexes titles (vol. 1) and authors (vol. 2) of the bibliographies in four of the *Shitong*, in the *Siku zongmu* itself and in four of its continuations and supplements. Arrangement is by stroke count. There are author/title stroke-count indexes.[16] These bibliographies are also fully indexed in a four-corner index (vol. 21 of the original Shangwu edition of the *Shitong*, 1937).

Many dynastic bibliographies and library catalogs were reprinted in *Shumu congbian* 書目叢編, 1st series, Guangwen, 1967.

9.5   *The Imperial Catalog*

Both in China and in Japan there is a long tradition of annotated library catalogs, which in China began at least in the Han and reached its height many centuries later with the carefully annotated catalog of the imperial library, the *Siku quanshu zongmu tiyao* 四庫全書總目提要 (*Siku zongmu* for short).

In 1771, at the command of the emperor, more than 350 eminent scholars began the work of collecting a definitive imperial library. They reviewed and annotated over 10,000 books

---

[16] *Siku jingji tiyao suoyin* (Index to the *Siku zongmu* and other bibliographies), 2 vols., Guoli zhongyang tushuguan, comp., and published, 1994. The works indexed are the *Jingjizhi* of the *Wenxian tongkao*, the *Xuwenxiantongkao*, the *Qingchao wenxian tongkao*, and of the *Qingchao xuwenxian tongkao* (see Table 25, chap. 26 on these works); *Siku zongmu*; *Xuxiu Siku quanshu tiyao*; *Siku zongmu buzheng*; *Siku zongmu bianzheng*; and the *Siku weishou shumu tiyao*.

and manuscripts from imperial collections, from collections all over the empire, and from the *Yongle dadian* 永樂大典 (the previously largest collection compiled for an emperor; see section 29). Some 3,000 works judged to be anti-Manchu were destroyed (the Qing dynasty saw more literary purges, more people imprisoned, and more books proscribed and burned than any other dynasty in Chinese history, a striking contrast with the contemporaneous Enlightenment going on in Europe). From the remaining 10,585 titles, 3,461 were selected for the imperial library, the *Siku quanshu* 四庫全書. All 2.3 million pages were transcribed by hand. The copyists (of whom there were 3,826) were not paid in cash but rewarded with official posts after they had transcribed a given number of words within a set time. Four copies were made for the use of the emperor in his palaces in the Zijincheng 紫禁城 (Forbidden City), the Yuanming yuan 圓明園 (Old Summer Palace), the secondary capital of Shengjing 盛京 (Shenyang 沈陽) and the summer retreat at Rehe 熱和 (Chengde 承德). The books were stored in specially constructed library buildings modeled after the Tianyige in Ningbo. In 1782, another three copies were ordered for deposit in Hangzhou, Zhenjiang, and Yangzhou. Unlike the four sets in the North, the emperor commanded that those in the South should be open to the public. Copies of the imperially commissioned encyclopaedia, the *Gujin tushu jicheng* 古今圖書集成 (29.3), were deposited in each of the seven libraries. Two of the *Siku quanshu* library buildings are still standing today, the *Wenyuange* 文淵閣 (Erudite Literature Pavilion, 1776) in the Forbidden City, and the Wenlange 文瀾閣 (Billowing Literature Pavilion, 1783) in Hangzhou, now part of the Zhejiang Provincial Museum. As to the books themselves, four of the seven copies are extant.[17]

---

[17] The copies of the *Siku quanshu* in the temples at Zhenjiang and Yangzhou were destroyed during the Taiping Rebellion. The copy in the Yuanming Yuan was largely burned by British troops during the Anglo-French attack on Beijing in 1860 although some volumes have since showed up in the sale rooms. The four remaining copies are in the Beitu

Footnote continued on next page

The master copy (*Wenyuange*) was photolithographically printed in 1,500 volumes in the 1980s.[18] It is now also available in a number of CD-ROM editions. Some of these have been entered from the originals using OCRs; others have been entered in modern type by hand. The former are known as *tuxingban* 圖形版. They are cheaper and less flexible to use; the latter are called *quanwenban* 全文版 and are preferrable.

All the titles in the works not included in the library, but noted in the catalog (*cunmu* 存目) are reprinted from the best available editions in reduced-size in the photo-facsimile collection, *Siku quanshu cunmu congshu* 四庫全書存目叢書. Finally, in order to complete the *Siku quanshu*, not only all those titles left out, but also newly discovered, or written between the eighteenth century and 1911, are being printed in the *Xuxiu Siku quanshu* 續修四庫全書 (Collectanea of works mentioned

---

(the Rehe copy), the Gansu Provincial Library (the Shenyang palace copy which was briefly captured by the Soviet Army in 1945), the Zhejiang Provincial Library (Hangzhou), and the Palace Museum, Taibei. It is this last copy, that of the Wenyuan ge 文淵閣, the first to be transcribed and the best preserved, which has been printed in photo-facsimile, see next note. For a detailed study of the compilation of the *Siku* and the political and scholarly background, see R. Kent Guy, *The Emperor's Four Treasuries: Scholars and the State in the Late Ch'ien-lung Era*, Council on East Asian Studies, Harvard University, 1987. See also *Zuanxiu Siku quanshu dang'an* 纂修四庫全書檔案 (Archives on the editing of the *Siku quanshu*), 10 vols., Yishiguan, eds., Shanghai guji, 1997.

[18] *Yingyin Wenyuange Siku quanshu* 影印文淵閣四庫全書 (Photofacsimile reprint of the Wenyuan Pavilion copy of the *Siku quanshu*), Taibei: Shangwu, 1983–86. Shanghai guji reprinted this in a reduced-size ed., 1,500 vols., 1987. There is a four-corner author/title index. Note also *Wenyuange siku quanshu shuming ji zhuzhe xingming suoyin* 文淵閣四庫全書書名及著者姓名索引 (Index to titles and authors' names in the Wenyuange *Siku quanshu*), Taibei: Shangwu, 1986; *Siku quanshu wenji pianmu fenlei suoyin* 四庫全書文集篇目分類索引 (Index to the entries on *wenji* by category), 5 vols., Taibei: Shangwu, 1989; *Siku quanshu zhuanji ziliao suoyin* 四庫全書傳記資料索引 (Index to biographical materials in the *Siku quanshu*), 2 vols., Taibei: Shangwu, 1991, with a third vol. index to *zihao* 字號, Taibei: Shangwu, 1990.

in the catalog but not included in the *Siku quanshu*), 1,200 vols., Qi-Lu, 1994–).

The editors of the *Siku quanshu*, under the chief editorship of Ji Yun 紀昀 (1724–1805), compiled an annotated catalog of all 3,461 books included in the library (*cunshu* 存書), together with brief notes on the 6,793 works not included (*cunmu* 存目). Work began in 1773. The first draft was ready by 1781, and the final draft was completed in 1798. The full title of the catalog is *Qinding Siku quanshu zongmu tiyao* 欽定四庫全書總目提要.[19] An entire industry of additions, comments and corrections to the *Siku zongmu* began almost as soon as it was printed. These have now been incorporated into the revised Zhonghua edition (1997), which makes it the most authoritative one. It is also by far the most convenient to use because it is set in a clear type, is fully punctuated, and has an author/title index with a *pinyin* first-character finding index.[20] Ji Yun 紀昀 also edited a simplified version, the *Siku quanshu jianming mulu* 四庫全書簡明目錄. The *Jianming mulu* includes brief sum-

---

[19] *Qinding Siku quanshu zongmu tiyao* or *Siku quanshu zongmu* 四庫全書總目 (Annotated catalog of the imperial library by command), 200 *zhuan*, Ji Yun, 1781; palace edition (*dianben* 殿本), 1789; Zhejiang edition, 1795; Canton edition, 1868; 2 vols., Zhonghua, 1965 (based on the Zhejiang edition); 5th prnt., 1995. In his preface to *H-Y Index* 7 (an author/title index to the *Siku zongmu*, 2 vols., Beiping, 1932), the editor in chief of the *H-Y Index* series, William Hung (Hong Ye 洪業), examines the editing and compilation of the *Siku quanshu zongmu tiyao*; see "Preface to an Index to *Ssu-k'u ch'üan-shu tsung-mu* and *Wei-shou shu-mu*," *HJAS* 4: 47–58 (1939).

[20] *Siku quanshu zongmu tiyao, zhengli ben* 整理本, rearranged ed., Lu Guangming 盧光明 et al., eds., 2 vols., Zhonghua, 1997 (based on the palace edition). This edition is fully punctuated and has an author/title index (with a *pinyin* and four-corner finding index) at the end of vol. 2. It incorporates the most important scholarship on the *Siku zongmu*, especially the corrections and additions of Yu Jiaxi 余嘉錫 (1883–1955), Hu Yujin 胡玉縉 (d. 1940) and Wang Xinfu 王欣夫, Li Yumin 李裕民, Cui Fuzhang 崔富章. Editions and present whereabouts of over 90 percent of the *cunmu* titles are indicated. Simplified characters are used except in places that could cause ambiguity.

maries of the annotations on the 3,461 works copied into the
Siku quanshu.[21]

The *Siku zongmu* is the largest book catalog to have been
compiled in traditional China. It is also the most important catalog, (1) because of the high quality of the annotations, which
give information on the nature and style of each work, including its table of contents in whole or in part, a brief biographical
sketch of the author (on first appearance), and an evaluation,
and (2) because it is the most comprehensive by far. Nevertheless, it is limited by the political constraints on the compilers of
the *Siku quanshu* who were obliged to leave out many works,
for example, of all those writers suspected of retaining sympathies with the Ming. Unless you have a special reason for using
the *Siku zongmu*, your first reference should be the *Siku da
cidian* (9.7).

9.6 Congshu 叢書

After printing became common in the Song, Chinese works often have been preserved in *congshu* 叢書. These are collections
of independent works published together to prevent their loss
or to gain them wider circulation. Publishers today in Europe
and America would call a *congshu* a reprint series or a library.
The phrase is often translated as *collectanea*.

There are over 2,000 *congshu*, containing a total of about
40,000 individual works. The indispensable index to these is the
Zhongguo congshu zonglu 中國叢書綜錄, which covers holdings
in 41 major Chinese libraries as of the first half of the 1950s. At

---

[21] *Siku quanshu jianming mulu* (Simplified annotated catalog of the
imperial library), Hangzhou, 1782; 2 vols., Shanghai guji, 1985, 1996.
There is a four-corner author/title index with stroke-count finding index.
For information on different editions of the works in the *Jianming mulu*,
use the bibliographic notes largely prepared by Shao Yichen 邵懿辰
(1810–61), *Zengding Siku quanshu jianming mulu biaozhu* 增訂四庫全書
簡明目錄標注 (Marginal notes to the simplified annotated catalog of the
imperial library), posthumously published in 1911; rev. and enlarged ed.,
Shanghai, 1959. There is a four-corner and stroke-count index.

an early stage of tracing a work, you should consult this catalog.[22] Vol. 1 (*zongmu* 總目) lists *congshu* by title. Arrangement
is by the four traditional bibliographic categories (*sibu* 四部).
The titles of individual works contained in each *congshu* are
shown. Altogether 2,086 *congshu* are listed in this way. An appendix shows which of the 41 libraries holds each of the *congshu* (including over 700 alternative editions). Vol. 2 (*zimu* 子目)
is arranged by the title of the 38,891 individual works contained in the *congshu*. Bibliographic details are given. Because
many titles appear in several *congshu* the total number of entries comes to about 70,000. Arrangement is by the four
branches further divided into subcategories based on those in
the *Siku quanshu*. Vol. 3 contains a 4-corner title index and
author index to vol. 2 (it also contains a *pinyin* and stroke-
count finding index). Note that the *Daozang* 道藏 is included
(1,500 works; see 33.4), but not the Buddhist Canon, *Da zangjing* 大藏經 (3,500 works; see 33.5).

The *Zhongguo congshu zonglu* has been supplemented and
corrected by a number of later works:

Zhongguo congshu mulu ji zimu suoyin huibian 中國叢書目錄及子目索引
匯編, Nanjing daxue tushuguan and Nanjing daxue lishixi ziliao shi,
comps., Nanjing daxue, 1982. This lists the contents of 977 traditional *congshu* omitted from the *Congshu zonglu*. There is a *congshu*
title index and an index to the titles of the individual works contained in each *congshu*. Unlike the *Zhongguo congshu zonglu*, it lacks a
table of contents.

Zhongguo congshu zonglu buzheng 中國叢書綜錄補正 (Corrections to the
Zhongguo congshu zonglu), Yang Haiqing 陽海清 and Jiang Xiaoda 蔣
校達, comps., Jiangsu guangling, 1984. This not only makes corrections to the *Congshu zonglu*, but also gives lists of reprints of *congshu*
between 1960 and 1982 as well as a useful index of alternative titles of
congshu.

---

[22] *Zhongguo congshu zonglu* (Bibliography of Chinese collectanea),
Shanghai Municipal Library, comp., 3 vols., Shanghai guji, 1959–62; reprinted with corrections, 1982–83; reduced-size ed., but clear print on
good quality paper, 1986; rpnt., 1993. The entire work comes to 2,938
double-column and 791 triple-column, pages.

Taiwan ge tushuguan xiancun congshu zimu suoyin 臺灣各圖書館現存叢
書子目索引 (Author/title index to *congshu* in Taiwan libraries),
Wang Baoxian 王寶先 comp., 3 vols., part 1, 2 vols., title index; part
2, author index, CMC, 1975–77. This is an index to the works included in over 1,500 *congshu* held by 10 libraries in Taiwan. Arrangement is by total stroke-count.

Chûgoku sôsho sôroku mishû Nichizô shomokukô 中國叢書總錄未收日藏
書目稿, Li Ruiqing 李鋭清, comp., Jimbun, 1995. Lists 852 titles in
Japanese collections not included in the *Congshu zonglu*.[23]

During the 1920s and 1930s many original sources and historical works were collected together and published in huge *cong-*
shu. The quickest way of finding the titles and authors of any
such series is to consult *Zhongguo congshu zonglu*, which lists
the titles of the *Sibu congkan*, for example, on pp. 285–97. Each
of the *congshu* listed below has its own annotated catalog:

Sibu congkan 四部叢刊. Large *congshu* of the main works of the Chinese
scholarly tradition photolithographed from Song, Yuan, Ming, and
early Qing editions issued in three series over a seventeen-year period
(1919–36). Arrangement, as the title suggests, is by the four branches,
jing, shi, zi and *ji*. In its advertisements, the publisher, Shangwu, emphasized that it had managed to avoid typesetting errors (found in
next item) by using photolithography. The *bona* 百衲 edition of the
Standard Histories (22.2) was included as a supplement. A separate
annotated catalog was issued for the first series thereafter the notes
were published after each title.[24]

Sibu beiyao 四部備要. Contains many of the same titles as in *Sibu cong-*
kan, but Zhonghua turned around its rival's, Shangwu's, claims, and
advertised that the ancestor of its owner, Lufei Chi 陸費墀, had been
chief collator of the *Siku quanshu*. The Zhonghua editors had carried

---

[23] For tracing original *congshu* in Japan, use the *Kanseki sôsho shozai*
mokuroku 漢籍叢書所在目錄 (Catalog of whereabouts of Chinese *collec-*
tanea), Tôyô bunko, 1965. It lists the whereabouts and contents of 1,990
congshu in seven Japanese collections.

[24] *Sibu congkan* (The four branches of literature collection), 3 series
(*chubian* 初編, 1919–22; rpnt., 1929; *xubian* 續編, 1934; and *sanbian* 三
編, 1936), containing 504 titles in 3,112 *ce*, Shangwu, 1919–36. See Karl
Lo, *A Guide to the Ssu-pu Ts'ung-k'an*, Univ. of Kansas Press, 1965; and
review by Elling O. Eide, *HJAS* 27: 266–286 (1967).

on this glorious family tradition and corrected the errors in old editions before the typesetting (using the characteristic "imitation Song-style type face" [*Fang-Songti* 仿宋體]). The publisher offered purchasers one dollar for every wrong character they could spot. Zhonghua had to pay out thousands of dollars, but was able to publish a second edition in 100 Western-style volumes with plenty of corrections in 1937. It is this edition that Zhonghua continues to re-issue to this day.[25]

Congshu jicheng 叢書集成. Over 4,100 titles taken from 100 previous *congshu*. The editors deliberately included works left out of the *Sibu congkan* and *Sibu beiyao*. The original intention was to print 4,000 volumes numbered 1 to 4,000. Because of the outbreak of the war, only 3,467 volumes were published. The series is mainly in movable type, and as a result there are many typesetting errors. The complete series of over 4,100 titles has been reprinted.[26] The *Baibu congshu jicheng* 百部叢書集成 is a re-creation of the *Congshu jicheng*, 1st series, Yiwen yinshuguan, 1965–70. It contains 4,144 titles, all reproduced from the original *congshu* and done in traditional format. The same publisher also put out *Congshu jicheng xubian*, 1970–71. It contains 774 titles in 1557 vols. in 176 cases.

Siku quanshu zhenben chuji 四庫全書珍本初集 (First collection of rare editions in four branches), Shangwu, 1934–5; 231 rare editions in 1,960 *ce*.

Wanyou wenku 萬有文庫, Shangwu, 2 collections, 1935–37. Includes more than 1,000 titles in 4,340 *ce*. The *Shitong* 十通 was printed in 20

---

[25] *Sibu beiyao* (Essentials of the four branches of literature), 336 titles in 2,500 *ce*, Zhonghua, 1920–33; corrected edition in 100 Western-style vols., 1935; repr., Taibei: Zhonghua, 1966–75; Zhonghua, 1990. *Sibu beiyao shumu tiyao* 四部備要書目提要 (Annotated catalog to the *Sibu beiyao*), Zhonghua, 1936; William C. Ju, *A Guide to the Ssu-pu pei-yao*, Taibei, 1971, is an index to the Taibei reprint giving author, title and subject.

[26] *Congshu jicheng chubian* (Collected collectanea, first series), 3,467 vols., Shangwu, 1935–7; Zhonghua, 1983; 1996 (including those titles not included in the original first series). *Congshu jicheng chubian mulu* 叢書集成初編目錄 (Index to the first series of the Collected collectanea), Shangwu, 1935; 1983. This in fact indexes the projected 4,107 titles. Also reprinted under the title *Congshu jicheng xinbian*, 129 vols., Xinwenfeng, 1986. A separate volume contains a table of contents arranged by modern categories as well as author/title indexes.

Western-style volumes with a new index (volume 21) and was included in the reference books attached to the second series.

Guoxue jiben congshu 國學基本叢書 (Basic sinological series), 400 titles, Shangwu, 1929–41, 100 titles reprinted during the 1950s. Typeset and punctuated editions of titles considered essential for the study of Chinese culture.

Despite the typesetting errors in items two and three above, works in these series are handy to use and were usually taken from good annotated editions. The advice used to be given to use and quote from works in major *congshu* series, since these are readily accessible. Nevertheless, there are now so many excellent editions of individual works, punctuated, annotated, and with "translations" into Modern Chinese, that the advice is no longer as forceful as when this was not the case.

9.7 Modern Annotated Bibliographies

At the end of the Qing and in the early days of the Republic, several scholars proposed updating and enlarging the *Siku zongmu* by including works deliberately left out for political reasons and by adding in all the books printed in the intervening years. Eventually, the Japanese Committee for Oriental Culture (Tôhô bunka jimu iinkai 東方文化事務委員會) decided to use part of the Boxer Indemnity Funds to edit a continuation to the *Siku zongmu* in its institute, the Beiping Renwen kexue yanjiusuo 人文科學研究所. Hashikawa Tokiô 橋川時雄 (1895–1982), the dean of the Institute, was put in charge of the project on the Japanese side, while the president of the Renwen and author of the *New History of the Yuan*, Ke Shaomin 柯劭忞 (1850–1933), took the lead on the Chinese side. Altogether, some 71 Chinese scholars participated in the project, including many of the leading historians, gazetteer compilers, and bibliophiles of the day.[27] The work started in

[27] In addition to Ke Shaomin, the group included other senior Chinese historians and bibliophiles such as Wang Shunan 王樹楠 (1851–1936), Luo Zhenyu 羅振玉 (1866–1940), Hu Yujin 胡玉縉 (d. 1940), and

Footnote continued on next page

1928 with the drawing up a list of those books left out of the *Siku quanshu* as well as those written between 1750 and 1911. The list of 32,000 titles was agreed upon by 1931. During the next three years, 32,960 abstracts were drafted (a few more titles had been added to the list). Next the slow work of checking and editing the drafts began. By 1940, they had completed 20,319.[28] The abstracts covered works not included in the *Siku zongmu*, especially by Ming and early Qing authors (the *Siku quanshu* did not include the works of contemporaries), Buddhist and Daoist works, as well as books, including 2,000 gazetteers, written between 1750 and 1911. The work of typing and mimeographing the abstracts began. Since the funds were low, only 10,080 were ready by the end of the war. The bulky draft was sent to the Tôhô bunka gakuin kenkyûjo in Kyoto.[29] The Renwen mimeograph was eventually published 30 years later in Taibei in 13 volumes with a total of 8,000 pages.[30]

The original notes and abstracts in Beijing, along with the Renwen library, were inherited in 1949 by the Chinese Academy of Sciences, which began putting them in order in 1983. In 1993 the notes on the works in the first of the four branches, Classics, was published. It includes annotations on 1,928 works from the Classics branch not included in the *Siku zongmu*, but

---

Yu Shaosong 余紹宋 (1883–1949), as well as recently graduated students such as Xiang Da 向達 (1900–1966), Xie Guozhen 謝國楨 (1901–82), Wang Zhongmin 王重民 (1903–75), Luo Fuyi 羅福頤 (1905–) and Tan Qixiang 譚其驤 (1911–91), many of whom later became well-known scholars.

[28] The breakdown was Classics: 3,878 titles; History: 8,363 titles; Philosophy: 5,082; and Belles-lettres: 2,996.

[29] Established in 1939, this was the forerunner of Kyoto University's Jimbun kagaku kenkyûjo; whose present name was adopted in 1949.

[30] *Xuxiu Siku quanshu zongmu tiyao* 續修四庫全書總目提要 (Revised continuation of the annotated catalog of the imperial library), Wang Yunwu 王雲五, ed. in chief, 13 vols., Taibei: Shangwu, 1971–72. A draft reprint was issued in 1996: *Xuxiu Siku quanshu zongmu tiyao gaoben* 續修四庫全書總目提要稿本 (Draft revised continuation of the annotated catalog of the imperial library), Library of the Academy of Sciences, eds., 38 vols., Pengyou and Qi-Lu, 1996.

as little more than a reprint of the original notes it was badly received.[31] At about the same time the decision was taken to re-edit the typed Renwen draft and combine it in a single work with a re-edited *Siku zongmu*. One hundred and seventy-five specialists worked on this new annotated bibliography. The title chosen for it was *Siku da cidian*.[32] It is the largest annotated bibliography of Chinese books available. It is also easy to use, and so should be the first reference for finding primary sources from all branches of Chinese literature, for getting a short summary of their contents, and for searching out editions. It covers nearly all the 10,254 works in the *Siku zongmu* plus another 10,070 appearing from mainly the late Ming to the early twentieth century, giving a total of more than 20,000 works. The *Siku da cidian* abstracts include basic information on the author (at first appearance), contents of the book, date of printing, and subsequent editions up to the 1980s. Arrangement is by the same main categories as in the *Siku zongmu*: Classics, History, Philosophers, and Belles-lettres. There is a four-corner title index with *pinyin* and stroke-count finding indexes attached to it.

There are many other modern Chinese encyclopaedic dictionaries of primary sources, arranged in the form of annotated bibliographies according to the four *Sibu* branches, but even the largest cover only a fraction of the works described in the *Siku da cidian*.

Zhongguo dang'an wenxian cidian 中國檔案文獻辭典 contains annotations on 3,985 compilations and publications containing archival materials and excerpts, including modern publications of archival documents from the pre-Qin to 1990.[33]

[31] *Xuxiu Siku quanshu zongmu tiyao: jingbu* 續修四庫全書總目提要經部 (Revised continuation of the annotated catalog of the imperial library: Classics), 2 vols., Zhonghua, 1993.

[32] *Siku da cidian* 四庫大辭典 (Large dictionary of Chinese books), Li Xueqin 李學勤 and Lü Wenyu 呂文郁, eds. in chief, 2 vols., Jilin daxue, 1996.

[33] *Zhongguo dang'an wenxian cidian* (Dictionary of archival literature), Zhu Jinfu 朱金甫, ed. in chief, Zhongguo renshi, 1994.

There are about 1,200 entries from the pre-Qin to 1911, with pride of place going to the Qing (see Box 7, chap. 20, for a fuller description of this useful work).

Japanese Annotated Guides to Primary Sources

There are some thorough Japanese annotated bibliographies of Chinese primary historical sources.[34] The most recent, *Chûgoku shiseki kaidai jiten* 中國史籍解題辞典, was edited by a team of 15 Japanese historians working under the editorship of Yamane Yukio 山根幸夫 and Kanda Nobuo 神田信夫.[35] It contains brief summaries of some 1,650 primary sources (not including *leishu*) from the earliest times to the end of the Qing. It is arranged by titles according to Japanese syllabary, but there is a *pinyin* title index, and the contributors have used *kanji* as much as possible in their notes to help those who do not read Japanese. This replaces all earlier such Japanese works. It is particularly useful for indicating Japanese indexes to Chinese primary sources, but it is neither as large nor as comprehensive as the *Siku da cidian* (which includes abstracts of 5,000 works in the History branch alone); nor are the notes as informative.

Western Annotated Guides to Primary Sources

The only guide to primary sources of all periods in English was the pioneering and unreliable work by Alexander Wylie, *Notes on Chinese Literature*, Kelly and Walsh, 1867; rpnt., Paragon, 1964. There are however excellent guides to the primary sources of particular periods—for example, *ECTBG* or *A Sung Bibliography*. These and others are listed in Part V.

---

[34] Katsura Isoo (Koson) 桂五十郎 (湖村), *Kanseki kaidai* 漢籍解題 (Annotated bibliography of Chinese works), 1ˢᵗ ed., Tokyo, 1905, and many later editions. Of more use are the similar works compiled by historians, of which the best prewar example was the *Kokushi Tôyôshi Seiyôshi shiseki kaidai* 國史東洋史西洋史籍解題 (Annotated bibliography of Japanese, Oriental, and Occidental history), Endô Motoo 遠藤元男 et al., eds., Heibonsha, 1936.

[35] Yamane Yukio and Kanda Nobuo, eds., *Chûgoku shiseki kaidai jiten* (Dictionary of annotations of Chinese historical sources), Ryôgen, 1989.

9.8 Rare, Lost, Recovered, Forged, and Banned Books

9.8.1   Rare Books

Rare books (*shanben* 善本) are normally defined as fine editions printed or copied in the Ming or earlier. For China itself, there is a union catalog listing 60,000 rare books held by 781 public libraries and institutions in China (not including private collections and not including Taiwan): *Zhongguo guji shanben shumu* 中國古籍善本書目.[36]

Wang Zhongmin 王重民, *Zhongguo shanben shu tiyao* 中國善本書提要 (Notes and annotations on Chinese rare books), Shanghai, 1983. Detailed, heavily annotated catalog of over 4,200 rare books inspected by the author, mainly at the Beitu 北圖 (but also at Peking University Library and the Library of Congress). It corrects errors in previous catalogs and indicates which library holds each item. There is an author/title index, and an index of woodblock carvers and of publishers. It has been updated in the same author's *Zhongguo shanben shu tiyao bubian* 中國善本書提要補編, Shumu wenxian, 1991, in which he adds annotations on a further 770 historical and 10 philosophical works.

Guji banben tiji suoyin 古籍版本題記索引 *Guji banben tiji suoyin* (Index to bibliographic notes on rare books), Luo Weiguo 羅偉國 and Hu Ping 胡平, eds., Shanghai shudian, 1991. Index to bibliographic notes on rare books as found in 102 public and private library catalogs, collections of colophons, and reading notes that appeared from the Song to the 1960s. There is a four-corner index with stroke-count and *pinyin* finding indexes.

Taiwan gongcang shanben shumu 臺灣公藏善本書目 (*Taiwan gongcang shanben shumu* (Catalog of rare books in Taiwan public collections), Guoli zhongyang tushuguan, comp., 2 vols., Taibei, 1971. Has stroke-count index. Indicates which library holds each item. Name

---

[36] *Zhongguo guji shanben shumu* (The China union catalog of rare books), Zhongguo guji shanben shumu bianji weiyuan hui, comp., Shanghai guji, *jingbu* 經部, 1986; rpnt., 1989; *congbu* 叢部, 1989; rpnt., 1990; *jibu* 集部, 1989; rpnt., 1997; *shibu* 史部, 1991; rpnt., 1993; *zibu* 子部, 1994. Each *bu* (branch) is in a separate *han* containing *ce* in traditional string binding. There are indexes indicating which institutions hold each item. Comprehensive author/title indexes are to be published separately.

index also compiled by the National Central Library, *Taiwan gong-cang shanben shumu renming suoyin* 臺灣公藏善本書目人名索引, Taibei, 1972. Lists the main public holdings of *shanben* in Taiwan.

Libraries fortunate enough to hold *shanben* not only compile special catalogs of such works but also publish facsimile reproductions or make them available on microfilm (chap. 11).

The Chinese Rare Books Project (CRBP) is in the process of establishing an online, international union catalog of Chinese rare books. The headquarters is at Princeton University, New Jersey (Department of East Asian Studies). By the end of the first quarter 1998, the project had created more than 12,000 full bibliographic records for Chinese rare books held in North America, China and Europe. Access is through the RLG Web site.[37]

9.8.2   Lost and Recovered Books

Over the centuries many books were lost, either because of some catastrophe, such as fire or pillage, or because they were banned, or simply because fashions and interests changed and a book was no longer copied or collected and so failed to be transmitted. Small wonder that only 85 of the 600 works in the *Hanshu* dynastic bibliography have survived, some of them only in part. Likewise, 86 percent of the titles in the *Suishu* bibliography have been lost. The losses declined after printing became more widespread in the Song and more copies were made. But those works that were still only made in one or two manuscript copies (such as the *Yongle dadian* 永樂大典 or the Veritable Records from the Tang to the Yuan) had a low survival rate.

Later scholars, particularly in the Qing, used much ingenuity in trying to recover such "lost" texts (*yishu* 逸[佚]書), often excerpt by excerpt or quotation by quotation from compilations such as *leishu*. Sometimes they succeeded in recovering the whole text (as with the *Jiu Wudaishi* 舊五代史, which was

---

[37] < http://www.rlg.org.eas/ > .

one of the 385 works recovered from the *Yongle dadian* 永樂大
典 by the *Siku* editors). Sometimes it was possible only to recover fragments of the lost work. Such "recovered," "reconstituted texts" or *rifacimenti* are called *jiben* 輯本 or *jiyishu* 輯
逸 [佚]書. For a catalog of *jiben*, see *Gu yishu jiben mulu (fu kaozheng)* 古佚書輯本目錄附考證.[38]

9.8.3   Forged Books

Controversy between the supporters of each version of the
Classics has been a major intellectual debate from the Han to
the Qing and early Republic.[39] Textual criticism (*choujiao* 讎校
or *jiaochou* 校讎 in the Han, and *jiaokan* 校勘 beginning in the
Six Dynasties; modern *jiaokanxue* 校勘學) focused on the cor-
rection and authentication of the various versions of texts,
principally those of the Confucian Classics. It covered everything from proofreading to editing. On textual criticism and
techniques of collation for the historian, see one of the numerous modern introductions such as Song Ziran, *Zhongguo gushu
jiaodufa* 中國古書校讀法,[40] or Zhang Shunhui 張舜徽, *Zhongguo gudai shiji jiaodufa* 中國古代史籍校讀法.[41] The marks and
colors used for collating texts are discussed in Susan Cherniack,

---

[38] *Gu yishu jiben mulu [fu kaozheng]* (Catalog of ancient recovered editions with scholarly apparatus), Sun Qizhi 孫啓治 and Chen Jianhua 陳
建華, Zhonghua, 1998.

[39] *ECTBG* contains notes on the authenticity and textual history of
64 Han and pre-Han works. The most convenient summary of the many
aspects and degrees of forgery, misrepresentation and misattribution
found in 1,105 titles is Zhang Xincheng 張心澂 *Weishu tongkao* 偽書通考
(General study of forgeries), 2 vols., Shangwu, 1939; 1954; rev. ed., 1957.
There is a four-corner authors/title index. Use in combination with
Zheng Liangshu 鄭良樹, *Xu Weishu tongkao* 續偽書通考 (General study
of forgeries, continued), 3 vols., Xuesheng, 1984.

[40] *Zhongguo gushu jiaodufa* (Techniques for the collation and reading
of old Chinese books), Ba-Shu, 1995.

[41] *Zhongguo gudai shiji jiaodufa* (Techniques for the collation and
reading of Chinese historical sources), Zhonghua, 1962; rpnt. with corrections, Shanghai guji, 1986.

"Book Culture and Textual Transmission in Sung China," *HJAS* 54.1: 5–125 (1994), 88–102.

The advances in textual criticism (*kaozheng* 考證) made by Qing scholars were very great. Although concentrating on the texts of the Classics, they also did much important work on later sources as well. Students should make sure, therefore, especially if working on an earlier text, that they have checked the Qing (and later) scholarship on it. Throughout the manual every effort has been made to draw attention to the best modern editions and reprints, which are by definition those that take account of, or are based on, the relevant Qing scholarship.[42]

9.8.4 Banned Books

Banned books (*jinshu* 禁書) have been a feature of Chinese political and intellectual life from the Warring States to the present day. For an introduction to the subject covering the Qin to the Qing, see *Zhongguo jinshu daguan* 中國禁書大觀. This contains a discussion of the reasons for banning books, based on 220 outstanding examples (including everything from the *Analects* and the *Odes* to the *Diamond Sutra* and the *Dream of the Red Chamber*). The book concludes with a list of 4,000 titles that the editors claim is a complete one of all the books banned in different periods up to the end of the Qing.[43] Note that four of the main earlier lists are indexed in *H-Y Index* 10 (see Table 14 for titles).

---

[42] On Qing textual criticism, see Benjamin Elman, *From Philosophy to Philology: Intellectual Aspects of Change in Late Imperial China*, Council on East Asian Studies, Harvard University, 1984, rpnt., 1990; on Qing historians and their contributions, see Du Weiyun 杜維運, *Qingdai shixue yu shijia* 清代史學與史家, Dongda tushu, 1984; Zhonghua, 1988.

[43] *Zhongguo jinshu daguan* (Overview of Chinese banned books), An Pingqiu 安平秋 and Zhang Peiheng 章培恒, eds., Shanghai wenhua, 1990; 4th prnt., 1991.

9.9 *Alternative and Difficult Book Titles*

A problem encountered throughout Chinese history is the use of more than one title for the same book, caused in the early days by the fact that books circulated as manuscripts in different versions with no fixed title or author (19.1). After the introduction of printing, new titles were often invented by publishers as a sales technique. Another reason why the titles of books changed was convenience. An enormous number were abbreviated. The more famous the work, the shorter the abbreviation (only a handful of the most ancient Confucian Classics were customarily known by one-word abbreviated titles, e.g., *Shu* 書, *Shi* 詩, *Yi* 易, see 19.2.1. Most well-known works circulated with disyllabic abbreviations, e.g., *Zuozhuan* 左傳, *Lunyu* 論語, *Shiji* 史紀, *Shuowen* 説文). Another reason why titles changed was the need to distinguish two books.[44] Often a reign period or dynastic name was added later. Yet another reason why titles changed was the need to avoid using characters in the title that had subsequently become taboo. If you have doubts about a title, check *Tongshu yiming tongjian* 同書異名通檢, which lists 6,000 books with different titles or *Tongming yishu tongjian* 同名異書通檢, which lists 3,500 different books with others having the same title.[45]

In choosing the title for a book, Chinese writers liked to use classical allusions, sometimes taken from the name of the study in which they wrote, sometimes not, but usually as a means of

[44] For example, the Song digest of laws known today as *Song xingtong* 宋刑通 began with the title *Song jianlong chongxiang ding xingtong* 宋建隆重詳定刑通. This was abbreviated to *Chongding xingtong* 重定刑通 or simply *Xingtong* 刑通. But at that point it became necessary to differentiate it from the *Xingtong* 刑通 compiled in the Later Zhou period, and so it acquired its present title of *Song xingtong* 宋刑通.

[45] *Tongshu yiming tongjian* (General investigation into books having different titles), Du Xinfu 杜信孚, comp., rev. and enl. ed., Jiangsu renmin, 1982; and *Tongming yishu tongjian* (General investigation into different books having the same title), Du Xinfu 杜信孚 and Mao Junyi 毛俊儀, eds., Jiangsu renmin, 1982.

expressing a personal point of view or whim. It is not always easy to fully understand the allusion unless it is explained in the preface. A good reference book such as the *Siku da cidian* will often give the author's reasons for choosing a particular title, but not always. Take an easy example, the title of a *biji* written by Lu Can 陸粲, *Gengji bian* 庚己編. If you did not know that the author lived at the beginning of the sixteenth century, you might not have guessed that it probably means "Written between 1510 and 1519" (i.e., between *Ming Zhengde gengwu nian* 明正德庚午年 and *Ming Zhengde jimao nian* 明正德己卯年. To take a more difficult example, a *biji* written by Zhu Guozhen 朱國禎 (1558–1632), *Yongchuang xiaopin* 湧幢小品. The original titles were *Xi Hong* 希洪 and later *Fang Hong xiaopin* 倣洪小品 (that is "A modest work in imitation of Hong [Mai's *Rongzhai suibi*]"). On reflection, Zhu decided that it would be presumptuous to compare his work with the famous Song *biji*, so he chose the present title based on the name of his study, "Springing from the oceans stele study trifles." Unless you read his preface, you could hardly guess the meaning (49.2, *Biji*).

When all else fails, or even before, check *Zhongguo gujin shuming shiyi cidian* 中國古今書名釋義辭典. This includes explanations of 3,200 difficult book titles (including the above two), from the earliest times to 1966. Arrangement is by stroke count. There is also a stroke-count table of contents.[46]

In order to find out if a source is extant and if so, in what library, the student should look through the published library catalogs of the major collections of Chinese books in China, Japan and the West (chap. 11). For recently published Chinese books, there are databases available on CD-ROM, for example, in China, the *Zhongguo guojia shumu guangpan* 中國國家書目光盤, 1988– . It is updated twice a year.

---

[46]*Zhongguo gujin shuming shiyi cidian* (Dictionary for clearing up doubts about book titles), Zhao Chuanren 趙傳仁 et al., eds., Shandong youyi, 1992. Briefly examines about 2,500 titles.

9.10   Indexes and Concordances

Chinese scholars compiled what amounted to general indexes
to the sum total of phrases and quotable quotes needed for literary composition (see, for example, the *Peiwen yunfu*; section
2.2). Such works were normally arranged by rhyme and sometimes by classifier. Encyclopaedias such as the *Taiping yulan*
(29.2) also served as detailed subject indexes to the contents of
previously printed books. Individual books, however, were
usually not indexed, although sometimes there was a table of
contents at the end of the last scroll (or at the end of sections)
as well as a postface. When printing became common in the
Song dynasty, the table of contents moved to the front of the
book, as did the postface (henceforward, preface; see note 30,
section 3.6).

The main reason why individual books were usually not
indexed was no doubt because the most widespread works,
such as the Confucian Classics, were learned by heart. A good
scholar did not need time-saving devices.

Indeed, Jia Sixie 賈思勰, the author of the *Qimin yaoshu* 齊
民要術 (35.1), felt that he had to apologize for cluttering up his
text with tables of contents (*mulu* 目錄) at the head of each
juan. The most famous table of contents (because it was the
first large-scale one for a major work) was that to the *Zizhi
tongjian* 資治通鑑 (see 21.3). To put things in perspective, it is
worth remembering that indexes to individual books began appearing in Europe only during the centuries after printing was
introduced, and even then they remained something of a rarity.
The first modern indexes were introduced in the nineteenth
century and in some countries, such as France, the index is still
seen as more of an indulgence to be avoided than as a necessity.

Because of the lack of indexes in Chinese books, a great deal
of time and effort can be saved by using the concordances and
indexes compiled in the twentieth century, not only for the
Classics, but also for many other Chinese printed sources. Particularly convenient are the growing number that are computer
generated and available on CD-ROM.

The most important set of concordances for classical works is the *ICS Ancient Chinese Texts Concordance Series* conceived by D.C. Lau (Liu Dianjue 劉殿爵) and produced at the Institute of Chinese Studies (ICS) at the Chinese University of Hong Kong.[47] The entire corpus of Classical Chinese, that is to say all 90 surviving works from pre-Han and Han times have been put on a computer database and are being published electronically, indexed on every character. In book form, the series comes to 65 volumes. Fifty-five volumes have been published or are in press. The entire series should be completed by mid-1999. The original texts (for the most part taken from *Sibu congkan* editions) are all included. Finding the use of a character or phrase in the text is rapidly done because the concordance is arranged by *pinyin*. There are character frequency counts and indexes by stroke count. All volumes are available on individual discs or one CD-ROM. The software allows searches across the entire corpus (which amounts to nine million characters). By their comprehensiveness, accuracy, and ease of use, the *ICS* concordances surpass all previous indexes and concordances of the Chinese Classics and other pre-Han and Han transmitted texts. They have the added advantage that revised editions can be easily issued in the form of corrected disks. References are made throughout the manual to the appropriate *ICS* concordance.

Now that all major extant Classical Chinese texts are on a computer database, it is possible to analyze Classical Chinese with a degree of accuracy not previously possible. The eventual inclusion of the newly excavated texts of certain classical works

---

[47] *Xian-Qin liang Han guji zhuzi suoyin congkan*, 先秦兩漢古籍逐字索引叢刊, D.C. Lau and Chen Fong Ching (Chen Fangzheng 陳方正), series eds.; He Zhihua 何志華, executive ed., and He Guojie 何國杰, director of computing; 1st series, HK: Shangwu, 1992; 2nd and 3rd series, HK: Shangwu, 1994–98. The title of the computer database is *Han da guji ziliaoku xian-Qin liang Han chuanshi guji* 漢達古籍資料庫先秦兩漢傳世古籍 ([Chinese Ancient Texts, CHANT] Database, Han and Pre-Han Traditional Chinese Texts), published by CHANT Center, ICS, the Chinese University of Hong Kong. Distributed by HK: Shangwu.

from tombs such as Mawangdui (18.2) will make the database even more comprehensive. The *ICS* concordance series is planned to cover all works from the end of the Han to the Sui.

Many more computer-based indexes and concordances are becoming available, including the entire corpus of the Standard Histories (22.2) and parts of the Daoist and Buddhist Canons (33.4 and 33.5).

The most important precomputer series of indexes and concordances for post-Han works is the *Harvard-Yenching Institute Sinological Index Series*, compiled under the general editorship of William Hung (Hong Ye 洪業, 1893–1980).[48] The series consists of two separately numbered groups; the first entitled Indices (*yinde* 引得, 41 works) and the second, Supplements (*yinde tekan* 引得特刊, 23 works). The latter include a number of concordances with complete texts as well as other materials. The Centre Franco-Chinois d'Etudes Sinologiques under the direction of Nie Chongqi 聶崇岐 and with the aid of the staff of the *H-Y Index Series*, who had been forced by the war to leave Yenching in 1942, published 13 volumes of indexes, Beiping, 1943–48. Of the total, 77 works covered by the *H-Y* and *CFC* concordance series, 25 classical works have now been superseded by the *ICS* concordance series. That still leaves 52 useful *H-Y* and *CFC* concordances and indexes of works from later periods. These are referred to in the appropriate sections.

A large number of indexes and concordances are compiled in Japan. These are usually produced by members of a seminar or study group collectively as a working aid (appearing under the senior member's name). As a rule a preliminary mimeographed version is circulated for a number of years before a revised printed edition is produced.

---

[48] William Hung, gen. ed., *Hafo-Yanjing xueshe yinde bianzuan chu* 哈佛燕京學社引得編纂處 (Harvard-Yenching Institute Sinological Index Series), 69 volumes, Yenching University, Beiping, 1931–50; rpnt., Zhonghua, 1960, 1966; CMC, Taibei, 1965–69; Shanghai guji, 1983–88. See Susan Chan Egan, *A Latterday Confucian: Reminiscences of William Hung (1893–1980)*, Harvard East Asian Monograph 131, 1980.

Two hundred and eighty-two precomputer indexes and concordances of Chinese texts from antiquity to 1900 are meticulously annotated in David L. McMullen, *Concordances and Indexes to Chinese Texts*, CMC, 1975.

10

Locating Secondary Sources

This chapter surveys comprehensive bibliographies of secondary sources (10.1); Chinese language bibliographies and journals (10.2); Japanese language bibliographies and journals (10.3); and finally Western language bibliographies and journals (10.4).

10.1 *Comprehensive Bibliographies*

At an early stage of research it is useful to find out what other historians are writing in your field, and also what has been written about it in the past. Computerized library catalogs can be useful, but their very comprehensiveness is a mixed blessing and they do not cover journal articles where most research first appears. So, it quickly pays to turn to the many specialized bibliographies available.

These can cover a single subject, a single period, a single type of historical source or the works of a particular scholar; many such selective bibliographies, as well as specialist journals, are listed in the appropriate section of the manual. Here the focus is on those bibliographies which cover the entire sweep of Chinese history. Those covering recent scholarship are listed first, followed by comprehensive bibliographies of past scholarship.

The most convenient way of gaining an overview of the entire field of Chinese studies in different languages is through the articles and review pages devoted to Chinese history in the main historical journals which are listed in this section.

Apart from these, there are four annual reviews. The first two cover research on Asian studies, including Chinese history.

They are comprehensive, but unannotated and appear with a delay of several years. The next two specialize in Chinese studies and are annotated. Each has particular strengths and weaknesses which makes it worthwhile to consult all four.

1. *Bibliography of Asian Studies*, published by the Association of Asian Studies (under various titles since 1936 and under the present title since 1956), gives a comprehensive listing of books and articles on China (as well as the rest of Asia) in Western languages, mainly English. The volume covering publications in 1991 appeared in 1997. It contained over 37,000 entries (for reviews rather than listings, see the *Journal of Asian Studies* itself). The BAS is available online via library subscription for the years 1971–1991 (plus numerous citations from more recent years, including all articles in the 100 most-used journals in Asian studies). Approximately 420,000 citations are included. For the years prior to 1970, see 10.4.1.

2. *Tôyôgaku kenkyû bunken ruimoku* 東洋學研究文獻類目 (Annual Bibliography of Oriental Studies).[1] For recent Japanese, Chinese and Korean scholarship, these are the most comprehensive of the annual bibliographies. They are compiled at the Jimbun (Western works, including Russian, are also listed). Books and articles are arranged according to language and further subdivided within each language group according to subject categories; full author indexes make this bibliography very easy to use. A unique feature is that it includes author's reviews, listed under work reviewed and also indexed by the author of the review. Note also the Tôhô Gakkai's *Books and Articles on Oriental Subjects* (10.3.2).

3. *Revue bibliographique de sinologie* (also, since 1997, *Review of Bibliography in Sinology*), Paris (1955– , annual).[2] The *RBS* is a selective annotated bibliography covering books and articles in Chinese, Japanese and European languages on all periods of Chinese history, including (since the 1997 issue) current affairs. *RBS* comes out rapidly, usually no more than a year after the year covered. Each book and article is briefly reviewed (either in French or in English). There are also (since the 1986 issue) occasional bibliographic essays on chosen topics. Has subject and author indexes.

---

[1] Between 1934 and 1964, the title was *Tôyôgaku bunken ruimoku*.

[2] *Revue bibliographique de sinologie*, 1st series, 15 vols., covering the years 1955–70, Paris, 1957–82; 2nd series, covering the years 1983 to the present, Paris, 1983– .

4. *China Review International*, University of Hawaii (1993–). This quarterly review is strong on new English-language scholarship on all aspects of Chinese studies.

The annual bibliographies and even journal reviews inevitably appear some time after the publication of articles and books. A more immediate way to keep up-to-date is to attend the annual conferences of the learned society or association covering your field of interest. The most important comprehensive Western one is the Association of Asian Studies. If you cannot attend the annual meeting, the abstracts have been published since 1992.³ The European Association of Chinese Studies (EACS) meets annually.

Another way of keeping up-to-date is to skim through the catalogs of publishers and bookstores. There are not all that many specializing in Chinese history (10.5). In America and Europe, only a handful of university presses have developed a tradition of publishing studies on Chinese history (11.5).

10.2   *Chinese Secondary Sources and Journals*

10.2.1   *Recent Scholarship*

For Chinese historical scholarship of the previous 12 months, use the following:

1. *Zhongguo lishixue nianjian* 中國歷史學年鑒.⁴ The survey carries essays on trends in selected fields, reports on conferences and on recent archaeological discoveries and bibliographies of books and articles appearing every year. Except for 1979, the year covered is that previous to the one in the title. Publication comes about 12 months after the year covered. Information in the annual survey is based on the society's quarterly *Shixue qingbao* 史學情報.

---

³ Association for Asian Studies, Inc., *Abstracts of the [year] Annual Meeting*, Association for Asian Studies, 1992– .

⁴ *Zhongguo lishixue nianjian* (Annual survey of Chinese historical studies), Chinese History Society, Zhongguo shixuehui 中國史學會, San-lian, 1980– .

2. *Zhongguoshi yanjiu dongtai* 中國史研究動態,[5] carries articles on recent trends in the field of Chinese history arranged in the form of brief state-of-the-field essays and book reviews. It is available on CD-ROM (item 3 below).

3. *Zhongguo xueshu qikan (guangpanban)* 中國學術期刊(光盤版).[6] The database includes articles appearing in many hundreds of scholarly and university journals. Coverage of science and technology journals is much better than the arts, but there are about a dozen historical and archaeological journals on the *Wenshizhe* 文史哲 disc. Those included are marked with an asterisk in the lists of archaeological journals in section 13.3 and of historical journals in subsection 10.2.3.

4. *Fuyin baokan ziliao* 復印報刊資料.[7] The main divisions of interest to the historian of China are: K-1, *Lishixue* 歷史學; K-2, *Zhongguo gudaishi* 中國古代史; K-3, *Zhongguo jindaishi* 中國近代史; K-21, *Xian-Qin Qin Hanshi* 先秦秦漢史; K-22, *Wei Jin Nan-Bei Chao Sui Tangshi* 魏晉南北朝隋唐史; K-23, *Song Liao Jin Yuanshi* 宋遼金元史; K-24, *Ming Qingshi* 明清史.

5. *Quanguo baokan suoyin* 全國報刊索引.[8] Reprints entire articles.

6. *Zhongguo shehui kexue wenxian tilu* 中國社會科學文獻提錄.[9] Contains summaries of articles on social science subjects, including history and archaeology.

---

[5] *Zhongguoshi yanjiu dongtai* (Trends in Chinese Historical Research), Shekeyuan 社科院, Lishisuo 歷史所, eds., monthly, 1978– .

[6] *Zhongguo xueshu qikan [guangpanban]* (Chinese academic journal CD publication), produced at Qinghua daxue guangpan guojia gongcheng yanjiu zhongxin 清華大學光盤國家工程研究中心 (Qinghua University reseach center for the national CD-ROM project) and the Xueshu dianzi chubanwu bianjibu 學術電子出版物編輯部 (Academic electronic publishing editorial department), 1996– .

[7] *Fuyin baokan ziliao* (Photocopied journal materials), Renmin daxue, bi-monthly, 1978– (and since 1985 for separate periods). Available on CD-ROM.

[8] *Quanguo baokan suoyin* 全國報刊索引 (1973– , bimonthly; appeared under the title *Quanguo zhuyao baokan suoyin* 全國主要報刊索引, 1955–56, monthly), Shanghai tushuguan, eds.

[9] *Zhongguo shehui kexue wenxian tilu* (Abstracts of article on Chinese social sciences), separate bimonthly issues on "History" and "Archeology," Zhongguo shehui kexue wenxian tilu editorial department eds., 1985– .

7. *Taiwan diqu Hanxue lunzhu xuanmu* 臺灣地區漢學論著選目.[10] The
    quarterly is called *Hanxue yanjiu tongxun* 漢學研究通訊.

For details, both biographic and bibliographic, on about 3,450
Chinese historians active in the twentieth century (including
110 working in Taiwan), see *Zhongguo dangdai lishixue xuezhe
cidian* 中國當代歷史學學者辭典.[11]

10.2.2 Previous Scholarship

For all books published in Chinese 1911–49, see *Minguo shiqi
zong shumu* 民國時期總書目 (Comprehensive catalog of Republican period books), 21 vols., Shumu wenxian, 1991. There
are two vols. on archaeology, history, geography and biography. They contain 11,029 titles. There is a *pinyin* index.

For the contents of nearly all Chinese periodicals and magazines published in Chinese 1857–1918, see *Zhongguo jindai qikan pianmu huilu* 中國近代期刊篇目匯錄 (Compendium of
the contents of modern Chinese periodicals), Shangtu, eds., 6
vols., 1965–84.

To locate Chinese historical monographs and books, check
Bashi nian lai shixue shumu 八十年來史學書目 *1900–1980*.[12] It
contains citations to over 12,400 Chinese books (including
Chinese translations) published from 1900–80 on China, world
history and archaeology. Arrangement is by subject. There is
an author index.

For an index of 20,000 books and articles on socioeconomic
history appearing in China, Taiwan and Hong Kong between
1900 and 1984, see *Zhongguo shehui jingjishi lunzhu mulu* 中國

---

[10] *Taiwan diqu Hanxue lunzhu xuanmu* (Selected Bibliography of Chinese Studies in Taiwan), Hanxue yanjiu zhongxin 漢學研究中心, comp.,
Taibei, 1982– .

[11] *Zhongguo dangdai lishixue xuezhe cidian* (Dictionary of contemporary Chinese historical scholars), Xibei daxue, 1993.

[12] *Bashi nian lai shixue shumu 1900–1980* (Bibliography of historical
books published in China during the last 80 years), Lishisuo, comp., Shehui kexue, 1984.

社會經濟史論著目錄.[13] See also Feng Erkang 馮爾康, *Zhong-guo shehuishi yanjiu gaishu* 中國社會史研究概述,[14] which covers primary sources on social history arranged by traditional categories as well as modern Chinese research on social history arranged by dynasty up to 1985.[15]

Between 1900 and 1976, over 100,000 articles on Chinese history appeared in Chinese journals and newspapers. They are indexed in the three-part *Zhongguo shixue lunwen suoyin* 中國史學論文索引.[16] The arrangement of all three parts is by extremely detailed subject categories as well as by period. These volumes now largely supersede earlier bibliographies.[17]

---

[13] *Zhongguo shehui jingjishi lunzhu mulu* (Index of books and articles on Chinese social and economic history), Shekeyuan, Jingjishizu 經濟史組 (Economic history group of CASS), comp., Qi-Lu, 1988.

[14] Feng Erkang et al., *Zhongguo shehuishi yanjiu gaishu* (Introduction to research on Chinese social history), Tianjin jiaoyu, 1988; Taibei rpnt., 1989.

[15] See also E-tu Zen Sun and J. de Francis, *Bibliography of Chinese Social History: A Selected and Critical List of Chinese Periodical Sources*, YUP, 1952. It lists and annotates 176 articles in Chinese on social history appearing mainly during the 1930s. Likewise, Richard C. Howard, *Index to Learned Chinese Periodicals*, G. K. Hall, 1962, which indexes 14 journals by journal and by subject.

[16] *Zhongguo shixue lunwen suoyin* (Index to Chinese Historical Articles), compiled by members of the Lishisuo and Beijing daxue lishixi 北京大學歷史系. Part 1 covers 1900–37 (2 vols., Kexue, 1957; rpnt., HK: Sanlian, 1980); Part 2 covers 1937 to 1949 (2 vols., Sanlian, 1980); Part 3 covers 1949 to 1976 (3 vols., Hong Kong: Zhonghua, 1995).

[17] See also Yu Ping-kuen (Yu Bingquan) 余秉權, *Chinese History: Index to Learned Articles, 1902–1962* (*Zhongguo shixue lunwen yinde* 中國史學論文引得), HKU Press, 1963; Taibei, 1968. Index of 10,325 articles in 355 journals (found in Hong Kong libraries) appearing between 1902 and 1962 and written by 3,392 authors. This should be used in conjunction with the same author's expansion: *Chinese History: Index to Learned Articles, 1905–64* (H-Y Library, 1970) in which many more journals (found in European and U. S. libraries) not included in the first volume were indexed. There is no duplication between the two volumes. The arrangement of both volumes is by total stroke count of authors' names; there is also a Wade-Giles index and a subject index.

Footnote continued on next page

Articles in collected essays (either by an individual or institution) often get left out of the bibliographies of journal articles and books. This gap can be made good with *1,522 zhong xueshu lunwenji shixue lunwen fenlei suoyin* 1,522 種學術論文集史學論文分類索引, which contains 34,146 articles and books published in scholarly collections between 1911 and 1986.[18]

Supplement the above bibliographies by looking through one of the bibliographic guides listed in section 10.1, or use the *Tôyôgaku kenkyû bunken ruimoku* or the *Revue bibliographique de sinologie.*[19]

The single best bibliographic introduction to scholarship on Chinese history in Taiwan and Hong Kong since 1949 is *Zhongguo lishi zhinan* 中國歷史指南.[20] For a book-length introduct-

---

Zhongguo gudaishi lunwen ziliao suoyin 中國古代史論文資料索引 (Index to articles and materials on Chinese ancient history), Fudan daxue lishixi, 2 vols., Shanghai renmin, 1985, covers articles appearing between 1949.10 and 1979.9 arranged by dynasty.

[18] *1,522 zhong xueshu lunwenji shixue lunwen fenlei suoyin*, Zhou Xun 周迅 and Li Fan 李凡, comps., Shumu wenxian, 1990. To a certain extent this is supplemented by *Jianguo yilai Zhongguo shixue lunwenji pianmu suoyin chubian* 建國以來中國史學論文集編目索引初編, Zhang Haihui 張海惠 and Wang Yuzhi 王玉芝, comps., Zhonghua, 1992. Indexes over 15,000 chapters and articles appearing in over 1,000 collections of scholarly writings on Chinese history published between 1949 and 1984 (not including those in Hong Kong and Taiwan). There is a clear arrangement by period and subject category. There is also an index of collections as well as an author index.

[19] See also Albert L. Feuerwerker and S. Cheng, *Chinese Communist Studies of Modern Chinese History*, HUP, 1961, in which some 500 books on Chinese history published in China between 1949 and 1959 are discussed under various broad subject headings. ("Modern" includes several works on the Ming). Also consult *Modern Chinese Society, 1644–1970: An Analytic Bibliography*, vol. 2, *Publications in Chinese*, G. W. Skinner and W. Hsieh, eds., SUP, 1973, for a critical, thoroughly arranged, annotated bibliography of Chinese publications covering this period.

[20] *Zhongguo lishi zhinan* (Guide to Chinese history), Gao Mingshi 高明士, ed., 5 vols., Lianjing, 1990 (see 8.2 for details).

ion to Chinese historical studies in Hong Kong, see *Dangdai Xianggang shixue yanjiu* 當代香港史學研究.[21]

10.2.3   *Main Chinese Language Historical Journals*

The abstract, excerpt and reprint journals listed under 10.2.1 are the best way of keeping up-to-date with the many dozens of Chinese journals publishing historical research. The following list is only a small selection of the main historical journals. Those marked with an asterisk are available on Qinghua University's *Zhongguo xueshu qikan (guangpanban)* 中國學術期刊 [光盤版] (10.2.1). Dozens of universities publish scholarly journals covering the humanities and social sciences. Such *xuebao* 學報 or *xuekan* 學刊 are far too numerous to list here despite the fact that they often carry articles of interest to the historian. For archaeological journals, see 14.4.

Beichao yanjiu 北朝研究 (45.5.2).

**Beijing daxue xuebao* 北京大學學報 (1955– , bimonthly).

Dang'an yu lishi 檔案與歷史 (1995– , quarterly), Shanghai.

Dunhuang Tulufan yanjiu 敦煌吐魯番研究 (46.3.3).

*Dunhuang yanjiu 敦煌研究 (46.3.3).

Dunhuangxue jikan 敦煌學輯刊 (46.3.3).

Gugong bowuyuan yuankan 故宮博物院院刊 (1958– , quarterly)

Guji zhengli yu yanjiu 古籍整理與研究 (1986– , irregular), Quanguo gaodeng yuanxiao guji zhengli yu yanjiu gongzuo weiyuanhui 全國高等院校古籍整理與研究工作委員會.

Gujin nongye 古今農業 (35.1).

Guoxue jikan 國學季刊 (1923–52, quarterly), Beijing daxue's Journal of sinological studies.

Guwenzi yanjiu 古文字研究 (12.2).

Jianduxue yanjiu 簡牘學研究 (18.1).

Lishi dang'an 歷史檔案 (1981– , quarterly).

[21] *Dangdai Xianggang shixue yanjiu* (Contemporary historical research in Hong Kong), Zhou Zhuirong 周佳榮 et al., HK: Sanlian, 1994.

Lishi dili 歷史地理 (1983– , irregular), Fudan daxue.

*Lishi yanjiu 歷史研究 (1954–66; 1974– , quarterly). This used to be the most important Chinese historical journal. Since the proliferation of new and specialized journals in the 1980s and 1990s, it has lost its leading position. It is edited at the Lishisuo. It has been weighted toward pre-1911 Chinese history. There is a n index of articles for the issues 1954–83.

Mingshi yanjiu 明史研究 (49.5.2).

Mingshi ziliao congkan 明史資料叢刊 (49.5.2).

Minzu yanjiu 民族研究 (40.2).

Minzu yanjiu dongtai (40.2).

Qinghua daxue xuebao (Zhexue shehui kexueban) 清華大學學報哲學社會科學版 (1955– , quarterly), Qinghua daxue, Beijing.

Qinghua xuebao 清華學報 (10.2.4).

Qingshi yanjiu 青史研究 (50.8.2).

Shijie zongjiao yanjiu 世界宗教研究 (33.2).

*Shixueshi yanjiu 史學史研究 (1979– , quarterly), Shifan daxue, Beijing. For the years 1979–81, the title was *Shixueshi ziliao* 史學史資料.

Songshi yanjiu tongxun 宋史研究通訊 (47.4).

Tang yanjiu 唐研究 (46.5.2).

Wenshi 文史 (1962–65, irregular), 4 vols., *Xin Jianshe* 新建設, eds.; vol. 5, 1978– , Zhonghua.

Wenxian 文獻 (1979– , triannual), Shumu wenxian chubanshe, Beijing.

Yanjing xuebao 燕京學報 (1927–51, quarterly; new series, 1995– , annual), Yanjing Yanjiuyuan, Beijing. The old series, *Yenching Journal of Chinese Studies*, was one of the four leading sinological (as well as historical) journals of the Republican era (the other three were Beida's *Guoxue jikan* 國學季刊, Qinghua's *Qinghua xuebao* 清華學報 and Academia Sinica's *Zhongyang yanjiuyuan Lishi yuyan yanjiusuo jikan* (10.2.4). The *Yanjing xuebao* was edited and published at the H-Y Institute for Chinese Studies at Yenching University, Beiping, which opened in 1928. Its editors included Rong Geng, Gu Jiegang, Hong Ye (William Hung), Qi Sihe 齊思和 (1907–81) and Wu Shichang 吳世昌 (1908–86). The journal also published a distinguished monograph series (23 vols.). The institute published the *H-Y Index Series* (see 9.10). For the titles of other major journals of this period plus a sampling of their contents, see E-tu Zen Sun and John de Francis (1952); and Richard C. Howard (1962).

Zhongguo jingjishi yanjiu 中國經濟史研究 (1986– , quarterly), Shekeyuan, Jingji yanjiusuo (Institute of Economic Research), Beijing.

Zhongguo keji shiliao 中國科技史料 (chap. 37).

Zhongguo lishi bowuguan guankan 中國歷史博物館館刊 (1979– , annual), Zhongguo lishi bowuguan, Beijing.

Zhongguo lishi dili luncong 中國歷史地理論叢 (1987– , quarterly), Shaanxi shifan daxue.

Zhongguo Mingshi xuehui tongxun 中國明史學會通訊 (49.5.2).

*Zhongguo nongshi 中國農史 (35.1).

Zhongguo shehui jingjishi yanjiu 中國社會經濟史研究 (1982– , quarterly), Xiamen daxue, lishixi.

Zhongguo shehui kexue 中國社會科學 (1979– , bimonthly), Shekeyuan. Articles from the research institutes of the Shekeyuan, including the Lishisuo. A selection of the best articles appear in translation in *Social Sciences in China*.

*Zhongguoshi yanjiu 中國史研究 (1979– , monthly), Lishisuo.

*Zhongguoshi yanjiu dongtai 中國史研究動態 (1978– , monthly), Lishisuo.

*Zhongguo zhexue nianjian 中國哲學年鑒 (1982– , annual), Shekeyuan, Zhexue yanjiusuo (Philosophy Research Institute), Beijing.

Zhonghua wenshi luncong 中華文史論叢 (1962– , annual), Shanghai guji chubanshe, Shanghai.

Ziran kexueshi yanjiu 自然科學史研究 (chap. 37).

*Zongjiaoxue yanjiu 宗教學研究 (33.2).

Hong Kong

Xinya xuebao 新亞學報 (1955– , irregular).

Chongji xuebao 崇基學報 (1960– , biannual), Chongchi College, Shatin.

Chongji lishixue jikan 崇基歷史學季刊 (1961– , biannual).

Zhongguo wenhua yanjiu zhongxin xuebao 中國文化研究中心學報 (1992– , annual). Previous title (1970–92): *Xianggang Zhongwen daxue Zhongguo wenhua yanjiu zhongxin xuebao* 香港中文大學中國文化研究中心學報.

10.2.4　Taiwan

Dalu zazhi 大陸雜志 (Continent magazine), 1950– , quarterly, Taibei.

Gugong jikan (1966– , quarterly), Taibei.

Hanxue yanjiu 漢學研究 (Chinese Culture), 1983– , quarterly, Taibei.

Jiandu xuebao 簡牘學報 (18.1).

Mingshi yanjiu zhuankan 明史研究專刊 (49.5.2).

Qinghua xuebao 清華學報 (Tsing Hua Journal of Chinese Studies, 1915–19; new series, 1924–47; 2nd series, 1956– , quarterly). Mainly contains articles by Chinese scholars working in Taiwan and the United States on all aspects of Chinese culture.

Shihuo yuekan 食貨月刊 (1971–88, monthly), specializing in economic and social history (as did its forerunner, the *Shihuo banyuekan* 食貨半月刊, 1934–37, rpnt. Daian, 1965; Shanghai shudian, 1982).

SYSJK: *Shiyusuo jikan* 史語所季刊 (short for *Zhongyang yanjiuyuan, Lishi yuyan yanjiusuo jikan* 中央研究院歷史語言研究所集刊. English title: Bulletin of the Institute of History and Philology, Academia Sinica), Nangang, 1928– , quarterly. In some of the earlier Western literature the abbreviation *BIHP* or *CYYY* is used. The leader of the four main sinological journals of the republican era (for the other three, see under 10.2.3, *Yanjing xuebao*). The *SYSJK* has continued to carry important articles to this day. Vols. 1–22 (1928–49) were reprinted by Zhonghua in 1987. For an index to all the articles (and their authors) published in vols. 1–66 (1928–1990), see *Zhongyang yanjiuyuan, Lishi yuyan yanjiusuo chubanpin mulu* 中央研究院歷史語言研究所出版品目錄, 1995.

Zhongguo lishi xuehui shixue jikan 中國歷史學會史學季刊, Taibei (1970– , quarterly).

Note that many of the top libraries in China are linked in an information network for academic journals. The following is a list of the catalogs of the newspaper and journal holdings of some of the largest Chinese libraries, starting with a union catalog:

1833–1949 quanguo Zhongwen qikan lianhe mulu zengdingben 1833–1949 全國中文期刊聯合目錄增訂本 (Union catalog of 19,115 periodicals in 50 Chinese libraries), Shumu wenxian, 1961; enlarged and rev. ed., 1981. There is a *pinyin* index.

Shanghai baokan tushuguan Zhongwen qikan mulu 上海報刊圖書館中文
期刊目錄 (Periodical and newspaper holdings of Shanghai newspaper
and periodical library), 2 vols. Shanghai, 1956–7. Vol. 1, 1888–1949,
8,037 titles; vol. 2, 1949–56, 1,300 titles.

Beijing tushuguan guancang baozhi mulu 北京圖書館館藏報紙目錄, Shumu wenxian (Catalog of newspaper holdings in Peking Library),
1981, provides holding information for some 1,800 Chinese and
1,000 foreign-language newspapers. Chinese-language titles are
grouped into pre-1949 and post-1949 sections and then arranged by
province. A separate section lists Hong Kong, Macao and overseas
Chinese titles, arranged by country. Foreign-language titles are also
arranged by country. Has stroke-count title indexes.

Shanghai tushuguan guancang Zhongwen baozhi mulu (1862–1949) 上海圖
書館館藏中文報紙目錄 (Catalog of Chinese newspaper holdings in
the Shanghai Library), Shanghai tushuguan, 1982, catalogs 3,543 Chinese newspaper titles. There is a *pinyin* index to the first character of
each title and an index of titles arranged by place of publication.

Shanghai tushuguan guancang Zhongwen baozhi fukan mulu (1898–1949)
上海圖書館館藏中文報紙復刊目錄 (Catalog of holdings of Chinese
newspaper supplements in the Shanghai Library), Shanghai tushuguan, 1985, is the companion volume to the above item. It catalogs
7,098 titles of supplements (special issues, magazine sections, photo-
gravure sections, etc.) to over 1,400 newspapers. There is a *pinyin* index to the first character of the title as well as an index of titles arranged by subject and an index of titles arranged by the title of the
newspaper in which the supplements appeared.

William C. Ju, *A Union List of Chinese Periodicals in Universities and Col-
leges in Taiwan*, CMC, 1975. Gives holding information for 2,487 periodicals in 104 institutions. Arranged in alphabetical order by romanized title. Has index of romanized titles and stroke-count title
index.

Zhongyang yanjiu yuan Zhong, Ri, Han wen qikan guancang lianhe mulu
中央研究院中日韓文期刊館藏聯合目錄 (Union catalog of Acade-
mia Sinica library's holdings of Chinese, Japanese and Korean serials), Zhongyan yanjiu yuan, Taibei, 1996. Well-indexed catalog of the
Academia Sinica's holdings of journals: 2,431 from Taiwan; 1,763
mainland and Hong Kong; 526 Japanese; and 85 Korean.

Periodicals and Newspapers in East Asian Languages in the Fung Ping Shan
[Feng Pingshan 馮平山] *Library of the University of Hong Kong*, Fung
Ping Shan Library Serials Section, comp., HKCU Press, 1990.

In order to locate Chinese journals in Western and Japanese libraries, the online catalogs have largely replaced the older checklists such as:

Union List of Chinese Periodicals in American Libraries, Zug, Switzerland: Xerox, Inter Documentation Co., 1968. This is a printing of the microfilm of the Library of Congress "Union Card File of Oriental Vernacular Series (Chinese)."

A Bibliography of Chinese Newspapers and Periodicals in European Libraries, CUP, 1975. Covers 102 collections, including holdings of libraries in Central and Eastern Europe and Russia.

Inventaire des Périodiques Chinois dans les bibliothèques Françaises, Michel Cartier, ed., Institut des Hautes Études Chinoises, Collège de France, 1984. Lists holdings of Chinese language journals in French libraries.

Chûgokubun zasshi shinbun sôgo mokuroku 中國文雜誌新聞總合目錄 (Union Catalog of Holdings of Chinese Periodicals and Newspapers), Ajia keizai kenkyûjo, 1985. Lists holdings of about 10,000 Chinese serials dating from the end of the Qing to the present in 40 Japanese collections.

10.3 Japanese Secondary Sources and Journals

Almost all Japanese academic writing on Chinese history appears first in journal articles. Authors frequently later assemble their articles and publish them as books. The standard form of the title of such works is *Nani nani no kenkyû* (collected researches on such and such; sometimes mistranslated as a study of such and such).

Festschrift volumes (*kinen ronbunshû* 紀念論文集) with contributions by pupils and friends are usually published to commemorate a distinguished scholar's sixtieth or seventieth birthday (*kanreki kinen* 還歷紀念 or *koki kinen* 古稀紀念) or death (*tsuito kinen* 追悼紀念). These frequently contain a short account of his life and a bibliography of his works. Yamane Yukio 山根幸夫, *Chûgokushi kenkyû nyûmon* 中國史研究入門 (8.2.2) lists 75 out of a total of no fewer than 700 such collections published on Oriental studies between the first year of Meiji and 1995.

There are two main types of bibliography available to help locate present and past work on a given subject or period. The first is usually in the form of an analytic bibliographic essay and includes the evaluations of the author. This type is called "academic trends" (*gakkai dôkô* 學界動向) or "history of research" (*kenkyûshi* 研究史) and serves to give the context of a given piece of research as well as the present state of the field. The second type is in the form of a straightforward, unannotated bibliography which attempts to list all publications on a given subject or period. This type is called "bibliography of secondary literature" (*bunken mokuroku* 文獻目錄). In Chinese history the usual arrangement in both types of bibliography is by dynasty, by neighboring peoples, and by special subject.

In this section only the most important bibliographies covering the whole of Chinese history are given. Thus for works examining Japanese scholarship on the Qing turn to section 50.8.3.

10.3.1 *Japanese Academic-Trends Bibliographies*

Meiji igo ni okeru rekishigaku no hattatsu 明治以後における歷史學の發達 contains bibliographic essays on Chinese history arranged by dynasty and by neighboring peoples (pp. 395–625). It is the standard reference covering work produced in Japan between ca. 1870 and 1926.[22]

For postwar trends several works are available. Most reliable is the annual summary of the previous year's historical writing which has appeared in the May issue (no.5) of *Shigaku zasshi* since vol. 60 (1950) under the tile "Nihon rekishi gakkai no kaiko to genjô 日本における歷史學界の回顧と現狀." It covers all periods. It has also been published in book form for the years 1949–85 under the title *Nihon rekishi gakkai no kaiko to*

---

[22] *Meiji igo ni okeru rekishigaku no hattatsu* (The development of historical studies since the Meiji period), Rekishi kyôiku kenkyûkai 歷史教育研究會 eds., Tokyo, 1933. Originally appeared in *Rekishi kyôiku*, vol. 7; vol. 9 (1932).

genjô 日本歴史學界の回顧と現狀.[23] Several English-language journals (e.g., *EC, JSYS* or *LIC*) publish translations of the *Shigaku zasshi* section on the period they cover.

The quinquennial volume of trends in Japanese historical writing which is published for the International Conference of Historical Sciences has English-language summaries: *Nihon ni okeru rekishigaku no hattatsu to genjô* 日本における歴史學の發達現狀. It has been published every five years since 1959 by Tokyo daigaku shuppansha or Yamakawa shuppansha.

Yamane's guide although not strictly speaking an academic-trends bibliography, contains annotated bibliographies giving major works in Japanese (and other languages) on all periods of Chinese history.

John Timothy Wixted, *Japanese Scholars of China: A Bibliographical Handbook*, Edwin Mellen Press, 1992, concentrates on the older generations of Japanese historians of China.[24]

10.3.2   Unannotated Bibliographies

In Japan, major publishing houses compete with each other to bring out multi-volume histories of the world (including China) or of China itself. These works usually contain thorough bibliographies focused on Japanese scholarship. For example, *Sekai rekishi taikei* 世界歴史大系 (Outlines of world history), 5 vols., Yamakawa, 1996–8; *Chûgoku shigaku no kihon mondai* 中國史學の基本問題 (Basic problems in Chinese historiography), 4 vols., Kyûko, 1997–8. These are usually edited by the leading scholars of the day and contain essays by younger specialists. For past scholarship, check a retrospective

---

[23] Shigakkai, eds., 25 vols., Yamakawa, 1987 (vols. 12–15 cover Chinese history from the Shang to the contemporary period).

[24] The years up to the 1950s are covered in *Japanese Studies on Japan and the Far East; a Short Biographical and Bibliographical Introduction*, Teng Ssu-yü, comp., with the collaboration of Masuda Kenji and Kaneda Hiromitsu, HKU Press, 1961. Arrangement is by authors (within broad subject categories). Many younger scholars were not included and the entries are not complete. There is an author/subject index.

bibliography such as (*Nihon ni okeru*) *Tôyôshi ronbun moku-roku* 日本における東洋史論文目錄 (English title: *Japanese Studies on Asian History: a Catalogue of Articles on Asia [Excluding Japan]*).[25]

Books and Articles on Oriental Subjects has appeared annually since 1956. There is always a long section on China.[26]

Both *Shigaku zasshi* and *Tôyôshi kenkyû* list the contents of other Japanese journals regularly throughout the year and thus provide a convenient way of keeping up-to-date with work as it is published (often in out-of-the-way journals).

An unannotated bibliography on Chinese economic history may be found in the annual bibliography of books and articles on Chinese economic history published by the journal *Keizaishi kenkyû*. The title since 1960 is *Keizaishi bunken kaidai* 經濟史文獻解題.[27]

---

[25] (*Nihon ni okeru*) *Tôyôshi ronbun mokuroku*, Tôyôshi ronbun mokuroku henshû iinkai, eds., 4 vols., Nippon gakujutsu shinkôkai, 1964-7. This lists all articles appearing in no less than 1,885 journals, periodicals, and collective publications between ca. 1880 and 1962. The arrangement is by journal, all articles in each issue being listed in turn. The fourth volume is an author index. The very wide coverage of this bibliography (which also includes an author's reviews) effectively puts out of business all previous unannotated, general bibliographies of Japanese studies of Chinese history and more than makes up for the lack of arrangement by subject categories.

[26] Tôhô gakkai (The Institute of Oriental Culture), *Books and Articles on Oriental Subjects*, Tokyo, 1956– . Each year covers the scholarship of the preceding year. It is less comprehensive, but comes out more quickly, than the Jimbun's *Tôyôgaku kenkyû bunken ruimoku* (10.1).

[27] The years 1933–38 were covered annually in the journal from vol. 11 (1934); after the war in book form under the title *Keizaishi nenkan* 經濟史年鑑, 3 vols. (Osaka), covering the years 1951–55 and under the title *Keizaishi bunken* 經濟史文獻 from 1956 to 1959.

10.3.3   Main Japanese Historical Journals

Those journals marked with an asterisk are indexed in the *Bibliography of Asian Studies*.

*Acta Asiatica (1960– , triannual to 1991, thereafter biannual) reprints English translations of Japanese articles on Chinese history, mainly by well-established scholars. From time to time an entire issue is devoted to the Japanese scholarship on a particular period or problem of Chinese history, e.g., *Sources of Manchu History* (*AA* 53, 1988); *Viewpoints on T'ang China* (*AA* 55, 1988).

*Annals of the Institute for Research in Humanities (1989– , annual), Jimbun, Kyoto University. From 1957–88, the title was *Zinbun*. Mainly carries English translations of articles appearing in *Tôhô gakuhô*.

*MTB   Memoirs of the Research Department of the Tôyô Bunko (1926– , annual since 1955) reprints translations of scholarly articles on Chinese historical geography and Chinese history by senior historians of the Tokyo school (English-language equivalent of the Tôyô bunko's *Tôyô gakuhô*).

Rekishigaku kenkyû 歷史學研究 (1933– , monthly), establishment Marxist historical journal.

Shigaku zasshi 史學雜誌 (1889– , monthly), Shigakkai, Tokyo University. The leading establishment historical journal in Japan; articles on all periods of history of all countries. Important annual bibliographic retrospect. The first 100 volumes (1889–1991) are indexed in *Shigaku zasshi sômokuroku* 史學雜誌總目錄, Yamakawa, 1993. It lists the tables of contents as well as providing an author index. Since 1983, the annual volume has English-language abstracts.

Tôyô bunka kenkyûjo kiyô 東洋文化研究所紀要 (1943– , triannual), Tôbunken, Tokyo University. Contains important articles on Chinese history and also on South and Southeast Asia.

Tôhô gaku 東方學 (1951– , biannual), Tôhô gakkai, Tokyo.

Tôhô gakuhô 東方學報 (1931– , annual), Jimbun, Kyoto University.

Tôyô gakuhô 東洋學報 (1910– , quarterly), Tôyô bunko, Tokyo. Scholarly contributions on Chinese history before the twentieth century. There is a comprehensive index covering issues 1 to 75 (1910–93): *Tôyô gakuhô sômokuroku* 東洋學報總目錄, Tôyô bunko, 1994.

Tôyôshi kenkyû 東洋史研究 (1935– , quarterly) carries many important articles on Chinese history, mainly before the twentieth century.

There are a great many other historical journals as well as the journals of many dozens of university history and other departments, all of which carry articles on Chinese history. There are also many specialist journals (on a particular period, on historical geography or on legal history). As a general rule it saves time to find out who are the historians who have published important work in a given field and who are those currently publishing in it; in Japan as in China there are closely knit schools which trace their line through the acknowledged leader in each generation. Thus the historians of China currently at Tôdai and other leading universities connected to Tôdai are the direct descendants in the fourth generation of the founder of the Tokyo school, Shiratori Kurakichi. This has implications not only for approaches and interpretations, but also for jobs.

In order to locate Japanese language periodicals and journals in Western collections, check the standard catalogs of periodicals but note the following:

National Union List of Current Japanese Serials in East Asian Libraries of North America, Committee on East Asian Libraries, A.A.S., 1992.

"Union Card File of Oriental Vernacular Series (Japanese)," Library of Congress, Washington, DC.

Check-list of Japanese Periodicals Held in British University and Research Libraries, S. M. Mandahl and P. W. Carnell, comps., Sheffield Univ. Press, 1971.

For names and addresses of Japanese scholars working on Chinese history, see Center for East Asian Cultural Studies of UNESCO, *Directory of Asian Studies in Japan*, Tôyô bunko, 1996.

10.4 Western Secondary Sources and Journals

10.4.1 Bibliography

The study of Chinese history in Europe began with the work of the Jesuit sinologists (33.7.1). It reached its peak in the first half of the twentieth century with French sinology. The center shifted from Europe to the United States with the development of area studies there in the 1950s.[28]

For names and addresses of many of those working in the field of Chinese history, see the Association of Asian Studies, *Membership Directory* (obtainable from 1021 East Huron Street, Ann Arbor, MI 48104 USA). The European Association of Chinese Studies publishes a quarterly newspaper entitled *EACS Newsletter*, which is also available on the Internet. Note that the *Guide to Asian Studies in Europe*, International Institute for Asian Studies, eds., Curzon, 1998, lists 5,000 European Asianists; 1,200 institutes and university departments; and 300 museums, organizations and newsletters.

The standard bibliography of 70,000 Western language works (both books and articles) on China up to 1921 was compiled by Henri Cordier, who, although he knew no Chinese, certainly knew the European and treaty-port publications on China extremely well: *Bibliotheca Sinica: dictionnaire bibliographique des ouvrages relatifs à l'Empire chinoise.*[29] There is a useful

---

[28] Arthur Wright, The Study of Chinese Civilization," *Journal of the History of Ideas* 2: 233–55 (1960). The autobiography of John King Fairbank (1907–91), a key figure in the development of China studies in the United States, is a good place to start: *Chinabound: A Fifty-Year Memoir*, Harper and Row, 1982; see also Paul A. Cohen, *Discovering History in China: American Historical Writing on the Recent Chinese Past*, Col. UP, 1984. This is in part an assessment of the Fairbank influence.

[29] *Bibliotheca Sinica*, 1893–95; rev. ed., 4 vols., Paris: Guilmoto, 1904–8; 4 vols., plus 1-vol. supplement, Paris: Geuthner, 1922–4; repr., Beiping, 1938; Taibei, 1966; New York: B. Franklin, 1968. See also John Lust, *Western Books on China Published up to 1850 in the Library of the School of Oriental and African Studies, University of London: A Descriptive Catalogue*, London: Bamboo Publishers, 1987. Contains citations to 1,283

Footnote continued on next page

but not entirely reliable *Author Index to the Bibliotheca Sinica of Henri Cordier*, East Asiatic Library, Columbia University, 1953. It was added to volume 5 of the 1966 Taibei reprint.

Four bibliographies bring Cordier up to the 1970s:

T'ung-li Yuan, *China in Western Literature: A Continuation of Cordier's Bibliotheca Sinica*, YUP, 1958, covers 18,000 books (not articles) appearing between 1921 and 1956; arrangement by subject category and contains author indexes.

John Lust: *Index Sinicus, A Catalogue of Articles Relating to China in Periodicals and Other Collective Publications, 1920–1955*, Heffer, 1964, covers 19,734 articles, reviews and obituary notices appearing between 1920 and 1955; arrangement by subject category and contains author indexes.

Books and articles on China in Western languages appearing between 1941 and 1970 (and therefore bringing Yuan and Lust up to 1970) are listed in *Cumulative Bibliography of Asian Studies, 1941–1965, Subject Bibliography*, 4 vols., G. K. Hall, 1970–1; *Cumulative Bibliography of Asian Studies, 1966–1970, Subject Bibliography*, 3 vols., 1972; *Author Bibliography*, 3 vols., 1973. This bibliography is based on the annual *Bibliography of Asian Studies*, which appears as a separate issue of the *Journal of Asian Studies* at year's end (10.1, item 1).

Modern Chinese Society 1644–1970: An Analytic Bibliography, vol. 1, *Publications in Western Languages*, G. W. Skinner and E. A. Winckler eds., SUP, 1973, for secondary works on the later empire.

The *Bibliography of Asian Studies* or the *Revue bibliographique de sinologie* should be used as a first reference for Western-language works appearing after 1970.

In addition, there are a number of selective, annotated bibliographies of Western works on all aspects of Chinese history and civilization available:

China: A Critical Bibliography, Charles O. Hucker, ed., UAP, 1962.

Premodern China, A Bibliographical Introduction, Chun-shu Chang, comp., CCS, Univ. of Michigan, 1971; updates previous item.

---

items, arranged by subject. Has title index, name index, supplementary subject index, and Chinese title index.

China, Peter Cheng, comp., *World Bibliographical Series*, Clio, 1983; rpnt., 1988. Covers books in English on all aspects of China, mainly published between 1970 and 1982. Serves to update previous item.

China: New Edition, Charles W. Hayford, comp., *World Bibliographical Series* 35, Clio Press, 1997. Contains more than 1,500 annotated entries, which refer to more than 2,200 book titles (mainly in English) on all aspects of China. Covers books mainly published in the 1980s and 1990s and therefore continues previous items.

American Historical Association Guide to Historical Literature, Mary Beth Norton, ed., 2 vols., OUP, 1995. Provides a selective and up-to-date bibliography. The chapters on Chinese history contain 750 works on the periods from the Shang to 1911, each entry with a short characterization of its content and value by a team of scholars. The chapter on China up to 1644 was edited by Patricia Buckley Ebrey and that on China after 1644 by James H. Cole. There are author and subject indexes. The *Guide* has the advantage of being regularly updated.

Doctoral Dissertations

For over 2,500 doctoral dissertations written in western languages between 1976 and 1990 dealing in one way or another with China before 1800, consult Shulman (1998), the first item below; to check theses written before 1976 and to keep up-to-date with those written after 1990, use the publications listed in item two.

Doctoral Dissertations on China and on Inner Asia, 1976–1990: An Annotated Bibliography of Studies in Western Languages, Frank Joseph Shulman, comp. and ed., with contributions by Patricia Polansky and Anna Leon Shulman, Greenwood Press, 1998. This is a multidisciplinary, classified, cross-referenced and indexed guide to 10,293 dissertations in western languages that in whole or in part are concerned with China, Mongolia, Tibet, Taiwan, Hong Kong, Macao and the overseas Chinese communities. Encompasses studies not only in every major discipline of the humanities, the social and behavioral sciences, but also in education, law, medicine, architecture, the natural sciences and engineering. The typical entry not only contains references to the thesis itself but also citations to one or more published thesis abstracts, statements indicating availability of copies, descriptive annotations, and bibliographical citations to one or more books and/or occasional papers published by the author that either constitute his published dissertation or are derived from his research. Indexes by author, by degree-awarding institution, and by subject.

Doctoral Dissertations on Asia published annually by the Association of Asian Studies since 1981.[30]

Russian Studies of China

The standard bibliography of early Russian-language publications on China (including Chinese history) is P. E. Skatchkov, *Bibliografiya Kitaya* (Systematic bibliography of books and journal articles on China in Russian published between 1730 and 1957), Nauka, 1960 (this revised and supplemented the original edition of 1932). The 19,551 entries are arranged under 25 broad subject categories. What amounts to an updated version (on filing cards) is available in the Sinological Department of the Institute of Scientific Information on Social Science (INION) of the Russian Academy of Sciences.

For a brief overview of present-day Russian sinology and Russian sources on Chinese history, see *Russia*, European Association of Chinese Studies, ed., 1996. See also the older C. Kiriloff, "Russian Sources," in Leslie, Mackerras and Wang, eds., *Essays on the Sources for Chinese History*, ANU Press, 1973, 188–202. See also T'ung-li Yuan, *Russian Works on China, 1918–1960, in American Libraries*, YUP, 1961, and Gilbert Rozman, ed., *Soviet Studies of Premodern China: Assessments of Recent Scholarship*, CCS, Univ. of Michigan, 1984. Fourteen signed bibliographical essays cover history (including archaeology) and literature from antiquity through to the Qing. There is an index of Soviet specialists on Asia as well as a general index.

Note also that the *Annual Bibliography of Oriental Studies* (Kyoto) and the *Bibliography of Asian Studies* both of which list recent publications in Russian on Chinese history, as does the

---

[30] Prior to 1981, use *Doctoral Dissertations on Asia: an Annotated Bibliographical Journal of Current International Research*, Univ. of Michigan, Ann Arbor, Winter 1975–80. Arrangement is chronological within subject and country categories. There is an author index. For earlier doctoral dissertations, see *Doctoral Dissertations on China: A Bibliography of Studies in Western Languages, 1945–1970*, L. H. D. Gordon and F. J. Shulman, eds., UWP, 1972, and *Doctoral Dissertations on China, 1971–1975*, UWP, 1978.

Revue bibliographique de sinologie, which is less comprehensive but provides brief reviews.

For a "bio-bibliographic dictionary" of 3,000 Soviet Orientalists, see *Biobibliografičeskij slovar' otechestvennyx vostokovedov c. 1917*, S. D. Miliband, comp., 2 vols., Nauka, 1995.

10.4.2   Main Western-Language Journals

To locate Western language journals, check the standard catalogs such as *Union List of Periodicals* (for the United States and Canada) and the China Library Group, *Union List of Current Chinese Serials in the UK* or *British Union Catalogue of Periodicals*. Efforts are being made to create a database of Chinese and sinological periodicals in major European libraries under the auspices of European Association of Chinese Studies.

The following list of 50 journals is by no means exhaustive. It only includes some of the main sinological and historical journals (all of which are indexed in the *Bibliography of Asian Studies*). Note in particular the journals of the various societies for the study of particular periods (*EC*, *TS*, *JSY*, *MS* and *LIC*). Similar societies with their own journals exist in China, Japan and Taiwan.

AA   *Acta Asiatica* (see 10.3.3).

AM   *Asia Major* (3rd series, 1988– , biannual). Leading German sinological journal (old series, Leipzig, 1923–33) until moving to London, where it became main the main British journal of sinology (new series, 1949–75). After a gap, it reopened in the United States, where it has been edited and published at Princeton University since 1988.

AO   *Archív Orientální* (1929– , quarterly), Prague. Index for 1929–92 in vol. 64.4 (1996).

AS   *Asiatische Studien/Études Asiatiques* (1947– , quarterly), Bern.

BEFEO   *Bulletin de l'École française d'Extrême-Orient* (1901– , annual), edited at Hanoi until 1955, then Saigon (1956.1) en route for Paris (1956.2–). Although it has always concentrated on Indo-China, it not infrequently has important articles on Chinese history.

BMFEA   *Bulletin of the Museum of Far Eastern Antiquities* (1929– , annual), edited in Stockholm, contains important articles of

Karlgren and his pupils. The Museum was founded by J. G. Andersson, the discoverer of the Yangshao culture in 1925. Karlgren was the Director from 1939–59.

BSEI   *Bulletin de la Société des études indochinoises* (1883–1925; n.s., 1932–75, quarterly), edited in Saigon; see comment on *BE-FEO*).

BSOAS   *Bulletin of the School of Oriental and African Studies* (1917– , quarterly) carries occasional important articles and reviews on Chinese history and linguistics. Edited at SOAS, University of London.

CA   *Cahiers d'Extrême-Asie* (1985– , annual). Bilingual journal of the Ecole Française d'Extrême Orient, Kyoto Section. Specializes mainly in the history of Daoism and Buddhism.

CAAD   *China Archaeology and Art Digest* (1996– , quarterly), indispensable way of keeping up-to-date with dozens of art and archaeological journals to many of which no Western and few libraries even in China have subscriptions (see 13.3).

CAJ   *Central Asiatic Journal* (1976– , biannual), Harrassowitz.

CLEAR   *Chinese Literature: Essays Articles Reviews* (1978– , annual). Editorial at Indiana University.

CQ   *The China Quarterly* (1960– , quarterly), SOAS, London. Although devoted to modern China, there are occasional reviews of historical works. Articles and reviews are indexed at the end of the fourth issue each year.

CR   *Chinese Repository*, 20 vols., Canton, 1832–51. Well-informed articles by the pioneer Protestant missionaries.

CS   *Chinese Science* (1975– , irregular), vols. 1–10; from volume 11 (1993–94), annual. Edited at the CCS, Univ. of California at Los Angeles.

CSH   *Chinese Studies in History* (1962– , annual). Translations into English of important Chinese articles on history. M. E. Sharp, Armonk, New York.

EAH   *East Asian History* (1991– , biannual), Canberra (from 1970–90, the title was *Papers on Far Eastern History*).

EC   *Early China* (1975– , annual). Publication of the Society for the Study of Pre-Han China (University of California, Berkeley).

Now named the Society for the Study of Early China (SSEC). From 1969–75 was called the society's *Newsletter*. See 12.2, *Societies, Yearbooks and Journals* for more on this journal.

EMC   *Early Medieval China* (1994– , irregular annual). Published at Western Michigan University in Kalamazoo, Michigan. All aspects of Han to Tang with special emphasis on the Six Dynasties period. Perhaps as a reflection of the relatively few Western scholars in this field, there have been many efforts to start a journal for this period. None have lasted long: *Newsletter of Nan-Pei-Ch'ao Studies*, CMC, 1977–78; *Nan-Pei-Ch'ao Studies* (1979–81); *Newsletter* of the *Early Medieval China Group* (1988).

ETC   *Études chinoises* (1983– , biannual), Paris.

HJAS   *Harvard Journal of Asiatic Studies* (1936– , biannual). The main journal in the United States for classical studies of China, Korea and Japan.

IJCL   *International Journal of Chinese Linguistics* (1996– , biannual). Hong Kong: John Benjamins.

JA   *Journal asiatique* (1922– , biannual) covers the whole of Asia, with focus on the ancient Near East; articles on Chinese history are less frequent than in the past.

JAOS   *Journal of the American Oriental Society* (1849– , quarterly) covers the entire "Orient," New Haven Connecticut.

JAH   *Journal of Asian History* (1966– , biannual), Harrassowitz. Specializes in Central Asian history.

JAS   *Journal of Asian Studies* (appeared 1941–55 under the title *Far Eastern Quarterly*). Journal of the Association for Asian Studies (AAS), Ann Arbor, Michigan. It covers North, South and East Asia and publishes many important articles and reviews on China. The focus is on modern China, and the reviews are mainly limited to books in English (and to a certain extent, other Western languages). Nevertheless this is the main Western journal devoted to Asian studies. It also carries important essays on the state of the field of sec-ondary scholarship in particular areas of Chinese historical studies. The *JAS* is available in full text from 1941 (*FEQ*) to 1993 on JSTOR at http://www.jstor.org. 1994 will be added in 1999 and 1995 in 2000.

JCL   *Journal of Chinese Linguistics* (1973– , biannual), University of California, Berkeley.

JCR   *Journal of Chinese Religions* (1983– , annual), Indiana University. From 1976 to 1983, the title was *Journal of the Society for the Study of Chinese Religions*; from 1998, also incorporates *Taoist Resources*.

JESHO   *Journal of the Economic and Social History of the Orient* (1957– , quarterly), Leiden. Attempts to cover the entire "Orient," and inevitably leaves some countries under-represented. This has normally been the case for China and Japan.

JOS   *Journal of Oriental Studies* (1954– , biannual). Hong Kong University. Articles in English or Chinese.

JOSoc   *Journal of the Oriental Society* (1968– , annual), Sydney.

JRAS   *Journal of the Royal Asiatic Society* (1823– , quarterly). Divided according to the various branches of the RAS, e.g., North China Branch (1857–1942: *JNCBRAS*); Malayan Branch, Hong Kong Branch. The *JNCBRAS* in particular is worth looking through. The *JRAS* is still published in London, and covers the whole of Asia, but the articles are mainly on the ancient Near East or other parts of Asia than China.

JSYS   *Journal of Song-Yuan Studies* (1989– , biannual). Started as *Sung Studies Newsletter*, 1969–80; changed title to *Bulletin of Sung-Yuan Studies*, 1980–8; adopted present title in 1989). A good way of keeping up-to-date with new work in this field. Albany, New York.

LIC   *Late Imperial China* (1985– , biannual). Started in 1965 under the title *Ch'ing-shih wen-t'i*. Society for Qing Studies, California Institute of Technology, Pasedena, California.

MingS   *Ming Studies* (1975– , annual), University of Minnesota, Minneapolis.

MTB   *Memoirs of the Research Department of the Tôyô Bunko* (see 10.3.3).

MS   *Monumenta Serica* (1935– , annual). German Catholic sinological journal, edited in Beijing (1935–48); Tokyo (1954–56); Nagoya (1957–62); Los Angeles (1963–71); since 1972 at Sankta Augusta, Germany.

NGNVO *Deutsche Gesellschaft für Natur und Völkerkunde Ostasiens, Nachrichten* (1926–); also *Mitteilungen* (1873–), currently edited (since 1951, biannual) at Hamburg.

OE   *Oriens Extremus* (1954– , biannual), edited at Hamburg.

OS   *Oriens Vostok* (1991– , bimonthly). Formerly *Narody Azii i Afriki* (Peoples of Asia and Africa, 1961–90). Edited at the Institute of Oriental Studies of the Russian Academy of Sciences, Moscow.

PCH   *Papers on Chinese History* (1991– , annual), Harvard University.

PV   *Peterburgskoye Vostokovedenye* (St. Petersburg Journal of Oriental Studies), 1992– , irregular; Institute of Oriental Studies of the Russian Academy of Sciences, St. Petersburg branch.

PEW *Philosophy East and West* (1951– , quarterly), UHP.

PDV *Problemy Dalnego Vostoka* (Problems of the Far East), incorporating *Sovetskoye Vostokovedenye* (Soviet Oriental Studies), 20 vols. (former Sinological Institute, Moscow), 1940–59.

RBS *Revue bibliographique de sinologie/Review of Bibliography in Sinology*, Paris (1957– , annual). See 10.1.

SL   *Sinologica* (1947–72), edited at Basel.

SSC *Social Sciences in China* (1980– , quarterly), see 10.2.3.

SYSJK Chinese acronym (*Shiyusuo jikan*) for the *Zhongyang yanjiuyuan, Lishi yuyan yanjiusuo jikan* 中央研究院歷史語言研究所集刊. Has occasional articles in English, see 10.2.4).

TP   *T'oung pao* (1890– , biannual), leading sinological journal in Europe. Edited in The Hague and Paris.

TR   *Taoist Resources* (1988– , irregular); see under *Journal of Chinese Religions*.

TS   *T'ang Studies* (1982– , annual). Journal of the T'ang Studies Society (editorial, Boulder Colorado).

11

Libraries

The present chapter introduces the most important libraries and collections of Chinese books in China (11.1), Taiwan (11.2), Japan (11.3), and the United States, Europe, and Russia (11.4). It concludes with a brief introduction on gaining access to these collections using the Internet (11.6) and a word on publishers and bookstores for Chinese historical works (11.5).

Note that the usefulness of a library for research depends as much on its quality and the ease of access to its collections as on the quantity of the books it contains.

11.1 China

Only the four largest libraries in China are given here.[1]

1. Beijing tushuguan 北京圖書館 (Peking Library), or Beitu 北圖 for short, is the national library of China and as such is the largest in the country, with a collection of over 20 million volumes (of which 45 percent are Chinese). It is open to the public free of charge with no special formalities. Three books may be called from the stacks at a time for reading on the premises. Beitu was founded in 1909 as the Jingshi tushuguan 京師圖書館 (Capital library), situated in Guanghua temple.[2] It opened for readers in 1912. It was endowed with part

---

[1] *Zhongguo tushuguan minglu* 中國圖書館名明錄 (Directory of Chinese libraries), Wu Renyong 吳仁勇 et al. Zhongguo xueshu, 1982.
[2] In 1917 it moved to the site of the 國子監 (Imperial academy), southern school. In 1928, it was renamed the Guoli Beiping tushuguan 國立北平圖書館 (National Library of Peiping); in 1931, it moved to new
Footnote continued on next page

of the book collections from the Grand Secretariat (Neige 內閣), the Hanlinyuan 翰林院 (Hanlin academy) and the Guozijian 國子監 (Imperial academy) which included portions of the imperial libraries of the Southern Song and Ming. In 1917 it acquired the copy of the *Siku quanshu* previously deposited in the palace at Chengde and a number of Qing private collections. Today the library possesses probably the finest collection of Chinese rare editions in the world.[3] There is a major *shanben* reprint series.[4] In addition, Beitu has the single largest collection of oracle-bone inscriptions in the world (over 34,500) and also more than 100,000 rubbings of stone inscriptions. Since it has been a deposit library since 1949, copies of all Chinese books, journals and newspapers published since then have been sent here. Beitu also has on deposit copies of all doctoral theses defended in China since 1949. The library has put 400,000 of its post-1975 acquisitions into an on-line catalog. It is also in the process of putting its post-1949 holdings on-line. There is a printed subject catalog of old Chinese books (mainly those published before 1911, but not including *shanben*): *Beijing tushuguan putong guji zongmu* 北京圖書館普通古籍總目 (Comprehensive catalog of ordinary, old Chinese books), 15 vols., Shumu wenxian, 1990–7. Each volume covers a separate subject category. Vol. 3 covers History and vol. 4, Geography. There are four-corner author/title indexes in each volume. The total number of titles listed comes to about 200,000.

2. The second largest library in China is the Shanghai tushuguan 上海圖書館 (Shanghai Library), or Shangtu 上圖 for short, with a collection of over 10 million books. It resides in a splendid new building with user-friendly reading rooms (ancient texts; genealogy etc.) and includes other important collections previously housed separately, e.g., the Shanghai baokan tushuguan 上海報刊圖書館 (Shanghai Newspapers and Periodicals Library) and the Shanghaishi lishi wenxian tushuguan 上海市歷史文獻圖書館 (Shanghai Library of Historical Documents).

---

premises near Beihai. In 1949, it acquired its present name and in 1983, it moved to its present location near the Purple Bamboo Park.

[3] *Beijing tushuguan guji shanben shumu* 北京圖書館古籍善本書目 (A Catalog of Rare Editions in the Beijing Library), 5 vols., Shumu wenxian, 1989. Lists 11,000 titles of rare editions collected since 1949.

[4] *Beijing tushuguan guji zhenben congkan* 北京圖書館古籍珍本叢刊, 117 vols., Shumu wenxian, 1988–91. Peking University also publishes a reprint series from its substantial holdings of rare editions: *Beijing daxue tushuguan shanben congkan* 北京大學圖書館善本叢刊, vols., 1–80, 1997.

3. The Nanjing tushuguan 南京圖書館 (Nanjing Library), or Nantu 南
    圖 for short, has a collection of 2.5 million volumes including the old
    Jiangsu shengli guoxue tushuguan 江蘇省立國學圖書館 (Jiangsu
    Provincial Sinological Library), which published one of the few gen-
    eral catalogs of a major Chinese collection.[5]

4. The library of the Shehui kexueyuan 社會科學院 (Shekeyuan, the
    Chinese Academy of Social Sciences, CASS), or Sheketu 社科圖 for
    short, is divided among the various institutes of the Academy. Alto-
    gether it contains 2.5 million volumes. The Academy inherited the
    collection of Chinese books which had been built up by the Beiping
    renwen kexue yanjiusuo (9.4) and numbered about 470,000 ce, includ-
    ing a considerable number of rare editions whose numbers were
    augmented after 1949. There is a published *shanben* catalog with
    8,496 entries.[6] For the Kaogusuo collection, see 13.3.

There are many other important libraries in China, mainly in
the older universities, starting with Peking University, and in
some of the provincial capitals (these latter often go back a long
way and have important collections).[7] Historical archival holdings are listed in Table 20, chap. 20 and chap. 50.1–3.

Note the following union catalogs for Chinese libraries:

Zhongguo congshu zonglu 中國叢書綜錄 (Bibliography of Chinese *Congshu*), Shanghai Municipal Library, comp., 3 vols., Shanghai guji,
1959–62; rpnt., 1983; reduced-size edition, but clear print on good
quality paper, 1986; rpnt., 1993.

Zhongguo guji shanben shumu 中國古籍善本書目 (9.8.1).

Zhongguo difangzhi lianhe mulu 中國地方志聯合目錄 (Union Catalog of
Chinese local gazetteers), Chinese Academy of Sciences, Beijing Observatory, Zhongguo kexueyuan, Beijing tianwentai 中國科學院北
京天文臺, ed., Zhonghua, 1985.

---

[5] *Jiangsu shengli guoxue tushuguan zongmu* 江蘇省立國學圖書館總
目, 44 *juan* plus *bubian*, 12 *juan*, Nanking, 1933–6; 1937 rpnt., 15 vols.,
Taibei, 1970.

[6] *Zhongguo kexueyuan tushuguan cang Zhongwen guji shanben shumu*
中國科學院圖書館藏中文古籍善本書目, Kexue, 1994.

[7] The largest university library is that of Peking University. There is
a published catalog of 7,800 rare books: *Beijing daxue tushuguan cang
shanben shumu* 北京大學圖書館藏善本書目, 2 vols., Beijing daxue, 1958.

Zhongguo jiapu zonghe mulu 中國家譜綜合目錄, Zhonghua, 1997, is a union catalog of 14,761 genealogies compiled before 1949 held in 400 Chinese collections.

Quanguo Zhongyi tushu lianhe mulu 全國中醫圖書聯合目錄 (Union catalog of works of traditional Chinese medicine), Zhongyi guji, 1991

1833–1949 Quanguo Zhongwen qikan lianhe mulu 全國中文期刊聯合 目錄 (Union Catalog of 19,115 Periodicals in 50 Chinese Libraries), Beijing, 1981. Revised edition of 1961 edition. Has *pinyin* index.

Increasingly provinces are publishing union catalogs—for example, *Sichuan sheng difangzhi lianhe mulu* 四川省地方志聯合目錄, Sichuan sheng zhongxin tushuguan, ed. and published, Chengdu, 1982.

To locate or contact a library in China, use Wang Enguang 王 恩光 et al., *Zhongguo tushuguan minglu* 中國圖書館名錄 (Directory of Chinese libraries), Zhongguo xueshu, 1982. The text is in Chinese and English. The directory is useful for providing the names and addresses of 2,887 libraries, but the details on names of the librarian, holdings statistics and telephone numbers for 658 of them are by now long since out-of-date. There is an institutional name index (arranged alphabetically by English translation).

Hong Kong

There is an efficient online service linking university library catalogs in Hong Kong, enabling searches in all the collections simultaneously. The largest academic library is that of the University of Hong Kong.

11.2 Taiwan

The Hanxue yanjiu zhongxin 漢學研究中心 (Center for Chinese studies) is situated in the National Central Library and offers assistance to visiting Chinese scholars.

1. National Central Library (Guoli zhongyang tushuguan 國立中央圖 書館). Includes portions of the holdings of the former National Central Library of Nanjing (founded 1928); the rare editions sent to the United States from the former National Library of Peiping and the

rare book collection of the former Northeastern University.[8] Splendidly housed; online catalog available.

2. Library of the National Palace Museum (*Guoli gugong bowuyuan* 國立故宮博物院). Includes many *shanben* plus important archival holdings representing 5–10 percent of the Qing palace records and Grand Council archives.

3. Various libraries attached to the Zhongyang yanjiu yuan 中央研究院 (Academia Sinica), Nangang 南港, Taibei. The Fu Sinian tushuguan 傅斯年圖書館 (Fu Sinian Library) was formerly the library of the Shiyusuo. It contains important collections, built up in the 1930s, of oracle bones, Ming-Qing state papers, Han wooden slips, and folk songs. It is well catuoged and maintained as a first-class research library.

4. Library of the Jindaishi yanjiusuo 近代史研究所 (Institute of Modern History). Contains important late Qing archive holdings, including the files of the Zongli Yamen and the Waiwubu (50.1.2).

Note the following union catalogs for Taiwan collections:

Taiwan ge tushuguan xiancun congshu zimu suoyin 臺灣各圖書館現存叢書子目索引 (Author/title indexes to *congshu* in Taiwan libraries), Wang Baoxian 王寶先 comp., 3 vols., part I, 2 vols., title index; part 2, author index, CMC., 1975–77. Both indexes are by stroke count.

Zhonghua minguo Taiwan diqu gongcang fangzhi mulu 中華民國臺灣地區公藏方志目錄 (Catalog of local gazetteers in the Republic of China [Taiwan District] Public Collections), Wang Deyi 王德毅, comp., Hanxue yanjiu ziliao ji fuwu zhongxin, 1985.

Taiwan gongcang zupu jieti 臺灣公藏族譜解題 (Annotated Bibliography of Genealogies in Taiwan Public Collections), Chang Bide 昌彼得, comp., Taibei, 1969.

Zhonghua minguo zhongwen qikan lianhe mulu 中華民國中文期刊聯合目錄, Guoli zhongyang tushuguan, comp., 2 vols., Taibei, 1980. Union catalog of Chinese periodicals giving holding information on 7,410 titles in 17 libraries in Taiwan as of December 1979. Arranged by stroke count. Has title index arranged by subject, plus Wade-Giles title index.

---

[8] *Guoli zhongyang tushuguan shanben shumu* 國立中央圖書館善本書目, 3 vols., Taibei, 1957–8; 2nd rev. ed., 4 vols., 1986.

Taiwanqu zupu mulu 臺灣區族譜目錄 (Catalog of Chinese genealogies in
Taiwan), Zhao Zhenji 趙振績 and Chen Meigui 陳美桂, eds., Taiwan
sheng gexing lishi yuanyuan fazhan yanjiu xiehui 臺灣省各姓歷史
淵源發展研究協會, 1987.

To locate or contact a library in Taiwan, use Guoli zhongyang
tushuguan, ed., *Zhonghua minguo Hanxue jigou lu* 中華民國漢
學機構錄 (Directory of institutes of Chinese studies in the Republic of China), Taibei, 1987. This gives details of 88 institutes, university departments, museums, and libraries. For each
is listed the address, phone number, director's name and detailed description (both in English and Chinese). It has institutional name indexes arranged by stroke count and alphabetically by English translation of name.

11.3 Japan

For an account of how some of the most important collections
of Chinese books in Japan were built up, see Yu-ying Brown,
"The Origins and Characteristics of Chinese Collections in Japan," *JOS*, 31.1: 19–31 (1983). Work has begun on a union catalog of Chinese books in Japan. Anything published after 1965
in Japanese can now be looked up on CD-ROM (J-BISC).
There is also an online interlibrary catalog system, *Toshokan
seibû kensaku shisutemu* 圖書館情報檢索システム (Online Public
Access Catalog, OPAC).

Note that Japan is the only country in which dozens of literary and historical sources which were lost in China have been
preserved. They began to be imported into Japan after Shôtoku
Taishi 聖德太子 (574–622) sent an embassy to the Sui in 607. In
the Edo Chinese literary, historical and philosophical works,
and also practical manuals—for example, on medicine or law or
geography—were imported in large numbers through the Chinese trading station at Nagasaki.

*Nihon ni okeru Kanseki no shûshû, Kanseki kankei mokuroku
shûsei* 日本における漢籍の蒐集漢籍關係目錄集成 is a biblio-
graphy of published catalogs of Chinese books in Japan which

includes 3,100 catalogs from the late nineteenth century to 1980.[9]

Tokyo

1. Tôyô bunko 東洋文庫 (Oriental Library). Originally established by Iwasaki Hisaya 岩崎久稱 in 1917, since 1948 it has been a branch of the National Diet Library. The Tôyô bunko contains one of the largest collections of old Chinese books in Japan and also functions as a focus of research on Chinese history. It is open to the public. There is not as yet a catalog of its overall holdings of old Chinese books, but there is a separate one for the History branch: *Tôyô bunko shozô Kanseki bunrui mokuroku shibu* 東洋文庫所藏漢籍分類目錄史部, Tôyô bunko, 1986. It has a title index. The Tôyô bunko has also published catalogs in the same series for its holdings in the *Congshu* (1967), Classics (1978) and Philosophy (1993) branches.

2. Tôyô bunka kenkyûjo 東洋文化研究所 (The Institute for Oriental Culture) at Tôdai 東大 (Tokyo University). The Tôbunken was established in 1929 and took its present form in 1948. The Chinese section has an excellent collection of books with important holdings in social and economic history. There are two up-to-date comprehensive catalogs of old Chinese books, and of post-1911 works. The former includes the holdings of the Institute's first main collection, the 45,000 volumes of Oki Kan'ichi 大木干一 (rich in Qing legal, economic and administrative history), as well as many other collections left it by distinguished scholars such as Matsumoto Tadao 松本忠雄, Nagasawa Kikuya 長澤規矩也 and Niida Noboru 仁井田陞, *Tôkyô daigaku Tôyô bunka kenkyûjo Kanseki bunrui mokuroku* 東京大學東洋文化研究所漢籍分類目錄. Part 1 lists 200,000 volumes; part 1 is a title index and part 2, an author index.[10] There is also a special catalog of holdings of land deeds and other economic documents, *Tôyô bunka kenkyûjo shozô Chûgoku tochi bunsho mokuroku*

[9] *Zôtei Nihon ni okeru Kanseki no shûshû. Kanseki kankei mokuroku shûsei* (Collections of Chinese books in Japan: a catalog of catalogs of Chinese books in public and private collections), Tôyô bunko, 1961; rev. and enl., Kyûko, 1982. Arrangement is by place. On the exchanges of books between China and Japan, see the volume *Dianji* 典籍 (books) in the series *Zhong-Ri wenhua jiaoliushi daxi* 中日文化交流史大系, Wang Yong 王勇 and Ôba Osamu 大庭脩, eds., Zhejiang renmin, 1996.

[10] *Tôkyô daigaku Tôyô bunka kenkyûjo Kanseki bunrui mokuroku* (Catalog of Chinese books in Tôbunken), 2 vols. 1973–5; reduced-size edition with corrections, 1 vol., 1981; rpnt., with corrections, Kyûko, 1996.

kaisetsu 東洋文化研究所藏中國土地文書目錄解說.[11] The catalog of modern Chinese books lists Chinese works published between 1912 and 1990: *Gendai Chûgokusho bunrui mokuroku* 現代中國書分類目錄, 2 vols., Uchiyama, 1996. The catalog of Tokyo University Library's collection of old Chinese books (built up since the near-complete destruction by the Taisho earthquake) has been published: *Tôkyô daigaku sôgo toshokan Kanseki mokuroku* 東京大學綜合圖書館漢籍目錄, Tôkyô daigaku, 1995. It is arranged by the five branches and includes a title index by stroke count.

Other important libraries in Tokyo (in alphabetic order):

3. Kokuritsu kokkai toshokan 國立國會圖書館 (National Diet Library). Published catalog of old Chinese books: *Kokuritsu kokkai toshokan Kanseki mokuroku* 國立國會圖書館漢籍目錄, Kokkai toshukan, 1987; and index to the catalog: *Kokuritsu kokkai toshokan Kanseki mokuroku, sakuin* 國立國會圖書館漢籍目錄索引, 2 vols, Kokkai toshokan, 1995. Note also the Diet Library's important collection of Chinese periodicals and newspapers, *Kokuritsu kokkai toshokan: Chûgoku, Chôsengo zasshi, shinbun mokuroku* 國立國會圖書館中國朝鮮雜誌新聞目錄, Kokkai toshukan, 1993. Open to the public without special formalities. Has excellent catalog (including online) and good, research-oriented reading rooms.

4. Kunaichô shoryôbu 宮內廳書陵部 (Imperial Household Library). Published catalog: *Wa-Kan tosho bunrui mokuroku* 和漢圖書分類目錄, 2 vols., plus index, plus continuation (1952–55).

5. Naikaku bunko 內閣文庫 (Cabinet Library). It was founded in 1884 on the basis of the Tokugawa government library. Holds 175,000 old Chinese books. Published catalog: *Naikaku bunko Kanseki bunrui mokuroku* 內閣文庫漢籍分類目錄, Tokyo, 1956; rev. ed., 1971. Includes title index.

6. Seikadô bunko 静嘉堂文庫. Published catalog of old Chinese books: *Seikadô bunko Kanseki bunrui mokuroku* 静嘉堂文庫漢籍分類目錄, Tokyo, 1930. Founded by Iwasaki Yanosuke 岩崎彌之助 and his son, Iwasaki Koyata 岩崎小彌太, in 1893. The collection has an

---

[11] Hamashita Takeshi 濱下武志 et al., *Tôyô bunka kenkyûjo shozô Chûgoku tochi bunsho mokuroku kaisetsu*, 2 vols., Tokyo, 1983–6. This contains (1) selections from 10 sets of Qing and Republican-period documents, with introductions and annotations and (2) a complete catalog of the 10 sets of documents (totalling 2,250 items).

enormous number of rare books of which the core is the Bi Song lou 皕宋樓 library of Lu Xinyuan 陸心源 (1834–94), one of the four finest private collections of the Qing. It was purchased in 1907. The lexicographer Morohashi Tetsuji 諸橋轍次 was appointed curator in 1921 and held this post until 1955. One of his first jobs was to edit the catalog. The observant user of Morohashi's great dictionary, the *Dai Kan-Wa jiten,* will notice that the decorations on the endpapers are from works held in the Seikadô (2.3). Rare book catalog: *Seikadô bunko Sô-Gen pan zuroku* 靜嘉堂文庫宋元版圖錄, 2 vols., Kyûko, 1992. Vol. 1 contains illustrations; vol. 2, notes. The Seikadô has been a branch of the National Diet Library since 1948.

7. Sonkeikaku bunko 尊經閣文庫. Published catalog of old Chinese books: *Sonkeikaku bunko Kanseki bunrui mokurodu* 尊經閣文庫漢籍分類目錄索引, Tokyo, 1934 (*mokuroku*), 1935 (*sakuin*).

Kyoto

Jimbun kagaku kenkyûjo 京都大學人文科學研究所 (Research Institute for Humanistic Studies), Kyôdai (Kyoto University). The Chinese section of the Jimbun contains the major sinological library in the Kansai region: *Kyôto daigaku Jimbun kagaku kenkyûjo Kanseki bunrui mokuroku* 京都大學人文科學研究所漢籍分類目錄 and *Kyôto daigaku Jimbun kagaku kenkyûjo Kanseki mokuroku* 京都大學人文科學研究所漢籍目錄.[12]

Tenri University 天理大學. Situated in Tenri (close to Kyoto), it has an excellent Chinese collection and a distinguished series of published catalogs.

Nagoya

Hôsa Bunko 蓬左文庫. Housed as a unit in the Nagoya city library. Published catalog of old Chinese books: *Nagoya shi Hôsa bunko Kanseki bunrui mokuroku* 名古屋市蓬左文庫漢籍分類目錄, 1975.

Note the following union catalogs of holdings of Chinese works in important Japanese libraries:

[12] *Kyôto daigaku Jimbun kagaku kenkyûjo Kanseki bunrui mokuroku,* 2 vols., 1964–5; *Kyôto daigaku Jimbun kagaku kenkyûjo Kanseki mokuroku* (Catalog of Chinese books in the Jimbun), 2 vols., 1979–80; reduced-size ed., 1981. The earlier catalog has collectanea arranged by subject: both catalogs include modern research works.

1. *Nihon genson* 日本現存 *Mindai chihôshi mokuroku* 明代地方志目錄 (Catalog of Ming gazetteers in Japanese collections), Yamane Yukio 山根幸夫, Kyûko, 1962; enl., 1971; new edition, 1995 (49.8).

2. *Zôtei Nihon genson* 日本現存 *Minjin bunshû mokuroku* 明人文集目錄 (Catalog of collected works of Ming writers extant in Japan), Yamane Yukio 山根幸夫 and Ogawa Takashi 小川尚, eds., 1978. Holdings of 10 libraries.

3. *Kanseki sôsho shozai mokuroku* 漢籍叢書所在目錄 (Catalog of whereabouts of Chinese *congshu*), Tokyo, 1965. Holdings of seven libraries.

4. *Chûgoku chihôshi sôgo mokuroku* 中國地方志綜合目錄 (Union catalog of Chinese local gazetteers in 14 major libraries and research institutes in Japan), Tokyo, 1969. Compiled by staff at the National Diet Library, it supersedes all previous catalogs of gazetteers in Japanese libraries. Holdings of 14 libraries.

5. *Tokushu bunko shozô maikurofurirumu rengô mokuroku* 特殊文庫所藏マイクロフイルム連合目錄 (A union list of microfilms of Japanese, Chinese, Korean, Manchu, Mongolian, Vietnamese and Tibetan books and manuscripts preserved in eight libraries), Tokyo, 1967.

6. *Nihonbun Chûgokubun Chôsenbun tô chikuji kankôbutsu mokuroku* 日本文中國文朝鮮文等逐次刊行物目錄 (Catalog of periodicals in Japanese, Chinese and Korean), Tokyo, 1963. Holdings of three libraries.

7. *Nihon shuyô kenkyû kikan toshokan shozô Chûgokubun shinbun zasshi sôgo mokuroku* 日本主要研究機關圖書館所藏中國文新聞雜誌總合目錄 (Union catalog of holdings of Chinese newspapers and periodicals in 23 important Japanese collections), Tokyo, 1959.

11.4 The United States, Europe and Russia

11.4.1 The United States

The major sinological collections outside of China and Japan, are in the United States. Note that in counting the number of books in Chinese collections it is common practice to count the number of volumes (*ce* or sometimes *juan*) rather than titles. The 11 main ones in the United States by order of size of holdings (as of June, 1996) are:

1. Library of Congress, Washington, DC, founded in 1861 (718,000 vols). Although the largest collection of Chinese and Japanese books in the United States, it is not open stack and not research-oriented.

The main catalog is online as is the subject catalog, a printed version of which is published annually.[13] There are a number of published catalogs of the huge Chinese and Japanese collections, including of *shanben* (the largest collection outside of China);[14] of local gazetteers (the largest collection in the United States);[15] of periodicals;[16] and of newspapers.[17] Library of Congress, Washington, DC: *Far Eastern Languages Catalog*, 22 vols., G. K. Hall, 1972. The Library has cards for the Union Catalog of Chinese books in the United States (which card catalog it circulates to the university libraries). For a history, see See Shu Chao Hu, *The Development of the Chinese Collection in the Library of Congress*, Westview, 1979.

2. Harvard: Harvard-Yenching Library. The leading research library for Chinese history in the United States (494,000 vols). Published catalog of cards: *Catalogs of the Harvard-Yenching Library: Chinese Catalog; Author-Title*, vols., 1–28; *Subject*, vols., 29–38; *Serial Records*, vol. 39, Garland, 1986. For a catalog of 1,431 Song to Ming editions in the library, see *An Annotated Catalog of Chinese Rare Books in the Harvard-Yenching Library*, Shanghai cishu, 1998.

3. Princeton University (380,000 vols). *A Catalogue of the Chinese Rare Books in the Gest Collection of the Princeton University Library*, Ch'ü

---

[13] This massive four-volume work is surprisingly detailed in some areas, less so in others. For example, there are 22 entries under "Chinese Cabbage," including alternative spellings and different Latin names for different varieties. Under "China History," all the dynasties are listed along the following lines, "Sung: Dynasty; Anecdotes, Humor."

[14] Wang Chung-min, *A Descriptive Catalog of Rare Chinese Books in the Library of Congress*, 2 vols., Library of Congress, Washington, DC, 1957.

[15] Chu Shih Chia, *A Catalog of Chinese Local Histories in the Library of Congress*, Washington, DC, 1942; rpnt., Zhonghua, 1991.

[16] Han Chu Huang and David H. G. Hsu, *Chinese Periodicals in the Library of Congress, A Bibliography*, Library of Congress, Washington, DC, 1988. Revised and expanded edition of 1978 original. Provides holding information on over 8,000 periodicals published 1864–1986. Arranged alphabetically by title. Gives call numbers.

[17] Han-chu Huang and Hseo-chin Jen, *Chinese Newspapers in the Library of Congress: A Bibliography*, Washington, DC, 1985. Provides holding information on some 1,200 newspapers published from the 1870s to the early 1980s. Arranged alphabetically by title. Has localities index and stroke-count index for first character in title.

Wanli, comp., Taibei: Yiwen, 1974; Lianjing rpnt., 1984 (includes *shanben* to the end of the Qianlong period).

4. Yale University (378,000 vols).

5. University of California, Berkeley (330,00 vols). Published catalog of library cards: *East Asiatic Library, University of California, Berkeley, Author-Title Catalog*, 13 vols.; *Subject Catalog*, 6 vols., G. K. Hall, 1968; *Author Catalog: First Supplement*, 2 vols., G. K. Hall, 1973; *Subject Catalog: First Supplement*, 2 vols., G. K. Hall, 1973.

6. University of Chicago (327,000 vols). *Catalogs of the Far Eastern Library, University of Chicago, Illinois: Author-Title Catalog of the Chinese Collection*, 18 vols., G. K. Hall, 1973; *First Supplement*, 4 vols., G. K. Hall, 1981.

7. Columbia University. C. V. Starr East Asian Library (305,000 vols).

8. University of Michigan (303,000 vols). *Catalogs of the Asia Library, University of Michigan, Ann Arbor: Chinese Catalog, Japanese Catalog*, 25 vols., G. K. Hall, 1978.

9. Cornell University (302,000 vols). *The Catalog of the Wason Collection on China and the Chinese, Cornell University Libraries, Part I, Serials Catalog*, Center for Chinese Research Materials, 1978; *Part II, Catalog of Monographs in Chinese, Japanese, and Western Languages*, 7 vols., 1980. *Supplement*, 1 vol., 1985.

10. Stanford University, Hoover Institute (222,000 vols). *The Library Catalogs of the Hoover Institution on War, Revolution, and Peace, Stanford University, Catalog of the Chinese Collection*, 13 vols., G. K. Hall, 1969; *First Supplement*, 2 vols., 1972.

11. University of Washington (220,000 vols).

Note that the Library of the University of British Columbia, Vancouver, contains 226,000 vols. of Chinese books.

For further details, consult *A Guide to East Asian Collections in North America*, Thomas H. Lee, comp., Greenwood, 1992.

11.4.2 Europe

See John T. Ma, *Chinese Collections in Europe: Survey of Their Technical and Readers' Service*, Zug, 1985, for one-page entries on 60 European Chinese collections, including names of librarians and telephone numbers. Some of the main libraries

and published catalogs are listed below. Most sinological libraries in Europe are in the process of converting their catalogs to
computer and in doing so are taking the opportunity to convert from earlier systems of romanization to *Hanyu pinyin*.
The European Association of Sinological Librarians meets
every year, usually just before the meeting of the European Association of Chinese Studies. The EACS has published national
or regional surveys of Chinese studies which include details of
sinological libraries.[18]

France: Bibliothèque Nationale, Paris.

Germany:

1. *Staatsbibliothek Preussischer Kulturbesitz Berlin: Katalog der Ostasien Abteilung*, 19 vols., Osnabrück: Biblio Verlag, 1983–85. Contains about 80,000 cards for the Chinese collection.

2. *Bayrische Staatsbibliotek, Katalog der Ostasiensammlung, China*, vols. 1–6, Wiesbaden: Dr. Ludwig Reichert Verlag, 1984–7.

UK: for background to the Chinese collections in the UK and to British sinology, see *Chinese Studies*, Frances Wood, ed., British Library, 1988.

1. London: *School of Oriental and African Studies, University of London, Library Catalogue*, 28 vols. (of which the *Chinese catalogue* occupies vols. 23–27), G. K. Hall, 1963. Same title, *First supplement*, 1968; *Second supplement*, 1973; *Third supplement*, 1973–78.

2. British Library.

3. Cambridge University: University Library. Online catalog of 45,000 titles in the Chinese collection. Also the Needham Research Institute, East Asian History of Science Library.

4. Oxford University.

[18] Italy (1984); France (1988); Germany (1990); the Nordic countries (1994); Russia and the CIS countries (1996); Central Europe (1996); the United Kingdom (1997).

11.4.3 Russia

The three main sinological libraries in Russia are:

1. Russian State Library (formerly the Lenin Library), Moscow.

2. The Institute of Oriental Studies of the Russian Academy of Sciences, St. Petersburg branch (formerly the Institute of the Peoples of Asia under the Academy of Social Sciences, Leningrad Branch). The collection began as the Asiatic Museum in 1818; it holds the S. F. Oldenburg collection of Dunhuang manuscripts (46.3).

3. Oriental Faculty of St. Petersburg University (formerly the collections of the Sinological Institute, Leningrad University).

Union catalogs of Chinese books and periodicals in Russia were previously published by the former Lenin Library.[19]

11.5 Publishers and Bookstores

In China itself, many publishers who do reprints of traditional historical sources and publish historical scholarship now keep up-to-date lists or catalogs.[20] Larger publishers specializing in history (for example, Zhonghua and Shanghai guji) publish retrospective, annotated catalogs in book form.[21] Zhonghua publishes a quarterly (*Shupin* 書品, 1986–) which contains scholarly reviews of its new books as well as short articles on literary and historical subjects. In the 1980s many *guji* 古籍 publishers were set up in the provinces. They mainly publish local works of history and those of an antiquarian interest.

[19] Consult *Soviet Studies of Premodern China*, Gilbert Rozman, ed., CCS, Univ. of Michigan, 1984.

[20] Zhonghua Shuju, Shanghai Guji Chubanshe (from 1958 to 1978 the Shanghai branch of Zhonghua Shuju), Zhonghua Shudian, Zhongguo Shudian, Zhongzhou Guji and many others. See *Directory of Publishers in China*, Jin Sheng 金聲, chief ed., FLP, 1992; rev. ed., 1996. There are 547 publishers listed with their addresses and telephone and fax numbers.

[21] *Zhonghua shuju tushu mulu 1949–1991*, 中華書局圖書目錄 (Catalog of books published by the Zhonghua Shuju), 1949–1991, Zhonghua, 1993; *Shanghai guji chubanshe sishi zhounian* 上海古籍出版社四十周年, 1956–1996 (The fortieth anniversary of the Shanghai Guji Chubanshe, 1956–1996), Shanghai guji, 1996.

The rule in China is that if you see a book, buy it, because it will not be there when you next go shopping and stores and publishers do not keep stocks. Many of the publishers have their own retail outlets. Because of the lack of distribution of academic books, ordering directly from the publisher is often more rewarding than browsing the large general bookstores, although the bookstore scene is changing so fast it is unwise to generalize.

Zhongguo tushu jinchukou zonggongsi 中國圖書進出口總共司 (National publications import and export co.) distributes its own catalog and takes orders. The company has offices in the United States, UK, Germany and Japan. The Zhongguo chuban fuwu gongsi 中國服務公司 (China publications service) is located in Chicago. It puts out an annual catalog of books by Chinese publishers (the 1998 catalog contains the titles of 680 books published in 1997). It can supply books, CD-ROMs, and microfilms.[22]

In America and Europe, only a handful of publishers have developed a list on Chinese history. They include the University presses of California, Columbia, Harvard, Stanford, Princeton, the State University of New York, Michigan, Oxford, Cambridge and such specialist publishers as M. E. Sharpe or E. J. Brill.

In Japan, there are over 20 bookstores specializing in Chinese books. Most are in Tokyo and Kyoto. A stroll through the half dozen in Kanda's Jimbochô 神田神保町 (including the one whose Shanghai branch was much patronized by Lu Xun in the 1930s) can reveal Chinese works which you might otherwise have missed or been unable to find in China. Several of these stores also publish book review magazines of Chinese books. Two of these reviews, those of Tôhô and Uchiyama, even include a section of dozens of forthcoming titles from Chinese publishers as well as lists of recent and forthcoming Japanese and Western works on China. Bookstores specializing in Chinese books include the following:

[22] P. O. Box 490614, Chicago, Illinois 60649; Fax (773) 288-8570.

Tôhô shoten 東方書店 (monthly book magazine: *Tôhô* 東方 [Eastern Book Review], 1975–); there are branches of the store in Kyoto and Osaka.

Uchiyama shoten 內山書店 (monthly book magazine: *Chûgoku tosho* 中國圖書, 1988–).

Yamamoto shoten 山本書店. Specializes in Japanese sinology.

Tôfuku shoten 東豐書店; just next to Yoyogi JNR station has such a huge stock of scholarly books from both China and Taiwan that it is almost impossible to move in the shop.

Rinrôkaku 琳琅閣 publishes extensive lists of rare and old books on China twice a year.

Ryôgen shoten 燎原書店 carries a stock of both mainland and Taiwan publications and also specializes in medical texts (monthly journal: *Ryôgen*, 1992–).

Taishûkan shoten 大修館書店 in Tokyo publishes the *Daikanwa jiten* and many other reference works (monthly journal: *Shinika* しにか, 1990–).

Kaifû shoten 海風書店, Tokyo, carries mainly pirated editions of mainland publications.

Kyûko shoin 汲古書院 is a publisher specializing in scholarly books on China which puts out a monthly magazine with news about books on China: *Kyûko* 汲古.

Chûbun shuppansha 中文出版社 in Kyoto carries mainly pirated editions of mainland publications.

Hôyû shoten 朋友書店 in Kyoto has a comprehensive collection of sinological works with the emphasis on scholarly works from China (monthly list, *Hôyû* 朋友, contains about 5,000 titles). Publishes a number of important Japanese scholarly works on China.

Tokyo Book Map (Shoseki seibosha, 1998), contains brief descriptions of 400 bookstores in Tokyo libraries. *Guide des libraries d'ancien* [sic] *de Kyoto* carries the same information for nearly 100 bookstores in Kyoto specializing in old books (including about 10 Chinese-book specialists). Despite the subtitle in French, it is in Japanese, *Kyôto koshoten meguri* 京都古書店巡り, Kyoto, 1995; rpnt., 1996.

11.6 *International Databases and Online Access*

For rapid access to library holdings of Chinese books, the wave of the future is the international database. At present there are two. The RLIN (Research Libraries Information Network) database is run by the Research Libraries Group (RLG), supported by a consortium of American university libraries and located in California.[23] The OCLC (Online Computer Library Center) database is maintained by an organization of that name in Ohio. Since the mid-1980s, most East Asian libraries in North America have begun to enter their bibliographical records on one or other of these databases, which in turn have begun to incorporate each other's records. As a result, either of them can offer access to the holdings of dozens of East Asian libraries (including all the major ones) and display them in full Chinese, Japanese, and Korean script as well as romanization. And both are increasing their coverage of East Asian libraries in Asia, Europe, and Australia. Already they contain hundreds of thousands of publications, mostly rather recent ones, but also several major collections of Chinese rare books and they are growing fast (for the RLG online database of Chinese rare books, see 9.8.1).

There are two problems. First, these are not open websites but proprietary databases accessible only to paying subscribers armed with a password. But because they can be consulted at almost any university library (though not always with Chinese, Japanese and Korean script), they are widely available. The second problem is that no major East Asian library has yet converted all its old records to machine-readable form and entered them in the databases, and so their coverage is fractional at best. In this respect Harvard-Yenching is the leader: it has about one-third of its Chinese, Japanese and Korean records online already and will complete the job in three or four years.

A growing number of East Asian libraries have home pages on the Internet that allow access to their online catalogs. The

---

[23] World Wide Web: < http://www.rlg.org.eas/ >.

best of them also offer descriptions of special collections, locally produced bibliographies and study aids, and an overview of sinological resources at the particular university. They also provide links to the home pages of other libraries and research organizations and to other sources of sinological information that are proliferating throughout the world. These include important indexes and databases, home pages devoted to particular areas of study and to individual texts, and a plethora of other information, for example you can search the 25 Histories full text database (22.2) through the home page of the Harvard-Yenching. Elsewhere you can search the catalogs of entire library systems from the University of California to Kyôdai.

Probably the most convenient gateway to this cyberworld in the United States is the home page of the Council on East Asian Libraries (CEAL) of the Association for Asian Studies. Another is the Asian Studies World Wide Web Virtual Library, based at the Australian National University but with outposts around the world.[24] The China branch of this resource is the Internet Guide for Chinese Studies based in Vienna.[25] Once you succeed in contacting one sinological site you should be able to contact them all, as they are mostly linked to one another, and you can spend weeks exploring them. If you lack the time for serendipity, you can contact the Virtual Library at ANU and subscribe to a mailing list that describes and evaluates websites.

Many of the innovations and new services are discussed in the pages of the *Journal of East Asian Libraries* (Association for Asian Studies, tri-annual) and in the *Bulletin* of the International Association of Oriental Libraries (1971– , quarterly).

[24] < http://coombs.anu.edu.au/wwwvl-AsianStudies.html >.
[25] < http://www.univie.ac.at/Sinologie/netguide.htm >.

II

Pre-Qin Sources

12

Introduction

Pre-Qin covers the Xia, Shang and Zhou, a period as long as that between the Qin and the Qing.[1] The main sources can be divided into three types: archaeological (chap. 13), epigraphic (chaps. 14–17) and textual (chaps. 18–19). It is one of the most exciting and one of the most difficult periods of Chinese history.

12.1 The Pre-Qin

The Pre-Qin is one of the most exciting periods because it deals with the various different traditions and civilizations in China leading up to the formation of the Han people and Chinese civilization and because, thanks to archaeology, so much new evidence has become, and is still becoming, available.[2] The new

---

[1] The benchmark for pre-Qin history in English is *The Cambridge History of Ancient China*, Michael Loewe and Edward L. Shaughnessy, eds., New York: CUP, 1999. *CHAC* contains 14 chapters by different authors on all aspects of pre-Qin history and archaeology. There are over 200 illustrations.

[2] The author of one of the chapters on archaeology in *CHAC*, Kwang-Chih Chang (Zhang Guangzhi 張光直, 1931–), also wrote what for many years was the standard book-length account in English of Chinese archaeology up to the Qin, *The Archaeology of Ancient China*, 4th ed., rev. and enl., YUP, 1986. This contains material up to 1985. For a manual of pre-Qin archaeology which takes account of discoveries announced up to the early 1990s, see Zhang Zhiheng 張之恒 and Zhou Yuxing 周裕興, *Xia, Shang, Zhou kaogu* 夏商周考古 (The archaeology of the Xia, Shang and Zhou), Nanjing daxue, 1995; rpnt., 1997. For other references to pre-Qin archaeology, see chap. 13.

archaeological data include artifacts, epigraphic sources and excavated texts. These have not only enabled a closer reading of the traditional textual sources, sometimes confirming their accuracy, they have also opened the entire field to new interpretations.[3]

The pre-Qin is one of the most difficult periods because of the limited number of textual sources, far fewer than for any later period, a shortage already noted for the pre-Zhou by Confucius in the fifth century BC (*Lunyu* 論語, iii.9). Texts which did survive were often partly lost or corrupted in transmission and had to be painstakingly reconstructed often centuries later. They were written in pre-classical and Classical Chinese, still recognizable to someone who reads Modern Chinese but nevertheless requiring special training to understand fully (see 1.1 for the different varieties of Classical and Literary Chinese). Moreover, however difficult the mastery of Classical Chinese may be, it is easy compared to the skills required to handle the earliest epigraphic sources for the pre-Qin which were written in an archaic language and in scripts which are difficult to read (16.4 and 16.5).

The plenitude of archaeological artifacts is in welcome contrast to the penury of textual and epigraphic sources, but the analysis and the formulation of new hypotheses are hard put to keep pace with the volume of archaeological discovery, and bridging the gap between the data and the written sources requires tremendous ingenuity going beyond traditional, speculative etymology.

The historicity of the Xia is now generally accepted in China although no specific evidence predating the Shang which identifies sites or artifacts with a kingdom or people or settlement known as Xia has been unearthed. A number of Bronze Age sites, however, have tentatively been identified as Xia, most important of which are the remains of a palace settlement at Erlitou 二里頭 in Henan (excavated 1952–59).

---

[3] Jessica Rawson, "Overturning Assumptions: Art and Culture in Ancient China," *Apollo* (March, 1997), 3–9.

A number of early Shang settlements have been excavated, notably, Yanshi 偃師 (1983; 1996–97), Erligang 二里崗 near Zhengzhou (1959); and Xiaoshuangqiao 小雙橋 (1990). The picture becomes clearer at the end of the second millennium BC with the first extant corpus of written evidence (on the oracle-bone inscriptions) and the material remains excavated from Shang settlements, cities, temples, palaces and tombs. But there are still many unanswered questions (not the least interesting being the origins and early development of the Chinese language, including Chinese writing; see chaps. 1 and 14–17).

The Western Zhou period is the first from which a few historical and literary texts survive (chaps. 18–19). Some of these transmitted texts (*chuanshi wenxian* 傳世文獻) can now be checked with excavated texts (*chutu wenxian* 出土文獻).[4]

Much more evidence survives from the Eastern Zhou, which saw the rise of numerous independent states as China entered the Iron Age. Their higher culture shared many common traits, but retained distinctive elements which in some cases can be traced back to regional Neolithic and Bronze Age cultures and tribes.[5]

Recent years have seen the first attempts to write comprehensive histories of regional cultures incorporating archaeological discoveries, the later histories of local kingdoms based

[4] Lothar von Falkenhausen, "Issues in Western Zhou Studies," *EC* 18: 139–226 (1993).

[5] Robert Bagley, "Shang Archaeology," *CHAC*, 124–231. See also the series published by Yale University Press entitled *Early Chinese Civilization*. The authors made full use of archaeological discoveries available as of the late 1970s: K. C. Chang, *Shang Civilization*, YUP, 1980, especially the introductory chapter, "Prolegomena: Five Doors to Shang," which discusses the main sources for Shang history, i.e., historical texts, bronze inscriptions, oracle-bone inscriptions and archaeology, as well as theoretical models; Cho-yun Hsu (Xu Zhoyun 許倬雲) and Katheryn M. Linduff, *Western Zhou Civilization*, YUP, 1988; Li Xueqin 李學勤, *Eastern Zhou and Qin Civilizations*, K. C. Chang, tr., YUP, 1985. The original Chinese edition (1984) was re-issued in a revised version, *Dong-Zhou yu Qindai wenming* 東周與秦代文明, Wenwu, 1991. See also *The Origins of Chinese Civilization*, David Keightley, ed., UCP, 1983.

on textual traditions, in some cases even tracing shared boundaries with the commanderies, circuits and provinces of the empire.[6] Increasingly, too, "dictionaries" of the archaeology and the history of a particular region have been appearing. Such reference works are especially useful because most Chinese books are still not indexed.

12.2 Research Tools

Different types of special-purpose reference works for Pre-Qin history are introduced in chaps. 13–19 and in other sections on particular subjects, for example, myth (33.1), or weights and measures (7.3). Below, only a handful of indispensable reference works on the pre-Qin are introduced.

Historical Encyclopaedia

Zhongguo lishi da cidian, Xian-Qin shi juan (Zhanguoqian) 中國歷史大辭典先秦史卷 (戰國前) (The great encyclopaedia of Chinese history, volume on pre-Qin), Li Xueqin 李學勤, ed. in chief, Meng Shikai 孟世凱 and Qiu Xigui 裘錫圭, deputy eds., Shanghai cishu, 1996. One of the best volumes in this 14-volume encyclopaedia of Chinese history (8.3.2), it contains 5,592 brief entries covering both history and archaeology.

Biographical Dictionary

Zhongguo shanggu renming cihui ji suoyin 中國上古人名詞彙及索引, Pan Ying 潘英 (Collection of ancient Chinese names and index), Mingwen, 1993.

Official Titles

For official titles in use in ancient China up to the Qin unification, see Zuo Yandong 左言東, *Xian-Qin zhiguan biao* 先秦職官表 (Tables of

---

[6] For example, *Chuxue wenku* 楚學文庫 (18.1.1); *Changjiang wenhuashi* 長江文化史 (History of Yangzi culture), Li Xueqin 李學勤 and Xu Jijun 徐吉軍, eds., Jiangxi jiaoyu, 1995; *Wu wenhua shicong* 吳文化史叢, 2 vols., Jiangsu renmin, 1995; Chen Ping 陳平, *Yanshi jishi biannian hui'an* 燕史記事編年會按 (Chronological collection of materials on the history of Yan arranged by topic), Shandong daxue, 1993.

official titles in the pre-Qin), Shangwu, 1994, which is thorough and indexed.

Xi-Zhou jinwen guanzhi yanjiu 西周金文官制研究 (Researches on the office system of Western Zhou bronze inscriptions), Zhang Yachu 張亞初 and Liu Yu 劉雨, Zhonghua, 1986, provides a convenient correlation with the *Zhouli* 周禮. For post-Qin titles and translations see the references in section 22.3 under *Official Posts and the Examination System*).

Geography

Zhongguo lishi ditu ji 中國歷史地圖集 (The Historical Atlas of China), Tan Qixiang 譚其驤, ed. in chief, vol. 1, *Yuanshi shehui, Xia, Shang, Xi-Zhou, Chunqiu, Zhanguo shiqi* 原始社會夏商西周春秋戰國時期 (Primitive society, the Xia, Shang, Western Zhou, *Chunqiu* and *Zhanguo*), Ditu, 1982; rpnt., 1985 (4.3.2).

Regional Reference Works

Of the many regional "dictionaries" available, three are cited as examples:

Chuguo lishi wenhua cidian 楚國歷史文化辭典 (Dictionary of the history and culture of the state of Chu), Shi Quan 石泉, ed. in chief, Wuhan daxue, 1996, contains 6,480 entries written by 59 scholars.

Zhongguo wenwu tuji 中國文物圖集 (Collected maps of China's cultural objects), Wenwu, eds. in chief, *Zhongguo ditu*, 1991– . See chap. 13, note 23 for more on this series.

Sichou zhi lu wenhua da cidian 絲綢之路文化大辭典 (A Dictionary of the Silk Road Culture), Wang Shangshou 王尚壽 and Ji Chengjia 季成家, eds., in chief, Hongqi, 1995. See 41.3.1 for details.

Chronology

Zhongguo xian-Qinshi libiao 中國先秦史曆表 (Calendrical concordance for pre-Qin history), Zhang Peiyu 張培瑜, comp., Qi-Lu, 1987, which extrapolates, using modern astronomical data, the first day and hour of winter equinoxes between 1,500 and 105 BC and gives the corresponding cyclical characters for the days; Part II gives the first day of each month and shows the position of the intercalary months from 722 to 105 BC in eight different calendars in use during these centuries. This allows the reader to chose the calendar equivalents according to the text being read. There are appendixes of technical tables, e.g., catalogs of solar eclipses which could have been seen from

Anyang 安陽 between 1,300 and 1,000 BC, and from Qufu during the Spring and Autumn period.

Xi-Zhou (Gonghe) zhi Xi-Han lipu 西周 (共和) 至西漢曆譜, Xu Xiqi 徐錫祺, ed., 2 vols., Beijing kexue jishu, 1997. Preface by Zhang Peiyu.

Shinpen Shiki Tô-Shû nenpyô 新編史記東周年表 (Newly edited *Shiji* Eastern Zhou chronological tables), Hirase Takao 平勢隆郎, comp., Tôbunken, Tokyo daigaku, 1995, is a chronological table from 841 to 221 BC with copious annotations seeking to correct the discrepancies and errors in the 10 chronological tables in the *Shiji*, the basic source on pre-Qin chronology.[7]

Zhongguo xian-Qinshi libiao 中國先秦史曆表 (Calendrical concordance for pre-Qin history), Zhang Peiyu 張培瑜 comp., Qi-Lu, 1987.

Some of the complexities of Pre-Qin chronology and time-keeping and further references are introduced in chaps. 5 and 6.

Textual Sources

ECTBG: *Early Chinese Texts: A Bibliographical Guide*, Michael Loewe, ed., *Early China* Special Monograph Series, SSEC and IEAS, 1993. *ECTBG* contains short articles by different specialists on the 64 main textual sources for the pre-Qin (and Han) covering their content, date of composition and authenticity, text history and editions, translations, studies, Japanese editions, research aids and indexes (19.1).

Indexes and Concordances

ICS: The main corpus of transmitted texts of the pre-Qin and Han are indexed character by character in the *ICS Ancient Chinese Texts Concordance Series* conceived by D. C. Lau (Liu Dianjue 劉殿爵), ICS, Chinese University of Hong Kong. The *ICS* concordances are also available on CD-ROM. For details see 9.10.

Paleographic Sources

NSECH: *New Sources of Early Chinese History: An Introduction to the Reading of Inscriptions and Manuscripts*, Edward L. Shaughnessy, ed.,

---

[7] See also Hirase Takao, *Chûgoku kodai kinen no kenkyû kara tenbun to ritsu no kentô* 中國古代 紀年の研究から天文と暦の檢討 (Researches on the chronology of ancient China—an examination of astronomy and the calendar), Tôbunken, Kyûko, 1996, which contains studies of the dating systems of the late Shang, Western Zhou and Spring and Autumn and Warring States with 150 pages of calendrical tables.

SSEC and IEAS, 1997. *NSECH* contains eight chapters by different authors on inscriptions on bronzes and oracle bones, stone, jade, bamboo, wood and silk and an introduction by the editor. The authors examine how the paleographic materials are read, and second, how they can be used to reconstruct ancient society. With few exceptions, no discoveries made after 1985 and no works published after the end of 1993 are covered.

Corpora Inscriptionarum

The main collections of inscriptions and pre-Qin manuscripts are listed in the following sections: pottery marks, chap. 14; oracle bones, chap. 15; bronze, stone, bones, shells, coins, jade, seals, pottery inscriptions (chap. 17); bamboo and silk manuscripts, chap. 18.

Illustrations

A Journey into China's Antiquity, vol. 1: *Palaeolithic–Spring and Autumn Period*; vol. 2: *Warring States–Northern and Southern Dynasties*, National Museum of Chinese History, eds., Morning Glory, 1997. Excellent colored photographs based on the collections of the Museum of Chinese History, including newly excavated artifacts, authoritative, brief explanations, and plentiful maps (see 8.2.1 on this series).

Qin wuzhi wenhuashi 秦物質文化史 (History of material culture during the Qin), Wang Xueli 王學理 et al., San-Qin, 1994, is an excellent introduction to Qin archaeology in the form of a copiously illustrated inventory of Qin artifacts from the earliest times to the fall of the Qin in 206 BC. There is also an extensive summary in English of the whole work.

Bibliographies

For archaeological bibliographies, see 13.3. In addition to these and the specialized references in chaps. 13 to 19, see the following:

CHAC : *The Cambridge History of Ancient China*, Michael Loewe and Edward L. Shaughnessy, eds., New York: CUP, 1999. Contains a bibliography with 3,000 references on all aspects of pre-Qin history in Chinese, Japanese and Western languages.

Xian-Qinshi yanjiu gaiyao 先秦史研究概要 (Survey of research on pre-Qin history), Zhu Fenghan 朱鳳瀚 and Xu Yong 徐勇, eds., Tianjin jiaoyu, 1996. Apart from introducing the sources on the Xia, Shang and Zhou, and surveying scholarly debates (1–475), it contains a bibliography of 4,000 references to Chinese secondary sources (up to

1991), arranged by period and by topic (518–764). In addition, there are 50 pages on Japanese scholarship as well as a brief outline of Western work (512–17).

For a much shorter survey, see Li Xueqin and Zheng Chao 鄭超, "Xian-Qin shiqi shiliao jieshao 先秦時期史料介紹" (Introduction to the sources of pre-Qin history) in *Zhongguo gudaishi daodu* 中國古代史導讀 (A guide to reading ancient Chinese history), Xiao Li 肖黎 and Li Guihai 李桂海 eds., Wenhui, 1991; rpnt., 1992, 1–76. See also the chapter on the pre-Qin in Yamane Yukio 山根幸夫 (1991), of which Tian Renlong 田人隆 (1994) and Gao Mingshi 高明士 (1990) are Chinese translations (8.2.1).

Xia, Shang, Zhou caizhengshi lunwen ziliao suoyin 夏商周財政史論文資料索引 (Index to articles on the history of public finance in the Xia, Shang and Zhou periods), in Wu Cailin 吳才麟 et al., *Zhongguo gudai caizhengshi yanjiu* 中國古代財政史研究 (Researches on the history of public finance in ancient China), Zhongguo caizheng, 1990, covers Chinese research published between 1948 and 1985.

Jiaguxue yu Shangshi lunzhu mulu 甲骨學與商史論著目錄 (Bibliography of works on oracle-bone studies and Shang history), Pu Maozuo 濮茅左, comp., Shanghai guji, 1991.

Xiashi Xia wenhua yanjiu shumu 夏史夏文化研究書目 (Bibliography of books on Xia history and culture), Zhou Hongxiang 周鴻翔, ed., Xianggang daxue 香港大學, Zhongwenxi 中文系, 1990.

Zhanguo Qin Han shi lunwen suoyin 戰國秦漢史論文索引 (Index of articles on the history of the Warring States, Qin and Han), Zhang Chuanxi 張傳璽, Hu Zhihong 胡志宏, Chen Keyun 陳柯雲, Liu Huazhu 劉華祝, Beijing daxue, 1983. This large-scale, unannotated bibliography of secondary scholarship on the Warring States covers articles written between 1900 and 1980 in China, Taiwan and Hong Kong, including articles appearing in all main archaeological journals. Arrangement is by period and by topic. A continuation covers books published from 1900 to 1990 and articles from 1981 to 1990: *Zhanguo Qin Han shi lunzhu suoyin; xubian lunwen 1981–90; quanzhu 1900–90* 戰國秦漢史論著索引, 續編論文 1981–90, 全著 1900–1990 (Continuation to index of articles and books on the history of the Warring States, Qin and Han; articles, 1981–90; books, 1900–1990), Beijing daxue, 1992.

The volumes on China of the latest Japanese scholarly, multi-volume history of the world usually contain up-to-date bibliographies of Japanese secondary scholarship—for example:

Sekai rekishi taikei 世界歴史大系 (World history series), *Senshi–Kô-Kan* 先史−后漢 (Pre-history to Later Han), Matsumaru Michio 松丸道雄 (1934–), ed., Yamakawa, 1998. This is vol. 1 of 5 vols. on China.

Archaeological journals often carry detailed bibliographies of a particular subject or region (13.3). On the textual sources for the pre-Qin, see chap. 19.

Societies, Yearbooks and Journals

Zhongguo shixuehui 中國史學會 (Chinese History Society), founded in 1979. The society compiles the *Zhongguo lishixue nianjian* 中國歴史學年鑒. It includes chapters on the state of the field in special subjects; state-of-the-field essays arranged by topic and by period, including the pre-Qin; brief reviews of new (and reprinted) books and monographs; a calendar of the main conferences; brief descriptions of the main archaeological discoveries arranged by province; obituaries; bibliography of books and articles arranged by period. The yearbook covers Chinese studies of world history as well as Chinese history.[8]

Zhongguo guwenzi yanjiuhui 中國古文字研究會 (Chinese Association for the Study of Pre-Qin Scripts), 1979. Since 1986, the association has published the annual journal *Guwenzi yanjiu* 古文字研究, Zhonghua, 1979– .

Nihon kôkotsugakkai 日本甲骨學會 (Japanese Association for the Study of Oracle-Bone Inscriptions), which publishes the journal *Kôkotsugaku* 甲骨學 (irregular, has bibliography of oracle-bone and bronze inscriptions), 1952– .

Xia-Shang xuehui 夏商學會, founded in 1982. Holds annual meetings.

Zhongguo xian-Qinshi xuehui 中國先秦史學會 (Society for the Study of Pre-Qin History), founded in 1982.

Zhongguo Yin-Shang wenhua xuehui 中國殷商文化學會 (Society for the Study of Yin Shang Culture), founded in 1989.

SSEC (The Society for the Study of Early China, University of California, Berkeley). Publishes *Early China* (1975– , annual), which began in 1969 as *Newsletter* of the Society for the Study of Pre-Han China. This is a lively and informative professional journal carrying articles, review articles, surveys of Chinese and Japanese scholarship (incl-

---

[8] *Zhongguo lishixue nianjian* (Yearbook of Chinese historical studies), Sanlian, 1980– . Appears about one year after the year covered.

uding a translation of the bibliographical review on early China appearing in the May issue of *Shigaku zasshi* 史學雜誌 every year). There is an annual bibliography as well as abstracts of Ph.D. dissertations. The society has published some important monographs and also puts out *Early China News*, which carries information about the profession.

13

Archaeology

Archaeology in the twentieth century has transformed the study of Chinese history and the process is still continuing.

13.1 Neolithic and Early Bronze Age Cultures

The discoveries of copious evidence of both Neolithic and advanced Bronze cultures from all over the China area have undermined the belief (which lasted from at least the time of Confucius to the present century) that the Chinese people were descended in a single direct line from the Three Sovereigns and the Five Emperors through the Three Dynasties, the Xia, Shang and Zhou, and that they came from one core region, namely the middle and lower reaches of the Yellow River. This belief could be termed "the Zhou interpretation of history" after the period in which it was first put forward. It is now regarded as a means of legitimizing the Zhou and later dynastic rulers, not as a description of reality.[1]

Paradoxically, therefore, modern Chinese archaeology has gone back two generations to the "doubting antiquity school" (Yigupai 疑古派).[2] It rejects the old accounts of the origins of

---

[1] Jessica Rawson, "Statesmen or Barbarians? The Western Zhou as Seen through their Bronzes," *Proceedings of the British Academy*, 75: 71–95 (1989); Robert W. Bagley, "Changjiang Bronzes and Shang Archaeology," *International Colloquium on Chinese Art History, Proceedings, Antiquities*, Part I, Taibei, 1992, 209–55.

[2] The "doubting antiquity school" emerged during the May Fourth Movement. It was initiated by Hu Shi 胡適 (1891–1962) and led by his

Footnote continued on next page

the Chinese people and Chinese civilization, but with the very important difference that it is continuously providing new evidence for the extension of history in China further back into antiquity and that it has a far richer variety of input from all over the China area than was ever dreamed possible in the past.

Human inhabitants (*Homo erectus*) may first have appeared in the area which later became China up to 1.7 million years ago but it was only at the very end of this period that the shift from the Paleolithic to the Neolithic began to take place. The change was coterminous with the end of the last Ice Age and was well under way by 10,000 BC. Subsequent developments were rapid.

To date, over 10,000 Neolithic sites have been discovered spanning a period stretching from the beginning of the tenth to the end of the third millennium BC.[3] Apart from the remains of the dead, the most characteristic artifacts are the pottery vessels whose different styles and colors help differentiate cultures and the relations between them. Enough have been excavated for archaeologists to group them into eight or so larger regions (covering many local cultures with similar characteristics and extending over an area equivalent to several modern provinces, see Table 15).

By about 3,000 BC, early Bronze Age cultures with permanent farming settlements emerging. Millet was the main crop in the North; rice in the South. Domestic animals were raised (pigs and dogs in the South; horse, cattle and sheep in the North). Bronze and stone implements were used for farming and for war. Many thousands of them are extant. Some of the

---

pupil, Gu Jiegang 顧頡剛 (1893–1980) and other historians. They began from 1920 onward by rejecting many previously revered Classics as later forgeries and soon cast doubt on the entire Zhou (Confucian) view of early Chinese history as being a series of later accretions of myth. See chap. 33.1–2.

[3] For secondary Chinese scholarship on Neolithic archaeology published between 1923 and 1989, see *Zhongguo xinshiqi shidai kaogu wenxian mulu* 中國新石器時代考古文獻目錄, Kexue, 1993.

*Table 15: Neolithic (ca. 6000– BC), *Chalcolithic (ca. 3000– BC)
and ** Bronze Age Cultures (ca. 2000– BC)*

	ca. BC–BC
1. Northeast (Mongolia, Heilongjiang, Jilin and Liaoning)	
Xinle 新樂	5300–4800
Zhaobaogou 趙寶溝	4500–4000
Hongshan 紅山	3500–2500
**Xiajiadian 夏家店	2000–300
2. Northwest or Upper Yellow River (Shaanxi, Gansu, Qinghai)	
Laogongtai 老宫臺 (incl. Gansu Yangshao 甘肅仰韶)	6000–5400
Majiayao 馬家窑, *Qijia 齊家	4500–2050
3. North Central or Central Yellow River (Henan, Hebei, Shanxi, Shaanxi)	
Cishan 磁山, Peiligang 裴李岡, Dadiwan 大地灣	6000–5400
Early Yangshao 仰韶 ("Painted pottery culture")	5000–3000
*Henan (or Central) Longshan 龍山 ("Black pottery culture")	2900–2000
**Erlitou 二里頭	1900–1500
4. Lower Yellow River (Shandong, East Henan, Jiangsu and Anhui)	
Qinglian'gang 青蓮岡 (incl. Beixin 北辛)	5400–4000
Dawenkou 大汶口	4300–2500
*Shandong Longshan 山東龍山	2500–2000
Yueshi 岳石	1900–1500
5. Southeast or Lower Yangzi (Zhejiang, Jiangsu)	
Hemudu 河姆渡	5000–4000
Majiabin 馬家浜 (incl. Songze 崧澤)	4300–3300
*Liangzhu 良渚 (incl. Maqiao 馬橋)	3300–2100
6. South Central or Central Yangzi (Hubei, E. Sichuan, N. Hunan)	
Pengtoushan 彭頭山	6000–5800
Daixi 大溪	4400–3300
Qujialing 屈家嶺	3000–2600
Hubei Longshan 湖北攏山 (Qinglongquan 青龍泉)	2500–2000
7. Southwest or Upper Yangzi (Guizhou, Yunnan, Sichuan)	
Baiyangcun 白陽村	2200–2100
Dalongtan 大龍潭	2100–2000
8. South (Fujian, Guangdong, Guangxi and Taiwan)	
Cord-marked cultures, e.g., Zengpiyan 甑皮岩	9500–5000
Coastal region painted pottery cultural sphere (e.g., Dapenkang 大坌坑, Shixia 石峽)	4000–1500

Note: Individual cultures are usually named after their place of discovery.

more exceptional cultures also produced elaborate jade carving
and silk weaving. Advanced Bronze cultures soon emerged
with a state system, a standing army and a writing system
(chaps. 14–17).

The discovery of many indigenous traces of early man and
many advanced Bronze Age cultures within the present-day
China area has led to the abandonment of simplistic diffusion
theories, which held that the key elements of early civilization
in China (for example, astronomy, crops, metallurgy, pottery,
writing, or music), were imported by invaders from Central
Asia or even from even further to the West. New archaeological discoveries, however, suggest that some elements of Bronze
Age culture in China may have come from the outside, either
by direct importation or by stimulus diffusion.[4]

The transition from Neolithic cultures to Chinese civilization is the subject of a long-running scholarly debate on the
origins of Chinese civilization (*Zhongguo wenming de qiyuan* 中
國文明的起源). It also involves the question of the origins of

---

[4] From the sixteenth to the early twentieth centuries, many, but by
no means all, Western scholars believed that Chinese civilization, if not
the Chinese people, had their origins in ancient Egypt, the ancient mid-
dle-East or India. Earlier theories and the most recent evidence are examined by Edwin G. Pulleyblank, "Early Contacts between Indo-Europeans
and Chinese," *International Review of Chinese Linguistics*, 1.1: 1–24
(1996). His main conclusion is that "the arrival of Indo-Europeans, with
their horse culture, in the northwestern frontier zone [of China] about
four thousand years ago must have been indirectly very important in the
formation of Chinese civilization; [but] the content of that civilization ...
mainly grew out of indigenous traditions ..." See also the same author's,
"The Chinese and their Neighbours in Prehistoric and Early Historic
Times," in *The Origins of Chinese Civilization*, David N. Keightley, ed.,
UCP, 1983. (1983), 411–66. Edward Shaughnessy in "Historic Perspectives on the Introduction of the Chariot into China," *HJAS* 48: 189–237
(1988), argues persuasively that the bronze chariot was introduced into
China in the late Shang around 1200 BC. This was precisely the time
from which the first Chinese writing survives although there is no evi-
dence that it was imported. On prehistoric routes to Central Asia and the
West via what was much later called the "Silk Road," see 41.3.1.

the Xia, Shang and Zhou peoples, the historicity of the Xia dynasty and the origins of the Chinese system of writing (since most consider writing as a defining element of civilization). The debate concentrates on five main questions: the definition of "culture" and of "civilization"; the definition of "Chinese civilization"; the identification of ancient peoples (and what can be discerned of their languages) with the different Neolithic and early Bronze Age cultures; the timing of the transition of these cultures from the Neolithic to the Bronze Age; and finally, the interactions of the different cultural areas. The new archaeological discoveries have made multiple-origin theories the new orthodoxy. Using different definitions of civilization, scholars have identified the Longshan, others Dawenkou, Xia (Erlitou) or Shang as being the key formative period in which Chinese civilization can first be identified.[5]

Already in 1935, the May Fourth intellectual, the first and longtime director of the Shiyusuo, Fu Sinian 傅斯年 (1896–1950), published an influential paper which argued that the prehistory of North China was deeply influenced by the interactions and struggles between two main groups of peoples: the Xia 夏 to the West (in the middle Yellow River valley) and the Yi 夷 to the East (in the lower Yellow River region).[6] The the-

---

[5] Kwang-Chih Chang, "China on the Eve of the Historical Period," *CHAC*, 37–73. Earlier the same author came down in favor of the late Longshan as seeing the transition to civilization on the basis of a preceding "interaction sphere" in which the main regional Neolithic cultures from all over China expanded and borrowed elements from one other (Chang, 1986, 234–94). See also David N. Keightley, "Early Civilization in China: Reflections on How it Became Chinese," in *Heritage of China*, Paul S. Ropp, ed., UCP, 1990, 15–54. *Zhongguo gudai wenming yu guojia xingcheng yanjiu* 中國古代文明與國家形成研究 (Researches on the formation of the ancient Chinese culture and nation), Li Xueqin 李學勤, ed. in chief, Yunnan renmin, 1997.

[6] Fu Sinian, "Yi-Xia dongxi shuo 夷夏東西説," in *Qingzhu Cai Yuanpei xiansheng liushiwu sui lunwenji* 慶祝蔡元培先生六十五歲論文集 (Papers presented to Mr. Ts'ai Yuan P'ei on his sixty-fifth birthday), Shiyusuo, 1933; rpnt., in *Fu Sinian xuanji* 傅斯年選集 (Selected works of Fu Sinian), Tianjin renmin, 1996, 247–92. The original meaning of Yi was

Footnote continued on next page

sis was in part based on the striking evidence of separate traditions suggested by the excavations of the Yangshao 仰韶 and Longshan 龍山 cultures, and it has in general been confirmed by later discoveries, but Fu Sinian's Yi-Xia thesis did not challenge the traditional conviction that Chinese civilization was generated in a single core area in the mid-Yellow River region.

Other scholars in the 1930s proposed a three-fold ethnic origin of the Chinese people namely, with the Yanhuang 炎黃 or Hua-Xia 華夏 in the center, the Dongyi 東夷 and Miao 苗 on the east coast and the Man 蠻 in the south. Later, each of the three were identified with separate cultures: the Hua-Xia with the Yangshao and other cultures of the Central Plains; the Dongyi with Hemudu, Liangzhu, Dawenkou and eastern Longshan cultures, and the Man with the Qujialing and Shijiahe cultures in the South. Out of the struggles between these three tribal groups the Hua-Xia eventually emerged as the single predominant leader, thus paving the way for the pre-eminence of the Xia at the end of the third millennium BC. Claims were also made that the peoples of the southeast coast were the originators of Chinese civilization, but it was not until the 1950s and 1960s that Chinese archaeology made a major and sustained push into new regions outside the Yellow River area, starting with the Yangzi and now extending to all of China. The resulting discoveries and excavations have created an infinitely more diverse and varied picture of prehistoric China by showing that there were indeed other core areas where late Neolithic and early Bronze Age cultures flourished. They, too, exerted an important influence on the formation of the Chinese people and the development of Chinese civilization. Indeed, some of the southern cultures may have been more advanced than those in the North. This is suggested by recent discoveries of some 60 rice-growing sites of Central and Lower Yangzi cultures, nota-

---

"the tribes living in the East." It was also used as a general term for barbarians, so the term Dongyi 東夷 was coined for the more specific meaning. For a summary of the archaeology of the Dongyi, see Luan Fengshi 欒豐實, *Dongyi kaogu* 東夷考古, Shandong daxue, 1996.

bly those around the Dongting lake such as Bashidang 八十當, Pengtoushan 彭頭山, Chengtoushan 城頭山 and Yuchanyan 玉蟾岩 (7000–6000 BC) or Hemudu 河姆渡 (Zhejiang, 5000–4000 BC). They almost certainly predated millet farming in the North.[7]

The Yi-Xia thesis has therefore now to be extended to include the interactions of at least eight major regional cultures and in particular of the rice-growing cultures of the Yangzi with the millet-growing cultures of the Yellow River and northeastern regions. These were the forces which eventually led to the creation of an advanced Bronze Age civilization at what is geographically almost the exact crossroads between the Yi and the Xia to be sure, but also at the meeting point of the cultures of the Yellow River and Yangzi regions.

Erlitou is the earliest Bronze culture known to date, but other, later ones have been unearthed in quite different parts of China in recent years.[8] Further discoveries will no doubt lead to many more surprises and more details on the pluralistic origins of the Chinese people and sources of Chinese civilization.

The interaction of the late Neolithic and Bronze Age peoples and their relations with their neighbors can only be reconstructed on the basis of archaeological analysis supplemented with the myths and legends recorded in the Zhou texts of the first millennium BC. This requires the ability to "read" objects

[7] *Huaxia kaogu* (1997.1). The paddy fields with irrigation systems that were excavated in 1992 at a Hemudu site (Caoxieshan 草鞋山, near Suzhou) are the oldest so far discovered in any country. A total of more than 80 Neolithic sites with traces of rice cultivation have been excavated from all over South China and from one or two places in Henan and Shaanxi (Xi'an). The northern sites date from the late Neolithic (4,000–3,000 BC). Chinese rice strains probably found their way to Japan directly from the Lower Yangzi region during the Jômon 繩文 period (1,000 BC) and to Korea during the Zhou dynasty.

[8] Robert Bagley, "Shang Archaeology," *CHAC*, 124–231. For a summary of the evidence of the bronze cultures of the various peoples in the China area and of their interaction, see Song Xinchao 宋新潮, *Yin-Shang wenhua quyu yanjiu* 殷商文化區域研究 (Research on the culture areas in the Yin-Shang period), Shaanxi renmin, 1991.

as well as to reconstruct styles and to decipher texts using the techniques of the archaeologist, the palaeographer, the linguist, the ethnographer, the mythologist, the art historian and the astronomer. Equally essential is the type of scholar who can bring all the disparate findings together.[9]

13.2 Archaeology Today

Jinshi 金石 (the study of bronze and stone inscriptions), since at least the Song primarily took the form of collecting and classifying antique bronze vessels and deciphering their inscriptions (chap. 17). The term *kaogu* 考古 was used in the general sense of the investigation of ancient things, chiefly inscriptions.[10] Little or no attempt was made to link the study of objects to the evidence derived from written documents. Both *jinshi* and *kaogu* remained one of the many activities of antiquarian scholars. Neither developed into a separate branch of study. Both *jinshi* and *kaogu* were turned into modern terms by adding *xue* 學 to form *jinshixue* 金石學 (epigraphy) and *kaoguxue* 考古學 (archaeology).

The first great period of modern Chinese archaeology, the 1920s and 1930s, saw the discovery of the late Neolithic cultures of Yangshao and Longshan,[11] of "Peking Man" (*H. erectus*

---

[9] K. C. Chang, *Art, Myth and Ritual: The Path to Political Authority in Ancient China*, HUP, 1983, 81–94; Lu Sixian 陸思賢, *Shenhua kaogu* 神話考古 (The archaeology of myths), Wenwu, 1995.

[10] The first use of the term is credited to Li Daoyuan 酈道元 in his *Shuijingzhu* 水經注 (Commentary on the *Shuijing*, 515–24 AD). The *Introduction* to K. C. Chang (1986) contains two short essays on the history of archaeology in China, "Traditional Historiography and Antiquarianism," and "Modern and Contemporary Archaeology," 4–21.

[11] For a monographic overview of prehistoric archaeology in China between 1895 and 1949, see Chen Xingcan 陳星燦, *Zhongguo shiqian kaoguxueshi yanjiu* (Research on the history of Chinese prehistoric archaeology, 1895 to 1949), Sanlian, 1997. For short articles on all aspects of Chinese archaeology, including biographies of 40 of China's leading archaeologists of the first and second generations, see *Zhongguo da baike quan-*

Footnote continued on next page

pekinensis or *Beijing zhili ren* 北京直立人 ca. 700,000– BC),[12] as well as the deciphering of the Shang oracle-bone inscriptions and the first excavations at the Shang capital near Anyang 安陽 in northern Henan.[13]

---

shu 中國大百科全書 (The great Chinese encyclopaedia), *Kaoguxue* 考古學 (Archaeology), Zhongguo da baike quanshu, 1986.

More than 1,000 Yangshao sites have been excavated since the first finding in 1921 in the village of Yangshao, Henan by the influential Swedish archaeologist J. Gunnar Andersson (1874–1960). In his memoirs (*Children of the Yellow Earth*, Kegan Paul, 1934; rpnt., MIT, 1973) he recounts how his search for prehistoric fossils led him to Henan and eventually to several visits to Yangshao during one of which he came across some shards of painted pottery. Andersson published a scholarly report of his findings under the title *Prehistory of the Chinese*, *BMFEA* 15 (1943).

The Longshan was discovered by a pupil of Li Ji, Wu Jinding 吳金鼎 (1901–48) in 1928 in a Shandong village of that name at the Chengziyai 城子崖 site and identified in 1930–1.

[12] Jia Lanpo 賈蘭坡 (1908–97) and Huang Weiwen 黃慰文, *The Story of Peking Man*, Yin Zhiqi, tr., FLP and HK: OUP, 1990. More than 700 Paleolithic sites have been unearthed. New discoveries and better dating techniques have pushed back the horizon for the appearance of hominids in China to as early as 1.7 million years ago. See X. Z. Wu (Wu Xinzhi 吳新智) and F. E. Poirier, *Human Evolution in China: A Metric Description of the Fossils and a Review of the Sites*, OUP, 1995. This is a thorough summary of the evidence with a bibliography of the main works in Chinese and English up to 1993.

[13] Planned excavations at Anyang began in 1928. This was to be the main training ground for the entire first generation of China's modern archaeologists, a generation whose last representatives stepped down in the 1970s and 1980s. Their pupils were also trained to high standards, but their work was interrupted for 10 years in the 1960s and 1970s by the Cultural Revolution and it is not yet clear that the successors will be able to maintain the same high standards.

For a well-illustrated and authoritative retrospective of 60 years work on Anyang, see *Yinxu de faxian yu yanjiu* 殷墟的發現與研究 (Archaeology, excavation and researches in the Yin ruins), Kaogusuo, eds., Kexue, 1994. For an earlier work by the Chinese pioneer archaeologist, see Li Ji 李濟 (1896–1979), *Anyang: A Chronicle of the Discovery and Excavations and Reconstructions of the Ancient Capital of the Shang Dynasty*, UWP, 1977, and for an evaluation of Li's work, see Hsü Cho-yün, "Commem-

Footnote continued on next page

The next period of discovery was in the 1950s and early 1960s. One of the most notable excavations was the first opening of an imperial tomb under controlled conditions, that of the Ming emperor Wanli 萬曆, the Ding Ling 定陵. Archaeological work here and elsewhere was interrupted by the Anti-Rightist campaign (1957). There was also a hiatus and much destruction during the Cultural Revolution (1966–72). Excavation reports were delayed for many years.[14]

The pace of excavation gathered momentum in the 1970s, and the volume of excavated sites is now without precedent and techniques of dating have also been improved.[15]

Some of the more spectacular finds have become household words—the unrifled tomb at Anyang of Fu Hao 婦好, one of the principal consorts of the great Shang king, Wu Ding 武丁 (1200–1181 BC); the complete set of 65 bronze chime bells in the tomb of Marquis Yi of Zeng 曾侯乙 (433 BC, see 39.3); the 7,000 warriors of the terracotta "underground army" found in the guard chambers to the tomb of Emperor Qin Shihuang (presaging who knows what splendors in the tomb itself, including if not copies of many of the burned books, then a cornu-

---

orating the Tenth Anniversary of Mr. Li Ji's Death," *Chinese Studies in History* 18.1: 11–17, 71 (1994).

[14] The excavation report of the Ding Ling was only published after a 30-year delay. See Yue Nan and Yang Shi, *The Dead Suffered Too: the Excavation of a Ming Tomb*, FLP, 1996, which tells the story of the excavation and (long before the cultural revolution) of "the interference by political movements, damage done unwittingly and, chiefly, the lack of knowledge and responsibility of the people involved" (the words are those of the leader of the excavation team), 276.

[15] See *Zhongguo kaoguxue zhong tan shisi niandai shuju ji* 中國考古學中碳十四年代數據集 (Collection of radiocarbon dates for Chinese archaeology, 1965–91), Wenwu, 1992. Updates of new radiocarbon dates are published in *Kaogu*. For a summary of the different scientific methods applied to archaeology, see the Kaogusuo's Kaogu keji shiyan yanjiu zhongxin 考古科技試驗研究中心 (Center of science and techniques in archaeology), "Kexue jishu zai kaoguxue zhong de yingyong 科學技術在考古學中的應用" (The application of scientific techniques in archaeology), *Kaogu*, 7: 1–11 (1996).

copia of medical and mantic texts on the techniques of acquiring longevity); the 2,100-year-old corpse of Xin Zhui 辛追, wife
of the Marquis of Dai 軑, Chancellor of the principality of
Changsha, perfectly preserved with its viscera, found in tomb
no. 1 (ca. 168 BC) at Mawangdui 馬王堆; and over two dozen
jade burial suits (three of which are complete) unearthed from
Han tombs, each made of between several hundred and 5,000
plaques of jade. They are like body armor intended to prevent
decay and to protect the wearer in the afterlife. The plaques
were stitched together with gold, silver, bronze wires or silk,
depending on the rank of the deceased. In form the suits were
not dissimilar to the early Chinese iron or leather armor worn
by the living.

Further back in time, the discoveries from the Neolithic are
equally striking: for example, the jade-using Hongshan culture
in present-day Liaoning province with elaborate altars and statues of naked pregnant figurines. They are similar to the
"Venus" fertility cult figurines of prehistoric Europe (*nüshen-
yong* 女神俑).[16] Another quite different center of jade carving,
the Liangzhu 良渚 culture, just to the south of the Lake Taihu
in Zhejiang (about 10 km west of Hangzhou), is typified by its
black pottery and finely carved jade. Fragments of silk and lacquer ware have also been found. Most famous of the Liangzhu
jades are the *yucong* 玉琮 (jade tubes), square on the outside and
round in the middle. They were certainly used as burial objects
and perhaps also as ritual or dance paraphernalia, but nobody
knows for sure. Some have argued that they symbolized the
unity of heaven (round) and earth (square), or the sun and the
moon. Some interpret the spirit and animal face motif on them
as representing the sun god. This motif is similar to the anthro-
pomorphic splayed animal-mask, the shamans or demon de-

---

[16] *Niuheliang Hongshan wenhua yizhi yu yuqi jingcui* 牛河梁紅山文
化遺址與玉器精粹 (Treasures and jades from the Niuheliang Hongshan
culture site), Liaoningsheng Kaogusuo, eds., Wenwu, 1997. Other female
fertility symbols were found 50 kms. away at another Hongshan site,
Dongshanzui 東山嘴 and also at Houtaizi 後臺子 in Hebei.

vourers of the Shang bronzes and may have been their stylistic forebear.[17]

Less striking because they were found scattered in many hundreds of sites, but equally interesting, are those objects such as the Neolithic carvings from all over China whose existence was not even suspected a generation ago.[18] Enough have been unearthed to justify a major inventory of prehistoric Chinese arts: *Zhongguo yuanshi yishu* 中國原始藝術.[19]

Other major discoveries from a later period are the elongated bronze figures with mask-like heads with eyes on stalks, straight nose, large mouth and ears and with gold foil stuck to their extraordinary puttied and limed features. They are from the sacrificial pits of Sanxingdui 三星堆 (2000–1700 BC), a Bronze culture found at Guanghan 廣漢 county, near Chengdu in Sichuan in 1986. Traces of another hitherto unknown Bronze culture were found in a tomb at Xin'gan 新干 in Dayangzhou 大陽洲, Jiangxi, in 1989.

[17] Sun Zhixin, "The Liangzhu Culture: Its Discovery and Its Jades," *EC* 18: 1–40 (1993); *Dongfang wenming zhi guang–Liangzhu wenhua faxian 60 zhounian jinian lunwenji* 東方文明之光–良渚文化發現 60 周年紀念論文集 (The Light of Oriental Civilization–Collected Essays in Celebration of the 60th Anniversary of the Discovery of Liangzhu Culture), Xu Huping 徐湖平, ed. in chief, Hainan guoji xinwen chuban zhongxin, 1996; Li Xueqin, "Liangzhu culture and the Shang Dynasty *Taotie* Motif," in *The Problem of Meaning in Early Chinese Ritual Bronzes*, Roderick Whitfield, ed., University of London, Percival David Foundation, SOAS, 1992, 56–66.

[18] Yang Xiaoneng 楊曉能, *Sculpture of Prehistoric China*, Tai Dao Publishing, 1988, contains 176 examples. The same author has also written *Sculpture of Xia and Shang China*, HK: Tai Dao Publishing [1988]. This contains illustrations of not only the monumental Shang funerary bronzes, but also a large number of lesser known, minor pieces of a surprising domesticity. For a general introduction to sculpture in China from the Shang to the present, including Buddhist sculpture, see "Sculpture for Tombs and Temples," in *The British Museum Book of Chinese Art*, Jessica Rawson, ed., British Museum, 1992, 134–67.

[19] *Zhongguo yuanshi yishu* (Chinese primitive art), Wu Shichi 吳詩池, Zijincheng, 1996.

The excavation of Neolithic and Bronze Age tombs has thrown new light on conditions in those days, including the population profile, life expectancy, diseases and early religious beliefs of the tribes who inhabited the area of what was later to become China.

There are also many other archaeological discoveries which are important for the historian. Some 100 large Yangshao and Longshan walled settlements, regarded by archaeologists as cities, have been identified in north China. All of the capitals of the principal Warring States kingdoms have also been found and reported on, as have the imperial capitals of Qin and the Former Han near Chang'an.[20]

New historical records have been found in large quantities; these include the oracle-bone and bronze inscriptions from the Shang and Zhou (chap. 15 and 17.1); Warring States manuscripts in the form of bundles of bamboo strips or rolls of silk, including portions of a Qin legal code predating the previous earliest known Chinese code (that of the Tang) by 1,000 years (44.3.2.1 and 27.2); maps on wood and paper (4.4); mantic, medical, astronomical and calendrical manuscripts on bamboo and silk (chaps. 36 and 5); 57,000 bone chits (*guqian* 骨簽) containing hundreds of thousands of characters recording in meticulous detail the inventories of Han centrally procured armaments and tribute from the empire (44.3.1); thousands of routine local documents on bamboo strips and wooden tablets dating from between the fourth century BC and the third century AD (44.3.2.2); a cache of bamboo and wood documents from the kingdom of Wu (220–280 AD), which contains more

---

[20] For a history of city planning which takes full account of archaeological discoveries, see He Yeju 賀業鉅, *Zhongguo gudai chengshi guihuashi* 中國古代城市規劃史 (A history of ancient Chinese city planning), Zhongguo jianzhu gongye, 1996. The first 300 pages cover the pre-Qin period. See also Nancy Shatzman Steinhardt, *Chinese Imperial City Planning*, UHP, 1990, one quarter of which despite the title is pre-Han; Shen Chen, "Early Urbanization in the Eastern Zhou in China (770–221 BC): An Archaeological View," *Antiquity* 68.261: 724–44 (1994); *China's Buried Kingdoms*, Alexandria, Va.: Time-Life Books, 1993.

than all previously discovered such documents (45.3); 40,000 manuscript items dating from the third to tenth centuries from a secret temple library (46.3); and huge quantities of stone inscriptions from later Chinese history (3.7, 16.3 and Part V).

Although the most spectacular archaeological finds have come from prehistoric and ancient China, archaeology, below ground, above ground and under water, has also contributed much to later Chinese history.[21] For example, the discovery (and equally important, the conservation) of tomb frescoes and tomb brick paintings, which have survived from every period from the Warring States through to the Yuan. They are fresh and life-like and far more detailed and down to earth (in the case of the brick paintings) than most of the surviving paintings or written descriptions from the scholar's brush.[22] There are

[21] The best first reference on Chinese archaeology of all periods is the *Kaoguxue* 考古學 (Archaeology) volume of the Great Chinese encyclopaedia (note 11). The articles contain material up to 1984 covering not only China, but also world archaeology, including short entries on the main cultures of China's neighbors. Arrangement is by *pinyin*; there is a *pinyin* index as well as a thematic table of contents. There are more than 250 color plates. See also the shorter *Zhongguo kaogu* 中國考古 (Chinese archaeology), An Jinhuai 安金槐, ed., Shanghai guji, 1992; rpnt., 1995.

There are an increasing number of introductions to the archaeology of single periods; for example, *Studies of Shang Archaeology*, K. C. Chang, ed., YUP, 1986; Song Zhimin 宋治民, *Zhanguo, Qin, Han kaogu* 戰國秦漢考古 (The archaeology of the Warring States, Qin and Han), Sichuan daxue, 1993. These are cited in Part V.

[22] For a good single-volume overview of the main recent discoveries up to the early 1990s, see the catalog of a major exhibition held in several European countries in 1995 and 1996, *Mysteries of Ancient China: New Discoveries from the Early Dynasties*, Jessica Rawson, ed., British Museum, 1996. See also the "dictionary" of 5,500 of the finest *objets d'art*, many recently excavated, edited by the Cultural Relics Department. Each treasure has a color photograph and a brief description. Arrangement is by material; for example, vol. 1 contains annotated photographs of metal, silver, jade and stone *objets*. *Zhongguo wenwu jinghua da cidian* 中國文物精華大辭典 (The large dictionary of the best of Chinese cultural relics), 4 vols., Cishu and HK: Shangwu, 1996. The 10 major archaeological discoveries of the 1970s and 1980s are presented in a superb series arranged

Footnote continued on next page

brief sections in each chapter of Part V giving some of the main archaeological sites and discoveries from the Qin to the Qing.

Every year during the 1990s, several hundred major new excavations have been undertaken. After the excavation comes the excavation report (many of which have been meticulous monographs). Two to three hundred book-length field reports and archaeological studies have been published annually and the archaeological journals (of which there are now well over 100) have carried 4,000 to 5,000 specialist reports and articles. New branches of archaeology are being developed, and are often linked to other disciplines—for example, the archaeology of science (chap. 37), the archaeology of agriculture (chap. 35), the archaeology of music (38.2), or the archaeology of religion (33.2). Ethno-archaeology of the non-Han peoples within China is also receiving increasing attention (chap. 40).

An increasing number of studies of the archaeology of individual provinces or regions are being published. In Henan, for example, between 1991 and 1995, there were 9,116 ancient tombs excavated and more than 100 studies and 1,000 articles written on the archaeology of the province. They are based on the wealth of new data usually turned up by accident in the course of ground clearing for infrastructure and building projects. To appreciate the growth in knowledge of regional archaeology, compare any summary on Sichuan or Chu archaeology written before 1960 with one written after 1990.[23]

There are 50 archaeological institutes or university departments of archaeology in China with over 1,500 full-time archaeologists. There are national research associations for most

_____

as a pictorial record of the excavations and inventory of the findings, *Zhongguo kaogu wenwu zhi mei* 中國考古文物之美 (The attraction of archaeological finds in China), 10 vols., Wenwu, 1994.

[23] For an attractive series covering archaeological sites by province, see *Zhongguo wenwu tuji* 中國文物圖集 (Collected maps of China's cultural objects), Wenwu, eds. in chief, Zhongguo ditu, 1991– . One of the best volumes in the series is the one on Henan (1991). It contains 235 maps indicating 3,653 ancient cultural sites in the province; 2,618 tombs; 2,118 ancient buildings; and 1,976 places with stone inscriptions.

historical periods, including ancient history and archaeology
(see 13.1 for pre-Qin associations). There are also provincial associations of cultural relics and archaeology managed by each
province's Cultural Relics and Archaeology Institute (Wenwu
kaogu yanjiusuo 文物考古研究所, Wenkaosuo for short).
Some of the larger cities also have their own archaeological departments. There are usually annual conferences on a specific
theme and these are occasions for exchanging news and views
long before it gets into the research publications let alone written up in book form. The general trend since the 1980s is for
the provincial and local institutes to gain more control over
their agendas than was the case when the Academy of Sciences
and the Kaogusuo under Guo Moruo 郭沫若 (1892–1978) were
all-powerful in the early years of the People's Republic.

Despite the many advances and despite the huge increase in
the inventory of excavated sites and objects, Chinese archaeology continues to take the culture-historical approach emphasizing the prehistory of the Chinese people within the borders
of modern China. So, the archaeology of China's neighbors
and their influence on China's prehistoric cultures remains a
neglected means of throwing light on what was truly distinctive
in Chinese prehistory.[24] For the time being, archaeology is still
a handmaid of nationalism. Influences from "outside," including diffusion, whether direct or stimulus, are therefore not examined. Moreover, it is assumed that economic and social arrangements need no further elucidation because they have long

[24] For a good overview which gets away from archaeology as the
anachronistic extension into prehistory of modern nationalistic concerns,
see Gina L. Barnes, *China, Korea and Japan, the Rise of Civilization in East
Asia*, Thames and Hudson, 1993; Sarah Milledge Nelson, *The Archaeology
of Northeast China*, Routledge, 1995, and by the same author, *The Archaeology of Korea*, CUP, 1993; Charles Higham, *The Archaeology of Mainland
Southeast Asia*, CUP, 1989; the same author rightly views South China
and mainland Southeast Asia as one huge region in his *The Bronze Age of
Southeast Asia*, CUP, 1996. See also, *Ancient Chinese Culture of South
China and Neighbouring Regions*, Centre for Chinese Archaeology and
Art, ICS and Chinese Univ. of Hong Kong, eds., HKCU Press, 1994.

since been revealed in the Marxist classics according to which pre-class society (pre-clan, matriarchal clan and patriarchal clan) is followed by class society (slave, feudal, semi-colonial, semi-feudal and capitalist). Small wonder that many of China's greatest archaeologists have concentrated on the meticulous description of excavated sites and objects leaving interpretation to historians.

Given the pace of economic and societal change in China today, and given the desire of a new generation of wealthy collectors to authenticate their collections to international standards it may not be long before the appearance of new analyses and their incorporation into the broader picture of a newly interpreted Chinese archaeology and history. But this will also depend on the training of a new generation of students in a discipline which is for the moment not finding it too easy to attract recruits.

Not surprisingly, general books on Chinese history do not always reflect the state of the field. Indeed, because of the volume of discoveries, and the decline of funding for research and publication, even within the archaeological profession itself there are often considerable delays and even at the best of times, the process from discovery to excavation to report to analysis can be a very long one. Most discoveries cannot be immediately excavated, and once started, excavations can take years, if not decades, if the site is a large one. The lack of funds for adequate facilities for preservation, storage and display means that a large proportion of known sites are not excavated.

13.3 Research Tools

Note that the best archaeological library in China is that of the Kaogusuo 考古所. It contains over 300,000 volumes.

Most major discoveries are conveniently listed by province in the *Annual Surveys* of the Archaeological Association and (in lesser detail) of the History Association, or in more detail in the retrospective and other bibliographies published by provincial archaeological institutes and museums.

There are two convenient ways of keeping up-to-date:

Zhongguo wenwubao 中國文物報 (1980–97, weekly; 1998– , biweekly), Wenhuabu, Wenwuju 文化部文物局 (Ministry of Culture, Cultural Relics Department), Beijing. This newspaper carries articles about all kinds of archaeological, museum and cultural news in more detail than in the ordinary press and more rapidly than in the archaeological journals.

CAAD: China Archaeology and Art Digest (1996– , quarterly), Bruce Gordon Doar and Susan Dewar, eds., HK: Art Text. This publication includes fairly full English summaries of articles in dozens of Chinese archaeological journals, many appearing in the same year as the publication of *CAAD*. There are also translations of longer articles on selected themes. An indispensable way of keeping up-to-date with many journals to which no Western libraries, and few even in China, have subscriptions.

Dictionary

Wenhua kaogu cidian, Ying-Han, Han-Ying 文化考古詞典, 英漢漢英 (A Dictionary of Culture and Archaeology: English-Chinese; Chinese-English), Han Xinghua 韓興華, ed. In chief, FLP, 1998.

Bibliographies

The *Revue bibliographique de sinologie* (see 10.1) carries short notices of selected archaeological books and articles and has done so since 1954.

Zhongguo kaoguxue wenxian mulu, 1900–1949 中國考古學文獻目錄, Wenwu, 1991, covers Chinese scholarship published up to 1949 in all fields of archaeology.

Zhongguo kaoguxue wenxian mulu, 1949–1966 中國考古學文獻目錄, Wenwu, 1978, covers Chinese scholarship published between 1949 and the outbreak of the Cultural Revolution in all fields of archaeology.

Zhongguo kaoguxue wenxian mulu, 1971–1982 中國考古學文獻目錄, Wenwu, 1998, covers Chinese scholarship published between 1971–82 in all fields of archaeology.

Wenwu kaogu gongzuo sanshi nian, 1949–1979 文物考古工作三十年, Wenwu, 1980, summarizes archaeological discoveries of the years 1949–79 by province with bibliographical notes; *Wenwu kaogu gongzuo shinian, 1979–1989* 文物考古工作十年, Wenwu, 1991, uses the same format for the years 1979–89. The years 1949–79 are also summed up by the Kaogusuo in *Xin Zhongguo de kaogu faxian he yanjiu* 新中國的考古發現和研究 (Archaeological Excavation and Researches in New China), Wenwu, 1984.

Chinese Archaeological Abstracts, 4 vols., Institute of Archaeology, Univ. of California at Los Angeles, 1978–85. About 1,200 articles appearing between 1963 and 1981 are summarized in English translation; vol. 1, edited by Richard C. Rudolph, covers articles in *Kaogu xuebao, Kaogu* and *Wenwu*; vols. 2–4, edited by Albert E. Dien, Jeffrey K. Riegel and Nancy T. Price, cover articles in *Kaogu* and *Wenwu*. Each volume has a comprehensive subject index.

Zhongguo xinshiqi shidai kaogu wenxian mulu 中國新石器時代考古文獻目錄, Miao Yajuan 繆雅娟 et al., eds., Kexue, 1993, covers Chinese scholarship published between 1923 and 1989 on the Neolithic.

The archaeologically richest provinces are well-served with separate bibliographies.[25] Note that university archaeological departments and provincial archaeological societies and museums publish bibliographies covering the secondary archaeological literature on their provinces or regions, often on special occasions, for example, the anniversary of the establishment of a provincial Kaogusuo or the anniversary of the discovery of a particular site or culture, for example, *Zhongguo kaoguxue luncong* 中國考古學論叢, Kexue, 1993; rpnt., 1995, a collection of research articles marking the 40th anniversary of the Kaogusuo.

A selection of the most important archaeological journals follows. Those marked with an asterisk are available on CD-ROM *Zhongguo xueshu qikan (guangpanban)* 中國學術期刊(光盤版); see 10.2.1 for details.[26]

---

[25] For example, *Henan Xinshiqi shidai tianye kaogu wenxian juyao* 河南新石器時代田野考古文獻舉要, Zhongzhou guji, 1997 lists 300 and summarizes 200 reports published 1923–96 on Neolithic sites excavated in Henan; *Henan wenbo kaogu wenxian xulu* 河南文博考古文獻叙錄, 2 vols., special publication of *Zhongyuan wenwu*, vol. 1 (1986) covers publications 1913–85; vol. 2 (1996), 1986–95; *Henan kaogu sishi nian* 河南考古四十年 (Forty years of archaeology in Henan), Henan renmin, 1994, covers archaeology activities in Henan between 1952 and 1992; *Luoyang kaogu sishinian* 洛陽考古四十年 (Forty years of archaeology in Luoyang, Ye Wansong 葉萬松, ed. in chief, Kexue, 1996.

[26] For an annotated list of well over 100 archaeological journals from all over China, see Lothar von Falkenhausen, "Serials on Chinese Archaeology," *EC* 17: 247–95 (1992). *Chinese Archaeology and Art Digest* also lists and annotates over 100 archaeological journals, including the main university journals.

Societies Yearbooks and Journals

Zhongguo kaogu xuehui 中國考古學會 (The Archaeological Society of China) was founded in its present form in 1979. It holds annual meetings. The proceedings are published in *Zhongguo kaogu xuehui nianhui lunwenji* 中國考古學會年會論文集, 1980– . The society compiles the following yearbook:

Zhongguo kaoguxue nianjian 中國考古學年鑒 (Yearbook of Chinese archaeology), Zhongguo kaoguxuehui, eds., Wenwu, 1983– . Covers activities and publications of each year, including state-of-the-field essays arranged by period; brief descriptions of new archaeological discoveries by province (200–300 pages); archaeological exhibitions and conferences; international scholarly exchanges; publications by subject and by province; details of the work of university and other archaeological departments; obituaries. Appears about a year or two (or even three) after the year covered.

Gugong bowuyuan yuankan 故宮博物院院刊 (1978– , quarterly), Palace Museum, Beijing.

Kaogu 考古 (Archaeology); appeared first under the title: *Kaogu tongxun* 考古通訊, 1955–58; thereafter under the present title, 1958–66; due to the cultural revolution did not appear 1966–71; 1972–82, bimonthly; 1983– , monthly), Shekeyuan 社科院, Kaogusuo 考古所, Beijing: Kaogu zazhishe 考古雜志社. Each year the December issue has an index by subject for the current year. All issues between 1955 and the end of 1996 (containing nearly 8,000 articles and 16,000 archaeological drawings) are available on CD-ROM: *Kaogu zazhi tuwen shujuku guangpan* 考古雜志圖文數據庫光盤 (CD-ROM database of illustrations and text from the journal Kaogu), 7 discs, 1997. There is a printed index to the first 200 issues, *Kaogu 200 qi zongmu suoyin, 1955.1–1984.5* 考古 200 期總目索引, Kexue, 1984.

Kaogu xuebao 考古學報 (Acta Archaeologica Sinica, 1978– , quarterly), Shekeyuan 社科院, Kaogusuo 考古所, Beijing. Began as *Anyang fajue kaogu* 安陽發掘考古, 1929–33; then changed to *Tianye kaogu baogao* in 1936; issues 2–4 (1947–49) appeared as *Zhongguo kaogu xuebao*; issue 5 appeared in 1952. In 1953, the present title was adopted; 1953–60 (quarterly); 1962–65 (biannual); 1960 (latter half), 1961 and 1966–71 did not appear; 1972–77 (biannual), Has English language abstracts Kaogu zazhishe.

Kaoguxue jikan 考古學季刊 (1981– , irregular, 11 vols., as of 1998). Kaogusuo, Beijing, Shehui kexue. Vol. 10 contains an index of the articles in vols. 1–10; vol. 11, Zhongguo da baike quanshu, 1998.

Nongye kaogu 農業考古 (Agricultural archaeology), 1981–90, biannual; thereafter, quarterly. Edited since 1990.2 by Jiangxi sheng Shehui kexueyuan, Lishisuo, Nanchang, Jiangxi.

Wenwu 文物 (1972– , monthly), Wenhuabu, Wenwuju 文化部文物局 (Cultural Relics Department, Ministry of Culture), Beijing. Each year, the December issue has an index by subject for the current year. Also, the issues of the previous year are bound together and published with a comprehensive index. There is also an index to the first 500 issues, *Wenwu 500 qi zongmu suoyin* 文物 500 期總目索引, Wenwu, 1998. It covers issues 1950.1–1998.1; arrangement is by topics and there is also an author index in *pinyin*.

After restarting in 1972, *Wenwu* became one of the main archaeological journals (earlier issues up to 1959 had few articles on archaeology). Unlike *Kaogu*, which is strictly for professional archaeologists, it includes papers on stone inscriptions, rare books and other cultural relics. In the 1990s the archaeological standards began to decline. Original title, *Wenwu cankao ziliao* 文物參考資料, 1950–8. Present title, 1959–66. 1966.6–1971, ceased publication.

Yindu xuekan 殷都學刊 (1989– , quarterly), Anyang shifan daxue, Henan.

The provincial Wenkaosuo and the larger provincial museums put out their own journals:

Beifang wenwu 北方文物 (1985– , quarterly), Heilongjiang Cultural Relics Administration.

Dongnan wenhua 東南文化 (Southeast Culture, 1978– , quarterly), Nanjing Museum, Nanjing.

Huaxia kaogu 華夏考古 (Huaxia Archaeology, 1987– , quarterly), Henan Wenkaosuo, Zhengzhou, Henan.

Jiang-Han kaogu 江漢考古 (1981– , quarterly), Hubei Wenkaosuo, Wuhan.

Kaogu yu wenwu 考古與文物 (1980– , bimonthly), Shaanxi Kaogusuo.

Liaohai wenwu xuekan 遼海文物學刊 (1992– , quarterly), Liaoning Wenkaosuo.

Nanfang wenwu 南方文物 (1992– , quarterly), Jiangxi Provincial Museum and Wenkaosuo.

Sichuan wenwu 四川文物 (1984– , bimonthly), Chengdu.

Zhongyuan wenwu 中原文物 (1978– , quarterly), Henan Provincial Museum, Zhengzhou.

14

Pre-Oracle Bone Signs and Symbols

The chance discovery of late Shang divinatory records written on bones and turtle shells has provided copious new evidence on the early development of Chinese characters (chap. 15). Only tantalizingly fragmentary signs and symbols have been found that pre-date the oracle-bone script. Their interpretation is controversial (this chapter). Many more epigraphic sources have survived from the Zhou and the Qin, notably on bronzes (17.1), on bamboo and wooden strips (18.1 and 44.3) and on silk (18.2).

14.1 Mnemonics

The earliest method of keeping records in China according to the *Yijing* 易經 was by tying knots in string (*jiesheng jishi* 結繩記事).[1] This technique has been found in many cultures from all over the world from ancient times to the present day and is not unknown to anyone who has ever tied a knot in a handkerchief or used a rosary. In China, according to an ancient commentary on the *Yijing*, large knots were used for important

---

[1] *Yijing*, "Xici," *xia* 易經.系辭下 (*Book of Changes*, commentary on the appended phrases, ii): "*Shanggu jiesheng er zhi* 上古結繩而治" (In very ancient times, good government was achieved by knotting string). This is the first known usage of the expression *shanggu*.

matters, small knots for lesser ones. The system could have been further elaborated by using different colored strings and by varying the number and length of the strings and the spaces between the knots. Some of the non-Han peoples in China until recently still used knot-tying as a mnemonic, usually for numbers or dates. The only traces to have survived in Han culture are possibly the characters (chiefly numerals) some of whose earliest forms may have been derived from representations of string knots (see, for example, 十 廿 卅 卌 千 世 系 which sometimes appear on the bronze script for *shi* 十, *nian* 廿, *sa* 卅, *xi* 卌 , *qian* 千, *shi* 世 and *xi* 系).

Various other origins for the characters are mentioned in the early texts: tallies; notches in bamboo or wood; or (in later sources) hexagrams. Indeed, traces of all of these have been excavated from Neolithic or Bronze Age sites and the first two were still in use for communication or for counting days by certain non-Han peoples in China until recently.[2]

But none of these "origins" helps explain when and how Chinese characters developed. Until the twentieth century, many believed that they were derived from cuneiform or hieroglyphs (see 13.1, note 4). Direct diffusion has long since been

---

[2] There have been an enormous number of more or less imaginative theories of the origin of Chinese characters. Graphological theories have been particularly popular, reflecting traditional methods of analyzing the characters and the importance attached to calligraphy. For example, the Song encyclopaedist Zheng Qiao 鄭樵 (29.1) argued that all Chinese characters were derived from a single horizontal stroke, *Tongzhi* 通志 (Comprehensive history of institutions), 1149, "Liushu lüe 六書略." A modern theory has the characters derived from pictures of fish heads (based on the designs found on Neolithic pottery, especially from Miaodigou 廟底溝), see *Zhongguo Hanzi wenhua daguan* 中國漢字文化大觀 (The culture of Chinese characters), He Jiuying 何九盈 et al., eds., Beijing daxue, 1995. Proponents of this theory do not find it a coincidence that according to the *Erya* 爾雅 (but not other sources), the first four of the *tiangan* 天干 (5.3) originally referred to parts of a fish. In fact, the characters for the *tiangan* were phonetic loans (*jiajiezi* 假借字, see 16.2). Therefore even if their original use had been for the words of fish parts, this would tell us little or nothing about the origin of the *tiangan*.

discarded (as also stimulus diffusion) as an explanation of the origin of most of the key elements of Chinese culture, including the characters. Nevertheless, despite all the archaeological excavations and discoveries from the 1920s to the present day, only a handful of characters have been discovered which predate the Shang oracle-bone script. What have been unearthed are considerable quantities of usually isolated signs and symbols on objects such as rocks, field marker stones, bones, turtle shells and jade. The earliest date from around the fifth millennium BC.

14.2 Pottery Marks

The most numerous of these signs are the pottery marks (*taoqi fuhao* 陶器符號) of the mid-Neolithic, starting from Yangshao 仰韶, with calibrated radio carbon dates of around 4770 BC.[3] Similar finds have been made from most of the major regional prehistoric cultures all over China right down to the third century BC. Judging from these finds, at a rough estimate one in every 30 or 40 pottery vessels had a single mark incised with a sharp object, often before the firing took place and usually at the rim.[4] Several hundred shards with marks have been found.

---

[3] The most complete inventory of the evidence from more than 50 prehistoric sites is in Li Jinglin (1995), see note 7. Rao Zongyi 饒宗頤 compares the pottery marks found in China with those from the Indus valley and the ancient Near East: *Fuhao, chuwen yu zimu—Hanzi shu* 符號, 初文與字母一漢字樹 (Marks, early writing and letters—the tree of Chinese characters), Hong Kong: Shangwu, 1998. See also Gao Ming 高明 (1926–), "Lüetan gudai taoqi fuhao, taoqi tuxiang he taoqi wenzi 略談古代陶器符號陶器圖像和陶器文字" (Brief discussion of ancient pottery marks, pictures and characters), *Xueshu jilin* 學術集林, vol. 2, Shanghai yuandong, 1994, 73–100; Qiu Xigui 裘錫圭 "Jiujing shibushi wenzi–tantan woguo xinshiqi shidai shiyong de fuhao 究竟是不是文字–談談我國新石器時代使用的符號" (Are they or are they not characters after all: a discussion on the marks in use in China's Neolithic), *Wenwu tiandi*, 2: 26–30 (1993).

[4] There were for example a total of 500,000 shards unearthed at Banpo 半坡 (of which 113 had a mark of one of 27 different types).

There are a total of about 100 separate types of mark, nearly all of which are geometric in form, consisting of simple straight lines or curves; some resemble the oracle-bone or bronze characters for numbers; some, notched tallies, for example, 刲刂 . About half consist of a single vertical line. Particular marks are usually found in the same place and on the same type of pot.

After the first finds in the 1930s, the influential palaeographer Tang Lan 唐蘭 (1900–78) proposed that the pottery marks gave Chinese characters a history of 6,000 to 7,000 years.[5] Scholars both inside China and out took up the same theme in the 1960s and 1970s after the publication of much more evidence, mainly from the Yangshao site at Banpo 半坡.[6] The clarity of the discussion has not been helped by lumping together pottery marks with pottery symbols (14.3) and pottery characters (14.4).

In recent years, scholars have been more cautious in their judgment, preferring to wait until more direct evidence is available and to use a stricter definition of what constitutes the difference between isolated symbols and a systematic writing sys-

[5] Tang Lan, *Guwenzixue daolun* 古文字學導論 (Introduction to the study of pre-Qin Chinese scripts), 1934, 27; rpnt., Qi-Lu, 1981, 77–8.

[6] Li Xiaoding 李孝定 (1918–): *Hanzi de qiyuan yu yanbian luncong* 漢字的起源與演變論叢 (Articles on the origin and development of Chinese characters), Lianjing, 1986 (the first article had appeared in 1969). Guo Moruo, the leading Marxist paleographer and historian of ancient China lent his influence to the view that the pottery marks were a direct forerunner of Chinese characters which *therefore* [my emphasis] could be said to have a 6,000 year history: "Gudai wenzi zhi bianzheng de fazhan 古代文字之辯證的發展" (The dialectic development of ancient Chinese writing), *Kaogu xuebao* 1: 1–13 (1972). This view was rapidly espoused by other leading scholars both in China and abroad, including Yu Xingwu 于省吾 (1896–1984), *Wenwu*, 1973.2; Ping-ti Ho (He Bingdi 何炳棣), *The Cradle of the East: An Enquiry into the Indigenous Origins of Techniques and Ideas of Neolithic and Early Historic China, 5,000–1,000 BC*, HKCU Press and UChP, 1975. Cheung Kwong-yue (Zhang Guangyu 張光裕) also tends toward the same view: "Recent Archaeological Evidence Relating to the Origin of Chinese Characters," in *The Origins of Chinese Civilization*, David N. Keightley, ed., UCP, 1983, 323–91.

tem representing sounds. One of the most thorough recent studies is by Li Jinglin 李荆林 who compares pottery marks and early pottery script with female writing (*nüshu* 女書, a curious script found only in one county of Hunan) and both with oracle-bone and bronze scripts as well with some of the oldest non-Han scripts and rock signs. Although his comparisons are not entirely convincing, his study contains the most complete illustrated inventory of pottery marks and script currently available.[7]

The stakes in the ongoing debate are not small: if indeed the pottery marks are forerunners of the Chinese characters, it could add another three thousand years to the history of Chinese writing making it as old or older than the first writing systems of Mesopotamia.

Nobody knows for sure the function of the pottery marks. Some have speculated that they represent the tribal owners of the pottery, or the hallmarks (or rather, "pottery marks") of their makers.[8] This may be nearer the truth. Dai 傣 potters in Yunnan have been observed scratching an identifying symbol, perhaps a number, on their pots with a fingernail before putting them into a shared kiln in order to identify theirs from those of other potters.[9] But one thing is clear. The pottery marks predate the earliest known Chinese characters by several

---

[7] "Taowen huilu 陶文彙錄" (Collected pottery script) in Li Jinglin, *Nüshu yu shiqian taowen yanjiu* 女書與史前陶文研究 (Research on female script and prehistoric pottery script), Zhuhai, 1995, 260–316. Li also conveniently tabulates the ancient scripts of 19 non-Han peoples as well as listing 1,300 characters of female writing. The weakness of claiming connections on the basis of the similarities of isolated symbols is illustrated by John DeFrancis who shows that the proofreaders' marks as listed in Webster's *Dictionary* bear a striking resemblance to 19 of the pottery marks; see his "Chinese Prehistoric Symbols and American Proofreaders' Marks," *Journal of Chinese Linguistics* 19.1: 116–121 (1991).

[8] K. C. Chang (1980, 241–48) concludes that most of the pottery inscriptions were the marks or emblems of social groups using the pottery.

[9] Wang Ningsheng 汪寧生, "Cong yuanshi jishi dao wenzi faming 從原始記事到文字發明" (From primitive ways of recording to the invention of characters), *Kaogu xuebao*, 1981.1.

millennia and then continue in use to the end of the Zhou (from which time characters were used to identify the maker, date and use of pottery and porcelain vessels). During all this time, they remained as they had been when they first appeared, limited in form, and limited in number to no more than 100 or so different types at the very most, essentially without development. The characters, on the other hand, from their first appearance in the late Shang, went through many changes during these centuries. Some were discarded and new ones developed. Overall, their numbers rose above 5,000. The conclusion is inescapable: the pottery scratch marks existed apart from and uninfluenced by the development of the characters.

14.3 Pottery Symbols

Another type of pottery mark began turning up in the 1950s at several of the Dawenkou 大汶口 Neolithic sites in Shandong. They are more like pictures. Sixteen vessels or shards have been found. Each has one symbol. Of the six different motifs, the two most common are 🜨 and 🪓 . The first appears to be the sun above what looks like a crescent moon or a three- or five-pointed altar or mountain; the second is an ax. They date from between 4200 and 2600 BC. They are similar to the sacred bird emblems found on half a dozen or so Liangzhu jades. We know from Zhou textual sources that the *yangniao* 陽鳥 (sun bird) was the talisman or totem of the peoples who inhabited the lower Yangzi region.[10] This suggests that Liangzhu symbols and possibly also those from Dawenkou may have served the same function as the clan emblems on early bronzes. Non-Han potters in Yunnan in modern times have been observed putting a circle above what looks like a crescent resting on a five-

---

[10] Wu Hung (Wu Hong 巫鴻), "Bird Motifs in Eastern Yi Art," *Orientations* 16,10: 30–41 (1985); Hayashi Minao 林巳奈夫, "Liangzhu wenhua he Dawenkou wenhua zhong de tuxiang jihao 良渚文化和大汶口文化中的圖像記號" (The pictographs and signs in the Liangzhu and Dawenkou cultures), *Dongnan wenhua*, 1991.3 and 4.

ramics. When asked its meaning, one potter replied that it showed that he had made the pot under the light of the sun and the moon; another said the mark showed the sun and the moon and a mountain and that storing grain in a pot like this would bring luck—a salutary warning, perhaps, against overinterpreting.[11]

Plenty of other symbols of fish (from the West) and birds (from the East) have been found painted on prehistoric pottery from sites all over China.[12] The birds almost certainly had mythical significance, possibly connected with the worship of the sun and the belief that the sun was carried by a bird. To take another example, the bird-eating-fish design (*niaoxianyu tu'an* 鳥銜魚圖案). The best known is on a Yangshao vase from Yancun 閻村 in Henan. It shows a cormorant holding a carp in its beak with a huge stone ax to the right (Chang, 1986, 137; Zhang, 1990, no. 1,682). This is often interpreted as a fu-

---

[11] Wang Hengjie 王恒杰, "Cong minzuxue faxian de xin cailiao kan Dawenkou wenhua taozun de 'wenzi', 從民族學發現的新材料看大汶口文化陶尊的'文字'" (The 'writing' on the Dawenkou *zun* as seen from the point of view of new materials from minority studies), *Kaogu*, 1991.12.

[12] The earliest Chinese prehistoric painted pottery comes from the Laoguantai 老官臺 culture in modern Gansu, Qinghai and Ningxia, some 5,000 to 6,000 years BC. An authoritative study is Zhang Mingchuan 張明川, *Zhongguo caitao tupu* 中國彩陶圖譜 (Illustrated catalog of Chinese painted pottery), Wenwu, 1990. This superbly printed work contains a 200-page introduction followed by meticulous, hand-painted illustrations of 2,009 prehistoric pots arranged geographically by place of discovery (there is a finding index for cultures at the end of the book). Appendixes contain a bibliography of research published between 1920 and 1982, also arranged by province; a table of carbon-14 dates; analysis of chemical composition and firing temperatures of selected pots from the main cultural sites; maps of sites; and finally a brief introduction to the 72 main cultures which produced painted pottery in prehistoric China. In his introduction the author analyzes the pottery from many different points of view, including the characteristics and technologies used in the main cultures; a systematic study of the symbols (showing, for example, how they moved from pictures to abstract designs based on the pictures); and the style of life reflected in the decorations of the pottery.

nerary vase for the leader of the tribe (the cormorant) who had used his power (the ax) to conquer his enemy (the carp). Others have compared all known examples of the design, down to those found in Later Han tombs, and have argued that it is a sexual symbol expressing transmigration sorcery. Before jumping to a conclusion, all known examples of a design should be compared and the date and time taken into account. It should not be assumed that only one interpretation is correct. It is quite possible that the designs held different meanings and that these may have changed over time.[13]

The pictures on the prehistoric pottery seem to develop into more abstract forms along similar lines to the earliest characters. But thereafter they become ever more abstract, ending up as pure design elements whose earlier meanings had probably long since been forgotten.

During excavations in 1991-92, a piece of Longshan pottery was found at a site at Dinggongcun, Zouping county 鄒平丁公村 in Shandong, dated to about 2,300 BC. On it were 11 symbols arranged in four rows. There is considerable controversy about this piece, partly because it was first noticed in the dig office, not on site. One hypothesis is that the symbols are an early form of Yi 夷 script, or at any rate, not directly related to the Shang oracle-bone script. Another is that they were scratched on a Longshan shard during the Warring States.

14.4 *The Earliest Pottery Characters*

Several recent finds of multiple marks on Liangzhu pottery fragments have been analyzed by Li Xueqin, who finds it "not easy to deny that they are characters" but later suggests that they may not have been directly connected with the Han char-

---

[13] For a wide-ranging summary of archaeological and pictographic evidence bearing on primitive beliefs, using insights from anthropology, astronomy and history, see Lu Sixian 陸思賢, *Shenhua kaogu* 神話考古 (The archaeology of myths), Wenwu, 1995. This work is more rigorous than the rapidly expanding number of fascinating but surely fanciful interpretations of the patterns and symbols on Neolithic utensils.

acters.[14] There have been occasional finds of Shang pottery characters over the years and new ones come up from time to time. The main sites are one each in Hebei and Jiangxi, and two in Henan.[15] A large number of the characters on these finds are immediately identifiable as Shang oracle-bone characters. The earliest, from Taixicun, Gaocheng county 藁城臺西村 in Henan, and from Wucheng 吳城 in Jiangxi, are contemporaneous with Erligang 二里岡 (early Shang) and thus predate the oracle bones (late Shang).[16] They are more pictographic than the ora-

---

[14] *Changjiang wenhuashi* 長江文化史 (History of Yangzi culture), Li Xueqin 李學勤 and Xu Jijun 徐吉軍, eds., Jiangxi jiaoyu, 1995, 56–60. Qiu (1993) is more skeptical. Liangzhu pottery marks and symbols are reproduced with a full bibliography in *Dongfang wenming zhi guang– Liangzhu wenhua faxian 60 zhounian jinian lunwenji* 東方文明之光–良渚文化發現60周年紀念論文集 (The Light of Oriental Civilization; Collected Essays in Celebration of the 60th Anniversary of the Discovery of Liang zhu Culture), Xu Huping 徐湖平, ed. in chief, Hainan guoji, 1996, 454–61.

[15] Gao Ming (1994), 85–90.

[16] Seventy-seven Taixi pieces were found in 1973, each with one or two characters, the total number of different characters coming to 22. Fifteen out of a total of 66 of the Wucheng pieces are contemporaneous with Erligang. They have more characters on them (up to 15). The remaining 24 pieces, like the later ones from Taixi, date from the late Shang, the same period as Anyang, which is the fourth main site from which Shang pottery characters have been unearthed. Eighty-two shards with writing on them (out of a total of 250,000 shards) were found at Xiaotun, Anyang during the first archaeological excavations there in 1928–29. The majority of the 82 have only one character scratched on them.

Gao Ming 高明, *Gu taowen huibian* 古陶文彙編 (Ancient pottery script), Zhonghua, 1990, contains exceptionally clear rubbings and transcriptions of 2,602 pre-Qin and Qin pottery shards with inscriptions on them discovered up to 1987, including 114 shards from Shang sites with 145 characters and 46 from the Western Zhou with 73 characters. The remaining 2,428 shards date from the Eastern Zhou and Qin and are arranged by province. An appendix contains an early version of Gao (1994) discussing and illustrating pottery marks and symbols (as distinct from pottery characters) from the Neolithic to the Warring States. The companion volume (Gao Ming and Ge Yinghui 葛英會, *Gu taowenzi zheng*

Footnote continued on next page

cle-bone characters, or similar to the earliest oracle-bone characters. For example, that for foot has three toes and one big toe whereas the oracle-bone character is much more stylized with three toes, one of which is larger. Another example is the character for field (*tian* 田), which is divided into six squares, not four. Many of the pottery characters are difficult to read, but they are similar to some of the Shang bronze characters (which are in general more archaic or pictographic than those on the oracle bones).

Several thousand pottery shards bearing characters (*taowen* 陶文) have survived from the sites of at least 30 Spring and Autumn and Warring States cities, but by that time there is plenty of other epigraphic evidence for the development of Chinese characters (17.1–2).

14.5 Conclusions

In the search for the origin of Chinese characters, other signs and symbols, apart from those on pottery, have been examined, including prehistoric rock art;[17] the markings on prehistoric

---

古陶文字徵 (Inquiry into ancient pottery characters), Zhonghua, 1991, is an annotated listing of the various forms (drawn by hand) of 1,823 different pottery characters, mainly as found on the shards illustrated in Gao (1990). Characters are transcribed into both seal and regular script. The main text lists 1,196 characters. At the end, 64 joined characters [*hewen* 合文] and 563 unknown characters are listed. The *hewen* are mostly special names, numbers or dates and common phrases for ritual offerings. They are read as polysyllabic words, e.g. *niu wu* 物, which originally was a *hewen* combining *niu* 牛 and *wu* 勿 meaning colored ox. The *hewen* was later borrowed for the word meaning "thing." There is a stroke-count index. For a similar listing of 1,700 pottery characters with 9,000 examples, see Xu Gufu 徐谷甫 and Wang Tinglin 王廷林, *Gu taozi hui* 古陶字彙 (Compendium of ancient pottery characters), Shanghai shudian, 1994; rpnt., 1996. This has the advantage that all the characters are reproductions of rubbings rather than drawings. There is a stroke-count index.

[17] Chinese rock art was first extensively cataloged in the sixth century AD by Li Daoyuan 酈道元 in his *Shuijingzhu* 水經注 (Commentary on the *Shuijing*,). He lists 20 different sites. Li is credited with the first use of the term *kaogu* 考古, meaning "the investigation of ancient things."

Footnote continued on next page

jades; the pictographic and other writing systems of non-Han peoples, such as the Naxi 納西 (related, according to some scholars, to the so-called Ba-Shu scripts or pictorial writing, *Ba-Shu wenzi* 巴蜀文字, of early Sichuan).[18] Despite many interesting discoveries, including the close similarity of some of the animals depicted in rock art with those in early pictographs, no major breakthrough on the origin of Chinese characters before their first appearance in large numbers on the late Shang oracle bones has been achieved as yet. The problem is the lack of evidence.

Just as with the three other ancient logographic writing systems, Sumerian, Egyptian and Hittite, Chinese writing appears to have been developed from pictorial recording (*tuhua jishi* 圖畫記事) and from symbols for numbers. As with the Egyptian hieroglyphs, the reason that little or no prior evidence of gestation of the system has been unearthed is presumably that writing was recorded mainly on perishable materials (indeed, at least one ancient Chinese source suggests that inscriptions on bronze and stone began because the ancient kings feared that their records on bamboo and silk would rot and be eaten by insects).[19]

For a comprehensive, modern study of Chinese rock art which also puts it in comparative perspective, see Gai Shanlin, 蓋山林, *Zhongguo yanhuaxue* 中國岩畫學 (The study of Chinese rock art), Shumu wenxian, 1995. For a more popular treatment with many excellent color photos, Song Yaoliang 宋耀良 *Zhongguo shiqian shenge renmian yanhua* 中國史前神格人面岩畫 (Mythical humans in China's prehistoric petroglyphs), HK: Sanlian, 1992. Note also Tang Huisheng, "Theory and Methods in Chinese Rock Art Studies," *Rock Art Research* 10.2: 83–90 (1993).

[18] "Gu Shuren de yuyan he wenhua 古蜀人的語言和文化" (The language and writing of the ancient peoples of Shu) in *Sanxingdui wenhua* 三星堆文化 (Sanxingdui Culture), Qu Xiaoqiang 屈小强, Li Dianyuan 李殿元 et al., eds., Sichuan renmin, 1993; rpnt., 1994, 421–74.

[19] Mozi 墨子 (468–376 BC), *Mozi, juan* 8, *Mingguixia* 明鬼下.*Mozi, juan* 8, *Mingguixia* 明鬼下. This is one of the several passages in which he discusses the use of writing to record good or bad conduct for the benefit of later generations.

The evidence for a wider use of writing in the Shang than for divination comes from the brief inscriptions on bronze vessels (including bronze seals) dating from the same period as the oracle-bone inscriptions themselves. In addition, there are fragmentary examples of Shang writing on stone, jade and pottery and traces of brush work on some of the later oracle bones. There are plenty of references on the oracle bones to *ce* 册 and *dian* 典 which appear to have been the records of important sacrificial rituals. In the later oracle-bone inscriptions, the phrase *zuoce* 作册 is usually taken to mean "recorder" or "scribe." There is also a reference in the *Documents* saying that "the Yin ancestors had *ce* and *dian*." It is generally assumed that the Spring and Autumn sense of *ce* (bamboo record) and *dian* (collection of important documents) already existed in the Shang.[20]

Another indication of a wider use of writing in the Shang comes from an analysis of the oracle-bone characters themselves. Some of the characters are compounds whose component parts are found neither on the oracle-bone inscriptions nor on the Shang bronze inscriptions. This suggests that the inscriptions contain only part of a larger Shang lexicon recorded on other media, including, presumably, bamboo and possibly even silk. It is perhaps also suggestive that the arrangement of characters on the late period oracle-bone inscriptions was the same as on the bamboo strips, that is in columns from top to bottom and from right to left (18.1).

---

[20] Jiang Hongyi 蔣紅毅 et al., "Shilun Yindai jiance de shiyong 試論殷代簡册的使用" (Examination of the use of bamboo documents in the Yin), *Yindu xuekan* 2: 11–14 (1992); also Li Xueqin (1985), 414–33.

Wang Yunzhi 王蘊智, *Yin-Zhou guwen tongyuan fenhua xianxiang tansuo* 殷周古文同源分化現象探索 (Investigation of the phenomenon of the division of cognate characters in Yin-Zhou scripts), Jilin renmin, 1996, 180–200, argues convincingly that in origin *dian* 典 and *ce* 册 were the same word (represented by the same character) meaning, "the records of important rituals"—for example, those conducted before the king went to war.

If the huge volume of archaeological discoveries going on today succeeds in unearthing precursors of the Shang oracle-bone script, they will almost certainly be on nonperishable materials such as stone, pottery or bone. But we should not expect that they will necessarily lead in a direct line backwards from the oracle bones discovered at Anyang. The pottery symbols from Dawenkou in the East, the Liangzhu symbols in the Southeast, the Ba-Shu scripts from Sichuan in the Southwest, even the pottery characters from Wucheng in the South, were used by peoples who still spoke different languages from the Shang. They may well represent traces of early writing systems which died out or were absorbed into the earliest forms of what later became Chinese characters.

The Shang kings extended their influence if not their direct rule over a considerable number of different peoples and tribes in lowland North China as well as further South. In doing so, they created the conditions and the need to unify into a single writing system what may well have been a number of mnemonic methods and early writing systems developed by the peoples over whom they ruled or with whom they came into contact.

Later history is filled with examples of rulers ordering the creation of new writing systems. In China and its neighbors, it was not uncommon for conquerors or founders of dynasties to do so. It is true of Songtsen Gampo, who sponsored the development of three different Tibetan scripts based on north Indian examples in the early seventh century. It is also true of the Khitan (920), the Tangut (early eleventh century), the Jurchen (early twelfth century), the Mongols (*hPhags-pa*, 1269), the Vietnamese (*Chunom*, fourteenth century) and the Manchu (*Manju*, 1599, a modified form of *hPhags-pa*), not to speak of the Koreans (*Hangkûl*, 1446). But it could be argued that by the time these scripts were promulgated the knowledge of different writing systems was widespread and it was possible to derive them from existing models.

The invention of the Chinese system of characters was credited to one of the scribes of the Yellow Emperor, Cang Jie 倉

頡. The first surviving mention of him dates from the third century BC. A Later Han writer suggests that he drew his inspiration from the realization that the tracks of birds and animals indicated in a consistent way different species and types.[21] There is no reliable evidence that such a person ever existed, although the first known users of the Chinese script were indeed, as the story suggests, court officials, namely the diviners and scribes of the Shang kings. This has led some scholars to hypothesize that it was the Shang diviners who were the first developers of the script.[22] One of the arguments for the timing that this implies is that the earliest oracle-bone script dates from some 30 years after the establishment of the Shang capital at Yin (Anyang). This suggests that there had not been much advance in the script since the only two known previous examples found at the mid-Shang capital of Erligang. The qualitative advance came only after the early Wu Ding period. If this is correct, it suggests that it is unlikely that archaeology will ever turn up examples of pre-Anyang oracle-bone script.[23] In this context, it may be significant that the earliest bronze vessels with writing on them were those found buried in the Fu Hao tomb (Wu Ding period), most of which simply bore the two characters of her name.

If divination was the first extensive use of the characters, this suggests a religious and political origin of Chinese writing rather than an economic one as with the writing in ancient

[21] The *Postface* to the *Shuowen jiezi* 說文解字 (2.2.1). The first legends about the invention of the Chinese characters are curiously late, see William G. Boltz, *The Origin and Early Development of the Chinese Writing System*, American Oriental Series, vol., 78, New Haven, Conn.: American Oriental Society, 1994, 129–38.

[22] Xu Zhongshu 徐中舒 (1898–1991) and Tang Jiahong 唐嘉弘, "Guanyu Xiadai wenzi de wenti 關于夏代文字的問題" (On the problem of Chinese characters in the Xia dynasty), *Xiashi luncong* 夏史論叢, Qi-Lu, 1985, 127, 140.

[23] Li Xueqin and Peng Yushang 彭裕商, *Yinxu jiagu fenqi yanjiu* 殷墟甲骨分期研究 (Researches on the periodization of Yinxu oracle bones), Shanghai guji, 1996, 410.

Mesopotamia.[24] It is a difficult theory to either prove or disprove because, as suggested above, the Shang almost certainly used writing for other purposes on other media, most of which have not survived.

That said, it is unlikely that the development of writing took place much before the late Shang because in its earliest known form, the oracle-bone script, it still displays signs of being a system in the early stages of evolution. For example, the forms, the size and the position of the characters were still not fixed and the proportion of pictographic characters was much greater than it later became. The origin of the characters as a system of writing is therefore most likely to have been in the mid- to late Shang, that is to say, around 1500–1100 BC.[25]

[24] K. C. Chang, "Writing as the Path to Authority," *Art, Myth and Ritual: the Path to Authority in Ancient China*, HUP, 1983, 81–94. On the other hand, Xu Shen seems to suggest an economic origin when he says that knot-making was replaced by writing when fraud increased due to the development of trade and crafts.

[25] For a comparative framework which suggests a relatively short gestation period, see Boltz (1994) and the same author's "Language and Writing," *CHAC*, 74–123.

15

Oracle-Bone Inscriptions

The chapter begins with the chance discovery of the oracle-bone inscriptions (15.1).[1] The earliest traces of pyromancy are briefly examined (15.2) before turning to the inscriptions themselves (15.3) and the guides, readers, research tools and reference works to assist in their decipherment and understanding (15.4).

15.1 The Discovery of the Oracle Bones

The first oracle-bone inscriptions to be recognized as such were unearthed at the very end of the nineteenth century from the buried ruins of the late Shang capital of Yin 殷, in the modern village of Xiaotun 小屯, three km to the northwest of Anyang in Henan province. The discovery of the bones was accidental and, unusually in China, unanticipated.

In the course of Chinese history, divination and fortune-telling have been omnipresent. Scapulimancy and plastromancy (divination using shoulder blades and turtle shells, respectively) were widespread from the Neolithic to the Western Zhou. As might be expected, there are many references to the earlier use

---

[1] "Oracle-bone script" (*jiaguwen* 甲骨文 or *jiawen* 甲文) is short for *guijia shougu wenzi* 龜甲獸骨文字 (turtle shell and animal bone script). In the early twentieth century, it was also called *qiwen* 契文 (inscribed script), *Yinxu shuqi* 殷墟書契 (Yin ruins inscriptions; *Yinqi* 殷契 for short), *zhenbu wenzi* 貞卜文字 (oracular script; *buci* 卜辭 for short) or *Yinxu buci* 殷墟卜辭 (Yin ruins oracular script). Yinxu 殷墟 was the name given since at least the Han to the last Shang capital of Yin after its destruction.

of turtle shells for divination in Han and pre-Qin texts, but no scholar appears to have suspected that the oracle bones had been written on during the Shang and that a royal archive of these records might have been preserved.[2]

During the Sui and the Tang, many people were buried at Anyang and some of the oracle bones were disturbed, but the grave diggers did not realize what they had found and reentered the oracle bones.

The modern discovery of the oracle bones was made by peasants digging in the fields around Anyang toward the end of the nineteenth century. Not realizing the value of their discovery, they used them as "dragon bones" (*longgu* 龍骨) for grinding into a tonic infusion or for poultices.[3] An antiques dealer from Tianjin named Fan Weiqing 范維卿 spotted them while buying bronzes in the neighborhood. He showed them to Wang Yirong 王懿榮 (1845–1900), a well-known scholar and collector in Beijing who was at that time the Chancellor of the Imperial Academy (Guozijian *jijiu* 國子監祭酒). Wang realized that the writing on the oracle bones was similar to that on ancient bronze inscriptions, of which he was an expert collector.[4]

---

[2] As Sima Qian 司馬遷 put it, "when the Xia and Yin wished to make divinations, they used yarrow and turtle," *Shiji* 史記, *juan* 128, but he makes no mention of any writing on the shells.

[3] "Dragon bones" and "dragon teeth" had been used in Chinese medicine for centuries. They were Tertiary and Pleistocene period fossils. Since the late nineteenth century, paleontologists, archaeologists and geologists often began their searches at famous sites of dragon bone deposits. The trail which eventually led to the discovery of Peking Man in 1926 began in this way.

[4] A second story about the discovery of the oracle bones began to circulate in the 1930s, according to which Wang Yirong, suffering from the ague, consulted one of the imperial physicians, who gave him a prescription requiring the use of "dragon bones." Wang sent a servant to an old pharmacy dating from the Ming, the Darentang (達仁堂), outside the Xuanwu gate, to get the medicine. On opening the package, he found to his astonishment that some of the dragon bones had strange writing on them, so he immediately sent the servant back to buy up the remaining stock. This is an unlikely story for various reasons, not the least being

Footnote continued on next page

He asked his house guest, Liu E 劉鶚 (1857–1909), to help him identify the inscriptions on the bones as Shang script. A few months after his discovery, Wang committed suicide by taking poison and throwing himself into a well the day after the Allied troops entered Beijing (he had shortly before reluctantly accepted the appointment as leader of the Boxer defense forces). His son sold the bones in 1902 to Liu, who published the first collection of rubbings of the inscriptions in 1903 under the title *Tieyun canggui* 鐵雲藏龜 (The turtles collected by Tieyun [Liu's studio name]), 6 *ce*, 1903.

Word spread, and antique dealers bought up more bones in Anyang but deliberately concealed where they were buying them. It was not until 1908 that a scholar named Luo Zhenyu 羅振玉 (1866–1940), who had first seen an oracle-bone rubbing in his friend Liu E's house in 1902, found out the real source and realized that this was the site of the last capital of the Shang. Meanwhile, the peasants continued to search for bones to sell to the dealers. By the time archaeological excavations were begun at Anyang in 1928, a large number of oracle bones had already been sold, many to foreign collectors.

At first there was a suspicion of forgery. But thanks to the efforts of a small but outstanding group of scholars, a specialized field of oracle-bone script studies developed. The four who created the new field were Luo Zhenyu; his pupil Wang Guowei 王國維 (1877–1927), considered by many to be the most outstanding Chinese classical scholar of the twentieth century;[5] Dong Zuobin 董作賓 (1895–1963);[6] and Guo Moruo.[7]

Wang used the oracle bones in 1917 to authenticate the names of Shang rulers as found in the *Shiji* king lists. He also

---

that there was no Darentang pharmacy outside the Xuanwu gate or indeed anywhere in Beijing. There was however, a pharmacy of this name in Tianjin.

[5] Joey Bonner, *Wang Kuo-wei: An Intellectual Biography*, HUP, 1986.

[6] *Jiaguxue wushi nian* 甲骨學五十年 (incompletely translated under the title *Fifty Years of Studies in Oracle Inscriptions*, Tôyô bunko, 1964).

[7] The first part of Guo Moruo's life is told in David Tod Roy, *Kuo Mo-jo: The Early Years*, HUP, 1971.

made major contributions to Shang chronology. Dong was the first to propose systematic criteria for dating the oracle bones and also to make a detailed study of the Shang calendar. Guo not only interpreted the inscriptions but also used them to write the first Marxist accounts of ancient China.

The main scholars of the next generation were Hu Houxuan 胡厚宣 (1911–95), and Yu Xingwu 于省吾 (1896–1984), both pupils of Dong Zuobin. They in turn trained the current generation of oracle-bone specialists.

15.2　Pyromancy

Scapulimancy began to emerge in China during the late Yangshao period (the earliest traces to be discovered so far date from about 4000 BC). By the time of the Longshan culture this method of divination (the generic term is pyromancy) was gradually spreading over the rest of north China and into Korea. By the Erlitou culture, its use was becoming more widespread. In all, nearly 200 prehistoric bones (usually shoulder blades of ox, sheep, deer, pigs or occasionally humans) used for pyromancy have been found at 35 sites in eight provinces. They are less well prepared than those of the Shang. Several have signs and symbols, but not characters on them. So far the earliest claim for a scapula that bears writing is from a Yueshi 岳石 culture site in Zibo county, Shandong, dated to between 1700 and 1500 BC. It has the characters *liubu* 六卜 incised on both sides.[8] Next come two bones from Erligang, Zhengzhou, dating from the early Shang. One has only one character; the other has 10 which await interpretation, unless indeed, as has been suggested, they have no meaning, being merely 10 characters incised for exercise.[9]

---

[8] *Zhongguo wenwu bao* 中國文物報 535: 1 (1997.5.18).

[9] On the archaeological evidence of divination practices using turtle shells before Shang, see Song Zhenhao 宋鎮豪, *Xia-Shang shehui shenghuoshi* 夏商社會生活史 (A history of social life in the Xia and Shang periods), Shehui kexue, 1994, rpnt., 1996, 514–22.

Turtles were worshipped for their magical properties in the East and in the South. Their plastrons are quite commonly found in Neolithic tombs from these areas, but they were not normally used for pyromancy. Then, in the late Shang, they too began to be used for divination (since the plastron rather than the carapace was usually used, the term is plastromancy). The application of scapulimancy to the divine medium of the turtle shell ushered in the golden age of oracle-bone divination. It started in the reign of Wu Ding 武丁 (ca. 1200–1181 BC) and lasted until the end of the dynasty (ca. 1045 BC).[10] The shells were first cleaned and then a small, oval-shaped hollow, prepared on the rough side, into which a red-hot bronze point or a heated stick of chaste wood (*jing* 荆) was inserted. This caused a fissure on the smooth side from which branched out horizontal cracks. These cracks were the omen (*buzhao* 卜兆) which the diviner interpreted as either auspicious or inauspicious responses to the "charge" (main question) he had posed. To take one example: if the king goes hunting on such and such a date, will he get a good bag? After the divination, in order to sort out which cracks belonged to which questions, the practice developed of incising the matter inquired about on the shell or bone with a bronze burin or knife. Occasionally a brush appears to have been used first.

Many of the questions were more elaborate and often contain three or four elements: the time of the divination and the name of the diviner; the question inquired about; and the judgment of the oracle and in some cases the outcome of the action. A few of the inscriptions simply record events. The king seems not to have taken even the smallest decision without consulting the oracle, especially as regards picking an auspicious day or time for religious sacrifices or ancestor worship or for his actions, including matters related to birth and marriage, illness or death, hunting, the weather, agriculture (especially the state of

---

[10] These dates are approximations. No absolute chronology has been established before 841 BC (see 5.2).

the harvest), appointments and dismissals and military campaigns.[11]

After the Shang and early Zhou, plastromancy continued in use, with the text of the divination at times written on bamboo strips, but by the Spring and Autumn period, the *Liji* 禮記 criticized the Shang people for attaching more importance to ghosts than to the rites (*Yinren ... xian gui er hou li* 殷人 ... 先鬼而後禮). And in the Warring States there were others who faulted the use of turtle shells for divination as being non-rational or inconsistent. Plastromancy never developed into an abstract system linked to a wisdom text and by the end of the Han, it had been almost totally replaced by the methods of divination descended from yarrow or milfoil stalk and later enshrined in the *Yijing* 易經 (*Book of Changes*).[12] There were, however, manuals still circulating in the Han dynasty on turtle-shell divination, one of which was the basis for much of Chapter 128 of the *Shiji*.

The enshrining of Confucianism as the official orthodoxy in the Han spelled the beginning of the end of the use of the turtle for divination, which from the golden days of the Shang had relied on court sponsorship. Some of the Han successor courts continued to practice the old arts and there was a brief revival at the beginning of the Tang, but thereafter they all but died out except among some of the non-Han peoples who con-

---

[11] David N. Keightley, "Late Shang Divination: The Magico-Religious Legacy," in *Explorations in Early Chinese Cosmology*, Henry Rosemont, Jr., ed., *Journal of the American Academy of Religious Studies*, 1984, 11–34.

[12] See Michael Loewe, "Divination by Shells, Bones and Stalks during the Han Period," in Loewe, *Divination, Mythology and Monarchy in Han China*, CUP, 1994, 160–90. See also, Léon Vandermeersch, "De la tortue à l'achillée," in *Divination et Rationalité*, J. Vernant et al., ed., Seuil, 1974, 29–51, and Li Ling 李零, "Zaoqi bushu de xin faxian 早期卜術的新發現" (New discoveries of early divination) in *Zhongguo fangshu kao* 中國方術考 (Studies on Chinese divinatory and medical arts), Renmin Zhongguo, 1993, 218–80, who summarizes divination practices, including those recorded on bamboo strips.

tinued, but with scapulimancy.[13] In the Shang and Zhou the turtle had been a rare item presented to the northern courts as tribute by the peoples of the Yangzi valley. By the later empire the center of gravity had long since shifted to the south and the turtle had lost its rarity value. It remained a symbol of longevity; it served as an ingredient in tonic dishes and potions, but in day-to-day language it was mainly used as a coarse scolding word for cuckold or penis.[14]

15.3 The Oracle-Bone Inscriptions

Of the total published corpus of approximately 155,000 oracle-bone inscriptions, 99.7 percent date from the late Shang and were found, or excavated at or near, the main Shang palace and temple complex in Xiaotun village. Less than 0.001 percent date from the early Shang or from other Shang cities. Less than 0.2 percent come from Western Zhou sites.[15]

---

[13] *Zhongguo gudai guibu wenhua* 中國古代龜卜文化 (The culture of turtle divination in ancient China), Liu Yujian 劉玉建, Guangxi shifan daxue, 1992; rpnt., 1993, assembles literary and historical references to turtle divination from the earliest times to its last revival in the early Tang. Even to this day some non-Han peoples in China practice various forms of scapulimancy. It was also practised in other parts of the world. In Scotland up to the eighteenth century it was called "sleinanachd," or in English, "reading the speal-bone." The blade-bone of a well-scraped shoulder of mutton rather than the carapace of a turtle was used.

[14] Cuckold: *guizi* 龜子, *gui'er* 龜兒, *gui sunzi* 龜孫子 or *wangba* 王 [忘] 八, *wangbadan* 王 [忘] 八蛋 (cuckold's egg); penis: *gui* 龜 or *guitou* 龜頭. *Guitou* was also used for brothel keeper in Mandarin. In Modern Chinese it is the term for glans penis.

[15] Today, there are 129,487 inscribed oracle bones in Chinese collections (at least 99,194 in China, possibly more; 30,204 in Taiwan and 89 in Hong Kong); and about 26,700 are held in 12 other countries around the world, mainly in Japan (12,443), Canada (7,802), the United Kingdom (3,355) and the United States (1,882). These figures may not be entirely accurate, as they are based on counts taken from dozens of publications of oracle-bone fragments from collections all over the world. There must be a significant number of duplicates and forgeries included in the total, although not nearly as many as the forgeries of ancient bronzes, which

Footnote continued on next page

The finds took place haphazardly from the end of the nineteenth century to 1928, by which time about 100,000 fragments
bearing inscriptions had fallen into the hands of private collectors. Thereafter, systematic archaeological excavations conducted at Anyang between 1928 and 1937 by the Shiyusuo and
by the Henan Provincial Museum (1929–30) turned up a total
of 28,575 inscriptions. In 1940–41, excavations were made by
archaeologists from Keio and Tokyo Universities and several
thousand more were found. By 1941, 96 percent of all oracle-
bone inscriptions known today had been unearthed. Since
1950, the Kaogusuo has continued excavations at Anyang. A
total of about 6,275 pieces with inscriptions had been excavated
as of 1998. The major finds were 5,335 pieces at Nandi, Xiaotun, in 1973–77 and 579 pieces (of which more than 300 complete shells, some with over 200 characters on them) excavated
in 1991 at Huayuanzhuang 花園莊, just south of Xiaotun, Anyang.

Of particular interest was the discovery in the 1950s and
1960s of several dozen oracle bones from Western Zhou capitals and feudal states, and in 1977–79 the major find of 296
Zhou oracle-bone inscriptions, 280 of which were from a cache
of approximately 17,000 pieces (mainly turtle shells) from the
excavations at a predynastic Zhou palace at the early Zhou cultic center of Qiyi 岐邑. This confirmed that the Zhou practiced
and recorded oracle-bone divination widely. The content is
much the same as the Shang inscriptions with the exception
that the Zhou ones include divination by trigrams. The inscriptions are much smaller than those of the Shang, sometimes so
minute that you need a magnifying glass to see them. The main
discovery was in the modern village of Fengchu 鳳雛 on what
is now called the Zhouyuan site (周原遺址, named after a line

---

for centuries have been highly prized collectors' items. The most thorough count of mainland collections is in Hu Houxuan, "Dalu xiancang
zhi jiaguwen 大陸現藏之甲骨文," *SYSJK* 67.4: 815–76 (1996). This article
also includes lists of rubbings and charts showing to where the early collections were dispersed.

from the *Shijing*), about 100 km to the West of Xi'an. Other discoveries were from nearby villages on the same site.[16]

Most of the Shang oracle-bone inscriptions are on fragments and are very short, some only one character. The longest is not much more than 200 characters. If the fragments were excavated from one pit they can often be rejoined into whole-plastron inscriptions. The characters are often in rough forms (unlike the bronze characters, which are more carefully written in ornate, formal, archaic scripts). Sometimes they point to the right, sometimes to the left. At times they are vertical, sometimes horizontal. The writing is usually recorded on segments of the shell, each segment arranged from top to bottom (and vice-versa on the scapula). Within each segment, the characters on late period oracle bones are usually incised in columns from top to bottom and from right to left, although sometimes in rows from left to right, depending on the contours and the position on the bone or shell. The vertical strokes were incised before the horizontal ones. In a few cases a single inscription covers several bones or shells. In all, the oracle bones discovered to date contain a total of several million characters, of which 4,500 to 5,000 are different characters. This latter figure includes alternative forms, so a more realistic estimate would probably be nearer 3,500.

The meanings of about 1,200 to 1,500 characters have been deciphered in a manner which meets with general acceptance by *jiaguwen* scholars. Opinions differ over the interpretation of

[16] Xu Xitai 徐錫臺, *Zhouyuan jiaguwen zongshu* 周原甲骨文綜述 (A Summary of Inscriptions of Bones of Zhouyuan), San-Qin, 1987, gives a thorough, printed introduction which is followed by a handwritten table comparing all the Zhouyuan characters with their Shang counterparts. There is a stroke-count index. See also, Wang Yuxin 王宇信, *Xi-Zhou jiagu tanlun* 西周甲骨探論 (An investigation of the oracle-bone writings of Western Zhou), Shehui kexue, 1984; Zhu Qixiang 朱歧祥, Zhouyuan jiagu yanjiu 周原甲骨研究 (Research on the Zhouyuan oracle bones), Xuesheng, 1997. Edward L. Shaughnessy, "Zhouyuan Oracle-Bone Inscriptions: Entering the Research Stage?" *EC* 12: 146–63; 182–94 (1985–87),

several hundred more. A further 1,500 characters can be identified and transcribed into Han chancery or regular script forms
(a step known as *liding* 隸定, *ligu* 隸古 or *lishi* 隸釋) but their
meanings and pronunciation are not known (many are per-
forming the functions of names of people or places). The remainder have not yet been deciphered in ways that are generally accepted. From time to time fanciful interpretations and
claims are made. These should be treated with the utmost skep-
ticism, especially when the new interpretation is used to fit a
character into a particular scheme or theory of history.

In China there are about 100 *jiaguwen* scholars; in Japan
about 50, in Korea some 20; and in the rest of the world no
more than a handful. Overall their numbers are dwindling.

The fascination of the oracle-bone inscriptions is that they
provide the earliest glimpse of the Chinese language and of
Chinese characters centuries before the previously known earliest evidence from the Zhou period. They also provide a
glimpse of Hua-Xia civilization before the Zhou version of
Chinese history, before the Confucian Classics, before the Qin
unification and before the Han consolidation of the institutions
of the early empire.

Until the oracle-bone script was deciphered, very little was
known about the Shang other than what was contained in the
account of the lineage of the Shang royal house in *Shiji* chapter
3 (Yin benji 殷本紀), written 1,000 years after the dynasty had
ended, largely on the basis of records that have long been lost.
The decipherment confirmed the credibility of the account in
the *Shiji*. It also dealt a severe blow to the skeptical approach to
records of the much earlier past, preserved in early Chinese
texts taken by the Yigupai 疑古派 (doubting antiquity school),
which had been in the ascendant in the 1920s. The oracle bones
provide a great deal of new information about the late Shang
period, including astronomy and the calendar, climate, animals
and plants, farming, local kingdoms, place-names, military expeditions, sacrifices, personalities, the royal house and religious
beliefs. Finally, it was the oracle bones which led to the discov-

ery and eventual excavation of the long-lost Shang capital of Yin.

Before their use as historical sources, the oracle-bone inscriptions have to be dated. Oracle-bone divination began only about 30 years after the capital was moved to Yin, reached its height not long thereafter, and continued another 120 years until the end of the dynasty. Absolute dating of the inscriptions is impossible so long as there is no absolute chronology for this period (5.3). Relative dating or sorting into periods can be done on the basis of the internal evidence contained in the inscriptions themselves and by using various archaeological criteria. Dong Zuobin's pioneer 1933 study establishing five main periods has been modified by later scholars, but his approach and his findings still set the framework for a debate which is by no means ended.[17]

15.4 Research Tools

For advice on studying Classical Chinese, see 1.3.5 and on ancient Chinese scripts, including *jiaguwen*, 16.5.

David N. Keightley, "Shang Oracle-bone Inscriptions," in *NSECH*, 15–56, is the best short introduction in English.

David N. Keightley, *Sources of Shang History: The Oracle-Bone Inscriptions of Bronze-Age China*, UCP, 1978; paperback rpnt. with minor revi-

---

[17] For a survey of the different theories on the dating of the oracle bones from the 1930s to the early 1990s, see Li Xueqin and Peng Yushang 彭裕商, *Yinxu jiagu fenqi yanjiu* 殷墟甲骨分期研究 (Researches on the periodization of Yinxu oracle bones), Shanghai guji, 1996. Dong's key study was "Jiaguwen duandai yanjiu 甲骨文斷代研究" (Researches on the periodization of the oracle bones), *SYSJK* special issue, 1.1: 323–424 (1933); later modifications were incorporated in his *Yin lipu* 殷曆譜 (Manual of the Yin calendar), 2 vols., Nanqi, Sichuan: Shiyusuo, special publication, 1945; rpnt., 1992. Dong's periodization and later interpretations up to 1970 are introduced in "Dating the Inscriptions: Relative Chronology," chap. 4 of Keightley, *Sources* (1978), 91–133. Edward L. Shaughnessy, "Recent Approaches to Oracle-Bone Periodization: A Review," *EC*, 8: 1–13 (1982–83), chiefly analyzes the impact of the Nandi finds on periodization.

sions, 1985. This is the standard work in English and an attractive guide to the subject.

There are many overviews in Chinese:

Jiaguxue yibai nian 甲骨學一百年 (One hundred years of oracle-bone studies), forthcoming. An authoritative retrospective prepared under the supervision of the leading oracle-bone scholars in China at the Lishisuo.

Chen Mengjia 陳夢家 (1911–66), *Yinxu buci zongshu* 殷墟卜辭綜述 (Comprehensive account of the divinatory inscriptions from Yinxu), Kexue, 1956; Zhonghua, rpnt., 1992. Although written a long time ago this remains in many ways the best overview.

Shima Kunio 島邦男 (1907–77), *Inkyo bokuji kenkyû* 殷墟甲骨研究, Hirosaki daigaku Chûgoku kenkyûkai, 1958. Chinese tr.: *Yinxu buci yanjiu* 殷墟卜辭研究, Wen Tianhe and Li Shoulin, Dingwen, 1975. Important overview by leading Japanese scholar.

The following are entry-level introductions:

Zhao Cheng, *Jiaguwen jianming cidian–buci fenlei duben* 甲骨文簡明詞典–卜辭分類讀本 (Concise dictionary of oracle-bone characters with topically arranged readings), Zhonghua, 1988; 3rd prnt., 1996, departs from the conventional arrangement by inscriptions, and instead examines the lexemes (usually characters) in 26 semantic fields (e.g., sacrifices, plants, time), with readings presented as examples of usage. There is a stroke-count index of the 2,000 different characters introduced.

Ma Rusen 馬如森 *Yinxu jiaguwen yinlun* 殷墟甲骨文引論 (Introduction to the oracle-bone script from the wastes of Yin), Dongbei shifan daxue, 1993, contains a small dictionary which illustrates and defines 1,056 oracle-bone characters (255–683). *Shuowen* definitions are given, plus examples of usage. There is a *pinyin* index and also an introduction to oracle-bone studies, 1–254.

Li Pu 李圃, *Jiaguwen wenzixue* 甲骨文文字學 (The study of oracle-bone script), Xuelin, 1995; 3rd prnt., 1997, is a good introductory textbook. It contains a thorough analysis of the construction of the oracle-bone characters including the 348 basic graphical units from which they were formed. The same author has also compiled a reader, *Jiaguwen xuanzhu* 甲骨文選注 (Selected oracle-bone inscriptions with notes), Shanghai guji, 1989; rpnt., 1993. This provides tracings of 60 pieces with transcriptions and translations into modern Chinese.

Jiaguwen jingcui xuandu 甲骨文精萃選讀 (Selected readings from the best of the oracle-bone script), Wang Yuxin 王宇信 et al., eds., Yuwen, 1989; rpnt., 1996, contains tracings and transcriptions of 692 pieces (611 from *Heji*; 49 from Nandi and 31 from the White collection). There is a concordance in an appendix. This work is intended not only as a reader but also as a convenient index. Arrangement is by period.

Gao Ming 高明, *Zhongguo guwenzixue tonglun* 中國古文字學通論 (General introduction to the study of Chinese palaeography), Wenwu, 1987; new rev. edition, Beijing daxue, 1996; rpnt., 1997, includes extensive readings of oracle-bone inscriptions (225–332), including those from Zhouyuan. Based on the author's lectures at Peking University.

The detailed interpretations of individual characters by leading scholars can serve as advanced introductions. For example:

Tang Lan 唐蘭, *Yinxu wenzi ji* 殷墟文字記 (Notes on Yinxu script), Peking University, 1934. Mimeo of the author's lecture notes; published ed., rev. with index, Zhonghua, 1981. Contains analysis of 74 characters.

Yu Xingwu 于省吾, *Jiagu wenzi shilin* 甲骨文字釋林, Zhonghua, 1979; rpnt., 1983. In the preface, Yu says that in more than 40 years of study he only managed to provide fresh interpretations of something less than 300 oracle-bone characters. But his meticulous scholarship has stood the test of time. Here he collects together and revises his main interpretations.

Kaizuka Shigeki 貝塚茂樹 (1904–1987) and Itô Michiharu 伊藤道治 (1925–), *Kôkotsu moji kenkyû* 甲骨文字研究 (Research on the oracle-bone characters), *Zuhan* 圖版 (rubbings), *Honbunhen* (本文篇), Dô-hôsha, 1980. This is the revised and renamed version of *Kyôto daigaku jimbun kagaku kenkyûjo shozô kôkotsu moji* 京都大學人文科學研究所所藏甲骨文字 (The oracle-bone inscriptions of the Institute for Humanistic Studies, Kyoto University), *Zuhan* 圖版 (rubbings), *Honbunhen* (本文篇) and Index, 3 vols., Jimbun, 1959, 1960 and 1968. Exemplary presentation and analysis of the Jimbun's collection of 3,426 oracle-bone inscriptions.

Corpus Inscriptionum

The complete corpus of oracle-bone inscriptions will eventually be available in the form of a computer database. The work is being done at the ICS at the Chinese University of Hong Kong. Until it is available, the most comprehensive corpus is

Jiaguwen heji 甲骨文合集 (Collected oracle-bone writings), Guo Moruo, ed., Hu Houxuan, ed. in chief, 13 large folio vols., Zhonghua, 1979–82; 3rd prnt., 1997.[18] The *Heji* contains 41,956 photographs of rubbings and lithographs of all main oracle-bone inscriptions discovered between 1899 and 1970. It is arranged under three subject categories (class and country; society and production; thought and culture) and 19 subcategories, which are set out in chronological order. Before the publication of the massive volumes of the *Heji*, illustrations of the oracle bones were scattered in more than 150 separate publications containing rubbings, drawings or photographs. There were also many scattered pieces in private collections. It was the chief editor, Hu Houxuan, who made it his lifetime work to bring together all this material from public and private collections, to examine individual inscriptions and to weed out the fakes. In the process he also visited many of the major foreign collections. It was Hu who proposed the *Heji* project already in 1956.[19] He guided the team which started the editorial work in 1961 and, despite interruptions from political campaigns, continued on it for the next 20 years. Additional volumes of explanations and indexes to the *Heji* are being readied for publication, including the following item.

Jiaguwen heji bubian 甲骨文合集補編 (Supplement to *Jiaguwen heji*), to be published in 1999 on the 100th anniversary of the discovery of the oracle bones. Contains rubbings and transcriptions of 15,000 inscribed oracle bones published since those included in *Heji*.

Since the publication of the *Heji*, a number of other collections have been published (some, such as the British and Tokyo collections, were largely included in the *Heji*, others, not). Supplement the *Heji* with these (listed below by date of publica-

---

[18] The *Heji* and Part I of the *Tunnan* collections were pirated in Taibei: *Shang-Zhou jiaguwen zongji* 商周甲骨文總集, 16 vols., Yiwen, 1984.

[19] Hu took the term *heji* from the most comprehensive collection of the works of Liang Qichao 梁啓超 (1873–1929), *Yinbingshi heji* 飲冰室合集, 40 vols., Zhonghua, 1936. It has the sense of a careful assemblage and collation of already published materials.

tion) and also with subsequent finds, notably those at Hua-yuanzhuang[20] and Zhouyuan.[21]

Tôkyô daigaku Tôyô bunka kenkyûjo shozô kôkotsu moji 東京大學東洋文化研究所藏甲骨文字 (Oracle-bone script in the Institute of Oriental Studies, Tokyo University), Matsumaru Michio 松丸道雄, comp., 1979 (1,315 inscriptions).

Huaiteshi deng suocang jiagu wenzi 懷特氏等所藏甲骨文字 (Oracle-bone script held by Mr. White and others), Xu Jinxiong 許進雄, Royal Ontario Museum, 1979 (1,915 inscriptions).

Xiaotun Nandi jiagu 小屯南地甲骨 (Oracle bones from Nandi, Xiaotun), Kaogusuo, eds., 2 parts in 5 large folio vols., with a supplement, Zhonghua, 1980, 1983; vol. 5 is an index. This work contains illustrations (Part I) and transcriptions (Part II) of 4,589 of the oracle bones discovered at Nandi in 1973 and another 23 in its neighborhood between 1975 and 1977. For a detailed review, see David N. Keightley, "Sources of Shang History: Two Major Oracle-Bone Collections Published in the People's Republic of China," *JAOS* 110.1: 39–59 (1990). Use Cai Fangpei, Edward L. Shaughnessy and James F. Shaughnessy, Jr., *A Concordance of the Xiaotun Nandi Oracle-Bone Inscriptions*, *EC* Special Monograph Series, no. 1, Chicago, 1988.

Collections d'inscriptions oraculaires en France, Jean A. Lefeuvre, ed., Variétés sinologiques, New Series, #70, Institut Ricci, 1985, which contains photos, transcriptions and translations of 64 pieces held in France.

Yingguo suocang jiagu ji 英國所藏甲骨集 (Oracle-bone collections in Great Britain), Qi Wenxin 齊文心, Sarah Allen and Li Xueqin 李學勤, eds., part 1 (rubbings), 2 vols., Zhonghua, 1985; part 2 (transcriptions, studies and index), 2 vols., Zhonghua, 1992 (2,674 inscriptions).

Tenri daigaku fuzoku Tenri sankôkan zô kôkotsu monji 天理大學附屬天理參考館藏甲骨文字 (Oracle-bone inscriptions stored in the Tenri reference library attached to Tenri University), Itô Michiharu 伊藤道治, ed., 1987.

---

[20] The total number of pieces discovered at Huayuanzhuang was 1,581. They date from the reign of Wu Ding and are mainly concerned with sacrifices, hunting, the weather and illness. The divinations were conducted for a prince, not the king, *Kaogu* 1993. 6.

Several Collections of Oracular Inscriptions in Germany, Switzerland, the Netherlands, Belgium, Jean A. Lefeuvre, ed., Variétés sinologiques, New Series, #77, Institut Ricci, 1997. For a review of this (plus Lefeuvre, 1985) dealing with the methodology of decipherment, see Takashima Ken'ichi, "*Several Collections of Oracular Inscriptions in Germany, Switzerland, the Netherlands, Belgium*: A Review in Metatheories," *TP* (1998).

The following collection was published before the *Heji*. It remains important, not least because of the editor's comments and a number of studies and translations made of it:

Xiaotun, Di'erben: Yinxu wenzi, Bingbian 小屯第二本殷墟文字丙編, (Xiaotun, vol. 2: Yinxu inscriptions, Part 3), 3 vols., 6 *ce*, Zhang Bingquan 張秉權, ed., Shiyusuo, 1957–72. These volumes contain 632 complete rejoined plastron inscriptions (a process made possible by the fact that the fragments were originally excavated from one pit).

  Takashima Ken'ichi 高嶋謙一 (1939–), *Commentaries to Fascicle Three of Inscriptions from the Yin Ruins: Palaeographical and Linguistic Studies*, forthcoming. These are notes to the translations in the following item.

  Translations of Fascicle Three of Inscriptions from the Yin Ruins, Paul L-M. Serruys and Takashima Ken'ichi, trs., forthcoming.

  Takashima Ken'ichi, *Yinxu wenzi Bingbian tongjian* 殷墟文字丙編通檢 (*A Concordance to Fascicle Three of Inscriptions from the Yin Ruins*), Shiyusuo, 1985.

Language and Dictionaries

On the language of the oracle-bone inscriptions, see:

Paul L-M. Serruys, "The Language of the Shang Oracle-Bone Inscriptions," *TP* 60: 12–120 (1974); "Basic Problems Underlying the Process of Identification of the Chinese Graphs of the Shang Oracular Inscriptions," *SYSJK* 53: 455–94 (1982); "Notes on the Grammar of the Oracular Inscriptions of Shang," in *Contributions to Sino-Tibetan Studies*, John McCoy and Timothy Light, eds., Brill, 1986, 203–57.

---

[21] For the Zhouyuan finds, see Xu Xitai (1987), Wang Yuxin (1984) and Zhu Qixiang (1997).

Itô Michiharu 伊藤道治 and Takashima Ken'ichi 高嶋謙一, *Studies in Early Chinese Civilization, Religion, Society, Language and Palaeography*, Hirakata, Osâka: Kansai Gaidai University Publications, 2 vols., 1996. Vol. I contains the text; vol. II, the tables, notes, bibliography and index. The chapters written by Itô are translated from his book *Chûgoku kodai ôchô no keisei* 中國古代王朝の形成 (The form of the ancient Chinese royal court), Sôbunsha, 1975, 1–133; those by Takashima are based on his articles on the language. There is also a lengthy bibliography of Japanese secondary scholarship on the Shang up to the 1980s.

Takashima Ken'ichi, "An Evaluation of the Theories Concerning the Shang Oracle-Bone Inscriptions," *The Journal of Intercultural Studies* (Kansai Gaidai University) 15–16: 11–54 (1988–89). This is a summary in English of the author's much longer article, "Indai teiboku gengo no honshitsu 殷代貞卜言語朝の本質" (The nature of the language of the Shang oracle-bone inscriptions), *Tôyô bunka kenkyûjo kiyô*, 110: 1–165 (1989).

Zhao Cheng 趙誠 mainly concentrates on the language in *Jiagu wenzixue gangyao* 甲骨文字學綱要 (Introduction to the study of oracle-bone script), Shangwu, 1993.

Jiaguwen zidian 甲骨文字典 (Dictionary of oracle-bone characters), Xu Zhongshu 徐中舒 et al., ed., Sichuan cishu, 1988; 4th prnt., 1995, is the leading *jiaguwen* dictionary available.[22] Arrangement is by *Shuowen* classifiers. An analysis of the form of each character (*jiezi* 解字) in one or all of the five periods of the development of the oracle-bone script is given. This is followed by an explanation of the meaning (*shiyi* 釋義), with an example of usage both in oracle-bone script and in modern characters. Most individual oracle-bone characters are included, even when their meanings or identifications are not known, so the total head characters comes to 2,938. There is a stroke-count index of characters in their *kaiti* forms at the front.

Zhang Yujin 張玉金, *Jiaguwen xuci cidian* 甲骨文虛詞辭典 (Dictionary of oracle-bone particles), Zhonghua, 1994, is a study of the particles found on the oracle-bone inscriptions arranged in dictionary form.

[22] The *Jiaguwen zidian* attempts to combine the strengths of Sun (1965) and Li Xiaoding (1965): *Jiaguwen bian* 甲骨文編 (Compilation of oracle-bone characters), Sun Haibo 孫海波 (1910–72), ed. in chief, 1934 (which contained 2,116 characters); rev. ed., Zhonghua, 1965 (which contained 4,672 characters); repr., 1982, 1989, 1997.

Collected Interpretations

There are two main works which assemble the different interpretations by modern scholars of the oracle-bone characters. The more comprehensive of the two is the first:

Kôkotsu moji jishaku sôran 甲骨文字字釋綜覽 (Synthetic Index for Interpretation of Oracle-Bone Characters), Matsumaru Michio 松丸道雄 and Takashima Ken'ichi 高嶋謙一, eds., Tôbunken, 1993, Tokyô daigaku, 1994. This gives regular script equivalents as found in the interpretations drawn from works published between 1904 and 1988 by 471 scholars in Chinese, Japanese, English, German, French, Russian and Korean (the list of these works which is appendixed amounts to a full bibliography of interpretations of oracle-bone characters up to 1988). In addition, the *Sôran* shows the different forms of the oracle-bone characters and also contains cross-references to the standard reference works as of 1988 (*Jiagu wenbian, Inkyo bokuji sôrui, Jiagu wenzi jishi, Jiaguwen zidian*). It is beautifully printed.

Jiagu wenzi gulin 甲骨文字詁林 (Collected commentaries on the oracle-bone characters), Yu Xingwu 于省吾, ed. in chief, Yao Xiaosui 姚孝遂 (1926–95) and Xiao Ding 肖丁 (Zhao Cheng 趙誠), gen. eds., 4 vols., Zhonghua, 1996. The authors have assembled the interpretations of 3,691 oracle-bone characters by the leading Chinese authorities (as of the end of 1989). The interpretations are arranged chronologically in the order in which they were written. For the most part contributions not written in Chinese are not included. There is neither a name nor title index. Unfortunately, this huge work (it runs to over 3,700 pages) is reproduced from handwriting, and is not always very clear.

These two works largely, but not entirely, supersede the similar, earlier reference by Li Xiaoding 李孝定, *Jiagu wenzi jishi* 甲骨文字集釋 (Collected explanations of the oracle-bone characters), 16 vols., Shiyusuo, special publication 50 (1965); rpnt., 8 vols., 1970; 1991.

Concordances

The most comprehensive concordance is:

Yinxu jiagu keci leizuan 殷墟甲骨刻辭類纂 (Concordance of Yin inscribed oracle bones), Yao Xiaosui and Xiao Ding, eds. in chief, 3 large folio vols., Zhonghua, 1989; rpnt., 1992. The *Leizuan* lists some 200,000 phrases and sentences in which the 1,473 head characters included occur. It also indicates *Heji* numbers. It thus not only shows the different contexts in which each character was used but can also serve as an index to the *Heji*. Vol. 3 contains a *pinyin* index in addition to classifier and stroke-count indexes.[23] By the simple fact that all transcriptions are given not only in oracle-bone script but also in *kaishu*, this work largely supersedes the previous standard concordance (Shima, 1971). Moreover, the *Leizuan* includes the important finds since Shima's work was compiled. It is handwritten, but clearly printed and easy to read.[24] However *Leizuan* does not treat key words consistently as pointed out by Qiu Xigui in his review in *Shupin* 1: 4–14 and 2: 2–9 (1990) and by David N. Keightley in "Graphs, Words and Meanings: Three Reference Works [*Leizuan, Zongji, Sôran*] for Shang Oracle-Bone Studies, with an Excursus on the Religious Roles of the Day or Sun," *JAOS* 117.3: 507–24 (1997).

Jiaguwen tongjian 甲骨文通檢 (A concordance to oracle-bone inscriptions), Rao Zongyi 饒宗頤, ed., 4 vols. to date, HKCU Press, 1989–95. This is a concordance to Heji and eight other collections arranged by categories, which, if they fit your research, is useful. Vol. 1 covers former kings, predynastic ancestors and diviners; vol. 2, place-names; vol. 3, astronomy and the weather; vol. 4, official posts and people. There is a finding list at the beginning of each volume in regular script, but the characters in the body of the work are in oracle-bone script. All references to each character or phrase are indicated by finding number in the *Heji* and supplementary collections.

Bibliography

For a comprehensive bibliography arranged by subject and listing both foreign and Chinese works published between 1898

---

[23] The *Leizuan* is based on *Yinxu jiagu keci moshi zongji* 殷墟甲骨刻辭摹釋總集 (Comprehensive copies and transcriptions [into *kaishu*] of inscribed oracle bones from Yinxu), Yao Xiaosui and Xiao Ding, eds. in chief, 2 large folio vols., Zhonghua, 1988; rpnt., 1992. This contains copies, transcriptions and an index of some 50,000 oracle-bone inscriptions found in *Heji* (1979–82); *Tunnan* (1980–83); *Yingguo* (1985–91); *Tôkyô* (1979) and *Huaiteshi* (1979). The transcriptions are handwritten and clearly readable in a standardized oracle-bone script and in *kaishu*. They follow the order of the plates.

[24] Shima Kunio 島邦男 (1907–77), *Inkyo bokuji sôrui* 殷墟卜辭綜類 (Comprehensive classification of the oracle-bone inscriptions from the wastes of Yin), Kyûko, 1967; 2nd rev. ed., 1971.

and 1987 on the oracle bones and on Shang dynasty history, see
Jiaguxue yu Shangshi lunzhu mulu 甲骨學與商史論著目錄 (Bibliography of works on oracle-bone studies and Shang history),
Pu Maozuo 濮茅左 comp., Shanghai guji, 1991.

　　Specialized journals such as *Early China, Guwenzi yanjiu* 古文字研究, *Kôkotsugaku* 甲骨學 or the archaeological and linguistic journals many of which contain articles and reviews of oracle-bone scholarship. These journals as well as yearbooks and other bibliographical references for early Chinese history are listed in 12.2 and 13.3.

16

The Characters:

Evolution and Structure

There is plenty of new evidence to trace the evolution of the different ways of writing the characters during the thousand years between the oracle-bone script and the emergence of Han chancery script (16.1). Characters were constructed in three main ways (16.2). A huge number of them are classified under surprisingly few classifiers (16.3). One of the main difficulties in reading any transmitted text written in the Han or before is the amount of orthographic variation. A situation that improves thereafter but remains a hazard, especially in manuscript sources (16.4). The chapter ends with some brief advice on studying ancient scripts (16.5).

16.1 Evolution of Scripts

The first special terms for the different scripts or character forms (*zixing* 字形) date from the Later Han, notably those in the *Shuowen jiezi* 説文解字 (2.2.1).[1] These terms can now be

---

[1] Zhan Jinxin 詹鄞鑫, *Hanzi shuolüe* 漢字説略 (Outline of Chinese characters), Hongye, 1995, 55–150; Qiu Xigui, *Wenzixue gaiyao* 文字學概要 (Essentials of paleography), Shangwu, 1988; 3rd prnt., with corrections, 1996, 40–96. For an English translation of Qiu, see *Chinese Writing*, Gilbert Mattos and Jerry Norman, trs., *Early China* Special Monograph Series, SSEC and IEAS, 1998.

elaborated and in some cases corrected using the writing on the oracle-bone and bronze inscriptions and on other excavated artifacts and texts. The new picture which emerges is summarized in Table 16.

Table 16: Main Script Forms

Form of Script (tr.), origin	Period of Use
Jiaguwen 甲骨文 (Oracle-bone, chap. 15)	Late Shang; W. Zhou
Jinwen 金文 (Bronze, chap. 17)	Late Shang; Zhou
Zhouwen 籀文 (Large-seal)	E. Zhou
Zhuanwen 篆文 (Seal)[2]	Warring States, W. Han
Lishu 隸書 (Chancery), cursive *zhuanwen*	4th c. BC (Qin)–4th AD
Caoshu 草書 (Cursive), cursive *lishu*[3]	Han
Xingshu 行書 (Running), cursive *lishu/caoshu*	E. Han (matures 4th c.)
Kaishu 楷書 (Model), from *xingshu*[4]	4th c. (matures 5th–6th c.)

[2] The term *zhuanwen* is first used in the *Shuowen*. It may simply have meant "carved script," but it is conventionally translated into English as "seal script." It is sometimes referred to as *xiaozhuan* 小篆 (small seal script) to distinguish it from *dazhuan* 大篆 (large seal script or *zhouwen* 籀文), the script found on Eastern Zhou bronzes.

During the Spring and Autumn and Warring States periods, a number of aesthetic forms of seal script were used mainly in the Yangzi kingdoms of Chu 楚, Yue 越 and Ba 巴 on bronze weapons as well as on insignia and seals, for which they are still popular to this day. They are known as *niaochongshu* 鳥蟲書 (bird and insect scripts). *Kedou* 蝌蚪 (tadpole) script was another variety of seal script used on bronzes. It was named after its appearance: heavy strokes at the top tapering off at the bottom.

[3] Han *caoshu* was termed *zhangcao* 章草 in the fourth century to distinguish it from *jincao* 今草 of that time. Wang Fang-yü (Wang Fangyu 王方宇), *Introduction to Chinese Cursive Script*, Far Eastern Publications, YUP, 1958; 7th prnt., 1972.

[4] *Kaishu* or *kaiti* after its emergence in the fourth century was used in parallel with *lishu* during the Wei and Jin before becoming the predominant style from the *Nan-Bei Chao*. *Kaishu* is also called *zhenshu* 真書 (true script), *zhengshu* 正書 (correct script). Variations on *kaishu* for block-printed books from the Song were based on the differing *kaishu* styles of famous calligraphers. In the later empire *zhengkai* 正楷 (correct model script) and *caoshu* 草書 were the two most common script forms.

The history of Chinese scripts can be broadly divided into two stages: *guwen* 古文 (the first four rows of Table 16), which were in use from the late Shang to Qin, and *jinwen* 今文, or *Li-Kai* 隸楷, from the Han to the present (the last four rows). The late Warring States to the early Han marks a transitional stage between the two. Modern typefaces are based on *kaishu*.[5]

Needless to say, the different scripts did not follow one after the other in orderly fashion, each growing from the previous one in a linear progression. They evolved over several centuries and often overlapped. A clear-cut profile of each of the main scripts was only established long afterwards when fine examples were taken as calligraphic models.

During the Warring States, two main scripts began to develop from *zhouwen* 籀文, namely *zhuanwen* 篆文 and *lishu* 隸書.[6] The first was more formal; the second was a cursive in day-to-day use by clerks and scribes, especially in the state of Qin. On the advice of his chancellor Li Si 李斯 (apart from his other accomplishments, a noted philologist and calligrapher), the first emperor standardized the characters (*shu tong wenzi* 書同文字). He made *Qinzhuan* 秦篆 (the Qin variety of seal script) the official standard for the whole country and suppressed the variant characters of the scripts of the six states (*liuguo wenzi* 六國文字). *Qinli* 秦隸 (Qin chancery script) continued in informal use in Qin. The unification laid the groundwork for an even bigger change, the shift from seal to chancery script.

[5] As relative terms, *guwen* 古文 and *jinwen* 今文 have changed their meanings many times. The second main usage refers to the Old and the New Text traditions (*guwen* and *jinwen*) and the schools of classical learning based on each (19.2); in addition, *guwen* is used for the *wenyan* style of writing introduced in the Tang by writers such as Han Yu 韓愈 (768–824) in contrast to the ornate *pianwen* 駢文 parallel prose of the Six Dynasties. *Guwen* is also sometimes used as a synonym for *Gudai Hanyu* embracing all forms of Classical and Literary Chinese before modern times (although strictly speaking, not *pianwen*).

[6] *Zhanguo guwen zidian* 戰國古文字典 (Dictionary of Warring States characters), He Linyi 何林義, ed., 2 vols., Zhonghua, 1998, arranges the *liuguo wenzi* as culled from epigraphic sources by rhyme groups.

This shift took place gradually with *lishu* 隸書 (variously translated as chancery, official or clerk's script) emerging in the Later Han as the standard. It was referred to as *jinwen* 今文 or *jinzi* 今字 (contemporary or modern script) to distinguish it from pre-Qin scripts, especially the *liuguo wenzi*, which were termed *guwen* 古文 or *guzi* 古字 (ancient scripts). Today, the term *guwen* is still used, but it has been extended to cover all pre-Qin scripts, including the oracle-bone script (which was no longer known in the Han).

The change to *lishu* (described since the late Tang as *libian* 隸變) was the biggest transformation of the Chinese writing system which has ever taken place. The old curvaceous *guwen* characters, many still clearly pictographic in inspiration, were finally replaced by *lishu* composed of geometric strokes in abstract patterns more easily and quickly written by brush.[7] A student today without special training would find it hard to read any of the *guwen* scripts. On the other hand *jinwen* (*lishu*) is sufficiently close to today's characters (Table 17) as to be recognizable.

Table 17: Modern Movable Typefaces

Kaiti 楷體 (devised for Shangwu)[8]	Since 1909
Songti 宋體[9]	Since early 20th c.
Fang-Songti 仿宋體[10]	Since 1916
Heiti 黑體 (bold typeface used for headlines)	Since early 20th c.
Jiantizi 簡體字 (Simplified characters)	1956; 1964 (rev., 1986)

[7] Zhao Pingan 趙平安, *Libian yanjiu* 隸變研究 (Research on the change to chancery script), Hebei daxue, 1993.

[8] Based on a Ming woodblock typeface. Also called *Zhengkai* 正楷. The typeface used in the manual is *Kaiti*.

[9] *Songti* 宋體 or (*jiangti* 匠體) was a Ming development of a Southern Song woodblock typeface. Hence its Japanese name *Minchôtai* 明朝體.

[10] *Fang-Songti* was based on the Wuyingdian (Qing imperial printing office) recreation of Northern Song woodblock typeface. Hence its Japanese name, *Sôchôtai* 宋朝體.

16.2 Structure

Analysis of the structure of a character has always been used as a way of providing clues to its original and later meanings and also as a technique for committing it to memory (1.3.2). The earliest evidence dates from the Spring and Autumn period, but the first systematic analysis came only after the shift to chancery script had been completed. One of the effects of the shift was that the structural elements of the characters became much less clear than they had been in small seal script. It was this which led Xu Shen 許慎 to compile the *Shuowen* 說文.

As a member of the Old Text school (19.2), his aim was to produce a standard for writing the characters and to define their correct meanings based on the analysis of their small seal components. In this way he felt orthographic and semantic confusion could be avoided and the link with old traditions as expressed in the *guwen* texts reestablished (prerequisites for good government). Not surprisingly, the *Shuowen* and all later philological works were placed in the Classics bibliographic classification (see Table 19, 19.2).

The basis of Xu's analysis was the *liushu* 六書 (six types of character composition theory).[11] His theory remained in use from the Later Han until the twentieth century, even though the definition and boundaries between the six categories are not entirely clear.[12]

---

[11] Xu's six categories should not be confused with *liushu* 六書, *liuti* 六體 or *liuwen* 六文, meaning the "six calligraphic scripts" variously defined from the Han onward.

[12] The six categories were *zhishi* 指事, *xiangxing* 象形, *xingsheng* 形聲, *huiyi* 會意, *zhuanzhu* 轉注 and *jiajie* 假借, conventionally translated respectively as symbols, pictographs, picto-phonetic compounds, compound ideographs, notative and phonetic loan characters. The phrase *liushu* 六書 appears in the *Zhouli* 周禮 without explanation. Apart from tradition, the reason that Xu chose to retain six categories was influenced by the prevailing fashion in the Han, inherited from the Qin, to regard six as a particularly fortunate number. See Zhao Cheng 趙誠, *Jiagu wenzixue gangyao* 甲骨文字學綱要, 140–56.

Footnote continued on next page

The title of the *Shuowen* reflects exactly the basic distinction drawn by Xu between single- and multiple-component characters, *wen* 文 and *zi* 字 (e.g., *shui* 水 and *he* 河). It is a distinction which is followed to this day (*dutizi* 獨體字 and *hetizi* 合體字); it determined that *wenzi* 文字 became the word for writing in Chinese (previously *ming* 名, *shu* 書 or *wen* 文 had been used); it was also the first work to arrange the characters in groups according to their significs (those components which gave a clue as to their meaning) hence called classifiers (often also called "radicals"), *bushou* 部首 (16.3).

Despite the modern discovery of new and earlier forms of writing on artifacts and in excavated texts, Xu's work is still the single most important historical source on ancient Chinese characters and on the written language as it had developed up to his day. It is used as the basis for most modern analyses of the structure of the characters which are frequently divided into three categories: (1) the form indicates the word and hence the sound; (2) a phonetic indicator suggests the word and hence the meaning and (3) is usually a combination of (1) and (2).[13]

Type-1 characters, *xingyizi* 形義字, are those in which the form indicates or symbolizes the meaning of words (*yixing biaoyi* 以形表義), usually for things. *Xingyizi* include Xu Shen's *zhishi*, *xiangxing* and *huiyi* categories (see note 12). For exam-

---

The eighteenth-century scholar Dai Zhen 戴震 (1723–77) modified the *liushu* to "four ways of constructing characters, two ways of using them," an approach many still use. Various new analyses were put forward in the 1930s, including a threefold division proposed by Tang Lan 唐蘭: pictographs (*xiangxing* 象形); ideographs (*xiangyi* 象意) and pictophonetic compounds (*xingsheng* 形聲). This was in turn modified by Chen Mengjia 陳夢家 who replaced *xiangyi* with *jiajie* 假借 (phonetic loans). Tang and Chen and later philologists were able to challenge Xu on the basis of newly discovered pre-Qin epigraphic sources not available in the Han.

[13] This threefold classification is based on Qiu (1996). See also William G. Boltz, *The Origin and Early Development of the Chinese Writing System*, American Oriental Series, vol. 78, New Haven, Conn.: American Oriental Society, 1994; Yin Binyong 尹斌庸, *Modern Chinese Characters*, John S. Rohsenow, tr., Sinolingua, 1994.

ple, pictographs such as the sun and moon, *ri* 日 and *yue* 月; or concepts, such as up and down, *shang* 上 and *xia* 下; or the numbers *yi* 一, *er* 二, *san* 三, *shi* 十, *nian* 廿, *sa* 卅.[14]

Pre-classical Chinese contains some 1,000 words represented by *xingyizi* (including about 300 which have not been deciphered), but that was about the limit as to how many words for things, let alone concepts, could be represented by characters derived from pictures, signs or symbols (Modern Chinese includes about 500 frequently used *xingyizi*). Ingenious ways were found of forming new characters based on the *xingyizi*, but the most important way was to borrow them.[15]

Type-2 characters, *yinyizi* 音義字 (that is, *jieyin biaoyi* 借音表義), are phonetic loans, formed according to a method used by the other writing systems of the ancient world (the so-called rebus principle whereby, for example, pictures of a cat and a log are borrowed for their sounds for the word pronounced "catalog"). Thus the word for "don't" (pronounced *wu* in modern standard Chinese) was represented by *mu* 母. The character was borrowed for its sound irrespective of its original meaning of mother.[16] *Yinyizi* were fairly common on oracle-bone and

---

[14] *Shi* 十, *nian* 廿 and *sa* 卅 in their oracle-bone script forms are simply 一, 二 and 三 written vertically, but in the bronze script they probably recall the knots in strings which may earlier have been used as a mnemonic in the conduct of government business (14.1). In both cases, they are considered *zhishizi* 指事字 (symbols). The other numerals (四, 五, 六, 七, 八 and 九) probably began as *zhishizi* before acquiring their present phonetic loan characters (an example of the fluidity in matching characters to words in the early stages of Chinese orthography, 1.6).

[15] Xu Jinxiong 許進雄 examines the forms, basic meanings and sounds of 830 type-1 characters and gives the *Shuowen* definitions, examples of usage and the number of *xieshengzi* in which the components feature: *Guwen xiesheng zigen* 古文諧聲字根 (The constituent roots of ancient Chinese phonetic compound characters), Taibei: Shangwu, 1995.

[16] Traditionally *yinyizi* are termed *jiajiezi* 假借字 (loan or borrowed characters). Those which were formed for words with no previous characters are mainly found on the oracle-bones and bronze inscriptions. Those which were borrowed for words with existing characters are called *tongjiazi* 通假字 (alternative characters). They became increasingly com-

Footnote continued on next page

bronze inscriptions when the development of new characters could hardly keep pace with the language, especially the requirement to find characters for proper names and abstract words such as numbers (甲, 乙, 丙, 丁), pronouns (我, 汝, 朕) or particles (毋, 勿, 不, 弗, 以, 于, 其).

In order to avoid the confusion arising when a character was borrowed to represent different words, small changes were made, for example, by adding strokes, dots and circles either singly or in combination (thus *wu* was written 毋 to distinguish it from 母). But as the number of characters grew, it became difficult to memorize all such changes. Eventually, the practice developed of adding a second component, the signific or determinative, in order to distinguish different words written with the same or a similar character. Likewise, a phonetic was often added to characters having the same or similar forms. This led to the third type.

Type-3 characters, *xingshengzi* 形聲字, are compounds usually of two parts, one of which, the signific (*xingfu* 形符), gives a clue to the meaning by suggesting in which broad category of things a word should be classified in (as with *mu* 木 "tree" in *song* 松 "pine"). It thus helps distinguish homonyms. The other part, the phonetic (*shengfu*), gives a hint of the sound (as with *gong* 公 in *song* 松).[17] *Xingshengzi* became the principal way of avoiding ambiguity and also of forming new characters. As a result, today most characters are of this type. As the name indicates, *xingshengzi* were typically formed by combining existing characters of types 1 and 2.

---

mon in the Warring States, the Qin and the Han for reasons explained in 16.4.4.

[17] *Xingshengzi* 形聲字 (picto-phonetic characters) are also called *xieshengzi* 諧聲字 (phonetic compound characters). *Xingfu* 形符 are also known as *xingpang* 形旁 or *yifu* 意符; *shengfu* 聲符 are sometimes referred to as *shengpang* 聲旁 or *yinpang* 音旁.

From the Han, the significs may properly be termed classifiers because from then on they were used as the basis of a system for organizing characters into groups according to semantic classifiers, *bushou* 部首 (radicals); see 16.3.

Only about 25 percent of the oracle-bone characters which have been deciphered to date were *xingshengzi* 形聲字 (of the remainder, more than half were *xingyizi* 形義字). About 40 percent of the bronze characters were *xingshengzi*; by the beginning of the second century AD, 80–85 percent of the small seal characters were *xingshengzi* and *xingyizi* had declined to less than 15 percent.[18] Ninety-nine percent of all new characters invented from the Han to the present day have been *xingsheng* compounds.

Although the relative number of Type-1 characters (*xingyizi*) declined during the Zhou as other types (especially Type-3 characters, *xingshengzi*) were formed, they are still among the most frequently used for three main reasons: as the first to be developed, they represent the words for basic things and concepts; second, arising from this, almost all significs were originally *xingyizi*, so *xingyizi* appear as one of the components in almost every character in the script; third, nearly all classifiers as well as a large number of phonetic indicators are *xingyizi*.[19]

16.3   Significs and Classifiers

Philologists have counted about 150 significs in use from the oracle-bone script to the centuries before the Qin unification. Many more have since been invented, but the original 150 are still in use today in thousands of the most frequently used characters. Words such as *shan* 山 (mountain), *shui* 水 (water), *niu* 牛 (ox), *ma* 馬 (horse) and numerals did not change their meaning from the late Shang to the present day. For these reasons the Shang lexical heritage dominates modern Chinese to an extent which may not always be fully recognized.

---

[18] Li Guoying 李國英, *Xiaozhuan xingshengzi yanjiu* 小篆形聲字研究 (Research on small seal *xingsheng* characters), Beijing shifan daxue, 1996.

[19] Another reason is that one type of *xingyizi*, the *huiyizi* 會意字, continued to be invented throughout Chinese history. For example, fire is *huo* 火; two fires are scorching hot, *yan* 炎; three are flames, *yan* 焱.

The core significs cover (1) man and parts of the body (the single most complete category);[20] (2) animals, insects, reptiles and their pelts and skins;[21] (3) trees, plants, wine and food;[22] (4) housing, clothing, utensils, equipment and weapons;[23] (5) the sun, the moon, topography and the elements;[24] (6) gods and divination.[25] As time went by, more and more words with extended meanings were placed in these categories. For example, the characters for mouth, ears, nose, eyes, tongue, heart, hands and feet were not only used for parts of the body, but also as significs in words related to eating, talking, hearing, smell, sight, taste, emotions, and actions using the hands and feet. Characters were associated now with one signific, now another as a result of similarities of meaning or of form between the significs. After several centuries of experimentation most characters eventually came to be placed under very few classifiers (significs) in dictionaries.[26] Even today, the 85,568 characters in

---

[20] 人亻儿大兒尸士女男父老子民臣首頁面耳目口自鼻彡身手又足勹骨肉血力

[21] 馬牛羊犬豕隹豸虎鹿鳥蟲魚黽龜龍羽毛角革

[22] 木竹艹禾食米酉鹵

[23] 門戶京瓦穴衣巾糸革帛韋舟車斤耒网工鼎鬲豆壺斗皿缶爵聿弓矢干戈刀矛殳

[24] 日月風雨山阜厂川田里邑行金玉石土水火

[25] 巫卜示鬼

[26] The characters classified under the five elements—*shui* 水 (water); *mu* 木 (wood); *jin* 金 (metal); *tu* 土 (earth); and *huo* 火 (fire)—account for 20 percent of the total 10,000 characters in the modern dictionary *Xinhua zidian* 新華字典. If you add three more of the most frequently used classifiers, the characters *kou* 口 (mouth), *shou* 手 (hand) and *cao* 艹 (grass or flower), these eight alone account for over one-third of all the characters in the dictionary and another 18 classifiers account for a second third. The same proportions hold for the *Kangxi zidian* 康熙字典, in which approximately two-thirds of the characters are listed under and contain the 25 most frequent classifiers. The remaining characters are scattered in small numbers under the other 150 classifiers.

On the graphic development of the characters, including a long section on the pre-Qin development of the classifiers, see Gao Ming 高明, *Zhongguo guwenzixue tonglun* 中國古文字學通論 (General introduction to the study of Chinese paleography), Wenwu, 1987; new rev. edition, Beijing daxue, 1996; rpnt., 1997. He uses hundreds of drawings and includes 200 pages of annotated, illustrated readings of ancient script (*gu-*

Footnote continued on next page

the *Zhonghua zihai* 中華字海 (Table 1, chap. 1) are classified under just 200 significs. This clearly indicates that the significs can only be very broad indicators of category.

16.4 Variants

One of the main difficulties in reading Classical Chinese is that the same character could be written in many different ways: there were graphic variants (*yitizi* 異體字, 16.4.1); a later way of writing a character often differed from an earlier way (*gujinzi* 古今字, 16.4.2); and variants with fewer strokes than the official ones were in popular use from the earliest times to the present day (*zhengsuzi* 正俗字, 16.4.3). Another type of difficulty is that one character could be used to represent two or more words with the same pronunciation (*tongjiazi* 通假字, 16.4.4), moreover, one character could have two or more different pronunciations (16.4.5). Finally, foreign loan words were written with all sorts of different characters (usually approximating the original sound, see 1.2.7).

There were also many special characters, for example, dialect characters (*fangyanzi* 方言字) unique to a particular dialect area;[27] characters used in a particular trade, *hangyu wenzi* 行語文字 (for example, *dangzi* 當字, pawnshop writing; see 7.1.2 for an example); magical and riddle characters, and many others.[28] It was forbidden to use such characters in official documents.

---

wenzi 古文字) forms. It should be read together with the same author's tabulated comparison of 3,056 characters in the different *guwen* scripts, *Guwenzi leibian* 古文字類編 (Ancient Chinese characters arranged by type), Zhonghua, 1980, Tôhô, 1987; 5th print., 1990. Both works are exceptionally clearly printed.

[27] Quite apart from such *fangyanzi*, some dialects have preserved Classical Chinese words and their characters (for example *zou* 走, *shi* 食 and *wen* 蚊 are still used in Cantonese instead of their *Putonghua* equivalents, *pao* 跑, *chi* 吃 and *wenzi* 蚊子). Even small dictionaries of Cantonese published in Hong Kong usually list several hundred Cantonese dialect characters (e.g., *mou* 冇 for *meiyou* 没有).

[28] Ireneus Laszlo Legeza, *Tao Magic: the Secret Language of Diagrams and Calligraphy*, Thames and Hudson, 1975; Liu Xiaoming 劉曉明,

Footnote continued on next page

Most of these variants arose because at the formative stages of the writing system communication between different centers of learning was poor and standardization of the characters was difficult during the two millennia before the invention of printing (and not so easily achieved after that).

As time went by, graphic variants declined: there are sometimes up to 50 different ways of writing a single character in the oracle-bone script, the golden age of *yitizi*. By the Han chancery script, their number was falling, largely as the result of official efforts to standardize the characters. The earliest known such attempt was the first emperor's decision to make the Qin small seal script the standard for the whole country. Efforts continued during the Han with the editing of authorized editions of the Classics in *lishu* for the imperial library and the carving of some of them on stone in the Later Han. Inclusion in the *Shuowen* was taken as the basis for recognition as a *zhengzi* 正字 (standard form of character) as opposed to *suzi* 俗字 (vulgar character). The Shuowen lists graphic varaiants for no less than 12 percent of the characters it contains. A practice followed in many later dictionaries and character primers. Tang scholars and the court worked on a standard form of *kaishu* to replace the chaotic variations which had developed during the *Nan-Bei Chao*. The examination system required candidates to use the standard forms of the characters. Indeed, one of the most popular Tang character primers was written to help scholars common variants and vulgar characters.[29] When printing became widespread in the Song, it too helped standardize the characters.. But there were still many variants and a large gap between printed and handwritten forms. In this respect, it is worth remembering that orthographic variation in Europe was common even within a single printed work until the early

---

Zhongguo fuzhou wenhua daguan 中國符咒文化大觀 (Overview of the culture of Chinese charms and spells), Baihuazhou wenyi, 1995.

[29] *Ganlu zishu* 干祿字書 (Character primer for office seekers), Yan Yuansun 顏元孫 (?–714).

seventeenth century. In China, different ways of writing and printing the characters continued into the twentieth century.

16.4.1 Graphic Variants

There was a huge amount of graphic variation in all the scripts (the sound in the standard Chinese of the day and the meaning were the same, only the form was different). The old terms for graphic variants are *chongwen* 重文 or *huoti* 或體, the modern one, *yitizi* 異體字.[29] In a different context, these are what we would call alternative spellings. *Yitizi* developed in many ways:

1. Characters for the same word were formed using more than one of the three main ways of forming characters, e.g., *jian* 奸 is a type-3 character, which was also written as a type-1 character with three *nü* 女 together: 姦.
2. Different significs (typically with closely related meanings) were assigned at different periods (or in different texts) to the same character, especially prior to the Qin-Han standardization, e.g., *yong* 咏 either with *kou* 口 or *yan* 言 as signific (咏 or 詠).
3. The same character, but with a different phonetic, e.g., *gu* 菰, with either 孤 or 姑 as phonetic.
4. The same character, but with the signific or phonetic put in different positions, e.g., *lüe* 略 with the 田 either at the left (略) or on top (畧).
5. Variant ways of writing a component part, e.g., *mu* 畝 written either with 久 or 厶 as the right-hand component (畝 or 畒).
6. Sometimes a *sutizi* 俗體字 became an *yitizi*, e.g., 吴 was used for 吳.
7. Previous ways of writing a character were held over long after the introduction of a major script reform. For example, *tu* 徒 (*lishu* for *tu* 徒) continued in use for centuries after *kaishu* had replaced *lishu*.

One special reason for creating graphic variants was the characters for taboo words, *huizi* 諱字, such as the personal names of

---

[29] *Yitizi zidian* 異體字字典 (Dictionary of graphic variants), Li Pu 李圃, ed. in chief, Xuelin, 1997, contains nearly 10,000 head characters and 50,000 variants of them drawn from 151 dictionaries and epigraphical works from the Shang dynasty to the present day. Arrangement is by *Shuowen* classifiers. There is a total stroke-count index of head characters and modern pronunciations are shown in *pinyin*.

members of the imperial family (3.3). Either a different character was used or scribes were required to drop a stroke (*xuan* 玄 for *xuan* 玄 or *zhao* 照 for *zhao* 照).

Large character dictionaries include *yitizi* (a) whose "correct" character, *zhengzi* 正字 (b), is normally indicated by the formula, *yitizi* (a) *tong* 同 *zhengzi* (b).

In 1955, the authorities forbade the use of 1,055 graphic variants (except in reprints of classical texts and other scholarly works, including dictionaries of Classical Chinese). Twenty-eight characters were reinstated in three subsequent revisions (the last in 1988), thus reducing the total proscribed graphic variants to 1,027.

Quite apart from graphic variants, characters were frequently written by mistake for another (*wuzi* 誤字, *huaizi* 壞字, *ezi* 訛字). As such they are regarded as textual errors resulting from the mistakes of copyists, or as ill-advised attempts to improve a text.[30]

Manuscripts also often contain large numbers of wrongly written, that is to say, non-existent, characters (*cuozi* 錯字).

16.4.2 *Ancient and Modern Characters* (gujinzi 古今字)

If a word was written with a type-1 or type-2 character (normally invented in the pre-Qin period) and later with a type 3 character (usually to distinguish one of its meanings), or if a type-3 character was later modified for the same reason, the pair was termed *gujinzi* 古今字 (ancient and modern characters), a description which has been in use since the Later Han. The modern term is *qubiezi* 區別字 (differentiated characters). For example, *yao* 腰 (waist) is a *jinzi* because it had a signific added later to differentiate it from the original character (*yao* 要, waist) which in the interim had acquired additional meanings. Sometimes for a period of centuries both the old and new forms of a character were in use interchangeably, but this was

---

[30] Susan Cherniack discusses textual errors (9–18) and lists six common types of them in the appendix to "Book Culture and Textual Transmission in Sung China," *HJAS* 54.1: 5–125 (1994), 102–25.

exceptional. Normally the pronunciation and meanings of *gu-jinzi* were closely related. A good dictionary such as the *Hanyu da cidian* will indicate the earlier form of a differentiated character: thus the entry for *yao* 要 reads, "*yao de guzi* 腰的古字."

16.4.3 Correct and Vulgar Characters (zhengsuzi 正俗字)

Characters have been written in simplified ways ever since they first appeared on the oracle-bone script. Often by dropping off one or other component, typically the classifier when these became common, the context making the meaning clear. Many Han and post-Han simplified characters were based on *xingshu* or *caoshu* forms.

After the Qin and Han script reforms, the distinction was drawn between *zhengzi* 正字 (standard characters), which were to be used in official writing, and *suzi* 俗字 (vulgar characters) which were banned but remained in everyday use. At the end of the nineteenth century, pioneer script reformers made efforts to make the *suzi* more respectable and they were renamed "simplified characters" (*jiantizi* 簡體字) as opposed to the *zhengzi*, renamed *fantizi* 繁體字 (complex characters).

A list of simplified characters was first made official in August 1935. The Harvard-Yenching Institute was quick off the mark in deciding to publish a dictionary of them, but by the time it was out, the government had withdrawn the list in February 1936.[31] A selection of *jiantizi* were finally made official on a national scale in 1956 (an enlarged list was gazetted in 1964).[32]

Plans to extend the list of simplified characters during the Cultural Revolution were shelved immediately after it was over and only minor adjustments have since appeared (in 1986). Today, the core number of simplified characters is 535 out of a total of 2,233 (for example, *ma* 马 is one of the 535 core charac-

---

[31] Rong Geng 容庚 (1894–1983), *Jianti zidian* 簡體字典 (Dictionary of simplified characters), H-Y Institute, 1936.

[32] Li Leyi 李樂毅 *Jianhuazi yuan* 簡化字源 (The origins of simplified Chinese characters), Sinolingua, 1996; Yin (1966), 56–61.

ters and also appears in its role as a classifier in many of the characters in the full list). Of the 535, one-third were already in circulation in pre-Qin and Han times; 40 percent date from between the Han and 1911. The Republic saw 12 percent invented and 20 percent were devised since 1949.

16.4.4　Alternative Characters (tongjiazi 通假字)

In Classical Chinese the same character can be used for different words. This can be the result of a type-1 character being used as a phonetic loan to stand for a word with no previous character (type-2 character, *jiajiezi* 假借字).[33]

A character (often type 3) can also be used to represent words which already have a character (*benzi* 本字). The second character has the same or a similar pronunciation to the first, but the meaning is different. For example, *shi* 矢 (arrow) was often used in place of *shi* 屎 (excrement), and *zao* 蚤 (flea) for *zao* 早 (early). Such alternative characters (*tongjiazi* 通假字) are distinguished from wrongly used characters (*biezi* 別字, *baizi* 白字) by the fact that they were recognized as alternatives (the conventional term means "generally used borrowed characters"). A character can have several *tongjiazi* and one *tongjiazi* can serve for several different characters (*shi* 矢, for example, also stood for *shi* 誓). *Tongjiazi* were not normally used interchangeably (矢 for 屎 or 誓, but never 屎 or 誓 for 矢), but this sometimes occurs (*ce* 策 for *ce* 冊 and vice-versa). *Tongjiazi* were already widespread on the Zhou bronzes and became increasingly so in the Warring States, Qin and Han. They appear in all types of words, including in personal and place names. These were the centuries that saw the biggest changes that have ever taken place in the writing system, including the rapid increase of picto-phonetic compound characters. But during these

---

[33] The definition of the same pronunciation is if the initial (*sheng* 聲), the rhyme (*yun* 韵) and tone (*diao* 調) are identical; similar refers to when two of these conditions are met, the sounds belonging to that period of the language in which the borrowing took place (normally Old Chinese).

centuries there was no uniform standard for the writing system, so it is understandable that a scribe might prefer a character with which he was more familiar—in other words, one whose pronunciation was closer to the local language in his kingdom or region. There was also a tendency to choose characters with fewer strokes.[34] More than 15,000 different *tongjiazi* have been counted. This does not include the large numbers found on new epigraphic sources such as bamboo strips and silk manuscripts. After the Tang and Song, new alternative characters tended to be regarded as *biezi* (wrongly used characters), but established *tongjiazi* continued in use until the script reforms of the twentieth century and have been retained in old texts to this day.[35]

Characters which appear to have been "borrowed" not so much for their sound, but for their similarity of form are generally regarded as *biezi*. For example, *yi* 已 instead of *ji* 己 or *wu* 戊 instead of *shu* 戌. *Biezi* and *suzi* are numerous in *baihua* fiction.

Had the use of *tongjiazi* continued to grow, thus downplaying the semantic component of characters, Chinese writing might have developed into a syllabic system. That it did not

[34] Zhao Ping'an (1993), 136–50. This study is based on the analysis of excavated manuscripts on bamboo and silk and also takes into account earlier work based on transmitted texts; for example, Bernhard Karlgren, *Loan Characters in Pre-Han Texts*, MFEA, 1967; originally appeared in *BMFEA* 35: 1–128 (1960).

[35] There are also specialized works, such as *Guzi tongjia huidian* 古字通假會典 (Compendium of ancient alternative characters), Gao Heng 高亨 comp., Dong Zhi'an 董治安, readied for publication, Qi-Lu, 1989; rpnt., 1997, which contains no less than 16,000 examples of *tongjiazi*, almost all from Han and pre-Han works, but not including new epigraphic sources. The compilers reached such a huge number by including *gujin*, *yiti* and *jianti* characters. Others using a stricter definition are on a more modest scale, e.g., *Gu Hanyu duoyong tongjia zidian* 古漢語多用通假字典 (Multi-use dictionary of *tongjiazi*), Zhang Jun 張軍 and Liu Naishu 劉乃叔, eds. in chief, Dongbei shifan daxue, 1991, contains 1,300 *tongjiazi* and indicates both ancient and modern pronunciation as well as giving definitions.

was because Old Chinese was mainly monosyllabic: every character normally stood for a syllable and each syllable was a
word with meaning. As William Boltz (1994, 171) puts it, "if a
language does not have syllables without meaning, why should
its speakers include in their writing system a way to write such
syllables?"

Tongjiazi are a pitfall for the unwary. If you come across an
apparently meaningless character in a phrase, especially in a
pre-Qin text, it may be a *tongjiazi*. To confirm it, check any
good dictionary. The formula under the entry of the borrowed
character (e.g., 蚤) is "通 [早]," or "(古) 同 [早]." *Tongjiazi* are
normally pronounced according to the *benzi* they replace, thus
tuo for 税 (通 [脱]), not *shui*.

16.4.5 Different Pronunciations

About 20 percent of the characters in Classical Chinese (and
10–15 percent in *Putonghua*) have more than one reading. This
is especially true of frequently used characters. The modern
term is polyphonic characters, *duoyinzi* 多音字.[36]

The changes in pronunciation or in tone can indicate different meanings and sometimes also different parts of speech
(1.2.2).

Both in standard Chinese and in the dialects there were often literary readings (*wendu* 文讀) and vernacular pronunciations (*baidu* 白讀) for the same character, for example, *ji* 給
(*wen*) as in *jiyu* 給予 (render, give) and *gei* 給 (*bai*) as in *gei ta* 給
他 or *xue* 血 (*wen*) and *xie* 血 (*bai*). Literary readings are sometimes retained in standard spoken Chinese in words that are in

[36] For a convenient dictionary of polyphonic characters, see *Shiyong
sucha duoyin zi cidian* 實用速查多音字詞典 (Practical quick reference
polyphonic character dictionary of compounds and phrases), Jiang Xue
江雪 and Chen Lin 陳琳, eds. in chief, Changchun, 1995; rpnt., 1996.
This includes 2,600 polyphonic characters both ancient and modern.
They are indexed in *pinyin* under all readings and (an unusual feature)
with copious examples of each character's different readings in compounds and phrases whether at the beginning, middle or end.

no sense literary, for example, *peiji* 配給 (ration) or *xuehong* 血紅 (blood-red).

When polyphonic characters (*duoyinzi* 多音字) have the same meaning, they are simply variant reading characters (*yiduzi* 異讀字) whose origins no doubt lie in changes in pronunciation over time and in different dialects and the differences between literary and vernacular pronunciations. It is possible that different pronunciations were most commonly given to characters which had no phonetic indicator (*shengfu* 聲符) or to borrowed characters (*jiajie*).

Polyphonic characters have been retained in the modern standard language when the change in pronunciation indicates a change in meaning. But when the change is simply a variant reading, they have generally been discarded except in a small number of cases where it is customary to use the old pronunciations.[37]

16.5 On Studying the Ancient Scripts

The paleographer Qiu Xigui 裘錫圭 (1936-) advises Chinese students against trying to jump straight into ancient scripts such as the oracle-bone or bronze inscriptions, simply relying on dictionaries. They should first get a good grounding in Classical Chinese by reading as much as possible (1.3.5).[38] Then do what Sima Qian 司馬遷, Sima Guang 司馬光 and countless other Chinese historians began by doing: read the *Zuozhuan* 左傳 with its commentaries. A knowledge of the context, as provided by archaeology and ancient history, is also essential, as is a thorough acquaintance with the *Shuowen*.

[37] The modern list of received pronunciations is *Putonghua yiduci shenyinbiao* 普通話異讀詞審音表 (List of authorized pronunciations for heterophonic words in Putonghua), Beijing, 1985.

[38] Qiu Xigui, "On the Methods of Studying Ancient Chinese Script," *Yuwen daobao* 語文導報, 1985.10; reprinted in the author's *Guwenzi luncong* 古文字論叢 (Collected papers on ancient characters), Zhonghua, 1992, 652–60, tr. by Lothar von Falkenhausen in *EC* 11–12: 301–16 (1985–87).

Gao Ming emphasizes four techniques (which also apply to the study of Classical Chinese). Compare the evolution of the forms of characters as they appear on different media and in different periods (not only as they appear in the *Shuowen*); compare the usage of characters in inscriptions with those found in contemporary texts; analyze the components of the characters and finally, examine their institutional context.[39]

For reference works and readers on the oracle-bone script, see 15.4. For a description of epigraphic sources on other media such as bronze, stone or jade, see chap. 17. General introductions to the different types of *guwen* usually contain annotated readings. One of the best is Gao Ming (1996). Another is *Shang-Zhou guwenzi duben* 商周古文字讀本.[40] This contains selected, annotated readings of oracle-bone, bronze, stone drums, jade and pottery inscriptions.

[39] Gao Ming (1996), 167–72; see also Edward L. Shaughnessy, "How to read a Western Zhou Bronze Inscription," in *Sources of Western Zhou History: Inscribed Bronze Vessels*, UCP, 1991, chap. 3, 63–105.

[40] *Shang-Zhou guwenzi duben* (Reader of ancient characters from the Shang and Zhou), Liu Xiang 劉翔 et al., Yuwen, 1989, 3rd print., 1996.

17

Epigraphy

The main inscriptional materials are bronze (17.1) and stone (17.3). In addition, inscriptions were recorded on all sorts of other materials and objects, including bone (chap. 15 and section 44.3.1), shell (chap. 15), jade, seals, coins, brick and pottery (17.2).

The antiquarian study of inscriptions dug up from the earth, particularly those on auspicious and valuable objects such as ancient bronze vessels or stone tablets, began in earnest in the Song dynasty, which first saw the use of the old phrase *jinshi* (金石) "[cast on] bronze and [carved on] stone" in this new sense.[1] It was mainly pursued by collectors and calligraphers. More than 500 ancient bronzes were dug up in the Northern Song. They were categorized and printed with illustrations and transcriptions in works such as *Kaogu lu* 考古錄, Lü Dalin 呂 大臨 (1046–92), comp., preface, 1092; and in the catalog of the emperor Huizong's collection of 839 bronzes, *Bogutu* 博古圖, Wang Fu 王黼 (1079–1126), ed., 1123. They not only categorized the bronze vessels according to formal criteria, but they also began the arduous task of reconstructing the forms and the meanings of the ancient characters found on some of the

---

[1] See Edward L. Shaughnessy, "Introduction," in *NSECH*, 1–14. For a general history of epigraphy, see Zhu Jianxin 朱劍心 *Jinshixue* 金石學 (The study of inscriptions on bronze and stone), Shanghai: Shangwu, 1955; rpnt., Wenwu, 1981.

Guides and research tools to particular epigraphic materials are listed at the end of 17.1, 17.2, and 17.3.

bronzes, many of which have long since been lost. In the Qing, the Qianlong emperor sponsored the publication of three works on the massive imperial collections of bronze vessels, which stimulated scholars to begin their own collections and to apply text critical methods to the study of the inscriptions (*jin-shi* 金石) which flourished as never before.[2]

The inscriptions were typically used to record the origin or the owner, or to commemorate important events or to record merit of one kind or another. They were highly valued.

Collections of epigraphy of particular periods or regions have been printed for many centuries. Today modern collections of newly unearthed bronze and stone inscriptions are also published in book form, often by region. Note that the *Zhong-guo kaoguxue nianjian* 中國考古學年鑑 (Yearbook of Chinese archaeology) includes over 30 double-column pages at the end indexing the inscriptions discovered the previous year, arranged by material, period and place.

17.1   Bronze Inscriptions

A very large number of elaborated decorated bronze vessels and objects of all sorts are extant today.[3] They are prized collectors'

---

[2] See Noel Barnard, "Records of Discoveries of Bronze Vessels in Literary Sources and Some Pertinent Remarks on Aspects of Chinese Historiography," *Journal of the Institute of Chinese Studies of the University of Hong Kong*, 6.1: 455–546 (1973).

[3] For introductions, see Jessica Rawson, *Chinese Bronzes: Art and Ritual*, British Museum, 1987; Li Xueqin, *The Wonder of Chinese Bronzes*, FLP, 1980. *The Art of the Houma Foundry*, Institute of Archaeology of Shanxi Province, eds., PUP and FLP, 1996, describes the workings and shows the remains of the largest Bronze Age foundry ever discovered in the world. On whether the bronze decorations have an iconographic meaning and if so, what, see *The Problem of Meaning in Early Chinese Ritual Bronzes*, Roderick Whitfield, ed., University of London, Percival David Foundation, SOAS, 1992. For an inventory of bronze vessels of every kind up to and including the Warring States, see *Gudai Zhongguo qingtongqi* 古代中國青銅器, Zhu Fenghan 朱鳳瀚, comp., Nankai daxue, 1995. Note Hayashi Minao 林巳奈夫, *In-Shû jidai seidôki sôran* 殷周

Footnote continued on next page

items not only in China but also in Japan and in the West, where from time to time sumptuous exhibitions are held of Shang and Zhou bronzes, introduced in monographic exhibition catalogs.[4] Collectors, too, publish scholarly catalogs.[5]

Only about 12,000 of the vessels and weapons have inscriptions (*jinwen* 金文 or *zhongdingwen* 鐘鼎文, "the writing on bells and caldrons," so-called since these were the most prestigious bronzes and therefore those upon which inscriptions were most frequently cast). Of the total of inscribed bronze vessels, about one-quarter date from the Yin Shang period, half from the Zhou and one-quarter from the Qin and Han. The nature of the inscriptions in each period is different. The Shang inscriptions start at the same time as the oracle-bone inscriptions (Wu Ding reign). They contain only two or three characters recording the name of the maker and an ancestor, often with a generation tag (*jiming jinwen* 記名金文). Some are emblems in the form of a single pictograph, probably representing a clan or lineage, or its settlement. Functionally such identifications may have been similar to the single marks found on prehistoric pottery vessels. The form of the writing on the early bronzes reflects the medium: the strokes are thicker than those on the oracle-bone inscriptions. The bronze characters are also more archaic, more pictographic, than the oracle-bone characters, which by comparison appear schematic and more simple. Most

---

時代青銅器綜覽 (Comprehensive studies on the bronze vessels of the Yin and Zhou), vols. 1 and 2 (Yin and Zhou), Tokyo, 1984, 1986; vol. 3 (Spring and Autumn and Warring States periods), Yoshikawa, 1989.

[4] See, for example, *The Great Bronze Age of China*, Wen C. Fong, ed., Metropolitan Museum, and Thames and Hudson, 1980.

[5] There are a large number of important monographic catalogs of bronze collections; see, for example, Robert Bagley, *Shang Ritual Bronzes from the Arthur M. Sackler Collections*, Arthur M. Sackler Museum and HUP, 1987; Jessica Rawson, *Western Zhou Bronzes from the Arthur M. Sackler Collections*, 2 vols., Arthur M. Sackler Museum and HUP, 1990; Jenny F. So, *Eastern Zhou Ritual Bronzes from the Arthur M. Sackler Collections*, same publishers, 1995.

of the Shang bronze inscriptions have been found in the vicinity of the late Shang capital at Anyang.

At the very end of the Shang and the beginning of the Zhou, bronze inscriptions of 30 or 40 characters began to appear. Gradually, in the Western Zhou the inscriptions grew longer and the forms of the characters became more simple and standardized. The longest inscription (497 characters) is that on the Maogong ding 毛公鼎, which is similar to a passage in the *Shangshu* 尚書 (*Book of Documents*). Its authenticity has been challenged but it is now generally regarded as dating from the late Western Zhou. It was discovered ca. 1840 at Qiyi, the cultic center of the Zhou, 90 km to the west of modern Xi'an.[6]

Bronze characters are called *jinwen* 金文 because *jin* 金 was used interchangeably with *tong* 銅 in Old Chinese. A total of about 4,000 separate bronze characters have been distinguished, of which 2,500 have been deciphered.

Many of the bronze inscriptions have been published in collections of rubbings or transcriptions by scholars both traditional and modern (see *Corpus Inscriptionum*, 17.4).

Note the large number of bronze weights and capacity measures, several of which are inscribed with regulations. The earliest extant today date from the Warring States.[7]

The most prestigious bronze vessels, the caldrons, were used in ancestral sacrifices and therefore heroic deeds and honors were recorded on them. Different ranks of the nobility were entitled to use different numbers of caldrons and other vessels and different sacrificial foods. The same applied to burials. The system as set out in the *Zhouli* and other ritual texts has been confirmed by archaeology. The emperor alone was entitled to use nine caldrons (*jiuding* 九鼎). These became the

---

[6] Shaughnessy (1991), 75, and on the question of authenticity of the bronzes in general, 43–62. The Maogong ding is in the Palace Museum, Taibei.

[7] For illustrations, rubbings and transcriptions, see Qiu Guangming 丘光明, *Zhongguo lidai duliangheng kao* 中國歷代度量衡考 (Research on Weights and Measures through the Ages in China), Kexue, 1992.

symbol of the ruler and of legitimate succession. The sacrificial bronze vessels were not only used by him as an expression of his power but also by lesser lords as a sign of their status and influence. The word for caldron also meant huge or solemn (it is a cognate of *zheng* 政, to rule). Symbolic *ding* 鼎 were not used for everyday cooking for which different vessels with different names were used. Most of the inscriptions record gifts bestowed by the monarch following some other kind of record such as orders of appointment to office, military campaigns, covenants, treaties or ceremonial events. The arrangement of the writing on the Zhou bronzes is more strict than on the oracle bones. The characters run from top to bottom in vertical rows reading from right to left. The characters themselves are in great seal script.

By the Warring States, the inscriptions once again became shorter, mainly recording the owners and the makers of the implements on which they were cast.

When the Western Zhou had left the scene, bronze vessels gradually lost their importance as the principal way of expressing status and power, although there are some remarkable Eastern Zhou ones. By the Han, stone stelae and monuments had become the main media for proclaiming political messages and for recording commemorative inscriptions of all sorts. Thus bronze inscriptions, or the rubbings taken from them, are important sources mainly for the earlier Zhou, while stone inscriptions are vital supplementary sources for the Qin, the Han and all subsequent periods.

Guides and Readers

The best short introductions to the Zhou bronze inscriptions with examples of how to read them as historical sources are:

Edward L. Shaughnessy, "Western Zhou Bronze Inscriptions" and Gilbert L. Mattos, "Eastern Zhou Bronze Inscriptions," both in *NSECH*, 57–84 and 85–124, respectively.

Edward L. Shaughnessy, *Sources of Western Zhou History: Inscribed Bronze Vessels*, UCP, 1991. The standard introduction in English; also contains advice on reading the inscriptions. For guidance in studying the ancient scripts (including bronze script), see 16.5.

On Shang bronze inscriptions as historical sources, see K. C. Chang, "Bronzes" in *Shang Civilization*, YUP, 1980, 20–31. Note also the use made of bronze inscriptions in Li Xueqin 李學勤, *Eastern Zhou and Qin Civilizations*, K. C. Chang, tr., YUP, 1985.

Corpus Inscriptionum

Yin-Zhou jinwen jicheng 殷周金文集成 (Complete collection of Yin Zhou bronze epigraphy), *Kaoguxue* special publication, 18 folio vols., Zhonghua, 1984–95, includes 11,984 inscription rubbings. There are transcriptions, explanations and an index. Arrangement is by 51 different vessel types (including five kinds of military weapons and tallies). Shorter inscriptions come first; longest, last. The largest number of inscriptions are found on caldrons (1,858). Work on this collection from conception in 1956 to the publication of the final volume took almost forty years. A supplementary volume of inscriptions not accepted for inclusion (either because they are illegible or because they are suspected of being forgeries) is forthcoming.

Shang-Zhou qingtongqi mingwen xuan 商周青銅器銘文選 (Selected inscriptions from Shang and Zhou bronze vessels), Ma Chengyuan 馬承原 et al., eds., 4 vols., Wenwu, 1986–91. Contains rubbings and transcriptions of 925 inscriptions conveniently arranged by topic and by period. Vol. 5 (forthcoming) is to contain an index to vols. 1–4.

The first important modern collection of rubbings of bronze inscriptions (from 4,800 vessels) was published by Luo Zhenyu: *Sandai jijin wencun* 三代吉金文存 (Collection of bronze inscriptions from the three dynasties), 1937. For a list of the "Major Catalogs of Inscribed Western Zhou Bronze Vessels," see Shaughnessy (1991), 289–92.

Examples of collections and studies of bronze inscriptions from particular provinces or ancient kingdoms:

Shaanxi chutu Shang-Zhou qingtongqi 陝西出土商周青銅器 (Excavated vessels from Shaanxi of the Shang and Zhou), 4 vols., Wenwu, 1978–82 (includes photographs of the vessels and rubbings of the inscriptions).

Hubei chutu Shang-Zhou wenzi jizheng 湖北出土商周文字輯證 (Collected texts and studies of Shang-Zhou excavated scripts from Hubei), Huang Xiquan 黃錫全, Wuhan daxue, 1992. Rubbings, transcriptions and explanations of nearly 1,700 inscriptions.

"Chuxi qingtongqi wenshi yanjiu 楚系青銅器紋飾研究" (Research on the decorations and writings on Chu style bronzes) and "Chuxi qingtongqi mingwen biannian kaoshu 楚系青銅器銘文編年考述" (Investigation of the chronology of Chu style bronze inscriptions), chaps. 5 and 6 of *Chuxi qingtongqi yanjiu* 楚系青銅器研究 (Researches on Chu-style bronzes), Liu Binhui 劉彬徽, ed., Hubei jiaoyu, 1995, 247–492.

Dictionaries, Concordances and Interpretations

Jinwen changyong zidian 金文常用字典 (Dictionary of frequently used bronze characters), Chen Chusheng 陳初生, comp., Shaanxi renmin, 1987. A good beginner's dictionary with examples of graphical variants and explanations of 1,000 frequently used bronze characters.

Kinbun tsûshaku 金文通釋 (Comprehensive interpretations of Bronze inscriptions), Shirakawa Shizuka 白川靜, *Hakutsuru bijutsukanshi* 白鶴美術館志, nos. 1–56, 1962–84. The single most important work interpreting the bronze inscriptions and also introducing the main alternative opinions.

Jinwen gulin 金文詁林 (An Etymological Dictionary of Ancient Chinese Bronze Inscriptions), Zhou Fagao 周法高 (1915–94), ed. in chief, Zhang Risheng 張日升 et al., comp., 16 vols., HKCU Press, 1974–75, with supplements, *Jinwen gulin futu* 金文詁林附圖, HKCU Press, 1977 (references are based on Luo, 1937); *Jinwen gulin bu* 金文詁林補 (Corrections and additions to the *Jinwen gulin*), 8 vols., Shiyusuo, 1982; rpnt., 1997. Li Xiaoding 李孝定, *Jinwen gulin duhou ji* 金文詁林讀後記 (Notes on reading the *Jinwen gulin*), Shiyusuo, 1982; rpnt., 1992. A concordance plus repertory of scholarly interpretations of bronze characters (including many of those of Shirakawa).

Jinwen bian 金文編 (A compilation of bronze characters), Rong Geng 容庚, ed., Yi'an tang 貽安堂, 1925; 2nd ed., rev. and expanded, Shangwu, 1939; 3rd ed., rev. and expanded, Kexue, 1959; 4th ed., rev. by Zhang Zhenlin 張振林 and Ma Guoquan 馬國權, 1985; 5th prnt., Zhonghua, 1996; Chen Hanping 陳漢平, *Jinwen bian dingbu* 金文編訂補 (Revisions to the *Jingwen bian*), Shehui kexue, 1993. A concordance to bronze characters of the Shang and Zhou. The 1985 revised edition is still considered the best listing. The author also published a continuation covering the Qin and Han.

Biographies

Jinwen renming huibian 金文人名匯編 (Compendium of personal names in bronze inscriptions), Wu Zhenfeng 吳鎮烽, comp., Zhonghua, 1987. Contains the names of 5,228 people found on the bronze inscriptions dating from the Shang to 221 BC discovered up to June 1985. The names recorded are normally those who commissioned the casting of the vessel. The names are rarely found in transmitted texts but when they are Wu gives the reference.

Bibliography

For a bibliography of secondary sources in Chinese (up to 1982) on bronze (and many other ancient inscriptional materials), see:

Qingtongqi lunwen suoyin 青銅器論文索引, Sun Zhichu 孫稚雛, comp., Zhonghua, 1986.

For studies appearing since then check the standard bibliographic references listed under 13.3.

17.2 Jade, Seal, Coin and Pottery Inscriptions

17.2.1   Jade Inscriptions

The earliest extant writing on jade is found on late Shang jade objects recording origin, ownership or an event.[8] The first long texts on jade record blood covenants (*mengshu* 盟書, *zaishu* 載書). There have been several finds, all from the ancient kingdom of Jin 晉. They probably date from the fifth century BC. The first were found in Wenxian 溫縣, Henan in the 1930s but have been lost. More turned up in 1942. Eleven of these narrow oblong tablets are now in the Kaogusuo (*Kaogu* 1966.5). The first major find (5,000 tablets), was made at Houma 侯馬, Shanxi in 1965–66 (*Wenwu*, 1975.5 and *Guwenzi yanjiu*, vol. 1, 1979). For photographs of 200 examples and transcriptions of the 656 legible inscriptions (kept in the Shanxi provincial museum), see *Houma mengshu* 侯馬盟書.[9] The second major find (10,000 tablets or fragments) was made in 1980–82, at Wenxian,

---

[8] Li Xueqin, "Jade and Stone Epigraphy from the Shang and Early Zhou Periods," in *Chinese Jades*, Rosemary E. Scott, ed., University of London, Percival David Foundation, SOAS, 1997, 99–104.

[9] *Houma mengshu* (Jade covenant inscriptions from Houma), Shanxi-sheng wenwu gongzuo weiyuanhui, eds., Wenwu, 1976. This work also includes a listing of all the characters in the inscriptions and their variants as well as a list of proper names occuring in the texts.

Henan. They are held in the Henan provincial museum at Zhengzhou (*Wenwu* 1983.3). They have not yet been published.[10] A separate cache of 50 jade strips in the same shape as bamboo strips was found in 1950 at Huixian 輝縣, Henan. They were ready for use but had not yet been written on.

The best introduction in English to the covenant texts is Susan Weld, "The Covenant Texts from Houma and Wenxian," in *NSECH* (1997), 125–60.

In later Chinese history, jade remained in use as a material for inscribed objects of special ceremonial importance or value, for example, the imperial seal, *yuxi* 玉璽 or the records of accession of an emperor.

17.2.2   Seal Inscriptions

Pre-Qin seals (*guxi* 古璽) were mainly used on clay. Red-ink seals came in from the Qin and Han. Letters or bundles were tied up with string and sealed with clay, upon which a seal was impressed (just as sealing wax was once used in the West). Many such clay seal impressions have survived, a few even from the Shang.[11]

---

[10] On the role of blood covenants in Zhou interstate relations and interlineage struggles, see Mark Edward Lewis, *Sanctioned Violence in Early China*, SUNY Press, 1990, 43–52. For additional readings, see Gao (1996), 418–30.

[11] *Gu fengni jicheng* 古封泥集成 (Collection of ancient clay seal impressions), Shanghai shudian, 1994; rpnt., 1996. For a short history of seals, see Wang Tingqia 王廷洽, *Zhongguo yinzhang shi* 中國印章史, Huadong shifan daxue, 1996. For a repertory of seal characters, see Luo Fuyi 羅福頤 (1905–81), *Guxi wenbian* 古璽文編 (A dictionary of ancient seal characters), Wenwu, 1981. Based on the author's earlier work of 1930; 2nd rpnt., 1994. It contains 2,773 characters. See also the same author's *Guxi huibian* 古璽匯編 (Ancient seals), Wenwu, 1981; rpnt., 1994, which contains beautifully executed impressions of 5,708 Warring States seals, mainly official ones. It is a useful source on local government.

17.2.3   Pottery Inscriptions

Pottery inscriptions (*taowen* 陶文 is the modern word) were utilitarian or informal. Most are found on shards, bricks and tiles. They are the marks and records (sometimes graffiti) left by builders, craftsmen, convicts and corvée laborers. As the least prestigious type of inscription, writing on pottery has received the least attention from collectors and scholars (the first collection was begun only in 1872).[12] Yet prehistoric pottery symbols and markings, as we saw in chap. 14 may yet hold the key to the origins of Chinese characters. Another reason why *taowen* inscriptions were ignored until recently is that they were typically very short. Among the rare exceptions is a Qin letter of investiture (*washu* 瓦書) of 119 characters dated 334 BC,[13] and the imperial decree on weights and measures of 221 BC (40 characters long), which was inscribed on all bronze weights and measures, as well as on those made of pottery.[14] *Taowen* is often exceedingly difficult to read because it was written by illiterate craftsmen who freely invented their own variants of the ancient scripts. Of a total of about 2,000 different pre-Qin pottery characters, about two-thirds have been deciphered.

[12] By Chen Jieqi 陳介祺 (1813–84), a scholar and famous collector of antiques from Weixian, Shandong.

[13] Yuan Zhongyi 袁仲一, *Qindai taowen* 秦代陶文 (Qin dynasty pottery script), San-Qin, 1987. Transcription and discussion of the *washu* 瓦書 on pages 75–84. There is a much clearer rubbing in Gao (1990), 513.

[14] The imperial decree has been found on pottery capacity measures, both complete and fragmented. For a transcription with notes, see *Shang-Zhou guwenzi duben* 商周古文字讀本 (Reader of ancient characters from the Shang and Zhou), Liu Xiang 劉翔 et al., comp., Yuwen, 1989, 3rd prnt., 1996, 174–5. See also A. F. Hulsewé, "Weights and Measures in Ch'in Law," in *State and law in East Asia: Festschrift Karl Bolger*, Dieter Eikemeier and Herbert Franke, eds., Harrassowitz, 1981, 25–39.

17.2.4 *Coin Inscriptions*

Starting from the Warring States, coin inscriptions (*quanwen* 泉文, *qianwen* 錢文, *huobiwen* 貨幣文) record the place they were cast or the denomination; from the fourth century AD, the era name was also recorded. For references to the history of Chinese coins and coinage, see 7.4.1.[15]

17.3 *Stone Inscriptions*

Stone has been used to keep records of many kinds for longer than any other material in China. Its use was widespread from the dawn of the first millennium to the present day. The most common form of stone inscription is the stele (*bei* 碑), an upright slab of stone bearing an inscription. They were used for commemorating talented writers and upright officials, for inscribing poems or statues, portraits, pictures and maps. Also, as any traveler in China knows there is hardly a famous mountain or scenic spot whose cliffs and rocks do not carry the calligraphy of emperors, statesmen and poets. Stone inscriptions were also used for more prosaic functions, such as marking the boundaries of fields (*jiebei* 界碑 or *sizhi* 四至); the details of ownership and construction; contracts and the names of contributors to public buildings such as temples, bridges, pagodas or wells and many other matters of great interest to the student of Chinese social and economic history, for example, guild rules.

It was in the Han that stone replaced wood for tomb stones and tomb inscriptions (*mubei* 墓碑 and *muzhi* 墓誌), which are one of the basic sources for Chinese biographical studies. The *muzhi* were usually placed in the tomb. Transcriptions of some 7,000 have been published and indexed (3.7).

Stone was also used for recording the Classics of Confucianism, Buddhism and Daoism.

[15] For a repertory of the characters found on pre-Qin coins, see *Xian-Qin huobi wenbian* 先秦貨幣文編, Shang Chengzuo 商承祚 (1902–91) et al., eds., Shumu wenxian, 1983.

Of the more than 100,000 stone inscriptions which are extant today only about 30,000 have had rubbings made or have been transcribed or published. Fewer still have been studied.

Tomb inscriptions and literary stelae from the Han to the Tang have been much studied, but those from later dynasties, including those with an economic interest, did not come within the purview of the literati collectors of inscriptions, who were more interested in ancient calligraphic models than the economic and social history of the later dynasties. In the twentieth century, too, historians have been slow to use this type of material. There have been some notable exceptions, however (see 50.4.5 for published collections of stelae of an economic interest, especially those dating from the Ming and Qing).

In general, most stone inscriptions from Shaanxi and the Central Plains date from the Sui and Tang (and to a lesser extent from the Han and Jin); those from the Northeast date from the Liao and Jin; those from the Northwest and the Southeast contain materials relative to the non-Han peoples; those from the Southeast date from the Ming and Qing.

Very few stone inscriptions survive from pre-Qin; about a dozen from the Former Han; 160 from the Later Han; several hundred from Wei, Jin, *Nan-Bei Chao* and Sui. Thereafter the numbers go up steeply: 4,000 to 5,000 tomb tablets from the Tang alone (46.4) and an unknown number of many thousands from late imperial China.

The few pre-Qin stone inscriptions so far discovered were all carved on rocks and stones in their natural state and hence termed *keshi* 刻石 rather than *shike* 石刻. Most famous are the 10 *jie* 碣 (drum-stones) of Qin (763 BC). They were discovered in the Tang dynasty in Shaanxi province and are today preserved in the Palace Museum. Each round-topped stone has a 70-character poem inscribed on it. Of the total of 700 characters, only 272 are still legible, but from rubbings made in the Song dynasty 501 characters have been preserved. They record in a script similar to Qin great seal the hunting and military expeditions of the Qin monarchs in a language similar to that of the *Odes*.[16]

The first emperor made five inspection tours or progresses and altogether had seven stone inscriptions carved extolling his accomplishments and his wise policies. They are said to have been written by his chancellor, Li Si 李斯. Parts of two of them have survived. One (the Langye 琅邪 inscription, 219 BC) is in the National Museum of Chinese History, Beijing. Subsequent emperors followed the same practice, but used specially-made stelae rather than natural rock faces. One of the most famous is the 13-meter-high stele on Mt. Tai in the Tang emperor Xuanzong's own hand recording his conduct of sacrifices there in 725. It can still be seen on the mountain to this day. Monumentally large stelae, their base one of several varieties of stone turtle (*guifu* 龜趺), mark the Qianlong emperor's visits wherever he went, especially in the temples and monuments around Beijing.

Throughout Chinese history, the ancient practice of writing characters on rocks and stones continued. Important visitors, for example, left their mark in the shape of an inscription naming the place, or mountain or grotto. This type of inscription is called *moyai* 摩崖. Subsequent less exalted or distinguished travellers, in addition to acquiring rubbings of the inscriptions, would seek to have their own comments and poems inscribed beneath or alongside the famous one or they would erect a stele. Not all found this urge to leave one's mark an improvement on the scenery. As one Ming official observed, "It is disgusting to see inscribed stone tablets cluttering the foothills ... The law provides regular punishments for those who rob mountains or open mines. Why is it that it does not prohibit the defiling and defacing of the spirit of the mountain by vulgar scholars?"[17] The writer of these words was no doubt well inten-

[16] Gilbert Mattos, *The Stone Drums of Ch'in*, Steyler, 1988.

[17] *The Travel Diaries of Hsu Hsia-k'o* [Xu Xiake 徐霞客 (1586–1641)], Li Chi, ed., HKCU Press, 1974., 62 (see 4.7, *Ming*). Such inscriptions are most numerous at the traditional scenic beauty spots of old China: for

Footnote continued on next page

tioned, but he was also misinformed in that at least since the Tang "officials who improperly set up stone monuments" were punished with one year of penal servitude (Article 134 of the Tang Code).[18]

When Confucianism was made the official state doctrine in the Later Han and seven Confucian Classics were selected (19.2), the complete text of 200,000 characters was inscribed onto 46 stelae each 2.5 meters high and 1 meter broad. It took eight years to carve them. They were placed outside the instruction hall of the Imperial Academy in Luoyang for everyone to see and copy. Only fragments remain today because they were soon broken or destroyed, but the practice of inscribing *shijing* 石經 (stone Classics) continued.[19] The best preserved was made on the occasion that the seven Classics were increased to twelve. The carving of the *Kaicheng shijing* 開成石 經 took four years and was completed in 837. The entire set is in the Forest of Stelae (*Beilin* 碑林), at Xi'an (see the list of *Collections of stelae* below). Subsequently three other *shijing* were inscribed, of these 85 stelae of the *Taixue shijing* (1131) and the *Qianlong shijing* (1794) have survived. This last was carved for display at the Imperial Academy in Beijing. It is now housed next door, behind the Confucian Temple. The set of 190 stelae contains just over 630,000 characters. The temple also has a copy made in the Qianlong period of two of the stone drums of Qin, as well as the originals of most of the 198 stelae upon

---

example, in the foothills around Hangzhou or Guilin, or along the paths right up to the summit of sacred mountains such as Taishan or Huashan. Even the large flat rocks along the banks of the upper reaches of the Yangzi have been carved, not only with records of high- water marks, but also with poems, in some cases since the first century AD (but those extant today date mainly from the Tang or post-Tang). All over China there were always many passersby who simply had carved for them that "So and so [of such and such rank] was here on such and such date."

[18] *The T'ang Code: Vol. II, Specific Articles*, Wallace Johnson, tr., PUP, 1997, 102–4.

[19] In 1980, 96 fragments were discovered on the site of the old Academy and more turned up later (*Zhongyuan wenwu*, 1988.2).

which were carved the names, native places and academies of the 50,000 people who passed the *jinshi* 進士 degree during the five centuries between the beginning of the Yuan and the end of the Qing.

The Buddhist and Daoist scriptures were also carved on stelae and on rocks. The largest collection of Buddhist *shijing* in the world, 14,278 stelae, is stored in caves on Stone Scripture Mt. in Fangshan county, southwest of Beijing (33.5).

The monumental *shijing* served two main purposes. The first was practical, especially in the early empire before the invention of printing: to establish standard texts of works, which otherwise circulated in many different versions and in less sturdy forms, and also to fix standard forms for the characters, most of which existed in a bewildering number of graphic variant. Accurate copies could easily be made by taking a rubbing. The second aim was to show esteem and devotion to canonical texts.

Guides and Research Tools

Zhongguo gudai shike gailun 中國古代石刻概論 (General introduction to Chinese stone inscriptions), Zhao Chao 趙超 Wenwu, 1997. A reliable introduction to all forms of stone inscription. There is a long chapter on the language of the inscriptions, including the set phrases which more and more characterized tomb tablets and memorial-stele inscriptions from the Tang on (168–258). There is also a chapter on how to distinguish fakes. Many thousands of alternative and unorthodox characters were used on the stone carvings. For a study of 12,844 such characters, see Qin Gong 秦公, *Bei biezi xinbian* 碑別字新編 The same author (with Liu Daxin 劉大新) adds a further 3,450 in *Guang Bei biezi* 廣碑別字.[20]

Shike tiba suoyin 石刻題跋索引 (Index to colophons on stone inscriptions), Yang Dianxun 楊殿珣, comp., Shangwu, 1940; enlarged ed., with index, 1957; rev., 1980; 2nd rpnt., 1995, indexes the colophons on stone inscriptions in 137 collections of inscriptions from the earli-

---

[20] *Bei biezi xinbian* (New edition of *Wrongly used characters on stelae*), Wenwu, 1985; *Guang Bei biezi* (Enlarged *Wrongly used characters on stelae*), Guoji wenhua, 1995; rpnt., 1997.

est times to the Yuan. It is arranged by category (tomb stones, tomb tablets, inscribed Classics, etc.). There is a four-corner index.

Published Collections of Stone Rubbings

Stone inscriptions such as *moyai* were written not only by powerful political figures, but also by renowned calligraphers, as were the *shijing*. Rubbings were taken as models for handwriting and circulated in bound sets, an early form of printing.[21] Thanks to this practice and thanks to *jinshixue*, a vast number of rubbings and transcriptions have survived, in special collections, arranged by style, period, medium, subject matter or place (often in local gazetteers); in collected works and other such sources. References to several of these collections are listed in the appropriate sections of the manual (especially in Part V). Many libraries have published collections of stone rubbings.

The largest collection of books of rubbings is held at Beitu 北圖:

Beijing tushuguan cang Zhongguo lidai shike taben huibian 北京圖書館藏中國歷代石刻拓本匯編 (Collection of rubbings of Chinese stone inscriptions held in the Beitu), 101 vols., Zhongzhou guji, 1989–91). Altogether, these 101 volumes contain over 20,000 rubbings (about one-fifth of the library's collection). They date from 475 BC to AD 1949, and include 2,182 funerary inscriptions; 270 epitaphs and 172 inscrip-

---

[21] Examples of the work of famous calligraphers were also inscribed onto stone blocks for making rubbings from which copybooks for calligraphic practice (*tie* 帖) were made. Casual writings (incl. letters) on small pieces of silk or paper came into vogue in the 3rd century. They too were used as calligraphic models. *Two Chinese Treatises on Calligraphy*, introduced, tr. and annotated by Chang Ch'ung-ho and Hans H. Frankel, YUP, 1995, presents the original texts and English translations of the seventh-century calligrapher Sun Guoting 孫過庭, *Shupu* 書譜 (Treatise on calligraphy), and Jiang Kui 姜夔, *Xu Shupu* 續書譜 (Sequel to *Shupu*). *Zhongguo beitie yishu lun* 中國碑帖藝術論 (On the art of China's stone-carved calligraphy), Jiang Wenguang 蔣文光 and Zhang Juying 張菊英, Zhongguo gongren, 1995, not only discusses the making of the copybooks, but gives a straightforward account of China's heritage of stone inscriptions as well. Zeng Yigong 曾毅公, *Shike kaogong lu* 石刻考工錄, Shumu wenxian, 1987, contains the names of nearly 1,800 stone carvers from the Han to the Qing.

tions related to guilds. The collection is arranged by period, which, incidentally, gives a good indication of the enormous amount of inscriptions which have survived from the Tang and the Ming and Qing. There are 195 inscriptions from the Warring States up to and including the Han; 1,182 from the period between the end of the Han and the Sui dynasty; 5,000 from the Sui, Tang and Five Dynasties; 1,500 from the Song; 567 from the Liao, Jin and Xi-Xia; 500 from the Yuan; 2,000 from the Ming; and 9,000 from the Qing. The last volume contains place and inscription indexes.

Shike shiliao xinbian 石刻史料新編 (Newly edited historical materials on stone inscriptions), 90 vols., Xinwenfeng, 1977, 1979, 1986. A collectanea of many of the important early collections of stone inscriptions, including the earlier *Shike shiliao congshu* 石刻史料叢書 (Collectanea of historical materials on stone inscriptions), Yan Gengwang 嚴耕望, ed., 420 *ce* in 60 cases, Yiwen, 1966. For indexes to authors and compilers in the *Shike shiliao xinbian*, see *Annotated Bibliography to the Shike shiliao xinbian*, Dieter Kuhn and Helga Stahl, comp., Forum, 1991.

Collections of inscriptions from a particular place were also published separately and continue to be—for example:

Dali congshu 大理叢書 (The Dali series), Zhang Shufang 張樹芳, ed., 10 vols., Shekeyuan, 1993. Inscriptions from Dali. Vol. 10 contains transcriptions.

Sichuan lidai beike 四川歷代碑刻 (Historical stone inscriptions from Sichuan), Gao Wen 高文 et al., eds., Sichuan daxue, 1990.

Yunnan gudai shike congkao 雲南古代石刻叢考 (Investigation into ancient stone inscriptions from Yunnan), Sun Taichu 孫太初, comp., Wenwu, 1983. Contains seventeen important inscriptions dating from the Han to the Qing.

Collections of Stelae

Major collections of stone inscriptions can be seen at:

Beijing shike yishu bowuguan 北京石刻藝術博物館 (Beijing Art Museum of Stone Carving). Housed at the Zhenjue temple 真覺寺 (also known as Wutasi 五塔寺, Five Pagoda Temple). Contains 1,500 stelae, of which 400 are on display.

Beijing, Yunjusi 雲居寺 (33.5).

Hangzhou beilin 杭州碑林 (Forest of Stelae, Hangzhou). Contains seven of the Confucian Classics from the Taixue *shijing*.

Luoyang shike yishu bowuguan 洛陽石刻藝術博物館 (Luoyang Art Museum of Stone Carving). Has the largest collection of tomb tablets in China (more than 5,000) from which rubbings of those dating from the Sui, Tang and Five Dynasties have been published (see 46.6 for details).

Qian-Tangzhi zhai 千唐誌齋 in Xin'an county 新安縣 near Luoyang, is the only museum dedicated to ancient tomb inscriptions of which it has 1,413. The greater number (1,209) date from the Tang (see 46.4 for details).

Nanmen beilin 南門碑林, Gaoxiong 高雄, Taiwan.

Qufu 曲阜 at the Confucian Temple (6,000–7,000 inscriptions).

Suzhou beike bowuguan 蘇州碑刻博物館 (Suzhou Museum of Inscribed Stelae) contains a special gallery which contains 226 inscriptions of an economic interest from the later empire. The museum is housed in the buildings of the Confucian School established by the Song man of letters Fan Zhongyan 范仲淹 in 1034. It also contains four unique Song dynasty maps, including the earliest star map carved on stone in the world (dating from 942) and a stone map of Pingjiang 平江 (Suzhou). See Chen Meidong 陳美東, *Zhongguo gu xingtu* (China's ancient star maps), Jilin jiaoyu, 1996.

Xi'an beilin bowuguan 西安碑林博物館 (Museum of Forest of Stelae, Xi'an) housed in the old Confucian Temple. The most famous of the beilin because it has the largest collection of early stone inscriptions including the Kaicheng *shijing* 開成石經, the earliest extant version of the Confucian Classics on stone.

Xichang dizhen beilin 西昌地震碑林 (Xichang Earthquake Museum, Sichuan (35.4.2, *Earthquakes*).

Apart from such special collections as these, all major historical museums, temples and ancient buildings and monuments in China have copious examples of stelae of every kind, and construction work continues to turn up large quantities of them.

18

The Earliest Manuscripts

Chinese manuscript and book production have gone through six main stages:

- A. Manuscripts written on bamboo strips and wooden tablets: Shang to Later Han
- B. Manuscripts written on silk: Warring States to Later Han
- C. Manuscripts written on paper: Later Han to Five Dynasties
- D. Woodblock printed books: seventh to nineteenth centuries
- E. Movable type printing: late nineteenth century to present

    [Electronic publishing: 1980s to present]

18.1 Bamboo Manuscripts

"[Those who are righteous are praised in their own times] but their deeds should also be written on bamboo and silk, inscribed on bronze and stone, and incised onto vessels in order to pass them down to later generations 又書其事於竹帛鏤之金石琢之盤盂傳遺後世子孫," *Mozi* 墨子 (468–376 BC), *Mozi, juan 27, Tianzhi zhong* 天志中.

A much handier and a cheaper medium for keeping records than shells, bones, jade, bronze or stone was bamboo or wood. The evidence that writing on bamboo had already begun at least during the later Shang is summarized in 15.5. Thereafter,

bamboo and wooden documents and other writings (*diance* 典
册, *jiance* 簡策) continued in use until the third and fourth centuries AD. This makes them a longer-serving medium for writing than paper.[1]

Up until at least the time of Confucius, texts were mainly
official records and documents not for circulation or general
use. They were usually written on strips (*jian* 簡) either of
bamboo (*zhujian* 竹簡) or of wood (*mujian* 木簡). The strips
normally held one, or sometimes two or more, rows of characters. When the individual strips were bound together they were
called a *ce* 册. They were either fastened together with a single
thread at the head of the strips (*pian* 篇) or bound together in a
bundle (*juan* 卷), usually with two threads.

Sometimes the binding was done after the writing (for example, for lists of funerary objects), but usually it was done be-
forehand. The writer would lay the bundle out horizontally before him to write on, starting from the right-hand strip. The
characters were written with a brush and ink vertically down
the strips following the grain, usually on the inside surface. After they were tied together, the strips were rolled up (from the
left to the right, as picture scrolls are to this day, so that the last
strip to be written on functioned as the spindle of the bundle
and the beginning of the text, on the first strip, was the first to
be unrolled). This way of writing and storing the strip bundles

---

[1] Tsuen-hsuin Tsien wrote an elegant and beautifully illustrated study
on Chinese writing and writing materials before the invention of paper
and printing. It is still the best introduction in English: Tsuen-hsuin
Tsien (Qian Cunxun 錢存訓), *Written on Bamboo and Silk: The Beginnings of Chinese Books and Inscriptions*, UChP, 1962. Revised and updated
Chinese edition: *Zhongguo gudai shu shi* 中國古代書史, HKCU Press,
1975. See also the same author's *Zhongguo shuji, zhimo ji yinshuashi lunwenji* 中國書籍紙墨及印刷史論文集 (Studies on the history of the Chi-
nese book, paper, ink and printing), HKCU Press, 1992. The medium-
size *Chuban cidian* 出版詞典 (Dictionary of publishing), Shanghai cishu,
1992. Contains short, up-to-date entries on all aspects of printing and
publishing from the earliest times to the present day, including the history of old books and information relating to inscriptions and writing.

helps explain why old Chinese records started at what for us to-day is the end. It was an arrangement which was retained when books began to be printed in the seventh century AD and it lasted until the 1950s. The only exception to this order of writing were counting-rod numerals, which were written horizontally from left to right (7.1.1).

Reading was a weighty matter; the first emperor is commended for his industriousness in getting through a large number of official documents every day, not in terms of the numbers of bundles or strips, but in terms of their weight (in this case 120 catties a day). Collections were measured by the cartload, a practice which continued to the third century AD. Hence the expression *xuefu wuche* 學富五車 (a learned man; literally to have five cartloads of learning). Because of the weight of the bamboo strips, texts did not widely circulate, and if they did, it must have been in a few bundles rather than as complete works.[2] A small number of copies were written for emperors and nobles on silk, which was less bulky than the strips, but much more expensive (18.2).

Apart from writing on bamboo and wooden strips, shorter documents, or those such as maps, which required a larger surface, were written on tablets, usually of wood (*du* 牘, *mudu* 木牘, *bandu* 版牘, *chidu* 尺牘, *gu* 觚, *ban* 板 or *fang* 方). They came into general use in the Han. The tablets were usually broader and shorter than the strips and could accommodate a short document with several rows of characters. For letters, two tablets were often notched into each other face-to-face and then tied together. The top tablet was used to record the addressee and the sender. Wooden tablets were also used as the table of contents of a bamboo record.

---

[2] The *Shiji* 史記 numbers 130 *pian* 篇 and has a total of 530,000 characters. If each strip contained 60 characters, the *Shiji* would have totalled 8,833 strips arranged into about 150–300 bundles (assuming 30–60 strips per bundle). Like other works of history or literature, the *Shiji* would also have been written on silk. Indeed, the 130 *pian* 篇 into which it is divided may probably refer to the number of silk rolls or to groups of rolls (or possibly sections).

Both the strips and the tablets varied in length according to the type of document. By the Han there were regulations that government laws should be written on strips of 3 *chi* 尺 (1 *chi* was about 23 cm); the Confucian Classics on 2.4 *chi* strips; and correspondence on tablets 1 *chi* long (hence the old name for letters, *chidu* 尺牘). In practice, we know from the excavated strips that there was considerable variation in length.[3]

There were many words and compounds for different types of writing. *Jiance* 簡策 (*ce* 冊) along with *jiandu* 簡牘 (strips and tablets), was one of the most common of the early words. Others included *dianji* 典籍, *jiance boshu* 簡冊帛書 or *jianbo* 簡帛, "writings on bamboo and silk", *shuji* 書籍, *shuce* 書冊 or *bandu* 版牘. *Dianji* only came to mean writing in general (perhaps even "books") after the Han. The principal meaning of the modern word for books, *tushu* 圖書, was "maps and documents" from its first appearance in the Zhou until after the Han.

Much of the vocabulary for books and publishing in use to-day reflects the bamboo and wooden origins of Chinese writing: the word for book or volume (*ce* 冊), for example, is often explained as a pictograph of two vertical bamboo or wooden strips held together with threads. Other such words include *dian* 典 (a pictograph of *ce* being placed on a stand); the *ji* 籍 in *dianji* 典籍 (originally a 2-foot bamboo strip) and *pian* 篇 (originally a swatch of bamboo or wooden strips secured with a thread, as opposed to a *juan* 卷 which was a longer rolled up section, or whole work, written on bamboo or silk). The old word for name card was *ci* 刺 because the name was carved on a bamboo or wooden strip. *Shan* 刪, as in *shanchu* 刪除 (to delete), originally meant to scrape the strips clean with a knife ready for writing on again, as also did *xiao* 削 and *kan* 刊, as in *kanwu* 刊誤, to cut out errors. Later *kan* also took on the meaning of carve, as on a wooden block for printing, hence eventually the modern word for publication, *kanwu* 刊物. Pop-

---

[3] See Michael Loewe, "Wood and Bamboo Administrative Documents of the Han Period," in *NSECH*, 161–92.

ulation registers were originally called *Huangji* 黃籍, probably after the color of the bamboo strips on which they were written. In the Ming and Qing the tradition was maintained by recording the population counts (for labor services) in thread-bound fascicles, with yellow covers known as *Huangce* 黃冊 (Yellow registers).

All of the Classics of the Spring and Autumn and Warring States periods were originally written in the form of what are conventionally called "bamboo records" (or on silk). How long and which ones were handed down by word of mouth before being written down is not known. Warring States bamboo writings were discovered twice during the Han, once during the Jin and once during the Qi. Several of the Classics written in ancient script (*guwen* 古文) on bamboo strips were found in 168 BC hidden in the wall of Confucius's house at Qufu, Shandong.[4] More *guwen* bamboo strips were found in a tomb in 73 BC. Several tens of cartloads of strips were discovered in AD 279 in the tomb of King Xiang of Wei 魏襄王 (died 296 BC) at Jixian 汲縣 in Henan. They were stored in the imperial library and transcribed from the Warring States original scripts (according to one source, tadpole script) to chancery script, but were later lost except for portions of the *Zhushu jinian* 竹書紀年 (*Bamboo Annals*) and the *Mu tianzi zhuan* 穆天子傳 (*Travels of Prince Mu*). More *guwen* strips were found in a Chu tomb in Xiangyang 襄陽 in AD 479.

Half a dozen minor discoveries are recorded up to the Song, but all have been lost. The first finds in modern times were not from tombs, but were made by Western and Japanese archaeologists and explorers at the beginning of the twentieth century in the Northwest among the ruins of the frontier posts of the empire along the Silk Road. Most of these military border documents dealt with administrative matters and dated from the Han, hence the name *Hanjian* 漢簡 (44.3.2.2–3).

---

[4] For the significance of these ancient-text editions, see Michael Nylan, "The *ku wen* Documents in Han Times," *TP* 81.1–3: 25–50 (1995).

The oldest documents and writings on silk and bamboo strips were not found in the Northwest, but in tombs in the central Yangzi kingdom of Chu 楚 (18.1.1). The finds included classical works written on *jiandu* and shorter documents on tablets. The texts placed in the tombs were not only Classics, but also practical works that the occupant (depending on his status and special interests or skills) was expected to need in the afterlife, including almanacs, mathematical, astronomical and divinatory texts, maps, laws and regulations and letters. Most tombs also included inventory lists of the funerary objects that were placed in them.

The bamboo strips from the Warring States and the Qin come almost entirely from tombs in the South, where the humidity kept them intact for 2,000 years. The Han *jiandu* administrative documents are usually of wood and have been mainly found in the Northwest, where it was the arid climate which preserved them. There have also been important finds of Former Han *jiandu* in the South. Most Later Han *jiandu* come from the Northwest. The finds from Wu, Wei and Jin come either from the far Northwest or from the South.

Altogether, over 180,000 *jiandu* have been discovered this century (of which 130,000 were found between 1975 and 1998). Some 8,500 date from the Warring States; 2,500 from the Qin; 70,000 from the Former Han; 800 from the Later Han; 92,000 from Wu; and 603 from the Wei and Jin.

Photographs and transcriptions of the *jiandu* have been published in dozens of different publications, but there is as yet no *corpus inscriptionum*, nor is there likely to be one because of the disparate nature of sources in the *jiandu*. In addition, new discoveries are constantly being made, and many of those that have been excavated are still being prepared for publication. The reasons for delays in publication, which are not uncommon, are varied. In some cases the strips were found by peasants and the negotiation of their purchase has been a protracted one. In a few cases they have been stored in small county museums. After they are brought to light, the strips, which are often out of order, stuck together, or fragmented, need to be treated sorted, reassembled, analyzed and transcribed. Once this has been done, reading them is by no means an easy matter, especially for the earlier ones. The Chu strips are in Chu Warring States small seal. The Qin ones are in Qin small seal and early Qin chancery script. The Han strips are mainly in chancery script and the Three Kingdoms strips are on the cusp between chancery and regular script. All the strips contain numerous graphic variants and wrong characters, especially those which were everyday administrative records rather than more carefully written documents.

Despite intensive studies of the different scripts found on the *jiandu* and *boshu* 帛書 (silk manuscripts), there are still a large number of characters which have not been identified.

Once the *jiandu* have been sorted they are transcribed and published in a preliminary form in one of the archaeological journals, usually *Wenwu*. The official excavation reports come some years later and sometimes include more authoritative transcriptions and photographs. Finally, separate studies are published for the more important finds with transcriptions and notes. Historians comb the new sources for the information they contain on particular subjects; for example, administration, particularly local administration; the law (27.2); the calendars in actual use at a particular period;[5] information on commodity prices; medicine; popular beliefs; the mantic arts; and geography. They can also be used to check transmitted texts or, in some notable cases, to supplement them with large quantities of new historical data.[6]

Quite apart from the historical and literary interest of the *jiandu*, they provide copious insights for paleographers (they have been used, for example, to show that *lishu* was in use at an

[5] Yu Zhongxin 俞忠鑫, *Hanjian kaoli* 漢簡考曆 (Calendrical records on the *Hanjian*), Wenjin, 1994. The Warring States almanacs discovered on bamboo strips are listed by place of discovery in this section; the Han ones at 44.3.2; see also 5.1.

[6] The most striking example of *jiandu* supplementing existing historical sources are the estimated 90,000 discovered at Zoumalou 走馬樓, near Changsha in 1996. See 45.3.

earlier date than had hitherto been known, see 16.1). They are also used as models for the calligrapher. Modern *jiandu* character exercise books are available.

For a bibliography of secondary scholarship on the *jiandu* (and silk manuscripts), published between 1905 and 1985, see "Qin-Han jiandu yu boshu yanjiu wenxian mulu 秦漢簡牘與帛書研究文獻目錄."[7] There are several compilations showing the forms of characters and their variants as found on *jiandu* and silk manuscripts.[8]

Journals

Jiandu xuebao 簡牘學報, Taibei (1970– , annual).

Jianduxue yanjiu 簡牘學研究, Lanzhou (1996– , irreg).

Chûgoku shutsudo shiriyô kenkyûkai kaihô 中國出土資料研究會會報 (Journal of the society for the study of Chinese excavated texts), Tôkyô daigaku bungakubu, irregular.

The *jiandu* are referred to either by the period from which they date or by the place in which they were found, or both;

---

[7] Xing Yitian 邢義田, *Qin-Han shi lungao* 秦漢史論稿, Dongda tushu gongsi, 1987, 569–635. Zheng Youguo 鄭有國, *Zhongguo Hanjianxue zonglun* 中國漢簡學綜論 (Comprehensive guide to the study of China's documents on bamboo and wood), Huadong shifan daxue, 1989. There is a bibliography of publications of reproductions of the strips and tablets, plus secondary literature up to 1988. See also Ôba Osamu 大庭脩, ed., *Kankan kenkyû no genjô to tenbô* 漢簡研究の現狀と展望 (Present state and prospects of research on bamboo documents), Kansai daigaku, 1993, and by the same author, *Kankan kenkyû* 漢簡研究 (Researches on *Hanjian*), Hôyû, 1992. The Shekeyuan's Jianbo yanjiu zhongxin 簡帛研究中心 (Center for research on bamboo and silk books) has published two collections of more recent articles: *Jianbo yanjiu* 簡帛研究, vols., 1 and 2, Falü, 1993, 1996.

[8] *Jiandu boshu zidian* 簡牘帛書字典 (Dictionary of bamboo and silk characters), Chen Jiangong 陳建貢 and Xu Min 徐敏 comp., Shanghai shuhua, 1991; Sano Kôichi 佐野光一, *Mokkan jiten* 木簡字典 (A dictionary of *Hanjian* characters), Yûzankaku, 1985. Neither of these works are dictionaries in the conventional sense, but rather collections of the different ways in which each bamboo character was written as a means of understanding their forms (*jiexing* 解形) and modern equivalents.

for example, *Zhanguojian* 戰國簡 (Warring States bamboo strips); *Chujian* 楚簡 (Bamboo strips from the kingdom of Chu); *Qinjian* 秦簡, *Hanjian* 漢簡 *Juyan Hanjian* 居延漢簡; and so forth.

Modern findings of Warring States *jiandu* are listed alphabetically in 18.1.1 (Chu *jiandu*) and 18.1.2 (non-Chu *jiandu*). Post-Qin unification and Han *Jiandu* are listed in 44.3.2. Three Kingdoms and Jin *jiandu* in 45.3. In the listings, the following distinctions are made:

Bamboo strips: *zhujian* 竹簡
Wooden strips: *mujian* 木簡
Bamboo and wooden strips: *jiandu* 簡牘
Bamboo tablets: *zhudu* 竹牘
Wooden tablets: *mudu* 木牘

18.1.1 *Warring States* Chujian 楚簡

The central Yangzi state of Chu, whose origins can be traced back to the Shang and Western Zhou, not only had a distinctive high culture, but also a spectacularly successful history of military expansion.[9] From the 10th to 3rd c. BC, it destroyed a total of 61 kingdoms thus becoming the largest kingdom in the Warring States period before eventually being destroyed by Qin in 223 BC. For over 400 years, from the end of the eighth (or the very beginning of the seventh) century to 278 BC, the capital was situated at Ying 郢, the site of which is located at the modern city of Ji'nan 記南, in the northern part of Jiangling 江陵 county, Hubei. As of 1998, over 6,000 Chu strips had been discovered at 30 separate sites containing a total of about 40,000 characters. In addition, Chu silk manuscripts with a total of about 1,000 characters have been discovered. Most of the

---

[9] The best series on all aspects of Chu history and culture is *Chuxue wenku* 楚學文庫 (Chu studies collection), Chu wenhua yanjiuhui 楚文化研究會 (Chu culture research society), eds., 18 vols., Hubei jiaoyu, 1993–96; *Chu kaogu wenhua da shiji* 楚考古文化大事記 (Main events in Chu archaeology), Wenwu, 1984, an index to Chu archaeological finds up to 1982. See also the literature on Mawangdui (18.2).

finds have been from tombs around the ancient capital of Ying
and later from around Changsha:

Li Yunfu 李運富, *Chuguo jianbo wenzi gouxing xitong yanjiu* 戰國簡帛文
字構形系統研究 (Systematic research into the forms of Chu bamboo
and silk characters), Qi-Lu, 1997. This study contains both a thorough description of the excavated manuscripts as well as a listing of
nearly 400 studies of them.

For compendia of Chu-style characters, see:

Chuxi jianbo wenzi bian 楚系簡帛文字編 (Compilation of Chu-style *jiandu* and silk manuscript characters), Teng Rensheng 滕壬生, comp.,
Hubei jiaoyu, 1995.

Zhanguo Chu zhujian huibian 戰國楚竹簡匯編 (Glossary of Chu Warring
States bamboo strips), Shang Chengzuo 商承祚, ed., Qi-Lu, 1995.

Note that the journal *Jiang-Han kaogu* carries many articles on
the *Chujian*. The following is a list of the main finds of *Chujian*
(arranged alphabetically by name of site):

Baoshan 包山, Jingmen 荆門, Hubei: 278 strips containing 12,472 characters. The largest find of Chujian. Excavated from tomb 2 in 1986 and
1987. The texts date from 323–292 BC. They are among the earliest
yet discovered and include records of events, legal works, divinatory
texts and lists of burial articles. For archaeological report, see *Baoshan
Chumu* 包山楚墓 (Chu tomb at Baoshan), Wenwu, 1991; for transcriptions, see *Baoshan Chujian* 包山楚簡 (Chu bamboo strips from
Baoshan), Wenwu, 1991; for listing of characters, see *Baoshan Chujian
wenzibian* 包山楚簡文字編 (Compilation of characters found on
Chu bamboo strips from Baoshan), Wenwu, 1996; for research, see
Chen Wei 陳偉, *Baoshan Chujian chutan* 包山楚簡初探 (Preliminary
investigations of the Chu bamboo strips from Baoshan), Wuhan
daxue, 1996; Li Ling 李零, "Formulaic Structure of Chu Divinatory
Bamboo Slips," *EC* 15: 71–86 (1990). *Jianghan kaogu* 1993.4; *Huaxia
kaogu* 1994.2; *Wenwu* 1996.12; *Nanfang wenwu* 1996.2 (on the legal
texts).

Changtaiguan 長臺關, Xinyang 信陽, Henan: 2 sets; the first (117 strips)
is part of a book; the second (29 strips) is a list of burial articles. Excavated in 1957. *Xinyang Chumu* 信陽楚墓 (The Chu graves at Xinyang), Wenwu, 1986.

Deshan Xiyangpo 德山夕陽坡, Changde 常德, Hunan: 2 strips with a
total of 54 characters recording events. Excavated in 1984 (tomb 2).

Fanjiapo 范家坡, Jiangling 江陵, Hubei: 1 strip from tomb 7, not yet published. Excavated in 1993.

Guodian 郭店, Jingmen, Hubei: of 804 strips in tomb 1, 730 with writing on them amounting to a total of over 13,000 characters. The strips record two Daoist works (one of which is the earliest known copy of about two-fifths of the modern *Laozi*, the fifth to have been unearthed to date) and several Confucian works. These are some of the earliest *jiandu* ever found. The texts are largely the same as the received copies but the order of the chapters is sometimes different. The strips are clearly reproduced and transcribed (with annotations by Qiu Xigui) in *Guodian Chumu zhujian* 郭店楚墓竹簡 (The bamboo strips from the Chu tomb at Guodian), Jingmenshi bowuguan, eds., Wenwu, 1998. Excavated in 1993, *Wenwu* 1997.7.

Jiudian 九店, Jiangling, Hubei: Total of 190 bamboo strips containing almanacs. Not yet published. See 5.1 on the almanacs of the Warring States, Qin and Han. Two tombs (56 and 621) excavated in 1981 and 1989.

Jiuli 九里, Linfeng 臨澧, Hunan: 10 strips excavated in 1980. Not yet published.

Mashan 馬山, Jiangling, Hubei: 1 strip from tomb 1 with 8 characters recording events. Also many textiles, including woven and embroidered silks (illustrated in Rawson, *Mysteries of Ancient China*, 1996, 144–49). Excavated in 1982.

Qinjiazui 秦家嘴, Jiangling, Hubei: Tomb 1 contains 7 strips and wooden tablets with divination and sacrificial records. Excavated in 1986.

Qinjiazui 秦家嘴, Jiangling, Hubei: Tomb 13 contains 18 damaged strips with divination and sacrificial records. Excavated in 1986.

Qinjiazui 秦家嘴, Jiangling, Hubei: Tomb 99 contains damaged strips with divination and sacrificial records. Excavated in 1986.

Shibancun 石板村, Cili 慈利, Hunan: Nearly 4,000 strips and wooden tablets recording events, mainly war between Wu and Yue (tomb 36). Not yet published. Excavated in 1987.

Tengdian 藤店, Jiangling 江陵, Hubei: 24 *zhujian* and *mudu*. Excavated from a tomb in 1973, badly damaged.

Tianxingguan 天星觀, Jiangling 江陵, Hubei: Over 70 *zhujian* and *mudu* containing records of events, divination and sacrificial records and lists of burial articles in a tomb; ca. 340 BC. Excavated in 1978.

Wangshan 望山, Jiangling, Hubei: 273 strips and wooden tablets in tomb 1 with records of events, divination and sacrificial records: *Wangshan*

Chujian 望山楚簡, Hubei Kaogusuo 湖北考古所 and Beida Zhong-wenxi 北大中文系, eds., Zhonghua, 1995. Includes illustrations of the originals; transcriptions; translations into modern Chinese; meticulous annotations and introductions. Excavated in 1965.

Wangshan 望山, Jiangling, Hubei: 66 strips with lists of burial articles. *Wangshan Chujian* (1995). Also contains tools for preparing bamboo strips, including a chopper, 2 splitting knives and a peeling knife, one of the uses of which was to scrape off old inscriptions (illustrated in Rawson, *Mysteries*, 1996, 151). "Jiangling Wangshan Chujian Zundui Chumu," *Wenwu*, 1996. Excavated in 1957 in tomb 2.

Wulipai 五里牌, Changsha, Hunan: 38 damaged strips with lists of burial articles. Excavated in 1951.

Yangjiawan 楊家灣, Changsha, Hunan: 72 strips. Excavated in 1953.

Yangtianhu 仰天湖, Changsha, Hunan: 43 *jiandu* with lists of burial articles. Excavated in 1953.

Zenghou Yi mu 曾侯乙墓, Suizhou 隨州, Hubei: Over 240 *zhujian* with 6,696 characters written on them were found in the tomb dating from 433 BC of Marquis Yi of Zeng. Lists of burial articles. Excavated in 1978.

Zhuanwachang 磚瓦廠, Jiangling, Hubei: 6 strips from tomb 370 with divination and sacrificial records. Excavated in 1992.

Zhulüguan 竹律管, Jiangling Yutaishan, Hubei: 4 strips with 38 characters of musical texts. Excavated in 1986.

There are 1,437 *Chujian* in the Shanghai Museum relating to fourth century BC. religious and intellectual life.

18.1.2   *Warring States* Jiandu 戰國簡牘: *Non-Chu*

Fangmatan 放馬灘, Tianshuishi 天水市, Gansu: 460 Qin bamboo strips with seven maps on wooden tablets and 2 almanacs dating from the end of the Warring States (see 4.2 for details of the maps). *Qin-Han jiandu lunwenji* 秦漢簡牘論文集, Gansu renmin, 1989; *Wenwu* 1990.4. Excavated from a Qin tomb in 1986.

Haojiaping 郝家坪, Qingchuan 青川 district, Sichuan: 2 wooden tablets, 1 on land law, the second indecipherable (*Wenwu* 1982.1; *Kaogu* 1988.8). Excavated from tomb 50 in 1979–80 (27.2).

18.2   Manuscripts Written on Silk

After bamboo and wood, silk was the other most commonly used writing material from at least the Warring States to the Tang. The expression *zhubo* 竹帛 "bamboo and silk" as indicated by the quotation at the beginning of this chapter had come to mean "books" by the fifth century BC. Because of the expense, silk was less widely used than bamboo were written on bamboo, not on silk). The arrangement of the characters on the silk follows the same order as on the bamboo strips.

Several books, as well as documents and maps, written on silk dating from the Warring States and Han periods have been excavated. The earliest was stolen from a Chu tomb at Zidanku 子彈庫, near Changsha in 1942, and is now held in the Arthur M. Sackler Museum in Washington, DC. It contained 900 characters and colored illustrations of the gods of the 12 months in the margins. Exposure to the light has made it faded and illegible.[10]

Most famous of the silk manuscripts are the dozen dating from the late Warring States and the Han found in Mawangdui (馬王堆) Former Han tomb 3 (168 BC) near Changsha. They contain over 120,000 characters and include two copies of *Laozi*

[10] See Noel Barnard, *The Ch'u Silk Manuscript–Translation and Commentary*, ANU Press, 1973. Over 75 books and articles have been published on this silk manuscript. For a bibliography of studies on the tomb, see Li Meilu 李梅鹿, *Mawangdui Hanmu yanjiu mulu* 馬王堆漢墓研究目錄, Hunansheng bowuguan, 1992, and for a brief bibliography of the texts, Li Ling 李零, *Zhongguo fangshu kao* 中國方術考 (Studies on Chinese divinatory and medical arts), Renmin Zhongguo, 1993, 167–85. See also the same author's *Changsha Zidanku Zhanguo Chu boshu yanjiu* 長沙子彈庫戰國楚帛書研究, Zhonghua, 1985 and *Zhujian boshu lunwen ji* 竹簡帛書論文集 (Collected articles on the books written on bamboo and silk), Zheng Liangshu 鄭良樹, eds., Zhonghua, 1982. For a listing of the characters in the manuscript, see *Changsha Chu boshu wenzibian* 長沙楚帛書文字編 (Compilation of the characters in the Changsha Chu silk manuscript), Zeng Xiantong 曾憲通, comp., Zhonghua, 1993, and for the larger context of Chu style characters as found on the Chu bamboo strips, see Teng Rensheng (1995).

老子.[11] They were written at the transition point between small seal and chancery scripts. There are several more works written on silk, including fragments of texts, which have been excavated from tombs elsewhere, but await publication.

The discoveries of manuscripts written on bamboo and silk have enabled comparison of the transmitted texts of literary works, which passed through many editorial hands over the centuries, with these older versions, sometimes untouched since their entombment in the Han or earlier.[12] In some cases lost works have been recovered and in other cases hitherto unknown works have been discovered.[13]

18.3   Manuscripts Written on Paper

Paper of a quality good enough to write on was produced in the second century AD and gradually came into general use dur-

---

[11] For transcriptions, see *Mawangdui Hanmu boshu* 馬王堆漢墓帛書 (The silk books from the Han tomb at Mawangdui), Mawangdui Hanmu boshu zhengli xiaozu 馬王堆漢墓帛書整理小組, 6 vols., Wenwu, 1980– . Vol. 1 contains the *Laozi* A and B texts; vol. 2, the *Yijing* 易經 (*Book of Changes*), not yet published; vol. 3 (titles added by the editors), the *Chunqiu shiyu* 春秋事語 (Deeds and words of the spring and autumn) and the *Zhanguo zonghengjia shu* 戰國縱橫家書 (Book of Warring States strategists), 1983; vol. 4 (1985); vols. 5 (astrology) and 6 (occult texts), forthcoming. The tomb also contained three tricolored maps on silk (4.2). *Mawangdui Hanmu wenwu* 馬王堆漢墓文物 (The cultural relics unearthed from the Han tombs at Mawangdui), Hunan, 1992, contains transcriptions of some of the silk texts not yet published in the *Mawangdui Hanmu boshu* series. Medical texts, including a silk painting showing 44 people doing *daoyin* 導引 (stretching and breathing) exercises, have been separately published (chap. 36). Robin D. S. Yates translates some of the philosophical texts in *Five Lost Classics: Tao, Huang-Lao and Yin-Yang in Han China*, Ballantine, 1996.

[12] William Boltz discusses manuscripts of transmitted texts on bamboo and silk in *NSECH* (1997), 253–84.

[13] Portions of *Sunzi bingfa* 孫子兵法 (*Sunzi: art of war*) and the previously lost *Sun Bin bingfa* 孫臏兵法 (*Sun Bin: art of war*) were found in 1972 in a Former Han tomb at Yinqueshan, Linyi county, Shandong (28.2).

ing the third and fourth centuries, replacing bamboo, wooden tablets and silk as it did so. Traditionally the discovery is credited to Cai Lun 蔡倫 (AD?–121), but descriptions of paper making using silk waste and scraps of paper made from fibers predating his birth have been found.

In AD 404, the self-appointed emperor of Chu, Huan Xuan 桓玄 (369–404) ordered that paper should be used instead of bamboo strips and wooden tablets. It is a sign of the beginning of the age of paper. A single book would consist of several scrolls. The scrolls were made by pasting together sheets of paper. Looking something up in a scroll dictionary or encyclopaedia would have taken a lot of time, but would have been a much less cumbersome affair than handling heavy bundles of bamboo. Books could also now be carried by hand rather than transported by cart. Literary culture with authors of individual works and different audiences of readers now became a feature of Chinese life.

Over 20,000 *juan* of manuscripts written on paper dating from AD 406 to 996 were discovered at the beginning of this century at Turpan and in the secret temple library at Dunhuang (46.3).[14]

Gradually scrolls were replaced in the ninth century by "sutra" binding (*jingzhezhuang* 經折裝) in which the leaves

---

[14] The authority on the history of paper and printed books in China is Tsuen-Hsuin Tsien, *Paper and Printing* in SCC, vol. V, part 1, *Chemistry and Chemical Technology*, CUP, 1985, 3rd prnt., rev., 1987; rpnt., 1993. Qian (Tsien), 1992, contains a bibliography of modern scholarship up to 1990, updating the huge bibliography in his SCC volume. These works update the Chinese side of the story told in Thomas F. Carter, *The Invention of Printing in China and its Spread Westward*, Col. UP, 1925; rev. ed., 1931; 2nd rev. ed., L. C. Goodrich, Ronald Press, 1955. Denis Twitchett, *Printing and Publishing in Medieval China*, London: Wynkyn de Worde Society, 1983, is a short, well-illustrated outline. See also Hok-lam Chan, *Control of Publishing in China: Past and Present*, ANU Press, 1987. For the wider context, see Lai Xinxia 來新夏, *Zhongguo gudai tushu shiyeshi* 中國古代圖書事業史 (A history of the book trade in ancient China), Shanghai renmin, 1990; rpnt., 1991.

were folded flat rather than rolled up. This may have begun in imitation of the palm-leaf books of Buddhist scriptures imported from India. It had the advantage that it was now possible to turn to a reference without unfolding the entire document. The next step was that the first and last leaves were pasted onto a single large sheet so the sheets were more secure (*xuanfeng zhuang* 旋風裝 "whirlwind binding"). The book opened like an accordion with both covers placed face downwards on the table. With the spread of printing, it became convenient to fold printed sheets into two to form pairs of facing pages that were bound together by pasting the backs of the folds (tenth-century *hudie zhuang* 蝴蝶裝 "butterfly binding"). The disadvantage was that every two pages the reader encountered two blank pages. By the thirteenth century this had been overcome by pasting together the edges of the pages so the reader encountered no blank pages (*baobei zhuang* 包背裝 "wrapped-back binding"). Thread stitching replaced pasting or paper for the binding in the late Ming, early Qing to produce the familiar thread-bound *ce* 冊 (fascicle) with soft covers (*xianzhuang* 綫裝). To protect these Chinese "paper-backs" and to make it easier to pull out a particular *ce* from a pile, sets of *ce* were boxed together in a protective case (*han* 函).[15]

18.4 Printed Books

Seals (*yin* 印) were in use at least from the late Shang. They gave their name to printing (*yinshua* 印刷). Books of paper rubbings taken from stone blocks incised with characters were made from the fourth century AD. This is generally considered a further step toward the invention of printing using wooden blocks (*banben* 版本), which started in the early seventh century using jujube or pear tree wood. The earliest example of printing in the world is a single sheet of a *dhâranî* (Buddhist spell) in Sanskrit, which was found in 1974 in a tomb in Xi'an.

---

[15] Edward Matinique, *Chinese Traditional Bookbinding*, CMC, 1983; Tsien (1987), 227–33.

It has been dated to 650–670. Another similar example was found in a stupa in 1966 in Pulguksa temple 佛國寺, Kyongju 慶州, the ancient capital of the Korean kingdom of Silla 新羅. It was probably printed in China sometime at the beginning of the eighth century. The oldest known *banben* is a printed manuscript of the Lotus Sutra (*Miaofa lianhua jing* 妙法蓮花經) discovered at Turpan in 1906. The earliest extant dated *banben* is a Diamond Sutra (*Jingang panruo boluomi jing* 金剛般若波羅密經) of 868 found at Dunhuang in 1907. It is in the form of a 14-foot-long illustrated scroll. It is held in the British Museum which also houses the first extant printed almanac in the world, the *Qianfu sinian lishu* 乾符四年曆書 (Almanac of 877).

Woodblock printing (*diaoban yinshua* 雕版印刷) probably started in Sichuan in the ninth century, if not earlier. It reached its height in the Song which saw the printing in 971 of the *Kaibao zangshu* 開寶藏書 (Kaibao *Tripitika*) in 1,076 ce. It was the largest work in the world at that date ever to have been printed and it was not to be surpassed until the Ming *Tripitika* in the fifteenth century (a copy of which is held at Beitu 北圖). It took 10 years to cut the 130,000 blocks which were required for the Song *Tripitika*.

Printing until the tenth century was mainly of Buddhist works. From the Song, printing was also used for secular texts such as the *Thirteen Classics* (done in Kaifeng and Chengdu) and the first official printing of the *Shiqishi* 十七史 (*Seventeen Histories*, see 22.1). It took 67 years to collate the Histories and to cut the blocks. The work was done in Sichuan.[16] Woodblock printing continued until the nineteenth century, although various methods of using movable type were invented and experimented with from the Song onward.

Movable type printing (*huozi yinshua* 活字印刷) was invented by Bi Sheng 畢升 in the eleventh century using clay but the invention was only rarely put to use. In the Yuan, movable type using wood was developed by Wang Zhen 王楨 in order

---

[16] Susan Cherniack, "Book Culture and Textual Transmission in Sung China," *HJAS* 54.1: 5–125 (1994).

to print his agricultural treatise, the *Nongshu* 農書 (1313). Eventually, this was printed for him using blocks but he added an appendix on the "Method of movable type printing using wood." It was not until the Ming that this technique became quite common and only in the Qing that it became widespread. The Ming also saw the beginnings of copper movable type.

During the Qing, the authorities printed books on a scale never before seen in China. The Qianlong emperor took a personal interest in movable woodtype printing. It was used for the largest book catalog ever printed in old China, the *Siku quanshu zongmu* 四庫全書總目 (The Imperial Catalog, 1789), on which see 9.5. The main government printing office, the Wuying dian (武英殿), used a specially cut set of movable copper type to print in 1727 the 852,408 pages of the *Gujin tushu jicheng* 古今圖書集成 (Imperial encyclopaedia, see 29.3), but it was not until the end of the nineteenth century that woodblocks and movable wood type were replaced.[17]

---

[17] For a thorough catalog of known woodblock publishers, both official and private, see Yang Shengxin 楊繩信, *Zhongguo banke zonglu* 中國版刻綜錄 (Catalog of Chinese woodblock publishers), Shaanxi renmin, 1983; rpnt., 1987. See also Sören Edgren, "Southern Song Printing at Hangzhou," *BMFEA* 61: 1–212 (1989); Lucille Chia, "The Development of the Jianyang Book Trade, Song-Yuan," *LIC* 17.1: 10–48 (1996); K. T. Wu, "Chinese Printing Under Four Alien Dynasties (916–1368)," *HJAS* 13: 447–523 (1950); Wu Kwang Tsing, "Ming Printing and Printers," *HJAS* 7: 203–60 (1943); Hiromitsu Kobayashi and Samantha Sabin, "The Great Age of Anhui Printing," in *Shadows of Mt. Huang: Chinese Painting and Printing of the Anhui School*, Berkeley: University Art Museum, 1981. There is a detailed account of the printing of the *Tushu jicheng*, see Richard C. Rudolph, *A Chinese Printing Manual, 1776*, Ward Ritchie Press, 1954. See also Shiow-jyu Lu Shaw, *The Imperial Printing of Early Ch'ing China, 1644–1805*, CMC, 1983.

19

Textual Sources

Pre-Qin texts are extremely rare. The most important ones are listed in Table 18 (19.1). The Confucian Classics are briefly introduced (19.2), including how they were classified (19.2.1).

19.1 Main Works and Their Translations

The Pre-Qin transmitted texts are referred to today as "books" with "titles" and in some cases "authors." This is misleading insofar as it implies that they were the deliberate creations of a single person. Whether they began as the sayings of a school of thought, as anthologies of poetry, as collections of documents or as court chronicles, they all had one thing in common: most had no fixed titles and no known authors, they were rather the work of many hands that compiled them over several centuries on the basis of oral traditions during which they were transmitted in different versions with only extremely limited circulation and access (scholars went to texts, not vice versa). Eventually, each was edited into a more definitive form (sometimes in the late Warring States, often during the Former Han). It was only then that they acquired the titles (and "authors") by which they were known in succeeding centuries right up to our own day.

The work of an editor in ancient China was more arduous than that of most editors today. First he had to arrange the bamboo or wooden strips in a coherent order into bundles (18.1). If, as often happened, the threads had perished, he had to reassemble the strips. Sometimes there were missing strips (*tuo-jian* 脱簡), or broken strips, and hence missing characters (*tuozi*

脱字), or a previous editor had put the strips in the wrong order (*cuojian* 錯簡), a common cause of confusion and variant
readings. Sometimes he would be tempted to add material at
the end of a bundle if there were blank strips left, thus creating
a puzzle for future editors. Next he had to assign to each bundle a heading (or, as we would say, a chapter title). This was often chosen from the key characters in the first sentence of the
first strip in each bundle.[1] Finally, the bundles had to be arranged into a coherent order. In the course of his work, the
editor often had to compare various editions usually with the
aim of producing a single reliable text, but in some cases recognizing the validity of several versions of a single work. Another
task was to chose the title from one of several available alternatives or to invent one and, in some cases, to attribute an
author.[2] One thing he did not have to do was to correct the
punctuation, since there was none (1.3.4).

During the Former Han, much of the editorial work was
handled by the court archivists, historians or librarians, who
on three occasions were charged with gathering together books
from all over the empire and putting into order the imperial
collection.[3] This was a formidable task after the depredations of
the Qin and it was one which came to be surrounded with the
greatest academic controversy in Chinese history (that between
the Old and the New Text traditions, see 19.2).

One of the first ancient works which appears to have been
conceived from start to finish as a complete "book" is credited
to Lü Buwei 呂不韋 (d. 235 BC), the *Lüshi chunqiu* 呂氏春秋
(see Table 18). It is an anthology of excerpts on many subjects

---

[1] For example, Chapter 1 of the *Lunyu* is entitled *Xue'er* 學而 after
the opening characters of the first sentence, 子曰, 學而時習之.
[2] For a good overview of pre-Qin books, see "The Problem of
Authorship" and "The Nature of the Work," in *Laozi* 老子 (*Chinese Classics, Tao Te Ching*, D. C. Lau, tr., HKCU Press, 1963; 1982, 2nd ed., 1989,
1996), Appendix I and II. In later Chinese history, many works continued to have alternative titles, but for different reasons (7.3).
[3] The three occasions were at the beginning of the dynasty in about
200 BC, in 124 BC and again in 26 BC.

apparently written by several scholars employed by Lü (who served at the end of his life as Chancellor of Qin). Subsequent Chinese history was to see not only an enormous number of such encyclopaedic compilations, but also books whose authorship was credited to senior officials, emperors or famous scholars, although their contribution to the actual writing may have been nil (a practice which is not unknown to this day). By the Han, the practice of a single author or compiler planning a book before beginning to compose it was becoming the norm for the first time. But even so, one of China's most famous books, whose authorship has never been in doubt, had no fixed title. Sima Qian may have indicated a title in his Postface (*Shiji*, *juan* 130), but it was only two centuries after his death that his work came to be known by the generic term *Shiji* (Historical record; see 44.1).

It follows from this that pre-Qin texts should be handled with extreme caution, with regard to both the text itself and its interpretation. For a start, it is vital to establish as far as possible which parts of it were written when and by whom (or by what school).

Some are nearly contemporaneous with the period they describe. Many contain materials written at different times, sometimes stretching over several centuries. Some were written later about an earlier period. Some were written as historical works (mainly court annals) or as compilations of official documents, others are classified as literature or philosophy, but contain material of interest to historians. It is not unlikely that the list of pre-Qin texts will grow longer as archaeology continues to turn up excavated texts (*chutu wenxian* 出土文獻) of transmitted works (*chuanshi wenxian* 傳世文獻), but also hitherto unknown works.[4] Problems of dates in pre-Qin texts are discussed in 16.3 and 19.2.

Ever since the Han, textual criticism as applied to the classical canon (broadly the pre-Qin and principal Han texts) has

---

[4] For example, those works found in Baoshan 包山, tomb 2 or Shuihudi 睡虎地, tomb 11 (see 18.1.1–18.1.3).

been one of the main activities and achievements of Chinese scholarship. After the collapse of the Chinese empire, modern scholars have continued the work in a more skeptical spirit and with the added advantage in some cases of being able to compare the transmitted texts with newly discovered Han and Warring States manuscripts on bamboo and silk. The result of all these efforts is that most of the early texts are now available in critical, annotated editions, although some of the old controversies have still not been resolved. Given the above, it is hardly surprising that few, if any, translations of pre-Qin works can be regarded as definitive although some have been translated hundreds of times.[5]

The best scholarly introduction to this philological minefield is *ECTBG*.[6] It contains short articles by different specialists on 64 of the main textual sources of the pre-Qin (and Han). The authors outline the content; date of composition and authenticity; text history and editions; translations; studies; Japanese editions; research aids; and indexes.

If you want to look something up in the main pre-Qin and Han sources, the most convenient way is to use the Institute of Chinese Studies, *ICS Ancient Chinese Texts Concordance Series*. This contains the full texts with punctuation added as well as character frequency counts and indexes by *pinyin* and strokecount. The *ICS* series is available not only in book form and disc, but also on a single CD-ROM, making it a most convenient and authoritative research tool (for more on the *ICS* concordances as well as other indexes, see 9.10).

For overall introductions to the main thinkers and schools of thought as reflected in the pre-Qin and Han texts, start with *CHAC*, or with A. C. Graham, *Disputers of the Tao*, Open

[5] For an instructive comparison of nine translations of one of the Confucian Classics into Western languages, see David S. Nivison, "On Translating Mencius," in *The Ways of Confucianism*, Open Court, 1996, 175–201. He comes down in favor of the Lau translation (Table 18).

[6] *Early Chinese Texts: A Bibliographical Guide*, Michael Loewe, ed., *Early China* Special Monograph Series, SSEC and IEAS, 1993. Liaoning jiaoyu published a Chinese translation in 1997.

Court, 1989, or with Kung-chuan Hsiao, *A History of Chinese Political Thought*.[7]

All the main pre-Qin and Han historical works are included in Table 18, but not all the philosophical works (for which, see also 19.2 and chap. 32).

Table 18: Main Textual Sources for Pre-Qin History

Note: A plus ("+") indicates the period(s) in which a work was written. An arrow ("⇦") indicates a work was written later about an earlier period. ICS refers to the number of the concordance in the *ICS Ancient Chinese Texts Concordance Series* (9.10).

Col. 1: 西周 (Western Zhou)
Col. 2: 春秋 (Spring and Autumn)
Col. 3: 戰國 (Warring States)
Col. 4: 漢代 (Han)

Title of book (*Translation*), translator, publisher	周	春	戰	漢	ICS
Shangshu 尚書 (*Book of Documents*), Bernhard Karlgren, Elanders, 1950; and by the same author, *Glosses on the Book of Documents*, Elanders, 1970; first issued in *BMFEA*, 20: 39–315 (1948) and 21: 63–206 (1949). See Shaughnessy in *ECTBG*, 376–89.	+	+	+	⇦	28
[*Yi*] *Zhoushu* [逸] 周書 ([Non-canonical] *Zhoushu*); originally entitled *Zhoushiji*, also called *Jizhong Zhoushu* 汲冢周書 (Ji tomb *Zhoushu*). Compilation of recorded comments and documents similar to those in the *Shangshu* dating from different periods. See Shaughnessy in *ECTBG*, 229–33.	+	+	+	⇦	12

Table continues

---

[7] David Shepherd Nivison, "The Classical Philosophical Writings," *CHAC*, 745–812; Donald Harper, "Warring States Natural Philosophy and Occult Thought," *CHAC*, 813–885; Kung-chuan Hsiao, *A History of Chinese Political Thought, Volume 1: From the Beginnings to the Sixth Century A.D*, F. W. Mote, tr., PUP, 1979 (from the original, 1945–46).

Table 18—Continued

Title of book (*Translation*), translator, publisher	周	春	戰	漢	ICS
Yijing 易經 (*The Classic of Changes: A New Translation of the I Ching as Interpreted by Wang Bi*), tr. by Richard John Lynn, Col. UP, 1994 (also available on CD-ROM); *I Ching, The Classic of Changes: The First English Translation of the Newly Discovered Second-Century B.C. Mawangdui Texts*, Edward L. Shaughnessy, Ballantine, 1996. See Shaughnessy in *ECTBG*, 216–28.	+				27
Shijing 詩經 (*Book of Odes [Songs]: Chinese Text, Transcription and Translation*), Bernhard Karlgren, *BMFEA*, 14, 16 and 18 (1942, 1944 and 1946); issued as a book, MFEA, 1950. See Loewe in *ECTBG*, 415–23.	+	+	+		29
Chunqiu 春秋 (*Spring and Autumn Annals*; *The Chinese Classics, The Ch'un Ts'ew with The Tso Chuen*), James Legge (1815–97), vol. 4, Parts 1 and 2, OUP, 1893–4; Göran Malmqvist, "Studies on the *Gongyang* and *Guuliang* commentaries," *BMFEA* 43: 67–222 (1971); 47: 19–69 (1975); 49: 33–215 (1977); see also section 21.1.	+	+	+ ⇐		30–32
Zhanguoce 戰國策 (*Chan-kuo-ts'e*), Liu Xiang 劉向, comp.; J. I. Crump, tr., Oxford: Clarendon Press, 1970; rev. with index, CCS, Univ. of Michigan, 1996; 3 vols.; Shanghai guji, 1978, also contains transcription of Mawangdui version. See Tsuen-hsuin Tsien in *ECTBG*, 1–11.				+	1
Lunyu 論語 (*Confucius, the Analects [Lun-yü]*), D. C. Lau, HKCU Press, 1979; 3rd rpnt., 1992. Bilingual text. *The Original Analects: Sayings of Confucius and His Successors*, E. Bruce Brooks and A. Taeko Brooks, Col. UP, 1997, attempts to show the text gradually taking shape during the centuries after the death of Confucius (551–479 BC). The *Analects* reached their definitive form in the first century AD. See Cheng in *ECTBG*, 313–23.				+	33

Table continues

Table 18—Continued

Title of book (*Translation*), translator, publisher	周	春	戰	漢	ICS
Mengzi 孟子 (*Meng tzu*), D. C. Lau, 2 vols., HKCU Press, 1979; 1984. Bilingual text. See Lau in *ECTBG*, 331–36.			+ ⇦		34
Mozi 墨子 (*The ethical and political works of Mo Tzu*), Yipao Mei, Probsthain, 1929; rpnt., Hyperion Press, 1973, tr. of chaps. 1–39 and 46–50. See Graham in *ECTBG*, 336–41.			+		54
Shangjunshu 商君書 (*Le livre du prince Shang*), Jean Levi, Flammarion, 1981. See Levi in *ECTBG*, 368–75.			+		3
Han Feizi 韓非子 (*The complete works of Han Fei Tzu*), W. K. Liao, vol. 1, Probsthain, 1939; rpnt., 1959; vol. 2, 1959. See Levi in *ECTBG*, 115–24.			+		56
Guanzi 管子 (*Guanzi*), W. Allyn Rickett, vol. 1, PUP, 1985 (tr. of chaps. I.1–XI.34); vol. 2, 1998. See Rickett in *ECTBG*, 244–51.			+		55
Laozi 老子 (*Chinese Classics, Tao Te Ching*), D. C. Lau, HKCU Press, 1963, 1982, 2nd ed., 1989; 1996. Bilingual text. Part I (tr. of Wang Bi text); Part II (tr. of Mawangdui texts). See Boltz in *ECTBG*, 269–92.			+		43
Zhuangzi 莊子 (*The Complete Works of Chuang-tzu*), putative author: Zhuangzi, ca. 370–301 BC; Burton Watson, Col. UP, 1968; 1996; A. C. Graham, *Chuang-tzu: The Inner Chapters*, Allen and Unwin, 1981. See Roth in *ECTBG*, 56–66.			+		57
Bingshu 兵書 (Military manuals): *Sun-tzu: The Art of Warfare: The First English Translation Incorporating the Yin-ch'üeh-shan Texts*, Roger T. Ames, Ballantine, 1993; see below under "Excavated texts" and also section 28.2.			+		11

Table continues

Table 18—Continued

Title of book (*Translation*), translator, publisher	周	春	戰	漢	ICS
Guoyu 國語 (Discourses of the states), records discourses from eight of the Warring States, authorship traditionally attributed to Zuo Qiuming 左丘明 (or Zuoqiu Ming, 5th c.), but more likely by several hands, possibly edited by Zuo. Regarded as a *waizhuan* 外傳 (informal commentary) on the *Chunqiu*. See Chang et al., in *ECTBG*, 263–268.				+ ⇦	53
Zhushu jinian 竹書紀年 (*Bamboo Annals*), in *The Chinese Classics*, James Legge, vol. 3, OUP, 1865, *Prolegomena*, chap. 4, 108–76. Edward L. Shaughnessy, "On the Authenticity of the *Bamboo Annals*," *HJAS* 46.1: 149–80 (1986). See also Nivison in *ECTBG*, 39–47.				+ ⇦	48
Shiben 世本 (Basics of hereditary lines), Liu Xiang 劉向; archive of Warring States descent lines; see *Shiben bazhong* 世本八種, Shangwu, 1957 3.5).				+ ⇦	47
Yili 儀禮 (*The I li, or Book of Etiquette and Ceremonial*), John Steele, 2 vols., Probsthain, 1917; Taibei rpnt., 1972. For a recently discovered *jiandu* version, see 46.3, item 7. See Boltz in *ECTBG*, 234–43.				+ ⇦	24
Zhouli 周禮 (*Institutes of Zhou*); *Le Tcheou-li ou Rites des Tcheou*, Edouard Biot, Imprimerie Nationale, 3 vols., 1851; rpnt., Chengwen, 1975. See Boltz in *ECTBG*, 24–32.				+ ⇦	13
Liji 禮記 (*Li Ki*), James Legge, in *Sacred Books of the East*, Max Müller, ed., vols., xxvii–xxviii, OUP, 1879–91, rpnt., 1926; 1967. See Riegel in *ECTBG*, 293–7.				+ ⇦	2
Chuci 楚辭 (*The Songs of the South: An Anthology of Ancient Chinese Poems by Qu Yuan* [屈原] *and Other Poets*), David Hawkes, Penguin, 1959; rev., 1985. See Hawkes in *ECTBG*, 48–55.				+ ⇦	59

Table continues

Table 18—Continued

Title of book (*Translation*), translator, publisher	周	春	戰	漢	ICS
Mu tianzi zhuan 穆天子傳 (*Le Mu Tianzi zhuan: traduction annotée: étude critique*), Rémi Mathieu, Collège de France, 1978. See the same scholar's contribution in *ECTBG*, 342–6.[8]			+	⇦	22
Shanhai jing 山海經 (*Étude sur la mythologie et l'ethnologie de la Chine ancienne*), Rémi Mathieu, vol. I *Traduction annotée*, vol. II *Index*, Collège de France, 1983. See Fracasso in *ECTBG*, 357–67.			+	⇦	22
Xunzi 荀子 (*Xunzi: A Translation and Study of the Complete Works*), John Knoblock, 3 vols., SUP, 1988–94. See Loewe in *ECTBG*, 178–88.			+	⇦	45
Lüshi chunqiu 呂氏春秋, ca. 239 BC (*Frühling und Herbst des Lü Bu We*), Richard Wilhelm (1873–1930), Diederichs, 1928; rpnt., 1971. See Carson and Loewe in *ECTBG*, 324–30.			+	⇦	23
Yanzi chunqiu 晏子春秋 (Spring and Autumn of Yan Ying). See Durrant in *ECTBG*, 483–9.			+	⇦	15
Excavated pre-Qin texts: a number have been unearthed from Warring States and Han tombs, notably the *Yili*, *Shijing*, *Yijing*, *Sun Bin* and *Sunzi bingfa*; see 18.2. and Boltz in *NSECH*.			+		
A number of Warring States maps have been unearthed; see 4.4.			+		
A number of Warring States and Qin legal works have been unearthed; see 18.1.3 and 27.2.			+		
For pre-Qin medical works, see chap. 36.			+		

Table continues

[8] See also Cheng Te-k'un, "The Travels of Emperor Mu," *JNCBRAS* 2nd series 64: 124–42 (1933); 65: 128–49 (1934); Deborah Lynn Porter, *From Deluge to Discourse: Myth, History, and the Generation of Chinese Fiction*, SUNY Press, 1996.

Table 18—Continued

Title of book (*Translation*), translator, publisher	周	春	戰	漢	ICS
A number of pre-Qin almanacs have been unearthed; see 18.1, 18.2 and 5.1.			+		
A pre-Qin mathematical text (*Suanshu shu* 算術書) has recently been unearthed (44.3.2.2).			+		
Jiuzhang suanshu 九章算術 (Nine chapters on the mathematical arts). See Cullen in *ECTBG*, 16–23.[9]				+ ⇐	62
Zhoubi suanjing 周髀算經 (The Zhou gnomon), tr. in Christopher Cullen, *Astronomy and Mathematics in Ancient China: The* Zhoubi Suanjing, CUP, 1996. See Cullen in *ECTBG*, 33–8				+ ⇐	62
Chunqiu fanlu 春秋繁露, credited to Dong Zhongshu 董仲舒 (?179–?104 BC), see Sarah A. Queen, *From Chronical to Canon: Luxuriant Gems of the Spring and Autumn*, CUP, 1996, also Davidson and Loewe in *ECTBG*, 77–87				+ ⇐	21
Lunheng 論衡, Wang Chong 王充 (AD 27–ca. 100): *Lun Heng*, Alfred Forke, 2 vols., Kelly and Walsh, 1907 and 1911; Paragon rpnt., 1962, see Pokora and Loewe in *ECTBG*, 309–312.				+ ⇐	41[10]
Huainanzi 淮南子: John S. Major, *Heaven and Earth in Early Han Thought*, chaps. 3–5 of the *Huainanzi*, SUNY Press, 1993; Harold D. Roth, *The Textual History of the Huai-nan Tzu*, MUP, 1992. See Le Blanc in *ECTBG*, 189–95.				+ ⇐	9

Table continues

[9] See Song Jie 宋杰, *Jiuzhang suanshu yu Handai shehui jingji* 九章算術與漢代社會經濟 (The *Jiuzhang suanshu* and the social economy of the Han), Shoudu shifan daxue, 1994.

[10] *Lunheng suoyin* 論衡索引, Cheng Xiangqing 程湘清 et al., comps., Zhonghua, 1994. A complete concordance with *pinyin*, stroke-count, classifier and four-corner indexes. Arrangement is by *pinyin*. The text is printed at the end.

Table 18—Continued

Title of book (*Translation*), translator, publisher	周	春	戰	漢	ICS
Fengsu tongyi 風俗通義, Ying Shao 應劭 (ca. 140– ca. 240): observations of Later Han cults and beliefs, see Nylan in *ECTBG*, 105–12.				+ ⇦	42
Shuowen jiezi 説文解字 (Explanation of single component graphs and analysis of composite characters), Xu Shen 許慎, see 2.2.1 and 16.2.				+ ⇦	63
Chu-Han Chunqiu 楚漢春秋, Lu Jia 陸賈 (ca. 240– 170), a high official of Liu Bang who recorded in chronicle form the rise to power of Xiang Yu 項羽 and Liu Bang 劉邦 and the reigns of Huidi 惠帝 and Wendi 文帝. One of the sources used by Sima Qian 司馬遷. Exists today only in a "recovered edition" (*jiben* 輯本).				+	
Shiji 史記 (*Records of the Grand Historian*); see 44.1.				+ ⇦	DB[11]
Hanshu 漢書 (History of the Former Han); see 44.1.				+ ⇦	DB[11]
Yuejue shu 越絕書 (Yue's destruction of Wu). Compiled in later Han. See Schuessler and Loewe in *ECTBG*, 490–93.				+ ⇦	17
Wu-Yue chunqiu 吳越春秋 (The Annals of Wu and Yue). Compiled in later Han by various hands. See Lagerwey in *ECTBG*, 473–6				+ ⇦	16

[11] The numerous indexes to the *Shiji* and the *Hanshu* are listed in 44.1. Both are also available on computer database: *Nianwushi quanwen ziliaoku* 廿五史全文資料庫 (25 Histories full text database), Shiyusuo, 1988. See 22.1 for further details.

19.2   *The Confucian Classics*

Four hundred years after the death of Confucius, the Han emperor Wudi 漢武帝 (140–88 BC) adopted the policy of *Bachu bojia duzun rushu* 罷黜百家獨尊儒術 (ban the hundred schools, only recognize the Confucians). The Confucian works were made state doctrine and their mastery, the entry to officialdom. The *Five Classics* (*Wujing* 五經) selected were the six mentioned by Confucius (minus the *Yue* 樂, *Book of Music*, which had been lost when the first emperor of Qin ordered the burning of the books). They were known for short as the *Shi* 詩 (*Odes*); the *Shu* 書 (*Documents*); the *Li* 禮 (*Rites*); the *Yi* 易 (*Book of Changes*); and the *Chunqiu* 春秋 (*Spring and Autumn Annals*).

In the Eastern Han, the *Xiaojing* 孝經 (*Classic of Filial Piety*) and the *Lunyu* 論語 (*Analects*) were added to make the *Seven Classics*. During the Tang, the number eventually rose to 12 (the *Li* and the *Chunqiu* were each split into three constituent parts and the *Erya* 爾雅 was added). These were the *Twelve Classics* inscribed on stelae and placed in the Imperial Academy in Chang'an (modern Xi'an); where they remain to this day. In the Song dynasty, the *Mengzi* 孟子 was added to make the *Shisanjing* 十三經 (*Thirteen Classics*).

The term *Sishu* 四書 (*Four Books*) dates from the Song, when Zhu Xi 朱熹 in 1190 edited in one book four of texts chosen from the Confucian Classics.[12] Thereafter, every Chinese examination candidate, if not schoolchild, had to remember them by heart (the *Four Books* were *Daxue* 大學, *Zhongyong* 中庸, *Lunyu* 論語 and *Mengzi* 孟子). The *Daxue* and *Zhongyong* are both short chapters of the *Liji*. The subject matter and brevity of the *Xiaojing* 孝經 (*Classic of Filial Piety*) made it the ideal basic textbook for children, not only in China, but also in Korea, Japan and Vietnam.

---

[12] On Zhu Xi's choice, see Daniel B. Gardner, "Principle and Pedagogy: Chu Hsi and the Four Books," *HJAS* 44.1: 57–81 (1984).

Table 19: The Thirteen Classics

1. *Yijing* or *Zhouyi* 易經, 周易 (*Book of Changes*); 24,000	*ICS* 27
2. *Shujing* or *Shangshu* 書經, 尚書 (*Documents*); 25,700	*ICS* 28
3. *Shijing* 詩經 (*Odes*); 39,200	*ICS* 29
4. *Zhouli* 周禮 (*Institutes of Zhou*); 45,800	*ICS* 13
5. *Yili* 儀禮 (*Book of Ceremonial*); 57,800	*ICS* 24
6. *Liji* 禮記 (*Rites*); 99,000	*ICS* 2
7. *Chunqiu Zuozhuan* 春秋左傳 (*Spring and Autumn Annals,* *Commentary of Zuo*); 178,000[13]	*ICS* 30
8. *Chunqiu Gongyangzhuan* 公羊傳 (*Commentary of Gongyang*)	*ICS* 31
9. *Chunqiu Guliang zhuan* 穀梁傳 (*Commentary of Guliang*)	*ICS* 32
10. *Lunyu* 論語 (*Analects*); 12,000	*ICS* 33
11. *Xiaojing* 孝經 (*Classic of Filial Piety*); 1,799	*ICS* 35
12. *Erya* 爾雅 (*Erya*); 10,900	*ICS* 35
13. *Mengzi* 孟子 (*Mencius*); 34,000	*ICS* 34

Note: the figures after each Classic refer to the total number of characters it contains; *ICS* numbers refer to the *ICS* concordances (9.10).

Many of the Classics had alternative titles for the reasons explained at the beginning of this chapter. For example, the original title of the *Zhouli* 周禮 was *Zhouguan* 周官. It was later known as the *Zhouguan jing* 周官經. It gained its present title only in the Eastern Han. The *Shangshu* 尚書 was originally called the *Shu* 書 and also *Shujing* 書經, which is still often used.[14]

The word *jing* 經 was added to titles only in the Former Han when the Confucian Classics were first made official. Later it was also used in a Buddhist context for "sutra." The first meaning of the word was silk warp. Later it was used in the extended sense of basic or long-lasting and of books it meant those which have high and permanent authority, as in the *Laozi* 老子 (*Daodejing* 道德經) or the *Shanhaijing* (山海經, Classic of mountains and seas).

---

[13] The *Chunqiujing* itself has 16,771 characters; the *Gongyang* and *Guliang* have 27,590 and 23,293 respectively.

[14] John B. Henderson, *Scripture, Canon, Commentary: A Comparison of Confucian and Western Exegesis*, PUP, 1991.

After the "burning of the books" by the first emperor in 213 BC and the destruction of the copies kept in the Qin academy in 207, many attempts were made to restore the pre-Qin Classics (only the Qin historical records and works on medicine, divination, agriculture, and forestry had been exempted). The two main rival schools in the Han were based on the Old and the New Text traditions (*guwen* 古文 and *jinwen* 今文). *Guwen* in this context referred to the discoveries in the Han of Classics written in Warring States seal script contrasted with the versions of them written in the contemporary Han chancery script (in this context, *jinwen*); see 16.1 on the different scripts, and 18.1 on the discoveries of the *guwen* texts. The controversy was revived again in the Qing.

The texts of the *Thirteen Classics* are for the most part very short; altogether they contain only 366,299 characters. If the three commentaries on the *Chunqiu* are included, the total comes to 589,283, which is only slightly longer than the *Shiji* (530,000) or 1.5 percent the length of the Standard Histories. Nevertheless, just to write 589,283 characters would have taken 9,821 strips (assuming 60 characters per strip). This would have made 300–500 bundles. Small wonder that the emphasis was on memorization: until the age of paper, manuscripts could only circulate with difficulty.

By the eighteenth century a huge body of commentary had accumulated amounting to more than 100 times the length of the *Thirteen Classics* themselves.[15] The earliest commentaries, for example, the *Zuozhuan* 左傳, had a tendency to become part of the classical canon. From the later Han, the terms *zhu* 注 or *jian* 箋 were used for commentary (along with other expressions such as *gu* 詁 or *zhuan* 傳). From the Tang, commentaries on the Classics, or on the Han commentaries, were termed *shu* 疏 (subcommentary). Large numbers of collected commentaries were also published (*jizhu* 集注, *jijie* 集解, *jishi* 集釋,

---

[15] The *Siku quanshu zongmu* lists 3,900 works in the Classics branch (*jingbu* 經部, see 19.2.1) in more than 50,000 *juan*. The Classics themselves contain 416 *juan*.

jiyi 集義). In Han and pre-Han works, the texts and commentaries circulated separately. From the Later Han commentaries began to be incorporated as interlinear notes, and from the Song, subcommentaries too were incorporated (hence the new expression *zhushu* 注疏).

19.2.1   Classification of the Classics

The Classics branch (*jingbu* 經部) ranked first in the traditional Chinese bibliographic classification (9.3). By the eighteenth century, it comprised 10 subbranches:

1. *Yi* 易 (*Book of Changes*).
2. *Shu* 書 (*Documents*).
3. *Shi* 詩 (*Odes*).
4. *Li* 禮 (*Rites*).
5. *Chunqiu* 春秋 (*Spring and Autumn Annals*).
6. *Xiao* 孝經 (*Classic of Filial Piety*).
7. *Wujing zongyi* 五經總義 (*Commentaries on the Five Classics*).
8. *Sishu* 四書 (*Four Books*).
9. *Yue* 樂 (*Music*).
10. *Xiaoxue* 小學 (The study of the characters).

Different editions are available for each of the Confucian Classics. They have also been printed and edited together as the *Shisanjing* 十三經 many times and with many of the commentaries and subcommentaries added by scholars down the ages.[16] There are plenty of modern editions which give the original text (often with the scholarly annotations of the modern editors). There are also numerous translations into modern Chinese. If you use one of these, make sure to choose one which gives the original text in full characters, not in their simplified

[16] One of the most popular editions of the *Shisanjing* published together with commentaries and sub-commentaries was *Shisanjing zhushu* 十三經注疏, Ruan Yuan 阮元, ed., 1815; Kaiming (with index), 1934; Zhonghua, 2 vols., with corrections, 1957; 4th prnt., 1980; separate index: *Shisanjing zhushu suoyin* 十三經注疏索引, Zhonghua, 1983; 5th prnt., 1996.

form. Texts of all the Classics are printed together with their concordances in the *ICS* series.

19.2.2   Dictionaries of Individual Works

In addition to the specialized dictionaries for ancient Chinese scripts *guwenzi* (chaps. 15 to 17) and the dictionaries of Classical Chinese discussed in chap. 2, note the sometimes useful dictionaries of a particular work of the classical period which are intended for readers who are not specialists, and are therefore useful for beginners.

Shijing cidian 詩經詞典 (Dictionary of the *Shijing*), Xiang Xi 向熹, comp., Sichuan renmin, 1986; Introduction by Wang Li 王力; 2nd ed., rev. and enlarged, 1997. Arrangement is by *pinyin*. All 2,826 individual characters in the *Shijing* as well as 510 alternative characters and almost 1,000 compounds are defined. More than 305 *Shijing* authorities from ancient times to the present are quoted in the definitions. An appendix contains the text of the odes with Old, Middle and Mandarin rhymes indicated. See also W. A. C. H. Dobson, *The Language of the Book of Songs*, University of Toronto Press, 1968.

Shikei kenkyû bunken mokuroku 詩經研究文獻目錄 (Index to scholarship on the *Shijing*), Matsuyama Yoshihiro 村山吉廣 and Eguchi Masayoshi 江口尚純, eds., Kyûko, 1992. Covers scholarship in Chinese written 1900–90 and in Japanese, 1868–90.

Chunqiu Zuozhuan cidian 春秋左傳詞典 (A dictionary of phrases in the *Spring and Autumn Annals* and *Zuozhuan*), Yang Bojun 楊伯峻 and Xu Ti 徐提, eds., Zhonghua, 1985.

Xian-Qin yaoji cidian 先秦要籍辭典 (Dictionary of some important pre-Qin sources), Wang Shishun 王世舜, ed. in chief, Xueyuan, 1997. Dictionary in three parts of the language of the *Liezi* 列子, *Shangjunshu* 商君書 and *Chunqiu Gongyangzhuan* 春秋公羊傳. Altogether 8,207 terms are defined.

Lao-Zhuang cidian 老莊辭典 (Dictionary of *Laozi* and *Zhuangzi*), Dong Zhi'an 董治安, ed. in chief, Shandong Jiaoyu, 1993; rpnt., 1995. Gives brief definitions for the characters in the *Laozi* and *Zhuangzi* separately, and also indicates how many times each character or phrase is used.

III

Historical Genres

20

Primary and Secondary Sources

In a country such as China with a long tradition of historical writing and compilation the distinction between a primary and a secondary source is not an easy one to make. Various archives have survived from the Qing (20.2), and more have been discovered this century, but "original" documents up to the Qing are typically preserved in whole or in part in compiled sources (Box 7). In general, the earlier the period, the fewer sources to have survived (20.1). Far fewer private documents survive than official ones (20.3). Not all Chinese historical writing was done by officials. There was also a strong tradition of private historical writing (20.5).

Part III deals with eleven of the fifteen categories listed in the History branch in the *Sibu* classification (Table 12, 9.3). The other four categories are covered in Part I: biographical writing (chap. 3); regulation of time (chaps. 5 and 6); geography (chap. 4) and bibliography (chap. 8). Part III also deals with two types of historical source classified by the *Siku* editors in the Philosophers' branch (Table 13, 9.3), namely military experts (chap. 28) and legal writers (chap. 27, also in chaps. 19 and 32).

20.1 Introduction

The earlier the period, the fewer the primary sources from the bottom of the pile listed in Box 6. In other words, more survives from each succeeding dynasty than from its predecessor: there are more primary sources from the Han than from the pre-Qin; more from the Tang than from the *Nan-Bei Chao*; more from the Song than from the Tang; and far more from the Ming than from the Song. By the time of the Qing, more survives than from all previous periods put together. Some notable exceptions to this rule are the archaeological or paleographic discoveries from earlier periods not matched later on, but these remain exceptions.

After the Qin and even more so after the Han, traditional historical sources become more plentiful, but for the most part they survive only in excerpted or condensed form (Box 7).

Thus the earlier Standard Histories down to the Tang are based on materials which have long since been lost, and as a result they are vital sources for the period. The reverse holds true for the post-Song Standard Histories, because many of the sources upon which they were based are still extant. This is even more true by the Ming and the Qing, for which periods sources such as the Court Diaries or the Veritable Records, not

---

Box 6: The Sources for Chinese History (Han to Qing)
Standard Histories
National Histories
Veritable Records
Court Diaries, Records of Current Government, Daily Calendars
Collections of important documents, statutes, laws and encyclopae-
dic compilations of primary materials
Edicts, memorials and other documents of the central government
Local official records (land and household registers, routine reports),
Local gazetteers, occasional finds from local archives
Nonofficial historical writings and inscriptions
Individual literary writings, family and business documents
Archaeological artifacts

to speak of over 6,000 local gazetteers, and historical, documentary, genealogical and literary sources of all kinds, have survived in enormous quantities (chaps. 49 and 50).

Box 7: Documents Preserved in Compilations

The earliest compilation of what purport to be selected historical documents is the *Shangshu* 尚書, the Book of Documents, one of the *Thirteen Classics*, parts of which were written in the Western Zhou (chap. 19). From that time to this day large numbers of compilations were made of every conceivable subject: of edicts and memorials; of laws and regulations, of bureaus and organs of central, provincial and local governments; of poetry and verse, of genres and styles; of people and places. Many of the most important of these are referred in the appropriate sections throughout the present manual.

A convenient, annotated inventory has been compiled of compilations containing archival materials and excerpts including modern publications (both books and journal articles) of archive documents and of materials extracted from them: *Zhongguo dang'an wenxian cidian* 中國檔案文獻辭典 (Dictionary of archival literature), Zhu Jinfu 朱金甫, ed. in chief, Zhongguo renshi, 1994. It contains annotations on 3,985 such compilations and publications from the pre-Qin to 1990. There are about 1,200 entries from the pre-Qin to the end of the Qing. The notes give a clear account of the contents and editions and the circumstances of compilation as well as basic biographic information on the premodern compilers. Arrangement is chronological by period and there is also a stroke-count index of titles. There is no compiler's name index.

To give an idea of the coverage in this useful work, and of the huge increase in availability of original documents from the Qing as opposed to earlier periods, there are entries on only 55 collections from the 320 years of the Song (including the main collected works of individual authors and statesmen containing documents such as edicts and memorials) as compared with 75 published collections of documents from the 13 years of the Yongzheng reign, including contemporary eighteenth-century collections, later Qing collections and modern publications from the central and local archives.

20.2 *Archives*

Governments in China have kept archives ever since they began to use writing. The earliest court documents to have survived are the Shang oracle-bone inscriptions. During the Spring and Autumn period, interstate treaties were kept in special archives called *mengfu* 盟府. Books and other documents were kept in *cefu* 册府 (*cefu* 策府). The practice continued in the Warring States period. We know that the different kingdoms kept archives containing maps of their territories, population registers and records of their ruling houses, treaties and other documents. Some of these archives were deliberately destroyed (as recommended by Mencius) to prevent their falling into enemy hands. Many more were destroyed by order of the first Qin emperor. The Qin imperial library itself and the Qin academy (which preserved unique copies of the burned books) were razed to the ground by Xiang Yu 項羽 (233–202 BC) when he captured the capital, Xianyang 咸陽, in 207. The *tuji* 圖籍 (military maps and population registers) in the Qin chancellor's archive however, were captured by Xiao He 蕭何 (d. 196 BC), who moved them to archives which he had especially constructed on the grounds of the Weiyang palace. For security against fire and thieves, water from a nearby canal was diverted to flow under and around one of the buildings, hence its name, the Shiquge 石渠閣 (Stone canal pavilion). This eventually housed not only the main Han central archive, but also part of the Han imperial library. Two hundred years later, the archive was deliberately destroyed during the fighting at the end of the Former Han. The site of the Weiyang palace, including the Shiquge, was excavated in the 1980s and can be visited today.[1]

---

[1] The site of the Shiquge (and of the Tianluge 天祿閣 and Qilinge 麒麟閣, the other two archives cum libraries built by Xiao He) are in the protected grounds of the Han capital about 2.5 km northwest of modern Xi'an. All that remains of the three are parts of their *terre pisé* (*hangtu* 夯土) foundations. A primary school exists on the site of the Tianluge. For a photograph of the Shiquge site, see *Han Chang'an cheng Weiyang-gong fajue baogao* 漢長安城未央宮發掘報告 (Excavation report: The Ever-

Footnote continued on next page

With the introduction of a civil service recruited by examination in the Sui and Tang, the government began keeping extensive personnel archives. The widespread use of paper from the Tang and printing from the Song led to the proliferation of archives. From the Song the most common classification system for documents was to arrange them chronologically divided into eight categories. Part of the series number for each document was also based on a character taken in order from the *Qianziwen* 千字文. This continued to be the most common system until the early Republic.[2]

By the Han an elaborate tradition of governmental compilation and history writing based on the archives had developed. As time went by this was continuously expanded. It is the compendia and books produced in this tradition which have survived in astonishing numbers from early imperial China, not usually the original archives. Considerable quantities of original documents have however survived from local archives (see Table 20 below).

The very efficiency with which the official historians produced excerpts, compilations and historical works based on the original documents led to an attitude after the Song that attached more value to the printed book than to the original manuscript documents. Another important reason why more manuscripts have not survived is that until the twentieth century it was cheaper to copy books by hand than to print them, so printed books, not manuscripts, were collector's items. In addition, it was expensive to keep documents in good condition. Special buildings had to be constructed and their contents regularly aired. From the Tang, government documents

---

lasting Palace of Han Chang'an), Kaogu yanjiusuo, eds., 2 vols., Zhongguo da baike quanshu chubanshe, 1996, vol. 2, plate VI. 2. One decorated, circular tile-end from the Shiquge survives. It bears the inscription *Shiqu qianqiu* 石渠千秋 (The stone moat pavilion lasts for ever).

[2] The eight categories were named after the first eight characters of the *Qianziwen*: *tian* 天, *di* 地, *yuan* 元 (or *xuan* 玄), *huang* 黄, *yu* 宇, *zhou* 宙, *hong* 洪, *huang* 荒. The inventor of the system was the Northern Song official Zhou Zhan 周湛.

were divided between those which were for long storage (*chang-liu* 常留) and those which could be destroyed after three years. Archives and libraries were constantly burning down by accident and at times of warfare as during the previous centuries they continued to be deliberately destroyed (the imperial collections went up in flames on at least a dozen occasions in the course of Chinese history). Quite apart from the depredations of fire and war, storage space had to be found for the new documents that the bureaucracy continuously produced. So, once the summaries or histories were written, even long-storage documents became superfluous and were often destroyed. For all these reasons, it is hardly surprising that in imperial China's 2,200 years of record keeping, with the outstanding exception of a part of the Qing central archives, only very few archives, either at the center or in the provinces, have survived. They did so by accident and were only opened or discovered in this century. So exceptional have these discoveries been that in many cases they have led to specialized fields of study, for example, *Jiaguxue* 甲骨學 (chap. 15); *Jianduxue* 簡牘學 (or *Hanjianxue* 漢簡學, 18.1 and 44.3); *Dunhuangxue* 敦煌學 (46.3); Huizhouxue 徽州學 (50.4.2); and *Ming-Qing dang'anxue* 明清檔案學 (49.3 and 50.1–3).

The value to the historian of the new archival sources varies as much as the materials themselves. At their best, they open the possibility of constructing a view of Chinese history unmediated by the efforts of Confucian historians, official compilers or modern theoreticians. They can often provide local detail on implementation and practice not found in the historical record.

For the earliest periods, the archaeological finds of books and archival sources are transforming ancient Chinese history because few textual sources were transmitted. At the end of the empire, the Qing central archives, because of their huge size, offer the chance of a closer look at decision making and historical events in general than is possible for any other period. They have not yet been fully utilized.

Table 20: Archives and Other Collections of Original Documents

1. The Shang central court oracle-bone inscriptions (chap. 15).
2. Records of events cast on bronze vessels, eleventh to third century BC (17.1).
3. Documents on jade from the state treaty archive (*mengfu* 盟府) of the Warring States kingdom of Jin (17.2).
4. Documents and books, mainly on bamboo strips, mainly private, but some from local archives (Chu and Qin), fifth century BC to third century AD (18.1).
5. Maps on silk, mainly from the kingdom of Chu (4.4).
6. Bone chits (*guqian* 骨签) from the Former Han (44.3.1).
7. Chu documents from tombs (44.3.2.1)
8. Han documents from tombs (44.3.2.2)
9. Han documents and maps, many from local archives at the Northwest border, mostly public, but some private (44.3.2.3).
10. Documents on bamboo strips from the Wei, Jin and Northern and Southern Kingdoms period from third to fourth century (45.3).
11. Manuscript documents from the fourth to the fourteenth centuries from tombs and ruined cities near Turpan in Xinjiang (46.3).
12. Manuscripts, mainly religious, but also some private and secular ones, temple library, Dunhuang, fourth to tenth century (46.3).
13. Xi-Xia documents in the Tangut script, eleventh to thirteenth (48.3).
14. Buddhist scriptures carved on stelae from all periods (17.2).
15. A small part of the Ming central archives (49.3).
16. About nine million documents from the Qing central archives and Shenyang archives (50.1–2).
17. Documents from the Ba county archive, Sichuan, eighteenth and nineteenth centuries (50.3).
18. Documents from the Danshui subprefecture and Xinzhu county archives, Taiwan, eighteenth and nineteenth century (50.3).
19. About three million documents in the Lhasa archives (50.3).
20. Documents from the nineteenth-century Canton provincial archive (50.3).
21. Documents from various late Qing provincial archives (50.3).

Needless to say, all the different archives present two challenges in common: first, understanding the system which produced the documents and for what purposes; second, decipherment.

20.3 Private Documents

Until recently, few archives and documents (as distinct from historical and literary compositions) of private individuals and businesses were known to have survived, but more have been turning up in recent years. The largest finds from the early years of Chinese history are from archaeological excavations of tombs. In addition, a considerable number of private documents were found among the documents on bamboo strips and wooden tablets. They date from the Warring States to the Tang. More private documents have survived from the late Ming and Qing, notably the Huizhou documents and the Sichuan Zigong salt works archive (the latter is strictly speaking not a private archive, 50.4).

Note the minor part played by family and kin, business and other association records. Although such nonofficial records and private documents were voluminous, few if any have escaped the ravages of time and fire (with the outstanding exception of several thousand genealogies from the Ming and Qing), because Chinese historians were primarily concerned to establish and to preserve the official record. Moreover, China had no corporations independent from the state as there were in Europe, each with its own private archive.

Although the literary output of China's elite has survived in very large quantities and although this includes private diaries, letters (3.6), notebooks (chap. 31) and other such writings, the only major nonliterary type of documents to have survived are chance finds such as those among (or on the back of) the Dunhuang and Turpan manuscripts (46.3) and in miscellaneous writings and on inscriptions. Contracts, land deeds, accounts and litigation of all kinds did not come within the purview of the traditional Chinese historian, and the owners of such documents usually guarded them jealously from prying eyes. Moreover, in the 1930s and 1940s, the burning of land deeds and IOUs was used as a way of mobilizing the peasantry. For these reasons, only scattered examples of this type of private document have been utilized or published. How many are still extant is unknown, but a great many must have been destroyed in the upheavals during the nineteenth and twentieth centuries.

20.4 Historiography

History was written by officials for officials—Etienne Balazs

One of the unique features of Chinese historical studies is that a very large number of the primary sources were works produced in or preserved by a conscious tradition of historical writing and compilation often by officials. The two most famous works of historical criticism (*shiping* 史評) were:

Liu Zhiji 劉知幾 (661–721), *Shitong* 史通 (Generalities on history), 710.[3]

Zhang Xuecheng 章學誠 (1738-1801), *Wenshi tongyi* 文史通義 (General meaning of historiography), 1832, Shanghai guji, 1993.[4]

Note also *Wenxin diaolong* 文心雕龍 (30.1).

Because of the long and sophisticated historiographical tradition in China, instead of working from official archives or private documents (as in post-Rankean European historiography), the modern student of Chinese history is liable to be handling historical works compiled by Chinese historians continuously over the last 3,000 years. In order to be able to assess the qualities and the biases of these works, clearly some knowledge of the aims and methods of the historians and compilers who produced them is essential.

Furthermore, in order to be able to start looking for primary sources on the topic of his choice, the student of Chinese

---

[3] Liu's work is discussed by Edwin G. Pulleyblank, "Chinese Historical Criticism, Liu Chih-chi and Ssu-ma Kuang," in *Historians of China and Japan*, William G. Beasley and Edwin G. Pulleyblank, eds., OUP, 1961, 135–66; David McMullen, *State and Scholarship in Tang China*, CUP, 1988, "History," 159–205. Guy Gagnon, *Concordance Combinée du Shitong et du Shitong xiaofan*, 2 vols., Maisonneuve, 1977. For a translation, see Stuart H. Sargent, "Liu Chih-chi: *Understanding History*: The Narration of Events," in *Renditions* 15: 27–35 (1981).

[4] On Zhang's work, see David S. Nivison, *The Life and Thought of Chang Hsüeh-ch'eng (1738–1801)*, SUP, 1966.

history will also need to know how traditional historians organized their materials and classified different types of sources.
This is a subject discussed in section 9.3.[5]

The characteristics of traditional Chinese historical writing
were as follows: (1) Chinese historians were typically Confucian literati, but more significantly, they were also officials.
Their primary focus was on politics defined as the affairs of
state, which meant the record of imperial government. In
common with officials in other societies, the final record that
they compiled was based on official documents and encoded
into bureaucratic (Confucian) categories. These were usually far
removed from actual transcripts of conversations or events.
From this follow the second, third, and fourth characteristics
of traditional historical writing: (2) its many close connections
with government and the orthodox ideology, as seen in the
theory of *zhengtong* 正統 (legitimate succession), which official
historians traced in an effort to legitimize new dynasties (see
Box 8 at the end of this chapter); also as seen in the compilation
of compendia of historical precedents as a guide to official action; (3) its strong moral didacticism, with the historian's duty
being to bestow *baobian* 褒貶 (praise and blame), using Confucian moral tenets as the yardstick; (4) its ruthless excision of
anything judged in conflict with the above two concerns (thus
not only a focus on the elite and its ideology but also a particularly narrow focus on that elite). Additional characteristics of

[5] Denis Twitchett, *The Writing of Official History under the T'ang*,
CUP, 1992, analyzes the process of official historical writing and compilation at a formative period. Beasley and Pulleyblank (1961) contains 11
papers on different aspects of Chinese traditional historical writing and
still forms the best interpretive introduction to the subject in a Western
language. *Essays on the Sources for Chinese History*, Donald Daniel Leslie,
Colin Mackerras and Wang Gungwu, eds., ANU, 1973; Univ. of South
Carolina Press, 1975, has some excellent chapters which are cited in the
appropriate chapters of the manual. Han Yu-shan, *Elements of Chinese
Historiography*, W. M. Hawley, 1955, contains a lot of basic information.
Charles S. Gardner (1900–66), *Chinese Traditional Historiography*, HUP,
1938; rev. ed., 1961, provides a brief overview.

China's traditional historical writing are: (5) its early elevation to the status of an activity differentiated form other branches of writing, to which great importance was attached for two millennia of continuous historical production;[6] (6) its development into many well defined genres and subgenres; (7) its scholarly attention to such ancillary disciplines as cataloguing, calendrical sciences, historical geography, ancient scripts and artifacts; and (8) its development of a philosophy of history.[7]

20.5 Private Historical Writing

In addition to official historical writing, a large amount of historical works were written privately (*sishi* 私史). Often they followed the main forms of the official histories, including annals, annals-biography, topically arranged histories and so forth (Table 12, section 9.3). Indeed, many of the most distinguished works in the official historical canon were credited to or written by private individuals, for example the *Zuozhuan* 左傳 or

---

[6] On the overlap between early historical and literary narrative, see David Derwei Wang, "Fictional History/Historical Fiction," in *Studies in Language and Literature* I (1985), 64–74; Anthony C. Yu, "History, Fiction and the Reading of Chinese Narrative," in *Chinese Literature: Essays, Articles, Reviews* X (1988), 1–19; Andrew H. Plaks, "Toward a Critical Theory of Chinese Narrative," in Plaks, *Chinese Narrative, Critical and Theoretical Essays*, PUP, 1977, 309–52; Sheldon Hsiao-peng Lu, *From Historicity to Fictionality: The Chinese Poetics of Narrative*, SUP, 1994; Henri Maspero, "Historical Romance in History," in *China in Antiquity*, Frank A. Kierman, Jr., tr., Univ. of Massachusetts Press, 1978, 357–65; and David Johnson, "Epic and History in Early China: The Matter of Wu Tzu-hsu," *JAS* 40.2: 255–71 (1981). See also studies of early historical works such as the *Zuozhuan* or the *Mu tianzi zhuan*.

[7] For an overview of Chinese historiography arranged by themes (for example, "talking straight and making a point by indirection," or "the advantages and disadvantages of national, informal and family histories"), see Qu Lindong 瞿林東, *Zhongguo gudai shixue piping zongheng* 中國古代史學批評縱橫 (An evaluation of historical criticism in ancient China), Zhonghua, 1994. For a bibliography of Chinese writing on historiography between 1900 and 1985, see *Zhongguo shixueshi yanjiu shuyao* 中國史學史研究述要, Yang Yixiang 楊翼驤 et al., eds., Tianjin jiaoyu, 1996.

the *Shiji* 史記. Private historical writing also took many other forms, including scholarly commentaries, studies of primary sources, and informal jottings (*biji* 筆記). There were special terms to distinguish privately written histories from official ones, for example, *bieshi* 別史, *zashi* 雜史 and *yeshi* 野史.

The definition of *bieshi* (lit. "separate history") changed over time. In general it was applied to nonofficial works which were not in annals or annals-biography form (*jizhuanti* 紀傳體). Sometimes it was used interchangeably with *zashi*, but normally the distinction between the two was that *bieshi* were considered more serious works, lying somewhere between *zhengshi* 正史 on the one hand and *zashi* on the other. *Zashi* (chap. 24) were often in the form of *biji* (chap. 31). *Baishi* 稗史 was a term sometimes used in book catalogs in the sense of record of folkways, otherwise just as another word for nonofficial history. The general expression *yeshi* 野史 was not used as a category in book catalogs. In ordinary language it meant nonofficial histories written about the dynasty of the day (private history, as opposed to official history). *Yeshi* flourished in the *Nan-Bei Chao*, in the Song and in the Ming. From the Qing onward they typically recount in a semifictional way life at the court. *Waishi* 外史 (informal history) was normally used in the titles of fictional narratives, the most famous example being the eighteenth-century satire *Rulin waishi* 儒林外史 (*The Scholars*).[8]

Shichao (historical excerpts) began to be published in the Song. They consist of quotations usually culled from the Standard Histories.

Zaiji (contemporary records) are the histories of states not regarded as legitimate. As recorded, for example, in *Wu-Yue chunqiu* (Table 18, section 19.1), in the *Shiliuguo chunqiu* (45.2) or in the *Manshu* (41.5.1).

Bieshi, *zaiji* or *baishi* were also often classified as *zashi*.

---

[8] Harold Kahn, *Monarchy in the Emperor's Eyes*, Univ. of Massachusetts Press, 1971; rpnt., 1978, contains a perceptive study of official and unofficial historiography of the later empire.

Box 8: *Five-Element Theory* (Wuxing 五行)
From the Warring States to the *Nan-Bei Chao*, it was considered vital
to correctly identify the pattern of the rise and fall of dynasties and
to identify each dynasty with the right one of the five elements or
agents.[8] At first these were ordered in a mutually overcoming cycle
(*xiangke* 相克) in which each element successively overcomes the
next one: water, fire, metal, wood, earth (*shui* 水, *huo* 火, *jin* 金, *mu*
木, *tu* 土). Then in the Han dynasty, the order was changed to a mutually producing cycle (*xiangsheng* 相生) in which each element produces its successor: wood, fire, earth, metal, water (*mu* 木, *huo* 火, *tu*
土, *jin* 金, *shui* 水). The debate on the legitimacy of the Northern
Wei dynasty turned on the choice of the right element;[9] the same
applied to the debate on the legitimacy of the Jin.[10] Thereafter, political legitimacy used other symbols, although the five elements
continued to be a popular means of ranking people and things (for
example, in the choice of the characters for siblings; see 3.2).

[8] L. S. Yang (Yang Liansheng 楊聯陞), "Toward a Study of Dynastic
Configurations in Chinese History," in his *Studies in Chinese Institutional
History*, HUP, 1963, 1–17; Rao Zongyi 饒宗頤, *Zhongguo shixue shang zhi
zhengtong lun* 中國史學上之正統論 (The theory of legitimate succession
in Chinese historiography), HKCU Press, 1977; rpnt., Shanghai yuandong, 1996, which is an anthology of 170 excerpts on the theme preceded
by a lengthy introduction.

[9] John Lee, From Five Elements to Five Agents: Wu-hsing in Chinese
History," in *Sages and Filial Sons*, Julia Ching and R. W. L. Guisso, eds.,
HKCUP, 1991, 163–78.

[10] Chan Hok-lam (Chen Xuelin 陳學林), "Patterns of Legitimation in
Imperial China," Part I of *Legitimation in Imperial China: Discussions under the Jurchen-Chin Dynasty*, Univ. of Washington Press, 1984, 19–48.
Chan returns to the same question in an article whose scope is wider
than the title implies, "'Ta Chin' (Great Golden): the Origin and Changing Interpretations of the Jurchen State Name," *TP* 77.4–5: 253–99 (1991).

21

Annals

The earliest and one of the most important methods of arranging historical materials throughout Chinese history began as a bare catalog of court events arranged chronologically: e.g., "on such and such a year, month, day, King X of Y went on a hunt." Much of the writing on the oracle bones (cf ap. 15), which predates the first extant historical work by many centuries, contains similar records of single events and actions, but the relations between court scapulimancy and the origins of a continuous process of record keeping are obscure. The court chronicler in early China was an important official charged with astronomical as well as archival functions; he played a key part in the arrangement and timing of royal ancestor worship and sacrificial rites and other ceremonies. He may also have had remonstrance functions, in light of his duties of keeping records of models worthy of emulation and of portents heralding disaster.

In later Chinese history the bare catalog of events at court was greatly expanded and elaborate composite chronicles of events throughout the empire began to appear, either written privately or under official sponsorship (although always with the major focus on the court and central government).

21.1 Chunqiu 春秋

The earliest extant example of a historical work in the annals style is the *Chunqiu* 春秋 (*Spring and Autumn Annals*), the court chronicle of the state of Lu.[1] It is only 17,000 characters long, but covers 242 years (722–481 BC), which works out at 70 characters per year; so events are tersely recorded. The longest entry is only 47 characters. The average is 10. The shortest is just one character under the year 715 BC: "*Ming* 螟" (pests).

Editorship was traditionally and implausibly attributed to Confucius. The *Chunqiu*'s title was later used to name the period 770–476.

The third of the three commentaries on the *Spring and Autumn Annals* to have survived, the *Zuozhuan* 左傳 (*Commentary of Zuo*), is much fuller and more lively than the *Annals* themselves and goes beyond the other two commentaries. It is the

[1] In the Western Zhou, *Chunqiu* meant "year" and was used as one of the generic terms for "annals." There are seven Warring States works with *chunqiu* in the title. Because of the connection with Confucius who also came from Lu, the *Lu chunqiu* 魯春秋 became one of the Classics and the only one to survive. The most convenient edition of the *Chunqiu* and its three commentaries is included in *ICS Concordances* 30–32. See also the older *H-Y Index*, Supplement 17. Note Bernard Karlgren, "Glosses on the Tso chuan," *BMFEA* (1969–70); for other references, see Anne Cheng in *ECHBG*, 67–76.

For translations, see Burton Watson, *The Tso chuan: Selections from China's Oldest Narrative History*, Col. UP, 1989; James Legge in *The Chinese Classics*, vol. 4 in 2 parts, HKU Press, 1960; Séraphin Couvreur, *Tch'ouen ts'iou et Tso tschouan*, 3 vols., Ho-kien fu, 1914; rpnt., Cathasia, 1951.

For stylistic analysis, see David Schaberg, "Foundations of Chinese Historiography: Literary Representation in *Zuo zhuan* and *Guoyu*," Ph.D., Harvard University, 1996; John C. Y. Wang, "Early Chinese Narrative: the *Tso-chuan* as Example," in Andrew H. Plaks, *Chinese Narrative, Critical and Theoretical Essays*, PUP, 1977. For a dictionary of the language, as well as a place name and personal-name index, see *Chunqiu zuozhuan cidian* 春秋左傳詞典, Yang Bojun 楊伯峻 and Xu Ti 徐提, eds., Zhonghua, 1985.

prime source on the history of the period 722–468 BC.[2] Another important early chronicle (mainly of the state of Wei) is the *Zhushu jinian* 竹書紀年 (Table 18, 19.1).

21.2 Annalistic Sources and Veritable Records

Annalistic writing was one of the main methods of arrangement adopted by Sima Qian in the *Shiji* (in the Basic Annals section) and it remained an integral part of the Standard Histories thereafter (see chap. 22). Xun Yue 荀悦 (148–209), *Hanji* 漢紀 was based on the *Hanshu*. It is the first annals of a single dynasty. From the Tang, the official writing of annalistic history had become standardized into the following types:

1. *Qijuzhu* 起居注 (Court Diaries), sometimes translated as diaries of activity and repose, imperial diaries or audience records. They record the decisions and actions of the emperor in the conduct of government business, normally as this occurred in formal sessions of the imperial court each morning. In periods when the emperor conducted the government informally or secretly, the *qijuzhu* were weak or nonexistent; the *qijuzhu* began in the Later Han and continued on and off until 1911. They were in no sense intended for publication. Only a tiny fraction survive up to the Qing, from which time the greater part, both in Chinese and Manchu, are extant in 12,000 *ce*.[3]

2. *Shizhengji* 時政記 (Records of Current Government), were in some periods confidential records compiled under the authority of ministers.

3. *Rili* 日曆 (Daily Calendars) were a condensation, arranged day by day, of the first two.

---

[2] Note that the first recorded title (in the *Hanshu* "Yiwenzhi," Zhonghua, 1,713) is *Zuoshizhuan* 左氏傳. It is usually referred to simply as the *Zuozhuan*.

[3] The Chinese versions of the following reigns have been printed: Kangxi, Yongzheng, Daoguang, Xianfeng, Tongzhi, and Guangxu (see 50.5 for details). The *Neige Manwen qijuzhu* 內閣滿文起居注 (Manchu versions of the *qijuzhu*) are available on microfilm at the Yishiguan in Beijing (50.2.1).

Only fragments of the Court Diaries, the Records of Current Government and the Daily Calendars have survived from before the Qing.

Given that the Court Diaries were composed almost immediately after the event, and were usually secret, they tend to be more reliable than other officially compiled sources, for example the Veritable Records, or even more so, the Standard Histories, which were compiled only after the downfall of a dynasty by its successor and therefore often came several hundred years after the event.

All three of the above were used as the chief source for the annalistic Veritable Records (*Shilu* 實錄), of which there was one for each emperor, as well as for the less detailed National Histories (*Guoshi* 國史), which were compiled in some periods for each reign. The keeping of *Shilu* began in the *Nan-Bei Chao* and continued until 1911. Less than 1 percent of the *Shilu* survive from before the Ming (a small part of the year 805 from the Tang and portions of the years 983 and 996 from the Song).[4]

The *Shilu* of the Ming and Qing covering the years 1368 to 1911 are extant in over 7,500 *juan*. They form an extremely important source for the Ming and for the Qing, but they were compiled only after the end of each reign, so they could come at some distance from what happened at the beginning of a long reign, and always with the risk of strong influence from participants (or their successors) in the events recorded.

Despite these drawbacks, the *Shilu* contain an extraordinarily detailed record, unequaled for any comparable period in any country. Many edicts, memorials and other documents, as well as day-to-day events, are preserved in them.[5] They constitute

[4] Denis Twitchett, *The Writing of Official History under the T'ang*, CUP, 1992.

[5] On the process of the compilation of the Veritable Records, see L. S. Yang (Yang Liansheng 楊聯陞), "The Organization of Chinese Official Historiography: Principles and Methods of the Standard Histories from the T'ang through the Ming Dynasty," in Beasley and Pulleyblank, 44–59, rpnt. in Yang's *Excursions in Sinology*, HUP, 1969, 96–111. Twitchett (1992), 119–59 examines the compilation of the Tang Veritable Records

Footnote continued on next page

the single most important source for the last 500 years of Chinese history.

21.3 Zizhi tongjian 資治通鑑

Although many annals and chronicles (not to mention Veritable Records) were written during and after the Han, it was not until the Song that a major step forward took place in this genre with the compilation of the *Zizhi tongjian* 資治通鑑 (Comprehensive mirror for aid in government) by Sima Guang 司馬光 (1019-86). This magisterially carries the history of China from 403 BC in continuous chronicle form over the following 1,362 years down to AD 959. In the catholicity of sources consulted, many since lost, in its discussion of disputed points where there was a divergence of evidence (*kaoyi* 考異), as well as in its huge table of contents (running to 74 pages in the Zhonghua edition), it marked an important new level for the chronicle form as well as for general historical methodology. It had an enormous influence on later Chinese historical writing, either directly or through its many abbreviations, continuations, and adaptations.[6] It remains an extraordinarily useful first reference for a quick and reliable coverage of events at a particular time.

In writing it, Sima Guang was assisted by three outstanding scholars: Fan Zuyu 范祖禹 who prepared the first draft on the Tang; Liu Shu 劉恕, who prepared the draft on the Wei, Jin

---

(no longer extant) and *ISMH*, 29-33, does the same for the Ming *Shilu*, which are extant. For editions of the Ming and Qing *Shilu*, see 49.1 and 50.5, respectively.

[6] On the compilation of Sima Guang's great work, see Edwin G. Pulleyblank, "Chinese Historical Criticism: Liu Chih-chi and Ssu-ma Kuang," in Beasley and Pulleyblank, 135-66; also Zhang Xu 張須, *Tong-jian xue* 通鑑學 (Studies on the Comprehensive Mirror), Shanghai: Kaiming shudian, 1948; rev., 1957; rev. and exp., Anhui renmin, 1981.

Chaps. 54 to 78 of the *Zizhi tongjian*, covering the last years of the Han and the Three Kingdoms, have been translated into English (45.2).

and *Nan-Bei Chao*; and Liu Ban 劉攽, who worked on the Han period. Sima Guang's son did the proofreading.

The best modern edition of the *Tongjian* is the punctuated, movable-type one prepared by a team of 12 editors led by Wang Chongwu 王崇武, Nie Chongqi 聶崇岐 and Gu Jiegang 顧頡剛. The text used was a Qing reprint of the Yuan dynasty edition of *Zizhi tongjian* by Hu Sanxing 胡三省 (1230–1302). Hu incorporated the *kaoyi* 考異 into the text as notes (they had originally been printed separately). Many of the sources quoted in them have since been lost. Hu also provided his own comments and corrections separately (appendix to vol. 20 of the Zhonghua edition, 1–190). The Zhonghua editors have incorporated the textual notes of Zhang Yu 章鈺 (1865–1937) which were taken from the most important Song, Yuan and Ming editions and added these and other Song commentaries in bracketed notes in the main text.[7]

Many adaptations and summaries of this massive 9,612 page chronicle were made. The most popular of all was a highly moralistic one entitled *Zizhi tongjian gangmu* 資治通鑑綱目. It was devised by Zhu Xi 朱熹 (1130–1200) and written by his pupils.[8] The *Siku* editors classified it under historiography (*shiping* 史評), nevertheless, because of Zhu Xi's name it was the *Gangmu* which was read in the Ming and Qing rather than the much longer and more rigorous *Tongjian*.[9] But it is the *Tong-*

[7] Sima Guang 司馬光, *Zizhi tongjian* 資治通鑑, Guji, 1956; 9th rpnt., 20 vols., Zhonghua, 1995; convenient and readable, two-volume, reduced-size reprint (four pages to the page with original page numbers indicated), 1997.

[8] Conrad Schirokauer, "Chu Hsi's Sense of History," in *Ordering the World: Approaches to State and Society in Sung Dynasty China*, Robert P. Hyams and Conrad Schirokauer, eds., UCP, 1993, 193–220.

[9] J. A. M. de Moyriac de Mailla's *Histoire générale de la Chine, ou annales de cet empire; traduites du Tong-Kien Kang-Mou*, 13 vols., Paris: Pierres et Clousier, 1777–85; Taibei rpnt., 1968 is an abridged translation from the Manchu version of Zhu Xi's *Zizhi tongjian gangmu* (Summary of the comprehensive mirror for aid in government) and its later continuations. It was the largest general history of China available in a West-

Footnote continued on next page

jian itself and the full continuations of it that are of interest to the modern historian.[10] The most important of these cover the Song and are listed in 47.1 and 47.2.

There is a dictionary to help find one's way around the *Tongjian*:

Zizhi tongjian da cidian 資治通鑑大辭典 (Great dictionary of the *Zizhi tongjian*), Shi Ding 施丁 and Shen Zhihua 深志華, eds. in chief, Jilin renmin, 1994.

Also indexes:

Shiji tsugan sakuin 資治通鑑索引, Saeki Tomi 佐伯富, ed., Tôyôshi ken-kyûkai, 1961.

Shiji tsugan kochû chimei sakuin 資治通鑑胡注地名索引, Araki Toshi-kazu 荒木敏一 and Yoneda Kenjirô 米田賢次郎 comps., Jimbun, 1967. An index to the place names in Hu Sanxing's notes.

---

ern language for two centuries (until the publication of *The Cambridge History of China*) and it was used by many later textbook writers.

[10] For example, Bi Yuan 畢沅 (1730–97) et al., *Xu Zizhi tongjian* 續資治通鑑, 12 vols., Beijing, 1957; 6th rpnt., 1988. Replaces the other continuations compiled in the Qing and covers the years 960–1370.

22

Standard Histories

The first great innovation in historical writing and departure from the early annals style was the work of Sima Tan 司馬談 (d. 110 BC) and his son, Sima Qian 司馬遷 (?145–86 BC), court astronomers and librarians during the second and at the beginning of the first century BC (44.2). They wrote what many centuries later was chosen as the first of the *zhengshi* 正史 (Standard Histories or Histories, for short). There was eventually one for each legitimate dynasty. In all, 24 Histories written over 1,832 years. They number just under 40,000,000 characters (*Hanzi* 漢字), of which 13,966 are different ones.

22.1 Structure, Contents and Titles

The *Shiji* is a history of China from the Yellow Emperor down to Han Wudi arranged in a manner which, with certain adaptations, was to set the form for a new way of writing history that came to be known as *Jizhuanti* 紀傳體 (annals-biography) after two of its most important parts. It was to be used in all of what later became known in the eighteenth century as the *Ershisishi* 二十四史 (The 24 histories).

The *Shiji* contains 130 chapters (*juan* 卷) divided into 12 *Benji* 本紀 (basic annals), 10 *Biao* 表 (tables), 8 *Shu* 書 (monographs), 30 *Shijia* 世家 (hereditary houses), and 70 *Liezhuan* 列傳 (collected biographies or memoirs). The two main innovations of Sima Qian were the monographs (*Shu* 書) and the memoirs (*Liezhuan* 列傳). The monographs (in later Standard

Histories usually called *Zhi* 志 and sometimes translated as treatises) cover the historical evolution of selected institutions such
as rituals, the calendar, astronomy or political economy (with
the emphasis on taxation and coinage). The memoirs are groups
of biographies or profiles of both famous and (some) less famous people (as well as foreign peoples) of each age. These two
sections of the *Shiji*, together with the older-style basic annals
(*Benji* 本紀) which carried on the court annals tradition, became the three major elements of the *jizhuan* genre of history
writing. In the Chinese historiographical tradition the annals
were considered the core and the biographies as illustrations of
the core. The monographs were entirely left out of eight of the
earlier Histories. They were considered belonging to a separate
tradition of institutional history writing. The other sections of
the *Shiji*, the *biao* and the *shijia* (which cover the history of the
major pre-Han states) were incorporated only sporadically or
not at all in the later Histories.

The most important difference between all the Standard
Histories from the *Hanshu* 漢書 onward and the *Shiji* was that
they covered only one dynasty and made no attempt to cover
the vast sweep of history (3,000 years) embraced by the *Shiji*.
The generic term is *duandaishi* 斷代史; as distinct from works
such as the *Shiji*, which are called *tongshi* 通史. Only the
monographs continued to cover periods of time extending earlier than the dynasty in question (see Table 23 for a list of the
different topics covered in the monographs in each of the Histories). Another important difference between the earlier and
later Standard Histories is that prior to the Tang, eight of what
later were recognized as Standard Histories were written by
private individuals and another seven were commissioned from
one or two individuals. After the Tang reorganization of the
Bureau of Historiography, the Histories (with some notable
exceptions) tended to become more and more standardized as
they became the final step in a cumulative process of compilation by committees of official historians (which History fell
into which category of authorial composition is indicated in
Table 21).

Explanation of Table 21

One asterisk indicates that the work was written by a private individual. Two asterisks indicate that the work was commissioned from one or two individuals.

Those Histories which were officially compiled (marked with three asterisks) had a nominal editor-in-chief (whose name is listed in the Table), but they were the work of many hands at the Historiography Bureau. They based themselves on materials compiled by the Bureau of the previous dynasty.

The numbering from 1–24 in the left-hand column is the same order as that in the *Siku quanshu zongmu*. With the exception of the *Nanshi* and the *Beishi*, it follows the chronological order of the dynasties. The numbering in brackets (1–26) is somewhat different because it shows the order according to the dates of compilation.

Table 21: The Standard Histories

Title	Author, editor (dates)	Compiled (presented or printed)	Period covered
*1 (1). *Shiji* 史記 (*The Records of the Grand Historian*)	Sima Tan 司馬談 (?180–110 BC) and Sima Qian 司馬遷 (?145–86 BC)	104–87 (91) BC	Earliest times to 95 BC
**2 (2). [*Qian*] *Hanshu* [前]漢書 (*History of the Former Han*)	Ban Gu 班固 (AD 32–92)	AD 58–76 (92)	206 BC – AD 24
*3 (4). *Hou Hanshu* 後漢書 (*History of the Later Han*)	Fan Ye 范曄 (398–445)	398–445 (445)	25–220
*4 (3). *Sanguozhi* 三國志 (*The Record of the History of the Three Kingdoms*)	Chen Shou 陳壽 (233–97)	285–97 (297)	Wei 221–65; Shu 221–64; Wu 222–80
***5 (13). *Jinshu* 晉書 (*History of the Jin*)	Fang Xuanling 房玄齡 (578–648)	644 (646)	265–419

Table continues

Table 21—continued

Title	Author, editor (dates)	Compiled (completed or printed)	Period covered
**6 (5). *Songshu* 宋書 (*History of the Song*)	Shen Yue 沈約 (441–513)	492–493	420–78
*7 (6). *Nan Qishu* 南齊書 (*History of Southern Qi*)	Xiao Zixian 蕭子顯 (489–537)	489–537 (537)	479–502
**8 (8). *Liangshu* 梁書 (*History of the Liang*)	Yao Cha 姚察 (533–606) and Yao Silian 姚思廉 (d. 637)	628–35 (636)	502–56
**9 (9). *Chenshu* 陳書 (*History of the Chen*)	Yao Cha 姚察 (533–606) and Yao Silian 姚思廉	622–29 (636)	557–89
**10 (7). *Weishu* 魏書 (*History of the Wei*)	Wei Shou 魏收 (506–72)	551–54 (554)	386–550
**11 (10). *Bei Qishu* 北齊書 (*History of the Northern Qi*)	Li Delin 李德林 (530–590) and Li Boyao 李百藥 (565–648)	627–36 (636)	550–77
***12 (11). *Zhoushu* 周書 (*History of the Zhou*)	Linghu Defen 令狐德棻 (583–661)	ca. 629 (636)	557–81
***13 (12). *Suishu* 隋書 (*History of Sui*)	Wei Zheng 魏徵 (580–643)	629–36 (636)	581–617
*14 (14). *Nanshi* 南史 (*History of the Southern Dynasties*)	Li Yanshou 李延壽 (fl. 618–76)	630–50 (659)	420–589
*15 (15). *Beishi* 北史 (*History of the Northern Dynasties*)	Li Yanshou 李延壽 (fl. 618–76)	630–50 (659)	368–618
***16 (16). *Jiu Tangshu* 舊唐書 (*Old History of the Tang*)	Liu Xu 劉昫 (887–946)	940–945 (945)	618–906

Table continues

Table 21—continued

Title	Author, editor (dates)	Compiled (completed or printed)	Period covered
**17 (18). *Xin Tangshu* 新唐書 (*New History of the Tang*)	Ouyang Xiu 歐陽修 (1007–72) and Song Qi 宋祁 (998–1061)	1043–60 (1060)	618–906
***18 (17). *Jiu Wudaishi* 舊五代史 (*Old History of the Five Dynasties*)	Xue Juzheng 薛居正 (912–81)	973–74 (974)	907–60
*19 (19). *Xin Wudaishi* 新五代史 (*New History of the Five Dynasties*). Original title: *Wudai shiji* 五代史記	Ouyang Xiu 歐陽修 (1007–72)	1044–60 (1072)	907–60
***20 (22). *Songshi* 宋史 (*History of the Song*)	Tuotuo (Toghto 脱脱) (1313–55)	1343–45 (1345)	960–1279
***21 (20). *Liaoshi* 遼史 (*History of the Liao*)	Same as *Songshi*	1343–44 (1344)	916–1125
****22 (21). *Jinshi* 金史 (*History of the Jin*)	Same as *Songshi*	1343–44 (1344)	1115–1234
***23 (23). *Yuanshi* 元史 (*History of the Yuan*)	Song Lian 宋濂 (1310–81)	1369–70 (1370)	1206–1369
***24 (24). *Mingshi* 明史 (*History of the Ming*)	Zhang Tingyu 張廷玉 (1672–1755)	1678–1735 (1739)	1368–1644
*25 (25). *Xin Yuanshi* 新元史 (*New History of the Yuan*)	Ke Shaomin 柯紹忞 (1850–1933)	1890–1920 (1920)	1206–1367
***26 (26). *Qingsh gao* 清史稿 (*Draft History of the Qing*)	Zhao Erxun 趙爾巽 (1844–1927)	1914–27 (1927)	1644–1911

The concept of a single Standard History for each successive dynasty emerged only very gradually. The term *zhengshi* 正史 itself was used for the first time in the Liang dynasty in AD 523 and incorporated into the *Suishu* "Jingjizhi 隋書經籍志" (*Standard History of the Sui*, monograph on dynastic bibliography) as a category distinct from *bashi* 霸史 (histories of dynasties not recognized as legitimate) or *bieshi* 別史 (not officially recognized history). As such it was applied to important historical works mainly in the *jizhuan* (and to some extent in the *biannian*) genres and it continued to be used in this sense until the Qing. The present usage to refer to the 24 (or 25, or 26) Histories became only the norm after the compilation of the *Siku quanshu* 四庫全書 in the eighteenth century (9.5).

Until the Tang, the usual reference was to the *Sanshi* 三史 (The three Histories): that is the *Shiji*, the *Hanshu* and the *Hou Hanshu* 後漢書 (replacing the *Dongguan Hanji* 東觀漢記). From the Tang, the *Sanguozhi* 三國志 was added to make the *Sishi* 四史 (The four Histories), or *Qian sishi* 前四史 (The first four Histories), terms still in use. During the Tang, six new Histories of different kingdoms of the preceding period were compiled by the Bureau of Historiography. Together with three privately written works this made a total of 13 works recognized as the main histories of China up to the end of the dynasty. They were referred to as the *Shisandai shi* 十三代史 (The Histories of thirteen dynasties). During the Northern Song, the *Nanshi* 南史 and *Beishi* 北史, which had been privately compiled in the Tang, were added to the Histories, as were the newly compiled *Xin Tangshu* 新唐書 (*New History of the Tang*) and *Xin Wudaishi* 新五代史 (*New History of the Five Dynasties*). This brought the total to 17. Thereafter new ones were added as they were officially compiled. At the end of the fourteenth century there were 21. The completion of the *Mingshi* 明史 (*Standard History of the Ming*) in 1735 raised the number to 22, to which were added at the time of the compilation of the *Siku Quanshu* the recovered editions of the *Jiu Tangshu* 舊唐書 (*Old History of the Tang*) and the *Jiu Wudaishi* 舊五代史 (*Old History of the Five Dynasties*). The number now stood at 24 and the phrase *Ershisishi* 二十四史 (*The 24 Histories*) was coined on the completion of the palace edition in 1775 (22.2). The number rose to 25 after the official addition of the *Xin Yuanshi* 新元史 (*New History of the Yuan*) in 1921. Although the *Qing-shi gao* 清史稿 (*Draft History of the Qing*) has not been officially included in the Histories, it is in the old tradition and is therefore included in Table 21 to bring the total to 26.

Although varying greatly in quality and length, the Standard Histories constitute a monumental *oeuvre*, the importance of which can hardly be exaggerated. They provide remarkably accurate coverage of over 2,000 years of Chinese history (from the official, Confucian standpoint, as seen from the imperial court), and they include historical profiles of the rulers, events, leading personalities, major institutions and administrative boundaries of each dynasty, as well as a considerable quantity of detailed information on the peoples of East, Central, and Southeast Asia. The value of the earlier Standard Histories is greatly enhanced by the fact that many of the sources upon which they were based have since been lost and alternative sources are lacking. For these reasons the scissors-and-paste methods of some of their editors should be regarded as an asset.

A huge literature exists on the Histories, especially on the first four, which are regarded as monuments of literary and historical excellence. A fraction of this literature is listed in the appropriate chapters of Part V. The following section notes various reference tools for the Histories as a whole.[1]

[1] *Zhongguo jizhuanti wenxian yanjiu* 中國紀傳體文獻研究 (Research on Chinese annals-biography literature), Wang Jingui 王錦貴, ed., Beijing daxue, 1996. *Chûgoku seishi kenkyû bunken mokuroku* 中國正史研究文獻目錄 (Bibliography of research on the Chinese Standard Histories), Kokusho kankôkai 國書刊行會, eds., Kokusho kankôkai, 1977. Covers books and articles in Japanese, Chinese and Korean from 1868 to 1977. Arranged by Standard History.

22.2 Editions and Research Tools

Editions

The best modern edition is the Zhonghua Shuju punctuated, collated edition (*dianjiao ben* 點校本), *Ershisishi* 二十四史, 241 vols., Zhonghua, 1962–75. It uses complex characters throughout. There are numerous later reprints including a convenient and readable reduced-size one (four pages to the page with original page numbers indicated), 20 vols., 1997; there is also a two-volume personal-name index to this edition. For a reprint of the *Qingshi gao* in a similar format, see 50.5.

Editorial work on the Zhonghua edition began in 1958 at the request of Mao Zedong. Senior historians were assigned to the task and worked full-time on it. The best previous editions and commentaries were consulted and modern punctuation and paragraphing added. It took more than twenty years to complete the editing. This was not just a scholarly task. On at least one occasion, a question of punctuation, and hence interpretation, had to be referred to the prime minister, Zhou Enlai, whose decision in this case was surely the right one.[2] Each History has a brief introduction, both on textual matters and on the authors. This edition is not only the standard one, it is also the most handy, in that the entire 177 volumes (almost 40 million characters) are now available in database form, searches and printouts from which are available on request from the Harvard-Yenching Library (and also from the East Asian Library at the University of Washington) free of charge. Access can be made through the home page of these libraries on the Internet.[3]

[2] Before committing suicide by hanging himself from the branch of a tree on Coal Hill, the Chongzhen emperor (Ming) is recorded as having written on the flap of his jacket the following phrase: 任賊分裂毋傷百姓一人 (*Mingshi* 明史, *juan* 24). The punctuator feared that if he put the stop where it should go after the first four characters, he would be accused of helping to place the emperor in a flattering light.

[3] Ten people worked for three years in Taibei at the Shiyusuo, keying the Zhonghua edition of the Standard Histories plus the *Qingshi gao*

Footnote continued on next page

Before the *Zhonghua*, the most commonly used uniform edition of the Histories was the *Bona* edition:

Bona ben ershisishi 百衲本二十四史, 820 *ce*, *Sibu conkan* series, Shangwu, 1930–37; 24 vols., 1958; Taibei rpnt., 1965. The title means "hundred patches edition," referring to the fact that each History was taken from the best Song and Yuan editions.

Other commonly used editions of the Histories are the many reprints of the 1739–75 *Wuying dianben* 武英殿本 (palace edition), *Ershisishi* 二十四史 (24 Histories), *dianben* for short:

Tongwen shuju 同文書局, *Ershisishi* 二十四史, 711 *ce*, Shanghai, 1894.

Wuzhou shuju 五洲書局, *Ershisishi* 二十四史, 524 *ce*, 1869–78.

Kaiming shudian 開明書店, *Ershiwushi* 二十五史, 9 vols., Shanghai, 1935, which added the *Xin Yuanshi*. References are listed at the end of each History to the most important of the very large number of corrections and supplements to the Standard Histories produced by traditional scholars. These were printed separately, see *Ershiwushi bubian*.

Annotations and comments on the Standard Histories from 245 works of traditional scholarship (mainly Qing) are brought together in two massive collections, the first published in the 1930s as a supplement to the Kaiming edition and the second appearing sixty years later. The two do not overlap:

Ershiwushi bubian 二十五史補編 *Ershiwushi bubian* (Supplements to the 25 Histories), 6 vols., Kaiming shudian, 1936–37; rpnt., Zhonghua, 1955; 1986.

Ershisishi dingbian 二十四史訂編 *Ershisishi dingbian* (Supplements to the 24 Histories), Xu Shu 徐蜀, comp., 12 vols., Shumu wenxian, 1996.

---

into a computer. The resultant *Nianwushi quanwen ziliaoku* 廿五史全文資料庫 (25 Histories full text database), 1988, is now available on CD-ROM from the Shiyusuo and on the Internet by subscription. See the Web Site of Academia Sinica Computing Center (Zhongyang yanjiuyuan jisuan zhongxin 中央研究院計算中心 for details of the Academy's expanding database of ancient texts: http://www.sinica.edu.tw/ftms-bin/ftmsw3.

Studies

During the Qing, the practice of carefully reading and comparing the Histories gave rise to three brilliant studies which combine textual acuity with a keen sense of the significance of the historical topics which they selected for attention:

Wang Mingsheng 王鳴盛 (1722–97), *Shiqishi shangque* 十七史商榷 (A critical study of the *Seventeen Histories*), 1787; 2 vols., punctuated ed., Shangwu, 1937; rpnt., 1959. Covers the 17 Standard Histories listed in Table 21 up to the *Xin Wudaishi*, but not including the *Jiu Tangshu* and the *Jiu Wudaishi*. It is indexed in *Chûgoku zuihitsu sakuin* 中國隨筆索引, Tôyôshi kenkyûkai, comp., Nihon gakujutsu shinkôkai, 1954.

Zhao Yi 趙翼 (1727–1814), *Nian'er shi zhaji* 廿二史劄記 (Critical notes on the 22 Histories), 1799. Covers the 24 Histories up to and including the *Mingshi* and including the *Jiu Tangshi* and the *Jiu Wudaishi* which the author preferred not to allude to in his title. Use the edition by Wang Shumin 王樹民, *Nian'er shi zhaji jiaozheng* 廿二史劄記校證, 2 vols., Zhonghua, 1984, and note also the critical edition by Du Weiyun 杜維運, Huashi, 1977. Of the three Qing studies of the Histories, this is the most interesting from the point of view of analytic insights, as opposed to philological expertise. Indexed in *Chûgoku zuihitsu sakuin*, 1954 (chap. 31).

Qian Daxin 錢大昕 (1728–1804), *Nian'er shi kaoyi* 廿二史考異 (Discrepencies in the 22 Histories), 1782; 2 vols., punctuated ed., Shangwu, 1937; rpnt., Shijie shuju, 1939; rpnt., Zhongguo shudian, 1987; rpnt., 1990. Covers the Histories up to and including the *Yuanshi* except for the *Jiu Tangshi* and the *Jiu Wudaishi*.

The best book-length study of the process of compilation which went into the production of a Standard History is Twitchett (1992), who takes the Tang dynasty as his period and the writing of the basic annals and monographs in the *Jiu Tangshu* as examples.[4]

---

[4] Note also L. S. Yang, *Excursions* (1969), and the same scholar's "A Theory about the Titles of the Twenty-four Dynastic Histories," also in Yang (1969), 87–93. See also Herbert Franke, "Some Remarks on the Interpretation of Chinese Dynastic Histories," *Oriens* 3: 113–22 (1950).

Indexes and Concordances

Indexes and concordances are indispensable in looking up names of people and places, official titles, book titles, and special terms. Apart from using the 25 Histories full text database (22.2) or the indexes to individual Histories or to parts of them (see Part V), note that there are a number of dictionaries or indexes which cover certain parts of all the Histories. An essential one is *Ershiwushi renming da cidian* 二十五史人名大辭典.[5] This biographical dictionary summarizes and indexes all the nearly 30,000 biographies in the 25 Histories as well as biographical materials on the several thousand more people found in other sections of the Histories. It also includes dates of birth and death and identifies ancient place names. Earlier indexes (including those published by Zhonghua and Shanghai guji) do not carry the same amount of information. The edition indexed is the Zhonghua (by page number, but *juan* references are also given, so it can be used with other editions).[6]

There are also indexes available to the monographs on dynastic bibliography, financial administration, penal law and official posts (22.3).

[5] *Ershiwushi renming da cidian* (Dictionary of personal names in the 25 Histories), Huang Huixian 黃惠賢, ed. in chief, 2 vols., Zhongzhou, 1997.

[6] *Ershisishi jizhuan renming suoyin* 二十四史紀傳人名索引 (Index to personal names in the biographies section of the 24 Histories), Zhang Chenshi 張忱石 and Wu Shuping 吳樹平, comp., Zhonghua, 1980; rpnt., 1985; *Ershiwushi jizhuan renming suoyin* 二十五史紀傳人名索引 (Index to personal names in the biographies section of the 24 Histories), Shanghai guji, 1990. Zhonghua also issued separate full biographical indexes to all of the 24 Standard Histories. They were published in reduced format in two volumes in 1998. They have now been superseded by the *Ershiwushi renming da cidian*. In their day the Zhonghua indexes replaced the earlier *Ershiwushi renming suoyin* 二十五史人名索引 (Biographical index to the twenty-five Histories), Kaiming shudian, 1935; Shanghai: Zhonghua, 1956.

Translations

An indispensable aid for locating translations from the first 19 Histories (excluding those for the first three) is Hans H. Frankel, *Catalogue of Translations from the Chinese Dynastic Histories for the Period 220–960*, UCP, 1957; rpnt., Greenwood, 1974. There have been a considerable number of translations since this catalog was compiled (see 41.4, note 20).

Excerpts

Particular sections from all the Histories are sometimes often published together, for example, the monographs on a given subject or the *lunzan* 論贊 (comments placed at the end of each chapter intended to express the personal view of the compilers).[7] So have the sections on non-Han peoples (41.1 and Table 27). Even the references to the sea have been excerpted: *Ershisishi de haiyang ziliao* 二十四史的海洋資料.[8]

22.3 Monographs in the Standard Histories

Administrative Geography

See 4.5.2.

Astronomy and the Calendar

For a punctuated uniform edition of the *Tianwen lülizhi* 天文律曆志 (monographs on astronomy and the calendar), see *Lidai tianwen lüli deng zhi huibian* 歷代天文律曆等志彙編 (5.1).

Financial Administration

Fifteen of the Standard Histories contain *Shihuozhi* 食貨志 (monographs on financial administration). They constitute the single most important source on the economic institutions (and economy in general) of each period and as a result they have been relatively intensively studied, translated, and indexed. The

---

[7] *Zhengshi lunzan* 正史論贊 (Authors' comments in the Standard Histories), Song Xi 宋晞, ed., 5 vols., Taibei, 1954–60.

[8] *Ershisishi de haiyang ziliao* (Materials in the 24 Histories on the oceans), Liu Pei 劉佩 et al., eds., Haiyang, 1995.

texts of the *Shihuozhi* have been published together several times.[9] The major studies and translations of individual *Shihuozhi* are listed in Part V. Note that several conveniently print the original text along with the notes and supplementary matter.

The standard combined index to the *Shihuozhi* is in *H-Y Index* 32. For a dictionary of special terms in them, see Hoshi Ayao 星斌夫, *Chûgoku shakai keizaishi goi* 中國社會經濟史語彙.[10] The brief explanations are based on the major Japanese studies and translations of the *Shihuozhi* as well as on 18 other important contributions of Japanese scholars to Chinese socioeconomic history.

Note also the *Hequzhi* 河渠志 (monographs on rivers and canals) in the *Shiji*, the *Hanshu*, *Songshi*, *Jinshi*, *Yuanshi*, *Mingshi* and *Qingshi gao*.[11]

Penal Law

The 15 *Xingfazhi* 刑法志 (monographs on penal law) have been annotated and published together several times, recently also with translations into modern Chinese.[12] Studies and translations of individual monographs on penal law are listed in the appropriate chapters of Part V. See Chap. 27 for more detailed sources on law than can be found in the monographs.

[9] For a convenient punctuated and annotated edition see, *Lidai shihuozhi zhushi* 歷代食貨志注釋, Wang Leiming 王雷鳴, ed., 5 vols., Nongye, 1985–93. See also, *Zhongguo lidai shihuozhi zhengbian* 中國歷代食貨志正編, Chengwen, 1971.

[10] *Chûgoku shakai keizaishi goi* (Glossary of Chinese socioeconomic history), Tôyô bunko, 1966; rev. ed., Kôbundô, 1976; continuation (*zokuhen* 曾編), Kôbundô, 1975; third collection (*sanhen* 三編), Kôbundô, 1988. The *zokuhen* and *sanhen* are drawn from more than 50 Japanese studies published between 1965 and 1983.

[11] *Ershiwushi hequzhi zhushi* 二十五史河渠志注釋 (Monographs on rivers and canals in the 25 Histories), Zhou Kuiyi 周魁一 et al., eds., Zhongguo shudian, 1990.

[12] See, for example, *Xingfazhi zhushi* 刑法志注釋 (Monographs on penal law, annotated and translated into modern Chinese), Jilin renmin, 1994.

Official Posts and the Examination System

All officials (*guan* 官) on the organization tables of the imperial government were a assigned a rank in a system known from AD 220 as the Nine ranks (*jiupin* 九品). The most senior was rank one. Each rank was further subdivided into upper (*zheng* 正) and lower (*cong* 從) grades (*deng* 等, also translated as classes or degrees). Thus the supervisor of the imperial secret service in the Ming, whose official post was eunuch director of the Directorate of Ceremonial (*Sili jian taijian* 司禮監太監), was ranked as *zheng sipin* 正四品 (Rank 4, upper grade, conventionally written "4a"). In some periods and for some posts the 18 grades were further divided into upper (*shang* 上) and lower (*xia* 下) echelons. If this is the case write 4a1 or 4a2.

The indispensable starting point is Charles O. Hucker, *A Dictionary of Official Titles in Imperial China*, SUP, 1985; SMC rpnt., 1988. *DOTIC* is the single best introduction in English to central and provincial administration in all periods of Chinese imperial history. As an added bonus, the Introduction gives an account of governmental organization from the Zhou to the Qing. *DOTIC* lists 8,291 titles, arranged alphabetically by Wade-Giles. There is an index to the English translations of the titles, plus a character index. If you cannot find a title in *DOTIC*, then either try an even larger comprehensive dictionary or one of the more specialized references for individual periods:

Zhongguo lidai guanzhi da cidian 中國歷代官制大辭典 has 21,659 entries from all periods up to 1911. It also has something missing in *DOTIC*, namely tables of the ranking systems used in each period, "Lidai zhiguan pinwei biao 歷代職官品位表," 871-915.[13]

Specialized references are listed for each period in Part I (pre-Qin) and in each chapter of Part V under *Research Tools, Official Titles and Office Holders*.

---

[13] *Zhongguo lidai guanzhi da cidian* (Large dictionary of Chinese official titles in different periods), Lü Zongli 呂宗力, ed. in chief, Beijing chubanshe, 1994; rpnt., 1995.

Sixteen of the Histories contain *Baiguanzhi* 百官志 or *Zhi-guanzhi* 職官志 (monographs on official posts); eight have *Xuanjuzhi* 選舉志 (monographs on the examination system; see Table 22). These are summaries of the organization of the bureaucracy in specific periods. Translations are listed in Part V.

Throughout Chinese history summaries of official posts of all periods were also compiled. The most complete was made in the Qing and served as the basis for modern dictionaries or directories of official posts such as *DOTIC* and Lü:

Lidai zhiguanbiao 歷代職官表 (Tables of official posts from the earliest times to the nineteenth century), Huang Benji 黃本驥, with introduction and glossary by Qu Tuiyuan 瞿蛻園, Zhonghua, 1965. This edition contains a four-corner index of titles; reprints include Shanghai guji, 1980. Huang produced his original table as a simplified version of the imperially sponsored work of the same title which had been compiled by Ji Yun 紀昀 and others in 1782.

For translations of official titles, mainly from these monographs, but also from the *Huidian* 會典 (institutes, i.e., compendia of administrative law), during individual dynasties, see the more detailed sources discussed in chaps. 26 to 28.

Table 22: Examination System of the Qing

Exam type	Tongshi 童試 juvenile[14]	Xiangshi 鄉試 local	Huishi 會試 metropolitan	Dianshi 殿試 palace
Time	annual	triennial; usually in the 8th month	triennial; 3rd month of the year after the xiangshi	triennial; after the huishi on 21/4
Place	xian 縣, fu 府 and xueyuan 學院	Provincial capitals; Beijing and Nanjing	Beijing and Nanjing	Beijing Taihedian 太和殿
Those eligible	tongsheng 童生	xiucai 秀才 (flourishing talents) and jiansheng 監生 (students of the Imperial Academy)	juren 舉人 (recommended man)	gongshi 貢士 (tribute students)
Content of exam	Classics; Histories; baguwen 八股文 (eight-legged essays); poetry composition	same	same	cewen 策問 (questions on policy)
Degree	shengyuan 生員 (also xiangsheng 庠生); popularly referred to as xiucai 秀才	juren 舉人 (popularly referred to as xiaoqing 孝廉; first ranked: jieyuan 解元. Juren 舉人 were eligible to serve as county magistrates or directors of county schools (zhixian 知縣 or jiaozhi 教職)	gongshi 貢士; first ranked: huiyuan 會元	jinshi 進士; (advanced scholar); first ranked: zhuangyuan 狀元; second: bangyan 榜眼; third: tanhua 探花. Jinshi were popularly known as laohuban 老虎班 (tiger class)

Note: The above in outline was the examination system (*kejuzhi* 科舉制) of the Qing as it had emerged after many centuries of evolution since the Han. The Ming system was broadly the same.[15]

[14] See section 1.3.2.

[15] Ichisada Miyazaki, *China's Examination Hell: The Civil Service Examinations of Imperial China*, Conrad Schirokauer, tr., Weatherill, 1976; Ping-ti Ho (He Bingdi 何炳棣), *The Ladder of Success in Imperial China: Aspects of Social Mobility, 1368–1911*, Col. UP, 1962.

Table 23: Monographs in the Standard Histories

History:	1	2	3	4	5	6	7	8	9	10	11	12	13	14	15	16	17	18	19	20	21	22	23	24	25	26
Ritual	x	x	x		x	x	x			x			x			x	x	x		x	x	x	x	x	x	x
Music	x	x			x	x	x			x			x			x	x	x		x	x	x	x	x	x	x
Harmony	x	x	x		x					x			x					x								
Calendar	x	x	x		x					x			x			x	x	x		x	x	x	x	x	x	x
Astronomy	x	x	x		x	x	x			x			x			x	x	x	x	x		x	x	x	x	x
Sacrifices	x	x	x																				x			
Rivers and canals	x	x																		x		x	x	x	x	x
Food and money	x	x			x					x			x			x	x	x		x	x	x	x	x	x	x
Law		x			x					x			x			x	x	x		x	x	x	x	x	x	x
Natural omens		x	x		x	x	x									x	x	x		x		x	x	x	x	x
Admin. geography		x	x		x	x	x			x			x			x	x	x	x	x	x	x	x	x	x	x
Bibliographies	x															x	x		x				x			x
Official posts			x		x	x	x			x			x			x	x	x		x	x	x	x	x	x	x
Sumptuary laws			x		x		x									x	x			x		x	x	x	x	x
Auspicious influences						x	x			x																
Buddhists, Daoists										x													x			
Imperial guards																x				x	x	x				
Exam system																x	x			x		x	x	x	x	x
Army																x				x	x	x	x	x	x	x
Border guards																				x						
Militia																				x						
Communications																										x
Foreign relations																										x

1. *Shiji* 史記
2. *Hanshu* 漢書
3. *Hou Hanshu* 後漢書
4. *Sanguozhi* 三國志
5. *Jinshu* 晉書
6. *Songshu* 宋書
7. *Nan-Qishu* 南齊書
8. *Liangshu* 梁書
9. *Chenshu* 陳書
10. *Weishu* 魏書
11. *Bei-Qishu* 北齊書
12. *Zhoushu* 周書
13. *Suishu* 隋書

14. *Nanshi* 南史
15. *Beishi* 北史
16. *Jiu Tangshu* 舊唐書
17. *Xin Tangshu* 新唐書
18. *Jiu Wudaishi* 舊五代史
19. *Xin Wudaishi* 新五代史
20. *Songshi* 宋史
21. *Liaoshi* 遼史
22. *Jinshi* 金史
23. *Yuanshi* 元史
24. *Mingshi* 明史
25. *Xin Yuanshi* 新元史
26. *Qingshi gao* 清史稿

23

Topically Arranged Histories

Until the Song, the two main forms of historical writing were *Biannianti* 編年體 (annals) and *Jizhuanti* 紀傳體 (annals-biographies, see chaps. 21 and 22). The disadvantages of these two forms was that in order to find out about one person or one event, the reader had either to search through many different entries in the rigid chronological frame of the Annals or to bring together information often scattered in the different parts of the composite Standard Histories. These difficulties were partially resolved when a twelfth-century Song scholar-official named Yuan Shu 袁樞 (1131–1205) rearranged all the chronological entries in Sima Guang's *Zizhi tongjian* into 239 topical entries and thus broke out of the strict Annals framework.

Yuan Shu called his rearrangement *Tongjian jishi benmo* 通鑑紀事本末.[1] He is generally credited with having developed the third major type of Chinese historical writing, *jishi benmo ti* 紀事本末體 (from beginning to ending of events or topically arranged style). There were many imitators, especially in the Qing, when *Fanglüe* 方略 (official histories of campaigns), became particularly popular (28.2), but for the most part, writers in this style only rearranged existing works (as had Yuan); they did not add new materials or interpretations. The single outstanding exception was Gu Yingtai 谷應泰 (d. 1689), who wrote his *Mingshi jishi benmo* 明史紀事本末 before the *Mingshi* had been compiled and thus made an important contribution to Ming history (49.6).

---

[1] *Tongjian jishi benmo* (The comprehensive mirror for aid in government, topically arranged), 1173; punctuated edition, 12 vols., Zhonghua, 1964; 1986.

The Zhonghua Shuju published the main *jishi benmo* titles in punctuated, collated editions in the 1970s and 1980s and re-issued them in 1997 in a reduced-type edition, *Lidai jishi ben-moti* 歷代 記事本末體, 2 vols.:

Tongjian jishi benmo 通鑑紀事本末 (see previous page).

Zuozhuan jishi benmo 左傳紀事本末 (The *Zuozhuan* topically arranged), Gao Shiqi 高士奇 (1645–1703), ed., 1690.

Songshi jishi benmo 明史紀事本末 (The *Songshi* topically arranged), Chen Bangchan 陳邦瞻 (1557–1602), 1605.

Liaoshi jishi benmo 明史紀事本末 (The *Liaoshi* topically arranged), Chen Bangchan 陳邦瞻, 1606.

Jinshi jishi benmo 明史紀事本末 (The *Jinshi* topically arranged), Chen Bangchan 陳邦瞻, 1606.

Yuanshi jishi benmo 明史紀事本末 (The *Yuanshi* topically arranged), Chen Bangchan 陳邦瞻, 1606.

Mingshi jishi benmo 明史紀事本末 (see previous page).

Sanfan jishi benmo 三蕃紀事本末 (The three feudatories topically arranged), Yang Lurong 楊陸榮 (dates not known), 1717.

24

Miscellaneous Histories

Zashi 雜史 (miscellaneous histories) is a residual biblio-graphical category, not a style of historical writing.

The definition of *zashi* changed after its introduction in the Tang, but in general, it included all those histori-cal works not fitting into the official categories and con-sidered less serious than the *Bieshi* 別史 (20.5). Many were also sometimes`classified under *Biji* 筆記 (miscel-laneous notes, chap. 31) or in the *Zajia* 雜家 (miscel-laneous writers), one of the subbranches of the Philoso-phers' branch. *Zashi* usually do not cover a whole dy-nasty, but rather a single event or a reign period or a particular institution. They are an extremely valuable type of source. Their wide scope is illustrated in the range of subjects covered in the 35 examples given be-low.

A number of Han and Pre-Qin works were cataloged as *Zashi* (for details, see Table 18, 19.1):

Yi Zhoushu 逸周書; *Guoyu* 國語; *Zhanguoce* 戰國策; *Yuejueshu* 越絕書; *Wu-Yue chunqiu* 吳越春秋; *Chu-Han chunqiu* 楚漢春秋.

Han to Tang

Gushi kao 古史考 (Investigation of ancient history), Qiao Zhou 譙周 (201–70). Exists today only in a recovered edition contained in vari-ous *congshu.*

Diwang shiji 帝王世紀 (Record of the lives of the emperors and kings), Huangfu Mi 皇甫謐 (215–82), Zhonghua, 1964. Ancient history us-ing sources long since lost.

Fengsu tongyi 風俗通義 (5.3.2).

Shishuo xinyu 世説新語 (45.2).

Tang

Zhenguan zhengyao 貞觀政要 (Essentials of government of the Zhenguan era), Wu Jing 吳兢 (670–749), Shanghai guji, 1978. Contains documents of senior officials of the Zhenguan period (627–49).

An Lushan shiji 安祿山事蹟 (46.2).

Dongguan zouji 東觀奏記 (Record of events from the Eastern Library), 891, Bei Tingyu 裴庭裕. Reminiscences of the Xuanzong 宣宗 court. The writer was a Hanlin scholar and one of those who attempted to compile the *Xuanzong shilu*. An important source for the later Tang.

Tang to Yuan

Nan Tang jinshi 南唐近事 (Recent events in Nan-Tang), Zheng Wenbao 鄭文寶 (953–1013). Recounts the events of 937–75.

Zhushi 麈史 (Chats on historical matters), Wang Dechen 王得臣 (1036–1116). Has details on the institutions of Northern Song (indexed in *Chûgoku zuihitsu zatcho sakuin*).

Qingxi kougui 青溪寇軌 (Traces of the bandits of Qingxi), Fang Shao 方勺 (1066–?). An independent account of the Fang La 方臘 rebellion, differing from that found in the *Songshi* 宋史 (Qingxi was the place in Zhejiang in which the rebellion occurred).

Chaoye leiyao 朝野類要 (Important affairs at court and in country), Zhao Sheng 趙陞. Defines terms from many areas of official life. See Stephen Yu, *Chaoye leiyao yinde* 朝野類要引得, (Index to the important affairs at court and in the country), CMC, 1974 (also indexed in *Chûgoku zuihitsu sakuin*).

Runan yishi 汝南遺事 (48.4).

Menggu bishi 蒙古秘史 (48.5.1).

Menggu yuanliu 蒙古源流 (Origins and devlopment of the Mongols), comp. in the early eighteenth century. The original Mongolian title is *Erdeni-yin tobci*; completed in 1662 by Sayang Secen (b. 1604), Nei Menggu renmin, 1980.

Zhanchi 站赤 (The postal relay system); recovered from the *Yongle dadian, juan* 19,416–19,426. Originally in *Jingshi dadian* 經世大典 and *Yuan dianzhang* 元典章. It was used as the basis for the coverage of this subject in the *Yuanshi, juan* 101. Describes the workings of the

Yuan horse-relay system, 1229–30. *Zhanchi* is a loan word from the Mongolian *Jamci* (4.1).

Changchun zhenren xiyouji 長春真人西遊記 (41.5.1, *Song*).

Ming and Qing

Guochu qunxiong shilüe 國初群雄事略 (Brief lives of the heroes at the beginning of the dynasty), Qian Qianyi 錢謙益 (1582–1664). Compilation of records on the rise of military leaders in the late Yuan and early Ming.

Xiyuan wenjianlu 西園聞見錄 (Heard and seen by Xiyuan), Zhang Xuan 張萱 (1557–?), 1632. Notes on the words and deeds of hundreds of Ming personalities. Includes gossip and observations of institutions at the end of the sixteenth century. Xiyuan was the *hao* of the late Ming scholar Zhang Xuan 張萱 (1558–1641). *DMB*, 78–79.

Chunming mengyu lu 春明夢餘錄 (see 49.2, *Biji*).

Beizheng lu 北征錄 (Record of the northern offensive), Jin Youzi 金幼孜 (1368–1431). Record in diary form of the Yongle emperor's Mongolian campaign between the second and seventh month, 1410, and again in 1414 (*Beizheng houlu* 北征後錄), Wenhai, *Zhongguo fangzhi congshu* 中國方志叢書 edition.

Fu'an dongyiji 撫安東夷記 (Record of pacification of the eastern barabarians), 1520, Ma Wensheng 馬文昇 (1426–1510). One of the earliest descriptions of Liaodong (1478).

Jiajing ping Wo zhiyi jilüe 嘉靖平倭祗役紀略 (Record of pacification of the pirates in the Jiajing era), Zhao Wenhua 趙文華 (?–1557), 1555, Yangzhou guji, 1959.

Jiajing Dongnan ping Wo tonglu 嘉靖東南平倭通錄 (Complete record of pacification of the southeast pirates in the Jiajing era), Xu Xueju 徐學聚 (*jinshi*, 1583). Excerpts from the author's *Guochao dianhui* 國朝典彙 (Compendium on the statutes of the dynasty) section on Japan, 1552–54, *Zhongguo lishi yanjiu ziliao congshu* 中國歷史研究資料叢書 edition, 1947.

Wanli wugonglu 萬曆武功錄 (Record of military affairs of the Wanli era), Qu Jiusi 瞿九思. Biographies of the Wanli emperor's military opponents.

Qizhen liangchao bofulu 啓禎兩朝剝膚錄 (Record of the calamities in the Tianqi 天啓 and Chongzhen 崇禎 reigns), Wu Yingji 吳應箕 (1594–1645). Chronicles the political struggles of 1624–8.

Liehuang xiaoshi 烈皇小識 (Brief notes on emperor Chongzhen 崇禎),
    Wen Bing 文秉 (1609–69); *Zhongguo lishi yanjiu ziliao congshu* 中國
    歷史研究資料叢書 edition, 1947.

Mingji beilüe 明季北略 (Brief account of the late Ming in the North) and
    Mingji nanlüe 明季南略 (Brief account of the late Ming in the South),
    Ji Liuqi 計六奇 (1622–87?). A history of the end of the Ming in *jishi
    benmo* style; the former covers the years 1595–1644; the latter, 1644–
    65, *Guoxue jiben congshu.*

Dongnan jishi 東南紀事 (Record of events in the Southeast) and *Xi'nan
    jishi* 西南紀事 (Record of events in the Southwest), Shao Tingcai 邵
    廷采 (1648–1711). Deals with the Southern Ming regime, *Zhongguo
    lishi yanjiu ziliao congshu* 中國歷史研究資料叢書 edition, 1946.

Suikou jilüe 綏寇紀略 (Record of insurrections), Wu Weiye 吳偉業
    (1609–71). Recounts the insurrections at the end of the Ming.

Official Communications

Since the beginning of the empire, there have been strict regulations as to the type of document to be used depending on the occasion, the addressee and the rank of the person whose name or seal was to appear on it. There have also been punishments for violation of name taboos and orthographic errors in documents, especially those submitted to the emperor.

By far the most numerous types of document were those from the top down (25.1), notably from the ruler to his officials, or to the people. One modern study lists 175 terms for top-down documents (edicts, *zhaoling* 詔令, became the generic term for these imperial commands); 64 for bottom-up (memorials *zouyi* 奏議, 25.2) and only 28 for documents between equal ranking officials or offices (25.3).

The names for different documents were often derived from the materials upon which they were originally written. Thus the ubiquitous *zha* 札 (small wooden tablet) came to mean "note" or "document."

The terms changed substantially over the dynasties and the same term was also used for different types of document. Some introductions to the different types of document are given in Box 9 at the end of the chapter.

25.1 Edicts

Tens of thousands of original documents have survived from the Ming and earlier dynasties and many more have been excerpted in whole or in part in various collections, historical works and official compilations. Approximately fifteen million original documents survive from the Qing. These documents are one of the most important basic materials used by historians in the past as well as today.

Most common of all were the proclamations or edicts (*zhao* 詔) of the ruler or his commands (*ling* 令). There were many different terms for edict apart from *zhao*, which during the Warring States had grown out of the expression *gao* 告 or *gao* 誥, meaning to call together to hear an announcement or proclamation. The first emperor standardized the terms for his edicts to *zhao* 詔 (or *zhaoshu* 詔書) and *zhi* 制 (particularly important pronouncements). These terms continued in use until 1911.

During the Han, edicts were composed in an elegant style unmatched in later history. There were many varieties: secret edicts (*mizhao* 密詔) or personally written edicts (*qinzhao* 親詔), for example. They were also called *zhaoce* 詔策 (*ce* 册), reflecting the material (*jiandu* 簡牘) on which the edicts were written. *Ce* 册 (or *ceshu* 册書 before the Han and *ce* 策, *ceshu* 策書 or *ceming* 策命 after the Han) is as old a term as *zhao* 詔 and in imperial times was used for different types of enfeoffment, investiture or appointment instruments such as letters patent. By the Qing, the material used, for example gold, silver, jade or paper, depended on the quality of the person being invested with a title or office. *Chi* 敕 was another term for documents of appointment, as in the expression *chiming* 敕命, which by the Qing was used for the letter of appointment of officials below grade 6. *Chi* was also used for rescript, as in *chizhi* 敕旨. It became a formal term in this sense during the Song. There were many other terms for imperial edicts or decrees, such as *shangyu* 上諭 or *shengzhi* 聖旨, as well as instructions from the emperor, such as *xun* 訓 or *yu* 諭 (*shengyu* 聖諭) or *jiao* 教. By the Ming, *yu* had become *yuzhi* 諭旨 (imperial rescript) and continued in use in this sense in the Qing. In the Ming, the emperor expressed his endorsement of a proposal with a *pida* 批答, which by the Qing was called a *zhupi* 硃批 (vermilion comment, from the color of the special ink reserved for use by the emperor).

Senior officials addressing an instruction to a subordinate in the Qing used a *yutie* 諭帖. To inform a wider public they used (as they still do today) a *gaoshi* 告示 or *bugao* 布告 (announcement), which the Qianlong emperor ordered "should be written in a style which women and children can understand." Other official communications to subordinates or inferior offices were called *zha* 劄 (*zhawen* 劄文; informally *zha* 札 was also used), *pai* 牌 or *feng* 封.

The practice of collecting together memorable edicts or imperial instructions (*shengxun* 聖訓) of a particular reign or dynasty began early, but the first large surviving collections were made during the Song, the most famous being the *Tang da zhaoling ji* 唐大詔令集 (46.2). Other collections of edicts are listed in the appropriate chapters of Part V. Many collections of Qing edicts and imperial instructions were published during the Qing, and tens of thousands of Qing edicts from the central Qing archives have been published in the course of the twentieth century and the process continues (50.2).

25.2 Memorials

Memorials (*zouyi* 奏議) were of many different types and were called by many different names in different periods. The earliest term was *shu* 書, which the first emperor had renamed *zou* 奏 although people continued to use *shu* 書 or *shu* 疏 (or *shangshu* 上書, *shangshu* 上疏). In the Han, a *zhang* 章 was used to make clear one's gratitude; a *zou* 奏 was used for reporting an investigation or to impeach; a *biao* 表 was used to express feelings; and an *yi* 議 was to express a contrary opinion. Other terms included *ce* 策 (a policy proposal). All could be used with *zou* 奏 prefixed to indicate they were directed to the emperor. A remonstrance was termed a *boyi* 駁議, or less formally, an *yi*

議 (opinion). These distinctions were not strictly adhered to in subsequent dynasties during the course of which additional terms were developed.

By the Ming, in theory, anybody (including non-officials) could submit a *zouben* 奏本 (personal memorial) to the emperor. *Tiben* 題本 (usually translated as "routine memorials") were reserved for official official matters. The Qing continued the Ming system, but the Kangxi emperor introduced secret palace memorials (*zouzhe* 奏摺, literally, "memorials written on folded paper"). The personal memorials (*zouben*) were abolished in 1748. The *tiben* gradually faded in importance until they too were abolished in 1901.[1]

The emperor would often add brief remarks to a memorial such as *zhidao le* 知道了 (as we would say, "noted"). Frequently, he just put a circle to show the same. This implied neither approval nor disapproval, merely that he had taken note.

The codes and statutes stipulated what terms could be used by officials of what rank to approve which documents.

Memorials and other bottom-up documents, form one of the basic sources of Chinese history, flowing in and up to all levels of the bureaucracy on all subjects. Many of the types of historical writing and documents so far discussed either quote from them in whole or in part or were based upon them.

As in all branches of Chinese historiography, the further back the period, the fewer such basic sources survive intact. Instead we have them in excerpted or adapted form in the Standard Histories or other compilations; the originals have long since been lost. If they have survived it is among the newly discovered documents (such as those on bamboo strips, *jiandu* 簡

---

[1] Silas Hsiu-liang Wu, "Transmission of Ming Memorials," *TP* 54: 275–87 (1968); Timothy Brook, "The transmission of state documents," in his chapter "Communications and Commerce," in *CHC*, vol. 8, CUP, 1998, 637–39; Silas Wu, "The Memorial Systems of the Ch'ing Dynasty," *HJAS* 27: 7–75 (1967); Beatrice S. Bartlett, *Monarchs and Ministers: The Grand Council in Mid-Ch'ing China, 1723–1820*, UCP, 1991. Further references to the Ming and Qing memorial systems are given in chaps. 49 and 50.

牘) or more usually, in an author's collected works (*bieji* 別集, 30.4). During the Ming it became common practice for the first time to publish collections of memorials (either of an individual, or of a given period or on a given subject). This practice was continued in the Qing. In the twentieth century the Qing central archives were opened and selections of memorials and other documents began to be edited and published from them. At a conservative estimate something in the order of 4 million late Qing memorials have yet to be published (50.1–2).

There is no easy way of tracing memorials on a particular subject or by a given author before the Ming.

The earliest comprehensive collection of memorials from all periods was the imperial-sponsored *Lidai mingchen zouyi* 歷代名臣奏議, Huang Huai 黃淮 (1367–1449) et al., comp., 1416. It includes 8,000 memorials. The Shanghai guji edition includes an author index.[2]

For a modern collection of 3,800 memorials of 2,200 personalities from the Warring States to the nineteenth century see *Zhongguo lidai zouyi dadian* 中國歷代奏議大典.[3]

The surest way of finding memorials by pre-Ming officials is first to check through their biographies and then to check through their collected works. The memorials of eminent officials were often collected and published together.

25.3 Lateral Communications

One of the earliest terms for lateral communications was *yi* 移 (or *yishu* 移書), with *yi* 移 changing to *yi* 遺 (or *yishu* 遺書) in the Warring States. Other expressions used later, included *guan* 關 (*guanwen* 關文). *Zi* 咨 (*ziwen* 咨文 or *zicheng* 咨呈) was used for communications between high-ranking offices or offi-

---

[2] *Lidai mingchen zouyi* (Memorials of leading officials of each period), 1416; 5 vols., Shanghai guji, 1989.

[3] *Zhongguo lidai zouyi dadian* 中國歷代奏議大典 (Large collection of memorials arranged by period), Ding Shouhe 丁守和 et al., eds., 4 vols., Heilongjiang renmin, 1994, which has notes and introductions and is indexed.

cials at the same level (for example during the Ming, for communications between ranking officials of the Six Boards). Everyday documents between offices were sent in the form of a *zhihui* 知會 (*zhaohui* 照會 during the Qing). The Grand Council used *jiaopian* 交片 for its everyday lateral communications.

Mengshu 盟書 was used for a covenant or treaty between two states (or two families). *Die* 牒 (*diewen* 牒文, *diecheng* 牒呈) began as a synonym for *zha* 札 (from the name of the wooden tablet on which it was originally written). It later came to mean note or record. Today it is still used, as in *tongdie* 通牒 (diplomatic note), or *zuihou tongdie* 最后通牒 (ultimatum). *Ci* 刺 (or *ye* 謁) was a namecard. *Han* 函 (*hanwen* 函文) by the Ming meant letter, both in public and private life, although in the former use, it was a letter signed by an individual official. The generic term for private letters was, and is, *shuxin* 書信 (3.6).

25.4 *Official Gazette*

Ever since the Tang, selected memorials and edicts were published in the capital as a form of gazette called *Jinzou yuan zhuangbao* 進奏院狀報 or *baozhuang* 報狀, *dibao* 邸報 or *zabao* 雜報.[4] In the Northern Song private *xiaobao* 小報 or *xinwen* 新聞 were for a short while published in the capital. From the mid-Ming, regular publication of news in the form of a *jingbao* 京報 (gazette) started. They were published in Beijing and Nanjing and other cities and carried selected edicts and memorials and official appointments. Fragments of the Ming gazettes were excerpted by a late Ming editor; otherwise, old-style gazettes are extant mainly from the late Qing.[5] Modern newspa-

---

[4] The *Jinzou yuan* in the Tang were the capital liaison offices of provincial officials, also referred to as liaison hostels (*di* 邸, *dishe* 邸社). In the Song they became formalized as the Memorial Office, charged inter alia with transmitting government documents between the center and the Circuit authorities (*DOTIC*, 1156).

[5] *Wanli dichao* 萬曆邸抄, Taibei: Guoli tushuguan, 1963; Yin Yungong 尹韵公, *Zhongguo Mingdai xinwen chuanboshi* 中國明代新聞傳播

Footnote continued on next page

pers in Chinese started at the beginning of the nineteenth century. The earliest were edited by Protestant missionaries, who
coined the word *xinwen* 新聞 for "news" after the same Song
term (which also gave Japanese its word for newspaper, *shim-
bun* 新聞).

Box 9: Introductions to Documentary Chinese

Gujin gongwen wenzhong huishi 古今公文文種匯釋 (Collected explanations of the different types of official correspondence, ancient and
modern), Liang Qinghai 梁清海 et al., eds., Sichuan daxue, 1992. Examples are given of the most important types of document with
summary translations into modern Chinese. The first two-thirds of
the book are on documents up to 1911; the last third is on documents from 1912 to the present day.

   Lishi wenshu yongyu cidian Ming-Qing, Minguo bufen 歷史文書用
語辭典明清民國部分 (Dictionary of documentary terms, Ming,
Qing and Republic periods), Liu Wenjie 劉文傑, ed., Sichuan renmin, 1988.

   A list of the many terms used for edicts and memorials is given
with brief annotations in E. D. Edwards, "A Classified Guide to the
Thirteen Classes of Chinese Prose," *BSOAS* 12: 777–88 (1948).

   For introductions to documentary Chinese of individual periods, see Part V (especially the Qing, 50.8.2).

史 (History of the spread of newspapers in the Ming dynasty), Qongqing,
1990.

26

Government Institutions

Very large quantities of official documents of all sorts were stored, collected and compiled under each dynasty. Some of the resulting printed collections are still extant. Broadest in coverage are the *Huiyao* 會要 (collections of important documents). They trace the history of institutions of a given dynasty using excerpts from contemporary documents (26.1). Other collections trace the history of governmental institutions over many dynasties. They served as repositories of precedents. The ten most famous are known as the *Shitong* 十通 (The ten encyclopaedic histories of institutions, 26.2). Both the *Huiyao* and the *Shitong* are listed as *zhengshu* 政書 (works relating to government) in the History branch of the *Sibu* classification as also were the codes, statutes and other works of law (chap. 27).

26.1 Huiyao 會要

The first *Huiyao* was compiled during the Tang and formed the basis of the *Tang huiyao* 唐會要 (Important documents of the Tang), Wang Pu 王溥 (922–82); the *Wudai huiyao* 五代會要 (Important documents of the Five Dynasties), Wang Pu 王溥; and the *Song huiyao* 宋會要 (Important documents of the Song), see below.[1] These three were compiled during the dyn-

---

[1]*Tang huiyao*, 3 vols., Zhonghua, 1955; 3rd rpnt., 2 vols., Shanghai guji, 1991; there is a name index: *Tang huiyao renming suoyin* 唐會要人名索
Footnote continued on next page

asty itself or shortly thereafter and, as a consequence, only they contain large amounts of primary materials not found in other sources.

Of the three, the third and by far the largest is the *Song huiyao jigao* 宋會要輯稿 (so called because it was recovered from the *Yongle dadian* 永樂大典 [Yongle encyclopaedia] in the early-nineteenth century [by Xu Song 徐松, 1781–1848]. It was only printed for the first time in 1936.[2]

The materials in the *Song huiyao* were taken from sources no longer extant such as the *Rili* 日曆 (Daily calendar). It is the largest collection of Song documents extant and the most important of the *Huiyao*. It and has been intensively studied and indexed by historians of the Song (47.2).

The *Huiyao* for the earlier dynasties were mainly compiled during the Qing. Although the sources on which they were based are often still extant today, they have a certain use in that the material they contain is organized systematically to cover the institutions of a particular dynasty—political, economic, military and cultural. It is, therefore, often easier to find things in them than in the sources from which they were taken.

For compendia containing similar information on governmental institutions, laws and regulations, see:

Administrative and Penal Law (chap. 27)
Encyclopaedic Histories of Institutions (26.2)
Monographs in the Standard Histories (22.3)

The main *Huiyao* are listed in Table 24:

引, Zhang Chenshi 張忱石, ed. in chief, Zhonghua, 1991; *Wudai huiyao*, Shanghai guji, 1978.

[2] *Song huiyao jigao* 宋會要輯稿, photolithographic reproduction, 200 *ce*, Peiping tushuguan, 1936; reduced-size, facsimile reproduction, 8 vols., Zhonghua, 1957; rpnt., 1987; Shanghai guji, 1986; Xinwenfeng, 1976.

Table 24: Huiyao 會要

Chunqiu huiyao 春秋會要, Yao Yanqu 姚彥渠 (Qing), punctuated ed., Zhonghua, 1955. Records gathered from existing sources under 98 subheadings.

Qiguo kao 七國考, Dong Yue 董說 (1620–86), punctuated ed., Zhonghua, 1956. Covers 14 subjects, including official posts, cities, palaces, music, clothing, weapons, laws, disasters of the Seven Kingdoms of the Warring States period.

Qin huiyao dingbu 秦會要訂補, Sun Kai 孫楷 (1871–1907), 1904; corrections by Xu Fu 徐復, punctuated ed., Zhonghua, 1959. Contains 336 entries covering the standard categories.

Xi-Han huiyao 西漢會要, Xu Tianlin 徐天麟 (twelfth–thirteenth century), 1211; punctuated ed., Zhonghua, 1955; Shanghai guji, 1977. The author used the *Tang huiyao* as his model. Sources are indicated.

Dong-Han huiyao 東漢會要, Xu Tianlin, 1226; punctuated ed., Zhonghua, 1955; Shanghai guji, punctuated ed., 1978.

Sanguo huiyao 三國會要, Yang Chen 楊晨 (late Qing), 1899; punctuated ed., Zhonghua, 1956. Since the Standard Histories of the Three Kingdoms have no monographs, this work is useful in rearranging under subject categories information scattered in many sources.

Gaoben Jin huiyao 稿本晉會要 (Draft of the *Jin huiyao*), Wang Zhaoyong 汪兆鏞 (1861–1939), punctuated ed., Shumu wenxuian, 1988. Similar categories to previous *huiyao* with the addition of inscriptions, the Classics and main events.

Nanchao Song huiyao 南朝宋會要, *Nanchao Qi huiyao* 南朝齊會要, *Nanchao Liang huiyao* 南朝梁會要, *Nanchao Chen huiyao* 南朝陳會要, Zhu Mingpan 朱銘盤 (1852–93), punctuated edition, Shanghai guji, 1984–86. These are useful sources on the institutions of these Southern Dynasties.

Tang huiyao 唐會要 (see previous page).

Wudai huiyao 五代會要 (see previous page).

Song huiyao jigao 宋會要輯稿 (see previous page).

Ming huiyao 明會要, Long Wenbin 龍文彬 (1821– ?), typeset, punctuated ed., Zhonghua, 1956; Shijie shuju, 2 vols., 1963.

26.2 Shitong 十通

The *Shitong* (The ten encyclopaedic histories of institutions) cover much the same subjects as the monographs in the Standard Histories (22.3). They were also written for the same purposes, that is, as guides and reference works to the administration and institutions of past periods for scholars and officials. In scope, however, they are often wider than the monographs; furthermore, the authors of the three most famous of them covered much longer periods and left the mark of their own individual views.

The work which was to set the model was Du You 杜佑 (735–812), *Tongdian* 通典. It lays greater emphasis on administration (Du had been chancellor three times) than on ritual as compared to the monographs in the Standard Histories up to that time. It is divided into nine main sections covering (1) Food and money; (2) the examination system; (3) official titles; (4) rites; (5) music; (6) the army; (7) punishments; (8) provincial administration; and (9) border defense. The value of the *Tongdian* lies not only in its assembling of many disparate sources under clear subject headings, but also in the fact that many of the sources used have since been lost.[3]

The two other most famous such works are Zheng Qiao 鄭樵 (1104–62), *Tongzhi* 通志,[4] and Ma Duanlin 馬端臨 (1254–1323) *Wenxian tongkao* 文獻通考.[5] The three were often published together and are usually referred to as the *Santong* 三通.

The following is a list of the main section headings of the *Wenxian tongkao* which gives some idea of the scope of the subjects covered: (1) land taxes; (2) currency; (3) population; (4) services and corvée; (5) customs and tolls; (6) official markets and purchases; (7) local tribute; (8) national expenditure; (9) ex-

[3] *Tongdian* (Encyclopaedic history of institutions), AD 801; 5 vols., punctuated edition, Zhonghua, 1988; 3rd prnt., 1996.

[4] *Tongzhi* (Comprehensive history of institutions), 1149; Zhonghua, 1987, rpnt., 1990.

[5] *Wenxian tongkao* (General history of institutions and critical examination of documents and studies), 1224; Zhonghua, 1986.

aminations and promotions; (10) schools; (11) government posts; (12) imperial sacrifices; (13) minor sacrifices; (14) imperial ancestral temple; (15) other temples and shrines; (16) court rites; (17) posthumous titles; (18) music; (19) the army; (20) penal law; (21) bibliography; (22) calligraphy; (23) imperial genealogy; (24) nobility; (25) the sun, the moon and the five planets; (26) freaks of nature; (27) geography; (28) foreign countries.

Six continuations were compiled during the eighteenth century and published together under the title *Jiutong* 九通. Although lacking the individual editorial touch and broad chronological sweep of the *Santong*, these six (plus a Ming and a late Qing one) are well arranged collections of sources. The best modern edition is the *Shitong* 十通 by the Shangwu Press. It has an index (vol. 21), essential for works with a combined total of over 20,000 triple pages.[6] The authors, titles and years covered by each of the *Tong* are shown in Table 25.

Wang Qi's *Xu Wenxian tongkao* contains some sections not found in the others, notably on clans and on Daoists and Buddhists; Liu Jinzao's *Qingchao xu wenxian tongkao* (the last in Table 25) contains sections on posts and communications, industry, constitutional government, and foreign affairs. Detailed tables of section and subsection headings to seven of the *Tong* (including Wang Qi) are available.[7]

Given the fact that in Chinese history different names were often used for the same institution in different periods and that likewise, an institution might change its functions but keep the same name, and given the added advantage that the *Shitong* are indexed, they are often used as a first step in sorting out the functions of institutions at different points in time.

---

[6] *Shitong* (The ten *Tong*), 21 vols., Shangwu, 1935–37; Xinxing, reduced-size version, 24 vols., 1963; Beijing neibu, 1965; Zhejiang guji, 1988; Taibei: Shangwu 3rd rpnt., 1994.

[7] *Bunken Tsûkô goshu sômokuroku, fu Tsûten, Tsûshi* 文獻通考五種總目錄附通典通志 (General index to the *Santong* and to the four continuations of the *Wenxian tongkao*), Tôyôshi kenkyûkai, 1954.

Table 25: Shitong 十通

1. Du You 杜佑, *Tongdian* 通典, 801, Zhonghua, 5 vols., punctuated ed., 1988. Earliest times to 755; important for pre-Tang institutions.

2. Zheng Qiao 鄭樵, *Tongzhi* 通志, 1149; Shangwu, 1935; rpnt., Zhonghua, 1990 (in *Shitong*); the 20 monographs (*lüe* 略) are the most original part. They were reprinted separately in *Sibu beiyao* under the title *Tongzhi lüe* 通志略, and thereafter many times, for example, by Shanghai guji in 1993 and by Zhonghua in 1995. They cover from earliest times to the end of the Tang. The "Yiwen lüe 藝文略" is the most detailed bibliographic scheme devised in pre-modern China.

3. Ma Duanlin 馬端臨, *Wenxian tongkao* 文獻通考, 1224; Shangwu, Shanghai, 1936. Earliest times to 1204; especially important for the Song (also contains a major bibliography, the "Jingjikao 經籍考."

Wang Qi 王圻, *Xu Wenxian tongkao* 續文獻通考, 1586. Not included in either *Jiutong* or *Shitong* editions; original edition only. Covers the years 907–1586; especially important for the Ming. Not superseded by no. 8.

4. *Xu Tongdian* 續通典. From 756 to end of the Ming.

5. *Qingchao Tongdian* 清朝通典. From 1644 to 1785 (original title: *Qinding huangchao tongdian* 欽定皇朝通典).

6. *Xu Tongzhi* 續通志. Monographs cover from 907 to 1644.

7. *Qingchao Tongzhi* 清朝通志. From 1644 to 1785 (original title: *Qinding huangchao tongzhi* 欽定皇朝通志).

8. *Xu Wenxian tongkao* 續文獻通考. From 1224 to 1644 (does not supersede Wang Qi).

9. *Qingchao Wenxian tongkao* 清朝文獻通考. From 1644 to 1785 (original title: *Qinding huangchao wenxian tongkao* 欽定皇朝文獻通考).

10. *Qingchao xu Wenxian tongkao* 清朝續文獻通考 (1921), Liu Jinzao 劉錦藻. From 1786 to 1911 (*Huangchao xu Wenxian tongkao* 皇朝續文獻通考). Highest quality of the Qing continuations.

Note: Nos. 4–9 were compiled under imperial sponsorship in the eighteenth century.

27

Penal and Administrative Law

Law in China was promulgated by the ruler and administered by his officials. There was no independendant judiciary. The emperor was both law-giver and supreme judge. The criminal codes and administrative regulations both included civil and economic laws. But there was no separate civil law code. From the Han, the laws became permeated with Confucian morality, which embodied the rites (*li* 禮) or customary law. For example, the punishment for lack of filial piety (a Confucian virtue) was unusually severe.

The present chapter introduces the different forms of law (27.1), then deals with criminal and administrative law up to the Tang (27.2), criminal law in the Tang and after (27.3), administrative law in the Tang and after (27.4) and finally, guides and handbooks for local magistrates and clerks (27.5).

Note that official works relating to law are usually listed as *zhengshu* 政書 in the History branch of the *Sibu* classification (Table 12, 9.3); unofficial legal works tend to appear in the *fajia* 法家 section of the Philosophers' branch (Table 13, 9.3).

27.1 Introduction

Penal law was set out in the codes (*lü* 律), which prescribed the action to be taken and the punishments to be inflicted for all infringements of the laws. Fragments of law codes have survived from as early as the Warring States (27.2), but the first complete one dates from the Tang. It formed the basis of all subsequent codes for the remainder of Chinese history (27.3), as also for China's neighbors.[1]

The most general form of codified administrative law was found in the *ling* 令 (statutes or commands), which were promulgated in most dynasties down to the *Da Ming ling* 大明令 (Great Ming statutes), 1368, the first collection of Ming law to be promulgated (27.4).

The division between the two types of law, penal and administrative (the *lü* and the *ling*) was not hard and fast, although it became much more so after the Tang. Both were modified or supplemented in the *ge* 格 (regulations) and their implementation was defined in the *shi* 式 (ordinances). They were also altered, expanded, and applied in the light of particular precedents or substatutes (*li* 例, *zeli* 則例, *shili* 事例), the most important of which are introduced below.

From the Tang dates the practice of compiling comprehensive handbooks on the structure and functions of the bureaucracy, referred to in what follows as *Huidian* 會典 (institutes) ultimately modeled on the *Zhouli* 周禮 (*Institutes of Zhou*).

The *lüling geshi* 律令格式, the edicts (*chi* 敕), and other decisions of the emperor, together with the precedents, are the basic sources for Chinese legal and institutional history. They are also important sources for all the many different areas of Chinese society with which they deal, either in the generalized terms of the codes, the statutes and other compendia of administrative law or in the more detailed commentaries, precedents, cases and handbooks which frequently illustrate the actual working of the law in concrete terms as it touched everyday

---

[1] For an outline see P. MacCormack, *Penal Law in Traditional China*, Edinburgh UP, 1990; R. P. Peerenboom, "The Victim in Chinese Criminal Theory and Practice: A Historical Survey," *Journal of Chinese Law* 7.1: 63–110 (1993). For translations, see *Chinese Law Past and Present: A Bibliography of Enactments and Commentaries in English Text*, Lin Fushun, comp., Col. UP, 1966.

life—for example, in laws of inheritance or divorce, or the laws and regulations governing ownership and contract (27.5 and 50.4.4).

On the different kinds of primary sources, both epigraphic and textual, for the history of Chinese law from the Zhou dynasty to the present day, see *Chûgoku hôseishi, kihon shiryô no kenkyû* 中國法制史基本資料の研究. It contains 28 chapters, each written by a specialist.[2]

Zhongguo zhenxi falü dianji jicheng 中國珍稀法律典籍集成 is a major collection of rare and important works of Chinese law from the oracle bones to the Qing. It is typeset, clearly printed and carefully annotated.[3]

27.2 Pre-Tang Law

The first code is traditionally supposed to have been promulgated at the beginning of the fourth century BC (Li Kui 李悝, *Fajing* 法經 [Canon of Laws]), but considerable doubt is attached to the later descriptions of this work.[4] There are also scattered references to the laws and to the punishments of the Xia and the Shang dynasties in early texts such as the *Shangshu* and the *Shiji*. These can now be supplemented with newly excavated sources. Oracle-bone and bronze inscriptions with in-

---

[2]*Chûgoku hôseishi, kihon shiryô no kenkyû* (Chinese legal history, studies on basic source materials), Shiga Shûzô 滋賀秀三, ed., Tokyo daigaku, 1993; rpnt., 1994; Brian E. McKnight, ed., *Law and the State in Traditional East Asia: Six Studies on the Sources of East Asian Law*, UHP, 1987; Zhang Weiren 張偉仁, ed. in chief, *Zhongguo fazhishi shumu* 中國法制史書目 (Bibliography of the history of Chinese law), 3 vols., Lishi yuyan yanjiusuo, *zhuankan* 67, 1976. Based on holdings in Taiwan libraries.

[3] *Zhongguo zhenxi falü dianji jicheng* (Collection of rare works of Chinese law), Liu Hainian 劉海年 and Yang Yifan 楊一凡, series eds., 14 vols., Kexue, 1994.

[4] See Timoteus Pokora, "The Canon of Laws of Li K'uei: A Double Falsification?" *Archiv Orientalni* 27: 96–121 (1959). Herrlee G. Creel, "Legal Institutions and Procedures during the Chou Dynasty," in *Essays on China's Legal Tradition*, Jerome A. Cohen, R. Randle Edwards and Fu-mei Chang Chen, eds., PUP, 1980, 26–55.

formation relating to punishments as well as laws, regulations and contracts are transcribed, punctuated, collated and translated into modern Chinese in *Jiaguwen jinwen jiandu falü wenxian* 甲骨文金文簡牘法律文獻.[5]

The study of Qin and Han law and regulations has been transformed by the discovery of laws, regulations and case books on bamboo and wooden strips. For an introduction to these new sources see A. F. P. Hulsewé, "Qin and Han Legal Manuscripts."[6] The earliest legal document so far discovered on bamboo or wood dates from 309 BC. It was found on a single wooden tablet at Haojiaping 郝家坪, Qingchuan 青川 district, near the border with Gansu in Sichuan. On the front is recorded the setting of a Qin statute on land law and on the back, various related matters (18.1.2). By far the most important breakthrough in the study of pre-Han law came in 1975–76 with the discovery at Shuihudi in Hubei of 612 legible bamboo strips mainly recording fragments of the long-lost Qin code and other legal or administrative works. They were found in the coffin of a Qin local judicial official named Xi 喜 (262–217 BC). Along with the Haojiaping land law they are transcribed, punctuated, collated, translated into modern Chinese and annotated in *Jiaguwen jinwen jiandu falü wenxian* (367–695).[7]

---

[5] *Jiaguwen jinwen jiandu falü wenxian* (Texts on law from oracle-bone and bronze inscriptions and bamboo MSS), Liu Hainian 劉海年, Yang Shengnan 楊陞南 and Wu Jiulong 吳九龍, eds. in chief; oracle-bone inscriptions (1–229); bronze inscriptions (231–362). This is vol. 1 of series 1 of *Zhongguo zhenxi falü dianji jicheng. Chûgoku hôseishi, kihon shiryô no kenkyû.* Chap. 1 has a bibliography of secondary literature on Western Zhou laws cast on bronze vessels.

[6] In *NSECH*, 193–221. The author does not cover the important finds of Qin law made since the late 1980s, notably those excavated from Yunmeng Longgang (see 44.3.2.1).

[7] This collection contains the best text of the Shuihudi legal works including *Qin lü shibazhong* 秦律十八種, *Xiaolü* 效律, *Falü dawen* 法律答問 and *Fengzhenshi* 封診式. It also includes the *Shoufa shouling deng shisan pian* 守法守令等十三篇 discovered at Yinqueshan 銀雀山 (44.3.2.2).

For a translation and studies of the Shuihudi texts, see A. F. P. Hulsewé, *Remnants of Ch'in Law: An Annotated Translation of the Ch'in Legal*

Footnote continued on next page

The basic source on Han law is the "Xingfazhi 刑法志" in the *Hanshu*, the first Standard History to contain such a monograph.[8] This should be supplemented with the growing body of Han legal texts and documents excavated from tombs (44.3.2.2) or found at the border posts along the Silk Road (44.3.2.3). See *Handai tunshu yijian falü zhi* 漢代屯戍遺簡法律志[9] for transcriptions of texts excerpted from published collections of *Hanjian* including the new Juyan documents. The texts are arranged under three headings: laws, edicts and punishments (1–304); judicial documents (305–425); other documents (427–607). There are copious annotations.

---

and *Administrative Rules of the 3rd Century BC Discovered in Yün-meng Prefecture, Hu-pei Province, in 1975*, Brill, 1985; by the same author, "The influence of the legalist government of Qin on the economy as reflected in the texts discovered in Yunmeng County," in *The scope of state power in China*, Stuart R. Schram, ed., London: SOAS and HKCU Press, 1985, 211–36; Katrina C. D. McLeod and Robin D. S. Yates, "Forms of Ch'in law: An Annotated Translation of the *Feng-chen shih*," *HJAS* 41.1: 111–63 (1981); Chen Gongrou 陳公柔, "Yunmeng Qinmu chutu *Falü dawen* jiance kaoshu 雲夢秦墓出土法律答問簡冊考述," (Study of the bamboo strips *Falü dawen* unearthed at Yunmeng), *Yanjing xuebao*, new series, 2: 171–212 (1996); A. F. P. Hulsewé, "The Legalists and the Laws of Ch'in." in *Leyden Studies in Sinology*, W. L. Idema, ed., Brill, 1981, 1–22; see also Li Jing 栗勁, *Qin lü tonglun* 秦律通論 (Introduction to Qin law), Shandong renmin, 1985.

[8] Note the following studies of A. F. P. Hulsewé, "Ch'in and Han Law," in the *CHC*, vol. 1, CUP, 1988, 520–44; "Introductory Studies," in *Remnants of Han Law*, Brill, 1955, 1–307; "The *Shuo-wen* dictionary as a source for ancient Chinese law," in *Studia Serica Bernhard Karlgren dedicata*, Sören Egerod and Else Glahn, eds., Copenhagen: Munksgaard, 1959, 239–58. See also Ôba Osamu 大庭脩, *Shin Kan hôseishi no kenkyû* 秦漢法制史の研究 (Research on the legal institutions of the Qin and Han), Sôbunsha, 1982; rpnt., 1985. Chinese version published by Shanghai renmin, 1991.

[9] *Handai tunshu yijian falü zhi* (Collection of legal documents from the Han border posts), Li Junming 李均明 and Liu Jun 劉軍, eds. Kexue, 1994. This is the second volume of series 1 of *Zhongguo zhenxi falü dianji jicheng*.

A pioneering attempt was made by Cheng Shude 程樹德 (1877–1944) in *Jiuchao lü kao* 九朝律考 to reconstruct the codes promulgated from the Han through to the Sui.[10] He uses the four monographs on law and the five monographs on official posts in the Standard Histories of these years as well as many other contemporary sources.

See Table 23 (22.3) for a list of the Standard Histories containing monographs on law and the chapters of Part V for studies and translations of them.

27.3 Penal Codes

During the Tang there were four main types of codified law, all of which had been inherited from the past. In addition to the *lü* 律 and the *ling* 令, there were the *ge* 格 (regulations) and the *shi* 式 (ordinances).[11]

The *Tang lü shuyi* 唐律疏議 (Tang code with commentary), 635, was the basis of all Chinese law codes down to the Qing.[12] For a complete, annotated translation with introduction, see Wallace Johnson, *The T'ang Code: Vol. I, General Principles*, PUP, 1979; *The T'ang Code: Vol. II, Specific Articles*, PUP, 1997. The same scholar also earlier compiled a concordance to the

---

[10] *Jiuchao lü kao* (A study of the penal statutes of nine dynasties), Changsha: Shangwu, 1927; Shanghai: Shangwu, 1934; 1955; Zhonghua, 1963; Taibei: Shangwu, 1965; Shanghai shudian, 1989.

[11] Shiga Shizô, "A Basic History of T'ang Legislative Forms," *AM* 3rd series, V.2: 97–127 (1992).

[12] Brian E. McKnight, "T'ang Law and Later Law: The Roots of Continuity," *JAOS* 115.3: 410–20 (1995). The text is in *Tang lü shuyi jianjie* 唐律疏議箋解 (Collected commentaries on the Tang code), Liu Junwen 劉俊文, ed., 2 vols., Zhonghua, 1996; see also Dai Yanhui 戴炎輝, *Tang lü tonglun* 唐律通論 (Comprehensive introduction to the Tang code) and *Tang lü ge lun* 唐律格論 (Discussions on the Tang code), Taibei, 1964; 1965. For a translation into Japanese, see *Tôritsu sogi* 唐律疏議, vols. 5, 6 and 7 of *Yakuchû Nihon ritsuryô* 譯注日本律令, Shiga Shûzô 滋賀秀三 et al., tr., Tôkyôdô, 1975. Niida Noboru, *Tô-Sô hôritsu bunsho no kenkyû* 唐宋法律文書の研究 (Researches on legal works of the Tang and Song dynasties), Tokyo, 1937.

code.[13] On the application of the code, see Wallace Johnson and Denis Twitchett, "Criminal Procedures in T'ang China," *AM* 3rd Series, 6.2: 113–46 (1993) and Denis Twitchett, "The Implementation of Law in Early T'ang China," *Civiltà Veneziana: Studi* 34: 57–84 (1978). A large amount of detailed research has been done using the fragments of laws discovered at Dunhuang and further to the west around Turpan.[14]

The Tang code was taken as the model for the codes of Japan, Korea and Vietnam.[15]

The *Song huiyao jigao* 宋會要輯稿, "Xingfa 刑法" section (*ce* 164–71), is an important source for Song legal history, as is also the *Song xingtong* 宋刑統 (Song repertory of penal law), 963, which was largely based on the Tang code and in use throughout the dynasty (for an evaluation and a study of the editions and secondary scholarship, see Okano Makoto 岡野誠, "*Sô keitsu* 宋刑統," in *Chûgoku hôseishi, kihon shiryô no kenkyû*, 281–318).

[13] Zhuang Weisi 莊爲斯, *Tang lü shuyi yinde* 唐律疏議引得 (Concordance to the Tang code with commentary), Wenhai, 1964.

[14] Legal texts from Dunhuang and Turpan are punctuated and collated in *Dunhuang fazhi wenshu* 敦煌法制文書 (Dunhuang legal documents), Tang Geng'ou 唐耕耦, ed. in chief, and in *Tulufan chutu falü wenxian* 吐魯番出土法律文獻 (Legal texts excavated at Turpan), Wu Zhen 吳震, ed. in chief, 1st series, vols. 3 and 4 of *Zhongguo zhenxi falü dianji jicheng*. Vol. 3 (Dunhuang) is a massive collection (1,630 pages) containing punctuated transcriptions of over 500 Dunhuang legal documents arranged according to subject matter. There are lengthy notes and summaries. Vol. 4 (Turpan) contains punctuated transcriptions of 63 fragments of laws, cases and judgments as well as 415 legal documents. For other references see the section on Dunhuang and Turpan (46.3).

[15] Niida Noboru, "Chinese Legal Institutions of the Sui and T'ang Periods and Their Influence on Surrounding East Asian Countries," in *Rapports II, Histoire des Continents*, Comité International des Sciences Historiques (Vienna, 1965), 113–31. For a study and translation of the Lê Dynasty code, which was modeled closely after the Tang code, see Nguyen Ngoc Huy et al., *The Lê Code: Law in Traditional Vietnam. A Comparative Sino-Vietnamese Legal Study with Historical-Juridical Analysis and Annotations*, 3 vols., Athens: Ohio UP, 1987.

Several collections of cases survive from the Song. They were intended to provide examples to assist county magistrates in reaching judicial decisions. The *Minggong shupan qingmingji* 名公書判清明集 (1260–65) was only rediscovered in the 1980s.[16] It contains a wealth of socioeconomic detail in the form of judgments and cases. It has been described as the most important new source on the Southern Song to have been found in this century. Another, the *Tangyin bishi* 棠陰比事 (1211), has been translated into English.[17] It cites cases from the whole of Chinese history up to that time.

None of the Liao or Jin codes are extant, although parts can be reconstructed on the basis of detailed studies of documents such as the monograph on penal law in the *Liaoshi* and *Jinshi*.[18]

---

[16] *Minggong shupan Qingmingji* (Collection of lucid decisions by celebrated judges), 14 *juan*, 1260–65; punctuated and collated edition of Song and Ming editions in *Zhongguo gudai shehui jingji shiziliao* 中國古代社會經濟史資料, Wang Zengyu 王曾瑜, Chen Zhichao 陳智超, Wu Tai 吳泰, eds., 1st collection, Fujian renmin, 1985; reprinted as *Minggong shupan qingmingji* 明公書判清明集, Zhonghua, 1987. This replaces the earlier photo reprint of a 1 *juan* fragment of a Song edition reprinted by the Koten kenkyûkai in 1964. For an evaluation and a study of the editions and secondary scholarship, see Takahashi Yoshirô 高橋芳郎, "Meikô shohan Seimeishô," 明公書判清明集, in *Chûgoku hôseishi, kihon shiryô no kenkyû*, 361–82.

[17] R. H. van Gulik, *T'ang-yin pi-shih, Parallel Cases from under the Peartree: A 13th Century Manual of Jurisprudence and Detection*, Brill, 1956.

[18] Herbert Franke, "The 'Treatise on Punishments' in the Liao History," *Central Asiatic Journal* 27: 9–38 (1983) and the same author's, "The Legal System of the Chin Dynasty," in *Collected Studies on Sung History Dedicated to Professor James T. C. Liu in Celebration of his Seventieth Birthday*, Tsuyoshi Kinugawa, ed., Dôhôsha, 1989, 387–409, and "Jurchen Customary Law and the Chinese Law of the Chin Dynasty," *State and Law in East Asia: Festschrift for Karl Bünger*, Dieter Eikemeier and Herbert Franke, eds., Harrassowitz, 1981, 215–33. Ye Qianzhao 葉潛昭, *Jin-lü zhi yanjiu* 金律之研究 (Researches on the Jin penal code), Taibei: Shangwu, 1972; Paul Ratchnevsky, *Un Code des Yuan*, vol., 1, Leroux, 1937; vol. 2, PUF, 1972; vol. 3, (with Françoise Aubin), *Index*, PUF, 1977; vol. 4, Collège de France: Institut des Hautes Etudes Chinoises, 1985. This is an annotated translation with a long introduction (vol. 1)

Footnote continued on next page

The Yuan never established a formal code. On Yuan law, see the monograph on law in the *Yuanshi* and the *Zhiyuan xinge* 至元新格 (48.5.2).

The first version of the *Da Ming lü* 大明律 (Great Ming code), 1373–74, was largely based on the Tang code as it had been transmitted down to the Yuan. The third version (1397), however, was completely revised and marks an important break from the 600-year tradition set by the Tang code. Its title was *Gengding Da Ming lü* 更訂大明律 but it is usually referred to as the *Da Ming lü* 大明律, or simply the *Ming lü* 明律. A very large number of editions of the 1397 version are extant; most include the itemized substatutes. After the 1585 edition they were made an integral part of the code, hence the title, *Ming lü jijie fuli* 明律集解附例.[19] Like the Tang code, it was extremely influential in Korea, Japan and Vietnam. Many commented editions were issed in these countries. It contained 460 articles covering general principles, personnel, revenue, rites, war, justice, and public works.[20]

Recently reprinted from a unique manuscript copy are the extremely detailed (5,000-page) substatutes, regulations, etc., used in the actual implementation of the code in the late fifteenth and early sixteenth centuries:

Huang Ming tiaofa shilei zuan 皇明條法事類纂, Dai Jin 戴金, comp., 1531–33; typeset, punctuated edition, Yang Yifan 楊一凡, ed. in chief, 2nd series, vols. 4–6, *Zhongguo zhenxi falü dianji jicheng* (based on the manuscript copy held in Tokyo University library which was earlier photolithographically reproduced by the Koten kenkyûkai, 2

---

and index (vol. 3) of the monograph on penal law of the *Yuanshi* (*juan* 102–105).

[19] See *ISMH*, 185–87, for an annotated list of 12 editions; rpnt. in *Huang Ming zhishu* 皇明制書, Zhang Lu 張鹵, ed., 1579; 2 vols., Koten kenkyûkai, 1966–67, vol. 2, 23–172; for a modern edition, see *Da Ming lü*, Huai Xiaofeng 懷效鋒, ed., Liao-Shen, 1990; for Japanese studies, see Satake Yasuhiko 佐藤邦憲 in *Chûgoku hôseishi, kihon shiryô no kenkyû*, 435–72.

[20] For details, see John D. Langlois, Jr., "Ming Law," in *CHC*, vol. 8, CUP, 1998, 172–220.

vols., 1966–67; rpnt., Wenhai, 1985. The *Zhenxi falü jicheng* edition is more convenient to use.

Collections of itemized substatutes (*tiaoli* 條例) have survived in greater numbers from the Qing (50.6.2).

The early version of the Qing code (1646) reached its final form in the expanded *Da Qing lüli* 大清律例 (Great Qing code with substatutes), 1740.[21] It was one of the first works studied and translated into English in the nineteenth century, albeit fairly freely.[22] An important new translation has recently been published, *The Great Qing Code*, William C. Jones, tr., Oxford: Clarendon Press, 1993. An introduction gives the legal background. The Jones translation replaces all previous ones into either English or French.[23] It is based on the text of the Code in the modern, punctuated edition of *Du li cunyi* 讀例存疑.[24]

For a translation from the largest Qing casebook, *Xing'an huilan* 刑案匯覽 (The conspectus of penal cases), see Bodde and

[21] For editions and extensive introductions to different aspects of the Qing code and penal law in the Qing, see Derk Bodde and Clarence Morris, *Law in Imperial China, Exemplified by 190 Ch'ing Dynasty Cases Translated from the Hsing-an hui-lan with Historical, Social, and Juridical Commentaries*, HUP, 1967; Zheng Qin, "Pursuing Perfection: Formation of the Qing code," *Modern China* 21.3: 310–344 (1995). See also Sybille van der Sprenkel, *Legal Institutions in Manchu China: A Sociological Analysis*, Athlone Press, 1962. See also T'ung-tsu Ch'ü, *Law and Society in Traditional China*, Mouton, 1961.

[22] George T. Staunton, *Ta Tsing Leu Lee*, 1810; Chengwen, 1967. For a translation of the Nguyễn code (1812), see P. L. F. Philastre, *Le Code annamite*, 2 vols., 1875; 2nd ed., 1909; rpnt., Chengwen, 1967. The Ngyuễn code was identical with the Qing code of 1740 save for 38 articles left out.

[23] Guy Boulais, *Manuel du Code chinois*, 2 vols., Variétés sinologiques, No. 55, Shanghai, 1924; Taibei rpnt., 1957. Leaves out portions of the original without indication, but does include translations of the Substatutes and also has the Chinese text on each page.

[24] *Du li cunyi* 讀例存疑, Huang Jingjia 黃靜嘉 ed., 5 vols., CMC, 1970. The *Du li cunyi* (1905) is a commentary on the code and its substatutes by one of the last presidents of the Board of Punishments, Xue Yunsheng 薛允昇 (1820–1901).

Morris (1967). The *Xing'an huilan* (1834; 1886) and its continuation have been reprinted: 11 vols., Taibei, 1968; and 10 vols., Taibei, 1970. For an interesting study of murder and adultery and the influence of Confucian morality, see M. J. Meijer, *Murder and Adultery in Late Imperial China: A Study of Law and Morality*, Brill, 1991.

27.4 Administrative Law

Although the monographs on official posts, examinations and law in the Tang and post-Tang Standard Histories contain useful overviews of administrative law, they are not mentioned in this section, which outlines instead the much more detailed sources that are increasingly available in the later dynasties.

None of the Statutes of the Tang are extant, but no fewer than 715 of the original 1,546 articles were reconstructed from other Chinese and Japanese sources in an important work by Niida Noboru 仁井田陞 (1904–66).[25]

Fragmentary remains of the regulations and ordinances of the Tang have been preserved in other compilations and in their original form among the manuscripts discovered at Dunhuang and other sites in northwest China (46.3). For an English translation of one of these fragments as well as a useful brief introduction to the different types of Tang administrative law, see Denis Twitchett, "The Fragment of the T'ang Ordinances of the Department of Waterways Discovered at Tun-Huang," *AM* 6.1: 23–79 (1957).

The earliest extant collection of administrative law was the *Tang liudian* 唐六典 (Compendium of administrative law of the six divisions of the Tang bureaucracy). It is based on all the

[25] Niida's famous work of scholarship is the *Tôryô shûi* 唐令拾遺 (Collected vestiges of the Tang statutes); Tokyo, 1933; 3rd rpnt., (reduced-size), 1993; rev. ed., Tôkô daigaku, 1997; Chinese translation of original edition: *Tang ling shiyi* 唐令拾遺, Changchun, 1989. For an evaluation and a study of the reconstructions of the *Tang ling* and secondary scholarship on it, see Ikeda On 池田温, "*Tôrei* 唐令," in *Chûgoku hôseishi, kihon shiryô no kenkyû*, 203–39.

different types of administrative law as these were applied in all branches of the bureaucracy in the early eighth century.[26]

During the Song, the division between penal and administrative law was made even more sharp by separating out the codes (*lü* 律) and their commentaries, substatutes, etc., and referring to administrative law under the fourfold division of edicts, statutes, regulations, and ordinances (*chiling geshi* 敕令 格式). Definitions of these four terms (as in other periods) were not strict and it would be a mistake to suppose that they represent exclusive categories.[27]

None of the Song statutes (inherited from the Tang) are extant but part of the most important compendium of Song administrative law, the *Qingyuan tiaofa shilei* 慶元條法事類 of 1203, has been preserved and in it about two-thirds of the Qingyuan Statutes.[28] The reason for making such a compilation is explained in the *Songshi*: "As few literati are proficient in

[26] *Da Tang liudian* 大唐六典, 738; Zhonghua facs. ed., 4 *ce*, 1984. The best Song edition was preserved in Japan and edited by Konoe Iehiro 近 衛家熙, *Kôtei Dai Tô rikuten* 考訂大唐六典, 1724; facs., *Da Tang liudian* 大唐六典, Wenhai, 1962; rpnt., 1974. For an introduction, see Wang Chao, "The Six Codes of the Tang Dynasty: China's Earliest Administrative Code," *Social Sciences in China* 2: 113–50 (1986), and Robert des Rotours, "Le *Tang Liou tien* d'êcrit-il exactement les institutions en usage sous les dynasties des Tangs?" *JA* 263: 183–201 (1975). On the extensive Japanese scholarship, see also Okamura Ikuzô 奥村郁三, "*Dai Tô rikuten* 大唐六典" in *Chûgoku hôseishi, kihon shiryô no kenkyû*, 263–80.

[27] Brian E. McKnight, "From Statute to Precedent: An Introduction to Song Law and its Transformation," in McKnight ed., *Law and the State in Traditional East Asia: Six Studies in the Sources of East Asian Law*, UHP, 1987, 111–31.

[28] *Qingyuan tiaofa shilei* (Compendium of administrative law of the Qingyuan period [1195–1200] arranged by categories), 80 *juan* (of which only 30 survive), 1203, Koten kenkyûkai photo reprint of Seikadô Library copy, 1960. For an evaluation and a study of the editions and secondary scholarship, see Kawamura "*Keigen jôhôi jirui to Sôdai hôden* 慶 元條法事類と宋代の法典," in *Chûgoku hôseishi, kihon shiryô no kenkyû*, 331–60. There is a glossary to this important text: *Keigen jôhô jirui goi shuran* 慶元條法事類語彙輯覽, Umehara Kaoru 梅原郁, comp., Jimbun, 1990.

law, if they just try and read up on it at the last moment they are often cheated by the clerks. Now if we compile a work by categories, literati officials can see all the pertinent laws when the need arises, and then the clerks cannot cheat."[29]

Many of the edicts, statutes, ordinances, regulations and substatutes of the Song, as of other periods, were excerpted or quoted in compilations such as the *Song huiyao* 宋會要 (Collections of important documents of the Song), see 26.1 and 47.1-2 for further references.

The main administrative compendium of the Yuan was the *Yuan dianzhang* 元典章 (Compendium of statutes and substatutes of the Yuan, or, more concisely, Institutes of the Yuan dynasty), 1303; revised and expanded edition, 1322. See 48.5.1 for comments on this work.

The *Da Ming ling* 大明令 (Great Ming statutes), 1368, are the first complete set to have survived.[30] They have been translated by Edward Farmer.[31] Several Ming handbooks of rules and regulations printed by individual branches of the administration are also extant.

During the Qing dynasty, no *ling* 令 were promulgated, but the Ming model for issuing detailed *huidian* 會典 (Institutes; also translated as Collected Statutes) was followed (the phrase is derived from *huiyao dianzhang* 會要典章, digest of regulations of government offices). There were five editions of such compendia of administrative law, all of which were entitled *Da*

---

[29] *Songshi quanwen xu Zizhi tongjian*, ch. 26, as quoted in Chikusa Masaaki, "Introduction to the Study of Five Dynasties and Sung History," Kenneth Chase, tr., in Peter Bol, *Research Tools for the Study of Sung History*, (Sung-Yuan Research Aids (II), Binghamton, 1990, 2nd ed., Albany, 1996, 134.

[30] The *Da Ming ling* was included in vol. 1 of *Huang Ming zhishu*. The *Da Ming ling* is much shorter than the previous ones are known to have been and was soon supplemented by such works as the *Zhusi zhizhang*, *Xian'gang shilei* 憲綱事類 (Regulations for the censorate), 1371, and other similar works all included in the *Huang Ming zhishu*.

[31] Edward L. Farmer, *Zhu Yuanzhang and Early Ming Legislation: The Reordering of Chinese Society Following the Era of Mongol Rule*, Brill, 1995.

Qing huidian 大清會典 (Institutes of the great Qing). Each also was published with "Supplementary precedents and regulations" (*shili* 事例). A very large number of other works of early Qing administrative law as well as many editions of the regulations and substatutes of individual departments of the bureaucracy are extant (on these *buli* 部例, *zeli* 則例 as well as the *huidian*, see, 50.6.2).

One of the unique features of Qing administrative law is that collections of provincial substatutes and cases (*shengli* 省例) relating only to a single province were printed. In addition, provincial yamen from the eighteenth century began issuing the regulations which they received from the central government in works usually called *dingli* 定例 (established regulations) or *tiaoli* 條例 (itemized regulations or substatutes), some of which have survived (50.6.2).

Detailed references to earlier fragments of statutes and compendia of administrative law as well as to the complete works of the later empire are given in Part V.

27.5 Guides and Handbooks

The guides to official documents for local officials and clerks (*guanzhen shu* 官箴書) contain a great deal of interesting supplementary material on the operation of the bureaucracy at the county level. Fragments of such a Qin Guide are translated and annotated in Hulsewé (1985). Other fragments have since been excavated (44.3.2.1–2). Many more have survived from the Song onward.

The tables of contents (or section headings) of 55 of these works dating from the Song to the end of the Qing have been indexed in *Kanshin mokuji sôgô sakuin* 官箴目次總合索引, mimeo, Kyoto daigaku, Tôyôshi kenkyûshitsu, 1950.

Note also:

Sô Gen kanshin sôgô sakuin 宋元官箴綜合索引 (Combined index to Song and Yuan *guanzhen*), Akagi Ryûji 赤城隆治 and Satake Yasuhiko 佐竹靖彦, comps., Kyûko, 1987.

Zhiyuan cuoyao 職源撮要: *Shokugen satsuyô sakuin* 職源撮要索引 (Index to the *Zhiyuan suoyao*), Tôyôshi kenkyûkai, 1956. This is a late twelfth-century work on the Song bureaucracy and its origins.

There is a translation of an important seventeenth-century handbook, Huang Liuhong 黃六鴻, *Fuhui quanshu* 福惠全書: Djang Chu (Zhang Chu 章楚), *A Complete Book Concerning Happiness and Benevolence: A Manual for Local Magistrates in Seventeenth-Century China*, AUP, 1984.[32]

Apart from such general guides to local administration, from the Qing there are also extant some practical handbooks containing regulations and procedures for secretarial assistants in charge of taxation under the local magistrates (*qian'gu* 錢穀).[33] Some were printed but they usually circulated in manuscript. The most famous printed handbook on taxation was Wang Youhuai, 王又槐 *Qiangu beiyao* 錢穀備要 (Essentials of taxation), 1793. It ran through many editions in the nineteenth century. Balazs translated parts of it.[34]

Handbooks of jurisprudence are also extant. No doubt they were intended for magistrates as well as for the secretarial assistants in charge of legal matters (*xingming* 刑名). A Song handbook on forensic medicine for coroners, the *Xiyuan jilu* 洗冤集錄 (Manual of forensic medicine), 1247 by Song Ci 宋慈 (1186–1249) has been translated by Brian E. McKnight under the title *The Washing Away of Wrongs*, CCS, UMP, 1981.[35] Many survive from the later empire.[36]

[32] On the administrative handbooks, see the introduction to the Kyoto index (1950) above by Miyazaki Ichisada; also Sybelle Van der Sprenkel, *Legal Institutions in Manchu China*, Athlone Press, 1962, 137–50.

[33] Philip Huang, "From the Perspective of Magistrates' Handbooks," in *Civil Justice in China: Representation and Practice in the Qing*, SUP, 1996, 198–222.

[34] Etienne Balazs, "A Handbook of Local Administrative Practice of 1793," in *Political Theory and Administrative Reality in Traditional China*, SOAS, 1965, 50–75.

[35] *Xiyuan jilu jiaoyi* 洗冤集錄校譯, Yang Fengkun 楊奉琨, ed., Qunzhong, 1980. The *Xiyuan jilu* was constantly revised and enlarged over

Footnote continued on next page

Ch'ing Administrative Terms: A Translation of the Terminology of the Six Boards with Explanatory Notes, E-tu Zen Sun, tr., HUP, 1961, is another example of this type of source; it is useful for understanding and translating administrative terminology. It was originally written for Manchu officials to help them find their way around the six boards of the Qing government in Beijing and has often been reprinted: *Liubu chengyu* 六部成語, 1742 (anon).

---

the centuries. Herbert Giles translated a late version dating from 1843: "The *Hsi Yuan Lu* (洗冤錄) or Instructions to Coroners," *The China Review* 3: 30–172 (1874–75); rpnt. in the *Proceedings of the Royal Society of Medicine* 17: 59–107 (1924); rpnt. together with McKnight (1981), Taibei, 1982.

For excerpts from handbooks of regulations for many varieties of local underling, see Cai Shenzhi 蔡申之, comp., *Qingdai zhouxian gushi* 清代州縣故事 (Informal materials on local government under the Qing dynasty), HKCU Press, 1968. T'ung-tsu Ch'ü in his *Local Government in China under the Ch'ing*, HUP, 1962, drew heavily on this type of source.

[36] Langlois, *CHC*, vol. 8, CUP, 1998, contains in Appendix A the titles of extant Ming commentaries on the code and handbooks of jurisprudence (211–13). Appendix B (by Thomas J. Nimick) contains notes on over 20 Ming handbooks for local magistrates (214–20).

28

Army Administration, Warfare and Uprisings

28.1 Army Administration

Studies on pre-Qin military affairs are able to use newly discovered epigraphic sources and archaeological artifacts to supplement the transmitted texts.[1]

For imperial China, a good starting point are the Standard Histories, eight of which have monographs on *bingwei* 兵衛,[2] *yiwei* 儀衛 (imperial guards)[3] or *yingwei* 營衛 (border guards).[4]

---

[1] The "General Introduction and Historical Overview" in Ralph D. Sawyer, *Sun Tzu: Art of War*, provides a good overview. See also Raimund Theodor Kolb, *Die Infanterie im Alten China: Ein Beitrag zur Militärgeschichte der Vor-Zhan-Guo-Zeit*, Mainz: Philipp von Zabern, 1991. For a review of these and other recent Western works, see Edward L. Shaughnessy, "Military Histories of Early China: A Review Article," *EC* 21 (1997), 159–82. See also, Song Zhenhao 宋鎮豪, "Shangdai junshi zhidu yanjiu 商代軍事制度研究," *Shaanxi lishi bowuguan guankan*, 1995.2; Chen Enlin 陳恩林, *Xian-Qin junshi zhidu yanjiu* 先秦軍事制度 研究, Jilin wenshi, 1992; Gao Rui 高銳, *Zhongguo shanggu junshishi* 中國上古 軍事史 (A history of Chinese military affairs in remote antiquity), Junshi kexue, 1995. Includes maps, chronology and illustrations.

[2] *Xin Tangshu* (whose monograph on the army is the subject of a scholarly study and translation by Robert des Rotours, see 46.1); also those in the *Songshi, Liaoshi, Jinshi, Yuanshi, Xin Yuanshi, Mingshi, Qingshi gao*.

[3] *Xin Tangshu*; also *Songshi, Liaoshi, Jinshi* and *Mingshi*.

[4] *Liaoshi*.

The monograph on law in the *Hanshu* deals with the army and the Han documents on wooden strips (44.3.2) are also mainly concerned with army administration.

The monographs on financial administration in the Standard Histories usually have itemized sections on the various forms of military expenditures which were a major part of state expenditure in most periods of Chinese history.[5]

28.2 *Warfare*

There is a very large group of writings that in the old catalogs was grouped under the general heading of Military Experts (*bingjia* 兵家), a subbranch of the Philosphers' branch (*zibu* 子部) in the fourfold bibliographic divisions (9.3). Start with Yang Hong, *Weapons in Ancient China*, which is a thorough survey of the subject through the Stone, Bronze and Iron Ages up to the invention of gunpowder; Herbert Franke, "Sources on Chinese Military Technology and History;" and the two *SCC* volumes investigating military technology.[6]

Next turn to one of the very thorough modern annotated catalogs of old Chinese writings on war and the military, for example Xu Baolin 許保林, *Zhongguo bingshu zhijianlu* 中國兵書知見錄.[7] This heavily annotated catalog arranges 3,380 works

---

[5] *Zhongguo junshi jingjishi* 中國軍事經濟史 (Economic history of Chinese military affairs), Zhang Zhenlong 張振龍, ed. in chief, Lantian, 1990. The first 400 pages cover from earliest times to the Taiping. The sources used are the obvious ones: monographs on the army and on financial administration from the Standard Histories and Encyclopaedias of Government.

[6] Yang Hong, *Weapons in Ancient China*, Kexue, 1992; Herbert Franke's paper is in *Chinese Ways in Warfare*, Frank A. Kierman and John K. Fairbank, eds., HUP, 1973, 195–201; *SCC*, vol. 5, Part 6: *Military Technology: Missiles and Sieges*; vol. 5, Part 7: *Military Technology: The Gunpowder Epic*, CUP, 1995 and 1986, respectively.

[7] *Zhongguo bingshu zhijianlu*, Jiefangjun, 1988. Liu Shenning 劉申寧, *Zhongguo bingshu zongmu* 中國兵書總目, Guofang daxue, 1990; rpnt., 1993, lists the location of no less than 4,221 works on the military found

Footnote continued on next page

by period. It indicates where each work is held and also contains references to modern research. The works include collected biographies of famous generals; histories of imperial and other campaigns; techniques of warfare (including weapons); strategy and tactics (cavalry and infantry); and accounts of sieges (techniques of city defense). Altogether 2,308 extant works are discussed.

The most famous Chinese work on strategy and tactics, Sun Wu 孫武, *Sunzi bingfa* 孫子兵法 (Sunzi: the art of war) dates from the Spring and Autumn period. It has been translated into Western languages almost as many times as Laozi's *Daode jing* (Napoleon is said to have carried on his campaigns the first European translation of *Sunzi*, that done by the Jesuit Jean-Joseph Marie Amiot [1718–93], Paris 1772). There are several new translations, plus also of the recently discovered manual by his descendant Sun Bin (*Sun Bin bingfa* 孫臏兵法), which also dates from the Warring States. The *Sunzi* 孫子 and three other militarists are in *ICS Concordance* 11.[8]

---

in 161 libraries and collections in China and nine in the rest of the world. Arrangement is by period. There is a stroke-count index.

[8] *Bingshu sizhong zhuzi suoyin* 兵書四種逐字索引 (Concordance to four military manuals), *ICS Concordance* 11, HK: Shangwu, 1992. Apart from *Sunzi*, the three other manuals are *Weiliaozi* 尉繚子, *Wuzi* 吳子 and *Simafa* 司馬法. On the text and editions of *Sunzi bingfa*, see Gawlikowski and Loewe in *ECHBG*, 446–455. Note Roger T. Ames, *Sun-tzu: The Art of Warfare: The First English Translation Incorporating the Yin-ch'üeh shan Texts*, Ballantine, 1993. The text of Sun Bin had been lost since the end of the Han and was only rediscovered written on bamboo strips along with *Sunzi* in a tomb excavated in Shandong in 1972. D. C. Lau and Roger T. Ames have translated it: *Sun Bin: the Art of Warfare*, Ballantine, 1996.

Ralph D. Sawyer, *The Seven Military Classics of China*, Westview, 1993, not only translates these works but has much interesting commentary. For the historical background to the military manuals of the Warring States period, see Mark Edward Lewis, *Sanctioned Violence in Early China*, SUNY Press, 1990, chap. 3, 97–135.

In 1996, there came word of the discovery of an original 82-*juan* version on bamboo strips which had allegedly been discovered in Xi'an in 1895. The owner and his sons had painstakingly copied it onto paper, so

Footnote continued on next page

There is a collectanea of 220 traditional works on warfare: *Zhongguo bingshu jicheng* 中國兵書集成.[9] For massive, heavily annotated chronological tables of all known battles in Chinese history from the earliest days to 1911, see *Lidai zhanzheng nianbiao* 歷代戰爭年表.[10] There are several dictionaries of Chinese military history. One is Wang Zheyue 王者悦, *Zhongguo gudai junshi da cidian* 中國古代軍事大辭典.[11]

For a study of strategic geography, see Zhang Xiaosheng 張曉生 *Bingjia bizheng zhi di* 兵家必爭之地,[12] and on the history of the Chinese navy (apart from the Ming and the late Qing, a relatively neglected subject), see Zhang Tieniu 張鐵牛, *Zhongguo gudai haijunshi* 中國古代海軍史.[13]

There are few histories of military campaigns in Western languages such as Herbert Franke, *Studien und Texte zur Kriegsgeschichte der südlichen Sungzeit*, Harrassowitz, 1987.

Many of the Qing *fanglüe* 方略 (Histories of imperial campaigns) have been reprinted in a special collectanea: *Zhongguo*

the story went; however, during the Cultural Revolution, the Red Guards had destroyed all but one of the bamboo strips (Yang Caiyu 楊才玉, *Shoucang* 收藏, 8, 1996). Indeed the *Hanshu* "Yiwenzhi" records the original *Sunzi* as having had 82 *juan*, but the Xi'an version was quickly shown to have been a fake.

[9] *Zhongguo bingshu jicheng* (Collectanea of Chinese books on war), 50 vols., Jiefangjun and Liao-Shen, 1987– .

[10] *Lidai zhanzheng nianbiao* (Tables of Chinese historic battles), 2 vols., Jiefangjun, 1985–6. The tables are annexed as a supplementary volume to the general history, *Zhongguo junshishi* 中國軍事史 (History of Chinese military affairs), 6 vols., Jiefangjun, 1983–91. Each volume covers the history of a different topic, e.g., military instutions (vol. 3); strategists (vol. 5). An even more thorough coverage is in *Zhongguo junshi tongshi* 中國軍事通史, 20 vols., 1996– .

[11] *Zhongguo gudai junshi da cidian* (Great Dictionary of Military Affairs in Ancient China), Guofang daxue, 1991.

[12] *Bingjia bizheng zhi di* (Land for which the strategist must fight), Jiefangjun, 1987.

[13] *Zhongguo gudai haijunshi* (History of China's navy in ancient times), Bayi, 1993; Also, *Ershisishi de haiyang ziliao* 二十四史的海洋資料 (Materials on the seas and oceans in the 24 histories), Liu Pei 劉佩 et al., eds., Haiyang, 1995.

fanglüe congshu 中國方略叢書, 1st and 2nd series, Taibei, 1968–71.[14] The historian and geographer, Wei Yuan 魏源 (1794–1856), in his general study of Qing military campaigns from the rise of the Manchu to the eve of the Opium War, wrote in the Preface, "[The book] is some 400 *juan* in length, so the gentry only stare at it with glazed eyes. Meanwhile the old generals are gradually fading away. How then will later generations be instructed? It is for this reason that I compiled this work," *Shengwuji* 聖武記.[15]

Copious materials from the archives on foreign encroachments and wars in the nineteenth century have been published, starting with the Opium War:

Yapian zhanzheng dang'an shiliao 鴉片戰爭檔案史料 (Historical materials from the archives on the Opium War), Yishiguan, eds., 7 vols., Shanghai renmin and Tianjin guji, 1987–92.

Yapian zhanzheng zai Zhejiang 鴉片戰爭在浙江 (The Opium War in Zhejiang), Yishiguan, eds., Zhejiang renmin, 1991.

Yapian zhanzheng zai Zhoushan shiliao xuanbian 鴉片戰爭在舟山史料選編 (Selected archival historical materials on the Opium War in Zhoushan), Yishiguan and Zhoushanshi Shekelian, eds., Zhejiang renmin, 1992.

Yapian zhanzheng wenxueji 鴉片戰爭文學集 (Collection of Materials for the study of the Opium War), 2 vols., Zhonghua, 1957.

Lin Zexu xingao 林則徐信稿 (Draft letters of Lin Zexu), Huang Zede 黃澤德, ed., Fujian renmin, 1985.

Lin Zexuji (zougao, riji, gongshu) 林則徐集 (奏稿, 日記, 公牘) (Lin Zexu collection: draft memorials, diary, public documents), Zhongshan daxue lishixi, eds., 4 vols., Zhonghua, 1962–65. Of which the fourth vol. is *Lin Zexu zougao gongdu riji bubian* 林則徐奏稿公牘日記補編 (Additions to Lin Zexu's draft memorials, public documents, and diary), Chen Xiqi 陳錫祺, ed. in chief, Zhongshan daxue, 1985.

[14] See "The Office of Military Archives," in Beatrice Bartlett, *Monarchs and Ministers: The Grand Council in Mid-Ch'ing China, 1723–1820*, UCP, 1991, 225–28.

[15] *Shengwuji* (Record of the campaigns of the holy warriors), 1842; Zhonghua, 1984.

Zhejiang yapian zhanzheng shiliao 浙江鴉片戰爭史料 (Historical materials on the Opium War in Zhejiang), Yishiguan and Ningboshi shehui kexuejie lianhehui, eds., Ningbo, 1997.

Di'erci Yapian zhanzheng 第二次鴉片戰爭 (The second Opium War), 6 vols., Gugong Ming-Qing dang'anbu, eds., Shanghai renmin, 1978–79.

For other materials on foreign wars, see 50.2.6.

28.3　Uprisings

In the 1950s, historical judgements were reversed and the study of court politics and culture was pushed into the background as the new regime officially proclaimed that "peasant uprisings were the major driving force of the development of China's feudal society." Accordingly, "peasant uprisings" became a top priority for historians and a large number of studies with supporting source materials were published.[16] As most soldiers fighting for or against any traditional state were generally peasants, the category "peasant uprising" can cover a wide range of disturbance. There is hardly a "peasant uprising" of any size in Chinese history for which there is not now a volume or several volumes of source materials—for example:

Qin-Han—Nan-Bei Chao

Qin-Han nongmin zhanzheng shiliao huibian 秦漢農民戰爭史料彙編 (Collection of historical materials on peasant wars in the Qin-Han), An Zuozhang 安作璋, ed., Zhonghua, 1982.

Wei, Jin, Nan-Bei Chao nongmin zhanzheng shiliao huibian 魏晉南北朝農民戰爭史料彙編 (Collection of historical materials on peasant wars in the Wei, Jin, *Nan-Bei Chao*), Zhang Zexian 張澤咸 and Zhu Dawei 朱大渭, eds., 2 vols., Zhonghua, 1980. Contains excerpts from Standard Histories, *biji* and funeral tablets.

---

[16] James P. Harrison, *The Communists and Chinese Peasant Rebellions: A Study in the Rewriting of History*, Atheneum, 1968.

Sui—Tang

Suimo nongmin zhanzheng shiliao huibian 隋末農民戰爭史料彙編 (Collection of historical materials on peasant wars at the end of the Sui), Wang Yongxing 王永興, ed., Zhonghua, 1980. Contains excerpts from the Standard Histories, and the *Tong jian.*

Tang-Wudai nongmin zhanzheng shiliao huibian 唐五代農民戰爭史料彙編 (Collection of historical materials on peasant wars in the Tang and Five Dynasties), Zhang Zexian 張澤咸, ed., 2 vols., Zhonghua, 1979. Contains excerpts from Standard Histories, *biji*, funeral inscriptions and *wenji.*

Song—Yuan

Liang Song nongmin zhanzheng shiliao huibian 兩宋農民戰爭史料彙編 (Collection of historical materials on peasant wars in the two Songs), He Zhuqi 何竹淇, ed., 4 vols., Zhonghua, 1976

Songdai sanci nongmin qiyi shiliao huibian 宋代三次農民起義史料彙編, (Collection of historical materials on the three peasant uprisings in the Song), Su Jinyuan 蘇金源, Li Chun pu 李春圃, eds., Zhonghua, 1963.

Yuandai nongmin zhanzheng shiliao huibian 元代農民戰爭史料彙編 (Collection of historical materials on peasant wars in the Yuan), Part 1, Yang Na 楊訥 and Chen Gaohua 陳高華, eds., Zhonghua, 1985. Covers uprisings between 1234 and 1350; Part 2, Yang Po 楊伯, Chen Gaohua 陳高華, eds., 2 vols., 1985, includes excerpts from 187 sources; Part 3, Chen Gaohua 陳高華, ed., 1985.

Ming—Qing

For the Ming, and even more so for the Qing, there are the rich resources of the archives.[17] For example:

Mingmo nongmin qiyi shiliao 明末農民起義史料 (Historical materials on peasant uprisings at the end of the Ming), Zheng Tianting 鄭天挺 et al., eds., Kaiming, 1952. Contains 220 documents dating from 1627–

---

[17] Susan Naquin, "True Confessions: Criminal Interrogations as Sources for Ch'ing History," *National Palace Museum Bulletin* 11.1: 1–17 (1976) and the same author's *Millenarian Rebellion in China: The Eight Trigrams Uprising of 1813*, YUP, 1976, which is based on documents relating to religious rebels (*jiaofei an* 教誹案) and their confessions (*gongci* 供詞).

48 dealing with the uprising of Li Zicheng. See James B. Parsons, *The Peasant Rebellions of the Late Ming Dynasty*, UAP, 1970.

Qingdai qianqi Miaomin qiyi dang'an shiliao huibian 清代前期苗民起義檔案史料彙編 (Archival historical materials on the Miao people's armed uprisings in the early Qing dynasty), Yishiguan and Guizhou sheng dang'an, eds., 3 vols., Guangming ribao, 1987.

Kangxi Qianlong shiqi chengxiang renmin fankang douzheng ziliao 康熙乾隆時期城鄉人民反抗斗爭資料 (Materials on uprisings by city and country folk during the Kangxi and Qianlong periods), Zhongguo renmin daxue, Qingshi yanjiusuo et al., eds., 2 vols., Zhonghua, 1979.

Bailianjiao

Qing zhongqi wusheng Bailianjiao qiyi ziliao 清中期五省白蓮教起義資料 (Materials on the White Lotus uprising in five provinces in the Qing), Lishisuo, eds., 5 vols., Jiangsu renmin, 1981–82.

Nian

Nianjun 捻軍 (The Nian army, 1814–1911), Zhongguoshi xuehui, 6 vols., Shanghai renmin, 1957. See Ssu-yu Teng, *The Nien Army and Their Guerrila Warfare, 1851–1868*, Mouton, 1961; Elizabeth Perry, *Chinese Perspectives on the Nien Rebellion*, Sharpe, 1981.

Muslim

There were a large number of major Muslim uprisings in the nineteenth century: in Yunnan, 1856–73; in Shaanxi and Gansu, 1862–78; in northern Xinjiang, 1873–78; and in the Gansu and Qinghai border regions, 1895, see, for example:

Huimin qiyi 回民起義 (The Muslim uprisings), Bai Shouyi 白壽彝, ed., 4 vols., Shenzhou guoguangshe, 1952. See Wen-djang Chu, *The Moslem Rebellon in North-West China, 1862–1878: A Study of Government Minority Policy*, Mouton, 1966.

Taiping

Taiping tianguo wenshu huibian 太平天國文書彙編 (Compendium of documents of the Taiping heavenly kingdom), Taiping tianguo lishi bowuguan, eds., Zhonghua, 1979. Franz Michael and Chung-li Chang, *The Taiping Rebellion: History and Documents*, 3 vols., UWP, 1966–71; Vincent Shih, *The Taiping Ideology, Its Sources, Interpretations and Influences*, UWP, 1967; Jonathan D. Spence, *God's Chinese Son: The Taiping Heavenly Kingdom of Hong Xiuquan*, Norton, 1996.

Taiping tianguo ziliao huibian 太平天國資料彙編 (Compendium of materials of the Taiping heavenly kingdom), Taiping tianguo lishi bowuguan, eds., Zhonghua, 1979–80.

Taiping tianguo wenxian shiliaoji 太平天國文獻史料集 (Collection of documents and historical data on the Taiping heavenly kingdom), Jinshisuo, eds., Shehui kexue, 1982.

Qing zhengfu zhenya Taiping tianguo dang'an shiliao 清政府鎮壓太平天國檔案史料 (Historical materials from the archives on the Qing government's suppression of the Taiping heavenly kingdom), Yishiguan, eds., 20 vols., Shehui kexue wenxian and Guangming ribao, 1990–94; 2 vols., Sheke wenxian, 1996.

Yihetuan

Yihetuan 義和團 (Militia united in righteousness, i.e., the Boxers), Zhongguoshi xuehui, 4 vols., Shanghai renmin, 1957. See Paul A. Cohen, *History in Three Keys: The Boxers as Event, Experience, and Myth*, Col. UP, 1997.

Yihetuan yundong shiliao congbian 義和團運動史料叢編 (Collection of historical materials on the Yihetuan movement), Beijing daxue lishixi, Zhongguo jindaishi jiaoyanshi, eds., 2 vols., Zhonghua, 1964.

Yihetuan dang'an shiliao 義和團檔案史料 (Historical materials on the Yihetuan from the archives), Guojia dang'anju Ming-Qing dang'an guan, eds., 2 vols., Zhonghua, 1959; rpnt., 1979.

Dongbei Yihetuan dang'an shiliao 東北義和團檔案史料 (Archival historical materials on the Yihetuan in the Northeast), Liaoning shehui kexueyuan, eds., Liaoning renmin, 1981.

Shandong Yihetuan anjuan 山東義和團案卷 (Archival files on Yihetuan cases in Shandong), Shekeyuan, Jindaishi yanjiusuo, eds., 2 vols., Qi-Lu, 1980.

Sichuan jiao'an yu Yihequan 四川教案與義和拳 (Missionary cases in Sichuan and the Yihetuan), Sichuan sheng dang'anguan, eds., Sichuan renmin, 1985.

Yihetuan yuanliu shiliao 義和團源流史料 (Historical materials on the origins of the Yihetuan), Lu Jingqi 陸景琪 et al., eds., Zhongguo renmin daxue, 1980.

Xiaodao

Fujian, Shanghai Xiaodaohui dang'an shiliao huibian 福建上海小刀會檔案史料彙編 (Collection of historical materials on the Small Sword Society in Fujian and Shanghai), Yishiguan and Shanghai shifan daxue, eds., Fujian renmin, 1993.

Wuchang

Wuchang qiyi dang'an shiliao xuanbian 武昌起義檔案史料選編 (Archival historical materials on the Wuchang uprising), Hubei sheng zhengxie et al., eds., 3 vols., Hubei renmin, 1981–83.

Much of the Qing archival material has been put on microfilm (50.2.1).

Bibliography

There is a large secondary literature on individual rebellions and peasant uprisings (some of the standard western studies have been indicated in the lists above). The Lishisuo is producing a multi-volume history of armed uprisings arranged by period under the title *Zhongguo nongmin zhanzhengshi* 中國農民戰爭史, Zhu Dawei 朱大渭, ed. in chief, Renmin, 1985– .

Protest and Crime in China: A Bibliography of Secret Associations, Popular Uprisings, Peasant Rebellions, Ssu-yü Teng, comp., Garland, 1981, lists nearly 4,000 citations to books and articles (of which 1,275 in Western languages and 2,725 in Chinese and Japanese). It is arranged alphabetically by author, with cross-references to titles, and has a subject index.

Frederic Wakeman, Jr., "Rebellion and Revolution: The Study of Popular Movements in Chinese History," *JAS* 36.2: 201–327 (1977).

Jean Chesneaux, ed., *Popular Movements and Secret Societies in China, 1840–1950*, SUP, 1972, "Bibliography," 279–88.

IV

Literary and Other Primary Sources

29

Leishu 類書

After a short introduction to *leishu* 類書 as a genre
(29.1), the discussion turns to general *leishu* (29.2); the
largest surviving general *leishu*, the *Gujin tushu jicheng*
古今圖書集成 or Imperial Encyclopaedia (29.3); and the
riyong leishu or encyclopaedias for daily use (29.4).[1]

29.1 Introduction

Many different kinds of *leishu* 類書 (lit., classified matters or
classified books, customarily translated as "encyclopaedia")
were compiled for many different purposes. Unlike a modern
encyclopaedia, the *leishu* typically consist of large numbers of
excerpts from primary sources rather than specially written articles. The excerpts are on a broad range of subjects arranged
under 20–30 headings and many hundreds of subdivisions. The
genre began as a reader of moral and political precedent to assist the emperor and his officials in government; it soon developed in other directions. Some were intended as elementary
primers or as the sum total of knowledge necessary to pass the
examinations to become an official. Some covered a particular

[1] On the *leishu* see Wolfgang Bauer, "The Encyclopaedia in China,"
Cahiers d'histoire mondiale 9: 665–91 (1966); also Teng Ssu-yü [Deng Siyu
鄧嗣禹] and Knight Biggerstaff, *An Annotated Bibliography of Selected
Chinese Reference Works*, 3rd rev. ed., H-Y Institute, 1971, 83–96. Zhang
Dihua 張滌華 *Leishu liubie* 類書流別 (On the different types of *leishu*),
1943; rev. ed., Shangwu, 1958, contains the important primary sources
on the compilation of *leishu* as well as an exhaustive list of over 400 lost
and extant *leishu* from all periods.

branch of literature (history or belles-lettres, for example), others covered all branches. Some were more literary and lexicographical and served as aids to composition, as vast repositories of well-turned phrases either general in application or devoted to specific models, such as letter writing or document drafting.

By the later Empire the tendency to include all existing human knowledge led to the compilation of monumental imperially sponsored *leishu* in which whole works, rather than excerpts, were copied into different categories.

Also in the later Empire, with the spreading of written knowledge to strata outside the literati, *riyong leishu* 日用類書 (Encyclopaedias for daily use) began to be compiled, summarizing practical information for townsfolk and others not primarily concerned with mastering the Confucian heritage.

The *leishu* are valuable to the historian for three main reasons:

1. Works which have long since been lost have often been preserved in whole or in part in the *leishu*. For example, the *Yiwen leiju* (see item 2 in the list below) has excerpts from 1,400 books written before the seventh century, of which only 140 are extant today. The *Yongle dadian* (beginning of the fifteenth century) contained no fewer than 385 complete books which had been lost by the eighteenth century. This has enabled scholars to recover works (or parts of them) which would otherwise have been lost (9.8.2).

2. The *leishu* not only provide a unique view of how Confucian education and knowledge were actually transmitted, they also provide a useful shortcut to materials on any given, traditionally defined subject.

3. The *riyong leishu* contain important materials on culture and attitudes of strata below the Confucian elite.

Besides these reasons, there are specific reasons why particular categories of *leishu* are still useful as works of reference. Thus the *Shitong* 十通 (26.2) provide easily accessible sources on all branches of the government, while some of the great encyclo-

paedias compiled as aids to literary composition are still useful
for placing characters or phrases in the contexts in which they
were used at different periods.

29.2 *General Encyclopaedias*

About 600 *leishu* were compiled between the Wei (third century AD) and the eighteenth century. Of these, 200 are extant
today and 10–20 are still used by historians. Seven of the most
important are introduced here (the order is chronological):

Beitang shuchao 北堂書鈔 (Excerpts from books in the Northern Hall),
   Yu Shinan 虞世南, (558–638), comp., 2 vols., Xinxing, 1978 (reprint
   of an 1888 collated edition); Zhonghua, punctuated ed., 1982. The
   earliest extant *leishu*. Divided into nineteen sections and many subsections. Deals mainly with government. Has quotations from many
   pre-Sui works long since lost. There is an index available.[2]

Yiwen leiju 藝文類聚 (Collection of literature arranged by categories),
   Ouyang Xun 歐陽詢 et al., comp., 100 *juan*, 604; *Yiwen leiju*, punctuated with corrections, 2 vols., Zhonghua, 1965; rpnt., Shanghai
   guji, 4 vols., 1982, has new index at end. Divided into 47 sections and
   many subsections. Criticised by the *Siku* editors as "of uneven quality
   and unsuitable categories." Nevertheless, the *Yiwen leiju* covers all
   subjects and contains many quotations from works long since lost
   and cites its sources.[3]

Chuxue ji 初學記 (Writings for elementary instruction), Xu Jian 徐堅 et
   al., comps., 713–42; 3 vols., Zhonghua, 1962, 3rd prnt., 1985. Background knowledge for beginning students. Divided into 23 main
   categories and 313 subcategories. Largely drawn from pre-Tang
   sources. There is an index available.[4]

---

[2] Yamada Hideo 山田英雄, *Hokudô shoshô insho sakuin* 北堂書鈔引
書索引 (Index to the books quoted in the *Beitang shuchao*), Nagoya: Saika
shorin, 1973.

[3] Nakatsuhama Wataru 中津濱涉, *Geibun ruijû insho sakuin* 藝文類
聚引書索引 (Index to the books quoted in the *Yiwen leiju*), rev. ed.,
Chûbun, 1974.

[4] *Chuxue ji suoyin* 初學記索引, Xu Yimin 許逸民 comp., Zhonghua,
1980. Has a four-corner as well as stroke-count index.

Taiping yulan 太平御覽 (Imperially reviewed encyclopaedia of the Taiping era), Li Fang 李昉 (925–96) et al., comps., 984; 4 vols., Zhonghua reprint of *Sibu congkan* 3rd series, 1960; 5th prnt., 1995. Important for Tang and Five Dynasties history. It took Li and 10 other scholars 10 years to compile the *Taiping yulan* and two years were needed to cut the woodblocks and do the printing. Divided into 55 main sections and 5,363 subsections. Quotations from over 1,690 sources, 70 of which have since been lost. *H-Y Index* 23.[5]

Cefu yuangui 册府元龜 (Outstanding models from the storehouse of literature), Wang Qinruo 王欽若 et al., eds., completed in 1013; photo-reprint of Song edition, 4 vols., Zhonghua, 1989; photo-reprint of 1642 ed., 12 vols., Zhonghua, 1960; 4th prnt., 1994. The Song edition is more reliable. Divided into 31 main sections and 1,104 subsections, covers from earliest times to the end of the Five Dynasties (960). Sources mainly the Standard Histories and, when not, often from works since lost. Particularly important for Tang and Five Dynasty history. There is an index to the names, titles, and technical terms in the sections on foreign countries and diplomatic affairs.[6]

Yuhai 玉海 (Ocean of jade), Wang Yinglin 王應麟 (1223–96), comp., Yuan edition, 1330–40; photo-reprint, Huawen, 1964; Zhejiang shuju, 1883; 6 vols., Jiangsu guji, 1987. Clumsily arranged but contains much important material for Song history, including quotations from the lost Song *Shilu*, National Histories and Daily Records. There is an index to the table of contents.[7] Wang Yinglin was also the author of a large number of scholarly and pedagogical works, including *Xiaoxue ganzhu* 小學紺珠 (Purple pearls for the beginner), 1299, on which see 2.6 and possibly the *Sanzijing* 三字經 (*Three Character Classic*), see 1.3.2.[8]

----

[5] See J. W. Haeger, "The Significance of Confusion: The Origins of the *T'ai-p'ing yü-lan*," *JAOS* 88.3: 401–10 (1968).

[6] *Sappu genki Hoshibu Gaishinbu sakuin* 册府元龜奉使部外臣部索引, Utsunomiya Kiyoyoshi 宇都宮清吉 and Naitô Shigenobu 内藤戊申 comps., Tôhô bunka kenkyûjo, 1938, with Wade-Giles index appended.

[7] *Gyokkai mokuroku* 玉海目錄, Yoshida Tora 吉田寅 and Tanada Naohiko 棚田直彦, comps., Kyôiku daigaku bungakubu, Tôyôshigaku kenkyûshitsu, Ajaishi kenkyûkai, 2 vols., 1957, 58.

[8] Hoyt Cleveland Tillman, "Encyclopaedias, Polymaths, and Taohsüeh Confucians: Preliminary Reflections with Special Reference to Chang Ju-yü," *Journal of Sung Yuan Studies* 22: 89–108 (1990–92), compares Zheng Qiao 鄭樵, Zhang Ruyu 章如愚 and Wang Yinglin 王應麟.

Yongle dadian 永樂大典 (Yongle encyclopaedia), 22,877 *juan* plus 60 *juan* index and preface; 11,095 *ce*, completed in 1408. The largest *leishu* ever compiled in China, with an estimated total of 370 million characters (compare the 26 Standard Histories, which contain a total of 40 million characters). Seven to eight thousand works from the Spring and Autumn period to the early Ming were copied by rhyme into this imperially-sponsored attempt to save for posterity the sum total of all Chinese written knowledge. Under the general editorship of Yao Guangxiao 姚廣孝, 2,169 scholars worked four years on the project. When it was completed, there was no money in the treasury to print it. A second manuscript copy was completed in 1567. The original manuscript was almost entirely lost by the end of the Ming. The eighteenth-century editors of the *Siku quanshu* took 385 works from the copy and also used in making annotations on works not included in the Imperial Library. A number of Qing scholars used it to recover lost works. By the eighteenth century, about 10 percent of the *Yongle dadian* had been lost. The Anglo-French forces took a considerable amount as souvenirs in 1860. By 1875, only 5,000 *ce* remained, less than half the complete work. By 1894, the number had dwindled to 800. During the occupation of Beijing in 1900 at the time of the Boxers, allied soldiers and officials took several hundred *ce* as souvenirs and many more were destroyed during the looting. By 1900, only 60 *ce* were left. The painstaking work of tracking down the dispersed *ce* which had escaped destruction has gone on for over 60 years. Different fragments were published between 1926 and 1983. Finally all of these (amounting to 3.5 percent of the original) have now been photo-lithographically reproduced as a set of 797 *juan*: *Yongle dadian*; Zhonghua, 10 folio vols., 1959; 3rd prnt., 1994; also Zhonghua, 1986, 222 *ce* in 22 *han*. There is a separate index: *Yongle dadian suoyin* 永樂大典索引, Luan Guiming 欒貴明, comp., Zuojia, 1997.

29.3 *The Imperial Encyclopaedia*

Gujin tushu jicheng 欽定古今圖書集成 (Imperially approved Synthesis of books and illustrations past and present), Chen Menglei 陳夢雷 et al., 10,000 *juan* plus 40 *juan* index, movable copper type edition, Beijing: Neifu 內府, 1726–28. By far the largest of the *leishu* to have been printed. It numbers 60 million characters on 852,408 pages and is divided into six main categories, 32 sections, and 6,109 subsections as shown in Table 26.

Table 26: The Imperial Encyclopaedia

Section (*dian* 典)	Number of (*juan* 卷)	Subsection (*bu* 部)
Category 1. Celestial Matters (*lixiang* 曆象)		
1 The Heavens (*qianxiang* 乾象)	21	100
2 The Year (*suigong* 歲功)	43	116
3 Astronomy and Mathematics (*lifa* 曆法)	6	140
4 Strange Phenomena (*shuzheng* 庶徵)	50	188
Category II. Geography (*fangyu* 方輿)		
5 The Earth (*kunyu* 坤輿)	21	140
6 Political Divisions (*zhifang* 職方)	223	544
7 Mountains and Rivers (*shanchuan* 山川)	401	320
8 Foreign Countries (*bianyi* 邊裔)	542	140
Category III. Human Relationships (*minglun* 明倫)		
9 The Emperor (*huangji* 皇極)	31	300
10 The Imperial Household (*gongwei* 宮闈)	15	140
11 The Government Service (*guanchang* 官常)	65	800
12 Family Relationships (*jiafan* 家範)	31	116
13 Social Intercourse (*jiaoyi* 交誼)	37	120
14 Clan and Family Names (*shizu* 氏族)	694	640
15 Man and his Attributes (*renshi* 人事)	97	112
16 Womankind (*guiyuan* 閨媛)	17	376
Category IV. Arts and Sciences (*bowu* 博物)		
17 Arts and Occupations (*yishu* 藝術)	43	824
18 Religion (*shenyi* 神異)	70	320
19 The Animal Kingdom (*qinchong* 禽蟲)	317	192
20 The Vegetable Kingdom (*caomu* 草木)	700	320
Category V. Confucianism and Literature (*lixue* 理學)		
21 Canonical and other Literature (*jingji* 經籍)	66	500
22 The Conduct of Life (*xuexing* 學行)	96	300
23 Branches of Literature (*wenxue* 文學)	49	260
24 Characters and Writing (*zixue* 字學)	24	160

Table continues

Table 26—Continued

Section (*dian* 典)	Number of (*juan* 卷)	Subsection (*bu* 部)
Category VI. Political Economy (*jingji* 經濟)		
25　The Examination System (*xuanju* 選舉)	29	136
26　The Official Career (*quanheng* 銓衡)	12	120
27　Foods and Traded Goods (*shihuo* 食貨)	83	360
28　Ceremonies (*liyi* 禮儀)	70	348
29　Music (*yuelü* 樂律)	46	136
30　Military Administration (*rongzheng* 戎政)	30	300
31　Law and Punishment (*xiangxing* 詳刑)	26	180
32　Industries and Manufactures (*kaogong* 考工)	154	252
Totals	6,109	10,000

Under each of the 6,109 subsections are sources gathered from the Zhou to the seventeenth century arranged under the following eight headings: (1) orthodox writings, especially the Classics; (2) other Confucian writings; (3) biographies; (4) literary works; (5) felicitous phrases and sentences; (6) historical works; (7) indirect reports; (8) anecdotes and myths.

Modern editions are available, including on CD-ROM. The most detailed index is that compiled for the 1985 Zhonghua and Ba-Shu edition, *Gujin tushu jicheng suoyin* 古今圖書集成索引.[9] This not only indexes the whereabouts of the subsections, but also contains separate indexes of illustrations, biographies, the political division section and the entries in the animal and vegetable kingdoms sections. The index also includes various additional notes on, for example, the sources of the *Tushu jicheng*.[10] There is also an excellent index to the translated titles of the subsections. It provides a convenient first entry point

[9] It accompanies the facsimile reproduction of the original edition, Shanghai: Zhonghua, 1934; rpnt., 82 vols., Zhonghua and Ba-Shu, 1985.

[10] Note also the name index of 20,000 Ming figures with biographical materials: *Tushu jicheng: Gujin tushu jicheng zhong Mingren zhuanji suoyin* 古今圖書集成中明人傳記索引, HKCU Press, 1963.

into this vast work: Lionel Giles (1875–1958), *Index to the Chinese Encyclopaedia*.[11]

The *Tushu jicheng* (as it is usually called) has frequently been used not only as a shortcut, but as the main and sometimes only route to primary sources. To use it this way is to risk becoming circumscribed by the biases of the eighteenth-century editors.

23.4 Encyclopaedias for Daily Use

From the Song, and increasingly from the Yuan and the Ming, encyclopaedias were compiled for a more popular audience than the emperor, the officials, and the literati. Such works as *Wanyong zhengzong* 萬用正宗, *Shilin guangji* 事林廣記 or *Wanbao quanshu* 萬寶全書 were issued in innumerable editions by the pulp publishers of Fujian and Jiangnan.[12] Their arrangement followed the literati *leishu*. There were sections on Heaven, Earth and Man, but the contents of these sections were concerned with current practical matters (e.g., advice to merchants and trade routes) rather than providing literary and historical models from the past. Many also contained sections on popular superstitions with instructions, for example, on how to select lucky days for different kinds of activity. Examples of such popular almanacs include *Jujia biyong shilei quanshu* 居家必用事類全書 (Guide to domestic operations), Yuan; or *Duonong bishi* 多能鄙事 (Various arts in everyday life), Ming. Many include brief outlines of the bureaucracy and the main administrative divisions of the Empire.

---

[11] British Museum, 1911; rpnt., Chengwen, 1969.

[12] *Wanyong zhengzong* (The all-purpose correct way), early sixteenth century; *Shilin guangji* (Wide gleanings of miscellaneous matters), Chen Yuanguan 陳元靚, ed.; end of the Song; 1322; rpnt. in 6 vols., Zhonghua, 1963; Chûbun, 1988. *Wanbao quanshu* (Complete book of 10,000 treasures). Many of these works have been photographically reproduced in *Chûgoku jitsuyô ruisho shusei* 中國日用類書集成 (Collection of Chinese encyclopaedias for everyday use), Kyûko, 1998.

These works form an important source on popular religion and attitudes, social practices, law and the economy not found in other extant sources. They have been intensively studied in Japan where many copies found their way in the Ming and Qing. Note, for example, the work of Sakai Tadao 酒井忠夫 on popular education;[13] of Niida Noboru on contracts,[14] and of Ogawa Yôichi 小川陽一 on vernacular novels.[15]

Certain miscellaneous notes, for example, *Wu zazu* 五雜俎 (49.1, *Biji*), are not dissimilar in content to the encyclopaedias for daily use.

[13] "Mindai no jitsuyô ruisho to shomin kyôiku 明代の日用類書と庶民教育" (Encyclopaedias for daily use and popular education in the Ming dynasty) in *Kinsei Chûgoku kyôikushi kenkyû* 近世中國教育史研究, Hayashi Tomoharu 林友春, ed., Kokudo, 1958, pp. 26-154; "Confucianism and Popular Educational Works," in *Self and Society in Ming Thought*, William T. De Bary, ed., Col. UP, 1970, 331-66.

[14] "Gen Min jidai no mura no kiyaku to kosaku shôsho nado, nichiyô hyakka zensho no rui nijûshu no naka kara 元明時代の村の規約と小作證書等日用百科全書の類二十種の中から" (Village regulations and wage laborer contracts in the Yuan and Ming as seen in twenty encyclopaedias for daily use) in his *Chûgoku hôseishi kenkyû* 中國法制史研究 (Collected papers on Chinese legal history), vol. 3, Tôbunken, 1962; 2nd ed., rev., 1980, pp. 741-829.

[15] *Nichiyô ruisho ni yoru Min-Shin shôsetsu no kenkyû* 日用類書による明清小説の研究 (Researches on Ming-Qing novels using everyday encyclopaedias), Kenbun, 1995.

30

Anthologies and Collected Works

Very large literary anthologies (*zongji* 總集) are extant from the sixth century onward. They contain memorials, letters and commemorative biographies by different hands as well as many other types of source material useful to the historian. By the Tang dynasty the practice of collecting together the prose and poetry of individual authors (called *bieji* 別集 to distinguish them from the *zongji*) was widespread and several have survived. After the Tang dynasty many hundreds of individual collected works (also called *wenji* 文集) are extant and the importance of the general anthologies for the historian declines as a result. This section introduces some useful reference tools for literature (30.1); the three most important general anthologies of Tang and pre-Tang prose literature (30.2); three examples of the massive poetry anthologies compiled (30.3); and reference tools for getting at the collected works of individual authors in the post-Tang period (30.4).

Both *zongji* and *bieji* are usually listed in the Belles-lettres branch (*jibu* 集部) of the *Sibu* classification (9.3).

30.1 Research Tools for Literature

The first comprehensive study of literary criticism in China was *Wenxin diaolong* 文心雕龍 by the scholar and monk, Liu Xie 劉勰 (ca. 465–522). Liu includes the first thorough discussion of literary genres, including historical writings, edicts, memorials, dispatches and letters. The translator traces the history of literary criticism in China up to Liu Xie whose life and work he also examines.[1]

The best available overall introduction and reference in English to Chinese literature is the *Indiana Companion to Traditional Chinese Literature*.[2] Over 160 scholars contributed. The scope is wide as shown by the range of introductory essays on Daoist literature, Buddhist literature, drama, fiction, literary criticism, poetry, popular literature, prose, rhetoric, and women's literature (Part I, 1–192). These are followed by the main body of the *Companion*, more than 500 entries on individual authors, works, schools and terms, each with bibliographical references (Part II, 195–969). Translations into English, French, German and Japanese are indicated where these exist. There are separate name, title and subject indexes. Beware the large number of printing mistakes.

On a smaller scale than the *Indiana Companion*, the best outline in English is *A Guide to Chinese Literature*, Wilt Idema and Lloyd Haft, comps., CCS, Univ. of Michigan, 1998. This is the English version of a guide originally published in Dutch. It replaces James Robert Hightower, *Topics in Chinese Literature: Outlines and Bibliographies*, rev. ed., H-Y Institute, 1953.

---

[1] Use Vincent Yu-chung Shih's bilingual Chinese-English edition, *The Literary Mind and the Carving of Dragons: A Study of Thought and Pattern in Chinese Literature*, HKCU Press, 1983. This supersedes the original edition published without Chinese text by Col. UP, 1959.

[2] William H. Nienhauser, Jr., editor and compiler; Charles Hartman, associate editor for poetry; Y. W. Ma, associate editor for fiction; Stephen H. West, associate editor for drama, IUP, 1986; rev. rpnt., SMC, 1988.

For a comprehensive, well-indexed, Chinese encyclopaedic dictionary of literature (33,000 entries), see *Zhongguo wenxue da cidian* 中國文學大詞典.[3] Vol. 1 contains a total stroke-count and a *pinyin* index.

Two excellent one-volume anthologies of Chinese literature in English translation are:

The Columbia Anthology of Traditional Chinese Literature, Victor Mair, ed., Col. UP, 1994. Four hundred translations by many hands. Belles-lettres are well represented, but in addition almost anything written in Chinese during the last 3,200 years is sampled from divination records to philosophical texts to anonymous folk ballads and marginal doodles of copyists. There is no index.

An Anthology of Chinese Literature, Beginnings to 1911, edited and tr. by Stephen Owen, Norton, 1996. The editor has not only done all the translations himself but has also provided up-to-date introductions to each major period of history and style of writing. Particularly interesting for anyone trying to understand the possibilities and constraints of the different genres of Chinese literature. The anthology is well indexed.

Note the journal *Renditions*. This is an attractive biannual of translations with contributions by leading sinologists from all over the world. Issues are often grouped around a theme—for example, "letters" or "classical prose." The Chinese text is usually printed after the translations. *Renditions* is published and edited at the Chinese University of Hong Kong.

There are a large number of Chinese dictionaries of the language found in various genres of literature as well as dictionaries of the language of specific periods and of individual works. Those covering *baihua* literature from the Tang to the Qing, especially vernacular fiction and specific periods, are listed in 34.3, *Dictionaries*.

---

[3] *Zhongguo wenxue da cidian*, Ma Liangchun 馬良春 and Li Futian 李福田, eds. in chief, 8 vols., Tianjin renmin, 1991.

30.2 *Anthologies and Collections of Prose*

Wenxuan 文選 (Anthology of Literature), compiled by Xiao Tong 蕭統, Crown Prince Zhaoming of Liang 梁昭明太子 (501–31). Divided into poetry and prose with the 761 prose excerpts further subdivided into 37 genres. Writing from the late Zhou to the Liang. A model for later anthologies as well as a textbook for examination candidates. A scholarly English language translation is in progress.[4]

Quan shanggu Sandai Qin Han Sanguo Liuchao wen 全上古三代秦漢三國六朝文 (Complete collection of prose literature from remote antiquity, the Three Dynasties, the Qin and Han, the Three Kingdoms, and the Six Dynasties), Yan Kejun 嚴可均, (1762–1843), comp., completed 1836; printed, Guangya shuju, 1893; rpnt., 4 vols., Zhonghua, 1951; 6th prnt., 1996. The compiler was not invited to join the editing of the *Quan Tang wen* (next item), so spent the following 27 years (1808–36) working on this huge collection (746 *juan*) of pre-Tang works of 3,497 writers. The contents were garnered from inscriptions and texts preserved in other works, not from obvious sources. There are indexes available.[5]

Quan Tang wen 全唐文 (Complete prose literature of the Tang), Dong Hao 董浩 (1740–1818), comp., 1814; 11 vols., Zhonghua, 1983; 3rd prnt., 1996; 4 vols., Shanghai guji, 1990. Contains 18,400 literary compositions of 3,042 named Tang authors (plus those of several hundred anonymous writers active in the Tang). There are indexes

---

[4] Three volumes of the projected eight-volume annotated translation by David R. Knechtges have been published under the title *Selections of Refined Literature. Volume One: Rhapsodies on Metropolises and Capitals; Volume Two: Rhapsodies on Sacrifices, Hunting, Travel, Sightseeing, Palaces and Halls, Rivers and Seas; Volume Three: Rhapsodies on Natural Phenomena, Birds and Animals, Aspirations and Feelings, Sorrowful Laments, Literature, Music, and Passions*, PUP, 1982; 1987; 1996. Note Shiba Rokurô 斯波六郎, *Monzen sakuin* 文選索引 (A Concordance to Wenxuan), *T'ang Civilization Reference Series*, 4 vols., Jimbun, 1957–59; Chûmon, 1995. This supersedes *H-Y Index* 25 to authors, titles, and works quoted in the anthology. There is a Chinese translation published by the Shanghai guji, 3 vols., 1997.

[5] *H-Y Index* 8 is an index to authors; *Quan shanggu Sandai Qin Han Sanguo Liuchao wen pianming mulu ji zuozhe suoyin* 全上古三代秦漢三國六朝文篇名目錄及作者索引, Zhonghua, 1958 [with corrections]; 6th rpnt., 1995; Chengwen, 1966. It includes an index to the table of contents as well as to the authors.

available.[6] A single large volume of excerpts of interest to the political and economic historian has been published: *Quan Tang wen zhengzhi jingji ziliao huibian* 全唐文政治經濟資料彙編.[7] There are other such collections of excerpts—for example, historical materials on Yunnan, or on Tibet.[8]

Quan Song wen 全宋文 (47.2, *Collections of Song Prose and Poetry*).

30.3   Collections of Poetry

"*Du qi shi zhi qi ren* 讀其詩知其人" (Know a man by his poetry), traditional saying.

A huge amount of poetry was written during the course of Chinese history, much to mark particular occasions. So poetry is an essential source for biography and atmosphere. Some forms of poetry (the Yuan *qu* 曲) are good sources for the colloquial language.[9] Of the many hundreds of poetry collections,

---

[6] Ma Xuchuan 馬緒傳, comp., *Quan Tang wen pianming mulu ji zuozhe suoyin* 全唐文篇名目錄及作者索引, Zhonghua, 1985. Also the *T'ang Civilization Reference Series*, vols. 3 and 10: *Tôdai no sanbun sakka* 唐代の散文作家 (Tang prose authors), Hiraoka Takeo 平岡武夫 et al., eds., Jimbun, 1954; Dôhôsha, 1977. Gives alternative names, floruit of author, and reference to his works in *Quan Tang wen* and its continuations; *Tôdai no sambun sakuhin* 唐代の散文作品 (Tang prose works), Hiraoka Takeo et al., ed., Jimbun, 1960; Dôhôsha, 1977. Indexes the works in *Tôdai no sanbun sakka* and gives the personal names found in the titles of the prose works. See also, *Quan Tang wen zhiguan congkao* 全唐文職官叢考 (Comprehensive study of officals in the *Quan Tang wen*), Chen Guocan 陳國燦 and Liu Jianming 劉建明, eds., Wuhan daxue, 1997.

[7] *Quan Tang wen zhengzhi jing ji ziliao huibian* (Collection of political and economic materials from the *Quan Tang wen*), Li Jiping 李季平, ed. in chief, San-Qin, 1992.

[8] *Quan Tang wen Yunnan shiliao jichao* 全唐文雲南史料輯抄, Yuan Renyun 袁任運, ed., Yunnan renmin, 1989; *Quan Tang wen Quan Tang shi Tubo shiliao* 全唐文全唐詩吐蕃史料, Fan Xuezong 范學宗 et al., comp., Xizang renmin, 1988.

[9] Zhang Xiang 張相, *Shi ci qu yuci huishi* 詩辭曲語詞匯釋 (Collected explications of the language of the *shi*, *ci* and *qu*), 2 vols., Zhonghua, 1953; 1978. Contains carefully researched definitions with copious examples of usage of 600 terms.

and leaving aside the *Shijing* 詩經, six examples are given below.

Yuefu shiji 樂府詩集 (Collection of Music-Bureau poems), Guo Maoqian 郭茂倩, comp., 12th century (on the *yuefu*, see section 34.2).

Yutai xinyong 玉臺新咏 (New songs from a jade terrace), Xu Ling 徐陵 (507–583), comp., ca. 545. Famous collection of 656 palace-style poems mainly written during the Southern Dynasties. Anne M. Birrell, *New Songs from Jade Terrace*, Allen and Unwin, 1982; rev. ed., Penguin 1986, is a complete annotated translation into English.[10]

Xian-Qin Han Wei Jin Nan-Bei Chao shi 先秦漢魏晉南北朝詩, 3 vols., Zhonghua, 1983; 3rd prnt., 1995, is a large collection of poetry up to the Sui arranged chronologically with short biographies of each poet. There is an index available.[11]

Tangshi jishi 唐詩記事, Ji Yugong 計有功 (*jinshi* 1121), comp. Ji's words are quoted at the head of this chapter. This anthology of Tang poetry is one of the earliest large-scale ones. In it he assembles the work of 1,100 poets together with anecdotes about the occasion for the writing of the poem. Many other poetry anthologies followed this *"jishi"* style. Three have *H-Y Indexes*.[12]

Quan Tang shi 全唐詩, Peng Dingqiu 彭定求 (1645–1719) et al., comp., 1705. The largest general anthology of Tang poetry. It contains 48,900 poems by 2,200 Tang authors. There is a database of the *Quan Tang shi* at the Academy of Social Sciences computer office which has used it to generate a multi-volume concordance on every character.[13] In addition, modern publishers of the *Quan Tang shi* usually include

---

[10] *Gyokudai shin'ei sakuin* 玉臺新咏索引, Obi Kôichi 小尾郊一 and Takashi Sadao 高志貞夫, comps., Yamamoto, 1976.

[11] *Xian-Qin Han Wei Jin Nan-Bei Chao shi zuozhe pianmu suoyin* 先秦漢魏晉南北朝詩作者篇目索引, Chang Zhenguo 常振國 et al., Zhonghua, 1988.

[12] *Tangshi jishi zhuzhe yinde* 唐詩記事著者引得; *Songshi jishi zhuzhe yinde* 宋詩記事著者引得; *Yuanshi jishi zhuzhe yinde* 元詩記事著者引得, *H-Y Indexes*, 18, 19, 20.

[13] *Quan Tang shi suoyin* 全唐詩索引, Luan Guiming 欒貴明, ed., Zhonghua and Xiandai, 1991– . Arrangement is by individual poets. There is a Zhonghua typeset edition of the *Quan Tang shi* in 25 *ce*, 1960; 5th prnt., 1992.

author/title indexes.[14] Personal names appearing in the titles, prefaces and annotations to the poems have also been indexed.[15] Finally, there is an index to occasional poetry in the *Quan Tang shi* (partings, gifts, visits, banquets and so forth).[16]

There have been numerous supplements to the *Quan Tang shi*, for example, *Quan Tang shi waibian* 全唐詩外編, Wang Zhongmin 王重民 et al., comps., 2 vols., Zhonghua, 1982, which includes poems discovered at Dunhuang; *Quan Tang shi bubian* 全唐詩補編, Chen Shangjun 陳尚君, comp., Zhonghua, 1992, which includes Tang poems newly discovered on tomb tablets. For an indexed catalog of anthologies of Tang poetry from the Tang to 1985, see *Tangshi shulu* 唐詩書錄.[17]

Quan Song shi 全宋詩 (47.2, *Collections of Song Prose and Poetry*).

30.4   *Collected Works*

Collected works of individual authors (*bieji* 別集 is the classificatory term used by the *Siku* editors) usually contain several of the following categories of writing: (1) prefaces to the collection; (2) memorials and other official writings; (3) congratulatory poetry for public occasions; (4) prefaces; (5) commentary on events, diaries; (6) letters; (7) commemorative biographies for tombstones, tomb tablets, encomia, accounts of conduct; (8)

---

[14] *Quan Tang shi suoyin* 全唐詩索引, Shi Cheng 史成, ed., Shanghai guji, 1990; *Quan Tang shi zuozhe suoyin* 全唐詩作者索引, Zhang Chenshi 張忱石, ed., Zhonghua, 1983. There is a Chinese translation of the Jimbun's *T'ang Civilization Reference Series* index 4 (Tang poets, 1960): *Tangdai de shiren* 唐代的詩人, Shanghai guji, 1991; indexes 11 and 12 (Tang poetry, 1964 and 1965): *Tangdai de shipian* 唐代的詩篇, 2 vols., Shanghai guji, 1990. Indexes 50,000 poems from all main collections of Tang poetry and includes lists of persons to whom poems were addressed as well an index of Five Dynasty poets.

[15] *Quan Tang shi renming kao* 全唐詩人名考, Wu Ruyu 吳汝煜 and Hu Kexian 胡可先, comp., Jiangsu jiaoyu, 1990. Sometimes a brief biography is supplied. There is a *pinyin* index at the end.

[16] Wu Ruyu 吳汝煜, *Tang-Wudai ren jiaowangshi suoyin* 唐五代人交往詩索引, Shanghai guji, 1993.

[17] *Tangshi shulu*, Chen Bohai 陳伯海 and Zhu Yi'an 朱易安, eds., Qi-Lu, 1988.

poems; (9) family instructions and (10) miscellaneous. Collected works do not necessarily include all the works of an author.

The titles of *bieji* normally begin with the author's name, alternative name, studio name, nickname or place of origin followed by the term *wenji* 文集, *ji* 集 or *quanji* 全集. But many other such descriptive terms were used. They are worth noting in order to be able to quickly spot a *bieji*. Alternative terms included simply *gao* 稿 (draft or manuscript), or

> *leigao* 類稿 (classified manuscripts)
> *shenggao* 剩稿 (remaining drafts)
> *weiding gao* 未定稿 (unedited manuscripts)
> *wenchao* 文鈔 (literary excerpts)
> *wencun* 文存 (preserved literary works)
> *wengao* 文稿 (draft literary works)
> *wenhui* 文匯 (literary collectanea)
> *yigao* 遺稿 (bequeathed draft or manuscripts)
> *yiji* 遺集 (bequeathed collection)
> *yishu* 遺書 (literary remains)

Of 904 *bieji* known to have been in existence in the Sui, 467 have been lost and the majority of Tang *bieji* have also been lost. Thanks to the invention of printing, 80 percent of the *bieji* of the Song have survived. About 1,500 *bieji* by Ming authors have survived and at least 5,000 by Qing authors.

Titles of an author's collected works are usually mentioned in his biography. Note that occasionally a part of the collected works of a particularly famous author will have an index or concordance made especially for it, Otherwise, there are reference works to help locate an author's collected works and also to use them rapidly. Some are catalogs, others detailed subject indexes. References to some of the main ones are given below. Further details and more indexes are given in Part V in the chapters indicated after each title below:

Tang
Tangji xulu 唐集叙錄 (46.2, *Bieji*).

Song
Xiancun Songren bieji banben mulu 現存宋人別集版本目錄 (47.2, *Bieji*).

Yuan

Yuanren wenji pianmu fenlei suoyin 元人文集篇目分類索引 (48.5.2, *Bie-ji*).

Ming

ISMH lists collected works if they contain three or more memorials.

Qing

Qingren wenji bielu 清人文集別錄 (50.6.6).

Qingdai wenji shulu 清代文集書錄 (50.6.6).

Biji 筆記

As Yuan Mei, the eighteenth-century poet observed of reading notes, when they have reached a certain bulk, "one is reluctant to keep them and equally reluctant to throw them away."[1] The solution was to publish them. Sometimes more or less as they were written, often meticulously rearranged according to topic, often maintaining a "notes and queries" form.

If *biji* only covered reading notes the category would be easy enough to understand. But it was used in other ways, to include, for example, short stories or to record anecdote and gossip. Reflecting the width of the definition, *biji* were classified under different *Sibu* categories, including *zashi* 雜史 or *dili* 地理 of the History branch and the *zajia* 雜家 or *xiaoshuo* 小説 of the Philosophy branch. They were often included in *congshu* 叢書.

The practice of writing *biji* had already begun after the Han dynasty but it became widespread only in the Tang and the Song. The *biji* 筆記 ("miscellanies" as they are sometimes called in English) often started as reading notes to which, fortunately, sometimes the author added his direct observations. Not a few were written in retirement and take the form of recollections of official and court life. They cover as wide a range of subjects

---

[1] Arthur Waley, *Yuan Mei: Eighteenth Century Chinese Poet*, Macmillan, 1956, 112–16.

as the individual interests and tastes of their authors. Some are purely fictional. Some are on scholastic points of history or philology; others simply record the flux of city life, including theatrical and other divertissements, local customs and practical guidebook-style advice. They often relate anecdotes, gossip and rumor, subjects considered unfit for more formal works but not infrequently essential for social history. The *biji* are therefore a useful corrective to the Standard Histories and other works of Confucian historiography and an important supplement to an author's *bieji* in which they were not normally included until long after his death. The quality and reliability of the *biji* are as varied as their subject matter.[2] Students of any post-Han period should make sure that they have found out the most important *biji* and glanced over them. It is often surprising what these works contain. Fifty of the most famous *biji* are listed in the relevant chapters of Part V.

In their titles, in addition to the terms *biji* and *suibi* 隨筆, many others were used, for example,

> *bitan* 筆談 (brush talk)
> *conghua* 叢話 (collected talk)
> *congtan* 叢談 (collected chats)
> *jianwenlu* 見聞錄 (record of things seen and heard)
> *jiuwen* 舊聞 (things heard long ago)
> *kehua* 客話 (the talk of guests) and many more.
> *suichao* 隨鈔 (miscellaneous excerpts)
> *suilu* 隨錄 (miscellaneous records)
> *suowen* 瑣聞 (trifles overheard)
> *xinyu* 新語 (new talk)
> *zalu* 雜錄 (miscellaneous records)
> *zazhi* 雜誌 (miscellaneous notes)
> *zhaji* 札記 (simplified notes)
> *zhaji* 劄記 (classified notes)

There are many collectanea of *biji* devoted to a single region. There are also a large number of collectanea which contain only *biji* novels, for example, *Biji xiaoshuo daguan* 筆記小

---

[2] For a general introduction to *biji* of all periods see Liu Yeqiu 劉葉秋 *Lidai biji gaishu* 歷代筆記概述, Zhonghua, 1980.

説大觀, many editions; e.g., 16 vols., Zhejiang guji, 1995. It contains over 200 fictional and other *biji* from the Tang and Song. Note the Yuan collection *Shuofu* 説郛 (48.5.2, *Biji*).

Zhonghua published 106 *biji* in excellent punctuated, annotated editions in the 1950s in three series of "historical materials *biji*" They were reprinted in the 1980s and again in 1997:

> *Tang-Song shiliao biji congkan* 唐宋史料筆記叢刊 (40 titles)
> *Yuan-Ming shiliao biji congkan* 元明史料筆記叢刊 (24 titles)
> *Qingdai shiliao biji congkan* 清代史料筆記叢刊 (42 titles).

There are a number of indexes to the key terms in *biji*. The two compiled under the direction of Saeki Tomi index the chapter headings, key words and important nouns found in 130 *biji*.[3] Umehara Kaoru indexed the five main *biji* on life in the two Song capitals (47.2).

Chidu 尺牘, *shujian* 書簡 (letters) or *daobi* 刀筆 (notes) can sometimes contain information on matters such as land prices (see for example, Ronald C. Egan, "Su Shih's 'Notes' as a Historical and Literary Source," *HJAS* 50.2: 561–88 (1990).

---

[3] Saeki Tomi 佐伯富 ed., *Chûgoku zuihitsu sakuin* 中國隨筆索引, Nihon gakujutsu shinkôkai, 1954; *Chûgoku zuihitsu zatcho sakuin* 中國隨筆雜著索引, Tôyôshi kenkyûkai, 1960.

32

Philosophical Works

Works listed under Philosophers in the *Imperial Catalog* cover a broad range including miscellaneous and incidental works:

The Philosophers' Branch in the Siku *Classification*

Confucian writers (chaps. 19, 32)	*rujia* 儒家
Military experts (28)	*bingjia* 兵家
Legal writers (19, 27 and 32)	*fajia* 法家
Writers on agriculture (35)	*nongjia* 農家
Writers on medicine (36)	*yijia* 醫家
Astronomy and math (5, 37)	*tianwen suanfa* 天文算法
Mantic arts (36, 37)	*shushu* 術數
The fine arts (38)	*yishu* 藝術
Manuals, e.g., on cooking (35.2)	*pulu* 譜錄
Miscellaneous writers (32)	*zajia* 雜家
Encyclopaedias (29)	*leishu* 類書
Essays and misc. works (34.3)	*xiaoshuo* 小説
Buddhists (33.5)	*shijia* 釋家
Daoists (33.4)	*daojia* 道家

Note: the numbers in brackets following each entry in the lefthand column refer to chapter and section numbers in the manual.

For the philosophers of the pre-Qin and Han, see Table 18, chap. 19 and for studies of the pre-Qin philosophers, see 19.1. For histories of Chinese philosophy in English, see

Kung-chuan Hsiao, *A History of Chinese Political Thought, Volume 1: From the Beginnings to the Sixth Century A.D*, F. W. Mote, tr. (from the Chinese original, 1945–46), PUP, 1979.

Fung Yu-lan (Feng Youlan 馮友蘭, 1895–1990), *A History of Chinese Philosophy*, Derk Bodde, tr. (from the Chinese original, 1931, 1934), 1937; PUP, 1952; vol. 2, 1953; rpnt., 1983.

For critical examinations of the lives and teachings of the later Confucian philosophers, see the three *Xue'an* 學案 collections. There are a number of indexes available, including a combined one (item 4 below):

Song-Yuan xue'an 宋元學案 (Major schools of Song and Yuan Confucians). The author, Huang Zongxi 黃宗羲 (1610–95) left this work uncompleted (it was modelled on his *Mingru xue'an*); finally completed and printed for the first time in 1838; 4 vols., Zhonghua, 1986; rpnt., 1990. Use *Song-Yuan lixue jia zhushu sheng zu nianbiao* 宋元理學家著書生卒年表 (Chronological table of bibliographical and biographical data of the Sung and Yuan Confucian philosophers), Mai Zhonggui 麥仲貴, comp., HKCU Press, 1968; *Sô-Gen gakuan, Sô-Gen gakuan hoi jinmei ji, gô, betsumei sakuin* 宋元學案, 宋元學案補遺人名字號別名索引 (Name index to *Song-Yuan xue'an* and its continuation), Kinugawa Tsuyoshi 衣川強, comp., Jimbun, 1974. For an English translation of Huang's *Mingyi daifang lu* 明夷待訪錄, 1662, see *Waiting for the Dawn: A Plan for the Prince*, Wm. Theodore de Bary (1918–), Col. UP, 1993.

Mingru xue'an 明儒學案 (Records of Ming Scholars), Huang Zongxi, 1700; 2 vols., Zhonghua, 1985. This has been partly translated by Julia Ching and Fang Chao-ying, eds., *The Records of Ming Scholars*, UHP, 1987.

清儒學案 (Records of Qing Scholars), Xu Shichang 徐世昌, comp., 1940; Zhongguo shudian rpnt., 1985.

Ming-Qing ruxuejia zhushu shengzu nianbiao 明清儒學家著述生卒年表 (Chronological table of bibliographical and biographical data of the Ming and Qing Confucian philosophers), Mai Zhonggui 麥仲貴, comp., Xuesheng, 1977.

Song-Yuan, Ming, Qing sichao xue'an suoyin 宋元明清四朝學案索引 (Index to the *xue'an* of the Song, Yuan, Ming and Qing dynasties), Chen Tiefan 陳鐵凡 comp., Yiwen, 1974.

Dictionaries

Zhongguo ruxue cidian 中國儒學辭典 (Dictionary of Confucianism), Zhao Jihui 趙吉惠 and Guo Houan 郭厚安, eds., Liaoning renmin, 1988. Contains over 2,200 signed entries, arranged in four sections:

biographies, texts, academies and schools of thought and philosophical terms. Has stroke-count index of names, titles and terms.

Zhongguo zhexue da cidian 中國哲學大辭典 (Large dictionary of Chinese philosophy), Fang Keli 方克立, ed., Shehui kexue, 1994, covers philosophers, their works and their concepts. Arrangement is by stroke count. There is a useful index of key concepts arranged by categories, i.e., schools of thought, personalities, works, concepts and the philosophy of the non-Han peoples. There is a *pinyin* index.

Translations and Excerpts

Sources of Chinese Tradition, William Theodore de Bary, Wing-tsit Chan (Chen Xuejie 陳學捷) and Chester Tan, 1960. An excellent selection of translated excerpts of Chinese thinkers arranged chronologically by subject.

A Sourcebook in Chinese Philosophy, Wing-tsit Chan, PUP, 1963; 4th prnt., 1973.

Reflections on Things at Hand: The Neo-Confucian Anthology, Wing-tsit Chan, tr., Col. UP, 1967. Translation of *Jin silu* 近思錄 by Zhu Xi 朱熹, 1130–1200 and Lü Zuqian 呂祖謙, 1137–81.

Neo Confucian Terms Explained (The Pei-hsi tsu-i 北溪字義 *by Ch'en Ch'un* [Chen Chun 陳淳], *1159–1237)*, Wing-tsit Chan, tr., ed. and introduced, Col. UP, 1988.

Bibliography

Guide to Chinese Philosophy, Charles Wei-hsin Wu and Wing-tsit Chan, Boston, 1978. An annotated bibliography of Western language books and articles.

"Chinese Philosophy: A Philosophical Essay on the State of the Art," Lin Tongqi, Henry Rosemont, Jr., and Roger T. Ames, *JAS* 54.3: 727–58 (1995), especially pages 745–58, where the authors argue that Chinese philosophy has suffered in translation from the use of Western words and terms already freighted with their own meanings. To avoid this problem they suggest using transliterations of Chinese concepts with explanations on first appearance.

Zhongguo zhexueshi lunwen suoyin 中國哲學史論文索引 (An index of articles on the history of Chinese philosophy), Fang Keli 方克立 et al., comps., 4 vols., Shehui kexue, 1986–91. Articles written in China between 1950 and 1985.

Journals

Philosophy East and West (1951– , quarterly), University of Hawaii.

Journal of Chinese Philosophy (1973– , quarterly), University of Hawaii.

There is an annual survey edited by the Shekeyuan, Zhexue yanjiu suo 哲學研究所 (Philosophy Institute of CASS), *Zhongguo zhexue nianjian* 中國哲學年鑒, Shanghai: Zhongguo baike quanshu, 1982–90; Beijing: Zhexue yanjiu zazhishe, 1991–). It includes coverage of current research on Chinese philosophy.

33

Myth and Religion

This chapter covers myth (33.1), religion in general (33.2), the common religion (33.3), Daoist works (33.4) and Buddhist works (33.5), including those of Tibetan Buddhism (33.5.1). There are also short sections on Islam (33.6), Christianity and Judaism (33.7).

33.1 *Myth*

Myths are the basis for understanding of any society for three main reasons: (1) they reveal the values and beliefs not only of the earliest peoples who lived in that society, but also of later generations who codified and passed down the elaborate mythology which generations of children learned from their mothers and wet nurses;[1] (2) an understanding of myth is essential in decoding symbols and art motifs (which can themselves provide in all periods, especially in the earliest ones for which other sources may be lacking, important keys to the understanding of values and beliefs);[2] (3) the relationship of myth and history, of fiction and fact lie at the heart of our understanding of the credibility of the earliest written records.

---

[1] On myth, I have drawn heavily on Anne M. Birrell, "Review Article: Studies in Chinese Myth since 1970: An Appraisal," Parts I and II, *History of Religions*, 39.4: 380–93 (1994); 39.5: 70–94 (1994). See also Whalen Lai, "Recent PRC Scholarship on Chinese Myths," *Asian Folklore Studies* 53.1: 151–63 (1994).

[2] K. C. Chang, *Art, Myth and Ritual: The Path to Political Authority in Ancient China*, HUP, 1983.

Sorting out what was genuinely an ancient myth from later inventions is no easy matter. In China, the work began in the twentieth century with the Yigupai 疑古派 (doubting antiquity school) led by Gu Jiegang 顧頡剛. Gu argued that China's earliest history was based on myths, with each successive layer adding more and more spurious detail to remoter and remoter ages in the past (*cenglei de zaocheng de Zhongguo gushi* 層累地造成的中國古史). He believed that these later accretions could be stripped away (thus reducing the length of China's history from 5,000 to 3,000 years) and analyzed as mythology.[3]

The first modern study of China's myths and legends using the findings of archaeologists was made by Xu Xusheng 徐旭生, *Zhongguo gushi de chuanshuo shidai* 中國古史的說傳時代.[4]

The best introductions to Chinese mythology in English are Anne M. Birrell, *Chinese Mythology: An Introduction*, and Derk Bodde, "Myths of Ancient China."[5] The contributions of Japanese studies of Chinese mythology are summarized in Wang Xiaolian 王孝廉, *Zhongguo de shenhua yu chuanshuo* 中國的神話與傳說 (Chinese myths and legends), Lianjing, 1977.

---

[3] The most influential works of the "Yigupai" were published in the series *Gushibian* 古史辨 (Debates on ancient history), 7 vols., 1926–41; several reprints, including Shanghai guji, 1982. In the *Preface* to vol. 1 of *Gushibian*, the young Gu wrote an account of his life up to that time (he was 33 in 1926). It has been translated under the title *The Autobiography of a Chinese Historian*, Arthur W. Hummel, Brill, tr., 1931; Taibei, 1966 and 1972. On Gu, see Laurence A. Schneider, *Ku Chieh-kang and China's New History: Nationalism and the Quest for Authoritative Traditions*, UCP, 1976.

[4] *Zhongguo gushi de chuanshuo shidai* (The legendary period of ancient Chinese history), 1943; rev. ed., Kexue, 1960, rpnt., Wenwu, 1985. The first Western study was Marcel Granet, *Danses et legendes de la Chine ancienne*, 3rd ed., corrected and annotated by Rémi Mathieu, PUF, 1994 [1926].

[5] Anne M. Birrell, *Chinese Mythology: An Introduction*, Johns Hopkins Univ. Press, 1993, and Derk Bodde, "Myths of Ancient China," in *Mythologies of the Ancient World*, S. N. Kramer, ed., Doubleday, 1961, 369–408.

Interpretations of Chinese society were until recently influenced by Confucian orthodoxy, which laid little store on popular religious beliefs. Not a few scholars even claimed that the Chinese were basically not a religious people and had no creation myths. Nothing could be further from the truth.

In "A Classification of Shang and Chou Myths," K. C. Chang examines the schemes proposed by previous scholars (up to 1961) and offers his own: (1) nature myths; (2) the world of gods and its separation from the world of humans; (3) natural calamities and human saviors; and (4) heroes and their descendants.[6]

The corpus of ancient Chinese myths is scattered in the written texts of the sixth to first centuries BC. These have been collected together in Yuan Ke 袁珂 (1916–), *Shenhua xuanyi baiti* 神話選譯百題 and in Yuan Ke and Zhou Ming 周明, eds., *Zhongguo shenhua ziliao cuibian* 中國神話資料萃編.[7]

Some of the main mythological texts have been translated, for example, the *Shanhaijing* 山海經 (Classic of mountains and seas), a mythogeography, parts of which were written in the Warring States period and part in the Han.[8] In the words of Ann Birrell, the *Shanhaijing* "constitutes a fabulous bestiary, a botanical thesaurus, a dictionary of natural science, a catalog of geological substances and rare jewels, a guide to portents and

---

[6] K. C. Chang, *Early Chinese Civilization: Anthropological Perspectives*, HUP, 1976, 149–73. Also Chang (1983).

[7] *Shenhua xuanyi baiti* (One hundred topics in Chinese mythology: An anthology with notes and translation), Shanghai guji, 1980, and in Yuan Ke and Zhou Ming, eds., *Zhongguo shenhua ziliao cuibian* (A source book of Chinese myth texts), Sichuan sheng Shekeyuan, 1985.

[8] See Rémi Mathieu, *Etude sur la mythologie et l'ethnologie de la Chine ancienne*, 2 vols., Collège de France, Institut des Hautes Etudes Chinoises, 1983, for an annotated translation (vol. 1) and index (vol. 2). *ICS Concordance* 23 replaces the earlier *CFC Index* 9. The best modern, annotated edition is Yuan Ke 袁珂, *Shanhaijing jiaozhu* 山海經校注 (Collated notes to the classic of mountains and seas), Shanghai guji, 1980; rpnt., 1983; Yuan Ke, *Shanhaijing jiaoyi* 山海經校譯 (The classic of mountains and seas, collated and translated), Shanghai guji, 1985.

omens, a register of medical ailments, an apothecary's hand-book, and a medley of folkloric and ethnological material."[9] The *Huainanzi* and another important later source on Chinese myths, the fourth-century AD *Bowu zhi* 博物志 (The treatise on research into nature), have also been translated into English.[10]

The interpretation of the evidence found in ancient tombs and other archaeological artifacts have provided powerful stim-uli to the study of ancient Chinese myths.[11] Ethnographic evi-dence drawn from the study of the beliefs of China's minority peoples is another means of tracing myths.[12]

There are several dictionaries of Chinese mythology. The earliest, by E. T. C. Werner, mixes myths and legends from all periods.[13] More to the point are Yuan Ke, *Zhongguo shenhua chuanshuo cidian* 中國神話傳説詞典 and Wolfgang Munke, *Die klassische chinesische Mythologie*, Stuttgart: Ernst Klett, 1976.[14]

[9] Anne M. Birrell (1994), p. 387.

[10] Roger Greatrex, *The Bowu Zhi: An Annotated Translation*, Stock-holm: Orientalska Studier, 1987.

[11] Lu Sixian 陸思賢, *Shenhua kaogu* 神話考古 (The archaeology of myths), Wenwu, 1995.

[12] See for example, Xiao Bing 蕭兵, *Chuci yu shenhua* 楚辭與神話 (Myth and the *Songs of Chu*), Jiangsu guji, 1986. The author finds traces of ancient myths in the cultures of many of today's minority peoples in south China.

[13] *A Dictionary of Chinese Mythology*, Kelly and Walsh, 1932; Taibei, 1961. A collection of popular beliefs in late nineteenth- and early twenti-eth-century China, but useless for earlier periods. The same could be said of Henri Doré, *Recherches sur les superstitions en Chine*, 18 vols., Shang-hai, 1911–38; English tr. by M. Kennelly, *Researches into Chinese Supersti-tions*, 5 vols., T'usewei Press, 1914–18; Taibei rpnt., 1966–67. This was based on data originally published by the Jesuit scholar Pierre Hoang (Huang Bolu 黄伯祿) under the title *Jishuo quanzhen* 集説詮真, Shang-hai, 1879; continuation, 1880; rpnt., 1884.

[14] *Zhongguo shenhua chuanshuo cidian* (A dictionary of Chinese myth and legend), Shanghai cishu, 1986. Has a thematic index (men, things, heaven and earth, books, events, others). Also lists in the bibliography, and briefly describes, the 175 works that are the main primary sources for the study of Chinese myth and legend.

33.2   Religion

To the extent that historians are concerned with questions of value and belief, they cannot afford to ignore the history of Chinese religion in all its many forms—popular or elite, public or private, formal or informal, common or esoteric, home-grown or imported, secret or open.

In China itself, as the this-worldly influence of the Confucian state ideology and examination system for officials fades ever further into the past, and after the failure of the state ideologies which succeeded it, there is a growing appreciation of the importance of religions, both as systems of belief and as a body of ritual and practice embedded in every nook and cranny of daily life. For the same reasons, the earlier Western interpretations of Chinese history and culture based on the self-view of Confucian officials that theirs was a rationalistic view of the world is now also increasingly questioned.[15]

Archaeology is providing huge amounts of new data from tombs, on oracle bones and in medical and mantic texts on silk and bamboo on the early religious beliefs and practices of the Han and non-Han peoples, particularly in the pre-Qin period.[16]

One interesting trend is the reinterpration of the major pre-Qin Classics using anthropological analysis, an approach pioneered by Marcel Granet in the 1920s. The difference today is that there is much more data available from the archaeological

[15] Stephen F. Teiser, "The Spirits of Chinese Religion," in *Religions of China in Practice*, Donald S. Lopez, Jr., ed., PUP, 1996, 3–37.

[16] For a convenient summary, see the series *Zhongguo yuanshi zong-jiao ziliao congbian* 中國原始宗教資料叢編, Lü Daji 呂大吉 et al, eds., Shanghai renmin, 1993– . Vol. 6, for example, contains copious materials on the Naxizu 納西族, Qiangzu 羌族, Dulongzu 獨龍族, Lisuzu 傈僳族 and Nuzu 怒族; volumes in the same series include other materials on the Manchus, Mongols and Tibetans (1997) and on the Dai, Hani and nine other Yunnan non-Han peoples (1997). See also in the same series, *Zhongguo ge minzu yuanshi zongjiao ziliao jicheng, kaogu juan* 中國各民族原始宗教資料集成，考古卷 (A series of source books on the primitive religions of China, archaeology), Yu Jinxiu 于錦繡 and Yang Shurong 楊淑荣, eds. in chief, Shehui kexue, 1996.

record. See, for example, the titles in the series *Zhongguo wenhua de renleixue poyi* 中國文化的人類學破譯 (An anthropological interpretation of Chinese culture), Ye Shuxian 葉舒憲, Xiao
Bing 蕭兵 and Wang Jianhui 王建輝, eds.:

Ye Shuxian 葉舒憲, *Shijing de wenhua chanshi* 詩經的文化闡釋 (A cultural hermeneutics of the *Shijing*), Hubei renmin, 1994; rpnt., 1996.

Xiao Bing 蕭兵, *Chuci de wenhua poyi* 楚辭的文化破譯 (A cultural interpretation of the *Chuci*), Hubei renmin, 1991; rpnt., 1997.

Xiao Bing 蕭兵 and Ye Shuxian 葉舒憲, *Laozi de wenhua jiedu* 老子的文
化解讀 (A cultural interpretation of the *Laozi*), Hubei renmin, 1994;
rpnt., 1996.

Ye Shuxian 葉舒憲, *Zhuangzi de wenhua jiexi* 莊子的文化解析 (A cultural analysis of the *Zhuangzi*), Hubei renmin, 1997.

Zang Kehe 臧克和, *Shuowen jiezi de wenhua shuojie* 說文解字的文化說
解 (A cultural interpretation of the *Shuowen jiezi*), Hubei renmin,
1995; rpnt., 1996.

Xiao Bing 蕭兵, *Zhongyong de wenhua shengcha* 中庸的文化省察 (A cultural perspective on the doctrine of the mean), Hubei renmin, 1997.

Wang Zijin 王子今, *Shiji de wenhua poyi* 史記的文化破譯 (A cultural interpretation of the *Shiji*), Hubei renmin, 1997.

Bibliographies

Laurence G. Thompson, *Chinese Religion in Western Languages: A Comprehensive and Classified Bibliography of Publications in English,
French, and German through 1980*, UAP, 1985; Continued, 1981–90,
Association for Asian Studies Monograph, 1993. Expanded versions
of 1976 original.

For surveys of the field of Han and pre-Qin religion, see Daniel L. Overmyer with David N. Keightley, Edward L. Shaughnessy, Constance
A. Cook and Donald Harper, "Chinese Religions: The State of the
Field, Part I, Early Religious Traditions: The Neolithic Period
through the Han Dynasty (ca. 4000 B.C.E. to 220 C.E.)," *JAS* 54.1:
124–60 (1995).

For state-of-the-field essays on religion in imperial China, see Daniel L.
Overmyer with Gary Arbuckle, Dru C. Gladney, John R. McRae,
Rodney L. Taylor, Stephen F. Teiser, and Franciscus Verellen, "Living Religious Traditions: Taoism, Confucianism, Buddhism, Islam
and Popular Religion," *JAS* 54.2: 314–95 (1995).

Alvin P. Cohen, "A Bibliography of Written Contributions to the Study of Chinese Folk Religion," *Journal of the American Academy of Religion* 43.2: 238–65 (June 1975). Western language books and articles, arranged alphabetically by author. There is no index.

Zong Li 宗力 and Liu Qun 劉群, *Zhongguo minjian zhushen* 中國民間諸神 (Chinese popular deities), Shijiazhuang, Hebei renmin, 1987. Contains information on over 200 folk deities, cited from primary sources. For example, the section on the city god (*chenghuang* 城隍), 194–206, consists of quotations from 24 sources, beginning with the *Liji*, plus an essay by the editors. There is no index.

Chûgoku bunka jinruigaku bunken kaidai 中國文化人類學文獻解體 (An annotated bibliography of anthropological studies of China), Suenari Michio 末成道男 et al, eds., Tokyo daigaku, 1995. Contains annotations on 600 books in all languages on Chinese anthropology, including the study of Chinese religion. There is an author index.

Anthologies

Religions of China in Practice, Donald S. Lopez, Jr., ed., PUP, 1996. One of the purposes of this excellent anthology is "to demonstrate that the 'three religions' of China—Confucianism, Daoism, and Buddhism (with a fourth, popular religion, sometimes added)—are not discrete, mutually exclusive traditions, but instead overlap and interact with each other," (p. xi). Accordingly, the selection of translated excerpts by 29 scholars includes ritual manuals, hagiographical and autobiographical works and folktales and many other texts not usually found in anthologies of Chinese religion.

Journals

Journal of Chinese Religions (10.4.2).

Tôhô shûkyô 東方宗教 (Eastern religions), Nippon Dôkyô Gakkai 日本道教學會 (Japan Society for Taoistic Research), 1951– .

Shijie zongjiao yanjiu 世界宗教研究 (Studies in world religions), Institute for the Study of World Religions, Shekeyuan, 1979– .

Cahiers d'Extrême-Asie (10.4.2).

Calendars

Buddhist and Muslim calendars were different from the ordinary Chinese calendar (for references to concordances for converting dates from the Muslim or other calendars to the Western or Chinese calendars, see 5.6).

33.3   Common Religion

Common religion is defined as those beliefs, and religious practices held in common by most members of society. Its definition changed over time as some elements may have fallen out of favor with one section of the population or another. It is a catch-all category for a huge range of activities and beliefs including animism; mountain cults;[17] totemism; festivals (5.7); the cult of the dead (ancestor worship); divination (chap. 15); the interpretation of dreams and other practices to secure good fortune and to avoid bad luck;[18] magic and other practices to protect against ghosts, including spellbinding;[19] the search for immortality;[20] geomancy (38.2); and belief in functional gods. It found expression in mythologies (33.1), folk literature (33.1) and all kinds of ritual and devotional practices.[21] The extent of these is hinted at in encyclopaedic studies such as *Zhonghua shenmi wenhua* 中華神秘文化,[22] in which there are chapters on all of the above plus Yinyang 陰陽 and *bagua* 八卦; climate, sacrifices, shamans (spirit mediums), Daoism, Buddhism and sexual and medicinal exercises (on these last, see chap. 36).

[17] Edouard Chavannes (1865–1918), *Le T'ai chan: Essai de monographie d'un culte chinois*, Annales du Musée Guimet 28, 1910; Kyohiko Munakata, *Sacred Mountains in Chinese Art*, Univ. of Illinois Press, 1991.

[18] Wolfgang Bauer, *China and the Search for Happiness*, tr. from the German by Michael Shaw, New York: Seabury Press, 1979; *Unruly Gods: Divinity and Society in China*, Meir Shahar and Robert P. Weller, eds., UHP, 1996.

[19] Donald Harper, "A Chinese Demonography of the Third Century BC," *HJAS* 45: 459–98 (1985).

[20] *SCC*, vol. 5, Parts 3 and 5 (see chap. 37); Michael Loewe, *Ways to Paradise: the Chinese Quest for Immortality*, Allen and Unwin, 1979; Ngo Van Xuyet, *Divination, magie, et politique dans la Chine ancienne: Essai suivi de la traduction des "Biographies des Magiciens" tirées de l'Histoire des Hans posterieurs*, PUF, 1976.

[21] *Religion and Ritual in Chinese Society*, Arthur P. Wolf, ed., SUP, 1974.

[22] *Zhonghua shenmi wenhua* (Chinese mystic culture), Wang Yude 王玉德 et al., eds., Hunan chubanshe, 1993.

Research into the common religion uses transmitted philosophical and religious texts as well as folk literature (33.1) and folk art; specialist texts, such as those of the *fangshu* 方術 (mystical and magical arts); other transmitted texts such as the observations of literati[23] or local gazetteers;[24] archaeological data (for example, on divination, sacrifices or burial practices) and finally, the all too few reports based on ethnographic, anthropological and sociological field research, for example, that done in the 1930s by the group from the Catholic University in Beijing led by W. A. Grootaers, whose inventories of temples, shrines and cult units are unique; see his

"Les temples villageois de la région au sudest de Tat'ong (Chansi Nord), leurs inscriptions et leur histoire," *Folklore Studies* 4: 161–212 (1945).

"Temples and History of Wanch'üan (Chahar): the Geographic Method Applied to Folklore," *MS* 13: 209–315 (1948).

"Rural Temples Around Hsüan-hua (South Chahar), Their Iconography and their History," *Folklore Studies* 10.2: 1–116 (1951).

The Sanctuaries in a North-China City. A Complete Survey of the Cultic Buildings in the City of Hsüan-hua (Chahar), William A. Grootaers, Li Shih-yü and Wang Fu-shih, comps., Mélanges Chinois et Bouddhiques, vol. 26, Bruxelles: Institut des Hautes Études Chinoises, 1995.

Japanese studies are summed up in Goto Kimpei, "Studies on Chinese Religion in Post-War Japan," *MS* 19: 384–402 (1960).

---

[23] Ying Shao 應劭 (ca. 140–206 AD), *Fengsu tongyi jiaoshi* 風俗通義校釋 (Explanations of social customs), Wu Shuping 吳樹平, collated and translated into modern Chinese, Tianjin renmin, 1980; Zhonghua, 1981. Indexed in *CFC Index* 3, 2 vols., 1943.

[24] *Zhongguo difangzhi minsu ziliao huibian* 中國地方志民俗資料匯編 (Collection of materials from Chinese gazetteers on popular customs), Ding Shiliang 丁世良 and Zhao Fang 趙放, eds., 11 vols., Shumu wenxian, 1989–95. The volumes on Huabei, Dongbei, and Xibei were published in 1989, Zhongnan and Xinan (both 2 vols.) followed in 1991 and Huadong in 1995. The first 11 vols. contain 5,500 pages of extracts from local gazetteers. There is a place index.

33.4 Daoism

The *Daodejing* 道德經 and the *Zhuangzi* 莊子 had become the classics of a Daoist religion by the end of the Eastern Han.[25] The religion spread rapidly in the Wei, Jin and *Nan-Bei Chao* and many new Daoist works were written. Their main repository (and a quantity of other works considered unorthodox) is the *Daozang* 道藏, which has grown over the centuries since it began to be put together in the fifth century AD.[26] By the Ming, this huge collection (like a Daoist *congshu*) contained 1,500 works from both philosophical and religious Daoism (*Daojia* 道家 and *Daojiao* 道教). It contains many materials not found elsewhere and is an important supplement to the various categories of Confucian historical and biographical writing.[27]

For annotated catalogs, see *Daozang tiyao* 道藏提要[28] and Kristofer Schipper and Franciscus Verellen, *Handbook of the Taoist Canon*, UChP, forthcoming.

[25] Isabelle Robinet, *Taoism: Growth of a Religion*, Phyllis Brooks, tr., SUP, 1997.

[26] See the *Indiana Companion to Traditional Chinese Literature*, section on "Taoist Literature, Part I: Through the T'ang Dynasty," 138–52, by Stephen R. Bokenkamp; "Part II: Five Dynasties to Ming," by Judith Magee Boltz, 152–74. Both authors have also published book-length studies: Stephen R. Bokenkamp, *Early Daoist Scriptures*, UCP, 1997; Judith M. Boltz, *A Survey of the Taoist Literature: Tenth to Seventeenth Centuries*, UCP, 1987.

[27] The only existing version of the *Daozang* today was the one compiled between 1436 and 1449 with an additional portion added in 1606: *Zhengtong daozang* 正統道藏 (Daoist canon compiled during the Zhengtong era) plus Wanli 萬曆 continuation. It survives in a 1920s reprint: *Daozang* 道藏, 1120 vols., Shangwu, 1923–26; rpnt., Yiwen, 1962; rpnt., Xinwenfeng, 60 vols., 1977 (includes as index: Schipper, [1975]); *Daozang* 道藏, 30 vols, Wenwu, 1985; *Zangwai daoshu* 藏外道書, Hu Daojing 胡道靜 et al., eds., 36 vols, Ba-Shu, 1992–94.

On the various versions of the *Daozang* from the post-Han, see Chen Guofu 陳國符 (1915–), *Daozang yuanliu kao* 道藏源流考, rev. and enlarged ed., of 1949 original, 2 vols., Zhonghua, 1963; Mingwen, 1983.

[28] *Daozang tiyao* (Descriptive notes on the *Daozang*), Ren Jiyu 任繼愈, ed. in chief, Shehui kexue, 1991; 2nd rev. ed., 1995. There is an index.

For an index, see *Daozang suoyin* 道藏索引, Shanghai shudian, 1996, which indexes five different editions, or the older *Combined Indices to the Authors and Titles of Books in Two Collections of Taoist Literature*, Weng Dujian 翁獨健, comp., *H-Y Index* 25; *Concordance du Tao-tsang: Titres des ouvrages*, Kristofer Schipper, comp., EFEO, 1975, which indexes all characters in the titles of all texts in the *Daozang*.

There is now a comprehensive catalog of Daoist works among the Dunhuang manuscripts.[29]

Dictionaries

A good test of Daoist dictionaries is to see if they cover both the *Daojia* 道家 and *Daojiao* 道教. Do they include book titles that only survive in the *Daozang*? Do they include temples? Do the definitions simply quote examples of usage or do they in addition use modern scholarship and language to define the meaning?

Daojiao da cidian 道教大辭典 (Dictionary of the Daoist religion), Zhongguo Daojiao xiehui 中國道教協會, eds., 1994; rpnt., Huaxia, 1995. A large-scale, scholarly work based on Daoist texts.

Zhonghua Daojiao da cidian 中華道教大辭典, Hu Fuchen 胡孚琛, ed., Shehui kexue, 1995.

Bibliographies

Franciscus Verellen, "Taoism," in *JAS* 54.2: 322–46 (1995).

Anna K. Seidel, "Chronicle of Taoist Studies in the West, 1950–90," *Cahiers d'Extrême-Asie*, 5: 223–347 (1989–90).

John Lagerwey in "Entre taoïsme et culture populaire," reviews recent work, *BEFEO* (1996), 438–61.

Julian F. Pas, *A Historical Dictionary of Taoism*, Scarecrow, 1998. Note the same author's earlier *Select Bibliography on Taoism*, SUNY Press, 1988, which contains Western-language books and articles, arranged by subject. There is an author index.

---

[29] Ôfuchi Ninji 大淵忍爾, comp., vol. 1, *Tonkô Dôkyô: mokuroku hen* 敦煌道經目錄編 (Catalog of Daoist Scriptures from Dunhuang); vol. 2, *Zurokuhen* 圖錄編 (Plates), Fukutake, 1978, 1979.

Biographies

Chen Yuan 陳垣, *Daojia jinshi lüe* 道家金石略 (Daoist figures on bronze and stone inscriptions), Wenwu, 1988. Posthumously published. Contains 1,538 inscriptions with biographical materials of Daoist figures from 133 BC to AD 1655, mostly from the Jin and Yuan. There is no index.

Journals

Taoist Resources (1988–1998, irregular); from 1998, incorporated into *Journal of Chinese Religions*.

33.5 Buddhism

Buddhism was introduced into China in the Later Han and spread rapidly during the period of disunion after the fall of the dynasty. The translation of 55 million words of Buddhist scriptures had an important influence on all aspects of Chinese life including the development of the language itself (1.1.2 and 1.2.7).[30]

The main repository of all branches of Buddhist scriptures as well as historical writings is the *San zangjing* 三藏經 (*Tripitaka*), so called because it contains the three main categories of the scriptures—Sutras (*jing* 經), Laws (*lü* 律) and Treatises (*lun* 論). Other names for the *Tripitika* include *Da zangjing* 大藏經, *Zangjing* 藏經 and *Yiqiejing* 一切經 (*Buddhist Canon*). The *Tripitaka* accumulated over a 2,000-year period. There are at least 23 different editions, each one larger than the last. The most recent one contains over 3,500 titles (including all categories of writings). In form the *Tripitaka* is like an enormous *congshu*. The *Taishô Tripitaka* is the most generally used.[31]

[30] Erik Zürcher, *The Buddhist Conquest of China*, 2 vols., Brill, 1959; rpnt., 1972.

[31] *Taishô shinshû Daizôkyô* (The *Tripitaka*, new compilation of the Taishô era), compiled under the direction of Takakusu Junjirô 高 楠順 次郎 (1866–1945) and Watanabe Kaikyoku 渡邊海旭 (1872–1932), Tokyo: Issaikyô kankôkai 一切經刊行會, vols. 1–85, 1924–34; Bekkan 別卷: Shôwa hôbô sômokuroku (Appendix: Shôwa era catalog of the jewel of law), vols., 1–3, Issaikyô kankôkai and Daizô shuppan, 1924–34.

There is a full concordance for each section: *Taishô shinshû Dai-zôkyô sakuin* 大正新修大藏經索引, 44 vols., Tokyo, 1975–88. It is arranged by detailed subject categories, and it is well in-dexed. Use vols. 1–55 with *H-Y Index* 11 and the general index, *Répertoire du Canon Bouddhique sino-japonais, Edition de Taishô*.[32] To look up the whereabouts of a work or Sutra in all major editions of the *Tripitaka* up to the Taishô edition, use the handy *Ershi'er zhong Da zangjing tongjian* 二十二種大藏經通劍.[33] It is indexed by *pinyin*, by stroke count and by Sanskrit and English titles; there are Chinese and English summaries of a total of 4,175 titles. Each title is translated and the names of the translators and the dates of translation are given.

The *Zhonghua Da zangjing (Hanwen bufen)* 中華大藏經 (漢文部分) began publication by Zhonghua in 1984 and was com-pleted in 1997. It contains 106 large volumes and it is now the main repository of Chinese Buddhist texts. The texts have been reproduced from original woodblock editions (unlike the *Tai-shô Tripitika* which is typeset).

The Buddhist (and Daoist) scriptures were not only printed, they were also carved on stelae and on rocks. The largest col-lection of Buddhist stone inscriptions (*shijing* 石經) in the world is stored in caves on the Mountain of Stone Scriptures at and near the temple of Yunzhu, Fangshan county, 75 km southwest of Beijing. The collection numbers 14,278 stelae and took 1,000 years to carve.[34]

---

[32] Fascicule Annexe du *Hôbôgirin*, 2nd rev. and enl. ed., Paul Dem-iéville, Hubert Durt, Anna Seidel, eds., Maisonneuve and Tokyo: Maison Franco-Japonaise, 1978. The *Hôbôgirin* is the EFEO encyclopaedia of Buddhism, see below under *Dictionaries*

[33] *Ershi'er zhong Da zangjing tongjian* (Index to 22 editions of the Buddhist Canon), Tong Wei 童瑋, comp., Zhonghua, 1997.

[34] The carving of the Buddhist scriptures began at the Yunjusi on the Shijingshan (房山縣石經山雲居寺) at the beginning of the seventh cen-tury and continued on and off until the early Qing. The 14,278 stelae re-cord 3,400 volumes of scriptures and 6,051 explanatory notes in a total of about 22.5 million characters. Many of them were carved in the Liao dy-nasty based on the *Qidan zang* 契丹藏 (Khitan Canon). The *Fangshan shi-*

Footnote continued on next page

For tracing manuscripts of Buddhist scriptures throughout the world in Sanskrit and Pâli, in Chinese, Tibetan, Mongolian, Manchu, Korean and Japanese as well as in the languages of Central Asia, use *Bibliographical Sources for Buddhist Studies*, Yasuhiro Sueki, comp., Tokyo: International Institute for Buddhist Studies, 1998. It provides not only details of catalogs of Buddhist collections but also references to the secondary literature on particular texts and book reviews.

Sources for the institutional history of Buddhism in Chinese society are not necessarily included in the *Tripitaka*, for example, the monograph on Buddhists and Daoists in the *Weishu* 魏書; the temple gazetteers, and also the extensive sections on temples found in most local gazetteers (4.6).

Note that the Dunhuang documents (46.3) are an important source for Tang and pre-Tang Buddhism.[35] The classic study on the economic role of Buddhism, in which the author used many of the documents in the Pelliot collection, is Jacques Gernet, *Buddhism in Chinese Society: An Economic History from the Fifth to the Tenth Centuries*.[36]

Unfortunately there is no guide to Buddhist historiography, but see Chen Yuan 陳垣 (1880–1971), *Zhongguo Fojiao shiji gailun* 中國佛教史籍概論, which not only outlines the Buddhist record, but also corrects errors in the *Siku tiyao*.[37]

The *Electronic Buddhist Text Initiative* (EBTI) was founded to coordinate the various projects involving the computer reading of Buddhist texts in all languages and in all traditions.

---

jing tiji huibian 房山石經題記匯編 (Collected inscriptions of Fangshan stone sutras), 22 vols., Shumu wenxian, 1987, contains reproductions of rubbings of the Liao and Jin scriptures and some of the Ming ones.

[35] Makita Tairyô 牧田諦亮, *Tonkô to Chûgoku Bukkyô* 敦煌と中國佛教, *Kôza Tonkô*, vol. 7, Daitô, 1984.

[36] Translated from the original French (*Les Aspects économiques du Bouddhisme*, Saigon: EFEO, 1956) by Franciscus Verellen, Col. UP, 1995.

[37] *Zhongguo Fojiao shiji gailun* (A survey of Chinese Buddhist historical books), Kexue, 1955; Zhonghua, 1962.

33.5.1   Tibetan Buddhism

The main non-Han tradition of Buddhism in the China area is found in Tibet. The Tibetan *Tripitika* is in the course of being collated based on the Derge edition: *Zhonghua Da zangjing Danzhu'er, Duikanben (Zangwen)* 中華大藏經丹珠爾對勘本[藏文].[38] The *Tanjur* part of the *Tripitaka* contains works written over the course of 1,000 years on philosophy, literature, art, language, astronomy, medicine and much else besides. The new edition is projected to fill 120 volumes with an average of about 1.5 million words per volume. About 100 monks and scholars are working on it in Chengdu. It will have a full author/title catalog. After the remaining 110 volumes are published, work will begin on the *Kanjur* section of the Tibetan *Tripitaka*.

The two most important collections of rare Tibetan Buddhist works are held at the Sakya monastery in Shigaze and the Yonghegong 雍和宮 (Lama Temple) in Beijing (into which were assembled the libraries of the 28 Lama temples of Beijing in the early 1950s). There are large collections of Tibetan texts in the United States thanks to the activities of the Library of Congress office in New Delhi. For introductions to Tibetan Buddhism, see

Donald S. Lopez, Jr., *Prisoners of Shangri-la: Tibetan Buddhism and the West*, UChP, 1998.

Religions of Tibet in Practice, Donald S. Lopez, Jr., ed., PUP, 1997.
    Thirty-six chapters with an introduction and translated texts.

Guiseppe Tucci, *The Religions of Tibet*, Routledge, 1980.

33.5.2   Zen Canonical Texts on CD-ROM

One day, the entire *Tripitaka* will be available on CD-ROM or on-line. The work has already begun in centers in China, Korea, Japan and North America, see for example, Urs App, "Reference Works for Ch'an Research: A Selective, Annotated Sur-

---

[38] *Zhonghua Da zangjing Danzhu'er, Duikanben (Zangwen)* (The Tibetan collated edition of the Chinese *Tripitaka: Tanjur*), Zhongguo Zangxue chubanshe, 10 vols., 1989–98.

vey," *Cahiers d'Extrême-Asie* 7: 357–409 (1993–94), and *ZenBase CD 1*, Kyoto, International Research Institute for Zen Buddhism, 1995. This contains many basic Zen texts as well as a bibliography of 20,000 books held at Hanazono University, built up by Yanagida Seizan 柳田聖山. On Zen research, see *Zengaku kenkyû nyûmon* 禪學研究入門.[39]

Dictionaries

Bussho kaisetsu daijiten 佛書解説大辭典 (Great dictionary of Buddhist works with explanations), Ono Genmyô 小野玄妙 (1883–1939), ed., 12 vols. Daitô shuppansha, 1933–6; rpnt., 1966; Chinese tr., Xin Wenfeng, 1983. This is the basic comprehensive reference on Buddhist works.

Hôbôgirin (法寶義林). *Dictionnaire encyclopédique du Bouddhisme d'après les sources chinoises et japonaises*, fascicules I–VIII, Académie des Inscriptions et Belles-Lettres, Institut de France, 1927–1999. This huge terminological encyclopaedia of Buddhist history and culture in China and Japan began under the guidance of Paul Demiéville. The first eight volumes cover the letters A–D. They took 72 years to compile. As the current editor, Hubert Durt, has remarked, "Great works take time." The articles are mainly written in French although some are in English. The *Hôbôgirin* covers Chinese, Japanese, Sanskrit and Pâli sources (but not Tibetan).[40]

A Dictionary of Chinese Buddhist Terms, W. E. Soothill and Louis Hodous, eds., London, 1937; rpnt., Curzon, 1995. Awaiting the completion of the *Hôbôgirin*, this early effort is all that is available in a Western language.

Encyclopedia of Religion, Mircea Eliade, ed. in chief, New York: Macmillan, 1987. Contains outline articles on Buddhism in East Asia, including in China and explanations of the main doctrinal terms.

Fojiao da cidian 佛教大辭典 (Dictionary of Buddhist phrases), Wu Rujun 吳汝鈞, ed., Taibei: Foguang, 1992; Shangwu International, 3rd prnt., 1995. The central focus is on Indian and Chinese Buddhist thought.

---

[39] *Zengaku kenkyû nyûmon* (Introduction to research in Zen studies), Tanaka Ryôshô 田中良昭, Daitô, 1994.

[40] *Index des caractères chinois dans les fasc. I–V du Hôbôgirin*, Antonino Forte, comp., Fascicule Annexe 2 du *Hôbôgirin*, Maisonneuve and Tokyo: Maison Franco-Japonaise, 1984.

A handy reference: the Sanskrit, Pâli or Tibetan originals of the phrases explained are given and indexed.

Fojiao wenhua cidian 佛教文化辭典, (Dictionary of Buddhist culture) Zhang Zhijiang 張治江, ed. in chief, Changchun, 1992.

Foxue da cidian 佛學大辭典 (The great Buddhist dictionary), Ding Fubao 丁福保, ed., Yixue, 1922; Wenwu, 1984; 2 vols., Taibei, 1986; Shanghai guji, 1991. Contains over 30,000 entries.

Mochizuki Bukkyô dai jiten 望月佛教大辭典 (The Mochizuki large Buddhist dictionary), Mochizuki Shinkô 望月信亨, ed., 10 vols., Tokyo: Sekai seiten kankô kyôkai 世界聖典刊行協會, 1955. The best dictionary. Indexes of Chinese, Japanese and Tibetan Buddhist terms.

Biographies

The best single work for finding the dates and also for locating biographical materials on Buddhist monks is Chen Yuan 陳垣, *Shishi yinian lu* 釋氏疑年錄 (Record of dubious dates of Buddhist monks), Shangwu, 1939; Zhonghua, 1964; Jiangsu guangling guji, 1991. It includes materials on 28,000 monks from the fourth to the seventeenth century. Based on 700 sources, it gives the monk's name, place name, temple name and dates of birth and death, native place, secular name (*suxing* 俗姓) and references to sources.[41]

Zhongguo Foxue renming cidian 中國佛學人名辭典 (Biographical dictionary of Chinese Buddhist names), Mingfu 明復, Fangchou, 1974; Zhonghua, 1988. Contains 5,326 detailed factual biographies of Chinese Buddhist monks and monks who came to China from the Han dynasty to the present. Based on Chen (1939).

Anthology

In addition to Lopez (1995), see *Buddhism in Practice*, Donald S. Lopez, Jr., ed., PUP, 1995. Contains readings on Buddhism in India, China, Tibet and Southeast Asia.

State of the Field

John R. McRae, "Buddhism," in *JAS* 54.2: 354–71 (1995).

---

[41] Compare Chen's entries and coverage with Zhang Zhizhe 張志哲, *Zhongguo Fojiao renwu da cidian* 中國佛教人物大辭典 (Dictionary of Chinese Buddhist personalities), Zhonghua, 1993. It gives biographies of over 14,000 people in 12,300 entries from the Han to the present with personal data and activities. There is a four-corner index.

33.6 Islam

Islam was introduced into China at the end of the Sui and the beginning of the Tang, no doubt by Arab merchants who settled in great ports such as Guangzhou and Quanzhou (42.3.2). Many more Muslims came to China during the Yuan dynasty, some of choice, some moved forcably by their Mongol conquerors. The Muslims were Muslims in China until the Yuan. By the Ming they had become transformed into Chinese Muslims and had produced the greatest admiral and explorer in Chinese history (Zheng He).[42]

The first extant copies of the Koran in China date to 1318. They are hand-written. The first introductions in Chinese to Islam are from the seventeenth century. The first translations of the Koran into Chinese were made in the nineteenth century. There were several large-scale Muslim uprisings in the nineteenth century (28.3). There are currently in China over 14 million Muslims. Note the following references:

Morris Rossabi, "Islam in China," in *The Encyclopedia of Religion*, Mircea Eliade, ed., Macmillan, 1987, vol. 7, 377–90.

Donald Daniel Leslie, *Islam in Traditional China: A Short History to 1800*, Canberra College of Advanced Education, 1986.

Zhongguo Yisilan baike quanshu 中國伊斯蘭百科全書 (Chinese Encyclopaedia of Islam), Sichuan cishu, 1994.

Bibliography

Dru C. Gladney, "Islam," in *JAS* 54.2: 371–77 (1995).

Donald Daniel Leslie, "Islam in China to 1800: A Bibliography," *Abr-Nahrain* 16: 16–48 (1976).

---

[42] See Donald Daniel Leslie, "Living with the Chinese: the Muslim Expansion in China, T'ang to Ming," in *Chinese Ideas About Nature and Society: Studies in Honour of Derk Bodde*, Charles Le Blanc and Susan Blader, eds., HKU Press, 1987, 175–94. Also Jianpang Wang, *The Hui Communities of Yunnan: Society in a Historical Perspective*, Univ. of Lund, 1996; for a case study of a single family, see under Pu Shougeng 蒲壽庚 (42.2, *Thirteenth Century*).

Islam in China: a Critical Bibliography, Raphael Israeli, comp., Green-wood, 1994, contains Western language works to 1992.

33.7   Christianity and Judaism

The first Christians to have left a trace in China are the Nesto-rians, of whom there was a community in Chang'an, the Tang capital. The so-called Nestorian monument, dated 781, can be seen to this day in the Museum of the Forest of Stelae, Xi'an. It is written in Syrian and Chinese.[43] Nestorians are also men-tioned in the Yuan dynasty (Khubilai Khan's mother was one). Other Christian visitors to China up to the Jesuits in the late sixteenth century are introduced in 42.1.

33.7.1   The Jesuits

Willard Peterson, "Learning from Heaven: The Introduction of Christianity and of Western Ideas into Late Ming China," chapter 12 of *CHC*, vol. 8, 1998, 789–839. For an overview of the Christian enterprise in China in the seventeenth century as seen from the Chinese point of view, see Jacques Gernet, *China and the Christian Impact: A Conflict of Cultures*, Janet Lloyd, tr., CUP, 1985; *The Chinese Rites Controversy: Its History and Mean-ing*, David E. Mungello, ed., Steiner, 1994; David E. Mungello, *The Forgotten Christians of Hangzhou*, UHP, 1994.[44]

The Jesuits were the first full-time professional observers to report on China to Europe. Much of their scholarly work went into letters and reports whose influence on the Western image of China was enormous. In many respects it is still felt today.[45]

---

[43] Paul Pelliot, *L'Inscription Nestorienne de Si-ngan-fou, Oeuvres post-humes de Paul Pelliot*, ed. with supplements by Antonino Forte, ISEAS and Collège de France, 1996; A. C. Moule, *Christians in China Before the Year 1550*, Macmillan, 1930.

[44] For a wide-ranging collection of research papers, see *Christianity in China: From the Eighteenth Century to the Present*, Daniel H. Bays, ed., SUP, 1996.

[45] For an evaluation of the key to their understanding of China and of their influence in the West, see Paul Rule, *K'ung-tzu or Confucius? The*

Footnote continued on next page

On being assigned to proselytizing missions in distant countries, including China, the Jesuits took a vow never to return, which in part explains why they made such efforts to study the language and customs of the country of their mission.[46] They rose higher in the imperial bureaucracy than any other Westerners before or since. The reformers of the astronomical system of China in the early Qing, Schall and Verbiest, were the *de facto* managers of the Bureau of Astronomy. Ignaz Koegler, was the first to be formally appointed Director of the Board in 1725. This was ironically the very year in which the Jesuits lost their case in Rome in the rites controversy, which eventually lead to the dissolution of the Jesuit Order in 1773. Nevertheless, Jesuits continued as Directors of Astronomy until the early nineteenth century. By that time, 456 Jesuits had worked in China in the "old mission" (the new mission began in the nineteenth century by which time the Protestant missionaries and other Catholic missions were also active; see 37.7.3).

The four leading Jesuits in the China mission were Matteo Ricci, Johann Adam Schall von Bell, Ferdinand Verbiest, and Antoine Gaubil:[47]

The history of the Jesuit mission in China by its founder, Matteo Ricci [Li Madou 利瑪竇] (1552–1610), with copious notes and Chinese characters: *Fonti Ricciane: Documenti originali concernenti Matteo Ricci e la storia delle prime relazioni tra l'Europa e la Cina (1579–1615)*, Pasquale d'Elia, ed., 3 vols., Libreria dello Stato, Rome: 1942–49. The text was completed after the death of Ricci by the Belgian Jesuit Ni-

Jesuit Interpretation of Confucianism, Sydney: Allen and Unwin, 1986; Lionel M. Jensen, "The Invention of 'Confucius' and His Chinese Other, 'Kong Fuzi,'" *Positions: East Asia Cultures Critique* 1.2: 414–59 (Fall, 1993); Thomas A. Wilson, *Genealogy of the Way: The Construction and Uses of the Confucian Tradition in Late Imperial China*, SUP, 1995.

[46] David E. Mungello, *Curious Land: Jesuit Accommodation and the Origins of Sinology*, Steiner, 1985; UHP, 1989.

[47] For a complete listing of all the Jesuits in the China mission, see Joseph Dehergne, *Répertoire des Jésuites de Chine de 1552 à 1800*, Bibliotheca Instituti Historici SI, vol. 37, Rome and Paris: Institutum Historicum and Letouzey & Ané, 1973.

colas Trigault [1577–1628] and published under the title *De Christiana Expeditione apud Sinas*, 1615; eventually translated into English under the title *China in the Sixteenth Century: The Journals of Matthew Ricci: 1583–1610*, Louis J. Gallagher, tr., Random House, 1953.

German Jesuit astronomer and scientist: Johann Adam Schall von Bell [Tang Ruowang 湯若望] (1591–1666). Senior official in the Bureau of Astronomy, 1645–66: *Lettres et Memoires d'Adam Schall, S.J.: Relation Historique*, Henri Bernard and Paul Bornet eds. and trs., Tianjin: Mission de Sienhsien, 1942; Alfons Väth, *Johann Adam Schall von Bell, S.J.*, Steyler, 1991.

Belgian Jesuit astronomer: Ferdinand Verbiest [Nan Huairen 南懷仁] (1623–88). Manager of the Bureau of Astronomy, 1669–88: *A Journey of the Emperor of China into East Tartary in the Year 1682*, Collins, 1686; Henri Josson and Louis Willaert, *Correspondance de Ferdinand Verbiest de la Compagnie de Jésus (1623–1688)*, Brussels: Palais des Acadamies, 1938; *Ferdinand Verbiest, S.J. (1623–1688): Jesuit Missionary, Scientist, Engineer and Diplomat*, John W. Wiket, ed., Steyler, 1994. Contains assessments of Verbiest as missionary, scientist, ballistics engineer, offical and diplomat. Verbiest was promoted to the brevet rank of Vice-Minister of the Right in the Board of Works in 1682. This was in recognition of his casting of 130 canon and writing a treatise on gunnery, not for his contributions to astronomy.

Learned French Jesuit, historian and astronomer, Antoine Gaubil [Song Junrong 宋君榮] (1689–1759): *Le P. Antoine Gaubil, S.J.: Correspondance de Pekin 1722–1759*, ed. by René Simon, Librairie Droz, 1970. There is a preface by Paul Demiéville and appendixes by Joseph Dehergne.

Jesuit letters: *Lettres édifiantes et curieuses écrites des missions étrangéres par quelques missionnaires de la Compagnie de Jésus*, 34 vols. Paris, 1702–76; new edition, 1780–83 (vols. 16 to 20 contain the letters from the China mission). There is a sampling of these in *Lettres édifiantes et curieuses de Chine par les missionnaires jésuites 1702–1776*, I. and J.-L. Vissière eds., Garnier-Flammarion, 1979.

Jesuit reports: *Mémoires concernant l'histoire, les sciences, les arts, les moeurs, les usages, etc. des Chinois*, 15 vols., Paris, 1776–96.

The old Jesuit cemetery (Shilan 柵欄) in Beijing contains 83 tombstones, including those of Matteo Ricci, Verbiest and Schall. It can be visited. The cemetery stands today on the grounds of the Beijing Party School. For a study of its history from the opening (1610) through the Cultural Revolution, when the stelae of Ricci and his colleagues were saved by the staff who buried them, see *Departed, Yet Present, Zhalan, The Oldest Christian Cemetery in Beijing*, Edward J. Malatesta, S. J., and Gao Zhiyu, eds., Instituto Cultural de Macau and Ricci Institute, University of San Francisco, 1995. Following a decision taken by the standing committee of the Politburo, the stelae were eventually re-erected and restored in 1979 (some had been smashed in 1900). The study contains photographs of each of the tombstones in the cemetery and transcriptions of the brief inscriptions on them in Latin and Chinese and, in some cases, also in Manchu.

There are five main bibliographies of Jesuit writings, the first two are general ones covering the Jesuit missions worldwide, the other three are specific to the China mission. Each is arranged differently, so they are complementary:

Robert Streit and Johannes Dindinger, *Bibliotheca Missionum*, vols 4, 5 and 7, Aachen: Franziskus Xaverius Missionsverein, 1928-31. Chronological arrangement, covers Jesuit missions worldwide, including China.

Carlos Sommervogel, *Bibliothèque de la compagnie de Jésus*, 12 vols., Brussels, 1890-1932; rpnt., Louvain, 1960. Arranged by name, covers Jesuit missions worldwide, including China.

Louis Pfister (1833-91), *Notices biographiques et bibliographiques sur les Jésuites de l'ancienne mission en Chine, 1552-1773*, 2 vols., Variétés sinologiques, 59-60, Shanghai: Imprimerie de la Mission Catholique, 1932-34; rpnt., CMC, 1976. Arranged by name. This has been translated into Chinese and at the same time extensively corrected by Geng Sheng 耿昇, *Zai Hua Yesu huishi liezhuan ji shumu bubian* 在華耶穌會士列傳及書目補編, 2 vols., Zhonghua, 1995.

Henri Cordier, *Bibliotheca Sinica* (10.4).

Erik Zürcher, Nicolas Standaert and Adrianus Dudink, *Bibliography of the Jesuit Mission in China, ca. 1580- ca. 1680*, Leiden Univ., 1991. Covers secondary literature in European languages on the first century of the Jesuit mission.

The Jesuits also translated many European works, both religious and scientific, into Chinese. These are listed in Henri Bernard, "Les adaptations chinoises d'ouvrages européens. Bibliographie chronologique depuis la venue des Portuguais à Canton jusqu' à la mission française de Pékin (1544-1688)," *MS* 10: 1-54; 309-88 (1945); and part 2, covering 1689-1799, *MS* 19:

349–83 (1960). The earlier translations into Chinese as well as those made in the nineteenth century are analyzed in Tsuen-hsuin Tsien, "Western Impact on China through Translation," *FEQ* 13: 305–27 (1954). Their contributions to Chinese technology and science is reassessed in J.Waley-Cohen, "China and Western Technology in the Late Eighteenth Century," *American Historical Review* 98: 1525–44 (1993); S-R. Du and Q. Han, "The Contributions of French Jesuits to Chinese Science in the Seventeenth and Eighteenth Centuries," *Impact of Science on Society* 167: 265–75 (1992).

Among the many aspects of European science, culture and faith which the Jesuits introduced to the Manchu court was Baroque music: for a CD of music by the Lazarist missionary to China Teodorico Pedrini (1671–1746) and the Jesuit Joseph-Marie Amiot (1718–93), see *Teodorico Pedrini, Baroque Concert at the Forbidden City*, Auvidis-Astrée, 1996.

33.7.2   Judaism in China

The first sources which mention Judaism in China relate to worshippers in Kaifeng from the Northern Song onward. The ources include four Ming and Qing stelae from the Kaifeng synagogue, local gazetteers, the *Yuanshi*, the observations of some of the early travellers to China,[48] as well as of Matteo Ricci and other Jesuits.[49] At that time a common name for Judaism was *Tiaojinjiao* 挑筋教 (the sect that plucks out the sinews).[50] Today it is called *Youtaijiao* 猶太教.

Pan Guangdan 潘光旦, *Zhongguo jingnei de yutairen de ruogan lishi wenti* 中國境內的猶太人的若干歷史問題 (Historical problems concerning the Jews in China), Beijing daxue, 1993. Originally written in 1953 but only published in summary form in 1983 and as a book in 1993.

---

[48] For example, Marco Polo or Aboul Zeyd al-Hassan, *Record of Observations in India and China* (see 42.2, *Ninth Century*).

[49] Joseph Dehergne and Donald Daniel Leslie, *Juifs de Chine à travers la correspondance inédite des jésuites du 17ᵉ siècle*, Institutum Historicum SI and Les Belles Lettres, 1980.

[50] After the Kashrut regulation that forbids the eating of the thigh muscle on the hip socket.

The 1983 version is translated in *Jews of Old China: Studies by Chinese Scholars*, Sidney Shapiro, tr., comp. and ed., New York: Hippocrene Books, 1984.

Donald Daniel Leslie, *The Survival of the Chinese Jews: The Jewish Community at Kaifeng*, Brill, 1972.

Michael Pollak, *The Jews of Dynastic China: A Critical Bibliography*, Cincinnati, Ohio: Hebrew Union College Press in association with the Sino-Judaic Institute, Menlo Park, 1993.

Yang Haijun, "Eighty Years of Research on Jews in China, *Social Sciences in China*," 1: 83–94 (1996).

33.7.3   The Protestants in China

The first Protestant missionary to arrive in China was Robert Morrison in 1807 (Box 2, chap. 2). It took nearly 60 years for their numbers to reach 112 (in 1865). In 1890, there were 1,296; in 1905, 3,445; by the 1920s, there were as many as 10,000 Protestant missionaries throughout the country. They were active in proseletyzing and good works (typically, teaching, publishing, medicine) and sinology.[51] In the nineteenth century those of them that wrote about the current scene in China, and there were many that did, often tended to take a more critical view than had the Catholic missionaries in the two previous centuries. There are several reasons why this was so. The arrival of industrialism in Europe and the United States in the nineteenth century suddenly made non-industrial countries like China seem extremely backward. And this was a time when China too was beginning to weaken. But perhaps most important of all for the individual protestant missionary was that he or she typically operated far from the court and the educated elite. They deliberately led less privileged lives than had the Jesuits. As a consequence they saw a much more impoverished and illiterate side of Chinese life.

There are several guides to missionary archives—for example, those listed in "Suggestions for additional reading," in

---

[51] Paul Cohen, "Christian Missions and their Impact to 1900," *CHC*, vol. 10, 1978, 543–590; 611–614.

Christian Missions in China: Evangelists of What? Jessie G. Lutz, ed., Boston: Heath, 1965. See also:

Alexander Wylie, *Memorials of Protestant missionaries to the Chinese: giving a list of their publications, and obituary notices of the deceased,* American Presbytarian Mission Press, 1867. Covers 1807–67.

The Missionary Enterprise in China and America, John King Fairbank, ed., HUP, 1970.

Archie R. Crouch, *Christianity in China: A Scholar's Guide to Resources in the Libraries and Archives of the United States,* M. E. Sharpe, 1989.

A Guide to the Archives and Records of the Protestant Christian Missions from the British Isles to China, Leslie R. Marchant, comp., Univ. of West Australia Press, 1966. Does not include the personal papers of missionaries.

Peter M. Mitchell, *A Guide to Archival Resources on Canadian Missionaries in East Asia: 1890–1960,* Univ. of Toronto-York, 1988.

Note the collections of Chinese sources on missionary cases *jiao'an* 教案 and the bibliography by Wu Shengde 吳盛德 and Chen Zenghui 陳增輝 (50.2.6).

34

Popular Literature

34.1 Folklore Studies

The Chinese literati recorded oral sources on legends, cults, popular beliefs and popular arts, festivals and customs and language in their miscellaneous and literary writings and sometimes in the gazetteers, but on the whole their interest was occasional rether than systemmatic. Note, for example, the type of sources from which Du Wenlan 杜文瀾 (1815–81) drew his enormous *Gu yaoyan* 古謠諺;[1] and likewise note that Zhang Yuan 張援 based his *Tianjian shi xuan* 田間詩選 mainly on works of scholarly poets.[2] For an annotated bibliography of 325 primary sources on the history of popular customs, see *Zhongguo minsu shiji juyao* 中國民俗史籍舉要, Liu Deren 劉德仁 et al., ed., Sichuan minzu, 1992. There is a comprehensive table of contents in lieu of an index. On folk literature, the pioneering study was that of Zheng Zhenduo 鄭振鐸, *Zhongguo suwenxueshi* 中國俗文學史.[3]

Early folklore research in China was the work of the missionaries or their converts. See, for example,

J. J. M. de Groot, *Les fêtes annuellement célébrées à Emoui [Amoy], étude concernant la religion populaire des chinois*, 2 vols., Paris: Annales du

---

[1] *Gu yaoyan* (Ancient songs and sayings), Zhou Shaoliang 周紹良, ed., Zhonghua, 1958; rpnt., 1984.

[2] *Tianjian shi xuan* (Selection of poems from the fields), Shangwu, 1929.

[3] *Zhongguo suwenxue shi* (History of Chinese popular literature), 2 vols., Shanghai, 1938; rpnt., Dongfang, 1996; see also Yang Yinshen 楊蔭深, *Zhongguo suwenxue gailun* 中國俗文學概論 (Outlines of Chinese popular literature), Shanghai: Shijie, 1946; Taibei, 1961.

Musée Guimet, vols. 11–12, 1886; rpnt., Leroux, 1977; English tr., *The Religious System of China*, 6 vols., Brill, 1892–1910; rpnt., SMC, 1982.

After the May Fourth Movement there developed considerable interest among Chinese researchers into folklore collection and anthropological studies. Special societies were set up and journals and reports were published; see Chao Wei-pang, "Modern Chinese Folklore Investigation," *Folklore Studies* 1: 55–76 (1942), 2: 79–88 (1943); and also Laurence A. Schneider, *Ku Chieh-kang and China's New History*, UCP, 1971, "The Folk Studies Movement and Its Populist Milieu," and "Popular Culture as a Modern Alternative," 121–52 and 153–87. Many of the publications of this period have recently been reprinted in Taiwan, where the original folk song and folk literature collections of the Shiyusuo are located. Note the following works:

Nai-tung Ting, *A Type Index of Classical Folktales in the Oral Tradition and Major Works of Non-religious Chinese Literature*, Academia Scientiarum Fennica FF Communications XCIV3 No. 223 (1978), Helsinki.

Chinese Fairy Tales and Folk Tales, Wolfram Eberhard, tr., Dutton, 1938 and 1958; also the same scholar's *Folktales of China*, UChP, 1965.

Legend, Lore and Religion in China: Essays in Honor of Wolfram Eberhard on his 70ᵗʰ Birthday, Sarah Allen and Alvin P. Cohen, eds., CMC, 1979.

A handful of Western folklorists and anthropologists also began field studies in this period (to 1949); see Morton Fried, "Community Studies in China," *FEQ* 14: 11–36 [1954–55]. Some specialized in popular religion (33.3).

During the 1950s and 1960s in China extensive oral history projects were launched and considerable attention was also paid to the recording of legends and popular tales. See Yen Chung-chiang, "Folklore Research in Communist China," *Folklore Studies* 26.2: 1–67 (1967).

34.2 Popular Literature

Popular literature consisted principally of mythology (33.1); legends; folk songs (and poems); short stories (and later novels); local operas and plays; and *chante-fables*. There were also many other forms, such as jokes and riddles.[4]

The *Shijing* 詩經 (*Odes*) contains 305 folk and ritual odes which have been used as primary sources for the popular beliefs and customs of the Zhou period.

In the second century the government set up an agency called the Yuefu 樂府 (Music Bureau) to collect popular tunes. Some of the ballads, love songs and laments which were collected have survived, and contain important materials for the study of the popular culture of the Han.[5]

After the Han, it may well have been the influence of Buddhism that led to the creation of a vernacular literature in China.[6] The earliest translations of the Buddhist texts are more in vernacular than *wenyanwen*, as are the popular stories on Buddhist themes (*bianwen* 變文) and secular ballads found at Dunhuang.[7] After the Tang, vernacular literature spread more

---

[4] "Popular Literature," in the *Indiana Companion to Traditional Chinese Literature*, William H. Nienhauser, Jr., ed, IUP, 1986; rev. rpnt., SMC, 1988, 75–92.

[5] See the extensive article on *Yuefu* by Ying-hsiung Chou in the *Indiana Companion*, 961–65; also, Anne M. Birrell, *Popular Songs and Ballads of Han China*, Unwin Hyman, 1988; rev. ed., UHP, 1993; Michael Loewe, "The Office of Music, c. 114–7 BC," *BSOAS* 36 (1973), 340–51.

[6] Victor H. Mair, "Buddhism and the Rise of the Written Vernacular in East Asia: The Making of National Languages," *JAS* 53.3: 707–51 (1994). The author has translated one of the earliest examples of non-Buddhist written vernacular. It is embedded in a poem by Ren Fang 任昉 (459–508), "Memorial of Indictment against Liu Cheng," see the *Columbia Anthology of Traditional Chinese Literature* (30.1), 542–7.

[7] *Bianwen* means transformation texts (hagiography was transformed into playlets and picture books); see Victor H. Mair, *Painting and Performance: Chinese Picture Recitation and Its Indian Genesis*, UHP, 1988; rpnt., 1996; Arthur Waley, *Ballads and Stories from Tun-huang*, Allen and Unwin, 1960. *Dunhuang bianwen jiaozhu* 敦煌變文校注 (Annotated and

Footnote continued on next page

widely, probably aided by the use of printing, more schools and a wealthy urban class looking for amusement. See, for example, the late tenth-century *Taiping guangji* 太平廣記, which contains sociological and mythological materials in the form of quotations from 485 titles, 240 of which have since been lost. The contents include fictional sources considered improper for inclusion in the *Taiping yulan* 太平御覽 (29.2).[8]

One of the most important of the new types of popular literature to emerge in the Song was the novel, which was rewritten in many different versions, from a storyteller's prompt book to finished literary product (34.3).

The main sources for the study of popular culture divide into four types: (1) vestiges of popular literature and legends in the elite literature; (2) extant works of popular literature (from the late Tang), including stories, dramas and local operas; (3) the records and direct observations of literati of "manners and customs," temples, cults and festivals; (4) popular tracts, devotional and other works of religion (chap. 33).

While the four types of source have by no means been fully utilized by modern historians, it would be misleading to suggest that the sources for the study of oral traditions and "popular culture" are rich, for they are not. As has already been pointed out, the recorders in traditional China were the Confucian literati who had scant respect for oral traditions. Nevertheless, these sources can to some extent be checked with and filled out using the reports and field studies of modern folklore researchers and anthropologists (see 33.2, *Bibliography*).

---

collated ballads from Dunhuang), Huang Zheng 黃徵 and Zhang Yong-quan 張涌泉, eds., Zhonghua, 1997.

[8] *Taiping guangji* 太平廣記 (Wide gleanings made in the Taiping era), comp. by Li Fang 李昉 (925–96) et al. 984, 1,000 *juan*; 10 vols., Zhonghua, 1961; 6th prnt., 1996. The most complete of several indexes is *Taiping guangji suoyin* 太平廣記索引 (Index to the *Taiping guangji*), Wang Xiumei 王秀梅 and Wang Hongbing 王泓冰, comps., Zhonghua, 1996. *H-Y Index* 15 is a title index.

34.3 Fiction and Drama

Chinese popular novels (*tongsu xiaoshuo* 通俗小説 or *baihua xiaoshuo* 白話小説) were not included in the Sibu classification. They can be of great interest to the historian.[9]

On the early history of Chinese fiction, see Robert Hegel, "Traditional Chinese Fiction: The State of the Field," *JAS* 53: 394–426 (1994); William H. Neinhauser, Jr., "The Origins of Chinese Fiction," *MS* 38: 191–219 (1988–89) and the references in note 6, section 20.4, on narrative in early historical and fictional sources.

The thirteenth to fifteenth centuries were the golden age of the drama combining singing, acrobatics and speech. The two main traditions were the *Yuanqu* 元曲 and the *Nanxi* 南戲, from the North and the South, respectively. See Wilt Idema and Stephen H. West, *Chinese Theater, 1100–1450: A Source Book*, Steiner, 1982 and James I. Crump, *Chinese Theater in the Days of Kublai Khan*, CCS, Michigan, 1990. See also section 38.2 on music.

Plot Summaries

Zhongguo tongsu xiaoshuo zongmu tiyao 中國通俗小説總目提要[10] contains plot summaries including chapter headings of all the 1,164 extant popular novels from the earliest surviving Song novel to the late Qing. It also includes brief biographies of the authors, when known, as well as publishing histories. It is more complete than any previous bibliography.[11]

---

[9] On the novels and stories as historical sources, see H. F. Schurmann, "On Social Themes in Sung Tales," *HJAS* 20: 239–61 (1957); Jaroslav Prusek, "Les contes chinoises du Moyen Age comme source de l'histoire économique et sociale sous les dynasties des Song et des Yuan," in *Chinese History and Literature*, Prague, 1970, 467–94.

[10] *Zhongguo tongsu xiaoshuo zongmu tiyao* (Annotated catalog of Chinese popular fiction), Ouyang Jian 歐陽健 and Xiao Xiangkai 蕭相愷, eds., Academy of Social Sciences, Jiangsu, Center for Ming-Qing Fiction, eds., Zhongguo wenlian, 1990.

[11] For an outline see Lu Xun, *A Brief History of Chinese Fiction*, tr. by Yang Hsien-yi and Gladys Yang, FLP, 1959.

Inventaire Analytique et Critique du Conte Chinois en Langue Vulgaire, André Levy and Michel Cartier, eds. in chief, 4 vols., Collège de France, 1978–91, is less comprehensive.

Bibliographies

For a bibliography listing both studies and translations into English, see Winston Yang, Peter Li and Nathan K. Mao, *Classical Chinese Fiction: A Guide to its Study and Appreciation, Essays and Bibliographies*, G. K. Hall, 1978. This includes both *wenyan* and *baihua* fiction and largely replaces the older *Chinese Fiction: A Bibliography of Books and Articles in Chinese and English*, Li Tien-yi, YUP, 1968. For earlier translations into English and other European languages (up to 1950), see Martha Davidson, *A List of Published Translations from Chinese into English, French and German, Vol. 1: Literature Exclusive of Poetry, Vol. 2: Poetry*, YUP, 1953; 1957.

Manuel D. Lopez, *Chinese Drama: An Annotated Bibliography of Commentary, Criticism, and Plays in English Translation*, Scarecrow, 1992.

Note the cumulative bibliography of works in all languages on all aspects of Chinese literature published at the end of each issue of *Chûgoku bungakuhô* 中國文學報, Jinbun, 1954– .

Dictionaries

Zhongguo huaben xiaoshuo suyu cidian 中國話本小説俗語辭典 (A Dictionary of Colloquial Terms and Expressions in Chinese Vernacualar Fictions [sic]), Tian Zongyao 田宗堯, comp., rev. and enlarged edition of the same author's 1983 work, Xinwenfeng, 1985 (see 2.5.2 for details of this and other bilingual dictionaries of the colloquial language).

Jindai Hanyu cidian 近代漢語辭典, Xu Shaofeng 許少峰, comp., Tuanjie, 1997. Covers the language of vernacular literature from the late Tang to the end of the Qing. All 25,000 entries include examples of usage with references cited. Arrangement is by *pinyin* with every phrase spelled out in full.

Jindai Hanyu duandai yuyan cidian xilie 近代漢語詞典系列 (Single-period dictionaries covering early Mandarin). There are separate volumes on the Tang-Wudai, Song and Yuan (for details, see 46.5.2, 47.4.2 and 48.5.4).

Jindai Hanyu cidian 近代漢語辭典, Gao Wenda 高文達, ed. in chief, Zhishi, 1992. A smaller dictionary (13,000 entries) of a similar nature to item 2.

Shi ci qu xiaoshuo yuci dadian 詩詞曲小說語詞大典.[12] Contains more than 20,000 entries explaining terms drawn from poetry and *baihua* literature from the Tang to the Qing.

Zhongguo gudai xiaoshuo renwu cidian 中國古代小說人物辭典 (Dictionary of characters in old Chinese fiction), Miao Zhuang 苗壯, ed., Qi-Lu, 1991. Includes some 1,700 persons, arranged according to genres.

There are now also any number of "dictionaries" of the language found in individual works (examples of these are given in the appropriate chapters). Here are some examples of dictionaries of the language (which in most cases also include the characters and places) of China's six greatest *baihua* novels. The best English translation is indicated:

Honglou meng 紅樓夢 (Dream of the red chamber), Cao Xueqin 曹雪芹, 1760: *Honglou meng yuyan cidian* 紅樓夢語言辭典 (Dictionary of the language of *Honglou meng*), Zhou Dingyi 周定一, ed. in chief, Shang-wu, 1995. The first part (1–1194) covers chaps. 1–80. The second part, chaps. 81–120 (1195–1445). According to the editor's foreword, the language of both parts of the novel is basically eighteenth-century Beijing dialect with some influence of Nanjing dialect but more from the language of the Northeast (which heavily influenced Beijing dialect at this time). The foreword is dated 1988.

> English translation: David Hawkes and John Minford, *The Story of the Stone*, 5 vols., Penguin Books, 1973–86.

Jin Ping Mei cidian 金瓶梅 (Gold, Vase, Plum or The Plum in the golden vase), anon, ca. 1618: *Jin Ping Mei cidian* 金瓶梅詞典 (Dictionary of *Jin Ping Mei*), Bai Weiguo 白維國, Zhonghua, ed., 1991; rpnt., 1994. Concentrates on difficult phrases from the spoken language rather than encyclopaedic coverage of personal and place names and so forth.

> Annotated English translation: David Tod Roy, *The Plum in the Golden Vase or Chin P'ing Mei, Volume one: The Gathering*, PUP, 1993.

Rulin waishi 儒林外史 (The scholars), Wu Jingzi 吳敬梓 (1701–54): *Rulin waishi cidian* 儒林外史辭典 (Dictionary of *Rulin waishi*), Chen Mei-lin 陳美林, ed. in chief, Nanjing daxue, 1994.

---

[12] *Shi ci qu xiaoshuo yuci dadian*, Wang Guiyuan 王貴元 and Ye Gui-gang 葉桂剛, eds. in chief, Qunyan, 1993.

English translation by Yang Hsien-yi and Gladys Yang, *The Scholars*, FLP, 1957.

Sanguozhi yanyi 三國志 (Romance of the three kingdoms), attrib. to Luo Guanzhong 羅貫中 (born ca. 1315): *Sanguo zhi yanyi cidian* 三國志演義辭典 (Dictionary of the *Three Kingdoms*), Zhang Shunhui 張舜徽 et al., eds., Shandong jiaoyu, 1992.

Annotated English translation with afterword: Moss Roberts, *Three Kingdoms: A Historical Novel*, 3 vols. FLP and UCP, 1991.

Shuihu cidian 水滸傳 (Water margin, or Outlaws of the marsh) *Shuihu cidian* 水滸詞典 (Dictionary of *Shuihuzhuan*), Hu Zhu'an 胡竹安, ed., Hanyu da cidian, 1989. Concentrates on difficult phrases from the spoken language rather than encyclopaedic coverage of personal and place names and so forth.

English translation: Sidney Shapiro, *Outlaws of the Marsh*, 3 vols., FLP, 1980. See also Richard G. Irwin, *The Evolution of a Chinese Novel, Shui-hu-chuan* [*Shuihuzhuan* 水滸傳], H-Y Institute, 1953.

Xiyouji cidian 西遊記 (Journey to the West or Monkey), attrib. to Wu Chengen 吳承恩 (ca. 1500–82), 1592: *Xiyouji cidian* 西遊記辭典 (Dictionary of *Xiyouji*), Zeng Shangyan 曾上炎, Henan renmin, 1994.

English translations: *Journey to the West*, William J. F. Jenner, tr., 2 vols., FLP, 1982–84; *The Journey to the West*, Anthony Yu, tr., 4 vols., UChP, 1977–83. See 41.5.1 for the original *Xiyouji* from which the story is derived.

Apart from the studies on narrative in historical writing and the novel cited in note 6, section 20.4, see the following introductory studies of the novels:

C. T. Hsia, *The Classic Chinese Novel: A Critical Introduction*, Col. UP, 1968.

Andrew Plaks, *Four Masterworks of the Ming Novel*, PUP, 1987.

35

Agriculture, Food and the Environment

Early farmers timed their tasks on the basis of periodic changes in natural and celestial phenomena (*Almanacs*, 35.1.1). From the Han, comprehensive agricultural treatises (*nongshu* 農書) on all aspects of agriculture, as well as specialized works on everything from crop systems to locust control, from pigeon raising to horse breeding, from irrigation to tea cultivation gradually became an established genre (35.1.2). Six hundred and fifty such treatises are extant, mainly from the later empire. Some quote from previous works; others are based on the experience and observation of their authors; some were officially sponsored (to popularize a new crop or technique, for example); and many were written by private authors (usually retired officials), discussing the agriculture of a single county, locality or estate. Most of the comprehensive agricultural treatises contain chapters on general principles of agriculture, crop types, the farming year, tools (often with illustrations) and side occupations. Taken as a whole, the *nongshu* are an important source for the history of Chinese agriculture and agricultural techniques, and taken singly some of them are good sources for the organization of agriculture in particular places at specific times.

The history of Chinese cooking can be traced using the *nongshu*, cookbooks, dietary treatises and *materia medica*. Much of what is commonly thought typical of Chinese food today is relatively recent in origin (35.3). Food production would have been impossible without water control (35.4). The chapter ends with a short section on the history of the environment and natural disasters (35.5). Medicine, disease and sex, all closely linked to the subjects of this chapter, are dealt with in chapter 36.

35.1 Almanacs and Agricultural Treatises

35.1.1   Almanacs

The earliest records relating to harvests and agriculture are scattered among the divinatory texts recorded on the oracle-bones.[1]

We know from later sources that pre-Qin farmers judged the changing seasons by closely observing natural phenomena that occur periodically such as hibernation, migration and blossoming. In addition to phenology, they also noted periodic changes in the weather and of celestial phenomena. These observations, called *wuhou* (物候), were collected together and eventually written down arranged by season and by month in almanacs. Several pre-Qin phenological calendars, or fragments, survive. The earliest has been preserved in the *Shijing*:

> *Shijing* 詩經 (*Odes*), "Qiyue, Binfeng 七月豳風" (Odes of Bin, July). A rhyming seasonal calendar, it gives in verse form the different farming and household tasks and seasonal sights and sounds ("In June the crickets start to skip out; in July they live in the fields; in August they live under the eaves; in September in the room they keep; in October under the bed they sleep," *The Book of Poetry*, Wang Rongpei and Ren Xiuhua, tr., and annotated, Liaoning jiaoyu, 1995, 616–

---

[1] Peng Bangjiong 彭邦炯, *Jiaguwen nongye ziliao kaobian yu yanjiu* 甲骨文農業資料考辨與研究 (Verification and research on agricultural materials in the oracle-bone inscriptions), Jilin wenshi, 1997.

617. Also translated slightly differently by Jeffrey Riegel in the *Columbia Anthology of Traditional Chinese Literature* (30.1), 158–60. A controversy has raged for centuries as to which calendar the poem is based on.

Other pre-Qin works with important chapters or fragments on the farming year include the following (bibliographic references in Table 18, chap. 19):

Lüshi chunqiu 呂氏春秋 (ca. 239 BC), *Shi'er ji* 十二季. Connects phenological observations with the 12 seasons (months).

Liji 禮記, "Yueling 月令" (Monthly ordinances). Combines farming advice with the type of information that was later included in popular encyclopaedias (23.4). The strictly farming features of the almanac were usually incorporated into the later *nongshu*; the calendrical information went into popular calendars (5.1). The heavenly phenomena were revised to fit the Tang calendar at the time of the carving of the Kaicheng stone Classics in 837 (17.3).

"Xia xiaozheng 夏小正." Similar to the "Yueling;" survived in a Han collection of mainly Warring States ritual texts similar to the *Liji* known as the *Da Dai liji* 大戴禮記; later circulated as a separate work. See Benedykt Grynpas, *Les écrits de Tai l'Ancien et le petit calendrier des Hia*, Paris, 1972.

Huainanzi 淮南子 (presented to the emperor in 139 BC), "Shize xun 時則訓" (On times and seasons). Includes the 24 *jieqi* more or less in the form in which they are still in use in the countryside today.

Yi Zhoushu 逸周書 (different *pian* date from different times), "Shixun jie 時訓解" (Interpretations of times and seasons). Includes the phenological basis for the system of 72 *hou*.

In the Former Han, phenological characteristics associated with each of 24 seasons (*jieqi* 節氣) were standardized into a system which has been used to the present day. The 72 minor periods of five days each (*hou* 候) were incorporated into the calendar in AD 520 (5.3.1).

Farmers and peasants strictly followed the traditional times as fixed with reference to the *jieqi* for planting, harvesting, pruning, and all the other main tasks of the farming year. Later, as the territory of China expanded to cover an area where the flowering, for example, of the apricot, occurred at least two months earlier in the South than in the North, adjustments were made to the phenological observations to fit them to different regions. These adjustments often featured in local *nongshu*, but many centuries passed before anybody openly criticized the practice of publishing official calendars for the whole of the country based on observations originally made in the Chang'an-Luoyang area during the Han. The first to do so was the seventeenth century geographer Liu Xianting 劉獻廷 (1658–95), who pointed out that different places had different *72 hou*. The Taiping calendar, however, was the first to include revised phenological observations (made in Nanjing).[2]

35.1.2   *Agricultural Treatises*

When reading agricultural treatises, as with other Chinese sources, it is essential to distinguish between what was based on the author's direct experience, observation or contemporary information and what was simply quoted, repeated or culled from previous writers, with or without acknowledgment.[3]

First Century AD

Fan Shengzhi shu 范勝之書 (Fan Shengzhi's work on agiculture). See Shih Sheng-han (Shi Shenghan 石聲漢, 1907–71), *On "Fan Sheng-chih shu,"* Science Press, 1959; 1963. Only fragments survive (3,500 characters preserved in encyclopaedias and in the next item). Based on farming in Guanzhong 關中 (Shaanxi).

Second Century

Cui Shi 崔寔, *Simin yueling* 四民月令 (Monthly ordinances for the four classes [scholars, farmers, artisans and merchants]). An important source for the economic history of the Later Han. Only fragments

---

[2] See Cao Wanru 曹婉如 in *Ancient China's Technology and Science*, FLP, 1987, 229–35.

[3] On both the early almanacs as well as the *nonshu*, see "Sources," in Francesca Bray, *SCC*, vol. 6, Part 2, *Agriculture*, CUP, 1984, 47–93. This includes a comparison of the Chinese sources with Greek, Roman and European agricultural works (85–93).

survive (preserved in *Qimin yaoshu*, see below).[4] Consists of instructions in the form of an almanac based on private-estate management. One of the earliest in this style, the forerunner of which is the "Yueling" (Monthly observances) sections of the *Liji*; the *Lüshi chunqiu* and the *Huai nanzi*. Farmers' almanacs have remained popular to this day. Most later agricultural treatises contained a calendrical section or diagram setting out the main tasks of the farming year.

Sixth Century

Jia Sixie 賈思勰 (b. end of fourth century in Shandong), *Qimin yaoshu* 齊民要術 (Techniques essential for the subsistence of common people). The first complete extant comprehensive agricultural treatise.[5] Although half the book is in the form of quotations from previous works (which have thereby been preserved), the rest is based on Jia Sixie's experience of farming in Shandong. He also has much material on eating and drinking habits during the Northern Wei.

Tenth Century

Sishi zuanyao 四時纂要 (Essentials of the four seasons), Han E 韓鄂. This is the only farming manual to survive from the seventh to tenth centuries. It was lost in China, but found in Japan in 1960 preserved in a Korean woodblock edition of 1590.[6]

Eleventh Century

Chen Fu 陳敷 (1076–1154), *Nongshu* 農書 (agricultural treatise), 1149. Based on paddy rice farming and sericulture in southern China.

---

[4] Patricia Buckley Ebrey, "Estate and Family Management in the Later Han as Seen in the *Monthly Instructions for the Four Classes of People*," *JESHO* 17: 173–205 (1974). *Simin yueling jishi* 四民月令集釋 (Annotated translation into modern Chinese of the *Simin yueling*), Miao Qiyu 繆啓愉, Nongye, 1981.

[5] Francesca Bray, *SCC*, vol. 6, Part 2, 55–59 (also includes a translation of the table of contents). See also Shih Sheng-han, *A Preliminary Survey of the Book* Ch'i Min Yao Shu: *An Agricultural Encyclopaedia of the 6th Century*, Kexue, 1958; 2nd ed., with corrections, 1962. See also Amano Motonosuke, "Dry Farming and the *Chi-min yao-shu*," in *Silver Jubilee Volume of the Zinbun-Kagaku-Kenkyusyo*, 1954, 451–66. For the original text punctuated and with translation into modern Chinese, see *Qimin yaoshu jiaoshi* 齊民要術校釋, Miao Qiyu 繆啓愉, ed., Nongye, 1982.

[6] *Sishi zuanyao jiaoshi* 四時纂要校釋, Miao Qiyu 繆啓愉, ed., Nongye, 1982 (based on the Japanese photo-reprint by Yamamoto, 1961).

Thirteenth Century

Nongsang jiyao 農桑輯要 (Essentials of agriculture and sericulture), 1273. Comprehensive, imperially sponsored. The earliest official agricultural treatise to have survived. Mainly quotations from previous works some of which have been lost.[7]

Fourteenth Century

Nongsang yishi cuoyao 農桑衣食撮要 (Essentials of agriculture, sericulture, clothing and food), compiled by a Uighur official, Lu Mingshan 魯明善. Important because written as an actual handbook for magistrates in their role as agricultural instructors. Arranged in almanac style.

Wang Zhen 王禎, *Nongshu* 農書 (agricultural treatise), Preface dated 1313, but probably written slightly earlier.[8] Important because based on the author's experience and observations as a county magistrate in Anhui and Jiangxi and travels in north China. The first two sections (on agriculture, sericulture and crops) are mainly based on previous works. The author however draws attention to differences in northern and southern agriculture. The third section, "Nongqi Tupu 農器圖譜" (Illustrations of agricultural implements), is unique and takes up most of the book. The drawings of all the main farming implements in use at that time are annotated. Compare these to the implements in use in the first part of the twentieth century as shown in *China at Work*.[9] Many are the same. In order to print the *Nongshu*

---

[7] *SCC*, vol. 6, Part 2, 71–72 (also includes a translation of the table of contents). For the Yuan text punctuated and with translation into modern Chinese, see *Yuanke Nongsang jiyao* 元刻農桑輯要, Miao Qiyu 繆啟愉, ed., Nongye, 1988.

[8] *SCC*, vol. 6, Part 2, 59–64 (also includes a translation of the table of contents). There is a heavily annotated edition of the original text with translation into modern Chinese in *Dong-Lu Wangshi nongshu yizhu* 東魯王氏農書譯注 (Mr. Wang of Eastern Lu's agricultural treatise, translated [into Modern Chinese] with notes), *Zhongguo gudai keji mingzhu yizhu congshu* 中國古代科技名著譯注叢書 (Collectanea of annotated famous Chinese works on science and technology done into modern Chinese), Miao Qiyu 繆啟愉, ed., Shanghai guji, 1994.

[9] Rudolph P. Hommel, *China at Work: An Illustrated Record of the Primitive Industries of China's Masses, Whose Life is Toil, and Thus an Account of Chinese Civilization*, New York: John Day & Company, 1937; MIT Press, 1969.

Wang developed the use of movable type using wood. Eventually it was printed for him using blocks but he added an appendix on the "Method of movable type printing using wood."

Seventeenth Century

Nongzheng quanshu 農政全書 (Comprehensive treatise on agricultural administration), Xu Guangqi 徐光啓 (1562–1633), comp., 1639. Important because it summed up the state of the art; it was highly popular in Tokugawa Japan. Xu was friendly with some of the Jesuit scholars and has included excerpts from European works on hydraulics.[10]

Tiangong kaiwu 天工開物 (chap. 37).

Bu Nongshu 補農書 (Addendum to [Mr Shen's] *Nongshu* of 1643), Zhang Luxiang 張履祥 (1611–74). Important because it contains advice on how to run a single estate in Tongxiang 桐鄉, Zhejiang.[11]

Zhang Ying 張英, *Hengchan suoyan* 恒產瑣言 (Remarks on real estate), c. 1697. Written for the benefit of his heirs (as indeed were many other such treatises which were more in the form of family instructions than farming manuals).[12]

Eighteenth Century

Shoushi tongkao 授時通考 (Comprehensive study of the farming year), imperially sponsored and distributed, 1747, Nongye, 1963. Almost entirely culled from previous works. See *SCC*, vol. 6, Part 2, 72–74 (also includes a translation of the table of contents).

---

[10] *SCC*, vol. 6, Part 2, 64–70 (also includes a translation of the table of contents). *Nongzheng quanshu jiaozhu* 農政全書校注 (Annotated and collated *Comprehensive Treatise on Agriculture*), Shi Shenghan 石聲漢, ed., 3 vols., Shanghai guji, 1979.

[11] Chen Hengli 陳恒力 (1911–78), *Bu Nongshu yanjiu* 補農書研究 (Studies on the *Bu Nongshu*), Zhonghua, 1958; Nongye, 1961. The same scholar also published a punctuated, annotated edition with translation into modern Chinese: *Bu Nongshu jiaoshi* 補農書校釋, Chen Hengli 陳恒力 and Wang Da 王達, eds., Nongye, 1983.

[12] Translated in Hilary J. Beattie, *Land and Lineage in China—A Study of T'ung-ch'eng County, Anhwei, in the Ming and Ch'ing Dynasties*, CUP, 1979, Appendix III, 140–51. Also by Clara Yu in *Chinese Civilization: A Sourcebook*, Patricia Ebrey, ed., 1981; 2nd ed., rev. and expanded, Free Press, 1993, 287–91.

Gengzhi tu 耕織圖 (Pictures of ploughing and weaving [agriculture and sericulture]), imperially sponsored.[13] Expanded from a Song original dating from 1210. The China Agriculture Museum in Beijing has reproduced pictures from this plus many other similar collections in *Zhongguo gudai gengzhitu* 中國古代耕織圖 (Farming and Weaving Pictures in Ancient China), Wang Chaosheng 王潮生, ed. in chief, Nongye, 1995. The explanatory text is in Chinese and English.

Nineteenth Century

Yang Xiuyuan 楊秀元, *Nongyan zhushi* 農言著實 (Practical advice on farming), in *Qin-Jin nongyan* 秦晉農言, Zhonghua, 1957.

Studies

In addition to the agricultural treatises, local gazetteers and the monographs on financial administration in the Standard Histories also contain information on Chinese agricultural history.

The best introduction to the history of Chinese agriculture in English is the substantial, well-illustrated work by Francesca Bray, *SCC*, vol. 6, Part 2, *Agriculture*, CUP, 1984.

There are a number of important studies and reference works on the history of Chinese agriculture published by the Nongye Chubanshe in Beijing:

Zhongguo nongye baike quanshu 中國農業百科全書: *Nongye lishijuan* 農業歷史卷 (Encyclopaedia of Chinese agriculture, agricultural history volume), Nongye, 1995. Contains articles on the history of each of the main Chinese crops; animal husbandry; irrigation; techniques; implements; land taxes; disaster relief and agricultural treatises (an annex lists 650 extant ones arranged in 11 categories). There are also articles on the agricultural history of each dynasty, the different regions of China and the main non-Han peoples both in China and abroad. The title of each of the 500 articles in the encyclopaedia are translated into English and there is also an English index. This is an excellent work of reference with over 150 color plates and numerous black and white illustrations. The other 30 vols. of this encyclopaedia all contain articles on the historical background to their subject.

---

[13] *Kêng tschi tu: Ackerbau und Seidengewinnung in China, ein kaiserliches Lehr- und Mahn-buch*, Otto Franke, tr., Hamburg: L. Friederichsen & Co., 1913.

Zhongguo nongye kexue jishu shigao 中國農業科學技術史稿 (Draft history of Chinese agricultural science and technology), Liang Jiamian 梁家勉, ed. in chief, Nongye, 1989; rpnt., 1992. Covers from Neolithic times to the end of the Han in 240 pages and thoroughly incorporates the findings of archaeology. It also contains a further 240 pages carrying the story to the end of the Qing. Appendix I summarizes the main innovations in agricultural technology in each period and in each field; appendix II gives the Latin and English names for all plants mentioned in the text and Appendix III is a bibliography of 750 primary and secondary sources used.

Zhongguo gudai nongye kejishi tushuo 中國古代農業科技史圖譜 *Zhongguo gudai nongye kejishi tupu* (Illustrations with commentary on the history of ancient Chinese agricultural science and technology), Chen Wenhua 陳文華, ed., Nongye, 1989; rpnt., 1991. Based on the historical displays in the Agricultural History Museum in Beijing. It covers crops, implements, animals and techniques and contains copious illustrations from archaeological reports and *nongshu* from prehistoric times to 1840.

The following studies examine the history of Chinese agriculture from the viewpoint of economists and historians:

Dwight H. Perkins, *Agricultural Development in China*, Aldine, 1969.

Kang Chao, *Man and Land in Chinese History, An Economic Analysis*, SUP, 1986.

Gang Deng, *Development Versus Stagnation: Technological Continuity and Agricultural Progress in Pre-Modern China*, Greenwood, 1993.

Mark Elvin, *The Pattern of the Chinese Past*, SUP, 1973.

Liu Ts'ui-jung (Liu Cuirong 劉翠溶), "Agricultural Change and Population Growth: A Brief Survey in the Case of China in Historical Perspective," *Academia Sinica Economic Papers* 14.1: 29–68 (1986).

Plant and Flower Names

To identify and check the English names of plants and flowers in Chinese works, in addition to the references cited above, use a compendium such as

Yangshi yuanyi zhiwu da mingdian 楊氏園藝植物大名典 *Yangshi yuanyi zhiwu da mingdian* (Yang's compendium of horticulture and plant names), Yang Gongyi 楊恭毅, comp., 9 vols., Taibei: Zhongguo huahui zazhishe 中國花卉雜志社, 1984. It contains color photographs of the trees, flowers and plants and the compiler indicates their Chinese,

English, Latin, French and German names as well as giving a synopsis of their history and their alternative names in Chinese.

Xinbian La, Han, Ying zhiwu mingcheng 新編拉漢英植物名稱 (Latin, Chinese and English plant names, newly edited), Zhongkeyuan Zhiwu yanjiusuo, comp., Hangkong gongye, 1996. Gives the Chinese and English equivalents of 55,800 plant names in Latin. It is alphabetically arranged by Latin name and also contains Chinese and English indexes.

Since the leaves, seeds and other parts of a huge variety of plants and flowers were used in Chinese medicine, medical dictionaries such as *Zhongyao da cidian* 中藥大辭典 (chap. 36, *Medical Terms*) can also be helpful.

There are also numerous specialized studies identifying the terminology found in the Classics and other early works, see for example,

Shijing 詩經: Wu Houyan 吳厚炎, *Shijing caomu huikao* 詩經草木匯考 (Invesigation of the vegetation in the *Shijing*), Guizhou renmin, 1992.

Michael E. Carr, *A Linguistic Study of the Flora and Fauna Sections of the Erh ya*, Ph.D., University of Arizona, 1972.

"Botanical Linguistics," *SCC*, vol. 6, part 1, CUP, 1986, 117–42.

Bibliography

Wang Yuhu 王毓瑚 (1907–80), *Zhongguo nongxue shulu* 中國農學書錄, is the basic bibliographic guide to all types of *nongshu* from all periods. The author arranges all known agricultural treatises (whether lost or extant) according to broad categories with bibliographic notes and summaries of the contents of each.[14]

---

[14] *Zhongguo nongxue shulu* (Annotated Catalogue of Chinese agricultural treatises), Nongye, 1964; rev. ed., 1979. Wang's work was reprinted and introduced by Amano Motonosuke 天野元之助, *Chûgoku nôgaku shoroku* 中國農學書錄 (Annotated catalog of Chinese agricultural treatises), Ryûkei, 1975, and commentated in the same author's *Chûgoku konôsho kô* 中國古農書考 (Researches on ancient Chinese agricultural works), Ryûkei, 1975. Amano's introduction formed the basis of the revised edition of Wang Yuhu (1979). See also Amano's *Chûgoku nôgyôshi kenkyû* 中國農業史研究 (Researches into Chinese agricultural history), Ochanomizu shobô, 1962; expanded edition, 1979. Amano (1975) was

Footnote continued on next page

William Y. Chen, *An Annotated Bibliography of Chinese Agriculture*, CMC, 1993, provides brief notes in English on 542 traditional works on agriculture (both lost and extant).

For 19,255 articles (including book reviews) on Chinese agricultural history published in China (as well as in Taiwan, Hong Kong and to a certain extent in Japan) between the late Qing and 1991, see *Zhongguo nongshi lunwen mulu suoyin* 中國農史論文目錄索引 (Index to articles on agricultural history), *Zhongguo nongye bowuguan ziliaoshi* 中國農業博物館資料室 (Documentation room of the museum of agricultural history), eds., Linye, 1993. This also includes studies of water control and transport, fertilizer, population, land systems, land taxes and trade in agricultural produce.

SCC, vol. 6, Part 2 contains a full bibliography of primary and secondary sources.

Journals

Gujin nongye 古今農業 (Ancient and Modern Agriculture of China), 1987– , bi-annual (1987– 90); thereafter, quarterly, China Agricultural Museum, Beijing.

Nongye kaogu 農業考古 (13.3).

Zhongguo nongshi 中國農史 (Chinese agricultural history), quarterly; since 1981, Nanjing nongye daxue et al., eds., Nanjing.

35.2 *Food*

35.2.1   *Variety and Changes in Chinese Cuisine*

There are at least four keys to the richness of the ever-changing Chinese cuisine. The first is the huge and expanding area from which it was able to draw its resources. Eventually this area included climate zones ranging from the subarctic to the tropical, each providing not only new ingredients, but often also cultures with distinct cooking traditions of their own. Chief among these are what can broadly be described as the northern and southern traditions. The southern traditions were based on rice, fish, domestic animals, vegetables and tropical fruits; those

---

translated into Chinese under the same title and published by Nongye, 1992.

of the North were typified by dry-land crops, the meat of wild animals and temparate fruits. Different eating habits of the various non-Han peoples within the China area were gradually absorbed into the two great traditions, for example, eating snakes, which was typical of the Yue 越, became part of the southern tradition.

The second key is the early development of an elaborate tradition of dietary and medicinal cooking. Food was seen as the basis of good health, provided the right amounts and combinations were taken. Eating the right ingredients could ensure a long life and potency (*yangsheng* 養生). Food was medicine and medicine, food.

The third key was the large number of demands from different patrons or groups for their own separate specialized cuisines. Such patrons included the court, rich households and scholar gourmands. Buddhists and Muslims also elaborated their own cuisines (*sucai* 素菜 and *qingzhen* 清真, respectively). Furthermore, by the later empire, there were enough wealthy businessmen and officials travelling or living away from their home towns to support restaurants catering to their tastes (35.2.4).

The fourth key (and it is related to the first two) was the continuous absorbtion for at least four thousand years of all sorts of foreign influences, including ingredients, cooking methods and recipes from Persia, Central Asia, India, Southeast Asia and the Americas, as well as from the peoples of the steppe, from the Xiongnu to the Manchus.

A growing and enormously varied resource base within China; the belief that the right foodstuffs could ensure good health and prolong life; the demand for specialized higher cuisines and the openness to imported foods and experimentation with foreign recipes and ingredients made Chinese cuisine the most varied in the world. More than is generally realized they also ensured that it was constantly changing. As a result, many of what are considered typical features today turn out to have been added relatively recently.

Today, open-door policies, greater wealth and new life-styles are accelerating changes in Chinese cooking methods, ingredients and eating habits, ever more influenced by the West, Japan and Hong Kong.[15]

35.2.2 *Pre-Qin Foodstuffs and Cooking*

In surveying the history of agriculture and food in China it is important to bear in mind that certain crops and ingredients may have been indigenous but not widely used, while the same import has been introduced on separate occasions, sometimes centuries apart. Walnuts, for example, have been found in Neolithic sites thousands of years before their supposed first introduction from Central Asia in the Han. The conclusion is that diffusion to different parts of the China area may not automatically have followed the introduction of a plant or crop, at least in the earlier centuries.

Rice cultivation had already spread from the Yangzi valley to the North as far as Shanxi and Henan in the late Neolithic.[16] It is only from sites seven or eight millennia later that wheat and barley begin to appear (in the late Shang, Western Zhou). Many assume that they were imported from the West. The main staple in the North, along with beans, was millet (*shuji* 黍稷). Cooking was mainly by boiling and steaming; the typical dish was a millet gruel or stew with mallow, turnips or radish and, for most people, only occasionally, meat, fish, or fruit.

---

[15] For good historical and cultural introductions, see *Food in Chinese History: Anthropological and Historical Perspectives*, K. C. Chang, ed., YUP, 1977; E. N. Anderson, *The Food of China*, YUP, 1988; and *Han-Tang yinshi wenhuashi* 漢唐飲食文化史 (History of food and beverages from the Han to the Tang), Li Hu 黎虎, ed., Beijing shifan daxue, 1998.

[16] Hui-lin Li, "The Domestication of Plants in China: Ecogeographical Considerations," and Te-tzu Chang, "The Origins and Early Cultures of the Cereal Grains and Food Legumes," in *The Origins of Chinese Civilization*, David Keightley, ed., UCP, 1983, 21–64 and 65–94. See also *Zhongguo shiqian yinshishi* 中國史前飲食史 (A history of Chinese prehistoric food and drink), Wang Renxiang 王仁湘, Qingdao chubanshe, 1997.

Soybeans are native to China. The early generic word for them was *shu* 菽 (modern *dadou* 大豆). The soybean began to be cultivated in the Spring and Autumn period. It was a major source of protein, especially for peasants and laborers.[17] Starting in the Yangzi valley, it was also used as the main flavoring. Berries and other native fruits provided vitamins. The main beverage was boiled water, or boiled rice water, ordinary people on special occasions drank fruit cordials and schnapps, the mighty took millet or rice ale.[18]

The leaves of the wild tea tree (indigenous to southwest China) had been used to make a medicinal drink since ancient times. Tea was called *tu* 荼 (*she* 蔎, *ming* 茗 or *chuan* 荈). The main cultivation centers were in the kingdoms of Ba and Shu. After the Qin conquest of Sichuan in 316 BC, tea planting and drinking spread to other parts of south China. The most famous work on tea was that written by the bachelor scholar Lu Yu 陸羽 (?–804) during the late Tang, when tea first became all the rage: *Chajing* 茶經 (Treatise on tea).[19]

The rulers of ancient China attached huge importance to the production of food. The main symbol of royal power was a massive cooking vessel, the *ding* 鼎 (caldron, see 17.1). At the Zhou court (according to the *Zhouli*), there were 21 different official posts with a total staff of 2,300 people involved in cooking and the preparation of food for banquets, ceremonies, ritu-

[17] *Siok* is the Old Chinese pronunciation of *shu*. It is supposed to be the origin of the word soya in European and other languages.

[18] David R. Knechtges, "A Literary Feast: Food in Early Chinese Literature, *JAOS* 106: 49–63 (1986); "Gradually Entering the Realm of Delight: Food and Drink in Early Medieval China," *JAOS* 117: 229–239 (1997).

[19] *Chajing qianshi* 茶經淺釋, Zhang Fangci 張芳賜 et al., tr. and annotated, Yunnan renmin, 1981. In most languages, the word for tea is either derived from the Mandarin pronunciation *cha* (e.g., Portuguese, Russian or Turkish), or from the Xiamen 廈門 pronunciation *te* (to rhyme with "say" as in Dutch and German *Tee* or French *thé*. This was also the first English pronunciation before tea, to rhyme with "see," became standard).

als and sacrifices. Indeed, the Zhou ritual texts are prime sources for the history of pre-Qin food and eating habits. One of the common words for cooking was *gepeng* 割烹 (to cut and cook) which possibly suggests the early appearance of one important characteristic of the Chinese cuisine, fine cutting of ingredients before cooking.

The *Shijing* 詩經 (*Odes*) mentions at least forty-four definite or probable food plants and most of the common domestic and wild animals and birds found in the North during the first millenium BC.[20] The ingredients of the southern cuisine are reflected in the other great anthology of ancient poetry, the *Chuci* 楚詞 and also in the "Benwei 本味" chapter of the *Lüshi chunqiu* 呂氏春秋. Pre-Qin recipes are found in the *Liji* 禮記 (*Rites*). Discoveries in tombs of actual foodstuffs and descriptions of their preparation have added much to the written sources.[21]

The vocabulary of pre-Qin cooking is minutely examined in the special dictionary *Zhongguo shanggu pengshi zidian* 中國上古烹食字典.[22]

---

[20] Hsüan Keng, "Economic Plants of Ancient North China as Mentioned in *Shih Ching*," *Economic Botany* 28, 4: 391–410. Keng's article is summarized in Anderson (1988), 30–35.

[21] Yü Yin-shih, "Han China," in Chang (1977), 55–58 describes the rich finds in Mawangdui, Tomb 1 (which incidentally corroborate the regulations in the *Liji*). He also outlines the evidence from Han mural paintings of kitchens and feasts.

[22] *Zhongguo shanggu pengshi zidian* (Dictionary of ancient Chinese cooking), Lin Yinsheng 林銀生 et al., eds., Shangye, 1993. In all, 940 words related to food and cooking are analyzed. They are drawn from the *Shuowen*, the *Erya* and the *Fangyan*. Note K. C. Chang, "Ancient China," in Chang (1977), 23–52; Donald Harper, "Gastronomy in Ancient China," *Parabola* 9.4 (1984) and Wang Shenxing 王慎行, "Lun Zhoudai de yinshi guan 論周代的飲食觀" (On the attitude to food and drink in the Zhou dynasty) in *Gu wenzi yu Yin-Zhou wenming* 古文字與殷周文明 (Ancient scripts and the culture of the Yin and Zhou), Shaanxi renmin jiaoyu, 1992, 280–95.

35.2.3   New Foodstuffs

During the four hundred years of the Han, cooking made great advances. One sign was the appearance of more elaborate cooking stoves. The meat stew remained popular; other methods of cooking meat included open roasting; deep frying; sun-drying; mud-baking; boiling; brazing and steaming. Thin slicing for eating raw was not uncommon. Fish sauce was used and noodles were introduced (called *bing* 餅 because they were made from flour and water). Soy beans remained an important source of protein.

The Han and the centuries up to and including the Tang saw the introduction and spread from Central Asia of the following ingredients, products and recipes. Many may have been imported earlier than their appearance in written sources suggests. The pomegranate, for example, has been found in third century BC graves. Nearly all of them originally betrayed their non-Chinese origin with the descriptive *hu* 胡 (barbarian from the Western Regions). By the Song, their foreign origin was forgotten and *hu* was dropped from all but four of their names:

> *anshiliu* 安石榴 (pomegranate, after Anxi guo 安息國, Parthia), modern *shiliu* 石榴
>
> *boleng* 菠薐 (spinach from Persia), modern *bocai* 菠菜
>
> *hu zhenzi* 胡榛子 or *ayue hunzi* 阿月渾子 (pistachio)
>
> *huchi* 胡豉 (fermented soy bean), modern *douchi* 豆豉
>
> *husui* 胡荽 (coriander), modern *xiangcai* 香菜
>
> *hucong* 胡葱 (green Chinese onion), modern *dacong* 大葱
>
> *hudou* 胡豆 (broad bean), modern *candou* 蠶豆
>
> *hugua* 胡瓜 (cucumber), modern *huanggua* 黃瓜
>
> *hujiao* 胡椒 (black pepper)
>
> *huluobo* 胡蘿卜 (carrot)
>
> *huma* 胡麻 (sesame), modern *zhima* 芝麻
>
> *husuan* 胡蒜 (garlic), modern *dasuan* 大蒜
>
> *hutao* 胡桃 (walnuts), modern *hetao* 核桃; used for desserts, in medicine and as a fixative for paintings
>
> *huyan* 胡鹽 (rock salt), also known as *rongyan* 戎鹽 or *qiangyan* 羌鹽
>
> *muxu* 苜蓿 (alfalfa, loan from *buksuk*, the name used in Ferghana, Dawan guo 大宛國, from which it was imported in the Former Han to feed the horses from the same place)

putao 葡萄 (grapes and grape wine); imported from Ferghana in the
Former Han; possibly a loan from putative early Persian *budâwa*
(a cognate of Greek *botros?*)
yuntai 蕓苔 (rape), modern *youcai* 油菜

The egg plant (*qiezi* 茄子) came to southwest China from
India in the Han along with Buddhism. By the Song, it had
gradually spread to the whole country.

Guangdong supplied tropical fruits and their Yue names
with them: *lizhi* 荔枝 (lychee), *longyan* 龍眼 (longan), *pipa*
枇杷 or *lujüe* 盧橘 (loquat), *jin'gan* 金柑 (cumquat). They are
attested in the literature as early as the Han, when unsuccessful
efforts were made to cultivate lychee in Chang'an and Luoyang. For most of the dynasty they were rushed post-haste to
the court as tribute. The cultivation of such fruits became widespread in Guangdong and Fujian only in the Tang and Song. In
the twentieth century, they reached China-town restaurants in
America, Europe and Japan before most people in North
China had ever seen them thanks to companies like the Amoy
Canning Corporation.[23]

Between the Han and the end of the Tang many sugar cane
varieties (as well as refining techniques) and spices (for example,
biba 蓽芨 or *bibo* 蓽撥, long pepper) and other ingredients,
such as ginger (*jiang* 姜) or betel leaf (*binlang* 檳榔 from Malay
pinang) were imported from India and Southeast Asia.[24]

Already, during the *Nan-Bei Chao*, the Chinese had the opportunity to observe and taste the cuisine of the northern
kingdoms, those ruled and partly settled by the *wuhu* 五胡 (five
barbarians). By the Sui and the Tang some of the *hushi* 胡食

[23] The English names for these fruits are usually derived from the
Cantonese or Min pronunciation, for example, *laiqi* gives lychee (not *lizhi*); *lukwat* gives loquat (not *lujüe*) and *kinkam* gives cumquat (not *jin-
gan*).

[24] On sugar, see Christian Daniels, *Agro-Industries and Forestry. Agro-
Industries: Sugarcane Technology, SCC*, vol. 6, Part 3 (1996). On imports
from India, see Liu Xinru, *Ancient India and Ancient China: Trade and
Religious Exchanges*, New Delhi: OUP, 1988. See also Edward H. Schafer,
The Golden Peaches of Samarkand: A Study of Tang Exotics, UCP, 1963.

(barbarian dishes) had become fashionable and were entering the mainstream. In some cases they probably originated in Persia or Central Asia but were introduced by the northern kingdoms.[25] They included the following:

> boiled lamb slices à la Qiang (Qiang *zhufa* 羌煮法, the forerunner of the northern dish of rinsed lamb (*shuanyangrou* 涮羊肉)
> clay-baked or mutton haggis (*hubao rou* 胡爆肉)
> *dimsam* (*dianxin* 點心), pastry snacks
> raw fish slices (Xi-Qiang *zhi* or *zha* 西羌鮓)
> roasted mutton slices seasoned with pickled cucumber and chopped fresh vegetables and then rolled in pancakes; a similar technique as is used for serving Peking duck today (*hufan* 胡飯)
> sesame buns (*hubing* 胡餅; modern *shaobing* 燒餅, a Chinese form of spiced wheat bread or *nan*)
> sheep stew (*hugeng* 胡羹)
> steamed bread rolls (*mantou* 饅頭)[26]
> whole-roasted lamb or calf (*mozhi* 貊炙)

Early ripening rice was imported from Champa to join local strains in the eleventh century. Bean curd (*doufu* 豆腐) is first mentioned in the Song (although credited to the uncle of Han

---

[25] The main primary source on food and cooking methods in the North during the *Nan-Bei Chao* is *Qimin yaoshu* 齊民要術 (36.1). See Lü Yifei 呂一飛, *Huzu xisu yu Sui-Tang fengyun* 胡族習俗與隋唐風韵 (The customs of the foreign tribes and the fashions of the Sui and Tang), Shumu wenxian, 1996. The author traces the influence of the non-Han peoples of the Wei, Jin and northern dynasties (including the Xiongnu) on the Sui and Tang in the fields of food and drink; clothing and body ornament; houses and transport; betrothal and marriage; song and dance and social customs.

[26] Zhuge Liang 諸葛亮 is said to have invented the *mantou* during his conquests in the south of China as a substitute for real human heads (used by Southerners for sacrifices), hence *mantou* 饅頭 meaning *mantou* 蠻頭 (the head of a southern barbarian). Another theory is that it is a loan from Turkish *mantu*. In the Song, *mantou* were very popular with students. Apart from snacks and as a staple in the North, they were used throughout the remainder of Chinese history as a sacrificial food at festivals, see Zhu Wei 朱偉, *Kaochi* 考吃 (Philological researches into eating), Zhonghua, 1997, 61–5.

Wudi, Liu An 劉安, ca. 179–122 BC, Prince of Huainan, a Daoist).

Liquor distillation using sorghum (*gaoliang* 高粱), the base of many of China's most famous spirits, became common only during the twelfth century. The Mongols and other northern rulers may not have introduced the firepot (*huoguo* 火鍋), but they probably helped enhance the popularity of lamb and stewed mutton in Beijing and the North with their own versions of old favorites introduced during the Northern Dynasties over a thousand years before.

New World crops made their way into China from the sixteenth century. They were usually brought in by way of Luzon and South China, but in some cases such as tobacco, they also came in through the North via Japan and Korea, or as in the case of maize (*yumi* 玉米), they were probably brought along the Silk Road and possibly also via the Southwest.

Importation during the Ming is often indicated by the character *fan* 番 (also written *fan* 蕃), another word for aboriginal or barbarian (it had been in use in this sense since the Zhou, became widespread in the Song and was extended to foodstuffs in the Ming; see 41.2.1). Just as with the earlier *hu* 胡, it was often attached to an existing plant or fruit name:

fangua 番瓜 (pumpkin, squash), modern *nangua* 南瓜
fanhonghua 番紅花 (saffron crocus), modern *xihonghua* 西紅花
fansuan 番蒜 (mango), modern *manguo* 芒果
fanjiang 番降 (Tanarius major), modern *jiangzhenxiang* 降真香
fanjiao 番椒 (capsicum, red pepper), modern *lajiao* 辣椒
fan longan 番龍眼 (Fiji longan)
fan lizhi 番荔枝 (sugar apple)
fanmai 番麥 (corn, maize), modern *yumi* 玉米
fanmugua 番木瓜 (papaya, also *mugua* 木瓜)
fanmubie 番木鱉 (vomic nut), modern *maqianzi* 馬錢子
fanqie 番茄 (tomato), modern *xihongshi* 西紅柿
fanqing 番青 (wild indigo), modern *huailan* 槐藍
fanshi 番石 (guava), *fan shiliu* 番石榴
fanshu 番薯 (sweet potato), modern *ganshu* 甘薯
fanxieshu 番瀉樹 (senna)
fanya 番鴨 (turkey)
fanyu 番芋 (sweet potato), modern *ganshu* 甘薯

Portuguese or Spanish food was called *fancai* 番菜 and *fancai guan* 番菜館 or *fanguan* 番館 were early words for western-style restaurants. *Fanguan* 番館 was also used for foreign-style hotel (compare the use of *fandian* 飯店 for "hotel"). *Fan* was changed to *xi* 西 in some of these words (e.g., *ximi* 西米, sago). The origin of later imports was also indicated in this way, or with *yang* 洋 or *hai* 海, as in *yangyu* 洋芋 (one of the early names for the white potato). In the southern dialects, *fan* has however often been retained; in Min dialect, for example, *fanjiang* 番姜, *fanke* 番客 and *fanshi* 番柿 are still used for *lajiao* 辣椒 (chili), *Huaqiao* 華僑 (overseas Chinese) and *xihongshi* 西紅柿 (tomato), respectively.

Two other major "characteristics" of Chinese cuisine, the bird's nest and shark's fin (i.e., sword fish), only entered China in the early Ming (they are said to have been brought back from Southeast Asia by the great eunuch Muslim admiral Zheng He).

Some of what until recently were typical dishes or sweets of the North, for example, the *saqima* 薩齊瑪 (薩其馬), are Manchu in origin. The ever-popular *baizhurou* 白煮肉, *shaguo bairou* 沙鍋白肉, *baipianrou* 白片肉 and other boiled pork recipes may have been derived from the Manchu practice of sacrificing pigs before shaman rituals.

Another "typical" but in fact very recent feature of Chinese cooking, monosodium glutamate, was invented in Japan in 1905. It was not until the 1920s and 1930s that it began turning up in every Chinese restaurant.

35.2.4 *Regional Cuisines*

In the later empire, variety was stimulated by gilds and meeting places in the capital and other major urban centers for fellow provincials away from home. They preferred to eat the dishes to which they were accustomed. This led to the greater awareness of regional cuisines, with their own styles and special dishes. Each was continuously developed using ideas and techniques borrowed from other regions (those who belong to the same language group ordinarily have similar food habits, but there is no strict correlation between dialect areas and regional cuisines). The main regional cuisines of today only took on their present form at the end of the empire.

Until the Song only two main regional cuisines were distinguished, the North (*beishi* 北食) and the South (*nanshi* 南食). In the Northern Song there is mention of restaurants in the capital, Bianliang 汴梁 (modern Kaifeng) specializing in both of these as well as in Sichuan dishes (*Chuanfan dian* 川飯店). Some of the dishes in the "*Chuanfan*" eating places had names identical to those still used in Sichuan today, but they cannot have been the same dish. One of the signatures of modern Sichuan cuisine (*Chuancai* 川菜 as it is called today) is the use of the Sichuan indigenous peppercorn (*huajiao* 花椒) mixed with chili to create the famous numbing and hot (*mala* 麻辣) effect. But chili was only imported to the province by Hunanese settlers in the eighteenth century. The first collection of recipes of a regional cuisine is devoted to Sichuan: the *Xingyuan lu* 醒園錄 (late eighteenth century). No dishes using *mala* appear in it. Many of what are today considered typical Sichuanese dishes were only introduced in the nineteenth century (for example, Sichuan hotpot, *huoguo* 火鍋, came in during the Daoguang reign and *Gongbao jiding* 宮保鷄丁 is said to be the invention of the famous late Qing governor of Sichuan, Ding Baozhen 丁寶楨, 1820–86). Indeed, all the elements that we associate with *Chuancai* today only came together at the end of the Qing. National prominence came during WW II when people from the rest of the country moved to the wartime capital of Chongqing.[27]

To take some other examples, duck was popular in Beijing in the Qing, but the dish we know as Peking duck was only invented in the nineteenth century by an ingenious restaurateur who combined existing methods and ingredients (from Nanjing and Shandong) to create the new dish. Oyster sauce, so impor-

[27] The *Chengdu tonglan* 成都通覽 (Guide to Chengdu), which appeared in the last years of the Qing, contains most of the ingredients and dishes which are now associated with *Chuancai*.

tant for preparing vegetables, especially in the Guangdong cuisine, was also first produced in the nineteenth century.

35.2.5   Cooking and Eating Implements

Chopsticks are one of the defining characteristics of Chinese culture. But even they had a long evolution before reaching their present familiar form and use. Since the Neolithic, small sticks or twigs were probably used as tongs (*jia* 梜) to put preheated stones into the cooking pot to heat up the water. Later such chopsticks were used along with spoons as a cooking utensil for taking morsels of food out of the gruel (the original name for chopsticks, *zhu* 箸, 筯 or 櫡 is a cognate of boil, *zhu* 煮). In other words, they were used for serving, not for eating, for which hands were still employed (along with bone spatulas, *bi* 匕, and later with pottery spoons and ladles *shao* 勺). It was only in the Former Han that chopsticks began to come into use for lifting food from small bowls into the mouth. Many centuries were to go by before they replaced the use of hands at the table. Until the Song, chopsticks were mainly used to place morsels of food in the mouth. The spoon was used for eating the staple. During the Ming, chopsticks came into normal use for both purposes and they also gained their modern name of *kuaizi* 筷子 (*zhu* is still used as the word for chopsticks in Fujian and in several of the other southern dialects. It is also retained in Japanese and Korean). Also from the Ming, the characteristic form of square at the head, round and tapered at the tip became more and more common.[28]

---

[28] A small number of bronze chopsticks were reported found in tombs at the Shang capital of Anyang and also some iron ones from Zhou burial sites. However, the most common material was bamboo or wood (ivory and lacquer were also used by the rich). *Zhongguo zhu wenhua daguan* 中國箸文化大觀 (Grand spectacle of Chinese chopstick culture), Liu Yun 劉雲, ed. in chief, Kexue, 1996. This also contains an interesting chapter tracing the development of the spatula and the spoon in China from Neolithic times. See also Xu Jinxiong 許進雄, *Gushi zatan* 古事雜談 (Random chats on old things), Shangwu, 1997, 123–128.

Woks (*guo* 鍋) may have been introduced during the Han, but they were mainly used for drying grains (as Tibetans prepare their roasted or parched barley meal, *rtsampa* [*zanba* 糌粑], to this day). Stir-frying (*chao* 炒) of meats, vegetables and eggs using a *wok* did not overtake boiling, steaming open roasting or deep-frying and other ways of preparing food (such as salting, pickling or fermenting) for many centuries, indeed it only began to become one of the more important cooking methods in the Ming. The sixteenth-century novel *Jin Ping Mei* 金瓶梅 only includes references to five or six stir-fry recipes out of a total of more than one hundred.[29] Even by the eighteenth century, *wok* dishes accounted for only 16% of the recipes in the most famous recipe book of the day, *Suiyuan shidan* 隨園食單 (see below).

All sorts of pictures of people eating and drinking have survived. They show that from the Han to the Qing square or oblong tables, either high or low, were used. Round tables, so typical of Chinese restaurants today, were not common until the late nineteenth century (they can be seen in the illustrations of late Qing novels). The "lazy Susan" (the rotating glass server on top of the table), is an American invention, adopted in Chinese restaurants in San Francisco (along with fortune cookies) and imported to China from there.

Bibliography

The history of Chinese eating habits up to the twentieth century can be traced in the pre-Qin works cited in 35.2, in agricultural treatises (35.1), recipe books and popular encyclopaedias as well as in miscellaneous notes and other literary sources.

After the Han, recipe books are called *shijing* 食經 (food treatises), and after the Tang, *shipu* 食譜 (recipe manuals) or *shidan* 食單 in the later empire. Most have been lost.

---

[29] *Jin Ping Mei fanshi pu* 金瓶梅飯食譜 (Recipes in the *Jin Ping Mei*), Hu Derong 胡德榮, ed., Jingji ribao, 1995.

The treatise on diet written for the Khan by the Muslim court doctor, Husihui 忽思慧, *Yinshan zhengyao* 飲膳正要, 1330, has been translated into English.[30]

Literati gourmands, the four most famous of whom were Su Shi 蘇軾 (1037–1101), Ni Zan 倪瓚 (1301–74), Xu Wei 徐渭 (1521–93) and Yuan Mei 袁枚 (1716–98), exerted a considerable influence on the development of a higher cuisine, especially when they compiled their own cookbooks as did Ni and Yuan.[31]

The main traditional cookbooks are reprinted in the punctuated series, *Zhongguo pengren guji congkan* 中國烹飪古籍叢刊, Shangye, 1984.

For a bibliography of 300 or so *shijing, shipu, nongshu* and other works containing materials on the Chinese diet and recipes in historical times, see the appendix to the largest collection of classical Chinese recipes, *Zhongguo gudian shipu* 中國古典食譜, a monumental collection of 3,249 historical recipes selected from a database of 11,000 compiled by the Chinese Classical Nutrition Research Institute (Zhongguo jingdian yingyang yanjiusuo 中國經典營養研究所).[32] Arrangement is according to main ingredient (e.g., the 484 fish recipes are grouped together and listed by alphabetical order). The earliest recipes are from the Zhou dynasty (as recorded in the *Liji* 禮記), the latest from the end of the Qing. There is a *pinyin* index. A special feature is that ingredients are also indicated by Latin names. The original texts are given, as well as translations into modern Chinese. Unfortunately there is no index by period. For which, see the

---

[30] *Yinshan zhengyao* (Essentials of eating and drinking); *A Soup for the Qan*, Paul D. Buell and Eugene N. Anderson, tr. and introduced, Kegan Paul Intl., 1997.

[31] Ni Zan, *Yunlintang yinshi zhidu ji* 雲林堂飲食制度集 (The food system of Yunlin); Yuan Mei, *Suiyuan shidan* 隨園食單 (The Suiyuan recipes), 1792, Shangye, 1984.

[32] *Zhongguo gudian shipu* (Chinese classical recipes) ed. Liu Daqi 劉大器, Shaanxi Lüyou, 1992.

Zhongguo pengren cidian 中國烹飪辭典.[33] This a convenient listing of some 2,000 recipes by dynasty with the sources indicated (303–410). Over 400 dishes of 31 non-Han peoples are given on pages 544–60. There is a stroke-count index.

Xiong Sizhi 熊四智 collects a large number of the references in poetry to food and drink from earliest times to the Qing arranged by period in *Zhongguo yinshi shiwen dadian* 中國飲食時文大典.[34]

Yan-kit So's *Classic Food of China*, Macmillan, 1992, contains a good introduction and 150 recipes (many of which are those of famous Chinese gourmands).

35.3 Water Control

No plant or human can exist without water. But water is rarely where you need it, when you need it and in the quantities required. Chinese civilization was characterized by small urban elites ruling over large rural populations engaged in intensive agriculture. Therefore one of the great themes of Chinese history is the channelling and control of water. Rivers, lakes and canals were also used as a principal means of transport. Finally, water was one of the main conduits for the rapid spread of disease (chap. 36).

There is a long tradition of Chinese geographical writing on natural river systems and lakes (35.3.1). There is an equally important tradition of practical works on the control of rivers and the digging of canals for many purposes, including irrigation, flood control and transport, both civil and military (35.3.2).

---

[33] *Zhongguo pengren cidian* (Dictionary of Chinese cooking), Xiao Fan 蕭帆, ed. in chief, Shangye, 1992.

[34] *Zhongguo yinshi shiwen dadian* (Dictionary of food and drink in Chinese poetry), Qingdao chubanshe, 1995 (in the series *Zhonghua yinshi wenku* 中華飲食文庫).

35.3.1   Geographical Works on River Systems

The earliest extant work on rivers is the *Shuijing* 水經 (Book of waterways), third century BC. It contains an inventory of 137 rivers and waterways. There is an extensive and important commentary by Li Daoyuan 酈道元 (d. 527) in what amounts to a separate work, the *Shuijingzhu* 水經注, edited ca. AD 515–24. Li greatly expanded the original with detailed comments on 1,252 rivers and waterways, land routes, famous products, antiquities, personalities and dialects, not to speak of providing the world's first inventory of rock art (14.5). He quotes from well over 400 books, many since lost, and he also records from over 300 stone inscriptions; see the introduction to the *H-Y Index* edition.[35] Two later examples of the genre are:

Shuidao tigang 水道提綱 (Essentials of waterways), Ji Zhaonan 齊召南, 1703–68.

Xiyu shuidaoji 西域水道記 (Record of waterways in the Western Regions), Xu Song 徐松 (Xu was the scholar who retrieved the *Song huiyao* 宋會要 from the *Yongle dadian* 永樂大典).

35.3.2   Works on Water Control

Zhongguo shuili shigao 中國水利史稿 contains references to 500 volumes of primary sources on water control.[36] Note also the bibliographies in *SCC*.[37] On the subject of water control in Chinese history, see Mark Elvin's introduction to the bibliography of Japanese studies on the history of water control in

[35] *Shuijingzhu yinde* 水經注引得 (Concordance of names in the *Shuijingzhu*), *H-Y Index* 17.

[36] *Zhongguo shuili shigao* (Draft history of Chinese water control), Shuili dianli kexue yanjiu xiaozu 水利水電科學研究小組, Shuili shuidian kexue yanjiuyuan 水利水電科學研究院, Wuhan, eds., 3 vols., Shuili dianli, 1979 and 1989.

[37] "The Literature on Civil Engineering and Water Conservancy," in *SCC*, vol. IV, Part 3, *Civil Engineering*, CUP, 1971, 323–9; also "Hydrographic books and Descriptions of the Coast," in *SCC*, vol. III, 514–17.

China.[38] This bibliography contains references to 600 Japanese works on water control in its widest sense, covering man-made systems of drainage, irrigation, urban systems of water supply, inland water transport and defence against floods and tidal incursions, together with the related technology and hydrological and hydraulic theories.

The monographs on rivers and canals in the Standard Histories contain important materials on irrigation and water control (22.3).[39] See also, for example:

Wuzhong shuili shu 吳中水利書, Dan E 單鍔 (Northern Song), based on the author's 30 years' of investigations of the water control works in the prefectures of Suzhou, Changzhou and Huzhou, *Congshu jicheng*, 1st series.

Xingshui jingjian 行水金鑑, Fu Zehong 傅澤洪, 1725; describes the river systems of China and their water control works from earliest times to 1721. *Xu Xingshui jingjian* 續行水金鑑 is a continuation compiled by Yu Zhengxie 俞正燮 (1775–1840). It covers the years 1721–1820.

The Yangzi River had on average a bad flood every 10 years between the Han and the end of the Qing.[40] The lower reaches of the Yellow River had six major, and 20 relatively large, changes of course in the last 3,000 years; each was the result of different combinations of natural and man-made causes. The destruction and loss of life was enormous. There is much material in the archives on the efforts made under the Qing to cope with such disasters, some of which has been published. See for example *Qingdai Huanghe honglao dang'an shiliao* 清代黃河洪澇檔案史

---

[38] Mark Elvin, Hiraoka Nishioka, Keiho Tamura and Joan Kwek, *Japanese Studies on the History of Water Control in China: A Selected Bibliography*, the Institute of Advanced Studies, ANU in conjunction with the Center for East Asian Cultural Studies for UNESCO, Tôyô bunko, 1994, 3–35.

[39] *Ershiwushi hequzhi zhushi* 二十五史河渠志注釋 (Monographs on rivers and canals in the 25 Standard Histories), Zhou Kuiyi 周魁一 et al., eds., Zhongguo shudian, 1990.

[40] Until the Six Dynasties, the Yangzi was known simple as the Jiang 江. Thereafter, as the Dajiang 大江 or the Changjiang 長江. See Lyman Van Slyke, *Yangtze: Nature, History and the River*, Addison-Wesley, 1988.

料.[41] This is in the archival series: *Jianghe dang'an shiliao conshu* 江河檔案史料叢書 (Collectanea of historical materials from the archives on rivers), which also includes the archives on the flooding of other rivers, including:

Qingdai Haihe Luanhe honglao dang'an shiliao 清代海河灤河洪澇檔案史料 (Qing dynasty historical materials from the archives on the flooding of the Haihe and Luanhe basins [Hebei]), Zhonghua, 1981. Covers 1736 to 1911.

Qingdai Huaihe honglao dang'an shiliao 清代淮河洪澇檔案史料 (Qing dynasty historical materials from the archives on the flooding of the Huai River), Zhonghua, 1988.

Major Water Control Works

Not a few of the large-scale water control works of ancient China can still be visited today, for example:

Dujiangyan 都江堰 (60 km northwest of Chengdu), 250 BC; built by Li Bing 李冰 in the kingdom of Shu after it had fallen to Qin. The largest irrigation works of ancient China.

Eleven canals were dug in the Warring States extending over a total of 1,000 km. The longest was that designed by Zheng Guo 鄭國 in Shaanxi to the north of Xianyang. Work began in 246 BC. Parts have been excavated.

Under the Sui, hundreds of thousands of people were mobilized to repair old canals and to dig new ones. The resultant system linked the North to the South using the five river systems of the Haihe 海河, Huanghe 黃河, Huaihe 淮河, Changjiang 長江 and Qiantangjiang 錢塘江. The canal was 40 paces wide, willow trees were planted on both sides, and granaries were built along the route as well as 40 imperial rest houses. From the Song the entire system was called the Grand Canal (Da yunhe 大運河). In the Yuan, a 1,000-mile canal was cut from the existing canal at Xuzhou north across Shandong via Jizhou 濟州, Linqing 臨清 and Haijin 海津 to Beijing. By the Ming 4,000,000 piculs of unhusked rice were being shipped up the canal every year under the supervision of 120,000 soldiers. The operation was financed locally as a surcharge on the land tax of which the grain

---

[41] *Qingdai Huanghe honglao dang'an shiliao* (Qing dynasty historical materials from the archives on the flooding of the Yellow River), Zhonghua, 1993.

was the principal payment. The bulk of the grain went to the imperial palace in Beijing and its huge numbers of retainers and dependents as well as a stipend to central government officials. Consult
chap. 5 of Dennis Twitchett, *Financial Administration Under the
T'ang Dynasty*, CUP, 1963; 2nd rev. ed., 1970; *The Ming Tribute Grain
System*, by Hoshi Ayao; Mark Elvin, tr., CCS, Ann Arbor, 1969;
Harold C. Hinton, *The Grain Tribute System of China*, HUP, 1956;
rpnt., 1970.

Quite apart from these huge canal and irrigation works, equally
impressive is the gradual extension of irrigation (using polders,
dykes, storage tanks, drainage channels, and terracing) to individual fields, at first in north China and then, after the Tang, to
the whole of the South.

Societies and Journals

Chûgoku suirishi kenkyû 中國水利史研究, 1970– , annual.

35.4 The Environment and Natural Disasters

35.4.1 Environmental History

Long-term natural processes combined with ever more intensive agriculture, deforestation, water control (and deliberate
acts of destruction at times of war) had huge impacts on the
Chinese environment. Environmental history studies these impacts over time and is concerned with "the interface where specifically human systems meet with other natural systems," as
Mark Elvin puts it in his introduction to the most thorough
collection of studies on various aspects of Chinese environmental history currently available.[42] See also J. R. McNeill's
chapter in the same collection, "China's Environmental His-

[42] *Sediments of Time: Environment and Society in Chinese History*,
Mark Elvin and Ts'ui-jung Liu (Liu Cuirong 劉翠溶) eds., CUP, 1998,
Introduction, 5. This large collection of studies first appeared in Chinese
under the title *Jijian suozhi: Zhongguo huanjingshi lunwenji* 積漸所至:中
國環境史論文集 (Collected essays on the history of the Chinese environment), 2 vols., Zhongyang yanjiuyuan, jingjisuo, 1995.

tory in World Perspective"[43] and Mark Elvin, "Three Thousand Years of Unsustainable Development: China's Environment from Archaic Times to the Present," *East Asian History* 6: 7–46 (1993). Note Georges Metailié, *Consolidated bibliography of the environment in China* (Laboratoire d'Ethnologie, Paris), forthcoming.

Recent years have seen more studies of individual environments or rivers or lakes over long periods of time. Many of these are referred to in the chapters in *Sediments of Time*.

Climate Change

For a comparative view of climate change in history, see

Climate and History: Studies in Past Climates and their Impact on Man, T. M. L. Wigley et al., eds., CUP, 1981.

The Climate of China and Global Climate: Proceedings of the Beijing International Symposium on Climate, Yu Duzheng et al., eds., Springer, 1988.

On climate change in China, the pioneer work (mainly based on data culled from local gazetteers) was done by Zhu Kezhen 竺可楨 who began publishing on the subject in 1925. For a summary of his work, see his "Zhongguo wuqian nian lai qihou biandong de chubu yanjiu 中國五千年來氣候變遷的初步研究" (Preliminary researches on climate change in China over the last 5,000 years, *Kaogu xuebao* (1972.1).

Later research using different methods has tended to confirm Zhu's findings:

Ren Zhenqiu 任振球, "Zhongguo jin wuqian nian lai qihou de yiqangqi ji qi tianwen chengyin tantao 中國近五千年來氣候的异常期及其天文成因探討" (An enquiry into the abnormal periods in China's climate during the last 5,000 years and contributing astronomical factors), *Nongye kaogu* 1 (1986); Wang Zichun 汪子春 and Gao Jian'guo 高建國, "Zhongguo jin erqian wubai nian lai zhiwu chonghua lishi jilu-zhi wuhou yanjiu 中國近二千五百年來植物重花歷史記錄之物候研究" (Phenological researches on historical records relating to the

[43] Elvin and Liu (1998), 31–49.

reflowering of plants in China during the last two thousand five hundred years), *Nongye kaogu* 1 and 2 (1982).

See also:

Zhang Jiacheng and Thomas B. Crowley, "Historical Climate Records in China and the Reconstruction of Past Climates," *Journal of Climate*, 2 (1989).

Zhang Peiyuan, "Extraction of Climate Information from Chinese Historical Writings," *LIC* 14.2: 96–106 (1993).

Brent Hinsch, "Climate Change and History in China," *JAH* 22: 131 59 (1988).

Quanguo qihou bianhua xueshu taolunhui wenji 全國氣候變化學術討論會文集 (Collected essays from the national symposium on climate change), Institute of Meteorology, comp., Kexue, 1981.

Zhongguo lishi shiqi zhiwu yu dongwu bianqian yanjiu 中國歷史時期植物與動物變遷研究 (Shifts of plants and animals in China in historical times), Wen Huanran 文煥然 et al., eds., Chongqing, 1995. Collection of twenty-two research papers on historical biogeography.

Liu Zhaomin 劉昭民, *Zhongguo lishi shang qihou zhi bianqian* 中國歷史上氣候之變遷 (Climate change in Chinese history), Taibei: Shangwu, 1981; rev., 1991.

Tian Wenrong 田文榕, *Zhongguo lishi shiqi dong ban'nian qihou lengnuan bianqian* 中國歷史時期冬半年氣候冷暖變遷 (Semi-annual changes in warm and cold in Chinese historical times of winter). Based on a close study of the changing appearance in different parts of China of different animals and plants.

Tianjia wuxing 田家五行 (Peasant proverbs on climate), Lou Yuanli 婁元禮, end of Yuan, beginning of Ming. Weather tips from around the Taihu 太湖 region.

Landscape, Culture, and Power in Chinese Society, Wen-hsin Yeh and Stephen West, eds., IEAS, UCP, 1997.

Forests

SCC, vol. VI, Part 3, Christian Daniels and Nicholas K. Menzies, *Agro-Industries and Forestry*, CUP, 1996.

35.4.2   Natural Disasters

The sections on omens and anomalies (*wuxing zhi* 五形志) in the Standard Histories and in the local gazetteers report on natural disasters. There are many tables and atlases showing droughts, floods, earthquakes and fires in Chinese history based on these and other sources. Many of the works dealing with climate change and the environment analyze and discuss natural disasters.

For the extremes to which hunger could drive people, see Key Rong Chong (鄭麒來), *Cannibalism in China*, Longwood Academic, 1990 (Chinese translation: *Zhongguo gudai de shiren* 中國古代的食人, Shehui kexue, 1994).

Zhongguo gudai zhongda ziran zaihai he yichang nianbiao zongji 中國古代重大自然災害和异常年表總集 (A comprehensive table of major natural disasters in Chinese ancient history), Song Zhenghai 宋正海 ed., Guangdong jiaoyu, 1992. Arrangement is chronological by types of disaster. The sources used are extensive.

Zhongguo lidai tianzai renhuo biao 中國歷代天災人禍表 (Table of historic natural disasters in China), Chen Gaofu 陳高傅 et al., comps., 2 vols., Shanghai shudian, 1986. Photo-reprint of 1939 original. Comprehensive. Arranged chronologically from 246 BC to 1911. Has appendix of statistical tables and charts.

Zhongguo zaihuang cidian 中國災荒辭典 (Dictionary of Chinese natural disasters), Meng Zhaohua 孟昭華 and Peng Farong 彭法榮 comp., Heilongjiang kexue jishu, 1989. Contains a 150 pages table in appendix listing natural disasters in China from the earliest times to 1911.

Zhongguo jin wubai nian hanlao fenbutu ji 中國近五百年旱澇分布圖集, (Yearly charts of draughts and floods in China during the last 500 years), Zhongyang qixiangju 中央氣象局 (State meterological administration), eds., Kexue, 1981.

Yao Shanyou 姚善友, "The chronological and seasonal distribution of floods and droughts in Chinese history, 206 BC–1911 AD," *HJAS* 6 (1942).

Yao Shanyou 姚善友, "Flood and drought data: *T'u-shu chi-ch'eng* and the *Ch'ing-shih kao*," *HJAS* 8 (1944).

Sichuan liangqian nian hongzai shiliao huibian 四川兩千年洪災史料匯編, Wenwu, 1993. Provides a tabulation of 4,000 records of floods in Sichuan from the Han to the Qing. There are also 288 stone inscriptions recording disasters listed in appendix.

Earthquakes

The first description of an earthquake in Chinese sources is in the *Shijing*: "Xiaoya 小牙," *Shiyue zhijiao* 十月之交. For quakes since then, see collections and atlases such as the following:

Zhongguo lishi qiang dizhen mulu 中國歷史強地震目錄 (Index of major Chinese earthquakes in history), Dizhen, 1995. Records 1,034 major quakes occurring between 2,300 BC and AD 1911.

Zhongguo dizhen lishi ziliao huibian 中國地震歷史資料匯編 (Collected historical materials on Chinese earthquakes), Xie Yushou 謝毓壽 and Cai Meibiao 蔡美彪 comp., 5 vols., Kexue, 1983-7. Vol. 1 covers up to the end of the Yuan, vol. 2, the Ming; and vol. 3, the Qing (2 books).

Zhongguo gujin dizhen zaiqing zonghui 中國古今地震災情總匯 (Comprehensive collection of Chinese ancient and modern earthquake disaster conditions), Lou Baotang 樓寶棠, ed. in chief, Dizhen, 1996. Has a good bibliography.

Qingdai dizhen dang'an shiliao 清代地震檔突史料 (Archival materials on earthquakes in the Qing), Ming-Qing dang'anguan, eds., Zhonghua, 1959.

Xizang dizhen shiliao huibian 西藏地震史料匯編 (Compendium of materials on earthquakes in Tibet), Xizang dang'anguan et al., eds., 2 vols., Xizang renmin, 1982.

Xichang dizhen beilin 西昌地震碑林 (Xichang Earthquake Museum), Sichuan. A unique collection containing 89 stelae and 20 stone rubbings of incsriptions related to the major earthquakes in Wuchang of 1536, 1732, and 1850.

Fires

Zhongguo huozai da dian 中國火災大典 (Grand collection of Chinese fires), 3 vols., Shanghai kexue jishu, 1998.

Journals

Chinese Environmental History Newsletter (biannual), Helen Dunstan, ed., 1994– . School of Asian Studies, University of Sydney, Sydney, Australia. English-language and Chinese-language versions available (E-mail address:helen.dunstan@asia.su.edu.au).

36

Medicine

The bones unearthed from Neolithic burial sites show that people died very young and often of disease. In particular they suffered from mouth diseases and decayed teeth as well as intestinal, gynecological and bone disorders. Infant mortality was high. Women began childbearing at puberty and had reached old age by 30. Average height was quite tall (men between 160 and 170 cm, and women between 150 and 160 cm).

In historical times, a large number of medical texts were written. Many of these are extant. Quite apart from being the main sources for the history of Chinese medicine, they are naturally also the essential sources for the history of Chinese disease. In the later empire, the local gazetteers supply details of the course of historical edpidemics and pandemics.[1]

---

[1] For an overview, see Angela Ki Che Leung, "Diseases of the Premodern Period in China," in the *Cambridge World History of Human Disease*, Kenneth Kiple, ed., CUP, 1993, 354–62; for case studies, see for example, Carol Benedict, *Bubonic Plague in 19th-Century China*, SUP, 1996, which traces an epidemic of bubonic plague that began in Yunnan in the late eighteenth century and spread to the rest of southeast China during the nineteenth century; Kerrie L. MacPherson, "Cholera in China, 1820–1930," and Zhang Yixia and Mark Elvin, "Environment and Tuberculosis in Modern China," chaps. 13 and 14 respectively of *Sediments of Time: Environment and Society in Chinese History*, Mark Elvin and Ts'ui-jung Liu (Liu Cuirong 劉翠溶) eds., CUP, 1998, 487–519; 520–542.

Life expectancy began to increase in the Bronze Age as a result of better living conditions, including settled life in houses which were regularly cleaned; the use of deep wells for clean drinking water; the introduction of regular eating habits (two meals a day); and the use of eating implements which were cleaned after use. Other hygienic practices such as washing and cleaning the teeth; delousing, cutting and combing the hair; and de-waxing the ears also became more widespread.

Archaeology has unearthed traces of the early use of medicinal plants and berries, the evidence for which increases in Shang tombs. An early form of acupuncture had been practiced from the Neolithic using pointed stone implements called *bian* 砭, which were also made of bone, ivory or bamboo. Moxibustion came into use at the same time. The medicinal use of liquor was recognized from at least the Shang.

There are over 500 references to diseases on the oracle bones of which 39 are separate ailments, among which parasites and tooth decay were the most common. The doctor (medicine man) in Shang times was the medium or shaman (*yi* 醫 = *wu* 巫) because it was believed that diseases were caused by vengeful ancestors and thus were cured by sacrifices, praying and exorcism.[2]

The earliest surviving medical texts are those found written on three silk rolls in an early Han tomb at Mawangdui in Hunan. They reflect a more this-worldly, body-centered approach to medicine than that of the Shang. It was an approach that by Zhou times had become the dominant tradition, although exorcism, using charms and spells remained a popular form of "alternative" medicine throughout Chinese dynastic history

[2] Song Zhenhao 宋鎮豪, "Yiliao baojian 醫療保健" (Medicine and health care), chap. 7 of *Xia-Shang shehui shenghuoshi* 夏商社會生活史 (A history of social life in the Xia and Shang periods), Shehui kexue, 1994, rpnt., 1996, 407–51; Shigehisa Kuriyama, "The Imagination of Winds and the Development of the Chinese Conception of the Body," in *Body, Subject & Power in China*, Angela Zito and Tani E. Barlow, eds., UChP, 1994, 23–41.

and the mainstream among some of the non-Han peoples within China. The 13 Mawangdui medical manuscripts include:

Maifa 脈法 (Methods of pulse feeling)

Wushi'er bing fang 五十二病方 (Prescriptions for 52 diseases)

Yin Yang shiyi mai jiujing 陰陽十一 脈灸經 (Eleven meridians for moxibustion of the Yin Yang system)[3]

Zubi shiyi mai jiujing 足臂十一脈灸經 (Eleven meridians for moxibustion of the arms and feet)

There are several thousand transmitted texts of traditional Chinese medicine (classified under subbranch five of the Philosophers' Branch of the Sibu. Below are 12 of the most famous:

Huangdi neijing 皇帝内經 or *Neijing* 内經 for short. Maoshing Ni, *The Yellow Emperor's Classic of Medicine*, Shambhala, 1995. A composite work which reached its present form at the end of the Warring States period in the third century BC, it is divided into two parts, *Suwen* 素問 (Plain questions) and *Zhenjing* 針經 (Classic of acupuncture; renamed *Lingshujing* 靈樞經 [Classic of the numinous pivot] in the eighth century). A third part, the *Taisu* 太素 (Great purity) was

---

[3] Donald J. Harper, *Early Chinese Medical Literature: The Mawangdui Medical Manuscripts*, Kegan Paul International, 1998. F. Nguyen Van, "Les ouvrages de médecine provenant de la tombe numéro trois de Mawangdui," *RBS* 1988/6: 297–301. All these works have been collated and transcribed in *Mawangdui Hanmu yishu jiaoshi* 馬王堆漢墓醫書校釋 (Transcription of the Mawangdui tomb medical works), 2 vols., Chengdu, 1992.

For other early texts, see Gao Dalun 高大倫, *Zhangjia shan Hanjian "maishu" jiaoshi* 張家山漢簡 '脈書' 校釋 (Transcription of the bamboo strip "book on the pulse" from Zhangjia shan), Chengdu, 1992. Parts of a *maishu* (medical book on the pulse) were also discovered at Mawangdui. See also the same author's *Zhangjia shan Hanjian "yinshu"* 張家山漢簡 "引書" (Researches on the bamboo strip *"Yinshu"* from Zhangjia shan), Ba-Shu, 1995. *Yinshu* were Daoist manuals of breathing exercises (*daoyin* 導引, stretching and contracting). A similar, badly damaged work was found at Mawangdui, as was a silk painting of the exercises. The author situates this type of manual in its historical and medical context as well as providing an annotated transcription of the text. There is an index of key terms.

added in the seventh century. See Yamada Kenji, "The formation of the Huang-ti nei-ching," *Acta Asiatica* 36: 67–89 (1979).

The *Shanhaijing* 山海經 (see section 33.1) has references to 132 drugs, including 28 based on plants; 23 on trees; 16 on animal products; 25 on birds; 30 on fish products; and 5 on minerals.

Shennong bencao jing 神農本草經 (Shennong's classic *materia medica*), compiled in the Qin and Han, is the earliest systematic pharmacology to have survived. It contains instructions on how to prescribe, administer and process 365 drugs which are divided according to their toxicity into three categories: superior, common and inferior.

Shang hanlun 傷寒論 (Treatise on febrile diseases caused by cold), Zhang Zhongjing 張仲景 (150–219). English tr.: *Treatise on Febrile Diseases Caused by Cold with 500 Cases*, Luo Xiwen, New World Press, 1985. The cases in this edition are mainly taken from the annals of modern medicine.

Jingui yaolüe 金匱要略 (*Jingui* collection of prescriptions), Zhang Zhongjing 張仲景. English tr.: *Synopsis of Prescriptions of the Golden Chamber with 300 Cases*, Luo Xiwen, New World Press, 1995. The cases are mainly taken from the annals of modern medicine.

Zhenjiu jiayijing 針灸甲乙經 (Classic ABC of acupuncture and moxibustion), Huangfu Mi 皇甫謐 (215–82); collated, punctuated and annotated edition in the series *Zhongyi guji zhengli congshu* 中醫古籍整理叢書 (Collection of re-edited ancient works of Chinese medicine), Renmin weisheng, 1996. Huangfu's work was also called *Huangdi sanbu zhenjiu jiayijing* 黃帝三部針灸甲乙經, or *Jiayijing* 甲乙經 for short.

Maijing 脈經 (Classic of the pulse), Wang Shuhe 王叔和. Drawn from previous works, including *Neijing* 內經. Although pulse feeling was already a well-tried technique of clinical examination, this was the first book-length treatment of the subject.

Beiji qianjin yaofang 備急千金要方 (Prescriptions worth a thousand gold pieces), also called *Qianjin yaofang* 千金要方, Sun Simiao 孫思邈 (581–682), Renmin weisheng, 1955. Also by the same author, *Qianjin yifang* 千金翼方 (Supplement to the Prescriptions worth a thousand gold pieces), Renmin weisheng, 1955.

Sanyin jiyibing zhengfang lun 三因極一病證方論 or 三因極一病源論粹, or simply *Sanyin fang* 三因方 (Prescriptions for the three types of disease), Chen Yan 陳言 (1131–89), Renmin weisheng, 1955.

Xi yuan jilu 洗冤集錄 (Manual of forensic medicine), Song Ci 宋慈 (1186–1249), 1247 (27.5).

Bencao gangmu 本草綱目 (Compendium of *materia medica*), Li Shizhen
李時珍 (1518–93), 1602. The most famous *materia medica* of them
all. It contains 1,892 varieties and 11,096 prescriptions and 1,110 illustrations; collated and punctuated edition, Renmin weisheng, 4 vols.,
1977.

Non-Han peoples had their own traditions of medicine. The
most elaborate is that of Tibetan medicine. It is similar to the
Han tradition but incorporates additional elements of its own
and from Nepal and India. See for example,

Tibetan Medical Thangka of the Four Medical Tantras, Byams-pa 'Phrin-las,
tr. and comp.; Cai Jingfeng, English tr., and annotator, People's Publishing House of Tibet, 1994. This is a reproduction of the illustrations and text of the eighth-century classic *rGyud-bzhi* as written
down in the late seventeenth century.

Medical Terms

In order to find translations of medical and biological terms,
start with Nathan S. Sivin, *Chinese Alchemy: Preliminary Studies*, HUP, 1968, 272–21. Next, try:

*Approaches to Traditional Chinese Medical Literature: Proceedings of an In-
ternational Symposium on Translation Methodologies and Terminolo-
gies*, ed. Paul U. Unschuld, Kluwer, 1989.

*Introductory Readings in Classical Chinese Medicine, Sixty Texts with Vo-
cabulary and Translation, a Guide to Research Aids and a General Glossary*, ed. Paul H. Unschuld, Kluwer, 1988.

The same author's *Learn to Read Chinese*, 2 vols., Paradigm Books, 1994,
complements item 2 above. Vol. 1 has 64 texts with translation into
English; vol. 2, grammatical explanations.

For a dictionary of traditional Chinese medicine, see *Zhongyao
da cidian* 中藥大辭典 (Dictionary of traditional Chinese medicine), Jiangsu xinyiyuan 江蘇新醫院, ed., 2 vols., Shanghai kexue jishu, 1986; 10th prnt., 1996. This has the advantage of identifying *materia medica*, including botanical names, with their
Latin names and also listing alternative Chinese names.

Bibliography

There are a large number of catalogs and guides to the original sources for traditional Chinese medicine. For a union catalog, see the first item in the following list, and for annotated guides to the primary sources, see the remainder:

Quanguo Zhongyi tushu lianhe mulu 全國中醫圖書聯合目錄 (Union catalog of works of traditional Chinese medicine), Zhongyi guji, 1991.

Zhongguo da baike quanshu 中國大百科全書 (The great Chinese encyclopaedia), *Chuantong yixue* 傳統醫學 (Traditional medicine), Zhongguo da baike quanshu, 1992, includes many articles on sources.

Zhongguo yiji tiyao 中國醫籍提要, Jilin renmin, 2 vols., rpnt., 1984.

Zhongguo yiji tongkao 中國醫籍通考, Yan Shiyun 嚴世蕓, ed. in chief, 4 vols., Shanghai Zhongyi xueyuan, 1990–93.

Zhongyi guji zhenben tiyao 中醫古籍珍本提要 (Notes on rare works on Chinese medicine), Yu Ying'ao 余瀛鰲 and Fu Jinghu 傅景華 eds., Zhongyi guji, 1992. Contains abstracts of more than 1,000 rare medical works.

Gujin tushu jicheng, yibu quanlu 古今圖書集成, 醫部全錄 (Complete records of the medical section of the *Tushu jicheng*), 12 vols., Renming weisheng, 1988–91.

For the secondary literature on Chinese medicine, see Nathan S. Sivin, "Science and Medicine in Imperial China: the State of the Field," *JAS* 47.1: 41–90 (1988). See also the same author's "An Introductory [annotated] Bibliography of Traditional Chinese Medicine: Books and Articles in Western Languages," in Sivin, *Medicine, Philosophy and Religion in Ancient China*, Variorum, 1995.

Note the following studies:

Liu Yanchi, *The Essential Book of Traditional Chinese Medicine*, 2 vols., Col. UP, 1988.

Paul U. Unschuld, *Medicine in China: A History of Ideas*, UCP, 1985. An appandix contains 100 pages of translated excerpts from primary sources.

Manfred Pokert, *The Theoretical Foundations of Chinese Medicine: Systems of Correspondence*, MIT Press, 1974.

Lu Gwei-Djen and Joseph Needham, *Celestial Lancets: A History and Rationale of Acupuncture and Moxa*, CUP, 1980. The *SCC* volume on medicine is unfinished.

Vivien Ng, *Madness in Late Imperial China: From Illness to Deviance*, University of Oklahoma Press, 1990.

Li Zhende 李貞德, "Han-Tang zhi jian yishu zhong de shengchang zhi dao 漢唐之間醫書的生廠之道" (Childbirth in late antiquity and early medieval China), *SYSJK* 67.3 (1996), 533—654; "Han-Tang zhi jian qiule yifang shitan—jianlun fuke jian yu xingbie lunshu 漢唐之間醫求了醫方試探-兼論婦科濫觴與性別論述" (Reproductive medicine in late antiquity and early medieval China: gender discourse and the birth of gynecology), *SYSJK* 68.2 (1997), 283-365. Li bases her reconstructions on a close reading of contemporary medical texts.

Note the Zhongguo yishi bowuguan 中國醫史博物館 (Chinese Museum for the History of Medicine) in Zhongguo Zhongyi yanjiu yuan 中國中醫研究 院, Beijing.

Sex

The works below (especially the first six) give some idea of the sources available for tracing Chinese sexual practices and attitudes towards sex. They range from sexual manuals and medical works to erotic art works and pornography:

Zhonghua xingxue guanzhi–Zhonghua xingyixue zhenji jicheng 中華性學 觀止-中華性醫學珍籍集成 (The best of Chinese sexology—a collection of original sources on Chinese traditional medicine sexology), Fen Youping 樊友平 et al., eds., Guangdong renmin, 1997. The first excerpt is from the Mawangdui sex manuscripts;[4] the remainder from 31 medical works.

Robert van Gulik, *Sexual Life in Ancient China: A Preliminary Survey of Chinese Sex and Society from ca. 1500 BC till 1644 AD*, Brill, 1961; 1964. See Charlotte Furth, "Rethinking Van Gulik: sexuality and reproduction in traditional Chinese medicine," in Christina K. Gilmartin et al., *Engendering China: Women, Culture and the State*," HUP, 1994, 125–46.

---

[4] Donald J. Harper, "The Sexual Arts of Ancient China as described in a manuscript of the second century BC," *HJAS* 47.2 (1987), 539–93. See also the chapter on esoteric texts by the same author in *NSECH*, 223–52.

Robert Van Gulik, *Erotic Colour Prints of the Ming Period, with an Essay on Chinese Sex Life from the Han to the Ch'ing Dynasty, 206 BC–AD 1644*, 3 vols., Tokyo, 1951; rpnt., Taibei, n.d.

Howard S. Levy, *Chinese Sex Jokes in Traditional Times*, The Orient Culture Service, 1974.

Howard S. Levy, *Chinese Footbinding: The History of a Curious Erotic Custom*, Rawls, 1966; rpnt. under the title *The Lotus Lovers*, Buffalo, NY: Prometheus, 1992.

Douglas Wile, *Art of the Bedchamber: The Chinese Sexual Yoga Classics Including Women's Solo Meditation Texts*, SUNY Press, 1992. On Daoist sexual practices with translated excerpts.

Liu Dalin 劉達臨, *Zhongguo gudai xing wenhua* 中國古代性文化 (Sex culture of ancient China), Ningxia renmin, 1993; rpnt., 1994. A wide-ranging historical survey, with much quotation of original sources.

Zheng Sili 鄭思禮 offers a Freudian analysis: *Zhongguo xing wenhua, yige qiannian bujie zhi jie* 中國性文化一個千年不解之結 (The sex culture of China: A thousand-year-old enigma), Zhongguo duiwai fanyi, 1994. Argues that sex, not culture or politics, was the original root of Chinese ritual and ethics.

Zhao Guohua 趙國華, *Shengzhi chongbai wenhua lun* 生殖崇拜文化論 (On fertility rites), Shehui kexue, 1990; 3rd prnt., 1996.

Li Ling 李零, *Zhongguo fangshu kao* 中國方術考 (Studies on Chinese divinatory and medical arts), Renmin Zhongguo, 1993, in the series 中國方術概觀.

Xu Jun 徐君 and Yang Hai 楊海, *Jinüshi* 妓女史 (A history of prostitution), Shanghai wenyi, 1995.

Bret Hinsch, *Passions of the Cut Sleeve: The Male Homosexual Tradition in China*, UCP, 1990.

37

Technology and Science

Technology and science were mainly listed under the Philosophers' branch of the *Siku*. The ordering can give some indication of the priority placed on different technologies in late imperial China: the military (chap. 29), agriculture and water control (chap. 35), medicine (chap. 36), astronomy and mathematics (chaps. 5 and 37), divination (chap. 15), architecture and building (37.3), mining and metallurgy (this section) and printing (18.4).

The best introductions to the primary sources for the history of most branches of technology and science in China remain the volumes of *Science and Civilisation in China* written or produced under the editorial direction of Joseph Needham (37.2).

37.1 Introduction

For a supposedly secular and pragmatic society such as that projected by the Confucian self-image, it is striking that many of the most famous Chinese inventions had their origins in magic and the mantic arts. For example, writing probably grew from the requirements of divination (14.5); printing, from the desire to gain merit by multiplying prayers and chants (18.4); magnetism, geology and the navigator's compass grew from the geomancer's arts (37.3); gunpowder for weapons developed from its use for fireworks to scare off evil spirits; astronomy was closely linked to astrology (6.1) and chemistry grew from alchemy.

A good single-volume introduction to Chinese works on science is *Ancient China's Technology and Science*, compiled at the Institute of the History of Natural Science, Chinese Academy of Sciences, FLP, 1983; 1987.[1] It contains 47 short chapters written by many leading historians of science. The guiding principle (found in many works on the history of science and technology) is to collect the great "achievements" with little or no attention paid to the broader intellectual, social or historical context, let alone to the "failures." The overall impression of this and many other works on the history of science is therefore rather like listening to a compact disk of the main themes of classical music divorced from the music itself.

The most comprehensive traditional work on industrial and agrarian arts was Song Yingxing 宋應星, *Tiangong kaiwu* 天工開物 (The Creations of Nature and Man), 1637. It has been translated into English.[2]

Song's chapters cover the growing of grains and their preparation; clothing materials; salt technology; sugar technology; ceramics; bronze casting; ships and carts; iron metallurgy; calcination of stones; vegetable oils and fats; paper making; metallurgy of silver, lead, tin, copper and zinc; military technology; vermilion and ink; yeast; pearls and gems. The principal manufacturing processes for all these are discussed and illustrated.

---

[1] Chinese original: *Zhongguo gudai keji chengjiu* 中國古代科技成就, Qingnian, 1978; rev. ed., 1995; 4th prnt., 1996.

[2] *Tien-kung kai-wu: Chinese Technology in the Seventeenth Century*, E-tu Zen Sun and Sun Shiou-chuan, tr. and annotated, Pennsylvania State Univ. Press, 1966; Dover, 1997. There are several excellent modern editions of the *Tiangong kaiwu*, e.g., Pan Jixing 潘吉星 *Tiangong kaiwu jiaozhu yu yanjiu* 天工開物校注與研究 (*Tiangong kaiwu* annotated and collected with research), Ba-Shu, 1989; rpnt. in the series *Zhongguo gudai keji mingzhu yizhu congshu* 中國古代科技名著譯注叢書 (Collectanea of annotated famous Chinese works on science and technology done into modern Chinese), Shanghai guji, 1993; See also the earlier collection of studies edited by Yabuuchi Kiyoshi 藪内清, *Tenkô kaibutsu no kenkyû* 天工開物の研究, Tokyo, 1953; Chinese tr. under the title *Tiangong kaiwu yanjiu lunwenji*, Shangwu, 1959.

Song concluded his preface by warning "An ambitious scholar will undoubtedly toss this book onto his desk and give it no further thought: it is a work that is in no way concerned with the art of advancement in officialdom," Sun and Sun, p. xiv. He knew what he was saying; despite repeated attempts he himself never succeeded in gaining the *jinshi* degree. Many of China's greatest mathematicians also failed to pass the exams to become officials. It is also worth noting that the reason that we know almost nothing about the inventor of printing with movable type (Bi Sheng 畢昇) is that he was a wealthy craftsman and businessman, not a scholar.[3] Another reason was that his invention had to wait many centuries until it was fully exploited. In the meantime labor intensive woodblock printing continued (section 18.4). The gap between tinker and thinker was a wide one.

The Standard Histories contain monographs covering astronomy-astrology, the calendar, mathematical harmonics and unusual phenomena.[4] Archaeologists in recent decades have turned up invaluable evidence of many ancient technologies.[5]

Many of the scientific classics have been republished photo-lithographically in the multivolume series *Zhongguo kexue jishu*

[3] In 1990, a stele dated 1052 was discovered in Hubei. It appears to be that of Bi Sheng. The designs on the stele suggest that he was a Manichaean. The attribution of the stele to Bi has been challenged, see *CAAD* 2.1 (1997), 69–71.

[4] *Lidai tianwen lüli deng zhi huibian* 歷代天文律曆等志彙編 (Collection of treatises on astronomy and the calendar from the Standard Histories), 10 vols., Zhonghua, 1975–76. See also the references on the history of Chinese astronomy cited at the beginning of chap. 5.

[5] For a collection of articles on archaeology and the history of science, see *Kaoguxue he kejishi* 考古學和科技史 (Archaeology and the history of science and technology), Xia Nai 夏鼐 (1910–85), Kexue, 1979. The articles were written between 1960 and 1976; *Keji kaogu luncong* 科技考古論叢 (Collected papers on the archaeology of science), Wang Zhenduo 王振鐸, Wenwu, 1989; *Keji kaogu luncong* 科技考古論叢 (Collected papers on the archaeology of science), Zhongguo kexue jishu daxue, 1991. Contains 41 papers delivered at the second conference on the archaeology of science.

dianji tonghui 中國科學技術典籍通彙.[6] The advantage of a collection like this is that you have works in the same genre easy to hand. The disadvantage is that there are many scholarly editions of individual texts available that most would prefer to use.

37.2 Science and Civilisation in China

Chinese primary and secondary sources (as well as Western nineteenth-century sources) on all aspects of technology and science are quoted and discussed throughout the volumes of Joseph Needham (1900–95), *Science and Civilisation in China* (*SCC*), as well as in the various works which grew out of it. Needham conceived the series in 1944 and the first volume appeared ten years later in 1954. The first 17 books appeared under his editorial direction. Although some of Needham's basic assumptions have since been questioned (see below, *Evaluation of SCC*) and research has also advanced, *SCC*, vols. 3–7, remain the best starting point:

Vol. I, *Introductory Orientations*, CUP, 1954, rpnt., 1961.

Vol. II, *History of Scientific Thought* (with Wang Ling 王鈴), CUP, 1956.

Vol. III, *Mathematics and the Sciences of the Heavens and the Earth* (with Wang Ling), CUP, 1959. On the earliest of the ten mathematical manuals (*Suanjing shishu* 算經十書) written between the Han and the Tang, the *Zhoubi suanjing* 周髀算經, see Christopher Cullen, *Astronomy and Mathematics in Ancient China: The Zhoubi Suanjing*, CUP, 1996. The most influential of the ten manuals was the Han *Jiuzhang suanshu* 九章算術 (Nine chapters on the mathematical arts). It has been translated many times. On the history of mathematics, in addition to Needham, see Jean-Claude Martzloff, *A History of Chinese Mathematics*, Springer, 1997 (tr. from the French original of 1987), and Li Yan 李儼 and Du Shiran 杜石然, *Chinese Mathematics: A Concise History*, John N. Crossley and Anthony W.-C. Lun, trs., Oxford: Clarendon Press, 1987; issue 16 (1993) of the journal *Extrême-Orient, Ex-*

---

[6] *Zhongguo kexue jishu dianji tonghui* (General collection of Chinese classical works on sciences and technology), Henan jiaoyu, 1993.

trême-Occident, contains articles that give a good indication of the efforts being made to trace the history of Chinese mathematics as it was conceived and used in historical contexts: *Sous les Nombres le Monde: Matériaux pour l'histoire culturelle du nombre en Chine ancienne*.

Vol. IV, *Physics*, Part 1, *Physics and Physical Technology* (with Kenneth Girdwood Robinson and Wang Ling), CUP, 1962.

Vol. IV, Part 2, *Mechanical Engineering* (with Kenneth Robinson and Wang Ling), CUP, 1965.

Vol. IV, Part 3, *Civil Engineering and Nautics* (with Wang Ling and Lu Gwei-Djen [Lu Guizhen 魯桂珍]), CUP, 1971.

Vol. V, *Chemistry and Chemical Technology*, Part 1 (Tsien Tsuen-Hsuin 錢存訓), *Paper and Printing*, CUP, 1985.

Vol. V, Part 2 (with Lu Gwei-Djen), *Spagyrical Discovery and Invention: Magisteries of Gold and Immortality*, CUP, 1974.

Vol. V, Part 3 (with Ho Ping-Yü [He Bingyu 何炳郁] and Lu Gwei-Djen), *Spagyrical Discovery and Invention: Historical Survey, from Cinnabar Elixirs to Synthetic Insulin*, CUP, 1976.

Vol. V, Part 4 (with Ho Ping-Yü, Lu Gwei-Djen and Nathan Sivin), *Spagyrical Discovery and Invention: Apparatus, Theories and Gifts*, CUP, 1980.

Vol. V, Part 5 (with Lu Gwei-Djen), *Spagyrical Discovery and Invention: Historical Physiological Alchemy*, CUP, 1983.

Vol. V, Part 6 (with Robin Yates, Krzysztof Gawlikowski, Edward McEwen, and Wang Ling), *Military Technology: Missiles and Sieges*, CUP, 1995.

Vol. V, Part 7 (with Ho Ping-Yü and Lu Gwei-Djen and Wang Ling), *Military Technology: The Gunpowder Epic*, CUP, 1986.

Vol. V, Part 9, Dieter Kuhn, *Textile Technology: Spinning and Reeling*, CUP, 1986. Note that considerable amounts of Chinese clothing have survived. Some was even found in Warring States tombs. For a comprehensive introduction, see *Zhongguo fuzhuangshi* 中國服裝史 (A history of Chinese clothing), Huang Nengfu 黃能馥, ed. in chief, Lüyou, 1995; rpnt., 1996; Zhou Xun 周汛 and Gao Chunming 高春明, *5,000 Years of Chinese Costumes*, HK: Shangwu, 1987; 2nd rpnt., 1988 (tr. of *Zhongguo fushi wuqian nian* 中國服飾五千年, Xuelin and HK: Shangwu 1984); Zhongguo yiguan fushi dacidian 中國衣冠服飾大辭典 (Dictionary of Chinese clothing and costumes), Zhou Xun 周汛, comp., Shanghai cishi, 1996. Verity Wilson, *Chinese Dress*, Victoria and Albert Museum, 1986. For scholarly catalogs of exhibitions of Qing offical clothing, see John E. Vollmer, *Decoding Dragons: Status Garments in Ch'ing Dynasty China*, Museum of Art, Univ. of Oregon, 1980; Julia White & Emma C. Bunker, *Adornment for Eternity: Status and Rank in Chinese Ornament*, Denver and Hong Kong, 1994.

Vol. V, Part 10, Dieter Kuhn, *Textile Technology: Weaving*, CUP, forthcoming.

Vol. V, Part 13, Peter Golas, *Mining*, CUP, 1998.

Vol. VI, *Biology and Biological Technology*, Part 1 (with Lu Gwei-Djen and Huang Hsing-Tsung (Huang Xingzong 黃興宗]), *Botany*, CUP, 1986.

Vol. VI, Part 2, Francesca Bray, *Agriculture*, CUP, 1984.

Vol. VI, Part 3, Christian Daniels and Nicholas K. Menzies, *Agro-Industries and Forestry*, CUP, 1996.

Vol. VI, Part 5, Huang Hsing-Tsung, *Biochemical Technology*, CUP, 1999.

Vol. VII, Part I, *Language and Logic in Traditional China*, Christoph Harbsmeier, CUP, 1998.

See also:

Joseph Needham, *The Development of Iron and Steel Technology in China*, Newcomen Society, 1958 (Compare with Donald B. Wagner, *Iron and Steel in Ancient China*, Brill, 1993).

Lu Gwei-Djen and Joseph Needham, *Celestial Lancets: A History and Rationale of Acupuncture and Moxa*, CUP, 1980.

Joseph Needham, Wang Ling and Derek Price, *Heavenly Clockwork: The Great Astronomical Clocks of Medieval China—A Missing Link in Horological Research*, CUP, 1960; rev., ed. 1986.

Joseph Needham, Lu Gwei-Djen, John H. Combridge and John S. Major, *The Hall of Heavenly Records: Korean Astronomical Instruments, 1380–1780*, CUP, 1986.

Explorations in the History of Science and Technology in China, comp. in honour of the 80th birthday of Dr. Joseph Needham, Shanghai Classics Publishing House, 1983.

Evaluation of SCC

At its best *SCC* is a cornucopia. Sometimes the quality or the detail varies. A reflection no doubt of the different approaches taken by the many scholars who contributed or wrote volumes in the series. Over the years the international scholarly community has had nothing but praise for the industry and insights displayed by Needham and his team of collaborators. He has been especially honored in China for drawing attention to some of the greatest achievements of Chinese civilization, hitherto (apart from the "four great discoveries" of paper, printing, the magnetic compass and gunpowder) somewhat overlooked. However, while nobody has doubted the importance of his work, several have questioned his teleological approach as embodied in the so-called "Needham question:" Why did no scientific and technical revolution occur in China, despite its notable early record in technology and science? Nowadays the view is increasingly that the emergence of modern science in Europe was exceptional and depended on particular historical circumstances there. So its non-emergence elsewhere hardly needs explanation.[7]

Needham has also been criticized for his over reliance on nineteenth-century missionary and Treaty-Port scholarship and for his anachronistic readings of Chinese texts, apparently based on his conviction that technology is the practical application of science, and therefore if the Chinese were good at making something there must have been a scientific theory to underpin it.[8]

Another weakness is his tendency to believe that because something was invented in China it must have contributed to

---

[7] Nathan Sivin examines the question and cites much of the literature in his "Why the Scientific Revolution Did Not Take Place in China—or Didn't It?" in *Explorations in the History of Science and Technology in China* (1983), 89–106; rpnt. in Sivin (1995). Francesca Bray, "Technology and Culture in Chinese History: An Introduction," *Chinese Science* 12: 13–17 (1995).

[8] Francesca Bray, "Eloge," *ISIS* 87.2: 312–17 (1996).

the similar later discovery in Europe (the reverse is not given such easy acceptance).[9]

Needham always intended that his final volume would take up the "Needham question," whose answer he felt lay in the influence of officialdom (bureaucratic feudalism). Vol. 7, part 2 of *SCC* (the final volume in the originally planned series) will contain Needham's "General Conclusions," together with other writings by him constituting his final reflections on the project.[10] Work was begun on the volume by Derk Bodde, who eventually published his findings as a separate book: *Chinese Thought, Society and Science: Intellectual and Social Background of Science and Technology in Pre-modern China*, UHP, 1991.

The Needham History of Science Project is continuing at the Needham Research Institute, Robinson College, Cambridge University.

Journals

Chinese Science, vols. 1–10, irregular; from vol. 11 (1993–94, annual). Edited at the University of California at Los Angeles.

Newsletter for the History of Chinese Science, 1988– , annual.

Zhongguo keji shiliao 中國科技史料 (1980– , quarterly), Beijing.

Ziran kexueshi yanjiu 自然科學史研究 (1992– , quarterly), Beijing. From 1958–66, the title was *Kexueshi jikan* 科學史季刊. The present title was adopted in 1967 (annual through 1985; quarterly since 1986).

Bibliography

Zhongguo gudai kejishi lunwen suoyin 中國古代科技史論文索引, Yan Dunjie 嚴敦傑 ed. in chief, Jiangsu kexue jishu, 1986. A bibliography of articles in Chinese on the history of science and technology in

[9] For balanced assessments, see Nathan Sivin and Shigeru Nakayama, eds., *Chinese Science: Explorations of an Ancient Tradition*, MIT, 1973, and Mark Elvin, ed., "The Work of Joseph Needham: A Symposium," *Past and Present* 87: 17–53 (1980).

[10] Needham's overall views as expressed in articles and speeches were published under the title *The Grand Titration: Science and Society in the East and the West*, George Allen and Unwin, 1969.

China written between 1900 and 1982 arranged by subject and by period.

Chinese Studies in the History and Philosophy of Science and Technology, Fan Dainian and Robert S. Cohen, eds. Kluwer, 1996. A broad selection of articles.

For a collection of the articles on science of one of the leading Chinese archaeologists, Xia Nai, written 1960–76, see *Kaoguxue he kejishi* 考古學和科技史 (Archaeology and the history of science and technology), Xia Nai 夏鼐, Kexue, 1979.

For an annotated bibliography of works in English, see Nathan Sivin, *Science in Ancient China: Researches and Reflections*, Variorum, 1995, IX, 1–17.

Note that the annual *Revue bibliographique de sinologie* (11.1) includes a section on Science and Technology.

37.3 Architecture and Geomancy

For the architecture of specific periods, see Part V. For general outlines see the following:

Liang Ssu-ch'eng (Liang Sicheng 梁思成), *A Pictorial History of Chinese Architecture*, Wilma Fairbank, ed., MIT Press, 1984. English version of Chinese original. Based on photographs taken by the author, the pioneer of Chinese architectural history, in the late 1920s and 1930s. The story of his life (and that of his wife Lin Whei-yin), and the conditions under which they worked on Chinese architecture are told in Wilma Fairbank, *Liang and Lin: Partners in Exploring China's Architectural Past*, Univ. of Pennsylvania Press, 1994.

Chinese Academy of Architecture, eds., *Ancient Chinese Architecture*, China Building Industry Press, 1982.

Ronald G. Knapp, *China's Traditional Rural Architecture*, UHP, 1986.

Ronald G. Knapp, *China's Vernacular Architecture: House Form and Culture*, UHP, 1989.

Zhongguo meishu quanji 中國美術全集, *Jianzhu yishu pian* 建築藝術篇, Jiangong, 6 vols., 1987–88. The same publisher also put out a lavish 10-vol. series: *Zhongguo gu jianzhu daxi* 中國古建築大系 (A grand collection of ancient Chinese architecture), 1993.

For an outline of Chinese city planning, see:

Nancy Shatzman Steinhardt, *Chinese Imperial City Planning*, UHP, 1990.

He Yeju 賀業鉅, *Zhongguo gudai chengshi guihuashi* 中國古代城市規劃史 (A history of ancient Chinese city planning), Zhongguo jianzhu gongye, 1996.

There is a large literature on palace construction and expenditures (not cited here) and various regulations of the Qing Board of Works are extant (50.6.2, *Zeli*). There are also more specialized texts on boat building and garden construction. Some of the basic texts used by Chinese architects have survived and several have been translated:

Yingzao fashi 營造法式 (Treatise on architectural methods), Li Jie 李誡 (? –1110), completed in 1100; prnt., 1103; rpnt., 1145; Wanyou wenku, 1925; Shangwu, 1953. The work of the architectural historian Liang Sicheng 梁思成 on this important classic has been published: *Yingzao fashi zhushi* 營造法式註釋 (Commentaries and notes on the *Yingzao fashi*), vol. 1, Zhongguo jianzhu gongye, 1983.

Frank J. Swetz, *The Sea Island Mathematical Manual, AD 263: Surveying and Mathematics in Ancient China*, Pennsylvania State Univ. Press, 1992.

Klaas Ruitenbeek, *Carpentry and Building in Late Imperial China: A Study of the 15th-Century Carpenter's Manual*, Lu Ban jing [魯班經], Brill, 1993.

Geomancy

Fengshui 風水 or *kanyu* 堪輿 (usually translated as geomancy) played an important role in Chinese architecture as a system of rules for siting man-made structures in the landscape (typically cities, tombs and buildings of all kinds). To assist him in his task, the diviner used a schematic representation of heaven and earth with a number of circles indicating the 24 directions (also used on Chinese navigating compasses when these evolved in the Tang and Song).[11]

---

[11] See *SCC*, vol. 4, part 1, *Physics*, 249 334; for additional material on the Han diviner's board set against Han ideas of cosmology, see Michael Loewe, *Ways to Paradise: The Chinese Quest for Immortality*, 1979; rpnt., SMC, 1994; on the geomancer's compass, see de Groot, J.J.M., *The Relig-*

Footnote continued on next page

The 24 compass-points (*ershisi fang* 二十四方, *ershisi wei* 二十四位, *ershisi xiang* 二十四向, or, in geomantic parlance, *ershisi shan* 二十四山) were set at 15° intervals (see 4.4, note 14). The geomantic compass (*luopan* 羅盤) evolved from the Han diviner's board (*shi* 式, 拭). For an architectural study of geomancy see:

Zhongguo gudai fengshui yu jianzhu xuanzhi 中國古代風水與建築選址 (Ancient Chinese *fengshui* and the choice of site for buildings), Yi Ding 一丁 et al., Hebei kexue jishu, 1995.

Gardens

There are many studies of the traditional Chinese garden; for three different approaches, see

Maggie Keswick, *The Chinese Garden: History, Art and Architecture*, with contributions and conclusion by Charles Jencks, London: Academy Editions, 1978; New York, St. Martin's Press, 1986. Also contains a list of selected gardens open to the visitor.

Craig Clunas, *Fruitful Sites: Garden Culture in Ming Dynasty China*, Reaktion, 1996. The work of a historian interested in the social and economic background.

Rolf A. Stein, *The World in Miniature: Container Gardens and Dwellings in Far Eastern Religious Thought*, tr. from the French original (1987) by Phyllis Brooks, SUP, 1990. Sums up a lifetime's reflection on the cosmological meanings of miniature gardens (Part I); dwelling places (Part II); and the world and architecture in religious thought (Part III).

---

ious System of China, vol. 3, bk. 1, part III, Chap. XII, 935–1056. See also Stephan Feuchtwang, *An Anthropological Analysis of Chinese Geomancy*, Vientiane: Vithagana, 1974.

38

Painting, Calligraphy
and Music

In addition to their aesthetic appeal, Chinese painting (and the other decorative and useful arts) can also provide the historian unique clues, and often evidence, of behavior, lifestyles, beliefs and attitudes at every period of Chinese history.[1] This is particularly true of the earlier dynasties for which other sources are scarce or nonexistent.[2] It goes without saying that the arts also provide vital evidence for other fields, such as the history of religion.

The present chapter introduces a number of reference works and studies related to painting and calligraphy, including forgeries, biographies, bibliography, mu-

---

[1] See the grouped entries on Chinese art in *The Grove Dictionary of Art*, Jane Turner, ed., Macmillan, 1997, vol. 6, 607–925; vol. 7, 1–162. *The British Museum Book of Chinese Art*, Jessica Rawson, ed., British Museum, 1992, has good, select bibliographies, including ones on jades and bronzes; painting, calligraphy and printing; sculpture; the decorative arts (silk and dress; lacquer; ivory carving; jade; gold, silver and jewelry; polychrome, cloisonné and enamelled wares; glass; snuff bottles; and miscellaneous); ceramics; and trade in art objects.

[2] See, for example, Wu Hung (Wu Hong 巫鴻), *The Wu Liang Shrine: The Ideology of Early Chinese Pictorial Art*, SUP, 1989. Compare this with the pioneering work of Edouard Chavannes, *La sculpture sur pierre en Chine au temps des deux dynasties Han*, Leroux, 1893; and Chavannes, *Mission archaéologique en Chine septontrionale*, 4 vols., Leroux, 1910–15. See also M. J. Powers, *Art and Political Expression in Early China*, YUP, 1991.

seums, exhibition catalogs and collections of illustrations, and Western painters and photographers. It concludes with a brief section on music (38.2).

38.1 Painting and Calligraphy

A number of universities have built up photographic data banks of Chinese painting (for example, at the Tôbunken or Princeton). Based on these, illustrated catalogs in the form of inventories have now been published. The illustrations are small but these works graphically index many thousands of paintings. They make the most convenient way of finding out what paintings survive of a particular painter or from a given period. Within China itself, there are catalogs of the main paintings and calligraphic works held in Chinese collections[3] and in addition, there is a comprehensive, illustrated catalog of all main frescoes in China.[4]

To find a painting held in a collection outside China first, consult Suzuki Kei 鈴木敬, *Chûgoku kaiga sôgô zuroku* 中國繪畫總合圖錄. The text is in Japanese and English.[5]

---

[3] *Zhongguo gudai shuhua tumu* 中國古代書畫圖目 (Illustrated Catalog of Selected Works of Ancient Chinese Painting and Calligraphy), 16 vols., Wenwu, 1986–97.

[4] *Zhongguo bihua quanji* 中國壁畫全集 (Comprehensive collection of Chinese frescoes), 34 vols., Tianjin renmin meishu and other provincial art publishers, 1989– .

[5] Suzuki Kei, *Chûgoku kaiga sôgô zuroku* (Comprehensive Illustrated Catalog of Chinese Paintings), 5 vols., Tokyo daigaku, 1982–83; rev. ed., 1998. Vol. 1 covers Chinese paintings in America and Canada; vol. 2, Southeast Asia and Europe; vols. 3 and 4, Japan; vol. 5 is an index. See also James Cahill, *An Index of Early Chinese Painters and Paintings: T'ang, Sung and Yuan*, UCP, 1980. This does not include frescoes. See also the lists in vols. 2 and 7 of Osvald Sirén's *Chinese Painting: Leading Masters and Principles*, Lund Humphries, 1958; New York: Hacker Art Books Inc., 1973. James Cahill's studies on Chinese painting from the thirteenth to the seventeenth centuries are the best introductions to these paintings: *Hills Beyond a River: Chinese Painting of the Yuan Dy-*

Footnote continued on next page

References such as *Zhongguo gudai shuhua tumu* or Suzuki, although relatively comprehensive, are not exhaustive. If you are particularly interested in the works of a painter, you should double-check with individual collections.

Many of the texts of Chinese connoisseurship have been translated into English:

W. R. B. Acker, *Some T'ang and Pre-T'ang Texts on Chinese Painting*, 2 vols., Brill, 1954–74

Susan Bush, *The Chinese Literati on Painting: Su Shih (1037–1101) to Tung Ch'i-ch'ang (1555–1636)*, HUP, 1971.

Susan Bush and Hsio-yen Shih, *Early Chinese Texts on Painting*, HUP, 1985.

Until recently the study of Chinese painting concentrated on aesthetic analysis. Now, its social and economic history is beginning to attract more attention. See, for example, Craig Clunas, *Art in China*, OUP, 1997 or Patricia Ebrey, *The Cambridge Illustrated History of China*, CUP, 1996.[6]

---

nasty, *1279–1368*, Weatherhill, 1976; *Parting at the Shore: Painting of the Early and Middle Ming Dynasty, 1368–1580*, Univ. Art Museum, Berkeley, 1978; *The Restless Landscape: Chinese Painting of the Late Ming Period*, Weatherhill, 1971; *The Compelling Image: Nature and Style in Seventeenth-Century Chinese Painting*, HUP, 1982.

[6] James Cahill, *The Painter's Practice: How Artists Lived and Worked in Traditional China*, Col. UP, 1994; Chu-tsing Li, James C. Y. Watt, *The Chinese Scholar's Studio: Artistic Life in the Late Ming Period*, Thames and Hudson and Asia Society Galleries, 1987; Chu-tsing Li et al., eds., *Artists and Patrons: Some Social and Economic Aspects of Chinese Painting*, Nelson-Atkins Museum of Art, Univ. Press of Kansas and the UWP, 1989 which includes Kuo, Jason Chi-sheng, "Hui-chou Merchants as Art Patrons in the Late Sixteenth and Early Eventeenth Centuries," 177–88; *Shadows of Mt. Huang: Chinese Painting and Printing of the Anhui School*, James Cahill, ed., Berkeley: University Art Museum, 1981; *Art and Power in Japan and China*, special number of *Asian Cultural Studies*, International Christian Univ. publications III-A, Tokyo, 1989.

Calligraphy

On the early history of Chinese writing, including its close connections to divination, see chaps. 14–17. In the empire, calligraphy contined to be highly prized. Indeed, it was regarded as more important than painting. Every child who went to school (and many who did not) learned to practice calligraphy by studying the works of famous calligraphers (1.3.2). On the importance of models of calligraphy carved on stone, see note 21, section 17.3. There are numerous introductions to calligraphy and reference works available, for example, Yuho Tseng, *A History of Chinese Calligraphy*, HKCUP, 1993. The *Sho no uchû* 書宇宙 collection is notable for the high quality of the photographs, including close-ups and analytical drawings. It also includes examples of many of the latest inscriptional and manuscript discoveries.[7]

Forgery

For a good introduction to the key question of forgery in Chinese calligraphy and painting, see

Xu Bangda 徐邦達, *Gu shuhua wei'e kaobian* 古書畫偽訛考辨 (Research into the forgery of ancient calligraphy and painting), 4 vols., Jiangsu guji, 1984. A carefully argued, scholarly work. Vols. 1–2, calligraphy; vol. 3, painting; vol. 4 (black and white illustrations).

Zhongguo gujin shuhua zhenwei tudian 中國古今書畫真偽圖典 (Genuine and fake illustrated dictionary of Chinese calligraphy and painting in every dynasty), Yang Renkai 楊仁愷, ed. in chief, Liaoning huabao, 1997.

Biographies

The standard English-language biographical dictionaries include painters, for example, vol. 4 of *Sung Biographies* deals with the main painters of the Song (3.4). For a specialized biographical dictionary, see

Zhongguo meishujia renming cidian 中國美術家人名辭典 (Dictionary of Chinese historical personalities in the arts), Yu Jianhua 俞劍華, comp., Shanghai renmin meishu, 1981; rev., 1987, 7th prnt., 1996. Contains biographies of 13,000 painters. Note that it was not un-

---

[7] *Sho no uchû* (Universe of calligraphy), 24 vols., Nigensha, 1996–98.

common for a single Chinese painter to use dozens of alternative names. If you cannot find an alternative name in this dictionary, which includes an appendix of them, then there is also a separate publication.[8]

There are also indexes and biographical dictionaries for specific periods—for example, *Tang-Song huajia renming cidian* 唐宋畫家人名辭典 (Personal name dictionary of Tang and Song painters), Zhu Zhuyu 朱鑄禹, comp., Zhongguo gudian yishu, 1958; *Song, Liao, Jin huajia shiliao* 宋遼金畫家史料 (Historical materials on Song, Liao and Jin painters), Chen Gaohua 陳高華, comp., Wenwu, 1984.

Bibliography

Jerome Silbergeld, "Chinese Painting Studies in the West," *JAS* 46.4: 849-97 (1987).

Museums

The imperial collections of paintings and art objects are held in the Palace Museums in Beijing and in Taibei. Numerous catalogs of the holdings are available.[9] The third largest portion of the old palace collections is held by the Liaoning Museum thanks to the scrolls brought to Shenyang by the last Qing Emperor, Pu Yi.

Apart from the Palace Museums, the best museums are the National Museum of Chinese History in Beijing (8.2, *Illustrations*); the new Shanghai Museum (opened in 1996); the various museums in Xi'an (46.4.1) and the provincial museums in He-

---

[8] *Zhongguo lidai shuhua zhuanke jia zihao suoyin* 中國歷代書畫篆刻家字號索引, Shang Chengzuo 商承祚 and Huang Hua 黃華 comps., 2 vols., Renmin meishu, 1960. This index contains alternative names of 16,000 painters and seal cutters from the Qin and Han periods to the Republic, and also gives birth and death dates, native place and so on. It has an index of names. See also, Nancy N. Seymour, *Index Dictionary of Chinese Artists, Collectors and Connoisseurs*, Scarecrow, 1988, which contains entries on over 5,000 persons from the Tang onward.

[9] *Gugong wenwu dadian* 故宮文物大典 (Antiques Canon: the Palace Museum), 4 folio vols., Fujian renmin, Jiangxi renmin, Zhejiang jiaoyu and Zijincheng, 1994; *Gugong shuhua tulu* 故宮書畫圖錄 (Illustrated Catalog of the Palace Museum), 15 vols., Taibei: Guoli gugong bowuyuan, 1989-95.

nan, Shanxi, Gansu, Liaoning, Hubei and Hunan. Several major museums have recently been rebuilt (Shaanxi, Shanghai and Henan) or are rebuilding (Liaoning). There is a series of large-scale, beautifully illustrated introductions to some of these collections. It is particularly strong on archaeological findings.[10] There are now also numerous museums of single archaeological sites well worth the detour, for example, the museum of the first site of the Western Zhou fief of Yan (Beijing) at Liulihe 琉璃河 or of the tomb of the prince of Nan-Yue (Nam-Viêt) in Guangzhou (44.4.1).

For a detailed, comprehensive guide to the museums of China, both large and small (including those in Taiwan, Hong Kong and Macao), many of which are of great interest to the historian, see *Zhongguo bowuguan zhi* 中國博物館志.[11]

Catalogs and Collections of Illustrations

Some of the most interesting writing on the Chinese arts appears not only in books and journals, but also in monographic catalogs of collections or exhibitions, which often have sumptuous illustrations. To take but four examples of major exhibition catalogs of Chinese art:

Mysteries of Ancient China: New Discoveries from the Early Dynasties, Jessica Rawson, ed., British Museum, 1996.

Possessing the Past: Treasures from the National Palace Museum (Taipei), Wen C. Fong and James C. Y. Watt, eds., Metropolitan Museum and the National Palace Museum, 1996.

The Chinese Exhibition: A Commemorative Catalogue of the International Exhibition of Chinese Art, Royal Academy of Arts, November 1935–

---

[10] *Zhongguo bowuguan* 中國博物館 (China's museums), 14 vols., Wenwu and Kodansha, 1991–94.

[11] *Zhongguo bowuguan zhi*, Zhongguo bowuguan xuehui 中國博物館學會 (Chinese Society of Museums), eds., Huaxia chubanshe, 1995. Arrangement is by province. Information on each museum includes details of the collections, main publications and serials, hours of opening, and average number of visitors per year. An English translation is given for each museum and there is an English index.

March 1936, Faber, 1936. This was the most comprehensive exhibition of Chinese art ever held outside of China before World War II.

A Descriptive Catalogue of the Chinese Collection, now exhibiting at St George's Place, Hyde Park Corner, London with condensed accounts of the genius, government, history, literature, agriculture, arts, trade, manners, customs & social life of the people of the Celestial Empire, William B. Langdon, ed., London, 1842. This is the first catalog of a Chinese exposition held in the West.

Old Chinese books were often illustrated and in some cases scholars collected illustrations of interesting artifacts, most notably Wang Qi 王圻 (*jinshi*, 1565), *Sancai tuhui* 三才圖會.[12] This contains maps, plans and sketches of everyday utensils and portraits.

For an enormous modern collection of illustrations of Chinese painting and artifacts, see *Zhongguo meishu quanji* 中國美術全集. It contains 15,000 plates in 59 folio volumes (vol. 60 is an index).[13] The first 21 volumes cover all forms of painting. Next come 13 volumes of sculpture, followed by 12 volumes of handicrafts and six volumes each of architecture and calligraphy and seals. Each volume has many hundreds of excellent color plates as well as smaller "inventory-style" black and white photographs with notes. The entire collection is available on CD-ROM. More managable is the sumptuous "dictionary" of 5,500 mainly recently excavated art objects, edited by the Wenwuju 文物局 (Cultural Relics Bureau).[14] Each treasure has a color photograph and a brief description. Arrangement is by mate-

[12] *Sancai tuhui* (Assembled pictures of the three realms [i.e., heaven, earth and man]), 1607; 3 vols., Shanghai guji, 1988.

[13] *Zhongguo meishu quanji* (Complete collection of Chinese arts), 60 vols., Wenwu and many other publishers, including Renmin meishu, Gongyi meishu, Zhongguo jianzhu gongye, 1984– . This collection is eventually planned to expand to 400 vols.

[14] *Zhongguo wenwu jinghua da cidian* 中國文物精華大全 (The complete collection of the best of Chinese cultural relics), 4 vols., Wenwu and HK: Shangwu, 1993–95; Cishu, 1995–96 (with the title 中國文物精華大辭典).

rial; for example, volume one contains annotated photographs of metal, silver, jade and stone objects.

Western Painters and Photographers

From the eighteenth century, there were several excellent missionary painters at the Qing court, as well as artists attached as recorders to the first embassies to China (42.3.1). The first photographs to have survived date from the 1850s (42.3.2).

38.2 Music

In Chinese music as in other fields, many features that today seem typical, for example, Peking opera or the *erhu* 二胡 (two-stringed fiddle), only took their present form or prominence, at the very end of the imperial period (Peking opera) or at the beginning of the twentieth century (the *erhu*).

The earliest musical instruments so far discovered are Neolithic whistles used for hunting: some were made of animal bone (*gushao* 骨哨, dated ca. 6000 BC from Hemudu), and some were globular pottery flutes (*taoxun* 陶塤, ca. 5000 BC from Yangshao sites). Sixteen seven-hole flutes (*qikong gudi* 七孔骨笛), made of bone and dating from the sixth millennium BC, were discovered in 1987 at a Yangshao site (Jiahu 賈湖, Wuyang 舞陽 in Henan). They produced a heptatonic scale and may have been used for dancing as well as for hunting. Neolithic chime bells as well as stone chimes from Anyang have been unearthed. Bronze chime bells were a characteristic feature of Chinese music for 2,000 years. Several huge sets dating from the Warring States have been unearthed in recent years. They fell out of use at the end of the Bronze Age.[15]

---

[15] Li Chunyi 李純一, *Zhongguo shanggu yueqi zongbian* 中國上古樂器綜編 (An overall survey of ancient Chinese musical instruments), Wenwu, 1996; Chen Cheng-yih (Cheng Zhenyi 程貞一), "Early Chinese Work on Acoustics," in *Early Chinese Work in Natural Science*, HKU Press, 1996, 19–112; Lothar von Falkenhausen, *Suspended Music: Chime Bells in the Culture of Bronze Age China*, UCP, 1993.

Seventeen of the Standard Histories have monographs on music.[16] Most of the encyclopaedias also have sections on it (chap. 29).

For a general introduction to the history of Chinese music, use the articles in the standard reference, *The New Grove Dictionary of Music and Musicians*, vol. 4, Macmillan, 1980, 245–83.

On the discoverer of equal temperament tuning, Zhu Zaiyu 朱載堉 (1536–1611), see Kenneth Robinson, *A Critical Study of Chu Tsai-yu's Contribution to Equal Temperament in Chinese Music*, Steiner, 1980.

For a collection of essays which examine the social uses of music in the later empire, see *Harmony and Counterpoint: Ritual Music in Chinese Context*, Bell Yung, Evelyn S. Rawski, and Rubie S. Watson, eds., SUP, 1996.

Colin P. Mackerras, *The Rise of the Peking Opera, 1770–1870*, Clarendon Press, 1972, is a study broader than the title might suggest. It touches on many aspects of the social and cultural life of the later empire.

Recordings

Only two pre-Song musical sources are extant in China today. The earlier of the two is a piece for the seven-string zither (*qin* 琴) ascribed to the sixth century.[17] The other is a set of 25 melodies for the four-string lute (*pipa* 琵琶). It was found among the Dunhuang manuscripts and has been dated to the early tenth century. Attempts have been made to reconstruct the sounds of these. Previous literature on the melodies plus new trancriptions and recordings can be found in *Dunhuang guyue* 敦煌古樂.[18] Echoes of the sonorous and slow rhythms of Tang court music and dances can be heard in Japanese *Gagaku* 雅樂 (imperial court music), which was based on Tang music. See Laurence Picken et al., *Music from the Tang Court*, 7 vols., CUP, 1981–97.

---

[16] See Michael Loewe, "The Office of Music, c. 114–7 BC," *BSOAS* 36 (1973), 340–51; Denis Twitchett, "A Note on the 'Monograph on Music' in *Chiu T'ang shu*," *AM*, 3rd series, 3.1: 51–62 (1990).

[17] Robert Van Gulik, *The Lore of the Chinese Lute: An Essay in Ch'in Ideology*, *MN* Monograph 3, Tokyo, 1940.

[18] *Dunhuang guyue* (Ancient music of Dunhuang), Dunhuang wenyi and Gansu yinxiang, 1992.

Much more Chinese music has survived from the Song and later dynasties.[19] For a CD of Qing court music as it sounded to a Lazarist and a Jesuits missionary, see 33.7.

Ancient Instruments

Zhonguo yinyue wenwu daxi 中國音樂文物大系 (Compendium of Chinese musical artifacts), Daxiang, 1995– .

Bibliographies

Walter Kaufmann, *Musical References in the Chinese Classics*, Info Coordinators, 1976. Gathers together with translations the references to music in the Confucian Classics (bilingual text).

Zhongguo gudai yinyue shumu 中國古代音樂書目 (Catalog of ancient Chinese books on music), first draft, Yinyue, 1961. Lists 1,400 works on Chinese music written before 1840.

Zhongguo yinyue shupuzhi 中國音樂書譜志 (Catalog of Chinese books on music), Renmin yinyue, 1984; rev. ed., 1994. Contains listings of 5,000 works on music from earliest times to 1949. Arrangement is by *pinyin*. There is a title index.

Western-language studies are discussed in François Picard, "La connaissance et l'étude de la musique chinoise: Une histoire brève," *RBS* 13: 265–72 (1996).

Biographies

Zhongguo yinyue wudao xiqu renming cidian 中國音樂舞蹈戲曲人名詞典, Cao Chousheng 曹惆生 (Dictionary of personal names of Chinese musicians, dancers and actors), Shangwu, 1959. Gives biographical notices of 5,201 persons connected with music, dance and the theater up the end of the Qing. Arrangement is by stroke count and classifier.

[19] Rulan Chao Pian, *Sonq Dynasty Musical Sources and Their Interpretation*, HUP, 1967.

Women's Studies

The sources for women's history in the pre-Qin are the same as for any other form of history of those centuries: archaeology, the oracle-bone and bronze inscriptions and the contemporary sources listed in Table 18, Chapter 19. Archaeology has unearthed new and fascinating evidence, including prehistoric statues of women possibly used in fertility rituals, but there is no consensus as to what light these finds throw on the role of women in society and attitudes towards them. In China the discussion normally turns round the question of the timing of the transition from matriarchal to patriarchal tribes according to the Morgan/Engels scheme.[1] The little evidence there is relates to women at the top of society and often seems to provide insufficient support for the conclusions reached.

There seems to be some evidence that women aristocrats in the late Shang had a powerful role in society, at least by comparison with their role in the Zhou period.

The ground becomes somewhat more solid for the study of women in Chinese imperial history. The direct primary sources can be divided between works written by women (39.1); works written about them (39.2); and

[1] Zhang Jing, "80 niandai yilai de xian-Qin funü shi yanjiu 80 年代以來的先秦婦女史研究" (Research since the 1980s on pre-Qin women's history), *Zhongguoshi yanjiu dongtai*, 1998.1, 2–8.

works written for them by both men and women (39.3). Modern interest in gender studies has led to a much closer study of these sources as well as the re-interpretation of standard primary sources, which are also important for studying the changing role of women in China.

On women's names and how they differed from those of men, see 3.2.1. On family and clan instructions, see 3.5. Sources on sex are also important for the history of women in China (chap. 36).

39.1 Works Written by Women

Since women were supposed to be educated for wifely tasks such as sewing and embroidery or running a household, they did not attend government schools nor did they sit the official exams (at no time were they eligible for public office). But in the course of Chinese history there were many outstanding women writers (typically of poetry), especially in the later empire.[2]

The most complete bibliography of works written by women is that of Hu Wenkai 胡文楷, *Lidai funü zhuzuo kao* 歷代婦女著作考.[3] In it he provides place of origin, family background, occupation, marital status and lists of all extant or known works for over 3,600 women writers from the Han to the Qing (mostly Qing).

Note the following anthologies and collections of materials:

---

[2] Sharon Shih-jiuan Hou, "Women's Literature," in the *Indiana Companion to Traditional Chinese Literature*, William H. Nienhauser Jr., ed, IUP, 1986; rev. rpnt., SMC, 1988, 175–94; *Writing Women in Late Imperial China*, Ellen Widmer and Kang-i Sun Chang, eds., SUP, 1997.

[3] *Lidai funü zhuzuo kao* (Study of the works of women throughout history), Shangwu, 1957; rev. ed., Shanghai guji, 1985.

Chinese Women Poets: An Anthology of Poetry and Criticism from Ancient Times to 1911, Kang-i Sun Chang and Haun Saussy, eds., SUP, forthcoming.

Views from the Jade Terrace: Chinese Women Artists, 1300–1912, Marsha Weidner et al., eds., IUP, 1988.

Jindai Zhongguo nüquan yundong shiliao 近代中國女權運動史料, 1842–1911 (Historical materials on the movements for women's rights, 1842-1911), Li Youning 李又寧 and Tan Yufa 譚玉法, eds., 2 vols., Longwen, 1995.

One unusual way in which women communicated with each other in Southern Hunan was by using *nüshu* 女書 (women's script). See William W. Chiang, *"We Know the Script: We Have Been Good Friends:" Linguistic and Social Analysis of the Women's Script Literacy in Southern Hunan, China*, Lanham: University Press of America Inc., 1995. Most of the texts are marriage congratulations. For a careful but more imaginative reconstruction of the early history of the *nüshu*, see Li Jinglin (1995), section 14.2; for a scholarly collection of papers at a national conference on the subject, *Qite de nüshu* 奇特的女書 (The mystery of the *nüshu*), Shi Jinbo 史金波 et al., eds., Beijing yuyan xueyuan, 1995.

39.2 Works Written for Women

Many works were written for the ethical and moral instruction of girls and women, starting with elementary-school primers and readers.[4] They normally either took the form of exemplary biographies of virtuous women or sets of rules and admonitions. The models for both these forms were written in the Han, one by a man, one by a woman:

Liu Xiang 劉向 (77?–6? BC), *Lienüzhuan* 列女傳. Contains the biographies of 125 women famous for their virtue who lived from the earliest times to the Former Han. Liu arranges the biographies into six groups according to the virtues exemplified and one group of pernicious and depraved (*niebi* 孽嬖) negative examples. His work was

---

[4] For example, the *Nü'er jing* 女兒經, the *Nü Lunyu* 女論語 or the *Gailiang Nü'er jing* 改良女兒經. Many of these are collected in *Chuantong nüzi mengdu xinbian* 傳統女子蒙讀新編 (Newly edited traditional primers for girls), Chen Ju 陳駒 et al., eds., Guangxi jiaoyu, 1992.

much imitated and many later collections were made right down to the later empire.[5]

Ban Zhao 班昭 (?48–?116), the most famous woman historian of China wrote a set of instructions for her daughters, *Nüjie* 女誡 AD 106. It is the earliest text on ideal womanhood and set the model for innumerable such works, some of which were eventually gathered together in the Qing as the *Nü sishu* 女四書.[6] For a translation and commentary on the *Nüjie*, Ban Zhao's most influential work, see Nancy Lee Swann, *Pan Chao, Foremost Woman Scholar of China, First Century A.D.*, Century Co., 1932; New York: Russell, 1960, chap. 5; her translation is reprinted in the *Columbia Anthology of Traditional Chinese Literature* (30.1), 534–541. See also Yu-shih Chen, "The Historical Template of Pan Chao's *Nü chieh*," *TP* 82: 229–97 (1996).

Note that women only feature explictly in one of the Confucian five relations (*wulun* 五倫), namely that between husband and wife (characterized by *bie* 別, separateness). Despite this the ideal relation between elder sister and younger sister and between two women friends was characterized along the same lines as the ideal for elder brother and younger brother and for

---

[5] *Lienüzhuan* (Biographies of famous women) has been translated (except for the introductions to each group of biographies) in *The Position of Women in Early China*, Albert Richard O'Hara, Catholic University of America, 1945; 2nd ed., 1955. There is an index with the original text appended: *Retsujoden sakuin (fu honbun)* 列女傳索引 (附本文), Miyamoto Masaru 宮本勝 and Mihashi Masanobu 三橋正信, comps., Tokyo, 1982. See also Katherine Carlitz, "The Social Uses of Female Virtue in Late Ming Editions of *Lienüzhuan*," *LIC* 12.2 (1991) 117–48; and on the numerous illustrations of the *Lienüzhuan*, see Julia K. Murray, "Didactic Art and Women," in *Flowering in the Shadows: Women in the History of Chinese and Japanese Painting*, Marsha Weidner, ed., UHP, 1990, 27–53; Mark Elvin, "Female Virtue and the State in China," in the author's *Another History: Essays on China from a European Perspective*, Wild Peony, 1996, 302–51 (originally appeared in *Past and Present* 104, 1984).

[6] Apart from the *Nüjie* itself, the *Nü sishu* (The four books for women) contained *Nü lunyu* 女論語 (The Woman's *Lunyu*), Tang; *Neixun* 內訓 (Instructions for the inner quarters), fifteenth century and *Nüfan jielu* 女範捷錄 (A concise account of basic regulations for women), Qing.

two friends, namely by *xu* 序, precedence, and by *xin* 信, trust, respectively.

As the status of women improved in the twentieth century, a special new character was invented for "she" (*ta* 她). At the same time, *tuo* 它 was borrowed for "it" (modern *ta*). Hitherto, *ta* 他 had been used for "he," "she," and "it."

39.3 Research Tools and Studies

Guide to Women's Studies in China, Gail Hershatter, Emily Honig, Susan Mann, and Lisa Rofel, comps. and eds., IEAS, UC, 1998.

Bibliographies

Richard W. Guisso and Stanley Johannesen, *Women in China: Current Directions in Historical Scholarship*, New York: Philo, 1981.

Lucie Cheng et al., *Women in China: Bibliography of Available English Language Materials*, UCP, 1984. Contains citations to 4,107 items, arranged by subject. Includes pre-1911 coverage. Has author index and "index of Chinese women as subjects."

Zhongguo funü wenxian conglan 中國婦女文獻叢覽 (Women's studies in China: a selected bibliography and resource guide from ancient times to the present), Qi Wenlei 齊文類, ed., Beijing daxue, 1995. Includes some references to pre-twentieth-century history and some inscriptional materials.

Biographical Dictionaries

Yuan Shaoying 袁韶瑩 and Yang Guizhen 楊瑰珍, *Zhongguo funü mingren cidian* 中國婦女名人辭典 (Dictionary of famous Chinese women), Beifang funü, 1989. Contains entries on some 4,100 women from all periods of Chinese history. Includes alternative names, dates and publications. Arranged by stroke count of name. Also has stroke-count name index arranged by occupation.

Excerpts

Excerpts on women from the *Ming Shilu* in the series *Ming Shilu leizuan* 明實錄類纂 (Veritable Records of the Ming by category), Li Guoxiang 李國祥 and Yang Chang 楊昶, eds., 1995. Useful if you are researching the history of women in the Ming dynasty.

Chen Peng 陳鵬, *Zhongguo hunyin shigao* 中國婚姻史稿 (Draft hisory of marriage in China), Zhonghua, 1990.

Studies

The following are examples of the growing number of studies in English of the role of women in Chinese history based on a close reading of standard sources:

Patricia Buckley Ebrey, "Women, Marriage, and the Family in Chinese History," in *Heritage of China: Contemporary Perspectives on Chinese Civilization*, Paul S. Ropp, ed., UCP, 1990, 197–223.

Rubie S. Watson and Patricia Buckley Ebrey, *Marriage and Inequality in Chinese Society*, UCP, 1991.

Ann-Marie Hsiung, "The Images of Women in Early Chinese Poetry: The *Book of Songs*, Han Ballads and Palace Style Verse of the Liang Dynasty," *Chinese Culture* 35.4: 81–90 (1994).

Julia Ch'ing, "Sung Philosophers on Women," *MS* 42 (1994), 259–74.

Kathryn Bernhardt draws the evidence for "The Inheritance Rights of Daughters: The Song Anomaly?" *Modern China* 21.3 (1995) 269–309, from the Song collection *Minggong shupan qingming ji* 名公書判清明集 (see 27.3 for details).

Patricia Ebrey, *The Inner Quarters: Marriage and the Lives of Chinese Women in the Sung Period*, UCP, 1993. One of the points made in this excellent study is that men could divorce women, but not vice-versa.

Priscilla Ching Chung, *Palace Women in the Northern Sung*, Brill, 1981.

Karl A. Wittfogel and Feng Chia-sheng, "Position of Women in Liao Society," in Wittfogel and Feng, *History of Chinese Society: Liao* Am. Philosophical Society, 1949, 199–202 (on this important study, see 48.2).

Lien-sheng Yang, "Women Rulers in Imperial China," *HJAS* 23: 47–61 (1960–61).

Herbert Franke, "Women under the Dynasties of Conquest," in Franke, *China under Mongol Rule*, Variorum, 1994, 23–43.

Charlotte Furth, "Poetry and Women's Culture in Late Imperial China," editor's introduction, *LIC* 13.1 (1992) 1–8.

Jonathan Spence, *The Death of Woman Wang*, Viking, 1978. Based on a manual for local magistrates (*Fuhui quanshu* 福惠全書, 27.5), local gazetteers and fiction.

Dorothy Ko, *Teachers of the Inner Chamber: Women and Culture in Seventeenth-Century China*, SUP, 1994.

Susan Mann, *Precious Records: Women in China's Long Eighteenth Century*, SUP, 1997.

Francesca Bray, *Technology and Gender: Fabrics of Power in Late Imperial China*, UCP, 1997.

Much good use has been made of popular novels, for example,

Keith McMahon, *Misers, Shrews and Polygamists: Sexuality and Male-Female Relations in Eighteenth-Century Chinese Fiction*, Duke Univ. Press, 1995. A rare study of polygamy in Qing fiction, setting the background out of which more famous novels such as the *Honglou-meng* or *Jin Ping Mei* grew.

Louise P. Edwards, *Men and Women in Qing China: Gender in the Dream of the Red Chamber*, Brill, 1994.

Eugene Cooper and Meng Zheng, "Patterns of Cousin Marriage in Rural Zhejiang and in the *Dream of the Red Chamber*," *JAS* 52.1 (1993), 90–106.

Yenna Wu, *The Chinese Virago: A Literary Theme*, HUP, 1995.

The Chinese Femme Fatale: Stories from the Ming Period, Anne E. McLaren, tr. and intoduced, Wild Peony, 1994.

40

Non-Han Peoples
(Inside China)

In the Chinese view, the peoples they encountered—whether the tribes of the South or the nomad and semi-nomad peoples of the North—were at a lower level of civilization than themselves. They divided them between those that had submitted and begun the process of acculturation and those that had not (the terms used were the cooked and the raw barbarians, the *shufan* 熟蕃 and the *shengfan* 生蕃).

Chapter 40 covers the cooked barbarians; chapter 41 deals with the sources on the raw ones and independent kingdoms and foreign states. Because many of the barbarians started outside of China and later settled inside, the distinction is not a hard and fast one (the Mongols or Manchus, for example, both began as tribal confederations that succeeded in conquering China. Thereafter, to a greater or lesser extent, they became ethnicities in China). So, chapters 40 and 41 should be read together.

This chapter begins with some comments on the question of ethnicity and the origins of the Chinese people (40.1). Next, one of the many research problems is selected for examination, namely the difficult question of accurately identifying non-Han peoples (40.2).

The rest of the chapter presents examples of the main sources and research tools on scripts and languages, biographies, excerpts from primary sources, archives, chronology, archaeology and bibliography (40.3).

40.1 Introduction

Ethnic consciousness as it is understood today was a late phenomenon in Chinese history. Ethnic terms such as Hanzu 漢族 (Hans), Manzu 滿族 (Manchus), Mengzu 蒙族 (Mongols) and Zangzu 藏族 (Tibetans) only entered the language under Western influence during the nineteenth century. *Minzu* 民族 came into Chinese from Japanese *minzoku* 民族 in 1895. The Stalinist generic "national minorities" (*shaoshu minzu* 少數民族) became orthodox in China in the 1950s. It remains so to this day, although the phrase is heard less and less. The normal way of referring to an ethnicity, for example the Miao 苗, is Miaozu 苗族.

In order to avoid injecting modern political sensitivities into the past, I have used the term "non-Han" rather than modern terms such as "national minority," "ethnic group," or "ethnicity." Even "non-Han" is obviously anachronistic for the pre-Han period (and for most of the remainder of Chinese history, because as explained in section 3.1, "Han" was not a common Chinese ethnonym until quite late in the imperial period). Although "non-Huaxia" would therefore be more appropriate, there is a point where accuracy risks becoming quaint, so I have used it only occasionally. One advantage of the term non-Han is that it accords quite well with the Chinese own view, which tended to define "savages" (aborigines) and "barbarians" alike in terms of the qualities they lacked.

One of the most contentious historical debates in China is on the origin of the Chinese people. It was a subject shrouded in myth until the archaeologists and linguists began turning up evidence that for the first time enabled the historians to begin to sort out fact from fantasy and to link tribal peoples and early kingdoms referred to in Zhou texts with archaeological remains. The last word has by no means been written, but the discussion serves as a reminder that the formation of the Chinese (or rather, Huaxia) evolved over millennia with contributions from many different peoples and tribes (13.1). Indeed, recent archaeology has shown that at the dawn of history in East Asia the peoples of the North and the South may also have farmed and have been as "civilized" as the peoples of the Yellow River and Yangzi.[1] As if to underline the diverse origins of Chinese civilization, recent studies have also shown that the peoples of north China are more closely related genetically to their northern neighbors outside of present-day China than they are to the peoples in south China. These are in turn more closely related to their southern neighbors in Southeast Asia than they are to the northern Chinese. Possibly reflecting a combination of these millennial differences combined with the influence of migration and invasion in historic times, the dialect map of China today also breaks down into two broad groups: the Mandarin-related dialects of the North and Northwest on the one hand, and the dialects of the Southeast and South on the other.

In direct contrast to the findings of archaeology and historical genetics, according to the Zhou interpretation of history (the orthodoxy until the twentieth century), the peoples outside the heartland areas of the Xia, Shang and Zhou were regarded as one or other form of non-settled, nomadic, warlike barbarian or savage, in bipolar contrast to the qualities of the Zhou (later the Han), who saw themselves as settled, civilized, moral, peace-loving farmers. Needless to say, the non-Huaxia were considered to have contributed little or nothing to the genesis of Chinese civilization. They were regarded as potential

---

[1] Nicola Di Cosmo, "Ancient Inner Asian Nomads: Their Economic Basis and Its Significance in Chinese History," *JAS* 53.4: 1092–1126 (1994); Nicola Di Cosmo, "The Northern Frontier in Pre-Imperial China," *CHAC*, 885–966; Sophia-Karin Psarras, "Exploring the North: Non-Chinese Cultures of the Late Warring States and Han," *MS* 42: 1–125 (1994) and the same author's *Han and Xiongnu*, forthcoming.

if not actual enemies, and scorned for their uncouth ways. Yet barbarians and savages, it was felt, if they submitted and studied, could become civilized (sinicized) and eventually accepted into the Huaxia melting pot.

Just as the Huaxia organized themselves hierarchically, so too they saw the rest of the world as a hierarchy: Huaxia; barbarians; animals. Within the category barbarian different degrees were recognized according to level of subjugation, proximity and sinicization (*Hanhua* 漢化 or more correctly, *Huahua* 華化; *laihua* 來華).[2]

40.2 Naming the Barbarians (1)

The barbarians were referred to by all sorts of collective terms such as the *siyi* 四夷[3] or (from the place where they lived) the *sihai* 四海. These and more prejudiced and informal terms are discussed in 41.2.[4]

---

[2] For a recent overview, see Ping-ti Ho, "In Defense of Sinicization: A Rebuttal of Evelyn Rawski's 'Reenvisioning the Qing,'" *JAS* 57.1: 123–55 (1998). Rawski's article appeared in *JAS* 55.4: 829–50 (1996). In part she argues that "sinicization—'the thesis that all of the non-Han peoples who have entered the Chinese realm have eventually been assimilated into Chinese culture'—is a twentieth century Han nationalist interpretation of China's past." For case studies of acculturation, see 33.6 (Jianpang Wang, 1996); 48.5.4 (Ch'en Yuan, 1966); 48.4 (Jing-shen Tao, 1976).

[3] The Siyi 四夷 were the Dong Yi 東夷, Bei Di 北狄, Xi Rong 西戎, Nan Man 南蠻. Most of these ethnonyms became generics for barbarian (41.2) and were also often used in combination (e.g., Rongdi 戎狄, Yidi 夷狄). See Ruth I. Meserve, "The Inhospitable Land of the Barbarian," *Journal of Asian History* 16: 51–89 (1982).

[4] The *Erya* defines *sihai* 四海 in the following way: *Jiuyi badi qirong liuman wei zhi sihai* 九夷八狄七戎六蠻謂之四海 (the nine Yi, eight Di, seven Rong, and six Man are called the four seas), *Erya* 爾雅, "Shidi 釋地." So, *sihai* meant the place where the barbarians lived, hence by extension, the barbarians. The expression *sihai zhinei* 四海之內 was used as a synonym for Zhongguo (the central states) as in the famous expression "*Sihai zhi nei jie xiongdi ye* 四海之內皆兄弟也" (all within the four seas

Footnote continued on next page

Well over 700 non-Han peoples and tribes are mentioned in Chinese sources. It is no easy matter to trace their history, not only because there are usually no non-Han sources and ethno-archaeology is in its infancy, but also because the names constantly changed. This is particularly true of the tribes and peoples of the North and West. Typically they themselves changed their names when they formed new confederations or alliances. Also, the Xiongnu, Turks, Uighur, Tibetan, Khitan, Jurchen, Mongols, and Manchus started as outsiders and ended by large numbers becoming acculturated (see 41.2.2 for the origins of their names). The situation was different in the South, where the "savages" usually never posed a threat to the Han state, but were gradually marginalized to the mountainous areas or absorbed as the Han farmers settled in the valleys (7.2.2).[5]

In order to trace the history of the non-Han peoples, it is necessary to accurately identify them in the Chinese sources. Chinese writers almost invariably represented the names of non-Han peoples (and their personal names), both inside and outside China, using loan words transcribing the sounds of the non-Han language (*yinyi* 音譯). Often different characters (with more or less the same sound) were used before a standard transcription emerged. To find the origin of an ethnonym loan a certain amount of detective work (sometimes termed linguistic ethnology) is required. For example, to trace the meaning behind the Luo-Yue 駱越 [粤] peoples (literally the "white-horse-with-black-mane Yue"), you have to know that the pre-Qin and Han sources stress the importance that this branch of the Yue attached to bronze drums (excavated from Luo-Yue sites from Yunnan to Vietnam). There is no record of them rearing white horses with black manes (*luo* 駱). So, *luo* is clearly used

---

are his brothers), *Lunyu*, 12.5 (referring to the gentleman who has no brothers of his own, but who treats people correctly).

[5] In the South more than in the North, there is the suspicion that Chinese observers did not always bother to accurately record the names of the peoples with whom they came into contact, often preferring to use a generic rather than a specific. For example, the Yi 彝 were often just called Manzi 蠻子 by Chinese observers.

for its sound, at that time pronounced *lak*. In Zhuang (one of the languages of the Luo-Yue descendants), there are four words meaning bronze drum, including *la*. This suggests that the meaning of Luo-Yue is "the Bronze-drum Yue." Whether the Luo-Yue themselves chose the ethnonym "Lac" for this reason is another matter altogether. They are presumably the same as the Lac who founded the first Vietnamese kingdom by the Red River near modern Hanoi (Ouluo 甌駱; Âu-Lac in Vietnamese) and there is no lack of different theories as to the meaning of *their* ethnonym.[6]

At the same time as finding characters to fit the sounds of a foreign word or name it is also possible to choose ones with a particular meaning, in the case of non-Han peoples and foreigners, usually a pejorative meaning. It was the practice, for example, to choose characters with an animal or reptile signific for southern non-Han peoples while many northern peoples were given characters for their names with the wolf, dog or leather hides signific. In origin this practice may have derived from the animal totems or tribal emblems typical of these peoples. This is not to deny that in later Chinese history such graphic pejoratives fitted neatly with Han convictions of the superiority of their own culture as compared to the uncultivated, hence animal-like savages and barbarians. Characters with animal significs were generally not used in formal correspondance. They were banned by the Qing and many were systematically altered during the script reforms of the 1950s.

To identify the ethnonyms, and personal and place names of non-Han tribes and peoples inside the area of what later became China, the ideal would be to know the pronunciation both in the original language and of the characters used for the

---

[6] *Lingnan gu Yueren mingcheng wenhua tanyuan* 嶺南古越人名稱文化探源 (Investigation into the origins of the culture of the names of the ancient Yue peoples of Lingnan), Qin Xiaohang 覃曉航, Zhongyang minzu daxue, 1994. The author shows how to trace the names of peoples, individuals, things and general vocabulary that have been transcribed or translated into Chinese characters from Zhuang-Dong 壯侗 languages.

transcription into Chinese. Unfortunately, there are usually insufficient records to reconstruct most of the non-Han languges,
but for Chinese, it is possible using references such as the first
three in section 2.5. The task becomes easier from the Song because Chinese begins to sound as it does today, and transcriptions of non-Han names are easier to recognize.

Non-Han languages were the source for many modern Chinese place names, including the names of five of the modern
provinces (Table 4, section 4.1).

40.3 Sources and Research Tools

Scripts and Languages

The languages of the non-Han peoples belong to the Indo-
European, Aramaic, Arabic and Sino-Tibetan language families.
Considerable amounts of written primary sources have sur-
vived in about 30 different scripts. The earliest is Karosthi.

The sources include Neolithic and later rock pictograms; inscriptions on stone and bronze and written sources of a religious, calendrical, legal or historical nature. There are also important archives from the Qing, principally in Manchu and Tibetan (see 50.2.5 and 50.3, respectively).

Before the 1920s, Han scholars showed little or no interest
in the languages of non-Han peoples in or around China, or indeed in foreign languages in general. Glossaries of Chinese into
Mongolian were officially compiled in the Southern Song. The
title of one that survives is *Menggu yiyu* 蒙古譯語. Others were
compiled in the Ming and Qing under the generic title *Huayi
yiyu* 華夷譯語 (Sino-barbarian glossary). They were arranged
according to subject categories. Four survive, the earliest dating
from 1389 (see David Kane, *The Sino-Jurchen Vocabulary of the
Bureau of Interpreters*, IUP, 1989). A number of Manchu glossaries were compiled in the Qing, including:

Yuding Qing wenjian 御定清文鑑, 1673–1708. The final version was enti-
    tled *Wuti Qingwen jian* 五體清文鑑. *Wuti Qingwen jian* (Five-
    language Manchu glossary), 1790; Minzu, 1957; rev., 1997. The five
    languages were Manchu (*Qingwen* 清文), Tibetan, Mongolian, Uig-
    hur and Chinese. Compare *Qinding Xiyu tongwenzhi* 欽定西域同

文志, 1763, which includes Manchu, Chinese, Mongolian, Tibetan, Xinjiang Mongolian and Uighur. There were also various Manchu-Chinese glossaries of official terms. The best known is the *Liubu chengyu* 六部成語. It has been translated into English (see 27.5).

In addition, several bilingual glossaries were compiled by non-Han peoples—for example,

Tangut-Chinese: *Wenhai* 文海, anon, compiled early twelfth century (48.3).

Tangut-Chinese: *Tongyin* 通音, anon, compiled early twelfth century (48.3).

Tibetan-Chinese: *Dingxiang zhang* 丁香帳, Rin-chen bkra-shis 仁欽扎西, comp., 1536; Minzu, 1981.

For modern studies of non-Han scripts, see S. Robert Ramsey, *The Languages of China*, PUP, 1987; rpnt., with corrections, 1989. Also:

Zhongguo minzu guwenzi tulu 中國民族古文字圖錄 (Ancient scripts of China's minorities. An illustrated catalog), Shehui kexue, 1990.

Zhongguo minzu guwenzi yanjiu 中國民族古文字 研究 (Researches on the ancient scripts of China's minorities), Shehui kexue, 1984.

Zhongguo shaoshu minzu guji lun 中國少數民族古籍論 (Essays on the ancient texts of China's national minorities), Li Jinyou 李晉有 et al., Ba-Shu, 1997.

Biographies

On the naming systems used for family names by 56 non-Han peoples, see Zhang Lianfang 張聯芳, *Zhongguoren de xingming* 中國人的姓名 (The names of Chinese people), Shehui kexue, 1992.

Zhongguo minzushi renwu cidian 中國民族史人物辭典 (Dictionary of personalities in the history of China's nationalities), Gao Wende 高文德 ed. in chief, Shehui kexue, 1990.

Bibliographies of Primary Sources

James S. Olson, *An Ethnohistorical Dictionary of China*, Greenwood, 1998.

Zhongguo minzu gongju wenxian cidian 中國民族工具文獻詞典 (Dictionary of reference works and literature on Chinese ethnic peoples), Liu Guanghong 劉光宏, ed. in chief, Gaige, 1995. There is a 160-page stroke-count index.

For an annotated bibliography of 1,653 primary historical sources and
828 modern reports and studies on the southern minorities, see *Nanfang minzu gushi shulu* 南方民族古史書錄 (Records from ancient historical works on the southern peoples), Lü Mingzhong 呂名中, ed. in
chief, Sichuan minzu, 1989. There is a title index arranged by stroke
count.

Zhongguo nanfang minzu shizhi yaoji tijie 中國南方民族史志要籍題解,
Wu Yongxin 吳永辛, Minzu, 1991. Contains notes on 120 primary
sources.

Excerpts

The Standard Histories and the Veritable Records as well as the
gazetteers carry important materials on the non-Han peoples.
Many have been excerpted, for example:

Ming Shilu youguan Yunnan lishi ziliao zhaiyao 明實錄有關雲南歷史資
料摘要 (Selected excerpts from the Veritable Records of the Ming on
the history of Yunnan), *Yunnan sheng shaoshu minzu shehui lishi yanjiusuo* 雲南省少數民族社會歷史研究所, Kunming, 1959.

Qing Shilu Yunnan shiliao jiyao 清實錄雲南史料輯要 (Historical materials on Yunnan from the *Qing Shilu*), 4 vols., Yunnan: Xinhua
shudian, 1986.

Qing Shilu Yizu shiliao jiyao 清實錄彝族史料輯要 (Selections from the
Qing Shilu on the Yi people), Yunnan minzu, 1986.

For similar volumes of excerpts on many other provinces, see
50.5 and on Tibet, section 41.4.1.

Zhongguo difangzhi minsu ziliao huibian 中國地方志民俗資料匯編 (Collection of materials from Chinese gazetteers on popular customs),
Ding Shiliang 丁世良 and Zhao Xiaozhong 趙曉鐘 eds., 11 vols.,
Shumu wenxian, 1989–95. The vols. on Huabei, Dongbei, and Xibei
were published in 1989, Zhongnan and Xinan (both 2 vols.) followed
in 1991 and Huadong in 1995. The series was reprinted by Beijing tushuguan chubanshe in 1997. The first 11 vols. contain 5,500 pages of
extracts from local gazetteers arranged under seven headings: rites,
festivals, living conditions, popular literature and art, language,
creeds and others. There is a place-name index. Future volumes will
cover the South.

There are other collections of excerpts from local gazetteers
specifically on non-Han peoples, often of a particular province
or region, for example,

Hu'nan difangzhi shaoshu minzu shiliao 湖南地方志少數民族史料 (Historical materials from Hunan local gazetteers on national minorities), Hunan sheng shaoshu minzu guji bangongshi, eds., 2 vols., Yuelu, 1991–2.

Archive Materials

Heilongjiang sheng shaoshu minzu dang'an shiliao xuanbian 黑龍江省少數民族檔案史料選編 (Selections of historical materials from the Heilongjiang provincial archives on national minorities), Heilongjiang dang'an guan, Heilongjiang sheng, 1985.

Qingdai Xibozu Manwen dang'an shiliao 清代錫伯族满文檔案史料 (Historical materials from the archives in Manchu on the Xibo people), Yishiguan, eds., 2 vols., Xinjiang renmin, 1987.

Qingdai Xibozu Hanwen dang'an shiliao xuanbian 清代錫伯族漢文檔案史料選編 (Selected archival historical materials in Chinese on the Xibo people in the Qing dynasty), Yishiguan, 2 vols., Liaoning minzu, 1989. Contains 647 documents in Manchu; 95 in Chinese.

Chronology

On the main non-Han calendars (Dai, Yi, Tibetan, Buddhist and Muslim) and the concordances to convert them to the Julian calendar, see 5.6.

Archaeology

The archaeology of the non-Han peoples in China is beginning to receive more attention. See for example,

Li Yangsong 李仰松, *Minzu kaoguxue lunwenji* 民族考古學論文集 (Treatises on ethno-archaeology), Kexue, 1998. The papers in this collection were used by the author as the basis of his courses in ethno-archaeology in the archaeology department of Peking University. Li did his field work in 1956–57 studying the Wa 佤 of Yunnan. His technique is to try and solve problems in Chinese prehistory using insights gained from the study of primitive peoples such as the Wa.

Minzu kaoguxue lunwenji 民族考古學論文集 (Collected articles on ethno-archaeology), Wang Ningsheng 王寧生, ed., Wenwu, 1989.

Zhongguo Xi-nan minzu kaogu 中國西南民族考古 (Archaeology of the peoples of southwest China), Zhang Zengqi 張增祺, Yunnan renmin, 1990.

Hou Shigui 侯石珪, *Xizang kaogu dagang* 西藏考古大綱 (Broad outlines of Tibetan archaeology), Xizang renmin, 1991.

Inscriptions

A number of collections of inscriptions either in Chinese or in non-Han languages have been published—for example,

Guangxi shaoshu minzu diqu shike beiwen ji 廣西少數民族地區石刻碑文集 (Collected stone inscriptions from the national minority areas in Guangxi), Guangxi renmin, 1982.

Tubo jinshi lu 吐蕃金石錄 (Record of Tibetan inscriptions on bronze and stone), Wang Yao 王堯, comp., Wenwu, 1982.

Mythology, Outline Histories and Case Studies

For a dictionary of mythology, see *Zhongguo minzu shenhua cidian* 中國民族神話辭典 (Dictionary of the mythology of China's nationalities), Yuan Ke 袁柯, ed., Sichuan shehui kexue, 1989.

Leo J. Moser, *The Chinese Mosaic: The Peoples and Provinces of China*, Westview, 1985. An introductory text. See also Wiens (7.2.2).

Zhongguo minzushi 中國民族史 (The history of Chinese nationalities), Wang Zhonghan 王鍾翰, ed. in chief, Shehui kexue, 1994.

Zhongguo minzu guanxishi yanjiu 中國民族關係史研究 (Research on the history of relations with the nationalities), Weng Dujian 翁獨健, ed., Shehui kexue, 1984, has an extensive bibliography, 525–66.

Shaoshu minzu yu Zhongguo wenhua 少數民族與中國文化 (The national minorities and Chinese culture), Tian Jizhou 田繼周 et al., ed., Shanghai renmin, 1996.

Pamela K. Crossley, "Thinking about Ethnicity in Early Modern China," *LIC* 1: 1–34 (1990).

Morris Rossabi, "Chinese Myths about the National Minorities: Khubilai Khan, a Case Study," *Central and Inner Asian Studies* I: 47–81 (1987).

Zhu Zhuxian 祝注先, *Zhongguo shaoshu minzu shigeshi* 中國少數民族詩歌史 (History of the songs and poetry of China's national minorities), Zhongyang minzu daxue, 1994. Few songs and poems of non-Han peoples survive, but from the Yuan onward the numbers increase as more and more they began taking a Chinese education.

Bibliographies of Secondary Sources

Guancang Zhongguo minzu yanjiu cankao jianmu 館藏中國民族研究參考簡目 (Reference bibliography to research materials in the library [of the Central Nationalities Academy] on the peoples of China), Zhongyang minzu xueyuan tushuguan 中央民族學院圖書館, eds. and pubs., 3 vols, 1985. Contains citations to 6,590 items dating from antiquity to 1949 (vol.1) and 6,155 items from 1951 to 1977 (vol. 2). Especially valuable for citations to historical materials. Volume 3 is a title index. There is a *pinyin* index.

Zhongguo minzu yu minsuxue yanjiu lunzhu mulu 中國民族與民俗學研究論著目錄 (Bibliography of research on China's ethnology and folklore), 3 vols., CCS, Taibei, 1997.

Zhongguo shaoshu minzu lunzhu suoyin 中國少數民族論著索引 (Articles and books on China's national minorities), Chen Ting 陳廷, Wang Ying 王應, comps., Xinjiang renmin, 1992, covers 3,088 books and 28,500 articles appearing between 1949 and 1988.

Alain Y. Dessaint, *Minorities of Southwest China: An Introduction to the Yi (Lolo) and Related Peoples and an Annotated Bibliography*, New Haven: HRAF, 1980.

Journals

Minzu yanjiu 民族研究 (1979– , bimonthly), Shehui kexue.

Minzu yanjiu dongtai 民族研究動態 (1983– , quarterly), Shekeyuan, Minzu yanjiusuo 社科院民族研究所 (from 1984 incorporates *Minzu yanjiu tongxun* 民族研究通訊, Zhongguo minzu xuehui 中國民族學會).

41

Non-Han Peoples
(Outside China)

Accounts of non-Han peoples outside of China are found in the Standard Histories (41.4); in the Veritable Records (41.4.1) and in various other sources, including records of journeys to foreign countries and diplomatic diaries (41.5). Some of the generics for barbarians or foreigners are dicussed in 41.1.1; ethnonyms for Tibetans, Uighurs, Mongols and Manchus are traced in 41.2.2 and some of the different meanings of the "West" are presented in 41.2.3. Extensive archival sources on negotiations with foreign states are extant only from the Qing (50.6). The chapter begins with some remarks on the Chinese world order (41.1).

41.1 The Chinese World Order

From the very earliest centuries of Chinese history the in-group visualized its relations with out-groups in hierarchical terms with the in-group at the top and center. The definition of the hierarchies and their number changed in each historical period according to the circumstances. The arrangements that governed the relations of the center with the various zones into which the rest of the territory was divided were also extended to the barbarians. The most famous example is the offering of gifts and the acceptance of tribute, expected alike from the Chinese as from the barbarian; from the feudatory to his lord, from the inferior to the superior; from a minor kingdom on the periphery of the empire to the emperor at the center.[1]

The Han established a system of diplomatic relations and alliances.[2] It was mainly developed to deal with the Xiongnu threat. It was based on the despatch of embassies; royal marriages; granting of titles; the taking of hostages (*zhi* 質), and above all, the exchange of gifts and tribute (*gong* 貢). All practices developed during the Warring States period.[3] The conduct of diplomacy was entrusted to permanent and specialized officials at the capital.[4] These officials handled not only relations with non-Han peoples and states, but also the visits of domestic princes and nobles to the capital.[5] In general, in the later empire, the Board of Rites handled peaceful relations with foreigners; the Board of War dealt with military relations. *Waiguo* 外國 (foreign country; abroad) came into use from the Tang to mean states outside China (during the Warring States it had re-

---

[1] *Zhongguo lidai gongpin daguan* 中國歷代貢品大觀 (Grand collection of historical tribute), Gong Yu 龔予 et al., eds., Shanghai Shekeyuan, 1992. Contains excerpts from the original sources recording over 3,000 tribute missions, with translations into modern Chinese. Under the empire, it was the duty of the Board of Rites to manage the tribute missions and to keep lists of them and of the tribute they presented and the presents received from them. These lists were written into the Veritable Records and later summarized in the Standard Histories (see 41.4.1).

[2] Yü Ying-shih, "Han Foreign Relations," *CHC* vol 1 (1986), 377–462; Li Hu 黎虎, *Han-Tang waijiao zhidushi* 漢唐外交制度史 (A history of diplomatic institutions from the Han to the Tang), Lanzhou daxue, 1998.

[3] Richard L. Walker, *The Multi-State System of Ancient China*, Shoestring Press, 1953. A study of interstate relations in the Warring States period.

[4] The Dianke 佃客 (Chamberlain for dependencies) of the Qin and early Han, superseded in 144 BC by the Da xingling 大行令 (Director of the messenger office), in turn superseded in 104 BC by the Da honglu 大鴻臚 (Chamberlain for dependencies).

[5] There is no thorough history of Chinese foreign relations or diplomacy from the Warring States through to modern times. But there are studies of individual periods. Most volumes of the *CHC* contain chapters or sections on foreign relations.

ferred to the territory of local lords outside the capital or to another of the Warring States).

Different foreign policies and models of how to conduct foreign relations were employed in China in different periods. No one model such as the tributary system fits all the Chinese historical experience.[6] Strategy was adjusted according to the strength of the adversary. Thus tribute (symbolizing a subservient relation) on many occasions was replaced by other forms of diplomacy, including the signing of treaties (implying some degree of equality). When they did encounter a country with a higher civilization such as Rome or India, the Chinese placed it in a different category other than savage or barbarian—but these encounters were at a distance and rare. Some of the most common terms used to describe different foreign policies:

> *Jimi* 羈縻 (loose reign policy)
> *Yiyi bianhua* 以夷變華 (*hua Hua* 化華; *lai Hua* 來華. See end of 41.1)
> *Yiyi zhiyi* 以夷制夷 (using barbarians to control barbarians)
> *Yiyi gongyi* 以夷功夷 or *yiyi fayi* 以夷伐夷 (using the barbarians to attack the barbarians)
> *Zhengfa* 征伐 (attack)
> *Heqin* 和親 (appeasement)[7]

41.2 Naming the Barbarians (2)

41.2.1   Terminology

The chief enemy of the Qin and Han empires was the Xiongnu 匈奴 confederation. The Xiongnu called themselves by a name earlier transcribed into Chinese with the character *hu* 胡. From

---

[6] Jing-shen Tao [Tao Jinsheng 陶晉生], "Foreign Relations in Ancient China," chap. 1 of *Two Sons of Heaven: Studies in Sung-Liao Relations*, UAP, 1988, 1–9. See also the studies in *China among Equals—The Middle Kingdom and Its Neighbors, 10th–14th centuries*, Morris Rossabi, ed., UCP, 1983.

[7] Lien-sheng Yang, "Historical Notes on the Chinese World Order," in *The Chinese World Order*, John K. Fairbank, ed., HUP, 1968. In the later empire *jimi zhouxian* 羈縻州縣 were governed by a local chieftan *tusi* 土司 (cf. modern autonomous prefectures and counties).

the Han, the Hu were termed Xiongnu 匈奴 (violent slaves). Typically, *Xiongnu* is transcribed in the sources with dozens of variant characters (one scholar has counted 32 different transcriptions). The name also illustrates the common tendency in naming barbarians to add a derogatory generic for them to a derogatory word such as slave, devil, caitiff or robber. Three of the most common generics were *Hu* 胡, *yi* 夷 and *fan* 蕃 (番) and *nu* 奴, *gui* 鬼 and *lu* 虜 were the most often used names. A list of the most popular derogative terms from all periods of Chinese history would include the following:

> *nu* 奴 (slaves) as in Xiongnu; *hunu* 胡奴 (barbarian slaves); *guinu* 鬼奴 (devil slaves); *heinu* 黑奴 (black slaves, Africans); *wonu* 倭奴 (dwarf slaves, Japanese)

> *lu* 虜 (caitiffs) as in Suolu 索虜 (the unkempt caitiffs, i.e., the Toba)

> *gui* 鬼 (devils) as in *heigui* 黑鬼 (black devils, Africans or Indians); *guinu* 鬼奴 (devil slaves); *guizi* 鬼子 (devils); *heiguinu* 黑鬼奴 (black devil slaves) or *baigui* 白鬼 (white devils); *fangui* 蕃(番)鬼 or the more recent *yangguizi* 洋鬼子 (foreign devils); *guailou* 鬼佬 (Cantonese pronunciation for *guilao*, devil men), the common Cantonese appellation for the western barbarians, from *fanguai lou* (*fanguilao* 蕃 [番] 鬼佬). Foreign women were called *guipo* 鬼婆.

Yi 夷 continued to be used in formal documents such as memorials right up to the end of the empire, for example, Yingyi 嘆夷 (the English barbarians).

Facial features, such as the length of the nose, skin color,[8] the color of the eyes, hair styles, hirsuteness, the size of the body or just general appearance were also used to nickname non-Han peoples—for example,

> *choulu* 丑虜 (ugly caitiff)

> *biyan wuxu* 碧眼烏須 (blue eyes and black beards, i.e., Central Asians). *Hu* as in *huzi* 胡子 (beard; moustache; whiskers) is an extended meaning of *hu* (barbarian)

> *wo* 倭 (dwarf; reserved almost exclusively for the Japanese in whose language it is pronounced *wa*, as in *wa* 和). It was used originally

[8] Frank Dikötter, *The Discourse of Race in Modern China*, Hurst, 1992. Pages 1–125 cover from earliest times to 1915.

in the *Hanshu* probably to refer to the inhabitants of Kyûshu and the Korean peninsula. Thereafter to the inhabitants of the Japanese archipelago; *Woguo* 倭國 (dwarfs' country); in offical documents Japan was called *Riben* 日本 after the Japanese starting using this name in the Tang dynasty); *Wonuguo* 倭奴國 (dwarf slaves' country); *wonu* 倭奴 (dwarf slaves); *Woren* 倭人 (dwarf men); *wozi* 倭子 (dwarf kids); *wokou* 倭寇 (dwarf pirates) was used from the fourteenth century; Chinese pirates were also tarred with the same brush.

hongmao yi 紅毛夷 (red-haired barbarians, i.e., the northern Europeans, particularly the Dutch)

chang bizi 長鼻子 or *da bizi* 大鼻子 (the long or big noses; i.e., Europeans and Americans)

Shendu 身毒 (early transcription of the Persian for "India"; the characters not only transcribe the sound but also literally mean "body poison;" the more neutral transcription "Yindu 印度" was introduced by Xuanzang 玄奘 (596–664), see 41.5.1.

Many of the Chinese names for barbarian peoples became in time generic words for "barbarian." This is true of Yi 夷, Rong 戎, Di 狄, and Man 蠻 and also of Hu 胡 (the same happened with names such as Hun or Vandal in English). Of all such generics, none has influenced the Chinese language more profoundly than *hu* 胡. A memory of the strange (barbarous) ways in which the non-Han spoke is no doubt reflected in the following expressions:

huche 胡扯 (talk nonsense)	*hushuo* 胡説 (drivel)
huchui 胡吹 (boast)	*hushuo badao* 胡説八道 (talk rubbish)
huchui luanpeng 胡吹亂捧 (boast)	*husi luanxiang* 胡思亂想 (fantasize)
hudaogu 胡叨咕 (blabber)	*huyan* 胡言 (nonsense)
huhua 胡話 (wild talk)	*huyan luanyu* 胡言亂語 (rave)
hujiao 胡攪 (pester; wrangle)	*huzhou* 胡謅 (tell tall stories)
hujiao manchan 胡攪蠻纏 (argue)	*huzhuan* 胡轉 (malapropism)

In addition, the memory of the barbarian's uncouth behavior is enshrined in expressions such as

huchi haisai 胡吃海塞 (eat anything and everything)
huchou 胡臭 (or *huchou* 狐臭; body [armpit] odor)
hugao 胡搞 (mess things up; be promiscuous)
huhua 胡花 (spend money foolishly)

huhun 胡混 (loaf around; *hunao* 胡鬧 horse around)
hulai 胡來 (bungle)
huluan 胡亂 (carelessly)
hurinong 胡日弄 (behave foolishly)
hutu 胡 [糊] 涂 (cheat; muddled; stupid)
hutuchong 胡 [糊] 涂蟲 (blunderer; *huwei* 胡爲, act recklessly)
huzuo feiwei 胡作非爲 (commit all kinds of outrages)

The word *fan* (Old Chinese *biuan*) has been in use since the Zhou to mean foreign or feudatory. During the course of Chinese history it was written with several alternative characters; *fan* 蕃 (luxuriant); *fan* 番 (barbarian, foreign); *fan* 藩 (protecting, feudatory). From about the Tang, and increasingly after the court moved to Hangzhou in the Southern Song, *fan* (OC *piuan*) 蕃 (*fan* 番) was also used as an alternative for *man* 蠻 (southern tribes; aboriginal, barbarian, foreign). From the Tang to the Qing, it was a common generic for barbarian or foreign, but it has not given the standard language nearly as many derogatives as *hu* 胡. This may reflect the more open culture of the Tang, a period when foreign was not necessarily regarded as synonymous with barbarous. Also, *fan* (*man*) originally applied to the savages of the South, who were far less of a threat than the dreaded northern enemy associated with *hu* 胡 (Xiongnu). Whatever the reasons may be, the following expressions sound more neutral:

zhufan 諸蕃 (foreigners)
fanbang 蕃(番)邦, *fandi* 番地 (foreign countries)
fanyu 蕃(番)語 (used for the speech of savages or foreigners)
fanshu 蕃書, *fanwen* 蕃文, or *fanzi* 蕃字 (foreign script)
fanshang 蕃商 (foreign merchants)
fanbo 蕃(番)舶 (foreign boats)
fanhuo 蕃貨 (foreign goods)
fanhan 蕃漢 (foreigners and Han; used from Song, cf. *Huayi* 華夷)

From the Han, *hu* 胡 was used in the names of many foodstuffs imported from foreign countries, especially from the Western Regions, often via the Silk Road; from the Ming, *fan* 蕃 (*fan* 番) was also used in the same way, especially for foodstuffs imported through the southern seaports (35.2.3). *Fan* continued to serve as a general term for foreign as long as Guangzhou was the main gateway for new products, but in the nineteenth century it was replaced by *yang* 洋 or *xi* 西, the more modern terms preferred in Shanghai.

41.2.2   Ethnonyms

The origins of the ethnonyms (and toponyms) for the Tibetans, Uighurs, Mongols and Manchu were as follows:

Tibetans

When the Tibetan peoples first united and began to call themselves "*Bod-pa" the Chinese referred to them as Bo 蕃 (a rarely used special pronunciation of *fan* 蕃). The Tibetan name for their kingdom was based on the same word and transliterated by the Tang as Tubo 吐蕃 (629–824).[9] This, or Xi-Bo 西蕃, was used in Chinese sources for the Tibetans (Tuboren 吐蕃人) and for the vast area in which they lived (Tibet proper as well as parts of modern Qinghai, Gansu, Sichuan and Yunnan) until the thirteenth century. Tubo is referred to in medieval Arabic sources from the ninth century as "al-Tibbat" from which "Tibet" in English and other western languages is presumably derived. But it is not the name for Tibet in Chinese itself. The Yuan divided up greater Tibet into separate administrative units and established an Office for the Pacification of central and southern Tibet proper naming it Wusizang 烏思藏 (from the Tibetan place names *dBus* "center," the Lhasa area; and *gTsang* "pure," the old name for the upper Brahmaputra river, whose valley had been the birthplace of Tibetan culture). The Ming used Xibo or the newer Wusizang for Tibet proper. In

---

[9] There is a controversy surrounding the meaning of "*Tu*," which is sometimes explained as derived from the Tibetan assumption of *Da* 大 (as in Da Tang 大唐) and the Tang turning it into a meaningless word. Others have suggested it might have come from Turpan (Tulufan 吐魯番). For a historical survey of the meanings of Tibet, see Melvyn Goldstein, "Change, Conflict and Continuity among a Community of Nomadic Pastoralists," in *Resistance and Reform in Tibet*, Robert Barnett and Shirin Akiner, eds., IUP, 1994, 76–90.

the Yongzheng period, Wu (seat of the Dalai Lama) was termed Qian-Zang 前藏 and Zang (seat of the Panchem Lama), Hou-Zang 後藏, terms still in use today. The switch to using Xizang 西藏 in official documents took place for the first time in 1663 and was imperially endorsed with the promulgation of the *Qinding Xizang zhangcheng* 欽定西藏章程 (Regulatons for Tibet). *Zang* 藏 eventually became the standard Chinese term both for the place (as in Xizang zizhiqu 西藏自治區) and the people of Tibet (as in Zangzu 藏族).

Uighurs

Uighur (meaning "united" in that language) is also ultimately derived from a Chinese approximation of the original sounds using characters (Weiwu'er 維吾爾).

Mongols

Mongol is derived from the Mengwu 蒙兀, a branch of the Shiwei 室韋 tribe whose name first appears in Chinese sources in the ninth century. Thereafter, they are referred to as Menggu 萌古, Menggu 朦骨, Mengguli 蒙古里, Menggusi 蒙古斯, Mangguzi 盲骨子 and so forth. The Mongols began using the name Menggu 蒙古 for all their tribes in the early thirteenth century. Chenghiz khan named his kingdom Da Menggu guo 大蒙古國 and from this time onward it was abbreviated in Chinese as Menggu 蒙古.

Manchus

There are numerous theories as to the origin of the neologism *Manju* (Manzhou 滿洲 in Chinese; Manchu in English). It appears first in the *Jiu Manzhou dang* 舊滿洲檔 (Old Manchu chronicles) in 1613 and was officially adopted in 1635 as part of the political effort to consolidate the newly emerging multi-ethnic confederation founded by Nurhaci (see Box 10, chap. 50).[10] In Manchu itself the word appears to be derived from the

---

[10] Pei Huang, "New Light on the Origin of the Manchus," *HJAS* 50.1: 239–82 (1990).

same root as the Mongolian word "Baatur" meaning "Brave" or "Hero."[11] But there is no certainty in the matter.

41.2.3   The "West"

Directional phrases such as *xifang* 西方 or *xitu* 西土 changed their meaning according to the position of the speaker and to the period. For much of Chinese imperial history, starting in the Han, Xiyu 西域 was the standard term for Central Asia (41.3.1). *Xi* 西 also had a strong Buddhist connotation. Thus *Xiguo* 西國 was India; *Xiyu* 西語, Sanskrit and *Xifang* 西方 was *pascime digbhâge* "the place where the sun goes down," as in *xifang jingtu* 西方淨土 (Sukhavati; Pure Land). Later in the nineteenth century, it was this phrase that was borrowed for what became the main word for the "West" or "Occident" (replacing the similar neologism, *Xitu* 西土). It also gave one of the many terms for "Westerner" (*Xifangren* 西方人).

During the Southern Song, a number of new geographic terms came into circulation. One was *Xiyang* 西洋 for the oceans and seas and countries along the coasts of Southeast Asia. It was still in use in this sense in the Ming (the voyages of Zheng He along these coasts and on through the Indian Ocean were described as going down to the western oceans (*xia Xiyang* 下西洋).

There was no general term for Westerners until quite late in Chinese history. There were plenty of foreign traders (*fanke* 蕃客 or *fanmin* 蕃民) from Arabia, Persia and Africa in Guangzhou during the Tang and in Quanzhou in the Song and Yuan,

---

[11] "Cong yuyan lunzheng Nüzhen, Manzhou zhi zucheng 從語言論證女真, 滿洲之族稱," (Examination of the tribal names of Jurchen and Manchu from the standpoint of language) in *Aixinjueluo shi sandai Manxue lunji* 愛新覺羅氏三代滿學論集 (Collected scholarly articles of three generations of the Aisingoros), Wulaxichun 烏拉西春 et al., Yuanfang, 1996, 381–8. See also Pamela Kyle Crossley, "An Introduction to the Qing Foundation Myth," *LIC* 6.2: 13–23 (1985); Liu Xiaomeng, *Manzu de buluo yu guojia* 滿族的部落與國家 (The tribes and state of the Manchu people), Jilin wenshi, 1995, stresses the Mongol influence on the early history of the Nüzhen.

but not from Europe.[12] The quarter or streets in which they lived were known as the *fanfang* 蕃坊 or *fanxiang* 蕃巷. The same terms were used until the Yuan. In the North, in the Yuan, foreigners were mainly from West or Central Asia and were called *semu* 色目 (42.1). *Xiyang* 西洋 was extended to cover the place where the Europeans (*Xiyangren* 西洋人) came from in the Ming and early Qing. The term *Da Xiyang* 大西洋 (lit. the Greater Western Ocean, i.e., the Atlantic) was coined by the Jesuits and their translators in the early seventeenth century. At first its use was controversial because of the presumption of using *da* 大 (normally reserved as a Chinese dynastic epithet or for the toponyms of respected countries). No connection was drawn between the *Xiyangren* and the people of the ancient empire of Da Qin 大秦 (Rome), which is first mentioned in the *Hou Hanshu*.[13]

In the early sixteenth century, Portugal was called Folangji 佛朗機, a term the Chinese took from Muslim traders (from the Persian for Europeans, Firangi, i.e., Franks). A *falangji* also meant a Portuguese canon (a confusion probably introduced by the third character in the transcription, *ji* 機, "instrument"). At the end of the sixteenth century, Spain was also dubbed Folangji. England was transcribed with many different characters for *Yingjili*, e.g., 嘆咭唎 or 英吉利. France was known as Falanxi 法蘭西 from Falanke 法蘭克 (Franks). America was called Yameilijia hezhongguo 亞美理駕合眾國, Meilige heshengguo 美理哥合省國 and so forth. Russia was called Luocha 羅剎 or Eluosi 俄羅斯.

Fortunately these early demotic transcriptions (and there were many variants at different times and in different parts of

---

[12] Several hundred tombstones in Quanzhou recording their deaths in ancient Arabic and Persian have been preserved (47.3).

[13] D. D. Leslie and K. J. H. Gardner, "All Roads Lead to Rome: Chinese Knowledge of the Roman Empire," *JAH* 26 (1992). The authors cite the copious previous scholarly literature on this subject. Note that Likan 犁軒 appears in the *Shiji* and refers to the Seleucid empire; Fulin 拂菻 is used in Sui and Tang sources for Byzantium.

China) followed one of the normal courses for loan words
(1.2.7) by becoming standardized in elegant Literary Chinese
abbreviated hybrids (effectively based on the first syllable of
the name): <u>Ying</u>guo 英國 (England); Faguo 法國 (from <u>Fa</u>-
lanke); <u>De</u>guo 德國 (<u>Deu</u>tschland); <u>Yi</u>dali 意大利 (<u>I</u>talia) or
<u>Mei</u>guo 美國 (abbreviated from Yameilijia hezhongguo). Unof-
ficially and not infrequently graphic pejoratives were added (as
when the character wolf, *lang* 狼, was written instead of *lan* 蘭
in Falanxi 法蘭西). Countries considered powerful usually
have *guo* 國 in their names, others not.

41.3 Main Routes To and From China

41.3.1   Overland Routes

The "Silk Road" was the main overland route to and from
China via Central Asia and Europe and India.[14] In imperial
times, it started from Chang'an (and later Luoyang, when the
capital moved there). From thence it led westward through the
Hexi zoulang 河西走廊 (i.e., the corridor west of the Yellow
River in modern Gansu), and on across the Western Regions
(Xiyu 西域). The route was formalized with settlements, post
stations and frontier walls for the first time during the second
century BC as a means of controlling the Xiongnu (44.3.2.3).[15]

---

[14] S. A. M. Adshead, *China in World History*, 1988; 2nd ed., Macmillan, 1995, contains convenient sections on "avenues of contact" between
China and the rest of the world from 200 BC to 1976 during six periods.

[15] The term *Xiyu* 西域 (the Western regions) was first recorded in the
Former Han. It was used in two different senses. In the narrowest sense it
meant the area East from Dunhuang to the Yumen pass on the western
borders of what is now the modern province of Xinjiang. In its broadest
sense it was used to refer to Central and West Asia, India, North Africa
and Eastern Europe. Which definition was used depended on the power
of the imperial government. In the Han, Tang and Qing it was used in a
somewhat broad sense. In the Yuan it reached its broadest extent. In
other periods the definition narrowed. The expression fell out of use in
the nineteenth century with the opening of sea routes to the West.

The route was in use long before historic times as attested by copious excavations of Paleolithic and Neolithic cultures along them.[16] Even Caucasian remains have been discovered.[17] In 1877, the German geographer Ferdinand Baron von Richthofen called these routes "die Seidenstrassen" (the silk routes; the customary, albeit mistranslation, into English is the "Silk Road").

The "Tubo Route" (Tubodao 吐蕃道) branched from the main Silk Road across the Qinghai plateau through Lhasa and Nepal to India.

For an informative dictionary of all aspects of the history and cultures of the Silk Road, see *Sichou zhi lu wenhua da cidian* 絲綢之路文化大辭典.[18] This contains 12,500 entries arranged topically, e.g., 86 double-column pages on archaeology: Paleolithic sites (23 entries); Neolithic sites and cultures (161); royal tombs (79); tombs of famous people (64); ruined cities (547); major finds of pottery, gold, silver and bronze vessels; coins and textiles. There are also detailed sections on primary sources including manuscripts on bamboo and paper; inscriptions on stone; Dunhuang, Turpan, Loulan and Xi-Xia manuscripts, and 82 foreign sources from Herodotus to the seventeenth century. There is a *pinyin* index.

One problem is the difficulty of correctly identifying place-names encountered in Chinese sources. Use references such as

Xiyu diming 西域地名 (Place-names of the Western Regions), Feng Chengjun 馮承鈞 (1885–1955), comp., Zhonghua, 1955; Lu Junling 陸峻嶺, enl., and corrected, 1980.

---

[16] See *Xiyu tongshi* 西域通史 (Comprehensive history of the Western Regions), Yu Taishan 余太山, ed. in chief, Zhongzhou guji, 1996, 1–45.

[17] Victor H. Mair, "The Mummified Remains Found in the Tarim Basin," *Journal of Indo-European Studies* 23.3–4 (1995), and 10 other articles in this issue on the subject; T. K. Chen and F. T. Hiebert, "The Late Prehistory of Xinjiang in Relation to its Neighbors," *Journal of World Prehistory* 9: 243–300 (1995).

[18] *Sichou zhi lu wenhua da cidian* (Dictionary of the Silk Road culture), Wang Shangshou 王尚壽 and Ji Chengjia 季成家, eds., in chief, Hongqi, 1995.

The "Southern Silk Road" (Yongchangdao 永昌道). Another important overland route to the West started from Xianyang and led via Chengdu in Sichuan through Yunnan (passing Kunming, Dali, Baoshan [Yongchang] and Tengchong 腾冲) before crossing into northern Burma and overland to India (or through southern Burma, to the sea). The Yunnan-Burma section was the same as the Dian-Mian gonglu 滇緬公路 (Burma road) of WW II.

The route to Korea either went overland through northeast China and over the Yalu river 鴨綠江, or across the bay of Bohai and then overland via the Yalu. The direct sea route went from the port of Dengzhou 登州 in Shandong to the mouth of the Yalu and then along the Korean coast before going overland to the capital of Silla.

41.3.2   The Maritime Routes

The main maritime routes from China to the rest of Asia started from the ports of Lüda 旅大, Tianjin 天津, Dengzhou 登州, Shanghai 上海, Ningbo 寧波, Fuzhou 福州, Quanzhou 泉州 and Guangzhou 廣州. Of these, Guangzhou served not only Southeast Asia, but also India, Africa, Arabia and Europe.[19] A Qin shipyard has been excavated in Guangzhou (Panyu 番禺 as it was then called), the busiest overseas trading port from at least that time until the Southern Song, when it was temporarily overtaken by Quanzhou. Of 56 Chinese monks who went to India or Ceylon to study Buddhism during the Tang, 34 travelled by ship from Guangzhou (the remainder

---

[19] *The Maritime Silk Route: 2,000 Years of Trade in the South China System*, produced by the Hong Kong Museum of History, HK: Urban Council, 1996. This is the well-illustrated catalog of a special exhibition with annotations and references to the literature. See also Wang Gungwu, *The Nanhai Trade: The Early History of Chinese Trade in the South China Sea*, Singapore: Times Academic Press, 1998 [1958]; Chen Yan 陳炎, *Haishang sichou zhilu yu Zhongwai wenhua jiaoliu* 海上絲綢之路與中外文化交流 (The maritime silk road and Sino-foreign cultural exchanges), Beijing daxue, 1996.

went overland by the Silk Road in the Northwest). From the early Ming there was a prohibition on foreign trade (*haijin* 海禁). In the Qing, after the recapture of Taiwan in 1683, four provinces were opened for overseas trade until the southern coast was closed in 1757, except for Guangzhou (a monopoly that it enjoyed until 1842 and again from 1949 to 1979). The trade had always been supervised and taxed by the central authorities, and not infrequently indirectly controlled using authorized Chinese merchants. In the Qing it came to be conducted and guaranteed through a monopoly guild of Cantonese merchants (the *shisan hang* 十三行, known better in English as the *Cohong*, an approximation of the Cantonese pronunciation of *gonghang* 公行, meaning combined merchant companies).

41.4 Accounts of Foreign Peoples

Works on border areas and foreign peoples are found in many different types of source, including in the Veritable Records, geographies, encyclopaedias, biographies of officials who served in or visited a country or territory on diplomatic mission (41.4.1) and in their collected prose or verse.

The Standard Histories also contain much material on foreign relations, both peaceful and warlike. They also usually have summaries on foreign peoples at the end of the *Liezhuan* 列傳 (Biographies) chapters (Table 27). In Western sinology there is a long tradition of studies of China's foreign relations based on annotated translations of these chapters, a practice known as "translating the barbarians."[20]

---

[20] Hans H. Frankel notes many of the early studies in *Catalogue of Translations from the Chinese Dynastic Histories for the Period 220–960*, UCP, 1957; rpnt. Greenwood, 1974; Ruth Dunnell contains an extensive list of translations (including many of the later ones) and also studies in "Central Asia," in *American Historical Association Guide to Historical Literature*, Mary Beth Norton, ed., 2 vols., New York: OUP, 1995, 263–83.

Table 27: Non-Han Peoples and Countries in the Standard Histories

1. *Shiji* 史記	Xiongnu 匈奴; Dongyue 東越; Nanyue 南越; Chaoxian 朝鮮; Xi'nanyi 西南夷
2. *Hanshu* 漢書	Xiongnu 匈奴; Xiyu 西域; Xi'nanyi 西南夷; Nanyue 南粵; Minyue 閩粵; Chao-xian 朝鮮
3. *Hou Hanshu* 後漢書	*Siyi* 四夷
4. *Sanguozhi* 三國志	
5. *Jinshu* 晉書	*Siyi* 四夷
6. *Songshu* 宋書	*Siyi* 四夷; *Suolu* 索虜 (the unkempt caitiffs, i.e., the Toba); *Hudi* 胡氏
7. *Nan-Qishu* 南齊書	*Weilu* 魏虜
8. *Liangshu* 梁書	*Zhuyi* 諸夷
9. *Chenshu* 陳書	
10. *Weishu* 魏書	
11. *Bei-Qishu* 北齊書	
12. *Zhoushu* 周書	*Yicheng* 異域
13. *Suishu* 隋書	Xiyu 西域; *Nanman Beidi* 南蠻北狄; Dongyi 東夷
14. *Nanshi* 南史	*Yimo* 夷貊
15. *Beishi* 北史	*Jianwei fuyong* 僭偽附庸
16. *Jiu Tangshu* 舊唐書	Xiyu 西域; *Nanman Beidi* 南蠻北狄; Dongyi 東夷
17. *Xin Tangshu* 新唐書	Xiyu 西域; *Nanman Beidi* 南蠻北狄; Dongyi 東夷
18. *Jiu Wudaishi* 舊五代史	*Waiguo* 外國
19. *Xin Wudaishi* 新五代史	*Siyi fulu* 四夷附錄
20. *Songshi* 宋史	*Waiguo Manyi* 外國蠻夷
21. *Liaoshi* 遼史	*Waiji* 外紀
22. *Jinshi* 金史	*Waiguo* 外國
23. *Yuanshi* 元史	*Waiguo* 外國
24. *Mingshi* 明史	Xiyu 西域; *Waiguo* 外國; *Tusi* 土司
25. *Xin Yuanshi* 新元史	*Waiguo* 外國
26. *Qingshigao* 清史稿	*Tusi fanbu shuguo* 土司藩部屬國

See *Niansan zhong zhengshi ji qingshi zhong ge zu shiliao huibian* 廿三種正史及清史中各族史料彙編, Rui Yifu 芮逸夫 et al., eds., 5 vols., Shiyusuo, 1973. All mentions of non-Han peoples in 23 Standard Histories plus the Draft History of the Qing are excerpted. Because of the name index this collection replaces earlier ones.

41.4.1   *Translations, Excerpts, Artifacts and Studies*

Exhibition catalogs are an excellent introduction to the archaeology the steppe. See, for example,

Adam T. Kessler, *Empires Beyond the Great Wall: the Heritage of Ghenghis Khan*, Natural History Museum of Los Angeles County, 1994. It covers briefly prehistoric origins of the steppe; the Eastern Hu and the Xiongnu; the Xianbei and the Wuhuan; the Qidan and the Liao Dynasty; North China during the pre-Mongol period and the Mongol Era and the Yuan Dynasty. It is based on an exhibition of artifacts from Inner Mongolia.

Ancient Chinese and Ordos Bronzes, Jessica Rawson and Emma Bunker, eds., Oriental Ceramic Society of Hong Kong, 1990.

Traders and Raiders on China's Northern Frontier, Jenny F. So and Emma C. Bunker, eds., Smithsonian Institution, 1995.

Most volumes of the *CHC* contain chapters or sections on foreign relations as well as bibliographic notes (see 41.4.3). Below follows a list of some of the main translations and collections of excerpts on foreign peoples.

A. F. P. Hulsewé and M. A. N. Loewe, *China in Central Asia: The Early Stage: 125 BC–AD 23*, Brill, 1979.

Rafe de Crespigny, *Northern Frontier: The Policies and Strategies of the Later Han Empire*, Faculty of Asian Studies, ANU, 1984.

Xiongnu: *Xiongnu shiliao huibian* 匈奴史料彙編 (Collection of historical materials on the Xiongnu), Lin Gan 林幹, 2 vols., Zhonghua, 1988. Includes excerpts from textual sources, archaeological materials and inscriptions. Vol. 1 covers from the Warring States to the third century AD; vol. 2, up to the Tang.

Turks: Edouard Chavannes, *Documents sur les Tou-kiue Turcs occidentaux*, 1903; rpnt. Maisonneuve, 1942; Cen Zhongmian 岑仲勉, ed., *Tujue jishi* 突厥集史, 2 vols., Zhonghua, 1958. Much of the same material is translated in *Die chinesischen Nachtrichten zur Geschichte der Ost-Türken (T'u-küe)*, 2 vols., Harrassowitz, 1958.

Uighurs: Colin Mackerras, *The Uighur Empire According to the T'ang Dynastic Histories*, 2nd ed., ANU Press, 1972.

Nanzhao: Charles Backus, *The Nan-chao Kingdom and T'ang China's Southwestern Frontier*, CUP, 1981 (uses many additional sources).

Tuyuhun: Gabriella Molè, *The T'u-yü-hun from the Northern Wei to the Time of the Five Dynasties*, Serie Orientale Roma, 41, 1970.

Southeast Asia: *Dongnan Ya gudaishi Zhongwen wenxian tiyao* 東南亞古代史文文獻提要 (Extracts from Chinese historical sources on Southeast Asian history), Gu Hai 顧海, comp., Xiamen daxue, 1990.

Philippines: *Zhongguo gujizhong youguan Feilübin ziliao huibian* 中國古籍中有關菲律賓資料匯編 (Collection of materials on the Philippines from old Chinese sources), Zhongshan daxue Dongnan Ya lishi yanjiusuo (Institute for SE Asian History, Zhongshan daxue), ed., Zhonghua, 1980. All mentions of the Philippines (Luzon, Sulu) in Chinese sources are excerpted. There are people- and place-name indexes as well as a listing of the works from which the excerpts are drawn.

Laos: *Zhongguo guji zhong youguan Laowo ziliao huibian* 中國古籍中有關老撾資料匯編 (Collection of materials on the kingdoms of Laos from old Chinese sources), Jing Zhenguo 景振國, ed., Zhongzhou guji, 1985.

Cambodia: *Zhongguo gujizhong youguan Jianbuzhai ziliao huibian* 中國古籍中有關東埔寨資料匯編 (Collection of materials on Cambodia from old Chinese sources), ed. and annotated by Lu Junling 陸峻岭 and Zhou Shaoquan 周紹泉, Zhonghua, 1986. Note the *Zhenla fengtu ji* 真臘風土記, Zhou Daguan 周達觀, 1297; Xia Nai 夏鼐, collated and annotated, Zhonghua, 1981. This is the fullest account of ancient Khmer ways of life in any language. *The Customs of Cambodia*, J. Paul, Siam Society, 1992; translation into English of French tr. by Paul Pelliot, *BEFEO* 2: 123–77 (1902). See also Stephen O. Murray, "A thirteenth-century imperial ethnography," *Anthropology Today* 10.5: 15–18 (1994).

Japan: *Zhong-Ri guanxishi ziliao huibian* 中日關係史資料匯編 (Collection of materials on the history of Sino-Japanese relations), Wang Xiangrong 汪向榮 and Xia Yingyuan 夏應元, eds., Zhonghua, 1984. Includes excerpts from Standard Histories from the Later Han onward and from encyclopaedias on Japan as well as excerpts from Japanese sources. See also Ryusaku Tsunoda, *Japan in the Chinese Dynastic Histories, Later Han through Ming Dynasties*, South Pasadena, 1951 (for archival documents on Sino-Japanese relations, see 50.26).

For the Ming and Qing, the Veritable Records are an important source on all aspects of external relations, including tribute missions. See for example,

Mindai Man-Mô shiryô Min jitsuroku shô, Manshûhen, Môkohen 明代満蒙史料明實錄抄滿洲篇蒙古篇 (Historical materials concerning Manchuria and Mongolia under the Ming selected from the Veritable Records of the Ming), Imanishi Shunju 今西春秋 and Mitamura Taisuke 三村泰助, eds., 17 vols., Kyôto daigaku, 1943–59. There is an itemized index: *Mindai Man-Mô shiryô, kômoku sôsakuin* 明代満蒙史料項目總合索引, Kyoto, 1959.

Watanabe Hiroshi, "An Index of Embassies and Tribute Missions from Islamic Countries to Ming China (1368–1644) as Recorded in the *Ming Shih-lu* 明實錄 Classified According to Geographic Area," *MTB* 33: 285–347 (1975); see also the volumes of excerpts from the *Ming Shilu* cited in 49.1 and from the *Qing Shilu* in 50.5.

Henry Serruys, *Sino-Mongol Relations During the Ming II: The tribute System and Diplomatic Missions (1400–1600)*, Brussels: *Mélanges chinois et bouddhiques* 14, 1967.

Roger Greatrex, "Tribute Missions from the Sichuan Borderlands to the Imperial Court (1400–1665)," *Acta Orientalia* 58: 75–151 (1997).

Henry Serruys, *The Mongols and Ming China: Customs and History*, Variorum, 1995.

Ming Shilu Zangzu shiliao 明實錄藏族史料 (Historical materials on the Tibetan people in the *Ming Shilu*), Gu Zucheng 顧祖成 et al., eds., Lhasa, Xizang renmin, vols., 1 and 2, 1982; vol. 3, 1985.

Ming-Qing Shilu zhong zhi Xizang shiliao 明清實錄中之西藏史料 (Historical materials on Tibet from the *Ming* and *Qing Shilu*), Luo Xianglin 羅香林, ed., HKCU Press, 1981.

Qing Shilu Zangzu shiliao xuan 清實錄藏族史料選 (Selection of historical materials on the Tibetan people from the *Qing Shilu*), Gu Zucheng 顧祖成 et al., eds., 10 vols., Xizang renmin, 1982; rpnt., 1993.

Yuan yilai Xizang difang yu zhongyang zhengfu guanxi dang'an shiliao huibian 元以來西藏地方與中央政府關係檔案史料匯編 (Collection of historical materials from the archives on the relationship between the Tibetan area with the central government since the Yuan), Zhongguo zangxue zhongxin et al., Zhongguo Zangxue, 1994.

Qing Shilu Taiwanshi ziliao xuanji 清實錄臺灣史資料選輯 (Selection of materials from the *Qing Shilu* on Taiwan), Fujian renmin, 1993.

Ming Shilu zhong zhi Dongnan Ya shiliao 明實錄中之東南亞史料 (Historical materials on Southeast Asia from the Veritable Records of the Ming), Chiu Ling-yeong (Zhao Lingyang 趙令揚) et al., 2 vols., Hsüeh-tsin press, 1968; 1976.

For sources on foreign countries in the Qing archives, see 50.2.6.

41.4.2   Transcription Conventions

The conventional systems for transcribing the languages of China's neighbors into English, are

Japanese: the Hepburn system.

Korean: the McLune-Reischauer system.

Manchu: Möllendorf system as adapted by Jerry Norman in *A Concise Manchu-English Lexicon*, UWP, 1978.

Mongolian: Antoine Mostaert, *Dictionnaire Ordos*, vol. 3, *Index des mots du mongol écrit et du Mongol ancien*, Peiping, 1944. The only derivations from this system are that *q* becomes *kh*; γ becomes *gh*; and the hacek (ˇ) is removed from above *j*, *c*, and *s*, which become *j*, *ch* and *sh*.

Tibetan: Turrell/Wylie, "A Standard System of Tibetan Transcription," *HJAS* 22: 261–67 (1959).

Vietnamese: the standard Quôc-ngu spelling. In non-specialst western works it is not uncommon to leave out both sets of diacritics (one for the tones, the other for vowel quality).

41.4.3   Bibliography

For a full bibliography of primary sources on border areas, see

Deng Yanlin 鄧衍林, *Zhongguo bianjiang tuji lu* 中國邊疆圖籍錄. (Catalog of maps and writings on China's border areas), Shangwu, 1958. Deng's work is arranged by place and it is also indexed; references to maps are included.

There are also bibliographies of particular border areas or regions, for example:

Western Regions

Cambridge History of Early Inner Asia, Denis I. Sinor, ed., CUP, 1990.

Chen Yanqi 陳延琪 et al., *Xiyu yanjiu shumu* 西域研究書目 (Bibliography of research on the Western regions), Xinjiang renmin, 1990; covers from the Qin to 1989.

Tibet

For an annotated bibliography of Tibetan sources, see *Tibetan Histories*, Dan Martin, London: Serindia, 1997, which contains notes on 700 Tibetan language sources from the earliest times (eighth century) onward. The most extensive local archive in China is held in Lhasa (50.3). Christopher Beckwith, *The Tibetan Empire*, PUP, 1987; rev. ed., 1993, also has a bibliography on Central Asia.

Note the secondary studies in *Zangxue shumu* 藏學書目 (*Catalog of Chinese Publications in Tibetan Studies, 1949–1991*), FLP, 1994; *Continuation* covering publications of 1992–95, FLP, 1997.

South

"Descriptions of Southern Regions and Foreign Countries," in *SCC*, vol. III, CUP, 1959, 510–14.

Southeast Asia: *Dongnan Ya yanjiu lunwen suoyin (1980–89)* 東南亞研究論文索引 (Index of research articles on Southeast Asia), Xiamen daxue Nanyang yanjiusuo ziliaoshi 厦門大學南洋研究所資料室, Xiamen daxue, 1993.

Dongnan Ya yanjiu shumu huibian 東南亞研究書目彙編 (Collection of books on research on Southeast Asia), Xiao Xinhuang 蕭新煌 and Lin Shuhui 林淑慧, Zhongyang yanjiuyuan 中央研究院, Dongnan Ya quyu yanjiu jihua 東南亞區域研究計劃, 1995.

Note that for Vietnam until about the tenth century the only major sources are all in Chinese and thereafter, if Vietnamese, then written in Chinese. See the sources cited in Keith Weller Taylor, *The Birth of Vietnam*, UCP, 1983.

Some of the *CHC* volumes have extensive bibliographic essays or notes on the border regions and foreign affairs covering both primary and secondary sources, notably,

"Liao, Xi-Xia, Jin and Yuan," *CHC*, vol. 6, 1994, 665–726.

"The Ming and Inner Asia," *CHC*, vol. 8, 1998, 987–89.

"Sino-Korean Tributary Relations under the Ming," vol. 8, 1998, 989–91.

"Ming Foreign Relations: Southeast Asia," vol. 8, 1998, 992–95.

"Relations with Maritime Europeans, 1514–1662," vol. 8, 1998, 995–98.

"The Canton Trade and the Opium War," *CHC*, 10, 1978, 599–601.

"The Creation of the Treaty System," *CHC*, 10, 1978, 601–603.

"Late Ch'ing Foreign Relations, 1866–1905," *CHC*, 11, 1980, 605–608.

"Changing Chinese Views of Western Relations, 1840–95," *CHC*, vol. 11, 1980, 608–610.

41.5 Travel and Sojourn Abroad

The first historical record of a Chinese traveler abroad is of Xu Shi 徐市, who went in search of the elixir of life to the islands in the East, Penglai 蓬萊 (as legend has it, Japan) during the Qin at the end of the third century BC.

As the man/land ratio began to decline in the Ming and Qing, an increasingly large number of Chinese, especially from the southern provinces of Guangdong and Fujian, began to settle abroad (41.5.2).

41.5.1   Travel Abroad

Zhonghua shuju has published 17 of the most famous Chinese overseas travel accounts, each work punctuated and annotated: *Zhongwai jiaotong shiji congkan* 中外交通史籍叢刊 (Collectanea of Chinese historical works on overseas travel), Zhonghua, 1961–96. A popular anthology of English translations from Chinese travel literature was edited by Jeanette Mirsky: *The Great Chinese Travelers*, Allen and Unwin, 1965.

Han

The first famous Chinese traveler abroad, Zhang Qian 張騫, led two expeditions to the Western regions in the second century BC. He spent 11 years abroad, married a Xiongnu wife and had children by her.[21]

---

[21] Mirsky (1965) reprints a translation of Sima Qian's account of his travels, 13–25. See also Ying-shi Yü, *Trade and Expansion in Han China: A Study in the Structure of Sino-Barbarian Economic Relations*, UCP, 1967.

Zhang had many successors. For a collection of 29 works (or excerpts) recounting voyages to the Xiyu, see *Gu Xixingji* 古西行記. There is a 60-page place-name index.[22]

Nan-Bei Chao

The travels of Chinese Buddhist pilgrims to India, starting with Faxian 法顯 (ca. 337–422), *Foguo ji* 佛國記 (Record of Buddhist kingdoms), have frequently been translated.[23] See Nancy E. Boulton, "Early Chinese Buddhist Travel Records as a Literary Genre," Ph.D. dissertation, Georgetown University, 1982.

Tang

Da Tang Xiyuji 大唐西域記 (Record of the Western Regions), Xuanzang 玄奘 (596–664), 646; use *Da Tang Xiyuji jiaozhu* 大唐西域記校注 (Punctuated and annotated edition of *Da Tang Xiyuji*), Zhonghua, 1985; 3rd prnt., 1995. Xuanzang's journey to India began in 629 and ended in 644. Alexander Leonhard Mayer et al., *Xuanzang's Leben und Werk*, Veröffentlichungen der Societas Uralo-Altaica, vol. 34, 5 parts, Harrassowitz, 1992; Arthur Waley, *The Real Tripitaka*, Allen and Unwin, 1932; *Si-yu-ki: Buddhist Records of the Western World*, Samuel Beal, tr., 2 vols., Trübner, 1884; CMC, 1976; New Delhi: Munshiram Manoharlal, 1983. Sally Hovey Wriggins, *Xuan-zang: A Buddhist Pilgrim on the Silk Road*, with a Foreword by Frederick W. Mote, Westview, 1996. Legends about Xuanzang formed the basis of the novel *Xiyouji* (34.3).

Manshu 蠻書, Fan Chuo 樊綽 (ninth century), Zhonghua, 1962; tr., G. H. Luce, *The Man Shu: Book of the Southern Barbarians*, Southeast Aia Program, Cornell University, 1961. Mainly on the kingdom of Nanzhao in Yunnan. The best Chinese edition is *Manshu jiaozhu* 蠻書校注, Xiang Da 向達, ed., Zhonghua, 1962. Fan was military and surveillance commissioner of Annam in the late Tang. Text retrieved from the *Yongle dadian* in the eighteenth century.

---

[22] *Gu Xixingji xuanzhu* (Selected and annotated ancient journeys to the Western regions), Yang Jianxin 楊建新, ed. in chief, Ningxia renmin, 1987; rpnt., 1996.

[23] *The Travels of Fa-hsien*, Herbert A. Giles, tr., CUP, 1923; rpnt., Routledge, 1956. SCC, vol. I, *Introductory Orientations*, CUP, 1954, rpnt., 1961, "The Buddhist Pilgrims," 207–11, for a brief summary.

Song

Changchun zhenren xiyouji 長春真人西遊記 (The Western journey of the sage of eternal spring), 1121–23, records in diary form of the journey of the Daoist master Qiu Chuji 丘處機, who was invited to visit Genghis Khan in the Hindu Kush; written by his disciple, Li Zhichang 李志常 (1193–1256). It contains the only eyewitness account of the founder of the Mongolian empire. See *The Travels of an Alchemist: The journey of the Taoist Ch'ang ch'un from China to the Hindukush at the Summons of Chinghiz Khan. Recorded by his Disciple Li Chih-ch'ang*, Arthur Waley, tr., Routledge, 1931, 1963; Paul Ratchnevsky, "The World Conqueror and the Taoist Monk," in *Genghis Khan, His Life and Legacy*, Blackwell, 1991, 134–6.

Song Diplomatic Diaries

There have been many studies and translations of individual diplomatic diaries, starting with Chavannes and continuing to the present. For a bibliography of these mission reports, see Herbert Franke's 1981 article cited below. Also the same author's "Sung Embassies: Some General Observations," in Morris Rossabi, *China among Equals—The Middle Kingdom and its Neighbors, 10ᵗʰ–14ᵗʰ Centuries*, UCP, 1983, 116–48. Christian Lamouroux has studied the eight extant reports of Song embassies to the Liao in the tenth century in "De L'étrangeté à la différence: Les récits des emissaires Song en pays Liao (XIᵉ s.)," in *Pérégrinations en Asie*, 101-26.

Edouard Chavannes, "Voyageur chinois chez les Khitan et les Jurchen," pt. 1, *JA* 9.9: 377–442 (1897); pt. 2, *JA* 9.11: 361–439 (1898); and by the same scholar, "Pei Yuan lou 北轅錄: Recit d'un voyage dans le Nord par Tcheou Chan 周燀," *TP* 5: 162–92 (1904).

Erik Haenisch, Yao Ts'ung-wu et al., tr., *Meng-Ta pei-lu* [*Mengda beilu* 蒙韃備錄] *und Hei-Ta shih-lüeh* [*Heida shilüe* 黑韃事略]: *chinesische Gesandtenberichte über die frühen Mongolen 1221 und 1237*, Harrassowitz, 1980.

Herbert Franke, "A Sung Embassy Diary of 1211–12: The *Shih Chin lu* [使金錄] of Ch'eng Cho [Cheng Zhuo 程卓]," *BEFEO* 69: 171–207 (1981).

James Hargett, "Fan Ch'eng-ta's *Lanpeilu*: A Southern Sung Embassy Account," *The Tsing Hua Journal of Chinese Studies* XVI.1-2: 119-177 (1984).

Song (others)

Zhufan zhi 諸蕃志, Zhao Rugua 趙汝适, 1242–58: *Chao Ju-Kua: His Work on the Chinese and Arab Trade in the Twelfth and Thirteenth Centuries, Entitled Chu-fan-chih*, Friedrich Hirth and William W. Rockhill, trs., St. Petersburg, 1911; Taibei rpnt., 1970. Zhao was Shibosi 市舶司 (Superintendant of shipping) at Quanzhou and based his account partly on information obtained from merchants there.

Yuan

Xi shiji 西使記, Liu Yu 劉郁. The author was on mission to Persia between 1259 and 1263.

Xi youlu 西遊錄, Yelü Chucai 耶律楚材 (1190–1244), Zhonghua, 1981. The author recorded his travels from Beijing to the Western regions. See Igor de Rachewiltz, "The *Hsi-yü lu* by Yeh-lü Ch'u-ts'ai," *MS*: 1–128 (1962).

Daoyi zhilüe 島夷志略 (also *Daoyizhi* 島夷志), Wang Dayuan 汪大淵 (ca. 1311– ?), 1350.

Voyager from Xanadu: Rabban Sauma and the First Journey from China to the West, Morris Rossabi, Kodansha Intl., 1993. Rabban was sent by the Ilkhan Arghun to Europe in 1287.

Ming

Yingyai shenglan 瀛涯勝覽, Ma Huan 馬歡. This is the most important account of Zheng He's voyages. Ma Huan was a participant and wrote in the colloquial. *Ying-yai Sheng-lan: The Overall Survey of the Ocean's Shores (1433)*, J. V. G. Mills, tr., Hakluyt Society, 1970; rpnt., White Lotus, 1997. Mills' scholarly translation has a gazetteer of more than 700 names mentioned in the text with their modern equivalents, as well as an index of conventional names of identified places. The translator also describes similar sources, 55–66. J. J. L. Duyvendak, *China's Discovery of Africa*, Probsthain, 1949.

Xingcha shenglan 星槎勝覽, Fei Xin 費信, 1436, is the second-most important account of Zheng He's voyages and was also written by a participant: *Hsing-ch'a Sheng-lan: The Overall Survey of the Star Raft by Fei Hsin*, J. V. G. Mills, tr., rev. and annotated by Roderich Ptak, Harrassowitz, 1995. This translation is based on the edition of Shen Jiefu 沈節甫, 1617; rpnt., Taibei: Yiwen, 1966.

Xiyang fanguo zhi 西洋番國志 (Gazetteer of the barbarian countries in the western oceans), Gong Zhen 鞏珍, Preface, 1434; Zhonghua, 1961. Supplements the above two accounts.

Zheng He xia Xiyang ziliao huibian 鄭和下西洋資料匯編 (Collection of materials on Zheng He's voyages to the southern seas), Zheng He-sheng 鄭鶴聲 and Zheng Yijun 鄭一鈞, eds., 3 vols., Qi-Lu, 1980–89. A huge collection of Ming sources on the subject.

Zhang Xie 張燮 (1574–1640), *Dong Xi yang kao* 東西洋考 (On the eastern and western oceans), 1618; Zhonghua, 1981, is the most comprehensive Ming description of the countries of Southeast Asia.

Xiyu xingchengji 西域行程記 (Record of travels in the western regions), Chen Cheng 陳誠. The author's travels began in 1414 and took him to present-day Samarkand and Herat. See Morris Rossabi, "Two Ming Envoys to Inner Asia," *TP* 62.3: 1–34 (1976), and the same scholar's "A translation of Ch'en Ch'eng's *Hsi-yu fan-kuo chih* [*Xiyu fanguo zhi* 西域番國志]," *Ming Studies* 17: 49–59 (1983).

Wanli xingchengji 萬里行程記 (Record of a long journey), Qi Yunshi 祁韻士 (1751–1815). Record of Qi's journey from Beijing to Yili.

Qing

Theodore Foss, "The European Sojourn of Philippe Couplet and Michael Shen Fuzung, 1683–92," in Philippe Couplet, S.J. (1623–93), *The Man Who Brought China to Europe*, Jerome Hendrickx, ed., Steyler, 1990.

Fan Shouyi 樊守義 (1682–1753), a Christian convert from Shanxi, accompanied the Kangxi emperor's special envoy to the vatican, the Jesuit Francesco Provanna (1662–1717). They went to Europe in 1707. Fan remained there until 1717 using the name Louis Fan. On the return voyage Provana died (a fragment of his tombstone survives: "Hic jacet P. Josephus Provana Societatis JESU Professus Sacerdos et Missionarius Sinensis"). Fan wrote the first Chinese account of Europe based on first-hand acquaintance: *Shenjian lu* 身見錄 (Seen with my own eyes), 1721. He was chiefly impressed by the magnificence of the royal palaces and also by the Vatican Library, St. Peter's and the other sights of Rome. For a study of John Hu, a near contemporary of Fan, who was in France from 1722 to 1725, see Jonathan D. Spence, *The Question of Hu*, Knopf, 1988.

Haiguo wenjian lu 海國聞見錄 (Record of things seen and heard about the maritime countries), Chen Lunjiong 陳倫炯 (fl. 1730).

Zhouju suozhi 舟車所至 (Places reached by land and by boat), Zheng Guangsu 鄭光祖 (b. 1775), 1843; Zhongguo, 1991. Account of the author's travels in China and Asia, including the Indian Ocean.

Hailu 海錄 (Maritime records), Xie Qinggao 謝清高 (1765–1822). Xie boarded a trading vessel (probably Portuguese) and sailed to America,

Europe and Asia. On losing his eyesight, he returned home and dictated his recollections in 1820 to Yang Bingnan. See Kenneth Ch'en, "*Hai Lu*: Forerunner of Chinese Travel Accounts of Western Countries," *MS* 7: 208–26 (1942). The work indicates how little was known at the beginning of the nineteenth century in China about the West (contrast Japanese knowledge at this time about not only the West, but also China).

Shuofang beisheng 朔方備乘 (Historical sources on the northern regions), He Qiutao 何秋濤 (1824–62), 80 *juan*, originally called *Beijiao huibian* 北徼彙編.

After the Opium War, demand for more information about foreign countries led to much more detailed travel accounts and to the publication of collectanea of Chinese and foreign works about travel and world geography such as the *Xiaofanghu zhai yudi congchao* 小方壺齋輿地叢鈔 (Collections of historical writings from the *Xiaofanghu* studio, 1897). The translation of foreign textbooks, including those on geography, also began at this time.

Haiguo tuzhi 海國圖志 (Gazetteer and maps of the maritime world), Wei Yuan 魏源, 50 *juan*, 1844; 60 *juan*, 1847; 100 *juan*, 1852. See Jane Kate Leonard, *Wei Yuan and China's Rediscovery of the Maritime World*, HUP, 1984. This work is remarkable for containing many early Western loan words, see section 1.2.7.

Yinghuan zhilüe 瀛環志略 (A Brief Description of the Ocean Circuit), Xu Jiyu 徐繼畬 (1795–1873), 1848. Based on Western geographic works. See Fred Drake, *China Charts the World: Hsü Chi-yü and His Geography of 1848*, HUP, 1975. Xu was much criticized for his progressive ideas and forced to retire in 1852. In 1865 he was recalled to be minister of the Zongli Yamen 總理衙門 and in 1866 made director of the Tongwen guan 同文館, the college for interpreters.

The First Chinese Embassy to the West, Translated from the Journals of Kuo Sung-t'ao, Liu Hsi-hung and Chang Te-yi, J. D. Frodsham, tr., OUP, 1974. Guo Songtao 郭嵩燾 (1818–91) set sail from Shanghai in 1876 to act as Minister to England (1877–78) and concurrently to France (1878).

The European Diary of Hsieh Fucheng (1838–94), Helen Hsieh Chien, tr., introduced and annotated by Douglas Howland, St. Martin's Press, 1993. Recounts Hsieh's travels in Europe, the United States and Asia in the years 1890–4.

See also *Land Without Ghosts: Chinese Impressions of America from the Mid-Nineteenth Century to the Present*, R. David Arkush and Leo O. Lee, tr., and ed., UCP, 1989.

41.5.2   Overseas Chinese

Huaqiaoshi lunwen ziliao suoyin 華僑史論文資料索引 (Index of articles on the history of the Huaqiao), Guangzhou, 1981. Covers secondary sources published in Chinese, 1895–1980.

Kajin Kakyô kankei bunken mokuroku 華人華僑關系文獻目錄 (Bibliography on overseas Chinese), Fukuzaki Hisakazu 福崎久一, ed., Ajia keizai kenkyû senta, 1996.

42

Foreign Accounts of China

Early travelers to China, whether from Japan, Korea, from the Arabic or Persian empires, or from Europe and later from North America, frequently left records of their stay. These make fascinating reading. In this chapter a tiny number are described, some written by monks or merchants, others by adventurers and explorers or by missionaries, diplomats or officials (42.2).[1] The most detailed accounts are those written by the Jesuits from the sixteenth to the eighteenth centuries (34.7).

In the eighteenth century, many closely observed paintings and sketches were made by European painters. The first photographs survive from the 1850s (42.3).

China is featured in official Korean, Ryûkyû and Vietnamese historical works based on the documentary sources of these countries. Some of the important works are briefly introduced (42.4).

There are a number of references for coping with the frequently encountered problem of knowing a foreign person's original name when the reference is in Chinese.[2] There are also more specialized references cover-

---

[1] *Visiteurs de l'Empire Céleste*, Réunion des Musées Nationaux, 1994, is the well-illustrated and scholarly catalog of an exhibition held at the Musée Guimet in Paris in 1994. It covers foreign visitors to China from the Tang to the Qing. See also the references in notes 3 and 4.

[2] *Jindai lai Hua waiguo renming cidian* 近代來華外國人名詞典 (Dictionary of the names of foreigners who came to China in modern times),

Footnote continued on next page

ing special categories of foreign visitors, for example, Christian missionaries (34.7) or diplomats coming to China (and sent abroad by the Qing) between 1843 and 1911 (50.5, *Biographies*).

The chapter begins by examining the various terms that outsiders have used for "China" and the "Chinese" (42.1).

42.1 The "Chinese" and "China"

42.1.1   The "Chinese"

Outsiders (including non-Han peoples living in the China area) usually called the Chinese by the name of the ruling dynasty as did the Chinese themselves (3.1). For example, during the Qin and the Han, the Xiongnu 匈奴 referred to the people of North China as the men of Qin (*Qinren* 秦人) or men of Han (*Hanren* 漢人).[3] As the Han dynasty grew weaker, the familiar terms *Han'er* 漢兒 or *Hanzi* 漢子 took on a pejorative sense.[4] After the fall of the Han, the alien kingdoms in the North of China continued often to refer to the people of the Southern Dynasties as *Hanzi*. Sometimes, they also used the old Zhou expression *daoyi* 島夷 (barbarians living in the islands off the East China coast). In return, the southerners referred to the people of the Nothern Dynasties as *Suolu* 索虜 (unkempt caitiffs).

During the Tang, several of the non-Han peoples in south China as well as foreigners referred to the inhabitants of the

Shekeyuan, Jindaishi yanjiusuo fanyishi 近代史研究所翻譯室, comp., Shehui kexue, 1981. Arrangement is by original names. Dates are given as well as the Chinese transcription of the name, and brief biographies. The transcriptions are indexed.

[3] For the origins of the patronym *Zhongguo* 中國, see Box 3, chap.4.

[4] *Hu'er* 胡兒 (barbarian weaklings) was the Han equivalent for referring to foreigners. It remained in use until the early twentieth century. This and other expressions for referring to foreigners are examined in section 41.2.

Central Plains (the Huaxia) as *Tangren* 唐人 (men of Tang), a practice which continued well into the Ming. *Tô* or *kara* (唐) in Japanese, or *Tang* 唐 in Korean, are used to this day in the sense of meaning "Chinese" or "foreign."[5]

Tangren was also adopted by overseas Chinese (especially Cantonese), who still often refer to themselves in this way, as well as to their Chinatowns as *Tangrenjie* 唐人街, to their (Cantonese) cuisine as "Tang food" and to old-style Chinese clothing as *Tangzhuang* 唐裝. China itself is called *Tangshan* 唐山 by many overseas Chinese (Guangdong's Tang connection comes from the fact that it was colonized from the Tang on. So modern Cantonese still shows traces of the variety of literary Chinese current in the late Tang dynasty, 1.2.1).

By the end of the Tang, *Hanren* or *Han'er* had lost any pejorative sense and *Hanzi* was no longer used to describe the Han people. Inside China it was used in the sense of "man" or "husband," but it still retained the pejorative sense of wrotten husband (*jian zhangfu* 賤丈夫) right up to the later empire.[6]

Among the Jin 金 elite, *Hanren* 漢人 was used to refer to the Chinese in the South. During the Yuan, conversely, *Hanren* or *Han'er* included all those of whatever ethnic background, who had been living in the North in Jin 金 territory, so the phrase included Han Chinese, Manchurians and Koreans. All those who had lived under the Southern Song were officially called *Nanren* 南人 (unofficially, *Manzi* 蠻子 or Nan Manzi 南蠻子, southern "savages" or "barbarians;" or Songren 宋人 or *xin furen* 新附人, "men of Song" or "newly submitted people"). *Nanren* were ranked after Mongols, *Semuren* 色目人 and *Hanren*. *Semuren* 色目人 in the Yuan referred to northwestern peoples, those living along the Silk Road in central and Western Asia as well as Europeans. The expression is usually

---

[5] E.g., *Tôbutsu* 唐物 (foreign goods); *karafû* 唐風 (Chinese style); *tôhon* 唐本 (books from China); *karamatsu* 唐松 ("Japanese" larch).

[6] Chen Shu 陳述, "Han'er Hanzi shuo 漢兒漢子説," (On *Han'er* and *Hanzi*), *Shehui kexue zhanxian* 1986.1: 290–97.

translated as "Western Asians" or "multi-origin people". They were also called *Zhuguoren* 諸國人—"people from all over".

Southerners referred politely to all those living in North China as *Beiren* 北人. For the first time the expression Beifanghua 北方話 (northern speech) appears.[7]

"Seres" (the silk people) may have been intended by some Roman writers to refer to the Chinese. "Silk" possibly came from Latin *Sericus*, itself in turn derived by way of Greek and Persian from the Old Chinese pronunciation *sie* for *si* 絲. The English word "Chinese" came from "China" and was used for the first time in the sixteenth century. "Chinaman" meant a dealer in porcelain in the eighteenth century; in the nineteenth century it became the slightly pejorative term for "Chinese."

42.1.2   "China"

In the European Middle Ages, China was known in Latin as Cathaya, a name derived via Central Asia from Qidan 契丹 (Khitan), the founders of the Liao dynasty. From whence came Slavonic, Turkic and Arabic words for China such as "*Kitaia*" or *Hitai* and eventually, the English "Cathay." At first Cathay referred to North China only. The South was known as the land of the Manzi 蠻子. Later, Cathay was retained as a poetic way of referring to all of China as in Tennyson's (1842) phrase "Better fifty years of Europe than a cycle of Cathay" (5.3.2).

The word "China" only entered European languages in the sixteenth and seventeenth centuries probably via Persian *Chînî*, (possibly based on the Sanskrit *Zhina* 支那, meaning the land of the Qin 秦 although this is now felt to be an unlikely provenance). "China" at first was used mainly to refer to what the Portuguese called "porcelain" (from its resemblance to polished Venus shell or cowrie). In the nineteenth century

---

[7] Jing-shen Tao [Tao Jinsheng 陶晉生], "Barbarians or Northerners: Northern Sung Images of the Khitans," in *China among Equals: The Middle Kingdom and Its Neighbors, 10th-14th centuries*, Morris Rossabi, ed., UCP, 1983, 66–88.

"China" became the main word for the country from which the porcelain came, that is, China.

Zhina 支那 entered Japanese as the "modern" word for China in the eighteenth century (prior to that, Tô 唐, Min 明 or Shin 清 were used). By the late nineteenth century Zhina was replacing Shin 清 and had become associated with Japan's colonial and imperial policies in China. As a result Shina 支那 and Shinajin 支那人 all but fell out of use after 1949 in Japan as also did the same words in Chinese.[8]

42.2 Travel Accounts and Reports

Many of the visitors from abroad came on tribute missions. The main entry points into China for foreign travellers, including tribute missions, throughout most of Chinese history were the Yumen pass on the Silk Road; the overland route from Korea and the ports of the eastern and southern coasts, notably Guangzhou. These entry points are listed in section 41.3.

Ninth and Tenth Centuries

Japanese monk, Ennin 圓仁, who visited Tang China in 840 and spent nine years there, mainly at Chang'an: Nit-Tô guhô junrei gyôki 入唐求法巡禮行記 (Account of a pilgrimage to Tang in search of the law), tr. into English as Ennin's Diary, Edwin O. Reischauer, Ronald Press, 1955. See also Reischauer's commentary in Ennin's Travels in Tang China, Ronald Press, 1955.[9] The text was only rediscovered in a hand-written copy in the twentieth century.

---

[8] Joshua Fogel, "The Sino-Japanese Controversy Over Shina as a Toponym for China," in The Cultural Dilemmas of Sino-Japanese Relations, Sharpe, 1994, 66–76.

[9] There were 19 Japanese embassies to China from the late sixth to early ninth centuries, most of which were of Buddhist monks. Ennin's is the longest and most interesting account to have survived. For a comprehensive study covering Japanese embassies to China, see Charlotte von Verschuer, Les relations officielles du Japon avec la Chine aux VIIIe et IXe siècles, Droz, 1985; also Joshua A. Fogel, "Travel in the Context of East Asia," chap. 1 of his The Literature of Travel in the Japanese Rediscovery of China, 1862–1945, SUP, 1996, 13–33.

Arab merchant: *Voyage du marchand arabe Sulayman en Inde et en Chine, rédigé en 851, suivi de remarques par Abu Zayd Hasan (vers 916)*, Gabriel Ferrand, tr., Paris: Editions Boissard, 1922. Also *Relation de la Chine et de l'Inde*, Jean Sauvaget, tr., Maisonneuve, 1949. Al-Hassan (Abu Zayd Hasan) visited Quanzhou just after the Huang Chao uprising, see *The Huang Ch'ao Rebellion*, Howard J. Levy, IEAS, 110–29. For other Arab sources on China, of which there are many, see the articles on "China" and "Djugrafiya" in the *Encyclopaedia of Islam*, 2nd edition, Lucazs and Brill, 1960– .

Eleventh Century

Japanese Buddhist pilgrim, Jôjin 成尋 (1011–81), *San Tendai Godai sanki* 叅天臺五臺山記 (An account of a pilgrimage to the Tiantai and Wudai Mountains); Charlotte von Verschuer, "Le voyage de Jin au mont Tiantai," *TP* 77:1–48 (1991). Rare glimpses of everyday life in Song China by a foreigner.

Twelfth Century

Arab merchant: *Sharaf Al-Zaman Tahir Marvazi on China, the Turks and India*, V. Minorsky, tr. from the Arabic, London: Royal Asiatic Society, 1942.

Thirteenth Century

Early European travelers: See Leonardo Olschki, *Marco Polo's Precursors*, Johns Hopkins Univ. Press, 1943.

Papal diplomats and priests: *Cathay and the Way Thither, Being a Collection of Medieval Notices of China*, Henry Yule, tr., London: Haklyut Society, 2 vols., 1866; rev. ed., Henri Cordier, ed., 4 vols., Haklyut Society, 1913–16, Taibei reprint, 1966. Igor de Rachewiltz, *Papal Envoys to the Great Khans*, Allen and Unwin, 1971.

Franciscan diplomats: *The Mongol Mission: Narratives and Letters of the Franciscan Missionaries in Mongolia and China in the Thirteenth and Fourteenth Centuries*, Christopher Dawson, ed., Sheed and Ward, 1955. Also, *The Mission of Friar William of Rubruck*, Peter Jackson and David Morgan, tr., Hakluyt Society, 1990.[10] William was sent by Louis IX of France to the Great Khan. He set out in 1253 and reached the Mongol capital of Karakhorum in 1254. He was a keen

---

[10] Replaces the old study *The Journey of William of Rubruck to the Eastern Parts of the World, 1253–55*, tr., William W. Rockhill, London: Hakluyt Society, 1900.

observer. Although he never reached China, he records the first description in a European source of the Chinese script, the postal system, the Southern Song empire and the kingdom of Korea. He also describes divination using the thigh-bone of a sheep (a form of pyromancy) at the Mongol court. While there he encountered a French goldsmith working for the Khan, see Leonardo Olschki, *Guillaume Boucher, A French Artist at the Court of the Khans*, Johns Hopkins Univ. Press, 1946. A predecessor of William's, Odorico of Pordenone contains in his *Recensione* the first mention in a Western language of Cantonese cuisine (snakes) and of foot-binding (see Yule, 1913–16).

Venetian merchant: *The Travels of Marco Polo*, Robert E. Latham, tr., Penguin Books, 1958. For two more scholarly editions, see *The Travels of Marco Polo: the Complete Yule-Cordier Edition*, 2 vols., Dover Publications reissue of the original Yule translation (1871 and 1875) as annotated by Cordier in 1903 and 1920; *Marco Polo: The Description of the World*, Arthur C. Moule and Paul Pelliot, tr. and annotated, 2 vols., Routledge, 1938, plus Paul Pelliot, *Notes on Marco Polo*, 3 vols., Imprimerie nationale, Maisonneuve, 1959, 1963, 1973. Polo is supposed to have arrived in China in 1275. Whether or not he himself went there (the question is raised in Frances Wood, *Did Marco Polo Go to China?*, Secker and Warburg, 1995), the fact remains that the work with which he is credited was widely circulated and was regarded as containing the sum total of European knowledge of China between the thirteenth and sixteenth centuries and was therefore immensely influential. It may leave out much (foot-binding, tea, chop-sticks, Chinese characters), but it also has many passages which ring true, whether based on what Polo himself had seen, or picked up from others.

Kuwabara Jitsuzô, "On P'u Shou-keng 蒲壽庚: A man of the Western regions who was the superintendent of the Trading Ships' Office in Ch'üan-chou toward the end of the Sung dynasty, together with a general sketch of trade with the Arabs in China during the T'ang and Sung eras," *MTB* 2: 1–79 (1928); 7: 1–104 (1935); Luo Xianglin 羅香林, *Pu Shougeng yanjiu* 蒲壽庚研究 (Research on Pu Shougeng), Hong Kong: Zhongguo xueshe, 1959, traces the fate of Pu and his descendants, who successfully acculturated.

Fourteenth Century

Islamic traveler: *Ibn Battuta: Travels in Asia and Africa 1325–54*, H. A. R. Gibb, tr., Routledge, 1929; rev. edition, 3 vols., Cambridge: Hakluyt Society, 1958, 1962, 1971. Ibn Battuta (1304–68) was one of the greatest world travellers before the European voyages of discovery.

Fifteenth Century

Shipwrecked Korean official: *Ch'oe Pu's Diary: A Record of Drifting Across the Sea* [*P'yohae-rok* 漂海錄, 1488], John Meskill, tr., UAP, 1965. Ch'oe Po 崔溥 (1454–1504) was caught in a storm and washed up on the Chinese coast near Ningbo. From there he was sent under escort to Beijing and repatriated overland via the Yalu. Many Koreans who visited China for one reason or another during the following centuries left interesting travel diaries usually recounting the sights and sounds of Beijing, Shenyang or Chengde (see *Eighteenth Century*, item 2 for another example).[11]

Influential fantasy in Europe: *Travels of Sir John Mandeville*, 1499. See John Higgins, Ian Macleod, *Writing East: The Travels of Sir John Mandeville*, Univ. of Pennsylvania Press, 1997, who argue persuasively that is a compilation of travel writings, first shaped by an unknown redactor, to which Sir John's name was later attached.

Sixteenth Century

Japanese monk: Diary of trips to Ming China, in Makita Tairyô 牧田諦亮, *Sakugen nyû Minki no kenkyû* 策彥入明記の研究, 2 vols., Hôzôkan, 1955, 1959. Sakugen was deputy chief of the Japanese embassy to China in 1539–41 and led the mission of 1547. His diaries were based on these two visits. See also Wang Yi-t'ung, *Official Relations between China and Japan 1368–1549*, HUP, 1953.

Shipwrecked Portuguese and Spanish travelers and clerics: *South China in the Sixteenth Century, Being the Narratives of Galiote Pereira, Fr. Gaspar da Cruz, O. P., Fr. Martin de Rada OESA*, Charles R. Boxer, tr., Haklyut Society, Series II, 1953; Kraus, 1967.

Spanish adventurer and missionary: Juan González de Mendoza, *The History of the Great and Mighty Kingdom of China*, Robert Parke, tr., 1588; Sir George Staunton, ed., 2 vols., London: Haklyut Society, 1853–54 (tr. of *Historia de la cosas más notables, ritos y costumbres del gran Reyno de las China*, Rome 1585). González' *History* (based on the works translated in Boxer, *South China*), was immensely influential in Europe as the first circumstantial account of China since Marco Polo.

---

[11] Gari Ledyard, "Korean Travelers in China over Four Hundred Years, 1488–1887," *Occasional Papers on Korea* 2: 1–42 (1974).

Seventeenth Century

Rumors at Nagasaki: *Ka-i hentai* 華夷變態, written by members of the Hayashi family (1644–77), 3 vols., Tôyô bunko, 1958–59, describes conditions during the Ming-Qing divide and in the subsequent decades. As the title indicates, the authors' sympathies were with the Ming. It was based on the reports of merchants from China visiting the Chinese trading station at Nagasaki (hence also the title of the continuation, *Kikô shôsetsu* 崎港商説, rpnt., Tôhô, 1981).

Shipwrecked Japanese boat crew: *Dattan hyôryûki* 韃靼漂流記 (An account of being shipwrecked among the Tartars). Takeuchi Tôemon 竹内藤右衛門 and 41 companions drifted onto the northeast China coast in the summer of 1644 and were sent to Shenyang and then to Beijing. In the following year they returned to Japan via Korea. The account of the adventure written by Captain Takeuchi includes much acute observation of the contemporary scene in China.[12]

The Jesuits were the most important foreign observers in China in the seventeenth and eighteenth centuries. Once established, they had plenty of opportunity to travel on cartographic assignment or as diplomatic interpreters. In Beijing itself, their entrée to the emperor was their expertise in the arts and sciences of Europe: music, painting, architecture and, more importantly, astronomy, horology, mathematics and ballistics. The four leading Jesuits in the China mission were Matteo Ricci, Johann Adam Schall von Bell, Ferdinand Verbiest and Antoine Gaubil. Details on them and their works, and of the two main collections of their letters and reports that circulated in Europe, are given in section 34.7.

Eighteenth Century

The Chronicles of the East India Company: Trading to China, 1638–1834, Hosea B. Morse (1855–1934), 3 vols., HUP, 1935.

Korean member of embassy to participate in the celebrations of Qianlong's 70th birthday in 1780: Pak Chi-won 朴趾源 (1737–1835), *Yorha ilgi* 熱河日記 (Chengde diary). Pak traveled to Rehe overland via Shengjing and Yanjing (modern Shenyang and Beijing) and in his diary compares conditions in Korea unfavorably with what he saw in China. There is a punctuated edition: *Rehe riji* 熱河日記, Shanghai

---

[12] Sonoda Kazuki 園田一龜, *Dattan hyôryûki no kenkyû* 韃靼漂流記の研究 (Researches on the *Record of Castaways* in Tartary), Fengtian: Mantetsu, 1936.

shudian, 1997. Several other Korean scholars wrote similar diaries at this time, for example, Hong Tae-yong 洪大容 (1731–83), *Yon-gi* 燕記 (Beijing diary).

British diplomat: *An Embassy to China; Being the Journal Kept by Lord Macartney during his Embassy to the Emperor Ch'ien-lung, 1793–1794*, edited with an introduction and notes by J. L. Cranmer-Byng, London: Longmans Green, 1962. See also Sir George Staunton (1781–1859), *Authentic Account of an Embassy from the King of Great Britain to the Emperor of China; Including Cursory Observations Made and Information Obtained, in Travelling through that Ancient Empire, and a Small Part of Chinese Tartary*, 2 vols. London: W. Bulmer and Co., 1797. Staunton accompanied his father as page to the ambassador, Lord Macartney. He was the only member of the embassy to be able to speak and write some Chinese (having picked it up on the long voyage out). He published a translation of the Qing code into English in 1810 (27.3).

Comptroller of the household in the Macartney Embassy: Sir John Barrow (1764–1848), *Travels in China*, London: Cadell and Davies, 1804; rpnt., Ch'engwen, 1972. Barrow absorbed much of the information contained in earlier accounts, including that of the Dutch East India ambassador, Johan Nieuhoff (1673) and Evert Ysbrants Ides, ambassador from the Czar of Muscovy (1706).

Nineteenth Century

Mamiya Rinzô 間宮林藏 visited Heilongjiang twice in 1808–9 and recorded his observations on the customs and trade of the local inhabitants in *Tôdatsu kikô* 東韃紀行, 1810; Chinese tr., under the same title, Shangwu, 1974.

British botanical collector of the Horticultural Society of London: Robert Fortune (1812–80), *Three Years' Wanderings in the Northern Provinces of China, Including a Visit to the Tea, Silk, Cotton Countries: With an Account of the Agriculture and Horticulture of the Chinese, New Plants etc.*, London, 1847. See also his later work, *A Residence Among the Chinese: Inland, on the Coast, and at Sea*, Murray, 1857.

French Lazarist missionaries: Evariste-Régis Huc (1813–60) and Joseph Gabet (1808–53), *Travels in Tartary, Thibet and China, 1844–46*, William Hazlitt, tr. from the French original of 1850, London, 1851; edited with an introduction by Paul Pelliot, Routledge, 2 vols., 1928; Dover rpnt., 1 vol., 1987. Huc followed up on this success with *The Empire of China*, New York: Harper Bros., 2 vols., 1855 (tr. from French original of 1854).

American Protestant missionary, diplomat and first professor of Chinese at Yale: Samuel Wells Williams (1812–84), *The Middle Kingdom*, 1848; rev. ed., Allen, 1883.

American Protestant missionary who spent the years 1850–64 in Fuzhou: Justus Doolittle (1824–80), *Social Life of the Chinese*, 2 vols., New York: Harper and Bros., 1865; rpnt., Graham Brash, 1986. Based on the author's popular "Jottings about the Chinese" that appeared in the Hong Kong newspaper *The China Mail*, 1861–64.

American Presbyterian in Shandong for 50 years: Arthur H. Smith (1845–1932), *Chinese Characteristics*, Shanghai: Kelly and Walsh; re. and enl. ed., New York: Fleming H. Revell, 1894. This began (as did much nineteenth-century Western commentary on China) as a series of articles in a Treaty-Port newspaper (*The North-China Daily News*, 1889). It soon became the most read book on China and the Chinese—in America and Europe as well as among expatriates in China, a status it retained until the 1920s. In its Japanese translation Smith's book deeply influenced Lu Xun 魯迅, helping him to formulate his own views on the theory of national character and to make the switch from medicine to writing.[13] Not a few of Smith's "characteristics" make an ironic appearance in Lu Xun's short story "A Q zheng zhuan A Q 正傳" (The true story of Ah Q).

See also Arthur Smith, *Proverbs and Common Sayings from the Chinese*, American Presbyterian Missionary Press, 1914; rpnt., Dover, 1965; Graham Brash, 1988 (under the new title *Pearls of Wisdom*). It contains explanations of 1,900 phrases and proverbs current in the latter part of the nineteenth century. Arrangement is by genre, with a running commentary in the learned but condescending tone of the nineteenth-century Protestant missionary.

American Protestant missionary and chief instructor at the Tongwen guan: W. A. P. Martin (1827–1926), *A Cycle of Cathay: Or, China, South and North, with Personal Reminiscences*, Revell, 1896; 3rd ed., 1900. He did his missionary work in Ningbo (1850–63), including a spell of translating for the first United States Minister to China, William Bradford Reed (1858). In 1863, Martin moved to Beijing and began teaching English at the Tongwen guan. He wrote an inflential introduction to science (*Gewu rumen* 格物入門, 1868) and made several important translations (e.g., of Wheaton's *International Law* (*Wanguo gongfa* 萬國公法).

[13] Lydia H. Liu, "Lu Xun and Arthur H. Smith," in *Translingual Practice*, SUP, 1995, 51–76.

One of the most thorough of the nineteenth-century commercial missions: *La mission lyonnaise d'exploration commerciale en Chine 1895–1897*, 2 vols., Lyons: A. Rey et Cie, 1898.

American botanist and plant hunter: E. H. Wilson, *A Naturalist in Western China*, 2 vols., Methuen, 1913.

The journals of the influential Inspector-General of the Imperial Maritime Customs: Robert Hart (1835–1911), *Entering China's Service: Robert Hart's Journals, 1854–1863*, Katherine F. Bruner, John K. Fairbank and Richard J. Smith, eds., Council on East Asian Studies, Harvard University, 1986; and *Robert Hart and China's Early Modernization: Robert Hart's Journals, 1863–1866*, Richard J. Smith, John K. Fairbank and Katherine F. Bruner, eds., HUP, 1991.

French consular official (in Ningbo and Fuzhou) and scholar: G. Eugène Simon (1829–96), *La Cité chinoise*, Paris: Nouvelle Revue, 1895; rpnt., Editions Kimé, 1992.

Hobson-Jobson: A Glossary of Colloquial Anglo-Indian Words and Phrases, and of Kindred Terms, Etymological, Historical, Geographical and Discursive, Henry Yule and A. C. Burnell, eds., 1887; new ed., William Crooke, ed., London: John Murray, 1903. This is more than a glossary of Anglo-Indian. It also includes many definitions and etymologies of the English words and phrases used in the Chinese Treaty Ports as well.

42.3 Paintings, Sketches and Photographs

Many of the earlier European accounts of China are beautifully illustrated as well as extensively introduced in Donald F. Lach's voluminous series, *Asia in the Making of Europe*, published by the UChP:

The Century of Discoveries, 2 vols., 1965 (covers up to 1600).

A Century of Wonder, 2 vols., 1970 (covers the sixteenth century); Book 2, *The Literary Arts*; Book 3, *The Scholarly Disciplines*, 1977.

A Century of Advance (with Edwin J. Van Kley), 4 vols., 1993 (covers up to 1700); Book 1 *Trade, Missions, Literature*; Book 2, *South Asia*; Book 3, *Southeast Asia*; Book 4, *East Asia*.

42.3.1   Paintings and Sketches

Before photographs began to be taken in the 1840s, the only visual representations of China were the sketches and paintings of Jesuit artists such as Giuseppe Castiglione or draughtsmen such as William Alexander, who accompanied the early embassies: [14]

Giuseppe Castiglione (1688–1766),[15] Dennis Attiret (1702–68) and other Jesuit painters not only made some fascinating paintings of Beijing and the court, they also had a considerable influence on a few Chinese painters.[16]

William Alexander (1767–1816), the junior draughtsman on the Macartney Embassy, filled three volumes of sketches; see *Image of China: William Alexander*, Susan Legouix, ed., Jupiter Books, 1980. In his lifetime he published several books of his prints (e.g., *The Costume of China*, William Miller, London, 1804; simplified version, Graham Brash, 1990). Selections from these and by another artist, George Henry Mason, were published under the title *Views of 18th-Century China*, Studio Editions, 1988. Alexander's are the most detailed sketches of the everyday life of ordinary people in China in the eighteenth century that exist. The originals are in the British Library.

British painter: George Chinnery (1774–1853). A student of Joshua Reynolds, he took up residence in Macao and eventually Hong Kong in order to escape his wife. He painted a large number of rustic, romantic scenes that greatly influenced the early photographers. See Patrick Conner, *George Chinnery, 1774–1852*, Antique Collectors' Club, 1993.

[14] Harrie Vanderstappen, "Chinese Art and the Jesuits in Peking," in Charles E. Ronan and Bonnie B. C. Oh, eds., *East Meets West, The Jesuits in China, 1582–1773*, HKCU Press, 1988 and Mayching Kao, "European Influences in Chinese Art, Sixteenth to Eighteenth Centuries," in *China and Europe: Images and Influences in Sixteenth to Eighteenth Centuries*, Thomas H. C. Lee, ed., HKCU Press, 1991, 251–304.

[15] Cécile Beurdeley and Michel Beurdeley, *Giuseppe Castiglione: A Jesuit Painter at the Court of the Chinese Emperors*, Tuttle, 1971; *Orientations* 19.11 (1988) is devoted to Castiglione.

[16] *Europa und die Kaiser von China (1240–1816)*, Berliner Festspiele, Insel Verlag, 1985, contains scholarly essays and reproductions of paintings and sketches of Europeans at the court of the Chinese emperors.

42.3.2   *Photographs*

The first surviving photographs of China date from the 1850s. The earliest are of the coastal areas around Hong Kong, but from the 1860s photographers began accompanying the troops and from the 1870s, the explorers. Beijing, North China and the interior provinces in addition to Canton, Shanghai and Hong Kong were extensively photographed by the likes of Felix Beato, Michael Miller and John Thomson, all of whom deromanticized the image of China. Their work circulated in stereographic form or was published in individual collections such as John Thomson (1837–1921), *Illustrations of China and Its People*, 4 vols. London, 1873–74. The works of early Chinese photographers are less well-known.[17] Several selections of early photographs of China have been published:

James Orange, *The Chater Collection, Pictures Relating to China, Hong Kong and Macao, 1655–1860, with Historical and Descriptive Letterpress*, London, Thornton, Butterworth, 1924.

Imperial China, Photographs 1850–1912, Pennwick Press, 1978; Scholar Press, 1979. The short account of "Photography in Early China," by Clark Worswick on pages 134–151 is excellent.

The Face of China as Seen by Photographers and Travellers, 1860–1912, with a preface by Luther Carrington Goodrich and historical commentary by Nigel Cameron, London: Aperture Books, 1978.

Caught in Time: Great Photographic Archives: China, Garnet Publishing, 1993. Photographs taken during the Russian research and trading expedition of 1874–75, now held in the St. Petersburg archives.

Photographs of China during the Boxer Rebellion, taken by James Ricalton, Christopher J. Lucas, ed., Edwin Mellen Press, 1990. The leading photographers of the many who covered the seige of Peking were Yamamoto and Killie.

On the Tracks of Manchu Culture: 1644–1994, Giovanni Stary et al., comps., Harrassowitz, 1995; 200 photographs and a bibliography.

---

[17] Hu Zhichuan 胡志川 et al., *Zhongguo sheyingshi* 中國攝影史 1840–1937 (A history of Chinese photography, 1840–1937), Zhongguo chubanshe, 1990.

China's Inner Asian Frontier: Photographs of the Wulsin Expedition to Northwest China in 1923, Mary Ellen Alonso, ed.; Historical text by Joseph Fletcher; Donald Freeman, design ed., Peabody Museum, HUP, 1979.

Hedda Morrison, *A Photographer in Old Peking*, OUP, 1985.

Beijing jiuying 北京舊影 (Old photos of Beijing), Renmin meishu, 1989.

Dijing jiuying 帝京舊影 (As Dusk Fell on the Imperial City), Zhu Jiati 朱家潛, ed., Zijincheng, 1992. Selections from the photographs made in 1900 by a mission from Tokyo Imperial University.

Jiujing daguan 舊京大觀 (Old Beijing in Panorama), Renmin Zhongguo, 1992.

Old Peking: The City and its People, Haifeng, 1993.

Shanghai: A Century in Photos, 1843–1949, Lynn Pan, ed., Haifeng, 1993.

Early Twentieth Century

Of all the many reports of archaeological expeditions which explored the inner Asian frontiers of China, including what was then called Chinese Turkestan, see Sir Mark Aurel Stein (1862–1943), *Ruins of Desert Cathay*, 2 vols., Macmillan, 1912, which includes his account of how he purchased a large part of the secret temple library of Dunhuang in the years 1906–8 (46.3).[18] Towards the end of his life, Stein summed up his life's work in *On Ancient Central Asian Tracks*, Macmillan, 1933; Pantheon, 1964.

42.4   China in East Asian Historical Records

Historical genres in Vietnam and Korea were closely modelled on those of the Chinese. They were mainly written in *wenyanwen*. Only a sample are given here.

Vietnamese Sources

Đại Việt sử-ký toàn thư 大越史記全書, 1479, is the Lê dynastic chronicle from the earliest times up to the late fifth century, with continuations up to the end of the seventeenth century. It contains much ma-

---

[18] The best popular account of the explorations of Hedin, Stein, Grünwedel, Von Le Coq, Ôtani and Pelliot is by Peter Hopkirk, *Foreign Devils on the Silk Road*, London: Murray, 1980; OUP, 1984.

terial on Vietnam's relations and negotiations with its neighbors, including China, during the Yuan dynasty.[19]

Đại Nam thực-lục 大南實錄 (The Veritable Records of the Nguyen dynasty 阮朝), 453 *juan*, completed in 1909.

Đại Nam liệt truyện 大南列傳 (Biographies of the Nguyen dynasty), 85 *juan*, Yurindô, 1962.

Việt-sử thông-giám cường-mục 越史通鑑綱目 (Outline complete mirror of government of the history of Vietnam), Historical office of the Nguyen dynasty 阮朝國史館, eds., 1856–84, covers from the earliest times to 1789.

Đại Nam hội-điển sử-lệ 大南會典事例 (Statutes and precedents of the Nguyen dynasty).

Korean Sources

See also those sources listed under 4.2.2.

Koryŏ sa 高麗史, Chong In-ji 鄭麟趾 et al., comps., 1454; 3 vols., Asea Munhwasa, 1972. Composed in chronicle form, it has especially full records on Koryŏ-Liao relations and also on Yuan China.

Nogoltae 老乞大 and *P'ak Tongsa* 朴通事 were early fourteenth century Koryŏ primers of Chinese intended for Koryŏ merchants. They both contain unique material on the social history of the Yuan capital of Dadu (Beijing).

Chosŏn wangjo sillok 朝鮮皇朝實錄 (or *Yijo sillok* 李朝實錄; Veritable records of the Yi dynasty), 1,893 *juan*, 1392–1863. Contains much material on China's relations with its neighbors in northeast Asia. Seoul Imperial University, 1930–2; 1953; Nihon gakushûin and Tôbunken, 50 vols., 1953; jointly published by the Academy of Sciences in China and Korea, 1959.

Chaoxian Lichao Shilu zhong de Zhongguo shiliao 朝鮮李朝實錄中的中國史料 (Excerpts on China from the Veritable Records of the Yi dynasty of Korea), Wu Han 吳晗, comp., 12 vols., Shangwu, 1930; Zhonghua, 1980. Important additional sources on the early history of the Manchus.

Mindai Man-Mô shiryô: Richô jitsuroku shô 明代滿蒙史料李朝實錄抄 (Manchurian and Mongolian materials on the Ming dynasty: Ex-

---

[19] On these and other Vietnamese sources, see Keith Weller Taylor, *The Birth of Vietnam*, UCP, 1983 and Alexander Woodside, *Vietnam and the Chinese Model*, HUP, 1971.

cerpts from the Yi Veritable Records), 18 vols., Tôkyô daigaku bun-gakubu, 1954–59.

Simyang changgye 瀋陽狀啓, in Chinese, 1636; Seoul Imperial University, 1935; covers the years 1637–43; contains information on life in Shen-yang and on the activities of the banner troops.

P'il I-je yugo pyonggyu 畢依齋遺稿拼庚. The author, P'il I-je, went on two embassies to China (1734 and 1750).

Zhong-Han guanxi shiliao jiyao 中韓關係史料輯要, Taibei, 1978, contains Korean accounts of Ming and Qing China.

Japanese Sources

See those sources listed under 4.2.2.

Ryûkyû 琉球 Sources

The Ryûkyû islands (Liuqiu) extend in a chain from south of Japan to Taiwan. From the Sui to the Yuan, Taiwan was nor-mally referred to as Liuqiu 琉球. Thereafter, the two were separated, Taiwan began to be so called and Ryûkyû became a regular tributary of China (in 1372); in 1609, the northern Ryûkyû islands were brought under the control of the Satsuma *han* 藩 and in 1879 all the Ryûkyûs were annexed by Japan and renamed Okinawa prefecture. Taiwan itself and the Pescadores were ceded to Japan in 1895.[20]

Rekidai hôan 歷代寶案, 1697 and continuations, *Lidai bao'an* 歷代寶案, 1697, with later continuations; Taiwan daxue, facsimile, 15 vols., 1972. Contains a large amount of original documents on Ryûkyû 琉球 relations with the Ming and Qing (covers the years 1424–1867).

Kyûyô 球陽 is a history of Ryûkyû from the founding there of the Chû-zan kingdom 中山國 in the fourteenth century to 1876.

Western Sources

For a full list of early Western writings on China, including travel accounts, see Henri Cordier, *Bibliotheca Sinica* (11.4). The second part is devoted to an exhaustive annotated list of

[20] *China's Island Frontier: Studies in the Historical Geography of Tai-wan*, Ronald G. Knapp, ed., UHP, 1980.

"Les étrangers en Chine, connaissances des peuples étrangers sur la Chine." Vol. 3, columns 1917–2091 cover foreign writing on China from Strabo to 1700; the remainder of the volume deals with the eighteenth and nineteenth centuries. The continuations to Cordier and the other standard bibliographies are listed in 10.4.1.

For an introduction to nineteenth-century non-Chinese sources such as treaty-port newspapers, diplomatic series, and European, American, Japanese and Russian national archives, use Andrew J. Nathan, *Modern China, 1840–1972: An Introduction to Sources and Research Aids*, CCS, Univ. of Michigan, 1973. This can be updated with:

Kindai Chûgoku kenkyû annai 近代中國研究案内 (Guide to research on modern China), Kojima Shinji 小島晋治 and Namiki Yorihisa 並木賴壽, comps., Iwanami, 1993. This handy guide to modern Chinese history covers 1840 to the present day and is organized into four parts: (1) research trends; (2) secondary sources (Japanese, Chinese and American); (3) primary sources; (4) statistical tables and a simple chronology from 1793 to 1949.

Chûgoku sankô tosho gaido Kingendaishi hen 中國叄考圖書ガイド近現代史編, Ichiko Kenji 市古健次, comp., Kyûko, 1997.

V

Primary Sources by Period

43

Introduction: Guides

Before starting to look for primary sources, it is essential to have developed an understanding of the different types of historical writing discussed in Parts II through IV. It is also essential to know how a certain type of source would have been classified by traditional historians; knowing where they would have placed source, or a work dealing with a specific subject, helps locate that source in catalogs of old Chinese books, which still follow the same classification scheme (see 9.3 for a discussion of classification and bibliography and 9.1 on locating an individual work).

The arrangement of each chapter of Part V is not identical because the sources available from each period differ greatly. Nevertheless, in general, the pattern followed is to put the basic historical works first followed by examples of other important primary sources. Next come newly discovered documentary sources (archival or excavated) and archaeological artifacts. Because both these categories are less well known, they are treated in greater detail than the traditional primary sources. Each chapter concludes by introducing guides to the primary sources of the period and a selection of research tools, usually under the following heads: language, biography, official titles and officeholders, geography, chronology, bibliographies, societies and journals.

Western Guides

There are a number of guides to the primary sources and research problems of individual periods. Their focus and scope differ widely. Details are given in the appropriate sections of Parts II and V. The titles of some of the main ones concentrating on primary sources are listed below.[1]

Sources of Shang History: The Oracle-Bone Inscriptions of Bronze-Age China, David N. Keightley (15.4).

Sources of Western Zhou History: Inscribed Bronze Vessels, Edward L. Shaughnessy (17.1).

NSECH   New Sources of Early Chinese History: An Introduction to the Reading of Inscriptions and Manuscripts, Edward L. Shaughnessy, ed. (12.2, Paleographic sources).

ECHBG   Early Chinese Texts: A Bibliographical Guide, Michael Loewe, ed. (19.1).

SB A Sung Bibliography, Yves Hervouet, ed. (47.4.2).

Research Tools for the Study of Sung History, Peter Bol, ed. (47.4.2).

ISMH   An Introduction to the Sources of Ming History, Wolfgang Franke, comp. (49.5.1).

Ming History: An Introductory Guide to Research, Edward L. Farmer, Romeyn Taylor and Ann Waltner, eds. (49.5.1).

Introduction to Ch'ing Documents, Philip Kuhn and John King Fairbank, eds. (50.8.2).

The main English-language biographical dictionaries cover the last thousand years of imperial China (3.4). They contain brief information on a large number of individual book titles because they record the main writings of their subjects:

Sung Biographies, Herbert Franke, ed. (47.4.2).

In the Service of the Kahn: Eminent Personalities of the Early Mongol Yuan Period (1200–1300), Igor de Rachewiltz et al., eds. (48.5.4).

---

[1] Introductions to Chinese historiography are discussed in 20.4. Annotated catalogs of primary sources are covered in 9.4, 9.5 and 9.7 and

Footnote continued on next page

DMB   *Dictionary of Ming Biography 1368-1644*, Luther Carrington Goodrich and Chaoyang Fang, eds. (49.5.1).

ECCP   *Eminent Chinese of the Ch'ing Period*, Arthur W. Hummel, ed. (50.8.3).

A great deal can be learned about what primary (and secondary) sources are available on a given problem or period by looking through *The Cambridge History of Ancient China* and *The Cambridge History of China*:

> *The Cambridge History of Ancient China*, Michael Loewe and Edward L. Shaughnessy, eds., New York: CUP, 1999.

> *The Cambridge History of China*, John K. Fairbank and Denis Twitchett, general editors, CUP, 1978– (abbreviated as *CHC*). Volume editors are given in the appropriate sections:
>
> Vol. 1, *The Ch'in and Han Empires, 221 BC–AD 220*, 1986.
>
> Vol. 2, *The Northern and Southern Kingdoms*, 1999.
>
> Vol. 3, *Sui and T'ang China, 589-906*, Part 1, 1979.
>
> Vol. 4, *Sui and T'ang China, 589-906*, Part 2, 1999.
>
> Vol. 5, *Sung China, 907-1267*, 1999.
>
> Vol. 6, *Alien Regimes and Border States, 907-1368*, 1994.
>
> Vol. 7, *The Ming Dynasty, 1368-1644*, Part 1, 1988.
>
> Vol. 8, *The Ming Dynasty, 1368-1644*, Part 2, 1998.
>
> Vol. 9, *Early Ch'ing, 1644-1800*, forthcoming.
>
> Vol. 10, *Late Ch'ing, 1800-1911*, Part 1, 1978.
>
> Vol. 11, *Late Ch'ing, 1800-1911*, Part 2, 1980.
>
> Vol. 12, *Republican China 1912-1949*, Part 1, 1983.
>
> Vol. 13, *Republican China 1912-1949*, Part 2, 1986.
>
> Vol. 14, *The People's Republic, Part 1: The Emergence of Revolutionary China 1949-1965*, 1987.
>
> Vol. 15, *The People's Republic, Part 2: Revolutions Within the Revolution 1966-1982*, 1991.

---

secondary sources in chap. 11. Guides to sinological reference works are given in 8.1.

In addition to the annotations to each chapter, many of the *CHC* volumes include bibliographic notes, and all have bibliographies. These are not all of the same standard and some are already showing signs of age. But in general they have the advantage that they cover not only the main primary sources, but also the research tools and secondary scholarship in Western languages as well as in Chinese and Japanese. After checking the *CHC*, turn to the following Chinese and Japanese works.

Chinese and Japanese Guides

There are numerous guides in Chinese and Japanese covering the whole of Chinese history. Some are arranged by individual period, some by genre. Details are given in 8.2.1 and 8.2.2. Five good ones are:

> *Zhongguoshi yanjiu zhinan* 中國史研究指南 (Guide to research on Chinese history), Gao Mingshi 高明士, ed. Arrangement is by dynasty. Covers both primary and secondary sources. Based on translation of the next item.

> *Chûgokushi kenkyû nyûmon* 中國史研究入門 (Handbook for research into Chinese history), Yamane Yukio 山根幸夫, ed. Arrangement is by dynasty.

> *Zhongguo gudaishi shiliaoxue* 中國古代史史料學 (The study of the primary source materials for ancient Chinese history), Chen Gaohua 陳高華 and Chen Zhichao 陳智超, eds. Arrangement is by dynasty.

> *Zhongguo gudaishi shiliaoxue* 中國古代史史料學 (The study of the primary source materials for ancient Chinese history), An Zuozhang 安作璋, ed. Arrangement is by genre.

In addition to these, there are also a number devoted to single periods. The volumes in the series *Xueshu yanjiu zhinan* 學術研究指南 (Guides to scholarly research) published by Tianjin Jiaoyu Chubanshe 天津教育出版社 in the 1980s and 1990s are an example. The titles and editors are listed below with section references.

> *Xian-Qinshi yanjiu gaiyao* 先秦史研究概要 (Guide to research on pre-Qin history), Zhu Fenghan 朱鳳瀚 and Xu Yong 徐勇 (12.2).

Sui, Tang, Wudai shi yanjiu gaiyao 隋唐五代史研究概要 (Guide to research on the history of the Sui, Tang and Five Dynasties), Zhang Guogang 張國剛 (46.5.2).

Yuanshixue gaishuo 元史學概説 (General introduction to the study of Yuan history), Yang Zhijiu 楊志玖 and Wang Xiao'an 王曉安 (48.5.4).

Mingshi yanjiu beilan 明史研究備覽 (Background to research on Ming history), Li Xiaolin 李小林 and Li Shengwen 李晟文 (49.5.1).

Qingshi yanjiu gaishuo 清史研究概説 (General introduction to research on Qing history), Chen Shengxi 陳生璽 (50.8.1).

The large-scale *Zhongguo tongshi* 中國通史 under the general editorship of Bai Shouyi 白壽彝 contains extensive essays on the primary sources of each period.[2]

For certain purposes it may be necessary to find out in greater detail than is possible from consulting modern historical guides what printed sources were in circulation at a given time and who their authors were. This can be done by looking through the most extensive bibliographies of primary sources, the "yiwenzhi" and their supplements in the Standard Histories (9.4), as well as other official and private catalogs.

Such catalogs of course do not contain references to the very important new types of documentary sources discovered in the twentieth century such as the oracle bones, the documents on bamboo strips and wooden tablets, the Dunhuang documents, the documents of the Huizhou merchants, the Ming-Qing archives and all the other new sources listed in Table 20, chap. 20.

[2] *Zhongguo tongshi* (General history of China), 20 vols., Shanghai renmin, 1994–98.

44

Qin and Han

Qin 秦[1]	221–206 BC
Han 漢[2]	202 BC–AD 220
Former Han 前漢 (also called Western Han)	202 BC–AD 23
Xin 新 (Wang Mang 王莽 interregnum)[3]	AD 9–23
Later Han 後漢 (also called Eastern Han)	AD 25–220

The history of the Qin and Han is based on transmitted texts, excavated texts and artifacts.

The Han saw the first large-scale histories ever written in China as well as the inauguration of the annals-biography form. Most history writing was the work of private historians, not officials. However, very few Qin and Former Han texts have survived and only about 10 percent of the works written in the Later Han are extant.

---

[1] The kingdom of Qin was established in 337 BC. It was named after the place in Shaanxi in which the king's ancestors had been enfeoffed. On the establishment of the empire in 221 BC, the name was retained.

[2] The dynastic name of Han was taken from Liu Bang's title, Prince of Han, which he had been granted in 206 on taking control of Hanzhong 漢中 (a Qin commandery) and the area further to the southwest, *CHC*, 1, 116.

[3] In AD 9 Wang Mang dismissed the imperial heir apparent and declared the beginning of the Xin 新 dynasty with himself as emperor. The name of the dynasty was taken from his title of Marquis of Xindu (新都侯). The interregnum lasted until AD 23 and is sometimes referred to as Xin Han 新漢 or Xin Mang 新莽.

The three main historical sources on the Former and Later Han are the *Shiji* 史記, the *Hanshu* 漢書 and the *Hou Hanshu* 後漢書 (the first three of what later were called the Standard Histories). The *Shiji* is also the main textual source on the Qin (44.1). Three dozen other transmitted texts are listed in 44.2. This is not intended as an exhaustive inventory. There is little or no comment on these well-known sources save to refer to the section in which they are mentioned elsewhere in the manual. Excavated texts and fragments, on the other hand, are given a great deal more attention since most have only recently been discovered and they have not yet been fully utilized (44.3). They are particularly important for economic, social and legal history (especially of the Qin, for which there are so few contemporary sources). The archaeology of the Qin and Han and stone inscriptions also provide important supplemental evidence (44.4). The chapter ends with a selection of guides to sources, readers and research tools not mentioned in the preceding sections (44.5).

44.1 Main Historical Works

Shiji 史記, Sima Qian 司馬遷 (145–86 BC), 130 *pian* 篇 (*juan* 卷), 530,000 characters.

Sima Qian fulfilled the request of his father Sima Tan 司馬談 (180–110? BC) to complete the project for which he had begun to gather the materials, a history of China from the earliest times to the reign of Han Wudi 漢武帝, a period of 3,000 years.[4] However, three-fifths of the work is on the pe-

---

[4] A. F. P. Hulsewé discusses the text history and early editions of the *Shiji* (of which there are at least 60), recent editions, translations, research aids and indexes in *ECTBG*, 405–14. He also examines one chapter in
Footnote continued on next page

riod between the reforms of Shang Yang 商鞅 (d. 338 BC) and Han Wudi (140–88 BC).

Sima Qian, to whom authorship is traditionally solely credited, refers to his work as *Taishigong shu* 太史公書. During the Han, this title was used, or *Taishigong* 太史公, *Taishigong zhuan* 太史公傳 or *Taishigongji* 太史公記 (from which the best known English title, the *Records of the Grand Historian*, is taken).[5] It was abbreviated in the second century AD to *Shiji* 史記 (The scribe's record), a generic term in the Han for history books, which suggests that only a century after its completion, Sima Qian's work was regarded as unique.[6]

For a brief description and an evaluation of the historiographical influence of this, the most famous of all Chinese historical works, see 22.1.

Use the Zhonghua punctuated, collated edition, *Shiji*, 10 vols., 1959; rev., 1985; 14th prnt., 1996; reduced-sized, 1997. At each printing typos and errors were corrected, so it is best to use the most recent printing. Another much-used edition (with notes in Chinese) is that of Takigawa Kametarô 瀧川龜太郎, *Shiki kaichû kôshô* 史記會注考證, 10

"The problem of the authenticity of *Shih-chi* chap. 123, the memoir on Ta Yuan," *TP* 61: 1–3: 83–147 (1975).

For a reconstruction of the sources used by Sima Qian (many of which have since been lost), see Jin Dejian 金德建, *Sima Qian suojian shu kao* 司馬遷所見書考, Shanghai renmin, 1963. For an index to the sources used by the three most important early commentators on the *Shiji*, see Duan Shu'an 段書安, *Shiji sanjia zhu yinshu suoyin* 史記三家注引書索引, Zhonghua, 1982.

[5] For a study of Sima Qian, see Burton Watson, *Ssu-ma Ch'ien: Grand Historian of China*, Col. UP, 1958; Stephen W. Durrant, *The Cloudy Mirror: Tension and Conflict in the Writings of Sima Qian*, SUNY Press, 1995; Li, Wai-Yee, "The Idea of Authority in the *Shih-chi* (Records of the Historian)," *HJAS* 54.2: 345–405 (1994); Willard J. Peterson, "Ssu-ma Ch'ien as Cultural Historian," in Willard J. Peterson et al., eds., *The Power of Culture: Studies in Chinese Cultural History*, HKCU Press, 1994, 70–79.

[6] Sima Qian uses the title *Shiji* in his work dozens of times as an abbreviation for the *Lieguo shiji* 列國史記, not to refer to his own work.

vols., Tôhô bunka gakuin, Tokyo kenkyûjo, 1932–34; rpnt., Beijing: Wenxue guji kanhangshe, 1955.

There are many different types of index to the *Shiji*. The most convenient are those based on the Zhonghua edition.

Nianwushi quanwen ziliaoku 廿五史全文資料庫 (25 Histories full text database), Shiyusuo, 1988. As soon as this database version of the Zhonghua edition becomes more widely and cheaply available, it will supersede all previous indexes not only to the *Shiji*, but also to *Hanshu*, the *Hou Hanshu* and later Standard Histories (22.1).

Shiji ji zhushi zonghe yinde 史記及注釋綜合引得 (Combined indexes to the *Shiji* and the notes of Pei Yin 裴駰, Sima Zhen 司馬貞, Zhang Shoujie 張守節 and Takigawa Kametarô 瀧川龜太郎), *H-Y Index* 40, 1940; 2nd ed., HUP, 1955. This concordance is based on the Tongwen edition.

Shiji suoyin 史記索引 (Index to the *Shiji*), Li Xiaoguang 李曉光 and Li Bo 李波, comps., Zhongguo guangbo dianshi, 1989. Complete index to the Zhonghua (1985) edition. Easier to use than the index with the same name compiled by Wong Fook-luen.[7]

Shiji cidian 史記辭典 (Dictionary of the *Shiji*), Cang Xiuliang 倉修良, ed. in chief, Shandong jiaoyu, 1991; rpnt., 1994. Includes proper names and place names and definitions of technical terms and phrases in the *Shiji*.

Shiji renming suoyin 史記人名索引 (Personal name index to the *Shiji*), Zhong Hua 鍾華, comp., Zhonghua, 1977.

Shiji diming suoyin 史記地名索引 (Place-name index to the *Shiji*), Ji Chao 嵇超 et al., comp., Zhonghua, 1990.

Translations from the Shiji

Leaving aside the 10 chapters of Tables (*biao* 表), 111 of the remaining total of 120 chapters of the *Shiji* have been translated in the first three of the following translations:

---

[7] *Shiji suoyin* 史記索引 (Subject Index to the Records of the Grand Historian), Wong Fook-luen (Huang Fuluan 黃福鑾), ed., HKCU Press, 1963, is an index by stroke count of terms, names, etc., arranged under 24 categories, with references to the *Sibu beiyao* and *Sibu congkan* (Bona) editions.

Les mémoires historiques de Se-ma Ts'ien, Edouard Chavannes, tr., 5 vols., Leroux, 1895–1905. The first 47 chapters of the *Shiji* are translated with an important introduction and supplementary matter in this monument of French sinology. It was reprinted with a sixth volume (*juan* 48–52), edited and completed by Paul Demiéville, Max Kaltenmark and Timoteus Pokora, Maisonneuve, 1967. This contains a full index and bibliography, as well as a list of translations from the *Shiji* into Western languages. The first five vols. were reprinted by Maisonneuve in 1969.

Records of the Grand Historian of China, Burton Watson, tr., 3 vols., Col. UP and *Renditions*, HKCU Press, 1994. Vol. 1 (on the Qin) is indexed and vols. 2 and 3 (on the Han, originally published by Col. UP, 1961) also have an index. Translation of 65 chapters (of which 46 are not included in Chavannes); 2 on the Qin, the rest on the Han.

Selections from Records of the Historian, Yang Hsien-yi and Gladys Yang, tr., FLP, 1979, contains 13 chapters translated neither by Chavannes nor Watson.

The Grand Scribe's Records, vol. I, *The Basic Annals of Pre-Han China by Ssu-ma Ch'ien*; vol. II, *The Memoirs of Pre-Han China by Ssu-ma Ch'ien*, William H. Nienhauser, Jr., ed., Tsai-fa Cheng, Zongli Lu (Lü Zongli 呂宗力), William H. Nienhauser, Jr. and Robert Reynolds, tr., IUP, 1994. This new translation of the *Shiji* started out as a translation of those chapters not translated by Chavannes and Watson. It is now attempting the more difficult aim of a full translation replacing previous efforts. Two-thirds of the way still remain before an evaluation is in order. In the meantime, for some of the pitfalls awaiting translators of the *Shiji*, see Michael Loewe's review in *TP* 84: 153–67 (1998).

Syma Cian, Istoriceskie zapiski–Siczi, Rudolph V. Viatkin and V. S. Taskin, trs., Nauka, 6 vols., 1972– .

Bibliographies of the Shiji

Shiji yanjiu de ziliao he lunwen suoyin 史記研究的資料和論文索引 (Index of research materials and articles on the *Shiji*), Zhongkeyuan, Lishisuo, comp., Kexue, 1957. Contains a detailed account of the editions, scholarship and comments on the *Shiji* down to 1937.

Shiji yanjiu ziliao suoyin he lunwen zhuanzhu tiyao 史記研究資料索引 和論文專著提要 (Index of research materials and summaries of articles and books on the *Shiji*), Yang Yanqi 楊燕起 and Yu

Zhanghua 俞樟華, comps., Lanzhou daxue, 1989. Continuation
of the previous item.

Sima Qian yu Shiji yanjiu lunzhu zhuanti suoyin 司馬遷與史記研究
論著專題索引 (Index of articles and books on research on Sima
Qian and the *Shiji*), Xu Xinghai 徐興海, ed. in chief, Shaanxi
renmin jiaoyu, 1995. Includes references to 236 books and 3,300
articles, mainly written in the 1980s and early 1990s.

Shiki gaku 50 nen 史記學 50 年, Ikeda Hideo 池田英男, comp., Meitoku, 1996. Covers publications in Japanese and Chinese between
1945 and 1995.

Hanshu 漢書 (*Standard History of the Han*), Ban Gu 班固 (AD
32–92) et al., 100 *pian* 篇 (120 *juan* 卷); 810,000 characters.

In order to distinguish it from the *Hou Hanshu*, the *Hanshu*
is sometimes called the *Qian Hanshu* 前漢書.[8] It covers the
Former Han from about 210 BC to AD 23. It is the first Standard History to cover a single dynasty. The arrangement of
the *Hanshu* is similar to that of the *Shiji*. It is divided into 12
Benji 本紀 (basic annals), 8 *Biao* 表 (tables), 10 *Zhi* 志
(monographs) and 70 *Liezhuan* 列傳 (collected biographies).
The section on *Shijia* 世家 (hereditary houses) and the biographies of rich merchants were dropped, but some very important new monographs were added, including the first
"Yiwenzhi 藝文志" (dynastic bibliography), "Xingfazhi 刑
法志" (penal law), "Dilizhi 地理志" (administrative geography) and "Baiguan gongqing biao 百官公卿表" (administration), all of which became familiar features of many of
the subsequent Histories. Like Sima Qian, Ban Gu set out
to complete a work begun by his father (the *Shiji houzhuan*
史記后傳, which he had begun in order to bring the story
to the end of the Former Han).[9] Ban Gu worked for twenty

---

[8] A. F. P. Hulsewé discusses the text history and early editions of the
Hanshu, recent editions, translations, research aids and indexes in
ECTBG, 129–36.

[9] For a comparison of the chapters on the Han in the *Hanshu* with
those in the *Shiji*, see Yves Hervouet, "La valeur relative des textes du
Che-ki et du *Han chou*," in *Mélanges de Sinologie offerts à Monsieur Paul*
Footnote continued on next page

years as a historian in the Lantai 蘭臺, one of the palace libraries. By the time of his execution he had almost finished. The tables were completed by his sister, Ban Zhao 班昭 (?48–?116),[10] and the monograph on astronomy by Ma Xu 馬續.

Use the Zhonghua punctuated, collated edition, *Hanshu*, 12 vols., 1962; 10th prnt., 1998; reduced-size, 1997. This was based on *Hanshu buzhu* 漢書補注, Wang Xianqian 王先謙 (1842–1918), ed., Changsha: Xushou tang 虛受堂, 1900; Yiwen, 1955. Wang's edition provides the most easily available notice of comments by Qing scholars.

The most convenient indexes are those based on the Zhonghua edition.

Nianwushi quanwen ziliaoku 廿五史全文資料庫 (25 Histories full text database), Shiyusuo, 1988.

Hanshu ji buzhu zonghe yinde 漢書及補注綜合引得 (Combined indexes to the *Hanshu* and the notes of Yan Shigu 顏師古 (581–645) and Wang Xianqian 王先謙), *H-Y Index* 36. This index of names and terms is based on the Tongwen edition.[11]

Hanshu cidian 漢書辭典 (Dictionary of the *Hanshu*), Cang Xiuliang 倉修良, ed., Shandong jiaoyu, 1994.

Hanshu renming suoyin 漢書人名索引 (Personal-name index to the *Hanshu*), Wei Lianke 魏連科, comp., Zhonghua, 1979.

Hanshu diming suoyin 漢書地名索引 (Place-name index to the *Hanshu*), Chen Jialin 陳家麟, comp., Zhonghua, 1990.

Demiéville, Bibliothèque de l'Institut des Hautes Etudes Chinoises, vol. 2, 1974, 55–76. For a book-length treatment of the same subject, see Park Chai-u 朴宰雨, '*Shiji*' '*Hanshu*' *bijiao yanjiu* 史記漢書比較研究 (Comparative research on the *Shiji* and the *Hanshu*), Zhongguo wenxue, 1994. There is a bibliography on pages 389–426.

[10] Nancy Lee Swann, *Pan Chao, Foremost Woman Scholar of China, First Century A.D.*, New York: Century Co., 1932; Russell, 1960.

[11] See also *Hanshu suoyin* 漢書索引 (Index to the *Hanshu*), Wong Fook-luen, comp., HKCU Press, 1966. This is an index by stroke count of terms, names, etc., arranged under 25 categories with references to the *Sibu beiyao* and *Sibu congkan* (Bona) editions.

Translations from the Hanshu

The following works translate 31 of the 90 chapters of text in the *Hanshu*:

The History of the Former Han Dynasty, Homer H. Dubs (1892–1969), tr., 3 vols., Baltimore: Waverly Press, 1938–55. Translation with notes of the first 12 chapters (the 12 basic annals) and chap. 99 (on Wang Mang).

Remnants of Han Law, A. F. P. Hulsewé, tr., vol. 1, Brill, 1955. An annotated translation of the "Xingfa zhi 刑法志" (chapters 22 and 23). Only vol. 1 of this monograph was finished.

Food and Money in Ancient China: The Earliest Economic History of China to A.D. 25, Han shu 24, with related texts, Han shu 91 and Shih-Chi 129, Nancy Lee Swann, tr., PUP, 1950. Reviewed by L. S. Yang, "Notes on Dr. Swann's *Food and money in ancient China*," *HJAS* 15: 507–21 (1952); rpnt. in *Studies in Chinese Institutional History*, HUP, 1963, 85–118. Yang points out the importance of the "Pingzhunshu 平準書" (*Shiji*) and "Shihuozhi 食貨志" (*Hanshu*): "Familiarity with certain passages from these chapters may be considered a requirement for every advanced student of Chinese history."

Rhea C. Blue, "The argumentation of the Shih-huo-chih chapters of the Han, Wei and Sui dynastic histories," *HJAS* 11.1 and 2: 1–118 (1948), includes a translation of the prefaces to the treatises on food and money in the *Shiji, Hanshu, Weishu* and *Suishu*.

Courtier and Commoner in Ancient China: Selections from the History of the Former Han by Pan Ku, Burton Watson, tr., Col. UP, 1974. Translation of 11 chapters (54, 63, 65, 67–68, 71, 74, 78, 92, 97A–B).

China in Central Asia; the early stage: 125 BC–AD 23. An annotated translation of chapters 61 and 96 of the History of the Former Han Dynasty, A. F. P. Hulsewé and M. A. N. Loewe, trs., Brill, 1979.

Po Hu T'ung, The Comprehensive Discussions in the White Tiger Hall, Tjan Tjoe Som, tr., vol. 1, Brill, 1949. Partial translation of chap. 88. The title of the original work is *Bohu tong* 白虎通 (or *Bohu tongyi* 白虎通義). *ICS Concordance* 40. Attributed to Ban Gu; a work of Confucian exegesis.

Hou Hanshu 後漢書 (*Standard History of the Later Han*), Fan Ye 范曄 (398–445), 120 *juan*, covers the years 25–220 AD.[12]

Of the 90 original *juan*, 10 are annals and 80 biographies. Later, 30 *juan* of monographs were added from another history of the Han written in the third century during the Western Jin by Sima Biao 司馬彪.[13]

Use the Zhonghua punctuated edition, *Hou Hanshu*; 12 vols, 1965; 8th prnt., 1996; reduced-size edition, 1997. The most convenient indexes are those based on this edition:

Nianwushi quanwen ziliaoku 廿五史全文資料庫 (25 Histories full text database), Shiyusuo, 1988.

Hou Hanshu ji zhushi zonghe yinde 後漢書及注釋綜合引得 (Combined indexes to the *Hou Hanshu* and the notes of Liu Zhao 劉昭 and Li Xian 李賢); *H-Y Index* 41. This index of names and terms is based on the Tongwen edition.[14]

Go-Kanjo goi shûsei 後漢書語彙集成 (Glossary of historical terms in the *Hou Hanshu*), 3 vols., Jimbun, 1960–2. Indexes some 15,000 names, geographical names, official titles and technical terms. This concordance is mainly based on the Bona edition.

Hou Hanshu cidian 後漢書辭典 (Dictionary of the *Hou Hanshu*), Zhang Shunhui 張舜徽, ed., Shandong jiaoyu, 1994.

Hou Hanshu renming suoyin 後漢書人名索引 (Personal-name index to the *Hou Hanshu*), Li Yumin 李裕民, comp., Zhonghua, 1979.

Hou Hanshu diming suoyin 後漢書地名索引 (Place-name index to the *Hou Hanshu*), Wang Tianliang 王天良, comp., Zhonghua, 1988.

---

[12] Hans Bielenstein, *The Restoration of the Han Dynasty, with Prolegomena on the Historiography of the Hou Han Shu*," 4 vols., *BMFEA*, 26: 1–209 (1954); 31: 1–287 (1959); 39: 1–198 (1967); 51: 1–300 (1979). See esp. 20–81 (1954).

[13] B. J. Mansvelt-Beck, *The Treatises of Later Han, Their Author, Sources, Contents and Place in Chinese Historiography*, Brill, 1990.

[14] *Hou Hanshu suoyin* 後漢書索引 (Index to the *Hou Hanshu*), Wong Fook-luen, comp., HKCU Press, 1971. This is an index by stroke count of terms, names, etc., arranged under 25 categories with references to the *Sibu beiyao* and *Sibu congkan* (Bona) editions.

44.2 *Other Textual Sources*

History

Sanguozhi 三國志 (for the end of the Han), see 45.1.

Hanji 漢紀 (or *Qian Hanji* 前漢紀), Xun Yue 荀悦 (148–209). This was the first chronicle of a single dynasty. The author rearranged the material in the *Hanshu* (including the Tables) in chronological order as well as adding from other sources. The period covered is from 209 BC to AD 22.

Hou Hanji 後漢紀, Yuan Hong 袁宏 (328–76). An annalistic history covering the years 23 to 220. It was based on many sources and was not entirely superseded by the *Hou Hanshu*.

Dongguan Hanji 東觀漢記. Until the Tang this was regarded as the standard work on the Later Han. It was used as a main source by Fan Ye for the *Hou Hanshu*. Sixty percent of it was retrieved from the *Yongle dadian* by the *Siku* editors (*ICS Concordance* 19).

Geography

Huayang guozhi 華陽國志 (45.2).

Shuijingzhu 水經注 (33.3).

Agriculture and the Economy

Simin yueling 四民月令 (35.1).

Fan Shengzhi shu 范勝之書 (35.1).

Yantielun 鹽鐵論, Huan Kuan 桓寬, comp., 1st c. BC. See *Discourses on Salt and Iron: A debate on State Control of Commerce and Industry in Ancient China; chapters I–XIX Translated from the Chinese of Huan K'uan with Introduction and Notes*, Esson M. Gale, tr., Brill, 1931; rpnt., Ch'engwen, 1967; Esson M. Gale, Peter A. Boodberg and T. C. Lin, "Discourses on salt and iron (*Yen T'ieh Lun*: chapters XX–XXVIII)," *JNCBRAS* 65: 73–110 (1934).[15] *Yantielun jiaozhu* 鹽鐵論校注, Wang Liqi 王利器, ed., 2 vols., Tianjin guji, 1983. For a concordance, see *ICS Concordance* 26.

[15] For a bibliography of Chinese and Japanese studies of the Chinese salt industry from the Han to the end of the Qing, see *Chûgoku engyôshi kenkyû bunken mokuroku* 中國鹽業史研究文獻目錄 (1926–88), Yoshida Tora 吉田寅, ed., Tokyo: Risshô daigaku Tôyôshigaku kenkyûshitsu, 1989.

Official Titles and Officeholders

Hanguan liuzhong 漢官六種 (*ICS Concordance* 18). Supplements material in the monographs on officials in the *Hanshu* and *Hou Hanshu*.[16]

Laws and Institutions

For the transmitted and excavated sources on Han dynasty law, see 27.2 and 44.3. Also:

Qin huiyao 秦會要 (Table 24, chap. 26).

Xi-Han huiyao 西漢會要 (Table 24, chap. 26).

Dong-Han huiyao 東漢會要 (Table 24, chap. 26).

Tongdian 通典 ("Shihuo 食貨", "Xuanju 選舉", "Zhiguan 職官" and "Dian 典"), 26.2.

Philosophy and Religion

Huainanzi 淮南子 (Table 18, chap.19).

Lunheng 論衡 (Table 18, chap.19).

Chunqiu fanlu 春秋繁露 (Table 18, chap.19).

Taiping jing 太平經. Daoist classic.

Fengsu tongyi 風俗通義 (5.3.2).

Bohu tong 白虎通 (see page 753).

Mathematics

Jiuzhang suanshu 九章算術 (Table 18, 19.1).

Zhoubi suanjing 周髀算經 (Table 18, 19.1).

Medicine

Shennong bencao jing 神農本草經 (39.1).

Shang hanlun 傷寒論 (36).

Jingui yaolüe 金匱要略 (36).

Literature

Yuefu shiji 樂府詩集 (30.3).

[16] Chen Tsu-lung (Chen Zuolong 陳祚龍), *Index du Han-kouan ts'i-tchong* 漢官七種通檢, Institut des Hautes Etudes Chinoises de l'Université de Paris, 1962.

Quan shanggu Sandai Qin Han Sanguo Liuchao wen 全上古三代秦漢三國六朝文 (30.2).

Xijing zaji 西京雜記, Liu Xin 劉歆 (d. AD 23). Former Han recovered miscellany on institutions and events linked to Chang'an.

Bowu zhi 博物志 (33.1).

Qilüe 七略 (9.3).

Language

Shiming 釋名 (2.2.2).

Shuowen jiezi 說文解字 (2.2.1 and 16.2).

Fangyan 方言 (1.1.1).

Jijiu pian 急就篇 (1.3.2).

44.3 Documents on Bone, Bamboo and Wood

44.3.1 Documents on Bone

During the excavations of the Weiyang Palace 未央宮 in Chang'an in 1980–89, archaeologists discovered over 60,000 Former Han "bone chits" or "bone tags" (*guqian* 骨簽), of which 57,000 are inscribed with records containing a total of several 100,000 characters. The material used is mainly ox bone. They are the first and only such massive find of writing on bone since the discovery at Zhouyuan in the 1970s of the oracle-bone documents dating from 900 years before (15.3). But the purpose of the *guqian* was completely different. They are inventories of tribute and goods (mainly weapons) manufactured and presented to the Han court throughout almost the entire Former Han period. It is not clear why these inventories were written on bone, but presumably it was desired to have a more lasting record than bamboo, wood or silk.[17]

---

[17] Many dozens of examples of the *guqian* are transcribed in vol. 1 of the excavation report and there are also 142 photographs in vol. 2 (Plates 107–44); see *Han Chang'an cheng Weiyanggong fajue baogao* 漢長安城未央宮發掘報告, Kaogu yanjiusuo, eds., vol. 1, text; vol. 2, plates, Zhongguo da baike quanshu, 1996.

44.3.2   Documents on Bamboo and Wood

For a general introduction to documents on bamboo strips and wooden tablets, see *jiandu* 簡牘, 18.1 and for those on silk, 18.2.

The Qin and Han *jiandu* are particularly interesting for the information they contain on administration, especially local administration,[18] the law,[19] the calendars in actual use at a particular period,[20] information on commodity prices (7.4), medicine, the mantic arts and geography. They can also be used to check received texts. Note that it is on the *jiandu* that some of the few private documents of the Qin and Han have been found.[21]

Below is a list of the main finds of Qin and Han *jiandu* (to date, 2,500 from the Qin; 70,000 from the Former Han; and 800 from the Later Han). The bamboo strips from the Qin come almost entirely from tombs in the South, where the humidity kept them intact for 2,000 years. The Han *jiandu* administrative documents are usually of wood and have been mainly found in the Northwest, where it was the arid climate, which preserved them (almost 60,000 are from just two of the three Han commanderies and guardposts along the Silk Road in modern Gansu, see 44.3.2.3). There have also been some finds of Former Han *jiandu* in the South. Most Later Han *jiandu* come from the Northwest.

The Qin strips are in Qin small seal and early Qin chancery script. The Han strips are mainly in chancery script. All the strips contain large numbers of graphic variants and wrong

---

[18] See Michael Loewe, "Wood and Bamboo Administrative Documents of the Han Period," in *NSECH*, 161–92.

[19] See A. F. P. Hulsewé, "Qin and Han Legal Manuscripts," in *NSECH*, 193–221. For more on excavated texts on Qin and Han laws, see 17.2.

[20] Yu Zhongxin 俞忠鑫, *Hanjian kaoli* 漢簡考曆 (Calendrical records on the *Hanjian*), Wenjin, 1994. The 12 almanacs discovered on bamboo strips are listed by place of discovery in 44.3.2.1–3. See also 5.1.

[21] See for example, A. F. P. Hulsewé, "Contracts of the Han Period," in *Il diritto in Cina*, L. Lanciotti, ed., Florence: Olschki, 1978, 11–38.

characters, especially those which were everyday administrative records rather than more carefully written documents.

In the listings, the following distinctions are made:

Bamboo strips: *zhujian* 竹簡
Wooden strips: *mujian* 木簡
Bamboo and wooden strips: *jiandu* 簡牘
Bamboo tablets: *zhudu* 竹牘
Wooden tablets: *mudu* 木牘

44.3.2.1   Qinjiandu 秦簡牘

Guanju 關沮, Hubei, Shashi 沙市, Hubei: 500 *zhujian* excavated in 1990 (some date from the Han).

Longgang 龍崗, Yunmeng 雲夢 county, Hubei (to the north of the Dongting lake just south of the Chu capital): 283 *zhujian* and one wooden tablet dating from the Warring States and (most) from the last years of Qin (excavated from tomb 6 in 1989 and 1991): legal texts on the management of roads, horses, sheep and cattle and taxation. See *Yunmeng Longgang Qinjian* 雲夢龍崗秦簡 (Qin bamboo strips from Longgang, Yunmeng county), Liu Xinfang 劉信芳 and Liang Gui 梁桂, eds., Kexue, 1997. See also Hu Pingsheng 胡平生, "Yunmeng Longgang Qinjian kaoshi jiaozheng 雲夢龍崗秦簡考釋校證," *Jianduxue yanjiu*, 1 (1996).

Shuihudi 睡虎地, Yunmeng, Hubei: the first Qin *zhujian* ever discovered. 1,155 strips dating from 217 BC were found in tomb 11 (excavation in 1975–76). The tomb is in the western suburbs of the county town; Longgang is a few km away in the southern suburbs. The strips record 10 works, written at different times from the end of the Warring States to the beginning of the Qin, including a lengthy portion of the lost Qin Code and other fragments of Qin laws and regulations (for references to research on these important texts, see 27.1); mantic texts and two almanacs. The tomb also contained two letters on wooden strips from two soldiers writing home to their families asking for clothes and money. They are the earliest private letters found so far. For archaeological report, see *Yunmeng Shuihudi Qinmu* 雲夢睡虎地秦墓 (The Qin tomb at Shuihudi, Yunmeng), Wenwu, 1981; for photographs, transcriptions, annotations and translations into modern Chinese, see *Shuihudi Qinmu zhujian* 睡虎地秦墓竹簡 (Bamboo strips from the Qin tomb at Shuihudi), Wenwu, 1990; transcriptions of the letters are not included (for them, see *Wenwu* 1976.9). For listing of characters, see *Shuihudi Qinjian wenzi-*

bian 睡虎地秦簡文字編 (Compilation of Qin bamboo strip characters from Shuihudi), Zhang Shouzhong 張守中, comp., Wenwu,
1994; for research, see *Yunmeng Qinjian yanjiu* 雲夢秦簡研究 (Research on the Qin bamboo strips from Yunmeng), Zhonghua, 1981;
Xu Fuchang 徐富昌, *Shuihudi Qinjian yanjiu* 睡虎地秦簡研究 (Research on the Qin bamboo strips from Shuihudi), Taibei: Wenshizhe,
1993; Wu Fuzhu 吳福助, *Shuihudi Qinjian lunkao* 睡虎地秦簡論考
(Discussion on the Qin bamboo strips from Shuihudi), Wenjin, 1994.

Yangjiashan 楊家山, Jingzhou 荆州, Hubei: 75 *zhujiandu* excavated from
tomb 135 in 1993. As important a find as Shuihudi. Not yet published.

Wangjiatai 王家臺, Jiangling, Hubei: more than 800 *zhujiandu* found in
Tomb 15 in 1993. Almanac.

44.3.2.2   *Han* Jiandu 漢簡牘 *from Tombs*

Bajiaolang 八角廊, Dingzhou 定州, Hebei: about 2,500 *zhujian* in the
tomb of Liu Xiu 劉修, King Huai of Zhongshan 中山懷王 (d. 55 BC).
They were burned by robbers at the end of the dynasty, making
most of the strips almost illegible. They include the earliest known
manuscript of the *Lunyu*, other Confucian works and an almanac
(*Wenwu* 1981.8). About a half of the text (7,576 characters on 620
mostly broken strips) of the *Lunyu* has now been deciphered and
punctuated and compared with the *jinwen* texts of the *Lunyu*; see
Dingzhou Hanmu zhujian Lunyu 定州漢墓竹簡論語 (The Dingzhou
Han tomb bamboo strip *Lunyu*), Dingzhou Hanmu zhujian zhengli
xiaozu, eds., Wenwu, 1997. In addition, 277 strips of the *Wenzi* 文子
have been deciphered (*Wenwu* 1995.12; *Wenwu* 1996.1). The tomb
was excavated in 1973.

Fenghuangshan 鳳凰山, Jiangling 江陵, Hubei: five Former Han tombs.
575 *jianmudu* excavated 1973–75, containing local population registers from five tombs (*Wenwu* 1974.7; *Wenwu* 1976.6). Two of the
tombs also included ink pellets and ink stones.

Gaotai 高臺, Jiangling 江陵, Hubei: four *mudu* from tomb 18 discovered
in 1990.

Huaguoshan 花果山, Lianyungang 連雲港, Jiangsu: Former Han. 13 *zhumu jiandu*.

Liujiaping 劉家坪, Hangu 旱谷, Gansu: 23 *mujian* discovered from Later
Han tomb in 1971. See *Hanjian yanjiu wenji* 漢簡研究文集 (Collect-
ed research articles on new documents on bamboo and wood [from
Dunhuang, Wuwei and Gansu]), Gansu renmin, 1984; 1988.

Luopowan 羅泊灣, Guixian 貴縣, Guangxi: 15 *mujiandu* discovered in 1976.

Mawangdui 馬王堆 *Chujian*, Changsha, Hunan: discovered in 1972 and 1973. Tomb 1 contained 361 *zhujian mudu* and there were 617 *zhumu jiandu* in tomb 3, mainly medical works and also lists of burial articles. For the medical works, see chap. 36. Also the earliest and most complete extant almanac ever found in China (dating from 129 BC). *Mawangdui Hanmu wenwu* 馬王堆漢墓文物 (The cultural relics unearthed from the Han tombs at Mawangdui), Hunan, 1992; Hunan sheng bowuguan, *Changsha Mawangdui yihao Hanmu* 長沙馬王堆一號漢墓 (Han tomb no. 1 from Mawangdui, Changsha), Wenwu, 1973. The important silk books found at Mawangdui are discussed in 18.2.

Shang Sunjiazhai 上孫家寨, Datong 大通, Qinghai: mainly military administration documents. More than 300 *mujian*; discovered in 1978 (*Wenwu* 1981.2).

Shuanggudui 雙古堆, Fuyang 阜陽, Anhui. Former Han tomb (165 BC) discovered in 1977. More than 6,000 *zhujian mudu* containing several Classics, the texts of which differ significantly from the transmitted texts, including the *Shijing*, the *Yijing* and the *Chuci*; an almanac; a manual on dogs; a text containing medicinal recipes; and fragments of one of the earliest character primers (the *Cang Jie pian* 倉頡篇, *Wenwu* 1983.2; *Jianbo yanjiu*, 2, 1996; see 1.3.2 for further references) and various medical texts: *Wenwu* 1978.8; 1983.1; 1984.8; 1988.4; 1989.1. Hu Pingsheng 胡平生 and Han Ziqiang 韓自強, *Fuyang Hanjian Shijing yanjiu* 阜陽漢簡詩經研究 (Researches on the Fuyang bamboo strip *Shijing*), Shanghai guji, 1988.

Wanghou Yuyang 王後漁陽, Changsha, Hunan: more than 100 wooden tomb tablets.

Weiyanggong 未央宮, Chang'an, Shaanxi: 98 badly burned *mujian* containing medical recipes and descriptions of events (discovered 1980–89): *Han Chang'an cheng Weiyanggong fajue baogao*, 1996, 238–48, for illustrations and transcriptions.

Yinqueshan 銀雀山, Linyi *xian* 臨沂縣, Shandong: Former Han tombs. 4,942 *zhujian* in tomb 1 and 32 in tomb 2. Portions of *Sunzi bing fa* 孫子兵法 (Sunzi: art of war) and the previously lost *Sun Bin bing fa* 孫臏兵法 (Sun Bin: art of war); *Yinqueshan Hanmu zhujian* 銀雀山漢墓竹簡 (Silver Sparrow Mt. Han tomb bamboo strips), vol. 1, Wenwu, 1985; Wu Jiulong 吳九龍, *Yinqueshan Hanjian shiwen* 銀雀山漢簡釋文 (Transcriptions of the Han bamboo strips from Silver Sparrow Mt.), Wenwu, 1985. Portions of the *Yanzi chunqiu* 晏子春秋.

Also an almanac dating from 174 BC found in tomb 2 (*Wenwu* 1974.3). Discovered in 1972.

Yinwan 尹灣 village, Lianyungang 連雲港 city, Jiangsu: Later Han tombs. 23 *mudu* and 133 *Hanjian* from the end of the Former Han from tomb 6 (the owner was Shi Rao 師饒, chief of the Labor Service section of the Donghai commandery 東海郡). The tablets are written on both sides (total more than 40,000 characters). They are the earliest extant traces of a commandery archive and contain details of the administration of Donghai in the last two decades BC. There are also almanacs and funerary texts; a silk funerary shawl, bronze vessels and objects, jade and pottery. Tomb 2 contained one wooden tablet consisting of a clothes list (the owner was a woman who died somewhat later than Shi Rao). For photographs and transcriptions, excavation report and maps, see *Yinwan Hanmu jiandu* 尹灣漢墓簡牘 (Wooden tablets and *Hanjian* from the Han tombs at Yinwan), Zhonghua, 1997; also *Wenwu* 1996.8, 10; 1997.1. Discovered and excavated in 1993.

Zhangjiashan 張家山, Jiangling, Hubei: Former Han tombs. About 1,000 *zhujian*, plus nine *mudu*. Early Han legal texts (tomb 247); two almanacs; medical and mathematical texts (discovered in 1983–84; *Wenwu* 1985.1). Transcriptions and studies of the medical works (on the pulse and on breathing exercises) have been published; see Gao Dalun, 1992 and 1995 (38.1). One of the legal texts is the *Zouyanshu* 奏言書 (Casebooks), which includes two cases from the Spring and Autumn period (*Wenwu* 1993.8; 1995.3; see 27.2 on Han law). About 500 *jian* of the Former Han code (*Hanlü* 漢律) await publication. The mathematical work is the oldest yet found. It predates the previous earliest known mathematical text, the *Jiuzhang suanshu* 九章算術 (37.2) by about 200 years. It has not yet been published.

44.3.2.3   Hanjian 漢簡 (Border Documents)

The overland routes from Northwest China to Central Asia along the "Silk Road" (41.3.1) were formalized for the first time following the successful efforts of the Han general Huo Qubing 霍去病 in 121 BC to drive the Xiongnu out of this region and to set up a line of frontier walls armed with guard houses and posting stations to protect it. The four commanderies established by Han Wudi a few years later (in 111 BC) were spread out over 600 km in the furthest stretch of the Hexi corridor in what is today the province of Gansu. The walled cities were at

Dunhuang 敦煌 (most distant; situated at the point at which the northern and southern branches of the Silk Road converge in the western part of Gansu), Jiuquan 酒泉, Zhangye 張掖 and Wuwei 武威. Two defense passes were also set up at Yangguan 陽關 and Yumen 玉門, the last stops within Chinese territory.

Finds of single *Hanjian* in Juyan 居延 (a border county in Zhangye) were reported in the Northern Zhou and again in the Northern Song. The first modern finds of *Hanjian* (dating from the Wei and the Jin) were made near the ancient buried city of Loulan 樓蘭 (modern Xinjiang) by the Swedish explorer Sven Hedin in 1901 and by the British explorer Sir Mark Aurel Stein in 1906–8 (for more details on both men, see 46.3). The *Hanjian* are listed below under the four main places around and in which they have been found in the twentieth century: Dunhuang 敦煌, Juyan 居延 (or Edsingol), Wuwei 武威 and Loulan 樓蘭.

Dunhuang 敦煌, Gansu. The second largest finds of bamboo and wooden documents from the Han. A total of about 27,400 *muzhu jiandu* were discovered between 1907 and 1992 (some from beacon towers, *fengsui* 烽燧 and some from tombs). Those from Dunhuang itself deal mainly with border administration; the 397 Jiuquan *mudu* include official reports, laws, letters, almanacs, medical and divination texts and the last testament of Han Wudi, which is not recorded in any other place. A further major find of more than 18,000 wooden tablets and strips was discovered at Xuanquan 懸泉, Dunhuang city, in 1990 and 1992. They include laws and regulations; divination and medical texts; and many documents on the Han postal system. Of the Dunhuang tablets, 2,484 (those discovered between 1907 and 1988) have been published in reproductions and transcribed. The most complete collection of the original materials is contained in *Dunhuang Hanjian* 敦煌漢簡 (Dunhuang *Hanjian*), Gansu sheng wenwu kaogu yanjiusuo ed., 2 vols., Zhonghua, 1990; vol. 1 contains photographs of 2,484 tablets and strips and vol. 2 the transcriptions. See also Wu Rengxiang 吳礽驤 et al., *Dunhuang Hanjian shiwen* 敦煌漢簡釋文 (Transcriptions of Dunhuang *Hanjian*), Gansu renmin, 1991, for annotated, punctuated transcriptions. Also Chen Zhi 陳直, *Dunhuang Hanjian pingyi* 敦煌漢簡評議 (A critical study of the Dunhuang *Hanjian*), Tianjin renmin, 1991. Rao Zongyi 饒宗頤, *Dunhuang Hanjian biannian kaozheng* 敦煌漢簡編年考證 (Studies on the chronology of the Dunhuang *Hanjian*), Xinwenfeng, 1995. The Xuanquan tablets have not yet been published although some have been exhibited.[22]

Juyan 居延, Gansu and Inner Mongolia. The largest finds of bamboo and wooden documents from the Han. Altogether there are about 32,200 strips and wooden tablets covering the century and a half from 119 BC to AD 167. These documents are mainly from 160 scattered sites along the 350 km of the Han Juyan 居延 and Jianshui 肩水 border defense lines. They include reports of fines and expenses, laws and regulations and a variety of other documents. The first large finds (10,100 *jiandu*) were made in 1930 and 1931 by the Sino-Swedish expedition led by Folke Bergman. The collection is housed in Taibei at the Shiyusuo.[23] The second, even larger finds in the Juyan area (19,637 *muzhu jiandu*) were made during excavations in 1973 and 1974 and sporadically thereafter. They were conducted by the Gansu province Juyan archaeological team. They date from 128 BC to AD 32.[24] There is a good introduction to the *Juyan Hanjian*: Xue Ying-

---

[22] *Zhongguo wenwu jingcui* 中國文物精粹 (Gems of China's Cultural Relics), 1997. Item 111 is a full-page photograph of a letter written on silk found at Xuanchuan and dated to 32–37 BC. The letter contains 370 characters and is the longest and best preserved private letter from the Han dynasty.

[23] *Juyan Hanjian jiayi bian* 居延漢簡甲乙編 (First and second collections of Han wooden strips from Juyan), Kaogusuo 考古所 ed., vol. 1, photographs; vol. 2, corrected transcriptions, Zhonghua, 1980. The most complete collection of original materials of the 1930s' Juyan finds; based on earlier publications, notably those of Lao Gan 勞幹, Shiyusuo, 2 vols., 1957–60; vol. 1 (photographs), rpnt., 1992; vol. 2 (transcriptions and commentary), rpnt., 1997. Xie Guihua 謝桂華 and Li Junming 李均明, *Juyan Hanjian shiwen hejiao* 居延漢簡釋文合校 (Collated transcriptions of Juyan documents on wood), 2 vols., Wenwu, 1987 contains corrected transcriptions of the old Juyan materials. For a pioneering study in English based on these documents, see Michael Loewe, *Records of Han Administration*; 2 vols., CUP, 1967.

Chen Zhi 陳直, *Juyan Hanjian yanjiu* 居延漢簡研究 (Researches on the Juyan *Hanjian*), Tianjin guji, 1986. For a thorough index to place names, contents and research on the old Juyan documents as well as some of the new ones, see *Kyoen kangen sakuin* 居延漢簡索引 (Index of Han Wooden Strips Found at Juyan, 1930-31 and 1973-74), Ôba Osamu 大庭脩, ed., Kansai daigaku, 1995.

[24] *Juyan xinjian* 居延新簡 (New documents on wood from Juyan), Gansu Wenkaosuo, Gansu Provincial Museum, Chinese Culture Re-

Footnote continued on next page

qun 薛英群, *Juyan Hanjian tonglun* 居延漢簡通論 (Survey of Han dynasty Juyan wooden documents), Gansu jiaoyu, 1991. It covers all the different finds at Juyan from Stein to the 1980s. See also Li Zhenhong 李振宏 and Sun Yingmin 孫英民 et al., *Juyan Hanjian ren-ming biannian* 居延漢簡人名編年 (Personal names on the Juyan *Hanjian* arranged by year), Shehui kexue, 1997. This is a major effort to place in chronological order the Juyan *Hanjian* despite the fact that many of the strips have only partial dates or none at all.

Wuwei 武威, Gansu. There have been seven finds at Wuwei coming to a total of 622 tablets and strips. Despite the smaller numbers, they are valuable because unlike the finds at Juyan and Dunhuang, they are either transmitted texts or rare medical works, not administrative documents. Four of the most important discoveries from sites at Wuwei were:

(i) Hantanpo 旱灘坡: 79 *mujiandu* discovered in 1972. Mainly medical texts from the Later Han: *Wuwei handai yijian* 武威漢代醫簡 (Wooden medical documents from Wuwei), Wenwu, 1975. Grass and Han chancery script is used, with an even larger share of *tong jiazi* than usual for this period.

(ii) Mozuizi 磨嘴子: 469 *zhumujian* excavated in 1959 from tomb 6 (dating from the time of Wang Mang 王莽), including complete rolls of strips (total 370) with annotations of the *Yili* 儀禮 (*Book of Ceremonial*). The text is slightly different from the transmitted version: *Wuwei Hanjian* 武威漢簡 (Wuwei *Hanjian*), Kexue, 1960.

(iii) Mozuizi: finds include 10 Daoist medical *mujian*. Discovered in tomb 18 (Later Han) in 1959, *Wuwei Hanjian*.

(iv) Mozuizi: 26 *mujian* were found in 1981 from a Han tomb with the *Wang Zhang zhaoling ce* 王仗詔令册; see *Hanjian yanjiu wenji* 漢簡研究文集 (1984; 1988).

---

search Institute and Lishisuo, eds., 2 vols., Zhonghua, 1994. This contains photographs and transcriptions of 7,000 *Hanjian*. *Juyan xinjian: jiaqu houguan yu disi sui* 居延新簡甲渠候官與第四燧 (New documents on wood from Jiaqu houguan, Juyan and the fourth beacon tower), Gansu Wenkaosuo et al., eds., 2 vols., Wenwu, 1990. Contains photographs to the original size (vol. 2) plus transcriptions (vol. 1) of the 8,409 *Hanjian* (mainly administrative documents) found between 1972 and 1982 at Jiaqu houguan (Juyan).

Loulan 樓蘭, Xinjiang: documents found by Hedin were translated by August Conrady;[25] documents found by Aurel Stein in Loulan were cataloged by Giles and by Ôba along with the Stein Dunhuang documents; in addition, 71 wooden documents dating from 49 to 8 BC were discovered at Loulan in 1930 and 1934. They are mainly laws and a copy of the *Analects*.[26] Most of the other documents were in other languages such as Turkish, Khotarian, Tibetan, Sanskrit and Karosthi.

44.4 Archaeology and Inscriptions

44.4.1 Archaeological Sites

The main archaeological sites of post-unification Qin and Han are as follows (detailed descriptions may be found in the *References* after this list):

Xianyang 咸陽 (capital of the first emperor of Qin, east of modern Xi'an).

Donghai xinggong 東海行宮 (Qin palace on the cliffs at modern Suizhong, Liaoning).

Museum of the Terracotta Army guarding the tomb of the First Emperor (Qin Shihuang bingmayong bowuguan 秦始皇兵馬俑博物館 at Lintong, 35 km east of modern Xi'an).

---

[25] August Conrady, *Die Chinesischen Handschriften–und sonstigen Kleinfunde Sven Hedins in Lou-lan*, Stockholm: Generalstatens Litografiska Anstalt, 1920. The documents and fragments mainly date from the Jin.

[26] Edouard Chavannes, *Les documents chinois découverts par Aurel Stein dans les sables du Turkestan oriental*, OUP, 1913. A translation with annotations of 991 documents, mainly on wood, brought back by Stein from his first and second expeditions (1906–1908). Of the 991 documents and fragments, 720 date from 98 BC to AD 153; 229 are from the Jin and 40 from the Tang; the 930 documents from Stein's third expedition (1913–16) are mainly from Turpan, and were cataloged and translated by Maspero (see 46.3.2); see also Ôba Osamu 大庭脩, *Dai-Ei hakubutsukan zô Tonkô Kankan* 大英博物館藏敦煌漢簡 (Dunhuang bamboo strips in the British Museum), Dôhôsha, 1990.

The city walls and site of the Former Han capital of Chang'an (just outside modern Xi'an).[27]

Later Han capital (at Luoyang).

Sections of Qin and Han Great Wall and guard posts and beacon towers extending into the Hexi 河西 corridor.

Non-Han archaeology (mainly artifacts from tombs in the North, Northwest and Southwest).

The Shaanxi History Museum (Shaanxi lishi bowuguan 陝西歷史博物館) has particularly fine collections.

Imperial Tombs of the Former Han (the 11 are scattered around modern Xi'an).

Imperial Tombs of the Later Han (the 12 are scattered around modern Luoyang).

Mawangdui 馬王堆, Changsha, Hunan: the three tombs of Li Cang 利蒼, the Marquis of Dai 軑 (d. 186 BC), his wife Xin Zhui 辛追 (d. ca. 168 BC) and probably their son; now in the Hunan Provincial Museum (44.3.2.2).

Tombs of Han princes and their wives (34 tombs from the Former Han; five from the Later Han).[28] Those with the richest finds (and they are spectacular) are the four that were not robbed in the course of the past 2,000 years, namely:

1. Mancheng 滿城, Hebei: the tomb of Liu Sheng 劉勝 (d. 113 BC), prince Jing of Zhongshan 中山靖王. Can be seen at the original site on a hilltop in Mancheng county.

2. Mancheng 滿城, Hebei: the tomb of the consort of Liu Sheng, prince of Zhongshan. She died sometime after her husband. Can be seen at the original site on a hilltop in Mancheng county.

3. Nan-Yue 南越, Canton: tomb of Zhao Mei 趙眛 (also known as 趙胡), 137–125 BC, the second king of Nan-Yue (207–111 BC). His grandfather, Zhao Tuo 趙佗 (?–137 BC; Triệu Đà in Vietnamese) was from Hebei. While head of the military forces of the Nanhai 南海 commandery, he had taken his opportunity during the con-

---

[27] *Xi'an lishi dituji* 西安歷史地圖集 (Historical atlas of Xi'an), Shi Nianhai 史念海, ed. in chief, Xi'an ditu, 1996.

[28] Huang Zhanyue 黃展岳, "Handai zhuhou wangmu lunshu 漢代諸侯王墓論述" (On princes' tombs of the Han period), *Kaogu xuebao* 128: 11–34 (1998.1).

fusion at the fall of the Qin to seize the principality of Ouluo 甌駱 (AD 257–208; Âu-Lạc in Vietnamese) and declare himself emperor (*di* 帝) of Nan-Yue (Nam-Việt, i.e., Vietnam). The territory extended over modern Guangdong, Guangxi and North Vietnam. The capital was Panyu 番禺 (just outside modern Guangzhou), the main port in the South already by the Qin. Excavations of the harbor and shipyard of Panyu have been made. The magnificent tomb is now in a special museum in Guangzhou: Xi-Han Nanyue Wang mu bowuguan 西漢南越王墓博物館.

4. Shuangrushan 雙乳山, Changqing 長清 county, Shandong: the tomb of Liu Hu 劉胡 (d. 98 BC), or Liu Kuan 劉寬 (d. 87 BC), prince of Qi-bei 齊北; excavated 1995–96, see *Kaogu* 354: 1–15 (1997.3).

44.4.2 *Archaeological References*

Song Zhimin 宋治民, *Zhanguo, Qin, Han kaogu* 戰國秦漢考古 (The archaeology of the Warring States, Qin and Han), Sichuan daxue, 1993. Contains references to the considerable number of reports and monographs on Qin and Han archaeology, including lesser known ones.

Wang Xueli 王學理 et al., *Qin wuzhi wenhuashi* 秦物質文化史 (History of material culture during the Qin), San-Qin, 1994. This is an excellent introduction to Qin archaeology in the form of a copiously illustrated survey of Qin artifacts from the earliest times to the fall of the Qin in 206 BC. There is a chronology of the main discoveries and excavations of Qin sites from 1933 to 1992 (397–417). There is also an extensive summary in English of the whole work.

Handai wuzhi wenhua ziliao tushuo 漢代物質文化資料圖說 (Annotated illustrations on the material culture of the Han dynasty), Sun Ji 孫機, comp., Wenwu, 1991. Almost an illustrated dictionary of Han terminology arranged under 110 topics (transport, clothing, hairstyles, farming, mining and so forth). Each topic is illustrated with between 5 and 20 line drawings traced from the originals (fully referenced). The notes quote from contemporary Han descriptions of the objects and also from the archaeological reports. Large numbers of crudely incised, broken tiles or bricks survive from the Han, especially from Yanshi, on the outskirts of Luoyang (Later Han). They provide a rare direct glimpse at the underside of Han rule.

A Journey into China's Antiquity, vol. 2: *Warring States–Northern and Southern Dynasties*, National Museum of Chinese History, eds.,

Morning Glory, 1998. See 8.2.1 on this authoritatively commented series of photographs of the collections of the museum.

The Land Within the Passes, Zou Zongxu, ed.; Susan Whitfield, tr. from Chinese original (1987), Penguin Viking, 1991.

Michèle Pirazzoli-t'Serstevens, *The Han Civilization of China*, Janet Seligman, tr. from the French original (1982), New York: Rizzoli, 1982.

There are a considerable number of works on Han stone reliefs (*huaxiangshi* 畫像石) found on tombs, shrines and other monuments, e.g., Wu Hung (Wu Hong 巫鴻), *The Wu Liang Shrine: The Ideology of Early Chinese Pictorial Art*, SUP, 1989, and other works cited in 38.1.

Zhongguo Handai huaxiangshi huaxiangzhuan wenxian mulu 中國漢代畫像石畫像磚文獻目錄 (Bibliography of works on Han dynasty stone and brick reliefs), Shenzhou bowuguan, eds., Wenwu, 1995. Covers books and articles written between 1900 and 1993.

44.4.3   Stone Inscriptions

Note that the earliest stone inscriptions of any length are from pre-imperial Qin (the stone-drum inscriptions). The fragments of the rock inscriptions, which the first emperor had inscribed, are also the earliest of this type to have survived (17.3).

Qindai taowen 秦代陶文 (Qin dynasty pottery script), Yuan Zhongyi 袁仲一, comp., San-Qin, 1987. Has 1,610 rubbings, which contain in all over 600 characters in rough forms of the Qin small seal script. Very few examples of Qin pottery script have survived from before 361 BC. The excavations of the ante-chambers of the tomb of the first emperor of Qin, however, turned up large quantities of pottery script, including names of corvée laborers who had worked on the tomb, funeral notices scratched onto tiles of those who had died during its construction and numbers on the statues of warriors and horses to put them in their right places.

Gao Wen 高文, *Hanbei jishi* 漢碑集釋, Henan daxue, 1985, is a study of 59 Han stelae with transcriptions and notes on the authors.

Wang Qingzheng 汪慶正, *Dong-Han shike wenzi zongshu* 東漢石刻文字綜述 (General description of the scripts carved on stone in the Later Han), *Shanghai bowuguan guankan*, 1. Collects materials of interest from stelae on economic, military and other topics.

Wu Tianying 吳天穎, "Handai maidi quan kao 漢代買地券考" (A study of Han land deeds), *Kaogu xuebao*, 1982.1.

Patricia Buckley Ebrey, "Later Han stone inscriptions," *HJAS*, 40: 325–53 (1980).

Hans Bielenstein, "Later Han Inscriptions and Dynastic Biographies: A Historiographical Comparison," in *Proceedings of the International Conference on Sinology, on History and Archaeology*, Nangang: Academia Sinica, 1981, 571–86.

Han, Wei, Nan-Bei Chao muzhi jishi 漢魏南北朝墓誌集釋 (Annotated transcriptions and originals of collected tomb tablets from the Han, Wei and *Nan-Bei Chao*), Zhao Wanli 趙萬里, ed., Kexue, 1956; Tianjin guji, 1992.

44.5 Guides and Research Tools

44.5.1   Guides to Sources and Readers

The main Han bibliographical work is the "Yiwenzhi 藝文志" in the *Hanshu* (9.4).

ECTBG   *Early Chinese Texts: A Bibliographical Guide*, Michael Loewe, ed., SSEC and IEAS, 1993. See 19.1.

NSECH   *New Sources of Early Chinese History: An Introduction to the Reading of Inscriptions and Manuscripts*, Edward L. Shaughnessy, ed., SSEC and IEAS, 1997. See chapters 15 and 16.

CHC   *The Cambridge History of China*, vol. 1, *The Ch'in and Han Empires, 221 BC–AD 220*, Denis Twitchett and Michael Loewe, eds., CUP, 1986; 3rd rpnt., 1995, 2–14, contains brief introductory essays on "The Written Sources and Their Problems," "Archaeology" and "Historical Scholarship."

Zhongguo lishi da cidian 中國歷史大辭典 (The great encyclopaedia of Chinese history), 14 vols., Shanghai cishu, 1983– , contains a separate volume on *Qin-Han shi* 秦漢史, 1990. See 8.3.2, item 2 for comments on this encyclopaedia.

A. F. P. Hulsewé, "Notes on the Historiography of the Han Period," in *Historians of China and Japan*, William G. Beasley and Edwin G. Pulleyblank, eds., OUP, 1961, 31–43.

For a shorter and more up-to-date introduction to primary (and secondary sources), see "Qin-Han shi bufen 秦漢史部分" (Section on Qin and Han history) in Xiao Li 肖黎 and Li Guihai 李桂海, gen. eds., *Zhongguo gudaishi daodu* 中國古代史導讀 (A guide to reading ancient Chinese history), Wenhui, 1991; rpnt., 1992, 77–136.

The History of the Han Dynasty: Selections with a Preface, Kan Lao (Lao Gan 勞幹), ed., 2 vols., Princeton Univ., Chinese Linguistics Project, 1983. Contains annotated readings from Han primary sources with the Chinese texts in volume 2.

T'ung-tsu Ch'ü, *Han Social Structure*, Jack L. Dull, ed., UWP, 1972, arranges numerous translated excerpts from Han primary sources by subject.

Cho-yun Hsü, *Han Agriculture*, Jack L. Dull, ed., UWP, 1980. The first part of the book discusses the topic. The second part (157–320) contains numerous translated excerpts from Han sources arranged by subject.

C. Martin Wilbur, *Slavery in China during the Former Han Dynasty*, Chicago: Field Museum of Natural History, 1943. After a thorough introduction to the subject the author assembles his evidence in the shape of numerous excerpts from Han primary sources in the original and with translations.

Qin-Han nongmin zhanzheng shiliao huibian 秦漢農民戰爭史料匯編 (28.3).

44.5.2   Research Tools

Different types of special-purpose reference works for Qin and Han history are introduced along with the main primary sources listed in 44.1. Note, too, special-purpose reference works for all of Chinese history, which are also useful for the Qin and Han, for example on weights and measures (7.3). Below are given a handful of reference works specifically for the Qin and Han.

Biographies

Liang Han bulie zhuan renming yunbian 兩漢不列傳人名韵編 (Index by rhymes of people not included in the *liezhuan* chapters of the *Shiji*, *Hanshu* and *Hou Hanshu*), Zhuang Dingyi 莊鼎彝, comp., Shangwu, 1935.

Qin, Former Han and Xin Dynasties Biographical Dictionary, Michael Loewe, forthcoming, Brill.

Later Han Biographical Dictionary, Rafe de Crespigny, forthcoming, Brill.

Official Titles and Officeholders

In addition to *DOTIC*, check Rafe de Crespigny, *Official Titles of the Former Han Dynasty*, ANU Press, 1967, and Homer H. Dubs and Rafe de Crespigny, *Official Titles of the Former Han Dynasty, An Index*, ANU Press, 1969.

Hans Bielenstein, *The Bureaucracy of Han Times*, CUP, 1980.

Geography

Zhongguo lishi dituji 中國歷史地圖集 (The Historical Atlas of China), Tan Qixiang 譚其驤, ed. in chief, vol. 2, *Qin-Han shiqi* 秦漢時期 (The Qin and Han periods), Ditu, 1982; rpnt., 1985.

Chronology

Zhongguo Xian-Qinshi libiao 中國先秦史曆表 (Calendrical concordance for pre-Qin history), Zhang Peiyu 張培瑜, comp., Qi-Lu, 1987.

Xi-Zhou (Gonghe) zhi Xi-Han lipu 西周 (共和) 至西漢曆譜, Xu Xiqi 徐錫祺, ed., 2 vols., Beijing kexue jishu, 1997. Preface by Zhang Peiyu.

Further details on these and other references on chronology and time-keeping are given in 5.6.

Indexes and Concordances

ICS Ancient Chinese Texts Concordance Series, conceived by D.C. Lau (Liu Dianjue 劉殿爵), produced at the ICS at the Chinese University of Hong Kong. The ICS *Concordances* are also available on CD-ROM. For further details see 9.10.

Bibliographies of Secondary Scholarship

Michael Loewe, "The History of the Early Empires," chap. 1 of Loewe, *Divination, Mythology and Monarchy in Han China*, CUP, 1994, is an essay on the state of the field in Qin and Han history arranged by subject categories.

CHC, vol. 1, contains a bibliography of secondary as well as primary sources, 879–920.

Zhanguo, Qin, Han shi lunwen suoyin 戰國秦漢史論文索引 (for details, see 12.2, *Bibliographies*).

Zhanguo, Qin, Han shi lunzhu suoyin; xubian lunwen 1981–90; zhuanzhu 1900–1990 戰國秦漢史論著索引續編論文 1981–1990; 專著 1900–1990 (a large-scale unannotated bibliography of Chinese twentieth-century scholarship on the Qin and Han; for details, see 12.2, *Bibliographies*).

Koga Noboru, "A Brief History of Ch'in and Han Studies in Japan," *Acta Asiatica* 58: 89–119 (1990).

Check also the bibliographies in one of the recent Japanese scholarly histories of China, for example Yamakawa Shuppansha 山川出版社, *Sekai rekishi taikei* 世界歴史大系 (World History Series).

Societies and Journals

The following are just some of the learned societies, which publish newsletters and/or collected articles based on conferences.

Qin-Hanshi yanjiuhui 秦漢史研究會 (Society for Research on Qin and Han History), Xi'an; founded in 1981.

Xian-Qinshi xuehui 先秦史學會 (Society for Pre-Qin history), Chengdu; founded in 1982.

The SSEC publishes the important journal *Early China* (12.2).

45

Wei, Jin, Nan-Bei Chao

220–581

Wei 魏, Jin 晉, *Nan-Bei Chao* 南北朝[1]	220–589
†*Sanguo* 三國 (three kingdoms)	220–280
Wei 魏 (also known as Cao Wei 曹魏)	220–265
Han 漢 (also known as Shu Han 蜀漢)	221–263
Wu 吳 (also known as Sun Wu 孫吳)	222–280
†Jin 晉	265–420
Western Jin 西晉	265–316
Eastern Jin 東晉	317–420
Six Dynasties 六朝[2]	222–589
Sixteen Kingdoms 十六國[3]	304–439
Nan-Bei Chao 南北朝	420–589
†Southern Dynasties 南朝	420–579
†Liu Song 劉宋	420–479

[1] This is the conventional term. More logical would be *Sanguo, liang-Jin, Nan-Bei Chao shiqi* 三國兩晉南北朝時期.

[2] The Six Dynasties (*Liuchao* 六朝) of the years 222–589 were Wu 吳, Dong Jin 東晉 and the four Southern dynasties of Song 宋, Qi 齊, Liang 梁 and Chen 陳. They were grouped together because they all had their capitals in the South at Jiankang 建康 (Nanjing). They are sometimes called the southern Six Dynasties to distinguish them from another definition of the term, the northern Six Dynasties (Wei, Xi-Jin, Hou-Wei, Bei-Qi, Bei-Zhou and Sui). Occasionally, too, the whole period of Wei, Jin, *Nan-Bei Chao* is also called the Six Dynasties.

[3] Conventional term for the sixteen states established over most of North China and Sichuan between 304 and 439, of which five were Xianbei 鮮卑; three Han 漢; three Xiongnu 匈奴; two Di 氐, and one each Qiang 羌, Jie 羯 and Badi 巴氐. Collectively the non-Han peoples who ruled in the North at this time were known as the "five barbarians" (*wuhu* 五胡). They were not counted in the legitimate succession of dynasties (*zhengtong* 正統); on which see 20.4.

†Qi 齊	479–502
†Liang 梁	502–557
†Chen 陳	557–589
†Northern Dynasties 北朝[4]	386–581
†Northern Wei 北魏[5]	386–534
Eastern Wei 東魏	534–550
Western Wei 西魏	535–556
†Northern Qi 北齊	550–577
†Northern Zhou 北周	557–581

Those dynasties for which a Standard History was compiled are indicated with a † (45.2).

Few historical sources other than the 11 Standard Histories have survived, which makes these compilations unusually important (45.1).

This was a period in which the annotation of texts, biography and geography flourished. Buddhist and Daoist works became widespread and collected works became an established form.

The discovery in 1996 of documents written on 90,000 bamboo strips dating from the third century marks an important new source for the period (45.2).

45.1 Main Historical Works

Many of the 11 Standard Histories listed below either have incomplete monographs or none at all. Qing scholars did much to make up this gap. Many of their corrections and additions and are published in *Ershiwushi bubian* and *Ershisishi dingbian* (22.2).

---

[4] The founders and rulers of the Northern Dynasties were all *Xianbei* 鮮卑 (a non-Han people), with the exception of the Northern Qi whose ruling house was founded by a Han from Bohai 渤海. Another convention is to date the Northern dynasties to the years 439–581 (from the Wei unification of North China to the establishment of the Sui dynasty).

[5] Also called *Tuoba* Wei 拓拔魏.

Works written by a private individual are indicated with a single asterisk. Those officially commissioned from one or two individuals are shown with double asterisks. Finally, those written by official historians are indicated with triple asterisks. In addition to the Standard Histories listed below, use also the *Hou Hanshu* (44.1) and the *Hou Hanji* (44.2) for the beginning of the period and the *Suishu* (46.1) for the end. Use the Zhonghua punctuated editions.

Sanguozhi 三國志 (*The Records of the Three Kingdoms**), Chen Shou 陳壽 (233–97), comp., 285–97.[6]

> *Sanguozhi ji Pei zhu zonghe yinde* 三國志及裴注綜合引得 (Combined indices to the Standard History of the *Sanguozhi* and the notes of Pei Songzhi), *H-Y Index* 33. Indexes proper names, place names, offices, titles, technical terms and titles of works in the standard commentary. Note the preface by Hong Ye 洪業.

> *Sanguozhi diming suoyin* 三國志地名索引 (Index of geographical names in the *Sanguozhi*), Wang Tianliang 王天良 ed., Zhonghua, 1980.

> Rafe de Crespigny, *The Records of the Three Kingdoms: A Study in the Historiography of the San Kuo Chih*, ANU Press, 1970.

Jinshu 晉書 (*Standard History of the Jin***), Fang Xuanling 房玄齡 (578–648) et al., comp., 644; covers the years 265–419.

> *Jinshu renming suoyin* 晉書人名索引, Zhang Chenshi 張忱石, ed., Zhonghua, 1977. Indexes the biographies in the Zhonghua punctuated edition.

> Lien-sheng Yang, "Notes on the Economic History of the Chin Dynasty," *HJAS* 8: 107–85 (1945–47), rpnt. in *Studies in Chinese Institutional History*, HUP, 1963, 119–97. Includes a translation of the "Shihuozhi" of the *Jinshu*, 137–97.

---

[6] *Sanguozhi* (History of the Three Kingdoms), 5 vols., Zhonghua, 1962. The *Sanguozhi jizhushi* 三國志集注譯 (Annotated and translated *Sanguozhi*), Fang Beichen 方北辰, 3 vols., Shanxi renmin, 1996. Includes a newly punctuated original text as well as correcting many mistakes in the Zhonghua edition and in the notes of Pei Songzhi 裴松之 (372–451), *Sanguozhi jijie* 三國志集解, Lu Bi 盧弼, Shanghai guji, 1957.

Southern Kingdoms

Songshu 宋書 (*Standard History of the Song***), Shen Yue 沈約 (441–513), comp., 492–93; covers the years 420–79.

Nan Qishu 南齊書 (*Standard History of the Southern Qi**), Xiao Zixian 蕭子顯 (489–537), comp., 489–537; covers the years 479–502.

Liangshu 梁書 (*Standard History of the Liang***), Yao Cha 姚察 (533–606) and Yao Silian 姚思廉 (d. 637), comp., 628–35; covers the years 502–56.

Chenshu 陳書 (*Standard History of the Chen***), Yao Cha 姚察 (533–606) and Yao Silian 姚思廉 (d. 637), comp., 622–29; covers the years 557–89.

Nanshi 南史 (*Standard History of the Southern Dynasties**), Li Yanshou 李延壽 (ca. 629), comp., 630–50; covers the years 420–589.

> *Nanchao wushi renming suoyin* 南朝五史人名索引, Zhang Chenshi 張忱石, 2 vols., Zhonghua, 1985. Indexes the biographies in the Zhonghua punctuated editions of the *Songshu*, *Nan Qishu*, *Liangshu*, *Chenshu* and the *Nanshi*.

Northern Kingdoms

Weishu 魏書 (*Standard History of the Wei***), Wei Shou 魏收 (506–72), comp., 551–54; covers the years 386–550.

Bei Qishu 北齊書 (*Standard History of the Northern Qi***), Li Delin 李德林 (530–90) and Li Boyao 李百藥 (565–648), comp., 627–36; covers the years 550–77.

Zhoushu 周書 (*Standard History of the Zhou****), Linghu Defen 令狐德棻 (583–661), comp., ca. 629; covers the years 557–581.

Beishi 北史 (*Standard History of the Northern Dynasties**), Li Yanshou 李延壽 (fl. 618–76), comp., 630–50; covers the years 368–618.

> *Beichao sishi renming suoyin* 北朝四史人名索引, Zhang Zhong'an 張仲安 et al., eds., Zhonghua, 1988. Indexes the biographies in the

Zhonghua punctuated editions of the *Weishu*, *Bei Qishu*, *Zhoushu* and *Beishi*.

On the composition of the above 11 Standard Histories (as well as the *Suishu* 隋書), see William Hung, "The T'ang *Kuo-shih kuan* before 708," *HJAS* 23: 93–107 (1960–61); L. S. Yang, "The Official History of the Chin Period," in Yang (1963), 119–24; J. R. Ware, "Notes on the History of the *Wei shu*," *JAOS* 52: 33–45 (1932).

Cheng Shude 程樹德 in *Jiuchao lü kao* 九朝律考 (27.2).

Translations

For earlier translations into Western languages from these Histories, see Hans H. Frankel, *Catalogue of Translations from the Chinese Dynastic Histories for the Period 220–960*, UCP, 1957; rpnt., Greenwood, 1974. There have been a considerable number of translations since this catalog was compiled (see 41.4, note 20).

Hans Bielenstein has prepared an annalistic political history based on the Standard Histories: "The Six Dynasties, Vol. I," *BMFEA* 68: 5–324 (1996); Vol. II, *BMFEA* 69 (1997).

45.2 Other Textual Sources

Wudai shizhi 五代史志 (compiled in the Tang as the monograph section of the *Suishu*).

Tongdian 通典 (26.2).

Zizhi tongjian 資治通鑑 (21.3). Many of the chapters covering the Later Han, Wei, Jin and *Nan-Bei Chao* have been translated into English, notably chapters 54 to 59 in *Emperor Huan and Emperor Ling, Being the Chronicle of Later Han for the Years 157–189 AD*, Rafe de Crespigny, tr. and annotated, vol. 1, *Text*; vol. 2, *Notes*, Faculty of Asian Studies, ANU, 1989; chapters 59–69 in *To Establish Peace, Being the Chronicle of Later Han for the Years 189–220 AD*, Rafe de Crespigny, tr. and annotated, 2 vols., ANU, 1997; and chapters 69–78 in *The Chronicles of the Three Kingdoms (220–265)*, Achilles Fang, tr. and annotated, 2 vols., HUP, 1952 and 1965. Fang's annotated translation is particularly useful in that the focus is on Sima Guang's sources for this period, thus providing a detailed view of his method of compilation.

Weilüe 魏略 (Brief history of Wei), Yu Huan 魚豢, privately written in Standard History form.

Huayang guozhi 華陽國志, Chang Qu 常璩, early gazetteer-like history cum topography of Sichuan; the Ba-Shu edition (1984) is punctuated and indexed.

Shiliuguo chunqiu 十六國春秋, Cui Hong 崔鴻, Northern Wei, is based on historical works of the 16 kingdoms.

Jiankang Shilu 建康實錄, Xu Song 許嵩, T'ang, has details on Jiankang (Nanjing). The Shanghai guji (1987) edition is punctuated.

Shuijingzhu 水經注 (4.4.1).

Wenxuan 文選 (30.2).

Quan shanggu Sandai Qin Han Sanguo Liuchao wen 全上古三代秦漢三國六朝文 (30.2).

Shishuo xinyu 世說新語 (A new account of tales of the world), comp. under the aegis of Liu Yiqing 劉義慶 (403–44). Richard B. Mather, tr., *A New Account of Tales of the World*, Univ. of Minnesota Press, 1976. Contains anecdotes about personalities and society, AD 150–420. Also important for recording the contemporary language.

Luoyang qielan ji 洛陽伽藍記 (Record of the monasteries of Luoyang), Yang Xuanzhi 楊衒之 (?–555), AD 530; Kexue, 1958. More than the title suggests; the earliest substantial account of a Chinese city to survive (in this case, Luoyang, the capital of the Northern Wei). *Memories of Loyang*, tr. with introduction by William Jenner, OUP, 1983. Contains a major study of the short-lived capital (pp. 1–138). See also, *A Record of Buddhist Monasteries in Lo-yang*, Wang Yi-t'ung, tr., PUP, 1984.

Qimin yaoshu 齊民要術 (35.1).

Yanshi jiaxun 顏氏家訓 (3.5).

Xian-Qin Han Wei Jin Nan-Bei Chao shi 先秦漢魏晉南北朝詩 (30.3).

Sanguo huiyao 三國會要 and *Gaoben Jin huiyao* 稿本晉會要 are more useful than the *Huiyao* for the Southern Dynasties compiled in the late Qing (26.1).

Chuxue ji 初學記 (29.2).

Taiping yulan 太平御覽 (29.2).

Yiwen leiju 藝文類聚 (29.2).

Beitang shuchao 北堂書鈔 (29.2).

Wei, Jin, Nan-Bei Chao nongmin zhanzheng shiliao huibian 魏晉南北朝農民戰爭史料彙編 (28.3).

45.3 Documents on Bamboo and Wood

Jiandu 簡牘 dating from the Wei and Jin were first found in modern times in Xinjiang at Loulan. They were transcribed and in some cases photographed and translated, along with Han *jiandu* finds from Dunhuang.[7]

A spectacular cache from the *Sanguo* kingdom of Wu (220–80) was discovered at a construction site at Zoumalou 走馬樓, Changsha, in 1996. It is equivalent to more than the number of all previously known *jiandu*. It includes 2,000 large wooden tablets half a meter in length each with 100 to 160 characters and an estimated 90,000 bamboo strips, each with about 20 characters, to give an estimated total of about 1.5 million legible characters (twice as long as the Standard History of Wu and longer than the *Sanguozhi*). The bamboo strips are mainly population registers (*huji* 戶籍). They also contain tax, rental, legal and administrative records. The strips were stored in what appears to be an underground grain silo. They survived because water seeped in. It will take many years to sort them. One of the main difficulties is that the tens of thousands of population strips have become out of sequence. Originally each family's register was tied together in a bundle with the family name only on the strip of the head of the household. In the course of time, the strings holding the strips together have rotted so it is extremely difficult to establish where the separate strips recording other family members (including wives and children) belong.

[7] Shulehe 疏勒河, near Shule (mod. Kashi 喀什, Kashgar), Xinjiang: Lin Meicun 林梅村 and Li Junming 李均明, *Shulehe liuyu chutu Hanjian* 疏勒河流域出土漢簡 (Bamboo strips excavated from the area of Shulehe), Wenwu, 1984.

Note that *Tulufan chutu wenshu* 吐魯番出土文書 (46.3.1), vols. 2 and 3, contain a considerable number of documents on wood from the Northern Wei.

45.4 *Archaeology and Inscriptions*

The archaeological record, although not yet as rich as that of the Qin and Han, is nevertheless an essential adjunct to make up for the paucity of historical sources. For an introduction, see Luo Zongzhen 羅宗真, *Liuchao kaogu* (Archaeology of the Six Dynasties), Nanjing daxue, 1994.

Archaeological Sites

Traces of the capital cities of the kingdoms of Wei (Yecheng 鄴城), Jin (Luoyang 洛陽), and Wu (Wuchang 武昌) have been excavated at modern Linzhangxian 臨漳縣 (Hebei), Luoyang and Echengxian 鄂城縣 (Hubei). No trace remains of the Six Dynasties capital of Jianye 建鄴 (Nanjing).

The capital of the Xiongnu kingdom of Xiaguo 夏國 or Da-Xia 大夏 (407–31) was called Tongwancheng 統萬城. It has been excavated at modern Jingbianxian 靖邊縣 (Shaanxi).

Many tombs of the Three Kingdoms, Jin and *Nan-Bei Chao* have been excavated.

All three of the great Buddhist cliff carvings began in this period: Mogao 莫高 (Dunhuang, Gansu); Yungang 雲岡 (Datong, Shanxi) and Longmen 龍門 (Luoyang, Henan).

There are many reproductions of the paintings at Dunhuang. Outstanding is *Caves of the Singing Sands: Dunhuang, Buddhist Art from the Silk Road*, text: Roderick Whitfield; photography: Seigo Otsuka, 2 vols., Textile and Art Publications, 1996.

Illustrations

A Journey into China's Antiquity, vol. 2: *Warring States–Northern and Southern Dynasties*, National Museum of Chinese History, eds., Morning Glory, 1998. See 8.2.1 on this authoritatively commented series of photographs based on the collections of the museum.

Stone Inscriptions

Han, Wei, Nan-Bei Chao muzhi jishi 漢魏南北朝墓誌集釋 (Annotated transcriptions and originals of collected tomb tablets from the Han, Wei and *Nan-Bei Chao*), Zhao Wanli 趙萬里, ed., 6 vols., Kexue, 1953–56; Tianjin guji, 1992.

Beichao muzhi yinghua 北朝墓誌英華 (The best of the tomb tablets of the Northern Dynasties), Zhang Boling 張伯齡, San-Qin, 1988.

Liuchao muzhi jianyao 六朝墓誌檢要 (Index to tomb tablets of the Six dynasties), Wang Zhuanghong 王壯弘 and Ma Chengming 馬成名, Shanghai shuhua, 1985; index with abbreviated summaries of about 1,800 tomb tablets from the Later Han to the Sui.

45.5 Guides and Research Tools

45.5.1 Guides to Sources

Sangokushi kenkyû yôran 三國志研究要覽 (Manual of research on the Three Kingdoms), Nakabayashi Shirô 中林史郎 and Watanabe Yoshihiro 渡邊義浩, eds., Tokyo: Jinbutsu ôraisha 人物未來社, 1996, contains an introduction on doing research on the Three Kingdoms as well as a bibliography of over 5,000 items of Japanese and Chinese secondary scholarship.

Zhongguo lishi da cidian 中國歷史大辭典 (The great encyclopaedia of Chinese history), 14 vols., Shanghai cishu, 1983– , contains a separate volume on *Wei, Jin, Nan-Bei Chao shi* 魏晉南北朝史, 1997. See 8.3.2, item 2 for comments on this encyclopaedia.

45.5.2 Research Tools

In addition to the indexes and other research tools listed under individual works above, note the following:

Geography

Zhongguo lishi dituji 中國歷史地圖集 (The Historical Atlas of China), Tan Qixiang 譚其驤, ed. in chief, vol. 3, *San Guo Xi-Jin shiqi* 三國西晉時期; vol. 4, *Dong-Jin Shiliuguo Nan-Bei Chao shiqi* 東晉十六國南北朝時期, 2nd rev. ed., 2nd prnt., Ditu, 1985.

Bibliography

Bibliography in *CHC*, vol. 2, *The Northern and Southern Dynasties*, Denis Twitchett, ed., CUP, 1999.

Societies and Journals

Wei, Jin, Nan-Bei Chao shi xuehui 魏晉南北朝史學會 (Society for the study of the history of the Wei, Jin and *Nan-Bei Chao*) founded in 1984; the headquarters is at the Lishisuo.

Early Medieval China (1994– , irreg. annual). All aspects of Han to Tang with special emphasis on the Six Dynasties period (see 10.4.2 for previous titles.

Beichao yanjiu 北朝 (1991– , quarterly), Pingcheng Beichao yanjiuhui 平城研究會, ed., Datong.

46

Sui, Tang and Five Dynasties

Sui 隋	581–618
Tang 唐	618–907
Wudai shiguo 五代十國	902–979
Five Dynasties 五代[1]	907–960
Ten Kingdoms 十國[2]	902–979

The official writing of history came of age in the Tang (21.2), which also saw the first major work on historiography (*Shitong* 史通, 20.4). Legal and institutional sources have survived intact, notably the *Tang lü* and the *Tang liudian* (chap. 27). The widespread use of paper encouraged individual authors to gather their collected works together. Not surprisingly, more Tang *bieji* are extant than for all of the preceding dynasties put together. Several geographical works are also extant as well as the beginnings of local gazetteers. The Tang is particularly rich in stone inscriptions (at least 6,000 are known to have survived, 46.4.2). Thanks to the preser-

---

[1] The Five Dynasties were Later Liang 後梁 (907–923); Later Tang 後唐 (*Shatuo* 沙陀, a Turkic people, 923–936); Later Jin 後晉 (*Shatuo* 沙陀, 936–946); Later Han 後漢 (*Shatuo* 沙陀, 947–950); and Later Zhou 後周 (951–960).

[2] The Ten Kingdoms were Wu 吳 (902–937); Nan Tang 南唐 (937–975); Wu-Yue 吳越 (907–978); Chu 楚 (907–951); Min 閩 (909–945); Nan Han 南漢 (917–971); Qian Shu 前蜀 (903–925); Hou Shu 後蜀 (933–965); Jingnan 荊南 (924–963); and Bei Han 北漢 (*Shatuo* 沙陀), 951–979. Most were conquered by the Song.

vation of the documents at Dunhuang and Turpan there is also a rich collection of religious works and popular literature, not to speak of a considerable number of local documents of a social and economic interest (46.3).

46.1 Main Historical Works

For the sake of convenience of presentation, the Standard Histories are listed first. As it was made clear in chap. 22, they are comprehensive summaries, compiled much after the event from many sources, which may themselves be just as important and often more detailed.

Suishu 隋書 (*Standard History of the Sui*), Wei Zheng 魏徵 (580–643) et al., comps., 629–36; 3 vols., Zhonghua, 1973. Covers the years 581–617.

> *Suishu renming suoyin* 隋書人名索引, Deng Jingyuan 鄧經元, comp., Zhonghua, 1979.

> Etienne Balazs, "Le Traité économique du *"Souei-chou,"* TP 42.3 and 4 (1953). Translation with notes and introduction of the *Suishu* "Shihuozhi."

> Etienne Balazs, *Le traité juridique du "Souei-chou,"* Brill, 1954. Annotated translation with introduction to the *Suishu* "Xingfazhi."

Jiu Tangshu 舊唐書 (*Old Standard History of the Tang*), Liu Xu 劉昫 (887–946) et al., comps., 940–45; 16 vols., Zhonghua, 1975. Covers the years 618–906.

> On the compilation of the *Jiu Tangshu*, see Denis C. Twitchett, *The Writing of Official History under the T'ang*, CUP, 1992.

> Denis Twitchett, "The Derivation of the Text of the *Shih-huo-chih* of the *Chiu T'ang-shu*," JOS 3: 48–62 (1956).

> Denis Twitchett, *Financial Administration under the T'ang Dynasty*, 1963; 2ⁿᵈ rev. ed., CUP, 1970. Introductory matter to (unpublished) translation of the monograph on financial administration in the *Jiu Tangshu*.

> Hans H. Frankel, "T'ang Literati: A Composite Biography," in *Confucian Personalities*, Arthur Wright and Denis Twitchett, eds.,

SUP, 1962, 65–83, a study of the biographical sketches in the "Garden of letters" section of the *Jiu Tangshu.*

Xin Tangshu 新唐書 (*New Standard History of the Tang*), Ou-yang Xiu 歐陽修 (1007–72), Song Qi 宋祁 (998–1061) et al., comps., 1043–60; 10 vols., Zhonghua, 1975. Covers the years 618–906.[3]

Xin-Jiu Tangshu renming suoyin 新舊唐書人名索引, Zhang Wanqi 張萬起, comp., 3 vols., Shanghai guji, 1986. Index to the Zhonghua edition.

Xin Tangshu zaixiang shixibiao yinde 新唐書宰相世繫表引得 (Index to the Genealogical Tables of Families of Chief Ministers in the New Standard History of the Tang), *H-Y Index* 16.

Karl Bünger, *Quellen zur Rechtsgeschichte der T'ang-zeit, MS* Monograph 9, Beijing, 1946. Annotated translation of the fifth and sixth of the monographs on penal law, those in the *Jiu Tangshu* and *Xin Tangshu.* It also includes the sections on law in *Tang hui-yao.*

Etienne Balazs, "Beiträge zur Wirtschaftsgeschichte der T'ang Zeit, 618–906," in *Mitteilungen des Seminars für orientalische Sprachen* 34: 1–92 (1931); 35: 1–73 (1932); 36: 1–62 (1933). Analytic study of Tang economy based on the "Shihuozhi" of both the *Jiu Tang-shu* and the *Xin Tangshu.*

Robert des Rotours, *Le traité des examens*, Leroux, 1932; rpnt., CMC, 1976. Annotated translation of the monograph on the examination system in the *Xin Tangshu* (*juan* 44 and 45).

Robert des Rotours, *Traité des fonctionnaires et traité de l'armée*, 2 vols., Brill, 1947–78; rpnt., CMC, 1974. Annotated translation of the monographs on officials and army in the *Xin Tangshu* (*juan* 46–50).

Hiraoka Takeo 平岡武夫, *Tôdai no gyôsei chiri* 唐代の行政地理 (Tang dynasty administrative geography), vol. 2 of *T'ang Civili-*

---

[3] The *Jiu Tangshu* is more reliable than the *Xin Tangshu*. The *XTS* has tables and better monographs, but much of the rest of the work was rewritten and contains many errors. For a comparison of the *Jiu* with the *Xin Tangshu*, see des Rotours (1932), 56–71; Twitchett and Johnson (1986), 32–35. On the author, see James T. C. Liu, *Ou-yang Hsiu, An Eleventh-Century Neo-Confucianist*, SUP, 1967.

zation Reference Series, Jimbun, 1954. Indexes the monographs on administrative geography in both the *Jiu* and *Xin Tangshu*; Chinese tr., *Tangdai de xingzheng dili* 唐代的行政地理, Shanghai guji, 1989.

Zizhi tongjian 資治通鑑 is the single most important source for Sui, Tang and *Wudai, Shiguo* history (21.3).

Tang lü shuyi 唐律疏議 (The Tang Code with commentaries). The first Chinese penal code to survive and of immense importance for both the Tang and later Chinese codes as well as those of its neighbors (27.3).

Tang liudian 唐六典 (27.4).

Tongdian 通典 (26.2).

Tang huiyao 唐會要 (26.1).[4]

Wudai huiyao 五代會要 (26.1).

Cefu yuangui 册府元龜 contains many Tang documents (29.2).

Wudai-Shiguo 五代十國

The Five Dynasties (and Ten Kingdoms) lasted just 77 years during which there was much fighting between the many kingdoms and regimes. Few historical sources have survived. Those that do were written in the Song or preserved in Song sources (chap. 47). There is a good brief introduction to the primary sources for the Five Dynasties in Chikusa Masaaki 竺沙雅章, "Five Dynasties and the Song."[5]

Jiu Wudaishi 舊五代史 (*The Old Standard History of the Five Dynasties*), Xue Juzheng 薛居正 (912–81), 6 vols., Zhonghua, 1976. Covers the years 907–60.

---

[4] *Tang huiyao renming suoyin* 唐會要人名索引, Zhang Chenshi 張忱石, ed. in chief, Zhonghua, 1991.

[5] English tr. by Kenneth Chase of Chikusa's chapter in *Ajia rekishi kenkyû nyûmon* アジア歴史研究入門 (8.3) in *Research Tools for the Study of Sung History*, Peter Bol, Sung-Yuan Research Aids (II), Binghamton, 1990, 2nd ed., Albany, 1996, 115–20.

Wang Gung-wu, "The *Chiu Wu-tai shih* and History-Writing during the Five Dynasties," *Asia Major* 6: 1–22 (1957–58), and on the period in general, the same author's *The Structure of Power in North China During the Five Dynasties*, Kuala Lumpur: Univ. of Malaya Press, 1963.

Xin Wudaishi 新五代史 (*The New Standard History of the Five Dynasties*), Ouyang Xiu 歐陽修 (1007–72), 2 vols., Zhonghua, 1976. Covers the years 907–60.[6]

> *Xin-Jiu Wudaishi renming suoyin* 新舊五代史人名索引, Zhang Wanqi 張萬起, comp., Shanghai guji, 1980. Index to the Zhonghua edition.

Jiuguo zhi 九國志, Lu Zhen 路振 (957–1014); the work was completed in the Song (1064) to cover all 10 kingdoms. Recovered from the *Yongle dadian* in the Qing. In *Congshu jicheng*, 1st series.

Nan Tangshu 南唐書. There are two works of this title. The first was by Ma Ling 馬令 (completed in 1105); the second was compiled by Lu You 陸游 (1125–1210) in 1184. Both are important sources for the history of the Kingdom of Southern Tang.

Shiguo chunqiu 十國春秋, Wu Renchen 吳任臣, 1669; punctuated and collated ed., 4 vols., Zhonghua, 1983.

46.2 Other Textual Sources

History

An Lushan shiji 安祿山事蹟 (Rebellion of An Lushan), Yao Runeng 姚汝能, Shanghai guji, 1983. Recounts the events of 703–62. For a translation, see *Histoire de Ngan Lou-chan* (*Ngan Lou-chan Che-tsi*), Robert des Rotours, tr., PUF, 1962.

Shitong 史通 (20.4).

[6] See Liu (1967).

Geography

Taiping huanyu ji [zhi] 太平寰宇記 [志] (Gazetteer of the world during the Taiping Period, 976–83), comprehensive geography written by Yue Shi 樂史, late tenth century. Largely based on Tang works and therefore an important source for Tang geography (4.5.3). There is an index available.[7]

Yuanhe junxian tuzhi 元和郡縣圖志 (4.5.3).

Yuanhe xingzuan 元和姓纂 (3.5.1).

Liang jing xinji 兩京新記, also called *Liang jing ji* 兩京記, *Dong-Xi jingji* 東西京記), Wei Shu 韋述 (? –757), 722. Indexed along with six other texts on the two Tang capitals, plus maps in *Tôdai no Chôan to Raku-yô* 唐代の長安と洛陽 (see 46.5.2, *Geography*).

Manshu 蠻書 (41.5.1).

Travel

Da Tang Xiyuji jiaozhu 大唐西域記校注 (41.5.1).

Nit-Tô guhô junrei gyôki 入唐求法巡禮行記 (42.2).

Laws and Institutions

Tang da zhaoling ji 唐大詔令集 (Collected edicts of the Tang), Song Min-qiu 宋敏求, 1070; Shangwu, 1959. Indexed in *T'ang Civilization Reference Series*, nos. 3 and 7.[8]

Dengkeji kao 登科記考 (3.8.2). See also Table 24, chap. 26 and chap. 27.

Encyclopaedias

Chuxue ji 初學記 (29.2).

Yiwen leiju 藝文類聚 (29.2).

Beitang shuchao 北堂書鈔 (29.2).

Yuhai 玉海 (29.2).

[7] *Taiping huanyu ji suoyin* 太平寰宇記索引, Wang Hui 王恢, comp., Wenhai, 1975.

[8] See also *Tôdai shôchoku mokuroku* 唐代詔敕目錄 (Catalog of imperial edicts under the Tang arranged in chronological order), Tôyô bunko Tôdaishi kenkyû iinkai eds., Tôyô bunko, 1981. Indexes 37 primary printed sources; 12 collections of epigraphy and five collections of Dunhuang and Turpan documents. Many edicts not included in this collection have been found on recently excavated stone inscriptions (46.4.2).

Agriculture

Chajing 茶經 (35.2).

Sishi zuanyao 四時纂要 (35.1).

Bieji 別集

Of 904 collected works of individual authors (*bieji* 別集) known to have been in existence in the Sui, 467 have been lost. Likewise, the majority of Tang *bieji* have also been lost. However, for a catalog of 108 extant Tang collected works, see *Tangji xulu* 唐集叙錄.[9] See also the large anthologies of Tang prose and poetry such as *Quan Tang wen* 全唐文, *Quan Tang shi* 全唐詩 or *Wenyuan yinghua* 文苑英華 and Tang wencui 唐文萃 (30.2).[10]

Biji 筆記

For a repertory of terminology in Tang *biji*, see *Tang-Song biji yuci huishi* 唐宋筆記語辭匯釋.[11] Arrangement is by *pinyin* with a stroke-count index (incomplete). There are also many printing mistakes. More useful, including for *biji*, is *Tang-Wudai yuyan cidian* 唐五代語言辭典 (see under 46.5.2, *Language*).

There is a name-index to Tang fictional *biji*: *Tang-Wudai wushi'er zhong biji xiaoshuo renming suoyin* 唐五代五十二種筆記小説人名索引.[12]

There follows a selection of five Tang *biji* (see also *Tang zashi* 唐雜史, chap. 24) and two later *biji* with Tang materials:

[9] *Tangji xulu* (Catalog of Tang collected works), Wan Man 萬曼, ed., Zhonghua, 1980.

[10] There are many other anthologies of Tang prose and poetry; for example, *Tang wencui* 唐文萃, which is sometimes more reliable than the *Wenyuan*. See William Nienhauser, Jnr., *Bibliography of Selected Western Works on T'ang Dynasty Literature*, CMC, 1988.

[11] *Tang-Song biji yuci huishi* (Collected notes on the language of Tang and Song miscellaneous notes), Wang Ying 王瑛, ed., Zhonghua, 1990.

[12] *Tang-Wudai wushi'er zhong biji xiaoshuo renming suoyin*, Fang Jiliu 方積六, comp., Zhonghua, 1992.

Fengshi wenjian ji 封氏聞見記 (Records of things heard and seen by Mr. Feng), Feng Yan 封演, completed in 800; Shangwu, 1933; punctuated ed., Zhonghua, 1985. *H-Y Index, Supplement 7.* Contains observations made during the second half of the eighth century on military institutions, court life, customs and local sights and the lives of the famous.

Tang zhiyan 唐摭言 (Picked-up words of Tang), Wang Dingbao 王定保 (870–941), Shanghai guji, 1978. Contains mainly anecdotes about the examination system and Tang literati. For some translated excerpts, see *Chinese Civilization: A Sourcebook*, Patricia Ebrey, ed., 1981; 2nd ed., rev. and expanded, Free Press, 1993, 128–31.

Beilizhi 北里志 (Anecdotes of the northern quarter), Sun Qi 孫棨, French translation by Robert des Rotours, *Courtisanes chinoises à la fin des T'ang*, Paris, 1968. The northern quarter was where the prostitutes gathered.

Beimeng suoyan 北夢瑣言 (Chit-chat of the northern dreamer [i.e., written at Jiangling 江陵]), Sun Guangxian 孫光憲 (ca. 900–968), punctuated ed., Shanghai guji, 1981. Notes on politics, institutions and customs at the Tang/Five Dynasties divide.

Youyang zazu 酉陽雜俎 (Miscellany of Youyang mountains), Duan Chengshi 段成式 (ca. 803–863), punctuated ed., Zhonghua, 2nd prnt., 1981. Wide-ranging *biji xiaoshuo*.

Taiping guangji 太平廣記 (Wide gleanings from the Taiping era), Li Fang 李昉 (925–96), Zhonghua, 1961; 6th prnt., 1996. Collection of fictional *biji* containing 475 *biji xiaoshuo* from Han to the Five Dynasties (34.1). Title index: *H-Y Index* 15; Zhonghua published an index in 1982; 10th prnt., 1996.

Shuofu 說郛 (48.5.2, Yuan *biji*).

46.3 Dunhuang and Turpan Documents

Toward the end of the nineteenth century, an ex-soldier from the Gansu border army, Wang Yuanlu 王元籙 (d. 1931), found refuge in one of the Mogao 莫高 temple caves at Dunhuang. There he practiced as a Daoist priest in order to make a living. He took an assistant named Yang, who one day early in 1900 discovered by accident a secret chamber, which turned out to be stacked with bundles of ancient manuscripts. Later research shows that the cave had most likely been sealed off in 1035, the year that the Xi-Xia occupied Dunhuang.

A few years before the discovery, Mark Aurel Stein (1862–1943), the Hungarian-born British archaeologist and explorer, had heard about the Caves of the Thousand Buddhas at Dunhuang (but not about the manuscripts) from his teacher, the head of the Hungarian geological survey who had been there in 1879. Stein finally visited during his second expedition to Central Asia in 1907 and then learned of Wang's discovery of "several cartloads" of ancient manuscripts. He persuaded Wang to let him see it: "The sight disclosed in the dim light of the priest's oil lamp," he later wrote, "made my eyes wide open. Heaped up in layers, but without any order, there appeared a solid mass of manuscript bundles rising to ten feet from the floor and filling, as subsequent measurement showed, close on five hundred cubic feet."[13]

The collection consisted mainly of Chinese manuscripts of the Confucian Classics and the literature of Buddhism, Daoism, Jingism and Monism as well as local records, account books, musical scores, astronomy, calendars, arithmetic, medical works and popular literature—stories, poems, biographies and travelogues. The main category was Buddhist sutras. There were also documents in Sanskrit, Sogdian, Tangut, Tubo (Tibetan), Turkic and Uighur. Stein paid Wang 300 *taels* (just over 200 1910 US$) for 10,000 manuscripts, which he sent back to the British Museum packed into 24 wooden crates. "The Chinese regard Stein and Pelliot as robbers," wrote the British sinologist Arthur Waley, whose opinion on the "sacking of the Dunhuang library," as he called it, is worth quoting at length since he had no particular ax to grind and he knew both men well and discussed the matter with them:

> I think the best way to understand [the feelings of the Chinese] on the subject is to imagine how we should feel if a Chinese archaeologist were to come to England, discover a cache of medieval manu-

<hr/>

[13] Aurel Stein, *On Ancient Central Asian Tracks*, 1941; rpnt., Pantheon, 1964, p. 179.

scripts at a ruined monastery, bribe the custodian to part with them and carry them off to Peking ... We have to remember that in the nineteenth century archaeology combined with a mild kind of espionage (consisting in little more than map-making) had been carried on extensively in Moslem countries where conversion to Islam had long ago completely divorced the inhabitants from their remote past ... Stein was of course aware that the Chinese were more interested in their own remote past than were, for example, the Bedouins. But I was never able to convince him that the Chinese scholars who in the eighteenth and nineteenth centuries wrote about the geography and antiquities of Central Asia were anything more than what he called 'arm-chair archaeologists'; though they had in fact, as Generals and administrators, spent far more time in Central Asia and traveled far more widely than Stein himself. Pelliot did, of course, after his return from Tun-huang, get in touch with Chinese scholars; but he had inherited so much of the nineteenth-century attitude about the right of Europeans to carry off 'finds' made in non-European lands that, like Stein, he seems never from the first to last to have had any qualms about the sacking of the Tun-huang library.[14]

The French sinologist referred to by Waley, Paul Pelliot (1878–1945), arrived in 1908 and spent three feverish weeks selecting the cream of what was left in the temple library. He paid 500 *taels* (about 340 US$ of that time) for just over 6,000 hand-picked manuscripts. Others quickly followed: assistants of Ôtani Kôzui (1876–1948) from Japan; Albert von Le Coq (1860–1930) from Germany; and Sergei Oldenburg (1863–1934) and Captain Petr Kuz'mich Kozlov (1863–1935) from Russia.[15] Altogether, about 25,000 manuscripts were collected from Dunhuang and neighboring sites and exported; the remainder were taken to Beijing or found their way into the hands of pri-

---

[14] Arthur Waley, *Ballads and Stories from Tun-huang*, Allen and Unwin, 1960, 237–38. For a biography, see Jeanette Mirsky, *Sir Aurel Stein: Archaeologist, Explorer*, UChP, 1977. For the views of the keeper of Chinese books at the British Museum, see Lionel Giles, *Six Centuries of Tun-huang*, British Museum, 1944.

[15] Peter Hopkirk, *Foreign Devils on the Silk Road*, John Murray, 1980; OUP, 1984; "The German Expeditions, 1902–1914," in *Along the Ancient Silk Routes: Central Asian Art from the West Berlin State Museum*, John P. O'Neill, ed. in chief, Metropolitan Museum of Art, 1982, 25–55.

vate collectors. The total number of Dunhuang manuscripts all over the world today comes to about 42,000 (including parts of documents). In addition, about 2,000 Tangut manuscripts were found in the ruined city of Kharakhoto (Halahetuo 哈拉何托) by Kozlov who took them back to St Petersburg.

The majority of the manuscripts are on paper. The earliest dates from 359, the latest from 1196. They form one of the largest collections of manuscripts on paper ever found in China. Their study has given rise to a new specialized field known as Dunhuang studies (*Dunhuangxue* 敦煌學).[16] In addition to the written documents, many thousands of Buddhist paintings are preserved on the walls of the Dunhuang and neighboring temples. Dunhuang has also been one of the main sites for the discovery of Han border documents (44.2.2.3).

Apart from the value of the Buddhist and Daoist texts, the Dunhuang manuscripts also include a considerable amount of popular literature. Because of the *baihua* 白話 movement in the decades after their discovery, it was the literary interest of the manuscripts that was emphasized. However, the sutras were often written on the back of all sorts of local documents, including fragments of ordinances, reports, purchase orders, contracts and other materials, which have led to some of the most de-

---

[16] As a general introduction to *Dunhuangxue* 敦煌學, see Denis Twitchett, "Chinese Social History; The Tun-huang Documents and their Implications," *Past and Present* 35: 28–53 (1966); Lin Jiaping 林家平 et al., *Zhongguo Dunhuang xueshi* 中國敦煌學史 (A history of Chinese Dunhuang studies), Beijing yuyan xueyuan, 1992.

For a bibliography of studies on Dunhuang documents, see *Tôrufan, Tonkô shutsudo Kanbun bunsho kenkyû bunken mokuroku* 吐魯番, 敦煌出土漢文文書研究文獻目錄 (Bibliography of Studies on Turpan and Tunhuang Chinese-language Documents), Tôyô bunko, 1990. This does not include scholarship on documents on bamboo strips or tomb inscriptions; see also, Kuang Shiyuan 鄺士元, *Dunhuangxue yanjiu lunzhu mulu* 敦煌學研究論著目錄 (A Review of Tun-huang Studies in the Past Century), Xinwenfeng, 1987, which contains citations to 6,084 works in Chinese, Japanese and Western languages arranged by topic. There is an author index and date of publication index (through 1984).

tailed researches into Chinese social and economic history of any period.

From 15,000 to 20,000 manuscripts on paper were also discovered at the end of the nineteenth and the beginning of the twentieth century near the modern city of Turpan (Tulufan 吐魯番) in Xinjiang, about 360 km to the northwest of Dunhuang. The documents date from the Jin to the Yuan. Between 1959 and 1975 another 2,000 documents were excavated mainly from tombs nearby, including several copies of the *Lunyu*, the *Qianziwen* 千字文, calendars and much else besides. They date from the fourth to eighth centuries.[17]

For many years the Dunhuang (and Turpan) manuscripts were almost inaccessible since they were scattered all over the world and the publishing of scholarly catalogs and transcriptions for the most part proceeded slowly. It was in the late 1950s that Ikeda, Dohi and other scholars at the Tôyô bunko in Tokyo, using microfilms, published a detailed catalog of non-Buddhist documents held in the British Museum. The second volume covered documents relating to the institutional and economic aspects of Buddhism.[18] Its two main subject categories

---

[17] Turpan is a transcription of the original Uighur name meaning "Low-lying ground." It is one of the lowest, hottest, driest places on earth. For centuries it was a key center on the silk road linking China to Persia. The more recently discovered manuscripts were found in several hundred tombs at Astana (Asitana 阿斯塔那) and in the ruins of the capital of the kingdom of Qoco (Gaochang 高昌, 460–640) and its successor cities, 40 km to the east of Turpan. On the question of dating the documents, see Wang Su 王素, *Tulufan chutu Gaochang wenxian biannian* 吐魯番出土高昌文獻編年 (Chronology of the documents excavated at Qoco, Turpan), Xinwenfeng, 1997.

[18] *Sutain Tonkô bunken oyobi kenkyû bunken ni in'yô shôkai seraretaru Saiiki shutsudo Kanbun bunken bunrui mokuroku shokô: Hi-Bukkyô no bu, komonjorui* スタイン敦煌文獻及び研究文獻に引用紹介せられたる西域出土漢文文獻分類目錄初稿非佛教之部古文書類 (Draft Classified Catalog of Dunhuang Manuscripts Collected by Sir Aurel Stein and of Chinese Manuscripts from Chinese Turkestan Described in Research: Section on Non-Buddhist Material, Ancient Documents); vol. 1 compiled by Ikeda On 池田温 and Kikuchi Hideo 菊池英夫, and vol. 2 by Dohi

Footnote continued on next page

are the administration of Buddhist monasteries and their economic organization. The classic study which used many of this type of document (in the Pelliot collection in Paris) was Jacques Gernet, *Buddhism in Chinese Society: An Economic History from the Fifth to the Tenth Centuries*.[19] At the same time as the work in Tokyo, scholars in Kyoto also produced some of the first studies of social and economic history.[20]

Today, the entire corpus of the Dunhuang manuscripts from collections all over the world has been published (46.3.2) and many transcriptions and studies of selected manuscripts on Buddhist, Daoist, literary and social and economic topics have appeared.

46.3.1   Catalogs of Dunhuang and Turpan Manuscripts

Bai Huawen 白化文, *Dunhuang wenwu mulu daolun* 敦煌文物目錄導論 (Guide to the Dunhuang catalogs), Taibei, 1991 (previously published by Hebei renmin in 1989). Good starting point through the mass of published catalogs of different parts of the Dunhuang documents.

Dunhuang yishu zuixin mulu 敦煌藝術最新目錄 (Latest catalog of manuscripts from Dunhuang), Huang Yongwu 黃永武, ed. in chief, Xin Wenfeng, 1986. The most comprehensive catalog to date. Index of titles to the manuscripts in the old Beiping, Stein, Pelliot, Leningrad and Ōtani collections, as well as 800 manuscripts in miscellaneous collections. It replaces the earlier *Dunhuang yishu zongmu suoyin* 敦煌

Yoshikazu 土肥義和, Tôyô bunko, 1964. The same series on the Stein manuscripts covered Daoism in vol. 3 and literature in vol. 4. In vol. 1, Dunhuang manuscripts are classified into categories of documents (Edicts; the Code; letters of appointment; certificates; passes; memorials relating to Dunhuang; and documents relating to administration). Stein also found 380 wooden tablets with Tibetan writing on them. They dated from the eighth and ninth centuries and were mainly from Lopnor.

[19] *Les Aspects économiques du Bouddhisme*, Saigon: EFEO, 1956, tr., Franciscus Verellen, Col. UP, 1995.

[20] *Tonkô Tôrufan shakai keizai shiryô* 敦煌吐魯番社會經濟史料 (Researches on Fragmentary Manuscripts on Chinese Socioeconomic History form Dunhuang and Turpan), *Saiiki bunka kenkyû* 西域文化研究 (*Monumenta Serindica*), vols., 2 and 3, Jimbun, 1959, 1960. Includes a bibliography and summary in English.

遺書總目索引 (Index to general catalog of manuscripts from Dunhuang), Shangwu, 1962; Tokyo, 1963; corrected edition, Zhonghua, 1981; 1983.

The main catalogs of individual collections are:

Peking Library: *Dunhuang jieyu lu* 敦煌劫餘錄 (An Analytical List of the Dunhuang manuscripts in the National Library of Beijing), Chen Yuan 陳垣, comp. Beijing, 1931. Contains bibliographic notes on each manuscript included (condition of text, colophons, dates, seals, etc.).

British Museum, London: *Descriptive Catalogue of the Chinese Manuscripts from Tunhuang in the British Museum*, Lionel Giles, comp., British Museum, 1957. Sections list Buddhist, Daoist and Manichean texts, as well as secular texts and printed documents in the Stein collection at the Museum.

British Museum: Turpan docs.: *Les documents chinois de la troisième expédition de Sir Aurel Stein en Asie centrale*, British Museum, 1953, Henri Maspero, tr. with annotations of 930 manuscripts (219 on wood and 711 on paper) found by Stein in Turpan in 1913–6.

Bibliothèque Nationale, Paris: Annotated catalog: *Catalogue des Manuscrits Chinois de Touen-Houang*, vol. 1 covering manuscripts nos. 2,001–2,500 (1970); vol. 3, 3,001–3,500 (1983); vol. 4, nos. 3,501–4,000 (1991); vol. 5, 4,001–6,040 (1995). The publication of vol. 2, which is to cover nos. 2,501–3,000, has been delayed for administrative reasons.

Institute of Oriental Studies of the Russian Academy of Sciences, St. Petersburg Branch (formerly the Institute of the Peoples of Asia under the Academy of Social Sciences, Leningrad branch): *Kitajskie rukopisi iz Dun'khuana* (Chinese Manuscripts from Dunhuang), L. N. Menshikov, 3 vols., 1963–83. Catalog of the documents originally collected by Oldenburg in the early twentieth century.

Ômiya Library, Ryûkoku University 龍谷大學大宮圖書館: *Ôtani monjo shûsei* 大谷文書集成 (The Ôtani Collection), Oda Yoshihisa 小田義久, comp., 2 vols., Hôzôkan, 1984, 1990. Includes documents from both Dunhuang and Turpan.

46.3.2 *Photographs of Dunhuang and Turpan Manuscripts*

For excellent photographs of the original Dunhuang manuscripts, see:

Beijing daxue cang Dunhuang wenxian 北京大學藏敦煌文獻 (Dunhuang documents held at Peking University), 2 vols., Shanghai guji, 1995.

E cang Dunhuang wenxian 俄藏敦煌文獻 (Dunhuang documents held in Russia [at the Institute of Oriental Studies of the Russian Academy of Sciences, St. Petersburg Branch]), 9 vols., Shanghai guji, 1995–99; vols. 10–15, forthcoming, 2000. Note also *E cang Dunhuang yishupin* 俄藏敦煌藝術品 (Dunhuang art objects held in Russia), 6 vols., Shanghai guji, 1997–99.

Facang Dunhuang Xiyu wenxian 法藏敦煌西域文獻 (Dunhuang and Western Region documents held in France), 8 vols., Shanghai guji, 1995–98.

Shanghai bowuguan cang Dunhuang Tulufan wenxian 上海博物館藏敦煌吐魯番文獻 (Dunhuang and Turpan documents held at the Shanghai Museum), 2 vols., Shanghai guji, 1995.

Shanghai tushuguan cang Dunhuang Tulufan wenxian 上海圖書館藏敦煌吐魯番文獻 (Dunhuang and Turpan documents held at the Shanghai Library), 2 vols., Shanghai guji, 1999.

Tianjinshi yishu bowuguan cang Dunhuang Tulufan wenxian 天津市藝術博物館藏敦煌吐魯番文獻 (Dunhuang and Turpan documents held at the Tianjin Art Museum), 7 vols., Shanghai guji, 1997–99.

Yingcang Dunhuang wenxian 英藏敦煌文獻 (Dunhuang Manuscripts in British Collections), 14 vols., Sichuan renmin and British Library, 1990–95. Non-Buddhist manuscripts rephotographed.

Dunhuang baozang 敦煌寶藏 (Treasures from Dunhuang), 140 vols., Xinwenfeng, 1981–6. Based on microfilm holdings from collections all over the world (except St. Petersburg). Not always legible, but is a major convenience until other series (e.g., that of Shanghai guji) are complete.

46.3.3 Social, Economic and Legal Dunhuang and Turpan Documents

Some of the most important collections of social, economic and legal documents and listed below:

Legal texts from Dunhuang and Turpan are typeset, punctuated and collated in *Zhongguo zhenxi falü dianji jicheng* 中國珍稀法律典籍集成 (Collection of rare works of Chinese law), 1st series, vols. 3 and 4 (see 27.3).

Chûgoku kodai shahon shikigo shûroku 中國古代寫本識語集錄 (Collected colophons of ancient Chinese manuscripts); Ikeda On, ed., Tôbunken, 1990. Includes 2,623 entries, of which 1,703 date from the Tang and are mainly Buddhist texts. See *Chinese Civilization: A Sourcebook*, Patricia Ebrey, ed., 1981; 2nd ed., rev. and expanded, Free Press, 1993, 102–4 for translations of five of them.

Dunhuang Tulufan wenshu chutan 敦煌吐魯番文書初探 (Preliminary investigations of Turpan documents), Tang Changru, ed. in chief, Wuhan daxue, 2 vols., 1983; 1990.

Dunhuang Tulufan wenxian yanjiu lunji 敦煌吐魯番文獻研究論集 (Collected research articles on Dunhuang and Turpan documents), Beijing daxue Zhongguo zhonggu yanjiu zhongxin, ed., Zhonghua, 1982; other research articles were published by the same center at Peking University under the same title in 1983, 1986, 1987 and 1990.

Dunhuang Tulufan chutu jingji wenshu yanjiu 敦煌吐魯番出土經濟文書研究 (Collected research articles on Dunhuang and Turpan economic documents), Han Guopan 韓國磐, ed., Xiamen daxue, 1986.

Liu Junwen 劉俊文, *Dunhuang Tulufan Tangdai fazhi wenshu kaoshi* 敦煌吐魯番唐代法制文書考釋 (Research on Tang dynasty Dunhuang and Turpan legal documents), Zhonghua, 1989.

Dunhuang shehui jingji wenxian zhenji Shilu 敦煌社會經濟文獻真蹟釋錄 (Photos and transcriptions of socioeconomic documents from Dunhuang), Shumu wenxian, 5 vols., 1986–90.

Dunhuang ziliao 敦煌資料 (Dunhuang Materials), 1st collection, Zhonghua, 1961; rpnt., Daian, 1963. Reproduces documents such as household, name and land registers and contracts. Transcriptions unreliable. Now largely superseded by the selections listed above.

Zhongguo gudai jizhang yanjiu 中國古代籍帳研究, Gong Zexian 龔澤銑, tr., (from the Japanese original of Ikeda On 池田温, 1977), Zhonghua, 1984.

46.3.4 Turpan Documents Only

Tulufan chutu wenshu 吐魯番出土文書 (Documents excavated at Turpan), Zhongguo wenwu yanjiusuo 中國文物研究所, eds., vol. 1 (*yi* 壹), 1992; vol. 2 (*er* 貳), 1994; vol. 3 (*san* 叄), 1996; vol. 4 (*si* 肆), Wenwu, 1997. Facsimiles (upper half of the page) plus transcriptions (lower half of the page). These contain transcriptions of about 1,600 documents including not only edicts and memorials but also private contracts and letters.

Tulufan chutu wenshu renming diming suoyin 吐魯番出土文書人名地名
索引 (Personal and place-name index to *Tulufan chutu wenshu* [1981–91]), Li Fang 李昉 and Wang Su 王素 comps., Wenwu, 1997.

Xinchu Tulufan chutu wenshu ji qi yanjiu 新出吐魯番出土文書及其研究
(Newly exavated documents from Tulufan andresearch on them), Liu Hongliang 劉洪亮, ed., Xinjiang, 1998. Documents discovered after 1975.

Berlin: the Le Coq Turpan manuscripts are being published in the series
Berliner Turfantexte, Akadamie-Verlag (many had been destroyed during WW II; about 6,000 Chinese documents survive and 8,000 Huihu ones).

46.3.5   Guides to the Dunhuang and Turpan Documents

The best overall introductions to the documents is the series *Tun-huang and Turpan Documents Concerning Social and Economic History*, edited by the Committee of Tunhuang Studies at the Tôyô bunko, 1978–87. Each consists of two volumes, (A) substantial introductions and notes (in English) on selected texts (transcriptions given) with bibliographies and (B) plates:

Legal Texts, Co-edited by Tatsuro Yamamoto, On Ikeda and Makoto Okano, 1978–80. Twenty-five legal texts.

Census Registers, Co-edited by Tatsuro Yamamoto and Yoshikazu Dohi, 1984–85. One hundred and five examples of census registers.

Contracts, Co-edited by Tatsuro Yamamoto and On Ikeda, 1986–7. Includes texts of 511 examples of all kinds of contracts including documents of sale and purchase, loans, leases, employment, adoption of sons, wills, divorce and so on.

Social and Related Documents, Co-edited by Tatsuro Yamamoto and Yoshikazu Dohi and Yusuku Ishida (forthcoming).

Other general introductions to the documents are also available; for example:

Wang Yongxing 王永興, *Dunhuang jingji wenshu daolun* 敦煌經濟文書
導論 (Introduction to Dunhuang economic documents), Xinwenfeng, 1994. Leaves out private documents (notably those of Buddhist temples).

Jiang Boqin 姜伯勤, *Dunhuang shehui wenshu daolun* 敦煌社會文書導論 (Introduction to Dunhuang social documents), Xinwenfeng, 1992.

Gao Guofan 高國藩, *Dunhuang minsu ziliao daolun* 敦煌民俗資料導論 (Introduction to Dunhuang materials on popular customs), Xinwenfeng, 1993.

The nine-volume series *Kôza Tonkô* 講座敦煌 contains detailed introductions to every aspect of Dunhuang by leading Japanese and Chinese scholars, including the geographical setting (vol. 1), history (vol. 2), society (vol. 3), Daoism (vol. 4), Chinese language documents (vol. 5), popular literature (vol. 6), Buddhism (vol. 7), Zen (vol. 8) and literature (vol. 9).[21] Volume 5, under the editorial responsibility of Ikeda On, is particularly valuable as a starting point to all the many categories of Chinese-language documents found in the Dunhuang library.[22]

Language

Dunhuang wenxian yuyan cidian 敦煌文獻語言詞典 (Dictionary of the language of Dunhuang documents), Jiang Lihong 蔣禮鴻, comp., Hangzhou daxue, 1994. Dictionary of the language found in Dunhuang and Turpan manuscripts.

Society and Journals

Dunhuang Tulufan xuehui 敦煌吐魯番學會 publishes proceedings every two years or so (1983–).

There are several specialist journals:

Dunhuang Tulufan yanjiu 敦煌吐魯番研究 (1995– , annual), Beida.

Dunhuangxue jikan 敦煌學輯刊 (1989– , irreg.), Lanzhou daxue lishixi.

Dunhuang yanjiu 敦煌研究 (1981– , biannual), Dunhuang yanjiuyuan (Dunhuang academy), Dunhuang.

---

[21] *Kôza Tonkô*, Daitô, 1980–92.
[22] Ikeda On, *Tonkô Kanbun bunken* 敦煌漢文文獻, *Kôza Tonkô*, 5, Daitô, 1992.

46.4 Archaeology and Inscriptions

46.4.1 Archaeology

On the Sui canals linking north and south China, see 36.3.

Xi'an (the Tang capital Chang'an) has outstanding Tang monuments—for example, the Greater Wild Goose Pagoda (Dayanta 大雁塔), which was originally built in 648. In 652, the just returned Xuanzang 玄奘 (596–664) (41.5.1) stored here the Buddhist scriptures he had brought back from India.

The city also has rich collections of Tang artifacts. These are mainly at the Shaanxi History Museum (Shaanxi lishi bowuguan 陝西歷史博物館). Treasures include detailed murals from the tombs of relatives of the Tang emperors and more than 2,000 tomb figurines. In addition there is the Xi'an-shi Tangdai yishu bowuguan 西安市唐代藝術博物館 (Museum of the art of the Tang Dynasty) as well as the Xi'an beilin bowuguan 西安碑林博物館 (Museum of the forest of stelae) housed in the old Confucian Temple. It contains the largest collection of early stone inscriptions in China including the *Kaicheng shijing* 開成石經 of 837 (17.4). Elsewhere, you can even bathe near the pool where Yang Guifei 楊貴妃 (719–56) took the waters in a stone pool fed by hot springs in the Huaqing palace 華清宮 (excavation report: *Wenwu* 1990.5; 1991.9 and 1995.11; *CAAD* 2.1, 1997, 23–25).

Parts of Tang Chang'an and Luoyang (alternative capital) have been excavated. So, too, has Yangzhou, an important Tang city (*Kaogu* 1990.1).

The tomb of the founding emperor of the Sui, Wendi 文帝, may be seen in the southeastern part of Fufeng county 扶風縣. The tombs of 18 of the Tang emperors lie scattered around Xi'an.

The Dunhuang murals and the carvings at the Longmen grottoes were mainly completed in the Sui and Tang.

Sui-Tang kaogu 隋唐考古 (Archaeology of the Sui and Tang), Qin Hao 秦浩, ed., Nanjing daxue, 1992; rpnt., 1996.

A Journey into China's Antiquity, vol. 3: *Sui-Tang-Song*, National Museum of Chinese History, eds., Morning Glory, 1998. See 8.2.1 on this authoritatively commented series of photographs of the collections of the museum.

Helga Stahl, *Gräber in Sichuan von der Tang bis zur Song-Zeit: Möglichkeiten einer Regionalgeschichte anhand von archäologischen Funden*, Forum, 1995.

46.4.2   *Stone Inscriptions*

The Tang is particularly rich in tomb inscriptions and more are being found all the time. They can be used to check or supplement the written record.[24]

For a comprehensive index of existing indexes, see *Tôdai boshi shozai sômokuroku* 唐代墓誌所在總目錄.[25] Arrangement is by date. There is no name index although the editor plans one. Altogether 5,826 tablets from 10 published collections are indexed, including the *Shike tiba suoyin* 石刻題跋索引 and *Beijing tushuguan cang Zhongguo lidai shike taben huibian* 北京圖書館藏中國歷代石刻拓本匯編 (17.3, *Guides and Research tools*). The other works indexed are:

Tangdai muzhi ming huibian fukao 唐代墓誌銘匯編附考, Mao Hanguang 毛漢光, ed., 18 vols., Shiyusuo, 1984–94 (3.7).

Qian-Tangzhi zhai 千唐誌齋, in Xin'an county 新安縣 near Luoyang, is the only museum dedicated to ancient tomb inscriptions, of which it has 1,413, the greater number of which (1,209) date from the Tang. The rubbings were published in *Qian-Tangzhi zhai cangzhi* 千唐誌齋藏誌, 2 vols., Wenwu, 1984; rpnt., 1991. There is also an index of the names of those recorded on the stelae, *Qian-Tangzhi zhai shizhizhu xingshi suoyin* 千唐誌齋石誌主姓氏索引 (An index to the names of those commemorated on the tomb tablets of the Tang thousand tomb inscriptions library).

[24] Han Lizhou 韓理洲, "Xin chutu mubei muzhi zai Tangdai wenshi yanjiu fangmian de xueshu jiazhi 新出土墓碑墓誌在唐代文史研究方面的學術價值," (The academic value of newly excavated Tang tomb inscriptions and tablets for the study of history and literature), *Xibei daxue xuebao* 3: 43–46 (1996).

[25] *Tôdai boshi shozai sômokuroku* (Comprehensive index to the whereabouts of Tang tomb tablets), Kigasawa Yasunari 氣賀澤保規, ed., Kyûko, 1997.

Inscriptions tombales des dynasties T'ang et Song (d'après le fonds d'inscription possédées par L'Ecole française d'Extrême Orient), Jao Tsung-I (Rao Zongyi 饒宗頤), ed., EFEO and HKCU Press, 1982. Annotated catalog of 388 tomb inscriptions, of which 370 are Tang, 5 Wudai and 13 Song (up to 1125). Includes the texts of the inscriptions plus photographs of the rubbings. Arranged chronologically. Has name index and chronological index (arranged by reign name).

Sui, Tang, Wudai muzhi huibian 隋唐五代墓誌匯編, 9 parts in 30 vols., Tianjin guji, 1991-2.

Luoyang chutu lidai muzhi jisheng 洛陽出土歷代墓誌輯繩 (3.7).

Tangdai muzhi huibian 唐代墓誌匯編, Zhou Shaoliang 周紹良, ed. in chief, 2 vols., Shanghai guji, 1992. Chronological arrangement with a four-corner finding index at the end of vol. 2. Contains rubbings of 5,000 tomb tablets.

Xin Zhongguo chutu muzhi 新中國出土墓誌 (3.7).

46.5 Guides and Research Tools

46.5.1   Guides to Sources and Readers

The Tang, as one of the high points of the Chinese empire, has always attracted special attention, not only in China, but also in Japan and Korea, which modeled much of their higher culture, laws and institutions on the Tang.

Denis Twitchett and Howard L. Goodman, *A Handbook for T'ang History*, 2 vols., Princeton Univ., Princeton Linguistic Studies, 1986. Contains a section on "Important T'ang Sources and T'ang Research Tools," 21-63. There are also annotated readings and notes on research topics, some general, but most linked to Tang history. Intended for beginning graduate students in Chinese studies.

Denis C. Twitchett, *The Writing of Official History under the T'ang*, CUP, 1992. Concentrates on the compilation of the *Jiu Tangshu*, but also has important things to say on official history writing in general.

Wu Feng 吳楓, *Sui-Tang lishi wenxian jishi* 隋唐歷史文獻集釋 (Collected historical texts of the Sui and Tang with notes), Zhongzhou guji, 1987. Contains bibliographic annotations on 200 traditional written sources for the Sui and Tang arranged under 10 categories such as annalistic sources, miscellaneous notes and so forth. An appendix lists the titles of more than 1,100 works written in the Tang arranged by

Sibu classification. The list was drawn from the *Zhongguo congshu zonglu*.

Sui,Tang,Wudai jingji shiliao huibian jiaozhu 隋唐五代經濟史料匯編校注 (Collection of annotated, collated economic sources on the history of the Sui, Tang and *Wudai*), Part 1, 2 vols., Wang Yongxing 王永興, comp., Zhonghua, 1987. Excerpts from *wenji*, *shiji*, *biji*, inscriptions, Dunhuang and Turpan manuscripts. The excerpts are divided into seven subject categories, of which the first two (classes and class relations) are covered in these volumes.

Suimo nongmin zhanzheng shiliao huibian 隋末農民戰爭史料匯編 (28.3).

Tang-Wudai nongmin zhanzheng shiliao huibian 唐五代農民戰爭史料匯編 (28.3).

Zhongguo lishi da cidian 中國歷史大辭典 contains a separate volume on *Sui, Tang, Wudai shi* 隋唐五代史, 1995. See 8.3.2, item 2 for comments on this encyclopaedia.

Guides to the Dunhuang and Turpan documents are listed at the end of 46.3.

46.5.2 Research Tools

Different types of special-purpose reference works for Sui, Tang and *Wudai-Shiguo* history have already been introduced in the previous sections. Note also special-purpose reference works for all of Chinese history, which are also useful for these periods, for example, on weights and measures (7.3). Below are given a handful of indispensable references for the Sui, Tang and *Wudai-Shiguo* on language, biography, official titles, geography, chronology, secondary sources and societies and journals.

Language

Tang-Wudai yuyan cidian 唐五代語言詞典 (Dictionary of the Tang and Five Dynasties language), Shanghai jiaoyu, 1997, Jiang Lansheng 江藍生 and Cao Guangshun 曹廣順, eds. This is in the series *Jindai Hanyu duandai yuyan cidian xilie* 近代漢語詞典系列 (Single-period dictionaries covering early Mandarin). The dictionary contains about 5,000 entries covering the language of Dunhuang *bianwen* 變文, *Chanzong yulu* 禪宗語錄 and poetry as well as *biji* 筆記, historical biographies, documents and so forth of the Tang and Five Dynasties. It is intended primarily for those interested in the development of the language between the seventh and tenth centuries and for readers of popular literature of the period. Arrangement is by *pinyin* and there is also a *pinyin* index.

Biographies

Tang-Wudai renwu zhuanji ziliao zonghe suoyin 唐五代人物傳記資料綜合索引, Fu Xuancong 傅璇琮, Zhang Chenshi 張忱石 and Xu Yimin 許逸民 eds., Zhonghua and Tôhô, 1982; rpnt., 1987. Thorough index to biographical materials in 86 primary sources on some 30,000 figures. Names arranged by four-corner index.

Tôdai no denki sakuin 唐代の人傳記索引, Jimbun, 1951. Indexes 17 works containing biographical information on Tang figures, in four categories: poets, Buddhists, Daoists and painters. Entries are listed in four-corner sequence, with supplementary indexes for stroke count and Wade-Giles alphabetical order.

Zhonguo wenxuejia da cidian 中國文學家大辭典 (Dictionary of Chinese writers), *Tang-Wudai* 唐五代, Zhou Zuzhuan 周祖撰, ed., Zhonghua, 1992.

Tangren hangdi lu 唐人行第錄 (Tang records of names by order of birth), Cen Zhongmian 岑仲勉, comp., 1962; Shanghai guji, 1978. Collects the names of many Tang literati with alternative names and has a finding table by stroke count.

Official Titles and Officeholders

In addition to *DOTIC*, see also the translations of Robert des Rotours, notably *Traité des fonctionnaires et traité de l' armée* (46.1).

Godai Sôsho hanchin nenpyô 五代宋初藩鎮年表 (Chronology of military commands in the Five Dynasties and the early Song), Kurihara Masuo 栗原益男, comp., Tôkyôdô, 1988.

Geography

Zhongguo lishi dituji 中國歷史地圖集 (The Historical Atlas of China), Tan Qixiang 譚其驤, ed. in chief, vol. 5, *Sui, Tang, Wudai shiqi* 隋唐五代時期, 2nd rev. ed., 2nd prnt., Ditu, 1985.

Tôdai no Chôan to Rakuyô 唐代の長安と洛陽 (Tang Dynasty Luoyang and Chang'an), Hiraoka Takeo 平岡武夫, ed., *T'ang Civilization Reference Series*, 3 vols., Jimbun, 1956. Collects a very large amount of formal and informal writings on the two capitals during the Tang, plus maps and an index; Chinese tr., *Tangdai de Chang'an yu Luoyang* 唐代的長安與洛陽, Shanghai guji, 1989.

Yan Gengwang, 嚴耕望, *Tangdai jiaotong tukao* 唐代交通圖考 (Critical maps of communications in the Tang), 5 vols., Shiyusuo, 1985–6.

Edward H. Schafer, *The Vermilion Bird: T'ang Images of the South*, UCP, 1967; rpnt., 1985.

Chronology

Tangdai de li 唐代的曆 (The Tang calendar), Hiraoka Takeo 平岡武夫, comp., Shanghai guji, 1990. (Chinese translation of Japanese original: *Tôdai no koyomi*, Jimbun, 1954). Tabulates cyclical characters for every day from February 1, 618 to July 12, 907, fitting 10 months on each page. The right-hand column indicates the first and last days of the Western calendar month equivalents, as well as cyclical characters for the day of the solstices and equinoxes.

Edward H. Schafer, *Pacing the Void: T'ang Approaches to the Stars*, UCP, 1977.

Bibliographies of Secondary Scholarship

Sui, Tang, Wudai shi yanjiu gaiyao 隋唐五代史概要 (Guide to the history of the Sui, Tang and Five Dynasties), Zhang Guogang 張國剛, ed. in chief, Tianjin jiaoyu, 1996. After a thorough discussion of the main themes in the history of these centuries with copious citation of modern Chinese scholarship (1–658), the authors introduce archaeology; Dunhuang studies, both in China and abroad (695–762); and historical sources and research tools (763–810). There follows a 374-page, unannotated bibliography of 8,000 books and articles of secondary scholarship in China (including Taiwan and Hong Kong), Japan and the West.

Sui, Tang, Wudai shi lunzhu mulu 隋唐五代史論著目錄, Lishi yanjiusuo, eds., Jiangsu guji, 1985. Covers articles written between 1900–1981. A continuation goes up to the end of 1995: *Sui, Tang, Wudai shi lunzhu mulu* 隋唐五代史論著目錄 1982–85, Hang Gaoling 杭高靈 et al., Shanxi shifan daxue, 1997.

CHC, vol. 4, *Sui and T'ang China*, Part II, Denis Twitchett, ed., CUP, 1999.

"Viewpoints on T'ang China," *Acta Asiatica* 55 (1988). Special issue summarizing Japanese scholarship.

Godaishi kenkyû bunken mokuroku 五代史研究文獻目錄 (Catalog of research on the history of the Five Dynasties), Yoshida Tora 古田寅 and Toriya Hiroaki 鳥谷弘昭, eds., Ritsumeikan daigaku, 1990. Covers 5,200 research articles and books in Japanese and Chinese up to 1988. There is an author index.

Bibliography on Parhae (Bohai-Bokkai): A Medieval State in the Far East, Norbert R. Adami, comp., Harrassowitz, 1994. Bohai (渤海), in northeast China, was an independent kingdom from 698 to 926.[26]

Societies and Journals

Zhongguo Tang shi xuehui 中國唐史學會 (Chinese society for Tang history), founded in 1980.

Tôdaishi kenkyûkai 唐代史研究會 (Research society for Tang dynasty history, Tokyo) has a publications series.

Tang yanjiu 唐研究 (1996–), Beida.

T'ang Studies (1982–). Journal of the T'ang Studies Society (Editorial, Boulder, Colorado).

[26] See also Johannes Reckel, *Bohai: Geschichte und Kultur eines mandschurisch-koreanischen Königsreiches der Tang-Zeit,* Harrassowitz, 1995.

47

Song

960–1279

| Northern Song 北宋 | 960–1127 |
| Southern Song 南宋 | 1127–1278 |

Most pre-Song and Song works survive today only in Song imprints and late copies and revisions of them. Indeed, it was the widespread use of printing that helped to ensure that more works (both official and private) survive from the Song than from any previous period.[1]

Throughout the Song there were alien dynastic regimes ruling over all or part of China. The sources for these regimes (Liao, Xi-Xia, Jin and Yuan) are also important for the history of the Song, and vice-versa. For ease of presentation, the four are placed together with the Yuan in chapter 48.

47.1 Main Historical Works

Song huiyao jigao 宋會要輯稿 (Draft recovered edition of the *Song huiyao*). The *Song huiyao* was recovered from the *Yongle dadian* in the early-nineteenth century under the direc-

---

[1] Susan Cherniack, "Book Culture and Textual Transmission in Song China, *HJAS* 54.1: 5–125 (1994). On the Song archival system, see Wang Jinyu 王金玉, *Songdai dang'an guanli yanjiu* 宋代檔案管理研究 (Research on the administration of the Song archives), Zhongguo Dang'an, 1997.

tion of Xu Song 徐松 (1781–1848), who also began the difficult task of trying to put it in order. Various other attempts
were made to edit it until eventually his manuscript was
published in a facsimile edition in 1936 under the title *Song
huiyao jigao*.[2] The materials in the *Song huiyao* were taken
from the Daily Records, no longer extant and the Veritable
Records, also no longer extant, as well as the documents of
the Six Ministries and of the Circuit Intendants.[3] It was
compiled throughout the dynasty by the Important Documents Bureau (*Huiyao suo* 會要所). It contains the largest
collection of documents from the Song with much information not available in the monographs of the *Songshi*, let
alone in the *Wenxian tongkao*, especially on the economy.
As such it has been intensively studied and indexed.[4] It is arranged in chronological order within institutional categories
and includes documents from 960 to 1220. There is an index
to the table of contents which indicates subsections and the
years covered in each, as well as the sources on which each
subsection was based; it is usable with any of the editions of
the *Song huiyao*:

[2]*Song huiyao jigao*, photolithographic reproduction, 200 *ce*, Peiping
tushuguan, 1936; reduced-size, facsimile reproduction, 8 vols., Zhonghua,
1957; 1987; Xinwenfeng, 1976.
 [3] See Wang Yunhai 王雲海, *Song huiyao jigao kaojiao* 宋會要輯稿考
校 (Study and collation of the *Song huiyao*), Shanghai guji, 1986; Chen
Zhichao 陳智超, *Jiekai Song huiyao zhi mi* 解開宋會要之謎 (Solving the
riddle of the *Song huiyao*), Shehui kexue wenxian, 1995.
 [4] For lists of the dates of all the documents in the *Song huiyao* in
chronological order, see *Sô kaiyô hennen sakuin* 宋會要編年索引 (Chronology of the *Song huiyao*), Umehara Kaoru 梅原郁, comp., Jimbun, 1995.
 For a personal-name index to the *Song huiyao*, see *Song huiyao jigao
renming suoyin* 宋會要輯稿人名索引, Wang Deyi 王德毅, comp., Xinwenfeng, 1978. There are also three Japanese indexes to the "Shihuozhi"
in the *Song huiyao*: *Sô kaiyô shûkô shokka sakuin* 宋會要輯稿食貨索引 (1)
personal names and book titles: *jinmei shomei-hen* 人名書名編; (2) dates
and imperial edicts: *nengappi shôchoku-hen* 年月日詔勅編; (3) bureaucratic terms: *shokkan-hen* 職官編, Tôyô bunko Sôdaishi kenkyû iinkai,
eds., Tôyô bunko, 1982, 1985, 1995.

Sô kaiyô kenkyû biyô-mokuroku 宋會要研究備要目錄 (Essentials for the study of the *Songhuiyao* table of contents), Tôyô bunko Sôdai-shi kenkyû iinkai, Tôyô bunko, 1970.

Wenxian tongkao 文獻通考 is most detailed in the sections covering the Song. See also the *Tongzhi* 通志 (26.2).

Xu Zizhi tongjian changbian 續資治通鑑長編 (Long draft of the continuation of the *Zizhi tongjian*), Li Tao 李燾 (1114–83), 34 vols., Zhonghua punctuated and collated edition, 1979–95. Covers the years 960–1100 (i.e., the Northern Song) in great detail. The author spent 40 years working on it, using all available sources.[5] In part it had to be recovered from the *Yongle dadian* during the course of editing the *Siku quanshu*.

Jianyan yilai xinian yaolu 建炎以來繫年要錄 (Record of important events in chronological order since the Jianyan reign period), Li Xinchuan 李心傳 (1166–1243), comp., 4 vols., Shanghai guji, 1993. This edition contains also a personal-name index. Covers the 36-year reign of Song Gaozong 宋高宗 (first emperor of Southern Song, 1127–63). Recovered from the *Yongle dadian* during the course of editing the *Siku quanshu*.[6]

---

[5] The first volume of the Zhonghua edition contains an index and materials on Li Tao's life. There is a computerized concordance to the *Changbian*: *Changbian quanwenben jiansuo xitong* 長編全文本檢索系統 (Complete computer concordance to the Changbian), Hebei daxue Lishi yanjiusuo 河北大學歷史研究所 and Hanzi xinxi chuli yanjiusuo 漢字信息處理研究所, 1996. Also, Shiyusuo digital library, forthcoming. See also *Zoku Shiji tsugan chôhen jinmei sakuin* 續資治通鑑長編人名索引 (Personal-name index to the *Changbian*), Umehara Kaoru 梅原郁, comp., Dôhôsha, 1978, and the same scholar's *Zoku Shiji tsugan chôhen goi sakuin* 續資治通鑑長編語彙索引 (Vocabulary index to the *Changbian*), Dôhôsha, 1989.

[6] John W. Chaffee discusses Li's work in his "The Historian as Critic: Li Hsin-ch'uan and the Dilemmas of Statecraft in Southern Sung China," in *Ordering the World: Approaches to State and Society in Sung Dynasty China*, UCP, 1993, 310–35. Vol. 4 of the Shanghai guji edition (1992) of the *Siku* edition of *Jianyan yilai* contains an index of personal names (17–

Footnote continued on next page

Jianyan yilai chaoye zaji 建炎以來朝野雜記 (Miscellaneous records of court and country since the Jianyan reign period), 1ˢᵗ collection, 1202; 2ⁿᵈ collection, 1216. Also by Li Xin-chuan 李心傳. Covers the last years of the Song.

Sanchao beimeng huibian 三朝北盟會編 (Collection of documents on the treaties with the North during three reigns), Xu Mengxin 徐夢莘 (1126–1207), comp., 250 *juan*, 4 vols., Wenhai, 1966.[7] This is an important source for the Song's relations with Jin during the years 1101–60 (the 3 reigns of the title).

Songshi 宋史 (*Standard History of the Song*); editorship was credited to the chancellor Tuotuo (Toghto 脱脱, 1313–55), but the compiling was done by a group of officials from his office and from the Yuan Guoshi yuan 國史院 (Yuan Historiography Academy), 1343–45; 40 vols., Zhonghua, 1977; 3ʳᵈ prnt., 1995. Covers the years 960–1279.[8] It is one of the largest of the 24 Standard Histories (thanks to the number of *guoshi* 國史 and documents which survived the fall of the Song) and it is particularly notable for the high standard of the monographs. Not surprisingly, the editors ensured that the coverage of the Yuan wars against the Song is seen more from a Yuan than a Song point of view. Despite the fact that the Zhonghua edition contains a certain number of mistakes, of both punctuation and wrong characters, it remains the best and most convenient to use.

---

508) and authors and book titles (509–614). See also *Ken'en irai kien yôroku jinmei sakuin* 建炎以來繫年要錄人名索引, Umehara Kaoru 梅原郁, comp., Dôhôsha, 1983.

[7] Name index to first 100 *juan*: "Sanchô hokumei kaihen jinmei sakuin 三朝北盟會編人名索引," Aso Mikio 安蘇幹夫, comp., *Hiroshima daigaku keizai ronsô* 廣島大學經濟論叢 1.4: 55–83 (1979) for *juan* 1–40; 2.1, 2, 3: 55–88 (1979.12) for *juan* 41–100.

[8] Chan Hok-lam (Chen Xuelin 陳學霖), "Chinese Official History at the Yuan Court: The Composition of the Liao, Chin and Sung Histories," in *China Under Mongol Rule*, John D. Langlois, ed., PUP, 1981, 56–106.

Note the punctuated, indexed and annotated editions to the monographs in all the Standard Histories (including the *Songshi*) given in 22.4. Below are listed a few of the translations and indexes for the monographs in the *Songshi* only:

Songshi shihuozhi buzheng 宋史食貨志補正 (Corrections and additions to the "Shihuozhi" of the *Songshi*), Liang Taiji 梁太濟 and Bao Weimin 包偉民, Hangzhou daxue, 1994. The authors have used many sources to supplement the *Songshi* text, principally material from the *Song huiyao jigao* 宋會要輯稿.

Sôshi shokkashi yakuchû 宋史食貨志譯註 (Translation with notes of three of the fourteen chapters of the "Shihuozhi" of the *Songshi*: *Songshi, juan* 173,174, 175), Wada Sei 和田清, ed., vol. 1, Tôyô bunko, 1960. This massive volume enlisted the aid of many experts on the Song economy; their work is in the tradition established by the leading Japanese economic historian of the Tokyo school of his generation, Katô Shigeshi 加藤繁 (1880–1946)—to produce integral translations of all the *Shihuozhi*. In the event only the revised translations of the monographs in the *Shiji* and in the *Qian Hanshu* and of those in the Standard Histories of the Tang and the Five Dynasties appeared in Katô's lifetime. The collective annotated translations edited by Wada of the "Shihuozhi" in the *Songshi* and in the *Mingshi* (49.2) are on a much grander scale. The detailed notes succeed in establishing the source for practically every statement in these monographs, which were themselves the longest and best compiled of the *Shihuozhi*. There are full indexes.[9]

Sôshi shokkanshi sakuin 宋史職官志索引 (Index to the monograph on official posts in the *Songshi*), Saeki Tomi 佐伯富, Tôyôshi kenkyûkai, 1963; for more on this index, see below under *Officeholders and Official Titles*.

Sôshi senkyoshi sakuin 宋史選舉志索引 (Index to the monograph on recruitment in the *Songshi*), Saeki Tomi 佐伯富, Dôhôsha, 1982.

[9] Sudô Yoshiyuki 周藤吉之, "The Relationships between the "Shihuozhi 食貨志" in the *Songchao guoshi* 宋朝國史 and the *Songshi* 宋史," *MTB* 19: 63–110 (1961); Deng Guangming 鄧廣銘, "*Songshi* 'Xingfazhi' kaozheng 宋史刑法志考正," (Critical study of the monograph on penal law in the *Songshi*), *SYSJK* 20.II: 123–73 (1949) and the same author's "*Songshi* 'Zhiguanzhi' kaozheng 宋史職官志考正," (Critical study of the monograph on official posts in the *Songshi*), *SYSJK* 10 (1948).

Songshi xingfazhi suoyin 宋史刑法志索引 (Index to the monograph on penal law in the *Songshi*), Saeki Tomi 佐伯富, Xuesheng, 1977.

Songshi bingzhi suoyin 宋史兵志索引 (Index to the monograph on the military system in the *Songshi*), Saeki Tomi 佐伯富, Huashi, 1978.

Sôshi karyôshi sakuin 宋史河渠志索引 (Index to the monograph on rivers and canals in the *Songshi*), Saeki Tomi 佐伯富, Seishin, 1979.

Songshi yiwenzhi, bu, fu pian, 宋史藝文志補附篇 (The *Songshi* "Yi-wenzhi," its supplement and related texts), Shangwu, 1957. Has author/title index.

Songshi yiwenzhi shibu yiji kao, 宋史藝文志史部佚籍考 (Study of lost works in the History branch of the *Songshi* "Yiwenzhi"), Liu Zhaoyou 劉兆祐, ed., 3 vols., Taibei: Guoli bianyiguan bianshen weiyuanhui 國立編譯館編審委員會, Zhonghua congshu 中華叢書, 1984. Also contains tables of lost and extant historical works in the Yiwenzhi and author/title indexes.

Songshi renming suoyin 宋史人名索引 (Personal-name index to the *Songshi*), Yu Ruyun 俞如雲, comp., 4 vols., Shanghai guji, 1992.

47.2 Other Textual Sources

The following list is in no sense intended to be exhaustive, but rather to give examples of the many additional Song sources available in different historical and literary genres.

History

Songshi quanwen xu Zizhi tongjian 宋史全文續資治通鑑, anon. Annalist-ic history of the entire dynasty. Particularly valuable for its last 50 years or so. There is a Wenhai photo-reprint edition, 5 vols., 1969.

Dongdu shilüe 東都事略, Wang Cheng 王稱. A twelfth-century *bian-nianti* type history of the Northern Song. In some respects (e.g., bi-ographies) it is more complete than the *Songshi*. There is a Wenhai photo-reprint edition, 4 vols., 1967; also 14 *ce*, Yangzhou guji, 1990.

Geography

(Songben) Lidai dili zhizhang tu (宋本)歷代地理指掌圖 (Song edition of administrative maps, chronologically arranged), Shanghai guji, 1989. This is a photo reproduction of an early Southern Song copy found

in the Tôyô bunko; it is the earliest extant work of administrative geography.

Taiping huanyu ji [*zhi*] 太平寰宇記 [志] (Universal geography of the Taiping era, 976–83). This is the first extant Song comprehensive gazetteer. It is discussed in 4.4.3. On this and other Song geographical works, see *SB*, 128–68.

Yuanfeng jiuyu zhi 元豐九域志 (Gazetteer of the nine regions during the Yuanfeng period, 1078–86), Wang Cun 王存, presented, 1080; published, 1085; 2 vols., Zhonghua, 1984. This edition includes an index.

Yudi jisheng 輿地紀勝 (Records of famous places), Wang Xiangzhi 王象之, 1227; 32 *juan* missing; 8 vols., Zhonghua, 1992. This photo reprint of a Qing edition includes a four-corner index to personal and place names and stone inscriptions. Describes the territories of the Southern Song with emphasis on culture. Arrangement is by *lu* 路, *zhou* 州 and *xian* 縣.

Fangyu shenglan 方輿勝覽 (Topography book for visiting places of scenic beauty), Zhu Mu 祝穆, 1239. There is a personal-name index attached to the Shanghai guji edition (1991).

Local Gazetteers

Fangzhi 方志: There are some 30 Song local gazetteers extant. Twenty-four are described in *SB*, 131–49, which also lists the titles of contents of each.[10] Personal names in them are indexed in *Songren zhuanji ziliao suoyin, zengdingben* (see 47.4.2, *Biographies*).

Travel and Diplomatic Missions

There are several famous Song accounts of trips inside China (4.8). Also, many of the Song embassies to neighboring regimes (Liao, Jin or Mongol) recorded the mission in diary form or wrote it up on return to China (41.5.1). Others based their descriptions of foreign countries on the accounts of merchants.

---

[10] See also James M. Hargett, "Song Dynasty Local Gazetteers," *HJAS* 56.2: 405–42 (1996). This article which contains in the appendix a listing of the 30 extant Song gazetteers. *Song-Yuan fangzhi congkan* 宋元方志叢刊 (Collection of Song and Yuan gazetteers), 8 vols., Zhonghua, 1990. Facsimiles of 37 Song and Yuan gazetteers; see also Dahua, 1979; 1988; plus *xubian* 續編, 1990 (under title *Song-Yuan difangzhi congshu*).

Foreign missions to Song China are listed in Robert Hartwell, *Tribute Missions to China, 960–1126*, Philadelphia: copyright by the author, 1983. The Japan section is not complete.

Laws and Institutions

Song huiyao jigao xingfa 宋會要輯稿刑法 (27.3).

Song xingtong 宋刑統 (27.3).

Minggong shupan qingmingji 名公書判清明集 (27.3).

Tangyin bishi 棠陰比事 (27.3).

Qingyuan tiaofa shilei 慶元條法事類 (27.4).

Zhiyuan cuoyao 職源撮要 (27.5).

Sô-Gen kanshin sôgô sakuin 宋元官箴綜合索引 (Combined index to Song and Yuan *guanzhen*), Akagi Ryûji 赤城隆治, Satake Yasuhiko 佐竹靖彥, comps., Kyûko, 1987. Index to seven Song local administrative handbooks (27.5).

Xiyuan jilu 洗冤集錄 (27.5).

Army

Wujing zongyao 武經總要 (Essentials of the military classics), Zeng Gongliang 曾公亮 (998–1078) and Ding Du 丁度 (990–1053), 1044; Jiefangjun, 1988. Important source on Song military institutions and strategic thinking (*SB*, 235–37).

Encyclopaedias

Taiping yulan 太平御覽 (29.2).

Cefu yuangui 册府元龜 (29.2).

Yuhai 玉海 (29.2).

Xiaoxue ganzhu 小學紺珠 (2.6, note 36).

For other Song encyclopaedias, of which there are several, as well as miscellaneous works, see *SB* 319–49.

Edicts and Memorials

Song da zhaoling ji 宋大詔令集 (Collected edicts of the Song), compiled 1131–62, Zhonghua, 1962. Out of the original 240 *juan*, 196 survive.

They contain over 3,800 edicts of the Northern Song emperors, many of which are not to be found elsewhere.[11]

Lidai mingchen zouyi 歷代名臣奏議 (Memorials of leading officials of each period), 1416; 5 vols., Shanghai guji, 1964; rpnt., 1989. This work contains excerpts from memorials and quotes from other sources down to the Yuan arranged in a somewhat over-categorized 67 divisions. The Song and Yuan memorials account for 70 percent of the total. The 1989 reprint includes a summary giving the tentative name for each memorial and its author's name, as well as an author index.

Collections of Song Prose and Poetry

Quan Song wen 全宋文 (Complete Song prose works), Zeng Zaozhuang 曾棗莊 and Liu Lin 劉琳, eds. in chief, Ba-Shu, 1988–89. Designed to include all known literary works in prose written during the Song in a planned 150 volumes (including memorials, prefaces, postfaces, obituaries, letters and so forth).

Quan Song shi 全宋詩 (Complete Song poetry), 60 vols., Beijing daxue, 1991– . Designed to include all poems written during the Song dynasty, arranged chronologically by author. It will contain more than 200,000 poems by 11,000 poets.

Tang-Song ci baike da cidian 唐宋詞百科大辭典 (Encyclopaedia of Tang and Song *ci*), Wang Hong 王洪 et al., comps., Xueyuan, 1990. Includes table of contents under headings such as literary terms or first lines, but also relating to content such as customs (*minsu* 民俗).

Bieji 別集

The collected works of nearly 750 Song individuals have survived (unlike earlier dynasties from which most have been lost). This is reckoned to be about 10–20 percent of the total of those that were printed. The following are the main indexes for finding Song *bieji* and their contents. Famous individual authors such as Su Shi 蘇軾 or Zhu Xi 朱熹 have their own in-

---

[11] Another Song collection of memorials is *Guochao zhuchen zouyi* 國朝諸臣奏議 (or *Zhuchen zouyi* 諸臣奏議 or *Song mingchen zouyi* 宋名臣奏議), Zhao Ruyu 趙汝愚 (1140–96), comp., Wenhai photo reprint available.

dexes, see Peter Bol, *Research Tools for the Study of Sung History* (the scope of this guide is described in 47.4.2).

Xiancun Songren bieji banben mulu 現存宋人別集版本目錄 (Catalog of extant collected works of Song individuals), Sichuan lianhe daxue guji zhengli yanjiusuo 四川聯合大學古籍整理研究所, ed., Ba-Shu, 1990. Arranged chronologically according to writer. Each entry includes title of extant work(s), edition(s) available (with details of *congshu* editions) and holding location. There are separate indexes for *congshu* collections based on the four-corner system; a list of holding libraries arranged by location (250 Chinese collections, 32 Japanese, and that of the Library of Congress); and authors' finding list by four-corner number.

Songren bieji xulu 宋人別集叙錄, Zhu Shangshu 祝尚書, Ba-Shu, 1997. More than 500 Song *bieji* in collections in China, Taiwan, Japan, Korea and the United States.

An Index to Sung Dynasty Titles Extant in Ts'ung-shu, Brian E. McKnight, comp., CMC, 1977. Lists 4,500 titles, incl. variants, by 1,664 authors as found in *Zhongguo congshu zonglu* 中國叢書綜錄 (9.9).

Songdai Shuren zhuzuo cunyi lu 宋代蜀人著作存佚錄 (Catalog of extant and lost writings by Sichuanese authors of the Song period), Xu Zhaoding 許肇鼎, comp., Ba-Shu, 1986.

Nihon genson 日本現存 *Sôjin bunshû mokuroku* 宋人文集目錄 (Catalog of collected works of Song Authors), Yoshida Tora 古田寅 et al., ed., Tokyo, 1959; rev. ed., Kyûko, 1972. Lists the works of 528 individuals whose *bieji* are held in Japanese collections.

Sôdai bunshû sakuin 宋代文集索引 (Index to Song collected works), compiled under the direction of Saeki Tomi 佐伯富, Tôyôshi kenkyûkai, 1970; rpnt., Zongqing tushu, 1986. Contains 70,000 entries to personal and place names, technical terms and key words in 10 major and 23 supplementary collections of 10 Song literary figures: Fan Zhongyan 范仲淹 (989–1052), Hong Gua 洪适 (1117–84), Ouyang Xiu 歐陽修 (1007–72), Sima Guang 司馬光 (1019–86), Ye Shi 葉適 (1150–1223), Yin Zhu 尹洙 (1001/2–42), Zeng Gong 曾鞏 (1019–83), Zhang Fangping 張方平 (1007–91), Zhen Dexiu 真德秀 (1178–1235) and Zhu Xi 朱熹 (1130–1200).

A Guide to Sources of Chinese Economic History, AD 618–1368, Robert Hartwell, comp., UChP, 1964. Annotated index to materials of interest to the economic historian drawn from 112 collected works of Tang, Song and Yuan authors mentioned in the *Imperial Catalog*.

Biji 筆記

Of the approximately 200 extant Song *biji* (see chap. 31 on this genre), 5 titles have been selected as examples here. There is a repertory of the terminology in Tang and Song *biji*, *Tang-Song biji yuci huishi* 唐宋筆記語辭匯釋.[12] There are also five indexes to headings in a total of 77 Song *biji*:

Rongzhai suibi wuji 容齋隨筆五集 (Tolerant Study notebooks, five collections), Hong Mai 洪邁 (1123–1202), 2 vols., Shanghai guji, 1978. *H-Y Index* 13: *Rongzhai suibi wuji zonghe yinde* 容齋隨筆五集綜合引得 (Combined indices to the five collections of *Tolerant Study Notebooks*). Also indexed in *Chûgoku zuihitsu sakuin*. Wide range of topics in 1,217 entries relating to civil service and intellectual life. There is a detailed description of the contents in *SB*, 292–308.

Dongjing menghualu 東京夢華錄 (The Eastern capital: A dream of splendors past), Meng Yuanlao 孟元老 (fl. 1090–50), 1148; annotated and punctuated, Deng Zhicheng 鄧之誠, ed., Zhonghua, 1959; indexed in *Chûgoku zuihitsu sakuin*. Lively and detailed descriptions of life in the Northern Song capital of Bianliang 汴梁 (Kaifeng) based on the authors reminiscences of his youthful years there. Umehara (1979) also indexes the *Dongjing menghualu* as well as the *Mengliang lu* and the *Wulin jiushi* and the other two key *biji* for the Southern Song capital of Lin'an 臨安 (Hangzhou), namely Nai Deweng 耐得翁, *Ducheng jisheng* 都城紀勝 (The famous sites of the capital) and Anon, *Xihu laoren fanshengji* 西湖老人繁勝記 (Description of the famous sites by the old man of the Western Lake), see *SB*, 150–52.

Mengliang lu 夢粱錄 (Record of the splendors of the capital city), Wu Zimu 吳自牧, Zhejiang renmin, 1983. Indexed in *Chûgoku zuihitsu sakuin* and Umehara (1979). Reminiscences of the Southern Song capital of Lin'an 臨安 (Hangzhou) modelled after *Menghualu*. See, for example, *Daily Life in China on the Eve of the Mongol Invasion, 1250–1276*, Jacques Gernet, Allen and Unwin, 1962; SUP, 1970 (French original, 1959).

Wulin jiushi 武林舊事 (Former events in Wulin [Hangzhou]), Zhou Mi 周密 (1232–99 or 1308), 1280. Reminiscences of the Southern Song

---

[12] See Wang Ying 王瑛, *Tang-Song biji yuci huishi* (Collected notes on the language of Tang and Song miscellaneous notes), Zhonghua, 1990. See under 46.2, *Biji*, for comments on this work.

capital. Indexed in *Chûgoku zuihitsu sakuin* and Umehara (1979), see *SB*, 155–56.

Mengxi bitan 夢溪筆談 (Jottings from the Mengxi), Shen Gua 沈括 (1031–95), 1089–93. Mengxi was an area in Zhenjiang, Jiangsu to which Shen retired to write in 1088. Newly punctuated and corrected edition, *Xin jiaozheng 'Mengxi bitan'*, Hu Daojing 胡道靜, ed., Zhonghua, 1957, 1975. One-third of the 507 notes record the author's observations of natural phenomena and the results of his experiments, see *SB*, 226–28. A major work in the history of Chinese invention. Contains the first reference to the magnetic compass.

Biji *Indexes*

In addition to the two Kyoto *biji* indexes (chap. 31), there are two especially for the Song:

Tôkei mukaroku Muryôroku tô goi sakuin 東京夢華錄夢梁錄等語彙索引, Umehara Kaoru 梅原郁, ed., Jimbun, 1979.

Liu Kuntai 劉坤太, *Diannaohua Songren biji jiansuo xitong* 電腦化宋人筆記檢索系統 (Computerized index to Song *biji*), The 50 titles in this database are listed in Bol (1996), 57 (47.4.2).

Nongshu 農書, Chen Fu 陳敷, ed. (35.1).

47.3 *Archaeology and Inscriptions*

On the beginnings of the antiquarian study of inscriptions in the Song, see chap. 17.

A Journey into China's Antiquity, vol. 3: *Sui-Tang-Song*, National Museum of Chinese History, eds., Morning Glory, 1998. See 8.2.1 on this authoritatively commented series of photographs of the collections of the museum.

Songling 宋陵 (Song tombs): the tombs of seven out of the nine emperors of the Northern Song may be visited at Gongyi city 鞏義市, Gong county 鞏縣, Henan about 130 km to the north of Kaifeng. The two emperors not buried here were Huizong 徽宗 and his eldest son and successor, Qinzong 欽宗. Having been taken captive by the Khitan in 1127, they died in captivity in the Northeast (Heilongjiang).

Valerie Hansen, "Inscriptions: Historical Sources for the Song," *Bulletin of Song-Yuan Studies* 19 (1987).

Angela Schottenhammer, *Grabinschriften in der Song-Dynastie*, Forum, 1995.

Angela Schottenhammer, "Characteristics of Song Epitaphs," in *Burial in Sung China*, Dieter Kuhn, ed., Forum, 1994, 253–306.

One of the largest collections of rubbings of inscriptions contains eight volumes of Song inscriptions: *Beijing tushuguan cang Zhongguo lidai shike taben huibian* 北京圖書館藏中國歷代石刻拓本匯編 (see 17.3).

Annotated Bibliography to the Shike shiliao xinbian [New Edition of Historical Materials Carved on Stone], Dieter Kuhn and Helga Stahl, eds., Forum, 1991. Listing of stone inscriptions from the Song, Liao and Jin. Arranged alphabetically by title; there is an author index.

Islamic Inscriptions in Quanzhou (Quanzhou Yisilanjiao shike 泉州伊斯蘭教石刻), Chen Dasheng 陳達生, ed., Chen Enming 陳恩明, tr., Yinchuan: Ningxia renmin and Fujian renmin, 1984. Contains transcriptions of more than 300 stelae with inscriptions in ancient Arabic and Persian from Quanzhou dating from the Song and Yuan with notes. In the 1990s, 20 more Islamic stelae were excavated in Quanzhou. They are mainly the tombstones of merchants.

Dieter Kuhn, *A Place for the Dead: An Archaeological Documentary on Graves and Tombs of the Song Dynasty (960–1279)*, Forum, 1996.

47.4 Guides and Research Tools

47.4.1 Guides

For library catalogs (e.g., *Songshi* 宋史 "Yiwenzhi 藝文志") and collections compiled in the Song and Yuan, see 9.2 and 9.4.

A Sung Bibliography, initiated by Etienne Balazs, Yves Hervouet, ed., HKCU Press, 1978. *SB* is an annotated catalog of about 450 works written during the Song, with detailed descriptions of the contents and authors. The entries (eighty percent of which are in English, the remainder in French) were written by 80 scholars from around the world. About 250 of the notices were written by Japanese contributors. Each entry outlines the nature of the work and gives bibliographic details. Yves Hervouet points out in his Introduction that the entries vary considerably in quality: "Some notices are outstanding, and are real miniature memoirs on the works described. Others are inadequate, and consist of a résumé of the notice in the *Ssu-k'u ch'üan-shu* or a re-writing of an article in a Japanese historical dictionary." Arrangement is by modified *Sibu* classification. There are separate indexes of books, personal names and subjects. Since *SB* only covers works written in the Song, there are no entries for works such as the *Songshi* 宋史 (compiled in the Yuan).

Zhongguo lishi da cidian 中國歷史大辭典 (The great encyclopaedia of Chinese history), 14 vols., Shanghai cishu, 1983– , contains a separate volume on *Songshi* 宋史, Deng Guangming 鄧廣銘 (1907–98) and Cheng Yingliu 程應鏐, eds., 1984. See 8.3.2, item 2 for comments on this encyclopaedia.

Jan Yun-hua, "Buddhist Historiography in Sung China," *ZDMG* 114: 360–81 (1964).

Judith M. Boltz, *A Survey of the Taoist Literature, Tenth to Seventeenth Centuries*, CCS, University of California, Berkeley, 1987.[13]

47.4.2 Research Tools

Research Tools for the Study of Sung History, Peter Bol, Sung-Yuan Research Aids (II), Binghamton, 1990, 2nd ed., Albany, 1996. A unique listing of indexes and other research tools for Song primary sources (1–82) plus bibliographies of secondary scholarship. There are Wade-Giles and Chinese indexes (83–99), followed by the chapter on the Song from *Ajia rekishi kenkyû nyûmon* アジア歴史研究入門 (8.3.3), which outlines both the primary sources and secondary scholarship (mainly Japanese) on the Song: Chikusa Masaaki 竺沙雅章, "Five Dynasties and the Song," Kenneth Chase, English tr. (103–41).

Language

Song yuyan cidian 宋語言詞典 (Dictionary of the language during the Song dynasty), Yuan Bin 袁賓, ed. in chief, Shanghai jiaoyu, 1997. This is in the series *Jindai Hanyu duandai yuyan cidian xilie* 近代漢語詞典系列 (Single-period dictionaries of early Mandarin). The dictionary contains over 4,000 entries covering mainly popular literature of the Song as well as *biji* 筆記, historical biographies, documents and so forth. It is intended both for historical linguists and for readers of the popular literature of the period. Arrangement is by *pinyin* and there is also a *pinyin* index.

Robert Hartwell, "A Guide to Documentary Sources of Middle Chinese History: Documentary Forms Contained in the Collected Papers (*wenji*) of 21 T'ang and Sung Writers," *Bulletin of Song and Yuan Studies* 18: 133–82 (1986).

---

[13] Piet van der Loon, *Taoist Books in the Libraries of the Sung Period*, London: Ithaca Press, 1984.

Note the appendix on Song official jargon in *Songdai guanzhi cidian* 宋代官制辭典 (Dictionary of Song dynasty official titles), Gong Yanming 龔延明, Zhonghua, 1997 (616–71).

Ō Anseki jiten 王安石事典 (Encyclopaedia of Wang Anshi), Higashi Ichio 東一夫, Kokusho kankōkai, 1980.

Biographies

If you cannot find a biography in one of the 441 included in *Sung Biographies* (item 4 below), then try items 1 and 2, which are indexes to biographical materials on well over 20,000 Song figures. Biographical materials on newly unearthed stone inscriptions are indexed in item 3, but since these are continually being found, check collections of inscriptions, which are often published for a place or for a long stretch of time covering several dynasties, not just for a particular place or dynasty (49.9). Remember, too, to search similar indexes for dynasties preceding, overlapping and succeeding the Song (46.3 and chap. 48):

Songren zhuanji ziliao suoyin, zengdingben 宋人傳記資料索引增訂本 (Index to biographical materials of Song figures), Chang Bide 昌彼德 et al., comps.; expanded by Wang Deyi 王德毅 and Cheng Yuanmin 程元敏, 6 vols., Taibei: Dingwen, 1976–80; Zhonghua, 1989, contains materials on 15,000 people, most with a short biographical notice.[14]

---

[14] It was based on two previous indexes: (1) *Song Biographical Index* compiled under the direction of Aoyama Sadao 青山定雄 by the Japanese Committee for the Song Project, *Sōjin denki sakuin* 宋人傳記索引, Tōyō bunko, 1968, which included dates (for some 8,000 Chinese who lived during the Song) as well as alternative names and the names of paternal ancestors for three generations if known (this last category not reproduced in the Chang Bide index). The materials indexed included biographies and commemorative writings found in a wide variety of sources including local gazetteers, collected works, encyclopaedias, collections of epigraphy, etc. There is a romanized index (Wade-Giles) at the end of the work; (2) *Sishiqi zhong Songdai zhuanji zonghe yinde* 四十七種宋代傳記綜合引得 (Combined indices to 47 Song dynasty biographical collections), *H-Y Index* 34. Altogether, 9,024 figures are included. This index is arranged by ordinary names and by alternative names but does not give the other types of information included in (1).

Songren zhuanji ziliao suoyin, zengdingben should be supplemented with *Songren zhuanji ziliao suoyin bubian* 宋人傳記資料索引補編, 3 vols., Sichuan daxue, 1994. Adds a further 14,000 names not found in item 1 as well as supplements 6,000 entries of the older work.[15]

Songren nianpu jimu, Songbian Songren nianpu xuankan 宋人年譜集目宋編宋人年譜選刊 (Bibliography of chronological biographies of Song personalities and selected Song *nianpu*), Wu Hongze, ed., Ba-Shu, 1995.

Sung Biographies, Herbert Franke, ed., 4 vols., Steiner, 1976. Includes biographies of 441 people.

Songren shengzu kao shili 宋人生卒考示例 (Verification of dates of birth and death of Song figures), Zheng Qian 鄭騫, Taibei: Huashi, 1977.

Tang-Song huajia renming cidian 唐宋畫家人名辭典 (Personal-name dictionary of Tang and Song painters), Zhu Zhuyu 朱鑄禹, Zhongguo gudian yishu, 1958.

Song, Liao, Jin huajia shiliao 宋遼金畫家史料 (Historical materials on Song, Liao and Jin painters), Chen Gaohua 陳高華, Wenwu, 1984.

Official Titles and Officeholders

Songdai guanzhi cidian 宋代官制辭典 (Dictionary of Song dynasty official titles), Gong Yanming 龔延明, ed., Zhonghua, 1997. The definitive reference work for Song official titles. It also contains an appendix on Song official jargon (616–71) as well as organization tables (672–731).

An Introduction to the Civil Service of Sung China: With Emphasis on Its Personnel Administration, Winston W. Lo, UHP, 1987. One of the important documents used by Lo is the *Libu tiaofa* 吏部條法 (Regulations of the Board of Personnel), of which nine chapters were reconstituted from the *Yongle dadian*. Edward Kracke, Jr., *Civil Service in Early Sung China*, HUP, 1953, includes the list of official titles and ranks of 1038.

Sôshi shokkanshi sakuin 宋史職官志索引 (Index to the monograph on official posts in the *Songshi*), Saeki Tomi 佐伯富, Tôyôshi kenkyûkai,

---

[15] It also indexes the gazetteers covered in Zhu shijia 朱士嘉, *Song-Yuan fangzhi zhuanji suoyin* 宋元方志傳記索引 (Index to the biographies in Song and Yuan local gazetteers), Zhonghua, 1963; rpnt., 1986, which includes 3,949 people in 33 gazetteers.

1963. Arranged by Japanese reading; has stroke-order index. There is a useful introduction by Miyazaki Ichisada 宮崎市定, "Sôdai kansei josetsu: *Sôshi* shokkanshi o ikani yomubeki ka 宋代官制序説:宋史職官志を如何に讀むべきか" (Introduction to the Song bureaucracy: How should the monograph on official posts in the *Songshi* be read?), 1–63. See also Umehara Kaoru, "Civil and Military Titles in Sung: The Chi-lu-kuan System," *Acta Asiatica* 50: 1–30 (1986). Useful for its chart showing ranking systems from different periods.

Les Fonctionnaires des Song, Index des Titres, Fu-jui Chang, Paris, 1962. Includes among the works indexed the *Songshi* "Zhiguanzhi 宋史職官志" (Monograph on officials in the *Songshi*).

Song zaifu biannian lu jiaobu 宋宰輔編年錄校補 (Chronology of Song chief and assisting counselors, revised), Wang Ruilai 王瑞來, ed., Zhonghua, 1986. Shows membership of the Council of State for the entire Song period, including documents of appointment and anecdotal information.

Bei-Song jing fu nianbiao 北宋經撫年表 (Chronological tables of Northern Song civil and military intendants); *Nan Song zhifu nianbiao* 南宋制撫年表 (Chronological tables of Southern Song civil and military intendants), Wu Tingxie 吳廷燮, punctuated and corrected by Zhang Chenshi 張忱石, Zhonghua, 1984. Includes all circuit-level intendants as well as prefects (*zhizhou* 知州) and gives dates of appointment. Arrangement by circuit and prefecture and by time. There is a personal-name index.

Geography

Zhongguo lishi dituji 中國歷史地圖集 (The Historical Atlas of China), Tan Qixiang 譚其驤, ed. in chief, vol. 6, *Song, Liao, Jin shiqi* 宋遼金時期, 2nd rev. ed., 2nd prnt., Ditu, 1985.

Tô-Sô jidai no kôtsû to chishi chizu no kenkyû 唐宋時代の交通と地志地圖の研究 (Collected studies on communications, gazetteers and maps of the Tang and Song), Aoyama Sadao 青山定雄, Yoshikawa kôbunkan, 1963. There are also maps of Song communications (roads, grain transport, etc., included).

Chronology

Zhongguo lishi dashi biannian: Wudai-Shiguo, Song, Liao, Xia, Jin 中國歷史大事編年五代十國宋遼夏金 (Chronology of major events in Chinese history: Five Dynasties, Ten Kingdoms, Song, Liao, Xia and Jin), Beijing, 1987.

Sôdaishi nenpyô 宋代史年表 (Chronological table of events of the Song dynasty), Aoyama Sadao 青山定雄, ed. in chief, vol. 1, *Hoku-Sô* 北宋 (Northern Song), Tôyô bunko, 1967; vol. 2, *Nan-Sô* 南宋 (Southern Song), Tôyô bunko, 1974. Gives year-by-year tables of important events and cultural matters as well as corresponding dates for Korea, Liao, Xi-Xia, Jin and Yuan. Based on the basic annals of the *Songshi*.

Bibliographies of Secondary Scholarship

Yang Weisheng, "A Brief Survey of Song Studies in Chinese over the Last Ten Years," Lee-fang Ch'ien, trs., *Bulletin of Song-Yuan Studies* 20 (1988), 1–17.

"Japanese Studies in Chinese History (Song, Yuan, Ming and Qing), 1973–83," Okazaki Hiroshi; Joseph McDermott, tr., Tokyo Center for East Asian Cultural Studies, 1986.

"Trends in Postwar Japanese Studies in Sung History: A Bibliographical Introduction," Hasegawa Yoshio, *Acta Asiatica* 50: 95–120 (1986).

Peter J. Golas, "Rural China in the Song," *JAS* 39.2: 291–325 (1980).

Bibliographie et index des travaux en chinois sur les Song 1900–1975, Chen Qinghao 陳慶浩, comp., Paris, 1979. Arranged by subject. Has subject and author indexes.

Societies and Journals

Journal of Song-Yuan Studies (began as *Sung Studies Newsletter*, 1969–80, changed title to *Bulletin of Sung-Yuan Studies*, 1980–88 and adopted present title in 1989). A good way of keeping up-to-date with new work on the Song. For example, it contains translations of the annual *Shigaku zasshi* state-of-the-field articles on Five Dynasties, Song and Yuan studies and also has regular bibliographical updates of Chinese, Japanese and Western scholarship on the Song period.

Songshi yanjiu tongxun 宋史研究通訊, 1985– , Shanghai shifan daxue.

Songshi yanjiu hui 宋史研究會 (Research society for Song history), Nanjing; founded in 1980. *Songshi yanjiu lunwenji* 宋史研究論文集 (Collected research articles on Song history). Has been published about two years after the annual meetings (held every other year) since 1982, publisher depending on the place of the meeting, 1982– .

48

Liao, Xi-Xia, Jin and Yuan

907–1368

Liao 遼 (*Qidan* 契丹, Khitan)[1]	916–1125
Xi-Xia 西夏 (*Dangxiang* 黨項, Tangut)[2]	1038–1227
Jin 金 (*Nüzhen* 女真, Jurchen)[3]	1115–1234
Yuan 元 (*Menggu* 蒙古, Mongol)[4]	1260–1368

[1] Khitan was replaced with the dynastic name Liao in 948. Liao was the name of the river from the area in modern Liaoning which the Khitan counted as their home.

[2] The ancestors of Li Yuanyi 李元昊, the founder of Da-Xia 大夏, were enfeoffed by the Tang as Dukes of Xia (Xiaguo gong 夏國公) in 883 and at the same time appointed governors-general of the three north-western prefectures of Xiazhou 夏州 (the capital of the short-lived Xiongnu kingdom of Da-Xia 大夏, 407–31), Suizhou 綏州 and Yinzhou 銀州. In 967, another ancestor was given the title King of Xia by the Song. Hence the choice of the dynastic name Da-Xia on the establishment of the new empire in 1038; see *CHC*, 6, 154–204. The main capital was Xingqing fucheng 興慶府城 near Yinzhou about 180 km to the west of Xiazhou. Given the geographic location of the new dynasty in relation to the Song it is called in Chinese sources Xi-Xia.

[3] "Anchuhu 按出虎" in Jurchen means "gold" after the Anchuhu River (present-day Ashihe 阿什河 in Heilongjiang province), which produces gold. This was the area from which the Jurchen came. Hence the dynastic name Jin 金. See Chan Hok-lam, "'Ta Chin' (Great Golden): The Origin and Changing Interpretations of the Jurchen State Name," *TP* 77.4–5: 253–99 (1991).

[4] Khubilai Khan adopted the concept "Fundamental force" (*Yuan* 元) for the name of his dynasty from the opening lines of the *Yijing* 易經, as pointed out by Zhao Yi 趙翼 (1727–1814), "Yuan jian guohao shiyong wenyi 元建國號始用文義" (In establishing their dynastic name the Yuan began the practice of using literary meanings), *Nian'er shi zhaji* 廿二史剳記 (Critical notes on the twenty-two Standard Histories), 1799, *juan* 29.

Footnote continued on next page

The difficulty of finding unbiased sources for the alien regimes of Liao, Xi-Xia, Jin and Yuan is compounded by the fact that the *Liaoshi* was written 200 years after the fall of the dynasty, long after its archives had been lost, and the Xi-Xia was never counted as a legitimate dynasty and so had no Standard History. Until recently it has not attracted the attention of historians. The *Yuanshi* is generally reckoned to be one of the worst, if not the worst, of all the Standard Histories.

Given that the Liao, Xi-Xia and Jin fought against and coexisted with the Song and that the Yuan attacked the Song for over 50 years, it goes without saying that the basic sources for the Song are also important for these dynasties (see 47.1 and 47.2), as are those of the Ming for the Yuan (49.1). Only when there is explicit overlap in sources or research tools are the works introduced in the chapters on the Song and the Ming (47 and 49) repeated here.

There are a number of earlier references which cover the Liao, Jin and Yuan—for example, biographical indexes.[5] Not infrequently these have been superseded by research tools for a single dynasty only.

Zhao's brief essay is translated in full in Chan (1991), 254–56. See also *CHC*, 6, 458. See also Herbert Franke, *From Tribal Chieftan to Universal God: The Legitimation of the Yuan Dynasty*, Bayrische Akedemie der Wissenschaften, 1978.

[5] *Liao, Jin, Yuan zhuanji sanshi zhong zonghe yinde* 遼金元傳記三十種綜合引得 (Combined indices to 30 Liao, Jin, and Yuan biographical collections), *H-Y Index* 35. To be used with the Song biographical indexes since the dynasties overlapped.

Ryô, Kin, Gen jin denki sakuin 遼金元人傳記索引, Umehara Kaoru 梅原郁 and Kinugawa Tsuyoshi 衣川強, comp., Jimbun, 1972. There are 3,200 individuals listed; 130 *wenji* were consulted.

48.1 Guides to Sources

Only those guides to two or more alien dynasties are listed in this section. Volume 6 of *CHC* is the best introduction to the history of the Liao, Xi-Xia, Jin and Yuan between two covers. It also contains good bibliographies:

"Bibliographical Essays," in *CHC*, vol. 6, *Alien Regimes and Border States, 907–1368*, Herbert Franke and Denis Twitchett, eds., CUP, 1994. These are a good introduction to the traditional sources, Qing scholarship and secondary sources (665–726).

Bu Liao Jin Yuan yiwenzhi 補遼金元藝文志 (9.4).

Zhongguo lishi da cidian 中國歷史大辭典 (The great encyclopaedia of Chinese history), 14 vols., Shanghai cishu, 1983– . Contains a separate volume on *Liao, Xia, Jin, Yuanshi* 遼夏金元史, Cai Meibiao 蔡美彪, ed., 1986. See 8.3.2, item 2 for comments.

48.2 Liao

Liaoshi 遼史, edited at the Yuan history office, 1343–44; 5 vols., Zhonghua, 1974; 6th prnt., 1996. It covers the years 916–1125.[6] The Liao dynasty (遼代, 916–1125) was only partially sinicized. It did not produce huge quantities of historical works in the first place and its conquerors, the Jurchen Jin, did not compile a Standard History of the Liao. By the time the *Liaoshi* was written the discussion of whether to include the dynasty in the legitimate succession had been going on for 200 years. The Liao archives were long since lost and no *guoshi* 國史 or documents survived for the Yuan editors to work on. Despite the fact that it is one of the weakest of the Standard Histories, the *Liaoshi* is an essential source for a dynasty from which almost no documents survive. The Zhonghua edition was produced under the supervision of the leading scholar of the Liao of his generation, Feng Jia-sheng 馮家昇. There is a full personal-name index[7] as well as

---

[6] "Bibliographical Essays, 1: The Liao," in *CHC*, vol. 6, 665–74.
[7] *Liaoshi renming suoyin* 遼史人名索引, Zhonghua, 1982.

a glossary.[8] The "Guoyujie 國語解" chapter (at the end of the "liezhuan 列傳") contains important materials on the Khitan language.[9]

Karl A. Wittfogel and Feng Chia-sheng (Feng Jiasheng 馮家昇), *History of Chinese Society: Liao (907–1125)*, Philadelphia: American Philosophical Society, *Transactions*, n.s., 26 (1949). A massive study on the social, economic and political institutions of the Liao period with many translated excerpts from the *Liaoshi* arranged by category. There is a thorough index.

"The 'Treatise on Punishments' in the Liao history," Herbert Franke, tr., *Central Asiatic Journal*, pp. 9–38 (1983), is a translation of the monograph on penal law in the *Liaoshi*.

Other Textual Sources

Qidan guozhi 契丹國志, Ye Longli 葉隆禮, *jinshi* 1247, was written on the basis of Song sources. It is the only text used by the editors of the *Liaoshi* to have survived.[10] There is an integral translation into Russian with introduction and commentary.[11]

Koryŏsa 高麗史: for this and other Korean sources, see 42.4.

Liaoshi huibian 遼史彙編 (Collected documents on the history of the Liao), Yang Jialuo 楊家駱, ed., 10 vols., Dingwen, 1973.

Liaoshi huibianbu 遼史彙編補 (Supplement to *Liaoshi huibian*), Yang Jialuo 楊家駱, ed., Dingwen, 1974.

Quan Liaowen 全遼文 (Complete Liao writings), Chen Shu 陳述, Zhonghua, 1982. Also includes inscriptions.

Qidan xiaozi yanjiu 契丹小字研究 (Researches on the Khitan script), Qingge'ertai 清格爾泰 et al., Shehui kexue, 1985.

---

[8] *Ryôshi sakuin* 遼史索引 (Index to the Standard History of the Liao), Jimbun, 1937. Cannot be relied upon for completeness.

[9] *Qinding Liao Jin Yuan sanshi Guoyujie suoyin* 欽訂遼金元三史國語解索引 (Index to the national language glossaries in the Liao, Jin and Yuan Histories), Taiwan: Shangwu, 1986.

[10] There is an index available: *Qidan guozhi tongjian* 契丹國志通檢, Wu Xiaoling 吳曉鈴 et al., comps., *CFS* 12, 1949; Chengwen, 1968.

[11] V. S. Taskin, *Istoriia gosudarstva Kidanei (Tsidan' go chzhi)*, Nauka, 1979.

Edouard Chavannes, "Voyageurs chinois chez les Khitans et les Jou-
tchen." (41.5.1).

Biographies

Liao, Jin, Yuan zhuanji sanshi zhong zonghe yinde 遼金元傳記三十種綜合
引得 (Combined indices to 30 Liao, Jin and Yuan biographical collections), *H-Y Index* 35. To be used with the Song biographical indexes, since the dynasties overlapped.

Ryô, Kin, Genjin denki sakuin 遼金元人傳記索引 (Index to biographies
of Liao, Jin and Yuan persons), Umehara Kaoru 梅原郁 and Kinugawa Tsuyoshi 衣川強 comp., Jimbun, 1972. There are 3,200 individuals listed; 130 *bieji* were consulted.

Archaeology

Liao art and artifacts, including excavated imperial capitals, imperial tombs, tomb frescoes and architectural remains, have
been intensively studied since the 1930s. The Liaoning Provincial Museum, one of the finest in China, includes a particularly
rich collection.

Xiang Chunsong 項春松, *Liaodai lishi yu kaogu* 遼代歷史與考古 (Liao
dynasty history and archaeology), Nei-Menggu renmin, 1996.

Liaodai shike wenbian 遼代石刻文編 (Liao dynasty inscriptions carved
on stone), Xiang Nan 向南, comp., Hebei jiaoyu, 1995, contains
transcriptions of more than 300 Liao inscriptions of all kinds, including many newly excavated.

Nancy Shatzman-Steinhardt, *Liao Architecture*, UHP, 1997.

Societies and Journals

Liao, Jin shi yanjiu hui 遼金史研究會 (Research society for Liao and Jin
history), Shenyang; founded in 1982.

48.3 Xi-Xia

The Xi-Xia (西夏, 1038–1227), a Tangut state established over a
huge part of the Northwest from Mongolia to Xinjiang, and
situated between the Song, Liao and Jin, lasted for almost 200

years.[12] It was never recognized as a legitimate dynasty and attracted little attention from historians. Original sources are almost non-existent. The main sources until modern times were the *liezhuan* chapters on the Xi-Xia in the *Songshi, Liaoshi* and *Yuanshi*. In the early twentieth century, quantities of Tangut language sources were discovered first at Kharakhota and Dunhuang and then later at other sites. Most of the early discoveries were made by Petr Kozlov who took them back to Russia, where they are now housed in St. Petersburg. The Tangut documents were deciphered only in the 1970s and 1980s. They are being published by Shanghai Guji:

E cang Heishuichen wenxian 俄藏黑水城文獻 (Tangut documents from Heishuicheng held in Russia), 9 vols., Shanghai guji, 1997–99.

These documents offer the first chance of seeing the Xi-Xia from the inside, a task made easier by the publication of a well-indexed dictionary containing definitions of 6,000 Tangut characters (including 107 variants) with explanations both in Chinese and in English.[13] For basic orientations, see *CHC*, vol. 6, especially the chapter by Ruth Dunnell ("The Hsi Hsia"), 154–204, as well as the following:

Ruth W, Dunnell, *The Great State of White and High: Buddhism and State Foundation in Eleventh-Century Xia*, UHP, 1996.

Ruth W, Dunnell, *Buddhism and the State in Eleventh Century Xia: Studies in the Sources of Early Tangut History*, UHP, 1995.

Xi-Xia xue gailun 西夏學概論 (Introduction to the study of the Xi-Xia), Wang Tianshun 王天順, ed. in chief, Gansu wenhua, 1995, covers the language, culture, history and archaeology of the Xi-Xia.

Shi Jinbo 史金波 et al., *Xi-Xia wenwu* 西夏文物 (Material culture of Xi-Xia), Wenwu, 1988.

[12] "Bibliographical Essays, 2: The Hsi Hsia," in *CHC*, vol. 6, 674–78; Ruth Dunnell, "Who Are the Tanguts? Remarks on Tangut Ethnogenesis and the Ethnonym Tangut," *JAH* 18: 78–89 (1984).
[13] Li Fanwen 李范文, *Xia-Han zidian* 夏漢字典 (Tangut-Han dictionary), Ningxia renmin, 1997. The same scholar also wrote *Tongyin yanjiu* 通音研究 (Research on the *Tongyin*), Ningxia renmin, 1986.

Wenhai yanjiu 文海研究, Shi Jinpo 史金波 et al., ed., Shehui kexue, 1983, contains a fragment of a rare Tangut-Chinese glossary, the *Wenhai* 文海 (anon, comp., 12th century) plus Chinese translation and index.

Li Fanwen 李範文, *Tongyin yanjiu* 通音研究 (Research on the *Tongyin*), Ningxia renmin, 1986. Tangut dictionary of homophones.

E. I. Kychanov, *Izmenennyi i zanovo utverzhdennyi kodeks deviza tsarst-vovaniia nebesnoe protsvetanie (1149–1169)*, vol.1, 1988; vol. 2, 1987; vol. 3, 1989; vol. 4, 1989. Translation and study of the almost complete Xia law code (*Tiansheng lüling* 天盛律令), of which a Chinese translation has been made.[14]

Evgenii I. Kycanov [Kychanov] and Herbert Franke, *Tangutische und chinesische Quellen zur Militärgesetzgebung des 11. Bis 13. Jahrhunderts*, Munich: Bayerischen Akademie der Wissenschaften, 1990.

Evgenii I. Kychanov, "Monuments of Tangut legislation (twelfth-thirteenth centuries)," in *Etudes tibétaines, Actes du XXIXe Congrès international des orientalistes*, July 1973, Paris: L'Asiathèque, 1976, 29–42.

48.4 Jin

Jinshi 金史, edited at the Yuan history office, 1343–44; punctuated and annotated edition, 8 vols., Zhonghua, 1975; 5th prnt., 1995. It covers the years 1115–1234.[15] One of the better edited of the Standard Histories thanks to the efforts of Wang E 王鶚 (1190–1273), a senior Jin official who ensured

---

[14] *Xi-Xia Tiansheng lüling* 西夏天盛律令 in *Zhongguo zhenxi falü dianji jicheng* 中國珍稀法律典籍集成 (Collection of rare works of Chinese law), Liu Hainian 劉海年 and Yang Yifan 楊一凡, eds., in chief, Kexue, 1994. See also Shi Jinbo 史金波, "Xi-Xia *Tiansheng lüling* lüelun 西夏天盛律令略論," *Ningxia shehui kexue* 1 (1993).

[15] Hok-lam Chan (Chen Xuelin 陳學林), "Bibliographical Essays, 3. The Chin Dynasty," in *CHC*, vol. 6, 678–89. Hok-lam Chan, "Chinese Official History at the Yuan Court: the Composition of the Liao, Chin and Sung Histories," in *China under Mongol Rule*, John D. Langlois, ed., PUP, 1981, 56–106. Hok-lam Chan, "Patterns of Legitimation in Imperial China," Part I of *Legitimation in Imperial China: Discussions under the Jurchen-Chin Dynasty*, Univ. of Washington Press, 1984, 19–48. Chan provides in Part III of this work a complete annotated translation of a Jin official collection of documents on the discussions on legitimate succession, 143–70.

that basic documents and historical works, including his own *Jinshi* 金史, were not lost at the fall of the Jin.[16] One feature not found in other Standard Histories is the table of foreign embassies received at the Jin court. Another feature is the "Jinguo yujie 金國語解" chapter at the end, which contains a list of non-Chinese names and terms with their Chinese equivalents. This is important for the study of the Jurchen language. There is a full personal-name index to the *Jinshi*[17] as well as a concordance of terms used in the entire work.[18]

> Herbert Franke, "Chinese Texts on the Jurchen: Translation of the Jurchen monograph in the *San ch'ao pei meng hui pien*," *Zentralasiatische Studien* 9: 119–86 (1975); "Chinese texts on the Jurchen II: A Translation of Chapter One of the *Chin shih*," *Zentralasiatische Studien* 12: 413–52 (1978).

Da Jin guozhi 大金國志 supplements *Jinshi*. Indexed.[19]

Wang E 王鶚, *Runan yishi* 汝南遺事 (Neglected facts from Runan).[20]

Da Jin zhaoling shizhu 大金詔令釋注 (Edicts of the Jin, annotated and translated into modern Chinese), Dong Kechang 董克昌, ed., Heilongjiang renmin, 1993.

Da Jin diaofa lu 大金弔伐錄 (Records of submission and attack under the great Jin), 1959. "A mine of information on the military and political situation during the collapse of the Northern Sung state," Chan (1994).

---

[16] See Hok-lam Chan, *The Fall of the Jurchen Chin: Wang E's Memoir of Ts'ai-chou under the Mongol Siege (1233–34)*, Steiner, 1996. This is a fully annotated translation of the *Runan yishi*. Runan was the ancient name of Caizhou 蔡州, to which the Jin court inadvisably fled having quit Kaifeng. The last emperor committed suicide and the Jin forces capitulated in February 1234.

[17] *Jinshi renming suoyin* 金史人名索引, Cen Wenyin 崔文印, comp., Zhonghua, 1980.

[18] *Kinshi goi shûsei* 金史語彙集成 (Index to Historical terms in the Standard History of the Jin), Onogawa Hidemi 小野川秀美, 3 vols., Jimbun, 1960–62. Based on the *Bona* edition.

[19] *Da Jin guozhi tongjian* 大金國志通檢, Wu Xiaoling 吳曉鈴 et al., comps., *CFS* 11, 1949; Chengwen, 1968.

[20] Chan (1996).

Comprehensive Literary Collection

Jinwen zui 金文最 (Complete collection of Jin literature), Zhang Jinwu 張金吾 (1787–1829), comp., 1895; rpnt., Chengwen, 1967.

Biji 筆記

Guiqian zhi 歸潛志 (Records written in retirement), Liu Qi 劉祁 (1203–50); Zhonghua, 1983. Life in Kaifeng during the last years of the Jin, including an eyewitness account of the Mongol siege.[21]

Biographies

Liao, Jin, Yuan zhuanji sanshi zhong zonghe yinde 遼金元傳記三十種綜合引得 (Combined indices to 30 Liao, Jin and Yuan biographical collections), *H-Y Index* 35. To be used with the Song biographical indexes, since the dynasties overlapped.

Ryô, Kin, Genjin denki sakuin 遼金元人傳記索引 (Index to biographies of Liao, Jin and Yuan persons), Umehara Kaoru 梅原郁 and Kinugawa Tsuyoshi 衣川強, comps., Jimbun, 1972. There are 3,200 individuals listed; 130 *wenji* were consulted.

Index to Biographical Material in Jin and Yuan Literary Works, Igor de Rachewiltz and Miyoko Nakano, comps., ANU Press, 1st series, 1970; 2nd and 3rd series (with May Wang), 1972 and 1979.

Archaeology

Russian studies of pre-dynastic Jurchen archaeology are summarized in A. P. Okladnikov and V. E. Medvedev, "Chzhurchzheni Priamur'ia po dannym arkheologii," *Problemy Dal'nego Vostoka* 4: 118–28 (1974).

Secondary Studies

Herbert Franke, "The Chin Dynasty," *CHC*, vol 6, 215–320.

Studies on the Jurchens and the Chin Dynasty, Herbert Franke, Hok-lam Chan, Variorum, 1997. Collected articles.

Jing-shen Tao, *The Jurchen in Twelfth-Century China: A Study of Sinicization*, UWP, 1976.

---

[21] Hok-lam Chan, "Liu Ch'i and his Kuei-ch'ien chih," in his *The Historiography of the Chin Dynasty: Three Studies*, Steiner, 1970, 121–88.

Societies and Journals

Liao, Jin shi yanjiu hui 遼金史研究會 (Research society for Liao and Jin history), Shenyang; founded in 1982.

48.5 Yuan

The main sources for the rise of the Mongol empire and the history of the Yuan dynasty (1260–1368) are in Mongolian, Chinese and Persian, supplemented by Korean works (in Literary Chinese) and Latin. The best introduction to the history of the rise of the Mongolian empire and to the Yuan dynasty are the chapters in *CHC*, vol. 6, 321–664.

48.5.1   Main Historical Works

Yuanshi 元史 (Standard History of the Yuan), Song Lian 宋濂 (1310–81) et al., comp., 1369–70; Zhonghua, 15 vols., 1976; 5th prnt., 1995. Covers the years 1206–1369. Edited in less than a year (faster than any other Standard History), it is incomplete and inaccurate (especially the *liezhuan*), yet nevertheless, in the words of Frederick Mote, it is "the modern historian's essential resource for the study of the Yuan period."[22] The fact that it is unpolished is a blessing in disguise in that many documents are preserved in their original or near-original state. This is especially true of the monographs. There is a concordance of terms used in the entire work.[23] There is also a personal-name index.[24]

> *Economic Structure of the Yuan Dynasty: Translation of chapters 93 and 94 of the Yüan shih*, Franz Schurmann, HUP, 1956; rpnt., 1967. This is an annotated translation of the "Shihuozhi" of the *Yuanshi* plus introductions and index.

[22] "A Note on Traditional Sources for Yüan History," p. 689.

[23] *Genshi goi shûsei* 元史語彙集成 (Index to historical terms in the *Yuanshi*), Tamura Jitsuzô 田村實造, comp., 3 vols., Jimbun, 1961–63. Cannot be relied upon for completeness.

[24] *Yuanshi renming suoyin* 元史人名索引, Yao Jing'an 姚景安, comp., Zhonghua, 1982.

Un Code des Yuan, Paul Ratchnevsky, vol., 1, Leroux, 1937; vol. 2 (PUF, 1972); vol. 3, (with Françoise Aubin), *Index* (PUF, 1977); vol. 4, Collège de France: Institut des Hautes Etudes Chinoises, 1985. This is an annotated translation with a long introduction (vol. 1) and index (vol. 3) of the monograph on penal law of the *Yuanshi* (*juan* 102–105).

The Military Establishment of the Yuan Dynasty, Ch'i-ch'ing Hsiao, HUP, 1978, contains a translation of *Yuanshi, juan* 98, "Bingzhi 兵制" (military system) and *juan* 99, "Zhenshu 陣屬" and "Suwei 宿衛" (imperial guards).

Yuanchao bishi 元朝秘史 (The secret history of the Mongols). A Mongolian account of their own history, essential for the reigns of Chinggis Khan and Ögödei. The Mongolian original having been lost, the text had to be reconstructed from a thirteenth-century phonetic transcription into Chinese characters.[25]

Shengwu qinzheng lu 聖武親征錄 (Record of the personal campaigns of the holy warrior) contains a more detailed chronological account of the reigns of Chinggis Khan and Ögödei than found in the *Yuanshi*.[26] It was based on a Mongolian chronicle which was also used by Rashîd al-Din in the preparation of his chronicle, *Jâmi 'al-Tavârîkh*. Parts of Rashîd (on Ögödei, Güyüg and Möngke) have been translated into

---

[25] *The secret history of the Mongols: For the First Time Done into English out of the Original Tongue, and Provided with an Exegetical Commentary*, Francis Woodman Cleaves (1911–95), tr., vol. 1, HUP, 1982 (set in type 1956). The author delayed publication for 26 years not wishing to disagree publicly with his teacher, William Hung, who had written some views on the *Secret History* in *HJAS* in 1951 with which he disagreed.

Igor de Rachewiltz, *Index to the Secret History of the Mongols*, IUP, 1972; the same author has also translated the *Secret History*. See also *Menggu bishi* 蒙古秘史 (The secret history of the Mongols), originally called *Tuobu chiyan* 脫卜赤顏 (*Yuanchao bishi* 元朝秘史), Menggu renmin, 1980. *Yuanchao bishi tongjian* 元朝秘史通檢), Zhonghua, 1986.

[26] *Histoire des campagnes de Gengis Khan*, Paul Pelliot and Louis Hambis, tr., Brill, 1951.

English in John Boyle, *The Successors of Ghenghis Khan: Translated from the Persian of Rashîd al-Din* , Col. UP, 1971.

Yuan dianzhang 元典章 (Compendium of Statutes and Sub-statutes of the Yuan, or, more concisely, Institutions of the Yuan dynasty), 1322; the Shen Jiaben 沈家本 (1908) edition was superseded in 1972 with the publication of a facsimile of the original revised and expanded 1303 edition.[27] "The text consists of a huge collection of codes, ordinances, precedents, cases and bureaucratic notes, thus reflecting the rich variety of the legal and social life of the Yuan dynasty."[28] Because so much of the text is "in the peculiar style of the Yüan period colloquial Chinese and further reflects, in many cases, the diction and grammar of Mongolian documents that underlie the Chinese texts, it has been difficult to read and also is offensive to cultivated Chinese because of the crudeness of its language."[29]

> *Gentenshô sakuin kô* 元典章索引稿 (Draft index to the *Yuan dianzhang*), 3 vols., Jimbun, 1957; Taibei rpnt., 1973.

> *Gentenshô nendai sakuin* 元典章年代索引 (Chronological index to the *Yuan dianzhang*), Uematsu Tadashi 植松正, comp., Dôhôsha, 1980.

48.5.2   Other Textual Sources

Da Yuan tongzhi tiaoge 大元通制條格 (Comprehensive Regulations and Statutes of the Yuan), 1321; 1930; rpnt., 2 vols., Taibei, 1968. There is a detailed but fragmentary index: *Tsûsei jôkaku. Kendai tsûki mokuji*

---

[27] *Da Yuan shengzheng guochao dianzhang* 大元聖政國朝典章, 16 *ce*, Taibei: Palace Museum, 1972. Uematsu Tadashi 植松正 reviews Japanese scholarship on the *Yuan dianzhang* in "Institutions of the Yuan Dynasty and Yuan Society," *Gest Library Journal* 5 (Spring 1992), 57–69.

[28] Paul Heng-chao Ch'en, *Chinese Legal Tradition under the Mongols: the Code of 1291 as Reconstructed*, PUP, 1979. This is a reconstruction and translation of the *Zhiyuan xinge* 至元新格, a set of regulations rather than a formal code (*lü* 律).

[29] Frederick W. Mote, "A Note on Traditional Sources for Yüan History," in *CHC*, vol. 6, 697–98.

sakuin 通制條格憲臺通記目次索引, mimeo, Kyoto, 1954. Annotated translation: *Tsûsei jôkaku no kenkyû yakuchû dai-issatsu* 通制條格の研究譯注第一册, Tokyo, 1964.

Jingshi dadian 經世大典 (Compendium for Administering the Empire), 1330–31. Only fragments survive.

Koryŏsa 高麗史: for this and other Korean sources, see 42.4.

Xin Yuanshi 新元史 (New Standard History of the Yuan), Ke Shaomin 柯劭忞 (1850–1933), 1922; Kaiming shudian, *Ershiwu shi*, Shanghai, 1935; Taibei, 1962–29. Covers the years 1206–1307.

Note the sources used and the bibliographies in Paul Ratchnevsky, *Genghis Khan, His Life and Legacy*, Blackwell, 1991 and Morris Rossabi, *Khubilai Khan: His Life and Times*, UCP, 1988.

Bieji 別集

Yuanren wenji pianmu fenlei suoyin 元人文集篇目分類索引, Lu Junling 陸峻嶺, Zhonghua, 1979. Contains detailed indexes to the tables of contents of the *bieji* of 151 Yuan authors; three general collections; and 16 early Ming *bieji*. The contents of all these collections are indexed under three major categories: (1) biographical; (2) historical; (3) literary and miscellaneous. The first section is subdivided into men, women, Buddhists, Daoists and those with a surname but no given name. The second contains items arranged under seven subdivisions, namely politics, taxes and labor service, education, army, law, manufacturing and peasant uprisings. The third is arranged by *Sibu* categories. The miscellaneous section is subdivided into birds, beasts, insects and fish; plants and trees; food and drink; utensils, and so forth.

Yuanren wenji banben mulu 元人文集版本目錄 (Catalog of editions of collected works of Yuan persons), Zhou Qingpeng 周清膨, Nanjing daxue, 1983.

Nihon genson 日本現存 *Genjin bunshû mokuroku* 元人文集目錄 (Catalog of collected works by Yuan authors extant in Japanese libraries), Yamane Yukio 山根幸夫 and Ogawa Takashi 小川尚 compiled and published, Tokyo, 1970.

Genjin bunshû shiryô sakuin 元人文集史料索引 (Index to Historical Materials in Yuan collected works), Jimbun, mimeo, 1960. Indexes some 4,000 proper names and historical terms from 23 Yuan collected works.

Biji 筆記

Yuan *biji* are discussed by Herbert Franke in "Some Aspects of Chinese Private Historiography in the Thirteenth and Fourteenth Century," in *Historians of China and Japan*, William G. Beasley and Edwin G. Pulleyblank, eds., OUP, 1961, 115–34. For an example of one type of information which can be drawn from them, the social history of the Yuan, see Shi Weimin 史衛民, *Yuandai shehui shenghuoshi* 元代社會生活史.[30]

Shanju xinhua 山居新話 (New talk from a mountain dwelling), Yang Yu 楊瑀 (1285–1361), Herbert Franke, tr., *Beiträge zur Kulturgeschichte Chinas unter der Mongolenherrschaft*, Steiner, 1956.

Gengshen waishi 庚申外史 (Unofficial history of [the emperor born in] 1320), Quan Heng 權衡 (second half of fourteenth century), 1369. *Das Keng-shen wai-shih: Eine Quelle zur späten Mongolenzeit*, Helmut Schulte-Uffelage, tr. and ed., Berlin: Akademie Verlag, 1963. Covers the years 1333–68 in annals style.

Chuogeng lu 輟耕錄 (Records compiled after returning from the farm), Tao Zongyi 陶宗儀 (1316–1403), c. 1366. *CFS Concordance* 13).[31]

Shuofu 說郛 (Sayings within a city wall), Tao Zongyi 陶宗儀. This massive compilation and its seventeenth-century continuation, *Shuofu xu* 說郛續 (Sequel to the *Shuofu*), contains abstracts of mainly fictional *biji* from earliest times to the fourteenth and sixteenth centuries.

Agriculture

Nongshu 農書, Wang Zhen 王禎, (35.1).

48.5.3   Archaeology

The Yuan capital of Shangdu 上都 (the Xanadu of Coleridge's poem "Kubla Khan," 1816) was the alternative capital to Dadu 大都 (Beijing) following a brief period (1260–63) when it was capital of the parts of China then controlled by Khubilai. It is situated near Zhenglan 正藍 in Inner Mongolia. In the 1950s

---

[30] *Yuandai shehui shenghuo shi* (History of social life in the Yuan dynasty), Shehui kexue, 1996.

[31] See Frederick W. Mote, *T'ao Tsung-i and His "Cho Keng Lu"*, Ph.D, Univ. of Washington, 1954.

military farms were built using the bricks from the city walls. Excavations of the palace at Shangdu were begun in 1992.

A Journey into China's Antiquity, vol. 4: *Yuan, Ming, Qing*, National Museum of Chinese History, eds., Morning Glory, 1998. See 8.2.1 on this authoritatively commented series of photographs of the collections of the museum.

48.5.4   Guides and Research Tools

The best introductions in English to the historiography of the Yuan are the "Bibliographical Essays" in *CHC*, vol. 6, 689–726. The first essay is "A Note on Traditional Sources for Yüan History," by Frederick W. Mote (689–99). See also Herbert Franke, "Chinese Historiography under Mongol Rule," in *China Under Mongol Rule*, Variorum, 1994, 15–26.

Yuanshixue gaishuo 元史學概説 (Introduction to the study of Yuan history), Yang Zhijiu 楊志玖, Li Zhi'an 李治安 and Wang Xiaoxin 王曉欣, eds., Tianjin jiaoyu, 1989. Introduces primary sources and gives the state of the field in Chinese Yuan studies.

David M. Farquhar, *The Government of China under Mongolian Rule, A Reference Guide*, Steiner, 1990. Contains brief but wide-ranging notes on all central and local government institutions.

Language

Yuan yuyan cidian 元語言詞典 (Dictionary of Yuan language), Yuan Bin 袁賓, ed., Shanghai jiaoyu, 1998. This is in the series *Jindai Hanyu duandai yuyan cidian xilie* 近代漢語詞典系列 (Single-period dictionaries of early Mandarin). The dictionary covers mainly popular literature of the Yuan as well as plays, poetry, *biji* 筆記, historical biographies and so forth. It is intended both for historical linguists and for readers of the popular literature of the period. It replaces the not too reliable *Song-Yuan yuyan cidian* 宋元語言詞典 (Dictionary of Song and Yuan language), Long Qian'an 龍潛庵, Shanghai cishu, 1985. Contains 11,000 entries drawn nearly one thousand Song and Yuan sources including plays, novels, *biji*, poetry and recorded sayings.

Biographies

In the Service of the Khan: Eminent Personalities of the Early Mongol Yuan Period (1200–1300), Igor de Rachewiltz, Hok-lam Chan, Hsiao Ch'i-ch'ing and Peter W. Grier, Harrassowitz, 1993. Includes extensive biographies of 37 people.

Repertory of Proper Names in Yuan Literary Sources, Igor de Rachewiltz and May Wang, 4 vols., SMC, 1988. Replaces two earlier indexes to biographical materials,[32] as well as complementing and supplementing other biographical indexes for the Yuan including:

Yuanren zhuanji ziliao suoyin 元人傳記資料索引 (Index to Biographical Materials of Yuan Figures), Wang Deyi 王德毅 and Li Rongcun 李榮村 et al., comp., Xin Wenfeng, 5 vols., 1979–82; Zhonghua, 1987. Contains materials on 16,000 people, from 800 sources. Volume 5 contains a stroke-count index of alternative names.

Ryô, Kin, Genjin denki sakuin 遼金元人傳記索引 (Index to biographies of Liao, Jin and Yuan persons), Umehara Kaoru 梅原郁 and Kinugawa Tsuyoshi 衣川強, comps., Jimbun, 1972. There are 3,200 individuals listed; 130 *bieji* were consulted.

Song-Yuan fangzhi zhuanji suoyin 宋元方志傳記索引 (Index to the Biographies in Song and Yuan local gazetteers), Zhu Shijia 朱士嘉, Beijing, 1963, which includes 3,949 people in 33 gazetteers.

Huizu renwu zhi, Yuandai 回族人物志·元代 (Biographies of Islamic people, Yuan dynasty), Bai Shouyi 白壽彝, Ningxia renmin, 1985. The first of four volumes of Islamic biographies.

Ch'en Yuan, *Westerners and Central Asians in China under the Mongols: their Transformation into Chinese*, tr. and annotated by Luther Carrington Goodrich, *MS* Monograph, Los Angeles: UCP, 1966; rpnt., Steyler, 1989.

Geography

Zhongguo lishi ditu ji 中國歷史地圖集 (The Historical Atlas of China), Tan Qixiang 譚其驤, ed. in chief, vol. 7, *Yuan-Ming shiqi* 元明時期, 2nd rev. ed., 2nd prnt., Ditu, 1985.

Eleven gazetteers are known to have been compiled in the Yuan. For their titles, see Zhang Guogan 張國淦, *Zhongguo gu fangzhi kao* 中國古方志考 (Critical notes on old Chinese gazetteers), Zhonghua, 1962.

Societies and Journals

Journal of Song-Yuan Studies (began as *Sung Studies Newsletter*, 1969–80, changed title to *Bulletin of Sung-Yuan Studies*, 1980–88; adopted the present title in 1989). A good way of keeping up-to-date with new

---

[32] See *H-Y Index* 35 for Yuan collections as well as Igor de Rachewiltz et al., comps., *Index to Biographical Material in Chin and Yuan Literary Works*, ANU Press, 3 vols., 1970–79.

work in this field. Contains translations of the annual *Shigaku zasshi* state-of-the-field articles on Five Dynasties, Song and Yuan.

Research Society for Yuan History (*Yuanshi yanjiu hui* 元史研究會), founded in 1980, Shekeyuan. Edits collected articles on Yuan history, see, for example, *Yuanshi luncong* 元史論叢 6, Shehui kexue, 1996.

49

Ming

1368–1644

The Ming is richly documented. It is the first dynasty from which the Veritable Records of most of the reigns survive. More than 200 works of official history and many more private ones were written. The collected works of some 1,500 Ming authors are extant. There are also about 1,000 Ming local gazetteers.[1] Ming land deeds, merchant records and other private documents are dealt with together with similar sources from the Qing (50.4).

49.1 Main Historical Works

Ming Shilu 明實錄 (Veritable Records of the Ming). Official title: *Da Ming Shilu* 大明實錄 or *Huang Ming Shilu* 皇明實錄. Given the fact that almost none of the Ming central government archives have survived, the single most important set of sources for Ming history are the Veritable Records of 13 of the 16 Ming reigns. They were compiled after the death of an emperor and were based on archival documents,

[1] Zhu Yuanzhang 朱元璋, the first emperor of the Ming 明, took the dynastic name Ming 明 from the title of his ward, the Red Turban leader Han Lin'er 韓林兒 (d. 1367), the Young Prince of Radiance (Xiaoming wang 小明王). It was a word filled with the promise of the reappearance of the light of Manichean (*Mingjiao* 明教) reversal and the coming of the Maitreya Buddha to rule the world; see *CHC*, 7, 51.

especially edicts and memorials. The Ming was unusual in that the *Qijuzhu* 起居注 (Court Diaries), were not kept for 200 years, presumably out of a desire to maintain secrecy by excluding the note takers (see next main entry, *Wanli qijuzhu*). The *Ming Shilu* are of an uneven quality because of the biases of their compilers and the responsible grand secretary. Although they were not intended for publication, various drafts circulated and have survived (including some that made their way to Japan during the Edo period). The best modern edition is the facsimile reproduction of the manuscript in the former National Library of Beiping and now in the Shiyusuo: *Ming Shilu* 明實錄, 3,045 *juan* in 133 vols., with appendixes (29 vols.) and corrections (21 vols.), Shiyusuo, 1961–66; rpnt., 1984; Zhonghua, 1987. See *ISMH*, 30–33; *CHC*, vol. 7, 746–52.

There are a number of modern collections of excerpts from the Veritable Records—for example:

Mindai Man-Mô shiryô Min jitsuroku shô, Manshuhen, Mokohen 明代滿蒙史料明實錄抄滿洲篇蒙古篇 (41.4.1).

Ming Shilu Beijing shiliao 明實錄北京史料 (Historical materials from the Veritable Records of the Ming on Beijing), Zhao Qichang 趙其昌, ed., 4 vols., Beijing guji, 1995.

Ming Shilu jingji ziliao xuanbian 明實錄經濟資料選編 (Economic materials from the Veritable Records of the Ming), Guo Hou'an 郭厚安, ed. in chief, Shehui kexue, 1989.

Ming Shilu leizuan 明實錄類纂 (Veritable Records of the Ming by category), Li Guoxiang 李國祥 and Yang Chang 楊昶, eds., 20 vols., Wuhan, 1990–96. This large-scale series contains volumes of excerpts on numerous subjects such as the economy, officials, law, foreign affairs, the examination system, science, natural disasters, biographies (more than 2,000 of them in the form in which they were entered in the *Shilu* under the date of their subject's death), Beijing, Anhui, Sichuan, Shandong and women.

Ming Shilu youguan Yunnan lishi ziliao zhaichao 明實錄有關雲南歷史資料摘抄 (see 39.3 and 40.3 under *Excerpts* for more titles).

Wanli qijuzhu 萬曆起居注 (Court Diaries of the Wanli era), 9 vols., Beijing daxue, 1988. These records, which had not been kept for the first 200 years of the Ming are an invaluable source for the years 1573–1615. They total 7,512 pages.

Mingshi 明史 (Standard History of the Ming), Zhang Tingyu 張廷玉 (1672–1755) et al., 1739, covers the years 1368–1644; 28 vols., Zhonghua, 1974; 5th prnt., 1995.[2] The sections on Ming relations with the Jianzhou 建州 Jurchen should be treated with care. There is a personal-name index.[3] There are also a number of translations of various parts of the *Mingshi*. Note especially:

Minshi Shokkashi yakuchû 明史食貨志譯注 (Integral translation with notes on the monograph on financial administration in the *Mingshi*), Wada Sei 和田清 (1890–1963) and pupils, trs. and eds., 2 vols., Tôyô bunko, 1957; new edition, edited by Yamane Yukio, Kyûko, 1996. The translation is in *Kanbun* while the notes are in current Japanese; the Chinese original is appended and there is an index. In the new edition, errors have been corrected, the old bibliography removed and updated references inserted into the text.

See also *Mingshi shihuozhi jiaozhu* 明史食貨志校注, Li Xun 李洵, ed., Zhonghua, 1982.

There are also indexes available to various sections of the *Mingshi*—for example, the monographs on penal law and on offices:

Minshi Keihôshi sakuin 明史刑法志索引, Noguchi Tetsurô 野口鐵郎, Kokusho kankôkai, 1981.

---

[2] Thomas A. Wilson, "Confucian Sectarianism and the Compilation of the Ming History," *LIC* 15.2: 53–84 (1994); Li Jinhua 李晉華, *Mingshi zuanxiu kao* 明史纂修考 (A History of the Compilation of the Standard History of the Ming), *Yenching Journal of Chinese Studies*, Monograph 3, 1933; rpnt., Shanghai shudian, 1992.

[3] *Mingshi renming suoyin* 明史人名索引 (Index to personal names in the *Mingshi*), Li Yumin 李裕民, comp., 2 vols., Zhonghua, 1985. Includes not only all Ming names, but names from Song, Yuan and Qing. References to *ce, juan* and page number of the Zhonghua punctuated edition of the *Mingshi* (1974).

Frank Münzel, *Strafrecht im alten China nach den Strafrechtskapiteln in den Ming-Annalen*, Harrassowitz, 1968. Annotated translation of the first section of *Mingshi* "Xingfazhi 刑法志."

Guoque 國榷 (Evaluation of the work of our dynasty), Tan Qian 談遷 (1594–1658), 1656; 6 vols., typeset ed., Guji, 1958. Useful for basic chronology. Also in some cases has a clearer account than the *Mingshi*, especially of Ming relations with the Jianzhou 建州 Jurchen.

Mingshi jishi benmo 明史紀事本末, Gu Yingtai 谷應泰 (1620–90), comp., 1658. Recounts 80 or so of the main events or *causes célèbres* of the dynasty.[4] Based in part on sources no longer extant.

Mingji 明紀, Chen He 陳鶴 (1757–1811) and Chen Kejia 陳克家 (d. 1860), 1871.

Ming tongjian 明通鑑, Xia Xie 夏燮 (1799–1875), 1873. In part corrects errors and omissions in the *Mingshi*; includes copious references to the sources used.[5]

49.2   Other Textual Sources

Geography

Da Ming yitongzhi 大明一統志 (Comprehensive gazetteer of the great Ming), Li Xian 李賢 et al., comp., 1461; photographic reprint of original palace edition, 10 vols., Taibei, 1965; 2 vols., San-Qin, 1990.

Tianxia junguo libing shu 天下郡國利病書 (4.5.4).

---

[4] Originally entitled *Mingchao* 明朝; later the title was changed to *Mingshi jishi benmo* 明史紀事本末 (The major events of Ming history), 10 vols., Shangwu, 1935–37; Taibei Wanyou wenku rpnt., 1956; Zhonghua, 1985.

[5] There is a partial French translation of one of the continuations of the *Zizhi tongjian gangmu* 資治通鑑綱目 by L. C. Delamarre, *Histoire de la dynastie des Ming*, Paris, 1865. It is a translation of the first part of *Zizhi tongjian gangmu sanbian* 資治通鑑綱目三編 (1746), the third continuation of the *Gangmu*.

Dushi fangyu jiyao 讀史方輿紀要 (4.5.4).

Local Gazetteers

About 1,000 gazetteers survive from the Ming. There is a listing of 900 of them in *ISMH*. Timothy Brook, *Geographical Sources of Ming-Qing History*, Michigan monographs in Chinese studies no. 58, Ann Arbor, 1988, covers also topographical and institutional gazetteers. Some gazetteers describe, or collect materials on, Nanjing and Beijing, for example, *Dijing jingwulüe* 帝京景物略 (Brief account of the sights of the imperial capital), Liu Tong 明劉侗 (1594–1637), 1635. It covers gardens, temples, imperial tombs, famous sites, rivers, bridges, flora and fauna, insects and fish, anecdotes and personalities of Beijing in the late Ming. There are also plenty of Ming *biji* recording city life (especially that of Nanjing, see below, *Biji*).

Tianyige cang Mingdai fangzhi xuankan 天一閣藏明代方志選刊 (Selected [107] Ming dynasty gazetteers from the Tianyige Library); 119 vols. Shanghai guji, 1963–65; 68 boxes, 1981–83. This famous, private Ningbo library originally held 435 Ming local gazetteers. Now the collection numbers 271. There is an index to biographical materials and personal names in these gazetteers, see below under *Biographies*.

Nihon genson 日本現存 *Mindai chihôshi mokuroku* 明代地方志目錄, Yamane Yukio 山根幸夫, ed., Tôyô bunko, 1962; enlarged, 1971; new edition, Kyûko, 1995. Arranged by province; contains references to 710 Ming dynasty gazetteers held in Japanese collections.

Merchant Route Books (Luchengshu 路程書)

See 50.4.3.

Travel

The most famous traveler inside China of the Ming was Xu Xiake 徐霞客 (1586–1641), *Xu Xiake [Xu Hongzu] youji* 徐霞客 [徐弘祖] 遊記 (4.6).

The most famous overseas Ming voyages were those of Zheng He 鄭和. The main sources on these and other Ming overseas travels are given in 41.5.1 (*Ming*).

Laws and Institutions

Start with John D. Langlois, Jr., "Ming Law," in *CHC*, vol. 8, CUP, 1998, 172–220.

Huang Ming zhishu 皇明制書, Zhang Lu 張鹵, ed., 1579; 2 vols., Koten kenkyûkai, 1966–67.

> *Ming Dagao yanjiu* 明大誥研究 (Research on the great pronouncements of the Ming), Yang Yifan 楊一凡, Jiangsu renmin, 1988. Reprints, collates and punctuates four different proclamations of the *Dagao*. See also the same author's *Hongwu falü dianji kaozheng* 洪武法律典籍考證 (Study of the legal codes of the Hongwu period), Falü, 1992.

Da Ming lü 大明律 (The great Ming code), 27.3.

Da Ming ling 大明令 (The great Ming statutes), 27.4.

Zhusi zhizhang 諸司職掌 (Statutes of the central administration), 1393 and 1458.

Mingdai tiaoli 明代條例 (Regulations and precedents of the Ming).

Huang Ming tiaofa shilei zuan 皇明條法事類纂 (27.3).

Ming huiyao 明會要 (Table 24, 26.1).

Da Ming huidian 大明會典 (Institutes of the great Ming).

> Four editions were compiled.[6] Two are extant: the first was completed in 1503 and revised in 1509 and printed in 1511 (the sixth year of *Zhengde* 正德). It is therefore referred to as the *Zhengde* edition. It covers the years 1368 to 1479.[7] The second was ordered in 1576 and printed in 1587 and it is therefore referred to as the *Wanli* 萬曆 edition. It covers the years 1479 to 1584.[8] The *huidian* were based on

[6] The first was ordered in 1474 and completed in 1479, but it was not printed and it has not survived; the third was ordered in 1529 and completed in 1550, but it has not survived.

[7] Rpnt., 3 vols., Kyûko, 1989.

[8] *Wanli huidian*, punctuated rpnt., 40 vols., Wanyou wenku, Shangwu, 1936; fac. rpnt. Taibei: Dongnan shubaoshe, 5 vols., 1963; Xinwenfeng, 1976; Zhonghua reduced-size edition, 1989. See Yamane Yukio 山根幸夫, "Min Shin no kaiten 明清の會典" (The institutes of the Ming and Qing), chap. 17 of *Chûgoku hôseishi kihon shiryô no kenkyû* 中國法制

Footnote continued on next page

early statutes and regulations such as the *Da Ming ling* (27.4). The *huidian* are not legal works, but collections of documents showing the workings of the main organs of government, their administrative procedures, precedents and historical development. As such they are very important sources for institutional and political history.

During the Ming dynasty, many individual branches of the administration printed their rules and regulations in handbooks such as the *Nanjing hubu zhi* 南京戶部志.[9] For a list of such works which have survived see *ISMH*, 181–84.

Xu Wenxian tongkao 續文獻通考, Wang Qi 王圻, comp. (26.2).

Edicts and Memorials

Memorials, edicts and many other documents may not have survived in the archives, but many thousands were collected and printed together during the Ming, either in general collections or in individual collections of an official (often in his collected works). *ISMH*, 119–75, lists approximately 300 collections of Ming memorials (arranged by author, by topic or by period). To supplement *ISMH*, check the collected works of the officials whose memorials are being traced (see below under *Bieji*).

Huang Ming jingshi wenbian 皇明經世文編 (Ming literature on statecraft), Chen Zilong 陳子龍 (1608–47) et al., comp., 1638. The most important topically arranged collection of Ming memorials (and other writings). The 3,145 entries (which are quoted in full) were selected from hundreds of *bieji* and other sources written by 430 senior officials during the course of the Ming, both in the central government and in the provinces. Many of the sources quoted have since been lost, hence the value of this collection. The intention of the chief compilers (childhood friends from the Yangzi delta and Ming loyalists) was to concentrate their readers'

史基本資料の研究 (Chinese legal history, studies on basic source materials), Shiga Shûzô 滋賀秀三, ed., Tokyo daigaku, 1993; rpnt., 1994.

[9] *Nanjing hubu zhi* (Monograph of the Nanjing board of finance), Xie Bin 謝彬, comp., 1550.

minds at a time of impending disaster. The emphasis therefore is on practical matters of government and administration, especially national security. The arrangement is by
author and by subject matter in a chronological frame. The
book was banned during the Qing.[10]

Huang Ming zhaoling 皇明詔令 (Edicts of the Ming), Fu Feng-
xiang 傅鳳翔, comp., 1539, 1548; 4 vols., Chengwen, 1967,
contains edicts of Ming emperors between 1366 and 1547.
For four other such collections, see *ISMH*, 199–200.

Bieji 別集

There are at least 1,500 extant collected works of individual
Ming authors. Note that *ISMH* (126–70) lists 209 Ming *bieji*
containing a minimum of three memorials.

Yuanren wenji pianmu fenlei suoyin 元人文集篇目分類索引, Lu Junling
陸峻嶺, Zhonghua, 1979. Contains detailed indexes to the tables of
contents of the *bieji* not only of Yuan authors, but also of 16 early
Ming *bieji*. For further details, see 48.4.

Zôtei Nihon genson 增訂日本現存 *Minjin bunshû mokuroku* 明人文集目
錄 (Catalog of collected works [by 1,400 Ming authors] extant in
Japanese collections), Yamane Yukio 山根幸夫, comp., enlarged and
rev., Tokyo joshi daigaku 東京女子大學, 1978.

Biji 筆記

ISMH (98–118), lists and comments on 75 Ming *biji* and *zashi*
presenting direct information on the political and social history
of the period. Xie Guozhen 謝國楨 in *Ming-Qing biji tancong*
明清筆記談叢 discusses 19.[11] Below are listed 18 outstanding

---

[10] *Ming jingshi wenbian* (based on four separate editions collated and
photolithographically printed), 6 vols., Zhonghua, 1962 (includes a name-
index); 3rd rpnt., 1997; Guofeng, photolithographic edition, 1964. Note
Mindai keiseibun bunrui mokuroku 明代經世文編分類目錄 (Classified
index to Ming literature on statecraft), Tôyô bunko, 1986. Indexes 11 of
the main Ming collections of essays on statecraft.

[11] *Ming-Qing biji tancong* (Collection of notes on Ming-Qing *biji*),
Shanghai: Zhonghua, 1960; enlarged ed., 1962; new ed., 1981. The author
discusses 48 *biji* of which 19 were written in the Ming.

Ming *biji* starting with several examples devoted to Nanjing (note also the examples of Ming *zashi* listed in chap. 24 and the Kyoto *biji* indexes in chap. 31):

Banqiao zaji 板橋雜記 (Miscellaneous records from the wooden bridge), Yu Huai 余懷 (1616–96), ca. 1695. Howard S. Levy, tr., *A Feast of Mist and Flowers*, Yokohama, 1966. Reminiscences of the Nanjing actors and singing girls encountered by the author in his youth before the Manchu conquest.

Chunming mengyu lu 春明夢余錄 (Record of dreams of the capital), Sun Chengze 孫承澤 (1592–1676), early Qing. Details on the buildings and institutions of Beijing in the Ming.

Diangu jiwen 典故紀聞 (Records of institutions and anecdotes), Yu Jideng 余繼登, Wanli; punctuated ed., Zhonghua, 1981. Exceptionally well informed. The author had access to the Wanli Court Diaries and Veritable Records of the previous reigns; covers first 200 years of Ming history.

Gengji bian 庚己編 (Written between 1510 and 1519), Lu Can 陸粲 (1494–1591); punctuated ed., Zhonghua, 1987. Printed together with *Kezuo zhuiyu* 客座贅語.

Jinling fancha zhi 金陵梵刹志 (Monographs on the Buddhist temples of Nanjing), 1627.

Jinling suoshi 金陵瑣事 (Nanjing trifles), Zhou Hui 周暉, 1610. Indexed in *Chûgoku zuihitsu zatcho sakuin*. Notes on life in Nanjing to 1607.

Jinyan 今言 (Contemporary words), Zheng Xiao 鄭曉 (1499–1566), 1566; punctuated ed., Zhonghua, 1984. Mainly court and institutional matters of early Ming.

Kezuo zhuiyu 客座贅語 (Idle talk with guests), Gu Qiyuan 顧起元 (1565–1628), 1617; punctuated ed., Zhonghua, 1987. Notes on life in Nanjing. Printed together with *Gengji bian* 庚己編.

Qixiu leigao 七修類稿 (Draft arranged in seven categories), Lang Ying 郎瑛 (1487–1566); punctuated ed., Zhonghua, 1959. Historical and political notes. For index, see *Chûgoku zuihitsu sakuin*.

Shaoshi shanfang bicong 少室山房筆叢 (Jottings from Shaoshi mountains study), Hu Yinglin 胡應麟 (1551–1602), punctuated ed., Zhonghua, 1958. The author's study was named after the Shaoshi mountains, Henan.

Shuidong riji 水東日記 (Diary written east of the river [Songjiang 淞江]), Ye Sheng 葉盛 (1420–74), punctuated ed., Zhonghua, 1980. Mainly historical and institutional subjects of early Ming plus snippets from Song, Yuan and Ming writers.

Songchuang mengyu 松窗夢語 (Sleep talk from a pine window), Zhang Han 張瀚 (1511-93). Thirty-three notes based on the author's experience as an official and also on conditions in his native Zhejiang. One of these notes, on merchants, has been translated (50.4.3).

[*Wanli*] *yehuo bian* 萬曆野獲編 (Harvested in the wilds [during the Wanli period]), Shen Defu 沈德符 (1578-1642), punctuated ed., 3 vols., Zhonghua, 1959; 2nd ed., 1980; *Chûgoku zuihitsu zatsusho sakuin*. One of the most famous of the Ming *biji*, it covers a wide variety of topics.

Wu zazu 五雜組 (Five assorted offerings), Xie Zhaozhe 謝肇淛 (1567-1624), punctuated ed., Zhonghua, 1955. The five categories referred to in the title are the traditional heaven, earth, man, things and events.

Yongchuang xiaopin 湧幢小品 (Springing from the oceans stele study trifles), Zhu Guozhen 朱國禎 (1558-1632), 1622; punctuated ed., Shanghai: Xinwenhua shushe 新文化書社, 1935; Zhonghua, 1959; *Chûgoku zuihitsu sakuin*. Written between 1609 and 1621. On this title, see 9.9.

Yueshi bian 閱世編 (Seeing the world), Ye Mengzhu 葉夢珠 (1624-ca. 1693), punctuated ed., Shanghai guji, 1981. Songjiang 松江 conditions and institutions in the late Ming, early Qing. His comments on taxes and labor service have been translated by Clara Yu in *Chinese Civilization: A Sourcebook*, Patricia Ebrey, ed., 1981; 2nd ed., rev. and expanded, Free Press, 1993, 282-6.

Yutang congyu 玉堂叢語 (Miscellaneous recordings from the Hanlin academy), Jiao Hong 焦竑 (1541-1620), 1618; punctuated ed., Zhonghua, 1981. The Yutang was one name for the academy.

Zaolin zazu 棗林雜俎 (Miscellaneous offerings from Zaolin), Tan Qian 談遷 (1594-1658), 1644; *Chûgoku zuihitsu zatsusho sakuin*. Notes on a wide variety of subjects. The author's ancestors had taken refuge on several occasions at Zaolin in Hainingxian 海寧縣.

Agriculture

Nongzheng quanshu 農政全書 (35.1).

Merchants

On Ming merchants and route books, see 50.4.3.

Technology and Science

Bencao gangmu 本草綱目 (chap. 36).

Tiangong kaiwu 天工開物 (37.1).

Lu Ban jing 魯班經 (37.3).

Foreign Works

The Korean Veritable Records (*Choson wangjo sillok* 朝鮮皇朝 實錄) were modeled after the Chinese and contain materials not found in Chinese sources. The Yi dynasty (1392–1910) covered almost the full span of the Ming and Qing. For excerpts on this and other sources, see 42.4.

49.3   *Central Archives*

The largest central archive during the Ming dynasty was the Houhuku 後湖庫 in Nanjing. It was built in 1381 under the personal supervision of the Hongwu emperor on the islands of the Back Lake (the Houhu, present-day Xuanwu Lake 玄武湖) for security and as a precaution against fire. Here were stored growing mountains of *huangce* 黄冊 (yellow registers), and *yulin tuce* 魚鱗圖冊 (fish-scale registers) population counts, used for calculating labor services and maps for calculating land taxes. At the beginning of the dynasty there were only six archive buildings. By the end of the sixteenth century there were 667 buildings holding 1,790,000 records, but the system was beginning to break down. The windows were not regularly opened and broken shelving was left unrepaired. The entire archive eventually went up in flames at the collapse of the dynasty.[12]

The most prestigious archives built by the Ming were the imperial historical archives (Huangshicheng 皇史宬) just to the east of the palace in Beijing. They were built in 1534–36 and are still standing today thanks to repairs carried out in 1568, 1807

---

[12] For a contemporary description of this archive at its height, see Zhao Weixian 趙惟賢, *Houhuzhi* 後湖志, preface dated 1513; punctuated ed., Jiangsu guangling guji, 1987.

and 1982. Only two windows light this massive brick and stone building whose vault-like construction resembles a tomb, built to protect the contents from fire, floods, thieves, bandits, insects and rats. The walls are two meters thick. The gables are open to the two high windows at either end of the vault to allow circulation of air. In the long interior the only furnishings are 152 huge gilded, copper-clad storage chests made of camphor wood. Each weighs 155 kilos. They rest on stone plinths like coffins. In them were stored imperial instructions (*xianxun* 賢訓), the *yudie* 玉牒 (Jade Registers, i.e., Imperial Genealogy), the Veritable Records of each reign; the one spare copy of the *Yongle dadian*; and various imperial portraits, congratulatory messages, seals and gifts of foreign rulers (from which came the alternative name of the archives, Biaozhangku 表章庫). The Ming contents of the Huangshicheng were deposited in the Grand Secretariat archive by the Qing emperors, who stored exactly the same types of documents and objects in the archive as had the Ming. The Huangshicheng was partly destroyed by looting during the occupation of Beijing by the Eight Powers in 1900; in 1933, the remainder of the contents were sent to Nanjing and in 1949, part of these went on to Taiwan, part eventually returned to Beijing. The Huangshicheng itself is today a museum open to the public. The original document chests stand empty. The remainder of the Qing contents are housed in the Yishiguan (50.1.1). Only about 3,600 Ming documents are extant, mainly from the Board of War dealing with the late Ming rebellion of Li Zicheng 李自成 and border defense against the Manchus. They were collected and stored in the early Qing in order to complete the Ming History. There are also some land and population records from the early Ming.[13]

In the Ming there were at least 300 provincial and prefectural archives. Most of their contents were destroyed in the fighting

[13] *Mingdai Liaodong dang'an huibian* 明代遼東檔案匯編, 2 vols., Liao-Shen shushe, 1985.

at the end of the dynasty. For lists of official Ming documents published in modern times, see 50.2.

49.4 Archaeology and Inscriptions

The founder of the dynasty, Ming Taizu 明太祖, is buried in the Xiaoling mausoleum (孝陵), Nanjing. The remainder of the Ming emperors are buried at the Ming tombs (Ming shisan ling 明十三陵) at Changping county 昌平縣, north of Beijing. For references to the excavation of the tomb of the Ming emperor Wanli, see 13.2, note 14.

Construction and archaeology have turned up hundreds of tomb inscriptions, including those who lived in the Ming (1,467 stelae are listed in one recent collection; see 3.7, Rong Li-hua, 1993). Collections of inscriptions of all kinds for individual provinces and cities have also been published. Since the Ming inscriptions are often published with those of the Qing, for convenience they are listed in 50.4.5.

Illustrations

Wang Qi 王圻, *Sancai tuhui* 三才圖會 (38.1).

A Journey into China's Antiquity, vol. 4: *Yuan, Ming and Qing*, National Museum of Chinese History, eds., Morning Glory, 1998. See 8.2.1 on this authoritatively commented series of photographs based on the collections of the museum.

49.5 Guides and Research Tools

49.5.1 Guides to Sources

ISMH An Introduction to the Sources of Ming History, Wolfgang Franke, Kuala Lumpur and Singapore: University of Malaya Press, 1968. *ISMH* is an indispensable annotated catalog of 800 primary sources written during the Ming. There is also an unannotated list of 900 Ming local gazetteers. No other work in a Western language contains such an extensive listing of Ming primary sources. The introduction and the discussions of the nine different categories of historical writing in which the book is arranged have been reprinted with minor revisions as a long chapter in *CHC*, vol. 7, *The Ming Dynasty, 1368–*

1644, Part I, Frederick Mote and Denis Twitchett, eds., CUP, 1988, "Historical Writing during the Ming," 726–82.

CHC The contributors to the *CHC* volume on the Ming have written interesting "Bibliographic Notes" to their chapters in which they discuss not only the main primary sources they have used, but also some of their intellectual debts (783–815).

DMB Dictionary of Ming Biography 1368–1644, L. Carrington Goodrich and Chaoying Fang, eds., 2 vols., Col. UP, 1976. Although the *DMB* is a biographical dictionary, it contains a great deal of information on a large number of the main works written or compiled during the Ming. There are detailed personal-name, book title and subject indexes.

Ming History: An Introductory Guide to Research, Edward L. Farmer, Romeyn Taylor and Ann Waltner, comps., University of Minnesota, Department of History, Ming Studies Research Series no. 3, 1994. Contains (1) explanations on such topics as the calendar, people and places (4–64); (2) main primary sources and reference works (65–125); (3) an annotated bibliography of secondary research (127–52); (4) 89 pages of selected Ming documents with 189 pages of vocabulary.

Mingshi yanjiu beilan 明史研究備覽 (Background to research on Ming history), Li Xiaolin 李小林 and Li Shengwen 李晟文, eds. in chief, Tianjin jiaoyu, 1988; rpnt., 1989. Contains an introduction to 330 primary sources, discussion of research themes and a bibliography of secondary scholarship from the Ming period itself up to 1985 (including scholarship in Taiwan, Hong Kong, Japan and the West).

Zhongguo lishi da cidian 中國歷史大辭典 (The great encyclopaedia of Chinese history), 14 vols., Shanghai cishu, 1983– , contains a separate volume on *Mingshi* 明史, Wang Yuquan 王毓銓 and Cao Guilin 曹貴林, eds., 1995. See 8.3.2, item 2 for comments on this encyclopaedia.

49.5.2   *Research Tools*

Biographies

The *DMB* is the first reference to check for biographical information on any Ming figure. It contains some 659 biographies with bibliographic notes and includes foreigners active in Ming China. See also:

Mingren zhuanji ziliao suoyin 明人傳記資料索引 (Index to Biographical Materials of Ming Figures), Chang Bide 昌彼德 et al., comp., 2 vols.,

Taibei: Zhongyang tushuguan 中央圖書館, 1965; 1978; Zhonghua, 1987. More than an index to biographical materials, these excellent volumes give short biographical sketches of some 10,000 individuals followed by detailed references to the sources (528 *bieji*; 65 historical biographies and *biji*, *nianpu*, accounts of conduct and so forth).

ECCP includes several biographies and much important material on the late Ming (50.8.3).

Bashijiu zhong Mingdai zhuanji zonghe yinde 八十九種明代傳記綜合引得 (Combined indices to 89 Ming dynasty biographical collections); 3 vols., *H-Y Index* 24. Ordinary names in vols. 2 and 3; alternative names in vol. 1; references to biographies of about 30,000 Ming figures.

Mingdai difangzhi zhuanji suoyin 明代地方志傳記索引, 2 vols., Dahua, 1986. Includes holdings of Taiwan and Japan and published material, thus expanding *Nihon genson* 日本現存 *Mindai chihôshi denki sakuin kô* 明代地方志傳記索引稿 (Draft index of people with biographies in Ming local gazetteers extant in Japanese collections), Yamane Yukio 山根幸夫, ed., Tôyô bunko, Mindai kenkyû shitsu, 1971, which had included references to biographies of some 30,000 people in 299 Ming gazetteers.

Tianyige cang Mingdai fangzhi xuankan: renwu ziliao renming suoyin 天一閣藏明代方志選刊: 人物資料人名索引 (Index to biographical materials and personal names in selected Ming dynasty gazetteers from the Tianyige Library), 2 vols., Huadong shifan daxue tushuguan gujibu 華東師範大學圖書館古籍部, eds., Shanghai shudian, 1997.

Ming-Qing jinshi timing beilu suoyin 明清進士題名錄索引 gives the names of the 51,624 *jinshi* of the Ming and the Qing and most usefully, also indicates where biographical sources on them may be found (see 3.8.2. On the examination system of the Qing, see Table 22, chap. 22).

Apart from checking the above items, remember to look in the index of *nianpu*, Xie Wei 謝巍, *Zhongguo lidai renwu nianpu kaolu* 中國歷代人物年譜考錄 (3.3). On genealogies, including those of the Ming, see 3.5.

Official Titles and Officeholders

For official titles, use *DOTIC*, which incorporates the author's earlier work on this subject.

For tables of *dufu* 督撫, use *Ming dufu nianbiao* 明督撫年表 (Table of Ming governors-general and governors), Wu Tingxie 吳廷燮, Zhonghua,

1982. This is based on the table in *Ershiwu shi bubian*, but with corrections and the addition of an index.

Geography

Zhongguo lishi dituji 中國歷史地圖集 (The Historical Atlas of China), Tan Qixiang 譚其驤, ed. in chief, vol. 7, *Yuan Ming shiqi* 元明時期, 2nd rev. ed., 2nd prnt., Ditu, 1985.

Mingdai zhengzhi dili yan'ge zongbiao 明代政治地理沿革總表 (Comprehensive tables of changing administrative areas in the Ming period), Niu Pinghan 牛平漢, Zhongguo ditu, 1997.

Chronology

A Synchronic Chinese-Western Daily Calendar, 1341–1661 AD, Keith H. Hazelton, Ming Studies Research Series no. 1, History Department, Univ. of Minnesota, 1984; rev., 1985, provides a computer-generated concordance for every day of the Ming dynasty using the Chinese calendar as the base. Each page contains one year.

Bibliographies and Catalogs of Primary Sources

The most important contemporary catalog of Ming books was the *Qianqingtang shumu* 千頃堂書目, Huang Yuji 黃虞稷 (1629–91). It was based on the author's own private library, which he built up from that of his father, and contains entries for 14,907 works by Ming writers as well as 3,000 works from the pre-Ming, many of which were lost as a result of the Qing literary purges. In the generally suspicious attitude toward the Ming, even this, the major catalog of books written during the Ming, had to circulate in manuscript form for 250 years and was printed only after the fall of the Qing (in the *Shiyuan congshu* 適園叢書, 2nd series, 1912; rpnt., Wenwu, 1992).[14]

The "Yiwenzhi" of the *Mingshi* was based on the *Qianqingtang shumu* and the Zhonghua edition includes four other late Ming/early Qing catalogs. It is also indexed (9.4). Unlike the "Yiwenzhi" in previous Standard Histories, it includes only works written in the Ming and therefore does not include pre-Ming works even if they were still circulating in the Ming.

[14] It has also been reprinted in *Shumu congbian* 書目叢編, 1st series, Guangwen, 1967. There is an author index available: *Senkeidô shomoku choshamei sakuin* 千頃堂書目著者名索引, Mindaishi kenkyû iinkai, Tôyô bunko, 1996.

Mingdai shumu tiba congkan 明代書目題跋叢刊 (Collection of prefaces and colophons from Ming dynasty book catalogs), Feng Huimin 馮惠民 and Li Wanjian 李萬健, comps., 2 vols., Shumu wenxian, 1994.

Xinbian Tianyige shumu 新編天一閣書目 (Newly edited catalog of the Tianyige library), Luo Zhaoping 駱兆平, Zhonghua, 1996, includes the actual library holdings and what it was able to offer in the past, including for the *Siku quanshu*. The Tianyige 天一閣 in Ningbo was built in the Ming. It is the earliest extant private library in China.[15]

Wan-Ming shiji kao 晚明史籍考, Xie Guozhen 謝國楨 (1901–82), Guoli Beiping tushuguan, 1933; rev. and enlarged ed., *Zengding Wan-Ming shiji kao* 增訂晚明史籍考, 3 vols., Shanghai guji, 1981, is an annotated bibliography of 1,400 primary sources for the history of the late Ming/early Qing (1621–62). Many of these sources do not appear in the standard Qing bibliographies. Xie also wrote various other works on Ming primary sources (see 49.2, *Biji*), as well as making collections of sources on *Mingdai shehui jingjishi ziliao xuanbian* 明代社會經濟史資料選編 (Selected social and economic materials from the Ming dynasty), 3 vols., Fujian renmin, 1980–81; *Mingdai nongmin qiyi shiliao xuanbian* 明代農民起義史料選編 (A selection of historical materials on peasant uprisings in the Ming), Fujian renmin, 1982.

Mingmo Qingchu shiliao xuankan 明末清初史料選刊, Zhejiang guji, 1982– .

Xuanlantang congshu 玄覽堂叢書, Zheng Zhenduo 鄭振鐸 (1897–1958), ed. Zheng was the pioneer scholar of popular literature. 1st series, Shanghai, 1941; 2nd series National Central Library, Nanjing; 3rd series, National Central Library, 1948; rpnt., 1955. This collectanea reprints 57 works mainly from the Ming. Zheng Zhenduo also edited another collectanea of rare Ming works (using his alternative name of Renqiu zhuren 紉秋主人), *Mingji shiliao congshu* 明季史料叢書, 1944.

Bibliographies of Secondary Sources

Zhongguo jin bashi nian Mingshi lunzhu mulu 中國近 80 年明史論著目錄 (Catalog of research on the Ming during the last 80 years), Lishisuo, Mingshi yanjiushi 明史研究室, comps., Jiangsu renmin, 1981. Contains citations to some 9,400 Chinese articles and some 600 Chinese

---

[15] The history of the Tianyige is told in Ulrich Stackmann, *Die Geschichte der chinesischen Bibliothek Tian Yi Ge vom 16. Jahrhundert bis in die Gegenwart*, Steiner, 1990.

books on the Ming published 1900–78. Includes Hong Kong and Taiwan publications. Arranged by subject (including historical geography and biography). Has author index.

Mindaishi kenkyû bunken mokuroku 明代史研究文獻目錄 (A Classified Bibliography of Ming Studies in Japan with Korean Ming Studies), Yamane Yukio 山根幸夫, comp., Kyûko, 1993. Includes references to 307 books in Japanese on the Ming and 5,000 articles mainly written between 1950 and 1993. In addition, 269 Korean articles and 6 books are cited. Has author index. Incorporates the Japanese scholarship in the author's earlier bibliography of Ming studies (same title, Tôyô bunko, 1960), but leaves out Chinese scholarship, because of the appearance of the preceding item. Supersedes Richard T. Wang, *Ming Studies in Japan 1961–1981: A Classified Bibliography*, Minneapolis, 1985.

There are a number of state-of-the-field essays on Ming studies—for example:

Evelyn S. Rawski, "Research Themes in Ming-Qing Socioeconomic History—The State of the Field," *JAS* 50.1: 84–111 (February, 1991).

Song Yuanqiang, "The Study of Regional Socio-Economic History in China: Retrospect and Prospects," *LIC* 12.1: 115–31 (June 1991). Surveys research in China.

Harriet T. Zurndorfer, "A Guide to the 'New' Chinese History: Recent Publications Concerning Chinese Social and Economic Development Before 1800," *International Review of Social History*; 33.2: 148–201 (1988). Covers from the Song to 1800. Includes a 16-page bibliography of Western books and articles published between 1970 and 1987.

William Rowe, "Approaches to Modern Chinese Social History," in Olivier Zunz, ed., *Reliving the Past: The Worlds of Social History*; Chapel Hill: Univ. North Carolina Press, 1985, 236–96.

Noriko Kamachi, "Feudalism or Absolute Monarchism?: Japanese Discourse on the Nature of the State and Society in Late Imperial China," *Modern China* 16.3: 330–70 (July 1990). Summarizes and evaluates Japanese historiographical debates since World War II. Includes an eight-page bibliography.

Mori Masao, "A Survey of Ming Historical Studies in Japan: Past and Present," *Ming Studies*, 27: 67–83 (Spring 1989).

State and Society in China: Japanese Perspectives on Ming-Qing Social and Economic History; Linda Grove and Christian Daniels, eds., Univ. of Tokyo Press, 1984.

Societies and Journals

Late Imperial China (*LIC*: began in 1965 under the title *Ch'ing-shih wen-t'i*; adopted present title in 1985, biannual), Society for Qing Studies, California Institute of Technology, Pasadena, California. Contains translations of *Shigaku zasshi* May issue review of Ming-Qing studies in Japan.

Mindaishi kenkyûkai 明代史研究會, Tokyo, 1967– . Journal: *Mindaishi kenkyû* 明代史研究 (1974–).

Ming Studies (1975– , biannual), University of Minnesota, Minneapolis.

Mingshi xuehui 明史學會 Society for the Study of Ming History (1980–).

Mingshi yanjiu 明史研究, Lishisuo, Mingshi yanjiushi, (1991– , annual), Huangshan shushe. Previously *Mingshi yanjiu luncong* 明史研究論叢 (1981–90, irreg.).

Mingshi yanjiu zhuankan 明史研究專刊, 1978– , Taibei: Zhongyang wenhua yanjiuyuan. Annual, 1978–82; thereafter, biannual.

Mingshi ziliao congkan 明史資料叢刊, Jiangsu guji, 1981– , annual. Reprints little-known Ming works.

Zhongguo Mingshi Xuehui Tongxun 中國明史學會通訊, 1990– .

50

Qing

1644–1912

Qing sources include over 10 million documents from
the central archives and a smaller number from local archives. All forms of official publication as well as historical and literary genres have also survived in larger
numbers than from the rest of Chinese history put together. There are also more non-Han language sources
than available in previous dynasties—Manchu, Mongolian, Uighur and Tibetan as well as Korean, Japanese
and Vietnamese sources written in *wenyanwen*. In general there are more sources from the later Qing (1840–
1911) than from the early Qing (1644–1840). European
and American sources become important in the nineteenth and twentieth centuries. That Qing sources are
so plentiful is no doubt due to the relative proximity in
time, the larger number of printed books in circulation
and the change in attitude toward archive documents
that gradually took hold in the twentieth century.

Attention turns directly to the Qing archives, both
central and local (50.1–2; 50.3) and then to private documents (50.4). The chapter ends with the main works in
the traditional historical and literary genres (50.5), archaeology and inscriptions (50.6) and guides to sources
and research tools not already mentioned in the preceding sections (50.7). Chapter subsections follow.

Qing scholars were active in many fields, including history, philology and phonology. Their studies are still important sources for earlier periods of Chinese history.

50.1 Central Archives

The imperial bureaucracy produced huge quantities of documents at the central government agencies, in the palace and at the provincial and local yamen 衙門.[1] At least half a dozen copies were made of every routine memorial (*tiben* 題本) as it made its way from the originating official to the emperor. Upwards of two thousand copies were made of important edicts and other imperial pronouncements for distribution to the Six Boards and to every provincial, prefectural and county yamen. Because of well-established traditions of compilation, a selection of these documents were excerpted or copied whole, particularly those considered to have a literary value.[2] But few

---

[1] The first use of the word *yamen* in the English language according to the *OED* was in 1747: "Each magistrate great or small has his Tribunal or Yamen." The yamen contained the offices for all aspects of official business at each level, not only legal affairs. One of the best-preserved provincial yamen is that of the governor-general of Hebei (Zhili Zongdu 直隸總督) at Baoding 保定, about 100 km south of Beijing. It was rebuilt in the early Qing and was the venue of many major national and international events in the late Qing and Republic.

For a brief introduction to the history of the Qing archives, see *Chinese Archives: An Introductory Guide*, Ye Wa and Joseph W. Esherick, eds., China Research Monograph 45, Institute of Asian Studies, CCS, UCP, 1996, 4–14. *Zhongguo dang'an guan minglu* 中國檔案館名錄 (Directory of Chinese archives), Dang'an, 1990, lists central and local archives with addresses and telephone numbers.

[2] The dictionary of compilations containing documents and excerpts as well as modern publications from the archives (*Zhongguo dang'an wenxian cidian* 中國檔案文獻辭典, chap. 20, Box 7) contains annotations on 2,785 such publications of Qing documents. This part of the book was edited by a team of historians and archivists led by Ni Daoshan 倪道善, the author of an earlier guide to the Ming-Qing archives. To give an idea

Footnote continued on next page

originals have survived from the Ming or earlier dynasties, either because of neglect or because of accidents such as fire or insects, or because they were deliberately destroyed to make storage space. Yet despite these hazards and despite all the fighting and destruction that preceded and followed the fall of the Qing, no fewer than 15 million original Qing documents have survived (mainly from archives in the capital, Beijing).[3] That they have done so is due to a number of different reasons, the most important being the new appreciation of the value of old government documents as antiquarian or historical items. This appreciation was nurtured by a small handful of collectors, bibliophiles and scholars during the early Republican period, who eventually won the support of the government. Since then the authorities both in Beijing and in Taibei have made efforts to collect, to preserve, to organize and to publish the documents on a scale which would have been unthinkable under the old regime.

In 1900, when the allied forces entered Beijing, 50 to 60 percent of the archives of the Six Boards[4] were destroyed, as well as a considerable portion of the contents of the imperial archive, the Huangshicheng 皇史宬. The Russian troops removed the archives of the office of the Heilongjiang Military

---

of the rich detail in the *Zhongguo dang'an wenxian cidian*, it lists and annotates 75 published collections of documents from the 13 years of the Yongzheng reign alone, including contemporary eighteenth-century collections, later Qing collections and modern publications from the Qing central and local archives.

[3] The best introduction to the Ming-Qing Archives is *Zhonghua Ming-Qing zhendang zhinan* 中華明清珍檔指南 (A guide to the Ming Qing archival treasures of China), Qin Guojing 秦國經, Renmin, 1994; rpnt., 1996. This supersedes the earlier factual introduction published on the 60th anniversary of the foundation of the archives, *Zhongguo diyi lishi dang'an guan cang dang'an gaishu* 中國第一歷史檔案館藏檔案概述 (Introduction to the archives held by the Yishiguan), Yishiguan, eds., Dang-an, 1985.

[4] Libu 吏部, Hubu 户部, Libu 禮部, Bingbu 兵部, Xingbu 刑部 and Gongbu 工部 (i.e., the Boards of Civil Office, Revenue, Rites, War, Punishments and Public Works).

Governor and of three other subordinate military archives in the Northeast.

At the fall of the dynasty in 1911, many millions of documents (mainly memorials, reports and rescripts and memorial copies) still remained in the archives of the Junjichu 軍機處 (lit. office of military plans, normally translated as Grand Council), the Neige 內閣 (Grand Secretariat), the palace archives (Gongzhong dang'an 宮中檔案) and the Liubu 六部 (Six Boards). Most dated from the middle and late Qing, but there were several thousand from the end of the Ming, as well as quantities of materials on early Manchu history and the Shunzhi and Kangxi reigns. In the first years of the Republic, the Grand Council and Grand Secretariat archives remained in the palace. The documents of the Six Boards were inherited by their successor ministries.

As an example of the precarious state of the imperial archives, the story is often told of how a large part of the Grand Secretariat archives (Neige daku 內閣大庫) were sold and later saved.[5] In 1909, most of these documents had been moved to temporary storage in a courtyard of the palace. To make space, it was proposed, in line with past practice, to burn them. Zhang Zhidong 張之洞 (1837–1909), who was at that time the Grand Councilor in charge of the Board of Education, memorialized that the books in the archive be transferred to establish a new library in the Board and sent one of his officials, the bibliophile, scholar and collector of ancient inscriptions, Luo Zhenyu 羅振玉 (1866–1940), to make the selection. While inspecting the books, Luo unscrolled some of the memorials and realized their worth as historical sources. So he persuaded Zhang to recommend storing the documents in order to prevent their being burned. As a result, not only the books found refuge in the Board's library (an early forerunner of the Beitu 北圖 housed at the Imperial Academy, Guozijian 國子監), but

---

[5] This account is based on Ni Daoshan 倪道善, *Ming-Qing dang'an gailun* 明清檔案概論 (An outline of the Ming-Qing archives), Sichuan daxue, 1990; rpnt., 1992, 1–10.

also the documents. In 1916, the library moved to the Palace. The documents were placed in a little courtyard near one of the northern palace gates (Duanmen 端門). For five years they lay neglected. There were rumors that there were Song editions and even the bones of emperors among them. Much pilfering took place by self-appointed archaeologists of the ministry of education. Some perfunctory sorting was done by short-term laborers armed with pointed sticks. Eventually, in 1921 the museum decided to follow the example of most of the other ministries and to sell off a large part of the less than perfect of its Ming and Qing documents to paper merchants as pulp. The documents (weighing an estimated 75 tons), which had been placed by the sorters into 8,000 sacks, were sold for 4,000 *yuan* to a used paper shop in Xidan. One day, Luo Zhenyu was buying books and antiques in Liulichang when he came across the original of a congratulatory message to the emperor from the king of Korea, which he realized could only have come from the Grand Secretariat archives. After making inquiries he found out about the sale and bought back the documents from the paper shop for three times the price they had paid. The whole matter had reached the proportions of a public scandal, which later drew the celebrated remark from Lu Xun 魯迅, "Chinese public property really is difficult to keep; if the authorities are incompetent they ruin it, but if they are competent they steal it."[6]

---

[6] Lu Xun wrote his comment in 1927 and it was published in a weekly magazine in January 1928: "Tan suowei 'Danei dang'an' 談所謂 大內檔案" (On the so-called "imperial archives"); rpnt., *Ming-Qing dang' an lunwen xuanbian* 明清檔案論文選編 (Selected articles on the Ming Qing archives), Dang'an, 1985, 1–6. This wide-ranging selection of scholarly articles from the 1920s to 1980s on the archives was published on their 60th anniversary. A similar collection was published in 1995 containing articles written on the archives between 1985 and 1994: *Ming-Qing dang'an yu lishi yanjiu lunwen xuan* 明清檔案與歷史研究論文選 (Selected articles on the Ming Qing archives and historical research), 2 vols., Guoji wenhua, 1995.

Lu Xun was referring not only to the incompetence of the early Republican officials responsible for the neglect of the documents, but also to the appropriation of rare items by senior officials and their authorization for sale of the routine documents as pulp. In doing so, they demonstrated the common attitude that rare books were valuable and that archival documents, especially of a defunct and in this case, alien, dynasty, were junk. Indeed, Lu Xun himself was more concerned with the fate of the rare books than with the archives.

Partly as a result of the scandal and partly as a result of the reorganization of the cultural agencies of the government after 1925, the work of cataloging the documents began for the first time; it was undertaken in the 1920s and 1930s mainly by the Documents Repository (Wenxianguan 文獻館, 1928), of the Palace Museum, which gradually acquired most of what was left of the central government and court archives. The Shiyusuo acquired in 1928 half of Luo's collection (for slightly more than he had paid for the whole); Peking University and Qinghua had also bought documents and began editing and publishing them. Luo and his son Luo Fuyi 羅福頤 sponsored publication and cataloging of the part of their collection that they had taken to Tianjin.

No sooner had the work of cataloging (and to a certain extent, publishing) begun than the War of Resistance against Japan broke out and the work was halted. In 1949, the republican government took a total of several hundred thousand Qing documents to Taiwan (50.1.2). Ninety-five percent of the Qing archives stayed in China. Today, the Yishiguan holds something to the order of 10 million documents and an estimated additional four million are on deposit in various provincial archives, notably in Shenyang (50.1.4) and in Lhasa (50.3).

50.1.1 Qing Documents in the Yishiguan

The First Historical Archives (Zhongguo Diyi lishi dang'an guan 中國第一歷史檔案館, Yishiguan 一史館 for short) are the main repository of Ming-Qing original documents in China. They are housed in modern buildings just inside the

Xihua gate (西華門) at the northern entrance to the Forbidden City.[7]

About 70 percent of the 10 million documents in the Yishiguan come from five of the main Qing central archives, those of the Grand Secretariat, the Grand Council, the palace, the Imperial Household and the Imperial Lineage. In addition, there are about 324,000 *juan* of documents from the Six Boards, mainly from the end of the dynasty and mostly from the Board of Punishments (320,000 *juan*), followed by the Army (2,500 *juan*) and the Board of Revenue, Hubu 戶部 (1,000 *juan*). There are also extensive records from the Zongli Yamen 總理衙門 (1861–1901) and the Waiwubu 外務部 (Foreign Ministry), many of which have been published.[8]

The most interesting archives for the economic historian are those of the financial and monetary departments (item II.B in the breakdown on pages 871–880), of which the most plentiful are those of the Board of Revenue. These include records of government finances, coinage, population, taxes, granaries and the salt industry.

For the social historian, as Ye and Esherick point out, the most interesting are probably the archives of the judiciary, supervisory and civil administrative departments (item II.E). Of these, those of the Board of Punishment (Xingbu 刑部) are the most extensive. They mainly date from 1870–1911. The materials are similar to the routine memorial copies in the censorial section of the Board of Punishments (Xingke 刑科 *tiben*) and

---

[7] The following description is mainly drawn from Ye and Esherick (1996), 35–45, and Qin (1996), 28–139. See also Beatrice S. Bartlett, "An Archival Revival: The Qing Central Government Archives in Peking Today," *Ch'ing-shih wen-t'i* 4.6 (1981), 81–110. The Yishiguan are the successor to the Wenxiangguan 文獻館 (Documents Repository) of the Palace Museum (in the 1950s, they were usually called the Ming-Qing Archives or the Ming-Qing Department of the Central Archives).

[8] Only a small part of the Ministry of Foreign Affairs archives covering the years 1901–11 are held at the Yishiguan. The larger part, as well as those of the Zongli Yamen, were taken to Taiwan in 1949 and are now housed in the Jinshisuo (50.1.2).

have been similarly reorganized according to research and publication priorities of Chinese historians as set in the first thirty years of the PRC. Thus there are sections, for example, on prosecutions of leaders of peasant uprisings and secret societies; records of urban strikes and tax protests; anti-missionary cases; minority affairs cases; and so on. There are also records on property and credit disputes, robbery and theft, marital and family disputes and corruption and smuggling.[9]

The full extent of the scope of the coverage of the Yishiguan may be appreciated at a glance at the 75 *quanzong* 全宗 (archive collections; record groups or *fonds*) into which the documents are divided [*quanzong* numbers are given in square brackets]. Ming documents (which are discussed in 49.4) are in *quanzong* 1: *Mingchao dang'an* 明朝檔案.[10] Note that each *quanzong* groups together the documents of a particular agency or person and therefore they vary in size between the largest (*quanzong* 2), the archives of the Neige with over 2.5 million documents, to that of *quanzong* 57, the mere handful of documents in the Imperial Stud archives.

The main breakdown is in the following broad categories:

I. Archives of the central organs of the imperial government (*Fubi huangdi de zhongshu jigou de dang'an* 輔弼皇帝的中樞機構的檔案).

II. Archives of the departments of the central government and of their dependent yamen (*Fen zhangguozheng ge buyuan yamen jiqi suoshu jigou de dang'an* 分掌國政各部院衙門及其所屬機構的檔案).

III. Archives of departments dealing with the imperial lineage and palace administration (*Zhangguan huangzu ji gongting shiwu jigou de dang'an* 掌管皇族及宮廷事務機構的檔案).

[9] Nancy Park and Robert Anthony, "Archival Research in Qing Legal History," *LIC* 14.1: 93–137 (1993).

[10] This list is based on Ni (1992), 36–45; Qin (1996), 243–46; and Ye and Esherick (1996), 35–45.

IV. Archives of local government organs, of individuals and of princely establishments (*Difang jiguan ji geren he wang fu dang'an* 地方機關及個人和王府檔案).

V. Maps and plans (*Yutu huiji* 輿圖匯集).

These five categories are broken down into the following sub-categories:

I. Archives of the central organs of the imperial government (*Fubi huangdi de zhongshu jigou de dang'an* 輔弼皇帝的中樞機構的檔案).

> 1. *Neige dang'an* 內閣檔案 (Grand Secretariat archives), [*quanzong* 2]. Grand Secretariat archives (Neige dang'an 內閣檔案): 2,714,851 edicts and memorials (Qin, 1996), of which the greater part are routine memorials (*tiben* 題本). About 1.5 million are in good condition (there are also a huge number of damaged ones). They cover all matters of civil and military government in great detail. They date from 1629–1911 and cover the years 1607–1911, with the majority falling towards the end of the period. Up to 1735, they are arranged by reign period and then divided topically. After 1735, they are grouped under each of the Six Boards, then arranged chronologically by reign, year or even month, and subdivided by topic. The Neige archives also contain documents dealing with daily matters of internal administration and of the various official compiling offices (for example, of the statutes, the Court Diaries and the Veritable Records). They also contain separate catalogs of yellow registers (*huangce* 黃册), the summaries of tax and head counts and other staistical matters attached to the routine memorials. There are more than 230 volumes of catalogs of the Neige documents. They are arranged by type of document, by period and by subject. Note that an additional 310,000 documents from the Neige archives are in the Shiyusuo in Taibei (50.1.2).

> 2. *Junjichu dang'an* 軍機處檔案 (Grand Council archives), [*quanzong* 3]. Grand Council archives (Junjichu dang'an 軍機處檔案) covering the period 1730–1911: 793,000 documents, of which about 600,000 are memorial reference copies (*lufu zouzhe*

錄副奏摺), many in running script.[11] They were kept in the Grand Council reference collection as a means of keeping track of what had been sent to the emperor for comment or what he had commented or commanded (the original memorial with comments was returned to the sender). These copies supplement (and may sometimes duplicate) the 500,000 original palace memorials or edicts with vermilion rescripts (*zhupi zouzhe* 硃批 奏摺 or *zhupi yuzhi* 硃批諭旨) kept in the palace collections described under item 3 below. In the 1950s they were organized according to eighteen subject categories: domestic administration; foreign affairs; military affairs; finance; agriculture; water control; industry; commerce; communications; construction; culture and education; law; non-Han peoples affairs; religion; astronomy and geography; suppression of revolutionary movements; imperialist aggression; miscellaneous. Several of these subject categories have been cataloged in whole or in subcategories. Routine memorials (*tiben*) normally entered the Grand Secretariat where comments on the matters they contained were noted on slips. These along with the memorial were then sent to the emperor. His reaction was then recorded in red on the memorial by the secretaries for transmission back to the Board or originator for action. Such *hongben* 紅本 as they were called are quite different from the palace memorials with vermilion rescripts in the emperor's own hand (*zhupi zouzhe*).

3. *Gongzhong gechu dang'an* 宮中各處檔案 (Documents of the palace archives), [*quanzong* 4]. Palace archives (Gongzhong dang 宮中檔): mainly imperial edicts with vermilion rescripts (*zhupi yuzhi*) of which there are 500,000 and memorials with imperial rescripts (*zhupi zouzhe*). These are divided into the same categories as the memorial copies in the Junjichu archives. Total: about 715,000 documents.[12]

4. *Zeren Neige dang'an* 責任內閣檔案 (Archives of the Cabinet), 6,000 documents, 1911.4 to 1911.12 [*quanzong* 7].

[11] The basic study of the operations of the Council is Beatrice S. Bartlett, *Monarchs and Ministers: The Grand Council in Mid-Ch'ing China, 1723–1820*, UCP, 1991.

[12] Beatrice S. Bartlett, "Imperial Notations on Ch'ing Official Documents in the Ch'ien-lung (1736–1795) and Chia-ch'ing (1796–1820) Reigns," *National Palace Museum Bulletin* 7.2 (1972), 1–13; 7.3 (1972), 1–13.

5. *Bideyuan dang'an* 弼德院檔案 (Archives of the Privy Council), 107 documents, 1911.4 to 1911.12 [*quanzong* 8].

6. *Zizhengyuan dang'an* 資政院檔案 (Archives of the National Assembly), very few documents, 1910–11 [*quanzong* 50].

7. *Huiyi zhengwuchu dang'an* 會議政務處檔案 (Archives of the Bureau on Government Affairs), few documents, 1901–11 [*quanzong* 35].

8. *Xianzheng bianchaguan dang'an* 憲政編查館檔案 (Archives of the Committee for Drawing up Regulations for Constitutional Government), 100 *juan*, 1905–11 [*quanzong* 9].

II. Archives of the departments of the central government and of their dependent yamen (*Fen zhangguozheng ge buyuan yamen jiqi suoshu jigou de dang'an* 分掌國政各部院衙門及其所屬機構的檔案).

A. Archives of the Board of Civil Office concerning appointments and transfers of civilian officials (*Zhangguan wenguan renmian de libu de dang'an* 掌管文官任免的吏部的檔案), over 1,000 *juan*, 1690–1911 [*quanzong* 12].

B. Archives of financial and monetary departments (*Zhangguan caizheng jinrong jigou de dang'an* 掌管財政金融機構的檔案).

1. *Hubu Duzhibu dang'an* 户部度支部檔案 (Archives of the Board of Revenue and of the Ministry of Finance), over 1,000 *juan*, 1631–1911 [*quanzong* 13].

2. *Huikaofu dang'an* 會考府檔案 (Archives of the department for checking money and grain), very few documents, 1723–25 [*quanzong* 63].

3. *Qingli caizhengchu dang'an* 清理財政處檔案 (Archives of the finance clearing section), very few documents, 1903–6 [*quanzong* 64].

4. *Shuiwuchu dang'an* 税務處檔案 (Archives of the section on tax affairs), 91 *juan*, 1906–11 [*quanzong* 44].

5. *Duban yanzhengchu dang'an* 督辦鹽政處檔案 (Archives of the salt supervisory division), very few documents, 1909–11 [*quanzong* 25].

6. *Da Qing yinhang dang'an* 大清銀行檔案 (Archives of the Great Qing Bank), 49 *juan*, 1908–11 [*quanzong* 24].

C. Archives of the rites departments (*Zhangguan liyi jisi jigou de dang'an* 掌管禮儀祭祀機構的檔案).

1. *Libu dang'an* 禮部檔案 (Archives of the Board of Rites), very incomplete, 1631–1911 [*quanzong* 14].

2. *Lingqin Libu dang'an* 陵寢禮部檔案 (Archives of the Imperial Mausoleum Department), very few, 1742–1911 [*quanzong* 56].

3. *Yuebu dang'an* 樂部檔案 (Archives of the Board of Music), very incomplete, 1738–1911 [*quanzong* 55].

4. *Taichangsi dang'an* 太常寺檔案 (Archives of the special service for sacrificial rites to altars and temples), 32 *juan*, 1644–1906 [*quanzong* 58].

5. *Guanglusi dang'an* 光祿寺檔案 (Archives of the special food supply service), very few, 1644–1906 [*quanzong* 59].

6. *Honglusi dang'an* 鴻臚寺檔案 (Archives of the state banquet service), very few, 1644–1906 [*quanzong* 60].

D. Archives of the military and patrol departments (*Zhangguan junshi jigou de dang'an* 掌管軍事機構的檔案).

1. *Bingbu Lujunbu dang'an* 兵部陸軍部檔案 (Archives of the Army Board, infantry department), 2,500 *juan*, incomplete [*quanzong* 15].

2. *Taipusi dang'an* 太僕寺檔案 (Archives of the Imperial Stud), very few, Guangxu [*quanzong* 57].

3. *Baqi dutong yamen dang'an* 八旗都統衙門檔案 (Archives of the Eight Banners yamen), over 900 *juan*, incomplete [*quanzong* 23].

4. *Bujun tongling yamen dang'an* 步軍統領衙門檔案 (Archives of the capital infantry guards), 49 *juan*, 1853–1911 [*quanzong* 51].

5. *Guanli qianfeng hujun deng yingshiwu dachenchu dang'an* 管理前鋒護軍等營事務大臣處檔案 (Archives of the office of the minister in charge of the administration of the vanguard and other divisions), very few, 1908–11 [*quanzong* 65].

6. *Jianruiying dang'an* 健銳營檔案 (Archives of the light division), very few and incomplete [*quanzong* 66].

7. *Huoqiying dang'an* 火器營檔案 (Archives of the artillery and musketry division), very few, 1908 [*quanzong* 67].

8. *Shenjiying dang'an* 神機營檔案 (Archives of the Peking Field Force [divine mechanism regiments]), very few, 1861–1911 [*quanzong* 40].

9. *Zongli lianbingchu dang'an* 總理練兵處檔案 (Archives of the central military training section), over 100 *juan*, 1908–11 [*quanzong* 39].

10. *Jingcheng xunfangchu dang'an* 京城巡防處檔案 (Archives of the capital patrol division), very few, 1853–55 [*quanzong* 71].

11. *Jingfangyingwuchu dang'an* 京防營務處檔案 (Archives of the capital guards division), very few, 1911 [*quanzong* 73].

12. *Jinji lujun ge zhendulian gongsuo dang'an* 近畿陸軍各鎮督練公所檔案 (Archives of the training boards of the metropolitan army garrisons), very few, 1907–11 [*quanzong* 42].

13. *Jinwei jun xunlianchu dang'an* 禁衛軍訓練處檔案 (Archives of the Guards Training Division), very few, 1908–11 [*quanzong* 70].

14. *Junzifu dang'an* 軍諮府檔案 (Archives of the General Staff Office), very few, 1906–11 [*quanzong* 49].

E. Archives of the judiciary, supervision and civil administration (*Zhangguan sifa jiancha jigou de dang'an* 掌管司法監察機構的檔案).

　1. *Xingbu Fabu dang'an* 刑部法部檔案 (Archives of the Board of Punishments and the Ministry of Justice), more than 32,000 *juan*, Kangxi to Xuantong, but mainly Guangxu and Xuantong [*quanzong* 16].

　2. *Daliyuan dang'an* 大理院檔案 (Archives of the Supreme Court), very few, 1908–11 [*quanzong* 62].

　3. *Xiuding Falüguan dang'an* 修訂法律館檔案 (Archives of the Legal Reform Office), 19 *juan*, 1905–11 [*quanzong* 10].

　4. *Duchayuan dang'an* 都察院檔案 (Archives of the Censorate Office), very few, Shunzhi to Xuantong [*quanzong* 48].

F. Archives of the departments administering public works, agriculture and commerce (*Zhangguan gongjiao nongshang jigou de dang'an* 掌管工交農商機構的檔案).

　1. *Gongbu dang'an* 工部檔案 (Archives of the Board of Works), more than 200 *juan*, very incomplete [*quanzong* 17].

2. *Nonggongshangbu dang'an* 農工商部檔案 (Archives of the Ministry of Commerce or the Ministry of Agriculture, Industry and Commerce), more than 300 *juan*, 1903–11 [*quanzong* 20].

3. *Youchuanbu dang'an* 郵傳部檔案 (Archives of the Ministry of Posts and Communications), 65 *juan*, incomplete [*quanzong* 22].

G. Archives of the departments dealing with civil affairs and police (*Zhangguan minzheng jingwu jigou de dang'an* 掌管民政警務機構的檔案).

1. *Jingcheng shanhou xiexun zongju dang'an* 京城善後協巡總局檔案 (Archives of the Board for Restoring Security), very few, 1901–2 [*quanzong* 72].

2. *Xunjingbu dang'an* 巡警部檔案 (Archives of the Ministry of Public Security), more than 400 *juan*, 1905–6 [*quanzong* 37].

3. *Minzhengbu dang'an* 民政部檔案 (Archives of the Ministry of Civil Affairs), 1,000 *juan*, 1906–11 [*quanzong* 21].

4. *Jinyan zongju dang'an* 禁烟總局檔案 (Archives of the Opium Prohibition Bureau), very few, 1902–11 [*quanzong* 74].

H. Archives of departments dealing with culture and education (*Zhangguan wenhua ji jiaoyu jigou de dang'an* 掌管文化及教育機構的檔案).

1. *Guozijian dang'an* 國子監檔案 (Archives of the Imperial Academy), few, 1740–1906 [*quanzong* 54].

2. *Xuebu dang'an* 學部檔案 (Archives of the Ministry of Education), 400 *juan*, Guangxu and Xuantong periods [*quanzong* 19].

3. *Qintianjian dang'an* 欽天監檔案 (Archives of the Meterological Division), very few, 1715–1908 [*quanzong* 53].

4. *Hanlinyuan dang'an* 翰林院檔案 (Archives of the Hanlin Academy), very few [*quanzong* 61].

5. *Guoshiguan dang'an* 國史館檔案 (Archives of the Historiography Institute), over 1,000 *juan*, mainly from after 1765; documents from 1703–1765 are in the Grand Secretariat archives [*quanzong* 11].

6. *Fanglüeguan dang'an* 方略館檔案 (Archives of the Military Campaigns Records Office) [*quanzong* 46].

I. Archives of minority and external affairs departments (*Zhangguan minzu, waijiao jigou de dang'an* 掌管民族外交機構的檔案).

1. *Lifanbu dang'an* 理藩部檔案 (Archives of the Board of Dependencies), 700 *juan*, 1873–1911 [*quanzong* 45].

2. *Waiwubu dang'an* 外務部檔案，包括總理各國事務衙門 (Archives of the Ministry of Foreign Affairs, including those of the Zongli Yamen), 5,000 *juan*, [*quanzong* 18].

III. *Zhangguan huangzu ji gongting shiwu jigou de dang'an* 掌管皇族及宮廷事務機構的檔案 (Archives of departments dealing with the imperial lineage and the imperial household).

    1. *Zongrenfu dang'an* 宗人府檔案 (Archives of the Imperial Lineage), 430,000 documents dating from Yongzheng to Xuantong. They include records of birth, marriage, enfeofment and genealogical records and also cover Pu Yi's temporary residence in the palace after 1911 [*quanzong* 6].[13]

    2. *Neiwufu dang'an* 內務府檔案 (Archives of the Imperial Household), 189,500 documents, 1654–1924 [*quanzong* 5]. All kinds of documents dealing with the life and activities of the imperial household, including the imperial lineage genealogies, as well as a large collection of maps originally attached to incoming memorials. Total: about 1.9 million documents.

    3. *Luanyiwei dang'an* 鑾儀衛檔案 (Archives of the Department of Protocol), over 500 *juan*, Qianlong to Xuantong [*quanzong* 36].

    4. *Shiweichu dang'an* 侍衛處檔案 (Archives of the Imperial Bodyguards), very few, 1892–1909 [*quanzong* 68].

    5. *Shangyu beiyongchu dang'an* 上虞備用處檔案 (Archives of the imperial parks), very few, incomplete [*quanzong* 69].

IV. Archives of local government organs, of individuals and of princely establishments (*Difang jiguan ji geren he wangfu dang'an* 地方機關及個人和王府檔案).

    A. Archives of local government organs (*Difang jiguan dang'an* 地方機關檔案).

        1. *Shuntianfu dang'an* 順天府檔案 (Archives of Shuntian prefecture), 300 *juan*, post-Tongzhi [*quanzong* 28].

[13] Beatrice S. Bartlett, "The Secret Memorials of the Yung-cheng Period (1723–1735): Archival and Published Versions," *National Palace Museum Bulletin* 9.4 (1974), 1–12.

2. *Jingshi gaodeng shenpanting jianchating dang'an* 京師高等審判廳檢察廳檔案 (Archives of the Peking high court and prosecuting attorneys' office), over 150 *juan*, 1907–11 [*quanzong* 41].

3. *Beiyang dulianchu dang'an* 北洋督練處檔案 (Archives of the Beiyang military training department), very few, 1886–1911 [*quanzong* 52].

4. *Shandong xunfu yamen dang'an* 山東巡撫衙門檔案 (Archives of the governor of Shandong), 200 *juan*, incomplete [*quanzong* 29].

5. *Heilongjiang jiangjun yamen dang'an* 黑龍江將軍衙門檔案 (Archives of the office of the Heilongjiang Military Governor), 14,000 *juan*, 1684–1900 [*quanzong* 30].

6. *Ningguta fudutong yamen dang'an* 寧古塔副都統衙門檔案 (Archives of the Ningguta Manchu Brigade-General's Office), 1,000 *juan*, 1675–1900 [*quanzong* 31].

7. *Alachuke fudutong yamen dang'an* 阿勒拉楚喀副都統衙門檔案 (Archives of the Alachuke Manchu Brigade-General's Office), 400 *juan*, 1866–1899 [*quanzong* 32].

8. *Hunchun fudutong yamen dang'an* 琿春副都統衙門檔案 (Archives of the Hunchun Manchu Brigade-General's Office), 500 *juan*, 1737–1900 [*quanzong* 33].

9. *Changlu yanyun shisi dang'an* 長蘆鹽運使司檔案 (Archives of the Changlu Salt Distribution Commissioner), 3,000 *juan*, 1768–1914 [*quanzong* 34].

B. Archives of individuals and of imperial relatives (*Geren ji wangfu dang'an* 個人及王府檔案).

1. *Qing feidi Puyi dang'an* 清廢帝溥儀檔案 (Archives of the deposed emperor Puyi, 1906–67), 3,000 *juan*, 1911–31 [*quanzong* 26].

2. *Duanfang dang'an* 端方檔案 (Archives of Duanfang, 1862–1911), 140,000 *juan*, [*quanzong* 27].

3. *Zhao Erxun dang'an* 趙爾巽檔案 (Archives of Zhao Erxun, 1844–1927), 622 *juan*, 1885–1912 [*quanzong* 75].

4. *Chun Qinwangfu dang'an* 醇親王府檔案 (Archives of Prince Chun, including Yihuan 奕譞, 1840–91 and Zaifeng 載灃, 1883–1951), 200 *juan*, 1875–1926 [*quanzong* 38].

V. *Yutu huiji* 輿圖匯集 (Maps and plans), 7,000 of which do not fit into any of the other *quanzong* [*quanzong* 47].

50.1.2 Qing Central Archives Held in Taibei

Of the many hundreds of thousands of documents shipped to Taibei in 1949, 346,776 are held at the Palace Museum.[14] The criteria for selection were that they be as old as possible and that they bore the emperor's personal handwriting. This is therefore a particularly valuable collection. They have been cataloged on cards and in a computer database enabling searches on the official memorializing, his office, the date and the contents.

Much of the Shiyusuo collection of Neige documents are available on microfilm; about one-fifth (60,000) have been published (50.2.2) and the remainder are due out on CD-ROM.[15]

---

[14] Beatrice Bartlett points out that statistics of the numbers of documents held in archives need careful evaluation. Some documents were as short as two lines, others were extremely lengthy. A record book may contain details of hundreds of documents covering a year, but is only counted as one item (personal communication). For other examples of the care with which statistical statements about Chinese history should be treated, see section 7.1.4. Many of the 153,215 palace memorials and 188,000 Grand Council reference copies (*lufu* 錄副) held at the Palace Museum have been published. Of the 39,824 record books none have been published except late Qing diaries; See Bartlett, "Ch'ing Documents in the National Palace Museum Archives. Part One, Document Registers: The *Sui-shou teng-chi*," *National Palace Museum Bulletin* 10.4 (1975), 1–17.

For a catalog of the collection, see *Guoli gugong bowuyuan Qingdai wenxian dang'an zongmu* 國立故宮博物院清代文獻檔案總目 (Catalog of Qing dynasty documentary archives in the National Palace Museum), Taibei: Gugong bowuyuan, 1982; Zhuang Jifa 莊吉發 describes the different types of document, their value for research and their shelving in *Gugong dang'an shuyao* 故宮檔案述要 (Basic account of the Palace Museum Archives), Gugong bowuyuan 故宮博物院, 1983.

[15] Susan Naquin, "The Grand Secretariat Archives at the Institute of History and Philology, Academia Sinica, Taiwan," *LIC* 8.2: 102–9 (1987).

In addition to the documents from the Palace Museum and Shiyusuo collections, the KMT also shipped the archives of the Ministry of Foreign Affairs and many rare books from the National Central Library, the National Palace Museum and the National Central Museum. The Jinshisuo has the Zongli yamen 總理衙門 (1860–1901) and Waiwubu 外務部 (Foreign Ministry) documents (1901–1911). About 10% have been published (see also 50.1.1, item I.2).

50.1.3   Qing Central Archives Held in Japan

Nihon shozai Shindai dô-an shiryô no shosô 日本所在清代檔案史料諸相 (On all aspects of Qing archive documents held in Japan), Kanda Nobuo 神田信夫, Tôyô bunko, 1993.

50.1.4   Shengjing Archives

Shengjing 盛京 (Shenyang) was the secondary capital of the Qing. Its Manchu name was Mukden. Documents relating to national as well as northeastern matters were stored in the archives there. Today, they are part of the Liaoning Provincial Archives, which have altogether about 200,000 Qing documents dating from 1789 to 1895. The Qing documents include 142 *juan* of imperial genealogy (*Yudie* 玉牒); 3,625 *juan* of Banner household and head counts (*Baqi bingding hukou ce* 八旗兵丁戶口冊) as well as other Banner documents; and 45,283 *juan* of northeastern documents. They also have a small holding of Ming documents (see 49.2).

50.2 Published Archive Documents

Just over 50 collections of documents from the Qing archives were published between the first collection put out by Luo Zhenyu in 1924 and 1948.[16] Since then more than 300 titles

---

[16] *Shiliao congkan chubian* 史料叢刊初編, Luo Zhenyu, ed., 10 *ce*, Shanghai, 1924; Taibei, 1964. Wide variety of early Qing documents from the Grand Secretariat archives.

have appeared, ranging from single volumes to series in several hundred volumes. There is a considerable amount of overlap and repetition, but in recent years efforts have been made to integrate the published holdings in Taibei with those in Beijing. Large portions of the archives are already available on microfilm and their publication on CD-ROM has also begun.[17] Eventually no doubt all the archives will be available on CD-ROM with complete indexes. For the time being, however, it is still necessary to look through a large number of catalogs and documents in order to track down those relevant to a particular research project.

From the earliest days there has been a twofold trend in publications from the archives, either to group documents around a theme or to publish them chronologically in a series. Indexes have also been compiled.

Common themes have been Sino-foreign relations; popular uprisings (28.3); religious cases; the Opium and other wars (28.2); missionary cases; the anti-foreign movement; the Taipings (28.3); the Reform Movement; the 1911 revolution; natural disasters (36.4); documents of a particular province or of a particular archive.

Important chronological publications have been many of the Qing Court Diaries; all the Veritable Records; and certain collected memorials of individual periods or individual officials (50.2.2).

A large number of indexes to the archives are available. For a start the documents were indexed as they came in or went out

---

[17] The Dang'an wenxian guangpan ku 檔案文獻光盤庫, 120 discs, Zhaoxing 超星, 1996. Part 1 (Zhongguo Ming-Qing dang'an ku 中國明清檔案庫, 10 disks) contains works already published by the Yishiguan in book form (e.g., the imperially endorsed palace memorials of the Kangxi and Yongzheng reigns; the edicts of Qianlong reign (see 50.2.2); already published archives on selected themes, e.g., Opium and Sino-Japanese wars as well as the journal Lishi dang'an 歷史檔案 (1981–95). The remaining 110 disks contain materials on the Republic (37 disks) and People's Republic (73 disks).

or were copied or read. Some of these indexes have been used in the compilation of modern indexes.[18]

50.2.1 Yishiguan *(Microfilms)*

Di'erci Yapian zhanzheng shiliao 第二次鴉片戰爭史料 (Historical materials on the Second Opium War), Yishiguan, comps., 14 reels, 1981. The records of the Second Opium War (1856–60) cover the years 1853–60.

Gongzhong liangjiadan 宮中糧價單 (Crop price reports; palace archives), Yishiguan, comps., 328 reels, 1990. Crop price reports covering each of the 28 provinces from Kangxi to 1911 (7.4).

Gongzhong lüli pian 宮中履歷片 (Curricula vitae of officials in the palace archives), Yishiguan, comps., 6 reels, 1985. These abbreviated curricula vitae of officials taking up, or leaving, office were prepared for the emperor and some contain his comments (from Kangxi reign to Xianfeng). They have been published in book form (50.2.4).

Gongzhong lüli yinjian zhe 宮中履歷引見摺 (Curricula vitae of officials in the palace archives), Yishiguan, comps., 27 reels, 1985. Curricula vitae of over 30,000 middle, and lower, ranking officials, prepared for the occasion of their taking up or leaving office. Covering the years 1721–1911; they have been published in book form (50.2.4).

Gongzhong zhupi zouzhe caizhenglei (Vermilion-rescripted memorials on financial matters in the palace archives), 宮中硃批奏摺財政類, Yishiguan, comps., 64 reels, 1986. These include 80,000 vermilion rescripted memorials on financial matters covering the years 1662 to 1911. The subjects covered are: land and other taxes, customs, salt monopoly, granaries, expenses, currency and so forth.

Heilongjiang jiang jun yamen dang'an 黑龍江將軍衙門檔案 (Archives of the Heilongjiang brigade general's office), Yishiguan, comps., 193

---

[18] For example, *Qing junjichu dang'an mulu* 清軍機處檔案目錄 (Catalog of record books in the Grand Council Archives), Beiping: Gugong wenxianguan, Gugong yinshuasuo, 1934. Lists year by year the record books (*dangce* 檔冊) and memorial bundles (*zhebao* 摺包) held by the Palace Museum; total of 7,969 of the former and 3,535 of the latter, containing some 800,000 documents in all. The memorials and other documents in this archive were copies of those passing to and from the emperor. A portion was removed to Taiwan.

reels, 1988. The archive has 12,800 records dating from 1684 to 1900. Most extensive are those of the Qianlong reign.

Hubu Duzhibu fengyin fengmi ce 戶部度支部俸銀俸米冊 (Board of Revenue, Revenue section records of tribute silver and grain), Yishiguan, comps., 7 reels, 1985. Records of the silver and rice received by bannermen from 1760 to 1913; in 2,306 volumes.

Junjichu lufu zouzhe nongmin yundong lei 軍機處錄副奏摺農民運動類 (Grand Council memorial copies in the peasant movement category), Yishiguan, comps., 7 reels, 1985.

Junjichu lufu zouzhe quanguo shuili yushui ziran zaihai ziliao 軍機處錄副奏摺全國水利雨水自然災害資料 (Memorial copies in the Grand Council archives concerning materials on water control, rainfall and natural calamities), Yishiguan, comps., 24 reels, 1992. Consists of 13,690 copies of weather reports covering the years 1736 to 1826. Includes also crop price reports.

Junjichu lufu zouzhe zhenya geming yundong lei 軍機處錄副奏摺鎮壓革命運動類 (Grand Council memorial copies in the suppression of revolutionary movements category), Yishiguan, comps., 49 reels, 1991. Memorial copies collected by subject. This collection includes the Nian army (1814–1911); Taiping heavenly kingdom (1850–1911); the 1911 revolution and the Boxers.

Junjichu shangyudang 軍機處上諭檔 (Grand Council edicts), Yishiguan, comps., 394 reels, 1980. Covers the years 1723–1911.

Libu zaosong fengzeng xingshi ce 吏部造送封贈姓氏冊 (Record of those receiving titles prepared by the Board of Civil Office), Yishiguan, comps., 7 reels, 1985. This archive records the names of those people who received titles between 1862 and 1874 (family details—e.g., names of fathers and mothers and grandparents—are also given).

Manwen laodang 滿文老檔 (The old Manchu archives), Yishiguan, comps., 14 reels, 1983. The original is held in Taibei; these reels are taken from one of the six copies made in the Qianlong reign, four of which are in the Yishiguan and two in the Shenyang archives.

Manwen neiguo zhi yuandang 滿文內國之院檔 (National history office Manchu archives), Yishiguan, comps., 3 reels, 1989. These are the archives of the early Neige bureau responsible for the compilation of the National History (*Guoshi* 國史). The archive is arranged chronologically and covers the years 1633–43.

Neige Hanwen qijuzhu 內閣漢文起居注 (Court Diaries in Chinese from the Grand Secretariat), Yishiguan, comps., 223 reels, 1982.

Neige jingchace 內閣京察冊 (Grand Secretariat capital investigation records), Yishiguan, comps., 80 reels, 1985.

Neige Kangxichao qijuzhu 內閣康熙朝起居注 (Kangxi Court Diaries from the Grand Secretariat), Yishiguan, comps., 16 reels, 1985.

Neige Manwen qijuzhu 內閣滿文起居注 (Court Diaries in Manchu from the Grand Secretariat), Yishiguan, comps., 7 reels, 1985.

Neige Qiushen tiben 內閣秋審題本 (Grand Secretariat Autumn Assizes memorials), Yishiguan, comps., 212 reels, 1989. Covers the years 1736–95.

Qingdai Liuqiu dang'an shiliao 清代琉球檔案史料 (Historical materials from the Qing dynasty archives on Liuqiu), Yishiguan, comps., 3 reels, 1992. Consists of 662 records taken from the memorial copies made in the Grand Council (1742–1898). For book publication, see 50.2.6, *Ryûkyû*.

Qingdai pudie dang'an 清代譜牒檔案 (Qing dynasty genealogies in the archives), Yishiguan, comps., 307 reels, 1983. Neiwufu personnel records covering 1754 to 1911 in 11,000 volumes. Details of the imperial house, bannermen, relatives, including not only family, but also economic conditions. Also palace personnel records, which cover everything from examination candidates to cases involving capital punishments in every province (1,200 volumes). Also Zongrenfu records, principally the imperial tree, which was revised every 10 years.

Xinhai geming dang'an shiliao 辛亥革命檔案史料 (Archive materials on the 1911 revolution), Yishiguan, comps., 4 reels, 1983. A selection of 640 documents (indexed) relating to the 1911 revolution, mainly from Qing official sources.

Zongrenfu hongqice 宗人府紅旗冊 (Red banner registers in the Office of the Imperial Lineage archives), Yishiguan, comps., 87 reels, 1985. The red registers record the family conditions (births, deaths, marriages) of bannermen related on the distaff side of the imperial house. Covers the years 1857–98 in 1,500 volumes.

See also "Qing Archival Materials for the No. 1 Historical Archives on Microfilm at the Genealogical Society of Utah," *LIC* 9.2: 86–114 (1988).

50.2.2 General Publications

Ming-Qing dang'an 明清檔案 (Ming-Qing archives), 324 vols., Taibei: Lianjing, 1986–95. The full title is *Zhongyang yanjiuyuan, Lishiyuyan yanjiusuo xiancun Qingdai Neige daku yuancang Ming-Qing dang'an* 中

央研究院歷史語言研究所現存清代內閣大庫原藏明清檔案. This se-
ries was planned to number 1,500 folio vols. containing all the
310,000 Neige documents in the Shiyusuo collection, arranged
chronologically and indexed and annotated. Having reached the 11th
year of Jiaqing (1806), the decision has been taken to produce the
remaining vols. on CD-ROM.

Ming-Qing dang'an cunzhen xuanji 明清檔案存真選輯 (Selected materials
from the Ming-Qing archives: documents of the late Ming, early
Qing photolithographically printed), Li Guangtao 李光濤 et al., 3
vols., Shiyusuo, 1959–75; 1st vol., rpnt., 1992. Vol. 2 contains Manchu documents.

Ming-Qing Neige daku shiliao 明清內閣大庫史料 (Historical materials
from the Grand Secretariat in the Ming and Qing), 1st collection,
Ming, 2 vols., Jin Yufu 金毓黻, ed., Dongbei tushuguan, 1949. Includes over 500 memorials dating from 1623–44; the remainder from
early Qing.

Ming-Qing shiliao 明清史料 (Ming-Qing historical materials), 100 vols., in
10 collections; first collection, Shiyusuo, 1930–1; rpnt., 1997; collections 2–4, Shangai: Shangwu; vols., 5–10, Shiyusuo, 1953–75; vol. 5,
rpnt., 1994. Consists of 8,200 typeset documents from the Grand
Secretariat dating from late Ming and early Qing from the collection
of the Shiyusuo.

Ming-Qing shiliao huibian 明清史料匯編 (Collection of Ming-Qing historical materials), Shen Yunlong 沈雲龍, ed., 93 vols., in nine collections, Wenhai, 1967–84. Reprints all sorts of historical materials, especially on the late Ming, early Qing.

Kangxichao Hanwen zhupi zouzhe huibian 康熙朝漢文硃批奏摺彙編
(Collection of Chinese-language vermilion-rescripted palace memorials of the Kangxi period), Yishiguan, 8 vols., Dang'an, 1984–85. Includes 3,119 memorials, of which 1,049 are in the Yishiguan and
2,070 are in the Palace Museum, Taibei, as published in the first
seven volumes of *Gongzhongdang Kangxichao zouzhe* 宮中檔康熙朝
奏摺 (Palace memorials of the Kangxi reign), Taibei: Gugong bowuyuan, eds., 9 vols., 1976. The last two volumes of this collection are
Yishiguan memorials in Manchu.

Yongzhengchao Hanwen zhupi zouzhe huibian 雍正朝漢文硃批奏摺彙編
(Collection of Chinese-language vermilion-rescripted palace memori-
als of the Yongzheng period), Yishiguan, 40 vols., Jiangsu guji, 1986.
Contains more than 35,000 memorials of 1,200 senior officials.
About 15,000 are from the Yishiguan; the remaining 20,000 are as re-
produced in *Gongzhongdang Yongzhengchao zouzhe* 宮中檔雍正朝奏

摺 (Palace memorials of the Yongzheng reign), Taibei: Gugong bo-wuyuan, eds., 32 vols., 1977–80. Note that already in the Yongzheng reign itself, an enormous collection of edicts was initiated: *Yong-zhengchao zhupi yuzhi* 雍正朝硃批諭旨, 1738. It contains 7,000 impe-rial-rescripted edicts.

Gongzhong dang Qianlongchao zouzhe 宮中檔乾隆朝奏摺 (Palace memo-rials of the Qianlong reign), Taibei: Gugong bowuyuan, eds., 68 vols., 1982–89. Contains 59,436 memorials arranged by date with un-dated ones placed at the end of the year.

Qianlongchao shangyu dang 乾隆朝上諭檔 (Archive of Qianlong reign imperial edicts), Yishiguan, eds., 18 vols., Zhongguo Dang'an, 1991; rpnt., 1998.

Guangxuchao zhupi zouzhe 光緒朝硃批奏摺 (Imperially rescripted palace memorials of the Guangxu reign), Yishiguan, 120 vols., Zhonghua, 1995–97. Arrangement of the more than 99,400 memorials (totalling 63 million characters) in this massive collection is by broad subject category. This includes the memorials in *Gongzhongdang Guangxu-chao zouzhe* 宮中檔光緒朝奏摺 (Palace memorials of the Guangxu reign), Taibei: Gugong bowuyuan, eds., 26 vols., 1973–75.

Xianfeng Tongzhi liangchao shangyu dang 光緒宣統兩朝上諭檔 (Archive of Xianfeng and Tongzhi imperial edicts), Yishiguan, eds., 24 vols., Guangxi shifan daxue, 1998.

Guangxu Xuantong liangchao shangyu dang 光緒宣統兩朝上諭檔 (Arch-ive of Guangxu and Xuangtong imperial edicts), 37 vols., Guangxi shifan daxue, 1996. The edicts cover the years 1875 to 1911 and the arrangement is chronological.

Neige daku shudang jiumu 內閣大庫書檔舊目 (Catalog of book lists and lists of documents in the Grand Secretariat archives), Beiping, 1933. *Supplement*, Shanghai, 1936. Based on record books (*dangce* 檔冊) and book lists in the Shiyusuo holdings; supplement contains similar ma-terials from Peking University and Palace Museum holdings.

Qingdai dang'an shiliao congbian 清代檔案史料叢編 (irregular serial), Yishiguan, 14 vols., Zhonghua, 1978–90. Each volume concentrates on two or three themes, e.g., the financial circumstances of the Qing government at the time of the Taipings.

Zhongguo xiandaishi diaocha mulu 中國現代史調查目錄 (Finding catalog for China's modern history), 11 vols., Jinshisuo, 1968–69.

Zhanggu congbian 掌故叢編 (Collected historical documents), 10 *ce*, Gu-gong wenxianguan, Heji yinshuaju, 1928–29; rpnt., Guofeng, 1964, mainly early Qing documents from Grand Council archives; after vol. 11, the name of the series was changed to *Wenxian congbian* 文獻叢編 (Collectanea from the historical records office), 44 *ce*, Gugong wenxianguan, Gugong yinshuasuo, 1930–42; rpnt., Guofeng, 1963. Arrangement is by themes, e.g., materials on customs duties levied during the Yongzheng period in vols. 10–11 and 17–19. Vol. 37 contains an index to the first 36 *ce*; *Qing sanfan shiliao* 清三藩史料 (Materials on the revolt of the three feudatories), 6 vols., Gugong bowuyuan, 1932–33, was a side publication of the series. In addition, the Wenxianguan also published a periodical, *Shiliao xunkan* 史料旬刊 (Historical documents published every 10 days), 40 *ce*, Gugong wenxianguan, Jinghua yinshuju, 1930–31; rpnt., Guofeng, 1963.

Qingmo choubei lixian dang'an shiliao 清末籌備立憲檔案史料 (Historical materials from the archives on the preparations for the establishment of a constitution at the end of the Qing), Yishiguan, eds., 2 vols., Zhonghua, 1979.

50.2.3   Economic Documents (Listed Alphabetically)

Diguozhuyi yu Zhongguo haiguan 帝國主義與中國海關 (Imperialism and the Chinese customs), Parts 1–15, Zhongguo jindai jingjishi ziliao congbian weiyuanhui, eds., Kexue and Zhonghua, 1952–65.

Gongzhong liangjiadan 宮中糧價單 (Crop price reports in the palace archives), see 50.2.1 (Microfilm, no. 13).

Gongzhong zhupi zouzhe caizhenglei 宮中硃批奏摺財政類 (Imperial re-scripted palace memorials on financial matters), see 50.2.1 (Microfilm, no. 12).

Guanyu Jiangning zhizao Caojia dang'an shiliao 關于江寧織造曹家檔案史料 (On the archives of the Cao family, Jiangning textile commissioner), Gugong Ming-Qing dang'anbu, eds., Zhonghua, 1975.

Haifang dang 海防檔 (Coastal defense archives), 9 vols., Jinshisuo, 1957.

Hanyeping gongsi 漢冶萍公司 (The Hanyeping Co.), vol. 1, Chen Xulu 陳旭麓 et al., Shanghai renmin, 1984.

Hubei kaicai meitie zongju, Jingmen kuangwu zongju 湖北開采煤鐵總局, 荊門礦務總局 (The Hubei iron and coal mine dept. and the Jingmen coal department), Chen Xulu 陳旭麓 et al., Shanghai renmin, 1981.

Jingji dang'an hanmu huibian 經濟檔案函目彙編 (Catalog of economic archives), Jinshisuo, eds., 10 vols., 1987.

Kuangwu dang 礦物檔 (Mining archives), Jinshisuo, eds., 8 vols., 1960.

Qing Neige jiucang Hanwen huangce lianhe mulu 清內閣舊藏漢文黃册聯合目錄 (Union catalog of yellow registers formerly stored in the archives of the Grand Secretariat), Wenxianguan, Beida wenke yanjiusuo and Shiyusuo, eds., 6 *ce.*, Beijing daxue yinshuasuo, 1952. The yellow books (*huangce* 黃册) included not only population counts (*huangce* 黃册) but also accounts relating to all types of labor service and payment. They were attached as numerical appendixes to memorials from officials working in any of the Six Boards or their subordinate departments. They often contain much fuller statistical materials than are found in the memorials themselves. This catalog includes a total of 17,033 *huangce*: 6,602 at Beida;[19] 7,000 at the Wenxianguan;[20] and 2,000 at the Shiyusuo. It is arranged by the Six Boards and then by subject matter. The introduction contains details of the subjects covered and numbers in each category. It has been reprinted in *Ming-Qing dang'an lunwen xuanbian* 明清檔案論文選編, 173–92.

Qingdai de kuangye 清代的礦業 (The mining industry in the Qing dynasty), 2 vols., Zhonghua, 1983.

Qingdai diqi dang'an shiliao (Jiaqing zhi Xuantong) 清代地契檔案史料嘉慶至宣統 (Historical materials on land deeds in the Qing dynasty), Xiong Jingfeng 熊敬馮, ed., Sichuan Xindu dang'anju and Dang'anguan, 1988. Consists of 196 deeds from Xindu, Sichuan dating from 1805 to 1911.

Qingdai diwang lingqin 清代帝王陵寝 (Imperial and royal tombs in the Qing dynasty), Yishiguan, eds., Dang'an, 1983.

Qingdai dizu boxue xingtai 清代地租剝削形態 (The exploitative land tax system in the Qing dynasty), Lishi yanjiusuo and Yishiguan, eds., 2 vols., Dang'an, 1981.

Qingdai Jilin dang'an shiliao xuanbian (gongye) 清代吉林檔案史料選編 (工業) (Selections from the Qing dynasty Jilin archival historical materials [industry]), Jilin dang'anguan, eds., 3 vols., Jilin dang'anguan, 1985.

[19] *Qing jiuchao jingsheng baoxiaoce mulu* 清九朝京省報銷册目錄 (Catalog of accounts forwarded to Beijing during nine reigns of the Qing dynasty), Qingdai neige daku dang'an zhengli weiyuanhui, eds., 1935. Only the *huangce* of the first two reigns were published.
[20] *Neige daku xiancun Qingdai Hanwen huangce mulu* 內閣大庫現存清代漢文黃册目錄 (Catalog of extant Yellow Registers in Chinese in the archive of the Grand Secretariat), Beijing, 1936.

Qingdai Jilin dang'an shiliao xuanbian 清代吉林檔案史料選編 (Selections from the Qing archives at Jilin), Jilin dang'anguan, eds., Jilin dang'anguan, 1987.

Qingdai zhupi zouzhe caizhenglei mulu 清代硃批奏摺財政類目錄 (Index of imperially rescripted memorials in the financial category), Yishiguan, 5 vols., Zhongguo caizheng, 1990–92.

Wu Xun dimuzhang 武訓地畝帳 (The land accounts of Wu Xun [1838–96]), Renmin, 1975.

Yuanming yuan 圓明園 (The summer palace), Yishiguan, 2 vols., Shanghai guji, 1991.

Zhongguo jindai bingqi gongye dang'an shiliao 中國近代兵器工業史料 (Historical materials on the history of the Chinese armaments industry in the Qing dynasty), Yishiguan, eds., Bingqi gongye, 1993.

Zhongguo jindai huobi jinrongshi ziliao 中國近代貨幣金融史資料 (Materials on the modern history of Chinese coins and currency), Zhongguo renmin yinhang canshishi, eds., 2 vols., Zhonghua, 1964.

Zigong yanye qiyue dang'an xuanji 自貢鹽業契約檔案選輯 (Selected contracts from the archives of the Zigong salt industry), Zigongshi dang'anguan, eds., Shehui kexue, 1985. The materials cover the period 1732–1949.

50.2.4   Biographical Material

Zhongguo Diyi lishi dang'an guancang 中國第一歷史檔案館藏, *Qingdai guanyuan lüli dang'an huibian*, 清代官員履歷檔案館匯編 (Holdings of the Yishiguan of curricula vitae of Qing officials), Zhang Guisu 張桂素 et al., eds., 30 vols., Huadong shifan daxue, 1997. Contains abbreviated curricula vitae of 55,883 individuals. The CV were prepared for the emperor to read before receiving an official for interview. Vol. 30 is a name index (both by stroke count and by the four-corner system). The Yishiguan holdings of these materials are also available on microfilm (50.2.1).

50.2.5   Documents in Manchu

The terms "Manchu" and "Qing" are briefly discussed in Box 10. There are between 1.6 and 2 million Qing documents in Manchu (representing about one-sixth the total extant number of central Qing documents). They are mainly held at the Yishiguan and the Shenyang archives. There is also an important collection of over 200 boxes at the Palace Museum, Taibei. The oldest Qing documents in the Yishiguan are the private day-to-day records of the Qing imperial house over the years 1607–36, the *Manwen laodang* 滿文老檔 (Old Manchu Archives). There are both modern Chinese and Japanese translations of the *Manwen laodang*. The Chinese translation (not yet completed) is being done both on the mainland and in Taibei; for the Japanese translation, see *Mambun rôtô* 滿文老檔.[21] They are an essential source for Manchu history before the conquest of China. The Yishiguan also contains the Manchu version of the Court Diaries in 6,479 volumes. The remainder of the Manchu documents (some of which are in both Manchu and Chinese), date mainly from the earlier part of the dynasty and deal with military matters or with Mongolia, Tibet or Xinjiang. Some have been translated into Chinese. Manchu materials in the archives are listed below in alphabetical order. Evaluations of the importance of Manchu documents as historical sources are given at the end of this subsection.

Hanyi Manwen jiudang 漢譯滿文舊檔 (Chinese translation of the old Manchu archives), Liaoning daxue lishixi, 3 vols., 1979. Translation in progress.

Jiu Manzhou dang 舊滿洲檔 (The old Manchu archives), Gugong bowu-yuan, 10 vols., Taibei, 1969. Photo-offset of the oldest version of this Manchu archive. Considerable portions have been translated into Chinese and published.

Manwen laodang 滿文老檔 (The old Manchu archives), 2 vols., Yishiguan and Shekeyuan, tr. and ed., Zhonghua, 1990. There are name- and place-indexes. This is a later version of the *Jiu Manzhou dang*. See Kanda Nobuo, "From *Man Wen Lao Tang* to *Chiu Man-chou Tang*," *MTB* 38 (1980).

Manwen laodang 滿文老檔 (The old Manchu archives), see 50.2.1 (Micro-film, no. 16).

Manwen neiguo zhi yuandang 滿文內國之院檔 (National history office Manchu archives), see 50.2.1 (Microfilm, no. 15).

[21] *Mambun rôtô* 滿文老檔 (The old Manchu archives), Kanda Nobuo 神田信夫, ed., 7 vols., Tôyô bunko, 1955–63.

Box 10: The Origins of "Manchu" and "Qing"

As a means of consolidating his power on the eve of the conquest of China and in order to avoid any unfortunate associations with the past, Abahai 阿巴海 (better known by his Chinese name, Huang Taiji 皇太極, 1592–1643), promulgated in 1632 a revision of the new script (of 1599) and in 1635 adopted a new title; changed the name of the dynasty and started a new era (*gaiyuan* 改元). The name of his people, Nüzhen 女真, was clearly no longer suitable for what was a fast-growing confederation including not only Jurchen, but also Mongols and Han, so the new name *Manju* (Manzhou 滿洲; Manchu in English) was chosen. There are many theories as to the origin of this name (41.2.2). The characters represented the sounds of the original non-Han word (possibly the Manchu for "brave") with the added twist that the characters chosen both had the water signific.

There is no surviving evidence to explain why Qing 清 (also with the water signific) was chosen to replace the previous dynastic name (*guohao* 國號) of Jin 金 (Hou-Jin 後金). The similarity in pronunciation of the two probably influenced the choice. Qing in Manchu (Csing) is almost the same as Jin (Cin) or xin (sin) as in *Aixin* (*jueluo*) 愛新覺羅 (*Aisin gioro*), the name adopted by Nurhaci. The meaning of Cin is gold. But even if this is correct, it still does not explain the choice of the character Qing 清. It is tempting to speculate that five-agent theory (*wuxing* 五行, Box 8, 20.4) played a decisive role. It had last been much used in the debate over the legitimacy of the Jin dynasty. By the Ming, *wuxing* had lost its saliency as a political symbol, but it was still much used in society, for example, to rank siblings (3.2). According to the ancient "mutually overcoming cycle", fire overcomes metal, so Ming 明 (an era of fire as suggested by the sun signific) was set to prevail over Jin 金 (the metal signific). On the other hand, water overcomes fire, so Qing 清 (with the water signific) would have been a preferable choice for the Manchu to attract followers to their banner in the overthrow of the Ming rather than sticking with Jin. Another possible reason why Qing was chosen was that the ceremonies marking the name changes took place at the time of the Qingming 清明 festival (fourth month), which may have put the character uppermost in people's minds.

We may never know for sure the reason for choosing Qing 清 due to the court's order to deliberately destroy the evidence in the sources, but the episode underlines the importance attached to choosing the right name and suggests some of the considerations that may have influenced the choice.

Manzhou midang xuanji 滿洲秘檔選輯 (Selected documents from the secret Manchu archives), Taiwan Yinhang 臺灣銀行, 1968.

Qing Taizuchao lao Manwen yuandang 清太祖朝老滿文原檔 (Original Manchu documents from the archives of the reign of Qing Taizu), Guang Lu 廣祿 et al., Shiyusuo, 2 vols., 1970–72.

Qingchu neiguo shiyuan Manwen dang'an yibian 清初內國史院滿文檔案譯編 (Translated excerpts from the Manchu archives of the early Qing History Bureau), Yishiguan, 3 vols., Guangming ribao, 1989.

Shengjing Manwen dang'an zhong de lüling ji shaoshu minzu falü 盛京滿文檔案中的律令及少數民族法律 (Codes and statutes and laws relating to the national minorities from the Manchu-language archives at Shengjing [Shenyang]), Zhang Ruizhi 張銳智 and Xu Lizhi 徐立志, eds. in chief, 3rd series, vol. 2 of *Zhongguo zhenxi falü dianji jicheng* 中國珍稀法律典籍集成 (Collection of rare works of Chinese law), Liu Hainian 劉海年 and Yang Yifan 楊一凡, series eds., 14 vols., Kexue, 1994. The Shengjing archive volume contains *Shengjing dang'an zhong de lüling* 盛京檔案中的律令 (Legal selections from laws in the Shengyang archives); *Menggu lüli* 蒙古律例 (Mongol laws and precedents); *Xining Qinghai fanyi chengli* 西寧青海藩夷成例 (Regulations for the Commander of Native Affairs of Xining and Qinghai); *Qinding Hui-Jiang zeli* 欽定回疆則例 (Imperially approved regulations for the Moslems of Xinjiang).

Qingdai Xibozu Manwen dang'an shiliao 清代錫伯族滿文檔案史料 (Historical materials from the archives in Manchu on the Xibo people), Yishiguan, eds., 2 vols., Minzu, 1987.

Zheng Chenggong Manwen dang'an shiliao xuanji 鄭成功滿文檔案史料選輯 (Selected translations from the archives on Zheng Chenggong in Manchu), Yishiguan, eds., Fujian renmin, 1987.

Kangxichao Manwen zhupi zouzhe quanyi 康熙朝滿文硃批奏摺全譯 (Complete translation of Manchu Kangxi vermilion-rescripted palace memorials), Yishiguan, eds., Shehui kexue, 1996. Includes more than 5,000 memorials, including those held in Taibei.

Manchu documents can be used to check and supplement Chinese sources. On their importance for the historian of the Qing, see:

Beatrice Bartlett, "Books of Revelations: The Importance of the Manchu Language Archival Books for Research on Ch'ing History," *LIC*, 6.2: 25–36 (1985).

Pamela K. Crossley and Evelyn S. Rawski, "A Profile of the Manchu Language in Ch'ing History," *HJAS* 53.1: 63–102 (1993).

Joseph Fletcher, "Manchu Sources," in Leslie, Mackerras and Wang (1973), 141–46.

Giovanni Stary, *Manchu Studies: An International Bibliography*, 3 vols., Harrassowitz, 1990 (vol. 3 is an author/subject index).

Hartmut Walravens, *Bibliographie der Bibliographien der mandjurischen Literatur*, Harrassowitz, 1996.

Chieh-hsien Chen, *Manchu Archival Materials*, Taibei: Linking Publishing Co., 1988.

50.2.6 Documents on Foreign Relations and Foreigners

This is simply a small selection of published archive documents and other collections of documents in Chinese on late Qing foreign affairs. For a much fuller listing, see *Zhongguo jindaishi wenxian bibei shumu* 中國近代史文獻必備書目 (Essential written sources for the history of modern China), Zhonghua, 1996, 22–29. For foreign sources on relations with the Qing, see 42.3 and 42.4. The extensive bibliographic essays on the border regions and foreign affairs covering both primary and secondary sources in the *CHC* volumes on the Qing are listed at the end of 41.4.

Chouban yiwu shimo 籌辦夷務始末 (The management of barbarian affairs from A to Z), Gugong bowuyuan, eds., 130 vols., 1930. Photo reprint of documents in the Palace Museum. A punctuated edition was put out by Zhonghua in 1964 (*Daoguangchao* 道光朝 *Chouban yiwu shimo*) and 1979 (*Xianfengchao* 咸豐朝 *Chouban yiwu shimo*); Beijing daxue, 9 vols., 1981. Vol. 1 is an index. See also David Nelson Rowe, *Index to Ch'ing Tai Ch'ou Pan I Wu Shih Mo*, Shoestring Press, 1960.

Daoguang, Xianfeng liangchao chouban yiwu shimo buyi 道光咸豐兩朝籌辦夷務始末補遺 (Additional materials from the reigns of Daoguang and Xianfeng on *Chouban yiwu shimo*), 6 vols., Jinshisuo, eds., 1966.

The West

Jindai Zhongguo dui Xifang ji lieqiang renshi ziliao huibian 近代中國對西方及列強認識資料彙編 (Compendium of materials on modern Chinese understanding of the West and the great powers), Jinshisuo, eds., 10 vols., 1972; 1984–90.

Kangxi yu Luoma shijie guanxi wenshu 康熙與羅馬使節關係文書 (Documents on the relations of Kangxi and the ambassadors of Rome), Gugong bowuyuan, eds., 1932.

Siguo xindang (E, Ying, Fa, Mei) 四國新檔 (俄, 英, 法, 美), (New archival materials on four countries, Russia, England, France, America), 4 vols., Jinshisuo, eds., 1966; 2 vols., 1992.

Qingdai waijiao shiliao, Jiaqing Daoguangchao 清代外交史料,嘉慶道光朝 (Historical materials on Qing diplomacy: The reigns of Jiaqing and Daoguang), Beiping: Gugong bowuyuan, eds., 10 vols., 1933. In the series *Waijiao dang'an mulu huibian* 外交檔案目錄彙編 (Collection of catalogs of the diplomatic archives).

Qingji geguo zhaohui mulu 清季各國照會目錄 (Catalog of the diplomatic notes of foreign states during the late Qing period), 4 vols., Gugong wenxianguan 故宮文獻館, eds., Gugong yinshuasuo, 1935–36. Contains 3,800 diplomatic notes. For a listing of all foreign consular and diplomatic officials posted to China between 1843 and 1911, see *Zhongwai shiling nianbiao* 清季中外使領年表 (50.5, *Biographies*).

England

See 28.2 for a sampling of published archives on the Opium War.

Yingshi Mage'erni fang Hua dang'an shiliao 馬戈爾尼訪華檔案史料選編 (Selected historical materials from the archive of the English Ambassador MaCartney's visit to China), Yishiguan, eds., Guoji wenhua, 1996.

France

Qing Guangxuchao Zhong-Fa jiaoshe shiliao 清光緒朝中法交涉史料 (Historical materials on Sino-French relations during the Guangxu period), 11 vols., Gugong wenxianguan 故宮文獻館, eds., Gugong yinshuasuo, 1933.

Zhong-Fa Yuenan jiaoshe dang 中法越南交涉檔 (Archive of Sino-French negotiations on Vietnam), 7 vols., Jinshisuo, eds., 1962.

Zhong-Fa zhanzheng 中法戰爭 (The Sino-French war [1883–85]), Gugong dang'an guan 故宮檔案館, eds., 7 vols., Xin zhishi, 1957. See Lloyd E. Eastman, *Throne and Mandarins: China's Search for a Policy During the Sino-French Controversy, 1880–1885*, HUP, 1967.

Zhong-Fa zhanzheng 中法戰爭 (The Sino-French war), 2 vols., Zhonghua, 1995–96. Includes not only Chinese, but also French archival materials.

Germany

Jiao'Ao zhuandang 胶澳專檔 (Special archives on Jiaozhou Bay), Jinshisuo, eds., 1991.

Deguo qinzhan Jiaozhouwan shiliao xuanbian 德國侵占胶州灣史料選編 (Selected historical materials on the German forced occupation of Jiaozhou Bay), Yishiguan, eds., Shandong renmin, 1987.

United States

Beatrice S. Bartlett, "Archive Materials in China on United States History," in *Guide to the Study of United States History outside the U.S. 1945–80*, Lewis H. Hanke, ed., White Plains, New York: Kraus International, 1985, vol. 1, 504–66. Despite the title, this chapter provides a good general survey of the Qing and Republic up to 1937.

Zhong-Mei guanxi shiliao 中美關係史料 (Historical materials on Sino-American relations), Jinshisuo, eds., 8 vols., 1968; 1988–90.

Missionary Cases

See 33.7.3 on the Protestants in China for further references.

Jiaowu jiao'an dang 教務教案檔 (Archives on church affairs and disputes involving missionaries and converts), 21 vols., Jinshisuo, eds., 1974–81. Contains 10,090 documents dating from the years 1855–99.

Qingji jiao'an shiliao 清季教案史料 (Historical materials on missionary cases during the late Qing), Gugong wenxianguan et al., eds., Part 1, 1937; Part 2, 1948.

Jiao'an shiliao bianmu 教案史料編目 (Bibliography of Chinese source materials dealing with local or international cases involving Christian missions), Wu Shengde 吳盛德 and Chen Zenghui 陳增輝, eds., Yanjing daxue, 1941.

Russia

For a recent study of Sino-Russian relations, see S. C. M. Paine, *Imperial Rivals: China, Russia, and Their Disputed Frontier*, Sharpe, 1996.

Gugong Ewen shiliao 故宮俄文史料 (Russian historical materials in the Palace Museum), Gugong Wenxianguan, eds., Gugong yinshuasuo,

1936. Consists of 23 documents in Russian dating from the early seventeenth and eighteenth centuries.

Gugong Ewen shiliao 故宮俄文史料 (Russian historical materials in the Palace Museum), *Lishi yanjiu* editorial dept., *Lishi yanjiu*, 1964. Of the 202 documents dating from 1670 to 1849 here translated into Chinese, only the 23 Kangxi period documents had already been printed in the previous item.

Qingdai Zhong-E guanxi dang'an shiliao xuanbian 清代中俄關係檔案史料選編 (Selection of historical materials from the archives on Sino-Russian relations during the Qing period), 1ˢᵗ and 3ʳᵈ collections, Yishiguan, eds., 5 vols., Zhonghua, 1979–81.

Zhong-E bianjie tiaoyue ji 中俄邊界條約集 (Collection of Sino-Russian border treaties), Shangwu, eds., Shangwu, 1973.

Zhong-E guanxi shiliao 中俄關係史料 (Historical materials on Sino-Russian relations), Jinshisuo, eds., 24 vols., 1959–75.

Zhongyijun kang E douzheng dang'an shiliao 忠義軍抗俄斗爭檔案史料 (Archival materials on the righteous army's struggle against the Russians), Liaoning sheng dang'an guan et al., eds., Liao-Shen, 1984.

Japan

There is a good guide to modern Sino-Japanese relations, which has very full citations for primary sources (both Chinese and Japanese): Yamane Yukio 山根幸夫 et al., *Kindai Nit-Chû kankeishi kenkyû nyûmon* 近代日中關係史研究入門, Kenbun shuppan, 1992; enlarged ed., 1996. The first two chapters cover 1868–1911.

Qing Guangxuchao Zhong-Ri jiaoshe shiliao 清光緒朝中日交涉史料 (Materials on Sino-Japanese negotiations during the Guangxu reign), 44 vols., Gugong bowuyuan, eds., 1932.

Zhong-Ri guanxi shiliao 中日關係史料 (Historical materials on Sino-Japanese relations), Jinshisuo, eds., 14 vols., 1974–80.

Jiawu Zhong-Ri zhanzheng 甲午中日戰爭 (The Sino-Japanese war of 1894–95), 2 vols., Shanghai renmin, 1982. From the papers of Sheng Xuanhuai 盛宣懷.

Zhong-Ri zhanzheng 中日戰爭 (The Sino-Japanese war), Shixuehui, 7 vols., Xinzhishi, 1956.

Zhong-Ri zhanzheng 中日戰爭 (The Sino-Japanese war), Qi Qizhang 戚其章, ed. in chief, Zhonghua, 1989– . Continuation of the previous item. Collection of documents held in the Yishiguan. There are 11 vols. planned.

Qingji Zhong-Ri-Han guanxi shiliao 清季中日韓關係史料 (Sino-Japanese-Korean relations during the late Qing period), Jinshisuo, eds., 11 vols., 1972.

Korea

Qingdai Zhong-Chao guanxi dang'an 清代中朝關系檔案 (Archives on Sino-Korean relations in the Qing period), Yishiguan, eds., Guoji wenhua, 1996.

Ryûkyû (Liuqiu) 琉球

Qingdai Zhong-Liu guanxi dang'an xuanbian 清代中琉關係檔案選編 (Selected historical materials from the archives on Sino-Ryûkyû relations during the Qing dynasty), Yishiguan, eds., Zhonghua, 1993; ... *xubian* 續編, 1994; ...*sanbian* 三編, 1996.

Others

Huagong chuguo shiliao huibian 華工出國史料匯編 (Compendium of historical materials on Chinese workers going abroad), Yishiguan et al., 4 vols., Zhonghua, 1985.

50.3 Provincial and County Archives

All provincial and county yamen kept extensive archives containing records of all aspects of official business and copies of official documents. Some idea of their extent can be gathered from the fragments of Qin and Han local archives, which have survived (44.3). They show that extremely detailed records were kept even in small border outposts.[22] In the Qing there

---

[22] Almost no trace of a local archive survives from the end of the Tang to the Qing. One exception are the letters and correspondence and office regulations from Huaining (Suzhou) prefectural archive for the years 1162–64, which were found on the reverse side of the pages of one edition of Wang Anshi's papers, but this was a rare find: *Songren yijian* 宋人佚簡 (Lost records of a Song writer), Shanghai guji, 1994. Understandably, modern librarians are unwilling to unstitch valuable, old edi-

Footnote continued on next page

were about 2,000 local yamen whose officials were responsible for a huge range of routine reporting. The filing itself was done by the yamen clerks, each of whom kept the records of his own specialty along the lines of the sixfold division of the Boards (*Li* 吏, *Hu* 户, *Li* 禮, *Bing* 兵, *Xing* 刑, *Gong* 工). In addition, various works of administrative law and regulations were also kept in the yamen.[23] Despite all this documentation, which is known to have been kept in original or in duplicate,[24] no single county or provincial archive is known to have survived intact. The volume of documents and the cost of constructing fire-, damp- and insect-proof buildings was so great that local archives even at the best of times cannot have long survived, and in the twentieth century the collection and preservation of local archives never got under way because of the disturbed conditions. Indeed, many archives must have been destroyed in the upheavals of the last 100 years.

Furthermore, there was hardly a single historian at the end of the Qing or in the first half of the twentieth century who used local archives or who saw their value, unless the archive was an ancient one dating back to the Han or Tang. Small wonder that relatively few local documents from the Qing have survived.[25]

The paucity of surviving documents from provincial or local archives is somewhat mitigated by the fact that centuries before historians in the West emphasized the importance of archival as opposed to literary sources, Chinese historians were still drawing upon a long tradition of handling and quoting

---

tions in order to retrieve what if anything may have been printed on the inside of the pages.

[23] T'ung-tsu Ch'ü, *Local Government in China Under the Ch'ing*, HUP, 1962.

[24] In 1729, as a security measure against fire losses, all yamen were ordered to make copies (*fuben* 副本) of all memorials, which were to be stored separately.

[25] One exception is Sidney D. Gamble, who uses a series of exchange rates (cash/silver) extracted from yamen documents in Ding county; see his *Ting Hsien: A North China Village*, SUP, 1954; rpnt., 1968.

from original documents; thus not a few local documents were preserved in compilations higher up the administrative and historiographical hierarchy (chap. 20, boxes 6 and 7). The same is also true of the local gazetteers (to a limited extent based on the local archives, although they were never intended to be a summary of them). They were compiled only on average two or three times a century and their primary purpose was to enshrine the people, places and literary output of a locality (4.5).

As of the late 1990s, an estimated three million Qing documents were known to be held in provincial or regional archives.[26] By far the largest number, 2.4 million, are preserved in Lhasa at the Archives of the Tibet Autonomous Region, where the cold and possibly also the relative security of Tibet helped preserve them. The earliest documents date from the Yuan. Most are from the Qing and over 90 percent are in Tibetan. The remainder are in Chinese, Manchu, English Russian and Japanese. Over half a million documents have been sorted; it is reckoned that it will take 150 years to complete the sorting. Seventy percent of the holdings are available to researchers, but about 30 percent are in a serious state of deterioration. A selection of over 100 documents are reproduced in color and translated into English and Chinese in *A Collection of the Historical Archives of Tibet*, Wenwu, 1995 (see also 34.5.1 for Tibetan religious archives).

Other major local archives include:

Ba county archive in Sichuan: 113,000 *juan* documents. Their survival was by accident. During World War II, they had been placed in a temple and were found again only in 1953. *Qingdai Qian dao Jia Baxian dang'an xuanbian* 清代乾到嘉巴縣檔案選編 (Selections from the Ba county archive, 1736–1850), 2 vols., Sichuan daxue, 1989 and 1996. They are now held in the Sichuan Provincial Archive at Chengdu. Other documents from the Ba county archives have also been published. See Madeline Zelin, "The Rights of Tenants in Mid-

---

[26] The principal aim of Ye and Esherick in *Chinese Archives: An Introductory Guide* is to describe many of the most important of the 3,500 archival collections in China today. The bulk of the contents of these archives is modern. Only a very small number (181) hold Qing documents.

Qing Sichuan: A Study of Land-related Lawsuits in the Baxian Archives," *JAS* 45.3: 499–526 (1986). On other Sichuan archives, see *Lishi dang'an* 歷史檔案 (1983.2 and 1990.3).

Landholding and tax assessment records (1,608 *juan* covering the years 1706–1911) from various Hebei counties, mainly Huailu 獲鹿. See *Lishi dang'an* 歷史檔案 (1988.1).

Guangdong provincial archives captured by British forces in 1858 (2,000 documents). They are cataloged in David Pong, *A Critical Guide to the Kwangtung Provincial Archives: Deposited at the Public Record Office of London*, HUP, East Asia Research Center, 1975. See also 歷史檔案 (1983.1).

Danshui 淡水 subprefecture; and the Xinzhu 新竹 county archive in northwest Taiwan (1,163 legal files dating from 1789–1895). *Dan-Xin dang'an* 淡新檔案, vol. 1, Taiwan daxue, 1993– . The originals are to be published in 12 vols. (plus notes and indexes in vols. 13 and 14). The archives contain materials relating to legal cases, including pleas, documentary evidence, summaries of testimony, warrants, judicial orders and decisions. See Mark A. Allee, "The Dan-Xin Archives," in *Law and Society in Late Imperial China*, SUP, 1994, 5–14, and the earlier David C. Buxbaum, "Some Aspects of Civil Procedure and Practice at the Trial Level in Tanshui and Hsinchu from 1789 to 1896," *JAS* 30.2: 255–79 (1971).

There are also more or less substantial holdings of Qing official documents, mainly from the end of the dynasty, in the Henan, Heilongjiang 歷史檔案, 1984.2), Yunnan, Gansu, Anhui (*Lishi dang'an* 歷史檔案, 1984.3), Jilin, Shandong (*Lishi dang'an* 歷史檔案, 1984.2) and Guizhou provincial archives. Some of these are available on microfilm or have been published (50.2.2). Parts of various provincial archives from Heilongjiang and Shandong are held at the Yishiguan (50.1.1, item IV).

The public papers of individuals were often published in their lifetimes, or posthumously. The Yishiguan holds extensive collections of the personal archives related to four individuals prominent at the end of the Qing. The documents consist mainly of memorials and official documents from 1875 to 1926 (50.1.1, item D.II).

50.4   Documents of Merchants and Landlords

50.4.1   Introduction

Various local groups of merchants rose to prominence in the Ming and Qing. Their networks eventually extended all over the country.[27] The Huishang 徽商 (Huizhou merchants) were one of the most powerful groups in the South; the Jinshang 晋商 (Shanxi merchants) in the North (50.4.2). Ming-Qing route books and merchant manuals are the focus of 50.4.3. Ming-Qing land deeds and tenancy contracts from various other sources have been transcribed and published (50.4.4). Documents on stone inscriptions with a social or economic interest form a distinct category (50.4.5).

The largest private archive in China is the family archive of the direct descendants of Confucius of which 9,110 *juan* are extant; the documents date from 1522 to 1948. Many volumes of excerpts have been published.[28] Most date from the Qing.

A large archive of a Sichuan salt manufactory has survived.[29] A few account books of shops are known to have survived.[30] Some, notably traditional pharmacies, were sufficiently pros-

---

[27] Their histories are told in the series *Zhongguo shida shangbang* 中國十大商幫 (The 10 merchant groups of China), Shanxi renmin.

[28] *Qufu Kongfu dang'an shiliao xuanbian* 曲阜孔府檔案史料選編 (Edited selections from the archives of the Confucian estate, Qufu), Qufu xian wenguanhui 曲阜縣文管會 et al., 24 vols., Qi-Lu, 1980; *Kongfu dang'an xuanbian* 孔府檔案選編 (Selections from the Confucius family archive), 2 vols., Zhonghua, 1982.

[29] *Zigong yanye qiyue dang'an xuanji* 自貢鹽業契約檔案選輯 (Selected contracts from the Zigong salt industry), Shehui kexue, 1985. There are 30,000 documents from this industry held at the Zigong Municipal Archives, Sichuan.

[30] In 1934, the Beijing Library was presented with 468 volumes of account books dating from the late eighteenth and first half of the nineteenth century from Hebei province. These are the accounts of some 10 shops in Ningjin county and Daliu market town and neighboring villages; see Yan Zhongping 嚴仲平, *Zhongguo jindai jingjishi tongji ziliao xuanji* 中國近代經濟史統計資料選輯 (Selected statistical materials on modern Chinese economic history), Kexue, 1955.

perous and long-lived to have left their mark. It is possible to trace back many of the leading Beijing pharmacies at least to the mid-nineteenth century. In some cases, even further. The Tongren tang 同仁堂, for example, was founded in the Ming and it is still operating.

It is only very rarely that the personal financial accounts of individuals have survived.[31]

50.4.2 Huizhou and Shanxi Merchants

The Huizhou merchants of Anhui reached their high point in the early Qing. They have left behind the single largest extant body of historical land deeds, some going back to the Ming and even earlier. See Joseph McDermott, *The Huizhou Documents—A Key to the Socio-economic History of Late Imperial China*, forthcoming.[32] Their historical background is analyzed and discussed in Harriet T. Zurndorfer, *Change and Continuity in Chinese Local History: The Development of Hui-chou Prefecture*, Brill, 1989. Many of the Huizhou documents have been published and there is also an annotated catalog:

Huizhou lishi dang'an zongmu tiyao 徽州歷史檔案總目提要 (Annotated catalog of Huizhou historical archives), Yan Guifu 嚴桂夫 et al., 2 vols., Huangshan shushe, 1996. The first vol. contains a description of the archives; the second, annotations on some 9,600 documents.

Huizhou qiannian qiyue wenshu 徽州千年契約文書 (A thousand years of contract documents from Huizhou), Zhou Shaoquan 周紹泉, ed. in chief, 40 vols, Huashan wenyi, 1991-93. Contains reproductions of

[31] Zhang Dechang 張德昌, *Qingji yige jingguan de shenghuo* 清季一個京官的生活 (The Life of a Court Official in the Late Qing Dynasty, A Study of Personal Income and Expenditure), HKCU Press, 1970, which tabulates the expenditures of Li Ciming 李慈銘 for the years 1854–94.

[32] See also Michel Cartier, "Naissance de la Huizhoulogie," *Revue bibiographique de sinologie* VIII: 94–100 (1990); and Kang Zhao, "New Data on Landownership Patterns in Ming-Ch'ing China—A Research Note," *JAS* 40.4: 719–33 (1981). The first sighting of the documents was in the 1940s. Fang Hao, Fuji Hiroshi, Fu Yiling 傅衣凌 (1911–88) and Ho Ping-ti wrote about the region in the 1950s and 1960s. The first report of the Huizhou documents was in 1957.

the Huizhou documents held at the Lishisuo. The first 20 volumes reproduce 1,811 documents dating from 1242 to the end of the Ming; the second set of 20 vols. has over 1,400 from the Qing and Republic.

Ming-Qing Huishang ziliao xuanbian 明清徽商資料選編 (Selected materials on the Ming-Qing Huizhou merchants), Zhang Haipeng 張海鵬 (1931–) and Wang Tingyuan 王廷元, eds., Huangshan shushe, 1985. This important collection contains 1,513 entries garnered from all kinds of sources, including Huizhou manuscripts and local genealogies.

Ming-Qing Huishang ziliao xuanbian 明清徽商資料續編 (Second selection of materials on the Ming-Qing Huizhou merchants), Zhang Haipeng 張海鵬 and Wang Tingyuan 王廷元, eds., Huangshan shushe, 1997.

Ming-Qing Huizhou shehui jingji ziliao congbian 明清徽州社會經濟資料從編 (Ming-Qing socioeconomic materials from Huizhou), Anhui sheng bowuguan eds., first selection, Shehui kexue, 1988; 2nd selection, Huizhou wenqi zhengli zu 徽州文契整理組, eds., Shehui kexue, 1990. The second selection contains transcriptions of 12 land purchase or sale deeds from Song and Yuan and 685 from the Ming (originals held at the Lishisuo).

Zhongguo lidai qiyue huibian kaoshi 中國歷代契約匯編考釋 contains many documents including those from Huizhou held in the Peking University library.

There are now many analyses of the operations of the Huizhou merchants. A selection follows:

Huishang fazhanshi 徽商發展史 (History of the development of the Huizhou merchants), Zhang Haipeng 張海鵬 and Wang Tingyuan 王廷元, Huangshan, 1997.

Ming-Qing Huishang yu Huaiyang shehui bianqian 明清徽商與淮楊社會變遷 (The Huizhou merchants and changes in the society of the Huaiyang region in the Ming-Qing), Wang Zhenzhong 王振忠, Sanlian, 1996.

Huishang yanjiu 徽商研究 (Researches on the Huizhou merchants), Zhang Haipeng 張海鵬 and Wang Tingyuan 王廷元, Anhui renmin, 1995.

Huizhou shehui jingjishi yanjiu yiwenji 徽州社會經濟史研究譯文集 (Collection of translated articles on the socioeconomic history of Huizhou), Liu Miao 劉淼, ed., Huangshan, 1988.

Ming-Qing Huizhou tudi guanxi yanjiu 明清徽州土地關係研究 (Land relations in Ming-Qing Huizhou), Zhang Youyi 章有義, ed., Shehui kexue, 1984.

Ming-Qing Huizhou nongcun shehui yu dianpuzhi 明清徽州農村社會與佃僕制 (Ming Qing Huizhou rural society and the tenant bondservant system), Ye Xian'en 葉顯恩, Anhui renmin, 1983. The first comprehensive study of the region.

On the Huizhou merchants as patrons of the arts, see 38.1, note 6.

The Jinshang 晋商 (Shanxi merchants), also called the Shanxi *piaohao* 山西票號 or *piaozhuang* 票莊 (Shanxi bankers) were one of the most powerful groups in the North. One of the main county towns from which the Jinshang operated is Pingyao 平遙. It was made a UNESCO world heritage site in 1998. Several of the Jinshang courtyard houses are still standing, see *Jinshang zhaiyuan* 晋商宅院.[33] One, the Qiao 橋 family house, featured in the Zhang Yimou 張藝謀 film *Raise the Red Lantern*. At the height of their prosperity in the eighteenth century, 70 Qiao family members lived here with 170 servants. They operated 18 businesses trading in oil and vegetables, 200 shops, several coal mines and a bank with 20 branches throughout China. The rise of Shanghai spelled the end of the Qiao and other Shanxi *piaohao* fortunes. See Zhang Zhengming 張正明, *Jin shang xingshuaishi* 晋商興衰史.[34]

50.4.3 *Ming-Qing Route Books and Manuals*

Route Books

Numerous merchant route books (*luchengshu* 路程書) and manuals were published in the Ming and Qing (for this type of work in general, see 4.7.2). For a thorough study containing a bibliography of more than 20 merchant manuals as well as of

---

[33] *Jinshang zhaiyuan* (The Shanxi merchant courtyard houses): Qiao 橋, Wang 王, Cao 曹 and Qu 渠, 4 vols., Shanxi renmin, 1997.

[34] *Jinshang xingshuaishi* (The history of the rise and fall of the Shanxi merchants), Shanxi guji, 1995; rpnt., 1996.

secondary scholarship in Chinese and Japanese on them, see Chen Xuewen 陳學文, *Ming-Qing shiqi shangye shu ji shangren shu zhi yanjiu* 明清時期商業書及商人書之研究.[35]

Yitong lucheng tuji 一統路程圖記 (Comprehensive maps and records of staging posts throughout the empire), Huang Bian 黃汴, preface, 1570; reprinted in: Yang Zhengtai 楊正泰, *Mingdai yizhan kao* 明代 驛站考 (Studies on the Ming postal relay system), Shanghai guji, 1994. *Tianxia shuilu lucheng* 天下水陸路程, Yang Zhengtai 楊正泰, ed., Shanxi renmin, 1992, is almost the same book.

Shuilu lucheng 水陸路程 (Land and water routes), Shang Jun 商濬, preface dated 1617, rpnt. in Yang Zhengtai (1992). Appeared in numerous popular encyclopaedias and under various titles.

Tianxia lucheng, Shiwo zhouxing 天下路程示我周行 (Guide to the routes of the empire). Combines two typical merchant route books, with many dozens of copies extant. The earliest edition is dated 1694. Many reprints appeared, often with different compilers or different titles.

Merchant Manuals

Shishang yaolan 士商要覽 (Essentials for scholar-merchants), early eighteenth century, Dan Yizi 儋漪子 ed. *Juan* 3 contains important materials on business ethics and methods of trading.

A Ming scholar's comments on merchants [from *Songchuang mengyu* 松窗夢語 (Sleep talk from a pine window), Zhang Han 張瀚 (1511–93)] has been translated by Lily Hwa in *Chinese Civilization: A Sourcebook*, Patricia Ebrey, ed., 1981; 2nd ed., rev. and expanded, Free Press, 1993, 216–18. See also Timothy Brook, "The Merchant Network in 16th Century China—A Discussion and Translation of Zhang Han's 'On Merchants.'" *JESHO* 24.2: 165–214 (1981).

Maoyi xuzhi 貿易須知 (Essentials for merchants), Wang Bingyuan 王秉 元, comp., mid-Qing, printed as appendix to Zhang Zhengming 張 正明, *Jin shang xingshuai shi* 晉商興衰史 (The history of the rise and fall of the Shanxi merchants), Shanxi guji, 1995; rpnt., 1996, 335–50.

---

[35] *Ming-Qing shiqi shangyeshu ji shangrenshu zhi yanjiu* (Research on business books and merchant books of the Ming and Qing periods), Hongye, 1997. See also Yamane Yukio 山根幸夫, "Mindai no roteisho ni tsuite 明代の路程書について" (On the route books of the Ming), *Mindaishi kenkyû* 4: 9–24 (1994).

Appears to be based on a late eighteenth-century manual for apprentices, *Shengyi shishi chujie* 生意世事初階 (First introduction to business), late eighteenth century, Wang Bingyuan 王秉元, comp., held at Nanjing daxue tushuguan 南京大學圖書館.

Dianye xuzhi 典業須知 (Essentials for the pawn industry), 1885, L. S. Yang, tr., *Xin Shihuo*, 1.4: 231–43 (1971).

Ming-Qing Merchant Culture

In addition to the copious literature generated by the debates on the buds of capitalism (*ziben zhuyi mengya* 資本主義萌芽), note the following studies of merchants and the rise of urban consumption in late imperial China:

Timothy Brook, *The Confusions of Pleasure: Commerce and Culture in Ming China*, UCP, 1998, and the same scholar's chapter "Communications and Commerce," in *CHC*, vol. 8, 579–707, especially "Merchants in Ming society," 699–707.

Craig Clunas, *Fruitful Sites: Garden Culture in Ming Dynasty China*, Reaktion, 1996.

Craig Clunas, *Superfluous Things: Material Culture and Social Status in Early Modern China*, Polity Press, 1991.

Ping-ti Ho, "The Salt Merchants of Yang-chou: A Study of commercial Capitalism in Eighteenth-Century China," *HJAS* XVII.1–2 (1954).

Chu-tsing Li and James C. Y. Watt, *The Chinese Scholar's Studio: Artistic Life in the Late Ming Period*, Thames and Hudson and Asia Society Galleries, 1987;

Richard John Lufrano, *Honorable Merchants: Commerce and Self-cultivation in Late Imperial China*, UHP, 1997.

50.4.4   Land Deeds and Tenancy Contracts

Selections of Ming and Qing private documents such as land deeds or tenancy agreements from areas other than Huizhou have been published. Some have been annotated and translated into modern Chinese; most have not. General collections of sources sometimes include Ming and Qing private documents. Collections of land deeds and other types of contracts usually include Ming and Qing contracts. Note the works of historians such as Fu Yiling. He began his career with the discovery of a chest of Ming land deeds in a Fujian village (the earliest dating from the beginning of the sixteenth century) and quickly went on to pioneer the use of the documents of the Huizhou merchants (50.4.2). Occasional genealogies also contain private documents relating to land or goods. Japanese historians have analyzed land tenantry in the Ming and Qing using rent books and other such private sources.[36]

Studies of Land Deeds and Tenancy Contracts

Valerie Hansen, *Negotiating Daily Life in Traditional China: How Ordinary People Used Contracts, 600–1400*, YUP, 1995. Analyzes all kinds of contracts in Chinese history from the Tang to the Ming. The first part deals with everyday life contracts, concentrating on the Dunhuang and Turpan materials; the second with afterlife contracts placed in tombs.

Zhongguo lidai qiyue huibian kaoshi 中國歷代契約會編考釋 (Collection of Chinese land deeds with notes and transcriptions), Zhang Chuanxi 張傳璽, ed., 2 vols., Beijing daxue, 1995. Includes 1,402 contracts from the Zhou dynasty to the Republic of China with transcriptions and translations into modern Chinese. The introduction draws on a long article by the same author on the different types of contracts used at different periods of Chinese history and their value as historical sources: "Qiyue wenti 契約問題" in *Qin Han wenti yanjiu* 秦漢問題研究 (Researches on the Qin and Han), rev. and enl. edition, Beijing daxue, 1995, 140–227.

Ming-Qing tudi qiyue wenshu yanjiu 明清土地契約文書研究 (Researches on Ming-Qing land deeds), Yang Guozhen 楊國楨, ed., Renmin, 1988.

Transcriptions of Land Deeds

Chûgoku tochi keiyaku monjoshû Kin-Shin 中國土地契約文書集·金-清 (Collection of texts of Chinese land deeds, Jin to Qing), Mindaishi kenkyûshitsu at the Tôyô bunko, eds., Tokyo, 1975. Gathers between two covers land deeds from 33 sources, including from Ming dynasty popular encyclopaedias.

Ming-Qing Suzhou nongcun jingji ziliao 明清蘇州農村經濟資料 (Economic materials from Suzhou villages in the Ming and Qing), Hong

---

[36] Muramatsu Yuji 村松祐次, *Kindai Kônan no sosen* 近代江南の租棧 (The bursaries of modern Jiangnan), Tokyo, 1970.

Huanchun 洪煥椿, ed., Jiangsu guji, 1988. Three hundred forty texts arranged under eight heads.

Ming-Qing Fujian jingji qiyue wenshu xuanji 明清福建經濟契約文書選輯 (Selected Ming-Qing economic contracts from Fujian), Shanghai shifan daxue, 1996.

Minnan qiyue wenshu zonglu 閩南契約文書綜錄 (Comprehensive account of land deeds in southern Fujian), *Zhongguo shehui jingjishi yanjiu*, 1990, special edition.

Qingdai diqi dang'an shiliao (Jiaqing zhi Xuantong) 清代地契檔案史料 嘉慶至宣統 (see 50.2.3).

Qing Hezhou qiwen huibian 清河州契文匯編, Gansu sheng Linxia huizu zizhizhou dang'an guan, 甘肅省臨夏回族自治州檔案館, Gansu renmin, 1993. Contains 588 land deeds dating from 1819–1911.

Tôyô bunka kenkyûjo shozô Chûgoku tochi monjo mokuroku kaisetsu 東洋 文化研究所藏中國土地文書目錄解説, Hamashita Takeshi 濱下武 志 et al., 2 vols., Tokyo, 1983–86. This contains (1) selections from 10 sets of Qing and Republican-period documents, with introductions and annotations and (2) a complete catalog of the 10 sets of documents (2,250 items in total).

Mizhixian Yangjiagou diaocha 米脂縣楊家溝調查 (Investigation of Yanjiagou, Mizhi county), Yan'an nongcun diaocha tuan 延安農村調查 團 (Yan'an investigation team), eds., Sanlian, 1957; rpnt., Renmin, 1980. Field study conducted in a north Shaanxi village in 1941.

Jing Su 景甦 and Luo Lun 羅崙 in their study of Shandong landlords, *Qingdai Shandong jingying dizhu de shehui xingzhi* 清代山東經營地 主底社會性質, Shandong renmin, 1959; Endymion Wilkinson, tr.: *Landlord and Labor in Late Imperial China*, HUP, 1980. Land deeds and other records of landlord enterprises were used in this study, some dating from the eighteenth century.

50.4.5 Stone Inscriptions of a Socioeconomic Interest

Eduard B. Vermeer, *Chinese Local History: Stone Inscriptions from Fukien in the Sung to Ch'ing Periods*, Westview, 1991. Transcribes, translates and comments 23 stone inscriptions.

Imahori Seiji 今堀誠二, *Chûgoku hôken shakai no kikô* 中國封建社會の 機構 (Chinese feudal society: An intensive investigation of social groups in a county town from the early Qing on), Nihon gakujutsu shinkôkai, 1955. The stelae are included in an appendix, 701–837.

Jiangsu sheng Ming-Qing yilai beike ziliao xuanji 江蘇省明清以來碑刻資料選集 (Selection of Jiangsu stone inscriptions from the Ming-Qing onward), Jiangsu sheng bowuguan, ed., 3 vols., Sanlian shudian, 1959; rpnt., Daian, 1967. Contains 370 transcriptions of stele texts of special interest to the economic historian.

Jiangxi chutu muzhi xuanbian 江西出土墓志選編 (A selection of funerary texts excavated in Jiangxi), Chen Baiquan 陳柏泉, ed., Jiangxi jiaoyu, 1991; also includes 220 land deeds from the Tang to the Qing.

Ming-Qing Foshan beike wenxian jingji ziliao 明清佛山碑刻文獻經濟資料 (Ming Qing economic materials from Foshan stele and documents), Guangdong renmin, 1987.

Ming-Qing Suzhou gongshangye beikeji 明清蘇州工商業碑刻集 (Collected Suzhou Ming-Qing stele on industry and commerce), Suzhou bowuyuan et al., comps., Jiangsu renmin, 1981.

Ming-Qing yilai Beijing gongshang huiguan beike xuanbian 明清以來北京工商會館碑刻選編 (Selected stele inscriptions from the Ming-Qing Beijing gild and *landsmannschaften*), Li Hua 李華, ed., Wenwu, 1980, 1990.

Niida Noboru hakase shû Pekin girudo kôshô shiryôshû 仁井田蹟博士輯北京工商ギルド資料集 (Materials on Beijing industrial and commercial guilds collected by Dr. Niida Noboru), 6 vols., Tôbunken, 1975–83.

Qingdai gongshang hangye beiwen jicui 清代工商行業碑文集粹 (Selection of the best Qing dynasty industrial and commercial gild stele and documents), Peng Zeyi 彭澤益, comp., Zhongzhou guji, 1997.

Shanghai beike ziliao xuanji 上海碑刻資料選輯 (Selections from Shanghai stele inscriptions), Shanghai renmin, 1980. Contains 245 transcriptions of stele texts from the Song to the Qing.

Taiwan nanbu beiwen jicheng 臺灣南部碑文集成, 6 vols., Taiwan yinhang, ed. and publisher, 1966; rpnt., 1994.

Taiwan zhongbu beiwen jicheng 臺灣中部碑文集成, Liu Zhiwan 劉枝萬, ed., Taiwan yinhang, 1962; rpnt., 1994.

50.5 Main Historical Works

Manwen laodang 滿文老檔 (The old Manchu archives), cover the years 1607–36. Six copies were made in the Qianlong reign. Today, four are in the Yishiguan and two in the Shenyang archives. The original is held in Taibei (see 50.2.5

for further details of these and other Manchu-language sources).

Qijuzhu 起居注. Starting from 1629, various Court Diaries were kept. These contained a daily account of the emperor's activities and utterances. The record keeping was regularized early in the reign of Kangxi (1670) and continued both in Manchu and in Chinese until the end of the dynasty, one volume per month, rising to two per month from Yongzheng onward. Altogether, more than 12,000 *ce* of the Court Diaries are extant, some held in Taibei, some in Beijing. They form one of the most important basic sources for the history of the Qing dynasty. The diaries were secret documents, in theory not open even to the emperor. They were held in the archives of the Inner Court. Written at the most one year after the events they record, they contain reliable details not found in more public documents, including the Veritable Records, which were to a large extent based on them. Some are available in draft form; the Chinese versions of the following reigns have been printed (the Manchu versions are available on microfilm (50.2.1).

Kangxichao qijuzhuce 康熙朝起居注册 (Court Diaries of the Kangxi reign), typeset, punctuated ed., 3 folio vols., Zhonghua, 1983.

Yongzhengchao qijuzhuce 雍正朝起居注册 (Court Diaries of the Yongzheng reign), photolithographic ed., Yishiguan, 5 vols., Zhonghua, 1993.

Daoguangchao qijuzhuce 道光朝起居注册 (Court Diaries of the Daoguang reign), photolithographic ed., 100 vols., Lianhebao wenhua jijinhui Guoxue wenxianguan, Taibei: Lianji chubanshiye gongsi, 1983.

Xianfengchao qijuzhuce 咸豊朝起居注册 (Court Diaries of the Xianfeng reign), photolithographic ed., 57 vols., Lianhebao wenhua jijinhui Guoxue wenxianguan, Taibei: Lianji chubanshiye gongsi, 1983.

Tongzhichao qijuzhuce 同治朝起居注册 (Court Diaries of the Tongzhi reign), photolithographic ed., 43 vols., Lianhebao wenhua jijinhui Guoxue wenxianguan, Taibei: Lianji chubanshiye gongsi, 1983.

Guangxuchao qijuzhuce 光緒朝起居注册 (Court Diaries of the Guangxu reign), photolithographic ed., 80 vols., Lianhebao wenhua jijinhui Guoxue wenxianguan, Taibei: Lianji chubanshiye gongsi, 1987.

The *Qing Shilu* 清實錄 (Veritable Records of the Qing; full title was *Da Qing lichao Shilu* 大清歷朝實錄), are another very important basic historical source for the Qing. They are 30 percent longer than the *Ming Shilu* totaling altogether 60 million characters. Veritable Records were compiled for all 12 Qing emperors, with the exception of Pu Yi's reign (1909–11), for which the similar work is called *Xuantong zhengji* 宣統政紀 (Political records of the Xuantong reign). Each *Shilu* was compiled by the new emperor for his predecessor. There are two printed editions of the *Shilu*:

> *Qing Shilu* 清實錄, 60 folio vols., Zhonghua, 1986–87. This is based on the original copy preserved in the Huangshicheng 皇史宬, Beijing (now in the Yishiguan), collated with various parts and drafts of the *Qing Shilu* held at Peking University, the Palace Museum and in the Liaoning (Shenyang) archives.

> *Tai Shin rekichô jitsuroku* 大清歷朝實錄, 4,485 *juan* in 120 *han*, 1,220 *ce*. 300 copies printed and published for the Manchuria-Japan Cultural Association, Ministry of Finance, Tokyo, 1934–36. This is a photographic reproduction of the copy of the Veritable Records kept at the Shengjing 盛京 (Shenyang) palace. A complete facsimile reprint was made of all the *Shilu* with the exception of the *Xuantong zhengji* by Huawen, Taibei, 93 vols., 1963–64; Liaoning Shekeyuan, 1980.

Other editions of the *Shilu* were edited, including trilingual Manchu, Chinese and Mongolian editions. Various portions were published separately, or especially for the government of Manchukuo (details may be found in the Introduction to the Zhonghua edition, which also discusses the process of drafting and publication of the *Qing Shilu*). Some have been reprinted.[37]

There are a considerable number of published excerpts from the *Qing Shilu*, which are potential time-savers—for example, *Qing Shilu jingjishi ziliao* 清實錄經濟史資料.[38] The

---

[37] *Qing Taizu gao huangdi Shilu, gaoben sanzhong* 清太祖高皇帝實錄, 稿本三種, Beijing, 1933–4.

[38] *Qing Shilu jingjishi ziliao* (Historical materials from the Veritable Records of the Qing), Chen Zhenhan 陳振漢 et al., comps., 3 vols., Bei-

Footnote continued on next page

first three volumes contain excerpts on agriculture for the period 1644–1820 (vol. 1, population and land; vol. 2, agricultural production; vol. 3, part 1, agricultural taxes and vol. 3, part 2 [in fact a fourth volume], living conditions and uprisings). Other selections of excerpts concentrate on individual provinces or regions—for example:

Qing Shilu Guangxi ziliao jilu 清實錄廣西資料輯錄 (Materials on Guangxi collected from the *Qing Shilu*), 5 vols., Guangxi renmin, 1988.

Qing Shilu Jiang-Zhe-Hu dizhu ziliao xuan 清實錄江浙滬地主資料選 (Selection of materials from the *Qing Shilu* on the landlords of Jiangsu, Zhejiang and Shanghai), Shanghai shehui kexueyuan, 1989. Has an index.

Qing Shilu Ningxia ziliao jilu 清實錄寧夏資料輯錄 (Selected materials on Ningxia from the *Qing Shilu*), 3 vols., Ningxia renmin, 1986.

Qing Shilu Shaanxi ziliao huibian 清實錄陝西資料匯編 (Collected materials on Shaanxi from the *Qing Shilu*), Shaanxi guji, 1996.

Qing Shilu Shandongshi ziliao xuan 清實錄山東史資料選 (Selected historical materials on Shandong from the *Qing Shilu*), 3 vols., Qi-Lu, 1984.

Qing Shilu Sichuan shiliao xuan 清實錄四川史料選 (Historical materials on Sichuan from the *Qing Shilu*), Dianzi keji daxue, 1988.

Qing Shilu Yunnan shiliao jiyao 清實錄雲南史料輯要 (40.2, *Historical excerpts*).

Qing Shilu Xinjiang ziliao jilu 清實錄新疆資料輯錄 (Selected materials on Xinjiang from the *Qing Shilu*), 12 vols., Xinjiang minzu yanjiusuo, 1978.

For excerpts on non-Han peoples from the *Qing Shilu*, see 40.2 and 41.4.1.

---

jing daxue, 1989–93. Another selection of economic source materials is *Qing Shilu jingji ziliao jiyao* 清實錄經濟資料輯要 (Excerpts from economic source materials from the *QingShilu*), Nankai daxue Lishixi 南開大學歷史系, eds., Zhonghua, 1959. It is arranged under 75 topics.

Donghua lu 東華錄 (Records from within the Eastern Gate of the palace compound), Jiang Liangqi 蔣良騏 (1723–89); punctuated edition, Zhonghua, 1980. This important annalistic source (covering from 1644 to the Yongzheng period) is so called from the fact that the first compiler, Jiang Liangqi, worked as an official in the Guoshi guan 國史館 (Historiography Institute), which after 1765 was situated inside the Donghua gate of the Forbidden City. The *Shiyichao Donghualu* 十一朝東華錄 covers the years 1644–1874 and the much fuller *Guangxuchao Donghualu* 光緒朝東華錄, 5 vols., punctuated ed., Zhonghua, 1958, covers the years 1875–1908. Although less detailed than the Veritable Records (upon which they were mainly based), the various *Donghua lu* are a quick way of finding sources in the Veritable Records.[39]

Qingshi gao 清史稿 (Draft Standard History of the Qing), Zhao Erxun 趙爾巽 (1844–1927) et al., comps., 48 vols., Zhonghua, 1976–77; 5th prnt., 1996. Covers the years 1644–1911. Work on the draft began at the instruction of Yuan Shikai 袁世凱 (1859–1916) in 1914.[40] The draft has never been fully accepted as one of the Standard Histories (indeed it was proscribed by the KMT) because it was compiled by Qing loyalists. Zhonghua published a punctuated edition in 1977 (reissued in reduced-size with biographical index, 4 vols., 1997). The monograph on penal law has also been published separately.[41] There is an annotated translation of part of the

[39] Knight Biggerstaff, "A Note on the *Tung-hua lu* and the *Shih-lu*," *HJAS* 4.2: 101–15 (1939).

[40] Thurston Griggs, "The Ch'ing Shih Kao: A Bibliographical Summary," *HJAS* 18: 105–23 (1955). Eric Haenisch, "*Das Ts'ing-shi-kao* und die sonstige chinesische Literatur zur Geschichte der letzten 300 Jahre," *AM* 6.4: 403–44 (1930). The biographies section was included among the materials indexed in *H-Y Index* 9.

[41] *Qingshi gao xingfa zhi zhujie* 清史稿刑法志註解 (Monograph on penal law from the *Qingshi gao*), Falü, 1957.

monograph on financial administration.[42] The Zhonghua edition of the *Qingshi gao* is fully indexed in the Shiyusuo's *Nianwushi quanwen ziliaoku* 廿五史全文資料庫 (25 Histories full text database), 1988 (see 22.2). There is a name index to the basic annals, tables and biographies sections: *Qingshi gao ji, biao, zhuan renming suoyin* 清史稿紀表傳人名索引.[43]

The *Qingshi* 清史 (History of the Qing) was completed in 1962 by a committee in Taiwan.[44] It is largely based on the *Qingshi gao*. It has a name index included in the last volume. Unfortunately, there are many errors. These were corrected in the *Renshou* edition of the Standard Histories.

Qing santong 清三通 (26.2):

> *Qingchao tongdian* 清朝通典; covers 1644–1785 (Table 25, 26.2).
>
> *Qingchao tongzhi* 清朝通志; covers 1644–1785 (Table 25, 26.2).
>
> *Qingchao wenxian tongkao* 清朝文獻通考; covers 1644–1785 (Table 25, 26.2).

Qingchao xu wenxian tongkao (1921), Liu Jinzao 劉錦藻. From 1786 to 1911. This is the highest quality of the Qing continuations of the *Shitong* (Table 25, 26.2).

Fanglüe 方略 (28.2). Official publications of imperial campaigns against enemies at home and abroad. The titles of these works usually are in the form of *Pingding* 平定 ... *fanglüe* 方略 (Strategy for the pacification of ...), hence the generic title *fanglüe*. They were normally written immediately after a campaign and based on edicts, memo-

---

[42] Hoshi Ayao 星斌夫, *Shinshikô sôunshi yakuchû* 清史稿漕運志譯註 (Annotated translation of the section on tribute transportation of the monograph on financial administration in the *Qingshi gao*), Kôbundô, 1962.

[43] *Qingshi gao ji, biao, zhuan renming suoyin* 清史稿紀表傳人名索引 (Name-index to the tables, and biographies sections of the Draft History of the Qing), He Yingfang 何英芳, comp., 2 vols., Zhonghua, 1996.

[44] *Qingshi*, 8 vols., Taibei: Guofang yanjiuyuan 國防研究院, 1961.

rials and battle reports. The form was *jishi benmo* (topically arranged).

50.6   Other Textual Sources

50.6.1   Geographical Works

Three comprehensive gazetteers of the empire were compiled during the Qing. The proposal to begin the first was agreed by the Kangxi emperor in 1672, but it was completed only in 1743 because of the time taken to newly compile the provincial gazetteers upon which it was based:

Da Qing yitongzhi 大清一統志, Xu Qianxue 徐乾學 et al., comps., completed 1746.

Da Qing yitongzhi 大清一統志, Heshen 和珅 et al., comps., presented in 1784 and printed in 1790.

Da Qing yitongzhi 大清一統志, Muzhang'a 穆彰阿 et al., comps., completed in 1820 at the end of the Jiaqing period and thus referred to as the *Jiaqing chongxiu da Qing yitongzhi* 嘉慶重修大清一統志, printed in 1842; Shangwu reprint with this title with an index, Shanghai, 1934; Taibei, 1967; Shanghai shudian, 1981–84. The *Jiaqing yitongzhi* was the largest and most accurate of this type of Comprehensive Gazetteer. From it may be gained a detailed picture of the administrative geography of the entire empire at the beginning of the nineteenth century; more detailed information on individual places is of course available in the many thousands of extant Qing local gazetteers.[45]

In addition to the more than 5,600 local gazetteers that were compiled during the Qing (70 percent of all extant gazetteers, see 4.6), many guides and accounts of individual cities, especially the capital, have survived, for example the two works below (see *Biji* for other titles):

[45] G. M. H. Playfair, *The Cities and Towns of China: A Geographical Dictionary* (Hong Kong, 1879; 2nd ed., Kelly and Walsh, 1910; rpnt., Chengwen, 1965) is based on the *Jiaqing yitongzhi* and is useful for locating better-known places, rivers, etc. (as of the late nineteenth century). It also gives coordinates.

Rixia jiuwen kao 日下舊聞考 (Historical studies of Beijing), Yu Min-zhong 于敏中 (1714–80), 1774; 4 vols., Beijing guji, 1985. Yu was the official in charge of the *Siku quanshu*. He expanded an earlier work, the *Rixia jiuwen* 日下舊聞 of Zhu Yizun 朱彝尊, 1629–1709, which quoted in 13 categories 1,449 sources on the history of Beijing from the earliest times to the end of the Ming.

Dumen zaji 都門雜記 (Miscellaneous notes on the capital), 1864. Issued under many different titles, it was intended as a guide to the capital for visiting scholars, officials and merchants.

Works on Border Areas

Materials on the border regions have been excerpted from the *Qing Shilu* (for titles of those on Ningxia, Yunnan and Xinjiang, see 50.5). Many topographical or historical studies of border regions or border peoples were also compiled in the Qing—for example:

Xinjiang zhilüe 新疆識略 (History of Xinjiang), Songyun 松筠 (1752–1835) et al., 1821; Tongwenguan movable-type ed., 1882.

Huangchao fanbu yaolüe 皇朝藩部要略 (Essentials on this august dynasty's barbarian territories [Mongolia, Xinjiang and Tibet]), Qi Yunshi 祁韻士 (1751–1815), 1845; Zhejiang shuju, 1884.

Menggu youmu ji 蒙古游牧記 (Record of nomad life in Mongolia), Zhang Mu 張穆 (1805–49); collated and added to by He Qiutao 何秋濤 (1824–62); completed, 1859; printed in 1867; included in *Guoxue jiben congshu* (9.6).

Shuofang beisheng 朔方備乘 (Historical sources on the Northern Regions), He Qiutao 何秋濤, 1881. First major study of Sino-Russian relations.

Qingdai bianjiang shidi lunzhu suoyin 清代邊疆史地論著索引 (Index of books and articles on the historical geography of the border areas in the Qing dynasty), Zhongguo renmin daxue, Qingshi yanjiusuo and Shekeyuan Zhongguo bianjiang shidi yanjiusuo, eds., Renmin daxue, 1988. Contains 8,000 articles and 1,200 books written 1900–86, including those published in Taiwan and Hong Kong. Arrangement is by categories and by area.

50.6.2 Laws and Regulations

Huidian 會典 *and zeli* 則例. During the Qing, no commands (*ling* 令) were promulgated, but the Ming model for issuing very detailed *Huidian* 會典 (institutes) was followed. There were five editions of such *Huidian*, all of which were entitled *Da Qing huidian* 大清會典 (Institutes of the great Qing dynasty). Each carried the important administrative law put in force since the previous edition (in the form of *zeli* 則例 or *shili* 事例, precedents and regulations, substatutes) and each is referred to by the reign name in which it was compiled (although in library catalogs they are entered under the actual title *Da Qing huidian* ... or *Qinding* 欽定 (Imperially authorized) *Da Qing huidian*:

Da Qing huidian 大清會典

Kangxi huidian 康熙會典, drafting began in 1684; completed in 1690, 162 *juan*, printed in 1696.

Yongzheng huidian 雍正會典, drafting began in 1624; completed in 1733, 250 *juan*, printed in 1734. Adds the institutions of 1687 to 1727 to the *Kangxi huidian*.

Qianlong huidian 乾隆會典, drafting began in 1747; completed in 1764; printed in 1768 + *Qinding da Qing huidian* 欽定大清會典, 100 *juan*, + *huidian zeli* 會典則例 (supplementary regulations and substatutes), 180 *juan*.

Jiaqing huidian 嘉慶會典, drafting began in 1801; completed in 1818; printed in 1822, 80 *juan* + *shili* 事例 (supplementary regulations and sub-statutes), 920 *juan* +*tu* 圖 (illustrations), 132 *juan*. Adds institutions since previous edition up to 1813.

Guangxu huidian 光緒會典, drafting began in 1886; completed in 1899, 100 *juan*; Shangwu, 1904 + *shili*, 1,220 *juan* +*tu*, 270 *juan*, rpnt., Zhonghua, 14 vols., 1991; 1995. Adds institutions, supplementary regulations and statutes between 1813 and 1896.

Zeli 則例

A very large number of works of early Qing administrative law as well as many editions of the Regulations and sub-statutes of individual departments (*buli* 部例, *zeli* 則例) are extant. The titles of some of the most important (omitting the prefix *Qinding* 欽定 ... "Imperially authorized ...") are:

Baqi zeli 八旗則例 (Regulations and precedents for the eight banners), 1739; Xuesheng shuju, 1968; Dongbei shifan daxue punctuated ed., 1985.

Gongbu zeli 工部則例 (Regulations and precedents of the Board of Works), 1749; 1798; 2nd rev., 1891; Jiaqing edition (1798), 20 vols. photolithographic ed., Beijing tushuguan, 1997.

Guochao gongshi 國朝宮史 (Palace regulations) completed in 1742; rewritten, 1769. One of the three MS copies was reprinted in a punctuated edition by Beijing guji in 1987. A continuation up to 1810 was finally published by the Palace Museum in 1932. See also the later *Gongzhong xianxing zeli* 宮中現行則例 (Presently applied regulations and precedents in the palace), 1856; 1888.

Hubu zeli 戶部則例 (Regulations and precedents of the Board of Revenue), 1776; thereafter 13 rev. eds. to 1851; 1864, Tongzhi rev. rpnt., Chengwen, 1966. More detailed regulations on different aspects of the work of the Board were also printed, for example, the *Hubu caoyun quanshu* 戶部漕運全書 (The Board of Revenue complete book of grain transport), 1735; 4th rev., 1876. Also the regulations for the separate provinces on customs; salt, famine relief and canals.

Libu zeli 禮部則例 (Regulations and precedents of the Board of Rites), 1794; 2nd rev., 1841; rpnt., Chengwen, 1966.

Libu zeli 吏部則例 (Regulations and precedents of the Board of Civil Office), 1734; rev., 1742; rev., 1783; Daoguang, Tongzhi and Guangxu revisions, Chengwen, 1966. More detailed regulations on different aspects of the work of the Board were also printed.

Lifanyuan zeli 理藩院則例 (Regulations and precedents of the Board of Colonial Affairs), 1789; 1817; 2nd rev., 1891; 1908.[46]

Zongrenfu zeli 宗人府則例 (Regulations and precedents of the Office of the Imperial Lineage), 1739; 3rd rev., 1888.

[46] Most of these works went through many editions and many other regulations were also published. Ma Fengchen 馬奉琛 lists and briefly describes 500 such works in his *Qingdai xingzheng zhidu yanjiu cankao shumu* 清代行政制度研究參考書目 (Reference catalog for research on the Qing administrative system), Beijing daxue, 1935.

Shengli 省例

One of the unique features of Qing administrative law is that collections of provincial sub-statutes and cases (*shengli* 省例) relating to a single province were printed. In addition to the *shengli*, provincial yamen from the eighteenth century began printing the official regulations, which they received from the central government in works usually called *dingli* 定例 (established regulations) or *tiaoli* 條例 (itemized regulations or sub-statutes), some of which have survived.[47] The regulations for particular institutions at the provincial level, for example the salt monopoly, have also survived, see under *Hubu zeli* above.

Fujian shengli 福建省例 (Substatutes of Fujian province), 1873; rpnt., Chengwen, 1967.

Hunan shengli cheng'an 湖南省例成案 (Substatutes and Leading Cases of Hunan province), Changsha, 1820. The largest and the most interesting.

Jiangsu shengli 江蘇省例 (Substatutes of Jiangsu province), Nanjing, 1869; continuations published in 1875, 1883 and 1890.

Jinzheng jiyao 晋政輯要 (Extracts for governing Shanxi Province).

Xijiang zhengyao 西江政要 (Essentials of government of Jiangxi province).

Yuedong shengli xinzuan 粤東省例新纂 (Newly edited Sub-statutes of Guangdong province), Huang Enzheng 黃恩正 comp., 1846, 2 vols., Taibei, 1968. Not as interesting a work as the *Yuedong cheng'an chubian* 粤東成案初編 (Criminal and civil cases decided in Guangdong province), Guangzhou, 1832.

Zhi Zhe chenggui 治浙成規 (Regulations for governing Zhejiang province).[48]

Da Qing lüli 大清律例 (27.2).

---

[47] See Fu-mei Chang Chen, "Provincial Documents of Laws and Regulations in the Ch'ing Period," *Ch'ing-shih wen-t'i*, vol. 3.6: 28–48 (1976).

[48] Terada Hiroaki 寺田浩明, "Shindai no shôrei 清代省例" (Provincial Sub-statutes and Cases in the Qing dynasty) in *Chûgoku hôseishi, kihon shiryô no kenkyû* (Chinese legal history: studies on basic source materials), Shiga Shûzô 滋賀秀三, ed., Tokyo daigaku, 1993; rpnt., 1994, 657–714.

Xing'an huilan 刑案匯覽 (27.2).

Fuhui quanshu 福惠全書 (27.4).

Qiangu beiyao 錢穀備要 (27.5).

50.6.3 Army and Uprisings

See chap. 28 for Qing sources on the army, wars (28.2) and uprisings (28.3).

50.6.4 Edicts and Memorials

Da Qing shichao shengxun 大清十朝聖訓 (Sacred instructions and edicts of 10 Qing emperors, 1880). Most comprehensive collection for Qing; covers the years 1616 to 1874 in 922 *juan*. Arranged by topics.

[Yongzheng] zhupi yuzhi 雍正硃批諭旨 (Vermilion-rescripted edicts of the Yongzheng period [1723–35], 1738, photolithographic rpnt., Beijing, 1930. Contains several thousand edicts directly dealt with by the emperor and carrying his personal comments and instructions in vermilion (hence the title).

Yongzheng shangyu neige 雍正上諭內閣 (Edicts of the Yongzheng emperor issued through the Grand Secretariat), 1731 and 1741, Beijing. Arranged chronologically.

Shangyu baqi 上諭八旗 (Edicts of the Yongzheng Emperor to do with the Eight Banners, 1741). Arranged chronologically.

Most leading officials of the late Qing had their memorials printed. Many of these collections are listed in Ma Fengchen 馬奉琛 (1935).

Huangchao jingshi wenbian 皇朝經世文編 (This august dynasty's memorials on statecraft). Altogether 16 were published during the Qing. These collections contain the important memorials of well over 2,000 Qing officials and they have been conveniently indexed by the Kindai Chûgoku kenkyûkai iinkai, *Keisei bunpen sômokuroku sakuin* 經世文編總目錄索引 (Seminar on Modern China at the Tôyô bunko), 3 vols., Tokyo, 1956. There is also an author index attached to volume three of the Zhonghua photolithographic edition: *Qing jingshi wenbian* 清經世文編, 3 vols., Zhonghua, 1992. The first volumes list the subject of each memorial (following the arrangement of the collections) while vol. 3 is an author index (with Wade-Giles finding list). Helen Dunstan, *Conflicting Counsels to Confuse the Age* (50.8.2) could serve as an excellent introduction to these documents.

There is no list comparable to the *ISMH* for the Qing; but see Fairbank (1965), I: 39–105, for a list of some major collections of memorials and also the memorial collections published from the Qing archives in the 1930s and later (50.8.2). For a fuller listing of published collections and catalogs of memorials, reports, etc. from the Qing archives, see 50.2.

The following guides and indexes to the titles of the memorials of high late Qing officials are available:

Guide to the Memorials of Seven Leading Officials of Nineteenth-Century China, Chung-li Chang and Stanley Spector, eds., UWP, 1955. Contains a useful subject index to the contents of the memorials of Zeng Guofan, Hu Linyi, Zuo Zongtang, Guo Songtao, Li Hongzhang, Zeng Guoquan and Zhang Zhidong.

Sa Sôtô, Chô Shidô, Setsu Fusei, Chô Ken sôgi mokuroku 左宗棠張之洞薛福成張謇奏議目錄 (Index of memorials by Zuo Zongtang, Zhang Zhidong, Xue Fucheng and Zhang Qian), Seminar on Modern China, ed., Tôyô bunko, 1955.

Sei Senkai, En Seigai sôgi mokuroku 盛宣懷袁世凱奏議目錄 (Index of Memorials presented to the emperor by Sheng Xuanhuai and Yuan Shikai), Seminar on Modern China, ed., Tôyô bunko, 1955.

50.6.5 Agriculture

Bu Nongshu 補農書 (35.1).
Hengchan suoyan 恒產瑣言 (35.1).
Shoushi tongkao 授時通考 (35.1).
Gengzhi tu 耕織圖 (35.1).
Nongyan zhushi 農言著實 (35.1).

50.6.6 Bieji 別集

The final count of extant Qing collected works (including both collected works of individual authors, *bieji* 別集 and literary anthologies, *zongji* 總集) has not yet been made. Estimates range as high as 13,000. The dynastic bibliographies of the *Qingshi gao* list over 5,000 titles. The contents of less than 1,000 have been indexed. The main published indexes are:

Qingren wenji bielu 清人文集別錄 (Additional notes on the collected works of Qing authors), Zhang Shunhui 張舜徽, 2 vols., Zhonghua, 1963, rpnt., 1980. The modest title of the author suggests an annotated catalog. But it is more than that. Zhang has selected 599 of the cream of Qing *bieji* (perhaps between five and 10 percent of the total) and uses his notes to describe the life and works of each author. There is a personal-name index.

Qingdai wenji pianmu fenlei suoyin 清代文集篇目分類索引 (Subject index to tables of contents of Qing collected works), Wang Zhongmin 王重民 et al., comps., Guoli Beiping tushuguan 國立北平圖書館, 1935; Zhonghua, 1965; Guofeng, 1965. Indexes tables of contents in 428 collected works of individual Qing authors and 12 general collections; particularly useful because arranged by subject under the three broad categories of scholarly, biographical and miscellaneous.

Qingdai wenji shulu 清代文集書錄 (Catalog of Qing dynasty *wenji*), Ke Yuchun 柯愈春, comp., Zhonghua, forthcoming. The largest index to date.

Nihon genzon 日本現存 *Shinjin bunshû mokuroku* 清人文集目錄 (Catalog of collected works by Qing authors extant in Japanese libraries), Nishimura Genshô 西村元照, ed., Tôyôshi kenkyûkai, 1972.

50.6.7 Biji 筆記

In the Qing, the full variety of *biji* writing continued, ranging from failed scholars writing colorful guides to the big cities to famous scholars and historians, including Gu Yanwu, Zhao Yi, Qian Daxin and Wang Mingsheng, recording some of their most interesting observations in their *biji*, often culled from a lifetime of reading (chap. 31).[49] The selection of 17 Qing *biji* given below reflects this variety. Note also the two examples of *biji* guides to the capital under *Geography* above and also the selection of Qing *zashi* 雜史 in chap. 24. The first seven listed below are the most famous Qing *kaozheng* 考證 (evidential research on historical and textual questions) *biji*.

---

[49] Zhang Shunhui 張舜徽 has published notes taken from 100 Qing *biji* in *Qingren biji tiaobian* 清人筆記條辨 (Analysis by subject matter of the *biji* of Qing writers), Zhonghua, 1986. See also Xie Guozhen's notes on Ming-Qing *biji* (49.2, *Biji*).

Gaiyu congkao 陔餘叢考 (Mourning period miscellaneous notes), Zhao Yi 趙翼 (1727-1814), 1790; punctuated ed., Hebei renmin, 1990.

Guisi leigao 癸巳類稿 (Categorized draft of 1813), Yu Zhengxie 俞正燮 (1775-1840), 1813. Notes on many subjects touching on history, anthropology, folklore, geography and the Classics, (see *ECCP*, 936); reprinted in *Guoxue jiben congshu* (9.6).

Guisi cungao 癸巳存稿 (Leftovers from *Guisi leigao*), Yu Zhengxie. Contains lighter subjects than the author selected for his first collection of notes.

Nian'er shi zhaji 廿二史劄記 (Classified notes on the twenty-two Standard Histories), Zhao Yi 趙翼, 1799; see 22.2.

Rizhilu 日知錄 (Record of knowledge gained day by day), Gu Yanwu 顧炎武 (1613-82), *Preface* dated 1676, published 1695. Use *Rizhilu jishi* 日知錄集釋 (Collected notes on the *Rizhilu*), Huang Rucheng 黃汝成, ed., Yuelu, 1992; rpnt., 1994. In his *Preface*, Gu explained the basis for including some subjects and not others: "Since my childhood studies, I have always noted down what I perceived and if it [turned out] to be incorrect, I revised it again and again, or if earlier men had said it before me, I omitted it entirely."[50] The book contains 1,020 entries divided roughly into philosophy, government, examination system, popular customs, astronomy and geography. It is indexed in *Chûgoku zuihitsu sakuin*.

Shijiazhai yangxin lu 十駕齋養新錄 (Record of self-renewal from the Ten yokes study), Qian Daxin 錢大昕 (1728-1804), 1804-1806; Shangwu, 1937; rpnt., Shanghai shudian, 1982. Careful notes on the Classics, phonology, philology, history, geography and much else besides.

Shiqishi shangque 十七史商榷, Wang Mingsheng 王鳴盛 (1722-97), see (22.2).

Chibei outan 池北偶談 (Chatting with visitors in the Chebei book depository),Wang Shizhen 王士禎 (1634-1711); 2 vols., Zhonghua, 1982 and 1984. Miscellaneous notes and comments by a famous scholar, poet and bibliophile.

[Dushutang] Xizheng suibi [讀書堂] 西征隨筆 (Notes of a western journey), Wang Jingqi 汪景祺 (1672-1726), 1723. Wang wrote these notes on his way to Shaanxi. His acerbic comments on the government and high officials including the emperor led to his execution in 1726.

[50] Liang Ch'i-chao, *Intellectual Trends in the Ch'ing Period*, tr. with introduction and notes by Immanuel C. Y. Hsü, HUP, 1959, p. 31.

Guangdong xinyu 廣東新語 (News from Guangdong), Qu Dajun 屈大均 (1630–96), 1680; punctuated ed., 2 vols., Zhonghua, 1985. Notes on conditions in Guangdong mainly in the Ming.

Qingbai leichao 清稗類鈔 (Classified collection of Qing notes), Xu Ke 徐 珂 (1869–1928), 13 vols., Zhonghua, 1984–86; rpnt., 1996. Gathers together excerpts from the author's observations and as well as reading notes in Qing *biji* and in late Qing and early Republican newspapers arranged by subject category. Indexed in *Chûgoku zuihitsu zatsusho sakuin*.

Shiqu yuji 石渠餘記 (Left-over notes from the Stone canal pavilion), Wang Qingyun 王慶雲 (1798–1862), completed in the 1850s, Beijing guji, 1985. Unofficial history of finance and tax during the Qing. The Shiqu library was the name of the famous imperial library of the Western Han (see 9.2).

Xiaoting zalu 嘯亭雜錄 (Miscellaneous records of Xiaoting), Zhaolian 昭 槤 (1776–1829), 1814 or 1815; *xulu* 續錄 (Continuation), written 1817–26. Important supplement for Qing history, especially the years 1736–1821; punctuated ed., Zhonghua, 1980.

Yangzhou huafang lu 揚州畫舫錄 (The decorated boats of Yangzhou), Li Dou 李斗, 1795; Zhonghua, 1960. The author was from Yangzhou and provides a detailed guide to the sights and personalities of this great eighteenth-century commercial center at the height of its prosperity. Lucie Borota translates excerpts in *Renditions* 46 (1996), 58–68. See also See Colin P. Mackerras, *The Rise of the Peking Opera, 1770–1870*, OUP, 1972, chap. 3. Li's 17th chapter is a handbook on garden architecture and carpentry. It is discussed in Klaas Ruitenbeek, *Carpentry and Building in Late Imperial China: A Study of the 15th-Century Carpenter's Manual*, Lu Banjing [.魯班經], Brill, 1993.

Yanpu zaji 簷曝雜記 (Miscellaneous records of Yanpu), Zhao Yi. A third collection of notes by the famous scholar-official.

Yuewei caotang biji 閱微草堂筆記 (Notes from the *Yuewei* hut), Ji Yun 紀昀 (1724–1805), 1800. Ji was one of the chief editors of the *Siku quanshu* (9.5). Towards the end of his life he wrote 1,200 fables and anecdotes many of them satirizing the pedantry and hypocrisy of his Song Neo-Confucian contemporaries. For a translation of more than 100 of the tales, see *Notes from the Hut for Examining the Subtle*, David L. Keenan, tr. and ed., Sharpe, 1998.

Zi buyu 子不語 (What the master did not say), Yuan Mei 袁枚 (1716–97), 1788; Yuelu, 1985; Renmin wenxue, 1996. The title refers to the seventh book of the *Analects*: "The Master never talked of wonders, feats of strength, disorders of nature or spirits" (*zi bu yu guaili luan-shen* 子不語怪力亂神). Yuan Mei, on the other hand, was particularly fond of such matters. *Censored by Confucius: Ghost Stories by Yuan Mei*, Kam Louie and Louise Edwards, tr., Sharpe, 1996. Yuan Mei arranged for his *Suibi* to be published after his death.

50.6.8   Encyclopaedias and Collectanea

Gujin tushu jicheng 古今圖書集成 (29.3).

Siku quanshu 四庫全書 (9.5).

50.6.9   Qing Fiction

See 34.3.

50.7   Archaeology and Inscriptions

Plenty of monuments survive from the Qing. Many were first built in previous dynasties, but like the Imperial Palace (Gugong 故宮) in Beijing, rebuilt or restored during the Qing. Others still carry some of the atmosphere of the Manchus—the palaces at Shengjing 盛京 (Shenyang) or Rehe 熱和 (Chengde), for example.

The Qing emperors are buried in four places: the ancestors of Nurhaci at Yongling town 永陵鎮 in the Xinbin Manchu self-governing county 新賓滿族自治縣, Liaoning. This is 100 km due east of Shenyang in the heart of what was Jianzhou 建州 Jurchen territory. After the founding of the Qing, a 1,000 km road was built from the tombs to Beijing to enable the emperors to pay their respects to their ancestors. Five km west of Yongling are the vestiges of Hetu'ala 赫圖阿拉, the first capital established by Nurhaci; the tomb of Nurhaci himself is at the Fuling 福陵, east of Shenyang; Huang Taiji is buried at the Zhaoling 昭陵 in Shenyang. The emperors Shunzhi, Kangxi, Qianlong, Xianfeng and Tongzhi are buried in the Eastern Qing tombs (Qing Dongling 清東陵) in Zunhua county 遵化縣, Hebei about 125 km to the east of Beijing. The empress dowager Ci Xi is also buried here. The Qing Dongling are the most magnificent and best preserved of all the Chinese imperial mausolea.

The emperors Yongzheng, Jiaqing, Daoguang and Guangxu are buried at the Western Qing tombs (Qing Xiling 清西陵) about 120 km to the west of Beijing in Yi county 易縣, Hebei. The decision to be buried 250 km away from his father was made by the Yongzheng emperor. The Xiling are in a rustic setting and still preserve a certain splendor and are well worth the detour. They also contain the second largest echoing wall in China after that of the Temple of Heaven.

Illustrations

The fourth illustrated volume of the collections of the National Museum of Chinese History (*A Journey into China's Antiquity*) covers the Yuan, Ming and Qing (see 8.2.1 on this series).

50.8 Guides and Research Tools

50.8.1 Guides to Primary Sources

ECCP Although a biographical dictionary (50.8.3), *ECCP* contains a great deal of information on a large number of the main works written or compiled during the Qing. There are detailed name, book title and subject indexes.

Qingshi yanjiu gaishuo 清史研究概説 (General introduction to research on Qing history), Chen Shengxi 陳生璽, ed., Tianjin jiaoyu, 1991. Covers secondary scholarship in China; research themes and primary sources.

For a brief introduction to early Qing sources see Xie Guozhen 謝國楨, "Ming-Qing shiliao yanjiu 明清史料研究" (Research in Ming-Qing historical materials), in his *Ming-Qing biji tancong* 明清筆記談叢 (Collection of notes on Ming-Qing miscellaneous notes), Zhonghua, 1962; Shanghai guji, 1981, 146–83. In this work he discusses 48 *biji*, of which 29 are from the Qing.

Du Weiyun 杜維運, *Qingdai shixue yu shijia* 清代史學與史家 (Qing historiography and historians), Dongda, 1984; Zhonghua, 1988.

Zhongguo jindaishi wenxian bibei shumu 中國近代史文獻必備書目 (Essential written sources for the history of modern China), Zhonghua, 1996, is a catalog of 5,600 published sources in Chinese for the period 1840 to 1919, mainly written between these years.

Zhongguo lishi da cidian 中國歷史大辭典 (The great encyclopaedia of Chinese history), 14 vols., Shanghai cishu, 1983– , has two volumes on the Qing: *Qingshi* 清史, vol. 1, Dai Yi 戴逸 and Luo Ming 羅明, eds.; vol. 2, Rong Mengyuan 榮孟源, ed., 1992. Vol. 1 contains just over 5,000 brief entries on the period 1644 to 1840; vol. 2 has the same number for the years 1840 to 1912. See 8.3.2 for comments.

Qing dynastic bibliographies are introduced in 9.4 and 9.5.

50.8.2   Readers

Introduction to Ch'ing Documents, Part One, Reading Documents: The Rebellion of Zhong Rongjie, vol. 1, *Introduction, Vocabulary and Notes*; vol. 2, *Chinese Texts*, Philip Kuhn and John King Fairbank, Fairbank Center, 1986; rev. ed., 1993. This republishes selected parts of the earlier now out of print *Ch'ing Documents: An Introductory Syllabus*, John King Fairbank, 1952; 3rd ed., rev. and enl., 2 vols., HUP, 1965; rpnt. with index, 1970.[51]

Conflicting Counsels to Confuse the Age: A Documentary Study of Political Economy in Qing China, 1644–1840, Helen Dunstan, CCS, Univ. of Michigan, 1996, is a carefully commented translation of 38 Qing documents dealing with political economy, more especially the management of the grain supply in relation to the subsistence of the population. It is designed for undergraduate instruction, both on the selected topics and on the language of the documents translated (whose originals are not however included).

Qingdai wenshu 清代文書 (Qing documents), Zhang Wode 張我德 et al., Renmin daxue, 1996, is the longtime textbook of the course on Qing archives at People's University. It contains examples of the main types of official communications in almost their original state (i.e., the minimum of punctuation has been added). There are introductions to each document as well as annotations and explanations of difficult phrases. In addition, there are brief but illuminating chapters on the mechanics of Qing documents, for example explanations not

---

[51] There are several important studies in English on the different types of documents in use in Qing government. See especially J. K. Fairbank and Teng Ssu-yü, *Ch'ing Administration: Three Studies*, HUP, 1960; Silas Wu, "Transmission of Ming Memorials," *TP* 54: 275–87 (1968); "The Memorial Systems of the Ch'ing Dynasty," *HJAS* (1967), 7–75; and the same author's *Communication and Imperial Control in China: Evolution of the Palace Memorial System 1693–1735*, HUP, 1971.

only of the main organs of government in which they were drafted, but on the people, the secretaries and assistants whose job it was to write them.

50.8.3   Research Tools

In addition to the research tools mentioned in the previous sections, note *Ch'ing Administrative Terms: A Translation of "The Terminology of the Six Boards with Explanatory Notes,"* E-tu Zen Sun, tr., HUP, 1961 (see 27.5).

Dictionary

Shinmatsu minshu monjo dokkai jiten, 清末民初文書讀解辞典 (Dictionary of documentary terminology used at the end of the Qing and beginning of the Republic), Yamakoshi Toshihiro 山腰敏寛, Kyûko, 1989. Contains definitions of some 4,900 terms and cites sources.

Biographies

ECCP Eminent Chinese of the Ch'ing Period, Arthur W. Hummel, ed., 2 vols., Washington, DC: Government Printing Office, 1943–44; SMC rpnt., 1991. *ECCP* includes authoritative biographies (many written by Fang Chaoying) of 800 leading officials, writers and personalities active during the Qing. There are detailed name, book title and subject indexes.

Qingdai zhuanji congkan suoyin 清代傳記叢刊索引, Zhou Junfu 周駿富, Mingwen, 1986, 3 vols. Now the most complete index to Qing biographies. Indexes the *Qingdai zhuanji congkan* 清代傳記叢刊 (a compendium of 150 separate Qing biographical collections reprinted under Zhou's editorship in 1985 in 202 vols.). The index gives citations to 46,955 people compared to 27,000 in the *Sanshisan zhong Qingdai zhuanji zonghe yinde* 三十三種清代傳記綜合引得 (Combined indices to 33 Qing dynasty biographical collections), *H-Y Index 9,* Beiping, 1932; 2nd ed., with corrections, Tôyô bunko, 1960.

Qingdai beizhuanwen tongjian 清代碑傳文通檢 (Index of Qing stele commemorative writings), Chen Naiqian 陳乃乾, comp., Shanghai: Zhonghua, 1959; pirated edition under the title *Qingren bieji qianzhong beizhuanwen yinde ji beizhuanzhu nianli pu* 清人別集千種碑傳文引得及碑傳主年里譜, Taibei, 1965. This important index (mainly of *muzhiming*) completely supersedes the sections on commemorative writings in *Qingdai wenji pianmu fenlei suoyin* 清代文集篇目分類索引 (Subject index to tables of contents of Qing collected works),

Wang Zhongmin 王重民 et al., comps., Guoli Beiping tushuguan, 1935; Zhonghua, 1965. Chen indexed more than twice as many collected works (altogether 1,025) and includes references to biographical materials on some 11,000 individuals, including those who died after 1644 or who were born before 1911. Dates are included.

Qingren shiming biecheng zihao suoyin 清人室名別稱字號索引 (Index to studio and alternative names of the Qing), Yang Tingfu 楊廷福 and Yang Tongfu 楊同甫, eds., 2 vols., Shanghai guji, 1988. Vol. 1 lists over 103,000 alternative names of 36,000 people. Vol. 2 is arranged by regular name and gives native place as well as alternative names. Arrangement in both parts is by stroke count.

Note the curricula vitae of 55,883 officials prepared for the emperor (50.2.1 and 50.2.4).

At least 1,000 Qing *nianpu* are extant (about one quarter of the total from all periods). Use the standard *nianpu* index (Xie Wei, 1992, section 3.8.3).

There is no comprehensive index to the biographies in Qing gazetteers. Despite this lack, it is fairly easy to find the biography of a person since it is usually (but not invariably) included in the gazetteer of the county in which the family claimed its domicile.

Hakki tsûshi retsuden sakuin 八旗通志列傳索引 (Index to the Biographies in the Gazetteer of the Eight Banners), Kanda Nobuo 神田信夫 et al., comps., Tôyô bunko, 1965.

Qingji Zhongwai shiling nianbiao 清季中外使領年表 (Tables of Chinese and foreign diplomats in the late Qing), Qin Guojing 秦國經 et al., eds., Zhonghua, 1986; rpnt., 1997. Lists foreign consuls (from 1843) and Ministers (from 1860) as well as Chinese diplomats going abroad (Ambassadors from 1875) and consuls (from 1877). There are personal-name indexes including for names in foreign languages.

Official Titles and Officeholders

Qingdai zhiguan nianbiao 清代職官年表 (Chronological tables of officeholders in the Qing dynasty), Qian Shifu 錢實甫, ed., 4 vols., Zhonghua, 1980; rpnt., 1997. This massive work contains tables showing all officeholders for 49 major posts. Useful both for biographical purposes as well as for understanding the functioning of the bureaucracy. There is a personal-name index starting from page 3,700.

Qingdai gedi jiangjun dutong dachen deng nianbiao 清代各地將軍都統大臣等年表 (Chronological tables of generals, commanders-in-chief and senior officials in every province), Zhang Bofeng 章伯鋒 et al., comps., Zhonghua, 1965. Covers the years 1796–1911.

The names of all holders of the *jinshi* degree in the Qing have been indexed in the *H-Y Index*, Supplement 19. For well indexed lists with the names of the 51,624 *jinshi* of the Ming and the Qing, see 3.8.2. On the examination system of the Qing, see Table 22, chap. 22.

Qingdai daxueshi nianbiao 清代大學士年表 (The Grand Secretaries in Ch'ing China: A chronological list), Hung-ting Ku (Gu Hongting 古鴻廷), CMC, 1980.

In addition to *DOTIC*, check *Present-Day Political Organization of China*, H. S. Brunnert and V. V. Hagelstrom, revised by N. Th. Kolessoff; A. Beltchenko and E. E. Moran, trs., Kelly and Walsh, 1912; rpnt., Taibei, 1960; Curzon, 1998. Based on *Da Qing huidian* 大清會典 (Institutes of the great Qing).

The Chinese Government, A Manual of Chinese Titles, Categorically Arranged and Explained with an Index, W. F. Mayers, ed., Kelly and Walsh, 1897; rpnt., Chengwen, 1967. Based on the *Da Qing huidian*.

Geography

Zhongguo lishi dituji 中國歷史地圖集 (The Historical Atlas of China), Tan Qixiang 譚其驤, ed. in chief, vol. 8, *Qing shiqi* 清時期, 2nd rev. ed., 2nd prnt., Ditu, 1985.

Qingdai dili yan'ge biao 清代地理沿革表 (Tables of administrative units in the Qing period), Zhao Quancheng 趙泉澄, 1941; Shanghai: Zhonghua, 1955.

Chronology

Jindai Zhongguo shishi rizhi 近代中國史事日志 (A daily chronology of events in modern Chinese history), Guo Tingyi 郭廷以, comp., Zhengzhong, 1963.

Jinshi Zhong-Xi shi ri duizhaobiao 近世中西史日對照表 (Daily concordance for modern Sino-Western history), Zheng Hesheng 鄭鶴聲, comp., Shangwu, Nanjing, 1936; Taibei: Shangwu, 1958; 3rd prnt., Zhonghua, 1985. Covers every day between 1516 (which saw the arrival of the first Portuguese by ship to Guangzhou) and 1941. Tables give Western calendar months, six months to a page, showing the equivalent date in the Chinese calendar, the day of the week and the *ganzhi* for each day, as well as indicating the *jieqi*. Easy to convert either way. The Taiping calendar (*Tianli* 天曆, 1851–64) is shown in an appendix with monthly and daily equivalents in both the Chinese and Western calendars (853–80).

Modern China: A Chronology from 1842 to the Present, Colin Mackerras, comp., Thames and Hudson, 1982.

Bibliographies of Secondary Scholarship

The bibliographical chapters and appendixes in the Qing volumes of the *CHC* are the best starting point, although some are already a shade out-of-date.

Andrew J. Nathan, *Modern China, 1840–1972: An Introduction to Sources and Research Aids*, CCS, Univ. of Michigan, 1973.

Kindai Chûgoku kenkyû annai 近代中國研究案内 (Guide to research on modern China), Kojima Shinji 小島晋治 and Namiki Yorihisa 並木 賴壽, Iwanami, 1993. Useful, mainly for secondary literature arranged around topics from 1840 to the present.

Chûgoku sankô tosho gaido Kingendaishi hen 中國參考圖書ガイデ近現代 史編 (Guide to reference works on China, modern and contemporary history section), Ichiko Kenji 市古健次, comp., Kyûko, 1997.

Modern Chinese Society, 1644–1970: An Analytical Bibliography, vol. 3, *Publications in Japanese*, G. W. Skinner and Shigeaki Tomita, comps., SUP, 1973.[52]

Qingshi lunwen suoyin 清史論文索引 (Index to articles on Qing history), Lishisuo and Renmin daxue lishixi 人民大學歷史系, comps., Zhonghua, 1984. Covers articles written between 1900–81 on the period 1644 to 1840. Taiwan and Hong Kong articles and books are included from 1949 onward. A total of 24,000 articles are indexed.

Societies and Journals

Late Imperial China (*LIC*: began in 1965 under the title *Ch'ing-shih wen-t'i*; adopted present title in 1985, biannual), Society for Qing Studies, California Institute of Technology, Pasadena, California. Contains

---

[52] Earlier Japanese scholarship on the late Qing is covered in *Japanese Studies of Modern China: A Bibliographical Guide to Historical and Social Science Research on the 19th and 20th Centuries*, John K. Fairbank et al., Tuttle, 1955; this is up-dated in *Japanese Studies of Modern China since 1953: A Bibliographical Guide to Historical and Social Science Research on the Nineteenth and Twentieth Century*, Noriko Kamachi et al., eds., HUP, 1975.

translations of *Shigaku zasshi* May issue review of Ming-Qing studies in Japan.

Qingshi luncong 清史論叢 (1979- , annual), Shekeyuan, Qingshi yanjiu-shi 清史研究室.

Qingshi yanjiu 清史研究 (1991- quarterly), Zhongguo renmin daxue Qingshi yanjiusuo 中國人民大學清史研究所; previous title, *Qingshi yanjiu tongxun* 清史研究通訊, 1981- .

Appendix

Appendix

Publishers

Academy Editions, London.
Aldine, Chicago.
Allen and Unwin, London.
American Philosophical Society, Philadelphia.
Anhui Renmin Chubanshe 安徽人民出版社, Hefei.
ANU Press, Australian National University Press, Canberra.
Aolinpike 奥林匹克, Beijing.
Athlone Press, University of London.
Atneneum, New York.
Aubier: Francoise Aubier, Paris.
Baihuazhou Wenyi Chubanshe 白花洲文藝出版社, Nanchang.
Ballantine Books, New York.
Ba-Shu Shushe 巴蜀書社, Chengdu.
Bayi Chubanshe 八一出版社, Beijing.
Beifang Funü Ertong Chubanshe 北方婦女兒童出版社, Changchun.
Beijing Chubanshe 北京出版社, Beijing.
Beijing Daxue Chubanshe 北京大學出版社, Beijing.
Beijing Haowang Shudian 北京好望書店, Beijing.
Beijing Yuyan Wenhua Daxue Chubanshe 中國文化語言大學出版社, Beijing.
Blackwell: Basil Blackwell, Oxford.
Brill: E. J. Brill, Amsterdam.
British Museum Press, London.
Carl Hauser Verlag, München/Wien.
Cehui Chubanshe 測繪出版社, Beijing.
Century Books, New York.
Ch'eng-wen, see Chengwen.
Changchun Chubanshe 長春出版社, Changchun.
Chengdu Chubanshe 成都出版社, Chengdu.
Chengwen 成文 Publishing Co., Taibei.
Chongqing Chubanshe 重慶出版社, Chongqing.
China Building Industry Press, see Zhongguo Jiancai Gongye Chubanshe
Chinese Language Research Association, Presidio, Monterey, California.
Chinese Materials Center, Taibei and San Francisco.
Chûbun Shuppansha 中文出版社, Kyoto.
Clarendon Press: Oxford University Press, Oxford.
Clio Press, Santa Barbara and Oxford.
Col. UP: Columbia University Press, New York City, New York.
Commercial Press, see under Shangwu.

Corn. UP: Cornell University Press, Ithaca, New York.

CUP: Cambridge University Press, Cambridge, England.

Curzon Press, Richmond, Surrey, England.

Dahua Shuju 大化書局, Taibei.

Daian 大安, Tokyo.

Daitô Shuppansha 大東出版社, Tokyo.

Dang'an Chubanshe 檔案出版社, Beijing.

Dianzi Keji Daxue Chubanshe 電子科技大學出版社, Chengdu.

Dingwen Shuju 鼎文書局, Taibei.

Ditu Chubanshe 地圖出版社, Beijing.

Dizhen Chubanshe 地震出版社, Beijing.

Dôhôsha 同朋舍, Kyoto.

Dôyûsha 同友舍, Kyoto.

Dongbei Shifan Daxue Chubanshe 東北師範大學出版社, Changchun.

Dongda: Dongda Tushu Youxian Gongsi, Taibei.

Doubleday Inc., New York.

Dover: Dover Publications, Inc., Mineola, New York.

Duke University Press, Durham, North Carolina.

Dunhuang Wenyi Chubanshe 敦煌文藝出版社, Lanzhou.

Edinburgh UP, Edinburgh University Press.

Editions Derouaux Ordina, Liège.

Elanders Boktryckeri Artiebolag, Göteborg.

Facts on File Inc., New York.

Falü Chubanshe 法律出版社, Beijing.

Fangzhou 房舟出版社, Taibei.

FLP: Foreign Languages Press (Waiwen Chubanshe 外文出版社), Beijing.

Forum, Edition Forum, Heidelberg.

Free Press, Glencoe, New York.

Fujian Renmin 福建人民, Fuzhou.

Fukutake Shoten 福武書店, Tokyo.

G. K. Hall, Boston, Mass.

Gansu Wenhua Chubanshe 甘肅文化出版社, Lanzhou.

Gansu Yinxiang Chubanshe 甘肅音像出版社, Lanzhou.

Garland Publishing, Inc., New York.

Gongyi Meishu Chubanshe 工藝美術出版社, Beijing.

Greenwood Press, Westport, Conn.

Guangdong Jiaoyu Chubanshe 廣東教育出版社, Guangzhou.

Guangdong Renmin Chubanshe 廣東人民出版社, Guangzhou.

Guangdongsheng Ditu Chubanshe 廣東省地圖出版社, Guangzhou.

Guangming Ribao Chubanshe 光明日報出版社, Beijing.

Guangwen Shuju 廣文書局, Taibei.

Guangxi Jiaoyu Chubanshe 廣西教育出版社, Nanning.

Guangxi Renmin Chubanshe 廣西人民出版社, Nanning, Guangxi.

Guangxi Shifan Daxue Chubanshe 師範大學出版社, Nanning.

Gudian Wenxue Chubanshe 古典文學出版社, Beijing.

Gugong Bowuyuan 故宮博物院, Taibei.

Guji Chubanshe 古籍出版社, Shanghai.

Guofang Daxue Chubanshe 國防大學出版社, Beijing.

Guofeng Chubanshe 國風出版社, Taibei.

Guoji Wenhua Chuban Gongsi 國際文化出版公司, Beijing.

Hacker Art Books Inc. New York

Hainan Guoji Xinwen Chuban Zhongxin 海南國際新聞出版中心, Haikou.

Haiyang Chubanshe 海洋出版社, Beijing.

Hakluyt Society, Cambridge and London.

Hanxue Yanjiu Ziliao ji Fuwu Zhongxin 漢學研究資料及服務中心, Taibei.

Hanyu Da Cidian Chubanshe 漢語大詞典出版社, Shanghai.

Harrassowitz: Otto Harrassowitz Verlag, Wiesbaden.

Hauser: see Carl Hauser Verlag.

Hebei Daxue Chubanshe 河北大學出版社, Shijiazhuang.

Heibonsha 平凡社, Tokyo.

Heilongjiang Kexue Jishu Chubanshe 黑龍江科學技術出版社, Harbin.

Heilongjiang Renmin Chubanshe 黑龍江人民出版社, Harbin.

Henan Daxue Chubanshe 河南大學出版社, Zhengzhou.

Henan Renmin Chubanshe 河南人民出版社, Kaifeng.

Heirakuji shoten 平樂寺書店, Tokyo.

HKCU Press: Chinese University Press, Shatin, N.T., Hong Kong.

HKU Press: Hong Kong University Press, Hong Kong.

Holos Verlag, Heidelburg.

Hongqi Chubanshe 紅旗出版社, Beijing.

Hongqiao Chubanshe 紅橋出版社, Taibei.

Hongye Wenhua Shiye Youxian Gongsi 洪葉文化事業有限公司, Taibei.

Hôzôkan 法藏館, Kyoto.

HRAF: Human Resource Area Files Press, New Haven.

Huadong Shifan Daxue Chubanshe 華東師範大學出版社, Shanghai.

Huangshan Shushe 黃山書社, Hefei.

Huashan wenyi cubanshe 華山文藝出版社, Hefei.

Huashi Chubanshe 華事出版社, Taibei.

Huawen shuju 華文書局, Taibei.

Huayu Jiaoxue Chubanshe 華語教學出版社, Beijing.

Huaxia Chubanshe 華夏出版社, Beijing.

Hubei Cishu Chubanshe 湖北辭書出版社, Wuhan.

Hubei Jiaoyu Chubanshe 湖北教育出版社, Wuhan.

Hunan Chubanshe 湖南出版社, Changsha.

Hunan Renmin Chubanshe 湖南人民出版社, Changsha.

HUP: Harvard University Press, Cambridge, Mass.

H-Y Institute: Harvard-Yenching Institute, Beiping and Cambridge, Mass.

IUP: Indiana Unversity Press, Bloomingdale, Indiana.

Iwanami Shoten 岩波書店, Tokyo.

Jiangong Chubanshe 建翠出版社, Beijing.

Jiangsu Guangling Guji Keyinshe 江蘇光陵古籍刻印社, Yangzhou.

Jiangsu Jiaoyu Chubanshe 江蘇教育出版社, Nanjing.

Jiangsu Kexue Jishu Chubanshe 江蘇科學技術出版社, Nanjing.

Jiangxi Jiaoyu Chubanshe 江西教育出版社, Nanchang.

Jiaotong Daxue Chubanshe 交通大學出版社, Shanghai.

Jiefangjun Chubanshe 解放軍出版社, Beijing.
Jilin Daxue Chubanshe 吉林大學出版社, Changchun.
Jilin Jiaoyu Chubanshe 吉林教育出版社, Changchun.
Jilin Kexue Jishu Chubanshe 吉林科學技術出版社, Changchun.
Jilin Wenshi Chubanshe 吉林文史出版社, Changchun.
Jimbun Kagaku Kenkyûjô 人文科學研究所, Kyoto.
Jingguan Jiaoyu Chubanshe 警官教育出版社, Beijing.
Jingji Ribao Chubanshe 經濟日報出版社, Beijing.
Kagaku Shoin 科學書院, Tokyo.
Kaiming Shudian 開明書店, Shanghai (unless otherwise indicated).
Kansai Daigaku Shupansha 關西大學出版社, Suida.
Kelly and Walsh, Shanghai.
Kenbun Shuppan 研文出版, Tokyo.
Kexue Chubanshe 科學出版社, Beijing.
Kluwer Academic Publishers, Dordrecht.
Knopf, New York.
Kôbundô Shoten 光文堂書店, Yamagata.
Kôdansha 講談社 Intl., Tokyo.
Kokudosha 國土社, Tokyo.
Kokusho Kankôkai, 國書刊行會, Tokyo.
Koten Kenkyûkai 古典研究會, Tokyo.
Kraus Reprint Ltd., Nendeln, Leichtenstein.
Kyûko Shoin 汲古書院, Tokyo.
Kyoto Daigaku Bungakubu 京都大學文學部, Tôyôshi kenkyûkai 東洋史
    研究會, Kyoto.
Lanzhou Daxue Chubanshe 蘭州大學出版社, Lanzhou.
Leroux: Ernest Leroux, Paris.
Lianjing: Lianjing Chuban Shiye Gongsi 聯經出版事業公司, Taibei.
Liaoning Jiaoyu Chubanshe 遼寧教育出版社, Shenyang.
Liaoning Minzu Chubanshe 遼寧民族出版社, Shenyang.
Liaoning Renmin Chubanshe 遼寧人民出版社, Shenyang.
Liao-Shen Shushe, 遼沈書社, Shenyang.
Lingnan daxue tushuguan 嶺南大學圖書館, Guangzhou.
Linye Chubanshe 林業出版社, Beijing.
Lund Humphries, London.
Lüyou Chubanshe 旅遊出版社, Beijing.
Macmillan, London.
Maisonneuve: Adrien-Maisonneuve, Paris.
Meitan Gongye Chubanshe 煤炭工業出版社, Beijing.
Meitoku Shobô 明德書房, Tokyo.
Metchuen, New Jersey.
Minglun Chubanshe 明論出版社, Taibei.
Mingwen shuju 明文書局, Taibei
MIT Press, Cambridge, Mass.
Morning Glory Publishers (Zhaohua Chubanshe 朝華出版社), Beijing.
Mouton de Gruyter, Berlin and New York.
Mouton et Cie, Paris and the Hague.

John Murray, London.
Museum of Far Eastern Antiquities (Östasiatiska Samlingarna), Stockholm.
Nanjing Daxue Chubanshe 南京大學出版社, Nanjing.
Nei Menggu Renmin Chubanshe 內蒙古出版社, Huhehaote.
New World Press, Beijing.
Nigensha 二玄社, Tokyo.
Nihon Gakujutsu Shinkôkai 日本學術新興會, Tokyo.
Ningxia Renmin Chubanshe 寧夏人民出版社, Yinchuan.
Nongye Chubanshe 農業出版社, Beijing.
Norton: W. W. Norton and Co., New York.
Ochanomizu Shobô 御茶の水書房, Tokyo.
Ohio University Press, Athens, Ohio.
Open Court, Chicago and La Salle, Illinois.
OUP, Oxford University Press, Oxford.
Paragon Book Reprint Corp., New York.
Penguin Books, Harmondsworth, Middlesex.
Pennsylvania State University Press, University Park, Pennsylvania.
People's China: see Renmin Zhongguo Chubanshe.
Praeger, New York.
Prentice Hall, Englewood Cliffs, N.J.
Probsthain: Arthur Probsthain, London.
PUF: Presses Universitaires de France, Paris.
PUP: Princeton University Press, Princeton, N.J.
Qi-Lu Shushe 齊魯書社, Jinan.
Qingdao Chubanshe 青島出版社, Qingdao.
Qingnian: see Zhongguo Qingnian Chubanshe.
Qunyan Chubanshe 群言出版社, Beijing.
Random House, New York.
Reaktion, London.
Renmin Chubanshe 人民出版社, Beijing.
Renmin Meishu 人民美術, Beijing.
Renmin Weisheng Chubanshe 人民衛生出版社, Beijing.
Renmin Zhongguo Chubanshe 人民中國出版社, Beijing.
Rider and Co., London.
Robalde: Ward Robalde Press, Los Angeles.
Ronald Press, New York.
Routledge & Kegan Paul, London.
Routledge Intl., London.
Ryôgen Shoten 燎原書店, Tokyo.
Ryûkei Shosha 龍溪書舍, Tokyo.
Saika Shorin 菜華樹林, Nagoya.
Sanlian: Shenghuo. Dushu. Xinzhi Sanlian Chubanshe 生活.讀書.新知三聯
  出版社, Beijing.
San-Qin Chubanshe 三秦出版社, Xi'an.
Science Press, see Kexue Chubanshe.
Seuil: Editions du Seuil, Paris.
Scarecrow Press, Metuchen, New York State.

Shaanxi Guji Chubanshe 陝西古籍出版社, Xi'an.
Shaanxi Lüyou Chubanshe 陝西旅遊出版社, Xian.
Shaanxi Renmin Jiaoyu Chubanshe 陝西人民出版社, Xi'an.
Shambala, Boston, Mass.
Shandong Daxue Chubanshe 山東大學出版社, Jinan.
Shandong Jiaoyu Chubanshe 山東教育出版社, Jinan.
Shandong Renmin Chubanshe 山東人民出版社, Jinan.
Shandong Wenyi Chubanshe 山東文藝出版社, Jinan.
Shandong Youyi Shushe 山東友誼出版社, Jinan.
Shanghai Cishu Chubanshe 上海辭書出版社, Shanghai.
Shanghai Guji Chubanshe 上海古籍出版社, Shanghai.
Shanghai Jiaoyu Chubanshe 上海出版社, Shanghai.
Shanghai Renmin Chubanshe 上海人民出版社, Shanghai.
Shanghai Shudian Chubanshe 上海書店出版社, Shanghai.
Shanghai Wenhua Chubanshe 上海文化出版社,
Shanghai Yuandong Chubanshe 上海遠東出版社, Shanhai.
Shangwu: Shangwu Yinshuguan 商務印書館, Beijing and Shanghai.
Shangwu Intl.: Shangwu Guoji Youxian Gongsi 商務國際有限公司, Beijing,
    Hong Kong, Taiwan, Singapore and Kual Lumpur.
Shanxi Shifan Daxue Chubanshe 山西師範大學出版社,
Sharpe: M. E. Sharpe, Armonk, New York.
Shehui Kexue Wenxian Chubanshe 社會科學出版社, Beijing.
Shehui Kexue Chubanshe: see Zhongguo Shehui Kexue Chubanshe.
Seishin Shobô 省心書房, Tokyo.
Shenzhou Guoguangshe 神州國光社, Shanghai.
Shijie Shuju 世界書局, Shanghai.
Shoestring Press, Hamden, Conn.
Shoseki Seibosha 書籍情報社, Tokyo.
Shogakukan Shuppansha 小學館出版社, Tokyo.
Shoudu Shifan Daxue Chubanshe 師範大學出版社,
Shumu Wenxian Chubanshe 書目文獻出版社, Beijing.
Sichuan Cishu Chubanshe 四川辭書出版社, Chengdu.
Sichuan Daxue Chubanshe 四川大學出版社, Chengdu.
Sichuan Renmin Chubanshe 四川人民出版社, Chengdu.
Sichuan Shehui Kexue Chubanshe 四川社會科學出版社, Chengdu.
Sinolingua, see Huayu Jiaoxue Chubanshe
SMC: Southern Materials Center, Inc., Taibei.
Sôbunsha 創文社, Tokyo.
Sôgensha 創元社, Kyoto.
Springer Verlag, Berlin and Hamburg.
St Martin's Press, London.
Steiner: Franz Steiner Verlag, Stuttgart.
Steyler: Franz Steyler Verlag, Nettetal.
Studio Editions, London.
SUNY Press: State University of New York Press, Albany, New York.
SUP: Stanford University Press, Stanford, California.
Suzhou Renmin Chubanshe 蘇州出版社,

Taishûkan shoten 大修館書店, Tokyo.
Thames and Hudson, London.
Tianjin Jiaoyu Chubanshe 天津教育出版社, Tianjin.
Tianjin Renmin Meishu Chubanshe 天津人民出版社, Tianjin.
Tianwa Chubanshe 天花出版社, Taibei.
Tôhô Shoten 東方書店, Tokyo.
Tôkyô Daigaku Shuppankai 東京大學出版會, Tokyo.
Tôkyôdô Shuppan 東京堂出版, Tokyo.
Tôsui Shobô 刀水書房, Tokyo.
Tôyô Bunko 東洋文庫, Tokyo.
Tuanjie Chubanshe 團結出版社, Beijing.
Tuttle: Charles E. Tuttle, Vermont and Tokyo.
Twayne, New York.
UAP: University of Arizona Press, Tucson.
UBC Press: University of British Columbia Press, Vancouver.
UChP: University of Chicago Press, Chicago.
UCP: University of California Press, Berkeley.
UHP: University of Hawaii Press, Honolulu.
UMP: University of Michigan Press, Ann Arbor, Michigan.
UWP: University of Washington Press, Seattle.
University of Kansas Press, Lawrence.
Unwin Hyman, London.
Variorum, Aldershot, England.
Vetch: Henri Vetch, Beiping and Hong Kong.
Waiyu Jiaoxue yu Yanjiu Chubanshe 外語教學與研究出版社, Beijing.
Weatherill, Tokyo and New York.
Wenhai Chubanshe 文海出版社, Taibei.
Wenjin Chubanshe 文浸出版社, Taibei.
Wenwu Chubanshe 文物出版社, Beijing.
Wenxing Shudian 文星書店, Beijing.
Westview Press, Boulder, Colorado, USA.
White Lotus Co. Ltd., Bangkok.
Wild Peony, Broadway, New South Wales, Australia.
Wiley: John Wiley, New York.
Wuhan Daxue Chubanshe 武漢大學出版社, Wuhan.
Xi'an Ditu Chubanshe 西安地圖出版社, Xi'an.
Xibei Daxue Chubanshe 西北大學出版社, Xian.
Xinhua Shudian 新華書店, Beijing.
Xin Wenfeng Chuban Gongsi 新文豐出版公司, Taibei.
Xinxing Chubanshe 新星出版社, Beijing.
Xizang Renmin Chubanshe 西藏人民出版社, Lhasa.
Xuelin Chubanshe 學林出版社, Shanghai.
Xuesheng Shuju 學生書局, Taibei.
Xueyuan Chuban Gongsi 學苑出版社, Beijing.
Yamakawa Shuppansha 山川出版社, Tokyo.
Yamamoto Shoten 山本書店, Tokyo.
Yiwen Yinshuguan 藝文印書館, Taibei.

Yoshikawa Kôbunkan 吉川弘文館, Tokyo.
Yuelu Shushe 岳麓書社, Changsha.
Yunnan Jiaoyu Chubanshe 雲南教育出版社, Kunming.
Yunnan Renmin Chubanshe 雲南人民出版社, Kunming.
YUP: Yale University Press, New Haven.
Yurindô 有鄰堂, Tokyo.
Yuwen Chubanshe 語文出版社, Beijing.
Yuzankaku 雄山閣, Tokyo.
Zhejiang Guji Chubanshe 浙江古籍出版社, Hangzhou.
Zhejiang Renmin Chubanshe 浙江人民出版社, Hangzhou.
Zhengzhong Shuju 正中書局, Taibei.
Zhishi Chubanshe 知識出版社, Shanghai.
Zhongguo Caizheng Jingji Chubanshe 中國財政經濟出版社, Beijing.
Zhongguo Chengshi Chubanshe 中國城市出版社, Beijing.
Zhongguo Da Baike Quanshu Chubanshe 中國大百科全書出版社, Beijing.
Zhongguo Ditu Chubanshe 中國地圖出版社, Beijing.
Zhongguo Duiwai Fanyi Chubanshe 中國對外翻譯出版社, Beijing.
Zhongguo Gongren Chubanshe 中國工人出版社, Beijing.
Zhongguo Guangbo Dianshi Chubanshe 中國廣播電視出版社, Beijing.
Zhongguo Guoji Guangbo Chubanshe 中國國際廣播出版社, Beijing.
Zhongguo Huaqiao Chubanshe 中國華僑出版社, Beijing.
Zhongguo Jiancai Gongye Chubanshe 中國建材工業出版社, Beijing.
Zhongguo Jianzhu Gongye Chubanshe 中國建築工業出版社, Beijing.
Zhongguo Kexueyuan, Beijing Tianwentai 中國科學院北京天文臺
Zhongguo Kuangye Daxue Chubanshe 中國礦業大學出版社, Hangzhou.
Zhongguo Qingnian Chubanshe 中國青年出版社, Beijing.
Zhongguo Renmin Daxue Chubanshe 中國人民大學出版社, Beijing.
Zhongguo Renmin Gong'an Daxue Chubanshe 中國人民公安大學出版社,
    Beijing.
Zhongguo Renshi Chubanshe 中國人事出版社, Beijing
Zhongguo Shangye Chubanshe 中國商業出版社, Beijing.
Zhongguo Shehui Kexue Chubanshu 中國社會科學出版社, Beijing.
Zhongguo Shudian 中國書店, Beijing.
Zhongguo Wenhua Yanjiusuo 中國文化研究所, Taibei.
Zhongguo Wenlian Chuban Gongsi 中國文聯出版公司, Tianjin.
Zhongguo Wenshi Chubanshe 中國文史出版社, Beijing.
Zhongguo Wenxue Chubanshe 中國文學出版社, Beijing.
Zhongguo Xueshu Chubanshe 中國學術出版社, Beijing.
Zhongguo Zangxue Chubanshe 中國藏學出版社, Beijing.
Zhonghua Ditu Xueshe 中華地圖學社, Shanghai.
Zhonghua: Zhonghua Shuju 中華書局, Beijing.
Zhongshan Daxue Chubanshe 中山大學出版社, Guangzhou.
Zhongyi Guji Chubanshe 中醫古籍出版社, Shanghai.
Zhongyi Xueyuan Chubanshe 中醫學院出版社, Shanghai.
Zhongzhou Guji Chubanshe 中州古籍出版社, Zhengzhou.
Zhuanji Wenxueshe 傳記文學舍, Taibei.
Zijincheng Chubanshe 紫禁城出版社, Beijing

Index of Names

Index of Names

Note: In general, authors of articles are not included in the index.

Index of Titles of Books

Index of Titles of Books

Subject Index

Subject Index

Harvard-Yenching Institute Monograph Series
(titles now in print)